Modern Jewish History
Robert Mandel, series editor

"Non-Germans" under the Third Reich:

*The Nazi Judicial and Administrative System
in Germany and Occupied Eastern Europe,
with Special Regard to Occupied Poland,
1939–1945*

DIEMUT MAJER

TRANSLATED BY
Peter Thomas Hill, Edward Vance Humphrey,
and Brian Levin

Texas Tech University Press

Published in Association with the
United States Holocaust Memorial Museum

Cover design by Ashley Beck
Cover photo: Einsatzkommando 3/V guarding Jews in Plonsk in Zichenau regional district, September 27, 1939. From a photo album of an unidentified official of Einsatzkommando 3/V and the Gestapo in Hohensalza. (*Instytut Pamieci Narodwej, courtesy of the US Holocaust Memorial Museum*)

Library of Congress Control Number: 2013947077

Printed in the United States of America
13   14   15   16   17   18   19   20   21 / 9   8   7   6   5   4   3   2   1

Texas Tech University Press
Box 41037
Lubbock, Texas 79409–1037 USA
800.832.4042
ttup@ttu.edu
www.ttupress.org

Published in association with the United States Holocaust Memorial Museum
100 Raoul Wallenberg Place, SW
Washington, DC 20024–2126

Contents

INTRODUCTION

PART ONE

The Principle of Special Law against "Non-Germans" in the Area of Public
Law (General and Internal Administration with Supplementary Areas)

SECTION ONE
The Implementation of *Völkisch* Inequality in the Altreich   79

PART TWO

The Principle of Special Law against "Non-Germans" in the Field of Justice

APPENDIXES

Illustrations follow page 322.

Preface to the English-Language Edition

The number of studies, conferences, and articles and the amount of research conducted in the United States and in other countries about the Holocaust is seemingly boundless. But this book is not a book *about* the Holocaust; it points the way *to* the Holocaust. It explains the history, legal status, and treatment of "non-Germans" (*Fremdvölkische,* or aliens), in the Third Reich from 1933 to 1945; it describes the judicial theories and the administrative systems and court decisions concerning the treatment of "non-Germans" in the spheres of civil law, penal law, police law, fiscal law, the social and cultural sectors, and the like. This treatment was based on the principle of "special law" (*Sonderrecht*), or on "racial" or "ethnic" inequality. This meant nothing other than the misuse—even the dissolution—of the general law by extralegal or contralegal means or by re-treating into secret directives of the administration or into single police actions.

An important part of the book is dedicated to the legal treatment of "non-Germans" in Eastern Europe, especially in occupied Poland from 1939 to 1945. These territories were the "field of experiment" for all future "racial" programs of the National Socialist government. At the same time, the Nazis' practices against Poles and Jews were an extreme extension of measures initiated in the territory of the Reich, which created a pernicious scale of discrimination from west to east.

My conclusion is that the National Socialist state practiced a "logic" system consisting of three elements: the Führer principle (the absolute power of the Führer); the monopoly status of the National Socialist German Workers' Party (Nationalsozialistische Deutsche Arbeiterpartei [NSDAP]) and its ideological ruling of the entire state, including intellectual and social spheres; and the principle of "racial *inequality*" for "non-Germans," which we may also call the principle of special law.

This principle of special law is the essential characteristic of the National Socialist state: no other authoritarian or totalitarian regime was so extremely focused on racial ideas. In practice, it meant the classification of German citizens and citizens of the occupied territories into "Aryans" and "non-Aryans," or "Germans" and "non-Germans," the separation in legal life and, as a consequence, the deprivation of all human rights and social protection for the so-called non-Germans. It amounted to reducing "non-Germans" to being deprived of paid labor without any public means—a psychic death before the physical death.

Of special interest is the role of the intellectuals, that is to say, those who emerged at the acme in the realms of science, politics, culture, business, justice, the military, and civil administration after the intellectual elite, especially those of Jewish extraction, had been dismissed or forced into exile, or both. These individuals acquired racist ideas from the Kaiserreich and in the powerful right-wing associations and parties of the Weimar Republic; they spread authoritarian or National Socialist ideas to their students and colleagues and in their own minds began to eliminate the "aliens" *before* the discriminatory measures started in practice. Their fascination with the Führer principle, their devotion and eagerness to serve the dictator without any moral or legal reservations, lay the groundwork for all of the pernicious legislation and administrative measures. This was facilitated by the fact that this racial thinking was given absolute priority by the National Socialist leadership and was encouraged in almost every official statement.

Why is the book of interest to an English-speaking audience?

In recent years countless publications and discussions concerning the Holocaust have inundated the media and dominated the discussions, promoted especially by the publication of Daniel J. Goldhagen's *Hitler's Willing Executioners* in 1997. The pros and cons concerning the role of anti-Semitism will certainly play an important part in future discussions.

This book puts these issues on a broader plain, one that transcends anti-Semitism and even racial thinking. It shows that at the core of National Socialist theories and legal practices was the elimination of the person as an individual— that is, the reduction of the person to a thing, from "he" or "she" to "it," a fact clearly shown in the National Socialist legal language. From this basis everything was possible, even physical extermination, because human rights are not applicable to "things." In this sense, not only Jews or other so-called non-Aryans, but all persons disliked by the regime for whatever reasons, represented potential victims. Thus, this book holds one of the most important keys to understanding the Holocaust. The numerous studies on law and justice in the Third

Reich published in Germany after the appearance of this book do not change these theses but rather confirm them.

This book, the preparation of which claimed twelve years, quotes or lists all materials available in West German and Polish archives at the time of the appearance of the first German edition. The annotation is abundant; I hope it is not confusing. In any case, it will give the reader an impression of the complicated and almost endless methods of "racial" and political discrimination carried out through law and police regulation. It also reflects the problems that administration and "justice" faced in establishing such a system *within* the framework of traditional law dealing with virtually every aspect of life. Thus the sinister atmosphere of those years of occupation (in Poland) shows through every source and through every report of the local or state authorities, of the police or Party offices, to the central offices of the Reich.

I am very much obliged to the University of Bern in Switzerland for accepting my book as a *Habilitation* after its prior submission in former West Berlin and also in (West) Germany. (A *Habilitation* is similar to a second Ph.D. dissertation and is a legal or de facto requirement for a university career.)

I am grateful to the Johns Hopkins University Press, especially to its executive editor, Henry Y. K. Tom, and to the United States Holocaust Memorial Museum, represented by Benton Arnovitz, head of its academic publications branch, for agreeing to publish the book for the English-speaking audience; I thank them for their patience with the numerous problems that often come with such a huge manuscript. Very helpful were the staff members of the United States Holocaust Memorial Museum, who completed the vetting of the manuscript and its preparation for transmittal to the publisher, especially Aleisa Fishman and Patricia Heberer. The late senior historian of the Museum, Sybil Milton, encouraged that institution's sponsorship of this project, for which she is owed special thanks. Special compliments to Lois Crum, the copy editor engaged by the Johns Hopkins University Press, who shaped the text, where necessary, in a most skillful was for the English-speaking audience.

I am grateful, further, to my translators, Ned Humphrey in the United States and Peter Hill and Brian Levin, both in Great Britain, whose brilliant abilities enabled them to cope with such a difficult manuscript and with the linguistic usages of a totalitarian state. That terminology does not exist in normal legal diction, so they often needed to create new expressions. Part 1 was translated by Ned Humphrey (with the exception of pages 237–316 of the German edition), part 2 by Peter Hill and Brian Levin; Brian Levin also translated pages 237–316 of part 1. The footnotes were translated by Peter Hill, as well as the index of places (consolidated with the subject index) and the index of persons; he also laid the basis for the glossary, which is new to this work. The glossary is unique because it includes a detailed survey of the most common traditional German legal terms and of the legal terms in the National Socialist phraseology. It is offered as a special service to the reader, so that he or she may understand the peculiarities of a highly bureaucratized, inhumane, and even inhuman language.

Most of all I am grateful to my cousin Albrecht Majer, senior teacher of English and Latin at the Claus-von-Stauffenberg-Schule, Rodgau, Germany, to his family, and to his team, who supported the preparation of the English edition (which took ten years) in many ways. Albrecht was manager, driving force, flying messenger between Frankfurt, Washington, and Baltimore, calming down the author who often got nervous considering the bulk of technical difficulties involved in such a huge project; he and his staff were also invaluable in meeting the problems of coordinating the texts of three translators, before the manuscript was sent to the editors in the United States.

Further, I am very much obliged to my assistants and friends Ursula Seybold-Schryro of Karlsruhe and Bijan Djawid of Dresden, who helped with technical assistance, which equally was a very considerable contribution in the preparation of the manuscript.

Diemut Majer

Karlsruhe, 2003

Foreword to the Second German Edition (1993)

Diemut Majer's book *"Fremdvölkische" im Dritten Reich* first appeared in 1981 in the Schriften des Bundesarchivs (Annals of the Federal Archives). It was widely acclaimed and received a large number of favorable reviews. Originally written as a law dissertation for the University of Bern, Switzerland, the text came into increasing demand in the wake of the upheavals in Central and Eastern Europe. The book had been out of print since 1991, and I decided on a new edition of it with an awareness of its ongoing practical value as a work of reference and documentation for courts of law, public prosecutors, social administration offices, and other welfare agencies.

The author has thoroughly revised the text and added a list of current literature. Not least, I am gratified that this book should once again be available to aid historical research of totalitarian systems in the communist field of influence. I have great respect for Diemut Majer's book as an important basis for comparative studies of administration and jurisdiction in the development and establishment of totalitarian systems.

I also thank my colleague Dr. Trumpp for editorial work on the new edition.

Professor Dr. Friedrich P. Kahlenberg
President of the Federal Archives
Koblenz, July 1993

Preface to the Second German Edition (1993)

The favorable reception that this book received in 1981 was due not least to its having been published under the auspices of the Federal Archives in Koblenz and its elegant presentation by the Harald Boldt Publishing House in Boppard on the Rhine, assisted by a printing subsidy from the Scientific Support Fund of VG Wort. I express my grateful thanks once again to all those who have participated in this work, especially the former president of the Federal Archives, Prof. Dr. Hans Booms, and his deputy, Dr. Heinz Boberach, director of the Archives. The positive reception by the scholarly media in Germany and abroad that the book enjoyed on its publication reflected the need for a systematic overview of the legal doctrine and practice of the Nazi state, for none had existed hitherto. The contemporary literature had concentrated primarily on the explicitly criminal aspects of the Nazi state: racial persecution, extermination policy, and so on, giving very little or no place to the legal theories and the legal and administrative practices that led up to these developments, nor to the everyday judicial events in the Nazi state. This was the first description of the constitutional and legal theory of the Nazi state based on systematic criteria, showing how they were applied in the domains of public law (state and administrative law), penal law, civil law in administrative practice, and the administration of justice. A further element that contributed to the ready acceptance of the book was its overview of the conditions in the occupied Polish territories (Annexed Eastern Territories and General Government) in each of the fields with which it dealt, illustrating how anti-Semitic legislative and administrative practice served as a model for the application of a racist policy against Eastern European populations in occupied territories.

The profound changes that have taken place in Germany since reunification in 1990 and since the collapse of the former Eastern bloc have set the stage for a new era of comparative law. Such studies should deal with totalitarian-authoritarian regimes and examine the function and procedures of state apparatus. It is the intention of the present new edition of the book, which has been out of print since 1991, to make a contribution in this direction. At the same time it will be valuable in helping to recognize in good time the dangers of authoritarian or totalitarian social systems, which the global threats represented by environmental disasters, national conflicts, and overpopulation make all too easy to forget. The historical dimension and the lessons of 1945 must be preserved for the future. The Koblenz Federal Archives and their president, Professor Dr. Friedrich P. Kahlenberg, deserve special thanks for having made this work available to the public once again.

Although a wealth of detailed documentation and general works have appeared since 1981 (see the addendum to the bibliography),** these do not include a comparable presentation of the overall system of the Nazi state. The main theses here remain uncontested and are almost fully substantiated by specific studies; indeed they should be emphasized even more strongly in many respects. The bibliography is up to date as of 1992 and includes all published works on the law, administration, and judicial practice of the Nazi state. In addition to the titles of monographs and general compilations, it cites individual articles in such compilations, for although they often are not recorded in library bibliographies, it is these in particular that document the scientific advances in the individual domains.

As seen in the bibliography, the main emphasis has been placed on the fields of constitutional law, administrative (police) law, penal law, civil law, and labor law. Related subjects such as juvenile law are dealt with in order to complete the different fields of law. Special fields such as military jurisdiction, which, although related to matters of justice, constitute an independent entity in themselves, have not been included.

Professor Dr. Diemut Majer
Karlsruhe, January 1993

*In this edition titled "Additions to the Bibliography (1993)"—Publisher.

Foreword to the First German Edition (1981)

Since its establishment in 1952, the German Federal Archives has assisted in atoning for National Socialist injustices and, where possible, has helped to make amends. It has done this by providing archival material and other information to courts, state's attorneys, and authorities charged with paying reparations. With the present study by a jurist, it would now like to contribute to the scholarly examination of this system of injustice, its methods, laws, and institutions.

The transformation of National Socialist racial ideology into practical politics, administration, and law has, to be sure, received abundant attention in the realms of journalism, judicial rulings, and contemporary history; yet until now there has been no work taking into account all aspects in a systematic and critical fashion and based on a broad array of sources. The discrimination against the so-called non-Germans (*Fremdvölkische*) in the Third Reich, up to and including their physical annihilation, took place, the author demonstrates, not by means of formal abrogation and substitution of the existing legal and administrative order or by arbitrary and haphazard introduction of a new set of special laws. Rather, it proceeded above all on the basis of a massive and thoroughgoing reinterpretation of traditional norms and their ensuing employment under the banner of ideological irrationality. National Socialist theory and practice was in its very approach fundamentally different from the laws concerning minorities and foreigners found in democratic systems of government. The present work documents in detail the self-contradictory and highly complex development of this system, using as its models the two groups most grievously afflicted by all forms of discriminatory treatment, Jews and Poles.

In addition to the documents available in the Federal Archives and in the Institute for Contemporary History—documents that have hitherto principally defined the discussion of these topics, Dr. Majer was able for the first time to draw upon the documentation gathered by the Central Office of the Administration of Justice of the *Länder,* located in Ludwigsburg. But most important were the relevant records and documents of the Polish Main Commission for the Investigation of Nazi Crimes, in Warsaw, and its district offices in Kraków and Posen, as well as the records and documents of the Institute for Western Studies, in Posen, and, last but not least, the records of German provenance in the State Archive in Posen. It is a testimony to the good and trusting relations between the German and the Polish archives that here for the first time sources from both Germany and Poland were made available for evaluation in this manner. The records of each have for years been open to researchers from both nations, and microfilms of archival material have been exchanged for some time now, to their mutual benefit.

Only the careful exposition and interpretation of a large number of sources such as we find in this work can refute the assertion, made repeatedly in the recent past, that many research findings in contemporary German history are the results of politically tendentious investigations lacking in methodological rigor and therefore unreliable.

Professor Dr. Hans Booms
President of the German Federal Archives
Koblenz, August 1980

Preface to the First German Edition (1981)

The present study attempts to contribute to the clarification of certain problems of significance to the position of law and administration under the National Socialist system of government. Reduced to a simple formula, it examines the question of how far the legal thought of the time, the structure of the traditional administration, and its bureaucratic elite fostered the development of power of, and lent stability to, the new political system.

The source material was generously made accessible to me by German and Polish institutions, in the form of files, archival material, and printed matter located in the Zentrale Stelle, Ludwigsburg; the Bundesarchiv, Koblenz; the Institut für Zeitgeschichte, Munich; the Instytut Zachodni, Posen; the Główna Komisja Badania Zbrodni Hitlerowskich w Polsce, Warsaw, in its Regional Commissions in Kraków and Posen; and the libraries of the Universities of Warsaw and Posen. By contrast, my application to inspect the material of the Reichsministerium des Innern in the Zentrales Staatsarchiv in Potsdam was denied by the authorities of the former German Democratic Republic (GDR). I have also evaluated previously published contemporary historical literature, the proclamations of the Reich authorities and Party offices in their respective official publications, and the relevant articles and judicial rulings in the standard law journals from 1933 to 1945. Finally, speeches and other statements by leading National Socialists have also been taken into account.

Two peculiarities also deserve mention. They concern the question of whether statements by leading National Socialists and published sources from the period between 1933 and 1945 are capable of providing an accurate picture of contemporary circumstances. This study shows that, contrary to what has occasionally been asserted,[1] these can by no means be viewed as empty and propagandistic clichés with no basis in reality; rather, they reveal, even where their demands are most radical, methods and modes of thought that were later put into practice with a logical consistency that could not initially have been surmised. A further objection concerns the question whether the published judicial rulings and scholarly statements can indeed reflect the juridical reality of the time, since the rules of press censorship prevented the publication of anything that might have been disagreeable to the regime. This may be countered by the relative frequency with which professional journals published opinions that were later subjected to harsh criticism by National Socialist authors. The same is true of the decisions discussed in the instructions to presiding judges (*Richterbriefe*) issued by the Reich Ministry of Justice; they were culled from all fields of law, so by considering them, a rather realistic picture of legal practice can indeed be pieced together. What is more, those decisions and scholarly statements that found the approval of the regime were themselves also part of judicial reality; indeed, under the totalitarian Führer state they must be given increased weight, since one must assume that anything that escaped censorship appeared "on official orders" or "with official approval," or on orders or with the approval of the professional legal organizations of the National Socialist German Workers' Party (NSDAP) and was—particularly as regards publications from the ranks of the ministerial bureaucracy—considered the officially prescribed policy and phraseology to which judicial decisions were expected to adhere. That the rulings and articles published in the literature are relatively representative, that they are both the reflection of and the model for the prevailing legal practice, is shown especially clearly by the comprehensive guidelines set forth for publications in the major professional journals *Deutsches Recht, Deutsche Justiz,* and *Juristische Wochenschrift.*[2] Even if one has recourse chiefly to the official publications, therefore, it is still possible in this way to correct the frequently quite stereotyped image of judicial practice under National Socialism by means of numerous individual "snapshots."[3]

The method followed by the present study had to be adapted to the peculiarities of the subject. It consisted, to reduce it to a simple formula, of considering and examining the accessible materials under the theoretical parameters introduced as premises at the outset. In view of the abundance of available sources, the materials have been classified according to special subjects. The emphasis is on the fields of internal administration and the judiciary.

Various formal aspects of the study remain to be underscored. The first pertains to language. Any work that concerns itself with totalitarian phenomena must confront the question of what terminology it ought to employ. If one utilizes exclusively today's nomenclature (oriented toward constitutional standards), it is possible that such phenomena might as a result be inadequately illuminated. For this reason the other route was chosen, namely, to describe the National Socialist regime using its own language,[4] which reveals a distinctive composite of different linguistic levels. To an extent, the years following 1933 saw a transition to the language of totalitarianism, one apparent most plainly in the terminology of racial policy;[5] for the most part, however, the legal nomenclature of the time-honored administration was retained. As a result the National Socialist state employed a kind of hybrid language compounded of both totalitarian and constitutional elements.

A comment is in order about the characterization of those responsible for the various legal policy guidelines. Frequent mention is made of the will of the political leadership. This is to be understood, according to specific context, as the declarations of intent by the chiefs of the ministries as well as of the Party and police leadership, since it was they who set forth and developed the relevant directives. Hitler's will, by contrast, is mentioned infrequently, since, as will be demonstrated, he had absolutely no interest in questions of law and administration and therefore expressed himself on such matters only rarely and then merely in passing.

In the course of dealing with such a complex set of questions, I had to disregard many historical and judicial topics of importance to an understanding of legal practice in the National Socialist state. However, to facilitate the reader's orientation in less well-known sets of problems, the sections dealing with the Annexed Eastern Territories and the General Government are each prefaced by a discussion summarizing the problems of National Socialist (administrative) policy.

This study was concluded in 1975.[6] I would like to take this opportunity to express my sincere thanks to all those who advanced it in word and deed. I owe particular thanks to the director of the Zentrale Stelle der Landesjustizverwaltungen in Ludwigsburg, Dr. A. Rückerl, and his colleagues; the director of the Institut für Zeitgeschichte in Munich, Prof. M. Broszat; and Mssrs. Dr. H. Boberach and Dr. K. Oldenhage of the Bundesarchiv in Koblenz. My researches in Poland were facilitated by the Instytut Zachodni, in Posen, more particularly by the late Dr. J. Rachocki, who allowed me to consult the files of administrative offices in the Annexed Eastern Territories. The director of the Główna Komisja Badania Zbrodni Hitlerowskich w Polsce, in Warsaw, Prof. Dr. Czesław Pilichowski, was kind enough to permit me access to pertinent materials from the files of the administration of the General Government.

Further, I would like to thank many individuals, who unfortunately cannot all be mentioned here, for their information, suggestions, and criticism. Particularly important in this regard were Federal Constitutional Judges Prof. Dr. W.

Geiger and M. Hirsch, Mssrs. Prof. Dr. A. Kamiński, State Prosecutor Lehmann, Prof. Dr. Cz. Madajczyk, Prof. Dr. A. Rajkiewicz, Presiding Judge at the Court of Appeals Dr. Th. Rasehorn, and Dr. E. Serwański. Great thanks, moreover, are due to the Rector of the University of Posen, Mr. Prof. Dr. Cz. Łuczak, as well as Mssrs. Dr. St. Nawrocki, Prof. Dr. R. Mußgnug, Prof. R. Löwenthal, and Prof. Dr. G. Kotowski, all of whom advanced the work in numerous ways. For their long and unstinting labor I am quite indebted to my mother, Mrs. Maria Majer, as well as Mrs. E. Görlich and Mr. H. Freckmann.

Diemut Majer

Karlsruhe, July 1980

Abbreviations

AcP	*Archiv für civilistische Praxis*
AG	Amtsgericht
	(district court)
AöR	*Archiv für öffentliches Recht*
ARS	Arbeitsrechtliche Sammlung
	(Collection of Court Decisions in Labor Law)
Art.	Artikel
	(article)
A.T.	Allgemeiner Teil
	(general part)
AuslPolVO	Ausländerpolizeiverordnung
	(Police Decree on Foreigners)
AV	Allgemeinverfügung
	(general decree)
AZ	Aktenzeichen
	(reference)
BA	Bundesarchiv, Koblenz
	(Federal Archive, Koblenz)
BadVGH	Badischer Verwaltungsgerichtshof
	(Supreme Administrative Court of Baden)
BBG	Berufsbeamtengesetz
	(Professional Civil Service Code)
Bd.	Band
	(volume)
BdO	Befehlshaber der Ordnungspolizei

	(commander of the Order Police)
BdS	Befehlshaber der Sicherheitspolizei und des Sicherheitsdienstes (SD) (commander of the Security Police and the Security Service)
BGB	Bürgerliches Gesetzbuch (Civil Code)
BGH	Bundesgerichtshof (Federal Supreme Court)
BGHSt	*Bundesgerichtshof Entscheidungen in Strafsachen*
BGHZ	*Bundesgerichtshof Entscheidungen in Zivilsachen*
BNSDJ	Bund Nationalsozialistischer Deutscher Juristen (League of National Socialist German Jurists)
BVerfGE	Entscheidungen des Bundesverfassungsgerichts (Amtliche Sammlung) (Decisions of the Federal Constitutional Court) (official compilation)
CdZ	Chef der Zivilverwaltung (head of civil administration)
DAF	Deutsche Arbeitsfront (German Labor Front)
DBG	German Civil Service Code
DGO	Deutsche Gemeindeordnung (German Municipal Law)
DJ	*Deutsche Justiz*
DJZ	*Deutsche Juristenzeitung*
Doc. Occ.	*Documenta Occupationis*
Dok	Dokument(e) (document[s])
DÖV	*Die Öffentliche Verwaltung*
DR	*Deutsches Recht*
DRG	Deutsches Richtergesetz (German Judicial Code)
Dt. Rechtswiss.	*Deutsche Rechtswissenschaft*
DRiZ	*Deutsche Richterzeitung*
DVerw	*Deutsche Verwaltung*
DVP	Deutsche Volkspartei (German People's Party, a liberal party in the Weimar Republic)

DVBl.	*Deutsches Verwaltungsblatt*
DVL	Deutsche Volksliste
	(German Ethnic Classification List)
DVO	Durchführungsverordnung
	(regulation)
DZA (Potsdam)	Zentrales Staatsarchiv, Historische Abteilung I
	(earlier Deutsches Zentralarchiv), Potsdam
EGH	Ehrengerichtshof der Rechtsanwaltkammer
	(Disciplinary Court of the Lawyers' Chamber)
EGHE	Entscheidungen des Ehrengerichtshofs der
	(Reichs-) Rechtsanwaltkammer
	(Decisions of the Disciplinary Court of the Lawyers' Chamber)
GBA	Generalbevollmächtigter für den Arbeitseinsatz
	(plenipotentiary general for labor allocation)
GBV	Generalbevollmächtigter für die Reichsverwaltung
	(plenipotentiary general for the Reich administration)
GG	Generalgouvernement (Polen)
	(General Government)
GGO	Combined Rules of Procedure for the Reich Ministries
GS	*Gesetzessammlung*
GStA	Generalstaatsanwalt
	(chief public prosecutor)
Gestapo	Geheime Staatspolizei
	(Secret State Police)
GVG	Gerichtsverfassungsgesetz
	(Judicature Law)
GWU	*Geschichte in Wissenschaft und Unterricht*
HGB	Commercial Code
HJ	Hitler Jugend
	(Hitler Youth)
HK	Hauptkommission zur Verfolgung von NS-Verbrechen in
	Polen, Warschau
	(Main Commission for the Investigation of Nazi Crimes in
	Poland, Warsaw)
HLKO	Haager Landkriegsordnung
	(Hague Convention on the Rules of Land Warfare)
HRR	*Höchstrichterliche Rechtsprechung*
	(Decisions of the Supreme Courts)

Hrsg.	Herausgeber
	(editor)
HSSPF	Höherer SS-und Polizeiführer
	(higher SS and police leader)
HTO	Haupttreuhandstelle Ost
	(Main Trustee Office East)
IfdT	*Informationen für die Truppe*
IfZ	Institut für Zeitgeschichte, Munich
	(Institute for Contemporary History, Munich)
IMT	Internationales Militärtribunal
	(International Military Tribunal)
JAO	Juristenausbildungsordnung
	(Procedural Regulation for the Education of Jurists)
JuS	*Juristische Schulung*
JW	*Juristische Wochenschrift*
KdO	Kommandeur der Ordnungspolizei
	(commander of the Order Police)
KdS	Kommandeur der Sicherheitspolizei und des SD
	(commander of the Security Police and the Security Service)
KG	Kammergericht Berlin
	(Supreme Court Berlin)
KJ	*Kritische Justiz*
KPD	Kommunistische Partei Deutschlands
	(German Communist Party)
Kripo	Kriminalpolizei
	(Criminal Police)
LAG	Landesarbeitsgericht
	(State Labor Court of Appeals)
LG	Landgericht
	(State Court of Appeals)
MDR	*Monatsschrift für Deutsches Recht*
MhAP	*Monatshefte für Auswärtige Politik*
MinbliV	*Ministerialblatt für die Preußische Innere Verwaltung* (bis 1936)
	Ministerialblatt des Reichs-und Preußischen Ministerium des Innern (1936–1941);
	Reichsministerialblatt der inneren Verwaltung (ab 1941)
Min.Rat	Ministerialrat
	(ministerial councilor)

NF	Neue Folge	
	(new series)	
NJW	*Neue Juristische Wochenschrift*	
NS	Nationalsozialismus	
	(National Socialism, also Nazism)	
NSBDT	Nationalsozialistischer Bund Deutscher Techniker	
	(National Socialist League of German Engineers)	
NSDAP	Nationalsozialistische Deutsche Arbeiterpartei	
	(National Socialist German Workers' Party)	
NSD-Ärzteb	Nationalsozialistischer Deutscher Ärztebund	
	(National Socialist German Physicians' League)	
NSD-Dozentenb	Nationalsozialistischer Deutscher Dozentenbund	
	(National Socialist German University Lecturers' League)	
NSDStB	Nationalsozialistischer Deutscher Studentenbund	
	(National Socialist German's Students' League)	
NSFK	Nationalsozialistisches Fliegerkorps	
	(National Socialist Flyers' Corps)	
NSKK	Nationalsozialistisches Kraftfahrerkorps	
	(National Socialist Motor Corps)	
NSKOV	Nationalsozialistische Kriegsopferversorgung	
	(National Socialist Support for War Victims)	
NSLB	Nationalsozialistischer Lehrerbund	
	(National Socialist Teachers' Organization)	
NSRB	Nationalsozialistischer Rechtswahrerbund	
	(National Socialistic Jurists' League)	
NSV	Nationalsozialistische Volkswohlfahrt	
	(National Socialist Welfare Organization)	
Nuremberg doc.	A series of documents of the International Military Tribunal and of the U.S. military courts in Nuremberg	
ObRA	Oberreichsanwalt	
	(state attorney general attached to the Supreme Court)	
OKH	Oberkommando des Heeres	
	(army high command)	
OKW	Oberkommando der Wehrmacht	
	(armed forces high command)	
OLG	Oberlandesgericht	
	(State Superior Court)	
Orpo	Ordnungspolizei	
	(Order Police)	

ORR   Oberregierungsrat
                (senior government councilor)
Ostdok.   Ostdokumentation
                (East Documents [reports of former officials of the General
                Government after 1945])
OVG   Preußisches Oberverwaltungsgericht
                (Prussian Administrative Supreme Court)
OVGE   Preußisches Oberverwaltungsgericht
                (Amtliche Entscheidungssammlung)
                (Official Compilation of the Decisions of the Prussian
                Administrative Supreme Court)
pr.   preußisch (e/r/s)
                (Prussian)
Präs.   Präsident
                (president)
PrGS   Preußische Gesetzessammlung
                (Compilation of Prussian Law)
PVG   Polizeiverwaltungsgesetz
                (Law of Police Administration)
PVS   *Politische Vierteljahresschrift*
RAG/RArbG   Reichsarbeitsgericht
                ([Reich] Supreme Labor Court)
RDB   Reichsverband Deutscher Beamter
                (Reich Association of German Civil Servants)
Rderlaß   Runderlaß
                ([circular] decree)
RDHE   Entscheidungen des Reichsdienststrafhofs (Amtliche
                Sammlung)
Reger   Entscheidungen der Gerichte und Verwaltungsbehörden aus
                dem Rechtsgebiete der inneren Verwaltung (1881 to 1943–44)
                (Decisions of the Courts and Authorities from the Law
                Branch of the Interior Administration [1881 to 1943–44])
RFHE   Entscheidungen des Reichsfinanzhofs
                (Amtliche Sammlung)
                (Decisions of the Reich Finance Court [Official Compilation])
RFSS   Reichsführer-SS
RFSS   Reichsführer-SS und Chef der deutschen Polizei im Reichs-
  uChddtPol   und Preußischen Ministerium des Innern

	(Reichsführer-SS and Chief of the German Police in the Reich Ministry of the Interior)
RG	Reichsgericht (Reich Supreme Court)
RGBl.	*Reichsgesetzblatt*
RGSt	Entscheidungen des Reichsgerichts in Strafsachen (Amtliche Sammlung) (Decisions of the Reich Supreme Court for Criminal Matters) (Official Collection)
RGZ	Entscheidungen des Reichsgerichts in Zivilsachen (Amtliche Sammlung) (Decisions of the Reich Supreme Court for Civil Matters/ Cares) (Official Compilation)
RKF=RKFDV	Reichskommissar für die Festigung deutschen Volkstums (Reich Commissioner for the Strengthening of German Nationhood)
RLB	Reichsluftschutzbund (Reich Air Defense League)
RMI	Reichs-und preußisches Ministerium des Innern/ Reichsinnenminister (Reich [and Prussian] Ministry of the Interior/Reich minister of the interior)
RMJ	Reichsjustizministerium/Reichsjustizminister (Reich Ministry of Justice/Reich minister of justice)
RMuChdRkzlei	Reichsminister und Chef der Reichskanzlei (Reich minister and chief of the Reich Chancellery)
RSHA	Reichssicherheitshauptamt (Reich Security Main Office)
RStBl.	*Reichssteuerblatt* (Reich Tax Gazette)
RuPreußMdI	Reichs- und Preußisches Ministerium des Innern (Reich and Prussian Ministry of the Interior)
RuSHA	Rasse-und Siedlungshauptamt
RuStAG	Reichs-und Staatsangehörigkeitsgesetz (Reich Nationality Law)
RV	Rundverfügung (circular letter)

xxxviii   List of Abbreviations

RVO	Reich Social Security Insurance Code
RVerwBl.	*Reichsverwaltungsblatt*
SA	Sturmabteilung
	(Storm Division, also Storm Troopers)
Schupo	Schutzpolizei
	(Municipal Police)
SD	Sicherheitsdienst
	(Security Service)
SG	Sondergericht
	(special court)
SIPO	Sicherheitspolizei
	(Security Police)
SPD	Sozialdemokratische Partei Deutschlands
	(German Social Democratic Party)
SS	Schutzstaffel
	(protective squad)
SSPF	SS-und Polizeiführer
	(SS and police leader)
StA	Staatsanwalt (schaft)
	(public prosecutor's office)
StF	Stellvertreter des Führers
	(deputy of the Führer)
StGB	Strafgesetzbuch
	(Penal Code)
StPÄG	Gesetz zur Änderung der Strafprozeßordnung
	(Law to Amend the Code of Criminal Procedure)
StPO	Strafprozeßordnung
	(Code of Criminal Procedure)
StS	Staatssekretär
	(state secretary)
TH	Technische Hochschule
	(technical university)
TOA	Tarifordnung für Angestellte
	(wage scale for employees)
UWZ	Umwandererzentralstelle
	(Central Resettlement Office)
VBl.GG	*Verordnungsblatt für das Generalgouvernement*
VGH	Verwaltungsgerichtshof
	(State Superior Administrative Court)

VGHE	Entscheidungen des Bayerischen Verwaltungsgerichtshofs, (Amtliche Sammlung) (Decisions of the Bavarian Administrative Court) (Official compilation)
VjhZ	*Vierteljahrshefte für Zeitgeschichte*
VO	Verordnung (decree)
Vorl.	vorläufig (provisional)
VVdStRL	*Veröffentlichungen der Vereinigung deutscher Staatsrechtslehrer*
WehrG	Wehrgesetz (National Defense Regulations)
WRV	Weimarer Reichsverfassung vom 19. August 1919 (Constitution of the Weimar Republic of August 19, 1919)
WVHA	Wirtschafts-und Verwaltungshauptamt der SS (Economic and Administrative Main Office)
ZAKfDtRecht	*Zeitschrift der Akademie für Deutsches Recht*
ZPO	Zivilprozeßordnung (Civil Procedure Act)
ZRP	*Zeitschrift für Rechtspolitik*
ZStW	*Zeitschrift für die gesamte Staatswissenschaft*
ZÖR	*Zeitschrift für öffentliches Recht*
ZS	Zentrale Stelle der Landesjustizverwaltungen in Ludwigsburg (Center of the State Administrations of Justice of the Länder in Ludwigsburg)
ZVR	*Zeitschrift für Völkerrecht*

Illustrations

H. H. Lammers and H. Stuckart
Execution of Polish citizens by German police

Maps are found in appendix 6.

"Non-Germans" under the Third Reich

Introduction

I. The Tense Relations between State Leadership and State Administration in the National Socialist System of Government

On August 1, 1941, in a nocturnal conversation at table in the Wolf's Lair, Hitler said of the bureaucracy:

> People are always asking me to say something in praise of the bureaucracy. I simply can't do so. Certainly, we have a decent administration, incorruptible, scrupulously precise. . . . But it is overorganized . . . ; they don't look to success, they don't know how to acknowledge specific responsibility for specific functions; rather, everything is contingent. And then the eternal clinging to positions. . . . The Wehrmacht provides the highest distinction for one who—acting against orders—salvages a situation by means of his own insight and determination. In the administration, deviating from the regulations always costs you your head. . . . That is also why they lack the courage for great responsibility.[1]

Later, Hitler expressed in even plainer terms his antipathy toward the administration, the judiciary that supported it,[2] and particularly the central ministerial bureaucracy. The judiciary, he said, should not be permitted to set too many rules, and the ministerial bureaucracy even fewer: "It was necessarily seldom that the Berlin ministries happened to hit upon the right thing in deciding individual cases . . . the men . . . in a ministry . . . were lacking any broadmindedness . . . [their] life element is thus their petty bureaucrat's egoism."[3] For him, therefore, political leadership and the administration were not only to be kept separate; they were necessarily antagonists. The danger was when the administration simultaneously wanted to be the state leadership. That initiated a rivalry "which had already caused the downfall of a whole series of formidable states."[4]

This addresses the tense relationship between state leadership and state administration, between politics and the Civil Service, one that is as old as states themselves. On the one hand, the administration is the instrument of the political leadership, having at its disposal the most effective means of carrying out the latter's will. On the other hand, if the administration does not accept the aims of the political leadership, a discrepancy may arise between political intent and administrative practice. The control of the administration thus becomes an existential question for any political system, since it is the natural opponent of any change; if such control is insufficient, the relationship is reversed, in that the administration forces its will upon the leadership, becoming the dominant factor within the state. In the history of Russia or of other centralist states (France, Spain), the special position of the bureaucracy as a social class with its own ideology is particularly evident. The struggle between political impetus and obstinate countermechanisms almost always ends in favor of the administration. Ultimately, any political system must adapt itself to the pace and stubbornness of its bureaucracy.[5]

This tense relationship becomes most evident in states with extreme or revolutionary aims, since, unless they are willing to abandon those aims, they are dependent for their very existence upon the quickest possible realization of their objectives by the administration. One could cite the example of the Soviet Union and the states it dominated: its revolutionary aims were crippled, indeed even brought to a standstill, by a lumbering and overly centralized administration;[6] however, developments there have not yet been concluded.[7] Since 1990, after the collapse of the Soviet Union, one can see that Russia and its former republics are in a state of transition between totalitarian/authoritarian and democratic structures.

One of the best examples of the antagonism between political aims and the judicial-administrative branch is offered by the National Socialist state.[8] On the basis of its development, we shall examine whether or not, and in what fashion, the bureaucracy put into practice the aims of the leadership.

II. Law and Administration as Partly Autonomous Powers in the National Socialist System of Government

1. Persistence and Continuity

Although National Socialism has been thoroughly analyzed, both as an overall phenomenon and as it relates to particular fields, there are still no comprehensive studies of the legal structure of the National Socialist regime or of the function of law and administration in the Third Reich. To be sure, the field of law and state administration has also been treated in the older literature, but merely as one among many that were suppressed or neutralized by National Socialist tyranny.[1] In recent years, now that well-founded conclusions are available regarding the National Socialist regime as a whole, and the significance of the administrative bureaucracy as an independent element within the Nazi system has gained an increasing measure of recognition, diverse studies on various aspects of the administration (Civil Service, local government, judiciary, police) and their positions within the Nazi state have begun to appear.[2] The major focus of these studies has been the power struggles between revolutionary forces (Party, police) and the traditional administration and judiciary, the resulting jurisdictional confusion, and the gradual overshadowing and corruption of the state organization by a multiplicity of extralegislative, state, and semistate offices derived solely from the power of the Führer.

In contrast, the evaluation of legal and administrative praxis from a system-immanent point of view, that is, on the basis of the judicial-administrative system of norms, has only just begun.[3] True, we have not a few investigations concerning law and administration in the Third Reich. Among them, however, one finds only a few dogmatic studies[4] and a mere handful of isolated works that demonstrate the firm integration of the judiciary and its leading representatives in the National Socialist state.[5] The majority take the form of descriptive collections of facts and reports on legal developments or the evolution of the legal professions, or of representations of an apologetic nature, a type that, up to the eighties, continued to appear.[6] These studies are often notable for their failure to establish the systematic or structural aspects of their chosen subjects. They are strongly influenced by contemporary research; as a result, legal history appears as a virtually uninterrupted series of illegal interventions by National Socialist tyranny. The main focus of these studies, too, is the dominance of the new revolutionary powers over the legal and judicial sector, a dominance whose destructive influences, embodied in the new powers represented by Party, SS, and police, are seen as having corrupted the law and, despite numerous attempts to reverse direction, as having brought about the paralysis or the downfall of the traditional order.[7]

This, however, does not do justice to the actual circumstances. As much as the normality of everyday law seemed to recede before the exceptional phenomena of the Nazi regime, the administrative and legal systems still managed, by and large, to preserve their essential structures. One of the tasks of this study is thus to show the differing extent to which the various areas of administration and law were influenced and infiltrated by the extraordinary powers of totalitarianism.

This infiltration met with particular difficulty in those branches of the administration that possessed a long and established tradition and that had developed a strong sense of cohesiveness. There the interference of the National Socialists was essentially limited only in kind, leaving the traditional organization and structure of the administrative apparatus largely undisturbed.[8] In the postwar period, this continuity of the state administration as an institution has frequently been brought up in connection with the question of the decline of the professional Civil Service in the Third Reich.[9] Above all, the ministerial bureaucracy of the Reich authorities in Berlin constituted a relatively closed circle, which from time immemorial had been accustomed to recruiting itself from among its own and was little influenced by the new regime. Not for nothing were so many complaints constantly directed by the Nazi leadership against the central administration in Berlin, about the members of which Hitler was in doubt as to whether they ever "happened to hit upon the right thing."[10]

Faced with such opposition, the new "political accountability" desired by the National Socialist leadership, one that would blindly carry out its every whim, could not be developed to the degree intended. An administration run by "active militant National Socialists" such as that envisioned and (at least in outline) realized by the Party leadership was in fact a contradiction in terms, since it was at the same time to have operated "nonbureaucratically," that is, without fixed norms and jurisdictional restrictions. It ultimately foundered because of the respective Party functionaries themselves, who generally lacked appropriate experience and whose own ineptitude was really what rendered them incapable of establishing a new, exclusively National Socialist administration.

Thus it is impossible to maintain the thesis, set forth in earlier studies, that the bureaucracy was totally dominated by political special powers or steeped in constant power struggle or antagonism. A further contribution to the stability of the administration was the paradoxical circumstance that, although theoretically the Führer state was ruled exclusively by the will of one man and everything, from top to bottom, was planned down to the smallest detail, the administration nevertheless enjoyed greater authority than even before. To this extent one must be somewhat wary of the frequently expressed premise that the state as a whole was shattered and enslaved by the National Socialist "Führer principle." For the emphasis on the personality of the leader and on personal responsibility, in conjunction with the removal of any parliamentary or judicial checks, reflected the glory of the power of the Führer upon anyone occupying a position of authority. Moreover, the very fact that the Führer principle was tailored to fit only one leader, who could not possibly manage every agency himself, necessarily meant a certain enhancement of the powers of the bureaucratic administration. The latter's importance was even further reinforced when the legislative responsibilities invested in the Reichstag (the German parliament) were de facto eliminated and the *right to make regulations* was granted also to the Reich government;[11] owing to the introduction of the Führer principle, the latter were now "not actually the supreme heads of the administration . . . [but] their range of activity and thus also their responsibility . . . [were] greater than ever."[12] Thanks to this initial situation, striking force (*Schlagkraft*) and efficiency, the twin ideals of any authoritarian administration, became the supreme principle of all administrative action; for the individual citizen, this meant the de facto abolition of all civil liberties, since they merely "interfered with" the administrative process; and a bureaucracy whose supervision has been removed can hardly resist the temptation to expand its own discretionary freedom until it runs the risk of abusing its powers.[13] Finally, the Nazi system increasingly replaced precise casuistic definitions of civil and criminal offenses with blanket clauses, and the state took upon itself ever more politically colored obligations, so that the scope of state activity grew in purely quantitative terms as well. All these factors meant that the administrative bureaucracy became invested with a discretionary latitude that was open to any and all politicization; the content and limitations of the politicization could be arbitrarily set by itself, that is, by the heads of the administration with the aid of their power to promulgate guidelines.[14] How far this latitude went was ultimately in the hands of the apparatus, namely, the department heads.

Therefore, although in a formal sense the absolute Führer principle was firmly anchored in the laws governing the Civil Service (unconditional obedience on the part of the Civil Service) and the administration remained largely shut out from "access to the man in power,"[15] in practice this only served to strengthen the administrative apparatus; indeed, even the traditional principles of administrative action could be maintained, although in theory these principles had been annulled by the exclusive validity of the Führer decree or the will of the Führer.

One further factor deserves mention: externally, the Nazi seizure of power altered but little, either in the structure or in the legal system to which the administration and the judiciary were bound. Here, too, tradition, customary methods of legal interpretation, and the conventional set of standards managed to hold their ground.

The system of abstract terminology that had developed out of judicial positivism, the various techniques of interpretation and subsumption, the methods of civil law scholarship devised for filtering life circumstances until they could be subsumed under a few general terms, all favored the implementation of National Socialist goals to a degree that not even the new leadership could have anticipated.

Since, until then, positive legislation was equated with binding law, and (over-positive/superpositive) legal principles were either not recognized at all or not acknowledged as binding, from the judicial standpoint it was also legitimate for the National Socialist legislature to annul previous fundamental standards by means of simple law (amendment to or breach of the constitution) or, even more frequently, to retain the old standards and charge them with new meaning.[16] With this methodology, civil law scholarship was in a position to bring about a fundamental shift in the legal situation and, without altering the doctrines of legal practice, deliver the required results.[17] The dominant legal thinking, which began its triumphal march in the fields of jurisprudence and public awareness under the banner of the "concrete philosophy of order" (using C. Schmitt's phrase),[18] viewed the established legal standards as "interchangeable termino-logical husks" that could be made to absorb any and all social and political cir-cumstances and value scales[19] and thus were open to the unrestrained influx of National Socialist ideology.[20] Since this meant that, according to prevailing thought, the principles of (state) law (legal guarantees and justice) were only functional terms without fixed meaning, the National Socialist state acquired, as leading National Socialist jurists were well aware, an "unheard-of liberty" in which "to realize" "its *völkisch* aims" (W. Best's terms). The fact that this *required no changes* in the established legal system but only the setting forth of new defi-nitions of meaning and revised guidelines (which were superimposed on the preexisting system of standards and so became binding immediately), has until now not been recognized in all its implications for the discussion of the problem of continuity in the Nazi period.[21]

The adaptability of the traditional legal apparatus was, moreover, consider-ably increased by the effective way in which the regime was able to appeal to the loyalty and collaboration of traditional leadership circles (bureaucracy, judiciary, and leaders of the army and industry).[22] The result, despite the fact that the neb-ulous ideas of National Socialism were totally opposed to the deliberately clear and orderly thinking of the judiciary and the Civil Service, was the evolution of a peculiar collusion between the administration and the new revolutionary powers, in which cause and effect became confused and can now hardly be dis-tinguished.

Once the basic premises of the regime were accepted as given, therefore, the high degree of adaptiveness of the administration contributed greatly to the suc-cessful realization of Nazi aims, despite all jurisdictional competition, conflict, and antagonism between the traditional order and the new political system. Hit-ler himself, although extremely antipathetic to the bureaucracy, boasted in a private conversation that "without this . . . vast array of good collaborators . . . he [would] not have come as far in his political work as was actually the case."[23] The National Socialist program was implemented thoroughly when the administration, with its high degree of efficiency and organization, identified with this program. Consequently, the decisive conflicts between bureaucracy and the new emergency powers do not break out until near the end of the totalitarian regime; but the roots of that regime were formed in the day-to-day work of the administration.[24] For it was not until the later war years, as we shall demonstrate, that the methodical adaptiveness of the established administrative and legal systems broke down under the demands of the regime,[25] when the war and the nature of tasks such as political repression and mass annihilation operations began to demand "nonbureaucratic action."

From the administration's ambivalent position toward the requirements of the political leadership, we may draw various conclusions. The relationship between the bureaucratic administration and National Socialist claims to power in many respects shows a high degree of congruence between political aims and their fulfillment; in others, however, there is a major discrepancy between political demands and actual performance. Individuals loyal to the constitution were found side by side with those who collaborated with a system that was as a whole corrupt.[26] Thus, the relationship between the administration and political power can be summed up neither as arbitrary execution of political aims nor under the heading of total confrontation. Rather, on the one hand it represents a dense web of conformity, coordination, and collaboration, and on the other hand one can observe numerous areas and phases marked by contrary tendencies, the undermining of jurisdictions, power struggles among rivals, and finally, too, many zones in which representatives of the administration abstained or actively resisted (bureaucratic sabotage). Overall, this relationship may perhaps best be characterized as compounded of collaboration and antagonism (referred to at the time as "Nazi contact sports"),[27] of traditional order and extraordinary revolutionary phenomena, of established jurisdictions and the extralegislative powers of the Führer. The fate of law and administration in the Third Reich was shaped not only by power struggles with the new regime but also, and perhaps even more, by long periods of close cooperation.

The fundamental question, therefore, is how the traditional administrative and legal system took up and dealt, case by case, with the National Socialist claim to power, which differed from anything previously experienced in the radical nature of its aims and demands and whose implementation in practice seemed at first impossible. But the traditional administration was also capable of integrating the "impossible" into its structure and praxis,[28] either implementing it by dint of excessive zeal and conformism or preventing it by delaying or not carrying out directives (bureaucratic sabotage).

The method most suited to apprehending this process of the integration of political aims is "system-immanent," that is, a phenomenological point of view that, starting with the aims announced by the Nazi leadership, examines how their implementation was represented from within, that is, from the standpoint of the *self-conception* of the time.[29]

Such a point of view, which the German Federal Constitutional Court has also followed in its earlier decision on the law subsequent to article 131 of the Basic Law and in the so-called Gestapo decision,[30] avoids the mistake of producing a commentary according to today's constitutional standards, which are themselves plainly a product of historical experience with the Nazi state. The point of departure for this study is therefore the structure of the legal situation of the period as expressed in written law; the individual regulations that defined the legal relationship of the individual to the state and their interpretation by judiciary and administration; and legal theory, both political and constitutional, as it was then represented by jurisprudence and put into practice under contemporary constitutional conditions.

Thus, if one regards the implementation of Nazi aims according to the standards of the time, it is plain that what seemed monstrous and new about National Socialist ideas loses some of its surreal quality when translated into the language of law or rendered into administrative practice; a process of functional "alienation" and abstraction obscures the original point of departure.

What also follows from such a system-immanent point of view is that, within this historical framework, the conflicts and antagonisms among the various powers within the Nazi state are presupposed and treated as *given* variables. Therefore, for the purposes of this study, it is generally of secondary significance whether the ideas of the political leadership were carried out by the administration in the course of the normal execution of duty or only after protracted confrontations with the political powers of the time (Party, SS, and police). Of sole importance here is whether and in some cases *how* the political ideas were at last put into practice. Such conflicts will be treated in more detail only to the extent that they were of fundamental importance and resulted in revolutionary changes in the practice of law and administration.

A study of this kind is, admittedly, fraught with serious difficulties. Since Nazism did not produce a comprehensive theory, it would appear that a discussion within the scholarly framework, such as is common for "normal" theories or doctrinal edifices, is hardly possible; it is particularly difficult for the student sifting through National Socialist literature to filter out from the murky state-ments of the Nazi jurists or the quite insubstantial discussions within the field of jurisprudence anything concrete enough to be conveyed as a juridical system.

In addition, the present-day student of these issues is constantly confronted with the question of how the muddled ideology of National Socialism was so eas-ily introduced into a system of jurisprudence that was, until 1933, an advocate of liberal constitutional principles. One answer could well be found in the recogni-tion that the influence of National Socialist literature and legal thinking has to date been greatly underestimated,[31] because from a "purely academic" point of view, it has not been taken seriously. The present-day critique of this legal think-ing, however, must not lead one to overlook the fact that it once enjoyed the positive endorsement of the prevailing school of jurisprudence in Germany and that the interpretation of the law as a whole took its cue from this legal thinking. Despite its irrationality, inconsistency, and absurdities, this thinking was of ne-cessity the background before which all public statements or academic disputes took place. One must ever be cognizant that the statements on the part of Nazi jurisprudence, just as with present-day judicial theories, were propagated via academic literature and were, in addition, deemed official guidelines for legal practice.[32] It is not so much that "the" legal scholars or judges were National So-cialists but that a knowledge of National Socialist literature was the ideological framework within which all further judicial developments occurred. Nazi litera-ture, therefore, had to have been absorbed and integrated into the universities, the judiciary, and the administration; otherwise, the dogmas and judicial rulings discussed in the present work could never have come into being.

An example of such integration is the surprising unity of the prescriptive language; in rulings and essays, the same turns of phrase occur over and over again. It is the vocabulary of conservative jurists with a largely German Nation-alist mindset, drafted into service by the National Socialists and retooled for their own purposes.[33]

2. Structural Elements

In order to portray the process by which the radical demands of National Socialism were integrated into the technical functionality and rationality of the established apparatus and judicial praxis, it would seem expedient to trace the evolution of this process and the various stages by which it took its course. Tak-ing the large view, it consisted in the establishment of generalized guidelines (derived from the maxims of Nazism) for judicial and administrative procedure that were set forth in generally binding regulations (laws, decrees of the Führer) and carried out by the administration and the judiciary. These guidelines, which are discussed in extenso, must be seen as the framework, as the guiding light according to which the standards were set and the policies executed. They represent structural elements, organizational schemata, which will provide the key to an understanding of the nature and position of judiciary and bureaucratic administration under the Nazi rule.

Therefore, the initial question must be, What were the legal and administrative principles of the Nazi state? or, better, Cannot its numerous totalitarian phenomena be traced back to certain basic elements? Let me anticipate the answer here as a premise. There were essentially three principles that were held to be axiomatic for the entire field of administration as well as the judiciary: the principle of absolute rule by a leader (the Führer principle), the principle of the authority of the Party over the state, and the influence of race as the fundamental principle guiding affairs of state ("racial inequality").

These three principles, however, are nowhere presented as a unified concept, as it were in a party platform, in programmatic regulations and articles, or in statements by the Nazi leadership or its adherents. They are the results of an analysis of the pertinent norms, standards, guidelines, judicial rulings, and official pronouncements and are thus to be understood as notional summaries of the National Socialist program for the administrative and judicial sectors.[34]

The focus of the present empirical study rests on its portrayal of the way in which the principle of racial inequality was put into practice, since this principle is doubtless the most important political idea of National Socialism and therefore the most important "legal principle" in administration and law.[35] Preceding this is a discussion of all three of the above-mentioned structural elements of the judicial and administrative system; for they are inseparable from one another, representing a dense web of parallel, intersecting, and intermeshed ideas and developments, such that the principle of racial inequality can be examined only together with the other two structural elements of the Nazi state.

III. Legal and Administrative Principles in the National Socialist State

1.   The Führer Principle

a.   The Concept

At the heart of National Socialist ideology was the Führer principle. This principle, which achieved its political breakthrough on January 30, 1933, rested, as Hitler had already revealed in *Mein Kampf,* on the principle that the entire nation (*Volk*), from the family to the central institutions of the state, was to be represented by one leader in possession of unlimited power.[1] It must be remembered that the Führer principle, although not specifically a National Socialist idea (but rather an essential feature of all hierarchic structures), had never before been taken to such an extreme by any modern state. At first this process took place virtually unnoticed, since even before 1933, tribute, mingled with mystical notions (leadership as "fullest mandate," "most unlimited jurisdiction"),[2] was rendered to the traditional idea of authoritarian leadership. The National Socialists were able to make an apparently seamless connection with these traditions.

The Führer principle, already broadly disseminated in so-called folkish (*völkisch*) literature and the press even in the Weimar period, derived from romantic-conservative notions that were in turn rooted in the longing for a unifying force; its model was above all the monarchist empire (*Kaisertum*) of the Teutonic period and the Middle Ages; the dream was to return to the "estate" system of the past and to its great leader-figures. In the political and economic turmoil after 1918, the Führer idea experienced an unanticipated renascence, one that extended also into the political realm, where the problem of leadership, that is, of a leader with comprehensive authority (*Reichspräsident*), now played a significant role.[3]

Of much graver import than its political significance, however, was the extent to which the Führer principle was rooted in the intellectual and social life of the governing classes. In the vacuum of a "state robbed of its monarch,"[4] all the difficulties that might have been attributed to the Kaiserreich and the war were laid at the feet of the republic; longing for the vanished authority of the Kaiser nourished antipathy against the parliamentary system, indeed against politics in general.[5] The Führer principle of the National Socialist government, which became state doctrine after January 30, 1933, seemed at first merely the continuation and the climax of the dominant "nationalist" mainstream zeitgeist.

In reality, however, there followed a profound transformation of the traditional leadership principle, the significance of which transformation, although it was set forth time and again in countless speeches, official pronouncements, and political rallies by leading National Socialists, often went unrecognized. Simply put, this transformation consisted of an open rejection of politics and all rules and customs of state life. It was considerably simplified by two factors.

First, the new Führer principle was nowhere formally or legally secured. Neither the party platform of the National Socialist German Workers' Party (NSDAP) of 1920 nor the "basic laws" enacted after 1933 proclaimed the absolute Führer principle. The latter could at best be inferred *indirectly* from the fundamental norms of National Socialism (such as, for instance, the Enabling Act).[6]

To that extent the Nazi regime had a free hand in utilizing for its own purposes the long-standing demands of the zeitgeist for a strong leader or central power. Thus, the National Socialists adopted only the outward forms of the traditional Führer principle, the rituals of leader and followers, of mass rallies, marches, processions, flag dedications, oath-takings, and so forth; those were augmented by the cult of violence and action (stylized as the antagonism between deed and thought), which exercised a peculiar attraction at that time.[7] However, the traditional idea of leadership and authority, which had previously been informed by community-oriented and *paternalistic* elements (responsibility, duty, public service, and so forth) as well as by the principle of *legal* restrictions placed on the powers of the leader, was in effect almost completely abandoned.

The rejection of these traditional elements was further facilitated by the fact that the Führer idea in National Socialism was entirely devoid of rational foundations; it was neither a political nor a judicial concept but a structure composed of equal parts of fantasy and wishful thinking. In Nazi ideology the world presented itself as a "colorful and spellbinding historical play,"[8] in which myths and dreams took the place of realities. It was precisely from these romanticizing, apolitical elements, which were proclaimed in the idiom of a quasi-religious doctrine of redemption,[9] that the new concept of leadership derived its irresistible fascination.[10]

For however disparate the positions of the so-called right-wing parties may have been regarding National Socialism, they were that much more in agreement with the Nazis in their rejection of parliamentary democracy and their struggle for a central leadership authority. In the Weimar period, therefore, all parties to the right of the Deutsche Volkspartei already actively, unanimously, and vehemently maligned the parliamentary form of government and the parties that supported it; using familiar generalizations to characterize the so-called party-ridden state as the scapegoat for each and every political and economic difficulty, the so-called national circles suggested that there was only one way out: the return to the old "authority" of preparliamentary times. Democracy, according to this view, was synonymous with all the contemporary negative symbols (Marxism, socialism, antinationalism, etc.); in this light, the Reich government was portrayed as the very embodiment of leaderlessness and weakness, as well as being blamed for the shameful past (the Treaty of Versailles, the revolution of 1918–19). The National Socialists merely turned such sentiments deftly to their own account.[11]

Accordingly, in the Weimar Republic—a society that had been unable to accept the idea of democracy—the degree to which hopes for a return to the political order of the Kaiserreich failed was precisely the extent to which desire for a towering leader-figure grew stronger: for a mythically intensified personage (possessed of qualities like "unerring certainty" and "prophetic glance") who would appear as a rescuer in dire need,[12] thus achieving an even greater impact.

Given this longing for security and subordination to the will of a single individual, the Führer idea became the unifying force that would bring the people together ("the German people agree that they need a leader on account of their disagreements").[13] It was thus only logical that when this idea crystallized and coalesced around the figure of the Führer and Reich chancellor, all social classes should have been carried along by the "momentum of the seizure of power,"[14] even though the aversion of Hitler and his adherents to the rational working criteria of the bureaucracy, more particularly to the judiciary, and indeed to any sort of intellectual activity whatsoever was to make itself felt only too quickly.[15]

b.   The Making of an Absolute

An immediate consequence of the apolitical nature of the National Socialist Führer principle, derived as it was from the realm of mysticism, is also one of its essential features: its vague and limitless character, one that had nothing in common with traditional concepts of leadership, that is, no normative definition of rights and obligations placed upon the office of leader by means of religion, law, tradition, privileges, or the like.[16] Accordingly, there is a lack of any serious scholarly analysis of the Führer's authority from the standpoint of origin, legitimacy,[17] meaning, or scope.

Made to serve as an explanation for the origin of the leader's authority was the presumption, impossible to prove by any means, of a historical or divine "calling"[18] (that is, usurpation) or "installation" of the Führer "from above."[19]

On the question of legitimacy, Hitler, those who paved the way for him, and those who aped him, all made it unmistakably clear that the only basis and justification for the Führer's authority was power and that they strove after power for its own sake.[20] The "objective right" of the Führer to take any given action was, according to Hitler, grounded in his own "necessity"; the "personal right" of the Führer lay in his success.[21] The only conceivable form of expression to be allowed the people in the Führer state, therefore, was acclamation, not in the sense of prior assent but as ex post facto consent to decisions already reached by the leadership.[22]

Hence the legitimation of the Führer's authority lay in a blatant tautology: the authority of the Führer was justified because it existed.

Above all else, National Socialist teaching declared any legal restriction upon the authority of the Führer to be an impossibility.[23] Only at the outset was half-hearted lip service paid to the idea that legal obligations were incumbent on the Führer; this was soon abandoned, to be replaced by the maxim that the authority of the supreme leader was *comprehensive, responsible to no one,* temporally and materially *unlimited,* and the wellspring of all law.[24] The inevitable consequences of this, to be sure, were correctly inferred by only a few, since in official parlance the term *authority* was used in place of the term *absolute power of the leader,*[25] thus making it appear as if the National Socialists had adopted the traditional concept of authority along with its moral and legal delimitation.

From the absolutism of the Führer principle, furthermore, it followed not only that commands of the leader were to be unconditionally obeyed but even that the simple *will* of the Führer was to be held as a binding principle.[26]

This obviated any necessity of tying expressions of the Führer's authority to statutory forms (laws, decrees) or indeed to any legal structure whatsoever.[27] Hence the will of the Führer was adopted by academics,[28] as well as by the head of the administration (the Reich minister of the interior), as "supreme law"[29] and declared to be the supreme axiom of all legal authority. The consequence was that even merely incidental statements of the Führer, in conversations or speeches, were made out to be binding standards, a consequence that was not only discussed in an academic way[30] but (in the latter years of the Third Reich) also became part of actual political practice.[31]

c.   Effects on the Governmental Sector

If National Socialism and its Führer principle ("the will to power") succeeded, with its cast of utter irrationality and its immoderate demands ("the will to create a new humanity"),[32] in mobilizing previously unheard-of energies in the domain of politics, its effects in the realm of law and the state remained always merely *destructive* and *negative.* The vagueness and totally antilegal nature of this concept[33] meant that all theories of public law lost their meaning and that the way was paved for an incursion of the irrational and emotional into public and constitutional law. To be sure, certain scholars did attempt to derive the Führer principle of National Socialism from the history of political ideas since the French Revolution of 1789 using traditional academic concepts.[34] To a far greater extent, however, these ideas were castigated as "rational" structures that ought to be abandoned as soon as possible.[35]

The debate over constitutional law was dominated not by rational criteria but by mysticism and emotion-laden catchwords (*feeling, beholding, intuiting,* etc.), as the following survey illustrates.

aa. Outlines of the "*Völkisch* Constitution"

Put in the place of established constitutional categories was a murky haze of core principles, guidelines, blanket clauses, and vague postulates.[36] Thus, according to the new doctrine, the Führer's authority could only be grasped "intuitively," since all constitutional concepts "foundered" on this phenomenon;[37] any legal limitation was declared impossible,[38] since this would have contradicted the "breadth and depth" of the "Führer concept."[39] Just as the outward splendor and purposefulness of National Socialist policies resonated with the general yearning for unity, discipline, and security,[40] the new concept of the Führer met the needs of a jurisprudence that was weary of "abstract" concepts and systems and sought to orient itself to the "concrete" "values of the community."[41] The new values of the Führer constitution, therefore, remained obscure, mysterious, shrouded by the squalls of History, veiled by their appeal to "Germanic community values" such as "honor, freedom, truthfulness, fidelity, readiness for sacrifice, purity of the blood,"[42] and cloaked by indefinite catchwords (*moral renewal, new spirit,* etc.) set in place of precise definitions.[43] Yet more important than organizational and constitutional changes, it was said, was the "inward change" in the organs of administration and judicature.[44] For above all the "basic state laws"[45] newly created by National Socialism stood the "unwritten constitution" of the "living order of the people's community (*Volksgemein-schaft*),"[46] the "*völkisch* constitution," which, as opposed to the "procedural" concepts of democracy, required no standardization.[47]

This "overall *völkisch* order," be it noted, is not to be understood as a system of legal concepts, since, owing to its fundamental irrationality, there could be no such thing as a dogmatics of National Socialist jurisprudence. Both academic and practicing jurists generally contented themselves with pillorying the "liberalistic principles" of the Weimar Republic,[48] holding its institutions up to ridicule, and underscoring the advantages of a Führer authority freed from "procedural" legal constraints. The result was—in conformity with the aims of the Nazi leadership[49]—no less than the categorical denial that legal and moral standards were applicable to the political realm.

The doctrine of the *völkisch* constitution did not exhaust itself in the repetition of empty blanket clauses or polemical attacks on the democratic past of the Weimar Republic; in fact it resulted in a profound redistribution in the relative importance and functions of state and law.

It was taken for granted that, in a societal order in which the Führer principle had been declared the supreme axiom of state action, the state as a legally *circumscribed* institution necessarily occupied the lowest rung in the hierarchy of the "community order."[50] According to the intentions of the Nazi leadership and their experts in jurisprudence, all that was to remain of it was the facade; its essential features—legal guarantees and the system of justice—were stripped of their constitutional meaning.[51]

Not only was the Führer's authority as such, along with its procedural and substantive unconditionality, adopted without reservation by the jurisprudence community,[52] but, with the stroke of a pen, the obvious conclusions were drawn regarding constitutional institutions as a whole. The principle of separation of powers was declared by National Socialism to have been "overcome";[53] all constitutional norms were tacitly annulled; the fundamental civic rights were mocked and pilloried as "objective features" of the bourgeois constitution and proclaimed "outdated."[54] The separation between constitution and law, between law and decree, between legal principle and administrative regulation,[55] as well as the principle of the hierarchy of standards, were all invalidated, and with them the traditional concept of the law and the principle of lawful administration were set aside.[56] The law became merely an "expression of the will of the Führer,"[57] and the obligation of the state organs to uphold the law was transformed into the duty to *smoothly carry out* the Führer's will.

Characteristic of the pseudolegality of the National Socialist system was the way in which *völkisch* constitutional doctrine retained the legal terminology of the liberal state, upon which, without any formal amendment, the content of the new Führer principle was superimposed. The decree promulgated by Reich Minister of Justice Otto Thierack when he took office on August 24, 1942, is a prime example of this seeming continuity, reflecting as it does the barely comprehensible manner in which all principles and ideas were intertwined with National Socialist thinking. It demonstrates how the Führer principle and its destructive consequences became so enmeshed in familiar aims of legal policy and in time-honored legal principles that, superficially at least, any responsible jurist could give his assent:

> The administration of justice does not mean the application of a trained understanding [to legal problems] but the ordering of life processes within the *Volk*. I do not wish to see judges whose art consists solely in the more or less sharp-witted application of the statutes on the books to the case before them. Let this be the occupation of legal scholars, from whom the *Volk* expects no judgments. That judge is best . . . whose rulings embody the sense of justice within the *Volk*. Statutory law is meant to help the judge in this process, but it must not dominate the judge to such

an extent that he thereby loses contact with the sense of justice of the *Volk*. Law is life, not the rigid form of a legal idea. The construction of law consists in the true-to-life application of the legal idea, not in the interpretation of dead letters. Real life must not be bent to shape dead letters. Anyone is at liberty to turn to me should he believe that the law forces him to reach a naive and unrealistic ruling. In such a contingency it will be my task to provide whatever law may be required.[58]

bb. The Führer Principle and State Organization

The Führer principle was, however, not merely a topic that dominated the field of public law doctrine but the basic idea behind the immediate reformation of state institutions. Failing to recognize the totalitarian claims of the Führer principle, the bureaucracy at first concluded that the principle offered an opportunity to restore the "authoritarian administration," in particular to strengthen and unify the leadership of the Reich administration under the direction of the Reich Ministry of the Interior (unity of administration).[59] However, the measures taken by the National Socialists soon put an end to such notions. To be sure, the Führer constitution did guarantee the much-invoked "unity of state leadership."[60] However, this unity referred solely to Hitler as the supreme leader of state and Party. Nothing was further from the minds of the Nazi leadership than strengthening the administration, which in their eyes never did anything but oppose any revolutionary innovations with doubts and delays;[61] consequently, it was to be atomized and as far as possible excluded from the process of political decision making. Hitler himself kept the bureaucracy at arm's length, and in so doing already weakened its influence, by setting up the Reich Chancellery as an intermediary that functioned as the coordination point and sole "information and command organ of the head of government," thus cutting off all direct contact between ministers and the Reich chancellor.[62]

A further decisive weakening of the administration was achieved through the destruction of municipal self-administration[63] as well as the coordination (*Gleichschaltung*) of the state (*Länder*) administrations and the annulment of the autonomy of all special authorities, institutions, and public corporations. At the same time, however, it should be noted that the central administration, that is, the departmental bureaucracy of the Reich ministries, in fact experienced a resurgence that was quite at odds with the intentions of the Nazi leadership. For the characteristic features of the Nazi legal system—global mandates, the disappearance of judicial controls, the creation of numerous blanket clauses with virtually unlimited scope, and the ever increasing tendency to assign politically colored tasks to the state—gave the highest Reich authorities a range of action and decision such as they had perhaps not enjoyed since the era of absolutism.[64] In their own political fiefdoms, by contrast, they were hard put to defend their positions against the intrusion of numerous new institutions of the Führer state.

These were, above all, the numerous special authorities within or parallel to the Reich administration, whose power was for the most part formulated in blanket clauses and thus was capable of expansive interpretation, in contrast to that of the respective administrative chiefs. Parallel to this, new "Führer" powers[65] were called into being, authorities that were not answerable to directives from the administration and indeed were in some cases in a position to issue instructions to it—for example, the office of the Reich Commissar for the Strengthening of German Nationhood (RKF) under Heinrich Himmler.

However, these new "Führer" powers did nothing to strengthen the administration; rather, they represented the most important means used by the Nazi leadership in its long-term attempts to undermine the administration and the bureaucracy,[66] to take away or dilute its powers, to multiply offices beyond all measure, and thus to ensure that the will of the Führer or of his chief administrator would be carried out in all cases; for within this jurisdictional chaos of official and semiofficial state agencies ("each one does or omits to do whatever he wants, since nowhere is there a strong central authority in place"),[67] in which, by the will of the Nazi leadership, the strongest agency, and thus the strongest and best forces, were supposed to prevail, there was always at least one agency to be found that would execute that will.[68] Thus it is understandable that the unlimited power of leadership under the Nazi system offers the easiest point of departure for post-1945 critiques,[69] since it was here that the break with constitutional traditions was at its plainest.

cc. The Führer Principle and the Administration of Justice

The absolute Führer principle also made grave incursions into the judicial system, although it, as an independent authority, seemed less immediately threatened by interventions on the part of the National Socialists,[70] as the following examples may serve to illustrate.

Although an (oral) agreement is said to have existed by which the rulers pledged not to violate the independence of the judiciary,[71] in the context of the Führer state this was of course nonsense. The function and organization of the justice system was fundamentally altered, and the Führer principle was introduced into the court constitution as well.[72] To be sure, the judge's material freedom from interference and his legal obligation to enforce formally enacted law (sec. 1, Judicature Code) were not formally rescinded.[73] However, the new "inner meaning" of material independence was, according to the doctrine of National Socialist legal reformers, unconstrained fervor and "legal interpretation borne by the National Socialist worldview." This meant that the responsibility of the judge to the "law" was held to endure, even though the Führer principle had brought with it the dissolution of the procedural concept of law. Law, therefore, was not identical with written legislation but rather with the expression of the declared will of the Führer. The administration of justice was no longer synonymous with interpretation of the law but was first and foremost the "search for" and "defense of" the unwritten law that was grounded in the *Volk*.[74]

It accorded well with the pseudolegal procedure by which the absolute Führer principle was to be put into effect in the judicial field that, in the early years of the Third Reich, judicial *independence* and all the principles and institutions that supported it were not simply allowed to be thrown overboard but instead had to be transformed "in the National Socialist spirit." Only in the later war years could the judicial leadership publicly announce that the term "judicial independence" was soon to vanish entirely, that judges, although not directly answerable to instructions from above, were nonetheless to be "guided" by controls imposed on the judicial system.[75] Admittedly, the "new guiding principles for the practice of law," as formulated by Carl Schmitt, were published in the professional journals as early as 1933,[76] well before the National Socialist Jurists' League (NSRB) published its own guidelines in 1936.[77] Schmitt's principles sought to harmonize the independence of the judge with the absolute Führer principle—a futile undertaking, since the Nazi jurists emphasized judicial independence even while proclaiming, in more or less veiled form, the obligation of the judge to the will of the Führer[78] ("the Führer is the supreme German judge, the German judge per se").[79]

This discrepancy between theory and practice, which runs like a recurring theme through all of National Socialist judicial policy, is particularly well illustrated by the question of the judicial *right of review* of acts of the legal system and of the administration.

To be sure, the freedom of the judge to test the validity of a legal standard and, when in doubt, not to apply it, was in principle still in effect, but in practice it had ceased to exist with the adoption of the Führer principle. Not only were Reich laws exempt from scrutiny (their examination was controversial even before 1933) but now such exemption also applied to standards of *Land* (state) law as well as decrees of the Reich government or of individual Reich ministers,[80] all of which had previously been open to judicial inquiry. This was because such norms were seen as being expressions of the will of the Führer, as "political acts" that were immune to judicial review by virtue of the "nature of the thing."[81]

Much more significant was the fact that judicial review was rejected even for acts of the *administration,* a prerogative that until then had never been contested. This struck at the core of all judicial activity. Here, too, in their usual equivocal fashion, scholars and the courts affirmed *"in principle"* the judicial examination of administrative acts while at the same time recognizing that there were numerous acts that defied judicial review. These included above all discretionary rulings, whose range of application had been significantly broadened (since in practice there were no limits set upon departmental discretion), as well as so-called political acts, since the "unity of political leadership" did not admit of any ex post facto control.[82] Although from the standpoint of *written law,* only those administrative decrees aimed at carrying out the National Socialist purges of the Civil Service (Civil Service Code)[83] and decrees of the Gestapo[84] were exempt from judicial review, as a result of the notion of "unrestricted interpretation" the practice increasingly was that *other* acts of the administration, in particular those of the (security) police, were declared to be immune to judicial review, since they were in any case political in character "by their very nature."

In so doing, the administration proceeded on the presumption of a substantive definition of what was "political." Thus the Reich minister of the interior declared all "political" acts (by the state) to be beyond the reach of the judiciary; and the decision as to when an act was political rested exclusively with the political authorities.[85] This differed from the legal practice of the Prussian Administrative Supreme Court (Oberverwaltungsgericht), which initially declared acts of the political police to be subject to judicial review, even if it did acknowledge that their discretionary latitude was "to extend as far as possible."[86] Nevertheless, it later shifted position in favor of a *formal* concept of the political, differentiating between (reviewable) acts of the regular police and (nonreviewable) acts of the special police (Gestapo).[87]

Ultimately, however, the judiciary too fell into line with the *substantive—*and thus unlimited—concept of what constituted "the political." As early as the precedent-setting ruling of March 19, 1938, the Prussian Administrative Supreme Court declared a police decree issued against a missionary to be "manifestly within the field of activity of the Gestapo" by its very "essence" and thus not subject to review, although it was promulgated by the prefect of a *Land* and not by the Gestapo.[88] In summing up a ruling of November 10, 1938, the court defined which administrative acts by the police were no longer subject to review on the basis of the law regulating the Secret State Police enacted February 10, 1936:[89] (1) any administrative act of the Gestapo, (2) any administrative act of the regular police authorities that was based on *particular* or *general* directives of the Gestapo, and (3) any administrative act that *substantively* belonged to the jurisdiction of the Gestapo.[90] The court reserved the right of review only over those administrative acts of the ordinary (general) police authorities that had no *inner* connection with the duties of the Gestapo.[91] This conferred upon the Gestapo the authority to remove from judicial control any aspect of life whatsoever, a practice that would lead to grotesque consequences.[92]

This development spelled the end of administrative jurisdiction[93] long before the administrative review process was at last formally abolished by a decree of the Führer and Reich chancellor dated September 28, 1939,[94] and replaced by an administrative appeals process, which provided for an appeal to the administrative courts only in exceptional cases. To the extent that its raison d'être was still formally recognized at all, the courts' administrative jurisdiction was no longer interpreted as being part of the *court system,* but rather as a part of the *administration.* The definition of the courts' scope of responsibility was such that administrative law (administrative courts) and administrative *discretion* were both equally obliged to carry out the will of the Führer (law); that is, they were held to be different in *degree* only, not in *kind.*[95] As tirelessly repeated in the literature, administrative jurisdiction was no longer a check on the administration, no longer an "institution for the protection of private interests," but rather a court of review considering the legality of administrative acts, not, as before, in the interests of the concerned parties but for the sake of ensuring *uniformity* of administration.[96] Thus, administrative jurisdiction, like all other legal principles, was stripped of any individual meaning and held to be a component and a "defender" of the so-called objective order of the constitution. Henceforth, therefore, there was to be no more balancing of public versus private interests in administrative court rulings—which, in the "authoritarian state," would of course always have been decided in the state's favor—unless such consideration was expressly permitted by special law; rather, the presupposition was that the state's interests always took precedence.[97] Put more succinctly, one could say that, as a rule, the courts have authority over the administration in questions of legality; in the Third Reich, however, the police authorities controlled the courts with a view toward expediency.[98]

Just as the Führer principle was aimed at transforming the practice of law into a kind of administrative activity, the policy regarding judicial personnel was fundamentally changed and judicial workers firmly locked into the National Socialist state. The call went out for a new, activist type of judge; in place of the judge who was "reserved in deed and full of scruples" came the German "champion of justice,"[99] and in place of the "professional pussyfooter," the "statutearchitect far removed from the *Volk,*" came the courageous, "dynamic" judge.[100]

These slogans too fell on fertile soil, for they corresponded almost word-for-word with aims long familiar in judicial politics. Only with difficulty could the jurists recognize that behind these catchwords was concealed the actual National Socialist call for the destruction of the judge as an independent entity. To the contrary: in the enthusiasm generated by the sense that they were setting out for new shores, they imagined that National Socialist law actually necessitated the "free judge," the freedom of such a judge being defined as the (quasiprescribed) commitment to and orientation toward National Socialist values (that is, the will of the Führer) and easily construed and legitimated with the aid of the theory of identity: the judge administered justice as the "agent of the people's community (*Volksgemeinschaft*)," whose view of justice was embodied in him as well as in the will of the Führer who promulgated the laws, thereby excluding the possibility of differences between the law and the views of the judge.

Thus, what was needed in a "free," National Socialist judge was a "strong leadership personality" who would not follow mass instincts but administer justice "from his elemental character and from his conscience, which in a true man can only be the expression of the people's conscience."[101]

In the later years of the Third Reich, however, the judge changed more and more from being the representative of the "community of the people" into a direct arm of the Führer's authority. The Führer system and its military structure were now transferred quite openly to the function of the judge; the judge was to be the "soldier of the Führer," the "Führer's agent" in the judicial domain.[102]

Indeed, overzealous judges even called for the elimination of the leading role of the Reich Ministry of Justice—saying that the judicial administration now had nothing but a "caretaker function"—and for the transfer of control of the judicial branch to the NSDAP; but these demands were rejected even by the most fanatical proponents of the new National Socialist judiciary.[103] "*Völkisch*" academics no longer viewed the judge "primarily as jurist" at all, but rather as a "member of the community"; they called for a political, a "*völkisch*" judge,[104] a judge who would be a mere "employee" and "executing organ" of the will of the Führer.[105]

Although these demands were a slap in the face to the bench as a whole and all its traditions, the National Socialist Führer principle was in fact accepted as it applied to personnel questions, since the Nazis cleverly made use of many justifiable concerns within the judicial administration. It was clearly recognized that National Socialism did not so much require a "renewal of law" as a "renewal of judges." Therefore, resorting to models from antiquity, National Socialist judicial reformers called for the renewed recognition of the "value of the personality," "common sense," and "modesty and folksiness" on the part of the judge,[106] all quite popular demands that were meant to find their fulfillment in the *ideal*

National Socialist judge ("soldierly in thought and deed," a "heroic being").[107]
Furthermore, the National Socialist judge would not only be "close to the people" but also politically drilled. Only men of a certain age and with a history of
successful Party work could become judges.[108] Thus the "Great Judicial Reform"[109] begun in 1942 by the Reich Ministry of Justice in collaboration with the
Academy of German Law was intended, first and foremost, to be a reform of the
idea of the judge and his public image, and only secondarily as an organizational
reform ("more than reform" we require "persons clear in thought and close to
the people"): "By reforming the judges to reform the law."[110]

In the later years of the Third Reich, when the judiciary was forced more
and more into the background by administration and police and even declared
completely superfluous in its previous form (formal independence) by the new
rulers, Party, police, and Security Service (SD)—or at very best considered to be
a instrument of the political leadership that could "be corrected" at any time[111]—
the Führer-dependence of the judge underwent yet another transformation: it
was now glorified with the term *immediately answerable to the Führer*. This was
a stratagem for the formal preservation of judicial independence, a way to avoid
equating judges with administrative officials. The judge was now, as it was formulated in a decree of the Reich Ministry of Justice, "liege of the Führer," acting
only in the name of the Führer and answerable to him alone,[112] so that intervention by "third parties" was in no case admissible. Making the judiciary directly
responsible to the Führer was indeed able to generate a certain amount of protection against those whose object was to abolish it altogether. However, as regards the actual position of the judge, it represented the climax of the destruction of judicial independence. For even a judiciary that was directly dependent
upon the will of the Führer remained a thorn in the side of Hitler and the Nazi
leadership, since, if we view the judiciary as an abstract entity, it reached its decisions as an institution based upon certain notions of justice (of whatever kind)
and not upon police *expediency,* and thus it contradicted, in its very *essence,* the
Führer principle's assertion of absolute authority. All corresponding National
Socialist reform plans were thus doomed to failure, since they were based upon
the Führer principle and at the same time tried somehow to preserve judicial
traditions. Just how irreconcilable the two principles were, and how deeply the
judicial administration was caught in the web of this insoluble contradiction, is
shown by the draft proposal of the Reich Ministry of Justice for a new law regulating judges dated June 15, 1944,[113] which on the one hand emphasized that the
Führer was the supreme legislator as well as the lawful magistrate in whose name
the judge administered justice and on the other hand declared that the legal order was the embodiment of the fundamental moral ideas of the people ("com-

radeship," "fidelity," etc.), which in turn were derived from National Socialism (and thus from the will of the Führer).

2.   The Principle of the Primacy of Party over State ("Politicized Administration")[1]

Section 1 of the Law to Secure the Unity of Party and State, dated December 1, 1933,[2] read: "After the victory of the National Socialist revolution, the National Socialist German Workers' Party has become the upholder of German state thinking and is indissolubly linked to the state." This consolidated the rule of the NSDAP and its Führer,[3] which had been outfitted by Hitler himself and his adherents[4] with a claim to infallibility borrowed directly from the Catholic church ("all-knowing and infallible institution"),[5] not only in the state sector but also in the entire domain of politics and philosophy (weltanschauung) as well.[6]

In practical terms, the totalitarian claims of the NSDAP, whose tight structure made it appear to be the perfect embodiment of the absolute Führer principle, climaxed in demands that the state apparatus be reduced to a mere implementing agency under the supervision of the NSDAP, which would issue the definitive orders; that there should be the closest possible integration, both in personnel and in organizational structure, between Party and state apparatus; that the Party should appoint the top leadership personnel (participation in state personnel policy) and oversee state affairs in their entirety (exertion of extralegislative influence by means of the press, propaganda, control over administrative departments or individuals, etc.).

a.   The Integration of Party and State Personnel

The close linkage between Party and state, quite imprecisely called the "unity of Party and state" in the National Socialist idiom, was put into practice in the most varied manner. The integration of personnel within the state apparatus was guaranteed after consolidation of offices made the political leadership largely identical with the administrative leadership.[7] Hitler himself, in his position as Führer of the NSDAP and Führer and Reich chancellor of the German government, best personified the principle of the identity of Party and state; this was the model for the *merging*—however imperfectly realized—of high offices of state with Party positions (and positions in the NSDAP-dominated corporative organizations)[8] from the *Länder/Reichsgau* level[9] on down to the intended, and in some cases realized, merging of the offices of *Landrat* and *Kreisleiter*.[10]

The principle of linked offices, coupled with the corresponding authority on the part of the Party leaders to issue directives to state agencies, meant, first of all, increased potential for the accomplishment of the revolutionary aims of National Socialism, since this could be done through a whole range of institutions, all of which shared a single leadership. But in the eyes of the Nazi leaders, the principle of multiple offices had still other purposes. If the hidebound administration proved unfit to carry through with radical political aims, such as the suppression of domestic opponents and policies of discrimination and annihilation in the occupied territories, the jurisdictional boundaries between state and Party authorities could, as later developments showed, be altered at any time by order of the Führer, and reliable "Old Fighters"[11] and Party formations could be brought in for such purposes. Although answerable only to Hitler, these latter were also empowered, by virtue of the institution of multiple offices, to enlist the aid of the respective state authorities.

An example of this is Hitler's declaration at the 1935 Party congress of the NSDAP that under certain conditions he would leave the solution of the Jewish question exclusively in the hands of the Party authorities. The struggle against the inner enemies of the nation, he said, should "never [be frustrated] by bureaucratic procedure"; "what the state because of its very nature is incapable of solving, will be solved by the Movement."[12] Explaining the plans of the state leadership for the Eastern Territories in a speech to the presiding judges of the high courts and chief public prosecutors on September 29, 1942, Reich Minister of Justice Thierack remarked that the East was Germany's colonial soil. This, he said, implied that "we must annihilate the peoples living there—I say this to you in all brutality—or at the least subdue them." In these Eastern Territories, he said, no courts should be established. Courts, he said, could "not destroy the peoples there"; that could only be done by "the Wehrmacht and the police."

b.   Organizational Integration of Party and State

The primacy of the NSDAP over the state found organizational expression in multiple enmeshments within the state apparatus. As the official state party,[13] the NSDAP grew, despite its status as a public corporation under state legal supervision,[14] into an uncontrollable system of multiple offices[15] modeled on state agencies, with their own budgetary allowances, jurisdictions, and sundry privileges, chief among which were the entitlement to the same protection as state institutions and the right to legal and official assistance[16] from the state. The director of the Party headquarters (the deputy of the Führer, later director of the Party Chancellery) was a member of the Reich government;[17] he was granted (de facto from the very beginning by Hitler, and after 1940 by formal act as well)

a decisive voice in all legislative questions (i.e., he held the position of a participating Reich minister), in the sense that all legislative proposals were subject to
his approval.[18] This pseudolegal situation alone indicates beyond doubt that the
"duality"[19] of Party and state, a concept derived from Hitler himself and celebrated as a "revolutionary innovation," was by no means to be understood as a
coexistence of Party and state. Rather, the NSDAP leadership had always made it
plain that the state sector was fundamentally subordinate to the Party, a principle that was unmistakably set forth[20] in the corresponding passages of the Civil
Service Code and that was tacitly or overtly accepted[21] by the judiciary (German
Supreme Court: "the *Volk*, not the state, is the decisive element") as well as by
the administration.[22]

But this also changed the purpose and function of the state itself. For Hitler
and the National Socialist leadership, dynamism and "movement," as exemplified in the Party, were everything; the state, as an expression of tradition and
constancy, nothing; occasional statements emphasizing the importance of state
continuity and the strict separation of Party and state[23] were merely tactical in
nature. According to the ideas of the Nazi leadership, the state was not an end in
itself, nor the origin of human culture, but merely a means to the evolution or
development of a "race capable of culture";[24] since this development was possible only with the aid of the Movement, the latter was avowed to be the antagonist of the state ("polarity between political movement and state bureaucracy"),[25]
one whose task it was, in a process of constant speeding up and slowing down of
the revolutionary forces opposing entrenched state power,[26] to advance the
"mission of the German people," following Hitler's ideas. The functions that the
state was to have *in the future* were, however, never clearly defined. Hitler himself made vacillating and mutually contradictory statements that depended entirely on the political occasion that gave rise to them.[27] As nearly as can be determined from his vague remarks, the Party "already bore within itself the
coming state" and, by its organization, would make available "to the state . . . in
days to come . . . the already perfected body of its own state."[28] The Party thus
became the primary element of "*völkisch* life" and the model for the structure of
the future state; in Nazi ideology, the state as presently constituted was merely
an institution to be utilized "until revoked."[29]

The image of this Party-state dualism as two opposing forces was also
adopted by post-1945 researchers, for whom it was associated with the further
question, not under discussion here, of the nature of and relationship between
regular and emergency powers.[30]

Be it noted in this regard merely that the term *dualism* is imprecise, because,
as already established, the very intentions of the Nazi leadership made dualism

between Party and state impossible and also because it was simply not implemented in practice. Important state agencies such as the SS, the police, and the judicial apparatus were closely intertwined with the Party in terms of personnel and to some extent structurally as well, a fact that Fraenkel rightly notes (in *The Dual State*). The result was an extraordinarily close connection between regular (state) power and the emergency power of the Party (despotism). The organs of the state became instruments of emergency power, whereas emergency power was integrated into the structure of the state (for example, the Nuremberg Laws). The emergency lost its exceptional character, becoming itself the rule and an integral part of the system.

It would be better to speak of graft (*Verklammerung*) in Party and state, something that is still best described by the image of the dual state put forward by Fraenkel. This personal and political enmeshment of Party and state was recognized in the Nazi period as well. E. R. Huber rightly commented that the National Socialist polity, the Third Reich, possessed an "intertwined, but double, structure . . . [consisting of] Party organization and state apparatus."[31] Both organizations, which were in fact a hopelessly confused tangle of parallel governmental, semiofficial, and Party bureaucracies—whose very confusion and intricacy had the effect of stabilizing the system and only served to strengthen the position of the supreme Führer[32]—exercised sovereign functions in practice.[33] The twofold structural organization was preserved merely for reasons of tradition and political expediency.[34]

c.   The Influence of the NSDAP on Government Personnel Policy

The destructive and corrosive influence of the principle of "politicized administration" made itself felt most of all in the area of personnel policy, which was far more vulnerable to the demands of the monopoly party than the organizational structure. The effect was particularly strong at the grassroots level (for instance in the area of municipal government).[35] From the outset, the Nazi leadership recognized the critical significance of personnel policy, which they were right in viewing as far more important than organizational reforms. After it became clear that there were not enough Party comrades to fill all leadership positions (from ministerial councillor on up),[36] the NSDAP obtained the participatory rights discussed below, which put them in a key position regarding overall personnel management.

Thus the appointment and promotion of any and all civil servants was contingent on Party approval. Legally, this mandate was backed by the Civil Service law requirement that made political allegiance an obligation and by the concept of personal "fitness" as expressed in section 26, paragraph 1, subparagraph 2, of the German Civil Service Code of 1937: the applicant was obliged to "guarantee" his willingness at any time "to stand up for the National Socialist state without reserve"[37]—a duty that the Civil Service took seriously and affirmed "at least to a considerable degree" (as was pointed out by the German Federal Constitutional Court).[38] The "least evidence" of a "non–National Socialist attitude" constituted malfeasance in office, even if the official did nothing more than to make such an attitude known "to any third party."[39] To be sure, determining personal fitness was still the responsibility of the appointing agency; however, there was now an additional necessary political certificate, the preparation of which was entrusted not to the agency itself, nor to the coordinated (gleichgeschaltet) civil servants' professional organization (the Reich Association of Civil Servants [Reichsbund der Beamten]),[40] but exclusively to the offices of the NSDAP.[41] The latter—bolstered by the right to a "hearing" to determine personal fitness in each case of hiring or promotion[42]—had sole responsibility for issuing the conclusive evaluation of the applicant.[43] According to regulations in effect, if the hiring agency did not want to be bound by the political certificate, the decision fell to the head office. In actual fact, however, neither a Civil Service appointment nor a promotion could be implemented against the vote of the monopoly party, because of the developments sketched below. The Party's rights to a hearing were significantly expanded by the fact that the NSDAP, like any totalitarian party, was not inclined to limit itself to its legally sanctioned powers. Originally, in fact, its rights pertaining to the appointment and promotion of civil servants were cloaked in the form of a negative veto power, or a statement that there were no objections to the fitness of the applicant (a "clean bill of health" [Unbedenklichkeitsbescheinigung, i.e., a certificate of nonobjection]).[44] Around 1937 the NSDAP transformed this veto power into a positive right of approval, with the justification that the need to confirm Civil Service appointments necessitated a positive evaluation (political certification).[45]

Membership in the NSDAP, naturally, played a considerable role in this process.[46] The material for such certification, which became part of the individual's permanent service record (and which represents in sum a treasure trove of contemporary terminology and rating categories for the researcher),[47] was not collected in an ad hoc fashion, from case to case, but was compiled from the beginning, and more than that: the Party offices accumulated materials on "all civil servants," "even when the appointment and promotion of a given individual was not yet[!] at issue."[48]

These usurped rights of approval provided the basis for massive political influence exerted by the monopoly party on government personnel policy; negative statements by the Party, even in the area of private law, could lead—without any written authority—to dismissal.[49]

This was true in any case of the top positions in the Reich Chancellery, the Reich ministries,[50] and the *Länder* but also of the rest of the internal administration sector, within which, as the Reich minister of the interior explained in an express letter to the Reich minister and head of the Reich Chancellery dated April 21, 1939, "the plan, from the very beginning, was to make use wherever possible of those candidates who had committed themselves to the Party even before the seizure of power."[51] Similar standards were employed in the judicial system, even if the number of judges who belonged to the NSDAP before 1933 was vanishingly small.[52] The numerous extralegal influences that the NSDAP was able to exert (arrangements with, desires of, and complaints from Party leaders and Gauleiter [the regional heads of the Party]) also played a large part, particularly in the judicial sphere[53]—notably in so-called difficult districts (such as the high courts in the districts of Cologne and Nuremberg), in which certain department heads had managed to preserve their sense of legal propriety and made either no concessions or insufficient ones, to the NSDAP.[54] From this direction also came the suggestion that a special high court be created for larger or "politically difficult" districts (*Gaue*), the head of which would need to be an "unconditionally reliable presiding judge on the high court with close ties to the Party, or else a chief public prosecutor with the same qualities."[55] However, appointments of "people with close Party affiliations" to such positions frequently failed to prove an entirely satisfactory choice, as shown, for instance, by the reports from the high court in the district of Cologne.[56]

Nevertheless, there was no wholesale replacement of personnel, if only because of the lack of applicants acceptable to the Party.[57] However, a far more important reason was that, as other studies have already established, the makeup and attitude of the (senior) Civil Service was in its overwhelming majority Protestant-conservative,[58] antiparliamentarian, authoritarian, and committed to the political right,[59] so that a large part of the staff from the Weimar period— even those in leadership positions—could for the moment be kept in place.[60] The consequence of this "metamorphosis," since the time of the Kaisers, of the attitude "of liberal dignitaries into the temperament of reserve officers,"[61] was that the Weimar Republic was inwardly rejected by the great majority of civil servants, who almost unanimously hailed the new government, since they thought they recognized in the promises of the new system (of "order," "authority," "duty," "honor," etc.) a return to the authoritarian order whose "decline" they had incessantly bemoaned in the Weimar period.

In the legally initiated transfer of power, therefore, they saw merely a shift in political leadership, not a change in the political system, since the existing laws and other legal foundations remained in force and the previous officeholders, as we have seen, largely retained their positions. Thus—according to the exclusive orientation to written law then prevailing—there was no reason to assume that any significant changes had taken place in the judicial-administrative sector itself.[62] As for the new regime's demands, programs, and desires, these were smoothly integrated into the existing legal and administrative system. Plainly illegal plans and actions on the part of the leadership (for instance, the abolition of the principle of *nulla poena sine lege*) were resolved by compromise— concessions granted in individual cases for the sake of salvaging jurisdiction as such. This, however, as will be confirmed further on, actually accomplished the opposite, ending in the forfeiture of the constitutions foundations of administration and justice. That is to say, the best possible preconditions for ideological *Gleichschaltung* were already in place in 1933.

d.   Coordination (*Gleichschaltung*) of the Reich Administration:
     The Example of the Judiciary

Examples of the domination of an administrative branch by the monopoly party without extensive changes in personnel are to be found, for instance, in the finance and economic administrations, the foreign service, and above all in the judiciary, which was the "first sovereign apparatus in the Third Reich" to carry out "the principle of the unity of Movement, people, and state in its personnel policy" (that is, transferring the professional judicial organizations to the corresponding corporative organizations of the Party, purging the personnel sector).[63] To be sure, the justice ministers of the *Länder* were replaced at the time of the Nazi seizure of power.[64] By contrast, the top-level positions in the Reich judicial administration (including the Reich minister of justice himself) show considerable continuity,[65] which was not interrupted until 1942–43 when there was a decisive changing of the guard at the head of the Reich Ministry of Justice.[66] Yet in this sector the initial lack of National Socialist leadership personnel is particularly obvious.[67]

As regards jurisdiction, too, a certain continuity was maintained, in that the presiding judge of the Reich Supreme Court, Dr. Erwin Bumke, who had held this office since 1929 and was highly regarded, remained at the head of the highest German court.[68] By contrast, a certain reshuffling at the top of the high court districts took place in 1933, inasmuch as this can be determined from existing documents.

This is in any case true of Prussia, which had been governed since 1919 (with brief interruptions) by the parties of the so-called Weimar coalition (the German Social Democratic Party [SPD], Zentrum, the Deutsche Demokratische Partei) and to which fully thirteen of the then twenty-six high court districts belonged; there, the greater part of the presiding judges on the high courts and the chief public prosecutors were eliminated.[69] Of the members of the Prussian Justice Examination Office, not one remained in office.[70] Whether decisive changes in personnel took place in 1933 in the non-Prussian *Länder* as well cannot be stated with certainty.[71] In any case, a change in officeholders can be shown to have happened only in the presiding judgeships of the high courts of Hamburg[72] and Zweibrücken, as well as in the offices of the chief public prosecutor for Hamburg and Darmstadt;[73] in all likelihood, such replacements hardly occurred in other high court districts or, if they did, then to a much lesser extent than in Prussia, since the other *Länder* had been governed before 1933 by majorities of the so-called right-wing parties. In some, such as Thüringen, Oldenburg, and Brunswick, the National Socialists already sat in the government,[74] so that presumably before 1933 NSDAP-loyal forces occupied the top positions, making any major reshuffling appear unnecessary.

Taken as a whole, then, the presumption seems justified that a significant, though not comprehensive, reshuffling of top positions in the high court districts took place in 1933; this was most likely true of judgeships to an even greater degree.[75] Profound restructuring did not occur until the power transition at the head of the Reich Ministry of Justice occurred, in 1942, when the chief positions in the high court districts were almost all occupied by jurists possessing long experience as frontline soldiers and so-called leadership characteristics ("the judge as soldier of the Führer"),[76] and numerous unpopular judges were dismissed.[77] In the remaining court hierarchy, as well, the *Gleichschaltung* of 1933 affected mainly department heads; the greater number of judges and public prosecutors remained in office.[78]

This partial retention of old personnel and partial reshuffling of leading positions meant that the judiciary was integrated relatively smoothly into the new system and was generally able to display a loyal, if not altogether approving, attitude toward the National Socialist government.

Interesting in this connection is the high degree of social homogeneity among leading judicial officials. The group was defined by a strong esprit de corps, which presumably also contributed to the largely conformist behavior of the judicial administration. Thus, the majority of presiding judges on the high courts and chief public prosecutors came from the so-called upper middle class, more precisely from academic families (see table 1).[79]

From this perspective it would seem less baffling that there were almost no

TABLE 1

Professions of the Fathers of Presiding Judges on the High Courts and Chief Public Prosecutors
(and, in Parentheses, of Their Wives' Fathers, Where Information Was Available)

Professions	Presiding Judges on the High Courts of the *Länder*	Chief Public Prosecutors
Judges, public prosecutors, and other legal professions	6 (3)	3 (5)
Civil servants (university teachers, 2; high school and other teachers, 6; officers, 1; diplomats, 1)	6 (1)	4 (–)
Technical professions (factory directors, 1; railroad engineers, 1; craftsmen [*Handwerker*], 1)	2 (1)	1 (1)
Business professions (manufacturers, 1; merchants, 7)	3 (8)	1 (1)
Liberal professions (physicians, 4; farmers, 4; journalists, 1)	5 (4)	4 (1)
Clerics	(–)	2 (–)
No information	3 (9)	(9)

known protests against the countless arbitrary measures by the Party and the police—neither against the purges of Jewish colleagues from judiciary and administration by SA terror groups in March and April 1933, nor against the murders of June 30 and July 1 and 2, 1934 (so-called Röhm Putsch), and the law promulgated in this connection, the Law on State Self-Defense (*Gesetz über Staatsnotwehr*) of July 3, 1934,[80] which declared the murders to be a matter of lawful "state self-defense"; neither against the abolition of the principle of *nulla poena sine lege* in connection with the Reichstag Fire trial, nor against the open attacks of the NSDAP on the corresponding December 23, 1933, ruling of the fourth high criminal court of the Supreme Court, which acquitted the defendant Torgler and his three Bulgarian Communist codefendants ("a plain miscarriage of justice").[81] All of this revealed the attitude toward the Hitler regime that was already characteristic of the judiciary: acceptance of, and compromise with, illegal practices in individual cases for the sake of preserving formal jurisdiction—an approach that, however, played right into the hands of National Socialism,[82] since it meant the piecemeal forfeiture of constitutional principles.

In addition, it was precisely those judges of the older "generation of jurists" not seen as being National Socialists by conviction who frequently made particularly persuasive attempts to prove their loyalty and willingness to collaborate, both by means of professions of political loyalty[83] and by administering justice in a way that managed to combine such loyalty with the traditional principles that codified the responsibility of the judge to the law (sec. 1, Judicature Code).[84]

Besides coercive measures on the part of the NSDAP and the control of positions by the Reich Ministry of Justice, deliberate internal measures were undertaken in personnel policy,[85] and massive influence was exerted by the judicial administrations of Reich and *Länder,* as well as by the professional organizations, all of them aimed, by means of ministerial decrees and appeals, at pressuring judges into joining, and more importantly actively supporting, the NSDAP.[86] The administrative boards, in contrast, either failed to adopt a clear position or else exerted pressure of their own to join the Party.[87] Such coercive measures, which accompanied the work of the courts from the beginning, became more drastic following the great "judicial crisis" of early 1942 that was triggered by Hitler's April 26, 1942, speech against the justice system in the Reichstag. The new Reich minister of justice, Thierack, openly appealed to the presiding judges on the high courts and the chief public prosecutors to name those judges who were "politically no longer supportable," without "regard for the persons concerned or their families." A secret injunction, he said, was about to be issued. No official was to be promoted who was not a member of the NSDAP. Young "high flyers" were to be encouraged; close collaboration with the Party was expected.[88] Numerous new instruments of control (instructions issued to presiding judges from the Reich Ministry of Justice [*Richterbriefe*],[89] the practice of reviewing court decisions both before and after trial, special directives, etc.)[90] replaced or supplemented previously existing measures of control, which, until that time, had been cloaked in the form of "advice" and "recommendations."

The Reich minister of justice did not shrink from targeting the very highest offices. For example, on August 27, 1943, a disciplinary action was brought against Dr. Drescher, the chief public prosecutor of Hamburg (who, in mid-August of the same year, had already been arrested in broad daylight at the initiative of the Gauleiter of Hamburg) on the grounds that he had given instructions, during the heavy aerial bombardments of Hamburg, to evacuate the prisons of that city, with the result that "felons and Communists" were able to escape. He was sentenced to four months in jail and after serving his time was retired at his own request as unfit to serve, in order to escape the certain outcome of pending disciplinary action (removal from service).[91] In early 1945, at the initiative of the Reich minister of justice, the presiding judge of the high court of Königsberg, Dr. Draeger, was sentenced to death by the People's Court (Volksgerichtshof) for cowardice and desertion and executed two days before the war's end, on the grounds that he had left the city without orders. The chief public prosecutor of Marienwerder, against whom proceedings had been initiated for the same offense, committed suicide.

Another source of the great influence of the totalitarian regime on the judiciary could well have been the fact that as a rule the agency heads themselves held high office in the Party, its subdivisions and auxiliaries, or the affiliated professional organizations,[92] and in many cases they owed their professional careers to the Party. The ties to the monopoly party NSDAP via membership or career in

TABLE 2

Party Memberships of Presiding Judges on the High Courts and Chief Public Prosecutors

	Presiding Judges on the High Courts of the *Länder*	Chief Public Prosecutors
Party Membership		
"Old fighters" (*Alte Kämpfer*) (before 1933)	8	3
Party entry in 1933	7	8
Party entry 1934–41	7	8
Nonmembership	1a	—
No information	2	1
Membership in Party organizations (*Parteigliederungen*)		
SS leaders	3	1
SA members	4 (3 SA leaders)	6 (2 SA leaders)
Funding or promoting SS members	5	5
Specific Party careers	5	7
Membership in Weimar Republic parties		
Zentrum (Catholic moderate party, part of the Weimar Coalition, 1921–28)	1 (Schwister)	—
Deutschnationale Volkspartei (DNVP) (right-wing, part of Hitler's coalition since 1933)	4	—
Deutsche Volkspartei (DVP) (right liberal party)	1	2
Deutsche Vaterlandspartei (right-wing party, till 1918; predecessor of DNVP)	2	—
German National Socialist party Eger (the NS Party in the Sudetengau after NS occupation of Czechoslovakia in March 1939)	—	1

The NSDAP had major problems with 13 of the presiding judges on the high courts and 4 of the chief public prosecutors, according to their personal files.

aThis was the presiding judge on the high court of Düsseldorf/Rheinland, Schwister, who before 1933 was a member of Zentrum, a Catholic moderate party. He was said to be one of leading heads of "Rhine Catholicism," which fought against the monopoly of the NSDAP in state and society. Schwister had many conflicts with the NSDAP and was forced to retire in 1943.

the Party are in any case particularly obvious in respect to the presiding judges on the high courts and the chief public prosecutors, especially when compared with the statistics on prior membership in one of the parties of the Weimar period (see table 2).[93]

If, in addition to these factors, one recognizes that restraint in questions of politics and fidelity to the state were traditionally regarded as the highest duties of judges and public prosecutors,[94] it seems a foreordained conclusion that, under the revolutionary circumstances of the time, this would lead to ever broader, tacitly condoned, if not, indeed, actively promoted, encroachment on the judicial sector by the totalitarian regime. The many allowances that had to be made within the judicial apparatus for colleagues and friends from student days and from the Party also contributed to making fluid, even invisible, the boundaries between traditional notions and the new thinking (which was not merely non-legal but antilegal) of the totalitarian power and to confirming its influence on matters of personal policy and thus also on the administration of justice. Therefore, the conclusion is certainly justified that, as in other branches of administration, the monopoly party NSDAP did not represent the sole dynamic force in the equation; rather, the judiciary itself, taken as a whole, acted with few exceptions as a compliant partner in carrying out the desires of the Party. On the basis of all these factors, then, the judicial system under the Nazi state, at least as regards positions of authority, presents much more the picture of an administrative branch dependent upon instructions from above than that of an independent judiciary. The political powers that be were able to infiltrate and dominate it almost without obstacle. This was the actual source of the corruption of the justice system in all areas of significance.

3. The Principle of *Völkisch* Inequality (Special Law)

    a. The National Socialist Idea of the *Volksgemeinschaft* as the Basis of *Völkisch* Inequality

If the Führer principle and the primacy of the Party were expressions of the Nazi leadership's claim to absolute power, the key terms of the Führer's authority from the point of view of the ruled are *followership (Gefolgschaft), community (Gemeinschaft),* and *national (or people's) community (Volksgemeinschaft).*[1] The Führer and his authority had sprung from the "*Volk* community," so that, in Nazi doctrine, the Führer principle and *Volksgemeinschaft* were declared to be coeval, indeed identical.[2] In adopting this doctrine of identity, National Socialism had abandoned the principle whereby every community is *represented* by a leader's authority, a principle that was the basis of all modern constitutions. National Socialist doctrine was incorrect in claiming, as justification, that National Socialism had restored the unity of *Volksgemeinschaft* and Führer, a unity it proclaimed had existed in the Germanic era. For the idea that the community was to merge itself with and be embodied in one supreme leader was, in fact, a denial of the very paramount significance given to the community (clan, *Landsgemeinde,* vassals and followers) in the Teutonic period. Furthermore, the identity of the Führer's authority with the (national) community put an end to any and all independent significance of the community; it lost its character as a legal subject or a legal personality and now merely had the task, as already mentioned, of giving its imprimatur to the will of the Führer by ex post facto acclamation. It accorded well with the obfuscatory tactics of the regime that the lost independence of the national community was tricked out and embellished with all sorts of mystical phrases. The Führer was the repository and "agent of community thinking," the "protagonist" in whom the individual rediscovered himself "in supreme perfection." The *Volksgemeinschaft* was declared to be the supreme value of all state affairs, the institution of the Führer the "unifying power" between *Volksgemein-schaft* and state organization.[3]

The link between Führer and community/followership was based not on written law but upon an indissoluble "invisible bond of fidelity."[4]

The National Socialists misused and falsified not only the concept of the unity of *Volksgemeinschaft* and Führer but also the idea of the (national) community itself. Experts in jurisprudence ceaselessly invoked so-called material or substantive community values, such as "duty," "fidelity," "honor," which were held up as essential characteristics of the *Volksgemeinschaft*. In reality, however, the concept of the National Socialist national community met neither the conditions for a true community in the traditional sense (traditional rulership) nor those for a society (rational rulership) but rather represented a union or federation (*Bund*) founded upon a charismatic rulership.[5] The basis of the National Socialist *Volksgemeinschaft* consisted rather, as will be demonstrated in detail further on, of a shallow racialist materialism. The supreme value in the doctrine of the primacy of the *Volksgemeinschaft* was race, its supreme goal the growth and expansion of the strongest race into a great state, something that was rationalized both historically and from the point of view of population policy.[6]

According to this doctrine, *community* could only consist in a community of the same race; people of different races could have no part in it. This essential feature, peculiar to Nazi ideology, can be defined as the racial principle or, more precisely, as the principle of racial or *völkisch* inequality among humans. In light of this principle, whose development is traced below, the profoundly antistate and antilegal structure of Nazi ideology becomes particularly obvious.

aa. The Racial Basis of the Term *Volksgemeinschaft*

The dominant role of the race concept in National Socialist doctrine originates with Hitler himself,[7] who during his time in Vienna absorbed the purely biologically based teachings of such radical anti-Semites as Jörg von Liebenfels, Georg Ritter von Schönerer, and Hans Lueger; these muddled notions he then combined in an abstruse mix with the politically and economically motivated anti-Semitism that had been widespread in the nations of Europe since the end of the nineteenth century.[8]

According to this doctrine, whatever race was stronger was therefore the better one, and the weaker therefore the worse; the stronger race's rule over the weaker was a necessity ordained by nature (a "basic aristocratic idea of nature").[9] The most valuable race was that of the Aryans; it alone was capable of creative labor and was therefore "called" to rule (the entire world). Thus, the essential feature of Nazi racial dogma was not the assertion of racial differences or the enumeration of unscientific racial terminology or the doctrine calling for the suppression of people of other races, but rather the *inference* drawn from this teaching: that the stronger race had the right to rule by virtue of destiny or natural law. The fact that these racial-biological doctrines, more particularly the National Socialist racial dogma, could in no way be defended scientifically and that any attempts to justify them by anthropological methods[10] were doomed to remain mired in addled racial mysticism, has already been sufficiently argued and requires no closer exposition here.[11]

Of paramount importance to this discussion is the *political effect* of this kind of racism, which transferred the Darwinian principle of the struggle for existence into the realm of the political. The effect was all the greater because the criteria applied to state affairs were now, on the one hand, supposedly measurable by *objective standards* (race) while, on the other, they were built—as was the Führer principle itself—upon irrational, logically unprovable foundations. The premise that one race—the Aryan—was superior to all others flattered the ego of the nation, precisely because it could not be proved but only believed and arbitrarily justified by means of the "eternal laws of nature," the "right of the stronger," the "heroic doctrine of the valuation of the blood . . . and the personality,"[12] the "will of the Almighty," "divine providence," "history," and so forth.[13]

Even the Nazi leaders themselves were probably aware from the outset that there was nothing to this racial theory but fabrications and insubstantial phrases.[14] Hitler himself rather early ceased to believe in his own racial ideas,[15] using them merely as a political means, as a way to obfuscate his plans for foreign domination.[16] For the seductive code word that held the German people to be "chosen" permitted National Socialism's claim to power and its actual "substance" (namely, the "dynamism of the Movement" and the "will to power" perse)[17] to be justified at any time and by any means. Already abandoned internally, the racial idea, that is, the notion of the rise of a new human type defined by "blood," continued to multiply its outward effects without interruption, unleashing—as did the Führer principle—previously unimagined destructive energies.[18]

The result was that the fundamental concepts of government and law, ideas such as, for instance, *nation* and *state,* since they were now "devoid of meaning" and "concerned merely with forms," could be broken down and replaced, Hitler said, by the "not yet politically exhausted concept of race."[19] According to this thinking, the state and its institutions had lost all independent meaning, not only in contrast to the Party but in general as well. The state had merely an instrumental purpose: to preserve the "type" (*Art*), the "*völkisch* substance" of the people,[20] a goal to which Hitler clung with stolid obduracy.[21] The judicial system operated on this same premise. In accord with Hitler's belief that the "state [was] only an organization of . . . the people" and that the people (*Volk*) alone were the "raison d'être of the state,"[22] the "democratic-bourgeois constitution" was declared to be a mere "organizational standard," not a "living order";[23] the latter could only be created in harmony with the needs of the "*Volk* community." This new order or constitution would, it followed, no longer be a set of rules by which the political game was played but the means "for the preservation and safeguarding of the *Volk* as the supreme value."[24] Consequently, the law was bound to lose its independent function as a set of regulations guiding the life of the state; Nazi legal doctrine saw in it merely a reflection, and thus held the law to be merely an *expression* of the race:[25] "Not the demons of Marxism and liberalism, but only the ethically correct, Nordic and National Socialist spirit [was] viewed as legally applicable. . . . The racial idea [was] at the core of the entire National Socialist worldview and therefore also of National Socialist legal doctrine."[26] The function of the law, it follows, was reduced to a mere means of preserving the power (of the race).[27] Accordingly, the theory and function of the law could now be determined only from a "*völkisch*-racial" point of view.

More particularly, the law of the National Socialist "*constitutional state*," which the former attorney Dr. Roland Freisler once compared to the "concentrated firepower" of a tank,[28] no longer required any kind of theological or philosophical justification. The law of the liberal state was rejected as being "exclusively formal-positivist" (that is, oriented solely to written law) in the sense of the "Paragraph State" ("The pure constitutional state . . . is the prototype of a community without honor and dignity").[29] According to the new doctrine of constitutional law, the law now in effect was that of the "substantive constitutional state," of the "state of substantive justice bound by the idea of the *Volk*."[30] Alfred Rosenberg expressed it in more popular form in 1934: "Justice and injustice do not go around saying: here we are. Justice is whatever Aryan men deem to be just."[31]

This meant nothing less than that the concept of justice was dissolved into vague circumlocutions,[32] which, as in Nazi mysticism as a whole, could neither be taught nor learned but only "found" and "inwardly beheld"—but, of course, only by those who, owing to their membership in the race, were possessed of the "correct spirit," that is, the "National Socialist spirit."[33] In place of legal guarantees and justice, which were repudiated as mere "abstract" formalisms, the doctrine now put "substantive justice pledged to the *Volk*," which from now on was to be construed and guaranteed by the "like-minded harmony of feeling and desire of all comrades under the law (*Rechtsgenossen*)."[34]

bb. The Reinterpretation of the Concept of Race as the Idea of the *Völkisch* and Its Delineation in Constitutional Theory

The political axiom of the Nazis that race was the sole foundation of the state required, of course, some camouflage and encryption of its own, since racial terminology and concepts could not well be directly employed in the fields of government and the law. However, such encoding could not be done on any serious scientific basis; for, since the racial concept itself was devoid of fixed meaning and characterized merely by muddled catchwords, there was a priori no foundation upon which scientific debate about its meaning and origin could take place. According to the express wish of the Party leadership, therefore, such debates were to be avoided altogether, in order not to endanger the "eternal truths" of the race idea and to prevent its turning "into a political encumbrance." The sole concern of National Socialist propaganda was to falsify history as "racial destiny" and to drum these articles of faith ceaselessly into the heads of the Germans.[35] Institutions whose job was to advance the race idea and the program of racial hygiene[36] were assigned the task of helping to fix the idea of Germany's "fateful" call to dominate other peoples firmly in the public consciousness.

Nonetheless, even the most radical race specialists among Party and administrative leaders were faced with the necessity of finding, at the very least, some sort of pseudoscientific or technically acceptable judicial periphrasis for the racial principle, since the introduction of the wholly irrational principles of racial ideology into juridical practice would inevitably lead to considerable difficulties. In particular, the fact that the German people "unfortunately no longer [rested] on a unified core," consisting rather of various "races,"[37] made for terminological difficulties that in turn would lead to numerous makeshift conclusions.

It was for this reason that talk of the "German race" was officially prohibited by order of the Party leadership.[38] However, in order still to define the German people as a racial community, the concept of race was given a correspondingly broad interpretation by the leading Nazi jurists,[39] and the unity of the *Volksgemeinschaft* was inferred, despite all racial differences, by declaring the various races ("Nordic, Dalo-Nordic, Dinaric, Alpine, East Baltic, Mediterranean races") to be similar to one another,[40] a scheme in which the noblest race, the Nordic, with (according to Hitler) its "master men" (*Herrenmenschen*) or "God-men" (*Gottmenschen*),[41] stood supreme. If it was at all possible, however, the concept of race was avoided altogether in administrative and legal language; one spoke instead of "equality of type," of people having the "same blood" or—in recollection of the Germanic idea of the *Blutsgemeinschaft*—of the "community of blood."[42]

In practice, however, the first term to be widely employed was of *Aryan descent;* yet from 1935 on, the expressions *German or related blood* or *German-bloodedness* were substituted, as the term *Aryan* was purely linguistic in origin and not capable of even pseudoscientific justification.[43] But these terms were just as imprecise as the terms previously used, *Aryan* and *non-Aryan,* for they either exhausted themselves in purely negative definitions (*non-Jewish, noncolored*),[44] or else they defined *German blood* as being the "blood of the various races" of which the German *Volk* was composed, as the blood of "peoples racially related" to it; but they never did define what *race* or *racially related* actually meant.[45]

In constitutional law doctrine, the key concept of the *Volk* or the *völkisch* (national or "folkish") was introduced in place of the idea of race (in contrast to Hitler, by the way, who consistently rejected the notion of the "*völkisch*" principle in favor of "racial" terminology);[46] and, unlike the Italian fascists (in whose doctrine the state was the all-important principle), this doctrine declared the *Volk* to be the supreme value in all matters of state.[47]

This reinterpretation of the idea of race under the heading of the *völkisch* or *Volkstum* (nation as defined by ethnicity) may perhaps be attributed to the facts that the racial ideas of the National Socialists were, at least initially, barely distinguishable from the *völkisch* ideas that were current before 1933 and that those ideas' terrible consequences were not recognized, not thought through to the end, or else understood merely as theoretical, abstract possibilities, not as a concrete political program. In the theory of constitutional law, in any case, this shift toward the concept of the *völkisch* resulted in the introduction of numerous elements of pre-1933 *völkisch* ideas into the racial principles of National Socialism. Only in this way can it be explained that any attempt at all was undertaken to integrate this racial principle into constitutional law.

In resurrecting the concept of the *völkisch,* the theorists harked back to its origins in the eighteenth century, attempting to create a link with the humanistic origins of the idea of nationhood (*Volkstum*), which the German Romantics (Herder, etc.) understood as the "ground that supports culture and the life of the state."[48]

This way of proceeding, however, was based on a thorough misperception of the racial ideology behind National Socialism. For one of the essential features of a community or a people in the concept of the *Volk* or of *Volkstum* as it had been understood since its origins in German Romanticism was that it was always oriented toward political characteristics, toward history, language, and culture, and never exclusively toward race in the sense of purely biological descent.

This misunderstanding of the National Socialist concept of race allowed the impression to take hold that National Socialism was the legitimate successor to the *völkisch* tradition in Germany, which had for the most part justified itself on cultural, political, and historical grounds.[49] Accordingly, the opinion affirmed in the literature was that the political concepts of the eighteenth and nineteenth centuries had been revived and—to give an example of the extent to which the theorists were capable of misunderstanding Nazi ideology—that the state was now to be restored to its "ancient glory."[50]

The result of this introduction of *völkisch* ideas into the Nazi racial concept was that the word *race* was supplanted by terms such as *type, equality of type, German blood*, and *völkisch substance*. Proponents of the new *völkisch* constitutional doctrine, whether they gave greater emphasis to the so-called vitalist element (as did writers such as Otto Koellreuter and Reinhard Höhn)[51] or to the supposed political factor within the race concept (as Carl Schmitt, Ernst R. Huber, and others did), were unanimous in reveling in the new "*völkisch* thinking."[52] Society or community became "*Volk* community," the state the embodiment of the *völkisch*. The talk now was of "*völkisch* law," the "*völkisch* constitution," and the "*völkisch* state," whose foundations were built on race ("blood") and soil.[53]

To be sure, the central concept of the *völkisch* (i.e., race) did require closer scientific distillation and elucidation in order to avoid the danger of replacing one ill-defined term (*Rasse*) with another equally vague (*the völkisch*). However, any explanation to the effect that the *völkisch* was an expression of the biological racial concept of National Socialism was—as we have seen—impossible, since this would have shut out any possibility of scientific explanation from the outset. Thus, in order to render it at all useful in theoretical debate within the theory of constitutional law, the concept of the *völkisch* (and therefore of race as well) was augmented by the introduction of political characteristics. A majority of the proponents of the so-called political constitutional theory[54] argued more or less as follows: a people made up of the same or related races was, admittedly, fundamental to the idea of the *Volk* community and the *völkisch*. This, however, ought not to lead to the presumption that the "biological element" alone was significant. Since the concept of the people in National Socialism, unlike that of liberalism, "reached down into the depths of the irrational forces of human life," other elements, such as having the same "vital consciousness," the same culture and history, were just as relevant; and in any case only due consideration of all factors could validate the (political) "unity of the people."[55] According to this doctrine, therefore, the political concept of the people was salvaged by declaring the "racially defined" people to be simultaneously a "political *Volk*," since "spirit and nature" were indivisible.[56] Not so the self-styled "vitalist" or *völkisch* faction among the constitutional theorists,[57] who openly championed the notion that the essential feature of the *völkisch* was the "organic" element, that is, "biological" racial equality, but who were unable to resolve either the question of the unifying political force within the state or the dilemma posed by the transfer of racial considerations into the judicial realm. Nevertheless, in order to come to some kind of resolution, the proponents of this school of thought concentrated more upon voluntary emotional (*emotional-voluntaristisch*) elements, attempting to describe the concept of race, which they defined as "equality of type" and as being the "vital consciousness of those of equal type," and to locate its origins in the mystical obscurity of Teutonic prehistory.[58] The nonexistent "equality of type" in the racial composition of the Germans was thus replaced with and cloaked by a putative "similarity" in the emotional sphere; its essence was said to consist of a "distinctive vital consciousness," of having the "same philosophical (*weltanschaulich*) desires."[59]

Thus, in the debate surrounding the question whether the *völkisch* (the racial principle) could best be legally codified using "political" or "vitalistic" (that is, biological) terminology, the proponents of the former school of thought attempted to put the generally accepted, if irrational, principles of Führer and race into some type of judicial system by introducing the concept of the political, thus lifting them, as it were, from the base racial level to the higher plane of constitutional legal theory. The latter school, meanwhile, attempted to develop a "*völkisch* constitutional theory" solely on the basis of the biological laws of nature. But these terminological debates, although carried on at great length, were ultimately without substance, circling as they did around nebulous fictions; they were in reality nothing but shadow play, since the race idea of National Socialism eluded any fixed definition. Such debates reveal merely that it was impossible to accept, on the one hand, irrational concepts like *race* (the *völkisch*), *equality of type* (German blood), and *related by race* (related blood) as being a priori axioms, granting them, after a fashion, the significance of natural law; and, on the other hand, to codify these same concepts into some kind of legal system. In terms of political reality, at least, these debates, which in any case had ceased almost entirely by 1938, were utterly without significance. By means of the double-dealing with which the concepts and principles of the old legal order were formally maintained, while at the same time irrational substrates such as the *völkisch* or racial principle were introduced as relevant criteria in law, and by virtue of the "generous negligence" with which violations of the principle of written law by the extralegislative power of the Führer were ignored or even encouraged,[60] constitutional law theory had become more and more entangled in insoluble contradictions, ultimately making itself supererogatory. This drying up and undermining of judicial theory becomes particularly evident when one considers that after 1940, at the latest, no serious scholarly works were published in the field of constitutional law. Those involved perhaps realized, not only in the end phase of the Nazi regime[61] but even in earlier years, what destructive consequences had resulted from their polemics against the traditional political and constitutional institutions of parliamentary democracy and from their abandonment of all constitutional principles.

b. The National Socialist Concept of *Völkisch* Equality

The difficulties involved in introducing pseudoscientific values into a legal system and the resulting pseudoscientific presentation of racial axioms became particularly plain when it came time to draw concrete conclusions from the concept of the primacy of the "*Volk* community." If "*völkisch* community" meant the community of those belonging to the same race ("persons of equal type"), then only those people could belong to it who "counted among [this] histori-cally formed blood-community of the Germans," that is, who were "of German or related blood."[62] From this it followed that only such persons enjoyed full le-gal rights, particularly as regarded any claim to equal treatment under the law. In place of civil equality, then, there was now "homogeneity of race" or ("sub-stantial") "equality of type."[63] Equality meant *völkisch* equality—this in full ac-cord with the demands of Hitler, for whom conventional equality was a "Jewish invention" and plain nonsense; in his view it was not a matter of "eliminating human inequality but, on the contrary, of intensifying it . . . and [buttressing] it behind barriers of insurmountable law," since only thus were domination (the German people as the "new master class" of the world) and development possi-ble.[64] Accordingly, *völkisch* constitutional doctrine considered the triad of Füh-rer, race, and "equality of type" the substance of the "*völkisch* constitution," and so also the essence of National Socialist equality.[65]

The relative ease with which racial axioms were integrated into constitu-tional doctrine can perhaps only be explained by the fact that racial thinking was by no means a novelty first brought forth by National Socialism. Rather, it was the continuation and extension of *völkisch*-racist currents that were already widespread in the Kaiserreich and the Weimar period, so that the racism of the National Socialists at first appeared, in the scholarly discussion as well, merely as a continuation of these traditions.

In the cultural sector, there are three currents that should be mentioned: a school of cultural philosophy built upon the works of Joseph de Gobineau and

Houston Chamberlain, which held a particular attraction for the intelligentsia; a literary-historical-philosophical school (characterized by authors such as Adolph Grimm, Moeller van den Bruck, Hans Freyer, and others), which enjoyed the broadest dissemination; and a current of natural science (represented by then very popular authors, such as Hans Kretschmer, Hans F. K. Günther, and others), which sought to classify the population of Germany according to physical-racial criteria and emphasized the importance of racial and genetic hygiene. Such racist thinking was also calamitously widespread in the political arena. The native soil of such thinking, that is, of political anti-Semitism, was particularly fecund in the right-wing parties, such as the Deutschnationale Volkspartei (DNVP), but it was also found in the Deutsche Volkspartei (DVP), in the influential *völkisch* associations (the All-German Association [Alldeutscher Verband] and the Federation of Farmers [Bund der Landwirte]), and in numerous other right-wing radical organizations.[66] Strong anti-Semitic tendencies also predominated in the youth movement and in the universities.[67]

The racist thinking of National Socialism differed significantly, however, from that expressed in the demands of the right-wing radical parties and societies, not in content but solely in the unyielding resolve with which it was put into practice.[68]

The legal form in which this thinking found its expression was the concept of *völkisch inequality*.[69] The judicial underpinnings of this concept were complex constructs designed to veil its racial content and replace it with so-called *völkisch* or political terminology. Just as the term *race* was not employed directly but rather entered the legal language indirectly via the terms *Volk community* or *the völkisch*, the term *völkisch equality* had to undergo systematic terminological transmutation before it was suitable and acceptable for use in the judicial administrative realm. Admittedly, this was also bound to have serious consequences in terms of the spirit of the law. For the principle that all citizens were equal in the eyes of the law was after all the copestone of the tradition of constitutionality as it then existed; indeed, legal scholars saw the struggle of the new "equality of type" against traditional "similarity" or "homogeny" (*Gleichartigkeit*) as the single most fundamental problem in National Socialist law.[70] However, just as only relatively few authors undertook a legal systematization of National Socialist terminology, fewer still attempted to develop a coherent theory of *völkisch* equality or *völkisch* inequality;[71] scholarly debates on the problem of equality are—with good reason—either lacking entirely or else can be found only in connection with other problems. Thus, what was meant by equality under Nazi constitutional doctrine cannot be extracted from a coherent set of teachings but must rather be pieced together from numerous scattered, individual statements. The one thing all agreed upon was that in place of the *abstract equality* (among citizens) invoked by liberalism, there was now the *concrete equality* of the "productive and faithful *Volksgenosse* (*Volk* comrade)."[72] This rejection of the standard legal construction was an expression of the idea (first developed by Schmitt and referring back to Hegel's philosophy of the state)[73] of the "concrete philosophy of distinctions," which he set against the "destruction" of liberalism.[74]

The significance of concrete *völkisch* equality, however, remained at first largely unexplained. Its features initially came into focus only in opposition to the liberalism of the Weimar period. And to be sure, opinion in scholarly publications was absolutely unanimous in its condemnation of the first German republic and its legal institutions ("formalism," "Jewish normativism," etc.). "Our sense of justice," one academic expostulated, "would be more profoundly injured by an insistence upon the *fiction* of equality, now recognized as fraudulent, than it ever could have been by an act of open, and therefore contestable, tyranny."[75] The young Turks among the Nazi jurists vied with one another in pillorying everything to do with the Weimar government, every aspect and type of order, as being "empty form" or "abstract normativism,"[76] since it was all seen as being oriented toward "abstract" equality and failed to take into account the concrete facts of "real life." Such polemics were directed above all against equality in the form of individual rights, against the concept of the free citizen without regard to origin and race, against personal equality before the law in criminal and civil cases, and against the equality of states in the law of nations.

Already much to be deplored was the "penetration," in the period before 1918, of the phrase "equality" into legislation, above all in civil law, and the ensuing "tendency toward . . . leveling thinking" that "rejected value-oriented [blood-centered, national and religious] differences"; but particularly ruinous was that the principle of equality had gained such allegiance among the legislators,[77] indeed that the idea of equality had become so prominent to begin with. This also held for the "liberal principle" of general human equality.[78] Today, so went the thinking, it is not a matter of abstract equality but of concrete differences between people in respect to ancestry, language, and so on: C. Schmitt's "philosophy of concrete distinctions"[79] was the order of the day. Under its influence, the principle of "liberalistic" equality was "fortunately now overcome," since it contradicted the naturally occurring inequalities among people.[80]

The wholesale rejection of the liberal legal system resulted simultaneously in the rejection of all rights of liberty and equality in the Nazi state. At issue now was merely whether the Weimar Constitution, with its guarantee of these rights, was already annulled with the Nazi seizure of power on January 30, 1933,[81] or not until later, at the time of the corresponding positive-law repeal (constitutional amendment).

The Reich president's Decree for the Protection of People and State dated February 28, 1933,[82] was seen above all as such an act of repeal, for although it *temporarily* suspended constitutional rights, it was generally considered the "end of subjective public rights,"[83] in addition to containing other provisions limiting constitutional rights.[84] The excuse for the proclamation of this decree was the Reichstag Fire of February 27, 1933, but in reality it was a matter of buttressing the National Socialist dictatorship for the long term. This is quite plainly evidenced by a decision of the Berlin State Appellate Court of November 1, 1933, according to which the decree deliberately instituted a state of emergency by repeal of constitutional laws, in order to permit the National Socialist state to become a reality.[85]

Disregarding the question of formal legality ("today's existing legislation has made use of the formal procedure of the Weimar Constitution . . . only for the sake of outward orderliness and peace [legality]; but it does not derive its justification therefrom"),[86] it was clear, both in theory and in practice, that constitutional rights and the constitution itself had lost their meaning in the Nazi state, whether because they were "in essence" incompatible with National Socialism; because they had lapsed at the time of the "seizure of power" and/or the decree of February 28, 1933,[87] or were considered to have been "overcome" by the "national community";[88] or because they were to be interpreted in the spirit of the "National Socialist worldview."[89] The continued validity of the Weimar Constitution as simple law was also negated in cases in which it was incompatible with the National Socialist conception of the state.[90] Breaches of and amendments to the constitution even in the absence of formal empowerment were declared to be legitimate under the most varied justifications imaginable;[91] in court rulings it was determined that the government was even permitted "to carry out reforms of constitutional law . . . by means of administrative directives and other measures of all kinds";[92] certain courts even viewed the party platform of the NSDAP as a kind of legal authority ("constitutional law") justifying breaches of the constitution and entertained the possibility of replacing the Weimar Constitution with said platform.[93] In any case, to the extent that constitutional rights were not seen as having been formally *annulled* (by the decree of February 28, 1933), the greater part of the literature accepted as a subsidiary principle (in the words of Schmitt) "the simple verdict that the Weimar Constitution is no longer in force."[94] This of course applied not merely to those constitutional rights that were expressly suspended by the decree of February 28, 1933 (personal liberty, freedom of expression, etc.), but also to those rights not expressly listed therein (for instance, the guarantee of due process and a fair trial, the principle of *nulla poena sine lege*, freedom of trade and profession, freedom of religion, and the employee's right of codetermination)[95]—up to and including the supposedly "dictatorship-proof" rights that, according to the constitution, were in no case (not even by means of Reich legislation) susceptible to amendment.[96]

Another (and most important) principle to be overturned was that of general equality, which was a right not subject to amendment or abridgement by legislative act (art. 109).[97] The "liberal ideas of equality" were now, in the common view, replaced by the "*völkisch* idea," a substitution that resulted in a fundamental shift in the relationship between *Volksgemeinschaft* (the state) and the individual. There could be no more talk of the right to equal treatment under law. Civil rights and guarantees were now replaced by the total incorporation and integration of the individual, in thought, action, and feeling, into the *Volksgemeinschaft* (national or people's community),[98] the contemporary term for which was *the total state*, in the sense of absolute "dominance over the soul."[99] And it was in that sense, too, that this concept was introduced into the administration of justice.[100]

This "integration and incorporation" of the individual into the *Volksgemeinschaft* meant not only the obligation of the former to the state (as scholarly opinion would have it) but, in essence, the destruction of the individual as a legal personality.[101] National Socialist doctrine, to be sure, did not follow National Socialist propaganda, which denied altogether the right or duty of the individual to existence,[102] or the opinion of Hitler and his côterie that the individual personality only achieved its "actual value" and development within the *Volksgemeinschaft*.[103] Yet the result was fundamentally the same when subtle juristic formulations were used to reconcile "community" and "individual," for example, by elevating the individual, as it were, onto a higher level by virtue of his membership in the community;[104] and likewise when even the theoreticians of the *total state* declared that, even within the confines of "community," the individual had to retain some scope or latitude for free development, since National Socialism set such store by the responsible (leader) personality.

As a result, therefore, the new status of the individual in the *Volksgemeinschaft* no longer had the least bit to do with any kind of *legal* status as a defense against state or government intervention. Attempts to salvage individual rights using the exception-to-the-rule mechanism in jurisprudence, that is, by the presumption that equality, though existing "in principle," was always subordinate[105] to the requirements of the *Volksgemeinschaft* (community-dependent rights of the individual), represented merely a gloss on the true situation: that individual or personal rights had become fundamentally untenable and were now, at best, interpreted (but not precisely defined) as the "privileges of the individual" (which could be suspended at any time).[106] More courageous souls than those constitutional law scholars who were still under the influence of the ethos of the liberal era openly announced the way in which the position of the individual was now to be conceived: "membership," total absorption by the *Volksgemeinschaft*, took the place of personal, subjective rights. "Organic, holistic thinking," embodied in the *Volksgemeinschaft*, "deep inner experience" rather than "empty abstraction," replaced the "unlucky star of individualism." Within this "organic thinking," the individual was by no means a nullity, as in the "leveling collective," but a "member of the community."[107]

At bottom, however, no one quite knew exactly what "the legal status of the national comrade" or "privileges within the national community"[108] were actually supposed to mean in concrete terms once equality had been destroyed as an individual right.

There were partial attempts to salvage the concept of equality by divesting it of its personal content and reformulating it as an *objective or impersonal* right, as an "essential structural element" of the constitution ("fundamental *völkisch* order").[109] This "objectification" was justified both by means of historical arguments and with an eye toward the constitutional systems of other nations where equality was not guaranteed as an individual subjective right but where the principle of equality obtained merely as an impersonal constitutional principle.[110] With the aid of this seemingly objective legal comparison and a reinterpretation of the concept of equality, there were those writing in the professional literature who propounded in all seriousness the belief that equality "as such" had not really been eliminated from the Nazi state but "merely" given a different *content*.[111] This construct, however, overlooked the fact that "objective [impersonal] equality" could exist only in a state that was pledged to its rigorous observance,[112] whereas, under the Nazi system, such an obligation on the part of the state to respect objective constitutional principles either was precisely what was denied[113] or else was recognized only in respect to any "positively constructive forces within the *Volk*."[114] Members of another school, in turn, proposed the idea that the state was committed to a "meaningfully just order of values,"[115] which, however, was an empty catchphrase, since it was possible to define said scale or order of values only from the standpoint of the primacy of the racially defined national community.

But the actual meaning of *völkisch* equality was approached, in the literature, by a different path; by way, so to speak, of its antithesis. Indeed, one could say that the new "equality" could be defined only from the point of view of its opposite, that is, from the standpoint of the common *civic duties and obligations—*

in itself sufficient proof that National Socialism was incapable of conceding any independent legal status whatsoever to the individual. Yet as soon as it came time, as in this case, to talk of integration, duties and obligations, liabilities, and thus of the repressive mechanism peculiar to National Socialism, however disguised by deliberate mystifications (such as Hitler's image of the "mystical triangle": "integration" into the "Labor Front" [*Arbeitsfront*], into the "Professional Estate" [*Berufsstand*], and into the "Party")[116]—then it suddenly became quite clear what was meant by "equality of national comrades (*Volksgenossen*)."[117] The mists of obscure terminology abruptly lifted; objective, impersonal "equality" once again became subjective, personal, focused on the individual. But the meaning and content of this new "equality" was the role of the individual as a *person subject to obligations:* his "rights" consisted of an equal distribution of burdens; and the individual was of concern solely in this regard. Now there was no more talk of rights or, if so, then as lip service only; "in the *völkisch* Reich" the fundamental obligations took precedence "over rights."[118] Taking their cue from Hitler ("equal rights can . . . never be anything more than the cheerful acceptance of equal obligations"),[119] the theoreticians of public and constitutional law talked expressly of an "all-encompassing socialism of obligations, never of rights."[120] The rights of the individual thus metamorphosed into the *right* of all *to the same obligations,*[121] which found their expression in countless legally mandated but also "voluntary" duties,[122] whose complete fulfillment was expected by the state "in reliance upon the German soul." Nonfulfillment of such "voluntary duties" was considered a violation of the common obligation to demonstrate fidelity to the Führer and could result in severe disciplinary or criminal sanctions.[123]

c.   The National Socialist Concept of *Völksch* Inequality: The Principle of Special Law

If the redefinition of *völkisch* equality in terms of constitutional and administrative theory was achieved with the utmost difficulty, how much more intractable was its necessary corollary, *völkisch* inequality, in regard to which the theorists either are almost entirely silent or else content themselves with a few vague insinuations. To be sure, it was possible to make a theoretical case that only racially equal "national comrades" enjoyed equal legal status, whereas all those of unequal or dissimilar race neither enjoyed equal rights nor were equal in the eyes of the law. Thus, for example, the administrative leadership (the head of the Reich Chancellery) openly declared that the "blood-determined" inequality among humans in all aspects of their "thought, feeling and action" resulted directly in their legal inequality ("just inequality").[124] The details of how this was to be accomplished and justified, however, no one was prepared to state with any degree of clarity. True, Hitler himself had plainly asserted that there was no such thing as equal rights for all,[125] but he provided no details as to how the concept of *völkisch* inequality should be put into practice. And the fourth, fifth, and ninth planks in the party platform of the NSDAP (equality of rights and obligations only for persons "of German blood") indicated that discrimination ("legislation regulating aliens") against people of other races (Jews and Gypsies) would generally be permitted but also failed to give more particulars. Similarly, the leading administrators barely took the trouble to look for "juristic" justifications, resorting instead to openly political arguments. Thus, according to the official commentary on the Law for the Protection of German Blood and German Honor of September 15, 1935 (the so-called Blood Protection Law [*Blutschutzgesetz*]), drafted by highly placed civil servants in the Reich Ministry of the Interior, the spirit of corruption and demoralization attributed to the Jews, their "assaults on German women," and their "presumption" were the reasons put forward for "legal segregation" (unequal treatment) of Germans and Jews.[126] Bernhard Lösener, who worked in the Department of Racial Affairs in the Reich Ministry of the Interior, spoke of the "fundamental recognition of the inequality of human races, in contrast to the smarmy liberal slogan touting the equality of anything possessing a human visage."[127] Even after the first concrete results of *völkisch* inequality became apparent, immediately after the Nazi seizure of power (purging of the Civil Service and the bar of persons of foreign race), the academic literature reveals only a few statements concerning the nature and scope of this new inequality, despite the enthusiastic acclaim with which the new state and its governmental order had been hailed.

This overwhelming silence in the literature may in part be explained by the recognition, current since the French Revolution, that the surrender of universal and general equality would necessarily lead to universal and general inequality (unabashed special law), and that this in turn could only result in violence and repression,[128] ending ultimately in despotism, as (in Rousseau's terms) the "final stage of inequality," "the blind obedience of slaves."[129] And indeed, such "blind" obedience was the supreme dictate of the Nazi system, under which all civil servants, soldiers, and other "followers" or "vassals" owed "fidelity unto death" to the Führer.

In order to bring about such a condition of universal inequality, the fetters of universal equality had to be discarded as quickly as practicable. The German people, one may read in the literature, must be rescued from their powerlessness by rejecting and overcoming democracy of the kind favored by Rousseau.[130]

Once again, this break with the constitutional concept of equality was veiled and disguised behind a kind of modified doctrine of identity. Just as the *Volksgemeinschaft* found its highest fulfillment in the supreme Führer, the place vacated by the principle of equality was to be taken up by "philosophical/ideological concurrence in the will and desires of all comrades enjoying protection of the law" (which was also embodied in the person of the Führer); in this fashion, "even the idea of inequality, so intolerable to liberalism," would lose "its terror."[131] *Völkisch* inequality thus gained general recognition as a necessary component of the prevailing legal order, dictated, as it were, by natural law.

With remarkable candor, even the highest members of the judiciary acknowledged this reduction in legal status on the grounds of racial policy. Whereas liberalism, for instance, granted civil rights even to the Jews, because it saw equality as a universal human right,[132] the German Supreme Court had already distanced itself from this view in a relatively early ruling of 1936, by in effect repudiating the idea that people of foreign race could have legal personality and indeed negating their very humanity:

> The earlier ["liberal"] idea of the legal meaning and content of the personality did not [make] any fundamental value judgments as to equality or dissimilarity of blood among the *beings with human visages*; it therefore rejected any legal classification and ranking or gradation of human beings according to racial criteria. In the National Socialist worldview, by contrast, it [was necessary] . . . to treat only those of German descent . . . as entitled to full legal status. This meant that fundamental distinctions in earlier laws pertaining to the rights of foreigners [were] revitalized, and ideas again adopted that in the past [had] recognized a distinction between persons of full legal capacity and persons *of lesser legal status*.[133]

The Reich Supreme Court here gave forthright expression to something that could be gleaned only indirectly from *völkisch* theoretical literature, namely, the actual substance of *völkisch* inequality. In general terms, it can be defined as being a status subject to different law, a *legally diminished* special position for "alien" persons. The judicial authority for this was supplied by the conception of *the political*, as developed by Schmitt and his school, according to which the constitutive feature of politics was the "philosophy" or "theory of concrete distinctions" between "friend" and "foe." This thinking, which originated in the doctrine that there existed acts of government not subject to judicial review,[134] as well as in the position of Germany after 1918 with respect to foreign policy and the law of nations,[135] started from the assumption that the existence of an abstract "foe" was a necessary precondition for all state activity; whether or not this foe existed in reality was of absolutely no import. A lack of content to the foe concept was therefore not a disadvantage but rather the purest, most absolute realization of *the political*,[136] since state power could thus remain flexible and the concept of the foe could be fleshed out at will with arbitrary meaning. From there it was only a small step to the equation of friend with "persons of the equal type" and foe with "alien"[137] and another small step to the corollary establishment of special law, or even no law at all (lawlessness), for the "foe" of the "national community."

Thus in 1933 it had already been determined that the "foe" stood outside the community, resulting in the demands that, "in execution of the distinction between friend and foe, all those should be weeded out" (that is, eliminated) who as "aliens and foes could no longer be tolerated."[138] Even the adherents of the "*völkisch*-vitalist" constitutional doctrine, who stood in opposition to this friend-foe dichotomy, came to the same conclusion. It was necessary, they said, to replace the equality clause in article 109, paragraph 1, of the Weimar Constitution by one that proclaimed "organic inequality"[139] and to insist upon "frank recognition of the fact" that, because of the necessarily racial definition of the concept of the *Volk*, "inequalities within this *Volk*" were unavoidable.[140] Such inequalities had far-reaching consequences: in an essay published in 1937, for instance, Hans Peter Ipsen expatiated upon the notion that "whoever . . . did not affirm it [the Nazi state] . . . had no place in German jurisprudence either."[141] Later authors also affirm the idea of *völkisch* inequality, if in some cases circuitously, either by their support for the discriminatory practices of the administration, known at the time as "accepting reality,"[142] or by arguing that every class of people had to be assigned its proper law.[143] To some extent, also, the exclusion of "aliens" from the utilization of public facilities was deemed not so much a permissible "exception" as, quite simply, the "fulfillment of the National Socialist principle of equality."[144]

There was, overall, a general agreement that "unequal treatment" of "aliens" was lawful and that it must "necessarily [result in] segregation of the alien elements from the German body politic, and their . . . differential treatment" in all areas of life, since equality between "racially identical and racially foreign persons [could] not be maintained in any essential social and legal relations."[145] The practical measures, too, as well as the race laws, such as those mandating the exclusion of Jews from public service, economic affairs, and culture ("absolute dissimilation"), were approved in more or less general terms.[146] To some extent, too, it was frankly admitted that this "exclusion" of "aliens" from the community was the expression of "true meaningful equality" in the sense of *suum cuique* (to each his own);[147] in part this "elimination" was also justified by saying that no breach of the equality principle (art. 109 of the Weimar Constitution) was involved, since the latter mandated equal treatment only for equal circumstances; and what "equal" meant was now to be left to the discretion of the guardians of the National Socialist worldview, according to which racial differences were the source of "unequal circumstances."[148] Thus, the principle of unequal treatment, or special law, becomes the (negative) central concept of National Socialist law. Be that as it may, however, the fact that this development had already been sketched out by earlier models was a decisive factor in the smooth manner in which völkisch inequality was integrated into the Nazi legal system.

The roots of this theory extend far back into the past. Demands for the suppression or neutralization of "aliens" (particularly Jews) from political, intellectual, and economic life were raised in quite specific form even before 1933 and especially after 1918 and were part of the established program of nationalist and völkisch circles (the All-German Federation and other organizations). There was no difference between these demands and those of the NSDAP; they had always insisted upon the same discriminatory policies that later were enshrined in and implemented by the Nuremberg Laws. The incorporation and adoption of the principle of discrimination in constitutional doctrine after 1933 was thus no innovation but merely the continuation of already existing anti-Semitic traditions and demands.

The only difference between the demands raised in the Weimar Republic and those of the "völkisch state" of the Nazis was that the principle of special law would now be put into legal practice. The specific result was the institution of an inferior legal status or exclusion from any legal status whatsoever. Here, too, attempts were made to disguise the true circumstances by means of empty slogans, which, in view of the overt discrimination practiced against racial and political minorities, could only bespeak a cynical, or at the very least, hypocritical policy. On January 30, 1934, in Berlin, Hitler himself declared that the racial idea did not lead to any "contempt for or lesser opinion of other peoples." Similar arguments were used both in theory and in practice. The race laws "deliberately [refrained] from judging the superiority of one race over the others."[149] There was talk of "mutual respect" for "foreign nations, and peoples of different blood,"[150] of "respect for the special quality of a people that is achieved by preserving the purity of the blood,"[151] of the necessity of "variations in type,"[152] and so forth, in order to justify the unequal legal treatment of "non-German" persons: "That which is contested against for political reasons is not therefore evil or ugly or harmful, and above all, not unjust. The political act takes place merely in order to combat the inimical, or, in a positive sense, to preserve one's own existence."[153]

The commentators of the race laws in the Reich Ministry of the Interior also tried to take an "objective" view of the prescribed regimen of racial hatred. There was, they said, no scale of racial value but only "differences in kind."[154] They protested in all seriousness that *völkisch* inequality did not denote any enmity toward other nations and peoples;[155] that special law directed against "people of foreign races" did not put them in an inferior position but merely emphasized "difference in kind," a "healthy, free foreignness";[156] that segregation (of the Jews) was a "generous solution to the Jewish and *Mischling* [persons of mixed descent] problem";[157] and that it simultaneously provided for (their) legal protection.[158]

But all this was merely a meager pretense cloaking the fact that the principle of special law, where its application is determined arbitrarily by governmental fiat, always means a retreat from legality, and fundamentally it brooks no restraint, since, in a situation where state power is unlimited, one can always find "objective" necessities to justify its expansion. If the inviolability of law is valid only under set conditions, then the principle of law is no longer in force, for "inviolability with reservations is the opposite of fundamentally acknowledged inviolability."[159] Therefore, such remarks on the supposed "foreignness" of those who did not belong to the "national community" signified nothing less than their basic "antagonism" toward the German people; and, since antagonists naturally must be combated, it provided the foundation for placing them under special law. Thus, the literature of the later years contains statements frankly expressing the idea that "differences" in "kind" imply "inferiority" and that "foreignness" results in "hostility" ("the Jews are not only foreign to us but also our enemies")[160]—that is, to the extent that such negative concepts and images were not from the very outset already implicit in the words *difference in kind*.[161]

Since this meant that the concept of the foreign was defined not legally but from a *völkisch*-racial standpoint, the concept of inequality was put beyond reach of any kind of legal delimitation and thus divested of any legitimate content whatsoever. The detailed structuring and implementation of the concept of special law was, it follows, a question not of *law* but of *political expediency*. This conclusion is expressed most plainly in an essay by the official legal adviser of the Gestapo, Werner Best, written in 1937. Best argued that the state indeed had to be free of all legal obligations. However, in his opinion this did not mean that any governmental actions ought to be executed without standards and at the discretion of individual representatives of state authority. Rather, in quite a number of areas it should be *expedient* for the state, of its own accord, to set forth precise standards for its future actions, to ensure that they will be predictable and that those affected will have the opportunity to act accordingly.[162]

However, this "self-restriction" of the state by means of standards set for its future behavior, that is, grants of legal protection, was only "appropriate with regard to any positively constructive forces within the *Volk*. These ought to be able to predict the actions of the state to the greatest possible extent, in order that their own works might be as fruitful as possible."[163]

Needless to say, according to this theory all racially desirable forces and energies were manifested in the "positive" forces; and, just as plainly, all non-Aryan subjects of the state (*Staatsangehörige*) were to be excluded from legal protection.[164] Depending upon the political requirements of the moment, therefore, such persons could "be granted" the benefits of German law in graduated form, that is, partially (inferior legal status); alternatively, they could be barred altogether (exclusion from the community of legal rights). For these groups, then, the principle of equality before the law was reinterpreted as proof of extraordinary favor and mercy, of which they had to prove themselves worthy[165] and in exchange for which those affected even had to pay financial compensation in the form of certain special taxes.[166]

Yet the reduction in or annulment of any and all legal status for unpopular minorities, a characteristic feature of all totalitarian forms of governance, was accomplished less by means of openly decreed special law than, first and foremost, on the authority of *prevailing* law (that is, without revoking the citizenship of German subjects of foreign descent).[167] In this manner, the practice of special law underwent a never-before-seen process of refinement and improvement, which the following examples may serve to illustrate.

Discrimination against "alien" persons took place on the basis of an interpretation of existing law that is most accurately described by Bernd Rüthers's term "*unlimited interpretation*." Such unequal treatment was justified with the excuse that the general principle under which all standards were interpreted in the "National Socialist spirit"[168] *implied* such differentiation *by its very nature*, since inequality based on racial origin was part of the National Socialist program.

This differentiation led, among other things, to the principle of judicial administration that held that every law contained an "unwritten *reservation*," namely, that its intention could never be to "provide [Jews] with any advantages or benefits or protect them from disadvantages or harm."[169] Thus the German Supreme Court, in an opinion handed down in the case of a Jewish attorney who filed suit to obtain an official document, made it clear that the (legally guaranteed) rights of the individual must be set aside where reasons of state security were involved[170] and that therefore the document could not be issued.

That "unlimited interpretation" would necessarily lead to the abandonment of the very idea of standardized law is proved by the fact that even in the early years of the Third Reich, "enemies of the national community" were discriminated against without the slightest legal foundation. In the realm of criminal justice, doubts were expressed as to whether or not a Jew could actually be said to possess "honor" in the sense required by the laws of slander and libel. The question was not whether he possessed "honor" in the Nazi sense, which only the "racially compatible" national comrade could possess; the discussion, rather, centered around whether he possessed what was termed "*Jewish honor*," which in the Nazi state could at best only be "recognized and protected to a very limited extent."[171] There were rulings in civil law that declared radio sets belonging to Jews to be leviable,[172] in contradiction to the prevailing practice, which held radio sets to be personal requisites and thus not attachable (sec. 811, no. 1, Code of Civil Procedure); or that considered eviction proceedings brought by Aryan landlords against Jewish tenants to be justified solely on the grounds of the latter's racial origins.[173]

Although no legal authority for the policy existed, sexual intercourse between German women and undesirable "persons of foreign race" (Negroes and others) could lead to the expulsion from the Reich of the colored partner, on the grounds that such relations contradicted "the views on the preservation of the purity of the German race," the dictates of "morality," and the "security of the Reich."[174] This exactly corresponded to the line propounded by Nazi ideologues such as Alfred Rosenberg, who had called for such relationships to be placed under the severest possible sanctions.[175] Discrimination against Gypsies of German nationality, too, was common from an early date, also without basis in law, although the administrative courts had plainly ruled that German Gypsies too enjoyed legal protection.[176]

Nevertheless, the physical annihilation of "alien" persons could not be justified by any legal standards, not even those of the National Socialists, and was therefore outside the administrative purview. Shortly before the commencement of the "Final Solution," therefore, German victims of National Socialist persecution were stripped of their citizenship upon "crossing the Reich frontiers"—that is, upon being deported[177]—so that, in the contemporary view, it could in all honesty be maintained that no German citizens died in the extermination camps, but only "stateless" "alien" persons.

d.   Targets for the Implementation of *Völkisch* Inequality

aa. Jews

The Jews were the primary targets of exploitation by the principle of *völkisch* inequality. National Socialist propaganda was in this regard able to tie into the virulent economic, political, and cultural-psychological anti-Semitism of the Kaiserreich and the Weimar period,[178] now putting the main emphasis on the racial factor. Since, however, there existed no clear definition of the term *Jew*, either from an anthropological or a cultural standpoint, the practical solution was simply to declare membership in the Jewish religion to be the relevant criterion,[179] thus focusing on that feature which is perhaps one of the deepest roots of anti-Semitism.[180] This departure from the pure doctrine of the racial principle was justified by the Reich internal administration in a circular of November 26, 1935, with the hair-splitting argument that "fundamentally, the decisive criterion is not membership in the Jewish *religion*, but in the Jewish *race*." "In order to avoid problems of argumentation and proof," said the same circular, it was, "however, expressly determined that a grandparent who belonged to the Jewish religion is held, without further ado, to be a member of the Jewish race"; counterevidence was inadmissible.[181] But the relevant literature continued to cling to the concept of race. The nature of the Jew was seen as being founded upon his "unfavorable and disharmonious," "extra-European" racial makeup, a tenet that was promoted above all by the so-called racial anthropologists[182] and the racial policymakers in the Reich leadership of the NSDAP and its associated organizations, by means of preposterous scientific theories.[183] The race experts in the Reich Ministry of the Interior, who in any case saw race mixing as the most harmful thing of all ("race bastards" are "characters torn by inner conflicts") and the Jewish "race mixture" more than any other as the most unfavorable imaginable form of race mixture,[184] also subscribed to this belief. Here, too, it is impossible not to recognize the continuity of pre-1933 anti-Semitic traditions.

All of the negative physical and psychological characteristics now ascribed to the Jew had been marked out in advance in anti-Semitic literature. Every cliché of the National Socialist period had been current for many years (race mixture resulted in psychological conflictedness; owing to his "foreignness," the Jew could not be truly "creative"; the "foreign" naturally and necessarily turned into "opposition," to "hate"; a plain solution could only bring about a "plain separation of the nations," and so forth).[185] Now that anti-Semitism had become state doctrine, such racial ideas were believed even more readily and were further refined, the more so as the negative characteristics of the Jew ("small stature," "shifty eyes," "Jewish nose," and so on) had long been considered "scientifically" proven.[186] But whereas the "scientific" anti-Semitic literature prior to 1933 had admitted, at least in part, that it labored under a total lack of certain historical knowledge and confined itself largely to speculative arguments,[187] much was now coarsened and falsified and always presented as if it were irrefutable scientific truth. Whereas in the past the characteristic feature of the Jew was not, or not solely, seen in his racial peculiarity but in his "consciousness of type" ("blood consciousness"),[188] it now lay in his racial distinctness, which was seen as representing a "particularly unfavorable" admixture.[189]

Hitler himself, as a matter of fact, only repeated time and again the same widespread clichés and commonplaces.[190] For him, the "Jewish essence" consisted quite simply in the fact that the Jews were "Asiatics" and therefore "inferior."[191] In his book *Mein Kampf*, which perhaps only a handful of contemporaries had read, much less taken seriously,[192] he emphasizes that Jewry, too, was a people with particular racial characteristics, a fact that the term *religion* only served to obscure, since the Jewish religion's primary function was to preserve the race;[193] but he failed to say what exactly these characteristics might be. In the final analysis, the term *Jew* was, in the eyes of the Nazi leadership, not an anthropological or cultural one but fundamentally a *concept of political expediency*.[194] The political leadership never tired of repeating that this concept was the polar opposite of the "German essence." The "Jewish" is seen as the quintessence of all bad qualities ("naked egoism," "incapability" of creating a culture, "parasitic way of life," "mendacity," "depravity," etc.), which were set against the good qualities of the "Aryan" ("idealism," "boundless honesty," "cleanliness," etc.).[195] The dichotomous pairing of "idealism" and "egoism," "dutifulness" and "parasitic way of life" and their transference onto the relationship between non-Jews and Jews are not only to be found in Hitler and Nazi propaganda but are also tirelessly repeated in the judicial literature[196] and in administrative proceedings; they are echoed particularly obtusely by the top jurists in the Reich administration. Historical reminiscences crop up: the Aryan is substituted for Teutonic or Germanic man. Only the Teuton, that is, the Germanic or Nordic man, has the will to perform his duty and to sacrifice for the "community" and the ability to "regard as freedom" his obligations to the national community.[197] The Jews, in contrast, since they are lacking in both the sense of sacrifice and idealism, are not merely a particularly "disharmonious" race but a thoroughly "inferior" one as well.[198]

The essence of this radical anti-Semitism, however, notwithstanding its constant references to Germanic or Teutonic man, was that it by no means limited itself to the conditions in Germany; rather, it was abstract, ahistorical, and universal. To be sure, in order to "prove" the destructive and parasitic nature of the Jews within whatever "host people" they afflicted, Hitler and his imitators were wont to describe the "life cycle" of the Jew in broad historical strokes, from the nomadic period to the Middle Ages in Germany to the nineteenth-century assimilation,[199] illustrating the whole with "scientific findings" that simply equated Jewry with criminality and iniquity of all kinds[200] and calling for its destruction. Yet in his remarks in *Mein Kampf*, and in his other statements as well, Hitler does not talk of a particular country or of particular peoples but only of the Jew as opposite number to the Aryan. The Jew was thus no concrete foe but a fiction, the embodiment of the counterman or antagonist. He was needed as the personification of evil, as the "enemy" principle, the "hereditary criminal," the symbol of the "plague" or "infection" that threatened the *Volksgemeinschaft*, against whom any measures taken in "self-defense" were justified.[201]

But the Nazi propagandists were in no way satisfied with this abstract demonization of Jewry: the *Volksgemeinschaft*, postulated as a value per se, needed a visible enemy as a permanent phenomenon; the racial threat was meant to have an integrative effect, aiming collective feelings of hatred at specified targets in all areas of life.[202] Hitler himself frankly admitted to his inner circle that if the Jew ceased to exist, he would have to be invented.[203]

Accordingly, Hitler himself made Jewry responsible for all the "humiliations" of the past (the Treaty of Versailles, liberalism, democracy, humanism, pacifism, Marxism-Bolshevism),[204] as well as for present difficulties and for World War II;[205] far-reaching decisions (such as the domestic policy of neutralizing the Jews and the acquisition of living space (*Lebensraum*) in the East) could be justified by Hitler at any time with the thesis of Jewry as the incarnation of evil itself and with sloganeering about the "international Jewish conspiracy."[206] A flood of anti-Semitic writings inundated the world of jurisprudence, all with the object of enlightening the reader about the "danger" of "penetration" and "sapping" carried on by Jews in the economy, the administration, and the judiciary.[207] Party organizations and academics (under Carl Schmitt's slogan "German jurisprudence in the fight against the Jewish spirit") called for the removal of all Jewish literature and all Jews from the academy.[208] A Jewish author could have "no authority, not even a purely academic one" in Germany. The necessary consequence was the removal of all jurists of Jewish descent from the judiciary and the administration.[209] For the Nazi leadership, however, Jewry was from the beginning no mere object of economic exploitation but also a potential target for physical destruction. For Hitler himself, and for the radical anti-Semites in the SS and the police, the Jews were not actually human but objects, treated arbitrarily as goods to be bargained over and traded, commodities with which to practice blackmail and extortion on foreign countries or cannon fodder in the coming war.[210] Thus, in theoretical anticipation of the "Final Solution," the Jews were referred to, in the language of the SS and the police, as pests, vermin, and so forth, who were to be disposed of as quickly as practicable and who could rightfully lay claim neither to life nor to legal protection.

The impact of such anti-Semitism was even greater in that the term *Jew*, though outwardly focused upon concretely identifiable minorities, was yet kept indefinite enough that any number of persons could be declared to be Jewish "race enemies," as the following examples will demonstrate.

Within the Reich itself, as already mentioned, the relevant criterion was fundamentally that of religious affiliation (sec. 7 of the First Decree subsequent to the Reich Citizenship Law dated November 14, 1935); but from the outset the leadership had allowed for exceptions (Hermann Göring said, "I will decide who is a Jew!"). In the so-called Occupied Eastern Territories, which were to become the center of the eastern German empire, the definition of the term *Jew* was, according to the above-mentioned section 7, infinitely broad ("A Jew is any person who professes the 'Jewish faith' . . . or otherwise professes or has ever professed to being a Jew or whose affiliation with Jewry can be established by *other* circumstances"), in order to encompass all racially or politically unpopular persons and include them in the campaign of racial extermination.

These two factors, its political function and its indeterminacy, lent anti-Semitism its extraordinary magnetism as a political program. Reminiscent in its simplicity of old legends and tribal myths, "it exerted . . . a powerful fascination."[211] It acted as a connecting link among all classes and levels of society, welding them together as those who could, by dint of "objective" racial characteristics, count themselves among the "chosen people."[212]

It is only from this starting point that we can begin to understand the nature and politically explosive force of the Nazi system, more particularly the intimate connection between race and politics, the equation of law with race law, the inseparable association of war (in the East) with race war[213] and of the politics of conquest with the extermination of the Jews.

bb. Other "Non-German" Minorities

The indeterminacy of the race concept in regard to Jewry already points up the fact that the race principle was fundamentally capable of unlimited interpretation and was consciously set up in such a way as to expand the range of application of *völkisch* inequality to cover more than just the Jews.[214] An indication of this was that even the first anti-Jewish measures (the Professional Civil Service Code) did not mention "Jewish descent" but rather "non-Aryan descent." This opened the door to numerous possibilities of subjecting other "foreign-race" persons as well to discriminations under special law, since, as already remarked, neither the term *Aryan* nor the term *non-Aryan* was ever satisfactorily defined. The objects of such discriminatory policies were, as in the ones practiced against the Jews, first and foremost the non-European races or racial mixtures that were considered to be undesirable, such as coloreds (Negroes); these were put on the same level as the Jews in regard to prohibitions on marriage and sexual intercourse with Germans. The policies toward Gypsies were similar:[215] even when Gypsies possessed German citizenship, they were held on account of their "work-dodging" and "asocial" character to be an "objective threat" ("Gypsy nuisance") and, on instructions from the Reich Ministry of the Interior, were now subjected to harsher and more rigorous treatment ("ruthless intervention").[216] As evidenced by the decisions handed down by the administrative courts, local administrative authorities acted similarly, even if there existed no legal authority for doing so.[217]

cc. "Non-Germans" in General

But all of these were merely borderline groups without statistical significance. The principle of *völkisch* inequality truly came into its own when its application was extended to the territories annexed and occupied by Germany. Since only a member of the racially defined *Volksgemeinschaft* was entitled to rights or privileges, the indigenous populations there were, where the Nazi leadership was concerned, not only a priori outside the German legal order but also outside any legal order whatsoever. This fundamental lack of all rights, which affected above all the peoples of Eastern Europe, could not, in the National Socialist view, stand in contradiction to the ideal of justice, since (as Roland Freisler said) "to each *Volk* was ordained its own right"[218] (one that was, of course, assigned to it by the Nazi leadership), and thus any substantive equality was, according to the literature, "a theoretical impossibility."[219]

In its treatment of "non-Germans," consequently, the National Socialist government and administration were not only free from any restraints imposed upon them in dealing with their own citizens but also free from any legal restraints or obligations whatsoever. The nonapplication of German law to "non-Germans" thus became the rule, its application the exception. When German law was utilized, it was presented as being a special legal benefaction and granted as a privilege to honor uncommon merit (for instance, pledging oneself to the German nation or military service in the German armed forces).

Since the preexisting indigenous law—at least in the Annexed Eastern European Territories—was not used because it was incompatible with "German sovereignty" and the application of German law was not even considered, the administration, as remains to be demonstrated, was faced with the problem of creating separate provisions for every aspect of life. The sole measure for the form these regulations was to take, and particularly for the decision as to which legal status was to be conceded to "non-Germans," was that of political-administrative expediency. This was determined by the degree of desirability or undesirability of the regulations from the standpoint of German interests, which in turn, as will be further shown, were primarily oriented toward the exploitation of the labor force and otherwise the suppression of the "non-Germans." Legal considerations, of course, were left altogether out of account.

Once theory and practice were committed to the essential significance of race as the central value motivating National Socialist ideology, the racial or *völkisch* aspect of the treatment of "non-Germans" under special law receded more and more into the background, indeed lost its meaning altogether, notwithstanding that this shift in meaning was still veiled behind racial arguments. The original racial foundation of *völkisch* inequality (special law) thus metamorphoses into a *political* principle.[220]

The ultimately political motivation behind the idea of special law for "non-Germans" is revealed in the mere fact that the "non-German" peoples of northern, western, and southern Europe enjoyed a "privileged" position, that is, were still allowed a certain legal status—ostensibly for reasons of race ("racially related peoples") but in actuality because of power politics (they were seen as allies or potential allies). Furthermore, various incentives were put in place, by decree or administrative provision, to encourage the complete integration of "non-German" but politically desirable persons into the German legal sphere. Thus, beginning in early 1942 it was possible to award German citizenship even to foreigners not domiciled within the borders of the Reich.[221] To boost the rate of population growth, particularly in order to gain conscripts for the German army, the Reich Ministry of the Interior had, moreover, drafted thorough legislative proposals according to which allies of "non-German" descent could be granted, by decree of the Führer, one of several documents (the *Adlerbrief*, the *Ehrenbrief*, the *Europabrief*, or the *Zusatzpaß*) as a reward for services rendered, thus achieving a status equal to that of the German citizen.[222] These proposals were elaborated during the war years to the point where they needed only a signature to become law, and they failed to receive the signature only because of the final outcome of hostilities.

The best example of the shift in meaning that occurred in the conception of *völkisch* inequality toward that of a political principle is seen in the position of the Eastern European peoples in the National Socialist scheme of things. From the outset, Hitler's particular hatred, and that of the Nazi leadership, was reserved for the so-called Slavic peoples, who were considered inferior and intended for the future slave class of Europe. From a purely racial standpoint, however, this was incapable of satisfactory proof, since even according to German ethnology it was impossible to speak of a Slavic race.[223] According to National Socialist doctrine, justification for discrimination against the Slavs lay rather in the "ethnic threat" presented by their fecundity. This is why Hitler quite early sketched precise outlines for the future "depopulation policy" in the East, which foresaw the annihilation of these peoples[224] and which was later carried out virtually to the letter by the civil administration and the police forces. Such arguments already imply that the treatment of the "non-Germans" under special law was actually justifiable only from the standpoint of (population) policy; nevertheless, the National Socialist leadership clung fast to the concept of racial value or lack thereof, in an attempt to concoct their policy on the basis of absolutely untenable racial arguments.

Where members of neutral or allied nations in (southern) Europe were concerned, of course, it was not possible to speak of inferiority; therefore, these peoples were either classified as "Southern Slavs," as "Dinarians" and thus as racially related;[225] or else they were simply not counted among the Slavs at all.[226] Members of enemy states, by contrast, were turned into "racial foes" as a means of justifying their classification under special law. Thus Hitler simply insinuated that the Czechs were (racially) inferior (descended from "Mongoloid tribes"), since he desired to rid himself of them in order to incorporate "Bohemia and Moravia" into the Reich; also "inferior" were Ukrainians, east-European Jews, Soviet Russians, Bulgarians,[227] Lithuanians, and members of other Eastern European peoples. Of course, this was nothing more than sloganeering and from a racial perspective not acceptable as justification even in the Nazi sense of the word. More imprecise than anything else was the position of the Soviet Russians in the Nazi racial scheme. Since they were declared to be political mortal enemies (as Bolshevists) while simultaneously being considered the incarnation of the *racial foe* (Jewry), Bolshevism and Jewry were flatly equated with one another, referred to as the "Jewish-Bolshevist threat," and made out to be the very quintessence of all types of inferiority.[228]

Analogously, no convincing race-theoretical explanation could be found to justify the discrimination against Poles. According to National Socialist racial doctrine, all European peoples belonged to the family of the Aryans and were thus fundamentally "racially equivalent," that is, recognized as equal before the law.[229] Discrimination against Poles was justified, however, because, like all Slavs, they represented a major *völkisch* and racial threat to Germany. Yet here, too, such reasoning was merely pretext. In his early statements on the Slavs, Hitler did not even mention the Poles, because at that time Poland was signatory to the Non-Aggression Treaty of 1934, and its position in the National Socialist scheme of conquest was not yet settled. The "ethnic threat" posed by the Poles was not discovered until the invasion of Poland. The placement of the Poles under rule of special law was done from fundamentally political motives, which were considerably intensified by the antipathy toward the Poles that, for reasons both political (voting disputes [Abstimmungskampf] in East and West Prussia, fighting in West Prussia and Upper Silesia, and the activities of the *Freikorps*) and religious, had been present in the eastern part of Germany in a particularly intense form since 1918. The main reason, however, was that the Nazi leadership considered the Poles to be the most dangerous of all peoples in Eastern Europe on account of their staunch insistence upon their national rights and identity as a people.[230] The race-political grounds for hatred of the Poles were merely the ideological mask justifying the National Socialist policy of violent force.[231]

The political basis for the systematically fomented hatred of and malice against Poles reveals itself in the thesis, invented ex post facto, of their "threat to the community," which then became the dominant argument in both theory and practice. According to this, the Poles had to be excluded from the European community of rights on account of their "Germanophobia" and their political incompetence and "lack of culture."[232] In contrast with this political argument, neither the racial window dressing of Nazi propaganda that commenced in 1939, according to which the Poles were "racial foes"[233] with regard to whom legal restraints were not to be observed, nor the elaborate attempts of the Race Policy Office to set up a racial classification of the Poles achieved much of an echo.[234]

Finally, the political basis for the unequal treatment of the peoples of Eastern Europe is seen in the about-face of the Nazi leadership when the fortunes of war were reversed and the labor of the "non-Germans" was required ever more urgently. On instructions from the Central Office of Propaganda of the NSDAP dated February 15, 1943, all chiefs of propaganda of the Reich *Gaue* were obliged, "within the framework of the war against Russia, for which the energies of all the peoples of Europe are required," to cease insulting the "Eastern nations" either directly or indirectly, and no longer characterize them as "beasts," "subhumans," and so forth, in order to gain their aid "in the struggle against Bolshevism."[235]

dd. "Racially Undesirable" Liaisons

The range of application of the principle of *völkisch* inequality was, however, not limited to the "non-Germans" in the German sphere of hegemony. Since, according to the National Socialist racial doctrine, the essential attribute of race was the *racial mixture*, upon which depended the degree of desirability or undesirability of particular persons for the German *Volksgemeinschaft*, the way was open for the race fanatics in leadership and administration to declare at their discretion any racial mixture, even *within* the German people, to be undesirable and therefore liable in principle to being dealt with under special law.

Practical approaches along these lines were certainly available, although they were perhaps not realized in thoroughgoing fashion by the administrative authorities. Thus, according to the views of the race experts in the Reich Ministry of the Interior, not only liaisons between Jews and Germans were "alien to type" and thus subject to a virtual marriage prohibition (sec. 6 of the First Implementing Order to the Blood Protection Law of November 14, 1935)[236] but also those mixtures involving "physical and mental differences," for instance, the liaison of a "tall and strong man" with a "woman of small and delicate race," since the physical health of the resulting child would "doubtlessly" be "endangered." The same could be expected in regard to "mental, psychological, and character difficulties for the child of such a marriage." Therefore, not only marriages between Germans and "non-German" persons (particularly people of color, Jews, and Gypsies) could be considered "foreign to type" in the sense of the Nazi race laws but even marriages between two persons of German blood whose external characteristics were unsuited to one another. Thus the marriage prohibitions in effect for Jews, including the regulation governing *Mischlinge*, also covered those persons who, according to the aforenamed criteria, exhibited an "alien" or "foreign-race" strain of blood (hereditary strain).[237]

A skeptic might well object that the exclusion of "alien" persons from the right of freely contracting marriage was merely an isolated phenomenon that says nothing much about the dismantling of the general legal status of "aliens." To this it must be countered that where racial policy is concerned, there were no isolated acts; nothing was left to chance; and that such discrimination was only the beginning of a process of total dissolution and adulteration of the law affecting such persons and their offspring, one that was single-mindedly pursued by the administrative leadership. Thus, for example, the plans and proposals drafted by the Reich Ministry of the Interior called for the future exclusion of all children of German citizens of "alien" descent from the German community of rights; that is, they would *ipso jure* no longer be able to obtain German citizenship. According to these plans, which in the case of the Jews at least were actually put into practice, the group of persons affected was to include not only children of Jewish citizens and Jewish *Mischlinge*, but also children of persons of other "alien" bloodlines.[238] If, therefore, one no longer interprets the concept of "alien origin" in the sense of biological descent but views it in connection with the fact that, quite simply, any otherwise undesirable liaison (irrespective of its racial classification) could be deemed "alien," the infinite expansability of the National Socialist racial ideas emerges in all clarity.

ee. "Undesirable" Persons or Groups: The Principle of Special Law as
the Central Concept of National Socialism

The above-described ability of the term *alien* to be infinitely expanded,
therefore, points far beyond the original racially oriented point of departure of
the concept of *völkisch* inequality. Although the racial-biological element had
largely disappeared from the concept of the alien, there was nothing to hinder
this process of legal undermining from being carried still further and being
completely divested of any racial or political content whatsoever. In this manner,
the concept of the alien gradually begins to replace that of the "foreign-racial" or
the "non-German," becoming at last a blanket clause behind which both racial
and political contents could be hidden. The concept of the alien now embodies
everything that was deemed foreign, strange, harmful, or undesirable. The judgment that one was alien could be passed upon anyone who did not conform to
the dominant type, that is, to the *Volksgemeinschaft*. Other terms used for this
were *foreign to the community* or *harmful to the community*, which were nothing
more than juristic expressions for the concept of the political foe.

This opened up the possibility, via "unlimited interpretation," of declaring
all undesirable or unpopular persons or groups to be alien or "foreign to the
community" and placing them under special law, particularly since anything
"foreign to the community" could be attacked from an exclusively political-
criminal point of view. Thus, criminal offenses that bore absolutely no relationship to political activities[239] (for example, sexual offenses, crimes involving currency violations, and others) could arbitrarily be declared political offenses,[240]
with the result that the accused could be remanded in custody indefinitely or
handed over to the Gestapo. Almost no matter or case was immune from the
intervention of special law practices, regardless of how trifling it may have been.

Thus, for example, the Bavarian Supreme Court in Munich remarked that
the name of a member of the executive board of a taxi owners' cooperative could
lawfully be struck from the register of associations if the police requested it.
Whether or not the man was "an enemy of the state or at least an enemy of the
state in the broader sense, [was] immaterial." "In the battle for self-assertion that
the German people are now forced to fight, there can no longer be, as there once
was, an area of life that is nonpolitical."[241] Significantly enough, the German
Supreme Court, in searching for matters that were immune from the intervention of political power, was unable to name anything other than the traffic
code.[242]

It was therefore quite accurate when, in the language of administration and law, the concept of special law also came to be described with the official phrase "special treatment,"[243] which originated in the secret idiom of the SS and the police (and was a code word for the liquidation of police prisoners).[244] Much more precisely than the phrase *special law*, it fittingly described the disappearance of any legal considerations in the treatment of undesirable persons. Discriminatory measures or special treatment thus became the common method for the disposal of any and all unpopular persons or groups.

The range of application of the principle of *völkisch* inequality was thus expanded ad infinitum. Not only racial, political, and clerical opponents were in practice deemed alien and thus "foreign to the community"; according to the dictates of political expediency, any persons or groups held to be undesirable for *other* reasons, regardless of their ancestry and/or citizenship, were characterized as criminal (see, for instance, the criminalization of the Catholic priesthood, which originated with Hitler himself)[245] or as "foreign to the community" and therefore fundamentally outside the community of rights. It thus became increasingly possible to dispense with proof of open antagonism or hostility to the regime. Objective criteria were neither necessary nor desirable. A "political enemy" (and therefore a person devoid of rights) was anyone whom the political authorities declared to be a political enemy. Nevertheless, as illustrated by the following examples, the term *Communist* was in practice the preferred way of characterizing "enemies" or unpopular persons, in order to give the impression that opposition to the regime was an objectively ascertainable offense. It was clearly stated, however, that the fight against Communism was not the actual *reason*, but only the *occasion* for the abandonment of "senseless" constitutional restraints.[246]

Just how limitless the group of potentially affected individuals could be is shown by the call, issued in the literature as early as 1933, for the expulsion from the community of rights not only of Communists but also of conscientious objectors, persons who made "Germanophobic statements" abroad, and "the politically heterodox." To be sure, this absolute deprivation of rights was disguised by saying that "heretics" belonged in principle "existentially" to the *Volk* and that no state could sunder this "fateful connection," that is, cast someone out of the "community." The individual member alone could exclude himself and "turn apostate." But then it became the duty of the state to exclude irrevocably such apostates from the *Volksgemeinschaft*, since with apostates, being different "always denotes enmity."[247] The courts consistently denied legal protection to members of the Jehovah's Witnesses sect, who pled the principle of religious freedom, on the grounds that they propagandized for conscientious objection.[248]

The most important, if not clearly the only, means of discrimination against all undesirable persons was the Reich president's Decree for the Protection of People and State dated February 28, 1933 (the so-called Reichstag Fire Decree),[249] which, in the words of the preamble, was promulgated to combat "Communist acts of violence." Despite this reservation, it soon became the legal authority for the indiscriminate persecution of all persons or groups supposedly foreign to the community.

The literature made it plain that the authorities were now free of "liberal fetters," and not only in the fight against Communism. Such restraints were "unreservedly set aside."[250] The principle of limiting the role of the police to defending against threats to public security and order and the principle of proportionality ("senseless and state-threatening . . . restraints")[251] were thereby abandoned. An implementing order of the Prussian minister of the interior dated March 3, 1933, determined that within the framework of the decree of February 28, 1933, the police authorities could extend their activities beyond the limitations set forth in sections 14 and 41 of the Law of Police Administration.[252]

Beginning about 1935, the decisions handed down by numerous superior courts—with the notable exception of the Prussian Administrative Supreme Court[253]—also maintained the position that this decree was promulgated not merely to achieve the concrete aims enumerated in the text itself; beyond that, it was interpreted to justify *all* measures taken by the executive "for the protection of the common interests of the *völkisch* community order."[254] With such judgments in hand, the lawfulness of police actions could be justified on grounds of "raison d'état," even in cases in which the offenses covered by the decree were not involved.[255] Accordingly, the Prussian implementing order dated March 3, 1933, was declared to be compatible with the spirit and intent of the decree of February 28, 1933, and therefore lawful; in all relevant decisions, however, it was emphasized by the courts that they were unable to test the necessity of the implementing order.[256]

Accordingly, the decree of February 28, 1933, was also employed in the fight against churches and sects, against the German youth movement *Wandervögel* (migratory birds), and against antivaccinationists, either because there were deemed to be no legal restraints upon police action or with the aid of the theory of the "imminent Communist threat."[257] In an (at the time isolated) opinion handed down on November 1, 1933, the Appellate Court of Berlin observed that "any . . . assaults directed against public security and order [were to be] considered as being Communist in the broadest sense of the term."[258] This theory was later to engender some very strange effects indeed.

For instance, the Bavarian Supreme Court in Munich upheld a prohibition by the Reich minister of the interior, based upon the decree of February 28, 1933, that made it a crime for any member of the clergy to publicly announce the names of those parishioners who had left the church, on the grounds that according to the named decree, "any measures . . . for the restoration of public security and order are permissible *without regard* to the source from which a disturbance . . . has emanated."[259] The Special Court of Hamburg reached a similar ruling in a case involving the Jehovah's Witnesses.[260] The Baden Administrative Court declared the dissolution of a church association for the care of the infirm to be permissible, since this association "doubtlessly caused considerable harm to the local women's association of the Red Cross in X." This fact alone was considered sufficient grounds for the dissolution: "If the minister of the interior declares that this . . . competition puts important state interests at a disadvantage . . . the Court is powerless . . . not to accept this declaration."[261] The dissolution of a publishing house belonging to the Watchtower Bible Tract Society was justified with the consideration that it "[could] also appear advantageous . . . to the defense against acts of Communist, state-threatening violence to ban such associations in which Communist sympathizers *might perhaps* be concealed without the knowledge of their directors."[262] In a case involving the members of a Catholic youth association who had staged group outings and sporting events and were therefore charged with violating a directive issued by the responsible district president based on the decree of February 28, 1933, the Prussian Supreme Court in Berlin declared that National Socialism (also) aimed to eliminate all tensions, since it was the true representative of the national community. The "way in which [the accused were charged with] emphasizing a split [contained] from the outset the germ of a demoralization of the German *Volk*, and *any* such demoralization [was], in turn, *likely* to provide *encouragement* to Communist activities and to support their aims." Personal opposition to Communism on the part of the accused did not exempt them from punishment: "For . . . the *individual opinion* thus paraded before the court can only too easily serve to incite adherents of or persons *sympathetic* to Communism who *perhaps* at present are still *undecided*, who then go out and spread . . . the opinion that the National Socialist state does not after all have the people behind it."[263]

The same court declared the statements of a pastor against the "German Christians" to be an "*indirect danger* to the state," since the dissatisfaction expressed in this manner prepared "the ground for the reemergence of Communist activities."[264] Finally, the indirect "fight against Communism" was made to provide legal authority for the prohibition of the antivaccinationists (by the Reich Supreme Court)[265] and for discrimination against the members of taxi owners' cooperatives.[266]

There were many other means used to implement the concept of *völkisch* inequality. Provisions for criminals and persons classified as asocial included "special treatment" in the form of preventive detention under criminal law, forced sterilization, or "protective or preventive custody" by the police; for persons deemed undesirable for reasons of race or population policy, there were special measures of "public health policy" (marriage prohibitions), followed by the actual annihilation programs (the euthanasia program, the extermination camps); and, finally, for all other persons considered unpopular, for whatever reasons, there were the concentration camps, which were elaborated into a system of indefinite incarceration.

"Protective custody" was not merely a phenomenon associated with the Nazi revolution, which would have meant that it was temporary in nature; rather, it was a means of *preservation* of the dictatorship of the NSDAP.[267] Experts in police law were of the opinion that the state, if it aspired to the "national attitude" (i.e., antidemocratic, pro-Nazi), must also have the necessary means of correction at its disposal. Protective custody was part of "the essence of a truly political state that is free of liberal fetters."[268] The thesis that protective custody was a means necessary for combating the "enemies of the state" was thus proved to be a fabrication.

In sum, if one considers the broad significance of the concept of special law, the *ultimate aim* of National Socialist legal policy can be said to have consisted in the destruction of the concept of common and equal rights, in the dissolution of all legal relationships between individual and community/state, in a tangled network of graduated (*völkisch*) rights and obligations, in a system of general inequality, that is, of arbitrary privilege and discrimination, in which each individual was assigned his position according to merit (to each his own [*Jedem das Seine*]) by the state leadership.

As an example of the system of privileges established to reward meritorious "national comrades," which was developed parallel to the elaborate discriminatory system,[269] one might mention the amnesties for the Old Guard (Alte Kämpfer),[270] who received remission of sentences for crimes committed during the so-called Period of Struggle prior to 1933. Perhaps because of the war, plans for further privileges, such as the suggestion of Hans Frank that the Party leadership corps be exempted altogether from the purview of common criminal law and placed under the exclusive legal jurisdiction of the Party,[271] were never put into practice.

For this system of unequal treatment, too, terms from legal history were misused—there was talk of "estate" law, of the "structured" body politic (*Volksganze*), and so on—all in order to veil the true character of a legal situation based upon "national comradeship" and create the illusion of continuity between National Socialism and the rest of German history, a continuity that in reality did not exist at all.

The firm ensconcing of the principle of special law in the legal system of the Nazi state, therefore, represented, by means of "legal dispensation," a de facto departure from any legal order whatsoever and was thus the best means for carrying out the "state of emergency" (C. Schmitt's term) against supposed internal enemies.[272] The system of absolute power of the Führer and the political monopoly enjoyed by the NSDAP ensured that this idea was rigidly centralized, both administratively and ideologically, and that it was enforced with all the efficiency the administration could muster. In connection with the two elements just discussed, therefore, the principle of special law, though it may have been principally (but not exclusively) directed at "non-German" persons and groups, also proves to be the decisive structural element in the Nazi system as a whole; it becomes the guiding principle according to which National Socialist society was to be structured and governed. This signified nothing more or less than the introduction of martial law at home;[273] and although order of a sort still obtained, its lack of any normative restraints meant that it no longer represented any kind of legal (much less just) order.

There is a direct line of descent leading from martial law at home to the horrible consequences of National Socialist despotism. For anyone whom the regime classified as alien, whether from the standpoint of political, criminal, racial, or population policy (the sick, the old, the weak), came to embody the polar opposite of the *Volksgemeinschaft*; that is, such persons were the "unworthy." The unworthy, as Nazi propaganda never tired of repeating, had to be exterminated or, at the very least, rendered harmless as "parasites" on the "healthy body of the *Volk*." Whereas, at first, many may have believed that "foreignness" brought with it merely an inferior legal status, one that was still within the German legal order, and whereas one might differentiate between the full legal status of the "racially acceptable" "ethnic comrades" and the limited legal status of alien "guests of the *Volk*," that is, "membership in a community of legal protection" for foreigners and persons of foreign descent,[274] the use of vocabulary like *subhumans* ought to have made it clear that the final consequence of the principle of *völkisch* inequality would necessarily be the "neutralization" and thus the extermination of all ethnically unworthy persons. With remarkable "judicial" logic and consistency, which was later to prove extremely prophetic as well, the German Supreme Court as early as 1936 compared the status of special law on grounds of race with (civil) death, with the utter "destruction of the legal personality."[275]

The fact that the precept of special law cannot be limited or restrained once it has been accepted on principle is shown most plainly in a draft bill of the Reich Ministry of the Interior that almost progressed to the stage of legislative enactment and which, in a manner of speaking, rips the shroud from all previous euphemisms describing the practice of special law.

This bill, which will be discussed in detail at a later time, contained a so-called Law on Aliens to the Community that was to take effect on January 1, 1945. Under this law, all "persons foreign to the community" were to be placed under *police statute* (detention in "police camps" or "reformatories," that is, in concentration camps or work houses).[276] Without benefit of *any* judicial rule, anyone was deemed "foreign to the community" who was classified as asocial or criminal by the offices of the Security Police. This meant that *anyone* could in fact be declared to be a "parasite," "good-for-nothing," "ne'er-do-well" (in the legal wording of the proposed bill) and excluded from the community of rights for *any* behavior.

The *völkisch* inequality of the Nazis thus became a generalized state of legal inequality; "foreign" became "foreign to the community," to such an extent that racial discrimination represents only an *isolated* instance of the application of the National Socialist policy of special law. The principle that all people are born with the same rights, embodied in the law of citizenship or in a minimum standard of elementary rights, is turned on its head: everyone was by nature without rights, fundamentally outside the law, "to the extent that nothing was determined to the contrary." According to this philosophy, the constitutional rights of the liberal era embodied the "selfishness of the individual vis-à-vis the state" and were "intolerable in the organic state."[277] In the Nazi state, the possession of legal status is declared a privilege, the state of rightlessness the normal case, the rule.

Ambitious administrative leaders developed outlandish ideas, negating all historical development, that lost themselves in the murky distances of Teutonic prehistory: the expulsion of all "undesirables" from the German community of rights was to be followed by the return to a mystical community of arms and labor composed of all fighting Germans, from which not only "foreigners" but also children, women, the infirm, and so forth, would be excluded. For just as there could be no equality of treatment between "national comrades" and "non—national comrades," legal equality of the sexes, of minors and the weak and infirm was unthinkable. Such ideas were by no means of theoretical interest only; they were not even specifically National Socialist in origin. Rather, they had already been current in *völkisch* circles before 1933, and after the Nazi seizure of power they fit even better into the "spirit of the times."[278] For even in the Nazi state, legislators and administrators were anxious to carry on with traditional ideas. If one takes this mechanism into account, it no longer appears astonishing that the later anti-Jewish measures reveal numerous similarities and parallels to plans from the early phase of the administration of the Nazi state, analogies that run from using the same terminology (*citizen of the Reich, alien descent, Nordic ancestry, race protection laws,* etc.) all the way to the precise tracing out of an Aryan classification of the population for purposes of future race legislation.[279]

The present study describes the most important case in which the principle of special law was applied, the treatment under special law of "non-German" persons, since research here is not restricted to plans and speculations but can fall back on a coherent system of actually enacted measures and laws. For the experimental field in the principle of special law was primarily the category of "non-Germans"; whereas the expansion of this principle to the extent just described, and as desired by the Nazi leadership, to include all other unpopular persons or groups, never took effect owing to the short duration of the Third Reich. In this respect, special law as used against "non-Germans" serves as a model for the kind of persecutional measures otherwise practiced by the Nazi state.

e.   Territorial Differences

In examining the special law used against "non-Germans," however, one comes upon significant regional differences. As a rough classification, there is an essential difference between the conditions in the Reich itself and those in the territories annexed or occupied by Germany. Where the latter are concerned, the most important caesura occurs between the occupied territories in Eastern Europe and the remaining parts of occupied Europe. Whereas the inhabitants of the occupied areas of western and northern Europe were treated by the Nazi leadership as political, not as racial, enemies, the Eastern European peoples, as already discussed, and particularly the Poles, were considered the very incarnation of inferior "non-Germans." And although here, too, the motivation was first and foremost political, the National Socialist propaganda machine made the Eastern Europeans appear as political and racial foes of the Nazi regime whose sole function was not only to serve German economic interests but also, and at all costs, to be (in part) exterminated and (in part) reduced to the lowest possible legal and social status.

In the following portrayal, therefore, I have chosen to divide the material along regional lines, in order to depict the development of special laws in its varying degrees of intensity. As far as the conditions in the area of the so-called Altreich (within the borders of 1937) are concerned, the first uncertain efforts at putting special law into effect were not altogether crowned with the success coveted by the political leadership, largely because of the constitutional traditions of the Reich administration, the ponderousness of the various ministerial departments, and the independence of the old, established bureaucracy. Outside the Reich itself, by contrast, in Occupied Eastern Europe, the obstacles posed by a conventional administration were not an issue; there, the political leadership had a free hand; there dwelt a "non-German" population with regard to which "constitutional inhibitions" could safely be disregarded. These areas therefore became the experimental arena of the "new *völkisch* order" of Europe, or the "parade ground of National Socialism," as it was more coarsely put by the Gauleiter of the Wartheland, Arthur Greiser. This holds true particularly for the annexed and occupied Polish territories (the Annexed Eastern Territories and the General Government for the occupied Polish territories), which, since they were occupied the longest, offer the best example of the experimental method and the art of the National Socialist policy of special law. Since the principle of special law was an essential component of the Nazi state, those areas may therefore be considered the ideal type of what was to have been the future rule of the Nazis over "non-German" peoples, and more: they are the *ideal type* of a National Socialist polity of graduated rights and obligations (beginning with the lowest level, the "non-Germans" as pariahs, and ending with the highest level, the political leadership corps).

Thanks to this regional comparison, one can see quite plainly how the character of special law as it developed in the occupied Polish territories contrasts with the legal regulations in the Reich, both as regards extent and severity. This should serve to make it clear that the regulations in effect in the Reich were not the normal case of special law, because it was there realized only imperfectly; rather, as will later be observed in detail, it is precisely the extreme regulations in the Polish sector that much better represent the actual character of special law. Thus the Annexed Eastern Territories (the Wartheland) became the model for a Reich administration within the Greater German Reich constructed upon special law, whereas the General Government was organized and cultivated as the model for a colonial administration founded upon special law. The administration of the General Government and the standards it promulgated thus possess exemplary character in the overall context of National Socialist occupation policy: of all the forms of administration in the occupied territories, it represented the purest prototype of the National Socialist politics of violence.[280]

Against the thesis that the practices of special law in the Polish territories according to National Socialist ideas were not the exception but rather represented their "normal state," the objection might be made that these practices in the East were indeed exceptional in character, since prevailing conditions were themselves exceptional on account of the war. This objection will not hold. The war in Poland ended with Poland's capitulation in October 1939. What was set in place there was not at all a military administration tailored to wartime conditions but rather a civil administration that according to National Socialist ideas was entirely oriented to "normalcy" and to the integration and/or annexation of these territories into the Reich.

In view of the massive amount of source material, of course, it is impossible to present a complete picture. Just as the aforementioned territories are merely models for the comprehensive nature of special law under the National Socialist regime, at least as it existed in the occupied territories of Eastern Europe, so, in regard to source material, only those territories are treated that are particularly exemplary of the implementation of special law. Such areas would include the fields of internal administration and the judiciary. And even limiting myself to areas, I have had to set certain limits so as not to overextend the framework of the study. Accordingly, only those areas are discussed at length in which the principle of special law had the most far-reaching and drastic effects, such as, for example, the laws governing civil servants, the professions, criminal prosecution, and marriages. However, one must constantly bear in mind that, in principle, the entire Nazi legal system is by nature shot through with and steeped in elements of special law. For the departmentalization and delimitation of the administrative and judicial sectors over against other sectors, I have employed uniform formal criteria, that is, first and foremost, the relevant organizational charts (*Geschäftsverteilungsplan*) of the Reich Ministry of the Interior[281] and the Reich Ministry of Justice[282] and those of the central authorities in the Annexed Eastern Territories and the General Government, as the basis for study. One pivotal question was whether or not the police were to be seen within this framework as part of the internal administration. If one applies the above-mentioned formal criteria, this question would have to be negated, since as early as 1936 the police had been placed under Himmler as *Reichsführer*-SS and so were removed from the jurisdiction of the Reich minister of the interior. Therefore, the police are not treated as part of the internal administration. Material having to do with extraneous departments (labor, revenues, commercial and cultural administration), which would require monographs of their own, has nonetheless been taken into account insofar as it involves areas of discrimination that bear a close formal or material relationship to internal administration or the judiciary (for instance, labor law as it relates to professional codes) or wherever it was necessary for the sake of completeness. The discussion of the practice of special law in the areas of internal administration and the judiciary makes it plain that, as imperfect and immature as the plans of the National Socialist leadership and their literal execution may have been, a system was nonetheless put in place that, in its legal-technical coherence, may well stand as an example of the overall method of rule of (National Socialist) totalitarian administration.

The Principle of Special Law against "Non-Germans" in the Area of Public Law (General and Internal Administration with Supplementary Areas)

Section One

The Implementation of *Völkisch* Inequality in the Altreich

I. General Outlines

In the process of implementing the principle of *völkisch* inequality in the area of constitutional law, the essential features of the legal policies of the new regime came into particularly sharp focus: first the regime provoked, promoted, and tolerated an unlawful state of emergency marked by tyranny and injustice; then it retroactively legalized that condition by means of legislative provisions; the legal norms were always catching up with the facts, as a result, and one-time, exceptional phenomena found their way retroactively into common "law." Besides the propagandistic advantages of such a procedure, the Nazi leaders also had a sure instinct for incorporating into their deliberations the traditional German legal thinking, where law was equated with legal principle and was never seen as an act of legalized injustice but always an act of legal security. Using this approach, they created a system of emergency regulations that ate their way into the domain of *common* law, thus forfeiting the color of emergency statutes standing outside of established law.[1] If it appeared in the *Reich Law Gazette (RGBl.)* so went the thinking, it could not be unjust.

The early stage of the implementation of special law is the best example for the way in which tyranny became the norm and centrally controlled "spontaneous" actions served to justify radical measures that were already on the agenda. In the very first weeks after the Nazi seizure of power, countless sudden and savage acts of violence, such as boycotts, abuse, and arrests, were committed under the leadership of the local NSDAP and the SA against "non-Germans." Targeted were political opponents, Jewish persons in the Civil Service (judges, public prosecutors, and university professors), Jewish attorneys-at-law, Jewish shops and synagogues,[2] and Polish citizens.[3] These actions, especially the central boycott that the Party leadership of the NSDAP ordered to take place on April 1, 1933,[4] against "Jewish shops, Jewish goods, Jewish physicians, and Jewish attorneys-at-law" and which was "lawfully" organized by so-called municipal boycott committees[5] could not help being temporary in nature, largely because of the manifestly disadvantageous consequences in terms of foreign policy and foreign trade that it brought upon the still uncertain regime; a second reason was that the popularization of the boycott measures by the National Socialist propaganda machine did not achieve the success desired by the NSDAP leadership.[6] Nevertheless, they created so much alarm, uncertainty, and confusion that the situation fairly cried out for legal controls, which were then embraced by the administration and broad segments of the population, even including the affected persons themselves, as the restoration of order and legal security.

What the administrative authorities whose job it was to prepare and promulgate such emergency regulations overlooked, condoned, or indeed even welcomed was that this emergency legislation by no means restored the status quo ante; rather, it undermined the principle of equality before the law and opened the door to much more effective discrimination against "non-Germans" or other unpopular persons than any so-called spontaneous actions from below. In many cases, too, the establishment of special law was explicitly hailed, and the departure from general equality made easy, because even in the highest ranks of the Reich administration there were those who, in complete ignorance of the nature of totalitarian rule, supposed that the matter would have an end with the legal norms already decreed, and further emergency laws could be prevented.[7] Although the constant moral defamation and discrimination practiced against the Jews by the NSDAP continued,[8] despite all legal restraints, and spoke in a clear idiom of things to come, they could not or did not wish to recognize that the National Socialist leadership was entirely innocent of legal philosophy, that for the Nazis conventional law at best possessed instrumental value, and that the first provisions adopted under special law were only the prelude to further emergency regulations.

From a terminological standpoint, the following phases (although they overlap at many points, both materially and temporally) may be distinguished in the day-to-day process of putting the principle of *völkisch* inequality into practice via legislation and administrative measures. Of primary concern to the National Socialist legislators was, first of all, the creation of a compliant and submissive instrument for carrying out their aims. As the most important repository of state thinking, the Civil Service thus had to be converted as quickly as possible to National Socialist ideology, that is, purged of political opponents and persons of "foreign race." In a later phase, the major concern was to *segregate* the "non-Germans" from the Germans constitutionally, to exclude them from the German state polity and thus from the principle of equal rights for all. Once the door was opened to the loss of citizenship or the establishment of different classes of citizen (the Reich Citizenship Law and subsequent regulations), the way was clear for the third step, genuine discrimination in the form of explicit special law. The political aim, meanwhile, as seen from the point of view of the

Reich administration, was "Aryanization"—the full-scale dispossession of the Jews with only nominal indemnification.[9] Therefore the corresponding legislative measures were aimed at ousting "non-Germans" from professional and economic life (which was justified as being in defense of public interests), robbing them of their reputations and fortunes, and forcing them down to the level of underpaid temporary day laborers and/or turning them into a pariah class (the "social proletariat")[10] dependent upon welfare services (to be provided from their own resources).

This underclass, lacking legal protection and defrauded of any and all material possessions, was now seized upon and slowly prepared to be the object of forced emigration and later "resettlement" (deportation to the East).[11] Preparations for resettlement were facilitated by a fourth set of measures, which henceforth, and in the full light of public view, excluded the Jews from the community of law and from social life of any kind. These included distinguishing marks (the Star of David), special names, prohibitions on residence in designated areas, and bans on the use of public transportation. Thus restricted to their places of residence, the Jews were kept under constant police surveillance, so that, when the day came for them to be resettled, they had only to be served with the necessary orders. In sum, these four phases, despite all misadventures and arbitrary acts involved in their implementation, still reveal a quite astonishing "object-oriented" methodicalness and logic, in the form, as it were, of a sequential scale.[12] Moreover, this was not merely good for the purposes of deprivation of legal rights by judicial means but, objectively speaking, led directly to the "Final Solution,"[13] regardless of whether it was called expulsion from economic and social life, emigration, or resettlement.

To be sure, as already observed in the introduction, this sequential scale will not be followed chronologically here—for such treatment the reader may have recourse to the chronicles already available[14]—but rather according to special subjects (jurisdictions), in order to provide a better foundation for our thesis concerning the orderliness and uniformity of the process of legal disfranchisement. According to the relevant official plans and orders of business, these special subjects (the Civil Service Code, regulations governing citizenship and public health, laws concerning professional accreditation, etc.) for the most part fall under the purview of the inner administration by virtue of their essential nature.[15] For reasons of material coherence and objective comparison, the professional code of the attorneys-at-law, although actually under the jurisdiction of the Reich Ministry of Justice, is discussed in the same section as the laws of professional accreditation. Moreover, the jurisdiction of the inner (general) administration over the special topics to be discussed was also given from a superordinate point of view: the Reich Ministry of the Interior (Department 1, Groups 5 and 6, and Department 4)[16] was *generally* responsible for "race laws and race policy" (particularly for the so-called Jewish questions) and was therefore, according to the intent of the Combined Rules of Procedure for the Reich ministries, the "participating" supreme Reich authority, even with regard to anti-Jewish measures in areas that belonged to the portfolios of other departments. The following (unfortunately cursory)[17] discussion of special law regarding race under the aspects of proprietary, commercial, and labor law and in the cultural field is therefore justified not only on grounds of the objective correlation but even according to the distribution of jurisdictions then in force.

These forms of "participation" by the Reich Ministry of the Interior in the promulgation of race-specific special law in matters that did not belong to its departmental brief were of various kinds. In all Reich laws involving special provisions (for instance, the Law on Admission to the Legal Profession and the Law Altering the Industrial Code, both dated April 7, 1933),[18] the Reich Ministry of the Interior, as the "model authority" in all questions of race, was the "participating supreme Reich authority," as mentioned above. Its agreement was necessary for the drafting of any pertinent regulations.[19] To a certain extent, however, the Reich Ministry of the Interior could also promulgate regulations in areas that did not belong to its portfolio per se, because it had by law certain general powers. Some examples would be the Reich minister of the interior's Third Decree to the Reich Citizenship Law of June 14, 1938 (definition of the term *Jewish commercial enterprise*), and the Thirteenth Decree to the Reich Citizenship Law dated July 1, 1943,[20] according to which "punishable offenses committed by Jews [would] in future be punished by the police," since the Reich minister of the interior was empowered by section 3 of the law to promulgate any "legal and administrative rules necessary for the implementation and completion of the law."

The Reich Ministry of the Interior was more or less forcefully engaged in drafting the special regulations in commercial and proprietary law as well. For example, the Decree on the Registration of Jewish Property dated April 26, 1938,[21] was issued *jointly* by Göring in his capacity as the plenipotentiary for the Four Year Plan and the Reich minister of the interior. But the decree of November 12, 1938, eliminating the Jews from German commercial life,[22] was issued by the plenipotentiary for the Four Year Plan without formal participation by other Reich authorities.[23] The Decree on the Utilization of Jewish Property dated December 3, 1938,[24] was adopted by the Reich minister of the economy "*in agreement* with the participating Reich ministers," that is, with the agreement of the Reich minister of the interior also.[25] Similarly, the Decree on the Employment of Jews dated October 3, 1941,[26] was issued by the plenipotentiary for the Four Year

Plan (not by the Reich minister of labor) on the basis of the powers granted him under the decree of October 18, 1936;[27] the Reich minister of labor was empowered merely to draft implementing regulations in agreement with the Reich minister of the interior and the Party Chancellery, which later were issued in the form of a corresponding implementing order dated October 31, 1941,[28] in agreement with the aforementioned offices.

In delineating the above-named special subjects, admittedly, it must be borne in mind that no general statements are possible regarding the implementation of measures of special law in individual cases. There is an almost total lack of court decisions that would provide insight into contemporary circumstances. For, as explained in the introduction, the extent of supervision over executive acts by administrative courts in the Third Reich was hardly worthy of mention. The reasons were as follows.

Either there was simply no provision for legal remedies against such measures, since in the Third Reich, too, the principle of enumeration, adopted from the Weimar period, was still formally in effect and, of course, did not provide legal recourse against such measures; or else the affected persons did not dare to appeal (this would most likely not have achieved the desired result anyway), since such measures commonly were viewed as political acts that, on the grounds of the unwritten reservation that political acts of state were not subject to review,[29] were seen as being not actionable. Finally, court decisions, even if they had sided with Jewish complainants, would hardly have been published to any significant extent, since this would have been in stark opposition to political objectives. A more precise picture could only be gained by means of individual studies using local archives, such as have been undertaken from time to time.[30]

For a study of the judicial practice in regard to "non-German" persons under constitutional law, therefore, only a few court rulings from the area of general police law and commercial law published in the juridical literature can be adduced, and almost all of them rejected the suits of the Jews involved. Hence the following discussion must concentrate primarily on the depiction of the legal situation according to the relevant norms and administrative guidelines.

II. Civil Service Law

The first set of measures under special law affected the restructuring of the Civil Service. The primary concern of the political leadership was certainly the reliability of the public officials, since it could be taken for granted "that from a purely superficial viewpoint, the task of a victorious revolution consists in creating an apparatus that carries out its functions in the service of revolutionary ideas."[1]

Accordingly, the Civil Service was subjected to a profound reorganization under public law. As noted in the so-called Civil Service ruling handed down by the German Federal Constitutional Court on December 17, 1953, the relationship of the civil servant to the state was transformed, in accordance with the Führer principle, from a politically neutral and impartial service committed to the public interest into a leader-follower relationship.[2] The new terms of service had nothing whatever to do with the conventional notion of the professional Civil Service: they were exclusively dependent upon the Führer; the previously secure legal position of the civil servant was abolished, as the rulings handed down by the disciplinary courts show. The civil servant no longer swore to uphold the constitution, instead pledging fealty to Führer and Reich. To the Führer he owed "fidelity unto death."[3] Every theorist of constitutional law between the years 1933 and 1945 agreed that the civil servant thus became "the instrument of the Führer's will" and that the previous neutrality of the Civil Service had been "utterly destroyed."[4] The "obligation to political fidelity," that is, the duty to act at all times on behalf of National Socialism, as well as unconditional obedience to the Führer, were requirements for public office[5] and were affirmed by the civil servants themselves "to a considerable degree" as being essential legal duties incumbent upon anyone enjoying the status of civil servant.[6]

Because the great majority of civil servants leaned toward nationalistic and conservative ideas, particularly in the higher echelons, there was actually little need, as we have already observed, of extensive personnel purges; the traditional loyalty of the civil servant, oriented as it was to the state per se, made rebellion of any kind appear impossible. The Civil Service had, from the tradition of nonpartisanship and neutrality, always regarded the Weimar Republic with distrust, or at least with reserve, and, even before 1933, had worked for a "monocratic administrative state in place of pluralistic democracy."[7] This attitude among the leading elements of the Civil Service was of major benefit to the National Socialist regime. Already in 1933 the literature contained quasi-mystical calls for training civil servants to be priests of the state and its worldview.[8] To this extent, the old state apparatus, taken as a whole, could be retained almost intact, or at least with no noticeable disruption.[9] What was required was merely the removal of politically and racially undesirable members of the public service; otherwise everything remained as it had always been.

This goal was single-mindedly tackled immediately following the coup d'état using the proven method: individual actions followed by legal codification. As early as February and March of 1933, extensive purges were carried out in the administration and the courts, in part involving violations of principles of Civil Service law, in part even by violent means.[10] In the Prussian judicial administration in particular, in which anti-Semitism was present to a greater degree than in other administrative departments, Jewish judges and civil servants were ousted even before legal regulations could be issued.[11] On March 31, 1933, one week before promulgation of the so-called Professional Civil Service Code, the National Socialist commissar for Prussian justice and later Prussian minister of justice, Hans Kerrl, who was also a SA *Gruppenführer* and a former *Justizoberrentmeister* (a low-grade civil servant in the administration of justice).[12] directed that Jewish judges be urged to "immediately hand in their requests for leave"; otherwise they were to be denied entry to the court building; Jewish public prosecutors as well as Jewish prison officials were suspended from office.[13]

1.   The Law for the Restoration of the Professional Civil Service, April 7, 1933

The legalization of these illegal acts was then set in motion by means of the Law for the Restoration of the Professional Civil Service dated April 7, 1933,[14] which can be viewed as a kind of preparation, in the personnel sector, for the institutional merging of state and Party offices that later occurred.[15] The law, which was no ad hoc effort but rather one for which the groundwork had been carefully laid with extensive preliminary work long before the Nazi seizure of power,[16] was designed to "restore a nationalist and professional Civil Service and to simplify the administration" by regulating the dismissal and compulsory retirement of civil servants without regard to the laws then in force (sec. 1).[17] According to section 4 of this law, which was applied analogously to workers and employees in the public sector as well (sec. 15), "civil servants who, judging by their prior *activities*, could not be counted upon to uphold the National Socialist state without reserve" (emphasis mine) could be dismissed from office. Their entire political history, particularly since November 9, 1918, was adjudged to be relevant.[18] According to section 2 of the law, dismissal was *mandatory* in the case of those civil servants who had entered public service since November 9, 1918, without having the necessary qualifications or aptitude[19] for their respective careers. Section 5 of the Professional Civil Service Code permitted a civil servant to be transferred for reasons of "official necessity" to a different office or department at the same seniority level or its equivalent; according to section 6 of the law, it was permissible to pension off a civil servant "to simplify the administration or in the interests of the service," even without proof that he was "unfit for service."

The removal of "alien" persons was set forth in the infamous Aryan Paragraph of section 3, in which the term *non-Aryan* makes its first appearance and which read as follows:[20]

> (1) Civil servants not of Aryan descent are to be pensioned off (secs. 8 ff.); honorary civil servants are to be dismissed from employment.
>
> (2) Par. 1 does not apply to civil servants who were already civil servants on or before August 1, 1914, or who fought at the front in the World War for the German Reich or for its allies, or whose fathers or sons fell in the World War. Further exceptions may be permitted by the Reich minister of the interior in agreement with the responsible departmental ministers or by the supreme state authorities for civil servants abroad.

This law was officially acclaimed as the means of creating "a Civil Service suited to the nationalist government"; and it received high praise on account of its elimination of Jewish civil servants in implementation of the "*völkisch* racial philosophy" ("there can be no higher task than preserving the purity of and promoting one's own ethnic comrades").[21] Ministerial director Hans Seel of the Reich Ministry of the Interior deemed this "Aryan legislation" to be nothing less than a "blazing torch" that had "forever cauterized the heads of this hydra [of Jewry]." Yet its intent was "never to discriminate against or degrade other peoples."[22] Internally, however, the implementation of the law caused no little disquiet. As early as April 25, 1933, Reich Minister of the Interior Wilhelm Frick was obliged to admit at a ministerial meeting that the law had "badly shaken" the legal security of the Civil Service,[23] particularly since according to sections 2–6 of the law there was no legal recourse against dismissal or pensioning off—which was also why it was valid only until September 30, 1933.[24] At this meeting the Prussian minister president, Göring, also emphasized the "particular difficulties" caused by the "weeding out of civil servants of non-Aryan descent," insisting, however, on the "most whole-hearted implementation of sec. 3," which was "absolutely necessary for the preservation of the purity of the blood of the German people."[25]

The Aryan Paragraph was indeed implemented "wholeheartedly," since section 3 was binding law, whereas dismissal for political reasons at least lay in the discretion of the administration ("civil servants . . . may be dismissed from service).[26] Therefore, it is not immediately apparent why historical research has set forth the thesis that "great restraint" was used, particularly by the central administration, in the application of the Professional Civil Service Code.[27] In such sweeping terms this thesis is certainly incorrect and must be revised in numerous respects.

Viewed objectively, the purges were carried out most extensively where the persons affected had the most contact with the public, where they were employed in administering examinations, and in the fields of education and instruction.[28] Viewed laterally, the purges were carried out quite speedily and comprehensively in the lower and middle echelons, that is, in the lower and ancillary clerical ranks of the Civil Service, as well as in the area of local administration,[29] whereas the ministerial bureaucracy and the high-ranking administrators at the level of the *Länder* remained virtually unchanged. There the endeavor was to satisfy the intent of the law more by means of transfer or retirement (secs. 5 and 6) than by direct dismissal with the attendant loss of all benefits, as indicated by the scattered materials available from the appellate court districts. For example, reports from Hamm show that disciplinary action taken against judges frequently took the form of promotions denied, involuntary retirement, or transfer to a lesser office.[30] Some light is also provided by statistics available from Hamburg from the general and inner administration, according to which the number of dismissals under sections 2 to 4 of the Professional Civil Service Code were relatively low, whereas the incidence of transfers (secs. 5 and 6) was relatively high.[31] The same conclusion may be drawn from statistics available from the higher judicial service in Prussia (100 cases under sec. 4 and a total of 482 cases under secs. 5 and 6 of the Professional Civil Service Code).[32]

Procedurally speaking, a civil servant's mere membership in a party from the Weimar period was insufficient justification for the assumption of "national unreliability" in the sense intended by section 4 of the Professional Civil Service Code, with the exception of membership in the German Communist Party (KPD) or in a "Communist support or front organization," which automatically led to dismissal on grounds of "unsuitability" under section 2 of the Professional Civil Service Code (First Implementing Decree to Professional Civil Service Code dated April 11, 1933).[33] Grounds for dismissal under section 4, paragraph 1, of the Professional Civil Service Code existed only in cases in which a civil servant, by means of his activities (in speech or writing or by other behavior), had "exhibited malice against the national movement, reviled its leaders, or misused his official position to persecute, discriminate against, or otherwise harm national-minded civil servants."[34] In practice, however, as shown by pertinent files in the appellate court districts[35] and in the Reich ministerial administration, even civil servants who had belonged to the SPD were removed from service (KPD and SPD members were given almost the same treatment throughout). Civil servants who had belonged to the Zentrum or other parties were in some instances removed as well or, at best, denied promotion, unless they could demonstrate uncommonly distinguished performance.[36] At least as far as the SPD was concerned, moreover, a decree circulated by the Reich Ministry of the

Interior on July 14, 1933, announced that, "given the manifestly treasonous character of social democratic aims . . . any further membership in the SPD on the part of civil servants, employees, and laborers in the public sector" was "irreconcilable." All members of the SPD were required to sign a declaration within three days' time stating that they had dissolved all relations to the SPD and its support and/or affiliated organizations.[37]

To this extent, then, the thesis proposed above can be applied only to the *reshuffling* of the reasons for dismissal—away from dismissal on political grounds (sec. 4) and toward transfer or retirement—whereas, in the case of section 3, which provided for the *mandatory* pensioning-off[38] of non-Aryan civil servants (with exceptions for frontline soldiers and those whose service was of long standing), there was no possibility of assisting those affected.

The legal authority for the application of section 3 rested in the directive of the Reich Ministry of the Interior that every civil servant was required to prove his Aryan ancestry to his departmental superiors. This was accomplished by means of a comprehensive questionnaire, to which as a rule it was necessary to append the appropriate documents or, in case of doubt, a certificate from the "adviser on race research" at the Reich Ministry of the Interior.[39] This was all the more true of candidates for Civil Service positions. In May 1933 the procedure for registering and "weeding out civil servants of non-Aryan descent" was simplified by the distribution of unified questionnaires for all departments; there were, nevertheless, still differences in the way these were used.[40] Beginning in 1935, proof of descent could also be furnished by means of the so-called certificate of ancestry, which could be used at all offices where proof of ancestry was required.[41] Civil servants who knowingly falsified information on the relevant questionnaire were generally dismissed.[42]

The use made of such proofs of ancestry in deciding on the appointment and dismissal of members of the public service differed from department to department.[43] Since the submission of the required documents (birth certificate, birth and marriage certificates of the parents, birth certificates of all grandparents) was a complicated and time-consuming undertaking, with court proceedings to adjudicate matters of descent further delaying the proceedings, a decree was finally issued by the Reich Ministry of the Interior on August 1, 1940, according to which proof of ancestry could be furnished through certification of the "German-bloodedness" of the applicant by either a Party office or a governmental agency.[44] This decree resulted, on the one hand, in increased power for the Party, in that determination of ancestry (and thus the fate) of the person concerned was now in its hands; on the other hand, the administration now secured the possibility of emergency protection for its civil servants by means of such certification—for example, in cases where not all the required documents could be obtained for submission. In any case, such proofs were not insisted upon in each and every instance; many administrations took a great deal of time in proving the Aryan descent of their civil servants, especially when qualified people were involved. For example, it was not until August 3, 1942, that the Reich Ministry of Justice noted that the Aryan descent of some of its high-level civil servants was not shown on the records.[45] Although there is no firm documentary evidence, some such cases, apparently, were handled by transfers to outstations (as long as those concerned were not "full Jews"); but retirement was frequently also the conclusion.[46]

The thesis that the Professional Civil Service Code was applied in any sense sparingly must be further qualified to the extent that, although the central administration may well have proceeded cautiously with dismissals and transfers, it still held in hand, as will be demonstrated in more detail, the most effective means of discriminating against civil servants on political or racial grounds—in the form of the disciplinary code.[47]

Precisely because the legality, scope, and application of the Professional Civil Service Code were controversial within the administration as well, no exact statistics on the number of civil servants dismissed and transferred were published; and numbers are even scarcer for Jewish civil servants dismissed under section 3.

Exact statistics were hardly possible, it seems, because the implementation of the Professional Civil Service Code was not completed until the German Civil Service Code of 1937 took effect. The submission of the proofs of descent was time-consuming and was also not treated as particularly urgent by some governmental agencies. What is in any case certain is that the number of dismissals from the universities ("whole-hearted enforcement of National Socialist personnel criteria") was relatively high.[48] In the area of general and inner administration, by contrast, the absolute number of those dismissed could be properly determined only according to the documents from the Reich and *Land* authorities that found their way to the Reich Ministry of the Interior; but these are either not accessible or else only partially preserved. An estimate of the number of Jewish civil servants involuntarily retired, expressed as a percentage, is just as difficult, since the information from the Reich Ministry of the Interior lumps together *all* cases of dismissal and retirement under the Professional Civil Service Code.

According to this, roughly 12.5 percent of the civil servants of the senior grade (211 civil servants out of a total of 1,663 permanent positions) retired under sections 2–4 of the Professional Civil Service Code; of these, local administration

Oberbürgermeister (lord mayors) and other municipal councilors and the police service were the ones most affected. In the other *Länder*, it was 4.5 percent of the senior-grade civil servants (106 civil servants out of 2,339 permanent posts). In the ancillary and lower service in Prussia, the figure was 1.13 percent (with the police service being the most affected), and in the other *Länder* 1.79 percent of all civil servants.[49]

For the ministerial level, too, I can give no precise statistics on the application of the Aryan Paragraph, because in the official statistics of the director of the personnel department (Department 2) in the Reich Ministry of the Interior, Erwin Schütze, which mention 317 senior-grade civil servants dismissed, the cases dealt with under section 3 of the code are not indicated separately, but rather *all* cases dealt with under sections 2–4 of the code are lumped together (whereas precise breakdowns are available from the Reich finance administration).[50] Moreover, there is reason to doubt whether these statistics are complete, that is, whether they cover the entire period during which the Professional Civil Service Code was implemented, from 1933 to 1937. In any case one can glean no information from them as to the implementation of the Aryan Paragraph. However, general experiential values permit the assumption that the number of non-Aryan civil servants retired under the code must have been quite low, not because of any sparing application of the law but because the circle of potentially affected persons at the ministerial level was presumably quite small.

This may have been particularly true of the number of non-Aryan civil servants in the Reich Ministry of the Interior, whether because this old, established administration in any case looked upon the admission of Jews with skepticism (except perhaps where baptized Jews were concerned) or because the tradition among non-Aryans generally led them to choose other careers (attorney, etc.).[51] Finally, to whatever extent Jewish civil servants may have worked in the Reich Ministry of the Interior (and, analogously, in the interior ministries of the *Länder*), it may be realistically presumed that most of them fell under the provision excepting frontline soldiers (sec. 3, par. 2, Professional Civil Service Code). For, since the majority of civil servants were not appointed to the prestigious and long-established Reich Ministry of the Interior until their middle or later years, they had either already been civil servants as of the cutoff date of August 1, 1914, or belonged in any case to the group of "frontline soldiers," the definition of which, moreover, was quite broadly worded.[52]

Finally, the thesis that the number of cases that fell under section 3 of the Professional Civil Service Code was probably quite small is supported by statistics from the Reich Ministry of the Interior on the changes undertaken in personnel matters under the code up to the end of 1933. Listed for the senior service are a mere five cases under section 4 (dismissal on political grounds), six cases under section 5 (transfer for official reasons), one case under section 6 (retirement for official reasons), and three temporary retirements under section 25 of the Reich Civil Service Code[53]—but not a single case under section 3 of the Professional Civil Service Code.

More precise statistics are available for the area of judicial administration. The official information provided by civil servants in the Reich Ministry of Justice contains comprehensive tables, broken down according to appellate court districts, regarding Jewish judges and state prosecutors ("Jews by race") eliminated under section 3 of the Professional Civil Service Code. According to these, by April 30, 1934, a total of 574 judges and state prosecutors had been retired by reason of the Aryan Paragraph.[54] This was engineered so that, at least in Prussia, the affected persons, to the extent that they were permitted to continue in office as "frontline soldiers," were initially transferred from the big cities to other appellate court districts[55] before being finally retired there, too, on the authority of the Nuremberg Laws of September 15, 1935 (by official count a total of 239 civil servants).[56] Broken down by *Land* or district, the picture is as follows.

In Prussia, according to the statistics of the Prussian ministry of justice,[57] there were 1,704 non-Aryans among the 41,302 judicial civil servants (including junior attorneys) in office on April 7, 1933 (i.e., 4.1%) (the proportion of non-Aryans in the senior judicial service was 7.6%). Of these, 1,114 civil servants (2.7% of all civil servants, 65.4% of the non-Aryan officials) were eliminated, whereas 331 civil servants (19.4% of the non-Aryan civil servants) remained in office by virtue of the exceptions granted in section 3, paragraph 2, of the Professional Civil Service Code.

Also available are isolated statistics from the appellate court districts. According to these, roughly 15 of the 571 career senior justice officials in the appellate court district of Cologne (2.6%) were of Jewish descent; of these, 9 were pensioned off and 6 remained in office temporarily under the exception granted to frontline soldiers by section 3.[58] In Hamburg, 31 non-Aryan judges and state prosecutors were retired, and 12 others were allowed to remain in office in subordinate positions under section 3, paragraph 2, Professional Civil Service Code.[59] Overall, by September 1933, 95 of the 280 judges and state prosecutors in Hamburg had been eliminated from office.[60] In the appellate court district of Hamm in 1933, 18 judges of Jewish descent were compelled to retire under the Professional Civil Service Code; another 13 Jewish judges remaining in office by virtue of the exceptions granted under section 3, paragraph 2, were eliminated after 1935 on the basis of the Reich Citizenship Law and its implementing regulations. Six judges were subjected to professional discrimination (denial of promotion, transfer to lesser offices, etc.) because they were married to Jewish women.[61]

Finally, if one surveys the entire field of reasons for dismissal under the Professional Civil Service Code, it would seem entirely justified to conclude that in the judiciary, the forced retirement of non-Aryan civil servants under section 3, paragraph 1, was implemented to the fullest extent, whereas, given the "vigorous [political] restraint" exercised by Reich Minister of Justice Gürtner[62] and the attitude, quite conservative in any case, of justice officials themselves, dismissals for political reasons under section 4 were in all probability not very numerous, with the exception of the first radical measures taken in early 1933.[63] Rather, in the cases of troublesome judges and state prosecutors, the preferred method was to make use of other means of neutralization—retirement or transfer to a lesser office—under sections 5 and 6 of the Professional Civil Service Code. This can be seen with particular clarity in the statistics from Prussia, according to which the number of retirements and transfers under sections 5 and 6 was several times that of dismissals under section 4.[64]

2.   The German Civil Service Code, January 26, 1937

The special legal treatment reserved for Jewish civil servants, who beginning in 1935 included both the so-called full Jews and the "persons of mixed descent of the first degree,"[65] was, however, not an isolated program that came to an end with the expiration of the Professional Civil Service Code. Rather, it was a process that took place in various stages,[66] all of them culminating in the German Civil Service Code of January 26, 1937.[67]

Prior to this, the Reich Citizenship Law of September 15, 1935,[68] which was in force in all territories incorporated into the German Reich,[69] determined that Jews might not hold public office; all Jewish civil servants who were permitted to remain in office for a time by virtue of the exceptions granted in section 3, paragraph 2, of the Professional Civil Service Code (those with long-standing service records and those who had been frontline soldiers), as well as all other persons of Jewish descent employed in public service, were thus eliminated on November 15, 1935, by means of forced retirement mandated by law no later than December 31, 1935 (sec. 4, pars. 1 and 2, of the First Decree to the Reich Citizenship Law, dated November 14, 1935).[70] In the Reich judicial administration alone, this affected 239 judges and state prosecutors.[71]

The pensions of retired Jewish civil servants were cut, in violation of every principle of the "well-earned rights" of civil servants (art. 129, par. 1, of the Weimar Constitution).[72] Jewish civil servants who were dismissed or forced to retire on political grounds received no monetary support (pension) from public funds whatsoever, unless they had served for more than ten years (sec. 8 of the Professional Civil Service Code). The size of the pensions granted differed as well. Among the Jewish civil servants whom the law forced into retirement, only those who had served as frontline soldiers received, until they reached the legal age limit, pensions equal to their full previous salaries; and even so they did not receive the usual advancement in degree of seniority. Others entitled to benefits and with more than ten years of service received reduced amounts. As early as 1938, however, the pensions of all (up to then) "privileged" Jewish civil servants who had legitimate claim to them were further reduced at the instigation of the Party leadership.[73] Even harsher regulations were introduced for Jewish employees, who (in contrast to civil servants) were not tenured and could be dismissed from public service according to "simple" labor law. Even if they had been frontline soldiers, they did not enjoy "these privileges";[74] that is, they were deprived of all benefits. Beginning in 1935, all former Jewish civil servants (those who had undergone compulsory retirement) who had no legitimate claim to pensions under the Professional Civil Service Code were granted, in cases of "worthiness" and "indigence," a "maintenance subsidy," cancelable at any time; of course this was not an adequate compensation.[75]

The final regulation in this matter was provided by the German Civil Service Code of January 26, 1937,[76] which replaced both the Reich Civil Service Code of 1873 and the Professional Civil Service Code of April 7, 1933. Although it adopted, to a great extent, the principles embodied in the Reich Civil Service Code, it nonetheless contained numerous political provisions and regulations on race law that in effect annulled those same principles.[77] The result was that all Civil Service positions were put on a new legal footing,[78] in total disregard of conflicting provisions under the Weimar Constitution.[79] From now on, only persons of "German or related blood" (sec. 25), who were citizens of the Reich as set forth under the Reich Citizenship Law of September 15, 1935, could become civil servants if they met the career requirements and were in a position to "ensure" that they would "at all times and without reserve act on behalf of the National Socialist state" (sec. 26).

Ever since the changes made in the Reich Civil Service Code by the law of June 30, 1933, which was also in force for the *Länder* and the municipalities,[80] non-Aryan persons could no longer be appointed to public service, either as Reich civil servants, employees, or laborers.[81] Therefore, proof of ancestry was an essential part of any application for admission to public service.[82] Beginning in April 1933 in Prussia, non-Aryans were not permitted to be Civil Service probationers, and after June 1, 1933, they were no longer admitted to the first or second state law examinations. Beginning in 1934, when jurisdiction was transferred to the Reich,[83] anyone in the entire Reich territory registering for the first state law examination had to furnish in advance a "certificate of Aryan descent" (showing four Aryan grandparents for the applicant as well as for his wife or fiancée);[84] otherwise he was excluded from taking the examinations.

A further requirement was introduced in that the spouse of the candidate also had to be of "Aryan descent," because according to the "theory of the *völkisch* community," the racial idea also extended to the family of the civil servant or applicant.[85]

The regulations governing dismissal on racial grounds, which were placed inconspicuously in the section entitled "Termination of Civil Service Status" (sec. 59, par. 1, subpar. 2c),[86] although they adopted the basic idea of the Aryan Paragraph of the Professional Civil Service Code of April 7, 1933, were pertinent only in those cases in which civil servants were at first mistakenly classified as Aryans, since all other Jewish civil servants had by law been eliminated by December 31, 1935. A novelty, however, was that marriage to a person of Jewish descent was now also grounds for dismissal (sec. 59, par. 1, German Civil Service Code). Persons to be dismissed under section 59 of the code forfeited (in contrast to earlier provisions) all legitimate claim to pension benefits;[87] only when there was no fault of the civil servant did the law provide, as a special act of charity, that he "merely" be forced to retire with pension benefits (sec. 72, par. 1, German Civil Service Code).[88]

Politically unreliable civil servants and persons of equivalent status (notaries, etc.) who were no longer in a position to "ensure" that they would "at all times act on behalf of the National Socialist state," could not, by contrast, simply be dismissed (and were to that extent treated more mildly than those subject to the German Civil Service Code). Rather, at the request of their administrative superiors, and with the consent of the Reich Ministry of the Interior, they could be forced to retire permanently or temporarily (sec. 71, German Civil Service Code); this granted the administration considerably more discretionary latitude in deciding the subsequent fate of civil servants than had earlier been the case. Moreover, all civil servants were now de facto frankly declared to be the executor of the will of the NSDAP (sec. 1, par. 2, and sec. 3, par. 2, German Civil Service Code),[89] and the principle of political neutrality in the career Civil Service was thereby set aside. A civil servant showed a poor National Socialist attitude by, for instance, maintaining relations with Jews,[90] "refus[ing] to give the German greeting ('Heil Hitler')," or making critical statements about the Führer or about the treatment of the Jews.[91] Be that as it may, there was relatively little use made of compulsory retirement under section 71 of the German Civil Service

Code,[92] since the political and racial purges of the Civil Service had already taken place; furthermore, the preferred method of disposing of politically troublesome civil servants, particularly in cases involving highly qualified specialists, was to transfer them rather than to pension them off,[93] the more so because the opportunities for transfer increased greatly during the war years.[94]

Moreover, the need for the sharp sword of dismissal or compulsory retirement under the provisions of this law was not so very great, since the Reich Code of Disciplinary Procedure, adopted simultaneously on January 26, 1937,[95] offered a much less spectacular, yet, because of the limitless definition of the duties of civil servants under section 30 of the German Civil Service Code,[96] just as effective a means of disciplinary action as the German Civil Service Code itself. This included, in particular, reduction or withdrawal of salary (or pension) (sec. 4, pars. 1, 7, 9, of the Reich Code of Disciplinary Procedure). Since the principle of the Supreme Disciplinary Court, developed and refined in the course of constant judicial practice, that any—even the most trifling—"exercise of a non-National Socialist attitude of whatever kind," even so much as a statement "to any third party whatever," represented malfeasance in office,[97] it is obvious that any "malfeasance" that went beyond this was subject to rigorous sanctions.

Thus, for example, withdrawal from the NSDAP, according to a decree circulated by the Reich minister of the interior dated February 27, 1936, was as a rule followed by dismissal, because such a civil servant lacked the "fervent affinity with the National Socialist state" or the "necessary sense of sacrifice."[98] In exceptional cases, however, there were also milder sanctions, such as being passed over for promotion[99] or having one's salary reduced.[100] A civil servant's expulsion from the Party also generally resulted in his dismissal,[101] although here too, "milder" disciplinary measures were possible in exceptional cases.[102] Mass dismissals of specialists not loyal to the Nazis were in any case impossible owing to the shortage of such personnel.[103] Even in the Reich Ministry of the Interior it was neither demanded nor expected that every civil servant be a member of the Party "under the currently existing conditions"; one was not even compelled to join the National League of German Civil Servants or the NSRB[104] even if, defacto, neither appointment nor promotion was possible in the absence of such membership. Nonetheless, such collective membership was by all means intended to be binding upon future generations of civil servants.[105] Accordingly, there was no express provision that required all civil servants to join the National Socialist Welfare Organization (NSV)—an "auxiliary unit" of the NSDAP; yet the disciplinary courts derived a duty to join from the general duty "to act without reserve on behalf of the National Socialist state," one whose violation could even be punished with dismissal.[106]

Further disciplinary sanctions consisted in the dismissal of civil servants who had troublesome religious affiliations (Jehovah's Witnesses) or who gave false answers on the questionnaires required under the German Civil Service Code.[107] Civil servants who maintained commercial relations with Jews were penalized by reductions in salary (or pension),[108] whereas retirees who were convicted of criminal offenses had their pensions withdrawn altogether.[109]

Such disciplinary measures as provided for in the German Civil Service Code and the Reich Code of Disciplinary Procedure were prerequisites for the effective implementation of Nazi aims and corresponding legal regulations. Added to this was intensive schooling in Party politics, both by the department chiefs[110] and by the Party itself, the support of which was incumbent on all department heads,[111] as was an obligation to put down any critical statements that were deemed, under the Civil Service decree circulated by the Reich minister of the interior on June 22, 1933, to be "defeatist" and a "continuation of Marxist agitation"; all civil servants with supervisory duties were expressly enjoined to report such cases.[112] It can therefore come as no surprise that the Civil Service, at least after the German Civil Service Code took effect, was populated either by the Nazi faithful or at the very least Nazi loyalists and that it lost no opportunity to demonstrate its loyalty in all things. Those civil servants who held reservations about political developments ventured at the very most to express doubts about issues of detail but did not dare criticize matters of principle, since above them, as seen in the records of the disciplinary courts,[113] dangled the Damoclean sword of immediate dismissal, transfer, or other disciplinary action.

The destiny of civil servants classified as "persons of mixed descent" was more complicated than that of full Jews. Persons of mixed descent of the first degree (half Jews), who, because of membership in the Jewish religion or marriage to a full Jew, were of equal status with the Jews ("legal Jews" in the sense of sec. 5, par. 2, of the First Decree to the Reich Citizenship Law, dated November 14, 1935),[114] were subject to the same provisions under special law as the Jews. Although persons of half-Jewish descent who were not considered Jews under the specified provisions (so-called *privileged* "persons of mixed descent of the first degree")—that is, persons who had only two Jewish grandparents and who were married to an Aryan—were permitted to remain in public service or even, to a limited extent, be appointed to public service,[115] they were excluded from careers as tenured civil servants, since the Reich Civil Service Code in the version adopted with the amending law of June 30, 1933,[116] barred even so-called one-quarter Jews (persons with one Jewish grandparent) from a career in civil service.

Persons of half-Jewish or quarter-Jewish descent (persons of mixed descent of the first degree and persons related by marriage to Jews who were already civil servants), as long as they were not legally equated with Jewish status or unable to provide a complete "Aryan certificate," were generally allowed to remain in office; however, if their positions were in the public eye, they were often transferred to other posts or to outstations, as long as this could be done without causing a stir. That such persons were in any case not dismissed is also underscored by the fact that as late as 1944, Himmler, in his capacity as Reich minister of the interior, issued a decree to all subordinate offices expressing the expectation that Jewish "persons of mixed descent" would no longer occupy "key positions."[117]

If civil servants of half-Jewish descent were simultaneously politically troublesome, however, there was really no keeping them. But their removal on political grounds then had to be initiated on the authority of the provisions concerning political reliability, since the special racial laws in the Professional Civil Service Code and the German Civil Service Code of 1937 did not apply to Jewish *Mischlinge*. However, in the wake of increasingly drastic anti-Jewish measures, especially those adopted after the beginning of the war, the attempt was made to subject Jewish "persons of mixed descent" in the public service sector as well to the special legal treatment already meted out to full Jews. The SS leadership in particular, having taken over more and more responsibility for anti-Jewish measures of all kinds, attempted to include *Mischlinge* under the purview of the anti-Jewish operations (for instance, equating them with Jews for purposes of the Final Solution)[118] or even pushing through special legal provisions for them.[119] These latter, however, never came into effect, whether for political reasons owing to fortunes of war or because the required administrative effort would have been prohibitive.[120] Nevertheless, no later than 1944 there were preparations under way for special treatment of the half-Jewish members of the public service, who until that time had been exempt from labor service duty; these preparations were undertaken with the same secrecy[121] that had characterized the anti-Jewish measures of 1933.[122]

As is common in the preparation of centralized (special) regulations, the first step, according to a decree signed by Undersecretary Hans Stuckart in 1944, was the registration and classification of everyone belonging to the affected group of persons. The decree required "reports broken down according to racial incrimination" on the following two questions: which and how many employees and laborers in the public service were "Jewish *Mischlinge*" of the first or second degree, and which civil servants, employees, and laborers in the public service were "related by marriage to Jewish *Mischlinge* of the first or second degree."[123]

What purpose these preparations served—whether "merely" removal from office or as groundwork for the sterilizations planned by Undersecretary

Stuckart,[124] or even as the first step toward the Final Solution—cannot be said with certainty. Whatever the case, it was plainly only the fortunes of war that prevented the meting out of special treatment to the Jewish "persons of mixed descent" in public service as well. Outside the public sector, to be sure, strictures against "non-Germans" were taken to much greater lengths.

III. Race Legislation in the Narrower Sense

Such strictures, in the form of actual race legislation, commenced immediately after the purges in public service. Superficially, they were presented as measures for the promotion of public hygiene and eugenics, having general effect and containing no particular provisions of special law directed against specific groups. The purpose, however, was manifestly to preserve "racial purity," which was synonymous with the advancement of the Aryan and the elimination of the non-Aryan races and other undersirable groups. Special treatment under the eugenics laws was provided for all those who did not fit into this framework. This consisted in the revocation of essential individual rights, more particularly in infringement of the right to freedom from bodily harm. These laws, which, to judge by the statements of leading National Socialists prior to 1933, had already been resolved upon long before the Nazi seizure of power,[1] initiated Nazi atrocities in the area of forced sterilizations and castrations and ultimately prepared the intellectual soil upon which the murderous actions of so-called euthanasia were committed.[2] In the process, the circle of persons who might be considered for such measures under special law was so broadly defined—with the aid of pseudomedical phraseology—that the authorities acquired an almost unlimited scope for deciding who, in each individual case, would be deemed to be among that set of people.

1.   The Law for the Prevention of Progeny with Hereditary Diseases
     (Eugenics Law), July 14, 1933

The opening salvo was the Law for the Prevention of Progeny with Hereditary Diseases of July 14, 1933,[3] which permitted the sterilization of a person suffering from "hereditary disease" when it was "in all probability to be expected that his or her descendants will suffer from grave physical or mental hereditary defects" (sec. 1, par. 1); mental and emotional disorders were included among the "hereditary diseases" covered by this law.[4] Application could be made, first and foremost, by the person who was to be sterilized; in case he or she was legally incapacitated, certified as feeble-minded, or of restricted legal competence, the legal guardian could sign with the approval of the Surrogate's Court (sec. 2). However, the medical examiner or the director of a hospital, sanatorium, nursing home, or penal institution could also make application for sterilization (sec. 3).

With this law the National Socialists had adopted an older Prussian bill, with the one essential difference that the Prussian bill had concerned itself exclusively with voluntary cases.

Since 1925 proposals on sterilization had been advanced several times in the Prussian representative assembly, but they had always been rejected. On June 2, 1932, a committee of the Prussian state health council published a draft sterilization law that provided for voluntary sterilization where it was eugenically indicated; this aroused considerable notice. Similar ideas were also being considered at the Reich level. The official draft of a General German Criminal Code of 1925 called for the legalization of sterilization (which until then was considered to be bodily injury under sec. 223 of the Penal Code) with the consent of the patient. Under section 229 of this proposal, consensual bodily injury was to be punished only in cases in which the act was offensive to good morals. In the relevant commentaries it was observed that sterilization on social grounds or for reasons of racial hygiene was permissible only when governed by a conscientious interpretation of the concept of public morals.[5] All official bills stressed voluntariness as being the sine qua non in any question of sterilization.

After passage of the law of July 14, 1933, however, the way was opened for *compulsory* sterilization, and not only upon application by the affected person's relatives but also at the instigation of the authorities. Moreover, the interpretation of the law, as it was expressed in the decree circulated by the Reich Ministry of the Interior on February 27, 1934, permitted interference with the right of individual freedom of movement for an indefinite period, in that so-called hereditarily diseased persons in living institutions could be confined there indefinitely.[6]

Responsible for decisions involving possible sterilization was the Hereditary Disease Court, which was attached to the respective municipal courts and consisted of a local judge (*Amtsrichter*) as presiding judge, a medical examiner, and another physician (sec. 6, par. 1).[7] The possibility of sterilization, for which the Reich Ministry of the Interior had vigorously campaigned,[8] was frequently used quite frivolously.[9] Nevertheless, because sterilization was applicable only to individual cases and required a formally regulated procedure, the race fanatics among the political leadership considered the eugenics law insufficient. If compulsory sterilization and forced indefinite confinement of "hereditarily diseased persons" in institutions was permissible, then, in the minds of the Nazi leaders, who were completely indifferent to moral and legal considerations, it was no great step to begin contemplating the deliberately planned obliteration of such persons. As early as 1929, Hitler had publicly toyed with the idea of killing all children with physical birth defects (he estimated their number at 700,000 to 800,000 annually).[10] For what was the point of keeping "diseased" people alive who were nothing but "useless" members of the *Volksgemeinschaft*? And whoever was "useless" was "by definition"—as shown by the treatment later meted out to the so-called asocials—not "worthy of life," but "unworthy of living." This planned "euthanasia,"[11] to be sure, could not be implemented by means of normative regulations, since even by the standards of the positivist legal thinking that predominated in National Socialism, such ideas were seen as not yet capable of being legalized.[12] However, the law of July 14, 1933, must be viewed as the immediate forerunner of that campaign, since it sought to overcome the "inhibitions" on the part of the public against straightforward killing of so-called inferior persons, in particular by constantly widening (and frequently quite arbitrarily defining) the circle of candidates for sterilization.[13] Even in the academic literature there were frank discussions of the question of killing "inferior" persons on racial grounds. Although such discussions at first took place "merely" in the context of punishing dangerous sex offenders under criminal law by emasculation, it was already clearly aimed at the eradication of so-called inferior persons in general. Thus, for example, one reads in a dissertation published in Göttingen in 1937:

> The value of the individual to the community is measured according to his racial makeup. Only a racially valuable person has the right to exist within the community. A person who, because of his inferiority, is useless, indeed harmful to the whole, on the other hand, must be eliminated. The specific way in which this is to be done is a question that depends on the climate of popular opinion. Whether or not the people can as yet find it within themselves to understand the elimination of the inferior individual by [legal] killing remains to be seen; but today, at least, they certainly welcome the eradication of the sex offender and thus the prevention of any asocial offspring. . . .
>
> The great task itself must not be inhibited nor its effectiveness impaired by any petty disputes over jurisdiction. It cannot be that the eugenic indication, and racial considerations as a whole, are left out of account in imposing the sentence of castration simply because in some circumstances the boundary between criminal and racial-hygienic measures might be become blurred as a result.[14]

Despite all efforts to popularize such ideas, however, plans for euthanasia were carried out under clandestine instructions from the Führer behind the veil of strictest (though perhaps never entirely successful) secrecy in hospitals and sanatoriums; roughly 190,000 persons fell victim to the program.[15] As the first large-scale murder operation on the part of the Nazi regime, euthanasia was the logical forerunner to the eradication of racially undesirable "non-Germans" in the East (where German legal principles were not in force and unwelcome attention was less to be feared), especially as implemented against the Jews (the Final Solution). This logical continuity is shown by, among other things, the fact that some of the personnel engaged in the euthanasia operations later found employment in the extermination camps in Poland.[16] True, the euthanasia campaign had to be broken off in 1941, because the conspicuously high number of death notices at the registry offices resulted in more and more questions from family members, protests by representatives of the Catholic and Protestant churches, and internal memos by individual judicial agencies.[17] In any case, the murder campaign of euthanasia shows, in the present context, what boundless possibilities had been opened up to a regime that was determined to take to its logical conclusion the fundamental idea built into the forced sterilization of undesirable persons, namely, that the state was at liberty to dispose of the individual as it saw fit.

2.   The Law for the Protection of German Blood and German Honor, September 15, 1935

The prevention of the birth of racially undesirable ("hereditarily diseased") children, however, was by itself not likely to bring about the desired triumph of the principle of "purity of German blood." The problem of undesirable offspring was attacked first only because there were existing proposals to fall back on as well as a broadly held conviction that eugenic measures were permissible in individual cases. The next step was to indict any liaison between racially undesirable persons as being morally objectionable, as "race defilement." Of course "mixed marriages" had already been subject to discrimination in the past; for example, beginning in 1933 the Reich Ministry of Finance had (without legal authority) excluded such marriages from marriage loans.[18] However, it now became a matter of preventing such liaisons altogether, especially those between Jews and "Germans." The ground for this had been prepared not only by an unbridled popular anti-Semitic propaganda campaign but also in the political[19] and in specialized academic[20] literature, as well as through the emphasis placed upon theoretical racial ("ethnological") instruction in the schools, where Jews were characterized not only as foreigners but also as enemies.[21]

This friend-foe theory of racial politics reached its zenith in the Law for the Protection of German Blood and German Honor (the Blood Protection Law), which was promulgated at the Nazi Party Congress in Nuremberg on September 15, 1935.[22] This law—which the commentaries put out by the Reich Ministry of the Interior celebrated, in all seriousness, as a "generous solution of the Jewish and *Mischling* problem"[23] and which, for the first time, used the term *Jew* in place of the term *non-Aryan* and introduced the expression "German or racially related *blood*"[24]—was worded in such a way that marriages between Jews[25] and "citizens of German or racially related blood" as well as any "extramarital intercourse" between them was flatly prohibited (secs. 1 and 2). Violations were punishable by a term in the penitentiary (of at least one year) or by a jail sentence or imprisonment (sec. 5). Jews were further prohibited from employing citizens "of German or racially related blood under forty-five years of age in their households" (sec. 3). This was meant to prevent the danger of the "undesirable mixture of races." They were also forbidden to "raise the Reich national flag or wear the Reich colors" (sec. 4),[26] a prohibition that, given the numerous parades and marches of the time, where showing the flag was compulsory, also served to facilitate the singling out and isolation of Jews for all to see.

In the period that followed, the Blood Protection Law underwent further expansion. Thus, the second implementing regulation to the Blood Protection Law broadened its prohibitions to cover those former Polish citizens who had acquired German citizenship—which affected primarily the so-called ethnic Germans[27]—whereas the prohibition against race mixing did not apply to the great mass of Poles (persons with so-called protected status, or politically reliable foreigners).[28] However, the Blood Protection Law was not aimed solely at Jews but also at other "undesirable" "non-Germans." Hence the call for racial purity, upon which the "inner unity" of a people was said to rest, targeted only superficially the neutralizing of the Jews; it actually took aim at "aliens" of all kinds.[29] Thus the prohibition on marriage, as already noted in the introduction, applied not only to marriages contracted between Jews (including Jewish *Mischlinge*) and "persons of German blood" and between Jews and *Mischlinge* of the second degree[30] but was also interpreted beyond the wording of the law as being a desideratum (de facto a requirement) for all marriages between "citizens of German or racially related blood" in cases in which "offspring that would endanger the preservation of the purity of German blood could be expected to result."[31] Such a threat was assumed to be latent in all liaisons between Germans and "inferior" "non-Germans," including Gypsies, blacks and their descendants, and later the peoples of Eastern Europe. In order to prove that this threat did not exist in liaisons between "partners of different races," it was necessary to obtain a "certificate of fitness for marriage" from the Public Health Office.[32] Poles, too, although in principle deemed to be among the Aryans, were included in the prohibition on race mixing. There was a de facto prohibition against marriage of (stateless) Poles and Germans as well as marriage of Poles who had acquired German citizenship and all other "non-Germans." There was no law enunciating such a prohibition. However, it was put into practice all the same by the tried-and-true method of internal administrative guidelines, which dictated that registry office officials simply should not record such marriages, in order (and this was of particular significance in the Annexed Eastern Territories) "to achieve a complete separation . . . [of the German citizens] from their Polish surroundings."[33]

Here, too, as usual under the Nazi system, actual practice far outstripped the legal mandates. Not until 1943 was this de facto marriage prohibition set forth in the form of a *universal* standard, in that the so-called Protected Status Order[34] prohibited marriages between Poles with protected status and *all* other persons (that is, they could marry neither Germans nor Poles registered in the German National Register nor any other "non-Germans" whatsoever), so that Poles were in effect allowed to marry only among themselves. This not only fulfilled the *Reichsführer*-SS's long-standing dream of total racial segregation[35] but contributed at the same time to the isolation of the Poles from all "extra-Polish" influences. Plans for such isolation, as will be shown in detail, were just as far-reaching as those for cutting off contact between the Jews and the outside world.

3. The Law for the Protection of the Hereditary Health of the German People (Marital Hygiene Law), October 18, 1935

The marriage prohibitions discussed above, however, were by no means restricted to persons "of foreign race." Indeed, as demonstrated in the introduction, the principle of placing such people under special law extended far beyond the circle of "non-Germans." Just one month after the promulgation of the Blood Protection Law as part of the new "*völkisch* legislation," the general outline of the marriage prohibitions was broadened to include all racially undesirable persons without regard to ancestry. The Law for the Protection of the Hereditary Health of the German People (Marital Hygiene Law) of October 18, 1935,[36] whose aim was to prevent the birth of any undesirable offspring, abrogated one of the most important individual rights—that of the free choice of one's mate—since, in a poorly defined multiplicity of cases, it made the contraction of marriage absolutely impossible. Marriage was prohibited, first of all, to any "person with hereditary disease" as defined under the Law for the Prevention of Progeny with Hereditary Diseases of July 14, 1933.[37] But it went further than that: marriage might not be contracted in any case in which "one of the persons engaged to be married suffered from a disease associated with the danger of contagion" that gave cause "to fear considerable harm to the health of the other party or of their offspring"; in which one of the persons engaged to be married was legally incompetent or under temporary guardianship; or in which one of the persons engaged to be married suffered "from a mental disturbance" causing "the marriage to be deemed undesirable for the ethnic community" (sec. 1). Such blanket clauses were open not only to unlimited interpretation but also to the most blatant kind of arbitrary rulings. The authorities were not required to show proof of the alleged harm; rather, the individual was expected to prove that such harm was *not* to be feared.

Such proof had to be furnished not only by any foreigner intending marriage;[38] henceforth, *anyone* harboring plans to marry, even a person "of German blood," was obliged to prove his or her fitness to marry by means of a "certificate of fitness for marriage" that was to be issued by "counseling bureaus for racial and marital hygiene"[39] that were set up under the offices of public health (sec. 2). Although this provision was never put into general effect, probably owing to the administrative expenditures it would have entailed,[40] and was later supplanted by the obligation to produce a "certificate of nonobjection to marriage,"[41] this example once again shows with particular clarity the true character of National Socialist (special) law. It was not the authorities who had to prove that legal restraints (marriage prohibitions) were applicable in any given case; rather, the individual had to prove that he did *not* fall under the prohibitions, that the general rules of civil liberty were valid for him. In principle, everything was forbidden unless it was expressly permitted, confirmed, or certified.

As for the scope of the Marital Hygiene Law, there were of course no specific provisions for "non-Germans," any more than had been the case in the Law for the Prevention of Progeny with Hereditary Diseases. There was simply no need for them, since the principle of racial discrimination affected every legal norm as a kind of generalized, universal legal proviso. What is more, following tried-and-true practice, the law was defined so broadly that anything could be subsumed under it. It is therefore obvious that "non-Germans" were the very first to be affected by the law. According to the general clause of section 1, it was first and foremost marriages between Germans and members of "inferior" races that could be obstructed, under the pretext of preventing the birth of undesirable offspring. Yet there was much more to it, namely the monstrous though (from a National Socialist point of view) logical idea of disallowing marriages between Germans and foreigners altogether. This concept may well have been taken from Italy, where the resolution of the Great Fascist Council (*Gran Consiglio del Fascismo*) dated October 7, 1938, prohibited not only marriages between Italian citizens and members of "Semitic" and "non-Aryan" races but also any marriages between members of the public service and foreign women, regardless of racial origin. Marriages between Italian citizens and foreigners in general depended upon permission from the Italian Ministry of the Interior.[42] It is possible that this idea was already haunting the minds of the Nazi leaders at the time the Marital Hygiene Law took effect; in any case the Reich administration began giving it serious consideration in 1938.[43]

Even though this plan for a general ban on marriages between German citizens and foreigners never came to fruition, a beginning was made in the form of regulations governing marriage by members of the SS, the Wehrmacht, and the Party as well as pressures brought to bear upon members of the public service.[44] Beginning in 1931, members of the SS needed to obtain permission to marry from the Reichführer-SS.[45] From 1936 on the Reich Security Main Office (RSHA), which had of course already excluded Jews from active military service,[46] required soldiers intending to marry to obtain authorization, which was granted only if the fiancée was "of German or racially related blood" and if both partners were "fit to be married" under the provisions of the Marital Hygiene Law of October 18, 1935.[47] The result was a complete halt to marriages between members of the armed services and "non-Germans" of any kind (and particularly Jews and Jewish Mischlinge).[48] These regulations were further stiffened during the war. According to a secret decree of the chief of the Armed Forces High Command dated January 26, 1942, members of the armed services were permitted to marry citizens of the Nordic states (Holland, Norway, Denmark, and Sweden), to which group Finland and Belgium were later added,[49] only with permission (obtained under degrading conditions) of the Führer.[50] To "preserve the purity . . . [of their] own racial and ethnic foundations," farmers who were members of the NSDAP were subject to a ban on marriages with Poles and Czechs, in order to "prevent . . . [the latter from] marrying into German farmsteads." Otherwise, all NSDAP members, as well as all members of its various organizations (the SA, the SS, the National Socialist Motor Corps, the Hitler Youth, the German Lecturers' Association, the National Socialist Student League, the Nazi Women's League) required permission from the local Gauleiter if they desired to marry "members of the Czech, Polish, or Magyar ethnic groups."[51] Although marrying without the required permission did not nullify the union (sec. 13 of the Marriage Law and sec. 14 of the First Implementing Decree), it did have disciplinary consequences. Members of the public service may not have been subject to any requirements for permission; but for a civil servant to marry a "non-German" person constituted malfeasance in office.[52] Furthermore, Party offices were instructed "unconditionally to prevent" "mixed marriages" on the part of members of the public service, political leaders of the NSDAP, officers, and persons active in the "instruction of the *Volk*."[53]

4. The Marriage Law, July 6, 1938

One important complement to the racial provisions under special law was the law of divorce, discussed in the second part of this book, which deals with judicial matters. However, in regard to its racially motivated provisions and its evolution, a brief summary is pertinent at this juncture, since, as previously observed, the Reich Ministry of the Interior had to be consulted in all regulations involving race law, even when the matters in question did not belong to the field of interior administration.

From a very early stage, every opportunity was taken to dissolve racially mixed marriages by means of a broad interpretation of civil law.[54] Ostensibly, this was done not for "moralistic reasons, but for the sake of racial hygiene." For this reason only, Jews were placed under the laws governing foreigners.[55] Accordingly, the German partner was permitted, without further ado, to contest the validity of the marriage on grounds of having made a mistake regarding a "personal characteristic" of the spouse under section 1333 of the Civil Code (old version), if at the time of the marriage he or she was unaware of the Jewish ancestry of the spouse[56] or of the possibility of such Jewish ancestry.[57] This was true in particular for the dissolution of marriages between German women and Jews, inasmuch as these liaisons were considered unusually offensive (as "race defilement").[58] Of course, the Marriage Law of July 6, 1938[59]—which was issued in the interests of harmonizing the law and in particular to supplant the Austrian law, which in divorce cases still made distinctions according to the religious affiliation of the spouses[60]—contained no explicit racial provisions. Rather, the racial aims of this law were veiled behind slogans (promotion of "genetic hygiene," etc.) or else appeared only in annotations to the commentaries or in the subsequent administrative guidelines. Thus, for example, divorce became easier to obtain since marriage was now seen more and more as an institution "in the interests of the continued existence of the German people," one in which the "individualistic interests of the spouses [were] no longer decisive."[61] For reasons of "eugenics," such as were seen to exist in cases of grave illness of mental or physical nature (secs. 7ff., 36 ff.), divorce or annulment of a marriage was made easier in that, for example, section 37 of the Marriage Law, as previously section 1333 of the Civil Code (old version), permitted mixed marriages to be contested on the basis of personal characteristics of one of the spouses. Similarly, divorce of German-Polish marriages was also facilitated, at least in the Annexed Eastern Territories, by means of a broad interpretation of section 4 of the Marriage Law,[62] which sustained divorce petitions by the German partner on grounds of so-called ethnic policy.

For the political leadership, however, the dissolution of marriages between non-Aryans and persons "of German or racially related blood" proceeded far too slowly. Moreover, it was dependent on the will of the persons affected: state authorities could intervene only in those cases where the marriage was legally invalid.[63] For this reason, means were sought by which to achieve a general dissolution or "drying-out" of all German-Jewish mixed marriages[64]—that is, a way of making divorce in such cases into a purely administrative procedure upon which the individuals themselves would have no influence. At a meeting held on March 6, 1942, at the Reich Security Main Office (RSHA), Undersecretary Stuckart of the Reich Ministry of the Interior proposed rigorous compulsory measures such as the forced sterilization of all "*Mischlinge* of the first degree" (the so-called half Jews), in order to prevent the birth of undesirable offspring; or, alternatively, the recognition of a general legal right to divorce on the part of the German partner. Since such a legal right to divorce was rejected by the Reich minister of propaganda, agreement was finally reached on the following procedure, which actually came quite close to the previously rejected idea: legislation was to be enacted to the effect that, upon application either by the German partner or the state prosecutor, divorce had to be granted in cases of "mixed marriage"; to mitigate the "impression of compulsory divorce," it was agreed that internal administrative guidelines would give the persons concerned a certain prescribed term during which to petition for divorce, after which the state prosecutor's office was to be instructed to begin divorce proceedings. Grounds for the divorce were to be—as the judiciary had proposed from the outset—solely the fact that one partner was a Jew or a (legally equivalent) Jewish *Mischling* as defined by section 5, paragraph 2, of the First Decree to the Reich Citizenship Law. Of decisive importance was that the *determination* of Jewishness was no longer up to the courts, nor the Reich minister of the interior, but was now settled by the chief of the Security Police and the Security Service, whose decision was binding on the courts as well.[65] This opened the floodgates to arbitrary rulings, since the police, as will be demonstrated, had no intention of sticking to the legal definition of who was or was not a Jew. Even though the planned regulation was never put into effect, such deliberations nevertheless show the radical manner in which the question of mixed marriages with "non-Germans" was to be settled. Once again, they plainly demonstrate the basic thrust of National Socialist race law: the pronounced way in which it was taken out of the hands of the judiciary and increasingly handed over to the political sphere and the police until, finally, it was almost completely removed from the jurisdiction of state administration.

IV. Citizenship Law

Parallel to the actual race legislation, the transformation of the law of citizenship was also undertaken. Since all domestic rights and responsibilities hinged upon citizenship, it represented a most important point of departure for the National Socialists to forsake the constitutional principle of equality and put *völkisch* inequality into effect in comprehensive form for all areas of law. It was the goal of the race fanatics in the political and administrative leadership to exclude all "non-Germans" from acquiring German citizenship or to revoke it where it had already been acquired—above all, of course, in the case of the Jews. Questions of citizenship, first and foremost among them being the closely related issue of ethnicity, thus attracted the particular attention of the authorities. Not only the interior administration but also numerous other agencies (the Party, the Reich Commissar for the Strengthening of German Nationhood [RKF], and others) were involved, so that the area became splintered into a labyrinthine jumble of competing jurisdictions.[1] Where the area of interior administration is concerned, the "final goal" of excluding all "non-Germans" from German citizenship was not achieved by a single legislative act but incrementally. To begin with, existing regulations were taken up and revised, and existing citizenship law was demolished in bits and pieces.

1.   The Law on the Revocation of Naturalization and the Deprivation of German Citizenship, July 14, 1933

From the outset, the National Socialist regime looked for ways and means to get rid of those citizens whom it deemed undesirable. As usual when laws were rewritten to fit the National Socialist program, they did not at first attack fundamental legal norms—in this case, the Reich Nationality Law of July 22, 1913 (RuStAG).[2] Instead, by means of various amending laws, its content was undermined to the point where the provisions in question became meaningless or were deemed to have been amended. They themselves remained as a facade or else their repeal appeared to be a matter of mere formality.[3]

The Law on the Revocation of Naturalization and the Deprivation of German Citizenship was passed as early as July 14, 1933.[4] According to it, naturalizations that took place between November 9, 1918, and January 30, 1933, could be revoked "if the naturalization [was] not deemed to be desirable."[5] This regulation directly contradicted the Reich Citizenship Law of 1913, because under the latter, naturalization was fundamentally irrevocable, and ex officio rescission of citizenship was limited to certain well-defined exceptional cases (for instance, failure to heed a summons to return to the homeland in case of war, etc. [secs. 27–29]). A further grave contravention of existing law lay in the fact that not only citizens by virtue of naturalization but also citizens by birth were threatened with the loss of citizenship. Under section 2, Reich citizens (*Reichsangehörige*) living abroad who had "harmed German interests" by violating their "obligation to show allegiance to Reich and *Volk*" (that is, persons who had fled for political or racial reasons or were otherwise troublesome) could be declared to have forfeited their German citizenship. Both possibilities of depriving citizenship were discriminatory policies that worked above all to the detriment of German citizens of Jewish descent. If grounds for racial and political "incrimination" coincided in one person, the administration apparently focused exclusively upon the political behavior rather than the racial extraction of the person concerned.[6]

As explained in the implementing regulations of the Reich minister of the interior dated July 26, 1933, the term *undesirable* as defined in section 1 of the law of July 14, 1933, was to be evaluated on a case-by-case basis according to "ethnic-national" principles, taking due account of all facts both before and after the naturalization;[7] that is to say, it was nothing other than a blanket clause that endowed the administration with unlimited means to proceed against any and all (racial) opponents of the regime, without the possibility of judicial review. Thus, as stated in those same implementing regulations, the primary targets to be considered for revocation of naturalization under section 1 were, logically enough, naturalized "eastern Jews" (*Ostjuden*) ("elements originating in Eastern and Southern Europe and their descendants"),[8] with exceptions made for those who had "fought in the World War or done particularly commendable service on behalf of Germany." Also targeted were persons who had "committed a serious crime or misdemeanor or otherwise [behaved] in a way that detracted from the welfare of *Volk* and state," that is, in a manner "disloyal to the Reich."[9] Racial discrimination is already expressed here in unambiguous form: naturalized "eastern Jews" were deemed undesirable solely by virtue of their origin. They did not need to display any "disloyal" behavior toward the Reich; to the contrary, they were expected to furnish proof of special merit in order to retain their citizenship.

Here the institution of *Sippenhaftung* enters the picture—that is, penalization of an (entire) family for (political) crimes or actions committed by one of its members. Revocation of naturalization automatically extended to all family members who would not otherwise have acquired German citizenship (wives and minor children [sec. 16, RuStAG]).[10] No reasons were given for revocation, the right of appeal was denied,[11] and revocation took effect upon proclamation in the *Reich Gazette* (sec. 2, par. 5, of the law of July 14, 1933).

The term *disloyal behavior* as it applied to forfeiture of German citizenship was even more broadly defined under section 2 of the law, which was also in force in the territories annexed to the German Reich beginning in 1938 (Austria and Sudetengau [or Sudetenland]).[12] As stated in the implementing regulations, this was defined as any behavior by which "a German encouraged propaganda inimical to Germany . . . or [sought to] demean Germany's standing or the actions of the national government"[13]—offenses that might be laid at the feet of all opponents living abroad but also of all fugitives (particularly Jews), since the very fact of their emigration or flight was proof of their critical attitude.

The financial repercussions were also far-reaching. Upon initiation of deprivation proceedings, the assets of the persons concerned could be confiscated for a period of up to two years; once proceedings were concluded, their assets could be made forfeit to the Reich (sec. 2, par. 1, of the law).[14] Moreover, according to a later law passed in 1937, persons whose German citizenship was forfeited under these provisions were not permitted to inherit anything from Germans; gifts to them by German citizens were prohibited and punishable by law, as was the acceptance of gifts.[15] Thus, what we have here are provisions that were, in every detail, the exact forerunner of the later collective expatriation of Jews; indeed, the anti-Jewish excesses of later years brought no fundamentally new developments.

Nevertheless, such legal preliminaries were by no means extensive enough for the radical forces within the political leadership. The tendency toward unrestrained interpretation of legal standards served to impel them onward to new deeds. As early as the promulgation of the Reich Citizenship Law, there were calls for revision of the regulations on acquisition and forfeiture of German citizenship, and in particular for abolition of the provisions governing acquisition, forfeiture, and change in citizenship by application of the individual. Such cases, suggested the official commentators in the Reich Ministry of the Interior, were now to be "codetermined" by the state.[16] Although no such new, comprehensively defined legal revision took place, a considerable amount had still been accomplished. Besides the individual regulations already mentioned, sections 1 and 2 of the Law to Amend Reich and State Citizenship of May 15, 1935,[17] voided all cases in which there was a legitimate claim to naturalization under the Reich Citizenship Law and left future naturalizations solely up to the discretion of the authorities.

2.   The Reich Citizenship Law, September 15, 1935 (*Reichsbürgergesetz*)

A further important pillar of this intended comprehensive revision was the
Reich Citizenship Law of September 15, 1935,[18] which implemented the demands
of the NSDAP program of 1920 ("Only national comrades can be citizens. Only
persons of German blood can be national comrades. . . . Therefore, no Jew can
be a national comrade").[19] And the thirteen decrees to the Reich Citizenship
Law laid the foundation for the later special legislation against the Jews.[20] This
law, like the simultaneously decreed Blood Protection Law, was effusively hailed
by its authors at the Race Policy Office of the Reich Ministry of the Interior as
"the result of a breakthrough recognition, put into real-life practice at the twelfth
hour, of the inequality of the human race, as opposed to the smarmy liberal slogan touting the equality of anything that has a human visage."[21] It was thereafter
considered an "anchoring and supporting foundation of the entire political-
ethnic order of the Third Reich."[22] Under it, the idea that "national comrade
equals citizen" was annulled and a distinction set up between persons "of German or racially related blood" and persons "of foreign racial ethnicity."[23]

Starting from a definition of the state as the "ethnic-political organization of
the living organism of the *Volk*," this law put citizenship on "an ethnic basis." At
its core was the principle of "like blood,"[24] that is, the notion that only within the
class of "like-blooded ethnic comrades" were racial-biological and constitutional
citizenship identical. For these people, a privileged class of citizenship was created, the so-called Right of Reich Citizenship (*Reichsbürgerrecht*). As usual with
key National Socialist ideas, its main feature was its indeterminacy, which resisted any legal definition. Nevertheless, because from the Nazi point of view the
idea of race or blood comprised both biological and political elements ("spiritual essence"),[25] the Right of Reich Citizenship was made up of two different
components. Thus, under the regulation in section 2, paragraph 1, of the Reich
Citizenship Law, only that "citizen of German or related blood who [proved] by
his conduct that he [was] willing and able to serve the German *Volk* and Reich
in fidelity" was considered a citizen of the Reich (*Reichsbürger*).[26]

Persons "of foreign blood" were thus automatically excluded from acquiring
the protection of the Right of Reich Citizenship. According to the commentators
in the Reich Ministry of the Interior, this meant, in Europe, only "Jews and Gypsies";[27] it was later amended to include members of certain Eastern European
peoples as well. That Jewish subjects of the state were excluded from the Right
of Reich Citizenship, however, was not stated in the law itself but only in the
First Decree to the Reich Citizenship Law dated November 14, 1935.[28]

Corresponding distinctions were made in the definition of the rights and obligations of *Reichsbürgers* and simple citizens. The latter's status in the Reich involved merely a "relationship of protection and obligation" (sec. 1, par. 1, of the Reich Citizenship Law), and thus they possessed a citizenship of inferior legal status. They enjoyed the protection of the state only within the framework—alterable at any time—of the prevailing laws.[29] Full possession of rights was guaranteed only by the Right of Reich Citizenship. Although, juristically speaking, quite a dubious phenomenon, one that was conceived ad hoc on Hitler's instructions during a few hours at the Nuremberg Party Congress of 1935 in order "to be able to show the beginning of *völkisch* legislation,"[30] the Right of Reich Citizenship was treated as a concept of substantive law and provided with vague glosses: on the basis of his ethnic membership in the *Volk*, which in turn was determined by ancestry and political belief,[31] "the *Reichsbürger* owed [the Reich] obedience and loyalty" and thus stood in relation to it "in total existential obligation."[32] Only the *Reichsbürger* enjoyed all political rights (sec. 2, par. 3, of the Reich Citizenship Law). Because only he was in a position "to feel, know, and distinguish" what was German, he alone was "the *Volksgenosse* endowed with full political rights,"[33] with legitimate claim to the protection and support of the state, *independent* of the framework of existing legal standards.

Outwardly, however, the distinction between citizens of the Reich (*Reichsbürger*) and subjects of the state (*Staatsangehörige*) was never completely realized. The Right of Reich Citizenship was to have been acquired by the bestowal of a so-called *Reichsbürger* Charter (*Reichsbürgerbrief*) (sec. 2, par. 2, of the Reich Citizenship Law). However, this was never issued. In the interim, all citizens "of German or racially related blood" who had possessed the right to vote in Reichstag elections at the time the Reich Citizenship Law took effect (September 15, 1935) were deemed to be *Reichsbürger*.[34] Pending proof to the contrary, the subjective requirement for the Right of Reich Citizenship, "the will to serve the German people and the Reich," was assumed to exist in citizens "of German or racially related blood."[35] By contrast, citizens who were not simultaneously members of the *Volk*, in violation of the guarantee of equal citizenship rights for all Germans (art. 109 of the Weimar Constitution), were deprived of their political rights, particularly the right to vote and the right to hold public office—a provision that, as evidenced by section 4 of the First Decree to the Reich Citizenship Law dated November 14, 1935, was first and foremost directed at Jews, as subjects of the German state.

Along with the creation of new terminology of Reich citizenship and state subject status went attempts to bring order to the muddle of ethnic-racial and traditional constitutional terms that had prevailed ever since the Nazi seizure of power.

Whereas the earlier provisions under special law had used the terms *Aryan descent* or *non-Aryan descent*, after the Nuremberg Laws of September 15, 1935, took effect, the only term in use was *German or racially related blood or non-German or racially unrelated blood*[36]—even though these terms were never officially defined.[37] Persons of "German or racially related blood" were in future to be grouped together under the expression *German-blooded*,[38] a term, however, that did not take hold to any great extent until the relevant regulations were promulgated beginning in 1939. Definitions of the terms *Jew* and *Jewish descent* were contained in section 5 of the First Decree to the Reich Citizenship Law dated November 14, 1935. Despite all attempts to find a racially based definition, it proved impossible to come up with an anthropological term;[39] rather, for reasons of documentation, religious faith alone offered a defining criterion.[40] Section 5 read as follows:

(1) A Jew is anyone descended from at least three racially Jewish grandparents. Section 2, paragraph 2, sentence 2, is applicable. [Sec. 2, par. 2, sentence 2, read, "A grandparent can safely be considered fully Jewish if he or she belonged to the Jewish religion."]

(2) Also considered to be a Jew is the citizen of mixed ancestry (*Mischling*) descended from two fully Jewish grandparents

a) who at the time the law was promulgated belonged to the Jewish religion or subsequently joins it;

b) who at the time the law was promulgated was married to a Jew or who subsequently marries one;

c) who is the offspring of a marriage to a Jew as defined in paragraph 1 that is contracted after the effective date of the Law for the Protection of German Blood and German Honor of September 15, 1935 [RGBl. I 1146];

d) who is the issue of extramarital intercourse with a Jew as defined in paragraph 1 and is born after July 31, 1936.

The definition of who was a member of the Jewish religion hinged on purely external factors, such as being named in the rolls of the Jewish religious community. In principle, therefore, subjective factors such as believing that one belonged to the Jewish religion were not determinative.[41]

Not considered to be Jews were half Jews, "*Mischlinge* of the first degree" who did not meet the criteria under section 5, paragraph 2, of the First Decree to the Reich Citizenship Law, that is, who were married to a person "of German blood" or who did not belong to the Jewish religion (so-called privileged *Mischlinge*, as well as so-called *Mischlinge* of the second degree, that is, persons having only one Jewish grandparent [quarter Jews]).

This concept of the Jew and of the Jewish *Mischling*, that is, the mere existence of a fixed definition, served at first to calm public debate and satisfy judicial misgivings. Yet this definition could not be regarded as final, since, as part of the preparations for the Final Solution, it was supplanted in the Occupied Eastern Territories by a broad new definition[42] in order to permit the apprehension of as many victims as possible—a procedure that in principle could also be applied in the Reich itself. Moreover, that the definition of the Jew was not conclusive is shown by the fact that the Führer, as the supreme legislator, was authorized to grant exceptions to the classification of a person as a Jew, the "indispensable principle" of National Socialism.[43] The processing of petitions for exemption was, however, discontinued by the Reich Ministry of the Interior in 1942,[44] probably so as not to disturb the progress of the deportations, which were then proceeding at full throttle. The classification of Jewish *Mischlinge*, too, was not settled once and for all. Whereas they did enjoy a certain protection within the bounds of the Altreich in the sense that anti-Jewish legislation was not applicable to them,[45] people belonging to other ethnic groups that were not considered "good races" were generally equated in legal status with the Jews. At least, such equivalent status was contemplated. Thus, in the opinion of the racial and ethnic experts in the Party headquarters of the NSDAP, Jewish *Mischlinge* from the Annexed Eastern Territories were to be deported just the same as Jews.[46] And in 1942 even the authorities in the Reich itself agreed that half Jews ("*Mischlinge* of the first degree") were in principle to be equated with Jews for purposes of the Final Solution;[47] the full implementation of this policy was prevented only by administrative and war-related difficulties.

In detail, the meaning and purpose of the Reich Citizenship Law consisted in laying the foundation for a comprehensive restructuring of the law of citizenship; starting from this point, the legal status of German citizens of Jewish descent could be made null and void. In the light of this objective, any attempts to define this new type of citizenship and to determine its actual meaning were of a purely formal nature, susceptible to any interpretation desired by the political powers. For, albeit the duties incurred by citizenship (not duties of "allegiance" but merely "outward obedience" [*Pflichtenverband*]) still evoked a concrete image, the legitimate claim of state subjects to the "protection of the Reich" (*Schutzverband*) "within the framework of the prevailing laws" was presently unmasked as an empty formula. Such protection was to have included life, property, and economic activity but not the possession of political rights;[48] yet it was in fact a pseudoprotection inasmuch as parliamentary and legislative procedure had been eliminated and the will of the Führer was supreme, able to overturn the "prevailing laws" at any time. For the rest, the circumscription of the set of legal protections served merely to distract from the fact that certain classes of people were—later by means of normative regulations as well—excluded or scheduled for exclusion from all political (and in fact from all cultural and economic) areas of life. As stated in Wilhelm Stuckart and Hans Globke's official commentary on the Reich Citizenship Law, Jews possessed freedom of religious observance, cultural activity, and economic life within the framework of the laws; however, "Jewish meddling in the formation of state, economic, and cultural policy of the Reich [was] made impossible"; the Jews "[would have to] accustom themselves to the fact that their influence upon the development of German life [was] finished once and for all."[49]

As demonstrated by subsequent anti-Jewish legislation, this supposed protection "within the framework of the laws" in fact existed only on paper. Although for reasons of domestic and foreign policy, Jews were still permitted the status of state subjects, the qualifications already mentioned made it increasingly formal and practically worthless. Whereas the general duties and obligations of state subjects of Jewish descent not only remained in force but were actually toughened (e.g., by changes in the tax law), they lost one legal protection after another. The state's part of the "social contract" (Schutzverband), whose advantages even Jewish state subjects were supposed to enjoy, was reduced to nothing, while the citizen's part (Pflichtenverband) became all-encompassing. In practice, state subject status under inferior law meant nothing less than participating in all public duties and obligations while being excluded from all legal guarantees (rights of political partnership), a development that had been sketched in advance, abstractly yet with great precision, in the judicial literature.

State subjects of this class, therefore, had a status very similar to that of foreigners living "as guests in Germany" and subject to "alien law."[50] That is to say, German state subject status was no protection at all from gradual civil and economic extinction, since the distinction between citizens of the Reich and state subjects had opened the way to unrestricted application of special-law provisions to all areas of life.

Nevertheless, the retention of German state subject status by those German Jews remaining within the bounds of the Reich meant that they also retained legal capacity and were thus deemed capable of owning property, being gainfully employed, and receiving inheritances. This meant that numerous persecutory measures had to be disguised as "restrictions" or comparative prohibitions on legal rights of Jewish state subjects that were considered still to exist in the abstract. As a result, even the Reich Citizenship Law appeared unsatisfactory to the radical anti-Semites in the National Socialist (administrative) leadership, since it still allowed these persons state subject status. Whereas the original assumption was that the issue would resolve itself as these persons died out, much broader considerations later came into play as to how to prevent the acquisition of German state subject status by Jews and other "aliens" in the future. From a technical standpoint, this required the creation of new regulations governing the acquisition of state subject status, since section 1, paragraph 2, of the Reich Citizenship Law had explicitly left the old procedures unaltered. What the administrators envisioned was a conclusive definition of various classes of state subjects, with graduated rights and duties, along the lines of those already set forth in the Reich Citizenship Law. These plans were justified by the presumed necessity of a comprehensive reorganization of the law of state subject status (*Staatsangehörigkeitsrecht*), the development of which is indicated below.

3.   Plans for New Regulations

On February 14, 1938, the Reich minister of the interior sent the other Reich ministers the draft of a new State Subject Law, whose purpose,[51] going even further than the Nuremberg Laws, was the future elimination of "Jews and aliens" as German state subjects,[52] although the draft contained no precise definition of the term *alien*. In particular, the naturalization of foreigners ("admission to the protection [*Schutzverband*] of the German Reich") was to be made more difficult. Required was, among other things, the taking of a so-called loyalty oath to the German Reich, in which the applicant—in imitation of feudal oaths—swore to be faithful and obedient for all time. The proposal further provided that legitimate children of Jews, Jewish *Mischlinge*, or "otherwise alien" persons who were the issue of marriages contracted between German state subjects after the law took effect could no longer (as previously under the Reich Nationality Law of 1913) acquire German state subject status by virtue of birth (an exception was children of approved *Mischling* marriages).

This harsher position on the offspring of "aliens" who nevertheless belonged to the German polity was most likely never approved by all the Reich departments,[53] since negotiations dragged on for more than three years. The issue, as far as the Reich Ministry of the Interior was concerned, was nothing less than the creation of (legal) congruence between the concept of belonging to the

German *Volk* and state subject status, that is, between *völkisch*-racial terminology (*völkisch equality, German or racially related blood*) and constitutional concepts, since, in fact, the Reich Citizenship Law had effected no change whatsoever in the law governing state subject status. The Jews retained their status as German state subjects, and the Right of Reich Citizenship was not further codified. The plan now was to get serious about the idea that only ethnic Germans could enjoy German state subject status, whereas all others were to be excluded from that status. In an express letter to the Supreme Reich Agencies dated June 16, 1941,[54] the Reich minister of the interior elucidated his proposal, since altered in several respects, for a state subject law that expanded and refined this idea. According to it, German state subject status was in the future to be divided into three categories: Reich citizenship (*Reichsbürgerschaft*), state subject status (*Staatsangehörigkeit*) and conditional state subject status (*Staatsangehörigkeit auf Widerruf*). Furthermore, in consideration of Germany's future colonial responsibilities in the conquered territories, there was to be a category known as "protected status" granting limited domestic rights; this was to be the status of the "majority of the peoples not ethnically related to the German *Volk*." Jews were to be excluded from the acquisition of both German state subject and protected status. This draft reflects, in abstract form, the rough ideas developed in 1940 by the *Reichsführer*-SS (in his capacity as Reich Commissar for the Strengthening of German Nationhood) regarding the status in public law of the ethnic groups living in the Annexed Eastern Territories.[55] However, the negotiations on this draft also bogged down, because the Reich Chancellery raised administrative scruples (objecting to too-brief probationary periods for the new classes of state subjects);[56] and no agreement could be reached[57] on an alternative draft thereupon presented by the Ministerial Council for the Defense of the Reich on January 20, 1942.[58]

Therefore, no comprehensive new regulation of state subject status came into being. The issues in question were much too broad and controversial to be settled by the promulgation of a single law. Yet partial results were achieved in that the question of *graduated* state subject status was separated from that of the state subject status of German Jews. When the question of the state subject status of the German Jews became compelling with the inception of deportations of Jews to the East in 1940, its solution, as is shown below, was given priority owing to the numerous questions of property rights that depended on it. The Reich Chancellery suggested that the issue of graduated state subject status, which had yet to be empirically tested in the Reich, could be temporarily deferred.[59] Pertinent regulations were not issued until April 1943.[60]

4. The Position under Constitutional Law of the Jews with German State
Subject Status Living Abroad: The Eleventh Decree to the Reich
Citizenship Law, November 25, 1941

The status of the Jews possessing German state subject status, as noted, had
occupied the Reich Ministry of the Interior for years. Beginning in 1940, efforts
were undertaken not only to exclude Jews from future acquisition of German
state subject status but also—the better to gain access to their property—to revoke the status of those who already were German citizens. Whereas the prohibition on future acquisition of German state subject status by Jews could not be
put into effect until 1943, together with a collection of other regulations,[61] the
revocation of German state subject status was achieved in relatively short order.

The original intent of the Reich Ministry of the Interior had been to issue a
decree to the Reich Citizenship Law that would make stateless all Jews of German state subject status living abroad and would degrade German Jews (*Inlands-
juden*) to protected status. The purpose was to avoid placing the Jews in a better
position than "racially related non-Germans" (who were initially declared stateless and were later supposed to receive no more than conditional state subject
status).[62] The Reich Chancellery opposed this on formal grounds, taking the position that of all persons, Jews should not have protected status in the Reich. The
chancellery advanced the suggestion, backed by the corresponding Führer decision, that forfeiture of German state subject status take place only upon forfeiture of inland residence.[63]

This suggestion carried the day. The new bill for a Decree regarding the
Property of Jews Living Abroad Who Forfeit German State Subject Status,[64] a
draft of which was presented by the Ministerial Council for the Defense of the
Reich at a meeting of state secretaries on January 15, 1941,[65] provided for the forfeiture of state subject status upon transfer of residence abroad, as well as the
forfeiture of all assets to the coffers of the Reich. With only minor alterations,
this later became the basis for the Eleventh Decree to the Reich Citizenship Law.

Notwithstanding this, the Reich Ministry of the Interior initially maintained
misgivings about the draft, which instituted the "outwardly visible segregation
of the Jews from the German body politic." Withdrawal of state subject status
only upon departing the Reich seemed inopportune; the Reich Ministry of the
Interior would have much preferred an earlier revocation,[66] for, as State Secretary Hans Pfundtner confided to the Reich Chancellery, the Reich Ministry of the
Interior wished to skirt the touchy problem of domestic policy involved in permitting, in full view of the public, the deportation and dispossession of German

state subjects.[67] If, however, the Jews had already become stateless at home, they would have been subject to the laws on immigration (e.g., the provisions for deportation under the Police Decree on Foreigners of August 22, 1938),[68] thus giving the police sole responsibility and sparing the general administration any involvement with all the irksome measures of resettlement or evacuation. Confiscation of property, too, in the eyes of the Reich Ministry of the Interior, would have been simpler if the Jews were considered stateless, since in that case it would no longer be necessary to furnish proof of "behavior detrimental to the Reich" as defined under the Law on the Revocation of Naturalization and the Deprivation of German Citizenship of July 14, 1933; seizure could then have been managed under the Law on the Seizure of Assets of Enemies of the People and State, also issued on July 14, 1933, by the expedient of treating Jewish assets, either singly or in general, as "property belonging to enemies of *Volk* and state."[69] But because the Reich Chancellery continued to regard the withdrawal of state subject status from German Jews as "unfortunate" and no agreement was reached with the Reich Ministry of the Interior,[70] a new "Führer decision" was issued that supported the position of the Reich Chancellery.[71]

The bill of the Reich minister of the interior, published on November 25, 1941, with appropriate amendments and thereupon approved by all departments as the Eleventh Decree to the Reich Citizenship Law[72] contained a compromise that more or less did justice to all interests, though with its far-reaching consequences in constitutional, property, and inheritance law it was in no way justifiable even by National Socialist legal standards.

True, all the elements of the decree (expatriation, forfeiture of assets to the Reich, and restrictions on the right of inheritance) were already outlined in previous regulations;[73] nevertheless, these had been tailored to individual cases. Now it was a question of collective measures, for example, the provisions regarding the confiscation and forfeiture of a person's *entire* fortune, which were inadmissible even under the suspension of constitutional rights brought about by the Reich president's February 28, 1933, Decree for the Protection of People and State[74]—which had, among other things, provided for restrictions on property and confiscation by extralegal means.

Jews whose customary residence was in a foreign country at the time the decree took effect forfeited their German state subject status at that time—not, as in the past, by means of an individual legal act but automatically under the law (sec. 2a).

Even more important was the provision under which Jews who later took up "customary residence" abroad forfeited their German state subject status upon transfer of their place of residence to a foreign country, that is to say, immediately upon crossing the border; they became stateless before ever taking up their new residence. German state subject status was irrevocably forfeited upon crossing the border; it could not be regained by returning to the Reich. However, such forfeiture did not extend to family members.[75] In the course of the enactment of this law, the term *place of residence* was completely redefined.[76] In the official interpretation of the Reich Ministry of the Interior, it was no longer linked, as was previously customary in citizenship law, to the *voluntarily* established domicile or place of residence;[77] rather, it was solely determined by "objective" standards; that is, it also encompassed changes in residence that took place against the will of the persons concerned and thus, as the Reich minister of the interior had desired, all changes in residence resulting from "expulsion" (deportation).[78] In order that the forfeiture of German citizenship by Jewish refugees and deportees might take effect with the greatest possible speed, the term *foreign country*, too, was given a broad interpretation, in a departure from the common usage. It included all areas outside the borders of the Reich,[79] all territories occupied by Germany, in particular the General Government (which usually was not considered foreign),[80] as well as the Reich commissariats Ostland and Ukraine, that is, the very regions that were designated as reception areas for deported Jews. For transparent reasons, even the concentration camp at Auschwitz, although situated on Reich territory, was for this purpose considered to be foreign terrain.[81] Thus it was that almost all of the extermination sites of the Final Solution, from a "juristic" standpoint, were situated abroad; those liquidated in them were not German state subjects but stateless persons of Jewish descent.

Financial consequences, too, were seamlessly regulated. When a Jew's state subject status was forfeited, his or her property fell to the Reich;[82] it was to be utilized "to further all purposes arising in connection with the solution of the Jewish question" (sec. 3 of the Eleventh Decree). The Reich assumed financial obligations only in the amount of the sale value of the affected Jews' goods and titles over which the Reich gained power of disposition; that is, property burdened by excessive debt was not assumed. Ruled out altogether was the assumption of debts "whose discharge by the Reich would violate the sensibilities of the *Volk*" (sec. 5 of the Eleventh Decree) and of legitimate claims for the support of third parties (e.g., family members) by Jews, although "Jewish [persons entitled to support]"[83] could be granted "compensation" (sec. 6 of the Eleventh Decree). All rights to pensions on the part of Jews were canceled; family members entitled to maintenance could, at the discretion of the administration, be granted a subsistence allowance (sec. 10 of the Eleventh Decree). Numerous other restrictions followed for the purpose—as one commentary described this organized state larceny—of "annulling the economic ties [of the Jews] to the Reich."[84] Thus,

Jews whose assets fell to the Reich were not allowed to inherit property from German state subjects, for testamentary gifts to such persons was prohibited (sec. 4 of the Eleventh Decree).

Not regulated by the decree was the treatment of Jewish *Mischlinge* and those Jews living in "privileged mixed marriages." This nonregulation met the desires of the *Reichsführer*-SS/RKF and the Party Chancellery, both of whom pleaded that there be no exceptions,[85] whereas the Reich minister of the interior wanted to exempt such persons from forfeiture of German state subject status. The omission of provisions for any exceptions whatsoever in the Eleventh Decree provided the Security Police (Gestapo) with broad discretion in whether these persons were to be treated in the same way as Jews, since the Gestapo alone made the decision whether the "requirements for forfeiture of assets" (that is, for deportation) were fulfilled.[86]

Collectively, these measures, which closely linked state subject status for Jews to their expulsion and made the forfeiture of such status solely dependent on the outward criterion of compulsory residence, represented a novelty in legal thinking, though they received barely any discussion in the academic literature.[87] In essence, the Eleventh Decree, by withdrawing all legal status and denying any basis for survival, effectively dissolved the law governing state subject status. It represented a pseudolegalization of the compulsory concentration in the ghettos of the East and was thus the direct administrative prelude to the Final Solution.[88]

5. The Constitutional Status of "Non-German" Inhabitants of the Reich and the Occupied Territories: Conditional State Subject Status, Protected Status, and the Consequences (Ethnic Gradation)

Despite efforts on the part of the Reich Ministry of the Interior to bring about a comprehensive revision of the law of state subject status, the question of the position of the remaining "non-German" inhabitants of the Reich and the occupied territories remained unresolved after it was tabled at the request of the Reich Chancellery to allow for prior clarification of the status of German Jews.[89] However, the regulation governing the status of Poles in the Annexed Eastern Territories in the decree of the *Reichsführer*-SS (RFSS)/RKF of September 12, 1942,[90] put in place a provisional regulation for these persons, who in principle were considered to be stateless;[91] it was finally sanctioned by the instituting of the German Ethnic Classification List of March 4, 1941.[92] In regard to the status of the other "non-German" inhabitants of the Reich and the territories it had occupied, however, no agreement was reached until 1943.

The Twelfth Decree to the Reich Citizenship Law, dated April 25, 1943,[93] which had been agreed upon in early 1943 among the participating Supreme Reich Agencies,[94] created the legal institution known as "conditional state subject status," which could be acquired either by general statute or by individual award. It could be acquired by "non-German" persons (except for Jews and Gypsies) who were considered from both the political and the racial standpoint to be "capable of Germanization," that is, who met the criteria for being "of German extraction." Parallel to this was the creation of the category known as protected status, which encompassed "those inhabitants of the German Reich not belonging to the German *Volk*" (except for Jews and Gypsies) "who are or . . . hereafter shall be granted protected status by general statute or by ruling in individual cases" (sec. 3). The particulars were regulated by decrees issued simultaneously on conditional state subject status and protected status.[95]

With the promulgation of the Twelfth Decree to the Reich Citizenship Law and related decrees, the three classes of state subject, the idea for which the Reich Ministry of the Interior had championed since 1938, were finally codified in law: (a) German state subject status, the particulars of which were drawn from the Reich Nationality Law of 1913, (b) conditional German state subject status for "non-Germans capable of Germanization," and (c) so-called protected status for "non-German" inhabitants of the German Reich who were willing to swear a loyalty oath to the German Reich.[96] The intent and purpose of these regulations was to create the constitutional foundations for the future colonial empire of the Greater German Reich.

At root, this was merely the judicial expression of ideas that Hitler had already developed prior to 1933 for a graduated social organization of the populations within the future German power sphere. Accordingly, the lowest level of the new hierarchy was formed of the great mass of stateless "non-Germans" subject to special law, that is, without any kind of legal status; next came the class of privileged "non-Germans" granted protected status as a reward for loyal behavior. "Non-Germans" found worthy of "Germanization" were to enjoy conditional German subject status. Slated for such experiments were, first and foremost, the native populations (i.e., "non-Germans") in the Occupied Eastern Territories, the General Government, and the Annexed Eastern Territories. Full German state subject status could be awarded to foreigners "of German extraction" on the basis of merit. The best example of this is the Führer decree dated May 19, 1943,[97] which was issued at the urging of the Armed Forces High Command (OKW) shortly after the promulgation of the Twelfth Decree; it granted unrestricted German state subject status by means of collective naturalization to all foreigners "of German extraction"[98] (with the exception of Poles and Czechs) who served in the Wehrmacht, the Waffen-SS, the Organisation Todt (the Reich agency that organized the compulsory labor in the occupied territories), and the police—as a way of recruiting volunteers from the non-German nations for service in the German ranks.[99]

The technical aspects of the semicolonial institutions of *conditional state subject* and *protected status* provide a foretaste of what the "non-Germans" in the occupied territories might have expected had this legislation been more fully implemented. In essence, they were police regulations that annulled the principle (still formally in effect even in the Nazi era) that the courts were not bound by administrative regulations, since they empowered the Reich Ministry of the Interior with administrative control over the legal standing of persons with protected status in a way that was binding even on the courts.[100] To be sure, this could only take place with the consent of the RFSS/RKF and the Party Chancellery, for the treatment accorded to "non-Germans" was a political question for whose solution (among other things, the "neutralization of the harmful influence of foreign population elements") the *Reichsführer*-SS in his capacity as Reich Commissar for the Strengthening of German Nationhood had been granted unlimited power by a secret Führer decree dated October 7, 1939;[101] and over this political matter the NSDAP, as the "guiding political force," naturally had authoritative influence. Thus, responsibility for questions regarding the state subject status of "non-Germans" was taken away from the Reich minister of the interior, who was henceforth obliged to seek participation and mutual agreement from the Party Chancellery and the RKF regarding all regulations.[102]

The first examples, and the legal consequences, of such graduated forms of state subject status reveal the procedural details of these regulations. These were admittedly issued primarily for the Poles in the Annexed Eastern Territories. Nevertheless, they belong to the realm of law governing questions of citizenship for the entire territory of the Reich, since most of the Poles who came to acquire German state subject status were transplanted to the Reich itself, and thus they can probably be considered a model for the future treatment of all "non-German" persons later to be accepted into the German polity.

On the basis of the decree instituting the German Ethnic Classification List of March 4, 1941,[103] the Polish population was divided into persons "capable of Germanization" (Class 3), persons "capable of re-Germanization" (Class 4), and persons with protected status. According to provisional regulations issued by the RFSS/RKF, persons "capable of Germanization" were those "of German descent" who had ties "to Polish culture" but who in their behavior inclined to German culture (including persons of Masurian, Kashubian, and Upper Silesian extraction). (Regulations that, according to the decree, were to be provided by the

Reich Ministry of the Interior "in consensus" with the RFSS/RKF were never issued owing to disagreement over the definition of *Polish* ethnicity, because the
former had approached the problem from the opposite end and, early on, had
already fixed the definition of *German* ethnicity.)[104] Considered capable of re-
Germanization were persons of German descent who had "merged politically
with Polish culture."[105] Persons "capable of Germanization" acquired conditional
state subject status upon registration in the German Ethnic Classification List,[106]
whereas that status had to be *granted* to persons "capable of re-Germanization."
All remaining inhabitants of the Eastern Territories were considered to be stateless—with protected status. The legal protection accorded the various classes
differed according to their status. We have already discussed the de facto prohibition on marriage, which had been in force since 1942 for marriages between
stateless Polish persons of protected status and German state subjects or Poles
"capable of Germanization,"[107] as well as the prohibition under section 8, paragraph 1, of the Decree on Protected Status of April 25, 1943,[108] which proscribed
marriage between persons of protected status and persons of other categories.
Such provisions clearly revealed the intent to restrict the intermingling of members of the Polish nation with other classes and ultimately to bring about its
extinction.

A dense system of graduated measures served to deepen the ostracism of
those with protected status from the privileged Poles listed in the German Ethnic Classification List, while simultaneously introducing a precise sequential hierarchy of rights and obligations among the diverse privileged classes. Thus,
Poles "inclined toward German ethnicity" in Class 3 of the German Ethnic Classification List (that is, Poles of German extraction) enjoyed a status that can only
be described as advantageous in comparison with that of Poles in Class 4, who
were merely "capable of re-Germanization"—if one uses the absolute lack of
rights accorded to "non-Germans" as the standard of measurement.

Thus, under directives issued by the *Reichsführer*-SS,[109] the Poles of Class 3
of the German Ethnic Classification List were subject to residential restrictions
"necessitated by the objective of Germanization." The goal was to uproot these
persons, to tear them loose from their old environment, and yet *not* to integrate
them fully into a new one. This put them under the Damoclean sword of losing
all rights if they failed to behave in an acceptable manner. Therefore, they were
in principle to be "utilized" only in the Altreich. Members of Class 3 of the German Ethnic Classification List already resettled (in the General Government)
were prohibited from returning home. Upon emigrating to the Altreich, their
farm holdings were subject to mandatory sale (exclusively to the offices of the
RKF or the Main Trustee Office East), in order "to prevent these persons from

taking root in the Eastern Territories." They were not permitted to join the Party or the Civil Service or take other "trusted or leading positions" in the public service; however, they could be admitted in subordinate, nonindependent capacities. The confiscation of their real property remained in effect pending expiration of the conditional quality of their state subject status (after no later than ten years); their agricultural holdings, taken away from them and occupied by German resettlers, were not to be "returned for the purpose of owner management and cultivation."[110] Nevertheless, public management and administration by commissariat of their property was discontinued upon their admission to the German Ethnic Classification List: "In the interests of Germanization, it [their property] should be protected as far as possible, to the extent that it could in any way be useful in establishing a livelihood in the Altreich."[111] Furthermore, certain modest cultural rights were preserved; thus, they were free to attend technical colleges, but they needed permission to matriculate at universities.[112] They were expected to meet considerable obligations, such as labor and military service.[113]

By contrast, the members of Class 4 of the German Ethnic Classification List, which in the terrible idiom of the offices of the *Reichsführer*-SS/RKF was comprised of "actively Polonized persons of German extraction,"[114] were subject to much harsher regulations,[115] however much they may have appeared to be "at an advantage" in comparison with those Poles who merely had protected status. In order to achieve "complete separation from the Polish environment," for example, this group was subject to compulsory resettlement in the Altreich, where they were liable for conscription into the armed services, with exception made for those selected out as racially inferior and/or politically incriminated, who were sent to concentration camps.[116] Prior to resettlement in the Altreich, they were subject to almost the same restrictions as stateless Poles in the Annexed Eastern Territories: no admission to the Party, no attendance at schools of higher learning or universities, and continued confiscation of property. The only area in which they were given equal status with Germans was that of food supply.[117] And even after their placement in the Altreich,[118] their property remained confiscated and was sold or otherwise turned to account by the office of the higher SS and police leader (HSSPF) in its capacity as deputy of the RKF. However, an amount not to exceed RM 2,000 per annum was placed at their disposal. One coercive measure was the provision that the confiscated property would be restored when "Germanization" was completed.

Other conditions imposed upon the Poles "capable of re-Germanization" by the offices of the Gestapo were as follows: that they promptly seek out and join an auxiliary unit of the NSDAP (children were to apply for membership in the

Hitler Youth), that during the first five years of residence in the Altreich they change their place of domicile only with permission from the responsible officer of the HSSPF, that they contract marriages and take up studies at institutions of higher learning only with permission of the HSSPF, that they assume no legal guardianship, and that any "non-German" names be replaced with German ones. Moreover, each family of Polish resettlers in this class was assigned a political watchdog, called an "adviser" for "aid in re-Germanization," whose job was to make regular reports on the political behavior of the family to the offices of the HSSPF and the responsible Gestapo office.

Severe penalties were imposed for those who dared to refuse the favor of "re-Germanization," preferring instead to remain Poles. In cases of "resistance to re-Germanization," application was to be made for revocation of naturalization; furthermore, this was to be brought to the attention of the responsible Gestapo office in order to initiate appropriate "state police measures" (internment in a concentration camp). In cases in which children were "detrimentally influenced by their parents" and said influence could not be removed by "state police measures" (police supervision or confinement in a concentration camp), the children were taken away from their parents and placed in "politically irreproachable families."[119] Taken all together, Poles deemed "capable of re-Germanization" were subject to hardships that were often far greater than those suffered by Polish persons of protected status.

Later on there were further gradations undertaken within individual classes, the aim being to provide persons who had actively taken the part of Germany with a better status than the total disfranchisement (of the person of protected status), since the system was dependent upon their labor and cooperation. Thus, in a directive dated January 3, 1944,[120] the *Reichsführer*-SS/RKF created the class of so-called *privileged persons of protected status*, which consisted of "German-Jewish *Mischlinge* who had actively taken the part of Germany," "Poles from Upper Silesia who have fought on the German side, and possibly also Ukrainians, Czechs in the Annexed Eastern Territories, and persons capable of Germanization." This gave them a status somewhere between that of stateless Poles and Poles listed in Class 4 of the German Ethnic Classification List.

In sum, it must be emphasized that "non-Germans" who were granted protected or conditional state subject status could by no means consider themselves in any way privileged. As was frequently the case with National Socialist legal constructs, this was a pseudoconcept behind which there was nothing, or at least very little, of legal substance. This is particularly true of the institution of protected status, which in reality afforded no protection whatsoever, as shown by the transportation of Polish civilian laborers into the Reich and the deportation of Poles from the Annexed Eastern Territories to the General Government.[121] Nor could the institution of conditional state subject status be seen as in any way equivalent to the legal position of German state subjects. In reality, all this was merely a means of implementing the all-dominating principle of dividing and segregating the various population groups (*divide et impera*). The privilege accorded to conditional state subjects consisted in being liable to the same duties and obligations as full state subjects, while equal rights were withheld by means of numerous prohibitions and injunctions on the grounds that the affected individual had to be integrated cautiously and gradually into the "German *Volk* community."[122]

V. Professional and Labor Law

The development of special-law provisions regulating the professions was initiated parallel to anti-Jewish measures introduced in the laws governing public service.[1] Like the laws directed against Jewish judicial and local officials, these laws brought about abuse and defamation of Jewish attorneys as well as bans on their entering judicial administration buildings, reported in many cities as early as April 1933.[2] Among the Jews murdered at that time there were numerous Jewish attorneys-at-law.[3]

The first measures taken under special law, then, were also initiated in April 1933. It requires no closer examination to show that each and every one of the following measures restricting or prohibiting "non-Germans" from free exercise of the professions under special law was unconstitutional, since they violated the guarantees of equal rights for all under article 109 and of professional freedom under article 151 of the Weimar Constitution, which was never formally suspended.[4] These measures therefore lacked any basis in law even by National Socialist standards. Even on the assumption that the enabling act of March 24, 1933,[5] which empowered the Reich government to enact regulations that deviated from the Weimar Constitution,[6] had effectively amended the latter, the result would be no different. For from the standpoint of procedure, even the Third Reich recognized the principle of the lawfulness of administration (despite countless violations in individual cases), according to which decrees required legal authorization, whereas implementing regulations required the authority of law or decree. But almost all measures prohibiting "non-Germans" from certain profession were either issued in the form of decrees lacking any foundation in Reich law,[7] or else they were ordered by internal administrative directives, some of which greatly overstepped the bounds of the authorizing regulation in law or decree.

1. Professions Subject to State Licensing

a. Attorneys and Related Professions

At the forefront of special-law measures were those taken against professions whose practitioners required special state accreditation or licensing, such as attorneys-at-law, notaries, physicians, and so forth, and were thus most easily subject to regulation by the state. The first target was, naturally enough, attorneys-at-law and related professions,[8] which, since they take the part of the individual and his interests against the state, are never highly regarded in totalitarian regimes.[9] The National Socialists, however, found particular reason to detest them in that a relatively high percentage of attorneys in the larger cities were of Jewish descent.[10] If the image of the attorney in National Socialist propaganda was generally negative in coloration—because he was, by virtue of debasing contact with Jews, greatly influenced by the idea of the "advocate . . . originating in the liberal era," who was held to be "selfish" and "gossipy," subsisting on the "labor of others" (according to Göring)[11]—how much more was the Jewish attorney seen as a "parasite" creeping into the soul of the "host people" in order to "poison" not only the legal profession but also the people as a whole.[12] As usual in the preparation of uniform special legislation, Jewish attorneys were to be neutralized, first by the creation of legal insecurity and uncertainty and confusion through numerous individual measures, demands, and arbitrary acts by state and Party offices, to the point where a set of centralized regulations would be hailed as a virtual restoration of legal guarantees—even if they contained still harsher measures than those of the ones they were designed to replace.

Thus, on March 14, 1933, the League of National Socialist German Jurists called for all judges of foreign race to be immediately purged from the courts and for a *ban on licensing* of any attorneys of "foreign race." Members of the KPD and the SPD were to lose their licenses effective immediately.[13] The National Socialist commissar for the Prussian judiciary and later Prussian minister of justice, Hans Kerrl, petitioned the courts to admit Jewish attorneys to the bar only in proportion "to the ratio of the Jewish population."[14] On April 1, 1933, Kerrl prohibited all Jewish notaries from exercising their occupation, and on April 4, 1933, he issued a preliminary general ban on representation by all non-Aryan attorneys in Prussia.[15] This was preceded as early as March of that year by a prohibition on their entering the buildings of the justice authorities.

After the boycott of April 1, 1933, the Reich Ministry of Justice issued an injunction signed by State Secretary Freisler in which (in a procedure that ran counter to all previous notions of constitutionality) the ministry undertook to engage in plain blackmail: every Jewish notary was immediately to declare "voluntarily" that he would refrain from all professional activity, failing which the ministry would be answerable for nothing, since "the people's outrage would no longer suffer official documents to be issued at the hands of Jewish notaries."[16] Also not officially published were further measures taken by the Prussian judicial administration, such as an order forbidding Jewish attorneys to sign written statements.[17] As with all writings by Jewish authors, the publications of Jewish attorneys were suppressed and, beginning in October 1936, ultimately taken out of circulation.[18]

The Reich Bar Association—formed by emergency decree of the Reich president dated March 18, 1933, and provided with new jurisdictional responsibility (i.e., disciplinary actions before a court of honor),[19] thus creating the Reich corporative representation long desired by members of the bar and entirely in keeping with the National Socialist system of strict centralization—issued "guidelines for the practice of the profession of attorney-at-law" in which attorneys "of German blood" were called upon to collaborate "in the great tasks of the *Volk*" and the National Socialist movement.[20]

With the ground thus prepared for revision of the law governing attorneys, the Law on Admission to the Legal Profession was promulgated on April 7, 1933,[21] at the same time as the so-called Professional Civil Service Code. The former was due to expire on September 30, 1933; thereafter, attorneys of non-Aryan descent as defined by the Professional Civil Service Code *could* have their licenses revoked (sec. 1); however, such revocation was *not mandatory*. Exceptions were granted to "frontline soldiers" and their next-of-kin, as well as to those attorneys who were already licensed on or before August 1, 1914—provisions similar to those of the Professional Civil Service Code. The judicial administrations were authorized to prohibit attorneys from representing clients pending revocation proceedings. Applications for new licenses by non-Aryans were to be rejected. New applicants were to furnish "proof of Aryan status."[22] Under section 3 of this law, revocation or denial of licensure was mandatory in cases in which the individual concerned had "been involved in Communist activities." This provision was not to be applied to non-Aryan attorneys who, prior to January 30, 1933, had joined an organization of the NSDAP or otherwise "proven" themselves to be "nationalists." Similar regulations were soon issued for patent attorneys.[23] Jewish tax consultants were also eliminated in the spring of 1933.[24]

Since these laws of April 1 and 4 effectively stripped non-Aryan attorneys and notaries of their licenses, all of them were obliged to take up the fight to re-new their accreditation. It was not up to the authorities to prove that the law was applicable; rather, the persons concerned had to show that they were not cov-ered by the new regulations. Accounts from affected persons report how ardu-ous, time-consuming, and degrading this fight could be, even if they were cov-ered by the exceptions provided for in the law.[25] For example, it was not enough for the applicant to present a police declaration to the effect that he had never engaged in Communist activities; rather, he was obliged to sign a sworn state-ment with the local bar association that he had neither belonged to the Com-munist Party nor ever represented Communists in court proceedings. If the statement was accepted, he had to wait almost three months before again being allowed to represent clients, as did non-Aryan notaries, provided they could prove that they had been frontline soldiers. However, troublesome non-Aryan notaries were dismissed under section 4 of the Professional Civil Service Code of April 7, 1933, no later than September 30, 1933, the deadline by which notary status had to be revoked. Among other grounds for dismissal was membership in one of the democratic parties of the Weimar Republic, if the party had en-tered into an election agreement with the SPD.[26]

Unlike cases involving non-Aryan civil servants, about whom official figures were never published (for fear of adverse publicity), successes in the case of the non-Aryan attorneys received lengthy notices in the judicial literature, accord-ing to which 1,500 attorneys were affected by these initial special legislative mea-sures; of those, a good third were from Berlin and 1,364 from Prussia as a whole.[27]

Harsher restrictions soon followed. Particularly significant was the law of July 20, 1933,[28] under section 6, paragraph 5, of which applicants who had been dismissed from service pursuant to the Professional Civil Service Code could be denied licensure; that is, dismissed administrative and judicial officials might be denied access to the profession of attorney. The Law to Amend the Reich Regu-lations on Attorneys of December 2, 1934,[29] pronounced a ban on the admission of Jewish attorneys to the Reich Bar Association; furthermore, Jewish attorneys whose licenses had been revoked could no longer use the professional title.

Here, too, however, legislative regulation was by no means the end of the matter; discrimination was carried well beyond the possibilities provided for in law. That the law could be amended by internal service directives was by 1933 already a given under the judicial leadership of the Führer state: a general in-junction of the Prussian Ministry of Justice dated April 24, 1933, regarding the "selection" of candidates for the bench and for the bar provided that, in future, "selection" of applicants "within the framework of Reich law" was to be made "also on the basis of an evaluation of the personality of the applicant as one who is conscious of his membership in the *Volk* as a whole." This evaluation was to have "equal weight beside the other, legally prescribed prerequisites."[30] But this in itself put the licensing procedure outside "the framework of Reich law." Although the attorney's claim to the respect due professional status was outwardly emphasized by a facade of individual regulations,[31] professional activities by attorneys of "foreign race" and the exercise of related occupations by Jews was systematically curtailed *extra legem* in other ways as well. The representation of German clients by Jewish attorneys was held to be "conscious sabotage,"[32] as it was "intolerable" for "Jews to play any sort of role in the administration of German law."[33]

Licensing regulations, too, were interpreted more strictly. In Prussia, at least, the discretionary provision of the law of April 7, 1933 ("the license may be withdrawn"), was, by decree of the Ministry of Justice, applied as if it were a mandatory regulation in cases in which the attorney in question was deemed generally politically undesirable (although sec. 3 of the law provided for compulsory expulsion only in case of "Communist activities"). Here, too, the guiding principle was that of every totalitarian regime: when in doubt, whatever was not permitted and/or confirmed was considered prohibited or suspicious. It was not up to the authorities to demonstrate the undesirability of the person concerned; rather, license was granted only when his political reliability was positively established. To this end, the authorities (the presiding judge of the Appellate Court) were to investigate ex officio. The same was true, mutatis mutandis, for new applicants.[34]

Critical remarks, even if made only in passing, and other vexatious behavior on the part of Jewish attorneys led to their expulsion from the bar and thus to the expiration of their licenses; the fact that they were Jews was seen as an aggravating factor in the offense.[35] (Jewish attorneys who were permitted to carry on in their profession were subject to increased duties and obligations.) Measures taken with respect to Jewish attorneys' offices (the sale or purchase of Jewish practices) or the maintenance of friendly relations between German attorneys and their Jewish staff were punished as (grave) "professional violations."[36]

In addition, as early as 1935 the Reich Ministry of Justice decreed that no public defense or legal aid cases brought in forma pauperis were to be assigned to Jewish attorneys, on the grounds that legal representation in public defense cases was similar to public office, from which Jews were excluded.[37] Suits brought on behalf of attorneys thus excluded remained unsuccessful.[38] Jews were also banned from other public occupations; for instance, the Reich Ministry of Justice forbade the appointment of Jews as administrators in cases of bankruptcy, financial settlement, or receivership.[39] Jews were also no longer permitted to be appointed as guardians, curators, or conservators.[40] And even more harassment was in store: Jewish attorneys were excluded from representing the principal heir courts set up by municipal courts in so-called hereditary farm disputes under the Reich Hereditary Farm Law. Written statements prepared by Jews were to be dismissed, even when they were signed by the Aryan client himself. When Jewish attorneys went on vacation, only Jewish colleagues could substitute for them, a requirement that led to the greatest difficulty in smaller towns and cities, where there were few or no other Jewish attorneys.[41] Aryan clients of Jewish attorneys were scared off by threats, coercion, and blackmail on the part of administrative offices.[42]

Particularly in the realm of legislation governing attorneys, it is clear that the regulation of Jewish attorneys under special law was not a closed circuit but merely provided the foundation for new complications directed at all members of the bar; indeed, this intention was openly proclaimed.[43] Accordingly, in the years after 1933 numerous new regulations were issued in the area of attorney legislation, all of which aimed at a "complete reordering" of the profession (the rescission of licensing entitlement,[44] the introduction of need testing [by way of the National Code on Attorneys-at-Law of 1936; this was a means for the state to control the lawyers by granting or refusing the license],[45] organizational restructuring, measures taken to relieve the overcrowding of the bar by expanding the professional domain of the attorney,[46] etc.). In 1938 new special legislative provisions were issued against Jews as, in the course of implementing the Nuremberg Laws, even those Jewish attorneys who until then had been allowed to continue to practice under the exemptions granted in the law of April 7, 1933 (so-called *Altjuden*, that is, frontline soldiers and attorneys licensed prior to the cut-off date), were eliminated. The Fifth Decree to the Reich Citizenship Law, dated September 27, 1938,[47] stipulated that the withdrawal of licenses from all Jewish attorneys was *mandatory* from December 1, 1938, onward; this affected an extremely high percentage of all members of the bar, no less than 16 percent.[48] Under section 1, number 1, of the decree, the names of the disbarred attorneys (on the so-called dead lists) were to be expunged from the register of the bar no later than December 31, 1938.[49]

Disbarred attorneys were prohibited from using the professional title *attorney* and forbidden to provide legal counsel under the Abuse of Legal Counsel Law of December 13, 1935.[50] With the elimination of Jewish attorneys, the contention of Hans Frank that "National Socialist laws [could] never be rightly applied by a Jewish judge or a Jewish attorney-at-law" was fulfilled, so that "the German attorney [could] once again . . . with pride . . . call himself attorney-at-law."[51] Professional activity on the part of Jewish colleagues was permitted only on behalf of Jewish clients, and then only in the capacity of "legal advisers"—an artifice of Franz Schlegelberger,[52] state secretary in the Reich Ministry of Justice—who were to be conditionally licensed by the judicial administration.

Petitions for licensing as a legal adviser were to be directed to the presiding judge of the appellate court, who then consulted with the president of the local bar association and the state police, as well as the board of the district court for which licensing was desired. The decision whether or not to license was up to the Reich minister of justice. Apart from being frontline soldiers or persons wounded in the World War, applicants—who as far as possible were to be drawn from the ranks of those frontline soldiers eliminated under section 1 of the Fifth Decree[53]—could also be given special consideration if they were married to "Aryan women."[54] The legal adviser was subject to supervision by the presiding judge of the responsible district court. The places where consultants could establish themselves were limited, as were their numbers, and special regulations were issued for the new professional title and the attorney's shingle.[55]

About the fate of the legal advisers hardly anything is known; but the assumption is justified that, beginning in 1938, at the start of harsher anti-Jewish measures, the number of Jews seeking legal counsel rapidly diminished and that the number of Jewish legal advisers sank commensurately. Nevertheless, some respected Jewish attorneys remained in Germany.[56] Whether or not they were spared deportation on account of their profession's formal standing—in contrast to the Jewish judges who were forced to retire and the Jewish attorneys who lost their licenses and were included in the deportations—is something that is yet to be determined.[57]

In view of the prevailing opinion that German legal affairs were "poisoned"[58] by any dealings with Jews, representation of Jews by German attorneys was also restricted, on the segregationist principle that reserved Aryan attorneys for Aryans only, legal advisers exclusively for Jews. However, legislation to bring about a general ban on representation of Jews by Aryan attorneys, corresponding to the strict prohibition on representation of Aryans by Jews, was never instituted—primarily for economic reasons. Such a prohibition was, as National Socialist jurists later explained, "undesirable" because otherwise Jewish attorneys would have achieved a "monopoly position" and a preponderance over German attorneys.[59] Despite all this, however, a de facto ban on such representation was instituted from the very beginning by means of special legislative practices and internal directives.

Discrimination against the attorneys of Jewish clients was a daily occurrence right from the outset. Fine-sounding phrases from official quarters about the freedom of the attorney meant little, since they were entirely unrealistic;[60] in actuality, such attorneys could look forward to the greatest difficulties. Just as in cases of politically troublesome attorneys, pressure was generally exerted on their clients.[61] Just as in cases in which an Aryan was represented by a Jewish attorney, care was taken that the latter (licensed with exceptional permission) received no more commissions, so, conversely, Aryan attorneys were also plagued with massive threats if they took on the cases of Jewish clients. In so doing, the NSRB (the National Socialist Jurists' League) made explicit reference to the fact that the principle "What is not expressly forbidden is permitted" from the "system period" (that is, from the Weimar Republic) was now no longer in force. Even in the absence of a lawful ban, any legal representation having to do with the protection of Jewish interests was proscribed. An attorney engaging in such was "altogether finished, both socially and as a person."[62]

According to rulings handed down by the disciplinary courts, taking on Jewish cases was, in certain instances, even considered a professional misdemeanor ("objectionable frequency of Jewish cases"). Later on this was also the case for representation of Jewish interests without explicit permission from the bar association, as mandated under a directive issued December 31, 1938, by the president of the Reich Bar Association.[63] The same was true of those who would represent the interests of Jews facing evacuation.[64] The representation of Jewish interests by those Jewish *Mischlinge* who remained in office was also a professional offense that could and did lead to expulsion from the bar.[65]

Naturally, Jewish attorneys faced considerable impediments to the daily practice of their profession, starting with the general duties imposed on attorneys, which (particularly in the realm of criminal defense) were made a great deal more severe. Of course, the new, stricter rules were to be applied with particular vehemence to Jewish attorneys.

Apart from Party and professional organizations, the Reich Ministry of Justice also continuously drummed it into the attorneys that the position of counsel for the defense was now another one altogether. Limits were now imposed upon the attorney in his defense strategy, limits that were set for the good of the *Volk*.[66] The attorney was the advocate of the law, not of his client; the latter notion originated with "the Jewish defense attorney," who was an extreme devotee of such individualistic ideas.[67] The Reich Ministry of Justice made this perfectly clear in an injunction, dated January 19, 1943, bemoaning the "increasing violations by attorneys of their professional obligations": "Rather than contributing, as organs of judicial administration, to determining the truth and reaching a verdict in full consciousness of their responsibilities, these defense attorneys take the position of accessories to the lawbreaker."[68] It goes without saying that Jewish defense counsel in particular were subject to the strongest imaginable pressures and were in fact hardly permitted to appear in criminal proceedings (this was certainly true for political criminal cases); but the same was also true of German attorneys representing Jews. Like anyone representing politically unpopular offenders, they had to face enormous consequences.[69] Even a note to a Jewish client reporting that the attorney was being attacked for taking on the defense was grounds for expulsion from the bar.[70]

As usual, these discriminatory policies were sanctioned in practice by means of various internal directives, either simultaneously or after the fact, aimed at placing considerable restrictions on the attorney's freedom of representation. The Reich Ministry of Justice refrained from issuing instructions of its own, preferring to leave such questions to the Party leadership and the professional organization (the Reich Bar Association), no doubt because it shared the opinion of the Party leadership that the issue of legal representation of Jews was "a political question" for which the "Party alone was responsible."[71] Thus, as early as 1934 the NSDAP was able to issue a ban on representation of Jews by any "ethnic comrades and jurists" who were *Party members*;[72] this was expanded in 1935 to include all *officeholders* in the NSRB and the directors of all legal administration offices of the NSRB. The remaining members of the NSRB were obligated to exercise "the greatest restraint" in taking on the cases of Jewish clients.[73] Only after the elimination of the last remaining Jewish attorneys under the Fifth Decree to the Reich Citizenship Law, dated September 27, 1938,[74] and in the wake of the anti-Jewish pogroms in November 1938 was there a noticeable departure from the principle of prohibiting or preventing the representation of Jewish clients at all costs. In the course of the state-sponsored plundering of Jewish property that began at this time, there arose a plethora of legal difficulties (the appointment of financial *curatores absentis*, trusteeships, liquidations, etc.) that had to be dealt with. All of a sudden, new regulations became necessary, for which—since it was again a matter of "purely political measures"—the Party alone was responsible, not the judiciary. Now it became downright imperative that "German jurists," and thoroughly politically reliable ones at that, take on the representation of Jews, in order to avoid "illicit transfers of assets, cover-ups," etc.

With the exception of such cases, however, representation of Jewish interests was now made impossible in all matters of consequence. In the literature we find bitter complaints that the promulgation of the Fifth Decree to the Reich Citizenship Law, dated September 27, 1938, forced many Jews to go to German attorneys without any justification, because the Jewish legal advisers were widely seen as no longer being "adequate legal representatives"—although "German authorities were, perhaps to too great an extent, entirely objective in all cases."[75] This had to change. The means for gaining complete control over the representation

of Jewish interests was a fundamental ban, with a proviso for granting exceptions. A directive from the deputy of the Führer dated December 19, 1938, and
one from the director of the Reich Legal Office of the NSDAP, Frank, dated January 2, 1939,[76] expanded the ban on representing Jews to the members of the
Party's affiliated organizations (the SS, the SA) and its auxiliary associations
(such as the NSV, the NSRB, and the German Labor Front [DAF]). To rule out
any potential advantages for attorneys outside the Nazi organizations, the Reich
Bar Association followed suit on December 31, 1938, and extended this ban to all
attorneys-at-law, including those "privileged *Mischlinge*" who remained licensed:
there was "now only one sort of attorney, all of whom [were] in equal measure
bound in fidelity to the Führer"; it was "the professional obligation of all attorneys to hold themselves aloof from Jews and Jewish enterprises" in their professional activity; representation of Jews was permitted only with special authorization.[77] If authorization was denied, there could be no legal remedy; appeals to
the supervisory authorities were without suspensive effect.[78] Not affected by the
ban on representation were German civil servants, notaries, and certified public
accountants, to the extent that they were engaged in official business, as well as
defense counsel before the special court in cases involving foul play and before
the People's Court.[79] However, the fundamental ban on representation of non-
Aryan persons was not limited exclusively to Jews. It also affected Gypsies and
Gypsy *Mischlinge*. The representation of Poles was not subject to formal prohibition, yet here, too, attorneys were expected to "carefully weigh the interests of
the *Volksgemeinschaft* and exercise maximum discretion."[80]

Taken as a whole, authorization (at least according to reports by Party representatives) was granted only sparingly,[81] the better to forge ahead with the disfranchisement of Jews and persons of equivalent status. Thus the Party exerted
strong pressures to limit the number of authorizations applied for as far as possible, since otherwise the suspicion might easily arise that the applicant was "a
stooge of the Jews" and "politically unreliable."

Evidence for political unreliability was already seen in the fact that the attorney was not even a member of the National Socialist Public Welfare Organization (NSV) or that he "pressed particularly actively for Jewish mandates."[82]
Such mandates were authorized from case to case only and on two conditions:
that representation of "non-German" clients (in court) be "in the German interest" and that the proposing attorney be considered politically reliable. Since all
matters concerning Jews were automatically of political interest, a "German interest" was assumed in all cases in which the authorities were involved, for example, those involving fiscal affairs, foreign currency, or eugenic health matters
and all other cases that had "political relevance" or in which the state was inter-

ested "for other reasons" (mainly economic).[83] Permission for mandates in lawsuits relating to (racial) origin was accorded to German attorneys only if the claim had some chance of success.[84] A German interest *was to be denied* in all cases in which exclusively Jewish interests were at stake, for example, in marital affairs, transfers of guardianships for Jewish wards, and so forth.[85] "Political reliability" was especially insisted upon.[86] Permission for such mandates was flatly denied to any attorneys regarded as having Jewish blood (*Mischlinge*) or who had "Jewish kinsmen." Attorneys who did not give in were quite openly threatened by Party functionaries with "personal troubles."[87] If an attorney was not regarded as being in tune with "the basis of the National Socialist ideology," not only was he refused permission for mandates in Jewish matters, but he was also threatened with the withdrawal of his general professional permit, a threat that was frequently put into practice on the initiative of the Party's regional office (*Gauleitung*).[88] The same happened when a licensed attorney who took the case of a Jewish client did not follow the instructions of the Party in the case or did not fulfill his obligation "to act primarily as a trustee for the German *Volksgemeinschaft.*"[89] Barring of the attorney was undertaken either by Party disciplinary measures (if he was a member of the Party) and/or by social honor or disciplinary measures aimed at excluding him from the (state licensed) Reich Chamber of Attorneys (a corporate body with compulsory membership for all attorneys of the Reich). But exclusion from the profession of attorney did not satisfy the demands of the Party: those who were in particular disfavor were denounced to the Gestapo and taken into "protective custody."[90] The state authorities were obliged to consider the lack of a permit for Jewish mandates ex officio, because they "could not disregard the political decision of the Party office responsible for the case."[91]

b.   Physicians and Related Professions

In parallel with the exclusion of Jewish attorneys, measures were also taken to exclude Jews from other liberal professions requiring a state permit. By the Decree on the Admission of Physicians to Health Insurance Activity of April 22, 1933,[92] non-Aryan physicians were removed from the panels of the health insurance institutions and no new admissions of non-Aryans were permitted. The same prohibition applied to Jewish dentists.[93] Analogous to the regulations concerning Jewish state officials, attorneys, and patent attorneys, exceptions were made for veterans of World War I, but such exceptional admissions were granted only on condition of at least one year's service after admittance to the health insurance schemes. Similarly, the *general* rules for the admission of physicians were amended in such a way that they abolished individual rights. The legal right to admission to the health insurance schemes for physicians, dentists, and dental technicians had already been suspended since November 1933, first for cities with over a million inhabitants; after May 1934 these rights were suspended for physicians in general, and after 1935 for dentists and dental technicians in general.[94] A new clause stated that admission was to be granted only if the applicant and his spouse were of Aryan descent.[95] Again, exceptions were made for "war veterans."[96]

Whereas the exclusion of Jewish physicians from the health insurance schemes put paid to the main source of income for many of them, the new rules for the implementation of the Reich Citizenship Law completely deprived them of a living. Here again events began in the public service. The new rules canceled de jure the contracts of all Jewish physicians in leading positions at public hospitals and hospitals of the welfare institutions as well as the contracts of all Jewish physicians serving the social welfare system (*Vertrauensärzte*), effective March 31, 1936 (sec. 6 of the Second Decree to the Reich Citizenship Law of December 21, 1935).[97] Here again the decree of December 21, 1935, was not a new constitutive measure but rather the legalization of previously existing (unlawful) practices, since Jewish physicians in those hospitals had already been dismissed before 1935 despite having valid contracts.[98]

The legal starting point for these dismissals was the question whether non-Aryan status was an adequate reason for dismissal without notice under the terms of section 626 of the Civil Code. This question could not, however, be settled in a uniform way; it was handled differently from case to case. The Reich Labor Supreme Court did not give a definitive answer to this question but in its decision, admittedly after 1935, pointed out that the contracts of the Jewish physicians in leading positions, who were not civil servants but employees under civil law and who were obliged to resign on March 31, 1936 (sec. 6, par. 1, of the Second Decree to the Reich Citizenship Law of December 21, 1935, in association with sec. 4, par. 1, of the First Decree to the Reich Citizenship Law of November 14, 1935), had expired *automatically*, so that the *contractual* basis for pension claims was also annulled.[99] In the literature jurists argued that for "public corporations Jewish descent [might] always be a major argument for dismissal."[100]

Further anti-Jewish regulations followed rapidly upon the decree of December 21, 1935. The exceptional admission to the health insurance schemes of Jewish physicians who were war veterans was definitively reversed in 1937; only Jewish physicians who were married to Aryan spouses were exempt from this regulation. Similar rules held for dentists and dental technicians.[101] Further, Jewish physicians always stood under the threat of having their license revoked by *individual* administrative act, because the *general* terms of the physician's code concerning the revocation of admissions were always interpreted more harshly in such cases.

More important were the Fourth and the Eighth Decrees to the Reich Citizenship Law, dated July 25, 1938, and January 17, 1939, respectively,[102] under the terms of which the licenses of all Jewish physicians, dentists, dental technicians, and veterinarians (including war veterans) for the medical treatment of Aryan patients expired definitively on September 30, 1938, and January 31, 1939, respectively, regardless of whether they were employees or had their own practice. These regulations abolished all claims for pensions (thus violating the most important principle of law, *pacta sunt servanda*). As with the regulations for Jewish attorneys, only those Jewish physicians who were war veterans could be granted a subsidy by the Reich Chamber of Physicians (a corporate body with compulsory membership for all physicians of the Reich) and then only if they were "in need and worthy." This subsidy could, however, be withdrawn at any time.[103] Jewish physicians whose approval had expired were "entitled" to give notice to vacate their rented homes and practices as of September 30, 1938. Similarly, the landlord could give notice to vacate for the same date, without right of objection on the part of the Jewish tenant (sec. 7 of the Fourth Decree to the Reich Citizenship Law).

So, like Jewish attorneys, Jewish physicians were thus pushed back to the small circle of family members and private Jewish patients,[104] but even here remaining dependent on the permission of the Reich minister of the interior, revocable at any time (secs. 2 and 3, par. 2, of the Fourth Decree to the Reich Citizenship Law). Jews were forbidden to use the title *physician*: if they practiced with special permission, they had to call themselves *medics* (*Krankenbehandler*), and the training of such medics was permitted only in Jewish medical training centers.[105] Further, the medical insurance coverage of Jewish patients was restricted by the fact that the Jewish medics were party to such coverage only with special permission of the Reich Panel Doctors' Association (*kassenärztliche Vereinigung*) (decree of October 6, 1938).[106] A year later, Jewish medics and "dental orderlies" (Jewish dentists) were granted membership in the health insurance system only with the special permission of the Reich minister of labor (decree of September 19, 1939),[107] so that Jewish physicians and dentists were subject to numerous reservations before they could practice. If—as was regularly the case— permission was denied, the only means of survival for Jewish physicians with a special permit was the medical care of private Jewish patients, whose number was constantly diminishing on account of emigration and economic restrictions after 1938. We must thus conclude that from the start Jewish physicians were gradually "strangled" economically by increasing restrictions, whether by way of legislation, arbitrary internal administrative regulations, or arbitrary individual administration acts.

A great blow had already been dealt in 1936 when, contrary to the existing law, internal administrative directives effectively excluded Jewish physicians from the medical care of patients in the public service.

A directive issued in the fall of 1936 by the Reich and Prussian minister of the interior in the name of all Reich ministers declared that the costs for the medical attendance of public servants by Jewish physicians and dentists would not be refunded or covered by emergency subsidies or by public welfare institutions (with few exceptions, e.g., when a Jewish physician had to be consulted in the event of danger to life). (Lawyers' consultation costs were treated in the same way.) Likewise, attestations by these physicians were no longer accepted by the public service subsidy offices (*Beihilfe*),[108] which generally refunded 50 percent of the costs of medical care.

A rigorous racial distinction was, of course, also practiced with respect to new permits. The new Reich Physicians Law of December 13, 1935 (sec. 3), and the new Reich Veterinary Law of April 3, 1936,[109] stated that non-Aryan physicians or veterinary surgeons and those married to non-Aryans would not be licensed (except when they were classed as state officials under the Professional Civil Service Code of April 7, 1933) if the percentage of the non-German physicians in relation to the total number of physicians was greater than the percentage of Jews in the German population (again exceptions were made only for World War I veterans). This was a very sophisticated method of considerably reducing the number of Jewish physicians, since the percentage of Jewish physicians in Germany was traditionally relatively high, whereas the percentage of Jews in the population was very low.

In the years 1938–39 the above-mentioned Fourth and Eighth Decrees to the Reich Citizenship Law of July 25, 1938, and January 17, 1939, definitely put an end to the licensing of all Jewish physicians, dentists, and veterinarians, *without exception.*[110]

In a similar manner, the activity of Jewish pharmacists was reduced, with the difference that the process of restrictions occurred at a slower pace. It began in 1934 with a change in the examination regulations, by which Jewish pharmacists would no longer be admitted to the professional examinations (this effectively prevented them from working).[111] From 1936 on, severe economic restrictions were imposed: Jewish pharmacists were forced to lease their businesses to German pharmacists but were forbidden to rent pharmacies owned by Germans.[112]

Existing licenses of Jewish pharmacists remained valid until the end of 1938 but generally expired on January 31, 1939, with the Eighth Decree to the Reich Citizenship Law of January 17, 1939.[113] Applicants for new licenses had to submit a certificate of Aryan descent,[114] with the consequence, of course, that Jewish applicants were excluded even more severely than in other professions. In addition to Jews in the "legal" sense, *Mischlinge* of the first degree (those of half-Jewish descent, according to a classification in the Reich Citizenship Law) were also refused licenses. *Mischlinge* of the second degree (of quarter-Jewish descent) were accepted only on decision of the Reich minister of the interior with the consent of the office of the deputy of the Führer.[115] Thus, the influence of the Party on racial policy in the professional field was ensured.

2.   Other Liberal Professions

In addition to the elimination of Jews from state-licensed professions, steps were taken to exclude them from all leading positions in the commercial field and all other activities of importance. This process was initiated immediately after the pogroms of November 1938 (*Reichskristallnacht*), because now the "Jewish question" had to be settled by central regulations. As Göring put it at a conference on November 12, 1938, "the screws also have to be tightened in the economic field, since the Jewish question is mainly an economic one."[116]

The decree on the exclusion of Jews from German economic life of November 12, 1938,[117] established that as of January 1, 1939, Jews could no longer be at the head of an enterprise under the terms of the Law for the Regulation of National Labor of January 20, 1934.[118] Jews were thus no longer permitted to be employers. The decree further prescribed that Jewish managers could be dismissed on six weeks' notice, after which period they lost all their contractual rights and all rights to pensions and indemnities (secs. 1 and 2). Jews were not allowed to be members of a cooperative (because this institution under German law was reserved for ethnic equals [*Volksgenossen*]) and automatically lost their membership on December 31, 1938 (sec. 3). They were further forbidden to run a retail shop, exercise an independent trade, or visit markets, fairs, and exhibitions for commercial purposes. In addition to these restrictions, from 1938 on Jews were barred from many other professions subject not to licensing but to registration. Through an amendment of the Commercial Code of July 6, 1938,[119] Jews were not allowed to work in the following businesses: detective agencies, security services, the administration of houses and estates, and commercial matrimonial agencies (with the exception of matchmaking for Jews and *Mischlinge* of the first degree);

they were also forbidden to work as real estate agents, brokers for real estate contracts and loans, or commercial tourist guides. With these measures all *autonomous* activities in the field of trade and industry became closed to Jews.

During this second wave of discrimination at the latest, the liberal professions in the cultural domain also became completely barred to non-Aryans. In the most important field, that of the press, their exclusion had been effected even earlier with the Law on Editors of October 4, 1933.[120] The barring of non-Aryans was implemented later in the fields of film, theater, and cinema, following administrative regulations attached to the various legislative acts (on movies, theaters, etc.).[121]

Once they had been ousted from public service, the liberal professions, and independent business, the only activities open to Jews from 1938 onward, apart from the very limited fields of legal adviser (*Rechtskonsulent*), medic (*Krankenbehandler*), or dental orderly (*Zahnbehandler*), were subordinate positions in commerce, industry, insurance, and banking. But here the doors were often closed to them, since many firms dismissed Jews on their own initiative and refused to recruit them.

3. Labor Law

a. Jewish Workers

As a consequence of the developments in the professional sector described above, Jewish workers were all the more in need of jobs in the private sector, because contracts with non-Aryans in the public service (which employed both state officials with special legal status [*Beamte*] and employees on the basis of private contracts) could in accordance with the Professional Civil Service Code of April 7, 1933, be rescinded (although not obligatorily), and no new recruitments were permitted.[122] Insofar as Jews obtained or kept a job in the private sector, they were also subject to far-reaching discriminatory treatment even in the field of labor laws,[123] which began to be passed in 1938. Virtually only low-level jobs were open to them, since positions in senior and middle management had been barred to them since 1934.[124]

As in other fields, the formal equality of Jewish workers to German workers under the law remained intact, while de facto pressure was exerted by the individual firms and through internal administrative regulations. The policy of the state authorities was aimed at separating Jews and Germans, registering all Jewish workers, and exploiting them to the maximum by what amounted to forced labor for minimum wages. To relieve the public funds of the additional burden of social welfare payments to unemployed Jews,[125] the president of the Reich Labor Exchange and Unemployment Insurance had been given extensive powers since 1934 in all questions of forced labor.[126] Under these powers and with the explicit approval of the plenipotentiary for the Four Year Plan, Göring, and the support of the deputy of the Führer, Hess,[127] he gave instructions that "an effort should be made to put all Jews who were unemployed and fit for work into service as quickly as possible" and asked public and private undertakings to prepare work projects to this end.[128] This initiative, which in fact was nothing other than a preparation of forced labor for Jews, led to the issuing of a decree a few months later (March 4, 1939) by the president of the Reich Labor Exchange, in agreement with the Reich minister for food and agriculture, according to which unemployed Jews were to be put to "hard physical work" and "segregated from non-Jews."[129] This did not yet mean the legal enforcement of generalized forced labor for Jews, but in order to avoid forced labor when unemployed, Jews were obliged to accept any work offered, whatever its nature. At the local level, nevertheless, things had gone further, and the prospect of forced labor loomed over the whole Jewish workforce, since Jews were sent on a short-term basis or permanently on work projects managed by the SS, usually in agriculture or forestry.[130] Instructions by Hitler blocked the planned allocation of Jewish workers in the Annexed Eastern Territories, foreseen in the Reich labor minister's decree of March 14, 1941,[131] since economic considerations always had to be secondary to the plans to deport Jews to the General Government.

With regard to the treatment of Jewish employees under actual labor law, they were kept subject to the general labor law for a relatively long time, since the racial legislation that had been enacted could not yet in principle be applied to Jewish employees in the private sector.[132]

This strict separation between the Civil Service with its rigorous racial regulations and the economic sector, to which the Aryan Paragraph did not in principle apply, was in many cases nothing but a technicality. Already by the spring of 1933 it had become extremely common for Jewish employees to be dismissed on racial grounds alone. Often they were axed without notice, because employers considered non-Aryan descent to be an important ground justifying dismissal in accordance with sec. 626 of the Civil Code,[133] which permitted dismissal without notice if continuation of the contract until the end of its regular term could not be expected from the party who issued the dismissal (in most cases the employer), that is, in cases in which the basis of confidence and/or reliability was seriously compromised. This clause was misused by employers, who claimed that the racial descent "contaminated" this reliability in a serious way— although racial descent had been of no consequence whatsoever before 1933. As a result of this practice, employers argued that legal claims by dismissed Jews should be refused solely on the grounds of the plaintiff's racial descent.[134] The Reich Supreme Labor Court adopted this argument because "the racial principles promulgated by the NSDAP were now widely acknowledged, even among those sectors of the population that did not belong to the Party."[135] (In practice this meant that claims by Jewish plaintiffs were in any case rejected as inadmissible without examination.)

Regarding the field of substantive law, the basic argument put forward for the dismissal of Jews, as pointed out in the draft for the reform of the labor law drawn up by the Academy of German Law, was that dismissal without notice could be considered in individual cases if "the party issuing the dismissal could not be expected to maintain the employment contract in accordance with the meaning and substance of the labor and business community, with due regard to the type of employment and mutual loyalty."[136] This principle was implemented mainly to justify dismissals of non-Aryan employees in highly placed positions and of non-Aryan salesmen or agents.[137] When non-Aryan descent did not justify dismissal without notice, the labor courts often approved regular dismissal. Petitions by the affected employees to have the dismissal revoked on the ground of "undue hardship" (according to the Law on Protection against Unjustified Dismissal) were usually unsuccessful[138] (thus "normal" legal protection had thus become the exception). This practice was the expression of a very broad and mostly arbitrary interpretation of the principles of dismissal developed mainly by the Reich Labor Court.

In sum, this interpretation argued as follows: employment contracts with Jewish employees could be dissolved by means of regular dismissal (which required consideration of certain terms, e.g., three or six months' notice). In answering the question whether non-Aryan descent justified dismissal without notice in accordance with sec. 626 of the Civil Code, the Reich Labor Court presented a differentiated approach. In a very early decision of November 25, 1933, which presumably established the main line of the subsequent judicature in labor law, the court pointed out that dismissal of non-Aryans without notice was legally valid only in the public service and not in the field of private business. Nevertheless, "because of the new attitude of the German people toward Jewry as a result of the national revolution, one [could] not ignore" the impact of this attitude on contracts in private business. (This was a de facto acknowledgment or justification of *extra legem*, illegal dismissals in the field of private business, the introduction of a racial ideology into private labor law.) The decisive point was therefore whether continuation of the employment contract could be expected (by the employer) until the expiry date for regular dismissal. The question whether racial descent was a major obstacle to the continuation of the contract always had to be answered according to the special circumstances of the individual case: the basis should in this context be the "enlightened attitudes of the present, . . . not the possibly premature judgments under the impact of political events."[139] (This was an evident allusion to the anti-Semitic excesses of spring 1933, by which the court obviously intended to put a stop to extreme anti-Semitic actions in the field of labor law; but by the acknowledgment *in principle* of racial thinking in labor law—*extra legem*—the court had opened the door to the illegal and arbitrary dismissal of Jewish employees.) In the legal literature, the opinions were equally in favor of a judgment according to the merits of the individual case.[140] (This was in any case implicit in the law; that individual considerations needed to be mentioned explicitly in the case of Jewish claims shows how legal thinking had perverted the law.)

In line with this manner of thinking, the Reich Labor Court denied Jewish employers whose businesses were seriously affected or even made bankrupt as a result of the anti-Jewish excesses, the right to dismiss employees without notice "for important reasons." In a judgment of February 1934 in which the court had to decide whether the dismissal of the head clerk of a non-Aryan lawyer and notary was lawful (the lawyer having established a practice together with another lawyer and having been dismissed from the notary's office on the strength of the Professional Civil Service Code of April 7, 1933), the court ruled in a strictly formal way, making a mockery of the actual situation of the Jewish employers. It was normal, the court ruled, that the risk of a business should be borne by the employer: economic losses did not therefore automatically entitle him to serve dismissals without notice. The extraordinary losses in the Jewish defendant's business after June 1933 (the date of the head clerk's dismissal) had not been "so catastrophic" that he could not have been expected to continue the employment contract with the head clerk until September 30, 1933, the date on which regular dismissal would have taken effect.[141] (The aim of this judgment was ostensibly to prolong the financial burdens for Jewish lawyers.)

Over and above this situation, an important question was whether and in what way the principle of reasonableness should be valid for Jewish employees of municipal authorities, too. In the literature, the dismissal without notice of such individuals on account of their race was always declared admissible.[142] In this context the legal argument was not based on the quality of non-Aryan descent as such, but on the "general viewpoint that had been growing up over the past years regarding the possibility of employing a Jew at a municipal agency."[143] (Thus, not only racial descent but even racial *thinking* was acknowledged as a legitimate argument for discriminatory measures.) The Reich Labor Court again confirmed its opinion, however, that only in the individual case could racial descent lead to a dismissal without notice, and it referred the case to the lower instance (decision of March 20, 1937).[144] In another case, however, the court did acknowledge as lawful the dismissal of a Jewish member of the communal orchestra because he had not been accepted in the Reich Chamber of Culture (ruling of February 6, 1937).[145]

The theory of reasonableness in the individual case developed by the courts certainly did open the way to less harsh actions toward Jews on the part of employers than in the public service, but it is doubtful that it was applied de facto to any significant extent.

As far as employees in managerial positions were concerned, their dismissal (on the basis of the above-mentioned "broad" interpretation of the existing labor law) had certainly become normal practice before 1938.[146]

A special provision for such dismissals was later created by the Decree on the Exclusion of Jews from German Economic Life of November 12, 1938, according to which senior Jewish staff could be dismissed at any time.

After 1937–38, especially following the pogroms of November 9, 1938, when thousands of Jews were taken into "police custody," that is, sent to concentration camps,[147] discrimination against all other Jewish employees was also stepped up by the labor courts. In many cases their decisions anticipated the later deprivation of Jews' rights.[148]

In this context it should be noted that Jewish employees were even denied the right to appeal against dismissal, an inadmissible situation, since sec. 56 of the National Labor Code (AOG) of January 24, 1934,[149] allowed such appeal in cases in which the plaintiff had worked for more than a year in the firm and the dismissal had particularly harsh effects and was not justified by the firm's situation.[150] A dismissal was ruled by the court to be justified by the situation of the firm when, for example, the employer feared that he would suffer loss of earnings or have poorer chances in the competitive situation of the Reich if he continued to employ Jewish personnel.[151]

When dismissals without notice on the ground of racial descent were sustained, there was a risk that the employees affected would lose all their pension entitlements. Much discussion revolved around the question whether the employer was bound by his earlier commitment to pay a pension to the dismissed employee. The Reich Labor Court decided on a case-by-case basis, presumably depending on the terms of the specific employment contract.

In the above-mentioned decision of March 20, 1937, the court stated that the question whether this dismissal (on racial grounds), which could not have been foreseen at the time the pension terms were formulated, should be treated as comparable to cases for which the pension was maintained. Through this ruling it became clear that dismissal without notice did not automatically lead to a loss of the pension. But in the decision of February 6, 1937, mentioned above, in the case of the dismissal of the Jewish member of the communal orchestra, the court ruled unequivocally that upon dismissal the person involved lost not only the right to any further wages but also the pension granted by the magisterial authority (this was a clear violation of the century-old principle of *pacta sunt servanda* and the principle of equal treatment of comparable cases established in the Civil Code). In the literature jurists also adhered to a restrictive interpretation. They argued that the main basis of the promise of pensions by the magisterial authority was to provide for subsistence in the event of old age or infirmity. Since this did not apply in the case of the dismissal of employees on racial grounds, the granting of a pension would not be applicable.[152]

In the context of discriminatory measures against Jewish employees, the question was discussed in the literature whether and under what circumstances (Jewish) pensioners who had retired in the normal way could subsequently be deprived of their pension for "important reasons." Several theories were developed, one of which was to apply the principles on dismissal without notice directly or analogously to such cases, because, as these jurists asserted, the legal basis of the pension was the employment contract, which expired with the dismissal.[153] (Such an argument was demonstrably unlawful, because retirement was the very opposite of dismissal, thus rendering any analogy impossible.) With regard to the excessive interpretation of sec. 626 of the Civil Code (dismissal without notice) mentioned above, on the one hand these theories effectively opened the way to depriving Jewish pensioners of their rights on account of their race. On the other hand, the courts argued in a more restrictive way that the withdrawal of pension rights had the quality of a punitive measure that hit the pensioner particularly hard. The judicature found the formula that revocation was justified only on the ground of such serious circumstances that a claim for a pension would be regarded as a violation of the rule of good faith.[154] Such a violation was acknowledged (again) in analogous implementation of the German Civil Service Code, 1937, sec. 67, according to which state officials continued to have certain obligations even after cessation of their active duty—when the pensioner behaved in an offensive or harmful way toward the employer. Another reason for withdrawal was seen in the fact—analogously to secs. 132 ff. of the German Civil Service Code, 1937 (revocation of pension, if the entitled person was sentenced to death or penitentiary for high treason [*Hochverrat*] or national betrayal [*Landesverrat*])—that the person had *acted* as a "traitor" (it was not clear whether punishment was necessary in these cases). Racial descent was not explicitly cited as a ground for nonpayment of pensions. The right to withhold a pension, it was argued, always had to be judged according to the "special circumstances of the case."[155]

The discriminatory practices did not concern only dismissals and pensions, however, and Jews were often refused other rights as employees. The Frankfurt/ Main Labor Court denied Jews the right to vacation[156] (in contrast to the Labor Court of Berlin as late as 1941).[157] The Labor Court of Appeal of Koblenz refused payment of wages to Jews on national holidays in a "law-making" manner,[158] thus anticipating the decree of October 3, 1941, referred to below.

These common discriminatory practices toward Jewish employees began to be "legalized" at the end of 1941, perhaps also in view of the forthcoming evacuation of Jews from the Reich (in preparation for "resettlement" and the Final Solution [see appendix 2, the Wannsee Protocol of January 20, 1941, which at this time was doubtless already decided upon at the highest political level]). This is certainly indicated by the coincidence of the events and the tendency of the special regulations to segregate Jewish workers from German workers and to establish forced labor for the former. Regarding Jewish workers with regular contracts, the Decree on Employment of Jews of October 3, 1941[159]—which was issued in parallel with the incipient massive deportation of Jews from the Reich territory—openly established the advent of special law. With the definition that "Jews employed in work have a work relationship of a special kind" (sui generis) (sec. 1), Jews were completely excluded from the (general) labor law, and the Reich minister of labor was empowered to create any type of special clauses whatsoever for the "special employment of Jews" (sec. 2), with the agreement of the minister of the interior and the Party Chancellery.

The main consequence of this special treatment was the provision that Jews no longer had the right to call themselves workers, this designation being reserved solely for Germans. "Alien" workers were designated as the "labor force." Further, the implementing order of October 31, 1941, attached to this decree, effectively established forced labor for all Jews and the principle of their segregation from German workers by obliging Jews to accept any work assigned to them and instructing the authorities to place Jews exclusively in "group employment," that is, the "closed" (forced) labor service, separated from other "personnel" (secs. 11 and 12).[160] As usual with special law, these clauses also lagged behind National Socialist practice. Forced labor for Jewish workers, as we have seen, was already commonly practiced before the decree of October 3, 1941, when only the most menial of jobs (road construction, garbage collection, clearing snow, etc.) for lower wages than for Germans, were of course considered appropriate to Jews.[161]

The special treatment of Jewish workers was effected by designating in the implementing regulations the fields of labor law from which Jews were excluded and leaving the details to administrative orders issued by the Reich minister of labor. For instance, although pay rules were formally still valid for Jews, the administrative orders had deprived them of all real substance de facto: payment was made only for work actually done; health benefits and holidays with pay ceased to exist; family and child allowances, marriage bonuses, death benefits, Christmas bonuses, maternity benefits, short-time work allowances, and so on all fell by the wayside. The Decree on the Protection of Labor of December 12, 1939,[162] was declared inapplicable to Jews. Unemployment benefits were granted to Jews only to cover "the absolute minimum to sustain life" (sec. 17). Protection against dismissal was abolished and replaced by a one-day notice with effect at the end of the next working day (secs. 3, 5, 6, 9, 15, and 18 ff. of the implementing order of December 12, 1939). Complaints arising out of work contracts were no longer dealt with by the labor tribunals but by a state agency (*Spruchstelle*) set up by the Ministry of Justice at which one judge sat (administrative order of the Reich Ministry of Justice, December 10, 1941).[163] When the disciplinary rules were breached, Jews—like other "loafers"—were sent to the SS and police "work training camps."[164]

b.   Excursus: The Special Treatment of the "Alien Workforce"

Provisions identical or similar to those discussed above also applied to the mass of "alien" workers who had come into the Reich since 1940,[165] indicating that the special treatment of Jews was basically only the thin end of the wedge that represented the discriminatory treatment of all non-Aryan workers.[166] The aim of this special treatment, constantly repeated at great propagandistic expense, was "total exploitation" (*restloser Einsatz*) to meet the goals of the war economy.[167] The general rules of the old German labor law, which was based on the principle of equal pay and equal social benefits for equal work, represented an obstacle for the political leaders, for whom the sole principle to be followed was to exploit "non-Germans" to the hilt. Furthermore, another purpose lurked behind these discriminatory measures in the minds of the political leadership, a favorite project of Hitler's: to uproot the "alien" workers from their familiar environment by harsh treatment, to weaken their fertility, and thus to decimate them without bloodshed.[168]

The forced labor system for "alien" workers is thus highly contradictory. Industry and the administration were on the whole in favor of the promotion or at least the upkeep of these workers, and for reasons of efficacy they consistently appealed "in the name of reason and not least pure expediency" for their good treatment,[169] in contrast to the radical ideas of the political leadership aimed at high output with the lowest possible living standards. As usual, political will prevailed over all arguments of economic reason: the sometimes draconian harshness of the special-law provisions mentioned hereafter[170] stood in contradiction to the need for technical efficiency, although in point of fact foreign workers were often treated better in practice than was provided for by the regulations, if only because employers could not otherwise have met their production targets.

The responsibility for labor regulations covering foreign workers, who according to official data numbered almost 5 million in 1942, including war prisoners in the labor service,[171] fell primarily to the offices of the Reich Ministry of Labor and the plenipotentiary general for labor allocation,[172] who were empowered by decree of the Führer to regulate the forced labor of foreign nationals in Germany.[173] The plenipotentiary general for labor allocation in particular had been invested with virtually unlimited powers.[174] On instruction from him, commissioners were appointed in the Occupied Eastern Territories with the task of "recruiting and securing" foreign workers for German agriculture and the armaments industry in these territories and in the Reich. To this end they intended to set up a "sound pay scale in favor of the *Großdeutsches Reich*" based on a piece-work and pay system with the aim of increasing output.[175] In the Reich territory itself, the plenipotentiary general for labor allocation appointed the regional heads of the Party (Gauleiter) as his commissioners in the *Gaue*, so that the competence for dealing with "alien" workers at the regional level rested with the Party (the political power). The agencies of the labor administration and the general and internal administrations were pledged to cooperate with the commissioners.[176]

The basis of all regulations was the instruction of the plenipotentiary general for labor allocation of October 25, 1942, according to which employers had to set up a piecework and premium system for workers from the occupied territories with a view to increasing output.[177] Even before this instruction was issued, particular emphasis had been placed on the introduction of such a system in the Annexed Eastern Territories and the Occupied Eastern (i.e., Soviet) Territories in order to increase results at all costs.[178] Such a system was often associated with premiums or allowances in order to prevent foreign workers from changing jobs. An instruction by the plenipotentiary general for labor allocation of June 11, 1942,[179] even needed to emphasize that it was forbidden to give foreigners better conditions of payment than those established for equivalent German workers.

An exception was made for Polish workers from the General Government and the Annexed Eastern Territories who, on account of the compulsory work imposed on them since 1940, had either voluntarily or by forced conscription since 1941–42 been brought to the Reich territory.[180] Technically speaking, these workers were in principle paid "equally" to German workers on the basis of the wage regulations of the given economic sector.[181] This equal treatment of Polish workers was a thorn in the side of the radical "racial fighters" in the administration and the Party: they complained that equal treatment was the basic rule in the Reich territory, so that conditions were generally better than in the East.[182] In point of fact, however, wages were anything but equal, on account of the many exceptions made. An instruction issued by the Reich trustee for labor dated October 5, 1941 (also valid in the Annexed Eastern Territories [sec. 17]), on the treatment of Polish workers in labor law[183] stated that the following instruments were not applicable to Poles: the Law for the Regulation of National Labor of January 20, 1934; the Law for the Regulation of Labor in Public Administrations and Institutions of March 23, 1934; the Law on Home Work of March 23, 1934, in the version of October 30, 1939; the Law on the Payment of Wages for the National Holiday of the German People (May 1) of April 26, 1934; the Law on Exceptional Holidays of April 17, 1939; and the Instruction on the Implementation of the Four Year Plan on Payment of Holidays of December 3, 1937.[184] In view of these numerous exceptions, equal pay was accorded only for the actual work done (similar to the situation for Jews [see above]); all payment for holidays, which was an integral part of the wage, was abolished. In addition, other restrictions comparable to those applied to Jews mentioned above were imposed.

These included, first, the 15 percent tax on wages for "social compensation" introduced by the instruction of October 5, 1941, mentioned above, and the abolition of premiums or allowances for holidays, family and children, maternity, and so forth, thus considerably diminishing the effective earnings of Poles. This instruction further entitled employers to pay Polish workers at the lowest level of wages usual in the firm (this was called the "lesser achievement clause").[185] Polish agricultural workers were generally paid less than their German counterparts.[186] But the lack of equal treatment was not confined to wages alone. Up to 1941 Polish workers had only one week's vacation, much less than the rules granted German workers;[187] old vacation rights were placed on hold until December 1, 1943, and could not be exercised until the end of the war.[188] The Reich labor minister took pains to point out that the provisions on maternity protection applied "in principle" to pregnant Polish women, as any other interpretation would violate "the fundamental laws of humanity"; the *scope* of the protection, however, might vary in relation to that accorded German women[189] (in line with the Nazi rule of law: upholding the principle in theory and opening the way to discriminatory measures in practice).

The discriminatory practices against the various groups of foreign workers applied to other fields of labor law, with considerable ethnic differentiation. For workers from Eastern Europe, conditions were very much harsher than for those from the occupied Western European territories or from neutral or friendly states, who (apart from the wage system) enjoyed equal treatment with Germans in matters of labor law.[190] The treatment received by the first-mentioned group, the so-called eastern workers, can serve as an example of the discriminations practiced. It was toward these people, workers from the Occupied Soviet Territories, that the program set up by the plenipotentiary general for labor allocation and the following special regulations were primarily oriented, with a view to their forced labor and "maximum exploitation."[191]

Like the Jews, the eastern workers (from the Occupied Soviet Territories) had an "employment relationship of a special kind" (sui generis). German labor law and the protective labor provisions were applicable only when they were explicitly stated in the corresponding clause[192] (the Nazi principle of legislation: whatever was not explicitly permitted was forbidden). And like the Jews, the eastern workers were paid only for the actual work done: no social benefits were granted, on the grounds that "many eastern workers did not need to take care of their families"; this seemed to mean that the German authorities had taken over this responsibility, but on a minimum level, through the compulsory "social compensation tax" (see below). Income tax had to be paid at the rate for class 1 (singles, the highest rate), whatever the actual family status. These workers, like Jews and Poles, were subject to a 15 percent tax on their income, a "social compensation tax," which went to the revenue offices "in order to provide benefits for needy eastern workers and their families."[193] Vacations of one week could be granted—not as a matter of right, of course—to eastern workers in their second year of employment, provided they had "proved themselves" in achievement and behavior.[194]

Other discriminatory rules were issued for all "non-German" workers, based on an instruction from the plenipotentiary general for labor allocation of October 2, 1943; these dealt with vacations, breaches of discipline, living accommodations, and board. To make sure that "alien" workers would return from home leave, a *collective responsibility* system was put into effect: groups of vacationers of the same nationality were formed, and if any members of the first group did not return, at least that number of the second group were held back; if all members of the third group did not return, a three-month ban on vacations was issued for *all* workers of the relevant nationality[195] (thus creating a system of "perfect" mutual dependence). These rules give a clear idea of what sort of conditions existed in practice.

So-called breaches of discipline by workers were in principle punished on the basis of the general rules,[196] which were implemented by the employer (warnings and fines) or the courts[197] (at the request of the labor agencies). In the event of infringements by "non-German" workers, however, the Reich labor trustees had been instructed by the Ministry of Labor not to demand a sentence as usual but "to request the intervention of the Gestapo."[198] In minor cases, the offender was put back to work; in all other cases—circumventing the competence of the courts[199]—they were sentenced to "heavy labor" at the so-called work training camps set up for "loafers" under the surveillance of the Gestapo.[200] In serious cases, they were committed to a concentration camp.[201]

Discriminatory (special) law was also applied to the treatment of foreign workers in other regards. Although the protective labor law and the rules on working hours of the industrial branches were also valid for foreign workers (with the exception of the eastern workers, for whom the protective labor law was suspended [see above]),[202] their housing, board, and other matters, which came under the competence of the labor administration with the consent of the highest Reich departments concerned, were regulated very differently.[203] As the German Labor Front leader Robert Ley put it, the aim of the regulations, which varied locally and from firm to firm, was to "exploit [foreign workers] to the hilt with a minimum of outlay," because "lesser races" needed "less room, less clothes, less food, and less culture than a superior race."[204]

The instructions of the plenipotentiary general for labor allocation with regard to the recruitment and treatment of workers in the occupied territories were even more discriminatory. There a merciless piecework system was practiced, which applied not only to wages and employment contracts ("only production-oriented contracts") but to all other fields too. In consequence, housing, food, and other matters were also managed on the "principle of productivity."[205]

Housing was organized in mass quarters segregated by nationality.[206] The administration of these camps was in the hands of the German Labor Front, whose camp commanders passed the instructions of the heads of the enterprises on to the workers.[207] Further disadvantages for "alien" workers compared with Germans were also practiced in the distribution of textiles, working clothes,[208] food, and so on. Regarding food supplies, only the Poles were treated equally to Germans; for the other foreign workers, the normal food rations merely served as a "basis" on which the Reich minister for food and agriculture established the actual allotments.[209]

All other regulations concerning the treatment of foreign workers, such as the relationship to the German population, time off, medical care, participation in cultural and church activities, and so forth, were no longer issued by the state labor administration: all these fields of competence had been usurped by the police forces through agreements or with the consent of the administration. This change in competence had long since ceased being a legal matter; it had become one of mere political opportunism, because the people concerned were in any case beyond the pale of German law and were completely at the behest of the needs of the "labor service." The corresponding regulations are therefore dealt with in the excursus titled "Police Law."

VI. The Cultural and Social Sector

The ousting of Jews from the liberal professions, public service, and the world of work as a whole was only the first step in the extensive moves "to eliminate Jews completely from the German Lebensraum."[1]

An important element of this aim was their elimination from the whole cultural sphere, this being one of the first sectors to be subject to *Gleichschaltung*, that is, centralized in the Reich Chamber of Culture and put under state censorship.[2] It is noteworthy, however, that—unlike the procedures set forth in the public service and the above-mentioned discriminatory decrees in the field of trade and industry (with the exception of the Law on Editors)[3]—the exclusion of non-Aryans was not explicitly provided for in the centralization acts or the corresponding implementing orders.[4] The basis of the exclusions rather was internal instructions requiring a certificate of Aryan descent[5] and demanding from every cultural performer obligatory membership in one of the departments of the Reich Chamber of Culture;[6] according to the general clauses of the above-mentioned implementing orders, the "required reliability and aptitude" also had to be certified by every applicant to one of the chambers.[7] The principle that Jews should not possess this aptitude was so taken for granted that explicit rules were no longer necessary, just as it was taken for granted that Jews should be portrayed in all films as representing evil and shamefulness, ridiculed, in short, as the incarnation of all the deadly sins (avarice, covetousness, hunger for power, perfidy, etc.).[8] On May 9, 1933, Paul Joseph Goebbels had already declared before German stage managers: "The Jew cannot be an interpreter of German *Volkstum*."[9]

The exclusion of Jews was achieved in practice through nonrenewal of existing contracts with non-Aryan artistic personnel or even the dissolution of contracts "by mutual agreement" (often under massive pressure by the Party). When no "agreement" could be reached, the contract was examined by the local committees of the specific chamber to decide whether the person involved could be dismissed with a view to enforcing the "principle of equity."[10] The judicature recognized a right to serve notice "for important reasons" on the part of the Aryan party (sec. 626 of the Civil Code) or a right to withdraw from the contract for reasons of good faith (given that the non-Aryan party was not capable of fulfilling the agreement) (secs. 346 and 347, in association with secs. 133 and 157, of the Civil Code). The following example illustrates the process clearly.

The Berlin Court of Appeal was called upon to decide whether the plaintiff, the famous German motion picture company UFA, could withdraw from a contract with a Swiss company on a manuscript, thereby acquiring all the rights to the novel *Odysseus* by the Jewish film director Eric Charell and his work on the scenario. In this contract, which had been concluded after the seizure of power by the National Socialists, the plaintiff had reserved the right to withdraw if the contract could not be fulfilled or if the director could not take over the management for reasons of illness, death, or "similar" circumstances. The court ruled that the plaintiff was entitled to withdraw in accordance with sections 346, 133, and 157 of the Civil Code. According to section 10 of the First Implementing Decree to the Reich Chamber of Culture Law, participation in a film production was reserved to Aryans, because the term *aptitude* (to participate in a movie production) was not to be understood exclusively in a technical sense. In a sophisticated argument, the court stated that it was not "the Jewish religion or the non-Aryan descent" of the Jewish director that was of consequence but the significance that the racial question had taken on for public life in Germany in the wake of the revolution of March 1933. In its ruling of June 27, 1936, the Reich Supreme Court confirmed this decision, seeing no "legal objections" to this interpretation of the clauses of the contract. Such an interpretation was consonant with the law and the "prevailing philosophy" on the racial question. With unparalleled frankness, the highest German court "without compunction" compared the racial descent of the director with death or illness as provided for by the clause on withdrawal:

The former ["liberal"] concept of the substance of a legal subject made no difference among human beings with a human face in terms of the similarity or difference of blood; it refused, therefore, a legal division and classification of people according to racial criteria. In line with the National Socialist ideology, however, only persons of

German descent (and any others legally assimilated to them) can be treated as having full legal rights in the German Reich. With this, the basic demarcations of the former law on foreigners are revived and concepts taken up again that were defined by a distinction between persons having full legal capacity and those with lesser legal capacity. Complete deprivation of rights was formerly assimilated . . . to physical death. If in point 6 of the manuscript contract of February 27, 1933, there is a question of Charell's not being "able to fulfill his contract as director by reason of illness, death, or a similar circumstance," this clause can without hesitation be assimilated to a change in the legal validity of the personality on the ground of legally accepted racial viewpoints, insofar as it prevents Charell from carrying out his stage manager activities in the same way as death or illness would.[11]

This "removal of Jewish influence in the spiritual field" was accompanied by limitations and expulsions of the Jews from the general education institutions[12] (later extended to other non-Aryan children). They were, of course, also excluded from the colleges and universities (after 1943, when the military situation was deteriorating, groups such as Slovenians and Ukrainians were exempted).[13] Jewish citizens were thus forced to return to the private Jewish schools and institutions,[14] which were definitively closed down in 1942.[15] The rabbinical seminars and Jewish libraries were closed or dissolved, and the land on which synagogues were built was expropriated. On an instruction by Goebbels, all paintings, collections, and books in Jewish hands that had "antique value" had to be declared and presumably surrendered.[16]

In addition, Jews were subject to numerous discriminations and prohibitions concerning free movement in public places and visits to cultural or sports events.[17] Jews were excluded from almost all state benefits such as public welfare, compensation benefits,[18] and so on, with the aim of gradually forcing them out of general economic and cultural life so as to achieve their complete impoverishment and psychological demoralization.[19]

In the streets, Jews were easy to recognize by their pale features and shabby clothes.[20] These humiliating measures by the administration in the cultural field were preceded by countless acts of discrimination in the public sector. From 1934 on, the notice "Jews not wanted" was to be seen on the doors of restaurants, at sports grounds, and on park benches. Social relations between Aryans and non-Aryans had almost completely ceased by this time. In effect, the Jewish citizens were in a total spiritual ghetto. Firms that had Jewish clients were pressed upon to abandon them.[21] From 1938 on, taxi drivers refused to transport Jewish passengers; schoolchildren bombarded the houses of Jews with stones and other projectiles under the guidance of their teachers; the names and addresses of

Jewish citizens were posted on public bulletin boards and in newspapers (e.g., in Frankfurt/Main).[22] According to eyewitnesses, these measures often evoked pity and a general unease rather than hatred for those affected.[23]

VII.   Commercial and Property Law

To accelerate this process of deprivation and humiliation of Jewish citizens, the political leadership was determined to get its hands not only on the work income of Jews but also on their resting assets. This meant to deprive them of all subsistence, to exclude them from the general law, and thus to provoke their "civil death" (*bürgerlicher Tod*, a term from the Middle Ages signifying the loss of all civil rights on entering a cloister).

1.   Measures for Dispossessing Jews of Their Property

The central element of the "special treatment" of non-Aryans was in the field of commercial and property law. It had always been a long-term goal of the political leadership to expropriate all Jewish property and to incorporate it into the National Socialist state. Hitler himself had early decided to confiscate Jewish assets for the benefit of the Reich. The Jews served as hostages against feared boycotts by the Western countries (some did occur), and from the start their property was potentially subject to seizure. When there was nothing left to take away from the Jews, the "precious Jewish life" could serve as a means of reprisal, that is, through hostage-taking.[1] The discriminatory treatment of the Jews, which had worsened since 1938, had thus long since been determined. The November 7, 1938, assassination of a member of the German embassy in Paris, Ernst vom Rath, by a Jew served as a convenient opportunity to move seriously to the drafts and suggestions for the dispossession of Jews and deprivation of their rights that had been slumbering in the drawers of the bureaucrats.[2] The Nazi leadership had the most radical ideas in this regard: as Göring stated at the important conference of Reich ministers of November 12, 1938,[3] the aim was to reduce the Jewish population to the status of pensioners by the expropriation ("Aryanization") of all their property, so that they would be dependent on state support, "which of course should be kept as low as possible." The sale to Aryans of Jewish businesses and property by the trustees at the current market value would bring in great riches to the German economy. In order to achieve this total impoverishment of the Jews, numerous regulations were issued,[4] so articulated among themselves that they could not help but achieve the desired aim.

a.   Dispossession Measures Following the *Reichskristallnacht*

Before the beginning of systematic expropriation of Jewish property, the *Reichskristallnacht* provided an opportunity to calm down the agitation among the public caused by the devastation of Jewish shops and synagogues initiated by the SA and the NSDAP in the course of the anti-Jewish pogroms of November 9, 1938.[5] By the decree of November 12, 1938, Jewish citizens became subject to an "expiatory tax" of RM 1 billion for the assassination of the German diplomat vom Rath by the Jew Herschl Grynszpan. This decree, which was apparently inspired by the compulsory payments imposed under medieval martial law, was accompanied by a decree on the "restoration of the appearance of the streets" (which were in a dreadful state after the devastation of Jewish shops) of the same date,[6] requiring the Jewish victims of the outrages to restore all damage; at the same time they were refused all insurance claims (these accrued to the Reich)—a harbinger of the expropriation policy that was to take hold in the weeks to come and a further demonstration of the National Socialist method of giving "legal" sanction to illegal practices by legislation after the fact.

b.   The Decree on the Registration of Jewish Property, April 26, 1938, and the Decree on the Utilization of Jewish Property, December 3, 1938

In preparation for the "legal" sanctioning (of these illegal actions), the Decree on the Registration of Jewish Property was passed on April 26, 1938,[7] subjecting all assets of Jews and their spouses (with the exception of household effects and personal belongings) to notification, in order "to safeguard Jewish property in accordance with the needs of the German economy" (sec. 7). *Safeguarding* was nothing other than a euphemism for the seizure of all Jewish property for the benefit of the Reich. The property owned had to be declared in detail on lengthy questionnaires. Any property not declared was subject to seizure.[8] The free disposal by Jewish employers of their own businesses had already been abolished by Göring in spring 1938, when the sales of all businesses were made subject to a permit from the state authorities[9] (to prevent employers from saving their property). The aim of the decree of April 26, 1938, the seizure of Jewish assets, was finally legalized through the Decree on the Utilization of Jewish Property of December 3, 1938,[10] issued by the minister of the economy and the Reich minister of the interior.

All Jews running a business (Jews' enterprises had had to be listed and registered since June 1938, according to the Third Decree to the Reich Citizenship

Law of June 14, 1938)[11] could be obliged by the authorities to sell or close their businesses within a set time limit. The same was true of agricultural and forestry undertakings or property, for all real estate, and other types of property (secs. 1 and 6).[12] Severely punished (generally by penitentiary) was the offense of "concealment of the Jewish character" (i.e., Jewish ownership) of a business.[13] This decree was the basis for the horrendous profits made by the German economy and the public authorities, and especially the offices of the plenipotentiary for the Four Year Plan, through the Aryanization of Jewish businesses.

The procedure was set up as follows: when a Jewish businessman or tradesman was ordered to sell his business, the authorities established state trustees to administer the transaction (sec. 2 of the Decree on the Utilization of Jewish Property). The trustees were to evaluate the business or the estate and to fix a compensation, which "had of course to be as low as possible."[14] Such administration by trustees offered German comrades unlimited opportunities to enrich themselves or "settle old accounts"; the trustees were then to transfer the item in question into Aryan hands at the normal price (needless to say without any possibility of legal protection for either the Jewish owner or those German competitors who were not successful in the race for acquisition).[15] This procedure caused enormous sums to be wasted, since the businesses sold were often not well run and were allowed to go to ruin. The net profit (the difference between the minimal compensation accorded the Jewish owner and the normal price paid by the German purchaser) was scooped up by the administration.[16]

The Decree on the Utilization of Jewish Property contained further discriminatory provisions, namely, that the acquisition of real estate was forbidden to Jews (sec. 7) and that all other dispositions of estates required authorization (sec. 8). In this regard, too, the decree merely rubber-stamped long-established practice. Jewish property owners were subject to enormous pressures from all sides (for example by Aryan competitors, creditors, etc.) to sell their land, especially when larger properties were at stake and when local notables, leading Party officials, or members of the police forces had their eye on the property. Extortion was resorted to without qualm: Jewish prisoners were released from concentration camp on condition that they sell their estates at a price to be fixed "later" by the government.[17]

Movable property, too, was subject to certain restraints. All securities in Jewish hands were made subject to compulsory deposit in a bank for foreign exchange, and all dispositions had to be licensed by the state (secs. 11 and 12). Any acquisition, whatever its legal basis, was forbidden, including donations[18] and all sales of objects of gold, precious metals, precious stones, or pearls of a value of more than one thousand reichsmarks (sec. 14). In spring 1939 all jewelry and precious-metal objects in Jewish hands had to be surrendered without compensation.[19] Since 1933 it had been generally forbidden to take along any money, securities, jewelry, or precious metals when emigrating.[20] If the individual did not have an emigration permit (when fleeing the country), such valuables were seized in accordance with the foreign exchange regulations, which were always applied more strictly to Jews.[21]

Through such illegal measures the state took possession of Jewish property. The proceeds either fell to the Reich authorities or were sold for a song into private hands. This blocking of foreign currency, the sale of real estate, and the negotiation of securities rendered emigration almost impossible for Jews, who were often able to retain only the clothes they wore and a few personal belongings. Frequently their baggage was seized and put up for auction.[22] The expression attributed to Hitler—that the Jews were allowed to leave "only with a backpack and ten marks" was not far from the truth.[23] Countless bureaucratic harassments (permits, certificates, authorizations, special taxes) ensured that every last mark was extorted from the emigrants.[24] Emigration became a form of banishment.

The decree of December 3, 1938, and all other regulations in context with it were not complete or were at least subject to misunderstanding, in that they contained no provisions on the legal consequences of the limitations on disposition or seizure. In reality, these measures constituted neither a temporary "safeguarding" of Jewish property nor its "administration" while preserving its substance, as the decree of December 3, 1938, would have us believe, but a full-blown appropriation ("utilization") of the real estate and movable property of Jews in favor of the state. The decrees were implemented by internal instructions, logged in the budget of the Reich finance minister, and served to enrich all branches of the administration.[25] The degree to which the concept of Jewish property was extended is indicated by the fact that in the Occupied Eastern Territories even Jewish manpower came under that heading, that is, was regarded as the property of the Reich.[26]

c.   The Eleventh Decree to the Reich Citizenship Law, November 25, 1941

The discriminatory treatment of Jews reached its climax in the Eleventh Decree to the Reich Citizenship Law of November 25, 1941,[27] issued in parallel to the deportations of Jews,[28] which were becoming numerous in the fall of 1941. According to this, the property of Jews deported beyond the borders of the Reich fell to the Reich in its entirety and was to be used "for the promotion of all the aims related to the solution of the Jewish question" (sec. 3).[29] The decision whether the conditions for forfeiture of property were fulfilled lay with the Security Police (sec. 8).

Forfeiture of property was accomplished by highly bureaucratic means as follows: before being deported, the persons involved had to prepare a detailed declaration of their property,[30] which served as the basis for the investigation carried out by the tax offices and the Gestapo. The seizure order, issued by the tax office and later by the Gestapo,[31] was delivered to the victim before deportation (in part by the court bailiff). The legal effect of such a seizure order was only of a declaratory nature, however, since the seizure was considered to be automatically in effect on the basis of section 8, paragraph 2, of the Eleventh Decree.[32]

d.   The Dispossession of Jewish Property on the Basis of Other Regulations

The Eleventh Decree was, as usual, only the legalization of an act of pillaging that had already come about. Whereas the decrees of April 26 and December 3, 1938, referred "only" to specific objects, other regulations had already been given a broad interpretation so as to confiscate the *whole property of Jews*.

The deportation of Jews began in spring 1940. The seizure and confiscation of Jewish property were originally carried out by the presidents of the districts (*Regierungspräsidenten*),[33] but later the Reich Security Main Office and the offices of the *Reichsführer*-SS took over these tasks.[34] This gave rise to a virtual tug-of-war among the authorities over the right to administer (and make use of) of Jewish property,[35] a contest that the administration won in this case.[36] Before the enactment of the Eleventh Decree to the Reich Citizenship Law, the basis for this wholesale confiscation of property had been the Law on the Seizure of Assets of Enemies of the People and State of July 14, 1933,[37] which was later also introduced in Austria and the occupied Czechoslovak territories (the German Sudeten Territories and the Protectorate of Bohemia and Moravia).[38] According to this law, the state could seize the property of any persons regarded as subversive, even when they were not deported (deportations started only in 1940). Also important here was the Law on the Revocation of Naturalization, published the same day;[39] it contained a clause authorizing the seizure of property of disfavored persons who were out of the country. Such dispossession occurred "in favor of the Reich" (instruction of the Führer and *Reichskanzler* of March 29, 1941),[40] based on the idea (which grew even stronger after the Eleventh Decree of November 25, 1941, had been issued)—at least in the eyes of the Security Police or the Party leadership—that Jewish property could *as a matter of principle* be regarded as "hostile" or "subversive" property,[41] although these terms were not defined. Furthermore, Jewish assets were even designated as objects of thieves, receivers of stolen goods, and hoarding[42] and thus *automatically the property of the Reich.*[43] Here too it was "juridically" concluded that the dispossession orders pursuant to the law were not constitutive but only declaratory. Such actions increasingly had the character of acts of pure revenge: acts of plunder in order to get hold of the property of rich Jews—in spite of the fact that this property existed only on paper, as a result of the total exchange embargo. When the victims applied for public relief, they were told to seek Jewish community support.[44]

In part, the (police) authorities waited until the Eleventh Decree of November 25, 1941, had been issued (because the above-mentioned laws on the confiscation "of hostile and subversive property" of July 14, 1933, did not refer explicitly to Jews but in general to "undesirable" persons, so that only "undesirable" Jews rather than Jews in general were affected) and then implemented the decree ex post facto (in order also to get their hands on the property of those Jews who had been deported before the decree had become effective).[45] To acquire the property of Jews to whom the decree was not applicable (those who had committed suicide or who had died in exile before November 25, 1941), the authorities applied the laws of July 14, 1933, mentioned above in parallel with the Eleventh Decree,[46] by an excessive interpretation: instructions from the Reich Security Main Office (RSHA) simply declared the "endeavors" of all deported Jews to whom the Eleventh Decree applied to be "hostile and subversive," thus satisfying the conditions of this law, with the aim of integrating the explicitly racial Eleventh Decree of 1941 into the "general" laws of 1933.[47] The police authorities did not succeed in getting their hands on Jewish property *abroad*. In order to "compensate for this loss," a "counteraccount" was opened up: since the property of Jews of foreign nationality deported from the Reich could allegedly not be seized in favor of the foreign state, the authorities (the Foreign Ministry and the Reich Security Main Office [RSHA]) proceeded to draw up a kind of "account" through which this property (although private) should be offered to the Reich and the property of German Jews abroad should be offered to the foreign state.[48] Whether this deal was carried through is unclear.

The fact that there were so many "legal" grounds for seizures of property meant in practice that the legal situation according to the Eleventh Decree did not correspond to reality. This decree exempted, de facto, German Jews—so long as they were not deported—from loss of their nationality and thus from forfeiture of their assets. In addition, immediately after the Eleventh Decree was issued, the Security Police (who increasingly encroached on the prerogatives of the internal administration) began to seize *all the property of the German Jews,* or whatever was left of it, in crass contrast to the terms of the Eleventh Decree.

All Jewish real estate had already been under state control since 1938, all securities were blocked, and gold, silver, and other valuable objects had had to be surrendered since 1939.[49] The appropriate authorities merely waived the normal procedure—normal at least by (normative) decree—because many Reich ministries would have had to be consulted, and it may be justifiably presumed that they preferred to leave such delicate questions to the Gestapo. Thus, the favored technique of secret directives used before the issue of the Eleventh Decree of 1941 continued to be used after it, "in order to prevent[!] Jews in the Reich from smuggling out their property."[50] The restrictions referred to below were therefore not based on the Eleventh Decree of 1941 but on the "proper competence" of the Security Police (in the context of its task to prepare for the emigration or deportation of the Jews);[51] in so doing they went far beyond the terms of the Eleventh Decree.

Shortly before the Eleventh Degree was published, a decree of the Reich Security Main Office dated November 13, 1941, ordered that all objects above a specified minimum value in the possession of Jews, such as typewriters, bicycles, optical apparatus, musical instruments, gramophone records, skis, or textiles, were to be registered and handed over;[52] these items were then seized by the Gestapo to equip the Gestapo offices in the overrun territories, as set out in an instruction by the Reich minister of finance.[53] The free disposition of objects of low value was prohibited, for could Jews destined to extermination still have any right to independent dispositions? This question was settled by a secret instruction of the Reich Security Main Office (RSHA) dated November 27, 1941, which at the request of the RSHA the Party Chancellery was to communicate to the "compatriots" (*Volksgenossen*), by which doubtless Party members were meant, by word of mouth only.[54] Whereas hitherto the blocking of dispositions had formally applied only to real estate, not to movables—with the exception of securities, gold, and jewelry—the restrictions were now extended to all dispositions of Jews, including their mobile property, and all such dispositions became subject to a "permit."

The disposition of movable objects (their sale, for example) had to be reported within a certain time limit so that the Gestapo could investigate whether "unjustified[!] moving of property [had] taken place."[55] Dispositions without permit were declared null and void; violations of the permit provisions were "naturally" punished by protective custody (in concentration camps) and the seizure of all property. Similar punishment was imposed on those of German blood who bought such Jewish property without authorization. The Reich minister of economics was to inform all banks and savings banks, and the postmaster-general was to inform all postal banking offices, of these police orders. Instructions issued by the Reich Association of Jews in Germany regulated the details.[56]

Here, too, of course, the instruments lagged behind the actual events, for before the enactment of the police instruction of November 27, 1941, Jews had been obliged to sell their property in order to survive. Such sales were possible only through the Jewish communities, with the consent of the Gestapo (no donations to Jewish family members were permitted).[57] The instruction of November 27, 1941, was therefore merely a confirmation of existing practices.

In addition, the term *permit* in the police instruction of November 27, 1941, was merely an empty formula masking the preparation for the total dispossession of Jewish property owners. The proper authority for real estate matters was no longer, as had been usual, the "normal" district agency (*höhere Verwaltungsbehörde, Regierungspräsidium*);[58] it was now the Gestapo, which never issued permits except in cases of "absolute necessity" (a situation recognized only when there were taxes to pay).[59]

Through such measures the entire property of Jews of German citizenship was seized and put at the disposal of the Reich. Since permits were issued only exceptionally, as we have seen, the "restrictions on the disposition of property" were in effect nothing other than a confiscation of the property, which their Jewish owners were permitted to use temporarily until it fell definitively to the Reich after their deportation. Very few usable objects were left to be handed over, however, for by 1942 Jewish citizens had been divested of every last possession of any value. As early as January 1942, all furs and woolen clothes had to be relinquished without compensation, and these were followed in the middle of that year by all other dispensable articles of clothing, all electrical appliances, and all other usable articles.[60] Thus, these restrictions cut the Jews off almost completely from everyday things. They were thus denied all means of subsistence, the allocation of fabric, shoes, and so forth, all of which were controlled with a legitimation paper called the clothing card (*Reichskleiderkart*)—not provided to Jews; further, they were refused allocations of fuel and entitlements to rations of vital foods and items such as coffee and tobacco.[61] In addition, food parcels from abroad were seized,[62] inconvenient shopping times for Jews were instituted,[63] and Jews were virtually completely excluded from public welfare benefits (this as early as 1938).[64] So the Jewish population of Germany sank to a class of pariahs without any independent means, having to turn to the Jewish communities for help.[65] This wearing down of their material existence was designed to prepare them mentally and physically for deportation.

2.   The Treatment of Polish Property in the Altreich

In the treatment of other non-Aryan property, the goal was the same as for that of the Jews. The job was easier and quicker in the case of these "aliens" from the occupied Polish territories, however, because here no questions of citizenship needed to be taken into consideration. The basis was the Decree on the Property of Persons of the Former Polish State, dated October 17, 1940,[66] which provided for the seizure of the property of all Jews who had their residence in the Annexed Eastern Territories in 1939. The same also applied to the property of such persons who resided in the Altreich territory.[67] Beginning in 1941, the Reich Ministry of Finance regarded this property as belonging to the Reich in principle,[68] so that Jewish proprietors had no legal rights whatsoever. The same decree also served as the basis for the confiscation of the property of Poles living in the Altreich who had fled from the Annexed Eastern Territories. Polish property in the Altreich was subject to the Decree on the Treatment of Enemy Property of January 15, 1940,[69] and the Decree on Guardianship for Absentees of October 11, 1939.[70]

EXCURSUS
Tax Law

The economic dispossession of Jews and other non-Aryans was further pursued and accelerated by discriminatory regulations in the field of tax law.[1] The goal of the fiscal policy was to squeeze as much tax revenue from the Jewish population as possible with a view to speeding up their economic ruin. At the theoretical level, the implementation of this goal met certain difficulties early on, however, because fiscal law had adhered closely to the principle of equality in taxation. There were no such difficulties in practice, however. The principle of equal taxation was in any case applied by the boards of assessment only with the aim of wringing as much as possible from taxpayers,[2] and in the taxation of "aliens" and all other people or associations that did not conform racially or politically (e.g., the freemasons),[3] it served only to make the fiscal rules harsher, even in contempt of the law as it stood.[4] But as soon as the question arose whether Jews should enjoy the same benefits or privileges as Germans or whether it would not be a good idea to enact special laws, the principle of equality in taxation was quickly forgotten. The relation in fiscal law between the state and the citizen was defined as a "relation of loyalty in public law" (*öffentlich-rechtliches Treueverhältnis*) for all "compatriots" (*Volksgenossen*),[5] in which the boards of assessment had the "power of command" over taxpayers.[6] Since Jewish citizens belonged neither to the German nationhood nor to the German *Volksgenossen* (i.e., were not a part of the German "community of law"), it was argued, they could not enjoy the principle of equality in taxation.

In regard to the first aspect, the discrimination of "aliens" in contempt of the existing law, many courts, and especially the Reich Finance Court, played an important and destructive role. A good example is the judicature of this court in the field of the so-called Reich Abandonment Tax. This tax, which had been created during the Weimar Republic,[7] was intended to provide a certain compensation to the state for the loss of taxes as a result of emigrations.[8] After 1933 it was, of course, applied to Jews, who were more or less forced to emigrate. In 1937 alone, over RM 80 million flowed to the Reich.[9] According to section 2, paragraph 3, of the relevant decree (issued December 8, 1931), the Reich Abandonment Tax was not exigible if the board of assessment decided that the abandonment of residence was "in the German interest" or economically justified. This rule was now turned on its head. The emigration of Jews had been always been justified in public discussions by its great interest for the state. When Jews desiring to emigrate claimed exemption from this tax in view of the prevailing anti-Semitism, however, the Reich Finance Court quite laughably declared that the enforcement of regulations did not take racial descent into consideration. It was not a matter of German interest in the emigration: what was relevant was whether the emigrant would promote German interests abroad, something that was quite out of the question in the case of Jews.[10] Under the terms of the law, furthermore, the Reich Abandonment Tax was not due if the emigrant remained abroad involuntarily. The Reich Finance Court, however, dismissed the argument by Jews that their emigration was involuntary: the fear of discrimination, the court argued, was not an immediate compulsion in the sense of precluding free will.[11] The same interpretation held, the court ruled, in the case of emigration resulting from the seizure of property or severe maltreatment (e.g., by the Gestapo).[12]

Regarding tax discrimination against Jewish associations, the Reich Finance Court passed a ruling in 1938, for example, concerning the validity of an anti-Jewish tax law. The law, issued on March 28, 1938,[13] withdrew the status of public-law corporation from the Jewish cultural organizations with respect to certain tax privileges they had enjoyed in common with other German associations. The court ruled not only that this law was valid but also that it was only of a declaratory nature: even without such rules, taxation had to follow this line.[14] Indeed the Reich Finance Court had acted in this sense even before this law became effective, by refusing (*contra legem*) the status of nonprofit organization to

Jewish cultural welfare associations and in so doing refusing them reduced taxes and fees as provided for by the Property Tax Law. Other courts had, however, applied the tax privileges correctly to Jewish associations on the basis of the existing law, at least until 1938.[15]

This practice of the Reich Finance Court was also applied to high schools, for example, on the strength of the argument that "the promotion of high school education for nationals of foreign race" was not in the interest of the German *Volksgemeinschaft*.[16] Jewish athletic clubs, hospitals, scientific associations, and so on, were also drawn into the net.[17] In 1937 an administrative order of the Reich ministerial authorities, adhered to by the Reich Finance Court, *contra legem*, withdraw all exemptions from administrative fees and court fees that had been enjoyed by Jewish charitable foundations, on the argument that charitable purposes (under the terms of the law) were only such purposes that "exclusively and directly" served needy German *Volksgenossen*.[18]

The Jewish missions run by the churches, which had hitherto enjoyed tax privileges as a valuable ecclesiastical activity (according to sec. 19 of the Tax Adjustment Law) lost their privileged status. The Reich Finance Court declared— consistently in "racial" terms—that Jewish missions were neither nonprofit nor charitable, since the "German people" saw "no benefit to their well-being"[19] in the conversion of Jews. Charity benefits accorded to Jews who under the terms of the law could formally be recognized as "worthy of support," that is, entitled to tax privileges (Tax Adaptation Law, 1934, sec. 18), were deprived of this "worthiness" by an amendment to the law. Here too the argument was a racial one: "charity" in the context of fiscal law meant only charity toward the German *Volksgenossen* (introductory law to the Real Tax Law [especially land tax]).[20] After 1938 even Jewish cemeteries were made subject to property tax, although cemeteries in general were exempt from taxation. Religious reasons, the Finance Court argued, were only "a personal circumstance," which did not exclude fiscal obligations.[21]

The courts ruled in a very restricted way where the possibility of tax reductions was concerned. As early as 1933, the Reich Finance Court had ruled that under the terms of the income tax laws,[22] Jews were not entitled to the usual deduction of professional expenses and special allowances. Other tax deductions, such as the reduced tax rate under section 34, paragraph 2, subparagraph 4, of the Income Tax Law were also denied to Jews, on the grounds that allowing the deductions would go against the "sound ethnic philosophy" of the German people.[23] The Jewish proprietor of a department store claiming special depreciation due to the increased trade risk resulting from his racial descent was only partially satisfied: the court decided that prejudices caused by the boycott of Jewish shops were not among the "objective conditions of the firm" (the basis of tax reductions) but were only a "personal" factor and therefore could not be taken into account.[24] The Reich Finance Court also denied Jews the higher tax-free allowance on property owned, which was normally granted when there was an incapacity to earn a living. The court did not consider the fact that unemployed Jews could not find work anywhere but ruled that the Jewish plaintiffs, though unemployed, were not unfit for work[25] (and therefore not entitled to tax reductions). However, the Supreme Finance Court granted people who had acquired Jewish property following the pogroms of November 1938 a general 50 percent reduction in the evaluation and thus a 50 percent tax reduction, because with "the retaliation measures of the German people . . . of November 1938 all supplies [had] diminished considerably in value and a statement of losses was not possible in the individual case."[26] By the same argument, the cheap acquisition of Jewish property in the cause of Aryanization (on the grounds of the Decree on the Utilization of Jewish Property of December 3, 1938) was met with a special "Aryanization tax" (sec. 15, par. 1, of the decree). The Reich Finance Court advanced the argument that an estate in Jewish hands would have a lower value than one in German hands but that the purchaser might not take advantage of this.[27]

In order to put the discrimination measures on a broader, more general level, explicit special regulations for non-Aryans were introduced by law or administrative rules at the beginning of the economic deprivation. These were summed up in an administrative order by the Reich minister of finance dated February 10, 1940,[28] on the special treatment of Jews in fiscal law. The following matters were dealt with: by a law of February 1, 1938,[29] the (usual) tax reductions granted to those bearing extraordinary child-care expenses (e.g., those who had children with disabilities) were denied to Jews if the children were considered Jewish by law.[30] From mid-1938 on, Jewish schools were refused all exemptions from taxation by administrative order of the Reich Ministry of Finance.[31] Emigrating Jews taking goods with them had to pay a tax to the gold discount bank that generally amounted to 100 percent of the value of the goods in question.[32] Jewish landowners were denied the usual possibilities of claiming exemption from land tax.[33] Jewish cultural organizations, as we have seen, lost their status as public-law corporations (and with that their tax privileges) by a law of March 28, 1938.[34] By the decree of September 20, 1941,[35] issued by the Reich minister of finance, a "social compensation tax" was imposed on all Poles (except for those capable of "Germanization" or living in an "ethnic mixed marriage") and Jews in the Reich territory. This tax consisted of a 50 percent increase in income tax, in no case deductible (for example as an extraordinary burden under the terms of the income tax law).

VIII.   Discrimination against "Non-Germans" in Public Life

Side by side with the economic robbery and ostracization in the cultural and professional domains, a huge propaganda campaign was waged with the aim of distinguishing Jews from *Volksgenossen* by external signs in order to isolate them from their surroundings and put them at the mercy of public contempt and the arbitrariness of state bodies and Party agencies, with a view to establishing the conditions for a Final Solution to the "Jewish question." As in the campaign to create economic impoverishment, the Jewish businesses were the first to be attacked, and this concept was based not on legal criteria but on actual features ("the dominating influence of the Jews").[1] These businesses had to be registered on the basis of the Third Decree to the Reich Citizenship Law of June 14, 1938,[2] and the Reich minister of economics, in agreement with the Reich minister of the interior and the deputy of the Führer, was empowered to order them to bear a distinguishing mark. At the same time a policy was instituted to mark individual Jewish citizens, after the efforts of previous years to openly declare Jews unwelcome in public offices had been prohibited by the Reich minister of the interior.[3] This campaign was carried out in the usual manner of first practicing discrimination against Jews in their relations with the authorities and subsequently carrying out the practice toward the general public.

1.   Identification Requirements

From 1934 on, Jews were not allowed to alter their names (circular of the Reich Ministry of the Interior of June 25, 1934).[4] In mid-1938 special identity cards were issued to all Jews, obliging them to indicate their Jewish status to authorities or Party offices without being asked and to indicate the place and date of issue of the identity cards.[5] These provisions obviously did not bring about the desired discrimination, because only a few weeks later, through a decree of August 17, 1938,[6] compulsory marking by the use of special names was imposed on all Jews of German citizenship—after previous proposals of the Reich Chancellery and the Reich Ministry of the Interior had proved not to be sufficiently radical.

In the beginning, in preparation for "consciously racial legislation," it was planned "only" to abolish all name changes since 1918 and to order the restoration of the former names, so as to distinguish more easily between Jews and non-Jews.[7] The decree of August 1938 went much further, however, permitting Jews to choose only such names as were listed in the Directives on the Use of Names for Jews of August 18, 1938,[8] published by the Reich Ministry of the Interior. From

January 1, 1939, on, any male Jew who did not have one of these names was obliged to add Israel to his name, and every female Jew the name Sara. These names had to be registered within one month at the proper registrar's office and the appropriate police station. A special designation was also required for the children of German citizens who were not Jews but of other "alien" descent (of "non-German nationhood"). Such persons were allowed to keep their ("alien") names, even when a German form for the name existed.[9]

The beginnings of discrimination in legal and business communications are to be found in section 3 of the decree of August 17, 1938, according to which Jewish first names (either the original or the imposed one) had to be used in all relevant documents, insofar as it was usual to include names—including family names—in such documents. A further decree of October 1938 required that the passports of Jewish citizens be inscribed with a *J* so as to make the owner immediately recognizable as a Jew to all authorities.[10] But in any case, passports were issued only in exceptional circumstances, in order to prevent Jews from fleeing.[11] The use of distinguishing marks for Jews in public began with the exclusion of Jews from air-raid exercises from October 1938 on[12] and from service in the voluntary fire brigade after 1939.[13] Three years later, the obligation for Jews to wear a distinguishing mark in public was established by the Police Decree on the Appearance of Jews in Public of September 1, 1941, issued by the chief of the Security Police.[14] Jews had to wear the Star of David not only on their everyday clothes but on their work clothes too:[15] this order revived the practice of labeling Jews that dated from medieval times. Violations of the decree were punished by a fine of up to RM 500 or a month's imprisonment. Jews married to a person of German blood were exempt from the obligation, very much against the will of the Party sections.[16] This obligation to wear a distinguishing mark—allegedly "welcomed" by the population but more likely perceived with considerable embarrassment[17]—was extended some months later (effective April 15, 1942) by an order that also all the homes of Jews were to display the Star of David in addition to the Jewish name.[18] Air-raid precautions were taken for Aryans' houses, but not for those owned by Jews, which were thus clearly recognizable.[19] Specific days and hours were fixed during which Jews had to do their shopping, and no shopping was permitted outside these times.[20]

2. Restrictions on Freedom of Personal Movement

By the measures mentioned above, the Jews were marked as outlaws of society: now all that was lacking was to restrict their freedom of movement so as to prepare for their deportation and put them totally at the mercy of the police.

Until 1941 freedom of movement was more or less guaranteed formally to Jews of German citizenship, notwithstanding that certain restrictions already obtained, such as a ban on participation in all cultural activities; a de facto total prohibition by the Reich minister of the interior against staying at health resorts (after mid-1939);[21] a ban on going out at night (from the fall of 1939);[22] and a ban on driving a car (from the end of 1938), with the requirement to surrender all driving licenses,[23] so that Jews were restricted to public transport. General restrictions on free movement did not yet exist in these years. It is true that the presidents of the administrative districts had been authorized by a police decree issued by the Reich authorities on November 28, 1938, to order restrictions of movement for Jews in their districts,[24] but this power was exerted only in Berlin, where the "Jew ban" (*Judenbann*) was imposed for all public cultural and sports places as well as the most important streets and squares.[25] But effective restrictions of free movement were the regular practice of the authorities, especially in the eastern parts of the Reich territory, where there was considerable pressure on housing on account of evacuation measures in other parts of the Reich. It was reported from Silesia, for example, that a whole Jewish quarter had been requisitioned by the authorities and had to be vacated by their Jewish tenants or owners under humiliating conditions in favor of Party or administration officials; the evicted Jews were put in camps on the outskirts of town or immediately deported eastward.[26] In the eyes of the National Socialist authorities, such actions did not formally constitute a restriction of personal movement, since all Jewish tenants and owners were forced to sign a declaration that they had left town voluntarily.[27]

As for Jews of Polish nationality in the Reich territory, who numbered some seven thousand in 1933,[28] special measures had already been taken in October 1938. These were the so-called Eastern Jews, whose expulsion had been the declared aim of the political leadership since 1933[29] in accordance with the policy that anyone who endangered "the purity of the German race" was to be removed from Reich territory. This concept applied to all "alien" foreigners (based on the Law on Expulsions from the Reich) and especially immigrant Jews.[30] The police decree on foreigners imposed a general ban on these Polish Jews and provided for their expulsion to Poland, as that country was preparing legislative measures to prevent their return.[31] Those Jews who were not taken in or were expatriated by Poland were treated by the Reich authorities as stateless until they were finally accepted in Poland or another country.[32]

The basic rule for the restrictions effective since fall 1941 was the above-mentioned September 1, 1941, police decree by the chief of the Security Police,[33] which in addition to the use of the compulsory identification marks imposed strict limits on residence. This decree is clearly indicative of the shift of power in favor of the Security Police over the regular police forces (*Ordnungspolizei*). For all questions relating to this decree, a circular from the Reich minister of the interior proclaimed that the regular police were no longer competent for matters having to do with foreign residents and that this authority was in the hands of the Security Police.[34]

The decree of September 1, 1941, rescinded in detail the freedom of movement for all Jews of German nationality and confined them to their local community, which they were permitted to leave only with the permission of the local police. The use of public transportation (except local) was in principle prohibited except by a special police permit,[35] and such permits were to be "limited to the strictest minimum."[36] Initially the special permit included the use of waiting rooms, station restaurants, and other transport utilities,[37] but it was repealed in July 1942 by a directive of the Reich minister of transport,[38] so that Jews with travel permits had the right to board and alight from the vehicle but no right to wait. Under the Reich minister of the interior's directives concerning the implementation of the decree of September 1, 1941,[39] Jews with a travel permit were allowed to sit down in a public vehicle only if the seat was not claimed by a German passenger: the use of sleeping cars and dining cars was forbidden. Jews were not allowed to use public transport during rush hours.

The publication of the decree of September 1, 1941, was followed by a number of further restrictions on movement.[40] On October 16, 1941, the Reich minister of the interior prohibited all Jews from using motor buses (interurban bus lines) run by the postal services.[41] After spring 1942, new restrictions were issued on the pretext of passengers' complaints that the inconveniences caused by the use of public transportation by Jews had become too great.

New restrictions came with the circular of March 24, 1942,[42] issued by the Reich minister of the interior. This required a permit for all journeys within the community of residence, issued for a specific mode of transport and for one year only, to Jewish workers who lived at least an hour's walk or seven kilometers away from their workplace, to Jewish schoolchildren if their distance from school was at least five kilometers or required them to walk at least an hour, and to Jewish "legal advisers" (lawyers), "medics" (doctors), and midwives; shortly afterward, this permission was restricted to Jewish workers and schoolchildren.[43] Violations of these provisions were punished with "protective custody" (thus even the minor offense of riding in a street car or bus without permission could carry the penalty of deportation to an SS concentration camp). The timing of these restrictions was not accidental but was chosen to coincide exactly with the start of the large-scale deportations to the East in the fall of 1941.[44] In the eastern parts of the Reich, the deportations were often justified by the "need for housing space" for Germans and were implemented under the cruelest conditions.[45] These restrictions thus created the best administrative conditions for preventing Jews from fleeing and the most "problem-free registration" of all concerned.

3.   "Non-German" Associations

With the abolition of personal freedom of "non-German" individuals came the destruction of "non-German" associations. From the beginning all events in the Jewish communities had been subject to registration and police supervision.[46] As we have seen above, the courts had denied Jewish institutions a public corporation status (with the consequence that they forfeited all tax privileges),[47] and this status was then definitively abolished by the decree of March 28, 1938,[48] which deprived the Jewish communities of the status of public-law corporations. Jewish cultural associations and their auxiliary organizations thus became incorporated societies under private law. The Jewish associations thus lost their autonomy, for all resolutions of any importance had to be sanctioned by the senior administration (presidents of the district administration). A year later, the Tenth Decree to the Reich Citizenship Law of July 4, 1939,[49] obliged all Jews living in the territory of the Reich to become members of the Reich Association of Jews in Germany. It had the form of an incorporated association, responsible for the Jewish school and welfare systems and serving as the central office for Jewish emigration (secs. 1 and 2).

With the establishment of this central office, the last ties between Jewish citizens and the authorities were severed: the central office was declared the sole addressee of commands related to the anti-Jewish regulations issued by the Reich authorities and the police; it was to pass those orders on to all members of the association. The Reich minister of the interior was charged with its technical and legal supervision and authorized to dissolve all Jewish associations, organizations, and foundations or to order their integration into the Reich Association (secs. 4 and 5 of the decree).

All Polish organizations in the territory of the Altreich were also completely abolished. The preparatory measures were secret, and as little as possible was published in order to prevent leaks. At a conference held in November 1939 at the Reich Ministry of the Interior only a few weeks after the outbreak of the war, it was agreed to dissolve the Polish organizations in the Reich territory immediately.[50] Their assets, about 7 to 8 million reichsmarks, were to be liquidated and to accrue to the Reich. It was planned to declare these assets as hostile under the terms of the Law on the Seizure of Assets of Enemies of the People and State of

July 14, 1933,[51] with a view to confiscating them, but this was not done for reasons of foreign policy.[52] The Polish associations in the Annexed Eastern Territories were not included in these regulations, because in these regions, where the
"national-racial struggle" had quite a different flavor, it was desired to introduce
"as little as possible" new (German) legislation. The closing down of the Polish
organizations was planned to take place on the basis of secret instructions issued with the consent of the Gestapo. It was planned to dissolve Polish commercial organizations on the basis of private law and Polish political and cultural
organizations on the basis of "national policy" principles. With regard to the
procedure followed, the Reich authorities concerned, who set a high value on an
orderly procedure, prevailed against the police, who would have liked to dissolve the organizations immediately. The dissolution of the Polish associations
was not to be implemented through police orders but by decree. The result of
the Ministry of the Interior conference mentioned above was the Decree on the
Organization of the Polish Ethnic Group in the German Reich of February 27,
1940.[53] This decree prohibited all activities of Polish organizations on Reich territory and declared their dissolution; a commissioner took charge of the liquidation of their assets, to the exclusion of all claims for damages.[54]

EXCURSUS
Police Law

Although the discriminatory rules issued by the general and internal administration were still confined to Jews, Gypsies, and Poles (relatively clearly defined groups), the police (who until 1936 operated as Department 3 within the
Reich Ministry of the Interior) extended the principle of special law without any
limits whatsoever. This was primarily related to the general development of the
police in the Nazi state.

In the same way, just as the new notion of police—without "restrictive"
norms—went far beyond the traditional notion of security and regular police,[1]
the powers of the police were in principle unlimited and covered everything that
was defined at that time as relating to internal security, especially the domains
in which discriminatory practices were the rule. The omnipotence of the police
on the internal front was such that the legal doctrine of police law postulated
that the traditional relationship of the police to the law should be replaced by a
limitation only to "suprapositive" law, which was defined by the political power
itself acting independently of the norms.[2]

This postulate merely referred to a situation in which the police no longer
needed a written law; written law had become subordinate to a policy of secret

instructions.[3] At the same time, as we have seen, the legal protection of the individual citizen by the administrative judiciary was either severely curtailed or completely abolished.[4]

This transformation of police law and the firm establishment of sweeping powers of the police over internal policy was effected mainly in the regulation of the organization and responsibilities[5] of the police (about which I will not go into further detail here), especially through the integration of the police into the SS in 1936.[6] In substantive law, however, only a few changes were made, according to the mixture of revolutionary ideas and conservative retention of the traditional forms of the law peculiar to the National Socialist system. Thus, the traditional law system remained in effect but was *interpreted in the spirit of National Socialist ideology.* The results were identical for traditionals and for radicals—the omnipotence of the police, the flouting of legal restrictions on the police. Only the arguments for this omnipotence were different.

The majority of traditional police-law jurists defined the unlimited powers of the police as belonging to the (traditional) fields of police activities—security, order, and danger—but other radical jurists postulated a new general clause, "free of normative restrictions," for police actions. (The latter argument was an abandonment of the century-old principle that interference by the state authorities in individual rights had to be based upon a law in the formal sense with clearly defined terms.) The difference between these two views lay less in the substance than in the formal way of arguing. With regard to practice, both sides based their arguments on the principle of unlimited powers of the police.[7]

The most important implementation of the omnipotence of the police was the introduction of so-called *protective or preventive custody* in 1936,[8] which is dealt with in more detail in part 2 of this volume. This police custody, implemented in the concentration camps, was accepted by the courts as legal,[9] though it did not have a general basis in written law in the Reich. (The corresponding Law on the Gestapo of February 10, 1936, referred only to Prussia but was implemented analogously throughout the Reich and was not contestable before the courts.)[10] In formal terms, the decree of the Reich minister of the interior of November 11, 1938,[11] is indicative of the boundless powers of the police, because it transferred the right to issue police decrees to *all the supreme Reich authorities* without any limitations on their type or content.

The terms for the new institutions and authorizations of the police, like those for police powers in general, were defined (according to the tried and tested method) not by normative regulations but only by internal administrative regulations with broad powers of discretion for the police. Thus, the police were entirely free to decide whether they should intervene from case to case.[12] This endless game of vague definitions and circumscriptions was the chosen means and the general method of every discriminatory action, especially in the police sector, thus reducing to a minimum or completely eliminating individual rights.[13] The method was used above all in the treatment of "non-Germans."

1.   Anti-Jewish Measures within the Purview of Traditional Police Law

The first attempts to replace the established terms of the law by vague definitions were made in the field of traditional police law. This concerned above all professional and commercial law, where the powers of the police were already rather wide. At the beginning of the National Socialist state, the juridical opinion followed the actual legislation, according to which the anti-Jewish legislation was valid only for the public service and did not concern trade and industry. Following the issue of the Nuremberg Laws (September 1935), two arguments were upheld: as the Reich minister of the economy pointed out in a circular,[14] racial descent alone did not justify a limitation on professional activities in trade and industry, limitations being restricted to the (actual) laws in effect.[15] Similarly, at the beginning the courts refused an analogous implementation of the Nuremberg Laws.[16] So the attempts by the police to act against Jews and Gypsies by means of commercial law on the sole ground of their racial descent were declared illegal: the Prussian Administrative Supreme Court in Berlin consistently ruled—against the strongest opposition[17]—that the fact of being Jewish did not in itself fulfill the conditions for unreliability in the sense of commercial law; the court argued on the ground (remarkable at that time) that the repeal and modification of laws was not within the responsibility of the judge.[18] Other courts, however, yielded as early as 1936, and increasingly from 1938 on, to the discriminatory practices of the police against Jewish traders. Their descent was used directly or indirectly by the police as a justification for professional interdictions.

For example, the District Administrative Court of Cologne ruled that "on the ground of century-old observations . . . and further from the National Socialist and the people's concept of legal and honest trade . . . it basically had to be said that Jewish tradesmen . . . are known to be generally unreliable and ought therefore to be got rid of . . . this on the basis of . . . the general sentiment of the people, respect for which is the most fundamental and absolute duty of all the public authorities."[19] The Württemberg Superior Administrative Court confirmed the police order forbidding a Jewish lay medical practitioner to take up his activity;[20] similarly, the Bavarian Superior Administrative Court confirmed this line of thinking in the case of a Jewish estate agent by construing two types of "commercial reliability" (which was the condition in the code of trade and industry that was required in order to undertake activities), a professional and a moral one, the latter to be judged by German standards of honor. On the basis of vague suppositions of an alleged morbid predisposition and the former conduct of the plaintiff, going back to the remote past, the court denied his moral reliability "because his racial foreignness [prevented] him from being able to adopt the German notion of honor."[21] Racial restrictions (a ban on the employment of German-blooded staff by non-Aryan innkeepers) could now also be imposed by subsequent injunctions; the relevant ministerial instructions of the "highest Reich authorities" were accepted without qualification in these cases, since, as was argued by the Bavarian Superior Administrative Court, though they were not normative, they were obligatory for everybody according to the principles of the Führer state.[22] There was now, and had been since 1938, a reversal of the burden of proof procedures: not the state authorities but the Jews themselves had to prove that in spite of being Jews they were reliable ("honorable") under the terms of the trade and industrial law (Bavarian Superior Administrative Court).[23] The ban on "relations" between Germans and Jews became the excuse for closing Jewish businesses because of the "danger to public security and order," and it was not the feared "excesses of the people" but the conduct of the Jewish businessman that was regarded, *contra legem*, as a danger to public security and order (Saxony Superior Administrative Court).[24]

For people who entered into business relationships with Jews, the treatment was somewhat less severe but nevertheless tougher than usual. The court challenge of a man whose itinerant trading license was withdrawn on account of alleged dealings with Jews was successful only because of lack of evidence (Supreme Administrative Court, Oldenburg).[25] An innkeeper succeeded in reversing the decision to revoke his license to sell alcoholic beverages because he had purchased goods from Jewish firms, on the ground that this fact justified unreliability under the terms of section 2 of the Law on Public Houses only when there was an abuse of confidence under the particular circumstances of the case (Bavarian Administrative Court of Appeal).[26]

2. Imposition of the Police Statutes on "Non-German" Workers in the Reich Territory

The major thrust of the discriminatory activities of the police was not, however, directed against Jews of German nationality, since here the leeway for transgressions was very small. Intervention on such a limited scale could not be sufficient for a National Socialist police leadership striving for internal hegemony unbound by any regulations. Unbridled activity under special law was

possible only in dealing with foreign and stateless subjects. Such people, classified as aliens, were automatically considered to be beyond the pale of the community of rights, so that the general administration disclaimed responsibility for
them. This domain fell rather to the police, especially insofar as "security risks"
due to aliens were concerned.

The primary target of the special laws enacted by the police was the millions of "non-German" workers who had come to the country since 1940, either
voluntarily or under coercion. In principle, the Foreign Police Decree of August
22, 1938,[27] and the Decree on the Treatment of Foreigners of September 5, 1939,[28]
which contained relatively firm definitions of offenses, were applicable to these
cases; and though they did not open the way for judicial review by the courts,
they allowed for appeals with the administration agencies against the decisions
of the foreign police. Application of these regulations was, however, by no means
in the interest of the police leadership, which was far more intent upon removing foreign workers completely from the purview of the law and subjecting them
exclusively to the decrees of the Security Police, thereby cutting out or at least
reducing or impeding the action of other authorities or branches of the administration. Accordingly, foreign civilian workers were removed from the ambit of
the Foreign Police Decree,[29] first tacitly and later by directives of a merely declaratory nature, and thus from the law in toto, since from then on there were
no articles of general law whatsoever that applied to them.

The new basis for the implementation of total police intervention was initially the circular instruction by the heads of the Security Police (SIPO) and the
SD proclaimed on September 3, 1939,[30] on "principles of internal state security
in wartime," following directives by Hitler, and subsequent police instructions,
which were not sufficient for this purpose, however, since they provided "only"
for the preventive detention of actual or potential opponents of the regime or
other undesirables.[31] Steps were quickly taken to establish a blanket authorization that could provide the boundless scope of discretion sought after. At the
time of the institution of forced labor in the Reich, Himmler received from
Göring in his capacity of plenipotentiary for the Four Year Plan on March 8,
1940, a secret authorization (to be discussed in more detail in part 2, below) to
regulate the "conduct" of Polish workers in the Reich territory with a view to
their "subjection."[32] This document, which was not made known to the administrative authorities, was to serve as the basis for all special directives on the treatment of "non-German" workers. A testimony to the thoroughness of the coordination and preparation of these special arrangements within the political
leadership is the fact that on the very same day the authorization was handed
over, a whole sheaf of directives concerning the conduct of (Polish) foreign

workers was issued by the office of the *Reichsführer*-SS and chief of the German police,[33] plus a police decree by the Ministry of the Interior concerning the imposition of a distinguishing mark for Polish workers in the Reich.[34] These decrees constituted a uniform policy toward Polish workers in both the territory of the Reich and the Eastern Territories and General Government.

The elaboration and preparation of these regulations was in the hands of the Security Police (RSHA—Department 4—Secret State Police—Group D—Foreign Worker Desk), who collaborated closely with the offices of the Ministry of Labor and later that of the commissioner general for forced labor. A liaison officer of the commissioner general for forced labor at the office of the *Reichsführer*-SS coordinated the recruitment of the compulsory labor force, later the numerous raids to round up labor in the occupied territories, and later still the organization and surveillance of transportation to the Reich border, thus rendering the labor directorate an invaluable service,[35] until finally the question of procuring labor became exclusively a "police matter."[36]

This arrangement of the various responsibilities indicates that already the organization of foreign labor had ceased to be dependent on labor law or even on the usual demands of police order; it was now exclusively a matter of state security in the then-current sense of the term. Since the existence of this foreign labor force represented a threat to "state security," it was logical that as a section of the Security Police the Gestapo should feel responsible for settling all matters concerning these people. Clearly, of course, matters of state security were only part of the question. In a circular order dated December 7, 1942, addressed to all Gestapo headquarters, the *Reichsführer*-SS and chief of the German police reiterated that the "defense against the risks of the recruitment of foreigners" was not only a matter of avoiding political danger to the Reich (terrorism, sabotage, etc.) but also of defense against "the risks for the racial continuity of the German people."[37] Seen in the light of this sweeping totalitarian definition of state security, the Reich administration, and especially the judicial administration, which was exhausted by the endless conflicts with the police, gradually came to tolerate the usurpation by the police of responsibility for foreign workers and finally even declare it to be justified.[38]

The various texts regulating the "conduct" of "non-German" workers in the Reich territory further illustrate the broad powers of the Gestapo, although they can in no way give a full picture of the discriminatory practices, which varied fitfully from one camp to another, one place to another, one factory to another, one economic sector to another and rather represented minimum regulations that had to be adhered to.

These texts show that, consonant with the racial connotations of state security already mentioned, the main interest of the Security Police was the relations between foreign workers and Germans. The regime feared nothing more than undesirable contacts between Germans and alien workers; those contacts had to be prevented at all costs. As early as March 1940, Himmler informed the office of the Führer's deputy that in the event of sexual intercourse or "other immoral acts" between Germans and Polish workers, he had ordered the immediate arrest of the responsible Germans.[39] Poles who had had sexual relations with German women were either executed ("special treatment") or, if they proved to be capable of Germanization, committed to preventive detention, depending on the personal decision of the *Reichsführer*-SS and chief of the German police.[40] If a Polish woman was involved, she was to be sent to a brothel.[41] Himmler further declared that such measures by no means implied a desire to "suppress the justified indignation of the German people at such shameful behavior": he found public defamation (through "spontaneous reactions of indignation") to be a powerful deterrent. He would have no compunction if in such cases "the hair of the German woman, say, was cropped in the presence of the girls of the village or she was led through the streets carrying a notice telling of her offence." But defamation should "more or less stay within such limits."[42] Initially a general ban on sexual intercourse between Germans and all foreign workers was even decreed.[43] As the labor shortage worsened, however, the terms of the ban were relaxed again by the circular order of December 7, 1942, referred to above, since for political reasons Italian workers and other foreigners coming from allied countries could not be included in it. This was also the case for the French, who were to be integrated as a nation in the "new Europe." Thus, sexual intercourse with people of these nationalities remained merely "undesirable," and intervention was envisaged only in the case of "intolerable conduct" (cohabitation, etc.), but externally this should under no circumstances appear to have any national or racial basis.[44]

In contrast, sexual relations between Germans and members of Eastern European nations were relentlessly prosecuted by the Gestapo on grounds of the "risks for the racial integrity of the German nation," and as usual only two sanctions were applied: committal to a concentration camp if the foreign offender was capable of being Germanized, or execution ("special treatment").[45] Preventive detention was demanded in the case of German offenders. This concerned above all Polish workers,[46] the first to arrive in the Reich, but also Polish prisoners of war, over whom hung the threat of committal to a concentration camp, at least provisionally.[47] A leaflet on the "duties of civilian workers . . . of Polish nationality" confirmed explicitly that the death sentence would be meted out for the offense of sexual intercourse with persons of German blood.[48] Russians

("Eastern workers"), Czechs, Serbs, and others later came to be included in this category, as will be discussed in detail later.[49]

The special regulations dealing with the conduct of the foreign workforce were amazingly similar to those concerning Jews, with the important difference that for political reasons they were not rendered public. They stated, in a word, that whatever was not explicitly permitted was forbidden. Though the regulations that followed nominally referred only to Polish workers, we may be sure that (through direct or analogous application or the addition of supplementary clauses) they were also used against other racially undesirable Eastern European workers, especially those coming from the Soviet Union.

In detail, the above-mentioned regulations forbade Polish workers to leave their place of domicile, to go out from their living quarters during the nightly curfew, or to use public transport, except locally, without authorization from the police. The police forces had instructions to bar Poles from German cultural, ecclesiastical, and social events and from frequenting German inns.[50] The isolation of Polish workers and their deprivation of all information from outside was assured by a ban on the possession of radios by Poles and on the purchase of printed matter of all kinds, including German newspapers.[51] Himmler suggested other supplementary prohibitions, which were left to the discretion of the police and which precisely matched the anti-Jewish regulations (for example the barring of certain streets on weekends for Poles, establishing specific shopping hours for Poles, etc.).[52] We do not know whether and to what extent these provisions were implemented by the local authorities.

Individual authorities proposed in addition quite senseless measures such as a general ban on smoking for Poles, or a ban on carrying pocket knives and matches. These were refused by Himmler because of the difficulty of supervising such prohibitions.[53] After 1943, however, further restrictions were effected by regulations of the central police command, such as a prohibition on riding bicycles, using a telephone, owning a camera or photographs, and attending athletic events or health meetings. All postal communications were censored.[54] Discriminatory practices were also frequent in the area of medical care and hospital visits (e.g., a prohibition on entering waiting rooms).[55]

Attending church services for Germans and religious instruction was also forbidden to Poles. However, the local police could issue authorizations to hold special services for Polish workers, the banning of which at any time "for general reasons or reasons connected with the labor service" could be used as a means of exerting pressure on them. In such services, which Poles were allowed to attend only once in a month, neither the Polish language nor Polish hymns were to be used.[56] In line with these police instructions, the Reich minister for ecclesiastical affairs forbade Polish clergymen to conduct confessions in Polish. The only people permitted to hold church services were a small number of politically selected "visiting" German chaplains (*Wanderseelsorger*) (on no account Polish clergymen), who were admonished by their superiors to strictly observe all "collective regulations," especially the ban on personal contact with Poles.[57] In some provinces, however, the authorities felt constrained to permit the care of individual souls beyond the limits of the services, following the intervention of German entrepreneurs anxious to pacify the Poles, who were showing great unrest in the face of these religious restrictions, and to promote their working capacity.[58]

Finally, supervision in the workplace was carried out exclusively according to police criteria. Offenses relating to work discipline were punished in the most minor cases by flogging, which employers or managers had authority to do on the basis of an "unwritten principle."[59] Other offenses, as mentioned above, were not handled by the responsible authorities (the employee's manager or the courts) but by the police, who issued a waring or assigned the offender to a "work training camp" or, in the most serious cases, to a concentration camp.[60] There was the same usurpation of power by the police with regard to criminal offenses, which were not passed over to the courts but first to the Gestapo.[61] "Lightning actions," that is to say, raids at the workplace by the Gestapo to catch "loafers,"[62] completed this system of total supervision by the police. Secret instructions by the *Reichsführer*-SS and chief of the German police repeated the above-mentioned prohibitions and enjoined all police posts to ensure that Polish workers did not forget that they had come to the Reich "voluntarily."[63]

As with Jewish workers, the principle of segregation was strictly implemented for these foreign workers, whose living accommodations always had to be separate from those for the German workers.[64] Like Jewish workers, too, all foreign workers were obliged to wear a mark to distinguish them from other workers. Poles had to wear a visible letter *P* on their work clothes from March 1940 on, and those from the Occupied Soviet Territories ("Eastern workers") the word *Ost* (east).[65] The degree to which these measures were taken for granted by the police authorities is illustrated by the corresponding directives of the RSHA mentioned above, which explicitly prescribed that these distinctions were to be worn both inside and outside the plant but that other marks were prohibited in order to "avoid discrimination."

In addition, Polish workers were subject to restrictions of food and clothing. Although the treatment of the Poles varied with the local conditions and was probably better in the rural areas than in the large industrial plants, the numerous reports by the administrative authorities and industrial managers (who cannot be suspected of pro-Polish sentiments) offer a devastating picture of the conditions under which Polish workers were kept, conditions that had a cata-strophic impact on their health and productivity.[66]

Later (from 1943 on) all alien workers were classified into four groups in line with internal police instructions, so as to establish a better and more detailed dis-tinction: Group 1, Germanic; Group 2, Non-Germanic from allied countries; Group 3, Non-Germanic under German control; Group 4, "eastern workers." De-tailed prescriptions were issued for every group.[67] This differentiation is illus-trated, for example, by the provisions of the directives of the chiefs of police that alien workers other than Poles and "eastern workers" could attend services for Germans and that the children of alien workers were admitted to primary schools, again with the exception of the children of Poles and "eastern workers." These prohibitions were complemented by a policy of separating families,[68] so as to reduce the birthrate, among Eastern European workers especially. Initially, in fact, the labor administration had favored keeping families together because they feared that social welfare would have to take responsibility for the unemployed family members who remained at home (e.g., in the General Government).

These prohibitions, together with a ban on all contacts with the German citizens around them, constituted a system of complete segregation of Eastern European workers not only from the social environment but also from their ori-gins, their families, and their homeland. Thus, it is anything but surprising that the treatment of these workers by the police was generally in open contradiction to the official promises and principles of the labor authorities and National So-cialist propaganda ("the most irreproachable, cleanest, and fairest principles"),[69] casting considerable doubt upon them and thwarting attempts by local agencies and industries to improve workers' conditions. Even less surprising are the re-ports from as early as 1940 that the motivation of foreign workers in Germany was very low.[70] only in 1943, as the military situation increasingly deteriorated, did the authorities try to change their policy. The principles for the treatment of alien workers were modified: now it had become important to maintain and promote their working capacity by providing adequate clothing and food, im-proved accommodations, "fair treatment," and access to cultural activities.[71] It is doubtful, however, that this change in policy was taken seriously by the admin-istrative authorities and heads of industry, after the out-and-out repression of foreign workers for so many years.

Conclusion

If we consider the practice of the principle of *völkisch* inequality on the ba-sis of the normative and administrative regulations as a whole, we must conclude that the special treatment of Jews and other aliens by the administrative authorities and the Security Police represented a seemingly coherent system of coordinated measures; as soon as the general political line was established, the administration and police apparatus functioned smoothly to put the system together. The respective provisions were carefully elaborated and coordinated by the proper authorities in line with the political and economic priorities: as regards Jewish citizens, first "purification" of the public service, then the anti-Jewish measures in the economic sector and public life; as regards the alien workers, first (or simultaneously with other measures) segregation from the community, then abolition of freedom of movement and complete severance of communications, restrictions in the cultural sector, and so forth. The system of special law regulated everything: nothing was to be left to chance, as the examples given show. When it came to the procedures for the implementation of special law, the simple device of administrative provisions for foreign workers was quite sufficient in the eyes of the administration and police authorities; specific legislation was not necessary, since they regarded these people as in principle being outside the realm of the (binding) provisions of the law. With regard to Jews of German nationality, special law had to be imposed, however, by the usual legislative process peculiar to the National Socialist state (laws issued by the Reich government and decrees issued by the Reich ministers), because regular (general) law was still applicable to them. These provisions, issued through the legislative channels, although blatantly unlawful, nevertheless contained remnants of some sort of correct procedure and did not fail to work. On the strength of the prevailing theory that the formal legislative process of law was identical with the terms of substantive law in the sense of "justice" (*Recht*), staunchly defended against all evidence even in the National Socialist era, these provisions were accepted by the administration as lawful and just. Further, the apparent regularity of these provisions misled the administrative authorities, even those at the highest levels of the Reich who elaborated these instruments, to the false conclusion that they were definitive and would preclude future restrictions; this could not have been further from the truth.

The reasons why the elaboration of the anti-Jewish regulations was assigned to the legislative powers can be found in foreign and internal policy considerations, which the regime had to observe. These considerations required a formal organization of the special (anti-Jewish) law system because the collective deprivation of the rights of a large number of persons of German nationality was at stake—an unheard-of event before that time in the German Reich as well as in the history of common (general) law.

In the eyes of the National Socialist leaders, such considerations were not necessary in the annexed and occupied territories, and especially in the overrun countries of Eastern Europe. The policy of eradication of aliens in the Altreich thus served the National Socialist authorities in the occupied territories as a model only with regard to the special fields to be regulated (because every authority charged with elaborating new rules naturally looks to precedent rules of the same or a similar kind) but not with regard to method and procedure. The choice of methods and procedures was rather arbitrary (and not bound by the rules of general law). It depended on the political aims (of the administration) and on the conditions in the respective territories, which differed considerably from those in the Altreich. Only against the background of these conditions is it possible to understand the special law for aliens in the Occupied Eastern Territories and in the General Government: not as a succession of more or less incidental isolated actions, but as an integral part of the National Socialist policy of special law. This system was established first in the territory of the Reich but took on its full development in the occupied East European territories. Thus, before examining the individual fields of special law, we must explain the underlying policy of the administration in these territories.

Section Two

The Implementation of *Völkisch* Inequality in the Annexed Eastern Territories

INTRODUCTION
Fundamentals of National Socialist Administrative Policy: The Exploitation
and Expulsion of "Non-Germans"

I. Objectives and Outlines of the Implementation of National Socialist Policy

Administrative policy outside the territory of the Altreich was the bureaucratic expression of the National Socialists' basic notion of how to shape the Europe of the future and the foreign territories still to be conquered. These notions
are best summarized under the term *National Socialist Grossraumpolitik*.[1] The
goal of this policy, often masked as the Lebensraum policy,[2] the acquisition of
areas with raw materials, and so forth, was the creation of a Greater German
Colonial Empire,[3] supposedly in imitation of the British. This concept, which
permeates all the special-law measures of the Civil Service, was by no means the
product of later years; it had been developed in its fundamentals even before the
seizure of power and was later rigorously adhered to, even if its implementation
in detail was ever oriented toward the politically expedient.[4]

About the outlines of this concept all political forces were unanimous. The
main protagonists—Hitler himself; the experts in agricultural and settlement
policy from Agriculture Minister Richard Walther Darré's staff; the SS and police leaders (Himmler, Heydrich); the Party leadership (the office of the deputy
of the Führer, later the Party Chancellery); as well as the heads of the Civil Service in the conquered territories, above all those in the occupied East European
regions—all started from the assumption that the issue at hand was the endur-
ing subordination of Greater Europe to the exclusion of the "outside" powers,
Great Britain and the USA. In *Mein Kampf* Hitler had already drawn a rough
sketch of the future Europe: Fascist Italy as an ally to the south, to the west a
France deprived of its power, Eastern Europe as Germany's future Lebensraum,
in *Mitteleuropa* a strong Empire of All the Germans (*Reich aller Deutschen*) going far beyond the borders of 1914.[5] In contrast to the structure of the British
Empire,[6] the dominant force in the National Socialist *Grossreich* was to be not

the Civil Service but, true to its role as the leading "movement," the Party[7]—as was later actually the case in the Annexed Eastern Territories and the occupied Soviet regions.

Regarding the status of the future colonies, however, the ideas of the political leadership and the Civil Service diverged. The Reich Ministry of Justice had since 1939–40 labored over numerous drafts for a "Reich colonial law" and on rules of jurisdiction in case of the reclamation of former colonies abroad,[8] such as Cameroon, German East Africa, German Southwest Africa, and New Guinea,[9] all of which planned a close emulation of the colonial law of the Kaiser era;[10] but, although great weight was given to considerations of detail such as the question of vacation for civil servants in the German colonies or a special colonial administrative career path for high-level officials,[11] the men of the political leadership knew with certainly during the pre-1933 period where the first German colonies were to lie: in the East.

As early as the summer of 1932, there was talk within the National Socialist leadership about the substance of a future German eastern policy, which now made concrete the vague concept of domination over Europe developed by Hitler in the early period of National Socialism.[12] There was to be a "federation of States" in Central Europe, whose core was to be made up of Germany, Bohemia, Moravia, and Austria as constituent parts,[13] surrounded by a wreath of small and medium-sized, dependent "state structures." Thus the Greater German *Grossreich* was to be built out of an encircling ring of satellite states, or structures half-colonial in status.

Seen as a natural precondition for this was the *dismemberment* of the Central European states, such as Czechoslovakia and "Jew-infested" Austria, which latter Hitler had included in his colonization plans from the very beginning.[14] As early as the fall of 1933 Hitler had laid out before his most intimate circle his concept of a future Europe from the Atlantic to the Caucasus:[15] Around Greater Germany (including Austria, Bohemia, Moravia, and western Poland), he envisioned not a federation of equal partners but a *Bund* of "auxiliary nations," without economies and polities of their own. To the west this would take the form of a *Westbund* (France, Flanders, Holland), to the north a *Nordbund* (Denmark, Norway, Sweden), to the east an *Ostbund* (the Baltic states, Poland, the Balkan states, the Ukraine, Georgia, and the Volga area).[16]

At stake here, therefore, was nothing more nor less than the *colonization* of the European nations, particularly those in Central, Eastern and Southern Europe. Indeed, to the National Socialist leadership the colonial status seemed the only appropriate one for conquered territories.[17] In this respect, the concept of colonization was not confined to certain regions alone; rather, the goal was expansion on all sides, not only to the east,[18] even if talk of colonization went mostly in that direction. In reality Hitler was thinking of "colonizing" all of Europe—with the exception of Italy.[19] The supposed necessity of gaining "room in the East" was, as Hitler declared in private, put forward only because the political leadership required freedom of action for the means of colonization, that is, for the coming war.[20]

The idea of "Lebensraum in the East" was thus justified less from a standpoint of population policy than from one of power politics, as a "precondition for the realization of the utopia of the supremacy of the master race," as the "temporally and spatially unlimited political freedom of action" of the Greater German Empire;[21] the arguments put forward for public consumption, for example the need for access to the sources of raw materials, for room for excess population, for economic autarky, albeit the expression of genuine interests that certainly played their part,[22] represented merely short-term objectives. Behind them stood military-political and security interests.[23] These latter were not nourished by rational calculation but rather had their roots in the (irrational)[24] weltanschauung of those who held them and so, as has already been stated in the introduction to this volume, cannot be rationally explained. At stake was nothing less than power at any cost. This was the actual "long-term goal" of National Socialist thought, quite apart from all national, economic, and military factors,[25] and it was much stronger than such considerations.

For in the struggle for power as such, a hunger for aggression and domination, for experience and action ("adventuresome colonial life"), which had long been building in Germany and was presently breaking loose under the National Socialist regime, now came to the fore.[26] It was reinforced precisely because the desire for expansion was not restricted to specific regions, because the long-term goal of the National Socialist leadership itself remained indeterminate and not limited to Europe.[27] The policy of "universal anxiety"[28] on the part of the National Socialist leadership offered all true believers, fellow travelers, and other enthusiasts unlimited opportunities to help themselves, to enrich themselves, to experience adventure. Add to this, moreover, that the mysticism of the East as encouraged in Germany (Eastern colonization, the Teutonic Order, etc.) allowed the sole objective of the leadership, power for its own sake, to be kept well out of sight. It was precisely from this lack of rational considerations,[29] then, that the National Socialist will to expand received its impetus, its fascination, and its irresistibility[30]—a fact whose emotional center of gravity was much better appreciated by contemporaries of Hitler than by subsequent generations.[31]

The addiction to power and domination at any price also helps to explain the ruthless colonization plans for and the treatment of even those nations who were "racially" related (such as the Austrians);[32] for, at root, neither racial nor other reasons were decisive for the policy in the conquered regions, but rather, and exclusively, the idea of domination, of the "universal drive for approval," the vague desire for a "new distribution of the earth," which coincided with the will to destroy all existing orders and create anarchy.[33] Of a federation of states dominated by Germany as talked about repeatedly within the National Socialist leadership, of a commonwealth after the British pattern, or of an extended area held together by alliances, there could be no question; according to the National Socialist leadership's own ideas, the only remaining path to supremacy lay through occupation sustained by the rule of force. As for the administrative policy to be cultivated in the conquered regions, whose practitioners openly re-adopted colonial terms and customs from the years prior to 1914 in order to create the impression of tradition and continuity in German foreign policy,[34] such irrational motives and goals among the leadership provided, however, no serviceable basis. For them the question was whether or not administratively defensible principles could be extrapolated from them, principles that would guide the Civil Service in the soon-to-be-conquered colonial territories.

The specific maxims of administrative policy in the conquered East European territories were total political *domination* and the greatest possible *exploitation* of all resources in the occupied countries. The domination was justified by saying that only those peoples were to be dominated who were incapable of governing themselves. Such peoples, that is, were only succumbing to their historically determined fate ("to each his own" [*jedem das Seine*]). For example, the Poles were said to lack a sense of how to fashion and maintain a state of their own.[35] National Socialist doctrine granted the right to rule over colonial peoples to the *Volk*—that is, Germany—who were capable of taking and keeping possession of a country.[36] From an economic perspective, the entire set of resources, industries, and arable land of the colonial territories consisted of "objects of exploitation" to be put at the disposal of the Reich;[37] anything at all movable was, in an excess of exploitation, to be transported into the Reich;[38] and the labor of the native population was to be utilized to the maximum degree.[39]

To achieve these objectives, both Hitler himself and his protégés in the civil administration and the police authorities of the occupied territories consistently advocated a policy of the "utmost severity" vis-à-vis subjugated peoples, opposing all practical considerations brought forward by administrative experts.[40] Autonomous statehood was ruled out altogether, the highest permissible level of self-administration being that of the municipality.[41]

That policy was correct which produced the most in terms of foodstuffs and labor; the "mild approach" was foolish and "starry-eyed."[42] Individual human lives were insignificant; how many of the natives died was a matter of absolutely no consequence, according to Hitler.[43] However, the exploitation of economic and human resources alone was, in the eyes of the National Socialist leadership, by no means sufficient; hand in glove with that went a systematic policy of separating non-Germans from the German *Herrenmenschen* (master men)[44] as well as one aimed at the greatest possible uprooting and depopulation, as a check to "Slavic fertility"[45] and in order to as far as possible drive out the resident population, since room had to be made for intended German settlement (Germanization [*Eindeutschung*]) of these regions.[46] Within the National Socialist leadership, there was at a very early date already the firm idea that the entire countryside was to come into German hands, while "foreign-race" farmers and workers were resettled to become migrant laborers for the Reich and unskilled workers for industry.[47]

At issue, therefore, was the forcing down of entire peoples to the status of helots,[48] that is, to the level of unskilled helpers, a level that Hitler himself described as the "modern form of bondage," as "slavery," which was necessary for the development of human culture.[49]

In conjunction with this, there were also reflections on whether to keep foreign peoples at a low level with respect to education and living standards (or if necessary reduce them to such a level); to prevent an "education toward the European standard"; to introduce only the "most necessary" of intellectual and technical achievements—that is, to institute merely an "education for order and work."[50] Such reflections belonged to the well-known repertoire of pan-Germanist and folkish thinking that was later copied in many ways by the National Socialists.[51] Hitler himself called for the needed "courage to [promote] illiteracy," since "education and knowledge" contained "certain dangers for the German master race"; knowledge must once again take on the "character of a secret science," for education is a "means of control."[52] The "non-German" may be given only as much knowledge as needed to understand German commands and traffic signs and the simplest elements of arithmetic; any educated person would be a future enemy.[53] The living conditions were to be kept as bad as possible, hygiene and health care deliberately neglected, the mortality rate kept high, and nutrition reduced to the barest minimum.[54] Furthermore, since "we shall indeed [one day] settle this entire . . . land with Germans," the plans of the National Socialist leadership were that alcoholism, the widespread availability of abortion, and poor sanitary conditions would be promoted, or at least tolerated.[55]

The legal consequences of these colonial plans consisted in the idea that the native population of the "colonial East" had lost its previous nationality, becoming, according to the German construction, merely a caste of stateless vassals whose labor and lives were seen as the exclusive object of exploitation by the occupying power. The means of their "suppression" was the practice of *völkisch* inequality in its two best-known forms: the strict separation between "Germans" and "non-Germans," embodied in the prohibition against "race mixing"[56] (euphemized under the slogan proclaiming "respect for the racial personality of nations"),[57] followed by special legal treatment in all areas of law according to political expediency. The latter was based on the principle of the absolute priority of German interests and, where these were not involved, on the idea of a certain "autonomy" for the indigenous population at the lowest administrative level, but one that was never to be confused with any form whatsoever of national autonomy.[58] In reality, therefore, despite numerous promises and consoling words from the German authorities,[59] there could be no talk of autonomy, however modest, for the resident populations, neither in the occupied Polish nor in the Occupied Soviet Territories (where the populations of Galicia and the Ukraine, especially, had great hopes that the Germans would free them from the Soviet policy of repression),[60] since nothing was so much feared as the eruption of national passions. As a result, the entire civil administration was taken over by the German occupation authorities.[61]

Yet it was still unclear what legal status ought to be accorded these colonial territories. This uncertainly did not arise merely because there was no agreement as to the legal and political fate of those regions; it also corresponded to a disinclination within the National Socialist leadership toward legal commitments of any kind. As long as everything hung in the balance, the government intended for the "colonial East" was most likely to succeed. Against all rules of international law, the occupied regions of Eastern Europe were therefore not treated as occupied territories according to the Hague Convention[62] but as colonies in which, according to the German construction, "all measures [were] permissible that appeared necessary and proper to the German administration in carrying out [its governmental authority]."[63] What is more, they often enough fell short even of colonial status, since, at least with respect to the Occupied Eastern Territories, the civil administration was almost completely decommissioned in favor of the almighty police and other central authorities[64] (as *Reichsführer-SS* and chief of the German police, Himmler coveted absolute authority with regard to all occupied territories, including the General Government and the Protectorate of Bohemia and Moravia);[65] that is, a colonial administration of the traditional type was never set in place to begin with. This procedure, a violation of international law, applied—with respect to the occupied territories—to the Wehrmacht as well, as demonstrated by the guidelines of the High Command of the Wehrmacht on the treatment of "non-Germans" and on the execution of hostages, "Communists," and "Commissars," as well as on the nonprosecution of crimes committed by members of the Wehrmacht.[66]

Such plans and practices were designed to create the conditions required for the new social order of National Socialism, in which the "non-Germans" were to form the lowest stratum as a class of slaves or helots. The actual design of this new order was, however, not fixed in all details but only vaguely hinted at. In this regard, as well, National Socialism was capable of developing detailed, concrete plans only in matters of destructiveness; it was incapable of clearly formulating new programs and goals, much less of constructively carrying them out.[67] This new social order,[68] which, like all other long-term considerations on the part of the National Socialist leadership, was not primarily nationalist or economic in character but rather justified exclusively in terms of power politics,[69] was based, as Hitler had already expounded to his intimate circle in 1933–34, on the idea of the *destruction* of all social orders and the melting down of all social and national distinctions.[70] To emerge in their place was a strictly hierarchic order, that is, a kind of modern slave-owners' society. At its apex stood a German "master race," selectively bred, much in the manner of horses, and drawing upon a gene pool made up of the SS, the peasantry, and the "good genetic makeup of the old aristocratic stock"[71] but also including those who "confessed belief" in this idea of the "master class."[72] After the caste of these new masters came the "mass of hierarchically ordered Party members" as the new middle class, then "the great mass of the anonymous, the collective of servants" (apparently the great mass of *Volksgenossen* who were not Party members). Consigned to the lowest rung of all, according to Hitler, was the "class of the subjugated foreign-born," the "modern slave-class,"[73] who, as shown above, were not to attain any level higher than that of merest subsistence.

Quite apart from its primitiveness, this conception meant the end of equal rights and opportunities and thus the end of any cultural and educational life for all those who did not belong to the new master class.[74] The implementation of the ideas for the domination of the "master race" over masses of "non-German" slaves and for gigantic shifts of whole populations was first to be undertaken in the East, since the East was to represent, in Hitler's own words, the "great field of experimentation"[75] of the new racial order, experimentation, that is, for the great melting-down and denationalization process of Europe under German rule. All terms and expressions, all traditions within these states that recalled their own political and cultural identity were systematically eradicated (while at the same time the Germans vaunted their "pioneering achievements" of earlier centuries),[76] in order to create the impression that Eastern Europe had at all times been culturally dominated by Germany and that nothing more was to be seen in the eastward expansion than the coming into their own of those who were from the first the legitimate heirs.[77]

Suited to this policy of denationalization were first and foremost the occupied Polish territories, since they had been held the longest and were the least impaired by the events of the war. The salient features of this policy were the ignorance and "downright naive" suppositions of the leadership about the traditions, history, and mentality of the country.[78] Compounding this was a politically motivated antipathy toward the Poles, which gradually grew into an utterly pathological hatred of their staunch national will to survive, a hatred for whose maintenance the resentments that had been in plentiful supply among the eastern German population since the period after 1918 (and stemming in particular from the fighting in Upper Silesia) were stirred up even more.[79]

In Poland, after the de facto incorporation into the German Reich[80] had been concluded and the colonization plans for Russia had miscarried, the occupants played through "on a small scale" what was to have served, later on, as the model colonial policy for all of Europe.[81] Thus Poland was the first colony within Europe, the proving ground for German "swiftness and brutality" in the political, military, and economic exploitation of the inhabitants.[82]

This policy of exploitation was primarily practiced in Poland's occupied western territories. By a decree of the Führer dated October 8, 1939,[83] these were incorporated into the German Reich as the Annexed Eastern Territories, in complete disregard of the principles of international law. As will be thoroughly demonstrated later on, it was the dominant opinion, both in theory and in practice, that the Polish state had been finished, *extinguished*, ever since September 1, 1939, or at the very latest upon Poland's capitulation, so that the Civil Service established in the Eastern Territories could not proceed on the basis of the "preservation of the previously existing state structure."[84] In consequence, the validity of any norms or standards of international law (as established at the Hague Convention and the Geneva Convention) within the Eastern Territories was denied and their inclusion in Germany's interior sphere of influence declared permissible[85]—all this in contravention of international law, which in cases in which a state was occupied initially presumed the continued existence of the occupied state, more especially when the occupation was brought about by aggression.[86] With the annexation the entire administrative policy became fixated on "Germanization," with a view toward making room for German settlement. The Warthegau district (or Wartheland) in particular, in the minds of the National Socialist leadership (who found their most zealous champion in the Gauleiter and Reich governor [*Reichsstatthalter*] of Posen [Poznań], Arthur Karl Greiser),[87] was to become a "living Eastern bulwark,"[88] a German "model district" (*Mustergau*), from which the greatest possible number of undesirable Poles were to be expelled and whose administration was meant to become the model for the later organization of the *Reichsgaue* within the Altreich itself.[89] The essential principles of this (Germanization) policy, which, however, depending on the audience, was paraphrased as a policy of "containing" the Poles (*Volkstumskampf*) or as a policy of building up "Germanness," consisted, first, in the liquidation of the property-owning and politically dominant classes or their expulsion ("resettlement") and replacement with German settlers,[90] while the remaining population was for the time being to be kept on as a source of cheap labor. The ultimate objective was the "utter removal of everything Polish," that is, in the long term, the deportation of all Poles and the final incorporation of these territories into the German state.[91] The second component or stage of the Polish policy consisted in the strictest possible separation between Germans and the resident population, while subjecting the latter to discriminatory measures with the aim of dramatizing German authority and obtaining the greatest possible work efforts (with the Poles as "more or less slave laborers") for the purposes of the Reich.[92]

The fulfillment of the objectives delineated here was approached exclusively from a standpoint of draconian severity.[93] Not surprisingly, the favorite slogan of this policy was the motto "harsh, but fair," which in reality meant harshness alone, and no fairness. For, as with "non-Germans" in general, what was expected from Poles and Jews in particular was nothing but obedience and labor; they were to be "honest and diligent" and submit in all things to German orders and directives. As in all authoritarian administrations, here, too, oppression was justified by assertions that it was also in the interests of the oppressed: "The broad mass of Poles feel," as *Reichsstatthalter* Greiser declared during a lecture in Kiel, "absolutely fine."[94]

One of the first measures taken was the registration of all those fit to work, enforced if necessary under compulsion (roundups);[95] the labor of the Jews, in particular, was exploited to the point of total exhaustion (as was noted with pride), because the procedure was "unbureaucratic," that is, SS and police units were used instead of administrative officials.[96] Further legal measures to enforce separation included raising the minimum age required for marriage among Poles; the maintenance of the existing poor living conditions through cuts in wages and salaries; and deliberate complications in the purchase or cuts in the distribution of foodstuffs and consumer goods,[97] leading to hoarding,[98] sinking labor productivity, and general dissatisfaction. Actual legal discrimination consisted, as is documented in detail below, in prohibitions on the use of the means of transportation and communication, choking off sources of information (newspaper, radio), introduction of special laws in the areas of criminal law, civil administration, and some parts of the labor laws—all exhibiting clear parallels to the legislation affecting Jews in the Reich itself. The final goal of the administrative "special treatment" of the Poles, as differentiated as it may have been in various areas, consisted in codifying the general principles for treatment of the "non-German" population in a system sui generis, in a special "Polish Codex" or set of legal statutes,[99] thus finalizing their removal from the German community of law by enshrining it in a special legislative act.

In addition, the "special treatment" of the Poles was perfected via numerous measures of psychological warfare, which are dealt with in detail later. Aside from measures exquisitely calculated to humiliate (such as mandatory salutation of Germans),[100] no propagandistic measure was spared to convince the Poles of the finality of their state's destruction, the victories of German arms, and the perpetual duration of German rule,[101] as well as to suppress with rigorous severity all signs of Polish resistance,[102] although these were, compared with those experienced in the General Government, relatively inconsequential. In order to secure the agreement of the German population, elements of which perceived the measures of persecution, in particular the resettlements, to be cruel and unjust, no kind of propaganda went untried that might provoke aversion and hate. Polish excesses committed against Germans in the first days of the war (the so-called September Murders) served as political justification, being laid at the door of the Poles as a collective guilt. Therefore, went the argument, Germany was free from any legal or political considerations.[103] Within the populace, these actions apparently met with only partial success, as demonstrated by the numerous complaints of friendly contacts between Germans and Poles and of "Polonophile behavior" among indigenous ethnic Germans.[104] Later on, the murder of thousands of Polish officers by Soviet troops at Katyn (the Katyn Murders) provided the Nazis with welcome grounds for excoriating the outrages of the Communists while distracting from their own plans for suppressing "non-Germans."

Thanks to regular reports on the mood of the populace, the living conditions, and the political situation received by the administrative authorities from subordinate departments and the Security Service,[105] there were numerous opportunities for adapting the administrative policy, turning the screw now looser, now tighter. Basically, however, a tough and inflexible course was pursued from the very beginning, not only in the speeches of the National Socialist leadership but also in practice—in reckless disregard of actual conditions. Since the official version held that Poles were fundamentally "cunning," "cheeky," and "underhanded," that is, born servants with whom anything but strong remedies were misplaced,[106] senseless measures were taken—such as, for instance, the public thrashing of Poles ("vigorous castigation")—which derived from colonial think-ing[107] and whose justification was traced to a firmly established "unwritten prin-ciple of law." This latter (then) experienced a corresponding revival in the East-ern Territories.[108] A further principle was never to allow Poles to take executive appointments or positions of trust.[109] The only things expected and demanded of them were underpaid work in subordinate positions and strict obedience. Trivialities were viewed as sabotage against German directives.[110] Because the mood and morale in the population were necessarily bad on account of the rig-orous anti-Polish measures,[111] this in turn was made to serve as the alibi for even sterner measures, so that both the mood of the "non-German" population and the measures directed against it mutually escalated; to this extent—and es-pecially in the Warthegau—one may speak of a "closed system" of anti-Polish measures, resolutely imposed.[112] Even when, toward the end of the war at the latest, a milder course would have been in their own best interests, the police leadership and the radical wing of the Party and the Civil Service stubbornly adhered to the previously determined path; they viewed the Annexed Eastern Territories as "German settlement land" for all time,[113] where a tough position was to be enforced under all circumstances. Leniency was taken for weakness, flexibility for indulgence. The only means of rule and the only language under-stood and practiced by these officials was that of violence and suppression.

The special-law policy directed against Poles and Jews (*Volkstumskampf*) was accompanied by substantial efforts at Germanization (the "German Re-structuring Effort"), the outlines of which can only be hinted at here. First and foremost in this category was the Germanization of place names and streets, the removal of Polish signs, and the Germanization (*Eindeutschung*) of the popula-tion[114] by resettling ethnic Germans from the Soviet Union and the Baltic states, who took possession of the property of the expelled Poles but whose identity as distinct ethnic groups was shattered and whose cultural individuality was stolen in order to breed the standardized "greater German man." In all this, the most important principle of the settlement policy was the partition of Polish-settled areas with German-settled strips that were to *smother* or prevent the spread of the Polish-settled areas.[115] In legal terms Germanization was reflected in the in-troduction of regulations adopted from the Reich,[116] particularly pertaining to economics, that favored the German population; in the creation of considerable tax advantages for the indigenous and incoming Germans; and in making the latter visually distinguishable from the Poles.[117] On the basis of such notions of settlement policy, the Annexed Eastern Territories were to develop into the model for future Eastern settlements, which in turn were to represent the agri-cultural reservoir ("breadbasket" of the Reich)[118] in addition to taking in soldiers and disabled veterans from the region of the Altreich. Germans reveled in historical reminiscences and intoxicated themselves with the "German Restructuring Effort," with their "admirable resettlement work," and with the riches that flowed into public coffers thanks to the expropriation of Polish possessions.[119] They invoked the new type of men, those destined "to be leaders of men," who were primarily to come from the ranks of former soldiers. The East required not only "professionally educated" personnel. If a man's "heart was in the right place" and his attitude correct, then he too could climb the career ladder in the East.[120]

II. The New Type of Administration in the Annexed Eastern Territories: The Primacy of the Party and the Separation of the Regional Administration from the Reich Administration

This radical administrative policy was decided on by the new revolutionary powers, the Party and the police, as both "racial struggle" and Germanization had been removed from the preserve of the administration, being declared instead issues "involving the leadership and guidance of people," that is, a matter for the Party (and the police).[1] The *Reichsstatthalter* (regional governors) of the new Eastern Territories, who also functioned as Gauleiter of their respective regions, certainly enjoyed excellent relations with the Party leadership and shared its taste for violent measures and the suppression of the Poles at all costs, its aversion to the stipulation of any legal status for "non-Germans," in fact its general dislike of bureaucratic methods and procedures. This developed into a "natural" opposition to the Reich administration, which although approving a tough anti-Polish line was still in favor of continuity and a degree of legal security for "non-Germans," albeit in its own interests. However, the policy of the Party, its obstinacy and arrogance, prevailed in the new Eastern districts (*Ostgaue*), whose administrative structure was much closer to the National Socialist ideal than the rigid system of the Altreich because it enjoyed the backing of the Gauleiter, Party Headquarters in the Reich, and ultimately Hitler himself,[2] whereas the administrative authorities could rely only on the weak Reich Ministry of the Interior, which was suffering from repeated attempts by the Party and the police to bring about its elimination and indeed whose continuous compromises made a not insubstantial contribution to the process of neutralization.

The dominance of the Party was evident in the close interrelationship between Party and state, from which emerged the new special powers (*Partikulargewalt*) that characterized the administrative model imposed on the Annexed Eastern Territories.[3] Though the administrative structure and institutional organization in the Annexed Eastern Territories corresponded, on the surface, to the law of the Reich,[4] a parallel Party apparatus was constructed alongside the governmental agencies, infiltrating them to such an extent that the Party was able to influence all action taken by the administration.[5] This not only took the form of the now well-established consultation procedures but was also implemented even more effectively: all measures of a fundamental nature, in particular those regarding the special treatment of Poles and Jews, required not only the tacit backing of the relevant Party office but also coordination with that office and its explicit approval.[6] On top of this, all key administrative positions were staffed by the leadership of the corresponding Party offices in a form of personal union.[7] This applied especially to the head of the administration, the *Reichsstatthalter*/Gauleiter, whose position of strength was justified by, among others things, the need for the powers of the Reich to appear in unified form,[8] so as to ensure their authority over the Poles and other "non-German races" and to prevent any public display of jurisdictional conflicts and the "undeniable" divergence of Party and state.[9] The heads of the state police regional headquarters were at the same time political advisers to the *Reichsstatthalter*.[10] The leading officials in the *Reichsstatthalter* offices performed key functions in the parallel Party organizations.[11] The political advisers in the district presidents' offices also headed the corresponding Gestapo district headquarters;[12] at the *Kreis* (county) level, the *Reichsstatthalter* had forced through the personal union of *Kreisleiter* (chief of the Party in a county) and *Landrat* (county administrator) in the vast majority of cases by provisionally empowering the *Kreisleiter* to assume the official duties of a *Landrat* and presenting the Reich Ministry of the Interior with a fait accompli.[13]

In contrast to the Reich, where the combined function of *Landrat* and *Kreisleiter* had been abolished for some time,[14] this personal union had been urged by the administrative heads of the Annexed Eastern Territories and the Party leadership to establish the authority of the Party at the grassroots level in order to make sure that the so-called political administrative leadership was retained by the Party in the face of the internal administration authorities,[15] which claimed these powers for the *Landräte*.[16] This was by no means guaranteed by the sole appointment of Party members to leading administration positions, because it was soon recognized that even with reliable Party members, a tendency to "drift off into the realms of the state" was evident as soon as they achieved office and rank in the administration.[17] To ensure that at least the professional administrative work was performed to a certain degree, attempts were made to appoint administrative officials who were also Party members, where no Party members with proven experience in Party work (but without administrative training) were available.[18] The poor quality of available personnel meant that the demands of the Party that the *Landräte* in the Eastern Territories should not only be reliable Party members but should also have been active in Party work proved to be of little help.[19] Nevertheless, the appointment of leading Party officials as *Landräte* was forced through by the *Reichsstatthalter* against the will of the Reich Ministry of the Interior.[20]

This development is an interesting example of the explosive nature of the so far practically unresearched personnel policy of the Nazi regime, the infiltration of the administration by the Party. Only eighteen months later, the Reich Ministry of the Interior could barely conceal its satisfaction at noting that this experiment had, not unexpectedly, been a complete failure. The ambition of the Party to appoint Party members without administrative experience had proved to be illusory. The result was "staggering." Many of these new *Kreisleiter/ Landräte*, including about half of those in the Warthegau, had either completely failed in their duties or had been unable "even once" to prove themselves in the eyes of the Party. If the administration there "had been makeshift," this was (solely) "thanks to the district governments (district presidents), who had increased their supervision to such an extent that they practically controlled the administration."[21]

The close integration of the administration with the organization of the NSDAP meant, of course, that administrative levels that did not fit into the scheme of the Party were restrained and robbed of their importance. The functions of the district presidents' offices (*Regierungspräsidien*), the pride of the Prussian administration, which had no corresponding Party organization and thus no personal union with Party offices,[22] were cut back heavily in the Annexed Eastern Territories in favor of the departments of the *Reichsstatthalter* and the *Landräte*,[23] as were the those of the regional presidents. The district presidents, the bulwark of the traditional administrative system, stood in the way of the political leadership; they were scheduled for abolition in the long term and were also eventually doomed to extinction in the Altreich.[24] The Reich Ministry of the Interior proved to be powerless against the undermining of its middle-ranking authorities; indeed, it had weakened its own position in the Eastern Territories through its constant acquiescence, countering only with empty protests in speeches and articles,[25] which were quite understandably not taken seriously by the leadership.

The prevailing influence of the Party was also reflected in the organization of legislative powers. Although these were formally the province of the Reich Ministry of the Interior in the new Reich districts (*Reichsgaue*), it required the consent of the Party Chancellery in all important matters, being largely robbed thereby of its liberty of action. This is shown, for instance, by the settlement of nationality questions, which required the consent of the Party Chancellery and the RFSS/RKF (*Reichsführer*-SS/Reich Commissar for the Strengthening of German Nationhood),[26] thus ensuring the decisive influence of the political powers. A further factor was that, ignoring all jurisdictional powers laid down by the law of the Reich, the departments of the RFSS/RKF had from the outset claimed supreme competence (*Generalzuständigkeit*) for all questions of the "establishment of German national identity (*Volkstum*)," which of course included principally the treatment of "non-Germans," as well as the corresponding authority to issue instructions to the general state administration.[27] The consequence of this was the not particularly reluctant withdrawal by the conventional administration from these issues, subject as they were to the arbitrary decisions of the departments of the RKF, which now felt itself responsible for the *Neuordnung* (New Order) of Europe in terms of ethnic policy. The (administrative) legislative powers of the *Reichsstatthalter* followed the same route. Although formally subject to the approval of the Reich minister of the interior,[28] in fact such powers were hardly used at all, as the same issues were settled by decrees issued arbitrarily by the *Reichsstatthalter*/Gauleiter, the new lords of the land.

The primacy of the Party was also evident in the nature of the administrative leadership in the Annexed Eastern Territories. Although formally responsible to the Reich minister of the interior and bound by his directives,[29] the *Reichsstatthalter*/Gauleiter of the Annexed Eastern Territories were autonomous administrative leaders and ruled to a certain extent independently of the Reich, in opposition to or parallel to the Reich authorities, if the line taken by the latter did not suit them.[30] This hybrid situation of the *Reichsstatthalter*, which was formally an executive organ of the Reich administration but de facto a semiautonomous central authority, is also evident in the complicated administrative structure and the regulations issued by their departments.[31]

The process of suppression of the Reich administration is illustrated by the political decision-making process in the disputes about the appointment of the *Gau* councils (*Gauräte*) in the new Reich *Gaue*.

Both the Ostmark Law and the Sudetengau Law, both of April 14, 1939,[32] applying to the corresponding Annexed Eastern Territories, had stipulated that the *Reichsstatthalter* should "be advised by *Gauräte* in matters of self-administration" but contained no provisions whatsoever about the size, composition, and selection of these bodies. Whereas the Reich Ministry of the Interior had principally envisaged Oberbürgermeister and *Landräte* as the members of the *Gauräte*, the intention of the deputy Führer was to appoint only full-time NSDAP functionaries. The protracted negotiations between the two authorities about the composition and powers of appointment of the *Gauräte* were totally fruitless. A Decree on the Administration of *Reichsgaue* as Self-Governing Bodies, drafted by the Reich Ministry of the Interior, collapsed in the face of the delaying tactics adopted by the deputy Führer, who saw in this relatively insignificant matter a fundamental issue of power. It was not so much a matter of administrative organization; more importantly, it raised the question of political leadership. Another conflict resulted from the question of the power of appointment. The Reich Ministry of the Interior held the view that the *Gauräte* should receive their certificates of appointment from, and be sworn into office by, the *Reichsstatthalter;* the deputy Führer, disagreeing, maintained that any swearing in was superfluous because the designated NSDAP candidates had already sworn an oath of loyalty to the Führer. Appointment by the deputy Führer was sufficient. When no agreement could be reached on this issue either, the deputy Führer presented the Reich Ministry of the Interior with a fait accompli, using tried and tested tactics, by starting to issue certificates of appointment to candidates of his choice. The Reich Ministry of the Interior, increasingly on the defensive, limited itself to recognizing the certificates but demanding their issue by the *Reichsstatthalter* as a constitutive act for the substantiation of the position of an (honorary) *Gaurat* under Civil Service law. Not surprisingly, this demand was unsuccessful. On the contrary, Martin Bormann once more went on the offensive by replacing the word *Following* by *On* in the wording of the certificate of appointment ("*On* your appointment by the deputy Führer . . . to the *Gaurat,* you are appointed an honorary officer under career Civil Service rules by virtue of this Certificate") and refusing any further debate on the subject. The issue was still unsettled by the end of the war.[33]

The development of the *Gauräte* is a perfect example of the successful efforts by the Party leadership to supplant the conventional bureaucracy and replace it by a system of *Führerherrschaft* (rule by the Führer) without fixed jurisdiction and accountability. The consequence was jurisdictional chaos, legal uncertainty, and helplessness, providing the most fertile ground for the system of emergency powers to which the NSDAP aspired in contrast to the legal homogeneity of the traditional Reich administration. The emergency powers kept the upper hand, but the price was the disintegration of the traditional administrative structure.[34]

What even the National Socialist leadership was unable to force through was the *complete* separation of the new National Socialist *Führerkorps* from the traditional Reich administration, because the shortcomings and poor professional and personal quality of the Party and the administrative personnel available for the Eastern Territories meant that the National Socialist leadership was still forced to depend on the Reich administration.[35] The dominance of the Party did, however, cause a weakening of the administrative machinery at middle (district president) and lower-ranking (municipal) levels, with the central *Reichsstatthalter's* office becoming a superauthority that acquired for itself as many powers as possible, governing everything and everybody itself and thus well on the way to actualizing Hitler's notions of the 'Führer's governors" in the East who as his deputies (*Reichsstatthalter*, Reich commissars, and governors, etc.) could do as they pleased.[36]

Faced with the massive pressure from the Party leadership, SS and police leaders, and the local administrative chiefs, all unanimously promoting the principle of independence from the Reich administration, the Reich administration, headed by the Reich Chancellery maneuvering in all directions, proved simply incapable of holding or developing any opposite standpoints. The attempt by the SS and police leaders mentioned above to seize for themselves the power vested by the *Immediatsprinzip*, originally designed for Hitler alone, that is, the authority to issue instructions to *all* civilian heads of administration, bypassing all Reich authorities, best shows how far the situation had progressed.[37]

In its reaction to this onslaught by the Party bureaucracy, the Reich Ministry of the Interior, which had general responsibility for the new Eastern Territories, picked the worst possible tactic. It initially reacted only in an "elastic defensive,"[38] despite verbally protesting the authority of the internal administration in all matters relating to the administration of the new Eastern Territories, instead of undertaking any positive action itself. If, as was normally the case, the deputy Führer or the *Reichsführer*-SS and chief of the German police proved to be uncompromising, the ministry retreated and limited itself to formal adjustments to political decisions that had already been made.[39] The sum total of the "participation" by the Reich internal administration was thus either that it was involved only via institutionalized information processes (which frequently served only the delaying and obstructing tactics of the Party leadership) or that it was simply confronted with a fait accompli.

In the areas where no agreement could be reached with Berlin about the policy of special rights for the local population, the endeavors of the Party leaders and the *Reichsstatthalter* in the Annexed Eastern Territories to achieve autonomy ultimately resulted in their frequently shying away from any trial of strength with the Reich Ministry of the Interior and protracted conflicts about jurisdiction, thereby simply excluding the Reich authorities. Berlin could complain as eloquently as it wished, but what effect did it have as long as the local authorities implemented the decrees of the *Reichsstatthalter*? Was it not the case that the *Reichsstatthalter*/Gauleiter, not Berlin, enjoyed all direct authority to issue instructions and thus true power, once the cumbersome legislative procedure had been abandoned and the more comfortable instrument of a *policy of issuing guidelines* had been adopted? The guideline policy therefore gradually became the most important instrument of totalitarian power in the Annexed Eastern Territories: it offered the advantage of bypassing the Reich authorities, secrecy, and the ability to change the relevant regulations at any time. This guideline policy offered particular advantages where "non-Germans" were concerned, since existing legal safeguards could be largely circumvented in the administrative procedure. Another favored tactic was to allow such people formal rights of appeal in guidelines but at the same time to issue instructions internally that all appeals should be rejected,[40] so as not to endanger the "authority of the German administration." The relevant authorities even went so far as to view the issue of guidelines as inappropriate because these were still stipulations that the Poles should not be allowed to cite.[41] The aim in the Warthegau (or Wartheland), achieved to a large extent, was the totalitarian ideal of the policy of ad hoc decisions and the absence of any binding nature whatsoever in acts of state.

Despite a superficial similarity to the Reich administration in organization,[42] a new model of totalitarian administration organization had thus evolved in the Annexed Eastern Territories, characterized by a semiautonomous status vis-à-vis the Reich authorities, the close personal and material integration of state and Party, the dominating influence of the Party, and a radical policy of special rights for the local population in the form of secret guidelines. This new administrative model thus stood about halfway between the traditional (Reich) form of administration and the colonial administration models established in the occupied territories of Eastern Europe, of which one, the administrative model in the General Government (Poland) is discussed in greater detail in section 3.

III. Results

The results of the Polish policy—predominantly drafted by the Party—in the German Eastern Territories, the overwhelming majority of whose population consisted of "non-Germans,"[1] require a differentiated assessment. Despite the aforementioned general guidelines, there can be no talk of any uniform Polish policy, because each of Hitler's "*Gau* kings" (*Reichsstatthalter,* or regional presidents) pursued his own policies in his own region. Although a stringent anti-Polish course was pursued in the Warthegau[2] and in the Zichenau administrative district, those regions with a strong mixed German-Polish population, such as Danzig–West Prussia and the annexed regions of Upper Silesia, experienced a policy of Germanization that took the form of the "alignment" of Polish living conditions with German conditions (e.g., an equal labor law status with Germans). This meant that the living conditions in these regions were relatively bearable, which led the Poles to the false conclusion that this was where the real Polish policy was being implemented and that the Warthegau was suffering from the rule of a "handful of radical *Polenfresser* ["eaters" of Poles]," who would not be able to prevail in the long term.[3] Especially in the "model district" of the Wartheland, however, the impact of the "ethnic policy" fell short of the expectations and notions of the National Socialist leadership.

The reasons for this lay not only in the organizational problems of the Party and administrative machineries mentioned above; a crucial factor in the failure of the ethnic policy was the critical personnel problem already cited, which led to innumerable complaints about the poor professional and personal suitability of administrative and Party personnel, to the recall of many appointees because of breach of service regulations or personal misconduct (drunken excesses, embezzlement, etc.),[4] and to many applications for transfer back to the Reich (being assigned service in the East was regarded as a "disciplinary transfer").[5]

Particular ill feeling arose because the personnel records of the seconded civil servants were not sent by their home authorities to the recipient authority, with the result that not all individuals appointed to positions of trust were thoroughly suited to the standards imposed upon them.[6]

Above all, however, as the responsible administrative authorities deplored repeatedly, the policy of segregation and "oppression" of the Poles was never properly grasped and consistently implemented by either the German authorities or the German population. In a report addressed to *Reichsstatthalter* Greiser concerning the current state of the Polish policy, and dated July 30, 1941, the head of ethnic policy in the office of the *Reichsstatthalter* Posen argued that the pre-1914 Prussian policy, oriented toward mutual understanding, had been wrong. The German population was no match for the "tactics of the Polish race," displayed not unity but a friendly attitude toward the Poles, and certainly did not maintain the prescribed personal distance.[7] Both this report and numerous other reports are full of complaints about fraternization between Germans (particularly members of the Wehrmacht) and Poles (particularly Polish women),[8] which was detrimental to the German race but did not decline even when unauthorized contact with Poles was punished by arrest by the Gestapo (i.e., mostly by committal to a concentration camp).[9] Germans helped Poles evade the German police on many occasions.[10]

Neither was the line taken by the individual authorities against the Poles consistent—at least in the Warthegau. The regular police, for instance, were explicitly prohibited from harassing the Poles.[11] In the *Reichsbahn,* 80 percent of whose employees were Poles, or in the labor administration, the prevailing conditions were largely dictated by economic considerations (i.e., preserving the workforce) rather than the principle of oppression at any cost. That situation prompted the radical ethnic politicians in the *Reichsstatthalter's* office to warn against actions hostile to the Germans and acts of sabotage by the Poles and to demand stronger ideological indoctrination on the Polish issue for civil servants and plant managers, indeed for the entire population.[12] According to the official line, the Poles were "rebellious" and "impudent" and must be treated harshly in every respect; even the slightest concession, according to the recommendation by the ethnic experts to the administrative leadership, would reinforce the Poles' hostile attitude toward the Germans. The administrative authorities always countered this policy with economic arguments, which were accepted as important but could have no effect on the ethnic policy objectives: in the long term, the Poles would have to be expelled from the Eastern Territories, but in the medium term the "Pole should be exploited as labor" "as much as possible and then left to his own devices," so that he "is no longer in a position . . . to reestablish himself ethnically and politically . . . with outside aid."[13]

A. The Principal Features of the National Socialist Policy of Special Law: The Segregation of Germans and "Non-Germans" and the Greatest Possible Discrimination against "Non-Germans"

The development and organization of the special regulations for isolation of and discrimination against "non-Germans" were linked to the practice already established in the Reich. The measures instituted against the Jews in the Altreich were implemented in comprehensive fashion in the Annexed Eastern Territories. This process of repression, under cover of the terms *racial struggle* and *German Restructuring Efforts (deutsche Aufbauarbeit)* cited before, was organized along the same lines in both the Altreich and all annexed and occupied territories: (1) the group to face discrimination was first *separated* and isolated from the other local population groups, and (2) *special regulations* were imposed upon this group, now placed outside the legal system (which frequently ended in the deprivation of all civil rights). The special regulations were frequently accompanied by the granting of explicit privileges to the German population.[1]

The measures implemented to separate the German and "non-German" races principally comprised the mandatory "Hitler-*Gruss*" (Hitler salute) and numerous compulsory identification regulations and rules of conduct for Poles designed to confront them daily with the ignominy of their defeat. These were a direct continuation of the "proven" models in the Reich instituted as part of the anti-Jewish persecution. The relevant measures in the Annexed Eastern Territories therefore display clear parallels with the anti-Jewish laws enforced in the Reich.

As to the Jews, the special regulations on Jewish names implemented in the Reich also applied, such as the obligation to adopt the first name or surname *Israel* or *Sara* in legal and commercial transactions and in all dealings with the authorities and public offices.[2] In the Wartheland, however, the authorities also came up with a special rule for the Poles. Along the same lines as the special treatment enforced for the Jews, a decree issued by the *Reichsstatthalter* on November 1, 1941, obliged all Poles to adopt a Polish name from an official list of names or to add the special name of *Kazimierz* to their own name,[3] so that all Poles could be immediately identified as such in dealings with the authorities. Although it is questionable whether this decree was implemented in practice, its very existence shows that there were proposals to subject Poles to the same treatment as the Jews.

In contrast, general compulsory identification of "non-Germans" was not introduced in the Annexed Eastern Territories (except for "non-German" forced laborers from Russia),[4] although the top administrators certainly had concrete plans: for instance, it was proposed that as with the Polish civilian laborers in the Altreich, all Poles in the Annexed Eastern Territories should wear an armband bearing a large *P*.[5] However, practical and political considerations made such a measure inappropriate. Instead, at least in the Warthegau, the objective of segregation and isolation of Poles and Germans was achieved by a different, much simpler method right from the outset—not the Poles, but the much less numerous local German population was obliged to wear a *Volksdeutsch* badge or another badge indicating their membership in the German race.[6] Anybody not wearing such a badge could automatically be identified as a "non-German." Overzealous Party offices also proposed compulsory identification for German staff in shops and inns so that "it is evident from the outset whether one is being served by a German or a Pole."[7] To prevent any form of disguise, the Poles themselves were strictly prohibited from wearing any form of badge or marking in the Warthegau,[8] which also included German, Austrian, and Polish medals and decorations, under a directive issued by the Reich Ministry of the Interior.[9] Poles were also forbidden to wear complete or partial German traditional costume (*Tracht*).[10] Although violations of the prohibition on the wearing of badges or decorations carried severe penalties, it is clear that these regulations were not always observed by the Poles.[11]

The mandatory Hitler-*Gruss* and the humiliating prohibitions ordered as

"disciplinary" measures by local head administrators in the first weeks of occupation proved more severe than these measures.[12] Although such regulations
were not deemed necessary in Danzig–West Prussia and the administrative district of Kattowitz (Katowice) in the Eastern Territories (although the Party leadership in Upper Silesia was convinced that the compulsory Hitler-*Gruss* had
been introduced for Poles),[13] the measures implemented at the local level in the
"model district" of the Wartheland were centralized and extended. As early as
November 1939, the HSSPF (higher SS and police leader) in Posen (Poznań) issued a directive that all male Poles should greet all German officials with the
Hitler-*Gruss* and that they must step aside if the sidewalks were "congested,"[14] a
directive that was to be enforced by all available means, including the imposition of forced labor on "recalcitrant" Poles.[15] Of course the local population did
not obey such an absurd directive, or at least not to the extent desired by its author.[16] Thus, despite the numerous exhortations from above to take a hard line,
the compulsory Hitler-*Gruss* was not administered very consistently in the Wartheland *Gau*. In some instances it was imposed by force, and in others it was not
practiced at all, because the Germans did not identify themselves by badges.[17]
There were also rural *Kreis* authorities who attached no importance to the compulsory Hitler-*Gruss;* they dispensed with it or simply did not introduce it in the
first place.[18] In contrast, there were authorities (in the railways and streetcars)
who actually demanded that Poles use military salutes. Ultimately, even the German security authorities in the Warthegau realized that although dispensing
with the compulsory Hitler-*Gruss* would be "further evidence of German weakness," the impossibility of enforcing the Hitler-*Gruss* consistently was damaging
the "prestige of the German nation, and in particular of the police." Therefore
they advocated its general abolition,[19] which, they stipulated, should not be implemented explicitly but merely by a tacit nonapplication. In turn, this experience induced the Party Chancellery and the SIPO to withdraw plans for the proposed introduction of a general compulsory Hitler-*Gruss* to Germans in uniform
in *all* annexed and occupied territories.[20]

Among the segregation measures was the practice of omitting the social title
Mr. in official correspondence with Poles,[21] the numerous measures to Germanize place names,[22] and the suppression of Polish terms and the Polish language
from public life as the language of the vanquished.[23] Extremist ethnic politicians
would have preferred to see the Polish language totally repressed and banned.[24]
Because this was impossible, bilingualism was introduced to the public sector
and hailed as a sign of "German superiority in the East."[25] The spread of the German language among those members of the (local) population of German origin who still could not speak German was encouraged by every means possible.[26]

The NSDAP *Gauleitung* Wartheland announced in December 1943 that all Germans in the Wartheland, including Poles of German origin recognized as capable of Germanization (*eindeutschungsfähig*) by entry of their names in the German Ethnic Classification List (*Deutsche Volksliste*) were required to learn German; if this did not occur voluntarily, pressure should be applied by threatening to revoke the German citizenship acquired by virtue of entry in the German Ethnic Classification List or by cancellation of the entry and the return of the resettlers to the Altreich ("forced repatriation").[27] Furthermore, it was the will of the leadership that "popular sentiment" as such would prevent any contact with the Polish neighbors. Leaflets, appeals, and posters continually urged vigilance, the maintaining of "distance from the Poles," who were the "eternal enemies."[28] Numerous articles and views published on the "Polish issue" advocated very radical measures far exceeding those actually implemented.[29] In contrast to the General Government, where a late change of course was attempted from 1943 on, the policy of segregation as such was maintained until the end of the war,[30] although a more lenient line was taken in Danzig–West Prussia and Upper Silesia than in the radically anti-Polish Warthegau and Zichenau administrative districts.

To clarify the full extent of the policy of segregation and discrimination, a number of regulations are described in detail below. These originate mostly from the *Reichsgau* Wartheland, officially termed the "model district" of the East because there the strictest ethnic segregation prevailed, the "non-German" population living as if in a large prison and completely isolated from the outside world. In this district, where all ethnic policy measures were agreed in minute detail between Party and administrative leadership, the decree issued by the *Reichsstatthalter* on September 25, 1940,[31] prevailed, in which the "principles of the coexistence" of Germans and Poles were specified; because it was impossible to implement fully the principle of total segregation because of the general housing shortage and the workplace conditions, the decree stipulated that contact with Poles should be limited to the minimum required for official or economic purposes. It warned against "repeated friendly contact" with Poles; in the event of sexual relations between German women and Polish men, the German partner was sent to a concentration camp; in the reverse case, the Polish woman was threatened with committal to a brothel. These measures, far exceeding the sanctions imposed by the Blood Protection Law, which punished only the man involved, were no empty threats but indeed were rigorously implemented.[32] Later on, as in the territory of the Reich, the Gestapo officially introduced the right of "first intervention" (by a decree of the RSHA) in all cases of sexual relations between Germans and Poles, including by circumventing the judicial system.[33] Corresponding, sometimes even more stringent instructions on the "absolute segregation" of Germans and Poles were issued to the administrative authorities, police authorities, and party offices.[34]

These examples alone show that especially in the Warthegau, the principle of ethnic segregation was extremely successful. Meticulously drafted police decrees and directions covering other areas also swamped the authorities. The National Socialist leadership had its eye especially on public socializing, as the uncontrolled opportunities this allowed for forming acquaintances and exchanging opinions were in any case particularly objectionable to the advocates of the "racial struggle," and they put their heart into this with their usual systematic approach. From mid-1940 on, all inns and restaurants in the Warthegau were divided into those for Germans and those for Poles, "to prevent an excessive mingling of the races."[35] German inns were identified as such and bore a special sign "Access for Poles prohibited."[36] The radical nature of these directives is a good example of the pigheadedness[37] with which the special regulations were railroaded through without any regard for reality—and the measures failed to achieve the desired results. Although Poles were prohibited from visiting German inns, Germans (with the exception of members of the Party or its divisions and affiliated associations) were essentially not forbidden to enter Polish inns,[38] a freedom exploited above all by members of the Wehrmacht; furthermore, the segregation resulted in considerable financial losses for the German inns because their Polish customers were absent.[39]

Another instance of the zealous special regulations of the authorities concerns the numerous police curfews and closing times for Poles and Jews[40] as well as the ban on Poles' buying spirits.[41] The policy of segregation also produced such exaggerations as the prohibitions on cinema performances for Poles on Saturdays and Sundays,[42] the ban on the showing of German fairy-tale films for Polish children ("The conveying of German sentimental values . . . appears . . . fundamentally questionable"),[43] the banning of Polish kindergartens,[44] the segregation of Germans and Poles during fire-fighting training and during ambulance transport,[45] and the closure of public baths to Poles.[46]

However, the policy of segregation had a serious impact not only in terms of ethnic policy and psychological effects but also when it came to administrative organization. One example is that of municipal law, which highlights particularly clearly the intentions of the regime as regards the segregation of Germans and "non-Germans."

After the occupation of Poland, Polish municipal constitutional law had been partially suspended,[47] but some elements remained in force—mostly for practical reasons—resulting in an inconsistent legal situation.[48] Despite this, the December 21, 1939, Decree on the Adoption of the German Municipal Code

(*Deutsche Gemeindeordnung*) in the Annexed Eastern Territories directly implemented German municipal law in the urban boroughs (*Stadtkreise*) only,[49]
whereas the law of the German Municipal Code could be granted to other municipalities by special decree of the *Reichsstatthalter* if the "ethnic policy conditions" existed, that is, if there was a "sufficient proportion of Germans" in the
population.[50] Until this occurred, the municipalities were administered by German municipal commissioners with the same function as local mayors.[51] German municipal law was not therefore introduced at once, which would have
corresponded to a policy of rapid Germanization, but rather decided from case
to case as a reward for a process of Germanization already completed.[52] In less
euphemistic terms, it was granted only after the completion of resettlement and
political "reallocation of land."[53] Opinions in the Annexed Eastern Territories
about exactly when a "sufficient proportion of Germans" had been reached in a
municipality, however, differed substantially.

As late as fall 1940, an inquiry by the Reich Ministry of the Interior as to
which municipalities had been granted the right to use the German Municipal
Code produced a near-zero return.[54] Only in Silesia, which had made strenuous
efforts to achieve Germanization, was the procedure more lenient, with the right
to use the German Municipal Code being granted at an early stage (1940) to
many municipalities, even where the proportion of Germans was low,[55] in order
to stimulate the settlement of Germans. The procedure in the Zichenau administrative district was also relatively flexible.[56] In Danzig–West Prussia, a minimum of 15 percent German population, where known, was required for the
granting of the German Municipal Code,[57] whereas in the Wartheland the "benefits" of German municipal law were reserved for the urban municipalities.[58]

For the "non-German" population, the special status of the "German" municipalities as a symbol of the integration of the municipality into the German
legal system entailed substantial discrimination. Local self-government was
abolished in favor of the Führer principle, and the Party was accorded farreach-
ing rights of participation,[59] leading to a form of "secondary administration" by
the NSDAP.[60] The only residents of the municipality with active and passive voting rights were Reich citizens and ethnic Germans, at least twenty-five years of
age, who had resided for a minimum of one year in the municipality and who
enjoyed civic rights; the "non-Germans" were merely "inhabitants" without any
legal status.[61]

Those municipalities in which German municipal law did not apply were
administered by municipal or town commissioners with varying qualifications
and enjoying substantial powers, in accordance with general instructions issued
by the *Landräte*. The provisions of general law (e.g., police law) regarding the

powers of the mayor did not apply.[62] However, the municipal or town commissioners, although local policy authorities, did not have their own administration. The police remained under the control of the (staunchly National Socialist) *Landräte*.[63] The Polish village headmen of the rural municipalities, who under no circumstances were allowed to be called mayors (Bürgermeister), because this was a term under German law,[64] were employed as assistants to the municipal commissioners or replaced by ethnic Germans. However, pertinent reports show that this rule by municipal commissioners appears to have been more lenient in the treatment of "non-Germans" than administration under the German Municipal Code: a "loyal" chief administrative official could therefore allow "humane impulses," that is, take the needs of the Polish and Jewish inhabitants much more into consideration, whereas in a municipality under the German Municipal Code, with its strong links to the Party, this was more difficult or even impossible. As far as these local administrators were concerned, the introduction of the German Municipal Code was therefore viewed as undesirable.[65]

The private sphere did not remain untouched by the general policy of segregation. Because of the numerous family ties between Germans and Poles, the policy led to extreme directives, thus encouraging—as demanded by the political leadership—not only the isolation of the "non-Germans" but also the severing of *all* inhabitants of the Warthegau from events in the Reich, establishing a veil behind which the administrative policy, with its aim of separation from the Reich administration and ruthless ethnic policies could proceed with as little outside attention as possible. At the request of especially the Party, visits to the Warthegau from outside were to be discouraged, especially during the late war years, to avoid any "undersirable contacts," and visits by Reich Germans to Polish relatives were to be prevented "wherever possible.[66] To force the departure of such undesirable visitors, the district president of Posen proposed exclusion orders by the Gestapo.[67] The *Landrat* of Schrimm simply banned such visits.[68] Of course, these administrative measures were not able to eliminate altogether the numerous family ties existing between Poles and Germans. Instead of a cautious, flexible policy of adaptation, the ethnic segregation policy was pursued stubbornly and systematically, producing far-reaching and cruel results. This is particularly evident from the treatment of illegitimate German-Polish children.

Because there were numerous contacts between Germans and Polish women producing illegitimate children (around two thousand by 1944) despite all the bans, state and Party agencies endeavored to implement a segregation of these children as well into ethnically "undesirable" and "desirable" (i.e., suitable for Germanization) children. If the Polish mothers were considered acceptable in terms of National Socialist ethnic policy, they could keep the children. But if the mothers proved to be "not desirable," the children were taken away from them. With no decision forthcoming from the RFSS/RKF (*Reichsführer*-SS and Reich Commissar for the Strengthening of German Nationhood), the Posen *Gau* Youth Welfare and *Gau* Social Welfare Offices suggested subjecting these "50 percent children" first to an "ethnic examination by the Racial and Settlement Office of the SS," which if positive, would result in the children's being sent initially to foster homes in the Wartheland and later to German foster parents in the Altreich.[69] The arrangement finally decided by the office of the Posen *Reichsstatthalter* envisaged the following graduated scheme: transfer of unmarried Polish mothers "suitable for Germanization" to the Altreich together with their children; ethnic examination of the remaining children, with "culling" of those "totally undesirable . . . for the German people"; gradual transfer of the remaining children classified as "desirable" to the *Gau* children's home in Kalisch (Kalisz) and thence to the Altreich, to avoid the removal of the children from their mothers, "principally due to the very adverse effect on the Poles."[70]

B. The Manifestations of Special Measures: Exceptional Regulations on the Basis of the General Law or Overt Special Legislation? (The Struggle over the Adoption of the Prussian Law of Police Administration)

The enactment of special legislative measures saw the political leadership facing the same question as before with the anti-Jewish laws in the Reich: should the appearance of nondiscrimination be maintained superficially and treatment under special legislation be implemented via special clauses, or could overt special legislation be adopted from the outset? Whereas the former path was chosen in the Altreich until 1938 for domestic and foreign political reasons (anti-Jewish laws in the form of general laws with special provisions, e.g., the Professional Civil Service Code), this approach was neither possible nor appropriate in the Eastern Territories. Nevertheless, it was understood that the technique of special legislation within the realm of general law could be implemented in the face of the vast majority of the local population only if the German element of the population was "fully oriented toward ethnic policies,"[1] that is, was convinced of the need for the repression of the Poles and the Jews and would be able to ensure that the special legislation could be strictly applied; as many ethnically aware authorities bemoaned, this was certainly not the case. However, this principle of special legislation was also superfluous because no foreign policy considerations prohibited "calling a spade a spade"—openly announcing the repression of the

Poles and the Jews as the objective of the policy. Furthermore, such consideration was viewed not only as no longer necessary but also as virtually a sign of weakness;[2] therefore, there was much pressure for the enactment of *overt* special legislation or administrative regulations as the only possible way, as had been pursued in the territory of the Altreich only with the adoption of overt anti-Jewish legislation from 1938.

This explains why German law was not adopted, or was adopted [*uno actu*] only from case to case,[3] although this method ran directly counter to the planned Germanization. The Reich Ministry of the Interior alleged that the new administrative structure was "not up to the global adoption of law" and neither was the general adoption of law appropriate "for reasons of population policy,"[4] arguments that barely concealed the true motive, the exclusion of the local population from the community of rights. The fields not affected by the adoption of law were correspondingly covered by overt special legislation in individual areas for Poles or Jews (the plan, cited above, for a comprehensive settlement of the legal situation of the Poles was never realized)[5] or—which was more often the case—remained completely unregulated and therefore had to be covered laboriously by the corresponding application of German law or acts of individual discretion (the application of "dubious principles"), which resulted in innumerable complaints and much irritation among the German population.[6] In particular, one issue never clarified during the entire period of occupation was that of the actual status of the "non-Germans" under special legislation, since only a few areas were legislated, the others being governed by internal guidelines.

The best example of the disputes surrounding the adoption of German law is provided by the struggle over the adoption of the Prussian Law of Police Administration in the Annexed Eastern Territories. This episode displays to the full the conflict between the traditional police authorities (Reich administration) and the revolutionary principles of the new *Partikulargewalten* (regional powers, e.g., *Reichsgaue*) in the Eastern Territories;[7] it was not only a struggle about authority but also a fundamental conflict about whether legal criteria or those of police policy should apply to the "non-Germans."

The initial position was that there were sufficient opportunities in legal terms to adopt Reich police law, as section 8 of the Decree of the Führer and Reich Chancellor on the Organization and Administration of the Eastern Territories, issued on October 8, 1939, entitled the Reich minister of the interior to adopt Reich law and Prussian state law by decree, in consultation with the Reich minister responsible, and also authorized him to issue all implementing and supplementary regulations.[8] The primacy of Reich law was ultimately reinforced, as the Reich minister of the interior explained to the *Reichsstatthalter* of

Danzing—West Prussia in a letter dated October 7, 1941, by the fact that the police regulations issued by the Reich minister on the basis of the Reich Police
Decree of November 14, 1938, automatically applied to the Annexed Eastern Territories as well.[9]

However, these decrees of the Reich minister concerned only peripheral areas. From the outset, political developments tended to concentrate the powers of
police law in the new *Partikulargewalten*.

As regards formal police law, the power of the administrative authorities in
the Eastern Territories to issue police regulations was not explicitly governed
anywhere, but it was tacitly claimed by the *Reichsstatthalter* on the basis of their
comprehensive jurisdiction for the administration;[10] district presidents and
Landrat offices also derived their powers to issue police regulations without any
formal basis in law, on the basis of the Prussian Law of Police Administration or
the Annexation Decree of October 8, 1939,[11] because there was a need for "more
rapid decisions, free from bureaucratic restraints."[12] In contrast, the municipal
commissioners, despite being local police authorities, were denied such a power
to issue police regulations for political reasons, counter to section 28 of the
Prussian Law of Police Administration.[13] However, the rural districts (*Landräte*)
and the district presidents played a significant role only early on and were subsequently limited to subordinate matters. The central authorities (*Reichsstatthalter*), who made every effort to gather as many powers as possible, were of much
greater importance. One example of this was the power, not customary under
Reich law, in force in the Wartheland to reserve approval of key police regulations, in particular of all police regulations concerning the treatment of Poles
and Jews. The formal justification used by the Posen (Poznań) *Reichsstatthalter*
was the argument that such regulations were of a fundamental nature requiring
harmonization throughout the entire *Gau*.[14]

In contrast, the organization of substantive police law hinged crucially on
the question of whether the police law in force in the Reich should also be observed in the Annexed Eastern Territories. An affirmative answer still meant
that there were certain limitations on police encroachment into the personal
sphere of "non-German" persons, as police law did not distinguish by race or
nationality in this respect. Rejection of the validity of the principles of Reich
police law meant that "non-German" inhabitants were ultimately deprived of
the principle of legitimacy of the administration, that is, the application of the
rule of law, and subject only to the political principles of police law enshrined in
the "racial struggle."

In concrete terms, the issue was whether the Prussian Law of Police Administration of 1931, in any case in force as state law in the territories incorporated

into the provinces of East Prussia and Silesia (the administrative districts of Zichenau and Kattowitz [Katowice]), should also be adopted in Danzing–West Prussia and the Warthegau. Both the Reich administration and the administrative authorities of the *Gaue* in question forcefully urged the adoption of the Prussian Law of Police Administration for reasons of law and order.[15] However, the Reich Ministry of the Interior was typically unwilling to assert itself against the new *Partikulargewalten* of the *Reichsstatthalter* (although it could have adopted the Prussian Law of Police Administration by simple decree on the basis of the Führer decree of October 8, 1939, cited above),[16] since the *Reichsstatthalter* rejected any commitment to Reich law, above all as regards its application to "non-Germans."

The issue was not so much the formal provisions of the Prussian Law of Police Administration regarding the authority to issue police regulations and police orders, which, as mentioned before, had a similar effect. Rather, it was whether the *substantive* provisions and principles of the Prussian Law of Police Administration (the principles of legitimacy of the administration, of the commensurability and necessity of instruments, of police coercion, of legal remedies against police orders, etc.), that is, whether the normative liability of police powers should also apply for the "non-German" population. The greatest resistance to such a direct adoption of the Prussian Law of Police Administration came from the Posen *Reichsstatthalter,* who saw his legislative authority to issue decrees (but only with the consent of the Reich ministers involved and the minister of the interior) affected and jealously insisted on his autonomy. For this reason, Greiser viewed rule by decree as adequate. However, after the Reich authorities had raised doubts about this procedure, he ultimately declared his willingness to accept the adoption of the Prussian Law of Police Administration through a decree, to be issued not by the Reich Ministry of the Interior but by himself.[17] But the corresponding draft decree contained only the jurisdictional provisions of the Prussian Law of Police Administration and left all substantive police law to be regulated through administrative channels by the *Reichsstatthalter.*[18]

None of the agencies involved was satisfied with the Posen draft. The Reich Ministry of the Interior opposed it because Greiser had no intention of complying with its request for the adoption of the police law issued for the Sudetengau (or Sudetenland) after consultation with the *Reichsstatthalter* for Danzig–West Prussia,[19] where no great importance was attached to this issue and police regulations were issued "as required as sovereign administrative decisions,"[20] ignoring formal legal principles. And of course the Reich Security Main Office (RSHA), which had received the draft six months earlier than the Reich Ministry of the Interior,[21] had objected sharply to the draft but for conflicting reasons. The aim of the policy of "police law replacement" pursued by the RSHA, termed as such in a letter to the Posen *Reichsstatthalter* dated October 18, 1941, was the elimination of the Prussian Law of Police Administration, because it was claimed that this did not do justice to the new police concept. The Posen draft represented "a certain legitimation of the Prussian Law of Police Administration by National Socialism" because it aimed at creating "a definitive situation." The RSHA was completely opposed to a new Law of Police Administration and deemed the *temporary* adoption of the Prussian Law of Police Administration in the Warthegau by a special decree as more than sufficient. "The emphasis on the temporary nature of this measure would avoid the edict" being capable of being "regarded as a legislative policy decision in favor of the Prussian Law of Police Administration,"[22] proposals that demonstrated that the police leadership under no circumstances intended to be bound to the constitutional principles of the Prussian Law of Police Administration. The police leadership was also supported by the deputy Führer and the NSDAP *Gau* leadership in the Wartheland, which had become seriously involved in the negotiations on Greiser's draft decree.[23] These agencies were completely opposed to the *general* adoption of the provisions of *Reich* law. If any dependence whatsoever upon Reich law proved to be necessary, the Prussian Law of Police Administration was to be formally adopted, but the *Reichsstatthalter* would be authorized to suspend certain provisions of importance to ethnic policy at his own discretion.

The Reich Ministry of the Interior was unwilling to stand up to the combined pressure of the political powers involved. The draft issued by the Posen *Reichsstatthalter*, who up until now had not given way an inch and had only with some difficulty been prevented by Berlin Party headquarters from proceeding with the issue of decrees without proper authority,[24] was dropped; instead, the Reich Ministry of the Interior took the bull by the horns, so as to preserve at least the principle of uniform regulation, and sent its own draft decree "with utmost respect" to the *Reichsstatthalter* (and district presidents) of the Eastern Territories on December 4, 1941, requesting a reaction as quickly as possible;[25] this draft incorporated almost every wish of the *Reichsführer*-SS and the Party leadership.

The draft envisaged the complete adoption of the Prussian Law of Police Administration in the Annexed Eastern Territories, subject to the provision of exemptions in the adoption decree. These exemptions, however, were quite extensive. For instance, appeals before an administrative court against a ruling refusing an appeal, against a police order by a district president under section 49 of the Prussian Law of Police Administration, and against the enforcement of an coercive act under section 57 of the Prussian Law of Police Administration were declared generally inadmissible, as was a petition for a court ruling against police penal orders under section 413 of the Code of Criminal Procedure. In addition, *all* legal remedies against police orders in security matters and against the enforcement of a coercive act were excluded. Furthermore—to open the floodgates for special legislation provisions—the *Reichsstatthalter* and the district presidents were empowered, with the consent of the Reich minister of the interior, to revoke the adoption of other regulations of the Prussian Law of Police Administration in the Annexed Eastern Territories, or adopt them only after a certain date, or to declare individual provisions applicable to certain ethnic groups only. Finally, there was also a proviso governed by the demands of ethnic policy that provisions of the Prussian Law of Police Administration "that cannot or can no longer be applied because of their wording . . . should be applied mutatis mutandis."

Reichsstatthalter Greiser had no objections to the adoption of the Prussian Law of Police Administration in this form; as regards the "non-Germans," however, he resisted the authorization to make regulations for individual ethnic groups by statutory provisions; the reason for this was that Greiser intended to exclude the Poles *arbitrarily* (e.g., by decree) from the German legal system and to exclude them from *all* legal remedies against police (penal) orders, well exceeding the remit of the draft. However, establishing this overtly did not (yet) seem feasible. Using the standard cover-up tactic, Greiser proposed that all police measures against Poles should simply be assigned to the province of the SIPO (the Gestapo), since its actions could not be challenged in any case. Specifically, he suggested that he should decide on the basis of an implementing decree to the adoption decree that police penal orders against Poles should, in principle, fall within the purview of the Security Police, "as in such cases, even if they were matters of a regular police nature, security policy aspects would always have priority." The integration of this structure into the interpretation of the adoption decree would thus disbar the Poles from *all* legal remedies against police action.[26]

The Reich Ministry of the Interior understood only too well that this would undermine the entire system of police administrative law as well as the system of legal remedies and withheld its consent. Greiser sought to no avail to convince Party headquarters in a detailed letter dated January 14, 1942, that the "treatment of the Poles" demanded "special regulations." Granting the Poles a right of appeal was "totally unacceptable." In particular the issue of legal remedies, but also that of the enforcement of coercive acts, should "be assessed not only from a police point of view but first and foremost from the position of the racial struggle." The Prussian Law of Police Administration did not meet these requirements at all; the authorities should not be bound by "restrictive provisions," because "more drastic instruments" were needed for the "strict segregation of the Germans from alien races."[27]

Negotiations still remained bogged down because the Posen *Reichsstatthalter* and the Security Police stuck to their position as described above and the Reich Ministry of the Interior did not give in.[28] Finally, Greiser stated quite plainly that he was no longer particularly interested in any centralized regulation of the issue, because he had in any case created a fait accompli even before the submission of the draft by the Reich Ministry of the Interior on December 4, 1941. In an urgent dispatch to the HSSPF (higher SS and police leader) in Posen dated December 10, 1941, he reported the implementation of his long-advocated intention: in the attached circular decree dated August 23, 1941, he had ordered the exclusion of Poles from *all forms* of legal remedies against police orders (i.e., also against orders issued by the regular police) as well as the abolition of all restrictions imposed on the enforcement of police coercive acts—allowing for forced labor instead of coercive detention—and was not disposed to cancel these (usurped) powers.[29] The Reich Ministry of the Interior was not willing to grant its consent under any circumstances to a general exclusion of legal remedies against orders issued by the Security Police and the exclusion of Poles from legal remedies against all police actions—especially not by the issue of a circular decree—this less because of any aspects of equality before the law for Germans and Poles than because any form of *Partikularrecht* (legislation by regional powers) ran counter to the plans for uniform legislation that the Reich Ministry of the Interior had been preparing for some time.

The uniform legislation proposed by the Reich Ministry of the Interior consisted of a reorganization of the entire administrative penal law for the Reich, to be implemented above all at the urging of the Security Police (the Gestapo) with the aim of extending still further the scope of police discretion not subject to review by the courts, that is, the latitude of the Gestapo to operate outside the law. Under the reorganization plans, all "nonjudicial violations" were to be punished by police penal orders, for which there would be recourse in the courts.[30] This is a further example of the phenomenon of Nazi legislative policy, already described, by which the special legislative measures against "non-Germans" were frequently only the beginning of wide-ranging plans to discriminate against the German population as well, or to remove them completely from the scope of the law. However, the corresponding draft decree of the Reich Ministry of the Interior was not adopted because of the difficulties and power struggles associated with such a comprehensive reorganization.[31] This ultimately resulted in victory for those forces representing *Partikularrecht*.

After being totally outplayed by the political authorities all along, the Reich

Ministry of the Interior subsequently retreated in the question of the adoption of the Prussian Law of Police Administration in the Eastern Territories and in February 1943 elaborated another draft decree but without submitting its own opinion (the clearest possible indication of its defeat), which took full account of the endeavors of the posen *Reichsstatthalter,* the police leadership, and the Party leadership to achieve special legislation and declared the Prussian Law of Police Administration applicable to Germans only.[32] This very brief draft, which envisaged the complete exclusion of legal remedies against all action by the Security Police (which consisted of the Gestapo and the *Kriminalpolizei* [the criminal police, as distinct from the political police (Gestapo)]) not only for Poles but also for Germans (something that had not been achieved in the Reich itself), was of course rejected by the Posen *Reichsstatthalter,* whose stance had been increasingly hardening with time. The NSDAP in the Wartheland also opposed the draft, but for other reasons. As it stated in a letter to the *Reichsstatthalter* on March 25, 1943, it believed that the draft was too far-reaching, because the exclusion of all legal remedies, particularly against the heavy actions of the Gestapo and the *Kriminalpolizei,* aroused a feeling of lawlessness in those affected and exposed them to the arbitrary despotism of the police, about which the Party, too, had no illusions.[33]

However, the situation had long since surpassed the need for centralized legislation of police law. The Reich Ministry of the Interior draft was not adopted. Posen continued to act independently after effectively sabotaging the adoption of the Prussian Law of Police Administration for good. In a further decree on March 22, 1943, Greiser issued precise instructions about the external form and specification of the means to enforce coercive acts in police regulations,[34] but he reserved internal guidelines for the application of the substantive provisions of the Prussian Law of Police Administration.[35] Not unnaturally, such guidelines were never issued, as the *Reichsstatthalter* did not even wish to commit himself within his own administration; at any rate, practical implementation implicitly understood that the Prussian Law of Police Administration was substantively applied "analogously" (i.e., with the right of derogation at any time). This principle applied in particular as regards the treatment of "non-Germans." Substantive police law in the Annexed Eastern Territories thus had no formal basis in either statutory or administrative provisions; as in every totalitarian regime, this legal uncertainty created the best breeding ground for special measures of every kind, which could now be enacted without being bound to any legislation or indeed to any form of regulations.

The imposition of coercive measures against Poles and Jews was therefore regulated without any basis in law, in contrast to the Prussian Law of Police Administration. On the basis of the original circular decree by the *Reichsstatthalter* on August 23, 1941,[36] administrative fines and coercive detention of unlimited amounts and duration could be imposed on Poles (sec. 55, Prussian Law of Police Administration, specified a maximum fine of RM 150 or a maximum detention of three weeks); the imposition of forced labor by police order was also permitted. The decree further ordered that action taken against Poles should be more severe than that against Germans, in particular in cases of violation of "ethnic principles," which included such serious crimes as the use of a railway compartment designated for Germans only. A circular decree by the *Reichsführer,*-SS and chief of the German police dated June 15, 1942,[37] had introduced the new penalties against Poles (and Jews) of prison camp (three to six months) and administrative fines of RM 3 to RM 10,000, which could also be imposed by police orders,[38] but the decree was ignored by the Posen *Reichsstatthalter,* who opposed any form of centralized regulatory scheme, regardless of its author; of course he had to issue his own scheme, which was incorporated into his own circulatory decree of March 22, 1943,[39] but which contained nothing new of any substance. It stated that police regulations applying to all inhabitants of the Eastern Territories should threaten the standard penalties of the Prussian Law of Police Administration (an administrative fine of up to RM 150, with up to three weeks coercive detention in the event of nonpayment); police regulations applying only to Poles and Jews, however, should threaten prison camp and financial penalties up to RM 10,000. As part of the same policy, Poles and Jews were illegally prohibited from filing appeals of any kind against police orders, as mentioned before.[40] The police ideal of total subjugation of the "non-Germans" was thus achieved, at least in the Warthegau (or Wartheland).

In line with the lack of any legal basis, substantive police law was also subjected to fundamental reorganization. The principles of legitimacy, necessity, and commensurability disappeared, replaced by lynch law based on the principles of the "racial struggle," subjugation at any price. The lack of any substantive basis was the reason why police intervention powers were extended infinitely and rules were made that customary principles would have deemed inadmissible, such as the aforementioned regulations about the obligation of Poles to salute Germans with the Hitler-*Gruss* or the prohibition on contacts between Germans and the local population, which were regarded as totally inadmissible under "ethnic policy."

The bulk of the special legislative restrictions for "non-Germans" discussed below were also based on the excessive expansion of police powers. These restrictions related to economic, cultural, constitutional, and labor discrimination and show that these police powers were first implemented comprehensively in the Eastern Territories.

The regulations cited below, principally from the Warthegau, originate from all areas of public administration, since—in contrast to the Reich— the *Reichsstatthalter* (district president), including the special administration offices, explicitly enjoyed jurisdiction in all matters in the Annexed Eastern Territories.[41]

C. Special Topics

I. The Social, Political, and Cultural Sector

1. The Transformation of State Pension Payments into "Welfare Subsidies"

The first example of special legislative regulations relates to social welfare measures, such as the freeze on state pension benefits and the exclusion of Poles from social security, accident and life insurance, and other benefits. According to comments by the office of the Posen (Poznań) *Reichsstatthalter,* the idea of making the Poles better off than before by granting them social security, benefits was "completely incomprehensible." The most important aspect of the "policy toward Non-Germans" was its "consistency." "Gradually backing off" would result in a drop in the labor performance of the Poles. And the granting of life insurance benefits to the Poles would not be "at all" in the interests of Germany, because of associated ethnic policy risks. In the event of a claim against such a policy, the family of the insured person would gain a certain amount of capital "without labor and effort." The same applied to accident insurance, which would only give the Poles the opportunity to collect benefits on the basis of high contributions and then escape compulsory labor.[1] Included in these measures was the elimination of old-age pensions and the reduction of welfare payments to an absolute minimum, since "the only interest in the Polish population was in the working elements"; those persons used as "slave laborers," as it were, should be "sufficiently paid"[2] in the form of "subsistence" sui generis but excluded from the benefits of the Reich Social Security Insurance Code (RVO); on retirement, however, they should in principle receive no retirement pay or pensions, at best welfare subsidies without any legal entitlement (with the exception of wardisabled Poles who had been wounded while fighting on the German or Austrian side between 1914 and 1918, because the Reich was not the legal successor to the Polish State).[3]

2. The Prohibition of Political and Church Activities

There should be no further need to explain that the public life of the "non-Germans" came to a complete standstill. As a matter of course, Polish newspapers,[4] gatherings, associations,[5] and all demonstrations were prohibited in the Annexed Eastern Territories from the outset; the prohibition also applied to larger funerals, which were regarded as demonstrations of Polish national sentiment.[6] For the same reason, local authorities banned priests from appearing in their robes of office.[7] The Catholic Church was in any case the target of the anger of the new rulers, who saw it as the bearer of Polish nationalism, and it was completely excluded. This has already been described at length elsewhere,[8] so extensive details are unnecessary here. Suffice it to say that the basis for the ruthless segregation and persecution of the Catholic Church in the Annexed Eastern Territories, where each *Reichsstatthalter* acted at his own discretion, was the fact that the concordat of July 20, 1933, between the Reich and the Vatican,[9] which guaranteed the Catholic Church freedom of religions, the status of a public corporation, the right of self-administration, the right to raise taxes, the preservation of its vested rights, and so forth, was *not* applied, although the status of the Eastern Territories as an integral part of the German Reich would have demanded the application of the concordat. As he stated quite unmistakably in nonpublic comments, Hitler unilaterally decided that the concordat was no more than a continuation of the concordats of the individual German *Länder* and had "actually become void" on their merger with the Reich, a legally untenable construction, since the concordat contained no provision for termination, stipulating an amicable settlement in the event of differences of opinion. The concordat certainly did not apply in the new *Reichsgau* districts, according to Hitler; church matters there were the "exclusive business" of the *Reichsstatthalter*.[10] On analysis of these unequivocal statements by Hitler, it can be regarded as a proven fact that he intended in any case to terminate the concordat unilaterally after the war[11] and replace it by the fragmentation of the Church ("regional arrangements") and the removal of all state subsidies.[12] The entire policy of church persecution in the Eastern Territories demonstrates the high degree of consistency of National Socialist policy goals and administrative practice: this region experienced the effects of what was later to become the general rule in the territory of the Reich.

The fate intended for the Evangelical (Protestant) churches in the Annexed Eastern Territories was only slightly better, with a sharp division between German and "non-German" Christians and, as far as the German Christians were concerned, a wretched existence as private associations.

The measures were most extreme in the Warthegau, attracting considerable attention in the Reich itself.[13] As in the case of the Roman Catholic Church, the Polish Protestant churches lost their status as public corporations and were declared extinct; as their legal successors, private religious associations "of German nationality" were created,[14] for which special application to the police was necessary, reversing the general principle of rule and exception, with nonmembership in a church as the rule and joining a church requiring a special act. This curtailment of the status of the Protestant churches caused a great deal of resentment among the ethnic Germans and settlers.[15] The new Protestant church associations were, of course, closed to Poles, who were thus not members of any church establishment and whose services were illegal and no more than tolerated by the police. This was demonstrated publicly by the fact that some Protestant churches bore notices "Germans Only" or "Polish Church."[16]

3.   Discrimination in the Education of "Non-Germans"

The same arbitrary policies and confusion reigned in all other cultural areas. The principal objective was to destroy all areas of Polish culture by segregation and discrimination,[17] ranging from the exclusion of non-Aryan creative artists (by the introduction of the Law on Editors and the Reich Chamber of Culture Law)[18] to the repression of "non-German" elements in education and language to below the minimum expected of civilized nations. Because the government was in any case of the opinion as regards German nationals that (primary) school teachers should not be too "comprehensively" trained and that children should not "be force-fed with everything,"[19] these maxims applied all the more to education for "non-Germans." In line with the goal of reducing the local population to an army of unskilled laborers, the people were practically excluded not only from all forms of higher education but also from the most elementary basic education; all they received was a rudimentary primary school education (without history and geography) and modest technical training for the recruitment of skilled laborers.[20]

In consequence, the University of Posen and all tertiary, technical, and vocational colleges, as well as all public and private libraries[21] in the Annexed Eastern Territories were closed at the beginning of the war.[22] A decree by the Reich minister for education and science on June 17, 1940,[23] ordered a general compulsory school education for Polish children and the teaching of Polish by Polish teachers, but the decree was not enforced in the Warthegau and Zichenau administrative districts;[24] only in Upper Silesia, where the majority of Poles were admitted to the German Ethnic Classification List *(Deutsche Volksliste)*, did Polish teachers teach in Polish in packed classes.[25] In Danzig–West Prussia there were Polish primary schools, in which classes were to be held in German "whenever possible."[26] In contrast, measures were much stricter in the Warthegau as part of the process of Germanization.[27]

In the Warthegau, all Polish teachers were dismissed without notice;[28] lessons in Polish schools were subsequently taught by poorly trained[29] German auxiliary teachers,[30] for whom an abbreviated training was quite sufficient since the education provided was of no more than a rudimentary nature (barely two hours per day).[31] It may be assumed that the quality of the lessons was poor from the outset, because in the view of the National Socialists, the only purpose of education for "non-German children" was to teach them to be "orderly, clean, disciplined, [and] honest." As reported in a circular from the Posen district president responsible for these matters, only an elementary knowledge of arithmetic, writing and reading was necessary for this purpose; the teaching of history was superfluous; therefore, two to two and a half hours of class per day in two shifts were all that was necessary.[32] The language of teaching was German,[33] and though German had also been the main subject during the reign of the military administration,[34] the subsequent teaching of German, as shown by a syllabus issued by the Hohensalza (Inowrocław) district president, was restricted to ensuring "that verbal instructions at the workplace could be understood without particular difficulty"; "no effort should be wasted ... in attempting to teach error-free German."[35] "Subjects intended to train the soul and the mind" (e.g., music, history, etc.) as well as physical education were not taught; however, great store was set on so-called work practice (collecting medicinal herbs—according to the former Posen SS and police leader [SSPF], Wilhelm Koppe, this was due to a particular interest of Himmler—waste material, weed control, etc.).[36]

Furthermore, Polish children were required to attend school only between the ages of ten and fourteen,[37] that is, a maximum of five years. To sever the influence of "Polishness," no German child should attend a Polish school, and no Polish child a German school; there was strict class segregation, even as regards classrooms.[38] Because the schooling age of Polish children was not standardized[39] and the number of Polish schools was inadequate, an awkward situation arose because many Polish children did not attend school at all, so the authorities themselves urgently endorsed the opening of additional schools to avoid the risk of the "total neglect and degeneration of Polish children of school age."[40] Poles were also prevented from gaining craft qualifications; although they were employed as apprentices, they did not receive any diplomas, learned only the "necessary minimum," and were not permitted to attend vocational colleges.[41]

II. The Economic and Commercial Sector

The short-sighted planning that prevailed in the education system also ruled in the economic and commercial realm.[1] Although the equal treatment of "non-Germans" with safeguards for their vested interests would have been vital to stabilize the situation and bring these territories into line with the rest of the Reich, the Germanization of these territories was interpreted in the first instance as no more than the confiscation and expropriation of all Polish assets of any importance for the Reich; this systematically robbed the local population of its economic existence. The parallels to the anti-Jewish laws (which also applied to Jews from the Reich in the Annexed Eastern Territories)[2] in the treatment of the Poles are all too obvious, as the schematics of the anti-Jewish laws—seizure, appointment of trustees, sale of assets to private persons (Aryanization) or their transfer to public ownership—were an excellent model that could be used as a precedent in all the occupied territories in Eastern Europe. Outside the Reich, however, the system of state asset robbery was accompanied and frequently undermined by countless unauthorized seizures.

As early as the first weeks of the war, the Wehrmacht and the chiefs of the civil administration in Posen (Poznań), Danzig (Gdańsk), and Kattowitz (Katowice) had issued extensive orders to confiscate the assets of "non-Germans," in particular land,[3] backed up by confiscation regulations issued by the local administrative authorities, in particular as regards Jewish assets;[4] as in the Reich, the confiscation of Jewish property was described as the "safeguarding of Jewish assets."[5] At the same time, however, there was a regular rush by Wehrmacht, state, and Party agencies to acquire Polish and Jewish assets[6] (quite apart from efforts by private individuals to line their own pockets,[7] with everyone taking what they felt like, ignoring all existing regulations), which resulted in "practically every house" and "every floor" being "searched" for valuable assets;[8] it was even admitted officially that "in tens of thousands of cases," "nondesignated" and "unauthorized agencies" had interfered with Poles, had misappropriated assets in many cases or removed them to their offices, and that very large numbers of "countless everyday articles" had disappeared[9]—in defiance of a central directive from the plenipotentiary for the Four Year Plan (Göring) prohibiting all "unauthorized confiscation."[10] Only in 1940 was the situation brought more or less under control by the civil administration and dealt with consistently, but even this could not quite put an end to the unauthorized confiscations.[11]

Seizure by the occupying power principally involved Polish *state* assets, which were "put into safe custody" in their entirety, that is, confiscated and administered in the name of the Reich.[12] The confiscation of private Polish and Jewish assets followed a few months later. The relevant Decree on the Property of Persons of the Former Polish State, dated September 17, 1940,[13] (the so-called Polish Assets Decree) contained the fundamental regulations about the legal "special treatment" of assets, the objective of which was "to make the Eastern Territories annexed to the Reich into German land." Under this decree, all Jewish assets were confiscated and treated as the property of the Reich;[14] this therefore involved not restrictions on disposal but permanent *expropriation*, so that from this time on, the Jews were no longer legal entities in terms of asset and property law. This decree also provided for the confiscation of the total assets of Poles who had already fled or been deported, as well as of other "non-Germans" in the Eastern Territories,[15] with massive proceeds from their sale accruing to the Main Trustee Office East *(Haupttreuhandstelle Ost),* specially established for this purpose.[16] The assets of the Poles still to be deported also fell to the public purse.[17] Special directives were also issued for the legal treatment of the assets of Jews to be resettled or deported.[18]

Under the Polish Assets Decree (sec. 2, par. 2), the remaining assets of Poles resident in the Annexed Eastern Territories were also open to seizure if they involved the assets of persons who had immigrated after October 1, 1918, or if the assets were required "for the public good," that is, were claimed to meet the needs of the administration of German resettlers. On the basis of this decree, it is evident that all Polish businesses and enterprises were confiscated, as any "decision not to confiscate from a Pole . . . was essentially excluded."[19] Under section 2, paragraph 4, of this decree, movables needed for personal existence were "regularly" exempt from confiscation, such as cash, bank balances, and securities up to a total value of RM 1,000. In practice, however, *all* bank balances, custody accounts, and safe deposit boxes of Polish nationals were initially confiscated on the basis of corresponding decrees issued by the head of the Main Trustee Office East, and cash assets up to RM 1,000 were released only on application, without any legal entitlement, where these involved so-called old assets (deposits before January 1, 1940). Deposits after December 31, 1939, were not subject to confiscation, to encourage savings.[20]

Only Poles who had remained in the Annexed Eastern Territories could make use of this personal allowance for "old assets"; those Poles who had fled or had been deported ("more than temporarily absent") (including those of Jewish descent) as well as "Polish Jews still present" were not normally granted this personal allowance.

As far as Polish real estate was concerned, agricultural and forestry land not owned by Germans was confiscated, whether its owner was present or not, under the Decree on the Public Administration of Agricultural and Forestry Enterprises and Land in the Annexed Eastern Territories, dated February 12, 1940 (the so-called Eastern Land Decree),[21] and transferred to public administration by the organizations established by the Reich minister of food and agriculture for this purpose.[22]

German settlers were appointed as trustees to manage this land; they could purchase it outright from 1942 on.[23] German trustees,[24] again often resettlers with prospects for acquisition at a later date,[25] were appointed to manage the other confiscated real estate and the commercial, trading, and industrial enterprises from which the Polish and Jewish owners had been evicted. The organization of manufacturing industry in the Reich was introduced here as well.[26] The numerous Polish textile enterprises were either liquidated on the eviction of the local owners or converted into munitions and weapons factories, with the destruction of the original plants and equipment.[27] Business activity was also largely interrupted.

Further restrictions followed. Under a decree issued on January 21, 1940, all real estate transactions were prohibited until further notice, and the establishment of all enterprises[28] was subject to approval, with the aim of hindering the remaining Poles from all free economic activities and reducing them to a subordinate position in the economy and the administration. This created a situation very similar to that conceived by German Foreign Office drafts for treatment of natives in the future colonies.[29]

The confiscation of private and public Polish assets, initially also used to pay welfare subsidies to Poles and Jews,[30] in fact represented nothing other than collective expropriation on a massive scale. Attempts were made to conceal this fact publicly by closely linking the concept of "trust administration" with that of confiscation. As with the earlier confiscation of Jewish assets in the Reich,[31] the confiscated assets of the Poles were put under "trust" "administration," in an attempt to give the impression that this was a temporary state of affairs, that is, "administration" and not expropriation. However, the impression that it was temporary was belied from the outset by the fact that an unbelievably complicated administrative machinery (the Main Trustee Office East) was established to implement this administration, which worked closely[32] with the departments of the RFSS/RKF (*Reichsführer*-SS/Reich Commissar for the Strengthening of German Nationhood) and was quite evidently intended and organized as a permanent establishment.[33] This machinery, with its countless decrees and directives[34] and with its powers intermingling and overlapping with those of the general administrative authorities and of police and RKF[35] departments, led to a completely entangled chaos of powers and administration.[36] Furthermore, the standards applied by the Main Trustee Office East made it quite clear that there could be no talk of "trust administration." The task of this "trust administration" was, of course, to manage and employ the confiscated assets not in the interests of their owners but solely in the interests of the National Socialist economic and settlement policy ("confiscated Polish assets" shall be "employed in the interests of the Reich, i.e., the public at large").[37] The aim of the exploitation, that is, of the collective expropriation, was so self-evident that in part the confiscation regulations themselves, but in any case the administrative practices, automatically assumed the loss of title of the rightful owners.

The owners of confiscated land and assets were not merely restricted in their rights of disposal (e.g., a prohibition on disposal or an approval proviso); they lost all rights of disposal and administration in toto.[38] In the case of the confiscated Polish state assets, the Reich was registered in the land register as the owner of all rights to the real estate. The relevant decree explicitly mentioned the "incorporation" of the rights of the former Polish state into the assets of the Reich.[39]

Under the guidelines issued by the head of the Main Trustee Office East, it could undertake the "irreversible assignment of title" to confiscated assets; compensation was "subject to special regulations,"[40] but these were never issued.[41] The Main Trustee Office East Property Stock Corporation, a subsidiary of the Main Trustee Office East, was empowered to "exploit [sell]" confiscated residential properties, among other activities.[42] The Reich Financial Administration not only regarded Jewish assets as being at the disposal of the Reich; it put private Polish estates in the same category and confiscated them as well.[43]

The fact that although many agencies were authorized to issue confiscation orders, their implementation was exclusively a matter for the Security Police (Gestapo), which also undertook the collection of the confiscated assets at the "special request" of the Main Trustee Office East,[44] offered a certain "guarantee" that practical implementation was controlled by the concept of expropriation. When it came to real estate belonging to the Polish state, the state administration—in this instance the Main Trustee Office East—had in any case been forced to assign to Himmler, in his capacity as Reich Commissar for the Strengthening of German Nationhood, the most important sector for the "reorganization of the Eastern Territories," the administration of agricultural real estate. In a letter dated February 15, 1940,[45] Himmler informed the Reich minister of food and agriculture that the Main Trustee Office East had "delegated" these powers to him with Göring's approval, and he requested that these properties be administered not by the trust offices but by the Reich Estates Administration, part of the

Reich Ministry of Food, as he was evidently confident of greater influence over this agency than over the local trust offices.

III. Civil Service Law

In contrast to the situation in the education and economic sectors, which required complete reorganization, Civil Service law was familiar ground, and the segregation and special legislation concept could be put into practice using the proven model. As in the Altreich, all "non-German" career civil servants in the Annexed Eastern Territories, that is, all Polish civil servants (including Jews) were sacked immediately, and all pension entitlements were annulled;[1] unless these individuals were deported to the General Government, they were forced into subordinate positions in the labor market. Because not all of them could be replaced by ethnic Germans, they frequently found employment as auxiliary personnel (messengers, drivers, low-level office clerks) in the German administration, very much to the displeasure of the high-echelon administration, which feared a strengthening of Polish espionage activity and attempted to keep Poles out of the public sector by means of considerable underpayment.[2]

Even in later days, Polish employees, at least in the Warthegau (or Wartheland), could not be paid at a higher rate than Group 7 in the wage scale for employees; in principle, they were only allowed to be paid 80 percent of the salary earned by Germans "because of their poor performance"; if their performance was "above average," they received 90 percent, and only "very highly qualified performance" earned them 100 percent.[3]

To implement the principle of segregation, a large number of directives were issued to carry the "racial struggle" into the public service. In the Warthegau, for instance, all members of the public service were instructed to practice the greatest restraint in official and private talks with Poles;[4] under a decree issued by the Reich Ministry of the Interior on February 12, 1941,[5] they were even obliged to avoid all dealings with Poles whatsoever. Sexual relations between members of the public service and Poles resulted in immediate dismissal and the annulment of all pension rights. Family relations with Poles also incurred drastic consequences; identical decrees issued by the Reich Ministry of the Interior[6] and the Reich Ministry of Justice[7] in summer 1941 at the suggestion of the champion of the radical "racial struggle" against the Poles, the *Reichsstatthalter* of Posen (Poznań) (which decrees were probably followed by the other ministries),[8] stipulated that all career civil servants, salaried employees, and workers at the relevant Reich authorities who were "related by blood or marriage" to Poles (i.e., the so-called Protected Subject Status Poles) were not to be transferred to the Annexed Eastern Territories or the General Government "in the interests of Germanization." All employees transferred to the Annexed Eastern Territories were required to submit a declaration of nonkinship with Poles, in much the same way as all civil servants, both in the Reich and in the Eastern Territories, had to submit proof of non-Jewish descent. This also applied to all employees of the Reich domestic administration working in these territories; any employee unable to furnish such evidence was to be replaced immediately.[9] In the Warthegau this procedure was even applied to the employees of all ministries;[10] in the other Eastern Territories, such declarations were also frequently required to avoid conflicts of loyalty.[11]

IV. Professional and Labor Law

1.   Professions Requiring State Licensing (Lawyers and Physicians)

The principle of segregation and discrimination was also implemented without exception outside the public service. It was self-evident that Poles of Jewish descent who had not fallen victim to the special-duties groups of the SIPO and had not been deported disappeared from all professions and were commandeered for forced labor, mostly in the form of labor troops in closed camps under extreme conditions, to enforce their complete isolation, not only from the Germans but also from their complete isolation, not only from the Germans but also from their Polish surroundings.[1] Severe restrictions were also imposed upon the Poles, who, if they were not deported to the General Government, were removed from all higher or self-employed positions in industry and commerce and were used only as employed workers (sometimes as auxiliary labor in their own, confiscated business).[2] Polish physicians and lawyers were subjected to a strict licensing procedure and strict political verification; if this proved negative, they were struck off the register of their respective professions. If not, they were permitted to continue working (under political supervision). Like the Jews in the Reich, Polish lawyers lost their professional titles, were assigned merely a *konsulentenähnliche* position (similar to the position of Jewish lawyers; see part 1, section 1, V, 1a of this volume ["Attorneys and Related Professions"]), and were entitled only to be called *advocates*.[3] In addition, they could be prohibited from giving legal advice on the grounds of "unsuitability."[4] Of course, they were completely dependent upon political clients and were forbidden from advising potential German clients. A ban on representing German clients was such a foregone conclusion under ethnic policy that there was not even any need for explicit prohibitions.

2. Labor Law and Working Conditions

The vast majority of the population in the Annexed Eastern Territories was used as unskilled industrial and agricultural labor. The long-term goal of labor market policy, in particular in the *Reichsgau* Wartheland, was to leave only the "good" workers in the Eastern Territories and to deport the "bad" to the General Government;[5] during the war, however, all available workers were needed,[6] but a large number of discriminatory measures separated the "non-German" workers from the German employees.[7]

One of the segregation measures implemented to the point of absurdity was to ensure that Poles were never made the superiors (e.g., supervisors) of German employees;[8] the principle of allowing qualified training (an apprenticeship) for Poles only if no German workers were available, and then only to the minimum extent possible,[9] was also implemented without exception in the Warthegau.

The official maxim that any parallels between Germans and "non-German workers" were impossible, in particular that all legal rights for the latter must be denied,[10] applied especially to wage conditions, and here above all for the Jewish workers, who (at least in the Warthegau) received only a fraction of their wage entitlement: 35 percent, with 65 percent being paid into a special account. The authorities also reserved the right to modify these rates depending on work performance and the costs of upkeep.[11] Polish workers were also exposed to substantial discrimination. Although they formally enjoyed wage parity with German workers, in practice they had to suffer numerous restrictions and deductions, as described in the following summary.

In terms of special treatment under labor law, the Poles were basically in a worse position than German employees,[12] since the corresponding provisions of Reich law were also applied in the Annexed Eastern Territories. Polish employees were subject to the regulations of the Reich minster of labor issued on October 5, 1941, cited above, which assigned a "special status" to Polish workers in the Reich because it "would not be compatible with the healthy sentiment of the *Volk*" "if they were also to participate without restriction in the social progress of the new Germany." The consequence was that they were excluded from numerous regulations regarding bonuses and wage payments on public holidays.[13] Wages were therefore paid only for work actually performed. Unless stated otherwise in a statutory wage regulation, Poles were always to be paid the lowest rates; however, performance bonuses were not excluded. Public holiday bonuses, family or child allowances, statutory maternity benefits (maternity relief), and pension agreements were prohibited.[14] The general vacation ban in the

Reich for Polish workers did not apply in the Eastern Territories,[15] however, so Polish workers were entitled to vacation time. Only the provisions in the statutory wage regulations regarding increased vacation on the basis of longer service were excluded. The special status of Polish workers was rounded off by the fact that Polish youths were not covered by the Juvenile Protection Law but by the Working Hours Decree of April 30, 1938, and other regulations applicable to adults and that the statutory period of notice was reduced to a maximum of two weeks; regulations to the contrary did not apply to Poles. As described above, the special status corresponded almost exactly to the status of Jewish workers in the Altreich in this respect.

These regulations of the Reich minister of labor, which, though they contained a large variety of special directives for Poles, clung to the principle of equal wages for equal work (albeit in heavily watered-down form), did not fit in any way into the concept of "racial struggle" promoted by the high-handed administrative chiefs of the Annexed Eastern Territories. Thus, no uniform line was taken in the Eastern Territories; the political and labor conditions differed too much.

In Danzing–West Prussia, for instance, the principle of equal wages for equal work was mostly observed,[16] whereas in the annexed territories of Upper Silesia, Polish workers were evidently treated harshly by the labor offices[17] (none of "this humanitarian nonsense") and the aforementioned Reich labor law principles were deliberately torpedoed. The "model district" of the Wartheland followed a similar course; the office of the *Reichsstatthalter* there had already complained, even before these Reich labor law regulations had been issued, that the policy of equal wages and the lack of discrimination against Poles in the statutory wage regulations for individual occupational categories was quite wrong, because the Polish workers displayed poor discipline and performance (only around 40–60% of the performance of German workers) and deliberately worked slowly, a claim that was completely at odds with the experience in all other Eastern Territories.[18]

The principle of equal (net) wages for Germans and Poles in the October 5, 1941, directive of the Reich minister of labor correspondingly met the stiffest resistance in the Warthegau. *Reichsstatthalter* Greiser flatly rejected the granting of equal wage rates for Poles. "No Reich minister was his superior, because he . . . had been granted far-reaching powers by the Führer, which no other individual was able to set aside. The Reich directive [of October 5, 1941] was therefore inoperative in the *Gau*." This was not an issue of labor law but of race.[19] Posen (Poznań) authorities continued, stating that it was exactly because of the "racial question" that it was vital to introduce a piece rate system based on work performance, to scrap vacation entitlements, and, if the labor administration filed any objection, to resort to the Party (DAF) to force through this plan.[20]

In the Reichsgau Wartheland, however, every effort was made to bypass the provisions of Reich law in other spheres as well. Polish workers were banned from taking vacations for the duration of the war. In the question of maternity protection, the tried and tested method of undermining existing regulations was applied. Under a directive issued by the Posen *Reichsstatthalter,* maternity protection should be applied to Polish women "in principle" but in compliance with the "general political policy toward Poles," with the result that maternity protection was undermined to such an extent that very little remained.[21] Furthermore, payment was below statutory rates in every instance, to keep operating over heads at a minimum,[22] and wages were depressed further by substantial deductions and the cutting of family and housing allowances to a far greater extent than allowed by Reich labor regulation.[23] In addition, it was evidently normal practice for individual employers to arbitrarily refuse to pay allowances normally included in wages if the workers proved themselves "unworthy of the wage conceded to them."[24] In the Zichenau administrative district, too, there was no attempt to comply with Reich law when wages were cut to 60 percent and later raised to 70 percent of normal rates (with the possibility of a performance bonus of up to 15%).[25]

This system of wage reductions came ever closer to the ideal of minimum wages or piece rates for Poles, which had been the favored idea of the Party and the political leadership from the outset.[26] With the same cool cynicism with which the leadership exploited the population as nothing more than a labor commodity, a wage freeze was ordered in the Warthegau on October 27, 1939, and in the subsequent years the wages of Polish workers were steadily changed by a system of wage deductions (up to 30%)[27] and allowances—but never with the effect of increasing wages, because of the opinion that wage increases would "weaken the German nation in the East."[28] In contrast, according to the reports from Upper Silesia, general wage cuts were not implemented there, in order to avoid the immediate drop in productivity this would cause;[29] industry in particular showed itself "interested" in the "reasonable" payment of those of its Polish workers who achieved their production target, because otherwise the will to work would drop even further.[30]

Poles were also discriminated against in the conditions of labor. Not only was there compulsory labor for Poles, which also covered Polish youths (aged 12 to 18) and, toward the end of the war, even children.[31] Even the choice of place of employment, still enjoyed to a certain extent by German employees (the chosen place of employment was subject to approval), was abolished by frequent police raids to round up Poles subject to compulsory labor,[32] after no further volunteers had been forthcoming since 1941 at the latest. Those rounded up were then assigned to compulsory employment in the Annexed Eastern Territories or in the Reich.[33] In the Warthegau during the last years of the war, the working hours for Poles were up to seventy-two hours per week, to offset the man-hours lost as a result of the high sickness rate (tuberculosis was prevalent) and the continuous arrests by the Gestapo; however, these long working hours could not be maintained because they caused an increase in the sickness rates.[34] It was no more than a natural consequence of the absurd policy of exploitation and the poor working conditions that there was a rapid decrease in employee morale[35] and the sickness rates were high; this did not result in any change in the "special treatment," although the catastrophic situation was clear to all involved.[36] Whereas the relevant authorities and industry had followed this policy with reluctance because they could see the consequences for the economy every day and urged—albeit too late—that remedial action be taken, even as late as 1944 the leadership in Posen doubted that any U-turn was necessary.[37] A number of concessions, such as the right of Poles to appeal punishments ordered by plant managers, were no more than illusory, having no real substance.[38]

V. Citizenship Law for Poles and Other "Non-Germans" (the German Ethnic Classification List)

One of the keynotes of the segregation and special legislation measures was in the area of citizenship, because membership in a particular state community is the basis of the status of the individual and his rights and obligations; if this bond is severed, the individual loses all rights of domicile and is thus no longer subject to the principles of common law but rather to aliens' law, that is, solely to considerations of state expediency. One of the first actions by the National Socialists in the Eastern European territories occupied by the Reich was therefore to dissolve the legal status of the "non-Germans."[1] In doing so, however, they proceeded initially less on the basis of racial than on political-ethnic grounds; they also incorporated by a collective act "non-German." population groups for reasons of population policy, so as to include as many people as possible in the German state community, either as Reich citizens or as mere state subjects.[2]

The inclusion of the local inhabitants of the occupied territories into the German state community, which was contrary to prevailing international law but led to intrastate consequences,[3] was implemented such that the formerly Austrian citizens of "related" extraction (including Czech extraction) became German state subjects and citizens of the Reich *uno acto* (Jews were excluded, of course),[4] the "long-established inhabitants of the Sudeten-German territories" became German state subjects,[5] and the "ethnic German inhabitants" of the Protectorate of Bohemia and Moravia became citizens of the Reich and state subjects (whereas the remaining population of the protectorate became so-called protectorate subjects),[6] as did those inhabitants of the Memel region who had lost their German citizenship in 1924 when the Memel region was annexed by Lithuania.[7] German state subject status was also granted to inhabitants of German extraction in Eupen, Malmédy, and Moresnet,[8] as well as in Alsace, Lorraine, and Luxembourg, if they had "proved" themselves with distinction.[9]

1. Point of Departure: Statelessness for All "Non-German" Inhabitants of the Annexed Eastern Territories

In the Annexed Eastern Territories, the linkage of *state subject status* and the *principle of extraction* was taken seriously for the first time, and all persons of "non-German" extraction, including the Poles, were proclaimed ineligible to acquire German state subject status (citizenship in the Reich) as a matter of principle.[10] As will be seen below, however, the Germanization policy with respect to the Poles in particular is an example of the blending of racial and political considerations, because the Poles could not be classified racially by the regime.

The basis for all citizenship law measures was the thesis of the collapse of the Polish state, which had automatically occurred on October 26, 1939, the effective date of the Annexation Decree of October 8, 1939. With the Decree issued by the Führer and Reich chancellor on October 12, 1939, on the Administration of the Occupied Polish Territories (the General Government), the local population had automatically lost its Polish citizenship.[11] Remarkably, this establishment of mass statelessness—again contrary to international law but an effective act in terms of intrastate law[12]—was never explicitly declared as such. It emerged as a converse conclusion from the existing regulations and became the dominating principle of administrative practice, as confirmed by the German Supreme Court.[13]

Apart from the special arrangement applying to Danzig (Gdańsk), the Decree on the Organization and Administration of the Annexed Eastern Territories, issued by the Führer and Reich chancellor on October 8, 1939,[14] provided that the inhabitants "of German or related" blood in the Annexed Eastern Territories became German state subjects effective October 26, 1939; from another provision of this degree, that the "ethnic Germans" in these territories simultaneously became citizens of the Reich, one could have drawn the conclusion that the Poles were also "of related extraction" and would therefore also become German state subjects, if the term "of related extraction" was only extended to a sufficient degree.

Indeed, this had been the original intention of the Reich Ministry of the Interior,[15] in the expectation that it would not be possible "to remove all members of alien races from the Annexed Eastern Territories and replace them with members of the German race"; thus the "desired population growth" should provide an opportunity to acquire German state subject status, and later Reich citizenship.[16] The Reich Ministry of the Interior therefore proposed that the ethnic Germans in the Annexed Eastern Territories would initially be distinguished from the Poles not by the possession of German state subject status but by the possession of Reich citizenship. However, because the question of who should be counted among the "desired population growth" had yet to be settled, a circular decree from the Reich Ministry of the Interior dated November 25, 1939,[17] provisionally stipulated that the general acquisition of state subject status by Poles could be considered only after the issue of definitive regulations, which could not currently be promulgated. Because there was no unity at that time on how the Poles should be treated, only the ethnic Germans (the *Volksdeutsche*)[18] in the Eastern Territories were allowed to become German state subjects and Reich citizens, with the citizenship of the Polish population remaining undecided for the time being; in practical terms, the Poles were treated as stateless, since in the German view the Polish state as a legal entity had disappeared on the capitulation of Poland.

This nonregulation of Poles' citizenship, like the nonregulation of their general legal status, still offered some advantages with regard to the radical goals of the political leadership, despite the great misgivings of the Reich administration.[19] With everything left in abeyance, the authorities could exercise infinite official discretion to treat the "non-Germans" as inhabitants of a colony without any rights and to govern not on the basis of binding judicial norms but by internal guidelines from case to case.

The statelessness of the "non-Germans" in the Annexed Eastern Territories particularly suited the wishes of the Party and the police, that is, the departments of the RFSS/RKF (*Reichsführer*-SS/Reich Commissar for the Strengthening of German Nationhood) and the local Party organizations, because these agencies operated a Germanization policy based purely on aspects of security policy—on the basis of the greatest possible blocking of citizenship for Poles (the "racial struggle")—in sharp contrast to the extensive interpretation of the concept of "membership of the German *Volk* in the interests of the largest possible number of Germanizations"[20] as understood by the Reich Ministry of the Interior. These agencies, which in any case regarded themselves as having sole authority in all

issues relating to non-German races (the Party, because these were political issues; the RKF agencies because they were responsible under the secret Führer decree of October 7, 1939),[21] were therefore not only satisfied with the consultation
rights they enjoyed in the matter of nationality;[22] they had also claimed crucial
rights. For instance, they almost completely ignored the relevant circular decree
of the Reich Ministry of the Interior of November 25, 1939, in which the review
of nationality and the establishment of German state subject status was assigned
to the lower administrative authorities. In both Danzig–West Prussia and Posen
(Poznań), ethnic Germans and Poles qualified for Germanization were registered solely by the Party offices and the Security Police, with the administration
being increasingly eased out of the whole field of nationality issues.[23]

Although the Party and police leadership would have preferred to maintain
this status of the indigenous population without any rights, statelessness raised
too many legal problems in the long term, and clarification of the nationality
status of the "non-German" population became increasingly urgent. In the disputes between the Reich Ministry of the Interior and the political leadership, the
ethnic-racial argument won the upper hand because of the political predomi-
nance of the Party and the police. The Reich Ministry of the Interior abandoned
its earlier standpoint, and "agreement" was reached on two principles for the
future legal status of the "non-Germans": (1) that German state subject status
was reserved for Germans only, and (2) that Poles with "German blood in the
family" should somehow be introduced into the German state community and
after a probationary period be granted German citizenship.[24] However, the varying procedures for the establishment of nationality in the Annexed Eastern Territories and the differences between the Reich Ministry of the Interior on the
one hand and the deputy Führer and Reich Commissar for the Strengthening of
German Nationhood on the other[25] delayed the conclusion of the negotiations.

2.   Decree on the German Ethnic Classification List and German
      Citizenship in the Annexed Eastern Territories, March 4, 1941

As was so often the case when no agreement with the Reich administration
appeared possible, the RFSS/RKF acted independently; this then forced the
Reich Ministry of the Interior to give way and more or less accept the reality of
the situation. The basic line taken by the RFSS/RKF was to establish various
mechanisms to separate those Poles "qualifying for Germanization" from the
rest and incorporate them into the Reich with a special status (as probationary
state subjects), whereas for the remaining Poles the so-called protected subject
status (discussed below) was established. The relevant decree of September 12,

1940,[26] issued not by the Reich Ministry of the Interior but by the RFSS/RKF and enjoying Hitler's basic approval,[27] divided the population of the Annexed Eastern Territories into four categories, based on the German Ethnic Classification List, and stipulated a procedure for ethnic-racial classification, the major principles of which had been practiced from the outset in the radical ethnic policy of the Warthegau,[28] regarded by the Racial Policy Office of the NSDAP and the deputy Führer as exemplary.[29]

The Reich Ministry of the Interior then swung into action. The Decree on the German Ethnic Classification List and German State Subject Status in the Annexed Eastern territories issued on March 4, 1941, in the version of the decree of January 31, 1942,[30] essentially adopted the decree of September 12, 1940, and was therefore, as was often the case with National Socialist legal innovations, no original act of the Reich interior administration but a legalization of practices long exercised, that is, the arbitrary practices of Himmler's departments. On the basis of this decree, whose substance was laboriously justified by borrowing from Germanic legal history, in which the "differences caused by blood" had been decisive,[31] the German Ethnic Classification List was created to establish membership in the German *Volk* and thus state subject status.

Groups 1 and 2 of the German Ethnic Classification List included those German members of the *Volk* who had been active in promoting Germanness (*Deutschtum*) or had "proved their Germanness" before September 1, 1939; at the same time, it confirmed that they had acquired German state subject status on October 26, 1939 (the effective date of the Führer decree of October 8, 1939), without any special act of conferment.[32] For Polish members of the *Volk,* the "probationary state subject status" (with ten days' notice of revocation) was created: Poles and other "non-Germans," if recognized as "capable of Germanization," could apply for inclusion in group 3 of the German Ethnic Classification List, acquiring probationary German state subject status on *registration.* Those Poles merely classified as "capable of re-Germanization" were registered in group 4 of the German Ethnic Classification List and acquired probationary German state subject status by a special *naturalization act.*[33] All other former state subjects of Poland and Danzig became "protected subjects of the German Reich" (sec. 7). Jews and Gypsies were not capable of either acquiring German state subject status on the basis of the German Ethnic Classification List or of becoming protected subjects of the German Reich.[34] All Jews and Gypsies living in the Annexed Eastern Territories thus had no legally defined status whatsoever.

The *conditions* for inclusion in group 3 of the German Ethnic Classification List were not contained in the decree of March 4, 1941, itself but set out in the implementing circular issued by Reich Ministry of the Interior on March 13,

1941.[35] This decree shows clearly the emasculation of the Reich Ministry of the Interior by the political authorities, since the Reich Ministry of the Interior was no longer, as before, exclusively responsible for all state subject status issues as regards "non-Germans"; it was obliged to seek the consent of the political authorities, which saw themselves as primarily responsible for "Non-German Racial Policy" (sec. 10, German Ethnic Classification List Decree), so that even this decree itself was issued only after gaining the consent of the deputy Führer and the RFSS/RKF.

Under this decree, persons "capable of Germanization" could be registered in group 3 of the German Ethnic Classification List: included were Poles and other "non-Germans" (Kashubians, Mazovians, the so-called *Wasserpolen,* and others) who were of "German extraction" ("of German stock") and who could demonstrate a "declared belief in Germanness" (not active participation) at the time of Polish "foreign rule," if the ties to the Polish nation could be dissolved; persons who were living in "mixed marriage" with a member of the German *Volk* in which the German element had prevailed, again if the ties to the Polish nation could be dissolved; and members of ethnic groups incapable of unambiguous classification but inclined toward Germanness (Mazovians, Kashubians, and others) (art. 2, clauses 2 and 6, of the implementing circular).

Group 4 was designated for "non-Germans" "capable of re-Germanization," that is, persons who were "of German stock" but who had "merged with the Polish nation" (who had in some way been "hostile to Germany" before 1939) (sec. 2, par. 7, of the decree). If the "German extraction" could no longer be demonstrated with certainty, an additional "racial examination" was prescribed (sec. 2, par. 2c, of the decree), which, as mentioned before, was performed not by the general administrative authorities (*Landrat*) but by the departments of the RFSS/RKF.

The other implementing regulations for the decree of March 4, 1941, and all associated questions clearly reflect the increasing exclusion of the Reich Ministry of the Interior; the regulations were issued either by the ministry *in conjunction with* the RFSS/RKF or, for the most part, solely by Himmler's departments or by the *Reichsstatthalter* for their own areas.

Among the issues covered by the individual regulations were the drawing up of the population figures and the planned future composition of the population in the Annexed Eastern Territories;[36] the preparation of criteria for the "selection of Polish families capable of Germanization,"[37] to be performed by special departments of the SS, the reimmigration offices (*Umwandererzentralen*); the question of the nationality of non-Polish "non-Germans" in the Annexed Eastern Territories; and the differing treatment of Germanized "non-Germans" and Altreich Germans.[38]

In particular, the more precise requirements for the acquisition of German state subject status on the basis of the decree of March 4, 1941, were covered in detail,[39] as was their implementation: for instance, the inclusion regulations for groups 1 and 2 of the German Ethnic Classification List, which were intended especially to keep out Jews;[40] the recording in the German Ethnic Classification List of registered ethnic Germans;[41] the regulations for the constitutional, asset, family, and police law treatment of Poles to be Germanized in groups 3 and 4,[42] as mentioned in part 1 of the regulations; and the procedure and competence of the Supreme Court of Review for Nationality Questions in the Annexed Eastern Territories.[43]

As mentioned above, a special portion of the implementing decree gave specific guidelines for determining who was to be included in group 3 of the German Ethnic Classification List.[44] An additional "racial inspection" ordered by the Reich Ministry of the Interior and the RFSS/RKF was to be carried out if the German extraction could no longer be demonstrated with certainty. Because of a conflict about jurisdiction, this met with protest from the *Reichsstatthalter* in the Warthegau, because the inspection declared numerous persons to be Poles who had already been classified as Germans on the basis of the political examination conducted by the administration (which relied on a person's declared belief in Germanness, etc.).[45]

3. Questions of Interpretation regarding the Decree of March 4, 1941:
    The Concept of Being Capable of Germanization

Despite the number of detailed regulations, the most important questions remained unsolved, with the result that the Germanization of "non-Germans" was *institutionalized* by the German Ethnic Classification List Decree but by no means *consistently implemented*.[46] The differences in the political authorities' interpretation of the nature and scope of the Germanization of the Eastern Territories were simply too great to allow any agreement on a consistent policy by the interior administration and the departments of the RFSS/RKF. These differences existed because the Reich administration had linked the question of who was "capable of Germanization or re-Germanization" to cultural-political criteria in the "ethnic sense" (declared belief in Germanness, solidarity with German culture, etc.), whereas the intervention of the departments of the SIPO and of the RFSS/RKF in the process of Germanization of the Eastern Territories threw the entire previous definition of national status into disarray. These powers, pursuing racial policies, were steadfastly persistent in their goal of replacing the political definitions until that time governing state subject status by racial definitions, or at least putting racial definitions on a par with the political concepts. Completely new terms, such as "non-German," "of German stock," "with German blood in the family," "capable of Germanization," and "capable of re-Germanization" now appeared in the implementation of the German Ethnic Classification List Decree. These were gradually adopted by the general administration as well, but they were not capable of definition and there was no agreement on their material substance. Indeed, these defects were an advantage in the eyes of the radical racial politicians, because they could proceed flexibly, depending on the "racial policy" situation, in other words, on the basis of ethnic-racial expediency.

There is also a rather curious phenomenon: in the Germanization of Poles, the Reich Ministry of the Interior pursued a liberal policy, in that for the two criteria "German extraction" and "bonds to Germanness" ("declared belief in Germanness"), it laid the emphasis on German extraction if evidence of a "declared belief in Germanness" proved difficult, with the aim of ensuring that "no German blood was lost" and "could be used by non-German *Volkstum*" (no. 2, par. 2, of the administrative decree of the Reich Ministry of the Interior of March 13, 1941);[47] it also included "Polonized" persons of German extraction. In contrast, the departments of the RFSS/RKF, otherwise the most forceful champions of the extraction (racial) principle, pursued a restrictive policy to exclude as many applicants as possible from German state subject status. In view of this restrictive policy, the practices of the interior administration were to be undermined and outmaneuvered by the requirement of additional racial examination of "non-German" persons whose German extraction was not unambiguous, as mentioned above (RFSS/RKF guidelines of September 12, 1940,[48] in conjunction with sec. 2, par. 2c, of the Reich Ministry of the Interior decree of March 13, 1941). It is obvious that this examination slowed down the process, since the concept of German extraction had not been defined and the interior administration decided in favor of the "reclamation of German blood" in case of doubt, whereas substantially fewer individuals were able to withstand the strict racial examination by the departments of the RFSS/RKF. To make the chaos complete, a complicating factor was that the heads of the administration in the Annexed Eastern Territories, insisting on their administrative autonomy, frequently rejected regulations from the center, whether they originated from the Reich Ministry of the Interior or the departments of the RFSS/RKF.

The consequence of all this was that the concepts and conditions for deciding Germanization remained unsolved, vague, and fluid right up to the end of the Third Reich, thereby making a substantial contribution to the conceptual chaos that characterized the National Socialist regime in the sphere of the (ethnic-racial) "New European Order." As it proved impossible in the Reich to define clearly the concept of "German or related blood" or the concept of the "non-German," so it proved impossible to agree on a consistent definition for the Annexed Eastern Territories of what percentage of German blood was necessary to classify an individual as "of German extraction" and thus "capable of Germanization" and which persons were to be deemed "non-Germans" and thus "not capable of Germanization."[49] Germanization practice in the new *Gaue* thus varied considerably. Each administrative chief of the new *Reichsgaue* acted independently on the basis of his own political notions.[50] The brutal classification of persons as "capable of Germanization" or "not capable of Germanization" often penetrated into individual families, exposing them to unbearable strains or even tearing them asunder indefinitely.[51]

In this era of general conceptual chaos, other key terms also remained unresolved. For instance, the terms *Pole* and *Polish ethnic origin* were never defined. As a result, the individual authorities often acted independently without mutual consultation. As the district president of Hohensalza (Inowrocław) in the Warthegau complained eloquently, the "inconsistency of the nationality policy" meant that the administrative authorities responsible for German Ethnic Classification List matters were still unaware in April 1942 (more than a year after the German Ethnic Classification List Decree) of the details of the racial examination procedure used by the Racial and Settlement Office (of the SS) in the Germanization of Poles, "which has been practiced here for some time" and "[should have] been coordinated with the German Ethnic Classification List procedure."[52] In essence, the concept of the Pole was and remained a political concept that could not be interpreted racially, so the administrative authorities spoke much more cautiously, not of Poles but of "members of the Polish nationality," of "members of the Polish *Volk*," or of "subjects of Polish ethnic origin." The Reich Ministry of the Interior was unable to specify definitively who was a Pole, on the one hand because questions of demarcation could not be solved in legal terms and on the other because the practice of the SIPO—counter to existing regulations—narrowed down to treating all Poles, including Poles registered in the German Ethnic Classification List, as Poles so long as they had not "proved" themselves.[53] All the Reich minister of the interior was able to rouse himself to do was to issue a negative definition of "nonmembership in the Polish *Volk*";[54] this did away with the need for a positive definition of the term *Pole* but also played into the hands of Himmler as head of the SS and police and Reich

Commissar for the Strengthening of German Nationhood, who was thus free to do as he pleased, as evidenced by the conflict about the treatment of persons who had applied for registration in the German Ethnic Classification List but whose applications had yet to be approved.[55]

The new institution of protected subject status was also unresolved; this was a stopgap category to deal with the fact that not all "non-German" Reich inhabitants could be incorporated into the German state community.[56] Although described as "a status of protection by and obligation to the German Reich under public law," it was never fixed in any law.[57] The literature allowed that protected subject status should involve granting those limited rights of resident nationals—the right of economic freedom and the right to protection by the state—to which stateless persons were entitled, as long as these did not run counter to "German interests,"[58] but this political proviso meant that the concept of protected subject status was at the total disposition of the state and thus no more than a formula without substance, a circumscription of the status, in principle, of statelessness.

The legal position of persons included in the German Ethnic Classification List was just as unclear and contradictory as the notions of the laws of nationality and citizenship themselves. There was no central regulation in political, economic, or legal terms. The Reich Ministry of the Interior should have been responsible for it, but such areas were subsequently usurped by the RFSS/RKF.[59] The consequence was that the proposed re-Germanization was delayed and the uncertainty of the administrative authorities increased.[60]

The practice reflected this uncertainty. Despite the formally equal status under constitutional law of the "Germanized" Poles in groups 3 and 4 of the German Ethnic Classification List and the "Reich Germans,"[61] complaints were voiced about the poor treatment of these new state subjects by the "Reich Germans";[62] the differences between the various categories of German state subjects could not be blurred so quickly, especially since the "ethnic Germans" living in the Annexed Eastern Territories could "under no circumstances" be termed "satisfactory," even in the opinion of the authorities of the day.[63] Furthermore, there was not a great amount of attention paid to the requirement of a "declared belief in Germanness" for inclusion in the German Ethnic Classification List; police departments reported that Polish members of the German Ethnic Classification List were "politically totally unreliable."[64] Neither do progress reports from training camps for children of members of groups 3 and 4 of the German Ethnic Classification List appear particularly encouraging.[65]

There were also many individuals whose application for registration in the German Ethnic Classification List depended more on political motives—that is, the progress of the war[66]—than their inner sense of Germanness, because the German Ethnic Classification List and the status of "half-Germans" (probationary state subject status) offered certain advantages, bringing as it did equality with the Germans in terms of labor law and rations and protection from deportation to the General Government.[67] However, the flood of applications to join the German Ethnic Classification List was not as large as had been expected.[68] As early as 1940, the office of the deputy Führer felt compelled to issue a directive[69] under which lower-level Party offices had to investigate in each individual instance why "so many Germans did not opt for the Reich after the 1914–18 war" but had preferred to adopt Polish citizenship and now wished to remain Poles. Even in 1942 the number of applications for the German Ethnic Classification List fell so far short of expectations that Himmler set May 31, 1942, as the final deadline for submitting applications.[70] As the course of the war started going against the Germans, there was an increase in the number of cases in which Poles neglected to submit their applications for inclusion in the German Ethnic Classification List or Polish persons who were included on the German Ethnic Classification List returned their identification documents or refused to accept identification documents in order to avoid the threat of military service.[71] The Gestapo reacted to this with coercive measures, cautions, brief detention, and later with committal to concentration camps.[72] At the end of 1944, Himmler even ordered the execution of such individuals.[73] Little remained of the originally intended voluntary nature of inclusion on the German Ethnic Classification List.

The Germanization policy in the Annexed Eastern Territories, officially conceived as the "reclamation of German blood," therefore did not achieve the desired level of success with those Poles "with German blood in the family." Despite formal equality with the full state subjects, probationary state subject status did not bring any genuine improvement in police practice: such persons were torn from their former environment but still not treated as Germans (they were subject to police supervision and the prohibition on attending higher education establishments, and their assets were still either confiscated or only partially returned, etc.). A further factor was the radicalism with which the racial and nationality fanatics in the Party, the SS, and the RKF proceeded, so that despite a number of specific advantages, the acquisition of German state subject status no longer appeared particularly desirable, at least after 1942. Even the later suggestions and advice of the Party about the increased reclamation of Poles for "Germanness"[74] testify more to the unbroken naïveté of the conquerors than to their sense of reality. The entire German Ethnic Classification List procedure—in particular as practiced in the "model district" of the Wartheland—resulted less in any genuine equality between the status of the Poles "of German extraction" and that of the German state subjects in the Altreich than in the separation, division, and segregation of the Polish population on the basis of the criterion of "desired population growth" in "ethnic-racial" terms; the Polish neighbors either became persons "capable of Germanization" but without the full legal status of German state subjects or "impure" "protected status subjects," regarded as a "permanent" danger to the *Volk*[75] and therefore to be repressed "by all means." This element of protected status subjects, accounting for around two-thirds of the local population, was the real object of the special legislative measures in the Annexed Eastern Territories, as described above, because those people did not enjoy any guaranteed protection (not even the status of stateless persons under the Aliens Police Decree of 1938). The institution of protected subject status therefore served merely to subject the mass of the "non-Germans" to unlimited discrimination behind the facade of a specious legal concept. This will be illuminated by the following examples.

VI. Marriage Law

For the policy of segregating Germans from "non-Germans," the classification of the population into those "capable of Germanization" and those "not capable of Germanization" was in itself not sufficient. It was far more important to avoid the "permanent danger to the *Volk*," namely, the mingling of the "non-Germans" either with other "non-Germans" or with Germans, in order to reduce their birthrates. As no models were available in the Altreich in this respect, new methods had to be found. Although the Blood Protection Law (the prohibition on marriage and sexual relations between persons of "German or related blood" and Jews) had been in force in the Annexed Eastern Territories since 1941, it was restricted to German state subjects and persons registered in the German Ethnic Classification List.[1]

The other provisions of Reich law that had been issued by the office of the deputy Führer or the Armed Forces High Command to prevent marriages between Party or Wehrmacht members and "non-Germans"[2] were also in force in the Annexed Eastern Territories but were by no means sufficient. Depending on the political line they pursued, the heads of administration in the *Gaue* issued a variety of regulations without any legal basis[3] (marriage law fell under the jurisdiction of the Reich Ministry of Justice),[4] whose scope far exceeded the other regulations mentioned above.

The most radical policy was implemented in the Zichenau administration district, in which *all* marriages were prohibited, at least until 1942.[5] The situation in the *Reichsgau* Wartheland was similar. *Reichsstatthalter* Greiser, deeply worried about the prospects of success of his Germanization policy, would have preferred to have no marriages at all between Poles allowed, so as to check Polish population growth.

Since 1940 the authorities had been complaining that the Poles, whether married or not, had been following Polish propaganda slogans to preserve "Polishness," to "reproduce in great numbers," and to "have large numbers of children without inhibition" and that pregnant Polish women were no longer registering with the welfare offices because they were afraid of (forced) abortions.[6] As early as November 7, 1939,[7] *Reichsstatthalter* Greiser had summarily stated in an order of the day that marriages between Poles and marriages between Jews were provisionally banned, that marraiges between ethnic Germans must "comply with the Nuremberg Race Laws," and that "if at all possible," there should be no marriages between Germans and Poles.

Of course, this general ban on marriages for Poles could not be maintained in the long term without a risk of causing severe unrest among the local population. However, racial segregation remained the foremost goal of the leadership. In March 1941, the same month as the issue of the decree on the German Ethnic Classification List, Greiser issued a secret circular on March 31 that took into consideration and supplemented the segregation concept of the German Ethnic Classification List Decree. It stated that marriages between "members of the German *Volk*" and "persons of recognized German extraction" (i.e., Poles on the German Ethnic Classification List) on the one hand and "members of the Polish *Volk*" (i.e., Poles with protected subject status) on the other were essentially prohibited (but there were no "ethnic policy reservations" about marriages between Poles).[8] In a further decree on September 10, 1941, possibly because legal reservations had emerged about his marriage ban, Greiser on his own authority raised the minimum marriageable age for Polish men, which had been 21 under Polish law (16 in exceptional cases),[9] to 28, and for Polish women he set the minimum age for marriage at 25,[10] in order at least to delay marriages that could not be prevented.

Reichsstatthalter Greiser was evidently the first to act in this independent fashion. The weak Reich Ministry of the Interior, which had seen the treatment of "non-Germans" slipping out of its hands more and more because of the single-minded activities of the departments of the RFSS/RKF[11] (and the radical racial politicians in the Annexed Eastern Territories), to which it had granted authority to issue instructions[12]—even to the authorities of the general state administration—ultimately had no option but to acknowledge the reality of the situation. In a meeting at the Reich Ministry of the Interior on January 21, 1943, it was established that the regulations in the other Annexed Eastern Territories should be harmonized with those in the Warthegau (or Wartheland) (although they had not achieved their original aim of restricting the "great fertility of the Poles")[13] and that at a later date a uniform marriageable age for Poles should be specified, "Preferably 25 or 28 years of age."[14] This was nothing but the retroactive legalization of the arbitrary actions of the *Reichsstatthalter* in Posen (Poznań) and was indeed subsequently implemented. A decree of January 10, 1944, by Himmler in his capacity as Reich minister of the interior,[15] based on the Decree on Protected Status of April 25, 1943, set forth a uniform marriageable age for Poles of 28 years for men and 25 years for women.

Section 8 of this Decree on Protected Status of April 25, 1943,[16] provided for drastic special regulations with regard to marriages between German state subjects and protected status subjects so as to prevent racial mingling between the Master Race and the subject races, a concept obviously based on colonial practices. The practical importance of these prohibitions principally affected the Poles in the Eastern Territories, because the institution of protected subject status was applied in administrative practice only in these regions. With the possibility of exemptions in individual instances, all marriages of protected status subjects and non-protected status subjects, in other words all marriages between (protected subject status) Poles in the Annexed Eastern Territories and other persons (Germans, stateless persons, foreigners), were prohibited. Marriages involving two protected subject status Poles were also subject to severe restriction by administrative guidelines issued by the departments of the RFSS/RKF, or even banned altogether.[17] These measures not only reflect the erroneous belief of the racial fanatics that by such means they would achieve the "choking-off of the foreign *Volkstum*"; the measures also cast a distinctive light on the simple-minded methods with which the local population was ruled. As was to be expected, the bans on marriage had no impact whatsoever on the birthrate; illegitimate births in particular rose steadily. As a result, additional measures were considered to counter the increasing Polish birthrate (e.g., obligation on the fathers' part to pay very high maintenance; withdrawal of welfare benefits from Polish mothers),[18] and these remained unimplemented only because of the shortage of time remaining. All the same, the authorities made every effort to effectively force down the undesired rise in the Polish birthrate. As late as fall 1944, the authorities in the Warthegau found time to consider how "measures could be introduced in good time" to prevent the "particularly high growth in the Polish population" that was to be expected from the use of the population to dig entrenchments.[19]

VII.   Freedom of Movement and Personal Liberty

The extensive restrictions on the freedom of movement and personal liberty of the "non-German" inhabitants of the Annexed Eastern Territories were based on the same policy of segregation and discrimination. Closely linked to the regulations on the wearing of badges and the compulsory Hitler-*Gruss* mentioned above, they were also intended to draw a highly visible line between the "non-Germans" and the privileged Germans, to demonstrate the German rule day by day to the "non-Germans," and to make absolutely clear to them their special status as nothing more than individuals living on the sufferance of the Germans, a mass of cheap labor completely dependent on the goodwill of the German authorities.

It is evident from relevant police regulations that the mildest restrictions were in force in the Kattowitz (Katowice) administrative district, to the extent that those Poles working in the municipal districts were subject to Reich police laws,[1] which contained well-defined statutory definitions of offenses as well as certain legal guarantees. In contrast, those Poles originating from the Annexed Eastern Territories and the General Government were explicitly excluded from the application of Reich police law; thus they could be subjected to further restrictions. Other "non-German" laborers were subject to strict supervision. The "Eastern workers" from the Occupied Soviet Territories, for instance, could leave the *parish* of their workplace only with police permission,[2] whereas all non-Polish "non-German" laborers from the Baltic states, the General Government, and the Annexed Eastern Territories[3] could move freely around the rural or municipal district in which they worked but could leave this only with the permission of the police.[4]

In contrast, the "non-Germans" in the "model district" of the Wartheland were liable to considerably more severe special legislative regulations. Not surprisingly, the Jews suffered most.[5] As early as November 1939, the HSSPF (higher SS and police leader) in Posen (Poznań) had issued a general migration and relocation ban for all Jews and Poles of the Warthegau and a ban on the entry of such persons from outside "to permit the conclusive registration of persons," under threat of "the stiffest punishment" in the event of violation.[6] These regulations were later relaxed somewhat. A police regulation issued by the HSSPF in Posen on June 26, 1941, as an "analogous application of the Prussian Law of Police Administration" stipulated that the permission of the local police authorities was required for any relocation within or outside the parish of residence.[7] For Posen, the future capital of the new Eastern Territories, particularly stringent regulations applied to ensure the creation of accommodation for Germans seeking houses and apartments.[8] As of November 1939, no further permits were issued to leave the city, and all relocations within the city were prohibited.[9] Toward the end of the war, Poles were also banned from the platforms of the Posen railway station,[10] with the aim of preventing any mass exodus.

In the Zichenau administrative district, local authorities faithfully emulated the special provisions of Reich law by frequently issuing even harsher regulations, such as the closure of certain roads and squares to Poles and Jews,[11] a ban on Jews' visiting markets, and the establishment of particular shopping hours and specific post office and other opening hours for Jews.[12] Undoubtedly, in the other parts of the Annexed Eastern Territories there were also restrictions on the freedom of movement of "non-Germans," but these are difficult to substantiate because of a lack of source material.

One example of the mentality applied by the political leadership to tackle the issues of freedom of movement and (compulsory) residence is the special treatment of a particular group of "non-Germans": Poles suffering from tuberculosis, whose number was put at 35,000 out of a total of 230,000 TB patients in the Warthegau.

As a consequence of the poor living and dietary conditions, a rapid increase in number of cases of open TB had been registered in the Warthegau since 1940, with the incidence among the German population three times higher, and among the Poles five to six times higher, than in the Altreich.[13] The authorities initially attempted to establish isolation facilities, but in view of the large number of Polish TB patients, these were by no means adequate.[14] *Reichsstatthalter* Greiser therefore hit upon the idea of resorting to "proven" models and arbitrarily proposed the "special treatment" (killing) of these persons, similar to the "special treatment of the approximately one hundred thousand Jews that will be completed in two to three months," because the "risk of infection is very great."[15] Himmler had no "fundamental" objections to this proposal but demanded the issue of certificates by medical officers confirming incurability in each individual case and ordered the strictest secrecy.[16] The deputy head of the Central Office for National Health of the NSDAP, Dr. Kurt Blome, also considered Greiser's proposal "the most practicable and simple solution," but he doubted whether Hitler would approve, since Hitler had already rejected the euthanasia program in the Reich "for practical reasons"; maintaining secrecy about the action would be impossible and foreign states would "stir up hatred."[17] Himmler then sided with Blome's misgivings and ordered that incurable TB patients should be sent to an isolated area and kept there under the strictest supervision.[18]

The residence restrictions on Poles and the compulsory concentration of

Jews were followed by a range of travel and transport restrictions as well as curfews, which further limited the freedom of movement of the "non-Germans" and ultimately isolated them almost completely from the outside world. Curfews for Poles (and Jews) were introduced in all rural districts of the Annexed Eastern Territories,[19] justified by the authorities on the grounds of security policy requirements and the need to make any participation in public occasions for Poles an impossibility.[20] No exceptions were tolerated, even for functions of minor importance.[21]

In contrast, no uniform policy about the use of public transport by "non-Germans" was pursued in the Annexed Eastern Territories because of the varied "racial situation," despite the advocating of uniform regulations by the RSHA. The Security Police authorities in Danzig (Gdańsk) and Breslau (Wrocław) in particular were opposed to such regulations because of the strong German-Polish mixed population in Upper Silesia and the mixed-race situation in the Danzig–West Prussia *Gau*, together with the impossibility of supervising such regulations.[22] Only with respect to the Jews is any uniform policy evident, to the extent that the special legislation in force in the Reich, which prohibited Jews in general from using all means of transport,[23] as well as from entering station restaurants, catering establishments, etc.,[24] also applied in the Annexed Eastern Territories. However, Poles in the Warthegau were also subject to similar restrictions, which although totally absurd in economic terms were "correct" in terms of "racial policy," because they rounded off the isolation of the local population from the outside world. For instance, "non-German" laborers without a pass *(Durchlaßschein)* were not allowed to return to the Warthegau, although this was an integral part of the Reich territory.[25] Poles arriving were subjected to strict controls.[26] Poles wishing to travel to the Altreich required a special permit, but this was no longer issued at all after 1942, even for urgent reasons (e.g., marriage), allegedly because of the difficult transport situation[27] but in fact to prevent Poles from establishing contacts outside the *Gau*. Although it is possible to identify certain variations among the other restrictions on travel applied in the individual administrative districts (Posen, Hohensalza [Inowrocław], Łódź), taken overall they represented a relatively uniform network of measures, with clear parallels to the travel restrictions for Jews in the Altreich, as demonstrated by the following examples.

From the outset, the district and local police authorities in the Warthegau had decreed a variety of transport restrictions for Poles (subject to approval), which were subsequently replaced by uniform regulations. As early as summer 1940, the *Reichsstatthalter* had issued a directive that prohibited the use of public transport by "non-Germans" and allowed exemptions (e.g., travel to one's workplace) only with police approval.[28] This was followed by corresponding police regulations in the individual administrative districts,[29] issued by the district presidents as the higher administrative and state police authority.[30]

However, in view of the traffic density caused by the already limited transport facilities and the heavy commuter traffic, these restrictions do not appear to have been particularly effective; the authorities were repeatedly admonished to supervise the travel regulations more closely because the "supervision of travel by non-German inhabitants of the Warthegau is an urgent political and Security Police requirement."[31] Toward the end of the war, the conditions were tightened even further, to prevent both resistance activities and the exodus of refugees.[32] Just a few months before, all males in the Warthegau between the ages of 16 and 65 had been banned altogether from traveling "to avoid population displacements";[33] the authorities had been given tighter guidelines regarding the issue of travel permits.[34]

Further restrictions followed in the *Reichsgau* Wartheland on the basis of the fundamental ban on travel (with possible exemptions). The issue of police rail travel permits was forbidden in particular cases or in general, to prevent Poles from traveling at all.[35] In addition, Poles were permitted only to use the lowest class of rail travel from 1942 at the latest, and Polish civilian laborers were forbidden access to express and fast trains without exception; otherwise, "justified complaints from the German population were to be expected."[36] The use of omnibuses by Poles, even if they possessed permits, was essentially illusory, because only a few routes were actually operating and Germans always enjoyed priority.[37] Furthermore, the *Reichsstatthalter* had ordered that for the whole *Gau* "the use of recreational craft on the Reich waterways between the Oder and the Vistula" or the use of "all motorized water craft" in the Posen district[38] was prohibited. Even use of the tram system, although generally not subject to approval,[39] was severely restricted for Poles in the Warthegau. Since 1940 Poles in the *Gau* capital of Posen were subjected to humiliating conditions, evidently based on the special legislative practice applied to Jews in the Reich and the General Government, partially or totally banning them from using the tram system, especially during peak periods.[40]

The Poles were seriously hindered in this way—or even excluded—from using urban public transport, but the authorities in the Warthegau eventually decided to attack the last means of transport open to the Poles, the *bicycle*, upon which the local population was ultimately dependent because of the restrictions on other forms of transport. On the grounds of eliminating illegal communications among the Poles, the use of bicycles was initially severely controlled or prohibited outright at the local level (the parish, the rural district) and later throughout the *Gau,* a measure that had not even been enforced against the Jews in the Reich. The forerunners at the municipality level[41] were then followed by a fundamental prohibition with provision for exemptions in the administrative districts via corresponding police regulations,[42] typical for National Socialist legal practice, banning all use of bicycles in principle and requiring a special police permit ("bicycle permit") for exemptions (given only for journeys of over two kilometers to and from the workplace and for professional travel on special occasions).

Of course, the issue of these bicycle permits, for which the local police authorities were responsible, was often turned over to the Gestapo, which proceeded with extreme pettiness, rejecting applications by Poles for the most paltry of reasons.[43] However, it is doubtful that these prohibitions were enforced in full, because complaints about the unauthorized use of bicycles by Poles did not cease.[44] That the prohibitions were not observed, at least in part, is demonstrated by the threat of severe penalties for violations and the appeals for increased alertness.[45] In any case, it is certain that bicycle traffic was severely curbed and that as many bicycles as possible were seized from the Poles, since bicycles for which no permit application had been submitted or for which an application had been rejected were confiscated and surrendered to the local police authorities for "safekeeping."[46] Of course, this did not mean "safekeeping" in the traditional sense but essentially expropriation, because the bicycles were then put to use for "public" purposes and put at the disposal of "public welfare" institutions, for example, various Party organizations, for an indefinite period.[47]

The purpose of the segregation of the "non-Germans" from the Germans, the isolation of the "non-Germans" from the outside world, and the restriction of their freedom of movement was, of course, not only to meet Security Police requirements, to supervise the population more easily, or to better control "labor management." This complex should be viewed more in the wider political context, and its significance can be properly understood only in this respect. In particular, these processes should be considered in conjunction with the mass deportations (resettlement) from the Eastern Territories that commenced in fall 1939. The particulars of these cannot be discussed in detail at this point, but they form the backdrop against which all restrictions on the residence rights of "non-Germans" should be viewed.

This applies in particular with regard to the Jewish population of the Eastern Territories, which was to be subjected to the phased residence restrictions set out in the anti-Jewish laws. In concrete terms, this entailed the herding of the Jews from the countryside to the towns and thence into ghettos, euphemistically termed "Jewish residential districts," where they were to be prepared for their "deportation" to the East (the Final Solution).[48] It is not the case that the policy of stipulating compulsory residence for the Jews was adopted by the SS and police leadership only at the Wannsee Conference; this had been the line taken from the outset. As early as September 1939, the head of the SIPO and the SD instructed all leaders of the "mobile killing units" (*Einsatzgruppen*) in a decree of September 21, 1939, to maintain the strictest secrecy about "anti-Jewish measures" and to proceed only "gradually" in the achievement of the "Final Objective" (the expulsion of the Jews);[49] they were to concentrate the Jews in the towns "for the time being," to consult closely with the civilian and military authorities with respect to all measures, and to report the latter on a continuous basis. Involved in the elimination of the freedom of movement of the Jewish population and its harassment[50] was not only the SIPO, which in any case no longer regarded the Jews as human beings but merely as a "commodity" to be deported,[51] but also the general administration, whose decrees it was that created the conditions under which the deportations and "resettlements" could proceed, with all their horrific consequences.[52] These were, of course, compounded by all the "normal" processes of harassment, such as the practice of forcing Jews to quit their homes to make way for members of the Party and the administration and sending them to camps in the countryside. As viewed by the National Socialists, however, this was no "resettlement" in the usual sense, because those affected were forced to sign a declaration that they were moving to the country "voluntarily."[53]

The policy of resettlement and "emigration," pursued by the departments of the RFSS/RKF in close cooperation with the general administrative authorities, affected not only the Jews but also the Poles.[54] To implement this resettlement, the enormous machinery of the "Resettlement Centers" was established, reporting directly to the RFSS/RKF. Nevertheless, it would be wrong to view this resettlement as the work only of the SS, implemented independently, as it were, of the authorities of the interior administration, because the senior administrators (*Reichsstatthalter*) were representatives of the RFSS/RKF.[55] Employees of the administration were used to establish the resettlement centers. At the local level, resettlement matters were the responsibility of the *Landrat* (Oberbürgermeister).[56]

After the liquidation of the ruling classes by the *Einsatzgruppen* of the SIPO or their transportation to concentration camps in fall 1939, key economic groups, criminals, and other undesirable individuals were resettled in the General Government, and those that remained were exploited as menial labor. For this reason, all "undesirable" Poles, such as the elderly, the sick, members of the propertied classes, and the intelligentsia were deported to the General Government on a massive scale.[57] The elimination of freedom of movement and the alleged need for a complete "registration of all persons" were, of course, closely linked to this, because they opened up optimum possibilities of registration, surveillance, and control of all individuals involved, measures that every totalitarian regime dreams of, and were thus the indispensable condition or consequence of all resettlement measures.

VIII.   Restrictions on Communication and Information Exchange among "Non-Germans" and the Confiscation of Cultural Goods.

Another consequence of the restrictions on the personal freedom of movement of the "non-Germans" was that almost all opportunities for communication were severed for the local population. This applied in the first instance to daily contacts, which were heavily restricted or even made impossible by the numerous curfews. It was compounded by the isolation from practically all information and news media.

The intensity of the special legislative measures differed in the various parts of the Annexed Eastern Territories, but it is certainly beyond doubt that all Jews were required to surrender radios and that early on in the occupation, radios were confiscated from Poles on a large scale to prevent their listening to Polish and foreign, in particular Allied, transmissions. Documents exist showing that "non-Germans" were required to register radios in upper Silesia, Danzig (Gdańsk)–West Prussia, and the Warthegau and that those belonging to Poles were normally subject to confiscation.[1] More details are available for the Warthegau, where the head of the civil administration had issued a corresponding directive as early as October 2, 1939,[2] after the local authorities in Posen (Poznań) had acted independently as soon as the city had been occupied.[3]

The confiscation of the radios was usually implemented by a duty to surrender these devices but also in part by raids ("surprise house searches").[4] Even before the Polish capitulation at the beginning of October 1939, however, the head of the civil administration in the office of the Posen military commandant and later *Reichsstatthalter* Greiser ordered the return of the radios because "it appears desirable to influence the Polish population . . . toward the Germans." Only a few days later, however, Greiser had changed his mind. It can be assumed that the radios confiscated on the basis of Greiser's original directive of October 2, 1939, and then returned were confiscated once again, as intended by Greiser;[5] an order of the day issued by the commander of the regular police in Posen shows that according to a directive by the Führer, all radios held by Poles and Jews were to be confiscated for good, including those previously registered but not confiscated.[6] This again was no temporary measure but expropriation, as the confiscated radios were released to the relevant agencies for distribution to *Volksgenossen* (*Volk* comrades).[7] Despite this, there must have been means to receive radio transmissions (in particular for those Poles working as ancillary labor in German offices or who had German landlords or tenants), as demonstrated by the complaints of administrative authorities or the harsh sentences passed by special courts against Poles for listening to foreign broadcasts.[8]

There were also special legislative restrictions on postal and telegraph communications. Local authorities had issued arbitrary prohibitions during the first weeks of the occupation (no handling of mail written in Polish),[9] but regulations issued by central authorities—at least in the Warthegau—are documented only from 1942 on. For instance, Poles were generally forbidden to send telegrams, with exemptions only with special police permission in "urgent cases" (deaths and severe illness).[10] Telegraph services were completely banned for Poles after April 1943; the reasons stated for "urgent cases" were no longer recognized.[11] Only Polish physicians providing medical care to the German population were exempt.[12] Shortly before, Poles in the Warthegau had also been prohibited from using public telephones, and even if they were allowed to telephone in exceptional cases with special permission, they were required to speak in German when they made the call.[13] However, even the *Reichsstatthalter* opposed the total telephone ban desired by radicals: because of the large number of Polish auxiliary personnel in the administration and the economy, this would be impossible, so exceptions must be permitted for urgent official or economic reasons;[14] more far-reaching restrictions than those measures already decreed were impossible because of the lack of sufficient surveillance facilities.[15] The receipt of mail was also restricted or monitored. As in the Reich territory, all mail to and from Poles was subject to censorship or confiscation by the Gestapo.[16] On the basis of a secret decree of the Reich Security Main Office of February 22, 1943, all packets and parcels from Portugal and Sweden addressed to Poles in the Reich and the General Government were confiscated, because the "headquarters of the Polish resistance movement" were located in these countries.[17]

The special legislative treatment of "non-Germans" also included the restriction and confiscation of everyday goods relating to one's quality of life and important for relaxation and leisure activities. There could, of course, be no further talk of continued "permitted retention" of these goods by Poles and Jews, to whom the function of mere slave laborers had now been accorded.

Available source documentation does not permit any consistent analysis of the individual procedures applied in the Annexed Eastern Territories, but there is evidence for the Wartheland that possession of such goods was regarded as completely superfluous for Poles (for Jews this was, of course, self-evident), even dangerous, and therefore prohibited. Apart from the general duty of surrender of certain goods important to the war effort,[18] the purchase by Poles of record players and accessories had been prohibited since 1941 in the Posen administrative district,[19] and probably in the other two administrative districts as well, and possession of phonographs and Polish records was generally prohibited for all. Such devices were confiscated and were supposed to be surrendered to the local police authorities.[20] In addition, all "Poles, enemy aliens, and stateless persons" (including Jews) were prohibited from possessing cameras and binoculars, which were also to be surrendered.[21] Such regulations were also in force in the Kattowitz (Katowice) administrative district from early 1942, which also banned all sales of film, cameras, and binoculars to Poles.[22] Overzealous authorities in the Wartheland also wanted to confiscate furs from the Poles during the Winter Relief Fund (*Winterhilfswerk*) collections for the Wehrmacht, in the same way that Germans had to surrender their furs; however, the *Reichsstatthalter* had made no generally binding decision in this matter because he feared that it would cause unrest among the Polish population, leaving it to the "tact and sensitivity," the "prudent discretion" of the *Landräte* to decide "which Polish furs they . . . believed they could take."[23]

IX. Food Supply

The deprivation of all means of communication and cultural goods would have been bearable in terms of sheer survival, but special legislative treatment of "non-Germans" ultimately assaulted the very basis of existence, the area of provisions and nutrition, where the parallels with anti-Jewish laws again cannot be ignored. In the Annexed Eastern Territories, the intensity of the implementation of these measures differed somewhat, as both the political and economic conditions and the political line adopted by the local administrative bosses (*Landräte* and district presidents) varied considerably. However, a fundamental feature was that Poles and Jews were almost invariably worse off than Germans; furthermore, "borrowings" from the special anti-Jewish legislation in the Altreich are evident. For instance, the segregation of shopping by Germans and Jews was strictly enforced, and food allowances for Jews were heavily reduced. A police regulation dated November 23, 1940, has survived from the Kattowitz (Katowice) administration district[1] (it was subsequently replaced by an identically worded police regulation dated December 20, 1942),[2] under which Jews were not permitted to make purchases at German and Polish retailers but only in specially marked Jewish shops, which were in turn prohibited for other "non-Germans."

Of course efforts were also made to segregate the Poles. One of the key principles was that—as in all other areas—the Germans, as the ruling class, were to receive preferential service; specially marked German shops were established, to which only Germans enjoyed access.

In particular in the Warthegau (or Wartheland), numerous regulations concerning shopping and opening hours for Poles were issued. In Posen (poznań), for instance, special opening hours in shops and markets were established at the beginning of 1940 for Poles and Germans, and these were strictly enforced by the police;[3] the corresponding regulations allocated the most inconvenient times to the "non-Germans" (after 10:00 A.M. in the summer; after 11:00 A.M. or in the afternoon in the winter) and the best shopping hours (early morning) to the Germans; this was of crucial importance when shopping for scarce goods *(Mangelwaren)*.[4] During the shopping hours for Germans, Poles were even prohibited from entering the grocery stores, butchers' shops, and weekly markets under a Posen police decree dated November 8, 1940.[5] Because of the differing situation in the individual districts of the city of Posen (population density, population mix, customers, etc.), however, these regulations were "treated flexibly" from shop to shop, as long as the fundamental principle of the regulation—preferential service for German customers—was observed.[6]

Special shopping hours for Poles are also recorded for other areas of the Warthegau;[7] the assumption that such special regulations existed in all *Kreise* is supported by a directive by the Central Chamber of Commerce of the Warthegau in June 1942 repeating the principles described above: Poles were permitted to shop for their personal needs only at specified times, and Polish employees were not permitted to shop for their German employers; German customers were always to be given preferential service.[8]

Again on the basis of documented sources relating to the Warthegau, a detailed system of special treatment for "non-Germans" had been developed with respect to the rationing of foodstuffs and other goods.[9] The first fact deserving mention is that Poles "naturally" received "far less coal" than the Germans, that there was no gas or electricity,[10] and that the Jews received no fuel rations whatsoever, with the result that the catastrophic shortage of fuel gave rise to fears of a "total collapse,"[11] and the ill feelings already rampant in the population because of the special shopping hours and other restrictions were reinforced further.[12] There were also restrictions on the supply to Poles of key commodities such as clothing, raw cotton, leather, soap, and medicines.[13] Despite this, there were numerous instances in which Poles received such goods despite the existing purchase restrictions, because—as the authorities complained—Polish sales staff were not adequately supervised and supported the Polish customers (by "fraud," helping with "hoarding," etc.) such that the Poles were, in part, "better supplied than the Germans."[14]

It is also evident that as far as food rationing was concerned, the protected subject status Poles received lower rations (they were even lower for Jews), which had a considerable impact on their mood and work performance.[15] Cases of Poles' receiving relatively adequate rations gave rise to complaints by "racially conscious" administrative officials of "extravagance" or demands for remedial action, because they were causing unrest and ill feeling among the German population.[16] After 1941 a number of rations for Poles were canceled altogether. In early 1941, for instance, the sale of wheat flour to Poles was forbidden, followed in fall 1941 by prohibitions on the sale of cakes, pies, and other wheat-based bakery products;[17] fruit could not be sold to Poles, with Posen "setting a good example" as early as fall 1940.[18] Poles were also forbidden to buy vegetables from 1942 on.[19] Local regulations went even further, forbidding Poles to buy other foods.[20] Poles were also banned from buying foodstuffs for sending to Polish prisoners of war.[21] A report from Upper Silesia states that the Poles were put on half rations for food in 1941.[22]

The consequences of these discriminatory measures were catastrophic, because they existed in an environment where—despite restrictions—*all* foodstuffs were very scarce and exorbitant prices prevailed.[23] The Poles were therefore left with only what the Germans did not want; the conditions were so bad that the authorities feared a general famine,[24] but they still did not cease their efforts to complain about the methods used by the local population to counter the privations (illegal purchases, substantial black market purchases, and hoarding),[25] which had become so rampant precisely because of the restrictions imposed by the authorities. However, as admitted at the time, what was regarded as even more serious than these illegal activities by Polish consumers was the fact that the authorities themselves had ruined any chance of cooperation, or even a prudent attitude, on the part of the Poles.[26] This was because the restrictions described above had affected the entire population; and even where there had been no impact, they had generated anti-German sentiments and activities.

Section Three

The Implementation of *Völkisch* Inequality in the General Government

INTRODUCTION
The Fundamentals of National Socialist Administrative Policy: The General
Government as a Model for Future German Colonies

I. Immediate Aims: A Military Staging Area, a Labor Reserve, and Economic Exploitation

In contrast to the Annexed Eastern Territories, whose purpose (Germanization) and status (annexation) was established from the outset, the legal status
and the fate of the occupied Polish territories (the General Government) were
never concretely clarified because the Nazi leadership itself had developed no
clear notions. In this respect, administrative policy and the treatment of "non-
Germans" also demonstrate variations and contradictions, reflected on the one
hand in an absurd policy of economic overexploitation and on the other in the
numerous measures to preserve the labor resources of the Poles. There was clarity only with regard to the immediate aims pursued at the time of the occupation of the General Government. From the beginning, Hitler had ordered that
the occupied Polish territories should serve as a military staging area for the
forth-coming war with the Soviet Union (the primary immediate aim) as well as
a reservoir of cheap labor for the Reich (the secondary immediate aim).[1] The
third immediate aim was to totally exploit all resources in the country to the
benefit of the Reich.[2] The prime maxims of administrative policy were therefore,
as Governor General Hans Frank repeatedly assured, to squeeze this region dry
of all possible resources by implementing the measures needed to achieve this
goal. This exclusively negative policy, according to Frank, would have "certain
consequences that are unpleasant to us National Socialists at the moment." The
General Government was no "extension of the Warthegau[!]." It must be ensured that the Poles are kept peaceful and quiet.[3] In contrast, all those of no use
to German interests (those who accomplished no work, or insufficient work)
should be "left to their own ends"—more or less left to starve.[4]

These were aims and precepts that had previously been applied only to colonies. And indeed, the General Government was destined to become the first

colony of the Reich, in the same way that the Warthegau was to become the model district of an annexed territory. German colonial lands did not start de facto to the east of the General Government,[5] as Governor General Frank considered, but to the east of the Annexed Eastern Territories. This colonial definition of the General Government became the basis of all administrative acts and a fixed component of internal and external officialese. It was reflected in a policy of economic exploitation, the cultural suppression of the Poles, and the liquidation of their intelligentsia, euphemistically circumscribed as a policy of "general pacification."[6] The Nazi occupation policy is thus characterized by a level of internal consistency and unity found in no other country occupied by Germany during World War II.[7] And the administrative leadership made no secret about the colonial designation of the General Government.

Even during the period of military administration, Frank, as head of the civil administration for the occupied Polish territories at the time, had stated to representatives of the military administration on October 3, 1939, that "Poland should be treated as a colony."[8] On December 2, 1939, he told his heads of departments that the criterion of the political leadership was the will of the Führer that "this territory was the first colonial territory of the German Nation," "the spoils of the German Reich";[9] at the opening of the German judicial system in the General Government on April 9, 1940, the German judges were called upon to "develop a colonial, imperial legal system" in the General Government.[10] The leaders of the Security Police talked of "methods [within the General Government] that England applied to non-European peoples [tin spoons and calico]."[11]

Statements for public consumption also borrowed heavily from the language of colonialism; in proclamations to the population of the occupied Polish territories of October 26, 1939, and to the population of Galicia on June 22, 1940, the population was accorded the same status as a native population "under the protection of the Reich" (the General Government was presented as the "Reich Protectorate of the Polish *Volkstum*").[12] The first "Report on the Development of the General Government," issued in July 1940 by the government of the General Government, spoke of the achievements of the administration as achievements that would do justice to the image of the Reich as "a new major colonial power."[13] In the sphere of justice, the terms *German Court* and *German Higher Court* already pointed toward the colonial status of the General Government (since these terms also appear in the drafts of the Foreign Office for the future colonial legislation), whereas with regard to the local Polish judicial system, there was overt mention of "native" jurisdiction.[14] The plans for the economic exports were totally oriented toward the "colonial structure" of the General Government.[15] Leading civil servants of the General Government presented papers on colonial administrative policy at the Colonial-Political Office of the NSDAP in Berlin,[16] because the General Government, as Reich Minister of Justice Franz Gürtner propounded in Kraków on December 15, 1940, was in the Reich "an example, a model, an exercise . . . of what we will often create in the Reich in future elsewhere, perhaps under different conditions but still with the same goal."[17] As Governor General Hans Frank repeatedly emphasized, the General Government served as a "laboratory for administrative studies and for the principles" of future colonial acquisitions, as a model of "how we can develop . . . colonial administrations in the first place."[18]

II. Ultimate Aims: German Colonial Rule

Despite the unambiguous nature of the immediate policy aims in the General Government, the notions about its ultimate fate remained unclear, lost in a vague future. Beyond dispute was only the principle that the General Government was more than temporarily occupied territory, that it was associated with the Reich in perpetuity and should be dependent upon it.[1] The crucial question, however, was whether the General Government, like the Eastern Territories, should be a German settlement area or not.[2] Although this was agreed in principle (the Vistula should become just as German as the Rhine), no set time frame was specified ("in the foreseeable decades"). Hitler, too, never committed himself unequivocally,[3] and Frank, the head of the administration, referred all relevant speculation to the time after the war or after the Germanization of the Eastern Territories and the "Southeastern Region."[4] In contrast, the radical racial experts in the departments of the *Reichsführer*-SS dreamed of mass deportations of the local "non-Germans" as soon as possible and "Greater German" settlement areas for members of the SS, discharged soldiers, deserving Party members,[5] and resettlers from Russia; they had already made a concrete start with the compulsory settlements and resettlements in the Lublin District.[6] Top secret deliberations by the SS had contemplated the monstrous notion of liquidating, or at any rate killing off, infirm resettlers and those unsuitable for resettlement, not only with regard to the "non-Germans" but also to the future German settlers.[7] In contrast, more detailed ideas about the future fate of the Poles were not developed. The extreme notions of the SS and police leadership were generally oriented toward deporting all Poles in the so-called Eastern region to western Siberia, since only 5 percent were "capable of Germanization" in any case, and space would have to be created there for the German settlers ("General Plan for the East" of the RFSS).[8]

However, this differed from the vision of the administrative authorities. The top departments in the General Government also agreed that in the long term the General Government should be settled by Germans.[9] In the "Eastern Region Plans" of the civil administration, vague and blurred though their suggestions might have been, there appeared the vision of a "Germanic East" with strong German settlement strongholds as a catchment area for the overpopulated Reich territory;[10] but in contrast to the Annexed Eastern Territories (where there was an emphasis on Germanization with agricultural settlements), it is evident that only the Germanization of the towns and cities, as centers of German rule, was proposed, with the local population merely segregated from the Germans and remaining on the land as labor.[11]

This plan therefore involved German rule, not in the sense of the total deportation or Germanization of the Poles but rather in the sense of (colonial) rule by a German "ruling class" over the mass of the "non-Germans," in the same way that ancient Sparta had ruled over its *perioikoi* and Helots. As expounded by the political leadership, this system of colonial rule, initially developed for the occupied Russian territories,[12] also represented the fundamental concept of administrative policy in the General Government.

III. Legal Status: Borderland (*Nebenland*) of the Reich or Part of Reich Territory?

On the basis of the aforementioned intended purpose of the General Government as an object of colonial exploitation, it would have been an obvious move to regulate its legal status conclusively, for instance as a formal colony or "protected territory." However, the relatively undefined long-term aims for the ultimate fate of the General Government made it difficult, indeed impossible, to define its legal status with the aid of conventional categories.[1] It therefore remained in legally ambiguous abeyance, a state that totally corresponded to the dislike of the National Socialist leadership for any legal stipulations whatsoever and offered the best conditions for the uninhibited development of the despotism of the National Socialist police and administrative authorities. The status of the General Government is a particularly good example of the minor role played by the legal sphere in National Socialism. Inspired by the revolutionary impetus and enthusiasm for "developing the East," they started by smashing what already existed, then got on with their own business and left it to the lawyers to find legal forms for the new "facts" that had been created.

But the search for a legal classification of the General Government within the conventional system remained fruitless. In view of the function of the General Government as the booty of the Reich, there was agreement in the leadership—and following it, jurisprudence[2]—only that the standards of international law did not apply to this territory. In the view of the National Socialists, the term "General Government for the occupied Polish territories," binding until July 12, 1940,[3] did not express any *occupatio bellica* after the end of military administration, a temporary occupation in terms of international law, but the subordination of this territory in perpetuity to German civil administration.[4] They believed that with the capitulation of Poland, the Polish state had ceased to exist;[5] its defeat should therefore be regarded as *debellatio* (extinction of the state) in terms of international law.[6] The disappearance of the Polish state as an object of international law, it was explained in the literature, resulted "principally from the fact that directly after September 1, 1939, no further traces of a system of government from Poland could be established."[7]

Even aside from the fact that such "traces" had been destroyed from the outset by the occupying power itself, this ran counter to all reality—the establishment of the Polish government in exile as well as the marshaling of Polish armed forces abroad, and so forth—but still remained the prevailing opinion of the jurisprudence of international law in Germany at the time, as long as the thesis of the collapse of the Polish state was repeated by the political leadership for a sufficiently long period in jurisprudence. The prevalent doctrine was not the slightest bit discomforted by the fact that its claim "that under recognized principles of international law . . . the German Reich as the victorious state had primarily acquired the right to dispose of the territory of the former Republic of Poland and its inhabitants"[8] was in open defiance of general international law, since in fact these "recognized principles" stated exactly the opposite, that "illegal" occupations (e.g., through aggression) did not lead to the extinction of the occupied state—at least not within such a brief period of time.[9] Under general international law, the theory of the nonextinction of the occupied state applied even when the occupying state intended to annex the territory of the occupied state, whereas for German jurisprudence it was just this intention of the German leadership (the breaking up of Poland)[10] that provided the justification for proceeding on the basis of the actual extinction of the Polish state.[11] The fact that the Western Powers had recognized the Polish government in exile in London was declared to be irrelevant by the Reich Chancellery itself,[12] since the National Socialist plans for empire did not permit the application of the rules of the international community of nations; as formulated by a representative of the Foreign Office, a mere *occupatio bellica* would have caused the rules of international law on the treatment of the local population to have gained ground, and Germany "unquestionably did not wish to submit to these."[13]

The treatment of the occupied Polish territories was thus viewed by the

National Socialist leadership as an *internal Reich* matter; with the doctrine of the "basic rights of states," in particular the right of a state to arm itself and the right of Lebensraum and of empire (*Grossraum*), to which a "leading power" was entitled (C. Schmitt),[14] National Socialist jurisprudence of international law supplied the corresponding theoretical foundations.[15] This rejection of the application of international law was already evident during the period of military administration in Poland, when the civil powers subordinate to that administration (heads of the civil administration, Party offices, local self-defense units), but above all the *Einsatzgruppen* of the SS and police, committed countless violations of the law, which, because the *occupatio bellica* under international law was still assumed at the time of the military administration,[16] were also crimes under international law from the German point of view; however, the rejection of the applicability of any international law was expressed after the end of the military administration, when attempts were made to justify the political decision to incorporate the General Government into the domestic territory of the National Socialist regime with vague formulas such as "affiliation" with the German Reich or the "actual edging closer . . . of this territory" to the German state community.[17]

The consequence of the rejection of the nature of the General Government as a territory occupied under international law was that the provisions of the Hague Warfare Convention and the Geneva Convention on the Treatment of Prisoners of War[18] were applied neither in the General Government nor in any other occupied territories in Eastern Europe. The rules of international law, now declared ineffective, primarily consisted of the regulations on the observance of state law, the protection of life and property of the inhabitants, the prohibition on the destruction of works of science and art, and the prohibition on the confiscation of the property of municipalities, churches, and charitable, scientific, and artistic associations (arts. 43, 46, 50, 53, and 56 of the Hague Convention). These provisions were systematically violated from the outset, since in the opinion of the Germans, civil administration in the General Government was exclusively an internal matter of the Reich. The violations of practically every rule of international law in the General Government—the confiscations, expropriations, destruction, and so on—were therefore nothing other than "legal measures of the internal German state powers in domestic German territories or those belonging to the German *Grossraum*."[19]

The question of the *constitutional* status of this territory subject to a German "claim of leadership" (Freisler), however, was difficult to answer, because the Decree of the Führer and Reich Chancellor on the Administration of the Occupied Polish Territories of October 12, 1939,[20] did not pronounce any formal incorporation. Although even members of the government of the General Government admitted that it was theoretically quite feasible to administer the General Government using the same administrative methods as in the Reich, the National Socialist doctrine of the "graduation in value and ranking of nations and the idea of a special system of rule to dominate the 'non-German' population"[21] ran counter to any formal incorporation. Treatment as a foreign territory was not possible, however, although the structure of the General Government and the comprehensive powers of the governor general (as well as his external relations) were modeled on the status of a foreign state, or at least that of an autonomous region,[22] since the General Government was part of the German dominions and thus could not at the same time be foreign territory. But it was also a land with a predominantly "non-German" population, so the only alternative was to create something quite new, something revolutionary. The ambitious aim of the authorities of the governor general was therefore to establish a new administrative and legal system, whose "guiding principles" should be only "the task at hand" and "National Socialist instinct,"[23] in order—as Reich Minister of Justice Gürtner observed in a speech in Kraków—"to show . . . for the first time, how we will live . . . with the non-German peoples."[24]

For the definition of the new form of mastery over "non-Germans," recourse was made first to the term *affiliation,* which was later used during the organization of the administration. The General Government was regarded as "affiliated" with the Reich, which was supposed to express both the association with the Reich and the autonomy of the affiliated territory. However, because affiliation was never defined precisely, it was of little use. The same applies to the concept of the General Government as a borderland (*Nebenland*) of the Reich, coined by Governor General Frank himself, or to the phrase "outpost of the Reich"[25] used by Hitler. In essence, the concept of the General Government represented new territory that could not be understood using the traditional categories of international law. There was less effort to achieve any legal *concretization* of its status, with commentators confining themselves to emphasizing the "historical task" of the General Government, the "original and unique nature" of its status (using the term *unique form*); the "proud central structure of Greater German life," the "unique, original creation . . . of National Socialist state thought," "a legislative and organizational creation of the first order," and so forth.[26]

Nevertheless, there was agreement that the General Government belonged to the "Greater German sphere of influence" (although the territory had not been annexed)[27] and that it represented the first case of the acknowledgment of "German sovereignty outside the Greater German Reich";[28] the few authors who made any comments at all on the status of the General Government invented the term *geopolitical thinking* (*"Raumdenken"*) to characterize this classification, which obviously borrowed from the concept of the empire (*Grossraum*).[29] However, it was not clear what this concept of *geopolitical sovereignty* (*"Raumhoheit"*) actually meant and what effect it would have on the conventional form of rule over foreign territories, for which only the term *territorial sovereignty* (*Gebietshoheit*) had previously been used.[30]

Consequently, the status of the General Government remained undefined. As was usual in the National Socialist system when no one knew what to do or how new structures should be defined, there was a retreat to negative definitions or vague circumscriptions. Court practice and jurisprudence agreed on what the General Government was *not,* that is, domestic territory; but they also agreed that it belonged to the "perpetual dominion" of the German *Grossraum.*[31] For "geopolitical thinking in terms of international law," the General Government therefore had a secular "political significance under international law";[32] it was the "first component" of a new "continental *Grossraum,*" whose era was now approaching and for which the historical models of Rome, the USA, Russia, and the colonial powers were adopted.[33] Put even more clearly by Governor General Frank, the General Government was the first step toward the "German Global Empire," a "land of the future."[34] At the same time, attention was always drawn to the fact that the National Socialist "*Grossraum* order," like the new structure of the General Government, was a completely new creation, neither a constitutional phenomenon nor one under international law; neither had it found its "final conceptual form."[35] As usual, when the instruments of legal policy could offer no answer, not jurisprudence but administrative practice was to produce the decisive solution.[36]

Indeed, the status of the General Government can be explained only by the established facts, with allowance for the political objectives. Thus it is evident that the General Government was essentially viewed by the administrative leadership as a component of the Reich, as Reich territory, despite its far-reaching administrative and legislative autonomy. Notwithstanding the zealous efforts of the governor general to prevent Reich authorities from "interfering" with the administration of the General Government,[37] Reich principles were still applied in the administration, the legislature, and the administration of justice, albeit in simplified form, as illustrated by the following examples.

The criminal law and the Civil Code of the Reich were adopted in full, or at least to a very substantial degree. The Reich authorities and the German authorities of the General Government provided each other with administrative assistance.[38] With regard to judicial assistance and the law of enforcement,[39] the General Government was regarded as Reich territory, in which Reich judgments could be enforced without further ado.[40] In terms of finance, appointments, and personnel, the General Government was completely dependent upon the Reich and integrated into the Reich financial administration.[41] In economic terms, too, the General Government was for all intents and purposes a part of the Reich. With the relocation of businesses, production, and armament factories to the General Government, the customs frontiers that existed formally were essentially eliminated, so that the differences with the Reich lay essentially only in the different price and wage levels, a number of import and export bans, and the foreign exchange and police frontiers.[42] Although the governor general continually insisted on his administrative autonomy, even with respect to agencies outside the General Government, he aspired to achieving the greatest possible harmonization of the General Government with the Reich for financial reasons, with the immediate aim of a customs and economic union.[43]

This de facto incorporation of the General Government into the Reich was also evident in the change in the terminology used by the administration[44] and the political leadership. For example, after meeting with criticism in the Reich, the term *Nebenland* was no longer used after the end of 1940 by order of Frank.[45] Instead, there was increasing talk of the General Government as a "component of the German sphere of influence" or of the "Greater German Reich."[46] Hitler himself regarded the General Government as part of the Reich[47] and declared the Austrian part of Galicia, which had been incorporated into the General Government in 1941, to be future "Reich territory."[48] The Reich Ministry of the Interior spoke of the "increasing amalgamation of the Reich territory with the General Government at all levels."[49]

The literature also recognized that the General Government had aligned itself with the Reich, was a "political structure that was integrated" into the state order of the Reich, and was in reality a "*component*" of the Reich.[50]

The incorporation of the General Government into the Reich was, however, no more than a principle, one that saw numerous exceptions in everyday practice. If the special legislative treatment of "non-Germans" could be enforced better if the General Government was deemed to be foreign territory, then it was not part of the Reich territory; conversely, it was reckoned as part of the Reich in cases in which "non-Germans" were to be subjected to German sovereign powers (e.g., in the area of criminal law).[51]

No doubt in connection with the long-term Germanization plans, there were also plans to reinforce the constitutional integration of the General Government into the Reich, but these never reached any concrete stage because the tensions between the Reich administration and the semiautonomous General Government prevented any attempts at implementation. As early as summer

1940, the governor general had submitted plans to the Reich Chancellery to incorporate the General Government in full into the German Reich by a Führer
decree; these plans were, of course, opposed by the Reich Ministry of the Interior as long as Frank stuck to his administrative autonomy.[52] Various Reich
agencies, however, above all the Reich Ministry of the Interior, themselves proposed in 1942 that the General Government be incorporated into the Reich (by
abolishing its administrative autonomy) in the form of three or five *Reichsgaue,*
because—as Governor General Frank quite correctly suspected—such a vague,
and worse still, autonomous structure as the General Government was a thorn
in the flesh of the well-oiled bureaucracy of the Reich.[53] But this proposal was
rejected by Hitler because of his aversion to the Reich administration and
Frank's urging against the "centralized bureaucracy." Because of these efforts,
however, Frank had commissioned his own state secretary, Joseph Bühler, to
prepare a secret study of the potential for a complete transfer of the General
Government to the Reich administration.[54] He even thought that the General
Government could someday become a "homogeneous *Reichsgau,*" "headed by a
Reichsstatthalter, who—as in the *Reichsgau* Wartheland—could try to cope with
the situation here," because the Reich administration was becoming increasingly
hostile to the autonomy of the General Government.[55]

IV. Principles of Administrative Policy and Their Results

The specifics of the efforts of the administration to cope with the conditions
in the General Government were oriented toward the definition of the General
Government as a colony and a de facto part of the Reich territory. This colonial
definition was also reflected in a policy of "oppression" and suppression, which
implemented the theory of the subhuman creature (*Untermensch*) by way of the
"racial" breakup of the local population, by way of its classification by special
law, or by way of deportation to concentration camps or to forced labor in the
Reich territory. The administration developed in the General Government thus
represented the purest form of National Socialist occupation administration,
not encountered in any other territory occupied by Germany.[1]

The policy of a relatively small German administration at the top that left the
Poles largely to themselves was correspondingly propagated. Hitler himself had
ordered in fall 1939 that no German "model administration" was to be developed in Poland; the "Polish economy" was to be left intact.[2] Originally, the administrative leadership in the General Government therefore had no more than
limited goals: the "maintenance of security and order," "ensuring that the population was fed," and "securing the total resources of the General Government for

the Reich."[3] In terms of legislation, this "securing" was to be achieved by allowing Polish law to continue in force where it did not contradict the "assumption of administration by the German Reich" (sec. 4 of the Führer decree of October 12, 1939).[4] The German administration was to be restricted to a few areas of public law:[5] where German security or economic interests were affected, German (special) law applied, for instance in the realms of police, criminal, and labor law; Polish law otherwise remained in force. Some examples of these German regulations deserving mention are the severe legal segregation of Germans and Poles and the exclusion of the Jews from the entire economy.[6] As regards the specific treatment of the "non-Germans," however, opinions differed sharply.

To avoid uprisings, the administrators and *Grossraum* experts of the old school warned—as history taught—against the self-deceit of treating the "non-German" peoples as Helots. All historical experience spoke against harsh treatment. Instead, they urged a patriarchal system under German sovereignty; although the local population must be segregated from the Germans and any assimilation prevented, these peoples must be *administered* and *supported* as much as possible within these limits.[7] Each of the "subject peoples" must be preserved in its "ethnic-racial sovereignty" and the "harmonious cohesion of national legislation sustained";[8] in contrast to the "imperialism of past epochs," the *Grossraum* must be oriented toward "racial principles" and should not be allowed to become a "cover for conquests."[9] Not only compulsion but also voluntary acts would hold the *Grossraum* together; it must be regarded by the "non-German" peoples as an "inner necessity.[10] The "*Führer Volk*" therefore had a duty to take precautions to ensure an adequate life for the "subject peoples" as well as their external defense.[11]

In reality, however, exactly the opposite occurred: the leadership acted stolidly on the concept that they had devised for the treatment of alien peoples and took everything into account apart from reality. All proclamations on respect for the "characteristic racial features" of the local population therefore proved to be empty phrases and concealed the true intentions of the regime. In its haste, blind zeal, and belief in force as the only means of rule, the Nazi leadership and its enforcers, the SS and the police, as well as the administrative leadership of the General Government itself (albeit to a lesser extent), reduced the Poles to the status of Helots through a ruthless policy of exploitation. In view of the high population surplus and the large number of jobless people in the General Government, there was no need to display any particular consideration in this policy of exploitation; on the contrary, they were able to act as they pleased, that is, work toward the greatest possible productivity of labor at the lowest possible cost.

The harsh anti-Polish policy of the administrative leadership of the General Government was expressed in a comprehensive catalog of special legislative restrictions, very similar to the regulations issued against the "non-Germans" in the Annexed Eastern Territories, as well as in a policy of "divide and conquer," which, in line with the National Socialist doctrine of the inequality of peoples, was intended to separate the individual ethnic groups in the General Government (Poles, Ukrainians, Górales). A particularly drastic policy was pursued in Galicia, earlier occupied by Soviet Russia, which was regarded as a Reich German settlement area and the incorporation of which had been dealt with by the head-quarters in Kraków even before the beginning of the war with Russia.[12] There the principle ruled, as expounded by the reigning governor of the Lemberg (L'vov) District at a conference, of not straying too far from the "harshness . . . applied by the Soviets," because ostensibly the population would have doubted the seriousness of the German instructions.[13] Unlike the situation in the Annexed Eastern Territories, however, there was no general policy of expulsion in the General Government because this region was to become a labor reservoir regardless of population density, in line with Hitler's axiom that the Poles were slaves born to perform menial labor;[14] neither was the extermination policy practiced in the Annexed Eastern Territories pursued to the same extent,[15] although large numbers of the "non-German" intelligentsia had been killed or abducted (via the AB Operation, etc.) with the backing of the administrative leadership.[16] However, it was a self-evident principle that the treatment of the Poles was not based on any humanitarian grounds but exclusively determined by considerations of expediency;[17] in this respect, the administrative leadership held the view that it was in their own properly understood interest to subject the Poles to severe special laws but at the same time to attempt to preserve their working capacity and morale, for instance by a certain level of welfare benefits for the nonworking population (e.g., support for Polish welfare organizations and for the Central Polish Aid Committee).[18]

But this principle of "preserving" the Polish workforce was misleading, because in terms of National Socialist theory, it meant only that the foreign laborers would not be allowed to starve to death immediately. All living conditions were to be organized in such a way that the Poles could do no more than *exist* as cheap labor, entailing the reduction of the population to or below the subsistence level ("emaciation status") as well as neglecting all its cultural and social needs.[19]

The consequences were far more catastrophic than in the Eastern Territories, because tens of thousands of deportees from the Eastern Territories were thronging into the densely populated General Government. Among the material consequences of the nonsensical administrative policies of the General Government authorities were the general undernourishment and exhaustion of the population, in particular of the "idle" persons unfit for work, whose rations were reduced *below* the subsistence level.[20] Jews received *no rations whatsoever* in any case and were totally dependent on the Jewish welfare organizations financed by the Jews themselves. A massive black market developed, which not only was tolerated by the German authorities but evolved into an indispensable feature of life, as food supplies could not have been maintained without it.

Faced with the growing importance of the General Government as an economic factor of the Reich, the growing impoverishment of the population, and the rise of the Polish resistance movement, the administrative leadership attempted to initiate a change in its Polish policy after 1943.[21] Numerous initiatives by the governor general to treat the Poles less harshly and grant greater administrative autonomy attempted to implement a change in Berlin's Polish policy.[22]

As was to be expected, these attempts met with no success because of the total lack of serious political will at the center. Berlin was not fundamentally opposed to a change of tactics,[23] and even the SS and police leadership had come to accept the need for a more lenient treatment of the Poles and seriously believed that it could still cooperate with the Polish Home Army (Armija Krajowa).[24] But only Hitler could make such a decision; and since he never made it, everything remained as it was. The central administration also tended to become bogged down in details; it was not prepared to abandon the "ultimate aim" of the future German settlement of the General Government; it insisted on retaining the segregation of Poles and Ukrainians because of a fear of the kindling of national passion, and it blocked the authorization of Polish priests who were "not acceptable."[25] Finally, the Reich Ministry of the Interior did not believe that the "time was ripe" for arrangements regarding Polish cooperation in the administration as a result of the Warsaw uprising and the poor military situation,[26] until it was too late for any changes.

Apart from this, both the timing and the substance of the planned change of policy demonstrated very markedly the "unstable enthusiasm"[27] of the governor general and the naive attitude of the authorities, who totally misjudged the impact of their propaganda and practice and were unable to comprehend that after a policy of total harshness and enslavement, it was impossible to put the clock back; the Poles could not be enlisted as allies overnight. Any credibility that could have made such attempts successful had already been gambled away, all the more because the tide would have been turned if the course of the war had run differently. Even if such attempts had not been steamrollered by the changing face of the war or had not incorporated tactical reservations, there had to be doubts about their seriousness because no genuine efforts were made to realize them; in fact the continuation of the same drastic measures as before merely gave the lie to them, with the governor general limiting himself to statements of good-will and nonbinding declarations.[28] Right until the end, therefore, the treatment of the Poles was determined exclusively by considerations of economic usefulness and not by political considerations, because the leadership had been blind to the realities of the situation from the outset and believed that it could continue its absurd policy of total exploitation ad infinitum.

V. Principles of Administrative Organization: The Principle of Unified Administration

With regard to the administrative organization of the new model of domination and administration of the "non-Germans" in the General Government, different tendencies are evident in theory and practice. The classical theory of administration based on the principles of the military administration of occupied territories was rejected,[1] and experiments were made with new forms of rule, as seen in countless reflections by the *Grossraum* experts on the nature of the future administration of the *Grossraum*.[2]

Whereas a continuation of the previous administrative practice under German suzerainty was planned and practiced in the occupied territories of Western Europe,[3] the principles of the administrative organization in the colonial East consisted of taking over the local administrative machinery, restructuring it to conform with Greater German colonial principles, and subjecting it to German control.[4] New terms (*Grossraum order, Grossraum administration, Grossraum territory, Grossraum Volk, Führervolk,*[5] subject peoples)[6] and a new typology of administrative forms appeared: administration in terms of "pacts" between the *Führervolk* and the *Grossraum Volk* (retaining the local administration and government); administration in the form of a "supervisory administration" (retention of the local administration under German supervision); "government administration" (occupation of the most important positions by the *Führervolk,* with other administrative tasks performed by the local self-administration);[7] and the "colonial administration" (occupation of all positions by the *Führervolk* and total supervision of the life of the local population).[8]

In administrative practice, however, these new forms of administration were never implemented. The efforts of the experts to systematize the new forms of rule, the development of abstract concepts, and their demarcation from one another show how strongly the new National Socialist *Grossraum* theory was tied to the organizational concept of the traditional administration as well as the extent to which it misjudged the revolutionary force of the National Socialist leadership in the occupied territories, averse as it was to any rigid legal structures. This shows particularly clearly the low importance, even irrelevance, of legal systems in the organization of National Socialist rule. The primacy of the policy, that is, of National Socialist radicalism, took no notice of the unity or expediency of a system but followed its own, self-driven gravity of political aims and the actual situation. The administrative forms in occupied Central and Eastern Europe were therefore mixtures of old and new elements that could not be harmonized with the aforementioned systems. The administration in the Protectorate of Bohemia and Moravia, for instance, lay somewhere between the "supervisory administration" and "government administration" types, and the administration in the General Government between the "government administration" and "colonial administration" types; in the Annexed Eastern Territories, an administrative structure was developed that was closest to the "colonial administration."[9]

In regard to the particulars of the administrative machinery established in the General Government, the plans for a German administration based on the Reich administration, drawn up in October 1939 by the central authorities in Berlin, had been rejected for political reasons (too complicated) during the era of the military administration.[10] These reasons certainly did not correspond to the ideas of the political leadership and the governor general, ideas of administrative leadership based on a colonial model. Officially, all top posts were to be staffed by Germans (because only in this way could Germany "become a global empire" and the "Polish danger" be eliminated),[11] with Poles being used merely as ancillary labor. Former Polish civil servants were therefore kept only as employees in subordinate positions;[12] the Polish intelligentsia was to be denied any activity wherever possible; it was feared as a standard-bearer of Polish national sentiment and rejected from the outset;[13] the potential for other forms of cooperation, especially at the local level and in rural areas, was not exploited and subsequently was gambled away recklessly.[14]

The policy of a small German administrative nucleus supervising an administration staffed with Polish ancillary workers never left the theoretical stage. In reality, starting in 1940, a German "model administration" was developed in the General Government contrary to Hitler's intentions;[15] the "Grossraum" administration was replaced by a closely woven network of authorities and regulations, in which the administration's tendency toward perfectionism[16] could unfold free from dependency on the Reich administration and totally unaffected by the course of the war.[17] There was no more talk of leaving the locals as far as possible to their own devices, as expounded in the colonial principle; of all the occupied territories, the local administration of the General Government was the one most comprehensively under German control. Only in matters of no interest to the German administration or in which financial burdens could be passed on was the Polish administration retained (e.g., in the area of welfare benefits).

The structure and lines of authority of the civil administration of the General Government were therefore somewhat inadequate from the beginning for any constructive Polish policy. In its expansion, its comprehensive jurisdiction, its quest for order and clarity, it was essentially no more than a mirror of the Reich administration, however strongly the top administrators in the general governor's office emphasized the unique features of their system compared to that of the Reich and the special authorities (e.g., the economic administration or the police).[18] The administration was headed by career civil servants with administrative experience from the Reich or the Austrian administration.[19] The administrative structure borrowed heavily from Reich law; in the words of the governor general, it represented "the last offshoot of an administration directly conducted using Reich methods."[20]

Compared with the increasing jurisdictional chaos in the Reich[21] or the legal vacuum and secret guidelines practiced in the Annexed Eastern Territories, the administration of the General Government still represented a certain degree of order. The judicial system was clearly structured, the administration organization had been developed along clear lines, at least at the beginning, and the administrative jurisdiction was not infested by Party authorities. The reason for this clarity was that the administrative structure of the General Government was based on a relatively simple basic pattern, described by the concept of the "Unified Administration." This pattern (which can be categorized as lying between the aforementioned "government administration" and "colonial administration" as coined by W. Best) was regarded as the ideal administrative from for colonial or semicolonial territories. Further, the Unified Administration was to create a strong centralized administration, compared with the cumbersome departmental administration of the Reich, and was to be the new administrative form of the future.[22] In a grotesque overestimation of his own limits, Governor General Frank, the most eager champion of the principle of the Unified Administration, regarded himself as a preceptor of the Reich administration, which his own administration must "educate."

The two characteristic features of the principle of the Unified Administration, which can only be outlined briefly, were revolutionary. They involved nothing less than the *elimination* of the departmental principle and of special administration and their consolidation under a single leadership.[23]

All levels of the administration in its entirety were headed by a chief administrator, who combined all responsibilities. The channels of decision of the specialist departments were placed under the control of the chief administrators of the various levels, and the entire administrative process was to be routed through these individuals. Initial attempts to implement this principle were already in place in the Reich—such as in the status of the Reich minister and head of the Reich Chancellery[24]—and had found strong advocates, especially in the Reich Ministry of the Interior, which assumed that the new central authority was the Reich *internal* administration and anticipated that implementation of the Unified Administration would result in the standardization and strengthening of the responsibilities it had lost to the Reich special administrations and the political special authorities.[25] However, the strong status of the departments prevented this principle from being implemented in the Reich. In contrast, the General Government was virgin territory where the Unified Administration could be tested without interference from the Reich administration.[26] Three administrative levels were developed: the office (later government) of the governor general as the central authority; the medium-level authority, roughly comparable to administrative districts, in the from of four (from 1941 five) districts (Kraków, Warsaw, Radom, Lublin, and Lemberg [Ľvov]) as well as forty (from 1941 fifty-five) rural *Kreise* and seven urban *Kreise*. Below *Kreis* level, the Polish administration of the towns and municipalities remained under German supervision. The chief administrators with comprehensive powers as mentioned above were the governor general for the central administration, the district chief (*Gouverneur*) in the districts, the *Kreishauptmann* in the rural *Kreise,* and the *Stadthauptmann* in the urban *Kreise.*[27] The specialist authorities were incorporated into the administrations of the *Kreishauptmann* and the district chief and of the governor general[28] and were directly responsible *not* to the internal administration but to the respective chief administrator. They lost their status as autonomous decision-making bodies and were reduced to the status of "executive and advisory bodies of the organ of sovereign power." For the administrative leadership of the General Government, Unified Administration was—as expressed in the bombastic language of the day—"not the supervision or dictatorship of the internal administration or any other branch of the administration over all others, but . . . the administrative policy direction of all branches of the administration as well as the elimination of all negative features in order to achieve the task placed upon us in a non-German settlement region in war and in peace."[29]

The strongest basis for the Unified Administration was to be above all the rural and urban *Kreise,* because the governor general had rightly realized that this from of administration could function and attract sufficient managerial staff only if the lower administrative levels had sufficient freedom of action and were not choked by a superbureaucracy at the center. In this respect, the governor general, sometimes even in opposition to his own administration, adhered to the principle of giving the medium and lower-level authorities as many powers "as could be tolerated" (and approved autonomous action by the lower-level authorities), because decentralization "helped develop personality" and was the basis of the "colonial administration of the East."[30]

The second characteristic of the principle of Unified Administration in the General Government consisted of the "politicization" of the administration in the sense that the administrative leadership was also the Party leadership;[31] thus the dualism of Party and state was abolished. This new function of the administration, one of the most important concerns of the governor general, whose relationship to the Party had been worse than poor from the start,[32] was to be a demonstration against the loss of authority[33] and standing by the administration in the Reich and in the occupied territories. It represented an attempt to harmonize the *political* aspirations of the Party with the *total administrative aspirations* of the administrative leadership, to simplify the administrative organization, and to increase its efficiency. This synthesis of politics and administration was to be supported by the ideal of every administration, the "antibureaucratic" chief administrator, in whom training and knowledge were less important than personality and the ability to get things done.[34] Above all at *Kreis* level as a *Kreishauptmann* or a *Stadthauptmann*—titles consciously linked to the models of the earlier Austrian administration (in Galicia)—he was to control a loose-knit administration, be flexible and no "desk man," be capable of acting independently and of enforcing his will, indeed of being "a real man"[35] in this "non-German region." This was the image of the administrative leader in the "typical colonial style" (according to Frank), with whom "German order" was to be established in the East.

This new definition of chief administrator certainly achieved its purpose. It appealed to the initiative and self-reliance of the individual, qualities that had no chance in the conventional administration. As a result, it initially attracted individuals who were offered opportunities for development that would never have been possible in the Reich. These individuals, from whom the team of *Kreishauptleute* and their offices were in part chosen, were dynamic forces from the economy, the Party, and the administration who were weary of the rigid bureaucracy of the Reich and the arrogance of the specialist administrations and came to the East to "experience something" but also to be "pioneers"; for the regime, they therefore represented a welcome pool of active, young executive personnel (government officials, lawyers, economic experts, graduates of NSDAP cadre schools, etc.).[36] However, this pool was by no means sufficient, especially for the specialist administration, whereas in the centralized authorities, the monopoly of legal specialists was tenaciously defended.[37] In contrast, the *top posts* were allocated to Party functionaries (mostly nonspecialists), some of them old friends of the governor general whom he had brought with him from the Reich judicial service, the Reich law office of the NSDAP, and the Academy of German Law.[38]

However, it was not possible to preserve the Unified Administration in the long term. It failed because of the political, administrative, and personnel situation and the inconsistency of its own administrative leadership. The principle of Unified Administration was not implemented at crucial points in the organizational field, which ultimately led to its downfall.

The police service led its own life separate from the civil administration with its own administrative structure and chain of command,[39] and from 1942 on, it wrested all police administration duties from the internal administration, delegating them to its own administration.[40] The "subordination" of the higher SS and police leader (HSSPF) to the governor general, and of the local SS and police leaders to the district chiefs set out in the governor general's decrees,[41] was meaningless, because the senior administrators had no authority to instruct these agencies and the "subordination" did not bring with it any disciplinary powers. Berlin continued to supervise and issue direct orders to the police, opening the door wide to arbitrary and despotic police acts.[42] Whether the local police chiefs obeyed instructions of the district chiefs or the *Kreishauptleute* depended on their personal relationship with the administration head involved and on their own policies.[43] Unified Administration was therefore doomed to failure because the administration had no means to enforce its instruction to the enforcement authorities.

The classic special administrations were not, as would have been necessary, incorporated into the unified authorities of the general administration; they led largely autonomous lives,[44] which gave rise to endless disputes because the administration heads (*Kreishauptleute* and *Stadthauptleute*) should, in theory, have been the "political leaders" of all branches of the administration, but they did not possess *ultimate authority*; that is, they were not the superior authority over the *special* administrations.[45] Particularly at the lower levels, this resulted in a good deal of administrative and jurisdictional chaos. The *Kreishauptmann* spent much of his time preventing turf wars between the various departments, which acted on the instructions of their own headquarters (the district administration or the central administration in Kraków) without notifying the *Kreishauptmann*.[46] Even within the departments reporting to the *Kreishauptmann*, tendencies to act as special administrations were soon evident.[47]

This all saw the concept of Unified Administration diluted and undermined. As time went by, the situation increasingly tended to emulate conditions reigning in the Reich: the independence of the specialist administrations and the existence of direct channels of decision from higher to lower *specialist authorities* (bypassing the medium-level authority, the district administration).[48] Relations between the various administrative levels (central and district) were also burdened by rivalries and tension.[49]

The district administrations jealously defended their independence from the central authorities in Kraków; they felt themselves to be the "Gauleiter of the General Government," advocated autonomous tendencies,[50] and complained bitterly about the arrogant ordering-around of the government of the General Government in totally irrelevant matters, whereas the districts were able to make their own decisions in major issues.[51] In turn, the central authorities tended toward expansion and started to dominate all lower-level authorities,[52] the worst consequences of which were overbureaucratization and "an unnecessary and senseless" jurisdictional chaos;[53] for instance, eighteen different agencies were responsible for trade permits in the General Government.[54]

Only at the beginning, when no regulations had been issued for many areas and the General Government was ruled by general instructions, was there relatively large scope for the much-hailed Unified Administration and the initiative of the administration.[55] This room for maneuver lasted until no later than fall 1940. After that, the reports by the administrative authorities in the districts and *Kreise* are full of complaints about friction with the special authorities (police), breaches of Unified Administration,[56] the "big-headed" central authorities, the red tape from the top,[57] the central authorities' administrative perfectionism[58] and unworldliness, and their inability or unwillingness to take account of the actual situation in the country[59] (although the lower-level authorities still had greater latitude than in the Reich territory).[60] The specialists at lower levels were completely tied up with blocking unnecessary or damaging directives from above and coping with the situation as it was.[61] Quite sensible proposals to achieve greater practical knowledge in the central authorities by exchanging staff[62] failed because of the reluctance and ponderous structure of the machinery.

It was therefore evident at an early stage that the (political) demand for "loose-knit" administrative leadership on the one hand, and the ambition of the German administration to supervise and control all areas on the other were totally incompatible. The heads of department in the central authorities and the districts wanted to rule, implement, control, and supervise everything and everyone themselves, imposing considerable strains and chaos on official business processes.[63] The office of the governor general administered but did not rule. As is normally the case with misgovernment, each department blamed another and passed responsibility down the line. But this did not have any effect on the appalling state of affairs. The governor general himself saw the chaos but did nothing to remedy it because he vacillated and was himself unable to pursue a consistent policy. He started to lose control, burying his head in the sand and agreeing with whoever last had his ear, for instance fighting against departmental autonomy (i.e., in favor of centralizing the administration) but still not disposed to tolerate the efforts by the general administrative authorities (district *Gouverneure*) to achieve independence.[64] It was an open secret throughout the entire administration that the principle of Unified Administration had been undermined, indeed abandoned, and was nothing more than a "pretty facade."[65]

IV. Actual Development: The Lack of Personnel and the Failure of the German Administration

Personnel problems also doomed the principle of Unified Administration to failure; the ideal of the chief administrator could not be realized because there were insufficient personnel, and in particular insufficient management personnel. As in the case of all staff employed in the East, the average number and quality of administrative staff in the General Government were well below those encountered in the Reich administration, blatantly contradicting the demands of the leadership that administrative officials "willing to make political decisions" should be brought to the General Government. Not "tired, shopworn file-shifters, comrades in bureaucracy" should work in the General Government but those "cast in the mold of true efficiency," "warriors totally dedicated to the liquidation of the Poles."[1] In practice, however, such "warriors" were almost totally lacking or proved to be failures whose characters were not up to the demands of the "life of luxury" in the East.

Because most civil servants had been drafted into the Wehrmacht, the Reich administration could only supply staff for individual specialist administrations in insufficient number, so that staff shortages became an everyday phenomenon.[2] Interest in the central authorities in Kraków and the districts, as well as for top positions in the urban *Kreise,* still remained relatively large because of the social and cultural attractions.[3] These levels thus received a disproportionately high number of personnel,[4] while the rural *Kreis* administrations suffered from permanent staff shortages and poor quality, which were even more noticeable given the high staff turnover[5] (apart from drafts to the Wehrmacht, there were also reassignments to the Reich and voluntary return because of the poor living conditions),[6] making any continuity in the administration impossible. The demands by the leadership that only the best people should be sent to the East contrasted with the ceaseless complaints about the poor professional and personal quality of the personnel, because—as seen by the administration of the General Government—the Reich administration was of the opinion that "anything was good enough for the East."[7] Feelings were particularly bitter that "elements" that had become "unpopular" in the Reich were to be employed in the General Government; "unpopular" in this context meant unpopular with the National Socialists. It was noted, for instance, that a civil servant was appointed vice governor in Lublin who had earlier been a Social Democrat.[8]

In terms of performance of duties,[9] the personnel disappointed even the lowest expectations: "a thousand kilometers and more away from home," even the most reliable civil servants failed and "went off the rails," as a former leading administrative official of the General Government put it.[10] Particularly in the field offices, numerous opportunities were available—and frequently used—to play the member of the "master race" in front of the "non-Germans" and indulge in the new colonial type, and even the SIPO (Gestapo), which behaved like an elite, was no exception.[11] Although the wealth of powers available to the lower-level authorities was in itself an opportunity to achieve at least a bearable, although hardly loyal, coexistence with the local population,[12] this opportunity was frittered away recklessly by personal shortcomings, as demonstrated by the numerous examples (especially from 1942 on) of unbelievable incompetence, inaction, and brutality by the senior staff, in particular in the *Kreishauptmann* offices.[13] It was an open secret that corruption and profiteering were the order of the day in the German departments and that in the General Government "not all principles of the homeland were preserved," whereby it is evident that a certain minimum level of misconduct was accepted as normal in view of the situation.[14] The security service was more straightforward. The notorious reports by the commander of the SIPO and the SD for the Galician District in Lemberg on the "conduct of the Reich Germans in the occupied territories" described with great relish the deplorable image of drunken excesses, bribery, profiteering, sexual offenses, and so on by members of the public administration and the police; their luxurious lifestyle; and their close contacts with the local Polish population, totally reprehensible in terms of racial policy, and—even worse—with Jews. These reports, which caused a tremendous stir and hit Berlin like a bomb,[15] resulted in the coining of the term *Polish disease* ("weakened morality") of the administration in the General Government and in calls for the dismissal of Governor General Frank.[16]

Against the backdrop of these shortcomings and the brutal actions of the SS and the police,[17] one gains the image of an administrative policy in which Eastern potentates were engaged in a futile struggle with the conventional administration, resulting in a strange conglomeration.

The victims were the Polish population, which was practically driven to resist the occupying powers by the contradictory policies of the various authorities. Only in 1944, when it was much too late for change in any case, was there any recognition or admission of the countless failures and mistakes with respect to the Polish population. On October 19, 1944, for instance, a report by the RSHA on "previous Polish policy and proposals for its relaxation or restructuring" noted that the "inadequate countermeasures adopted by the Germans [support] resistance activities very strongly. Politically incorrect measures [resettlement of Poles in Zamość, labor roundups, etc.] [had increased] the Polish will to resist." The treatment of a people "with methods (tin bowls and calico) used by England against non-European peoples" was therefore out of the question for the Poles from the outset(!).[18]

Essentially, this situation merely reflected the style and policies of the leadership itself, and its loud complaints about the administration, personnel, and police interference demonstrated its double standards, since poor examples had already been set and abuses tolerated.[19] Characteristic of this is not only the vacillating, insecure personality of Governor General and Chief Administrator Frank, with his weak leadership and contradictory management of the administration;[20] the arrogance and incompetence of his officials and large numbers of senior personnel also played a crucial role.[21] These attitudes and utterings show clearly that counter to the thesis repeatedly brought forward until very recently,[22] the administration in the General Government did not fail because of "tight control from the outside" and the restricted room for maneuver of the authorities but first and foremost because of the corruption and indecisive leadership of its top officials and its unimaginative policy of brutal repression. In its blind actionism and short-sighted attitudes, the leadership of the General Government and its subordinate authorities pursued the totally insupportable notions that it had conceived about the "colonial East" and the treatment of subjugated peoples, completely ignoring the actual circumstances and refusing to make any effort, as a former high official in the General Government put it, "to understand the psyche of the subjugated peoples and drew the appropriate conclusions."[23] It therefore foundered less on any external threat than essentially on its own incompetence and shortsightedness.[24] The consequence of these factors, combined with the extravagance and perfectionism of the administrative machinery, its inconsistency and jurisdictional chaos, was that the administration in the General Government neither was an administration in the conventional sense, nor did it meet the conditions for a real colonial administration; it was nothing more than an unimaginative ruinous administration on the greatest possible scale, politically, economically, and psychologically.[25]

A. Fundamentals: The Segregation of Germans and "Non-Germans" and the Discrimination against "Non-Germans" as Far as "Necessary"

---

1. Jews

The methods and intensity of the treatment of the local population needed for this predatory administration differed depending on whether Poles or other "non-Germans" were involved or Poles of Jewish extraction. For the Jewish Poles, whose proportion of the total population of the General Government was relatively high (1.6 million) and whose influence in commerce and the professions was considerable,[1] a special system of legal rules was devised, the details of which are discussed below. This system of legal rules had become necessary because in contrast to the Annexed Eastern Territories, in which Jews were no more than a temporary phenomenon (deportations and ghettoization had largely been completed in 1940–41), it was expected that the local Jews would remain in the General Government for a longer time; furthermore, this region was designated as the catchment area for all Jews deported from Western Europe, so special rules were needed covering all areas of life. The basic policy of the treatment of the Jews consisted of utmost harshness, because Jews, as in general in the East, were barely regarded by the administration any more as persons (legal entities) or groups but rather as troublesome "parasites," the more so where "Eastern Jews" were concerned, who were viewed as the embodiment of the "Jewish essence" and of corruption.

Although the concept of the Jew was harmonized with the concept prevailing in the Reich territory,[2] the office of the governor general was contemplating far-reaching plans to foil efforts by the Jews to be excluded from the official concept of the Jew. In the legislation office of the governor general, a plan was drafted to introduce a general prohibition on the baptism of Jews,[3] but this was never implemented. The compulsory wearing of badges by Jews (irrespective of their citizenship) was introduced as early as November 1939, long before the corresponding regulation in the Reich.[4] At the end of October 1940, the emigration of Jews from the General Government was finally halted because it was only reinforcing "world Jewry."[5] To prevent them from enjoying any rights whatsoever,

Jews were prohibited from acting on their own behalf with respect to the authorities.[6] When submitting applications, Jews paid double the fees charged to Poles.[7] An uninhibited anti-Semitic propaganda campaign flooded the General Government, whereas a certain amount of restraint was practiced in dealing with the Polish population, on whose labor the Germans depended. Countless anti-Semitic posters, publications, and photos about the Jewish slums, the Jewish markets and ghettos, the "Jewish wealth" and "Jewish dissipation" were in circulation in the General Government and the Reich;[8] anti-Semitic exhibitions were organized to "prove" the long list of bad qualities and features attributed to the Jews (they were considered "born dealers," marked by "dissipation," etc.),[9] characteristics to which they had been more or less driven by the actions of the German administration described below. These actions had been carefully prepared and implemented in a phased plan. They were designed to prepare the population for what was to come, namely, the elimination of personal freedom and the evacuation and resettlement of the Jews until they were reduced to indifference and oblivion behind the ghetto walls,[10] a state that frequently occurred.

These measures, which, as in the Reich, mostly fell under the jurisdiction of the internal administration,[11] aimed at the quickest possible total deprivation of all rights of the Jews. Mostly small-scale craftsmen and merchants whose traditions and lifestyle often differed substantially from those of the Poles, the Jews, living in poverty and not suspecting their fate, were reduced to a condition of absolute privation by the rigorous practices of the German agencies; they were hardly capable of living, to say nothing of working.[12] With single-minded purpose, anti-Jewish special laws were promulgated in the first weeks of the civil administration; the first official act by the German authorities in the General Government was the introduction of forced labor for Jews. The reason for the speed with which this special law appeared was that numerous models were already available in the Reich that could be borrowed or adopted.[13] In all, four phases of anti-Jewish legislation can be identified.[14] The first phase was segregation and *discrimination* compared with the rest of the population (forced labor, compulsory wearing of badges, etc.).[15] The second phase involved *extension* of the isolation measures, starting as usual with numerous reporting and registration obligations and ending with residence restrictions and restrictions on the use of public facilities and transport;[16] it served the purpose of "marshaling" the Jews by the authorities. The third phase was the *total isolation* of the Jews from their environment. This included directives that Jews must reside in a particular residential district (the Jewish quarter, the ghetto) and sealing this off hermetically from the outside world, with total administrative and police special law reigning inside the ghetto walls.[17] Ghettoization was the preliminary to the fourth phase, the resettlement or evacuation[18] of the Jews to the extermination camps in the process of the Final Solution, for which the SS and the police were responsible, collaborating closely with the administrative authorities.[19]

II. Poles

The treatment of the Poles followed different rules. Their treatment under special law did not aim to eradicate their physical and economic existence but "merely" to reduce their existence to the level of a leaderless pool of unskilled labor for the purposes of the Reich.[20] Because the treatment of the Poles was thus determined by pragmatic rather than systematic considerations, it is not possible to identify any set phases in an orderly, unwavering sequence dictated by racial hatred alone—in contrast to the treatment of the Jews. The key factor for the special legislation was solely the "real" needs of political opportuneness. These comprised first denationalization—the extermination of the economic, political, and cultural lives of the Poles—then their greatest possible isolation from the German "ruling class," and finally the reduction in the Polish standard of living where this was necessary in the interests of the German economy.

If at all possible, any memories of the era of the Polish nation-state were to be eradicated. Expressions of this objective included the prohibition on the wearing of Polish decorations and insignia, the prohibition on the use of Polish national emblems, and the removal of Polish monuments and places of remembrance, including such things as memorial plaques in the churches,[21] which was a particularly painful blow to the Poles. Comprehensive research work was intended to prove that German superiority had always existed in all domains.[22] Fanciful plans to rebuild the larger Polish cities were intended to immortalize the "German character" of these places.[23] This was all accompanied by broad-ranging segregation and special legislation that, as in the Eastern Territories, was meant to emphasize the subordinate status of the "non-Germans" and the special status of the Germans in everyday life. Absolute segregation was also to be universally enforced in the economic and private spheres.

Examples of this are the compulsory identification of German and Polish businesses; the compulsory wearing of insignia by members of the Party and its organizations; the compulsory Hitler-*Gruss* between persons in uniform and members of the public administration, which served to segregate the Germans from the "non-Germans" and encourage German solidarity; and the compulsory Hitler-*Gruss* to NSDAP flags;[24] in contrast to the practice in the Annexed Eastern Territories, no compulsory Hitler-*Gruss* by Poles to Germans was introduced because it was impossible to control this. The compulsory Hitler-*Gruss* by Jews to all Germans (especially those in uniform), introduced in some areas at *Kreis* level, had to be repealed because it was "undesirable" for Germans to be greeted by Jews at all.[25] All Germans, in particular members of the German administration, were instructed to avoid all private contacts with Poles and Jews, as well as all opportunities for making such contacts. Attendance at Polish church services was also incompatible with the conduct of an "honor-conscious" *Volksgenosse*.[26]

Further examples of the segregation policy are the "identification measures" for "non-Germans" issued on the first day of the civil administration, which always represented the first stage of special law. As one of his first legislative acts, the governor general had introduced compulsory identification cards for all "non-German" inhabitants of the General Government above the age of 15, except for foreigners, on October 26, 1939.[27] It was not so much the compulsory identification cards themselves that represented the actual special legislative character but rather their administration: for Jews and Gypsies, yellow ID cards with a black *J* or *Z* (for *Zigeuner* [Gypsy]) were designated; for minorities (Górales, Ukrainians, etc.), blue cards; and for all other persons, that is, Poles, gray cards.[28] Whether the compulsory identification cards were actually implemented in full is a matter of doubt, since for technical reasons they were not issued until 1941.[29]

B. The Nature of the System of Special Law: A Normative System instead of Secret Guidelines

With regard to the techniques of the special legislative measures, the administrative leadership in the General Government had an easier start than that in the occupied territories, because the General Government was a new colonial territory in which the administration enjoyed complete autonomy.[1] In this respect, the General Government offered limitless opportunities for special-law practices; totally new ground could be broken in terms of racial policy and the treatment of "non-Germans" without being bound to the principles of Reich law ("The methods"—the "implementation of a hard racial struggle"—"will be irreconcilable with our other principles").[2]

With regard to the organization of the details of a special legislative system, however, there soon arose a deep contradiction among the original political objectives, practical requirements, and the plans followed by the administrative leadership of the General Government.[3] Whereas Hitler himself was convinced that "all ideas of consolidation . . . have been eliminated"[4] because of the designated purpose of the occupied Polish territories as a military staging area, Governor General Frank, unable to conceal his legal background, prepared to develop a new National Socialist order in the General Government, or at least some sort of order, and did exactly what should not have been done according to Hitler's will (there was to be no "model province or a model state based on German order."[5]

In contrast to the Annexed Eastern Territories, with their often chaotic legal situation, the General Government saw an orderly system of legal rules, carefully matched and formulated,[6] a system that was undoubtedly envisaged as a model for legislation in countries not scheduled as colonies. Technically, the organization of a system of special law in the General Government was much easier to achieve than in the Annexed Eastern Territories, where special legislative provisions had to be either incorporated into Reich law or established *alongside* Reich law; in the General Government, with its approximately 10.5 million inhabitants, over 90 percent of whom were "non-Germans,"[7] there was no competition with Reich law from the outset, so almost the entire legal system had the nature of special law. The form of special law chosen by the leadership of the General Government also offered more order and thus more legal security in the formal sense than the totalitarian omnibus provisions and the secret guidelines in the Annexed Eastern Territories.[8] On the basis of its extensive legal and administrative autonomy (sec. 5 of the Führer decree of October 12, 1939),[9] almost all provisions of special law were issued not in the form of guidelines but by *legal rules,* decrees, which—although the General Government was essentially dependent upon the Reich authorities[10]—were largely based on Reich law and each of which was also formally published.[11] However, these decrees, as well as their associated administrative acts, were not subject to review by administrative courts,[12] in contrast to the situation in the Reich, where a court review of state acts was possible under the enumeration principle, albeit to no more than a modest extent. The principles of the legislative *process* of the Reich (with a heavy emphasis on the Fühere principle)[13] were similarly applied with a zeal sometimes approaching perfectionism.[14] A stabilizing factor of the legal system was also the fact that the pernicious influence of the Party was almost totally excluded in the General Government;[15] many of the radical special regulations in the Annexed Eastern Territories can be traced back to Party pressure or influence,[16] which took the view that the "non-Germans" were best dominated not by legal rules but by guidelines.

C. Special Topics

This description of the practice of special law in the individual sectors is structured using the same classification as in section 2 on the Annexed Eastern Territories, because the top administration in the General Government (the governor general) also controlled *all* branches of the administration (he had global jurisdiction).[1] Nonetheless, only the most important sectors of the internal administration will be covered; the vast number of regulations in the special administrations (cultural, economic, and labor administrations)[2] precludes anything more than a brief survey. The practical importance of the activities in these special administrations was also in the forefront in the General Government in the early days. As with the Annexed Eastern Territories, this survey will therefore be given precedence, with the internal administration covered thereafter.

I. The Cultural Sector

The principal aim of the policy of denationalization mentioned previously, which aimed to prepare the Poles for the status of leaderless laborers, was to promote German interests (by granting privileges to Germans) and extinguish or repress Polish cultural life as far as possible (through discrimination). In this context, Polish cultural life was regarded as the "main enemy of *Deutschtum*," to be destroyed as soon as possible, as were all nation-state traditions in Eastern Europe.[3] Whereas the authorities dedicated substantial personnel and financial resources[4] to the organization of German culture[5] and sports,[6] to show that "German Man" was the more superior bearer of culture,[7] Polish education and culture were largely extinguished. After much uncontrolled looting (by departments of the RFSS),[8] Polish art treasures were confiscated and some of them removed to the Reich.[9] Cultural policy was decided by the "cultural policy guidelines" issued by the governor general in 1940, under which Polish cultural life was not to be encouraged but was still to be permitted as long as it "serves a primitive need for entertainment and diversion"; the Jews, however, were forbidden all cultural activities.[10] The cultural life of the Poles was therefore tolerated only to the extent that it could be expected to keep the workers in line and show them that "the fate of their *Volk* offered no future prospects"; all that could be considered was "at the most poor-quality films or films that demonstrate the size and strength of the German Reich";[11] for the same reasons, the Poles were permitted limited access to information via censored press publications.[12] Of course, these restricted activities, described as "autonomy" (which also met stiff resistance from the police),[13] were no autonomy in the proper sense; in fact, the situation was just the opposite, with the aim to extinguish all cultural life at a higher level and to achieve strict control of the remaining minimal cultural program.

In all the measures adopted, there was an almost panicky fear of a revival of the "Polish intelligentsia," which had always been regarded as "hostile to Germany";[14] until around 1942, however, an understanding with the working and peasant classes was believed quite possible and was even practiced.[15] The key concepts for the special legislative measures in the education sector are described below.[16]

All Polish high schools, higher education establishments, and seminaries[17] were closed, but this did not achieve the intended purpose because it only resulted in the development of a widespread underground education system;[18] after being closed for a brief period in 1940, the technical, industrial, and vocational colleges were reopened in the interests of gaining skilled workers; private schools and private tuition required the approval of the authorities.[19] The Polish primary schools, which had initially been closed, were also reopened, but the segregation principle was strictly maintained, and only the basics were to be taught, under German supervision and in accordance with German guidelines;[20] the shortage of teaching aids and teachers (caused in part by the Germans) as well as increased class sizes[21] were destined to make school education "poor of its own accord."[22]

Other cultural facilities and activities of the "non-Germans" were totally suppressed or permitted only to a limited extent. All registered and unregistered Polish clubs and associations were dissolved on August 1, 1940; they could receive a special "confirmation" from the German authorities to continue their activities if these involved German interests.[23] All foundations and religious sects[24] were also dissolved.

The policy of the National Socialist authorities on cultural institutions was essentially that all valuable institutions and collections were treated as de facto German property, and the authorities behaved as if an independent Polish culture had never existed. Polish literature in public libraries was seized, and the collections of important libraries were removed to the Reich.[25] All Polish theaters and cinemas were also confiscated; they were released only on a limited scale.[26]

The printing and distribution of Polish newspapers was heavily restricted and placed under the strictest supervision.[27] German propaganda (book exhibitions, poetry readings, publicity events, etc.),[28] particularly for the rural population (by loudspeakers, posters, wall newspapers),[29] increased considerably.

All cultural activities were placed under German supervision or were subject to approval;[30] public music performances were completely forbidden; the ownership and continued operation of printing establishments and publishing houses, the publication of printed matter of any sort, and the continued operation of bookstores required the approval of the authorities; the publication of books and independent newspapers and (from 1942) the manufacture of paper products of any kind (e.g., exercise books) were prohibited; the distribution of "philosophical or political" literature was banned but not that of "entertainment or technical books."[31]

The regulations governing mandatory approval for cultural activities and the publishing of printed matter were mostly of a general nature and did not distinguish between German and "non-German"; the special-law character of these regulations was inherent, since their main purpose was to create bans, controls, and supervision of the activities of the "non-Germans." This is shown by the fact that it was not the internal administration or the Central Department for Education and Adult Education but the (Central) Department for *Education of the people and Propaganda* that was responsible for the supervision and approval requirements described above,[32] the latter being one of the prime proponents of a severe anti-Polish line, and authorized to issue implementing regulations to the corresponding decrees of the governor general.[33]

Church life was not affected, in contrast to the Annexed Eastern Territories, because the church was required as a steadying and disciplinary factor. The Polish Church retained its status as a public corporation and the Polish seminaries were reopened.[34] But, according to the principle of segregation, the Polish-German ("racially mixed") Evangelical Protestant congregations were dissolved; the reduction of the Evangelical congregations to private associations, as in the Warthegau (or Wartheland), did not, however, occur; again, the principle of segregation was applied, with the governor general ordering the establishment of "German" and "non-German" congregations.[35]

II. The Economic and Commercial Sector

In the same way as in the cultural sector, a policy of oppression was pursued in the areas of economic administration and economic law; but in contrast to the intentions for the Annexed Eastern Territories, this did not aim to *extinguish* the economic life of the Poles but to reduce it to such a level (subsistence level) that the Poles could be used only as labor.

The consequence of this attitude for general economic policy was that the General Government, in any case poor and dependent on imports, was pillaged, with everything of value transported to the Reich;[1] later, when the General

Government produced no further "spoils of war," production was revived, but for the sole purpose of squeezing the country dry once again of "everything that could be extracted."[2] The British system of colonial administration, allegedly the role model for the National Socialists, was not practiced at all, with the development of an economy for Poles themselves deliberately neglected;[3] instead, an expensive centralized economic bureaucracy was installed,[4] but this was unable to achieve its goal of the supervision of the "non-German" economy because of its cumbersome structure.[5] All possible assets were exploited by this bloated economic administration[6] exclusively in the interests of the Reich.[7] Contrary to the announcements of the governor general, the original priority status awarded to Galicia was implemented to no more than a minimal degree and soon gave way to the general policy of exploitation;[8] the governor general himself once said that the relationship with the Poles in the General Government was "the relationship between an ant and a greenfly."[9] The predatory exploitation of human and material resources that ensued never reached its set objectives and merely led to the complete impoverishment of the colony of the General Government.[10]

With regard to the details of the implementation of this policy, there was no general policy of expropriation as practiced in the Annexed Eastern Territories. State assets were confiscated and expropriated, but not *private* assets,[11] because the Germans were dependent upon the willingness of the Polish population to work. However, sufficient opportunities were created to oust the Poles from their property and block all possibility of acquiring assets. In this instance as well, the administration was able to make use of relevant regulations under Reich special law.

1.   Polish Assets

The Decree on the Confiscation of Private Assets in the General Government of January 24, 1940,[12] had given the governor general and the subordinate authorities (the district chief, the *Kreishauptmann*) the opportunity to order confiscations by *single decree* from case to case "to fulfill tasks in the public interest." No compensation was generally envisaged, but this could be granted at the discretion of the administration for damages resulting from the implementation of the decree.[13] At any rate, the decree created a degree of legal certainty by preventing controlled seizure by all types of authorities as was the order of the day in the Annexed Eastern Territories. Under certain circumstances, it was even possible to appeal to the courts against confiscation orders.[14]

A decree issued by the governor general on March 27, 1940, stipulated a *requirement of official approval* for the disposal of real estate in order to "safeguard an appropriate regional policy and economic system"; although this had a *global* effect, it did, of course, principally relate to the Poles. All acquisitions of enterprises and warehouses were also subject to official approval, intended to restrict the economic activities of the Poles and ensure control over them.[15] As in the Reich, Jews were not permitted to acquire either real estate or real property rights under this decree. From the beginning of 1943, the administration was also able to order the merger and closure of enterprises (without any right of appeal or entitlement to compensation).[16]

The police, of course, enjoyed substantially greater powers. Under a decree issued on January 24, 1940, the HSSPF (higher SS and police leader) had declared a right of seizure "in exceptional cases" with the aim of "increasing the power of the regular police and the armed SS," in particular with regard to objects "directly linked to criminal acts" (secs. 12 ff.). This wording is yet another example of the boundless omnibus provisions found in National Socialist law, on the basis of which the (security) police could do as they pleased: under the conditions reigning at that time, was there anything that could not be linked "to criminal acts"?

At any rate, this right of seizure was no more than a weak remnant of the original plans of the RFSS, who as Reich Commissar for the Strengthening of German Nationhood had presented a draft decree on October 11, 1939, "under which *all* real estate of Polish land owners will be expropriated and confiscated" (this amounted to a ban on disposal of property) and "given in its entirety to the [German] settlers without compensation."[17] Both this plan and efforts by the police to achieve a *general expropriation* of the "non-Germans" were curbed by the administration as far as possible for reasons of economic policy.

To preempt the police, however, the administration itself had drawn up a decree on the expropriation of real estate, which it presented as a draft in October 1942.[18] The draft was a response to a draft expropriation decree submitted by Higher SS and Police Leader (HSSPF) Friedrich Wilhelm Krüger in his capacity as commissioner of the RFSS/RKF, which was based on Himmler's own ideas as set out above and went so far as to remove from the internal administration all general jurisdiction for expropriations, since these involved "racial and settlement policy plans," for which the RFSS was responsible as Reich Commissar for the Strengthening of German Nationhood.[19] Neither of the two drafts was adopted, however, because at the latest in 1942, the administrative leadership was unable to enforce anything of importance against the will of the police, and the extremist notions of the police in turn met the delaying passive resistance of the bureaucracy.

This meant that the confiscation decree of January 24, 1940, continued in force; it met the needs of expropriations to almost the same degree, because sei-zures under this decree resulted not only in *restrictions on disposal* but also in the *loss* of all rights in rem and rights in personam giving title.[20] In the case of expropriations ordered under this decree, the assets seized were subject to the complete *power of disposal* of the German administration.[21] Despite the lack of any legal basis, these confiscated assets were frequently impounded in favor of the General Government;[22] the favored argument of the administration at that time, that the ownership status was not affected by the confiscation but was "merely" subject to restrictions on disposal,[23] thus flew in the face of reality. However, if German statements on the matter are to be believed, only very few assets were confiscated "for economic or political reasons."[24] Unless confiscated, the assets of private Polish individuals remained relatively protected for the same "political reasons" (preservation of willingness to work) as long as the *administration* (and not the police) had jurisdiction.

2.   Jewish Assets

These principles did not apply to Poles of Jewish extraction;[25] they were subject to the principle of special law and overt discrimination in all its harsh-ness. With the aim of segregating Polish and Jewish economic life (in the termi-nology of the day, "eliminating" the earlier Jewish influence on the economy),[26] their total assets were subject to compulsory registration, as in the Reich: the acquisition of foreign currency, gold, and other precious metals was rendered de facto impossible;[27] all accounts were blocked; unregistered assets were im-pounded as ownerless;[28] and the almost total exclusion of Jews from "industry, wholesaling, import and export activities, the ownership of land, and the bank-ing, insurance, and transport sectors" was ordered. As was explained quite frankly within the administration itself, Jews were still permitted to engage in "retailing" and "strictly controlled craft and trade sectors" because they were "still" required to supply the population.[29] In other words, all Jewish enterprises were confiscated—first the large businesses (smaller enterprises remained provi-sionally open) and Jewish real estate.[30] The earnings from the confiscated enter-prises and goods flowed into German pockets, and the confiscated real estate was used to meet the demands of the administration for accommodation and office space. Reports of the day make a subtle distinction between confiscations per se, which were seen as quite proper, and their implementation, which was evidently so brutal and arbitrary that it had given the "impression[!] of arbitrary acts and lawlessness" and had damaged the reputation of the Germans.[31]

This "impression" was quite correct because the legal basis of such mass seizures and confiscations was more than questionable. The only possible basis was the confiscation decree of January 24, 1940[32] (confiscation "in the public interest"), with the robbery of the Jewish population obviously regarded as the "fulfillment of tasks in the public interest," as described in a budget meeting in the governor general's office.[33] However, it is questionable whether the decree of January 24, 1940, was ever used. The evidence tends to show that the administration shared the prevailing view in the Reich that Jewish property was ownerless as it was and could therefore be occupied without a specific basis in law. This ambiguity is an indication that there was essentially only one aim: the comprehensive implementation of the robbery of assets by the state and the seizure of Jewish assets as quickly as possible.

Implementation of this robbery of assets by the state was based very heavily on models from Reich law. The confiscated Jewish assets were under provisional administration, but they were allowed to deteriorate quickly, because they were administered by German and Polish trustees at district level (District Trust Agencies), who were frequently a bad choice of individuals, interested only in personal gain; they had been appointed during the military administration and had no desire to preserve the Jewish enterprises entrusted to them but regarded them merely as a fat living to line their own pockets.[34] The countless cases of personal enrichment and the deterioration of the operating assets resulted in a deplorable state of affairs in many enterprises. Even the offices of the government of the General Government complained about the "scandalous conditions" and the "uncontrollable plundering" by the trustees, whose large number was in inverse proportion to their efficiency[35] and who succeeded in creating a situation whereby as early as 1940, the majority of the confiscated Jewish enterprises were no longer competitive because of the lack of capital and the incompetence of the trustees and had become run down to the point of bankruptcy and sold off for a minimal amount to private or state buyers. In Warsaw, for instance, the "administration" of Jewish rented property swallowed up the entire rental income of 88 million złoty. Of a thousand Jewish enterprises seized in Warsaw, only three hundred were still functioning in 1940.[36]

The profits and proceeds from the "utilization" of Jewish assets accrued to the administration,[37] in particular at the *Kreis* level (*Kreishauptleute* and *Stadthauptleute*); those individuals also benefited from the use and exploitation of the confiscated Jewish real estate, since much of it (seized by the government of the General Government), representing enormous financial resources,[38] as stated by the head of the Central Department of Economics in the office of the governor general, was, "as it were, given away to the municipalities,"[39] which at the same time were burdened with the cost of upkeep.[40]

As usual, there was friction with the police, but this time the administration came out on top. The *Reichsführer*-SS, in his capacity as Reich Commissar for the Strengthening of German Nationhood, also had his eye on these assets and—when the planned expropriation decree mentioned above did not come to fruition—issued a corresponding directive on December 15, 1942,[41] instructing the higher SS and police leader in the East (HSSPF *Ost*) to dispose of all Jewish real property assets following the registration of the entire assets of the deported Jews (Action Reinhard)[42] and to make these available for German settlers. This immediately caused a storm of indignation in the administration. Governor General Frank insisted on his jurisdiction and declared the decree and the measures implemented thereunder to be void. As "ownerless goods," all Jewish property was the property of the state; only when this was recognized in principle could negotiations be initiated with the Reich Commissar for the Strengthening of German Nationhood.[43] However, Himmler had no intention of accepting this view, and the matter therefore remained in abeyance.[44] The result was that the confiscated real estate of Jewish owners was not used and lost value because maintenance work was neglected. Formally at least, this property and real estate continued to be administered by the District Trust Agencies, but if it exceeded the needs of the German administration, it was sold off to private individuals at giveaway prices. The blocked Jewish accounts and securities portfolios at the banks were not surrendered to the police but remained at the banks, which refused to surrender them because jurisdiction for their release had not been clarified.[45] The RFSS/RKF was thus unable to achieve complete success with his objective of bringing all Jewish assets under his control. However, the police acted first. As the deportations of the Jewish population increased and with them the jurisdictional scope of the police, there was a rise in the number of unauthorized seizures and disposals of Jewish real estate by the police. After a personal meeting between Frank and Himmler in February 1944,[46] Himmler yielded only to the extent that he instructed the SS Central Office to put *movable* Jewish assets at the disposal of the governor general; cash was to be used for settlement purposes. The question of who was ultimately to have the use of the Jewish real estate remained unsolved at the end of the war.

EXCURSUS
Tax Law

The fiscal "special treatment" of the "non-Germans," outlined below, ran parallel to the special legislative treatment in the commercial sector. Besides the existing taxes levied under Polish law, the "non-Germans" were subject to spe-

cial taxes, levied and collected by the Polish tax authorities under German supervision.[47] Whereas German state subjects and ethnic Germans in the General
Government were basically taxed under Reich law,[48] new sources of tax revenue
were tapped (in addition to the 50% increase in the land tax)[49] by making all
inhabitants of the Polish municipalities age 18 and over liable to a special tax
from the beginning of 1940; it was a municipal tax, the so-called Resident's Tax,
which ranged from 15 to 20 złoty per annum depending on the municipality
concerned, and was principally envisaged to fund municipal welfare services, in
particular for the homeless Poles and Jews deported from the Annexed Eastern
Territories. Two-thirds of tax revenues accrued to the Reich, and one-third was
retained by the municipalities.[50] Germans, who had initially been liable to this
tax, were exempt from the Resident's Tax from 1942.[51]

This special tax was later increased substantially (to 50–100 złoty per person per annum) but shortly thereafter reduced again;[52] the revenue distribution
ratio was also changed, with 20 percent of revenues now to be transferred to the
central administration in Kraków and 40 percent to the *Kreishauptleute;* the
municipalities also received 40 percent of the revenues to reduce the chronic
cash shortage of the municipal authorities.[53] From 1942 an additional "war surcharge" of 200 percent of the Resident's Tax was levied on the Resident's Tax
(minimum rate of 36 złoty per annum),[54] which represented an appreciable burden in view of the extremely low wages. The Jews were liable to even greater income restrictions. In addition to the taxes described above, they also paid a 50
percent surcharge on trade tax;[55] it was merely a matter of course that—as in the
Reich—all tax allowances for Jewish corporations and associations had been
abolished in November 1939.[56]

III. Civil Service Law

In contrast to the cultural and commercial sectors, where the Poles suffered
heavy discrimination, the public service sector was initially characterized by segregation rules. The objective was to demonstrate the unity of *Deutschtum* to the
"non-Germans." As in many other areas of the Eastern Territories, the administrative leadership in the General Government emphasized unremittingly that all
personal contacts with Poles must be avoided, with this being impressed upon
the civil servants in numerous instructions,[1] because in the words of Governor
General Frank, "*Deutschtum* in the General Government as a self-contained entity in all its expressions was subject . . . to the law of the National Socialist
weltanschauung" [the principle of racial segregation—Author].[2] As in the Annexed Eastern Territories, the overwhelming number of Polish personnel in the

German departments did not, of course, permit any strict observance of the strict segregation that had been ordered; the situation forced them to close ranks. As a consequence, the reports of the police and administrative authorities are full of complaints about very far-reaching "fraternization" between Germans and Poles, particularly in the countryside, where personal contacts were completely unavoidable. It must be questioned whether the severest "official sanctions" threatened for social contact with "non-Germans" were of great importance.[3] The same probably applies to the threat of sacking civil servants without notice who married or had sexual relations with "non-German" persons.[4] Apart from the aforementioned segregation from German staff, a further special legislative treatment of the Polish civil servants and salaried employees[5] still employed was that although they received the same salary as before, this salary represented a blatant underpayment barely covering the minimum required for subsistence, compared with the German personnel, paid under Reich rates, and in view of the general inflation.[6]

A formal adoption of the principles of Reich (racial) special law did not take effect until the beginning of 1941; from this time on, all German members of the public service in the General Government were required to submit the *Ariernachweis* (proof of Aryan descent), in particular senior members of the Civil Service.[7] Under a decree issued by the governor general on July 31, 1942, at the same times as the start of the mass deportations of the Jews to the extermination camps, Polish civil servants still employed in 1942 were to be dismissed if they or their spouses were of Jewish descent or were "Jewish half-breed[s]" or were no longer capable of "ruthless obedience."[8] There was also a comprehensive shake-up of civil servants employed before 1939; a directive that "non-German" civil servants still employed should be retired after completing at least fifteen years' service was intended to free positions for employees loyal to the occupying power.

Of much greater significance than the measures applied to pay and employment policy was the principle of the "subjugation" of the Poles; this was applied to a lesser extent than in the Annexed Eastern Territories because of the personnel shortage, but still it was enforced with the greatest severity. Poles lost their managerial posts in the administration and were not readmitted to these posts later because of a fear of sabotage (expressed as "uncertainty about the future") and a revival of the Polish intelligentsia. The failure of this stubborn policy of subjugation by removing former senior Polish state and municipal civil servants from their posts or placing them under German supervisory bodies was soon very evident, because the very consequences that the Germans feared were bound to, and did indeed, ensue. But in its most characteristic shortsightedness and naïveté, the administrative leadership obviously did not realize this; it seriously held the view that the policy of debarring Poles from leading positions "had been quite right"[9] (especially after the retreat in the East) but that "no humiliation of the Poles" had thereby been intended.

IV. Professional and Labor Law

1.   Professions Requiring State Licensing (Lawyers, Physicians, Etc.)

The same principles of segregation and subjugation were applied to employment law in the professions, especially with regard to the accreditation of lawyers.[1] German attorneys in the General Government, who, like members of related professions,[2] were subject to strict supervision and were accredited only if they were politically reliable and exercised their profession exclusively in the General Government (as "ambassadors of *Deutschtum* in the outpost of the Eastern lands"),[3] felt the impact of the concept of segregation in two ways: not only was acceptance of Jewish clients "of course" out of the question, but the acceptance of Polish clients was also undesirable; this was only unobjectionable if not forbidden by "the nature of the matter."[4] Prohibited, for instance, was the representation of a Polish client in an action against a German agency (in other words, the representation of Polish interests against confiscation and robbery by the authorities);[5] desirable was the representation of Poles by German attorneys in criminal cases heard before German courts, because it was assumed that this would "better serve the establishment of truth."[6] Apart from the representation of Reich and ethnic Germans, German attorneys were totally forbidden to appear in the "non-German" courts.[7]

Of course the "non-German" attorneys were placed under a much stricter system of control, based on Reich law practice. In contrast to the practice in the Reich, however, all corresponding control measures were implemented *without* any legal basis and solely on the basis of internal directives: it is evident that the issue and publication of corresponding normative legal regulations was felt to be superfluous, since impingement on the rights of stateless "non-Germans" did not require such a basis. The first right to be affected was their accreditation as attorneys. This was canceled for all "non-German" attorneys—in accord with the motto of every totalitarian regime that everything was prohibited that was not explicitly permitted. Reaccreditation by the relevant German authorities for admission before Polish and German courts was issued only to politically reliable Polish attorneys, with the strictest standards being applied;[8] in Warsaw, for instance, around half of the approximately fourteen hundred attorneys were reaccredited.[9] According to a directive issued by the Central Department of Justice, "non-German" attorneys were no longer entitled to bear the title *attorney at law;* as in the Annexed Eastern Territories, they were allowed to use only the term *advocate.*[10] The numerous Jewish attorneys did not, of course, receive reaccreditation, since most of them had already been removed in 1939;[11] German and Polish attorneys took over the free practices. The remaining Jewish attorneys *with dispensations* were permitted only to conclude current business before their accreditation was withdrawn. As the head of the Department of Justice in the office of the governor general put it during an internal meeting, because of the "move" to exclude Jews from all economic activities, "there was no requirement for Jewish legal advisers in the German legal system."[12] Numerous members of the Polish legal profession, who had protested the exclusion of their Jewish colleagues without any basis in law, not only lost their accreditation but were also "treated by the Security Police," that is, arrested and sent to prison or a concentration camp.[13] Despite the sanctions imposed, the German Security Service (SD) did not let the matter rest in the light of this demonstration of solidarity, as this would have run counter to the propaganda thesis of the hatred toward the Jews among the Polish population as well, which was frequently used to justify anti-Jewish measures in order to conceal the aims of the Germans. In the internal situation reports of the SD destined for the administrative authorities in the Reich, the reactions of the Polish legal profession were rephrased as support for the German measures ("gratitude for the nonaccreditation of the Jews") by means of transparent manipulation of the figures.[14]

The treatment of the other professions was also based to a large extent on models from the Reich. The Polish medical boards of registration were dissolved, their were assets confiscated, and they were consolidated to form the Chamber of Health of the General Government under the control of the Health Services Office in the (Central) Department of the Interior Administration.[15] Although the "non-German" physicians were generally allowed to retain their licenses, the usual special legislative restrictions still applied: Aryan (German) physicians were, of course, prohibited from treating Jews; physicians violating this prohibition could expect prosecution by the police, with removal from the General Government as the mildest form of punishment. The prohibition on treating Jews also applied to Polish physicians, who could lose their license by violating the ban. A further policy of the radically anti-Polish health administration was also to enforce the unequal treatment of Polish and German *patients.* The well-known case of the German physician Dr. Hagen, who provided the same treatment to Polish and German TB patients in a Warsaw hospital, sheds some light on the situation prevailing at that time;[16] it resulted in a full-blown confrontation between Dr. Hagen and the responsible authorities, and he was saved from the clutches of Himmler and the Security Police only by the intervention of the Reich chief health officer, Dr. Conti.[17] Additional employment restrictions on members of the Polish medical professions (physicians, dentists, pharmacists, etc.) consisted of their being subject to forced service within a particular district and with a particular residence (the emergency service obligation).[18]

The most severe special-law measures were, of course, issued with regard to Jewish physicians. In view of the large number of Jewish physicians,[19] a drastic measure to segregate Aryans from non-Aryans was the directive, based on Reich regulations, that Jewish physicians were prohibited from bearing the professional designation *physician* and could only term themselves *medical practitioners*. It goes without saying that the prohibition on treating Aryans also applied to them, so they were solely dependent on Jewish patients. In addition, they were left with few opportunities for work; under a directive issued by the head of the Health Services Office in the Department of the Interior Administration of the government of the General Government in 1939, they had been deprived of all medical equipment;[20] furthermore, during the course of the implementation of the aforementioned directive, they were also deprived of *all other* items (household effects, carpets, kitchen utensils, furniture, valuables, etc.) if these were of use to the private and professional requirements of German physicians.[21]

There was similar drastic "segregation" between Poles and Jews on the one hand and Poles and Germans on the other in other professional employment regulations. Whereas the Poles were merely expelled from senior positions under the principle of "no senior positions for Poles" but had only been excluded down to middle-management level because of the lack of replacement German staff, Jews lost their posts in all professions, as well as jobs in industry and commerce (except retailing) and in the banking and insurance sectors.[22] As was to be expected, the only result of these measures was to cripple and ruin trade and industry because the "absent Jews" could not be replaced.[23]

2.   Labor Law

   a.   Polish and Jewish Personnel

Whereas the expulsion measures described above more or less represented the closure of the senior levels of the professional hierarchy to "non-Germans," an extensive administrative and legislative machinery was set in motion to achieve the desired ultimate goal, the quickest possible reduction of the local population to a leaderless mass of cheap labor for the objectives of the Reich.[1] Under the leadership of the Central Department of Labor, with its field offices in the districts and the *Kreise,* which were the first civil authorities to function and certainly the most important administrative agencies in the General Government, a completely new system of labor law was developed "to replace the existing individualistic foundations."[2] Its principal features comprised the introduction of the piece-rate and bonus system to achieve the "greatest possible output," setting the minimum working hours per week at fifty-four, the requirement of the "strictest work discipline," and so forth.[3] As mentioned above, the General Government was treated in practice sometimes as Reich territory and at other times as foreign territory, depending on requirements. In this case it appeared expedient not to regard the General Government as a part of the Reich in order to bypass any obligations to the principles of Reich labor law. The treatment of the "non-Germans" was therefore oriented solely toward the objective of the mobilization of labor (*Arbeitseinsatz* [forced-labor squads]) and the availability of the General Government for the economy of the Greater German Reich. In contrast, the local Germans were treated as if the General Government was an immediate part of the Reich, in that they were paid German rates.

A condition for the introduction of the new system, which resulted in fundamental changes to the structure of the labor market and the social structure,[4] was the introduction of compulsory labor for all Poles age 14 and over,[5] which was justified in all seriousness by Governor General Frank with the argument that this served as compensation for the damage caused by the Poles "because they had abducted Polish money abroad."[6] The special legislative treatment of Poles was not so much found in the compulsory labor[7] in all its forms (which included "construction service")[8] and further obligations to perform services, to which the Germans were also liable to a certain extent,[9] but related to the sphere of working conditions and individual regulations of labor law,[10] which, in conjunction with the lack of provisions, contributed greatly to the impoverishment of the workers, the poor efficiency, and work performance, which was estimated at 50 percent of German labor productivity. Contemporary reports by German authorities speak of working conditions that were rarely encountered in the Reich, and of "nigger-like" working methods.[11]

The wages paid to Polish compulsory laborers differed from those of German employees. The standard wage system based on fixed statutory wage scales was abandoned; instead, the Compulsory Labor Decree of October 26, 1939, provided for remuneration "by rates appearing to be equitable,"[12] but these were never specified in a binding new standard wage structure, so that wages could be changed at any time to meet labor market conditions. Polish workers and their families were no longer entitled to welfare benefits; these were merely to be "safeguarded" wherever possible.[13]

However, the new wage system was not introduced *uno actu*; in contrast to what was done in the Annexed Eastern Territories, the former Polish regulations remained provisionally in force; deviations from the earlier statutory wages and salaries required the approval of the district chief[14] and, if they were also to apply outside the district, the approval of the Central Department of Labor in the governor general's office, with the aim of preventing uncontrolled wage changes. The district chiefs and the head of the Central Department of Labor themselves were also authorized to issue new statutory wage scales for individual enterprises or groups of enterprises.[15] However, such revisions were issued in a relatively large number only from the beginning of 1942;[16] they introduced the piece-rate system and thus complied with the policy of the governor general and his departments that the Poles should be paid less than normal rates and without further benefits: remuneration (net wage) was to be paid only for work *actually* performed—exactly the wording of the piece-rate and bonus system[17]—as was the practice for Poles and Jews in the Reich. In fact, the new wage system now practiced, namely, the rejection of the function of the wage to safeguard a "socially balanced standard of living" and the introduction of the piece-rate and bonus system,[18] was more than a break with the system of guaranteed minimum wages, because of the hope that it would reduce costs and bring about a substantial rise in productivity.

Poles were also gradually placed under the provisions of special law in other areas of labor law, with the tacit abolition of Polish regulations. The Polish vacation regulations[19] were suspended for the year 1940, all vacation entitlement was dismissed, and (as in the Reich) the "granting" of a vacation of normally six paid working days was ordered. The periods of notice for "non-German" employees were reduced, opportunities to extend working hours were introduced, maternity protection regulations for Polish and Jewish women were abolished, and severe sanctions were threatened—but only in 1943—for violations of labor law regulations.[20] From 1942, in addition to the existing compulsory labor, general compulsory service for all "non-German" inhabitants of the General Government was ordered for "urgent tasks of particular importance to the state," soon followed by a general compulsory service for all German state subjects in the General Government.[21]

The Poles were thus subject to mixed law, that is, partly Polish law, partly the new (special) law of the German civil administration, but Poles of Jewish extraction were subject exclusively to special law,[22] which suspended all previous regulations and far exceeded the regulations in force in the Reich. The most significant feature was the introduction of forced labor for all Jews between the ages of 14 and 16 in the form of guarded forced-labor squads (*Arbeitseinsatz*) with "camp accommodation" or by employment in free jobs.[23] The introduction of forced labor, with which the freedom of movement of those affected was also abolished, marks the beginning of the unrestricted police power over the Jews, since the organization of forced labor (and thus of residence: ghettoization) was no longer exclusively the province of the administration but also a matter of the HSSPF (there was a change in jurisdiction).

The segregation concept of the Forced Labor Decree of October 26, 1939, applied not only to Germans but also to Jews and Poles, such that Jewish workers were always to be segregated from Polish workers.[24]

The forced labor itself was dominated by rigorous, previously nonexistent practices, which even went so far as the proposal to hang Jews who did not work hard enough.[25] The working conditions were kept below the Polish level as far as possible. Originally, the Jews received no wages whatsoever but depended on support from the Jewish Council. When these funds were exhausted, guidelines issued by the head of the Department of Labor in the Governor General's Office dated July 5, 1940,[26] stipulated that the Jews conscripted for forced labor should receive no remuneration but only performance bonuses; Jews placed in free employment were granted a wage on the basis of piece rates, which had to be 20 percent below the wage for Polish workers. A decree of December 15, 1941,[27] refined this practice so that—as in the Reich—Jews received wages only for work actually performed (not for vacations or inability to work due to illness or accident), and all wage supplements (for overtime, qualifications, incentive payments, benefits, family allowances, etc.) were abolished. The period of notice was reduced to *one day,* and the regulations on the employment of women and young persons were declared inapplicable to Jews. The same applied to regulations governing working hours. A directive had already been issued in 1940 that Jews must work on Jewish holidays.[28] The value of Jewish laborers, which was considerable in view of their craft and trade skills (resulting in a permanent tug-of-war between the labor administration and the police), was thus much higher than that of the Polish laborers, because of the low costs involved.[29]

Needy Jews did not, of course, receive any welfare benefits from the Germans but were dependent upon the Jewish welfare agencies.[30] From 1942 on, when the Jewish labor camps were wrested from the jurisdiction of the German labor administration and placed under the responsibility of the police because the latter themselves now undertook the "exploitation" of Jewish "labor,"[31] the conditions in the labor camps, catastrophic in any case, deteriorated even further because these camps were now operated as satellite camps of the concentration camps, with the selective exploitation of labor organized as the penultimate station before final liquidation.[32]

b.   Consequences of the *Arbeitseinsatz* (Labor Allocation) Policy

The implementation of compulsory labor for Poles and Jews had brought considerable gains for the labor market in the General Government and the Reich territory in terms of nominal figures. The Department of Labor in the Governor General's Office noted with pride that the Poles formed the basis of the "German war economy," a factor that was also acknowledged in the Reich itself.[33] At the end of 1941, the proportion of the foreign labor force in the Reich accounted for by Poles was put at 47 percent.[34] However, these results arose only because voluntary registration for *Arbeitseinsatz* had dropped since 1939-40 as a result of a number of factors including deterring reports about the treatment ("calumny") of the Poles in the Reich and the expected resettlements and evacuations by the RKF (as the Reich Chancellery established without any pretense at embellishment); the police, increasingly reacting to requests from the labor administration itself—inspired by the ambition to fulfill the excessive demands of the Reich at all costs—rounded up the industrial conscripts in raids and ensured their forced deportation to the Reich or the *Arbeitseinsatz* facilities in the General Government.[35]

The administrative leadership had mixed feelings about these measures,[36] implemented as they were with unbelievable brutality, because on the one hand it did not dare to forcefully oppose the excessive demands of the Reich and its own labor authorities, and on the other, these measures jeopardized economic life in the General Government because they caused considerable economic problems and numerous complaints by lower-level administrative authorities. For instance, the police actions were a major cause of problems: the willingness to work had sunk to a new low; the administration had lost the last remnant of any credibility it had enjoyed, including in the countryside; and there had been a considerable growth in Polish resistance activities, even in areas that had previously been relatively calm.[37] The brutal policy of "registering" workers by the police thus proved to be absurd in the long term and without any positive result whatsoever. The administration authorities recognized early on that no "positive" cooperation by the Poles could be expected,[38] but they either intentionally left matters as they were or were unable to do anything about the police hunt for workers, which was controlled centrally and enforced without any consideration at all for the economic situation.

The consequence of the police terror and the special labor law treatment was that the actual value of "non-German" labor in the General Government fell further and further. The legal uncertainty surrounding the erratic wage system for

Poles and the difference between the remuneration of German workers (paid in reichsmarks on Reich German pay scales) and that of Polish workers had reached an "unbearable disparity," as the authorities complained;[39] a complicating factor was that the supply situation was catastrophic ("starvation status"), because the General Government had been looted to supply the Reich;[40] as a result, only certain (war-priority) groups were recognized as eligible for supplies;[41] those Poles no longer used as labor received in the words of Governor General Frank "only the little left over" (with the Jews at the bottom of the pile, receiving minimal or even no rations whatsoever).[42] The result was a rapid rise in black market prices, and inflation shot up rapidly, so that the value of the wages paid to the Poles—in any case minimal—shrank more and could be compensated only by allocating additional supplies of food rations to industry.[43]

EXCURSUS
Social Welfare Law

With the wages paid to working Poles worse than inadequate, this applied all the more to other benefits under labor law and to welfare benefits for the non-working population, people who were of no practical use to German interests, the support of whom was thus reduced to an absolute minimum. After a temporary drop, health insurance and pension insurance benefits reached prewar levels (according to German claims), and certain social facilities were established to preserve the Polish labor capacity (again according to German claims), but all these benefits were provided at the discretion of the administration.[44] The payment *obligations* of health and pension insurers were turned into *optional* provisions, and maximum rates were stipulated for pensions (Jews were totally excluded from such benefits); in addition, war pensions were reduced to around half of 80 percent of the Polish rates.[45] Furthermore, Polish unemployment benefit law had been suspended in December 1939—apart from the liability for contributions; all entitlements to unemployment relief were abolished, the amount paid was restricted to minimum rates, and its granting was subject to the discretion of the administration.[46]

The responsibility for welfare benefits for Poles in need of assistance was delegated to the Polish municipalities without specific benefit rates being set.[47] For financial reasons, social relief for the "non-Germans" (for refugees and children) was detached from welfare benefits, an artificial division because social relief functions frequently overlapped with other welfare tasks. For the central organization of social relief measures, a "voluntary social relief work" association of the Central Polish Aid Committee, with a branch in the seat of government of each *Kreishauptmann,* was established because German agencies were totally uninterested in these functions, and the state "could not possibly" assume these responsibilities for financial reasons.[48] This committee, financed by public subsidies and donations, thus assumed "social relief responsibilities" for the Poles;[49] the Jewish mutual aid organizations had the same functions for the Jews, but these were also responsible for welfare benefits and received no public subsidies at all, surviving only through "mutual aid" and donations from outside.[50]

V. The Legal Status of "Non-Germans"

As regards special-law practice in the sphere of the general and internal administration, whose responsibilities more or less corresponded to those of the internal administration of the Reich,[1] the same policy of ruthless exploitation already described was implemented.

It should be noted, however, that the actual and most extreme forms of special law, in the form of the countless, extensive police measures against "non-Germans," were removed from the jurisdiction of the general administration because they had been usurped by the police—who regarded them as their own province—and because numerous special duties were assigned to special authorities by way of special powers. Among the areas usurped by the police (who merely followed their regular practice under Reich law) was the regulation of Jewish affairs and ghetto matters, to be discussed later; the resettlement and evacuation of "non-Germans" to and within the General Government (and now to all Occupied Eastern Territories),[2] one of the prime everyday administrative tasks, was undertaken by the departments of the RFSS, in his capacity as Reich Commissar for the Strengthening of German Nationhood, on the basis of a special authorization by the Führer, in close cooperation with the internal administration.[3] These measures were intentionally implemented in the midst of the war, because, as Himmler said, they "were easier to digest in time of war."[4] The crucial factor, however, was that—going far beyond the organization in the Reich—all police powers were removed from the administration and integrated into the agencies of the higher SS and police leader (HSSPF),[5] who was in practice independent of the administrative leadership; all that remained under the jurisdiction of the administration itself (until 1943) were the so-called administrative police matters.[6] Both the unmistakable changes in jurisdiction implemented in the organizational structure of the authorities and the focus of the administration itself thus resulted in the practically limitless omnipotence of the SS and police agencies in the General Government.[7]

Although the internal administration lagged behind the police with its special-law measures, it still achieved a high degree of radicalism, because like the police measures, the special-law measures were implemented largely without any formal legal basis, since the constitutional status of the "non-Germans" made any consideration of the principles of Reich law (such as the principle of the legitimacy of the administration), indeed of any normative principles whatsoever, quite superfluous. A condition for the designation on the one hand of the Poles as a dependent mass of laborers and on the other of the Jews as objects of exploitation only tolerated in the General Government on a temporary basis was that the administration could do as it pleased, free from any legal restraints. The legal status of the "non-German" population therefore had to be abolished and their capacity as the bearers of subjective rights eliminated.

In contrast to the situation in the Annexed Eastern Territories, where the expulsion of the Poles was accompanied by the "reclamation of German blood," the inhabitants of the General Government were therefore not subject to a phased legal status depending on their extraction: their legal status was destroyed for good. This was all justified by the thesis that at the latest with the capitulation of Poland, Polish state authority and thus Polish citizenship had disappeared. Neither could a new citizenship appear, because the General Government was neither a state or a parastatal entity but practically a part (a "dependency") of the Reich. Its inhabitants were therefore stateless and must remain so.[8] In the view of the Germans, such persons as were deported to the General Government, such as Poles from the Annexed Eastern Territories, also lost their citizenship; however, this applied above all to the Jews deported from Germany, because under the Eleventh Decree to the Reich Citizenship Law of November 25, 1941, Jews who were German state subjects lost their state subject status on crossing the German state border, and the General Government (although a part of the Reich) was regarded in this case (as with the Annexed Eastern Territories) as non-German Territory (de facto as foreign territory).[9] During the course of the German occupation, no changes were made to the stateless status of the inhabitants of the General Government, although the police leadership showed itself interested in the Germanization of Poles "of German blood."[10] This was because on the one hand—in contrast to the practice in the Annexed Eastern Territories, where the Germanization of the "non-Germans" of German extraction was hurried along at all costs—no Germanization in the General Government was intended by the political leadership (at least during the war)[11] and on the other hand because the deprivation of rights of the population most closely corresponded to the practical requirements of the authorities.

Nonetheless, various measures were initiated to achieve some form of compensation for the nonintroduction of the German Ethnic Classification List in the General Government, with the aim of registering German blood and raising it above its "non-German" environment. For instance, the registration was started of persons belonging to the German *Volk* ("ethnic Germans"), who were to be naturalized as soon as possible.[12] Integrated into *Deutschtum,* for instance, were around one hundred thousand so-called persons of German origin (corresponding to those in group 4 of the German Ethnic Classification List),[13] who were raised "out of their Polish environment" (awakening "pride in their origins"),[14] with the intention of naturalizing them *later* "on behalf and by order of the Reich."[15] As in the Annexed Eastern Territories, persons resisting naturalization were threatened with protective custody,[16] essentially because the authorities were dependent on every instance of naturalization since the military service was associated with naturalization.

However, this hunt for "German blood" and "German nature" met with no more than moderate success.[17] The old unsettled differences of opinion between the administration and the SS and police leadership about who should be regarded as an ethnic German flared up again; and the declared belief in *Deutschtum* on the part of the individuals in question was not particularly great.[18] Because of these difficulties, the number of naturalizations was relatively small. Only the "ethnic Germans" were naturalized,[19] and the countless bureaucratic conditions and examinations to which Poles "of German extraction" were subjected meant that these persons were not naturalized at all;[20] on the orders of the RFSS/RKF, they therefore remained stateless unless they volunteered for service in the Wehrmacht;[21] but they were treated as Germans by being subject to German personal, family, and criminal law as well as to German jurisdiction.[22] However, the issue that was much more critical at that time, their treatment with regard to food rations, welfare benefits, and so forth, was never settled.[23]

With the administrative segregation of Germans and "non-Germans" now in place, the actual special legislation itself could be implemented. It was much milder than in the Annexed Eastern Territories, because the dependence on Polish labor and the uncertainty about the constitutional status of the population *after* the was meant that much was omitted that was enforced at all costs in the Annexed Eastern Territories to achieve rapid Germanization. This is shown, for instance, in the fact that where the coexistence of Germans and "non-Germans" was involved, the prime principle applied was not that of subjugation at all costs (Jews excepted) but initially the principle of segregation.

VI. Marriage Law

In particular with regard to marriage law, which, together with the identification and segregation measures, formed one of the cornerstones of *völkisch* inequality, many of the restrictions introduced in the Annexed Eastern Territories were not adopted in the General Government. For instance, there were no general prohibitions on marriages between Germans and "non-Germans" (except for Jews), as long as there were no objections from the "racial aspect." Germans who married Polish women were forced to leave the General Government,[1] so that the official line of the segregation of Germans and "non-Germans" could be maintained. Marriages between civil servants of the General Government and "non-Germans" were regarded as undesirable, but marriages to Ukrainian and Polish partners were normally approved if the result of the racial examination of the "non-German" partner was positive, but a number of sanctions applied to such marriages: these persons too had to leave the General Government; they were also threatened with dismissal from office and the loss of all pension entitlements.[2] Marriages between Poles were also probably regarded as undesirable in line with the political principle of checking the Polish birthrate as much as possible; at least this can be derived as a converse conclusion, taking into account the maxim "what is not allowed is prohibited" applied by the SS agencies, from a circular decree of the RFSS/RKF of January 10,1944, under which no restrictions were placed on marriages between Poles—that is, as in the Reich, between Poles registered in the German Ethnic Classification List and protected subject status Poles.[3] According to another circular decree of August 4, 1944, neither were there any reservations about marriages between Ukrainians; marriages between Poles and Ukrainians, however, were undesirable because this would not achieve any "fragmentation of Polishness," since the "children were normally brought up as Poles." The marriageable age also remained unchanged in the General Government, only being raised—in line with the regulations in the Annexed Eastern Territories—to 28 (for men) and 25 (for women) by the central authorities of the SS (for the purpose of "weakening Polishness").[4]

VII. Public Health

Whereas the segregation concept governing marriage law largely avoided any form of discrimination (in the sense of general prohibitions), measures were tightened appreciably when it came to the treatment of "non-Germans" in routine administrative matters, where the concept of *völkisch* inequality led not only to segregation but also to overt discrimination in favor of German state subjects or ethnic Germans, true to the aforementioned policy of the political leadership that the population of occupied territories in the East should be reduced to the lowest possible standard. This applied all the more where areas were involved that were of no direct use for the German *Arbeitseinsatz* but served the subsistence of the local population itself. A characteristic example is the health sector, which originally came under the jurisdiction of the internal administration and was expanded in 1943 to an autonomous central department in the government of the General Government.[1] Apart from the general search for undesirable persons in terms of health policy,[2] there was initially a policy of unequal treatment for the German and Polish population to the extent that the nonlicensing of Polish physicians and the small number of Polish physicians allowed into medical training meant that medical support and provision was withdrawn to a very large extent,[3] causing a rapid rise in the sickness rate and the risk of epidemics, which—in view of the low number of Polish physicians, decimated still further by arrests—was of crucial importance.[4] The facilities for controlling tuberculosis were deliberately reduced. In Kraków, for instance, only three Polish hospitals, with a total of around one hundred beds, were licensed for this purpose. According to the testimony of Polish physicians, the Health Services Department had also prohibited prophylactic medical and dental examinations of "non-German" children and mothers;[5] according to this testimony, medical experiments (measurements and examinations of "racial purity"), including forced gynecological examinations, were conducted on Polish girls.[6] For the Jewish population, nothing was done to provide medical treatment; existing treatment facilities were eliminated or drastically reduced. As with medical practices, Jewish hospitals were robbed of almost their entire supply of medical and other equipment. Jews were prohibited from seeking medical assistance in any hospital.[7]

However, there was more in the public health sector than the mere reduction of the local population to the lowest possible level of provision; the prime objective was rather to prepare and conceal the subsequent drastic special measures against the Jews under the innocuous guise of medical prophylaxis against epidemics and diseases and thus ultimately to increase the sickness and death rates. In this respect, the exclusion of the Jews from any medical attention was only the first step on the long road to isolation, ghettoization, and deportation.

In preparation for the subsequent Final Solution, the risk of epidemics (e.g., typhus) spread by the Jews was invented or considerably exaggerated; it was used primarily to justify all anti-Jewish measures right up to the ghettoization of the Jews, because the pretense that precautionary medical measures had to be adopted was most readily believed and accepted by the public. Even in the Central Department of Interior Administration, however, it was known that the head of the health department was merely "painting a picture" of the "risk of epidemics"[8] to find an excuse for the plans to lock up the Jews. Based on the practice in the Reich, "actions" were first initiated under this camouflage; their main purpose was to denounce the Jews as the cause of dangerous epidemics; anti-Semitic posters portrayed the Jews as typhus carriers,[9] to justify to the public their drastic segregation from the rest of the population (exclusion from public transport and communications, residence bans, etc.) right up to their total isolation in the ghettos.[10] That these pretenses were absurd is obvious, but they do show the reversal of cause and effect so characteristic of National Socialist tactics. It was not the Jews themselves but the very overpopulation in the ghettos that was the cause of epidemics. Even Josef Walbaum, the head of the Health Services Department in the Governor General's Office, was forced to admit the "unbelievable result" of a very *low* rate of typhus in the General Government in early 1940, before Jewish "residential quarters" were established.[11] However, the Jews were now herded together in the ghettos to promote the outbreak of epidemics through overpopulation and thereby provide further proof of the "typhoidal" Jews;[12] once the ghettos had been established, numerous complaints had been raised about the risk of epidemics they posed, and ever more measures were demanded and adopted, which appeared to those contemporaries who believed the propaganda as a consistent consequence of the health policy "precautions" adopted by the administration; the "non-German" population, however, had no illusions about the real intentions concealed behind the camouflage of health policy. The isolation of the Jews in the ghettos was still being justified to the outside world by the pretense of protection against typhus, but this was no longer an adequate guise *inside* the administration as early as 1941. At a conference in Krynica on October 13–16, 1941, the head of the Health Services Department proposed, to the acclaim of those present, that since the ghettos were the sources of typhus, the only possible measure to control this risk was to shoot the Jews, as the "German *Volk*" should not be allowed to be "infected by the parasites."[13]

VIII. Freedom of Movement and Personal Liberty

The aforementioned practices in the public health sector should be viewed in conjunction with restrictions on freedom of movement, whose actual target was the Jews—against the background of their pending resettlement or evacuation (deportation to the extermination camps).[1] There is no evidence of general residence bans and restrictions on entry or change of residence for Polish "non-

Germans," as existed frequently in the Annexed Eastern Territories, except in cases of eviction for the establishment of Jewish residential quarters.

1.   Residential Restrictions and Ghettoization of the Jewish Population

Jews had been prohibited since December 1939 from leaving or changing their place of residence without police approval and from using public paths, roads, and squares between 9 P.M. and 5 A.M. without permission, unless they could demonstrate a "public or personal emergency."[2] However, the corresponding directive of December 11, 1939, was issued not by the internal administration, responsible for residence issues, but by the HSSPF *Ost* (in Kraków), for under a decree on forced labor for Jews issued by the governor general on October 26, 1939, the HSSPF was empowered to issue implementing regulations, including those with regard to residence. In this respect, the jurisdiction of the police, which was to usurp all Jewish affairs at a later date, had already been firmly established in the most important area, residence rights for Jews (ghettoization). Additional *general* residence restrictions or restrictions for particular groups,[3] authority to issue which had been given to the *Kreishauptleute (Stadthauptleute),* the district chiefs, or the Central Department of Interior Administration (depending on the scope of the restrictions) under the First Decree on Residence Restrictions in the General Government of September 13, 1940, were not affected by the directive of December 11, 1939.[4] This authorization was merely a neutrally worded circumscription of the powers of the administration to establish ghettos ("Jewish residential quarters"),[5] use of which was made from the first months of the civil administration, with experiments first in the *Kreishauptmann* towns[6] and later in the larger towns and cities of the General Government from the fall of 1940,[7] in particular in Warsaw, where the largest ghetto in the General Government was established.[8] The official pretenses for the establishment of ghettos were principally the protection of the Germans and the Poles against infectious diseases (e.g., typhus), the exclusion of the Jews from economic life, the need to restrict the freedom of movement of the Jews because of the risk of black market activities, and so forth.[9]

From the outset, both the administration and the police had jurisdiction over the residence of the Jews. The decree of September 13, 1940, served not only as a "legal basis" for the establishment of the ghettos themselves but more and more as a general authorization for regulating *all* issues relating to the treatment of the Jews (the prohibition on the use of public streets and transport, etc.).[10] But even in those towns where ghettos had yet to be established, the Jews had been tied to their place of residence from the beginning by the decree of the HSSPF

mentioned above and had thus become easily manageable "material" for rounding up for forced labor and ghettoization. Violations of residence prohibitions
issued on the basis of the decree of September 13, 1940, in particular leaving the
ghetto without authorization, were punished severely, initially by administrative
penal proceedings instituted by the relevant *Kreishauptmann*[11] and, after the infamous Third Decree on Residence Restrictions in the General Government of
October 15,1941,[12] even by death following sentencing by the special courts. The
same applied to any assistance provided to fugitive Jews and—after internal consultation—to unauthorized entry into the ghetto by "non-Jews."[13] These measures, although put into more concrete form by specific regulations issued by
the district chiefs,[14] were the source of growing friction between the justice authorities and the police, because the justice authorities regarded the death penalty as too harsh a punishment and would rather have handed over all such matters to the Security Police,[15] whereas for the police, the judicial machinery was
far too slow; the ultimate consequence was that the police increasingly took the
punishment of the Jews into their own hands and simply shot all Jews found
outside the ghetto "without permission" on the basis of a secret order of the
BdO (senior police officer) in Kraków.[16]

The definitive isolation of the Jews from the outside world took place in
1942—with the start of the deportations to the extermination camps—by the issue of numerous additional regulations about the establishment of Jewish residential quarters, forcing the Jews to take up residence there and obliging the
former inhabitants to leave these districts. It should be noted that these regulations were no longer issued in the form of directives (*Anordnungen*) or proclamations (*Bekanntmachungen*) of the internal administration (the *Kreishauptmann* and the district chief) on the basis of the powers conferred by the First
Decree on Residence Restrictions of September 13, 1940;[17] in this instance, the
latent jurisdiction of the police over Jewish affairs had already developed to the
point where *police regulations* of the HSSPF now intervened. Their only "legal"
basis was the general authorization set out in section 3 of the Decree on Security
and Public Order in the General Government of October 26, 1939,[18] which contained no indication of the object, nature, and scope of the subject and regulations to be adopted ("the Senior SS and Police Officer is authorized to issue police regulations") and thus opened the floodgates to the boundless discretion of
the police and continuous jurisdictional conflicts with the administration. This
blanket authorization and the regulations issued on its basis show clearly that *at
the latest* on this date, the police leadership had assumed control of the solution
of all issues connected with the establishment of ghettos and had increasingly
outplayed the internal administration (with either its overt approval or its tacit

consent), because the police—as was recorded at a police meeting—had a very strong interest "in the Jewish question for obvious reasons."[19] The regulations on the establishment of ghettos in specific districts of Warsaw, Kraków, Radom, Lublin, and Lemberg (L'vov) issued by the HSSPF in 1942 thus replaced de facto the existing regulations of the administrative authorities governing "Jewish residential quarters," or created "original" new "law" where no such previous regulations had existed.[20] Evidently, clarification of the jurisdiction to establish ghettos in accordance with the letter of the law was regarded as superfluous, since the stronger power—the police—had already prevailed: the rule of "might has right" was confirmed.

Equally unclear, and of much more far-reaching importance, was the problem—never settled—of who was responsible for regulating matters *inside* the ghetto. Under the general regulations, this should have been the Interior Administration, as the Jewish "residential quarters" did not represent any formal exception;[21] however, the police regarded the ghettos as the exclusive domain of the Security Police outside the jurisdiction of any regular administration (and the administration was increasingly ousted from such jurisdiction),[22] as demonstrated particularly clearly by the situation in the Warsaw Ghetto. The pretense adopted was the usual argument that the police, responsible for supervising the forced labor by the Jews, must also control the ghetto.[23] The consequence of this trend was ultimately that the police undermined the jurisdiction of the Interior Administration[24] and monopolized or had the major say in all Jewish affairs, because most of the Jews had been deported to the ghettos after the end of 1941.

2.   Other Restrictions on Personal Freedom of Movement

The total isolation of the Jewish population in "Jewish residential quarters" was prepared for and accompanied by a total elimination of all personal freedom of movement—again with the aim of fettering the Jews to their place of residence so that they would be more easily managed for police measures. Countless travel and usage prohibitions for public transport systems were issued, which had a particularly grotesque impact because under the aforementioned decree of the HSSPF of December 11, 1939, Jews could not leave their place of residence in any case. These prohibitions can thus be regarded as no more than an attempt to give the public impression that the Jews could "essentially" move around freely within the General Government with the exception of a few restrictions; these restrictions were, however, comprehensive. For instance, Jews were in principle forbidden to use the railway and other public transport for "reasons of security and epidemiological policy" as well as for "general policy reasons."[25] The fees for special permits from the police were set extortionately high so that "unsubstan-tiated applications as well as avoidable journeys were suppressed wherever pos-sible";[26] fees of between 20 and 100 złoty (between RM 10 and 50 in nominal terms) were demanded,[27] thus making travel impossible for many Jews, even for urgent reasons. Even stricter regulations were imposed in the individual districts, such as a prohibition on the use of *all* private and public transport, the use of pub-lic streets and squares, and so forth.[28] The restrictions on the freedom of move-ment of Jews were thus subject to two sets of rules. Jews could enjoy a minimum standard of personal freedom of movement only if the police approved an excep-tion to the general residence restrictions (to the Jewish residential quarters) and an exception to the general restriction on the use of all forms of transport. It is quite obvious that such special permits for Jews, who had long since lost the status of legal entities, were never issued for personal reasons; they were issued only if there was an "urgent public interest": "illness," forced labor conscription, and "re-settlement and evacuation."[29] The consistent consequence was that in this self-contained system of administrative regulations, even the road to forced labor, de-portation, and extermination was paved with official "licenses" and "permits."

The Poles, in contrast, were in many respects treated more leniently, as more consideration had to be taken of them in the interests of trouble-free *Ar-beitseinsatz*. The restrictions to which they were subject were thus primarily re-lated to segregation from the Germans, as shown by the prohibition on Poles' use of railway compartments reserved for Germans.[30] The use of public trans-port remained in other respects relatively free. Although the Poles were forbid-den to use the Eastern Railway (Ostbahn) without special permission in 1941, probably at the initiative of the district administration in Warsaw, this ban had to be lifted several months later because it was obstructing *Arbeitseinsatz* and food supplies.[31] Police attempts to introduce a regulation enforcing a general prohibition on Poles using the railways were frustrated at the last minute[32] by the Central Department of Interior Administration in 1943 when that depart-ment invoked the supply problems prevailing at the time, in view of the fact that the railway was the only functioning means of transport during adverse weather conditions and also the means of transport upon which the Poles were solely dependent, private transport (motor traffic) having been banned in the General Government since the end of 1939.[33] However, after failing to achieve conces-sions from the administration, the police—as usual—acted independently. As a form of substitute for their failure in 1941 to enforce a general prohibition on the use of the *Ostbahn* without a special permit, the police reintroduced this very same general prohibition by a regulation of October 18, 1943, and made the use of the *Ostbahn* subject to the issue of a permit by the local police authorities;[34]

for the police, allowing long-distance and commuter traffic without any control was an intolerable situation. In addition, a directive issued by the government of the General Government prohibited all official agencies from carrying Poles in motor vehicles,[35] with the aim of excluding the Poles from all means of transport other than the *Ostbahn*. In contrast, such petty regulations as the prohibition on using the tram service, either globally or at certain times, as was customary in parts of the Annexed Eastern Territories, were not introduced. The exception to this rule was Warsaw, where special streetcar sections were designated for Germans, Poles, and Jews.[36] As in the Warthegau (or Wartheland), the use of bicycles was prohibited except with a special permit. No doubt with the intention of preventing illegal communications among the Poles, all bicycles were required to be registered (with the exception of bicycles owned by Germans) under a police regulation issued by the higher SS and police leader (HSSPF) on August 3, 1942;[37] and after August 30, 1942, bicycles could be used only with a police permit (issued exclusively for occupational purposes and other important reasons); in addition, they could be confiscated or expropriated for German agencies at any time.[38]

IX. Restrictions on Communication and Information Exchange among "Non-Germans"

The restrictions on external personal freedom of movement corresponded to restrictions on the use of communication and news media, to "ensure" the segregation and insulation of the "non-Germans" from information and the social environment.

Until 1942 postal services remained free from intervention. Only then, according to a decree issued by the governor general, were "non-Germans" limited to a maximum of two letters a month per person, each letter a maximum of two pages long (there was no restriction on postcards); correspondence was permitted only with non-enemy countries.[1] There were additional restrictions on telecommunications and on sending and receiving parcels. To facilitate censorship, the full name and address of the sender had to appear on each sheet of paper.[2] The Armed Forces High Command was also authorized to order restrictions on domestic mail services "for the prosecution of the war" under the same decree.[3] Polish postal workers suffered severe penalties for mail offenses, imposed by the courts from case to case without any consideration of the statutory range of punishments.[4] The desire for additional restrictions on postal services for "non-Germans" expressed by the head of the Security Police and the Security Service in November 1943 in the Security Service Reports on Domestic Issues should be seen as a means of combating the activities of the Polish underground movement, which was particularly active among Polish postal workers; the reasons given were that the Polish underground was growing in strength via correspondence with Poles in the General Government, hostile propaganda was being spread by post, reports on conditions in the Altreich were reaching the General Government, and the risk of theft, black market activities, and so forth was in- creased.[5] Because of the course of the war, however, the proposed countermeasures did not result in any further restrictions, at least not any directed by the governor general.

Jews, of course, were subject to additional special laws. They had been completely excluded from telegraph services since August 1940,[6] as well as from telephone communications and the possession of telephones. In December 1941 the post no longer accepted packets, parcels, or insured parcels from Jews "*to avoid the risk of epidemics.*"[7]

News media privately owned by "non-Germans" were also subject to far-reaching restrictions. Numerous prohibitions were issued early on, restricting radio reception; these were of dubious effect, however, as stated in the aforementioned Security Service Reports on Domestic Issues. During the military administration, foreign radio sets held by poles who were "suspected of listening to Allied broadcasts" were confiscated, as were those owned by persons who were "notorious Polish chauvinists."[8] The civil administration rapidly followed suit and—backed up by corresponding proclamations in the *kreise*[9]—decreed in December 1939 that all radios held by Poles and Jews be confiscated, to be collected by January 25, 1940, and that all "superfluous aerials" be removed;[10] the responsible administrative authority (*Kreishauptmann or stadthauptmann*) could issue exemptions from the duty of surrender in individual instances to members of the Ukrainian and Góral population in a phased "racial" approach (i.e., for political "good conduct"); Reich and ethnic Germans could keep their radios but were required to register all sets.[11]

As was to be expected, the duty of surrender was not obeyed in all cases; according to a report by SS-*Sturmbahnführer* Joseph Meisinger on the security situation in the Warsaw District at a meeting of the Reich Defense Committee on March 2, 1940, only 87,000 out of a total of around 140,000 radio sets in Warsaw had been surrendered; many radios had been destroyed in the fighting, but many others were being hidden.[12] In view of the low number of available police officers, the situation is likely to have been similar in the other districts.

For other luxury goods, such as binoculars, cameras, and so on, there were no central confiscation regulations and surrender obligations as were common, for instance in the *Reichsgau* Wartheland; all that can be proved is the registration and confiscation of film equipment, skis, and ski boots for the use of the Wehrmacht.[13] No doubt more extensive individual regulations were issued by the district and *Kreis* administrations on the basis of the Confiscation Decree of January 26,1940, or by single acts of the police for "the public benefit" in line with the principle that, whenever the German civil authorities had a requirement, they could seize the private property of the "non-Germans" without objection.

A concluding survey of the discriminatory measures in these areas highlights two specific features: compared with the radical practices common in parts of the Annexed Eastern Territories and in the parts of eastern Poland occupied by the Soviet Union, relatively tolerable living conditions reigned in the General Government.[14] However, this applied only to the Polish population; the legal and administrative extinction of the Jews, based on the model of the Reich, was tackled with single-minded determination. Whereas in the Warthegau, for instance, a radical isolation of the Polish population from the outside world (travel bans) and from key information media, cultural goods, and commodities was implemented down to humiliating, petty harassment, there still existed in the General Government—despite the restrictions in force—an opportunity for personal freedom of movement, freedom of communication and information, and protection of private property, either because the regulations in force were not so far-reaching or because there were simply no facilities for supervising their observance. Nevertheless, the practice of special law, especially in the professional and labor law sectors, led to predatory policies running counter to all principles of economic reason. As could be expected, these policies therefore implemented their own objectives (the General Government as an inexhaustible supplier of willing labor, industrial goods, and foodstuffs) ad absurdum. As a report of the Military District Command of the General Government of January 7, 1943, soberly ascertained, the consequences of the isolation and expulsion measures, of the "psychologically mistaken treatment," of the "erroneous harshness" and the "complete disregard [for the Poles] in conjunction with poor social welfare," were the ruin of trade and industry, poor labor productivity, falling production figures, failure to meet the quotas imposed by the Reich, and at an early date (since around 1941 and to a larger extent since 1942) an increasingly anti-German mood in all areas,[15] which was only reinforced by the professional and moral failure, the corruption, and the "master-race attitude" of the leadership and numerous departments.[16] The most paralyzing and destructive factors, however, were the largely contrary policies of the administration and the police, the jurisdictional chaos and legal uncertainty in this strained relationship, and the lack of any solid line by the administrative leadership against the claims to power of the police or in the question of the treatment of the "non-Germans."

These conflicts did not affect the relationship between the administration and the police in all areas. In particular, the fact should not be ignored that they collaborated closely in many areas of the treatment of "non-Germans." The administrative leadership of the General Government, which had developed in an atmosphere of anti-Polish sentiment,[17] was also convinced in the beginning, as were the police, that it could establish a *permanent* colonial regime on the basis of pure repression. The numerous resettlement and evacuation measures, the indiscriminate taking of hostages and executions, and the ruthless collection of laborers right up to manhunts demonstrate that system of blind failure to appreciate facts that was so characteristic of the Nazi regime. As established by the aforementioned report of the Military District Command of the General Government, these actions created the best conditions for acts of desperation, criminal gangs, and so forth, leading to the Poles' fear that "all rights to exist were to be taken from them and that they were to meet the same fate as the Jews."[18] When the difficulties became insurmountable, there were calls by the police for increasingly drastic measures, as shown by the recruitment of labor, which in turn strengthened the Polish resistance. When it was too late, the need for a change of course was recognized, but it never passed the stage of promises and small changes to the "*Fremdvolk* policy," and nothing at all was done to curb the omnipotence of the police.

For instance, the government of the General Government attempted to win back the powers of the police, which it had initially transferred so generously—in particular the infinite police administrative law in section 3 of the Decree on Security and Public Order in the General Government of October 26, 1939.[19] A draft unified police administrative law in the General Government submitted in 1941 eliminated the police administrative law of the SS and police; the ranks of the regular police performing specific duties (gendarmerie and uniformed police) were no longer to be subordinate to the head of the regular police, and above him the HSSPF, but to the *Kreis* authorities and *Stadthauptleute*.[20] However, as with all other efforts to curb the growing powers of the police, it was too late. The HSSPF had no intention of giving up the powers transferred to him;[21] in addition, as regards its application to "non-Germans," substantive police law gradually lost its—in any case minor—importance.

The needs of the moment in the eyes of the police were more than ever the proven means of guidelines and specific directives, requiring no legal basis for authorization and for which neither the consent nor the notification of the administrative authorities was necessary. Furthermore, from 1943 on, the treatment of the "non-Germans" was increasingly enforced in the form of acts of terror. The governor general, who had been concerned about preserving his own powers since the replacement of HSSPF Friedrich Wilhelm Krüger by SS-*Obergruppenführer* Wilhelm Koppe in fall 1943, and with an eye to the security situation, which was "falling to pieces," allied himself ever more closely with the police and indeed supported their approval for the hardest possible line against the Poles. For this reason the governor general had given the police unheard-of powers in 1943, far exceeding their already extensive jurisdiction (e.g., jurisdiction for courts-martial).[22] These included the Decree on the Combating of Attacks on the German (*Aufbauwerk*) of October 2, 1943,[23] through which it was hoped to gain the upper hand over the Polish resistance movement.[24] This decree entailed the complete annulment of all concepts of police law by instituting the death penalty without any court proceedings for any violation of any directive by German agencies, treating any prejudicial conduct as an "attack on the German (*Aufbauwerk*)."[25]

With this decree, the police obtained what they regarded as the *ideal police law,* with one single offense and infinite omnibus provisions, as well as a single penalty, the death sentence, which could be used as the basis for all forms of police action, particularly for raids, including the execution of hostages, resistance fighters, and so on. As usual, the governor general considered curbing these powers again when it was discovered that the situation was not markedly improved by the rigorous approach adopted by the police.[26] And as usual, it was too late to recall the furies that had been let loose.

The predatory practice of the administration had thus not only successfully prevented the realization of its own goals within the shortest possible period, but it had incurred the enmity of all sections of the population and reduced the country to a "total starvation level" (according to Frank), both culturally and economically. Its transfer of extensive powers to the police had also robbed it of any opportunity to influence the treatment of the "non-Germans," had crucially strengthened the Polish will to resist,[27] had assisted the revolutionary violence of the police in all key aspects, and had thus cooperated in the elimination of all conventional concepts and forms of administrative acts in favor of a regime of pure brutality, which left behind it nothing but destruction and ruins.

Gesamt-

der Durchführung des Gesetzes zur Wiederherstellung des
Statistik des Preußischen

Ergebnis

Berufsbeamtentums vom 7. April 1933 (— RG. Bl. I S. 175 —
Justizministeriums — 1962), 730 ff. —

FIG. 1   Statistical survey of the Prussian Ministry of Justice, 1934. Reproduced in H. Schorn, *Der Richter im Dritten Reich* (Frankfurt/Main, 1959), 730 f., from original in Geheimen Staatsarchiv Preussischer Kulturbesitz, Rep. 84a.

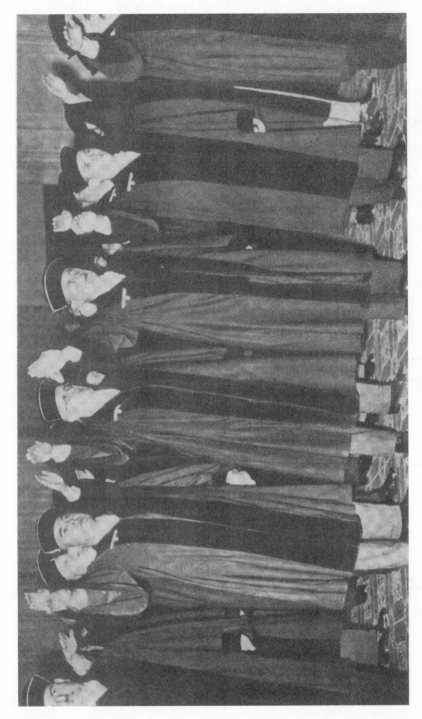

FIG. 2   Celebration of the presentation of the national emblem swastika pin to be worn on the justices' robes in the Criminal Court Berlin-Moabit, October 1, 1936. Ullstein Bilderdienst.

FIG. 3   Reich Minister of Justice Gürtner at the induction of the president of the Posen State Superior Court, April 1940. Archiwum Państwowe Poznań.

FIG. 4   Reich Minister of the Interior Frick in Prague during a tour through the Protectorate of Bohemia and Moravia, October 30, 1940. Bundesarchiv, Bild 1/80/62.

III.Kps.80/46

<u>odpis z odpisu</u>

B l a t t 2.

Unter Bezug auf das Protokoll vom 29.9.39 wird auf dem dort
näher nachgewiesenen Sachverhalt verwiesen / Ermordung des
Volksdeutschen Rausch in Nitsche bei Schmiegel / Es wird
nochmals der Befehl des Chefs Einsatzgruppe VI verlesen,
indem der Befehl des Chefs der Zivilverwaltung SS Brigadeführer u. Senatspräsident Greiser auf Erschiessung von
16 Polen erhalten ist.
Es wurden folgende Polen vorgeführt:

1/ Wydra Ladislaus geb.am 20.1.94 zu Zywiec wohnhaft Kosten
   Kreisschulinspektor
2/ Fabiszczak Stanislaus, geb. am 18.4.06 in Katowiecko
   wohnhaft Kosten. Postdirektor
3/ Kaczmarek Ludwig, geb. am 7.8.21 in Kosten wohnhaft
   Kosten, Jugendführer der Pfadfinder. Militärische
   Vorbildung
4/ Wenski Ludwig, geb. am 4.8.82 in Zodby, wohnhaft in Kosten
   Grosskfm. Vorsitzender des Sokolverbandes in Kosten
5/ Cichowszewski Ludwig, geb. am 20.7.15 zu Ickern, wohnhaft
   Kokoschyn, Präses des nationalen Lagers, berüchtigter Hetzer.
6/ Szynkiewski Josef, geb. am 19.3.82 zu Posen, wohnhaft
   Czempin Vorsitzender des Sokolverbandes. Mitglied des
   Westmarkenverbandes
7/ Obaro Franz, geb. am 2.12.95 zu Otwa, wohnhaft zu Kosten
   Kleinbahndirektor
8/ von Koscielski Wladislaus, geb. am 15.8.79 zu Sepno,
   wohnhaft zu Sepno, Gutsbesitzer.

===================== ==

B l a t t 3

Das Standgericht ist sich schlüssig dolgende Polen zu
erschiessen
1/ Nr. 1 Es handelt sich um einen massgebenden Mann aus der Stadt
   Kosten, als Hetzer bekannt.
2/ Nr. 2 Ein Übel beleumendeter Pole
3/ Nr. 3 Judendführer
4/ Nr. 4 Vorsitzerder des Sokolverbandes übler Deutschen-Hasser
5/ Nr. 5 Berüchtigter Hetzer
6/ Nr. 6 Mitglied des Westmarkenvereins
7/ Nr. 7 Gehört zur geistigen Führerschicht
8/ Nr. 8 Gutsbesitzer, übler Hetzer

SS Untersturmführer Apfelstädt erhielt den Befehl, die
oben aufgeführten Polen sofort zu erschiessen.
Der zuständige Landrat Dr. Liese und der Ortskommandant
Hauptmann Dekan wurden benachrichtigt. Ebenfalls wurde der
Bürgermeister S.A. Sturmführer Szitter. Die Sitzung wurde
um 13^{19} Uhr unterbrochen.
Die Sitzung wurde fortgesetzt um 13^{30} Uhr.
Die Sitzung wurde geschlossen um 13^{35} Uhr, nachdem der Bürger-
meister angewiesen worden war den zu erschiessenden 8 Polen
zu eröffnrn, dass sie auf Grund der in der Nacht vom29. zum
30.9. begannennen Ermordung eines Deutschen erschossen werden.
Gleichzeitig ist der Bürgermeister angewiesen worden in der
Stadt die Erschiessung bekannt zu geben.

Beisitzer   Vorsitzender   Beisitzer

FIG. 5   Protocol from a hearing of the court-martial attached to Einsatzkommando 14 of
Einsatzgruppe VI in Kosten, government district Posen. The hearing took place before two SS-
Sturmbannführer, one a government councillor and the other a counselor of the Criminal Police,
and an SS-*Obersturmbannführer* (who was also a superintendent of the Criminal Police). They
were assisted by an ethnic German teacher as "regional consultant." Kreiskommission zur Verfolgung von NS-Verbrechen in Polen, Posen, II/4/21 K 73.

FIG. 6 Einsatzkommando 3/V guarding Jews in Płonsk in the regional district Zichenau, September 27, 1939. From a photo album of an unidentified official of Einsatzkommando 3/V and the Gestapo in Hohensalza, Główna Komisja Badania Zbrodni Hitlerowskich w Polsce, Warsaw, reproduced in *Der Stern* 47 (1979): 112.

FIG. 7 Sentencing by an unidentified court-martial of the security police and SD, 1939–40. Bundesarchiv, Bild 3/79/67.

FIG. 8 Płonsk, September 1939. From a photo album of an unidentified official of Einsatzkommando 3/V and the Gestapo in Hohensalza, Główna Komisja Badania Zbrodni Hitlerowskich w Polsce, Warsaw, reproduced in *Der Stern* 47 (1979): 106 f.

Plock, den 8. Februar 1940.

S t a n d g e r i c h t :

Am 8. Februar 1940 trat auf der Dienststelle der Geheimen
Staatspolizei in Plock das Standgericht zusammen:

Den Vorsitz des Standgerichtes führte:
H-Oberführer Dr. R a s c h.

Als Beisitzer amtierten:
Krim.Sek.u.H-Unterstuf. B a n d o w,
Krim.Ass. u.H-Oberscharführer L e r c h.

Zur Sache:

Der Pole C z a b l i n s k i Tadeusz, geb. 13.1.1898
Wola Mlocke Kreis Zichenau geb. verh., Plock Bahnhofstrasse
Nr. 40 wohnhaft, war aktives Mitglied der P.O.W. Vom Jahre
1931 bis 1936 war er Sekretär dieser Vereinigung in Plock.
Bei Ihm wurden Abzeichen von verschiedenen polnischen Ver-
einigungen und Armbinden, sowie auch verschiedenes Propaganda-
material der P.O.W. vorgefunden. Vertraulichen Mitteilungen
von hiesigen Volksdeutschen zufolge sollen auch in der letzten Zeit
bei Czablinski Zusammenkünfte von Polen stattgefunden haben.

r gilt allgemein als polnischer Intelligenzler und es ist
anzunehmen, daß er auch heute noch   seine früheren
Verbindungen aufrecht erhalten hat.

XXXXXXXXXX

Der Sachverhalt wird vorgetragen. Der Besch. wird dazu
gehört.

Es wird das

U r t e i l

verkündet.

Der Besch. wird zum Tode verurteilt.

H-Oberführer.

H-Untersturmführer.   H-Oberscharführer

FIG. 9 Protocol from a hearing of the court-martial attached to the Gestapo office Zichenau/
Schröttersburg, February 8, 1940. Główna Komisja Badania Zbrodni Hitlerowskich w Polsce,
Warsaw, II/470.

Der Oberamtsrichter
- 41 -

An den
Herrn L a n d r a t
in W o l l s t e i n

Wollstein,den 8. April 1941
Tel.58

Vertraulich!

Betrifft: Kenntlichmachung der Liege-
stellen standrechtlich er-
schossener Polen ausserhalb
der öffentlichen Begräbnisstätten

Im Kreise Wollstein dürften ausserhalb der amtlichen Begräbnisstätten mehrere standrechtlich erschos-
sene Polen liegen.

Es besteht die nahe Wahrscheinlichkeit,dass frü-
her oder später durch Raubtiere (Füchse) oder beim Ackern,
Roden oder sonstigen Arbeiten solche Leichen aufgedeckt
werden.Es wird dann Polizei,Gericht und Staatsanwaltschaft
in Bewegung gesetzt werden.

Um für alle Zeiten sicherzustellen,dass von irgendwelchen Ermittlungen bei Leichenfunden dieser Art ab-
gesehen wird,schlage ich vor,alle solche Grabstellen nach
Art und Lage festzustellen,in eine Liste und eine Karte
einzutragen.Karten und Listen dürften zweckmässig in 2
Stücken gefertigtwerden,von denen die eine bei den Geheim-
sachen des Amtsgerichts,die andere bei den Geheimakten des
Landratsamts aufbewahrt werden.Auf diese Weise würde in
späteren Jahren zeitraubende,aber völlig unnötige Ermittlungen erspart bleiben.Über die betreffenden Stellen im
Kreise Wollstein dürften am besten der Gendarmeriemeister
Pätzold und der frühere SA.-Sturmbannführer Auskunft geben können.

FIG. 10 Memorandum from the superior district court judge in Wollstein, government district Posen, to the district magistrate, April 8, 1941. Archiwum Państwowe Poznań, Landgericht Posen, no. 14.

Der Landrat des Kreises
Kempen.
Gesch. Zeich: K A VI.

Kempen (Wartheland), den 18. Juni 1941.

Verteiler:
Bürgermeister der Stadt Kempen,
Amtskommissare des **K r e i s e s**.

R u n d v e r f ü g u n g.

Betrifft: Arbeitseinsatz von Juden; hier Abführung von Lohnteilen.

Nach einer Anordnung des Herrn Reichsstatthalters vom 27.7.40 müssen die Arbeitgeber von Juden den jeweils tarifmäßigen Arbeitslohn zahlen, von dem der Jude 35% erhält, während 65% auf ein von mir einzurichtendes Sonderkonto abzuführen ist.

Sollten innerhalb Ihres Amtsbezirkes künftig einmal Juden beschäftigt werden, ist dementsprechend zu verfahren. Auch ist mir dann zu berichten, ob der für die Juden bestimmte Anteil für ihre Ernährung und für die Erhaltung ihrer Arbeitsfähigkeit ausreicht. Desgleichen ist mir beim Arbeitseinsatz von Juden mitzuteilen, wie die Arbeitgeber mit der Arbeitsleistung zufrieden sind und welche durchschnittliche Unterhaltungskosten für einen Juden entstehen.

In Vertretung.
gez. Wolf.
Regierungsinspektor.

Beglaubigt:
Büroangestellte.

1) Der Lohnabteilung zur Kenntnis und Beachtung
2) z.d.A.

FIG. 11 Circular decree of the district magistrate of the district Kempen, government district Łódź, June 18, 1941. Instytut Zachodni Poznań.

RK 14387 B - 20KT 1941

Der Chef der Sicherheitspolizei und des SD

II A 1 Nr.305 II/41-15/-.

Berlin SW 11, am 18.September 1941
Prinz-Albrecht-Straße 8

An den

Herrn Reichsminister
und Chef der Reichskanzlei Dr. L a m m e r s

B e r l i n W 8
Voßstrasse 6

Sehr verehrter Herr Reichsminister!

Bezugnehmend auf mein letztes Telefongespräch das Generalgouvernement betreffend darf ich nochmals zusammen- fassend vortragen:

Durch Führererlass sind die Chefs der Zivilverwaltung und die ihnen gleichgestellten Verwaltungschefs im deutschen Machtbereich von der Jeisungsgewalt der Reichszentralbehörden befreit und lediglich den Jeisungen des Führers unterstellt worden.

Während ursprünglich von dieser ulleinigen Unterstellung unter das Jeisungsrecht des Führers lediglich zu Gunsten des Reichsmarschalls in seiner Eigenschaft als Beauftragter für den Vierjahresplan eine Ausnahme gemacht worden ist, sind, wie ich aus Mitteilungen des Herrn Reichsministers des Innern vom 19. und 27. März 1941 entnehme, auch der Reichsverkehrs- minister und der Reichspostminister ermächtigt worden, im Rahmen ihrer Zuständigkeiten Jeisungen an die Chefs der Zivilverwaltung und die ihnen gleichgestellten Verwaltungs- chefs zu erteilen.

Nun ist aber die polizeiliche Sicherung des Reiches, der Schutz seiner Grenzen durch die Grenzpolizei, die Bekämpfung der Spionage und der politischen Zersetzung

Ostgebiete hervorgeht, das Jeisungsrecht des Reichs- führers-# gegenüber den Zivilverwaltungen hinsichtlich der inneren Sicherung der betreffenden Gebiete sicher- gestellt.

Ich würde es für dringend wünschenswert halten, dass der Führer in einem Erlass, der dem Erlass über die polizeiliche Sicherung der neu besetzten Ostgebiete vom 17. Juli 1941 nachgebildet ist, auch für die übrigen Gebiete, in denen eine deutsche Zivilverwaltung besteht, dem Reichsführer-# eine entsprechende Stellung verleiht. Ich habe mir gestattet, einen entsprechenden Entwurf beizufügen.

Ich darf Sie daher sehr herzlich bitten, beim Führer unter Hinweis auf seinen oben erwähnten Erlass vom 17. Juli 1941 diese erstlichen und die Sicherheit des Reiches im ganzen gefährdenden Verhältnisse vorzutragen und auch für den Reichsführer-# und die ihm unterstellten Zentraldienststellen das Jeisungsrecht an die Chefs der Zivilverwaltung und die ihnen gleichgestellten Verwaltungs- chefs in deutschen Machtbereich zu erwirken. Ich glaube zu wissen, dass der Führer diese Aufgabe und Befugnis als schon bestehend annimmt. Da es auch um die Sicherheit des Reiches selbst geht, wäre ich Ihnen für einen recht baldigen Vortrag beim Führer in dieser Angelegenheit dankbar.

FIG. 12 Memorandum from SS-Gruppenführer Heydrich to Reich Minister Lammers with handwritten notation from Lammers: "I have promised the R(eichs) F(ührer) SS to give a lecture on this. Please examine [the] matter promptly. Proceedings with W. in the F(ührer's) h(ead)qu(arters) in V-M [i.e., lecture file]." September 18–October 4, 1941. Bundesarchiv R 43 II/396.

E n t w u r f

Erlass des Führers

Über die polizeiliche Sicherung des Generalgouvernements, des Protektorats Böhmen und Mähren sowie der von Reichskommissaren oder Chefs der Zivilverwaltung verwalteten Gebiete.

Vom .... 1941.

I.

Die innenpolitische Sicherung des Generalgouvernements, des Protektorats Böhmen und Mähren sowie der von Reichskommissaren oder Chefs der Zivilverwaltung verwalteten Gebiete ist Aufgabe des Reichsführers-SS und Chefs der Deutschen Polizei.

II.

Im Rahmen der unter I bezeichneten Aufgabe ist der Reichsführer-SS und Chef der Deutschen Polizei berechtigt, den Generalgouverneur, dem Reichsprotektor, den Reichskommissaren und den Chefs der Zivilverwaltung sowie den ihnen nachgeordneten Stellen Weisungen zu erteilen.

Soweit sich die Weisungen an die nachgeordneten Stellen richten, sind sie im Benehmen mit dem Generalgouverneur, dem Reichsprotektor, den Reichskommissuren oder Chefs der Zivilverwaltung zu erteilen, es sei denn, dass es sich um die Abwendung einer unmittelbar drohenden Gefahr handelt. Das innenpolizeiliche Weisungsrecht des Reichsführers-SS bleibt davon unberührt.

III.

Zur Durchführung der polizeilichen Sicherung tritt zu dem Generalgouverneur, zu dem Reichsprotektor sowie zu jedem Reichskommissar oder Chef der Zivilverwaltung ein höherer SS- und Polizeiführer, der dem Generalgouverneur,

FIG. 13   Draft of a Führer decree (not promulgated) from the Reich Security Main Office (RSHA) (enclosure to memorandum in FIG. 12), September 18, 1941. Bundesarchiv R 43 II/396.

2.) Herrn RKabR.Dr.Willuhn
erg.m.d.Bitte um Mitzeichnung.

3.) Herrn R e i c h s m i n i s t e r
gehorsamst weisungsgemäß vorgelegt.

Die Angelegenheit dürfte zunächst grundsätzlich beim Führer zur Sprache zu bringen sein. Stimmt der Führer dem Wunsche des Chefs der Sicherheitspolizei grundsätzlich zu, so wird ein entsprechender Erlaß von hier aus vorzubereiten sein.

JT 108

1.) Ich habe die Angelegenheit gestern mit dem Reichsführer-SS besprochen. Wir sind dahin übereingekommen, daß ich den von mir beabsichtigten Vortrag beim Führer vorerst noch zurückstelle.

2.) a/Herrn MinDir.Kritzinger
b/Herrn RKabR.Dr.Willuhn
c/Herrn RKabR.Dr.Ficker
erg.m.d.Bitte um Kenntnisnahme.
zu c/auch m.d.Bitte um Rücksprache.

3.) W.15.11.41.   FHQ., den 23.10.41.

FIG. 14   Notation from the Reich Chancellery renouncing further pursuit of the suggestion of the Reich Security Main Office (RSHA), October 23, 1941. Bundesarchiv R 43 II/396.

FIG. 15   Execution of three death sentences carried out by officials of Hohensalsa Gestapo in Kutno on the orders of the Special Court Leslau; the three victims had been convicted of black-marketeering in flour and sugar, June 9, 1941. From a photo album of an unidentified official of Einsatzkommando 3/V and the Gestapo in Hohensalza, Główna Komisja Badania Zbrodni Hitlerowskich w Polsce, Warsaw, reproduced in *Der Stern 47* (1979): 108 f.

Folgo 3

Informationsblatt

Streng vertraulich!

Gemeinschaft mit Polen gibt es nicht

Dieser immer wieder betonte Grundsatz wird nicht von allen Deutschen mit der gleichen Selbstverständlichkeit befolgt. Mancher Deutsche,
sei es, dass er mitten in polnischer Umgebung aufgewachsen ist, sei es,
dass ihm als Binnendeutscher der Volkstumskampf noch kein klarer Begriff ist, muss gelegentlich zu volksbewusster Haltung gegenüber Polen
gemahnt werden. Dasselbe gilt besonders von Kindern und Jugendlichen,
die in ihrer Ahnungslosigkeit von Polen nur zu leicht für deutschfeind-
liche Zwecke ausgenutzt werden können. Das Sondergericht in Posen hatte sich kürzlich mit folgendem Sachverhalt zu beschäftigen: Ein 13 jähriger volksdeutscher Schüler, der der
Hitlerjugend angehört, war aus früherer Zeit mit einem etwas älteren
Polen bekannt. Er lieh dem Polen, der damit Einlass in ein Kino erlan-
gen wollte sein HJ-Abzeichen und den HJ-Meldeschein. Der Pole besuchte
die Kinovorstellung und lief auch noch einige Tage später mit dem Abzeichen herum. Bei dem Versuch, sich als Deutscher getarnt, den Kauf von
Zigaretten zu erleichtern, wurde er festgenommen. Er wurde vom Sondergericht zu 1 Jahr 6 Monaten Straflager verurteilt.

Der Fall zeigt eine Gefahrenquelle in der Volkstumslinie, die -
auch im Interesse unserer Jugend - die Aufmerksamkeit aller Deutschen
verdient.

FIG. 16 Information sheet of the *Gau* press agency of the *Gau* leadership Wartheland concerning court decisions, series 3, March 16, 1942. Archiwum Państwowe Poznań, Reichsstatthalter No.
468.

Garmeriezug Warschau
Distrikt Warschau

348.

Warschau, den 22. Februar 1943.

1.) An

die Gendarmerie-Hauptmannschaft Warschau

in J a r s c h a u .

Betrifft: Tägliche Schnellmeldung.

Nach den bestehenden Richtlinien verfahren.

20.2.43	Tluszcz (Gend. Posten Tluszcz)	1 Jüdin.
21.2.43	Falenica (Gend. Post. Rembertow)	2 Juden (1 männl. u. 1 weibl.)
21.2.43	Marki (Gend. Post. Warschau)	2 Juden.
21.2.43	Kempa-Falenica (Gend. Post. Warschau)	1 Jude.

A.B.

2.) z.d.A.

Leiter der Gendarmerie.

FIG. 17 Report concerning the shooting by the police of a Jew fleeing from the Warsaw ghetto;
the shooting occurred without legal proceeding ("nach den bestehenden Richtlinien verfahren"
[according to existing instructions]), February 22, 1943. Instytut Zachodni Poznań.

dann das langsame Abziehen nach Kalisch im Benehmen mit dem
SD und dem Gauamt für Volkstumsfragen durchgeführt wird. Die
Außenstelle Litzmannstadt des Rasse- und Siedlungshauptamtes 4
ist mit dieser Regelung einverstanden.

Bei dem jetzt geplanten Tempo ist eine Unterbringung in Friedenszeiten an anderen Stellen des Gaues wie mir zugegeben wurde
auch nicht möglich.

Der Erlaß an die Jugendämter wird mir zur Mitzeichnung vorgelegt und dann an die Landräte und Oberbürgermeister gegeben.

I/50
140/3-5

Posen, den 10. Juni 1944.

Geheim

Aktenvermerk:

Am 8. Juni 1944 hatte ich eine Besprechung mit Herrn
Gauverwaltungsdirektor Dr. B a r t e l s von der Gauselbst-
verwaltung über die Frage der Behandlung der unehelichen
Kinder polnischer Mütter mit deutschen Vätern.

1) Es wurde dabei festgestellt, daß es sich insgesamt um
eine Zahl von etwa 2000 Kindern handelt. Schätzungsweise
20 % dieser Kinder werden mit ihren Müttern, da diese
eindeutschungsfähig sind, ins Altreich verbracht werden.
Der Rest von etwa 80 % wird im Laufe der Zeit durch bestimmte rassische und psychologische Methoden untersucht.
Dabei werden die ausgemerzt, bei denen von vornherein fest-
steht, daß sie für das deutsche Volk keinen erwünschten
Bevölkerungszuwachs bedeuten sondern völlig unerwünscht
sind. Es werden danach etwa 1200 Kinder übrig bleiben.
Eine Unterbringung im Altreich in einer geschlossenen Aktion ist völlig unmöglich.

2) Wir kamen überein, diese Kinder langsam nach Kalisch
einzuberufen, und zwar die ersten in etwa 3 Monaten, und
sie dann nach der üblichen Beobachtungszeit in Kalisch
einzeln ins Altreich zu geben. Damit wird vor allen Din-
gen vermieden, daß im jetzigen Augenblick in Großen ein
Wegnehmen der Kinder von ihren polnischen Müttern erfolgt.
Ich habe besonders darauf hingewiesen, daß dies auf die
Polen einen recht ungünstigen Einfluß haben könnte.

3) Bis die Auslese in Kalisch erfolgt, werden die Kinder
als Polen behandelt. Die Jugendämter werden durch einen
entsprechenden Erlaß darauf hingewiesen, die 50 % deutschen Kinder gelegentlich zu beobachten und wenn sie
merken, daß in einer Familie besonders grobe Mißstände
auftauchen, werden diese Kinder im Einzelfall besonders
schnell nach Kalisch geholt.

4) Der Ablauf der Aktion ist also der, daß zunächst eine
Untersuchung überhaupt durch das Rasse- und Siedlungs-
hauptamt-SS, Außenstelle Litzmannstadt, erfolgt und daß

-2-

FIG. 18   Notation from the director of Section I/50 in the office of the *Reichsstatthalter* in the Warthegau in Posen, SS-*Sturmbahnführer* Höppner, concerning the Germanization of Polish children with instructions for submission of the same to the director of Department I and "resubmission after acknowledgment of the decree to the Youth Welfare Offices, presumably 1 July 1944," June 10, 1944. Archiwum Państwowe Poznań, Reichsstatthalter No. 1174.

FIG. 19   Dr. Franz Schlegelberger, secretary of state in the Reich Ministry of Justice, 1933–40, acting Reich minister of justice, 1941–42, after the death of Reich Minister of Justice Dr. Franz Gürtner in January 1941. Photograph by Heinrich Hoffmann, courtesy of Bayerische Staatsbibliothek München.

FIG. 20 The "*Gau*-kings" of the Reichsgaue, Erich Koch of East Prussia (*left, next to General Karl Bodenschatz of the Luftwaffe*) and Franz Schwede-Coburg of Pomerania (*right*) in discussion with Reich Minister of the Interior Wilhelm Frick (*second from right*). Photograph by Heinrich Hoffmann, courtesy of Bayerische Staatsbibliothek München.

FIG. 21 Fritz Sauckel, plenipotentiary general for labor allocation, who was in charge of organizing the system of forced labor in all occupied territories. Courtsey of United States Holocaust Memorial Museum Photo Archives.

FIG. 22 Erich Koch, Gauleiter (highest NSDAP official in a Party district) of Eastern Prussia, became Reich commissar for the Ukraine in 1941. In 1959 Koch was sentenced to death by the Polish Supreme Court. The sentence was later changed to life imprisonment. He died in a Polish prison in 1986. The picture shows him as a defendant before the Polish Supreme Court in 1946. Nederlands Instituut voor Oorlogsdocumentatie, courtesy of United States Holocaust Memorial Museum Photo Archives.

FIG. 23 The Reich minister and head of the Reich Chancellery, H. H. Lammers (*left*) and Secretary of State H. Stuckart of the Reich Ministry of the Interior (*right*) in discussion with Adolf Hitler (not pictured). Photograph by Heinrich Hoffmann, courtesy of Bayerische Staats-bibliothek München.

FIG. 24   An execution of Polish citizens by German police forces in German-occupied Polish territory, presumably 1939. Archiwum Państwowe Inowrocław, 1549 Sign. 1557.

PART TWO

The Principle of Special Law against "Non-Germans" in the Field of Justice

Section One

The Implementation of *Völkisch* Inequality in the Altreich

A. Penal Law

I. The General Thrust of National Socialist Policy in Penal Law

In the implementation of *völkisch* inequality in the field of justice, the main emphasis was naturally on criminal law, for it is there that the mechanisms of suppression inherent in the National Socialist system were most visible and the treatment of "non-Germans" reached its peak of unbridled terror. At first, however, *völkisch* inequality—or the "special treatment" of Jews, as the terminology originally had it—could not be implemented in the Reich territory by legislative means on any great scale, except by way of exceptional measures such as the Blood Protection Law.[1] For in accordance with section 3, paragraph 1 of the Penal Code, all offenses committed by German nationals, including Jews who had German nationality (*Personalprinzip*), were to be judged by the established laws,[2] and there was great reluctance to amend this basic regulation. It was thus possible to implement special penal provisions only if in formal terms they could be encompassed within the framework of general criminal law. Therefore the name of the game was to incorporate the discriminatory intentions of the political leadership into the terms and objectives of the general criminal legislative and judicial policy, without amending the actual texts as written. Once the special criteria had become generally established, they could be "interpreted" to apply to each individual case as required. The application of such general discriminatory measures was thus effected in two stages: first through directives, recommendations, and suggestions by the judicial authorities (with no change in legislative intent); and second, in concrete cases, through extensive court interpretation of the offenses and by a harsher evaluation of culpability. It is important to bear this sequence in mind in order to understand how the treatment of "non-Germans" under special law was able to function so smoothly. We shall now review the sequence in more detail.

1.   Rejection of the Established Principles of Law

It should not be forgotten that this harsher treatment of "non-Germans" was part of an overriding general trend to tighten up and extend the interpretation of criminal offenses, which included cases involving Germans. The policy of rendering criminal proceedings more stringent had already been applied by the Nazi leadership in peacetime in many ways: [3] through the enactment of a large number of new penal provisions amending the Penal Code in both content and form (especially in the field of political and so-called martial criminal law);[4] through a tightening up of the existing legislation and legal sanctions (extension of the death penalty);[5] through the introduction of the principles of public security and correction;[6] through the creation of new branches of the law with stronger powers to award punishment, such as the special courts and the People's Court;[7] and through the abolition of procedural safeguards.[8] A reshuffling within the Reich Ministry of Justice put State Secretary Freisler, the most radical proponent of the Nazi legal policy, in charge of all the criminal and other important departments, while State Secretary Franz Schlegelberger, originally a specialist in commercial law, managed the less crucial sectors. This constellation guaranteed that the criminal procedure policy would remain extremely tough.[9]

The tactic of a general tightening up of penal law and the criminalization of large segments of everyday life can be traced back to the National Socialist concept of a new penal law,[10] which it was intended to implement through extensive penal reform in the broader framework of general legal reform.[11] In this context the fulfillment of old plans for a reform of the judiciary were of major importance, and they made strange bedfellows with the Nazi ideology. The combination was not successful at all, since the Ministry of Justice was not ready to give up its traditional legal perfectionism; the conflict ultimately led to the ruin of the ministry.[12] Championed at the political level primarily by the judicial directorate of the NSDAP under Hans Frank,[13] this drive for reform picked up the strands left by the Weimar Republic, which had developed a number of texts ready for enactment,[14] thus maintaining an appearance of continuity. [15] But although the Prussian and Reich justice ministries had worked on the reform since 1933 and had presented complete draft bills,[16] it made little progress. At the May 1937 meeting of the Reich cabinet, which was to be its last, the movement was shelved once and for all, because fundamentally the political leadership was not interested in radical reform, which would have established defined legal regulations limiting the power of the state to determine the status of suspects or defendants, tying it down to rules of procedure and so on. For a regime that was characterized above all by irrationality and arbitrariness and thus needed to be constantly in movement, such reform would have meant immobility and so could not be tolerated. The political leadership had decided that the best way to achieve its aims was to alter the criminal code by the enactment of single statutes, which would follow a harsher or a more lenient line according to the political expediency of the moment, thus effectively concealing the long-term erosion and destruction of the legal regime inherited from the liberal period, the form of which remained intact.

2.   The Main Contours of the National Socialist "Authoritarian Penal Law"

Of what, then, was the National Socialist concept of criminal law composed? How was the new penal code to appear? It is best described as an "authoritarian Penal law,"[17] the central idea of which was the racist ethnic community, the *Volksgemeinschaft*.

Nazi criminal law was determined by a reversal of all the previous theories of punishment and guilt and, above all, the principles of education and resocialization. They were replaced by a pragmatic penal code that stressed the absolute priority of the greater good of the ethnic community (as determined by the NSDAP), with the aim of "severe repression of disobedient elements," since the National Socialist state was determined to put an end to the "liberalistic behavior of the criminals, especially habitual criminals."[18] On that basis, everything that went against the ethnic community was liable to punishment ("whatever served the community was right"), and the purpose of punishment was intimidation. The basic principle of "no crime without a law" was invalidated and replaced by the concept of analogy.[19] In accordance with this "community proviso," the very nature of guilt changed. From the National Socialist viewpoint, guilt was defined not by the knowledge of the individual act, but by awareness of the damage to the community.[20] The boundaries between political crimes (treason) and everyday criminal acts thus became increasingly tenuous.[21] Any "hostile attitude," as the literature put it, was a crime against the state.[22] Thus, any criminal act could be declared a violation of state security and a political crime. Since the masses would not understand this exclusively political approach, the discrimination should be given a moralistic flavor. One should act as though purification were being effected in the political *and* moral sense.[23]

A criminal act was therefore at the same time a breach of faith toward the ethnic community[24] and a morally objectionable act, and in consequence punishment was not merely an expiation but was designed to strip the offender of his honor and exclude him from the community,[25] with consequent loss of all rights.

Significantly, the official draft of a penal code by the Grand Penal Law Commission of the Ministry of Justice in 1936 contained the new sanction, drawn from Germanic law, of *Ächtung* (outlawing, banishment) for particularly serious offenses, whereby the offender was to be imprisoned for an unlimited period of time in a similar manner to protective custody.

The clearest expression of a penal code as conceived by the Nazi leadership was the planned Law on Aliens to the Community initiated by the Reich Security Main Office (RSHA) through the Reich Ministry of the Interior, without the participation of the Reich Ministry of Justice, and which was to become effective on January 1, 1945. The purpose of this attempt to legalize the secret protective custody practice of the police by a statute was to assimilate the concept of a punishable act with acts that were "dangerous to the community" or "asocial."[26]

The absolute priority given to the "interests of the community" over and above all individual concerns and the consequent abandonment of every principle of the rule of law found their (first) typical application in the special law against "non-Germans," who, as we have seen, stood outside the ethnic community and were therefore foreign to it. From here to the concept of "enemy of the people" was but a short step. It therefore seems logical that the notion of "non-German" should from the start be associated or even equated with the negative idea of an asocial person,[27] with the developments in the general penal code we have described as natural consequence. Thus, mere objective appurtenance to a foreign nation could be sufficient to render a punishment more severe, or even serve as the crime itself.

II. "Non-German" Offenders

1. The Introduction of Standards of Special Law

Although the interpolation of elements of special law into established law was accomplished primarily by means of administrative regulations, "recommendations" (to the courts), and specific directives (to public prosecutors) on the part of the judicial administration, several fundamental special regulations were nonetheless enacted as laws in order to lend them greater significance. The first special penal law was the Law for the Protection of German Blood and German Honor (the so-called Blood Protection Law or *Blutschutzgesetz*) of 1935.[1]

This provided mandatory criminal penalties for marriages between Jews and "people of German blood," as well as for those between other "aliens" and "people of German blood" in cases in which "offspring that would imperil the continued purity of German bloodlines [could] be expected."[2] Furthermore, sexual intercourse outside marriage between Jews and "citizens of German or racially related blood," or so-called race defilement, was punishable by imprisonment or jail of up to two years—although only the man was penalized, regardless of whether or not he was Jewish (secs. 2, 5, par. 2), while the woman went unpunished.[3] Jews who employed female domestic servants "of German blood" under forty-five years of age in their households were also liable for punishment of up to one year in jail or fines, or both, if a Jewish man was a member of the household (secs. 3, 5, par. 2).

The application of this law (an "expression of the racial consciousness of the German people")[4] varied; what is remarkable is that the number of initiated proceedings was considerably higher than that of final convictions;[5] that is to say, a large number of proceedings were dropped. Whereas application of the law was relatively restrained until around 1937 (i.e., more or less correct), the period thereafter saw a phase of harsher interpretation, one that may be attributed largely to the constant appeals for harsher penalties from the Reich Ministry of Justice[6] and the "official" statements on the race question issuing from the Reich Ministry of the Interior.[7] This practice was sustained above all by the superior courts, and most especially by the Reich Supreme Court,[8] whose "law-framing" activity set it further and further apart from the actual legislative intent. This may be illustrated by the following examples.

Contrary to principles of criminal procedure, forensic evidence and indications of guilt were not taken into consideration when they might benefit the case of the accused. Thus, indications of Jewishness (belonging to the Jewish religious community)[9] were interpreted as broadly as possible. In the opinion of the Reich Supreme Court, outward characteristics were all that mattered, not the attitude of the accused.[10] In order to treat the accused as a Jew, it was therefore sufficient for him to know or have reason to know of his membership in the Jewish religious community; this was true even if he had long since inwardly repudiated the Jewish religion.[11] The term *sexual intercourse* was extended far beyond the legally defined concept of *coitus*[12] to cover all sexual activities carried out with the intent to "satisfy the sexual urge of at least one of the partners."[13] If this in fact already equates sexual intercourse with "lewd" acts, the Reich Supreme Court would ultimately expand the term *sexual intercourse* to such an extent that its definition as an act was annulled, so that even simply *looking at* another "with lascivious intent" was punishable as "race defilement."[14] How this could still be considered a "threat to German blood" remained the secret of the nation's highest judges and their interpretive arts; one has only to read the nonsensical opinions with which culpability was construed in such cases.[15]

Along the same lines, the definition of *attempted* "race defilement" was expanded beyond all bounds, in order to extend the spectrum of punishable acts as far as possible into the realm of the intent or preparation to commit an act. Even amorous caresses exchanged prior to intended intercourse by the persons involved were held to be attempted "race defilement," indeed even mere casual physical contact *without* the intent of procuring "sexual gratification."[16] This breakdown in the concept of a legally punishable act reached its peak in decisions of the Reich Supreme Court according to which merely verbal expressions, together with preparatory acts (in themselves not seen as punishable)—indeed even a mere verbal invitation to participate in sexual intercourse—were punished as attempted race defilement, because they were held to have an "immediate affinity with the sexual act."[17]

Mitigating circumstances were given to consideration,[18] a position for which the judicial system found some very far-fetched justifications. Thus, if sexual intercourse took place at the instigation of the German woman, the Reich Supreme Court did not consider such "racially forgetful behavior of the participating woman" as an extenuating circumstance, because the law did not protect the "sexual honor of the individual" but was rather intended to "secure the ethnic community from any threat to German blood and German honor."[19] Also deemed irrelevant were the measure of personal guilt or the motives of the accused, because the only essential consideration was the quality of "race defilement" as a "crime of endangerment." This "objectification" of "race defilement" also ruled out any exculpatory or mitigating error of judgement on the part of the accused.[20]

Even the place where the act occurred no longer played a part in the evaluation of culpability. Even since the Jewish emigration from Germany had set in, liability was no longer limited to acts committed within its borders; now any relations between Germans and Jews, no matter where they were undertaken, were covered under the concept of the so-called crime committed abroad, since they, too, represented "an immediate violation of German blood . . . in the sense of an organism unified by blood-ties."[21] This, too, contradicted the principles of common criminal law. For according to section 3, paragraph 2, of the Penal Code, crimes committed by German nationals abroad that were not illegal under the law of the country where they occurred were not prosecuted—a circumstance that exactly fit the "crime" of "race defilement" on foreign soil.

In matters of sentencing, too, actual practice became a good deal more drastic. Following the general trend, penalties were largely set with a view toward deterrence.[22] Thus, even in "normal" cases, the Reich Supreme Court usually sentenced Jews to terms in prison (whereas Germans were given jail sentences), although section 5, paragraph 2, of the law provided the option of prison versus jail terms. This judicial practice originated in a directive of the Reich Ministry of Justice to the chief state prosecutors dated April 2, 1936, according to which prison sentences were the sole appropriate penalty for race defilement committed by Jews; furthermore, average cases were to be treated as aggravated cases. In the great majority of cases, the courts followed the recommendations of the prosecution, although they often reduced the length of the requested sentences. At least, this was the case in Hamburg, Cologne, and Frankfurt on Main; the average prison sentences was still quite long, however. Many sentences for first-time convictions were close to the maximum permissible sentence of two years in prison;[23] repeat offenders generally received much longer sentences. According to a report in the organ of the Warthegau (or Wartheland) NSDAP dated July 20, 1942, the Special Court in Łódź sentenced a German defendant, a cobbler charged with two counts of "race defilement" with a Jewess from the local ghetto, to six years in prison and six years' loss of civil rights. The State Court of Appeals in Hamburg, too, sentenced repeat offenders to prison terms of up to six years.[24] During the war, there were even several cases in which the *death penalty* was imposed. Since the Blood Protection Law itself did not provide for the death penalty, the courts constructed a so-called nominal concurrence (sec. 73, Penal Code) with crimes that were punishable by death.

The examples that have come to light thus far are the verdict of the Special Court of Cologne dated July 8, 1942, which sentenced a Jewish waiter to death as a "dangerous habitual criminal" on seven counts of "race defilement," in the sense of section 20a of the Penal Code;[25] the verdict of the Special Court of Kassel dated April 20, 1943, which sentenced W. Holländer, a Hungarian Protestant, to death as a "dangerous habitual criminal"[26] on seven counts of "race defilement," resulting in Holländer's execution on May 30, 1943; and the death sentence imposed by the third Special Court of Berlin against the Jewish defendant Berkheim dated April 9, 1943[27] (this sentence resulting from the plea of nullity entered by the Reich chief prosecutor, in response to which the Reich Supreme Court set aside the original sentence of seven years in prison). From Breslau comes the report of the case of the defendant B. Zadik, who was sentenced to death for "race defilement," grievous bodily injury, and theft.[28] From Hamburg two cases are known: that of a defendant sentenced to death as a dangerous habitual criminal solely for several counts of race defilement,[29] and that of the inland skipper C., sentenced to death on April 29, 1941 (retroactively), under the violent criminals decree of December 5, 1939, for rape in concurrence with race defilement.[30] This murderous justice reached its "high water mark" with the notorious verdict of the Special Court of Nuremberg dated March 13, 1942, against the Jewish defendant Katzenberger, which sentenced him to death under the Blood Protection Law in combination with section 4 of the Decree on Parasites upon the *Volk* of September 5, 1939, because he had committed "race defilement under cover of the black-out," although not even the objective facts of the case were proved to a reasonable certainty.[31]

Further special laws were created by the Decree on the Administration of Penal Justice against Poles and Jews (the Decree on Penal Law for Poles) dated December 4, 1941.[32] This decree, whose vast generalities and provisions dismantled any guarantees under procedural or substantive law, represented a novelty even by National Socialist standards and constituted an open breach of existing law.[33] The tone was set by the general clause of item 1, which read:

> (1) Poles and Jews in the Annexed Eastern Territories are expected to behave in accord with German law and the directives issued for them by the German authorities. They are to refrain from any actions detrimental to the sovereignty of the German Reich and the good name of the German people. . . .
>
> (2) . . . .
>
> (3) They are punishable by death, or, in less serious cases, by imprisonment, for expressing anti-German sentiment by means of malicious or seditious activities, in particular for anti-German statements or the removal or defacement of public notices by German authorities or offices, or for disparaging or damaging the good name or the welfare of the German Reich or the German people by any other actions.
>
> (4) [contains definitions of particular offenses]

Since in this wording there is absolutely no indication as to exactly what actions might constitute the offense of "anti-German" activities, the floodgates of unlimited interpretation were now opened. And this legal uncertainty was mirrored in actual practice. Overly harsh sentences stand in stark contrast to attempts to correct draconian punishments retroactively by granting pardons, a practice that was strongly censured by the Reich Ministry of Justice.[34]

For the dogmatically inclined, the predominant tendency was to entirely remove crimes committed by Poles from the framework of common criminal law and to present them as offenses sui generis, to which the principles of German criminal law were not applicable. The purpose of this was to prevent the application of those principles of criminal law that, under common law, would have worked in favor of the accused, in order to obtain the harshest possible penalties for so-called Polish offenses.[35]

At the same time, to judge by the verdicts handed down by the Reich Supreme Court, the already limitless general clauses of the decree were meant to be interpreted as broadly as possible. Thus, for instance, the regulation in clause 1, paragraph 2, of the decree, which made "acts of violence" committed against Germans by Poles and Jews "because of their membership in the German race" punishable by death, was interpreted such that an "act of violence," contrary to general practice, was understood to mean not an act of particular gravity, but rather *any* criminal action "committed by use of force,"[36] so that the concept of the act of violence came more and more to resemble simple bodily injury, or indeed even the much less serious crime of intimidation or duress.[37]

One high point of such innovative legal interpretation was the tendency to punish Poles for behavior that was legally irrelevant according to the German-imposed Polish criminal statutes. Thus, it was generally agreed that sexual intercourse between Germans and Poles, even in cases where no criminal enticement was involved (sec. 176, no. 3, Penal Code), constituted a criminal act analogous to "race defilement," one that was punishable as "anti-German behavior" where the implicated Polish man was concerned (clause, 1, par. 3, Decree on Penal Law for Poles). The interpretation of this clause took on truly grotesque features in the ruling by certain special courts that sexual intercourse with Germans was "anti-German" because it represented an "attack on the *honor* of German womanhood" and thus was " an action detrimental to the *sovereignty* of the German Reich and the good name of the German people."[38] The courts generally presumed the existence of such an "attack" even when the sexual intercourse was consensual or indeed even initiated[39] by the German woman. Overzealous special courts even imposed the death penalty for sexual intercourse engaged in by "non-Germans" among themselves.[40] However, the question whether, in cases of sexual intercourse between German men and "non-German" women, the women should also be punishable, remained unresolved.[41]

2. Discrimination against "Non-German" Offenders by a Harsher Interpretation of the Regular Law

The creation of special laws notwithstanding, the discrimination against "non-Germans" in penal law came about mainly through a harsher application of general criminal law, for this made it possible to stick to the basic form while nevertheless obeying the tenets of National Socialist thought,[42] even when these went against the letter of the law. Discrimination was practiced chiefly in the Special Part of the penal code; the General Part offered few such opportunities.[43] The following examples will illustrate how far this tightening up of the law went.

The analogy provision of section 2 of the new version of the Penal Code was often quoted as the legal foundation for discriminatory practice; under its terms acts not normally liable to punishment could be punished when this was required by the "sound thinking of the people." A considerable number of regulations were used as analogous "criminal statutes"[44] to punish acts that otherwise would not carry a penalty, in order to prevent (as the Reich Supreme Court pointed out) "someone who has committed a punishable act from slipping through a loophole in the law or being punished too leniently."[45] The analogy was particularly favored for Poles.[46] A telling example is a decision by the Reich Supreme Court, which on the strength of section 4 of the Military Installations Defense Decree of November 25, 1939,[47] in conjunction with section 2 of the Penal Code, condemned a Catholic priest who had described prisoners of war as a model of Christianity for incitement to disaffection, although section 4 of said decree spoke only of fraternization with prisoners of war.[48]

The discrimination against "non-Germans" was also achieved, however, simply by an extensive interpretation of the law—even contradicting its content—as was also commonly practiced against German defendants in order to outlaw undesirable behavior.[49] Thus, the regulations on defamation (secs. 185 ff., Penal Code) were not applied in favor of Jews to the same extent as they were in favor of Germans, since " a Jew. . . . [could] not enjoy the same protection of his honor as a Reich citizen."[50] Abusive language by Poles against ethnic Germans was punished under section 134a of the Penal Code in the Annexed Eastern Territories, although the text in question spoke only of "abusive language against the Reich."[51] The foreign race of an offender was of course particularly taken into account as a major aggravating factor in the case of sexual offenses.[52]

The provisions on theft were also interpreted more harshly. In a ruling by the Reich Supreme Court, Polish agricultural workers could not be classified as domestic staff under the terms of section 247, Penal Code, so that the privilege provided for in the law (prosecution only at the suit of the plaintiff) did not apply. Thus, petty theft was punished without any action being brought by the employer.[53] The term *domestic staff*, it was claimed, presumed residence with the employer "analogous to that of the family." This was held not to apply to Poles, who belonged to a people that had "placed itself outside any cultural community and the German *Volksgemeinschaft*."[54]

The homicide provisions were also tightened up. In 1940 the Nuremberg Special Court passed the death penalty on a Polish mother who had killed her newborn baby, although section 214 of the Penal Code on infanticide provided only for imprisonment.[55]

In spite of this tendency toward harsher interpretation, the law also continued to be applied correctly, even when it conflicted with the prevalent racial philosophy. Such judgements were, however, sharply reproved by the ministry ("incomprehensible lenience," "outrageous mistakes," etc.), which circulated its disapproval among judges and public prosecutors in the *Richterbriefe*.[56]

The ministry was particularly incensed by a district court decision sentencing a Jew to two years' imprisonment and a fine of nine thousand reichsmarks for a currency offense (failure to declare foreign income), since in weighing the mitigating and aggravating circumstances the court had treated him like a German. This was wrong, it was claimed: the Jew was "the enemy of the German people," a member not only of a different race but of an "inferior race." It was only fair that the racial viewpoint should not judge different things by the same measure.[57]

In addition to the broad interpretation of criminal offenses, the tightening-up process in the treatment of "non-Germans" also stretched to sentencing practice. It clearly came naturally to punish offenses committed by non-Aryans more severely than equivalent offenses by Aryans, although opinions differed as to the penalty that should be imposed. This was justified in legal terms by stating that such offenses should always be seen as both severe transgressions against the German *Volksgemeinschaft* (the national community) and a violation of the "laws of hospitality" granted in Germany. This principle was supplemented by the further principle that Aryans should never receive less favorable treatment than non-Aryans in a comparable situation; this was so even when it contradicted the law. Instructive examples are the cases of a Jewish retired professor and an Aryan baker. Both the Jew and the German had touched women's backsides with lewd intent in the same store in 1936. Although this was not the Aryan baker's first offense, the lay assessor's court of Frankfurt on Main sentenced him to one month's imprisonment for an outrage upon decency, whereas the Jewish defendant was given a cumulative sentence of ten months for two offenses of assault with intent to insult. The commentary on the judgment expressed the racial hatred built into the judicial practice of the time in exceptionally invective terms:

The defendant is in his 56th year. He is a Jew and was dismissed from state employment in . . . on October 1, 1933, under the terms of the Law for the Restoration of the Professional Civil Service. His last position was as a teacher at the higher modern school of. . . . The defendant's plea states that on the day in question he had a domestic upset, then went into the town on some errands. Among other stores, he visited Woolworth's on the street *auf der Zeil* in Frankfurt on Main. He claims to have touched the witnesses' clothing only lightly with his hand, just as one brushes past a garden fence. He states that he had not been in command of himself at the time and had apparently lost his mental capacity. He had not intended to cause offense. This plea by the defendant shows true Jewish deviousness, as taught in the Talmud.[58]

The two witness do not present the case in such an anodyne manner as the learned Jew, however. . . . It is striking that in a private appraisal requested by Aryan defense counsel Dr. Z. in the preliminary proceedings, the Jewish physician Dr.

Hermann G. declared the defendant not to be criminally responsible. . . . As an aggravating circumstance, it will be noted that the accused tries to play down his actions in a typically talmudic way and to present them as innocent, believing that he will be let off with a fine, as used to be the case. Furthermore, by his actions the accused most grossly abuses the laws and regulations of the State and Party in a country in which he merely enjoys hospitality rights. As a Jew he must know that since the enactment of the Nuremberg Laws, a clear line of demarcation has been drawn between Aryans and Jews. If he nevertheless abuses the honor of German women and thus German honor, he cannot be reprimanded severely enough, especially as Jews are continually committing such moral violations of women and girls of their host nations. The Jew must be shown by exemplary punishments that he has to keep within the limits set for him by the state.[59]

Following an appeal by the defendant, the Frankfurt District Court did, however, reverse the aforementioned decision and reduce the sentence to four months' imprisonment with explicit reference to the more lenient punishment imposed on the Aryan baker. In this connection it should be mentioned that on February 1, 1937, the *Strafsenat* of the Frankfurt Court of Appeal canceled the arrest warrant against the Jewish defendant, since there was no risk that he would abscond, whereupon on February 20 the lay assessor's court in Frankfurt on Main also reversed the arrest warrant against the Aryan baker ex officio, with a similar justification, although reasons for arrest still existed. The commentary on this decision reads as follows:

It is inadmissible to keep and Aryan under arrest while the Jew . . . runs free. . . . The ordinary national comrade with his healthy sense of justice cannot understand such a situation. He wants to see fair justice done and quite instinctively sees such an offense on the part of a Jew as more insupportable than a similar lapse by an Aryan. . . . Every German is outraged when a Jew touches a German woman, for such an action is equally an attack on German honor. The people are again aware of how supranational powers and Jewish lackeys have long distorted the sense of honor, and experience it is an unacceptable insult against the whole nation that an arrogant and impertinent member of the Jewish bastard race, pernicious to all other peoples, should touch a German woman.[60]

Such discriminatory criteria were applied in considerably severer form in the field of so-called martial penal law. Here, where draconian harshness was already inflicted upon German offenders,[61] discrimination against "non-Germans" reached its peak; as early as 1941 the Reich minister of justice in office, Schlegelberger, had complained that the administration of justice showed an "incomprehensibly considerate attitude toward the Polish people, who are irreconcilably hostile to us," and thus presented a danger to public safety. He expressed the hope that from now on "the heaviest punishments [would] be inflicted on Polish criminals."[62] His successor, Otto Thierack, constantly pressed for a harsher line.

The severest practice is to be found with respect to political cases—in the then current (extensive) interpretation of the term—which were to be handled in close cooperation with the Secret Police.[63] High treason and national betrayal (secs. 80 ff., Penal Code) were always tried before the People's Court, although an indictment was also possible before the court of appeal. But as a political special court, the People's Court offered the best guarantee of "absolute severity" and in this respect was surpassed by no other type of court.[64] But the special courts, too, which dealt with the conviction of other political offenses ("espionage," "incitement to disaffection," etc.),[65] frequently made extensive use of their powers. Particularly with respect to "incitement to subversion" in the broader sense (sabotage, fraternization with prisoners of war, etc.),[66] which after 1944 was centrally managed by a special adviser at the Reich Ministry of Justice,[67] the harshest measures imaginable were directed against "non-German" offenders.[68]

But the jurisdiction also attacked "non-German" offenders with excessive harshness with respect to all the other so-called war offenses in the Nazi sense. After 1940 these offenses were in principle tried before the special courts,[69] backed by constant appeals from the ministry for the "most severe punishment" ("unrelenting struggle . . . against all war criminals").[70] Under the so-called War Economy Penal Code particularly, in which extremely heavy prison sentences were imposed for quite mild violations, the ministry called for the most stringent measures on account of the "insolent and presumptuous behavior" of Jews.[71]

The best example of the persecution of "non-Germans" in this context was the so-called Decree on Parasites upon the *Volk* of September 5, 1939.[72] This decree punished looting with death (sec. 1), whereas its section 4 imposed a term of life imprisonment on "all other offenses committed by taking advantage of the special circumstances brought about by the war." The death sentence was called for if "the sound thinking of the people in the face of such particularly reprehensible crimes" demanded it.

Though the ministry constantly admonished the courts to punish even German offenders very severely,[73] the Decree on Parasites upon the *Volk* was extended beyond all limits where "non-Germans" were concerned. Thus, as it stated in its circular of July 24, 1941—probably written as the result of pressure on the part of the public prosecutor's office—the ministry held the application of section 4 (the administration of the death sentence) to be justified for Poles as the general rule and urged the courts to proceed accordingly.[74] The ministry claimed in justification that the staff shortage resulting from the war made it impossible to keep the Poles under adequate surveillance; thus a lack of adequate surveillance was equated with "exploitation of the special circumstances brought about by the war" and thereby acknowledged as a criterion justifying punishment. The decree was directed above all toward sexual offenses by Poles, which in principle were covered not by the provisions of the Penal Code but by the Decree on Parasites upon the *Volk*, which provided for the death penalty.[75] It was already deemed an "exploitation of the special circumstances brought about by the war" if a Pole as the only male worker on a farm committed a sexual offense. Even the attempt at such an offense was awarded the death sentence by the Reich Supreme Court.[76]

The recommendations of the Reich Ministry of Justice did not fall on deaf ears. Thus the *Führerinformationen*, which the minister of justice sent to Hitler and the heads of the Party Chancellery (Bormann) and the Reich Chancellery from mid-1942 on, reported the justice branch's "successes" to the Führer in the various districts.

In the Hamm Court of Appeal district, in particular, political arguments were openly used to justify the death penalty as a matter of principle for all offenses by Poles. Since the Poles had killed sixty thousand Germans, offenses by Poles were "not simply normal offenses" but were defined by the "inherent criminality of the Poles against the German Reich" (thus, the very fact of being a Pole became a ground for punishment) and the "way in which the Poles waged war." So criminal offenses committed by Poles, especially "political offenses" (in the current broad sense) and offenses against Germans, were invariably an "exploitation of the special circumstances brought about by the war," to which was added the pretext of inadequate surveillance in the midst of German national comrades. The public prosecutors of the district were accordingly instructed to call for the death penalty on principle for all "political" offenses by Poles or for offenses against Germans or their property.[77] With this development the interpretation of section 4 of the Decree on Parasites upon the *Volk*, which had been enacted as an extraordinary provision, was extended without limit. This practice is matched only by the system introduced in the Annexed Eastern Territories, where all offenses by Poles were deemed to be covered by a "permanent state of emergency," justifying the harshest penalties.[78]

Finally, the stricter regulations concerning so-called violent and habitual offenders (the Decree against Violent Criminals of December 5, 1939),[79] were applied extensively against "non-Germans" through the Penal Code Amendment Law of September 4, 1941.[80] Section 1 of the latter threatened the death sentence for all criminal offenses committed with violence or the use of a dangerous instrument by a "dangerous habitual criminal" under the terms of section 20a of the Penal Code, "if protection of the community or the need for fair retribution required it," when applied to "non-Germans." Here too the ministry never failed to call for "a tireless struggle" against "professional and habitual criminals," "asocial persons," "parasites," and so forth, and to demand the death sentence as standard punishment.[81] This demand corresponded precisely with Hitler's viewpoint that the death sentence was preferable to a long term of imprisonment in such cases. This was necessary "in order to set an example."[82]

The rulings of supreme justice complied in full with these demands.[83] The broad interpretation of the term *dangerous instrument* by the Reich Supreme Court is of particular note. Unlike the rulings of the local courts, which made the natural distinction between the body and an instrument,[84] the Supreme Court included the mere physical force of the offender under this term, so that cases analogous to simple bodily harm or robbery could be stamped as meriting the death penalty.[85] Thus, the criterion was on longer the commission of the offense, but only the "inferiority" of the offender and the deterrent policy, which justified the death penalty ("extirpation") in virtually all cases of violent offenses.[86] This was particularly true for Polish offenders, against whom the Reich Supreme Court as a general rule pronounced "neutralization."[87] In particular, the death penalty was "generally called for in the event of a sexual offense by a Pole against a German woman," since most Polish workers in Germany constituted a "racial threat."[88] The only question was whether the death penalty should be based on the need to "protect the *Volksgemeinschaft*" or the "need for just punishment"; in general the Supreme Court opted for the needs of the *Volksgemeinschaft*, so that it became a moot point whether "the need for just punishment requires the death penalty,"[89] and the question of the appropriateness of the punishment was also avoided.

In summary, it may be noted that in the intention of the justice authorities, "non-German" defendants were always—that is, without exception—to be punished more severely than Germans. That this was so is largely borne out by the published and otherwise recorded judgments,[90] but only after 1942 and above all in the jurisdiction of the special courts.

Nevertheless, a number of examples testify to the fact that before the enactment of the Decree on Penal Law for Poles, that is, in 1941–42, the sentences awarded remained within the limits normal for German offenders, in spite of the fact that even at this time the Reich Ministry of Justice had pressed for harsher penalties for Jews and Poles and was soon to present draconian judgments as "successes."[91] But even at this time, the majority of the death penalties imposed by the special courts were directed against "non-Germans" (above all Poles), just as the majority of the accused before the special courts were "non-Germans" (so-called immigrant workers).[92] The regular courts, in contrast, generally brought "more lenient" judgments; that is to say, they applied the standards prevailing for Germans to "non-Germans" too. Conviction of Poles to relatively short terms of imprisonment by the lower courts for minor bodily harm or sexual offenses appears to have been relatively common before the fall of 1941,[93] since such rulings were the object of much criticism in the Security Service's reports ("The people consider the penalties to be too mild, since imprisonment is useless for Poles").[94] But the higher courts were not exempt from such criticism, which sometimes came from the highest authorities. Massive reprimands against specific department chiefs were not uncommon ("regrettably lenient penalties," and so on), coupled with the "expectation" of strong influence on judges,[95] although such reproofs did not lead to disciplinary measures.[96] As late as 1944, the ministry found time to go into detail on the subject of quite ludicrous incidents, especially when they concerned "non-Germans,"[97] and it was particularly displeased if the law was applied fairly to Jews.[98] The Security Service also voiced complaints that criminal justice did not act with "the expected rigor" against Poles, since a number of judges were unable "to see the need for differential treatment of Poles and Germans." Many judges were not capable of awarding "better" judgments because of a "misconceived independence."[99]

After the passing of the Decree on Penal Law for Poles, however, the constant pressures (control measures) on the part of the ministry (directives, "recommendations," obligation to report, previews and reviews, etc.,)[100] began in early 1942 to bear fruit, even though central control of the administration of justice can only have been partially successful on account of the reticence on the part of the judges.[101] Later, the pressure became more overt, and during the Thierack era it was further directed at the courts, employing all means to gain complete control of the judiciary. The spring and summer of 1942 can generally be regarded as something of a transition period, for by then at the latest the political prestige of the justice branch was at its lowest ebb. Given the "crisis of justice" brought about by Hitler's sharp Reichstag speech of April 26, 1942, the judiciary was fighting to retain its public image and its own self-assurance and was struggling to demonstrate its toughness by dint of greater zeal.[102] With Schlegelberger's appeal to the judiciary to "fully integrate with the National Socialist state,"[103] the general discriminatory treatment of "non-Germans" was finally endorsed from on high.

Thus, what would normally have been classed as standard offenses were now regularly regarded as serious when they were committed by Jews, with accordingly harsher penalties. State Secretary Schlegelberger, at this time charged with the office of the minister justice after Gürtner's death in January 1941, exhorted the courts in the strongest terms to always administer "exemplary punishment" to Jews.[104]

The same was true for the treatment of "non-German" "habitual criminals" and asocial individuals, in that Hitler, and consequently the justice administration too, had always called for " merciless severity" toward these social groups,[105] and so much more so if they were of " alien race." Now the individual circumstances of the event were no longer a consideration, since only the principle of "extirpation" from the *Volksgemeinschaft* held good. When the police murdered a polish woman who was not criminally responsible, the only basis the Reich minister of justice in office, State Secretary Schlegelberger, could find to criticize the action of the police was that the judiciary was already sufficiently tough.

In a letter to Himmler as *Reichsführer*-SS and chief of the German police dated June 13, 1942,[106] Schlegelberger stated that the courts no longer considered the individual aspects of the offense in their judgments but basically adhered to the objective principle, that is, protection of the *Volksgemeinschaft* from its enemies; therefore, under the terms of section 51 of the Penal Code, they condemned to death offenders who were not criminally responsible or were only partly criminally responsible, because such offenders (so-called psychopaths) were "eligible for death" and a reduction of the sentence could not be considered. The courts acted in this way since the promulgation of the Decree on Penal Law for Poles, so that no intervention by the police was necessary.

Consequently, from the middle of 1942, a great number of extremely stringent sentences were passed, many of which are on record through having been discussed in the *Richterbriefe,* first published by the Reich minister of justice in October 1942.[107] Thierack, the former president of the People's Court, had through a systematic personnel policy created the basis for strict implementation of the will of the political leadership, and after he came into office on February 20, 1942, the persecution of "non-Germans" became even more consistent,[108] It is enough to say that in fields in which the jurisdiction already proceeded extremely strongly against Germans,[109] it was carried to excess in the case of 'non-Germans."[110] Thus, certain judgments in the field of so-called political penal law, which was dealt with centrally by the Reich Ministry of Justice,[111] and in war criminal law, even went beyond the harshness demanded by the justice administration, because the order of the day was unlimited interpretation of the law and imposition of the death sentence whenever possible for its deterrent effect. Nonetheless, sentences have come down in which a balance was sought between the seriousness of the act and the punishment inflicted and which, as we have seen, were criticized by the ministry as being completely inadequate.[112] This vacillation in the administration of justice reflects the uncertainty of the judiciary regarding the (special) treatment of "non-German" defendants, since the innumerable directives, recommendations, and instructions from above referred only to specific problems; the most important questions, such as the usurping of the Decree on Penal Law for Poles by the police or the relationship between that decree and general German penal law, were hardly touched upon, let alone clarified. But this same lack of clarity made it possible for judges with legal scruples to undermine the terror in relative safety.

III. The Situation of "Non-Germans" in Procedural Law

It is more difficult to prove discriminatory practices against "non-German" defendants in procedural law than in material penal law, because the characteristic of the former as *jus cogens* (strict law) runs counter to such discrimination.

1.   The Tightening Up of the Technical Jurisdiction Regulations
     (Discriminatory Jurisdiction)

A basis for discriminatory practices already existed, however, in the fact that the public prosecutor had relatively broad freedom in the legal classification of offenses at the time of the indictment, so that with the change in the competence of the court before which the case was to come, there was also a change toward stricter procedural practice: minor offenses were advanced to the status of criminal offenses; minor trials were conducted by the district court rather than the local court; cases of some importance were dealt with by the special courts,[1] which during the war had become the main instrument for the administration of justice and were above all responsible for the adjudication of "non-German" defendants.[2]

There is no evidence of direct discrimination against "non-German" in procedural law in the court decisions published during the early years of the Third Reich; the practice became apparent only with the tightening up of the legislation concerning Jews from 1938–39 onward. Thus, for example, in a judgment passed in 1939, the Reich Supreme Court ruled that the removal of a Jew from the courtroom did not constitute a violation of the principle of the public nature of the hearing, since such an action by the presiding judge contributed to maintaining order in court.[3] The literature began to contain discussions whether Jews should be allowed to benefit at all from the procedural regulations in favor of the defendant; the real purpose of criminal procedure, it was claimed, was to punish Jews, not to provide advantages for them.[4] When the competence of the various courts was in doubt, it was argued that such conflict was harmful to the legal process "if a Jew benefited from the conflict." As such, these were "questions of lesser importance."[5]

2. The Situation of "Non-German" Defendants and Witnesses in the Penal Process

Following Hitler's inflammatory speech against the judiciary on April 26, 1942, which led to a general crisis of justice, the Reich Ministry of Justice took matters in hand more energetically. Procedural discrimination within the bounds of the established rules was considered in order to prove to the Führer that the justice branch intended to follow a hard line against "non-German" in procedural matters too. The early measures in this regard were designed to limit the means of defense available to "non-Germans."

A general directive issued by the Reich Ministry of Justice for the Annexed Eastern Territories in May 1942 prohibited court-appointed defense for Polish and Jewish defendants,[6] except when "the public German interest" required it (and when would such interest ever require the defense of a "non-German"?). The order was based on the right to a "free procedural structure," as was anchored explicitly in the Decree on Penal Law for Poles, but it was applicable only in the Annexed Eastern Territories. The intention of the ministry was to amend the Decree on Penal Law for Poles such that this exemption from the standard regulations would be extended to the Reich territory as a whole, where the appointment of counsel by the court was still obligatory in certain cases. According to Reich Minister of Justice Thierack, the matter of court-appointed defense would then depend on the "dutiful decision of the judge" from case to case.[7]

Since no such amendment of the Decree on Penal Law for Poles came about, however, the minister of justice tried at least to outlaw the choice of legal defense in the case of Poles and Jews. Notwithstanding the terms of section 137 of the Code of Criminal Procedure, according to which the defendant could have a legal counsel of his choice at any phase in the proceedings, the Reich Ministry of Justice circular of May 25, 1942,[8] explicitly forbade the representation of Poles and Jews before the court by German lawyers, a move that met with criticism not only from the lawyers but also from the justice authorities, since it was feared that it would complicate procedure.[9]

Difficulties were also placed in the way of Poles and Jews acting as witnesses to a trial. Here, too, the model was the Decree on Penal Law for Poles, under which Poles and Jews could no longer be sworn in as witnesses (clause 9 in conjunction with the Amending Decree of January 31, 1942), with a view to reducing the value of their evidence and indeed making it completely worthless. It was now intended to apply this principle throughout the Reich. The ministry's viewpoint was set out in a circular signed by State Secretary Freisler, dated August 7, 1942,[10] according to which Poles and Jews were no longer to be examined as witnesses in the trial process.[11]

3. Final Objective: Exclusion of "Non-German" from the Whole Penal Procedure and Judicial Criminal Prosecution (Thirteenth Decree to the Reich Citizenship Law)

But from 1942, on, directives issued piecemeal were no longer sufficient to satisfy the ministry's plans for the discrimination against Jews, for it wanted no less than published special law pertaining to Jews, including procedural law. A ministry draft of a decree on the limitation of legal recourse for Jews of August 3, 1942, provided that in criminal prosecutions, Jews were no longer permitted to apply for judicial review or to lodge appeals or formal objections.[12] These efforts conflicted with the plan of the police authorities to transfer the criminal jurisdiction of Jews to the Security Police.[13] Negotiations between the Reich Ministry of Justice and the *Reichsführer*-SS and chief of the German police resulted in the principle, approved by Hitler, that "nothing stood in the way" of handing over the criminal prosecution of Jews and Gypsies to the police.[14] Thus, when it was finally enacted on July 1, 1943, the Thirteenth Decree to the Reich Citizenship Law[15] went much further than the exclusion of Jews from legal recourse: its section 1 removed Jews entirely from the judicial criminal prosecution process ("punishable acts committed by Jews shall be dealt with by the police. Assets accrue to the Reich after death").[16]

Apart from Jews, however, millions of other "non-Germans" lived in the Reich as part of the labor force, to whom the general German law of criminal procedure still applied de jure. For the justice administration this was an untenable situation. Once the ministry's draft of August 3, 1942, on the limitation of legal recourse to Jews had been superseded by the Thirteenth Decree, Minister of Justice Thierack was able to establish discriminatory procedural law for "non-Germans" by way of internal instructions and recommendations, on the model of the limitations imposed on Poles. As the minister stated at the meeting of the Court of Appeal presiding judges and chief public prosecutors in Berlin on February 10–11, 1943, even "without a legal basis," hostile "non-Germans" (i.e., nationals of "hostile states") were not to appear as witnesses in trials of German citizens, a rule that was to apply not only to Poles but now also to Russians, Ukrainians, and so on.[17] Poles also could not be employed as translators. Nor did the infringements of the law called for by the minister stop there: in addition to reducing the minimum penalty of three month's prison camp as set out in the Decree on Penal Law for Poles to one month, with a view to allaying the serious manpower shortage, summary punishment awards against Poles should become effective and implemented immediately without appeal (in violation of sec. 400, Code of Criminal Procedure, old version).[18] However, ever more drastic discriminations were planned by the Reich Ministry of Justice. As the ministry representative stated at the February meeting just referred to, the severance from all procedural regulations in line with the Decree on Penal Law for Poles should be extended not only to criminal proceedings but also to all judicial proceedings against "non-Germans."[19]

EXCURSUS

The "Rectification" of Justice by the NSDAP, the SS, and the Police

1.   The Influence of the Party

The treatment of "non-Germans" through legislation and jurisdiction can only be understood in the light of the judiciary's position vis-à-vis the two predominant forces in the National Socialist state, the Party and the police.[1] At the institutional level, the influence of the Party on judicial practice was enormous.

In the introduction to this volume we have already seen the important role played by the Party in legislation.[2] To this must be added a strong influence on matters of pardon, decisions on which were basically in the hands of Hitler as the Supreme Führer (of the Party).[3] With the involvement of the Gestapo, these decisions took on a major political slant at an early stage.[4] Where Party members were concerned, the Gauleiter of the relevant district also had a say in the matter. From 1942 on, the Party's involvement was extended to all questions of pardon.[5] An order by Hitler required approval by the Gauleiter in all cases in which clemency was requested by the minister of justice.[6]

In addition to such technical arrangements, the relations between the judiciary and the Party had an informal aspect,[7] which gave the National Socialist movement sufficient leeway to ensure that its self-interest was served. It can be best described as a system of constant pressures on the courts by way of the Party press and the influence of top Party officials, with a view to influencing the judges in the National Socialist spirit. For the NSDAP, as the ideological leadership and "bearer of the German state philosophy,"[8] it was above all important to wean the judiciary away from the idea of justice for all and to replace this by a generally accepted practice of *vökisch* inequality. Given the ubiquity of the totalitarian propaganda machine and ignorance of the administrative legalities, much hope was placed at first on a centralized education effort.[9] The party or its auxiliary League of National Socialist German Jurists, later renamed the National Socialist Association of Law Officers (NSRB), was charged with training judges and the upcoming generation of lawmen "in the spirit of National Socialism," to strengthen the "community awareness" of the "guardians of the law" through meetings, "comradeship evenings," weekend training courses, training camps, and so forth.[10] The success of this great effort was relatively meager. The romanticism of blood and soil, the rigid drilling in the communal camps, the level of "ideological training," plus the additional load of legal training in the form of so-called *Volk* studies[11] were often experienced as a burdensome obligation or a necessary evil. Criticism was expressed both openly and covertly,[12] and relations between the Party and the judges, especially among junior barristers and the younger judges, in whom much hope had originally been placed, were strained. With the outbreak of the war, therefore, the excessive political training effort was curbed, to be replaced by the communal "experience" at events involving the "whole nation."[13] Both the Party and the judiciary subsequently attached more importance to technical training,[14] close consultation between the Party and the ministry in these matters,[15] and future training reform measures.[16] In addition, efforts were made to enhance the influence of the Party and judicial leadership on court rulings by way of a concentrated personnel policy, which was seen as the main problem of the judiciary.[17]

In parallel with general training, direct pressure was exerted by the Party to push through the Nazi jurisdiction it wanted. After 1933 attacks by Party agencies on individual judges who fell out of favor and interference in current procedures were everyday occurrences (especially on the part of the SA).[18] The *Diensttagebuch* records of the early years 1933–35 or special lists of such interventions by the Party describe in detail the spying operations, suggestions made to lower justice officials and court employees, accusations, threats of arrest to specific judges, "consultations" between Party agencies and the justice authorities, intimidation of witnesses, false statements, delaying tactics, and so forth.[19]

The conditions for exerting such pressure were, however, provided not least by the forbearance and compliance of department chiefs and the ministry in the face of such activity,[20] but above all they were made possible by the fact that members of the NSDAP and their friends at the local level regularly reported important proceedings in progress (especially "particularly crass and to our mind incomprehensible court rulings") to their superiors. The *Gauleitung* for its part passed on such information to the Party leadership (the deputy of the Führer) with a view to "discussions" with the ministry.[21] From 1941 on, internal Party directives expressly included the obligation to report information on cases in which judges did not award the death penalty where it was "deserved," so as to ensure that the situation could be "rectified" by the Ministry of Justice.[22] Thus, it is fair to assume that the Party leadership was constantly kept informed of all proceedings of note and was able to exert its influence when it desired.

The Party leadership, including Hitler, true to the ambivalent language characteristic of the Third Reich, continually stressed the monopoly of the justice branch on criminal prosecution; at the same time they spoke of the possibility of "exerting influence" where "doubts" arose. In this way it presented the appearance of supporting the judiciary as an institution, all the while sowing insecurity and confusion through this political proviso. How the leadership saw the role of the judiciary comes out clearly in the internal instructions issued by Hitler and Party headquarters: although in principle jurisdiction was in the hands of the judiciary, in all "fundamental or politically important" matters, the justice authorities' power of decision was revoked and the outcomes of the proceedings were to depend on a decision at the highest level, that is, by Hitler himself or by the Reich Ministry of Justice.[23]

The specific pressures exerted on the judiciary are illustrated particularly well by the Party's attack on the judgment pronounced by the Fourth Criminal Division of the Reich Supreme Court in the Reichstag fire trial on December 23, 1933, in which four accused were acquitted. The official Party line was that of "a blatant miscarriage of justice" caught up in the rut of a "hidebound, alien-spirited, liberalistic philosophy," indicating the "need for a fundamental reform of our legal system."[24] Pressure was probably exerted most frequently in cases involving Party members, whether "ordinary" or serious,[25] and in situations where the Party could present itself as the guardian of the "law of the people" and the champion of anti-Jewish activities.[26]

This was the case in matters of enforcement,[27] for example, where pressure was applied on a particular court to place Jewish plaintiffs or defendants at a disadvantage,[28] especially when Party members were involved.[29] Party officials who were sued by Jews did everything in their power to persuade the plaintiff to withdraw his action, often openly threatening to have Jewish plaintiffs sent to concentration camp if they pursued the case.[30] Similarly, in cases in which Poles appeared as creditors of Germans,[31] "overly lenient" judgments against "non-Germans" were "corrected" after the lodging of a complaint by the Gauleiter.[32]

Such piecemeal interventions were far from satisfying the ambitious plans of the political leadership, however. In the totalitarian Nazi system, in which everything was politicized, the duty of the administration of justice was also first and foremost political. The final objective of the Party, as internal circulars openly demanded, was total control of the justice apparatus, "a National Socialist orientation of justice and justice officials."[33] The Party came a lot closer to realizing this intent when on August 29, 1942, it put its own man, Thierack, in the office of Reich minister of justice. Thierack was in tune with the system. Political training was explicitly proclaimed to be the "privilege of the Party," while a very vague line existed between such activity and the responsibility of the justice administration over its staff.[34] The Party's interventions in judicial matters became formally recognized and centralized. It was now no longer a matter of influencing individual court decisions as they occurred, but of imposing the overall primacy of the Party in all questions of control and training within the judicial establishment, with the blessing of the new Reich minister of justice. Arbitrariness became the system, and pressure and string-pulling were institutionalized. A circular from the Reich Chancellery dated August 27, 1942, informed all Party offices that the administration of justice was now possible "only in close collaboration with the Party," which was to help the new minister of justice "build a strong National Socialist system of justice."[35] For this task he had received full powers with the Führer decree of August 20.[36] All public criticism of judges and individual rulings was further suppressed. Such criticism was indeed no longer needed in the individual case, because from now on the hold of the Party on the justice branch was exerted centrally at the highest level through the head of the department himself; the Party Chancellery "discussed the necessary details" with the minister in all objectionable cases.[37]

To this end the Party leadership was now far more comprehensively informed on the major decisions and measures taken by the judiciary authorities than it had been in the past. The Party leadership had hitherto depended on its own sources for information, but the flow of information was now centralized. Both Hitler and the Party Chancellery received the *Führerinformationen*, issued by the Reich Ministry of Justice starting in May 1942, [38] the purpose of which was to demonstrate the "hard line" of the judiciary to the supreme leadership. An additional medium of information for the top Party members was the *Richterbriefe* we have already mentioned, which first appeared on October 1, 1942, dreamed up by Thierack as a new instrument of control for the judiciary, in which court rulings were discussed critically or approved by the ministry.[39] Although these broadsheets were expressly declared secret and destined only for the various courts,[40] they were also passed on to the Gauleiter by Bormann to keep them abreast of the dispensation of justice, with a request for "rectification" proposals.[41] It is possible that the *Richterbriefe* were even passed down the line as far as the *Kreisleiter*, for one *Kreisleiter* had the idea of requesting them directly from the ministry, since "it was not always possible to borrow them from the Gauleiter."[42] Thus, with the advent of the *Richterbriefe*, not only the ministry had means of keeping tabs on the courts, but such possibilities were now available to the Party leadership also.

In addition, the NSDAP built up its own competitive information apparatus, doubtless because it did not consider the selection of "suitable" cases presented by the ministry to be sufficient to strengthen its political influence on the judiciary. Just as the Reich minister of justice demanded appropriate rulings from the subordinate justice authorities for inclusion in the *Richterbriefe*,[43] the Party Chancellery instructed its offices to send in "good and bad court decisions" so that "rectifications" could be proposed to the ministry.[44]

The overall political primacy in all matters of judicial control demanded by the Party and its agencies affected above all the major questions of the treatment of "non-Germans." Although since 1933 the Party had attempted by every variety of direct and indirect pressure to induce the judiciary to rule against Jews, the office of the Führer's deputy and later the Party Chancellery had from the begining of the war, with the agreement of the SS and the Party leadership, demanded that all "non-German," as nonmembers of the German *Volksgemeinschaft*, be severed from the German process of law and handed over to the police (the *Reichsführer*-SS and chief of the German police), and this did indeed become the case with the advent of the Thirteenth Decree of July 1, 1943, to the Reich Citizenship Law.[45] As a result, complaints came pouring into the Reich Ministry of Justice concerning the leniency of penalties meted out in "non-German penal law," down to the pettiest cases, with reference to which a tedious correspondence shuttled back and forth at the highest level between the Party Chancellery and the ministry.[46]

2.   The Influence of Hitler, the SS, and the Police Command

     a.   The Ousting of the Judiciary from the Field of General
          Criminal Jurisdiction

With an executive power at its immediate disposal, the police posed a greater threat to the activity and existence of the judiciary than did the Party, and the police were thus its major opponent.[1] The origin of the totalitarian powers of the police, which reached across all branches of the traditional administration, was to be found in its wide-ranging jurisdiction, although this had no basis in theory. The most visible manifestation of this power was the activity of the Gestapo, regarded as the "central hub in the struggle against all enemies of the state."[2] The Gestapo operated something like a state within the state and never bowed to the principle of control of police action by the courts.[3]

After the police and the SS were unified at the central level in 1936,[4] the police leadership became the principal force in the country. In common with the Party, the police held the view that the question of "non-German" could not be left in the hands of the judiciary. For this was a "political" matter, a field ominously widened in scope by the legal doctrine and which, according to the prevailing opinion, in no way came into the purview of the judiciary (starting with section 7 of the Prussian Law on the Gestapo of February 10, 1936, which ruled out all control of the Gestapo's activities by the administrative tribunals).[5] The abandonment of the principle of judicial control of police actions led to the situation in the Nazi system whereby "determined intervention" by the police carried more weight than "desperate clinging to legal principles."[6] Spurred on by Hitler's revulsion and disdain for all legal activity,[7] the police leadership basically considered the judiciary to be expendable, because "its completely different principles of thought and action were detrimental to the purposeful running of an effective administration."[8]

This rise in power of the police was by no means a makeshift affair, however. Each phase of the escalating confrontation with the judicial authorities was meticulously prepared, in parallel with the campaign by the Party offices against the judiciary described above.

The first phase was a broad-based campaign in the press and malicious agitation against individual court rulings.

The second phase was direct intervention in the jurisdiction itself. This included applying "protective custody" unrestrictedly,[9] a measure that had nothing to do with actual protective custody as provided for in general police law and which as such was governed by strict conditions (sec. 15 of the Prussian Police Administration Law), nor the protective custody described in section 20 of the Reich president's decree of February 4, 1933.[10] Bereft of all legal foundation and based only on the revocation of the basic rights anchored in the Reich president's Decree of February 28, 1933, on the Protection of People and State and on Ministry of the Interior decrees,[11] it was recognized in theory and practice as a "preventive measure" by the police, an admissible measure of constraint by the Gestapo in the defense against "actions by enemies of the people and the state."[12] In the present context, the way in which protective (or preventive) custody was implemented was to take suspects into custody before completion of the penal process and to commit them to a concentration camp, thus effectively removing them from the purview of the judiciary. This led to the grotesque situation whereby many courts chose to impose long-term imprisonment or apply a broad interpretation of the prevailing regulations in order to protect the accused from the Gestapo.[13] To these cases must be added the far greater number of arrests that never came before the courts.[14] In the view of the police, preventive/protective custody was the ideal "punishment," especially for "non-Germans."

The third phase of the police advance was the "rectification of rulings" (Urteilskorrekturen) on the personal order of Hitler or Himmler, with the result that people who had been sentenced to imprisonment were executed out of hand by the police.[15] These shootings were frequently explained by "attempted escape" or "resistance" on the part of the prisoner,[16] although neither the courts nor the population were taken in by such pretexts.[17]

Such practices were naturally directed first and foremost against "non-Germans," who in any case were not considered to come under the protection of the law. The "rectification" of justice was exercised from the very beginning of the war,[18] once it had been shown that no great resistance to the use of protective custody was to be expected from the judiciary. As the section head of the SD Inland (Interior), Otto Ohlendorf, explained to his subordinates in 1941, the new function of the police in wartime was to adapt jurisdiction once and for all to the political requisites of the national organization; the judiciary had not done its part "in removing the inadequacies in the legal system in the interests of the Volksgemeinschaft," so that rulings that were " in blatant contradiction with the sound thinking of the people" had to be "repaired,"[19]

In the final phase of the usurpation of criminal prosecution powers by the police, which began around the middle of 1941—the earlier "rectification measures" continuing unabated all the while—an increasing number of ordinary offenders were handed over to the Gestapo before judgment had been passed.[20] At the same time the police exerted pressure on the judiciary to contest objectional rulings of its own accord.[21]

A far more important development, however, was that from now on the police no longer limited themselves to correcting individual court decisions, but began to call the whole judicial institution into question in all politically important cases, major criminality, and offenses by "non-Germans." Was a system of justice necessary at all to prosecute "state and racial enemies"? Had the judiciary lived up to the expectations of the political of leadership? In the Nazi state, where all institutions and regulations were held in contempt, there was only one possible answer to such questions, because the principle of the rule of law was not compatible with that of authoritarian leadership. In the eyes of the radical champions of the Führer state, the regular justice system had failed, because it always dealt with individual cases and took individual viewpoints into account, and "for these reasons alone" it always found too leniently (" in blatant contradiction to the demands of a rigorous administration of criminal justice in time of war"— so said the head of the Secret Police and SD of the Party Chancellery on October 22, 1942).[22] Consequences needed to be drawn, new advances made. The process was made all the easier in that the weak leadership of the ministry showed little serious resistance to any of the moves by the SS and the police to increase their hold. As an illustration of the powerlessness of the judiciary, State Secretary Curt Rothenberger of the Reich Ministry of Justice had to "request" the *Reichsführer* -SS and chief of the German police to at least no publish press reports on the execution of people "who could not be sentenced to death" by the courts, "in order not to undermine court authority." The best he achieved was that Himmler expressed his readiness to check personally whether such reports should or should not appear in the future,[23] though, significantly, he forbade press reports on the execution of people who had not been tried by the courts at all.[24]

b. The Judiciary's Part in the Process of Its Displacement by the Police

To understand this systematic process of displacement of the judiciary by the police, it is important to look at the part played by the judiciary apparatus itself, for it then becomes clear that the judiciary largely contributed to its own demise.

This process had already begun in Franz Gürtner's era,[25] and it reached its zenith when Thierack took over the ministry on August 29, 1942. Thierack's declared aim was to remove objectionable categories of people from the criminal jurisdiction of the courts and to put them in the hands of the police. Thus it would not be a fair representation of events to assign responsibility for the fading role of the judiciary solely to the police, repeating the commonly held theory that the judiciary was simply an innocent victim. This is disproved by the (albeit rare) cases in which the justice chiefs protested energetically, and successfully, against the practice of protective custody for their detainees.[26] Nor did the judicial leadership stand by passively in the usurpation of its legal powers. Indeed, from the beginning it actively promoted the takeover by close cooperation with the police. On the one hand, the justice authorities maintained extremely good relations with the police in many districts through personal contacts, exchanges of information, and so forth—beyond the call of duty—at least until the early years of the war.[27] On the other, their protests—if indeed any were forthcoming—against the countless cases of police intervention were ineffectual,[28] or they simply voiced complaints about such details as the number of people taken into protective custody or its imposition on certain individuals.[29] This did not, of course, get them very far, because the judiciary and the court decisions themselves acknowledged the admissibility of the new regime's practices "in principle,"[30] provided that a formal distinction was maintained between a penalty and police "preventive measures."[31] Thus, from early on the police leadership was generally able to dismiss the judiciary's protests and continue its advance unabated.

In a great many cases, furthermore, the judicial authorities not only tolerated the protective custody practice of the police, but they went out of their way to support it. An instruction from the ministry to the chief public prosecutors stated that as far as possible people under protective custody should not be detained in German prisons.[32] In many cases in which an arrest warrant was rescinded, the judiciary actually handed the individual over to the Gestapo,[33] either at the Gestapo's request from case to case, or on the basis of "agreements" and contacts between the judiciary and the Gestapo or "good relations" between the committing magistrate and the Gestapop.[34] The Reich Ministry of Justice expressly encouraged the department chiefs to maintain such relations.[35] In some cases the contacts were even closer: from Hamburg it was reported that the public prosecutor directly informed the Gestapo of convictions in no small number of cases,[36] so that it " occurred to" the district court president that the public prosecutor was "apparently" working together with the Gestapo, having defendants committed to concentration camp whenever the ruling by a court did not suit him.[37] The police authorities were sometimes instructed by the relevant Gestapo directorate to inform them of "political cases" before the trial, so that an arrest warrant could be issued and the accused brought to court or before the Gestapo on the basis of the latter's instructions.[38]

aa. Institutionalized Cooperation: The Obligation to Provide Information and Channels of Information between the Judiciary and the Police and Party

Thus, whereas collaboration between the justice authorities and the police was largely a function of local circumstances, the passage of information to the police about forthcoming judicial measures occurred on a much broader scale, organized centrally as it was.

The first thing to mention is the general obligation of the justice authorities to keep the Gestapo informed. The decree of May 28, 1937,[39] instructed the chief public prosecutors to appoint an official to the corresponding court of appeal as a "political defense representative" with whom the Gestapo could engage discussion of state police matters at any time; at the suggestion of the Reich minister of justice, almost all the chief public prosecutors assumed this office themselves.[40]

As of late 1937 the Ministry of justice itself housed an official whose brief was to assure the connection with the Reich Security Main Office (RSHA).[41] After 1942 the justice authorities were obliged to provide the Security Service with information on request in the same way as other offices, since the SD was "also in the service of the state."[42] Mere lip service was paid to the Reich minister of justice's claim to a reciprocal arrangement with the SD: as a secret organization, the Security Service was able to keep information from the judiciary at will.[43] Well before this, of course, the SD had its informers in the judiciary offices and regularly sent police officers to hearings, whose anonymous secret reports were then read by the Party and the ministry.[44]

Considerable efforts were also made to establish a basis of direct cooperation between justice officials and the Security Service. In his administrative instructions of August 3, 1942, the Reich minister of justice made the point that in terms of its staff and organization, the Security Service was a unit of the Party.[45] Cooperation with the Security Service was "equivalent to activity in the Party" and, like the latter, was "of course possible for all officials and employees of the Reich judicial administration." An example of such cooperation was provided by the change of office at the head of the ministry in August 1942: the Security Service contacted most (if not all) chief public prosecutors with the request to report their approval of this change "among wide circles, especially lawyers and most especially judges." Although the chief public prosecutors responded to this request, they did not do so in writing, but only by word of mouth.[46]

Here we need to mention the close cooperation between the judiciary and the Party itself, for the close links between Party and police provided the latter with a mine of information on judicial matters. Ministerial directives required that the Party be informed of all penal and disciplinary cases involving members of the public service and members of the Party and its subdivisions.[47] In other cases all the major Party and Party subdivision offices further had almost unlimited right of access to files and other information "on justified request";[48] for whether a request was justified or not was decided on political criteria, determined in the last resort by the Party, the leading power of the state, with which the justice authorities could not afford to get into trouble.

As time went on, the ties between the Party and the judiciary became ever closer as a result of pressure from above. After the "crisis of justice" in early 1942, the Reich minister of justice in office reported to the Führer that he had "personally made the justice chief responsible for the closest collaboration with the high officials of the Party."[49] It is consonant with the Party's advance at that time that the Party Chancellery and the *Reichsführer*-SS and chief of the German police should agree to recruit Party members to the auxiliary police force to watch over foreign workers from the East and to spy on fellow Germans and "note lapses of any sort."[50] Finally, toward the end of the Third Reich, Party functionaries officially took on duties as auxiliary officials in the public prosecutor's office (sec. 152, Law of Judicial Organization, old version); and following a September 1944 agreement on "closer cooperation" between the police and the Party, the political chiefs of the Party's structural divisions were given auxiliary police duties to detect "defeatists and rumor-mongers"; "suitable party members" got honorary positions in the Security Police.[51]

Conversely, however, the judiciary was not informed of the decrees and instructions issued by the police, or only at a very late juncture, nor did it have any official sources of information within the Party. On account of the absence of appropriate guidelines, any information generally reached the judiciary "by the courtesy" of the local police authorities. Only at Thierack's request in 1943 did the record of Secret Police orders, which contained all the decrees issued by the Reichsführer-SS and chief of the German police, go to the chief public prosecutors and attorneys general in addition to the Reich Ministry of Justice, although not to the presiding judges of the courts of appeal. Finally, we may mention the collaboration between the judiciary and the police in a number of technical fields and regarding certain classes of people, which went far beyond the general consultation we have spoken of.

First and foremost among these, of course, were the political cases, which were dealt with in close collaboration between the judiciary and the police.[52] Very shortly after the seizure of power, instructions were circulated in the Länder on the basis of a decree issued by the Reich minister of justice,[53] according to which the political police were to be notified of all cases in which political detainees were on the point of the being released after imprisonment or detention in pretrial confinement. Such notification was required four weeks before the release, so that the need for protective custody could be considered. Under the terms of the decree, people who had been arrested for "behavior hostile to the state" were to be released from pretrial confinement once strong suspicion no longer held, but only after a hearing before the political police. The arrangements whereby the police were to be informed were reiterated in an instruction from the Reich Ministry of Justice to the prison directors dated October 29, 1935.[54] "At the request" of the Reichsführer-SS and chief of the German police, the Reich Ministry of Justice issued two further decrees on June 3 and October 17, 1936, requiring that in addition to the Gestapo, the Security Service was to be notified of the imminent release of political prisoners.[55]

With the unification in 1936 of the SS and the police under a common head, the Reichsführer-SS and chief of the German police, the regulations became centralized. The Ministry of Justice first issued a circular on January 18, 1937,[56] instructing the public prosecutor's office to inform the police unit that had undertaken the investigation of all proceedings concerning treason,[57] so that the police could investigate whether protective custody was necessary after the term of imprisonment or release from pretrial confinement. At the same time it made explicit that this procedure was also applicable to people who had been charged prior to January 30, 1933, but who had been condemned since that date. Only a few weeks later, a decree issued by the *Reichsführer*-SS and chief of the German police on February 18, 1937, transferred all "state police affairs" from the regular police (criminal police, gendarmerie, *Schutzpolizei58* over to the Gestapo.[59] The Reich Ministry of Justice expressly approved the decree of February 18, 1937, on the mere condition that no "delay in the proceedings" should result from this change,[60] so that with a stroke of the pen an administrative guideline demolished the principle that the investigating authority was always the public prosecutor, with the police being authorized to act only as an auxiliary organ thereto (sec. 160, Code of Criminal Procedure; sec. 152, Law of Judicial Organization).[61] For once the Gestapo became the master of so-called state police affairs ("treasonable activities"), it had the power to sever the direct channel of information between the regular police authorities and the public prosecutor's office. Instructions from the Gestapo exist forbidding investigations by all police units and reserving them exclusively for the Gestapo.[62]

At the same time, the notion of "state police affairs" kept becoming broader. On July 2, 1937, the ministry issued a further order, under which the obligation of the prison authorities to report to the Gestapo and the SD was extended to the imminent release of Jehovah's Witnesses.[63] With a further order dated March 8, 1938, the ministry decreed that the release of "race defilement" offenders should also be reported to the Gestapo six weeks ahead of time, with "a copy of the judgment and grounds" appended.[64]

Already at this early stage of police expansion, the judiciary was entrenched in two mechanisms in its relations with the police that greatly contributed to its dislodgement from a broad field of action.

The first of these was the continued practice, however illogical it may seem, of not defining legal concepts, such as "state police affairs," just mentioned, but of merely describing them, apparently on the assumption that a unified legal terminology would continue to exist in its substantive content in relation to the political authorities, just as it had before 1933. How wrong this assumption was, giving as it did the totalitarian police organization the possibility of extending the interpretation of legal terms quite boundlessly, is proved by the continual extension of the categories of people liable to protective custody.

Whereas in its circular decree of January 18, 1937, the judiciary had provided that only political offenses in the narrow sense would be passed on to the Gestapo for it to examine the need for protective custody, the police early extended the concept of "political offense" such that all offenses were construed as acts against the *Volksgemeinschaft* and thus were political. For example, the Reich Ministry of the Interior circular of December 14, 1937, included what were called "professional criminals" and "asocial" persons in general (persons whose asocial behavior presented a danger to the community) among protective custody candidates, whether or not they had been convicted.[65]

The second mechanism that considerably weakened the judiciary's position was to provide the police with detailed information on all criminal investigations and proceedings in progress, with no quid pro quo from the police. Thus, as reports by the judicial authorities complained, the circular of January 18, 1937, permitting a protective custody evaluation for political offenders,[66] gave the police "complete freedom to obtain information on all such proceedings and to take police measures"[67] (that is, protective custody). At the same time, the ministry itself continually broadened the circle of people automatically qualifying for such consideration of protective custody. The decree of July 2, 1937, extended it to Jehovah's Witnesses[68] and that of March 8, 1938, to people who had been convicted for "race defilement."[69] We must presume, however, that such people were committed to a concentration camp, even if they had been acquitted or proceedings had been suspended.

Of course the very possibility of imposing protective custody offered by these decrees was interpreted by the police as an authorization to do so whenever it suited them. Protective custody following release was therefore not limited to political offenders in the narrow sense but was applied as a general principle to "jailbirds," Jehovah's Witnesses, and those convicted for "race defilement."[70] More generally, it must also be presumed that even before 1937 the Gestapo was regularly informed of all imminent releases so that it could undertake its investigations.[71]

This was particularly true for protective custody detainees regarded as "asocial."[72] Here the enforcement agency was directed to obtain the "comments" of the competent Security Police authority (criminal police) before ordering their release;[73] in effect, such release depended on police permission. The same directive, however, vetoed releases generally: if they nevertheless did occur, the individual was to be put into protective custody immediately,[74] so that whatever happened he continued to be detained.

At the end of the war, court prosecutions were restricted even more to the advantage of the police, "for reasons of simplification. " Toward the end of 1941, the prison authorities—doubtless in connection with the "resettlement" of Jews in the East that began in this period—were instructed to report the imminent release of all Jewish prisoners to the local Gestapo,[75] whereas eight months earlier these reports had gone to the local criminal police.[76] All these agencies were to take a stand on the release of such prisoners and the imposition of protective custody.[77] Here, too, protective custody was the general rule, and in the case of Jews invariably so. Finally, as the war drew on, protective custody took absolute priority, a sign of the incipient general discrimination that came to include Germans too. "Community regulations" issued by the Reich minister of justice and the *Reichsführer*-SS and chief of the German police in late 1944 instructed that criminal proceedings "of a minor nature" should not longer be instituted against people in protective or preventive custody. The execution of sentences of previously convicted persons detained in a concentration camp was suspended, and the *Reichsführer*-SS—although only at the request of the senior executive authority—waived the restitution of prisoners for whom protective custody was planned after their sentence had been served. In such cases, protective custody was to be served in the prisons of the justice branch.[78]

Collaboration between the judicial authorities and the (political) police was not limited to reporting the imminent release of prisoners, however. It also involved the decision not to institute criminal proceedings when this appeared necessary for political reasons, a practice that became increasingly common in the latter years of the war but was by no means confined to them. For example, the Reich Ministry of Justice instructed the public prosecutors to pursue investigations concerning the events of the *Reichskristallnacht* only in particularly serious cases and to drop all others.[79]

The purpose of all these concatenations between the judiciary and the police was to gradually bring the justice system under political control and influence. One indirect way of achieving this was to have senior police officials present at discussions and meetings of the head of the judicial administration. Top police representatives lectured senior district justice officials on the political duties of the courts;[80] Gestapo men spoke at meetings of senior judicial officials on problems of political criminal cases,[81] and their speeches were reported in the districts. At the order of the Reich Ministry of Justice, all judges and public prosecutors were informed of a speech by the *Reichsführer*-SS on May 20, 1944, before the presiding judges of the courts of appeal and the chief public prosecutors in Cochem, where he spoke of the development and aims of the SS and especially the significance of the race question. The presiding judges of the courts of appeal were required to report on how the speech had been received by the judges.[82]

bb. Reactions of the Judicial Administration to Police Intervention: Basic Acceptance and Specific Criticism

Although at an institutional level the judicial administration permitted intervention by the police in its affairs in a number of ways, the question arises how it reacted to such growing interference in specific cases. The increasingly sharp tone of the National Socialist press since 1937, the countless arbitrary instances of protective custody and interference in ongoing proceedings by local Party functionaries and the police, and the many attacks on justice officials were a sign of how far it was possible to go without having to fear serious resistance from the justice authorities.[83] Weighed down by regulations, the justice apparatus seemed to have little chance of defying an opponent that was so much more agile, had the whole executive in its hands,[84] was able to act rapidly and ruthlessly, and whose chief, Himmler, abominated all rules: in his own words, "if a paragraph didn's suit our ends, I couldn't care a damn; I do what my conscience and common sense dictate in order to fulfill my task."[85] Although the ministry strongly protested the invectives published in the press, its stance was solely defensive and limited to the technical press,[86] so that it had no political impact whatsoever. Fundamental objections on the part of the judiciary against the illegal acts by the police were merely internal,[87] and very few were directed at those who were really concerned, the various organs of the political police, even at a time when the position of the judiciary was in no way jeopardized.

The Reich minister of justice carried considerable responsibility for the passivity of the judicial administration, occasionally expressing his regret about certain "awkward" cases but otherwise doing nothing.[88] At best, he instructed the presiding judges of the courts of appeal to ensure that arrests by the Gestapo did not take place in the courtroom at least,[89] and to report "rectification measures" to him.[90]

At the lower echelons of the judiciary, in contrast, the threat was felt much more clearly.[91] The authorities simply relayed protests without commenting upon them, and they did so for a reason. The Reich Ministry of Justice and the authorities had reached a consensus that police Ministry of Justice and the authorities had reached a consensus that police measures such as imposition of protective custody were "purely preventive" and had nothing to do with justice. "Rectification," however, was not held to be permissible.[92] Yet the judicial authorities certainly could have achieved something with a determined efforts, since energetic protests did have the effect of getting prisoners released from protective custody.[93] The justice authorities' position made it impossible for the courts to prove the illegality of Gestapo procedures, for where was the proof of illegal "rectification"? Even when the victim was detained immediately on release, the police could always claim that the measure was a preventive one and served the "interests of the community." Thus, the courts, feeling that they had been abandoned by their superiors, were largely resigned to police practices, so long as they stuck to the form of and declared the arrests to be preventive measures. As a result, the judicial process was regularly passed over in the case of certain offenders[94] whom the police took for granted were theirs and whose arrest was in any case imminent. [95] In an attempt to prevent the imposition of protective or preventive custody by the police, the judiciary also tightened up its own custody and penal practice. It became common to carry out arrests without a warrant or to impose "sufficiently" long prison sentences to keep the offender out of the reach of the Security Police.[96] But there also are cases in which even the summary execution of offenders—irrespective of whether a judgment had been passed against them—excited either no protest at all or merely one limited to formal aspects of the case, claiming that the judiciary was capable of striking just as fast and as hard as the police[97] or demanding a "legal settlement" with participation of the courts in executions, which were permissible as such.[98]

Though the reaction of the judicial authorities to the "rectification" of judgments by the police was generally one of *passive* acceptance, the judiciary responded to *criticism* of court rulings by the political leadership with excessive zeal.[99] From the early days the ministry had lost its independence, once it had conceded that "it was the Führer and only the Führer" who decided on legal matters.[100]

Its response to other statements by Hitler on the justice system and its actions is, equally, more like that of a subordinate agency than an independent department, even judged by the criteria of the day.[101] Thus, after Hitler's Reichstag speech on December 11, 1941, in which he announced "merciless severity . . . in the struggle for the survival of our people," Schlegelberger issued a decree (December 15, 1941) appealing to the judicial authorities for rigor and expediency "on the internal front" and gave instructions to have the most important passage of the speech immediately circulated to all judges and public prosecutors.[102]

When Hitler renewed his criticism in his Reichstag speech of April 26 of the following year, the judiciary did not limit itself to passive acquiescence or an appeal for harsher action. Its whole existence now appeared to be at risk, and such a danger could only be met with a doubling of zeal. With the support of the Reich Chancellery,[103] the minister of justice now proposed unparalleled changes, abandoning the principle of the independent administration of justice and acknowledging the function of the Führer as the highest instance of appeal. The project[104] provided for a right of confirmation by the Führer and Reich Chancellor on all rulings. If Hitler did not choose to exercise this right personally, it was to be delegated to the minister of justice, who in turn could delegate it to the presiding judges of the courts of appeal; if the ruling was not confirmed, the presiding judges could reassess the sentence. In this way it was assured that the sentencing practice of the courts "would not give cause for complaint." Furthermore, the Reich minister of justice was to have the right to transfer a case to a different court at any time, as soon as it was clear that the court "was not equal to it." But as was to be expected, these proposals did not prove acceptable, because their bureaucratic approach could never be radical enough for the Führer. Hitler was of course unable to oversee all court decisions, but he was not going to pass on the right of confirmation to the hated judiciary, nor would he accept a formal arrangement about the right of assent. So it was natural that he should issue a clear rejection of the proposals through the Reich Chancellery. In a letter dated June 10, 1942, Bormann informed the Reich minister of justice in office that as of April 26 the Führer had a right to intervene in all rulings "over and above all existing formal arrangements"; furthermore, the Reich Ministry of Justice and the presiding judges of the courts of appeal could not be expected to exercise the "necessary sense of responsibility and harshness," let alone "adequate rigorous action" against "recalcitrant or incompetent judges."[105]

cc. Flight Forward as Response: Tightening Up Sentencing Practice

The only "reaction" of the judicial leadership in the face of the arbitrariness of the police operations and the usurpation of those of its powers that had any significance was an attitude of compliance and enforced zeal; contrary to its hopes, this only accelerated the exclusion of the judiciary as an independent entity within the Reich administration. The judiciary increasingly compromised its position and allowed its actions to be dictated by the other side without developing a firm standpoint or taking any initiatives. It gave up consolidated positions without receiving any goodwill on the part of the political directorate, for it was never able to follow the regime's radical actions without losing its own credibility. All that remained was uncertain maneuvering, a constant shifting of ground through the tangles of police directives and arbitrary moves. In the totalitarian tradition of constant adaptation to the will of the top leadership, and in the vain hope of getting it right, the judicial administration confined itself to recommending that its officers go along with events and prove that they too could "hit hard." As such, the Reich Ministry of Justice set the example.

This was true above all with respect to the tightening up of penal practice in the fields of middle-grade and serious criminality, the "cowardly handling" of which by the justice department the Party and police never failed to castigate. A good example is the legislation of November 24, 1933, introducing preventive detention.[106] State Secretary Freisler, true to form, endorsed increased use of the new instrument of preventive detention in an article in *Deutsche Justiz* in 1938.[107] This practice, which was tantamount to prolonging the prison sentence, had originally been intended to remove out of harm's way for a protracted period those prisoners whom it was impossible to reintegrate into society. It should now, said Freisler, be used as a political weapon, a "sharp blade in the struggle against professional and habitual criminals and the criminal mentality." And since the Law against Dangerous Habitual Criminals of November 24, 1933,[108] admitted a prolongation of preventive detention when there was a danger to "public security," a political-ideological view of preventive detention was irresistible. Freisler's "recommendations" did not fall on deaf ears: the chronological relationship between the campaign waged on the judiciary, the ministry's recommendations, and the growing number of preventive detention cases speak for themselves. Whereas their number had fallen in 1937 to 765 cases, the figure climbed to 964 in 1938, to 1,827 in 1939, and to 1,916 in 1940; the figures declined again after 1941,[109] because the Penal Code Amendment Law of September 4, 1941,[110] against "dangerous habitual criminals" allowed the death sentence, an option that was frequently used at the demand of Hitler,[111] and because from about this time the police took people suspected of serious crimes directly into their own preventive detention, thus rendering them inaccessible to the courts.

Another example of the compliance of the judiciary with political demands is the general instruction issued on March 3, 1938, by the Reich Ministry of Justice,[112] introducing the participation of the police in legal affairs and the revocation of preventive detention in defiance of the fact that under the law this came under the competence of the judges. The instruction called for an "opinion" from the relevant Security Police authorities (the criminal police) before a prisoner was released, with the result that releases came about only with their permission, after which the prisoner was usually committed to a concentration camp. During the war, the release tended not to be granted.[113]

The so-called *Führerinformationen* are a further illustration of the placating policy of the justice branch. Following the failure of Schlegelberger's proposals to introduce a right of confirmation for the Führer or the Reich Ministry of Justice concerning all court rulings during the "crisis of justice" of early 1942,[114] the Reich Ministry of Justice looked for other ways to persuade the Führer that the judiciary meant business. The top people in the ministry knew that Hitler had only a tenuous understanding of the justice machine and that the sketchy and untimely information based on unqualified press reports that he received from Bormann only served to increase his anger against the system.[115] His invectives before the Reichstag of April 26, 1942, were also due to an incomplete press report (the Schlitt case). The ministry, completely unsettled by these attacks and deciding that things had to change, took steps to enhance its image, which had fallen to rock bottom. It thus sought a direct connection with Hitler and the Party Chancellery through which to inform them firsthand of the "achievements of the judiciary" and its activities in general,[116] in the hope of stemming the rebukes from on high and countering the influence of the Party and the police. Thus the *Führerinformationen* came into being.[117] These were published weekly from May 15, 1942, until February 15, 1945, and were to be transmitted to Hitler by way of the head of the Party Chancellery.[118] Top secret, only four copies were printed.[119] In line with their avowed purpose, the *Führerinformationen* contained a wealth of information that was not otherwise accessible, "interesting court decisions and events, as well as measures taken and projects of the Reich minister of justice."[120] Above all they included reports on investigations and criminal proceedings,[121] especially in the field of criminal law (People's Court),[122] of war criminal law, and of homicide and sexual offenses.[123] Information on the number of final death sentences passed was intended to show Hitler that the judiciary was now "hitting hard" against the most minor offenses and to demonstrate how tough they acted in the matter of clemency.[124] Other information outside the narrower field of legal practice concerned "achievements" such as the prisons, execution of sentences, forced labor of prisoners, and instructions and control measures by the Reich minister of justice relating to the "punishment of war criminals," "Communist high treason," and so forth.[125]

Whether the *Führerinformationen* achieved their aim remains unclear. There is even some doubt that they actually reached Hitler, possibly being held back by the Party Chancellery.[126] Apart from this possibility, it is difficult to imagine that such a publication could change Hitler's opinion of the "total incompetence" or even the superfluity of the judiciary in dealing with certain offenses, especially political ones.[127]

With the declining course of the war after 1939, Hitler lost interest in the judiciary and its plans for reform. From late 1942 Himmler built up a large "counterjustice" apparatus, doubtless with the Führer's knowledge and consent, which took on increasing importance as a competitor to the regular justice system.

dd. The Justice System Comes under the Control of the Police Command in 1942: Systematization

The creation of this "counterjustice" system was facilitated above all by the fact that Gürtner's successor to the ministry, Thierack, who took over on August 20, 1942, was a trusted Party man who worked closely with the Security Police (Himmler, Heydrich). Despite Schlegelberger's opinion that he himself was "under Party orders,"[128] the appointment of Thierack, who had a clean record in the judiciary and the Party and who as president of the People's Court had fostered good relations with the Security Police, found a welcome on all sides.[129]

The judiciary hoped that Thierack's close connections with the Party and the police would reduced the pressure on it. The police took encouragement from the rumor that during the air raids on Berlin he had appeared personally at prisons and ordered the immediate execution of numerous prisoners, staying to ensure that the order was carried out, and the police approved of him "as a man who doesn't get lost in the paragraph jungle,. . . . but takes ruthless and rapid action on the basis of state considerations."[130] The Party leaders took note of Thierack's appointment "with satisfaction" and declared themselves ready "to work together with the courts in confidence."[131]

The new minister came up to expectations. Actions that previously had been seen as police interventions were now decided upon through "agreements." Arbitrary action became the system, chaos the order of the day.

Seen from outside, the situation had become calm. The omnipotence of the police was institutionalized; the status quo was legalized and ready to be extended. In real terms, this meant both a multiplication of police interventions in the form of the "rectification" of court rulings and a confirmation and extension of criminal prosecution by the police. The "rectification" of rulings was thus no longer a matter of police autocracy but was an established instrument of police control, endorsed by the judicial administration. The guiding principles were laid down by Thierack at a meeting with Himmler on September 18, 1942, only a few weeks after he took office.[132] In addition to the introduction of punitive innovations such as flogging,[133] the heads of the judiciary and the police agreed "no longer to burden" the Führer with matters of "rectification," "inadequate rulings," and so on, but to settle them between the *Reichsführer*-SS and the ministry in the form of a centralized procedure and to have recourse to the head of the Party Chancellery if they could not come to an understanding. On this basis the head of the Security Police and the Security Service could either "propose" a rectification of certain rulings to the judiciary (by lodging a plea of nullity) or make a formal "application" for rectification and have the prisoner handed over to them. Whole lists of "contested" judgments were now regularly communicated to the Reich Ministry of Justice. For his part, the minister of justice could "suggest" to the Security Police that police custody be imposed against convicted people after they had served their sentence.[134]

The stronger position thus obtained by the police meant that "rectification" in the form of the execution ("special treatment") of prisoners of justice now became regular practice and was no longer regarded as the exception. The matter was settled in discussions between Thierack and Himmler on September 18, 1942; they agreed that such corrections should become the instrument to change "unsatisfactory" rulings. A certain "concession" by the police would be the rule that the minister of justice and not the police should decide on the question of "special police treatment" (execution) as a measure of "balancing out overly lenient sentences." If he and the *Reichsführer*-SS agreed about "special treatment," it was carried out. Otherwise the head of the Party Chancellery was called in.[135] The procedure was similar to that for applications for rectification of judgements: the head of the Security Police and the Security Service provided the Reich minister of justice, by way of the Party Chancellery, with regular lists of the names of people sentenced to imprisonment with an application for "special treatment." The applications contained brief explanations.[136]

Himmler received further additional powers from the Reich minister of justice. In particular, this concerned jurisdiction over so-called asocial individuals, which had long since lost all relation to the prosecution of criminal acts. In the discussion of September 18, 1942, the result of which was explicitly sanctioned by Hitler and was in line with his own wishes,[137] Himmler and Thierack agreed to hand over "asocial elements" to the Gestapo for "destruction through work";[138] "in this war of survival," it was "insupportable that a large number of asocial elements enjoy security" in German prisons and protective custody, and there was "no call to feed and treat these prisoners as had been done in the past."[139]

"Asocial elements" in this sense above all referred to people in protective custody, of whom there were 6,716 in June 1942,[140] and penitentiary inmates serving long sentences, who in the opinion of the minister had "placed themselves out of the community of the German people" through their acts and numerous previous convictions. All convicted Germans and Czechs who had been sentenced to more than eight years' imprisonment were handed over to the Gestapo,[141] followed by other groups of prisoners held by the judiciary (see the following section).

3.   Police "Rectification" Measures in the Prosecution of "Non-Germans"

   a.   Collaboration between the Reich Ministry of Justice and the
         Police:"Non-Germans" Are Handed Over to the Gestapo

To date, the "rectification" measures of the Gestapo, however far they went, were never enough for the police leadership, since they were isolated instances that left the judiciary as an institution intact. At least as regards the imposition of protective custody, all judicial acts such as the finality of the decision still required the seal of the justice branch. What the police wanted, in spite of all the successes they had obtained so far, was to take over the authority of the judiciary de jure and de facto for certain offenses ("political and serious criminality") and certain categories of people ("non-Germans," "habitual criminals," etc.). Their efforts to achieve this centered on the prosecution of "non-Germans," particularly Jews and other "asocial" foreigners, since this fitted best into the racial concept of the day and had the best chance of acceptance. Since, furthermore, these categories were in any case considered inferior and nefarious to the community, and it was easy to brand them with the Nazi theories of enmity or asocial behavior typical of offenders who were foreign to the race or the community, scant resistance was to be expected from the judicial leadership to efforts by the police to take over the prosecution of the offenses they committed. Indeed, in his agreement with Himmler of September 18, 1942, the Reich minister of justice expressly approved these plans.[1] "Asocial" individuals, as understood in that agreement, included Jews and "non-Germans" from the East (Poles, Russians, Gypsies, etc.), whatever their offense. The agreement must be seen as one element of the over-all aim pursued by the police leadership and the judical authorities to make justice available exclusively to Germans, leaving the police generally responsible for "hostile aliens."[2] In other words, the fundamental tenet of penal law of punishing the individual act according to the specific motives of the offender should be reserved for Germans, whereas "hostile aliens" were to be dealt with by the police without any consideration of personal motives, but exclusively from the viewpoint of their danger to public security and order.[3]

This plan was successfully resisted by the Reich governors in the Annexed Eastern Territories, who feared that handing over Polish prisoners of justice could cause unrest among the people. In a discussion with Thierack and State Secretary Wilhelm Stuckart from the Reich Ministry of the Interior on November 13, 1942, they firmly refused the project,[4] whereupon on December 13 Himmler surprisingly informed Thierack that, given the circumstances, he was no longer interested in settling the question "in the form discussed."[5]

b.   Usurpation of Sentencing Powers in Specific Domains

For the police, however, the failure of this plan was only a matter of form, since the Thirteenth Decree to the Reich Citizenship Law,[6] legalizing the police procedures with respect to the prosecution of Jews, had made the agreement of September 18, 1942, dispensable. But Himmler was not a man to allow pragmatic objections to get in the way of his intention of having other "non-German" "offenders" handed over. Since an agreement had not sufficed to bring about the delimitation of the jurisdiction, the Security Police resorted to the well-tried maneuver of eroding the authority of the judiciary by secret decrees issued without the latter's knowledge. Thus, the method covered police operations with a veneer of legality and had the advantage of avoiding disputes about jurisdiction while nevertheless sowing uncertainty and confusion in the ranks of the judiciary.

Regarding "non-Germans," Himmler could be sure of forbearance or even tolerance on the part of the Reich minister of justice. At the meeting of December 13, 1942, the two had agreed in principle that the basis for the new prosecution of "non-Germans" should no longer be the German Penal Code but rather decrees issued by the *Reichsführer*-SS.[7] The "legal basis" for the developing practice of the Security Police was the secret decree of March 8, 1940,[8] issued by Hermann Göring in his capacity as plenipotentiary for the Four Year Plan, empowering the *Reichsführer*-SS and chief of the German police to "secure" the conduct of Polish civilian workers in the Reich territory by way of administrative instruments. Himmler had always interpreted this as a general license to circumvent the powers of the judiciary, and he had instructed all Security Police units to punish every "digression" by Polish workers with police measures only, applying "special treatment" (execution) in the most serious cases.[9] As time went on, the police unilaterally extended this authorization, which had originally been conceived only for Polish civilian workers, to all "non-German" workers in the Reich, including those from Western and Northern Europe in addition to Eastern Europeans.[10]

aa.   So-Called Political Crimes (Including *Nacht und Nebel* Cases and Racial and Sexual Offenses)

In this context we are focusing especially on so-called political crimes (in the contemporary broad sense of the term), which from the very beginning had been dealt with primarily by the Gestapo; that is to say they were not brought before the courts. The rule was the execution of the prisoner or "custody" in a concentration camp for an unspecified period.[11]

The so-called *Nacht und Nebel* (night and fog) regulations related to quite general offenses (i.e., not only those endangering military security) committed by "non-Germans" in certain occupied territories, as well as to "political" ones.[12] The procedure was originally in the hands of the judiciary but was increasingly taken over by the police.

The *Nacht und Nebel* proceedings were based exclusively on Führer decrees and directives issued by Hitler personally, especially his instruction of December 1, 1941, which in the form of a decree of December 7, 1941, signed by Wilhelm Keitel as chief of the Wehrmacht Supreme Command, became known as the *Nacht und Nebel* decree.[13] Under its terms and the corresponding directives issued on the same date, all "non-Germans" in the occupied territories in the West and the North (Belgium, Netherlands, occupied France, Norway) who had committed an offense against the German occupying power were to be tried by the special courts or, in the case of "serious political crimes" (secs. 80 ff., Penal Code), to be brought before the People's Court in the Reich territory (so as to avoid unrest in the local population), except when the military courts adjudicated the case on the spot.[14] In line with Hitler"s wish, the death penalty was in principle imposed in *Nacht und Nebel* cases.[15]

The essential element of these proceedings, which were processed by Department 4 (criminal jurisdiction) in the Reich Ministry of Justice, was absolute secrecy[16]—this in contrast to the special criminal law for Poles, which for deterrent purposes enjoyed a certain degree of publicity both within the judiciary and outside. This was an insidious form of justice perfectly described by the German alliterative phrase *Nacht und Nebel* (night and fog).[17]

It is not surprising that the SS and the police took over this most "political" of all discriminatory legislation and ensured that "non-Germans" should come less often before the courts for trial, for on account of the formal independence of the judiciary, there was always the risk of a "miscarriage of justice" (i.e., acquittal). The ground gained by the police had been prepared (probably from the very start) by the fact that on instructions by the Reich Ministry of Justice, defendants who were acquitted or who, having been convicted, had served their sentence were to be handed over to the Gestapo, which decided on the "further measures" to be taken.[18] Although the special courts of Kiel, Essen, Cologne, Dortmund, and Berlin,[19] which were responsible for the jurisdiction of *Nacht und Nebel* matters, and the People's Court worked extremely fast,[20] awarding hundreds of death sentences,[21] the special courts were active in *Nacht und Nebel* cases only for about two years. In the fall of 1944, Hitler ordered that the proceedings should no longer be undertaken by the courts-martial and special courts but that the prisoners should be immediately given over to the Gestapo.[22]

Once a person was caught up in a *Nacht und Nebel* procedure, there was no chance of saving his or her life or freedom.[23]

Another item on the priorities list of the police was to gain jurisdiction over all "other dangerous offenses committed by 'non-Germans' threatening the German *Volksgemeinschaft*." This included all contacts between Germans and prisoners of war and sexual offenses by "non-Germans," in which Himmler as the *Reichsführer*-SS had always shown particular interest. Under the terms of a secret decree issued on March 11, 1942, by the *Reichsführer*-SS and chief of the German police, all reports of an offense were to be transmitted to the appropriate Gestapo directorate.[24] If the offender was "racially undesirable," he or she was generally executed ("special treatment"),[25] or at best (i.e., if the racial evaluation was positive) such offenders were "punished" with detention in a concentration camp, a principle applied above all to "racially undesirable" members of East European nations.[26] In an effort to "take care of the continued racial existence of the German nation," the *Reichsführer*-SS and chief of the German police created by way of an unpublished circular decree dated December 7, 1942,[27] the new "offense" of unauthorized sexual intercourse, punishable by death.[28] This decree was, however, only a repetition of earlier orders of September 1940 and July 5, 1941, under which it already carried the death penalty. The corresponding directives had called for the execution not only of "non-German" offenders from the East but also of offenders of Western origin, that is, from France, Belgium, and Britain,[29] whereas the circular decree of December 1942 excluded these last from the death penalty. In order to "maintain the ethnic entity (*Volkstum*)," the decree outlawed sexual intercourse between Germans and Poles, Russians, and other "Eastern workers"; it was permitted but "undesirable" in the case of other nationals. With this move Himmler found himself in agreement with the viewpoint of the judiciary, for which, as we have seen, indecency and sexual relations between Poles and Germans had since 1942 been prosecuted as anti-German behavior under the terms of clause 1, par. 3, of the Decree on Penal Law for Poles, provided the man was not a German.[30] Such cases rarely came before the courts, however. From the beginning of the war, the great majority of cases were dealt with by the police on the basis of the directives mentioned, without the judiciary being involved or informed. Such offenders were generally executed publicly as a deterrent measure.[31]

bb. Labor Law Offenses

A further category of offenses that were prosecuted exclusively by the police were so-called breaches of labor contract and "disciplinary problems" involving "non-German" workers in the workplace. Because the police declared such matters to be a question of internal security, they were generally removed from the jurisdiction of the Reich Labor Administration and the judiciary and dealt with by the Gestapo. This argument also met with substantial agreement on the part of the labor administration, since it considered security matters to be outside its normal purview and in any case "non-Germans" were always seen as such. Disciplinary labor offenses thus no longer carried a relatively mild sanction (an administrative penalty, a fine, or imprisonment) but were regularly punished by committal to a concentration camp or "work camp."[32]

c.   General Usurpation of Jurisdiction

Starting with the total responsibility for "hostile" "non-Germans" by the police, it was inevitable that this usurpation of jurisdiction should be extended to the entire prosecution of "non-Germans."[33]

aa.   Decree of the *Reichsführer*-SS and Chief of the German Police, January 19, 1942

The major step in this process was Himmler's decree of January 19, 1942, according to which all criminal acts by Polish civilian workers were to be dealt with by the Gestapo, to which the relevant information was to be sent immediately, and not by the public prosecutor.[34] The Gestapo was then free to pass on the affair to the judicial authorities or to deal with it itself. In the latter case—which was the rule—the usual sanctions (concentration camp or "special treatment" in the case of serious offenses) were then imposed.[35] This decree needs to be viewed in connection with the Decree on Penal Law for Poles of December 4, 1941,[36] which, though it introduced a whole discriminatory legislation for Poles and Jews, had at least maintained the jurisdiction of the lower courts and the special courts, so that the later decree may be regarded as a substitute for the unsuccessful attempts of the police leadership to get hold of direct jurisdiction over "non-Germans." It is significant that no one objected to the contradiction with the Decree on Penal Law for Poles. In line with the complete absence of the checks and balances of the rule of law, the decree did not in fact mark the beginning of the autocratic activity of the Gestapo but—like other relevant decrees—was rather a legalization after the fact of practices that had long been established.

A further secret decree issued by Himmler as *Reichsführer*-SS and chief of the German police, dated February 20, 1942, extended the Gestapo's general jurisdiction to the workforce of the Occupied Soviet Territories (so-called Eastern workers)."Serious" offenses were punished by concentration camp or "special treatment" (hanging). Similar treatment was meted out to all workers of "Polish" and "non-Polish" nationality from the General Government and the Annexed Eastern Territories.[37]

The category of serious offenses comprised above all political acts ("hostile tendencies against the state"), violent crime, sexual offenses, and "sabotage," all of which were comprehensively interpreted by the police, without which the list would have been mere enumeration. Rather, the reason for the listing was simply that, under the terms of the decree, all these cases were in principle subject to "special treatment" and that their surrender to the courts could only be considered when it was certain that the death sentence would be obtained. If, "against expectation," the death sentence was not passed, the *Reichsführer*-SS and chief of the German police was to be informed and a copy of the ruling sent to him. He then demanded delivery of the prisoner in order that "special treatment" could be exercised. Poles and Jews who had committed "milder" ("purely criminal") offenses were to be handed over to the public prosecutor, on the proviso that in the event of a massive increase in crime, only "State Police measures" were to be taken with a view to their deterrent effect.[38] Thus, here too the involvement of the judiciary depended on the Gestapo's judgment.

bb. The Circular of June 30, 1943, by the Reich Security Main Office (RSHA)

All these regulations made it possible for Himmler, on the pretext of "foregoing" agreements with the Reich minister of justice,[39] to maintain the appearance that the competence for the prosecution of "non-Germans" in principle remained with the judiciary and that the police intervened only in the case of specific categories of cases. But this still could not satisfy the boundless demands on the part of the police leadership as time went on. A secret circular decree issued by the Reich Security Main Office (RSHA) on June 30, 1943,[40] of which the Reich minister of justice informed the chief prosecutor at the Reich Supreme Court and the chief public prosecutors by way of the decree of August 27, 1943,[41] assigned the jurisdiction of all criminality among Polish and Soviet Russian civilian workers and other "Eastern workers" in the Reich to the Security Police as a matter of principle.[42] The decree quoted an alleged agreement of September 18, 1942, between the *Reichsführer*-SS and the Reich minister of justice on the transfer of the entire administration of penal justice for "non-Germans," an agreement that, as we have seen, was never instituted. Legal proceedings against "non-Germans" were only possible "when the police so desired." "Only cases in which adjudication by the courts appears desirable for propaganda reasons and it has been confirmed by prior contacts that the court will award the death penalty" were to be passed on to the judiciary.

In attempting to draw a picture, in conclusion, of the jurisdiction of "non-Germans" following the total usurpation of the penal authority by the police in the later years of the war, the first observation is confusion and lack of clarity. For all the various secret agreements between the judiciary and the police and the latter's secret decrees were not made known to the lower judicial authorities. Even the presiding judges of the courts of appeal and the chief public prosecutors were informed of the instructions of the police leadership only in February 1943, by word of mouth at the ministry. Basically, therefore, the judicial authorities were not clear about the treatment of "non-Germans" and were dependent on secondhand information, unofficial communications, or "gestures" on the part of the police. It took a long time for the judicial administration to confront the situation: far too late, on August 27, 1943, it issued a decree to the chief public prosecutors (but not the presiding judges of the courts of appeal) informing them that following Göring's decree of March 8, 1940, in his capacity of plenipotentiary for the Four Year Plan and subsequent arrangements, "the securing of faultless behavior of civilian workers of Polish nationality and Soviet workers in the Reich territory (with the exception of the Annexed Eastern Territories) had been transferred to the police."[43] The decree produced more confusion than clarity, however, since it was couched in only general terms and gave no details of the penal powers of the police.[44] The picture seen by the prosecution authorities and the courts was thus that of competitive two-track jurisdiction by the judiciary and the police, with definitions and boundaries that were unclear and impossible to overview. The legal insecurity increased, with the balance more and more in favor of the Security Police. How did this picture appear to the judiciary in detail?

4.   Judicial Consequences of the Usurpation of the Prosecution of "Non-Germans" by the Police

The judiciary did what it could to retaliate in the face of the profound inroads in its jurisdiction made by the police, which were particularly blatant with respect to sexual offenses and breaches of labor contracts by "non-Germans." The Hamm chief public prosecutor, for example, who in his situation report of January 29, 1941, spelled out the legal insecurity caused by the competitive activities of the Gestapo, issued directives to the attorneys general of the district to the effect that the adjudication of Polish civilians was a matter for the regular system of justice, which needed to "act energetically," and demanded that the police authorities inform the public prosecutor of criminal offenses by Polish civilian workers.[45] Such reactions occurred only at the local level, however, and were by no means uniform.

The legal insecurity was further increased by the absence of standard instructions, information, or recommendations governing the treatment of "non-Germans," especially foreign workers, because the Ministry of Justice was incapable of a clear line of action. Schlegelberger's term of office (January 1941 to August 1942), was a period in which the judicial authorities were in any case constantly at odds with the Party and the police on account of the introduction of German penal law in the Annexed Eastern Territories, and though "in principle" they recognized the need for as harsh as possible treatment of "non-Germans," their only reaction to the demands of the police was to make studied concessions that merely increased them, or to exercise greater harshness in the courts. The judiciary was neither willing nor able to recognize that the Gestapo's encroachments were not local arbitrary acts but part of a huge, ambitious plan to completely take over the criminal prosecution of "non-Germans," and perhaps ultimately even to exclude the justice branch from the prosecution of Germans.[46] The judiciary was not at first informed either of Göring's authorization of March 8, 1940, permitting Himmler to deal with the situation of Polish workers in the Reich territory, or of the subsequent police decrees extending said authorization to all "non-German" workers, so that the judiciary and the police were constantly in one another's hair when in 1940 the first voluntary or deported foreign workers arrived in the Reich, on account of how they should be dealt with under the law.[47]

But after all the invectives against the judiciary in the Party press (*Schwarzes Korps, Stürmer*) since 1937–38, and the already commonplace interference of the Party and the police in current proceedings, it needed more than good faith not to perceive a general attack on the judiciary's authority in such actions. According to its official statements, however, the judiciary—to which the idea occurred only in December 1942 that "centralized instructions from the *Reichsführer*-SS existed"[48]—claimed to have knowledge of the precise extent of the powers usurped by the police only at a very late juncture. At the decisive meeting of the presiding judges of the courts of appeal and chief public prosecutors in Berlin on February 10–11, 1943, the relevant decrees by the *Reichsführer*-SS and chief of the German police and the chiefs of the Security Police and Security Service were made known (but not handed out), having until then been kept from the Reich Ministry of Justice on the flimsiest of pretexts—that they had been issued before Minister of Justice Thierack came into office.[49]

He and the ministry, as Reich Minister of Justice Thierack explained, had not known what was going on and had only heard of "incomprehensible events"; only now, in early 1943, had he, the minister, found the "solution to the puzzle," the empowerment of the *Reichsführer*-SS and chief of the German police by the plenipotentiary for the Four Year Plan through the decree of March 8, 1940.[50] These statements are all the more revealing in that the situation reports by the presiding judges of the courts of appeal and the chief public prosecutors had been full of complaints about police interventions, so that the ministry, as Thierack himself explicitly stated, was very aware of the "countless reports and complaints" from the districts and of the systematic actions of the police.[51] In addition, on the strength of his long connections with the Security Police,[52] he doubtless had access to official information sources. The ministry's explanation of why the police regulations had not filtered through to the heads of the districts is equally dubious: the ministry, as the responsible official stated at the meeting of February 1943, had studied the wording of the police decrees but did not yet feel "in a position" (this in 1943) to inform its field offices, because it first wanted to come to an "acceptable arrangement" with the *Reichsführer*-SS and chief of the German police.[53]

But certainly two things were achieved after Thierack took over the ministry. First, the penal prosecution of "non-Germans" was thoroughly discussed at least once with the heads of the field offices (at the Berlin meeting in February)—precious little, but nevertheless something in a time of general legal uncertainty and lack of information. Second, Thierack—the keenest proponent of the harshest possible line in "penal law for aliens"—did attempt to obtain a delimitation of the respective jurisdiction powers through internal "agreements" with the *Reichsführer*-SS and chief of the German police, so that there would at least be some clarity about the reigning lawless conditions.

This clarification took the form of guidelines on criminal law for "non-Germans," which, significantly, were transmitted to the heads of the justice department by word of mouth only at the February meeting.[54] These guidelines were nothing other than the defensive reaction of the judiciary to the encroachments of the police; they confirmed the status quo, marking less the existing jurisdiction powers of the judiciary than the position the police had carved out for themselves, without dealing with the whole extent of the loss of competence. For Thierack, who in the matter of dealing with "non-Germans" had always gone along with the police leadership, did not dream of disputing the usurped powers with the police. On the contrary, he pressed for the transfer of still further powers. He agreed with Himmler that now that some seven million people of foreign descent were living in the Reich, the judiciary was in no position to "keep down this mass of people" by itself.[55] It is revealing of the attitude of the judicial leadership that at the meeting of the judiciary heads in Berlin, Thierack did not give the true reasons for the failure of the plan to put all "non-Germans" from the East, that is, Poles, Jews, Gypsies, and Russians, under the control of the police[56] (protests by the Gauleiter in the Annexed Eastern Territories and by the Reich minister regarding the Occupied Eastern Territories),[57] but spoke of a return to legality, the maintenance of the "non-German" workforce, and consideration for the foreign units in the Wehrmacht. In early 1943, the minister (he who as late as October 1942 had told the Party Chancellery that the judiciary could contribute to the extermination "only in a small measure)[58] proclaimed that the situation was different from that of the previous fall, because "today we cannot go along with the idea that we should somehow exterminate these people," if only because "many Easterners are fighting on our side." So it was necessary to guarantee these "non-Germans" some sort of "court proceedings."[59]

According to his statement,[60] the situation regarding the penal treatment of "non-Germans" since 1941 was as follows:

a. Minor offenses were dealt with by the police, if it so wished: when workers were housed in camps, adjudication could take place in so-called camp courts, as was already partly the case in the East.

b. In line with the wishes of the ministry, the police dealt with all political offenses, as well as collective criminality by "non-Germans," e.g., "outrages against Germans," "forming gangs," etc. The minister himself demanded "extreme harshness" in the "suppression and deterrence of whatever was hostile to Germans" punishment must follow close on the heels of the act, with or without summary court proceedings by the police, so that the hanging of such perpetrators by the police was "nothing special."[61]

c. The judiciary thus retained only the jurisdiction of serious isolated offenses by "non-Germans," known as "middle grade" criminality, for which the minister demanded extreme harshness, just as "absolute severity" was now practiced against the Poles.[62] In real terms, however, here as elsewhere the police still had unlimited powers of intervention. As a representative of the ministry explained with respect to the refractory behavior of the Poles, which was already quite substantial in the Altreich (where Poles "banded together" in the villages and openly sung Polish songs), the judiciary was capable of proceeding "with the harshest measures," but such matters would not even come into its hands, and it was well so.[63]

As comprehensive as the guidelines on criminal law for "non-Germans" were regarding the status quo, they were less precise when it came to future action, if the police continued to take the law into its own hands. Minister Thierack was unable to recommend anything better to his chiefs of departments than to carry on as before, until things "finally sort themselves out,"[64] not that this was ever the case, given the fundamental differences of opinion between the police leadership and the judiciary. *Ministerialdirigent* L. Schäfer, the responsible department head and rapporteur, expressed himself somewhat more clearly, although still not very explicitly: generally speaking, the line between the judiciary and the police should be drawn after "reasonable consideration of the prevailing circumstances" and should be based only on expediency; at the same time it should be not be forgotten that foreigners were needed for the workforce or even as soldiers in the East, so that, for example, workers from the Soviet Union needed to be treated differently.[65]

Regarding workers from the West and the North and the Italians, the police regulations "might as well" stay put. As for the Eastern workers, especially the Russians, involvement of both the police and the judiciary was "unbearable" in the long term. Since there was no question of letting the police take over completely, a delimitation of powers needed to be established. In cases such as moderate offenses by these people ("banding together," for example) the jurisdiction should remain in the hands of the police, since in any case the judiciary did not have the necessary strong and speedy executive available. The same was true for minor offenses (e.g., violations of the work requirement and discipline) by Eastern workers, Poles and Jews, which could be "dealt with" by the police in order not to burden the courts.

An exception to the instructions on the treatment of Eastern workers was made for the Poles in the Annexed Eastern Territories. There the Decree on Penal Law for Poles exclusively applied, so that offenses by Poles would be punished either in the courts, by the police (summary police courts),[66] or by specific police order prescribing prison camp.[67] Punishment by the Gestapo alone was not permissible, because the empowerment of March 8, 1940, of the *Reichsführer*-SS by the plenipotentiary for the Four Year Plan did not apply to the Annexed Eastern Territories. All these differentiations were mere lip service, because "punishment" by the summary police courts always meant execution or committal to a concentration camp and because the prison camps where the police penal orders were executed were exclusively under the control of the police and as such were hardly different from concentration camps themselves.

Similar uncertainty reigned regarding procedure in the prosecution of "non-Germans." At the Berlin meeting in February 1943, *Ministerialdirigent* Schäfer gave the instruction on behalf of the minister that in cases in which the police "claimed" a prosecution, there should be no attempt to hold onto the proceedings, an instruction that left it entirely up to the police to decide whether or not they would respect the jurisdiction of the judiciary.

In contrast, "serious criminality," especially acts of violence against Germans, sexual offenses, assault, or threats against German employers, should, according to Schäfer, remain in the hands of the justice branch[68]—a demand that the police had long not been bothered about, as we have seen. Things had even come to such a head that the rapporteur felt in necessary to stress how important it was that the judiciary should "avoid guaranteeing" to the police a particular outcome such as the death penalty in such cases.

In respect, too, of the normal obligation of the police authorities to leave investigations to the public prosecutor, the procedural rules had been turned on their head: from now on, as Schäfer put it, the judicial authorities were to "request" the police to pass on the defendant and the investigation procedure and to report to the ministry in the event of a refusal. Conversely, when the police demanded that the defendant be handed over by the judiciary, the instruction was anything but clear, only a report to the ministry being required.[69]

When all is said and done, all these instructions were a lost cause, designed to give the impression that the judiciary still had some influence in these matters. "Requests" by the judiciary to hand over a procedure or an individual or a report to the ministry had long cut no ice with the police; equally ineffectual were appeals to the chief presiding judges and the chief public prosecutors to point to "the legal situation" in the face of police interventions,[70] for the police were far from taking such admonitions seriously, and matters had progressed much further than that. The vagueness of the ministry's explanations shows how deeply the judiciary had been corrupted by police arbitrariness and how far advanced was the final dissolution of the whole legal framework. It also shows how necessary it was to conceal a situation that was experienced daily but which could never be stated out loud: that the judiciary was almost completely cut out from the prosecution of "non-Germans" (as well as of Germans in quite a number of areas), living off the crumbs thrown to it by the police, and that a "reasonable attitude toward the existing conditions" was nothing other than an endorsement of the arbitrariness of the Security Police. As early as 1941 the judiciary had wondered "to what extent the administration of justice still made sense."[71] The ministry's assurances that the situation was being clarified with the *Reichsführer*-SS and chief of the German police, after which "the friction would hopefully stop," was but proof of the judiciary's complete ignorance of police tactics. Clarification meant taking a stand, something that the police leadership abhorred. The ministry's recommendation to the department chiefs "to steer their way through" as best they could[72] until the situation became clear was a miracle of vague formulation that well described matters as they stood: a permanent need to steer their way through the tangled thickets of police powers and adaptation to escalating demands, ultimately leading to the almost complete abandonment of the prosecution of "non-Germans" to the police. Thus, legislative measures such as the Thirteenth Decree to the Reich Citizenship Law of July 1, 1943,[73] which sanctioned the responsibility of the police for offenses by Jews, were quite unnecessary, since the hegemony of the police was such that— apart from the occasional exception—criminal cases were no longer brought to the notice of the judicial authorities of the Old Reich.

B.   Civil Law

I.   Main Elements of the Transformation of Civil Law on an Ethnic Basis

Compared with criminal law, civil law was a minor political concern in the Third Reich. The legal ideology in the Nazi period, based as it was on the collectivistic principle of the national community (*Volksgemeinschaft*), regarded civil proceedings with distaste as a "social evil" and rejected the idea of their use as a means of settling conflicts between individuals.[1] Civil law also lacked the impact that led to incisive changes in legislative procedure, and its precise definitions of offenses and rigid procedural rules rendered it less suitable for ideological manipulation than the value-laden criminal law, with its greater scope for interpretation. A complete revision of the whole fabric of civil law was contemplated in the long term, but it never saw completion.

Influential in matters of both theory and practice, the reformers at the Academy for German Law,[2] with their hazy concepts of community, continued to work on a new national law (*Volksrecht*)[3] on the corporate state (*ständisch*) model in the form of a Code of National Law,[4] and as early as 1937 Schlegelberger published a book with the nostalgic title *Abschied vom* BGB (Farewell, Civil Code);[5] all this was difficult to reconcile with the body of civil law, with its emphasis on precision; and as the war wore on, the work on comprehensive reform of the Civil Code finally came completely to a halt. The major principles and institutions of the Civil Code (freedom of contract and trade, property, etc.) were thus not amended.[6] A number of reforms were effected in certain specific areas, however, partly on account of the war itself,[7] partly in order to anchor the ideology of race and community in the most important fields at least (marriage law, inheritance law, law of entail, labor law).[8] At the same time there was no way the civil law could remain a repository of the legal principles that had come down from the liberal period, safe from the influence of Nazi legal ideology. However, the transformation came about not by way of spectacular statutory modifications but rather through the practice of "boundless" interpretation of the law by the administration and the courts,[9] with "the spirit of National Socialist ideology" as the watchword.[10] In particular, the numerous general provisions of the Civil Code, such as "public morality" (sec. 138, Civil Code),[11] "good faith" (sec. 242, Civil Code), "immorality" (sec. 826, Civil Code), and so on, which C. Schmitt's "Five Principles for Legal Practice" expressly subordinated to the Nazi ideology,[12] served as a spearhead for the predominant legal dogma, including the "community values" of the Party,[13] and were thus, in the expression of the time, a "cuckoo's egg in the liberal legal nest."[14]

This process of "boundless interpretation" was based on the maxim of the absolute priority of the authoritarian state and the national community over the interests of the individual. In the words of the literature of the period, it was thus possible that "with a sympathetic approach to the overall ideas of the new state constitution, even typically liberal laws need not be an insurmountable obstacle, but [could] be brought into line with the requirements of the time."[15] Furthermore, the basic tenets of the new *Volksrecht* designed to replace the Civil Code, propounded in a great many publications,[16] placed even greater emphasis on the National Socialist concepts of race and community,[17] with the result that these ideas became the absolute principle underlying current legal practice. Since, however, the concepts were based exclusively on racist ideas, the inherent principle of unequal treatment of all who were foreign to the *Volksgemeinschaft* (i.e., of a different race) very rapidly infiltrated civil law.[18] Nor did the process stop there, for the reformers intended that this principle should become the over-riding basis of all civil law; euphemistically designated "corporate state law" (*ständisches Recht*),[19] its intention was to abolish equality before the law. Significantly, the literature described the new concept as nothing other than a "special order."[20]

II. The Principle of Völkisch Inequality in the Domain of Substantive Law

1. General Principles

The first tenet of this ideology of discriminatory law, from 1933 on, was that Jews and other undesirables should be treated in a different way from Germans, as an expression of "public morality," that is, of the "sentiments of all right-thinking people."

Although as a rule the courts refused to admit a general racist proviso covering all legal norms, such that they automatically had to give way whenever they conflicted with Nazi dogma,[1] unequal treatment was considered permissible, and indeed even obligatory, in the individual case. Strict observance of the law in its concrete application to Jews was thus even considered an error and as such was sharply criticized in the Nazi literature.[2] In such cases the judge had a legal obligation to deliver unequal treatment of the Jewish party to a suit. Thus, a decision of the Berlin District Court of November 7, 1938, stated:

> The problem in dispute here cannot be solved by an interpretation of the Protection of Tenants Act. Its significance stretches far beyond the bounds of this legislation. This is not a matter that can be solved by interpreting the Protection of Tenants Act, but a matter of ideology. . . . The view that every single measure against Jews can only be by order of the government is not correct. If this were the case, no interpretation of the law detrimental to Jews would be possible and Jews would have special protection. It is clear that this is not in the spirit of the matter.[3]

The Reich Supreme Court upheld the refusal of a registry officer to issue a birth certificate to a Jewish lawyer on the ground that this right, laid down in section 16, paragraph 2, of the Law on Civil Status, ceased to apply if it conflicted with state security.[4] The commentary of the Düsseldorf Labor Court was couched in even more general terms: every statutory rule contained a "tacit proviso" that Jews should under no circumstances obtain a benefit from it; that is to say that the law should operate only to the disadvantage of Jews, never in their favor.[5] Noteworthy in this regard is a judgment by the Reich Supreme Court of June 27, 1936, holding that Jewishness was a "legally recognized politico-racial criterion" justifying revocation of a contract.[6] As such, the judgment was probably representative of the Supreme Court practice of interpreting established legal norms to the disadvantage of Jewish parties. Some examples of the contestation and nullification of contracts will illustrate the extent to which this acknowledgment of racial discrimination was practiced.

Agreements with Jews were on principle contestable if the Aryan party was unaware that his partner was a Jew. The error concerning membership in the Jewish race was thus considered an error of judgment about an "essential aspect" of the person, according to section 119, Civil Code, which could justify contesting the legality of the business. The characteristics of the individual case were, however, the determining factor. Thus, several municipal courts ruled that contracts of sale between Jewish buyers and Aryan vendors could not automatically be contested on the grounds of an error of judgment under the terms of section 119 of the Civil Code; the courts allowed the action of the Jewish plaintiff.[7] But the refusal of an SS man to pay his debt to a Jewish company was upheld and the firm's action rejected, because National Socialists "fundamentally" refused to enter into a business relationship with Jews, "even if it is not forbidden for them to do so."[8] A teaching contract drawn up in January 1933 between a National Socialist and the Jewish owner of a private school, concerning the preparation of an examination, was deemed a voidable transaction under the terms of section 119.[9] Business between a newspaper and "Jews and persons of Jewish ancestry" related to advertising was held not only to be contestable but even null and void on account of "immorality" (sec. 138, Civil Code).[10] A contract of guarantee between an SS officer and a Jewish creditor was declared contestable on the ground of malicious intent to deceive (sec. 123, Civil Code); deception on the part of the creditor was found not only in the fact that he bore a German instead of a Jewish name but also because he had accompanied the debtor into his SS office.[11]

Attempts were also made to further the principle of *völkisch* inequality on the basis of the established law, over and above the confines of the regulations on contestable dealings.

Jewish creditors were not allowed garnishment of salary claims while the debtor was serving at the front, even if his family could afford it.[12] The Reich Labor Court recognized patronage of a Jewish store by family members of a public service employee, who was a member of the NSDAP and the SA, as a ground for immediate dismissal, because "the principles" of the NSDAP also applied to "the off-duty conduct" of its members.[13] The lack of German ancestry by a partner of a company supplying state departments was, in the view of the Reich Supreme Court, sufficient to justify termination of the contract for important reasons.[14] The new proprietors of an "Aryanized" Jewish insurance company were permitted to repudiate all insurance contracts with the company without notice, because the agreements on the term of the contracts were not deemed to be effective.[15] Associations constituted under civil law could, following the resignation of their Jewish board of management, be visited by a state commissioner who was deemed an associate under the terms of section 29, Civil Code (section 29 governs "emergency appointments," that is, the appointment, at the request of an associate, of a board of management by the court of first instance in the absence of a board) and who could be appointed to the board on his own proposal.[16] As a commentary on this decision noted, "even typically liberalistic laws are not an obstacle, but can be brought into line with the requirements of the period."[17] A similarly "sympathetic" approach will be found in judgments of cases in which the relatives of Jewish deceased persons sued for survivor's and compensation claims. In the view of the Reich Supreme Court, although claims for widow's benefits by relatives of Jewish employees were anchored in the law and could not be completely denied, the amount granted could be reduced on grounds of "good faith" (secs. 157, 242, Civil Code), where the reduction, termed "appropriateness" in the legal jargon, depended on whether or not the widow was Jewish.[18]

The concept of *völkisch* inequality was particularly blatant in the field of civil status. In the opinion of some courts, registrars of vital statistics had the right to refuse to undertake official acts to which they were otherwise committed by law. Even before the passage of the Nuremberg Laws on September 15, 1935, "the registrar [was] not obliged to publish the banns of a mixed marriage,"[19] despite the fact that marriages between Jews and "non-Jews" were not forbidden at the time.

When the registrar was ordered by a lower court to perform the act in accordance with the law,[20] in the absence of any obstacles to the marriage under the terms of sections 1305–15 and 1348 of the Civil Code, the order was quashed by a race-conscious district court following an appeal by the administration, *contralegem*, because the terms of the Civil Code covered only marriages "that by their nature are in harmony with the ideological tenets of our *völkisch* legal system and are thus basically sanctioned by it."[21] Similarly, the supervisory Prussian Supreme Court in Berlin upheld and appeal against a decision of the lower court ordering the registrar to issue an extract from the register of births, because the supervisory authority had to ensure that the registrar did not injure "the public interest"—that is, the Nazi principles of racial discrimination.[22] The Reich Supreme Court also confirmed that the refusal of a registrar to issue a document to an emigrant was legal, because a regular court could not be expected to decide which administrative measures were necessary for the maintenance of state security.[23]

The principle of inequality before the law according to ethnic or political criteria even went to the extreme that the state of mind of the claimant made a difference.

An article by E. Wendt in the *Juristische Wochenschrift*, 1934, entitled "It Can Also Be of Significance for the Civil Judge Whether Someone Seeking the Protection of the Law Is a Marxist or Communist" (page 18), illustrates the concerns of the literature of the time. The discussion revolved around whether the suspension of a threatened compulsory sale on account of financial difficulties through no fault of the applicant should be accorded equally to a National Socialist innkeeper (whose turnover had diminished since 1933 because his establishment had until then been mainly patronized by socialists) and a Communist innkeeper (whose turnover had also diminished). A distinction was made as follows: whoever was a member of parties that laid stress on the national community was a "good innkeeper," whereas anyone who followed the "shady ways" of parties that "destroyed the *Volksgemeinschaft*" did so at his own risk. In the opinion of the court, therefore, the Nazi innkeeper should be allowed his claim, but not the Communist.

2. The Main Areas of Discriminatory Practices

The main areas in which discriminatory legislation was applied were family law, inheritance law, tenancy law, and labor law, all of which dealt with situations involving close legal and personal relationships and so lent themselves particularly well to the principle of the separation of Jews and non-Jews.

a. Family Law

Within the ambit of family law, the application of special law was naturally concentrated on laws relating to marriage and divorce. The so-called Blood Protection Law of September 15, 1935,[24] had outlawed marriages between Jews and people of "German or related blood," declaring any such existing marriages null and void and "other racially unrelated blood mixtures" an obstacle to matrimony.[25] Even a valid engagement between a "citizen of German blood and a Jew" was not permissible.[26] The Marriage Law of July 6, 1938,[27] brought with it a revision of the grounds for divorce, and consequently these were now to be interpreted in terms of the racial principle.[28] This applied above all to existing German-Jewish "mixed marriages," which were deemed highly "undesirable."[29] Though it was not possible to oblige anybody to divorce, since the ban on marriage in the Blood Protection Law was not retroactive,[30] the judiciary and especially the Reich Supreme Court did everything in its power to dissolves such marriages by encouraging a broad interpretation of the divorce laws.[31] The principal legal basis for this was provided by the provisions of sections 1333 and 1337 of the Civil Code, which were later taken up in an expanded, "objectivized" form in section 37 of the Marriage Law.[32] The reason for this broad interpretation, according to the official preamble, was "to prevent an overly narrow interpretation of the concept of personal characteristics" and to introduce an "objective standard derived exclusively from the concept of marriage as understood by the state of today."[33] This can be illustrated by the following examples.

1. The error of judgment regarding the Jewishness of a marriage partner was generally recognized as an error of judgment pertaining to a personal characteristic under the terms of section 1333 of the Civil Code, old version,[34] in spite of

the fact that under the law, the term *personal characteristic* referred only to characteristics of the person himself and not to his objective circumstances (nationality, membership in a particular religious community, ill repute, etc.). At first the court rulings had been uncertain and in some cases had allowed a marriage to be contested only when the factual aspect of the spouse's race was in question, since only facts were contestable.[35] But as early as 1934 it became the predominant practice to include errors about the significance of this fact among errors of judgment justifying dissolution of the marriage under the terms of section 1333 of the Civil Code, since according to the Reich Supreme Court, "as a natural way of looking at it," the error pertained to an "essential feature of the personality."[36] But even the most sophisticated art of legal interpretation was not capable of explaining why such questions of appraisal ("significance of the different races") should be put on the same footing as contestable facts.

This was either stated in so many words[37] or it was claimed that the significance of the race question was "common knowledge."[38] If a justification was ever sought, it was found in "ethnic considerations," held to be of prime importance in marriage law. Under the jurisdiction of the Reich Supreme Court, "moral appraisal of a marriage" should no longer take account of the concerns of the couple involved but should give priority to ethnic considerations.[39] Only "purerace" marriages could satisfy these considerations, however. It was thus "often justified to sacrifice a long-standing marriage in order thereby to open the way to the institution of a marriage valuable to the nation."[40]

2. The original time limit for contesting a marriage on the basis of section 1333 of the Civil Code, which was one year from the acquisition of the knowledge of the grounds for contestation (sec. 1333, Civil Code) was a short one, that is to say it was interpreted in the spirit of maintaining existing German-Jewish marriages.[41] But from mid-1934 on, at the latest, the time limit was no longer taken so seriously. A particular difficulty was determining the beginning of the period. Some courts took the stand that in the case of an error of judgment regarding the non-Aryan descent of a marriage partner, the time period was set into motion only by the legislation of 1933,[42] and especially by the implementation of the so-called Law for the Restoration of the Professional Civil Service of April 7,1933.[43] Later annulment of the marriage was sometimes permitted even without consideration of the time limit, given that the beginning of the period could no longer be ascertained.[44] In addition, a number of courts attempted to circumvent forfeiture of the right of rescission (continuation of the marriage with knowledge of the grounds for annulment) in order to achieve the highest possible divorce rate among so-called mixed marriages.[45]

3. The greater ease of obtaining divorce brought in by the Marriage Law of

1938 was employed not only against Jews but also against other "aliens," thus proving, as we have seen, that the discriminatory legislation constituted a general principle of National Socialism, directed not only against Jews but also against all other racially undesirable persons. Thus, in 1942 in Breslau, a German-Polish "mixed marriage" was annulled at the request of the public prosecutor (sec. 607, Code of Civil Procedure) despite the absence of fault, because in 1939 the husband had played a leading role in the Polish national movement. "The previous record of the marriage" (sec. 37, par. 2, Marriage Law) was not relevant, in the view of the Breslau Court of Appeal, if considerations of the greater public good were in question. It was thus "in the public interest" to annul the marriage.[46]

4. The special-law principle was also wielded with a firm hand in the field of custody and maintenance. In this respect general law, that is to say the tenets of the Nazi state, was already evoked to justify withdrawal of the right to custody when the children were not brought up on the desired path. Thus, an education in the spirit of Jehovah's Witnesses represented "a most serious risk to the mental health of the children," and removal of the right to custody was therefore justified (District Court, Hamburg).[47] The same was true for a Catholic (Court of First Instance, Frankfurt-Hoechst),[48] Communist, or atheist upbringing (Court of First Instance, Berlin-Lichterfelde).[49] The refusal of a father to send his children to the *Hitlerjugend* was an "abuse of the right to custody" that justified taking the children into a welfare institution (Court of First Instance, Wilster).[50] However, a woman did not lose the right of custody to her children because she was a prostitute (Hamburg Court of First Instance).[51]

These principles were of course applied even more rigorously to the custody rights of non-Aryan parents. The right of custody to Aryan children following the divorce of a "mixed marriage" was granted to the Aryan partner, even if he or she was the sole guilty party,[52] notwithstanding section 1635 of the Civil Code, which fundamentally provided for custody by the nonguilty party. This was justified by the argument that leaving the child with the non-Aryan parent was a mental or emotional "hazard for the child" within the meaning of section 1666 of the Civil Code, which provided an exception to the rule set out in section 1635. The children were also given over to the custody of the Aryan parent, irrespective of guilt, in a case of "*Mischlinge* of the second degree" ("quarter-Jews") even though the divorced Jewish parent, who had been raised as a Christian, promised to have the children brought up in a Christian institution.[53] Similarly, the Prussian Supreme Court in Berlin refused the action of a Jewish father who had custody to recover the children from his noncustodial Aryan wife, using an alleged danger to the child as a pretext to withdraw his right of custody.[54] A Jewish "mixed marriage" divorcée was refused access at her home to her child, who had been brought up in the father's house on Christian principles.[55] Even if the child was only a quarter Jewish, it should not be put into the hands of the Jewish parent, in order to save "German blood."[56] In another case a German mother who had "given herself to a Jew" was deprived of the custody and her right to represent the child.[57] The right to care and custody of Jewish parents who had adopted an "Aryan child" was withdrawn illegally (although they still had to pay maintenance costs), because in this case the law was subordinate to the Party program. The commentary on the decision stated: "Now that the German ideology has been helped to victory, legal technicalities must not be allowed to stand in the way of the application of German principles. . . . Above all, the overriding principle of 'the public weal before self-interest' is also valid for German nationals of Jewish descent." (The "self-interest" on the part of the Jewish parents was that "the father kept the child in full cognizance of the racial laws," although according to the regulations in force, he could not have done otherwise.[58]

Thus, although everything was done to ensure that children with partly German blood should be removed from the Jewish parent and their upbringing put into the hands of the parent of German blood, the fact that a Jewish child was given a German upbringing was not sufficient to prove that the child was a member of the German nation. For example, the Prussian Supreme Court in Berlin found that "in the question of the endangerment of his [the child's] mental well-being, it is of no legal consequence whether a Jewish child of German nationality receives a German upbringing abroad."[59] Conversely, the rights of care and custody, guardianship, and maintenance remained intact when the beneficiaries of these rights were of German and the ward or recipient of the upbringing was of Jewish ancestry. Thus a "German-blooded" father was not deprived of the right to represent his half-Jewish child before the law on the strength of the later's racial characteristic alone.[60]

Similar principles were applied in the matter of maintenance. The Reich Supreme Court denied a claim for compensation by a non-Aryan family outside of Germany that maintained an illegitimate Aryan child against the wishes of the Aryan father, who was responsible for the child's maintenance. The court stated that it was not "in the father's interest" that the child should be taken care of abroad in a Jewish family.[61] A divorced Jewish mother was in principle granted a maintenance claim against the Aryan father, but "her racial identity" was taken into account in calculation of the payment, tantamount in real terms to a reduction of the claim.[62]

Actions concerning descent (secs. 256, 640, Code of Civil Procedure) to establish racial identity with respect to parent-child relations were permitted on the broadest possible scale in order to promote the race ideology. Thus, even after expiry of the one-year time limit (sec. 1594, Civil Code) for contesting the legitimacy of the child, the Reich Supreme Court allowed the possibility of determining the "blood-line" descent in the contrary sense.[63] The apparently frequent actions for a declaratory judgment brought with the aim of certifying "uncertain" descent, which would allow actual determination of Jewish descent to be circumvented, were deemed inadmissible by the Reich Supreme Court, because the courts could "under no circumstances be misused in order to conceal even the slightest possibility of Jewish descent."[64] The procedure was particularly rigorous in the case of an action brought to prove the Aryan descent of a child who had been classified as a *Mischling*. An administrative directive issued by the Reich Ministry of Justice demanded more stringent requirements (blood tests, hereditary and racial appraisals, recourse to the opinion of the Gestapo) for such actions; on no account was the mother's statement sufficient. Only when all the evidence was positive could a claim be allowed.[65]

The principle of maximum segregation of Germans and Jews was also upheld in the field of guardianship and tutelage. It was applied, however, only to legal relations between Germans and Jews, not those between Jews themselves. For example, a Jew who was to be placed in the care of a guardian was not accorded the right to request that the guardian be Jewish.[66] In contrast, a court of guardianship refused to approve an apprenticeship contract between a German apprentice and the German subsidiary of a Jewish undertaking.[67]

As early as 1935, the Reich Supreme Court had stated that the "raising of a young person of Aryan descent to an ethnicity-and race-conscious citizen cannot be guaranteed if the foster father is not Aryan, even if the foster mother is," thereby opening the way for the authorities to revoke permission to keep a foster child.[68] Non-Aryan guardians of Aryan wards could be dismissed by sole virtue of their race, and the Prussian Supreme Court in Berlin construed the possibility of such dismissal in a very broad interpretation "out of due consideration for the religious confession of the ward" (secs. 1779, par. 2, and 1915, Civil Code).[69] Such dismissal was even imposed if the guardian was only a half-Jew (*Mischling* of the first degree);[70] such persons were as a matter of principle not to be appointed guardians of Aryan wards (Hamburg District Court),[71] since a Jew was "fundamentally unsuited to the office of guardian."[72]

The doctrine of segregating Germans and Jews was only a part of an extensive policy of ethnic division and discrimination, which had particularly devastating effects with respect to family law. Just as, in accordance with Reich Ministry of the Interior guidelines, Aryan wards and foster children could under no circumstances be taken into so-called mixed-marriage households or remain there, and quarter-Jewish children could not be raised by the Jewish parent, in order to save "German blood,"[73] the long-term strategy of the "ethnicity" experts in the internal administration, the office of the *Reichsführer*-SS and the National Directorate of the NSDAP, was to withdraw the raising of all "valuable blood" among conquered nations from those naturally qualified to fulfill the task and to put it into Aryan hands. This strategy was designed on the one hand to weaken foreign populations and on the other to provide the German Reich with "racially desirable" offspring ("useful members of the *Volksgemeinschaft*") and to create new reserves of a young generation available for work and military service.[74] Similar actions (Germanization) proposed by the Nazi offices in their search for "good blood"[75] were undertaken in a number of countries, but they concentrated above all on Eastern Europe.[76] Such actions of course increased in intensity once the losses sustained by the Wehrmacht on all fronts, and especially in the Russian arena, could no longer be made good by national resources; the full implementation of the search for racially desirable children was prevented only by the outcome of the war.[77]

The "legal basis" for these Germanization actions undertaken by the offices of the Reich Commissar for the Strengthening of German Nationhood (RKF) under the banner of the ethnic struggle was the Decree on the German Ethnic Classification List of March 4, 1941,[78] the prime objective of which was to recover all "German blood." By virtue of this decree, Himmler ordered (as a first measure) that all legitimate and illegitimate children in the Reich district of the Wartheland whose fathers had been killed in action or whose parents had otherwise died should undergo racial and psychological screening by the Central Resettlement Office of the SS and its outposts.[79] "Racially desirable children" were to be forcibly removed from their mothers on the pretext of health endangerment and transferred to the Altreich after a provisional period in a children's home in their district.[80] The only exceptions possible were for Polish mothers "of good race" as understood by the SS, who were to be brought into the Altreich with their children and given German nationality and German names.[81] In order to eradicate all traces of their national origin, the children were designated "German orphans from the recovered Eastern Territories" by order of the RKF.[82] A similar policy was followed for racially desirable children of non-German women brought into the Reich from Eastern Europe (Polish and so-called Eastern workers): the children were taken away from their mothers, who continued to serve in the workforce, although it was not clearly established whether the children of Eastern workers were to die or be adopted.[83] The children of German women and Polish or other foreign men were to remain with the mother, as such children were considered racially valuable; only when the (male) foreigner was "particularly inferior" was a(compulsory) abortion undertaken by order of the RKF.[84]

No accurate estimation of the number of children affected by these resettlement and Germanization programs is now possible,[85] nor of the extent of such actions, since much of the documentation was destroyed.[86] The family law status of orphans brought into the Reich territory from the Occupied Eastern Territories is also unclear. The removal of the children from their mothers signified in practice the permanent withdrawal of the right to custody along with the decision to Germanize then (a decision that could be taken solely by the RKF and the administrative authority),[87] apparently without recourse to the guardianship courts competent to order such removal. Whatever the case may be, we may presume that Poles were not allowed to adopt such children[88] and that before their adoption by German families, the children were put under ex officio guardianship by the youth welfare office, as prescribed by civil law, either by virtue of the law or through an explicit order.[89]

b.   Inheritance Law

The same policy of strict segregation of Germans and Jews was also followed in succession matters. Here special law was used to openly amend the legislation, for the Eleventh Decree to the Reich Citizenship Law of November 25, 1941,[90] proscribed the right of succession (sec. 4) to all German Jews living abroad, in addition to depriving them of citizenship (with which their assets fell to the Reich). Legal practice followed a harsh line and declared all exceptions inadmissible.[91]

The general inheritance regulations were also interpreted to the detriment of Jews. Particular outrage was occasioned when a Jew was named as beneficiary over the heads of close relatives; this was considered a gross violation of "the considerations . . . that a responsible testator should have toward his family and the *Volksgemeinschaft*," contrary to the "sound thinking of the people" (sec. 48, par.2, Testament Law).[92]

Such a judgment must be viewed against the natural tendency of the judiciary to find that passing over the legal heirs contradicted the "sound thinking of the people."[93] It was, further, an infringement of the moral code for a testator to nominate his second (Jewish) wife as heir, passing over the children of the first marriage, and such a will was declared null and void.[94] Following the promulgation of the Nuremberg Laws, the greatest offense was taken, and the will nullified, if an Aryan testatrix gave precedence to her Jewish lover over her own family, since "the content, motivation, and purpose" of such a disposition was in contradiction to "the thinking of the people founded on the National Socialist ideology."[95]

Jewish executors were not allowed to continue in that role; upon the application of an Aryan heir, they were to be relieved of this duty by the sole virtue of their race; this was construed as a grave reason (sec. 1227, Civil Code), since, in the view of the Reich Supreme Court, "a German comrade cannot be expected to tolerate the management of an inheritance by a Jew against his will," except in exceptional circumstances.[96] Grounds for the dismissal of Jewish executors were not admitted, however, if the heirs were half-Jewish.[97]

c.   Law of Tenancy

The special-law principle of the segregation of Aryans from non-Aryans was also rigorously enforced in tenancy matters. A regular practice began only with the second wave of anti-Jewish legislation after 1938; until then the question whether discrimination against Jewish tenants was justified on the basis of their race had been answered in a variety of ways.[98] Until that time all court rulings had applied the Protection of Tenants Law of 1928 in cases involving Germans and Jews.[99]

Since 1938 the "ideological postulate" ruled that all joint relations with Jews should be terminated as rapidly as possible, and it was in this direction that extensive interpretation of the law was practiced.[100] The application of the Protection of Tenants Law of 1928 to Jewish tenants was now flatly refused on "ideological grounds," and eviction actions by private and public landlords were allowed.[101] Conversely, Aryan tenants were permitted immediate termination of a lease with a Jewish landlord " if the landlord had let out a flat to him and at the same time had let a flat in the same house to a Jew."[102] This was founded on the "interests of the community of occupants,"[103] which was suddenly considered an essential feature of the tenancy relationship, "directly inspired," as the literature put it, by the community concept of National Socialism;[104] according to the Reich Supreme Court, a true community of occupants could only be "composed of German-thinking people and inhabitants of Aryan descent with a common viewpoint"; living in the same house with Jews could thus not be expected of the German tenant, who was entitled to give notice (in application of secs. 2 and 4, Protection of Tenants Law), since the presence of Jews was a burden and a disturbance within the meaning of these regulations.[105]

Following the lead of the Reich Supreme Court, the Berlin District Court offered the following commentary on a decision of November 7, 1938:

The Protection of Tenants Law makes the revocation of tenancy agreements with Jews difficult and even impossible in certain cases. This, however, conflicts with the ideological demand that *all* joint relations with Jews be curtailed as rapidly as possible. The application of the Protection of Tenants Law to Jewish tenants is therefore inadmissible. . . . It is not true to say that the Nuremberg Laws have settled the situation of Jews once and for all. The Nuremberg Laws were only a start. The process has not finished. In addition, the view that every single measure against Jews can only be by order of the government is not correct. . . . Though it may be true that, as a result of the termination of contracts, a large number of Jews in Germany have become homeless, that is not the point. These dwellings are made available to German comrades, and this can only be welcome given the present housing shortage.[106]

The Nuremberg Court of First Instance was even harsher in the formulation of its decision of November 26, 1938, declaring termination without notice to be admissible on the grounds of the racial characteristic of the Jewish tenant:

I. The Nuremberg Court of First Instance, *like the whole of legal practice*, has hitherto held that the Protection of Tenants Law is to be applied in cases concerning German landlords and Jewish tenants. . . . the conscientious judge can no longer uphold this standpoint. . . . 1. . . . The liberal principle of the free play of market forces is replaced in the field of housing by the principle of the link between property and the community. . . . By the will of the National Socialist legislators, the Protection of Tenants Law is the legal realization of the community of the people in the housing domain, and as such is the legal expression of the Party program's demand that the public weal should come before self-interest. 2. Since, therefore, the purpose of the Protection of Tenants Law is to serve the community of the German people, it can only be applicable to those who belong to the community of the German people or who are assimilated to it by their blood. It would therefore be a contradiction of the aim pursued by the National Socialist legislators in maintaining and enlarging the law if the protective clauses were to be applied to persons who are outside the community of the German people and who can never belong to it. This is the case for Jews. . . . It thus follows that the protective provisions of the Protection of Tenants Law cannot apply to Jewish tenants in their relations with German landlords. . . . The fact that the issue has not yet been explicitly settled by the legislator is not an obstacle to such a legal viewpoint on the part of the judge. For the circumstance that the government has not yet formally changed a legal position that is incompatible with National Socialist views does not preclude the judge from refusing to recognize this position in his decision, which of necessity he must do. . . .
II. . . . In principle the Civil Code grants the landlord the right of termination of the tenancy contract without notice only in cases to which sections 553 and 554

apply. Neither of these is applicable here. Legal practice has, however, for a long time developed the principle that the legal concept embodied in the terms of sections 553, 626, and 723 of the Civil Code is quite generally valid for long-term obligations. Accordingly, such obligations can be terminated without notice if an important reason is given. . . . The presence of Jews in the house he lives in is a nuisance for any German; it is embarrassing for him to meet them, to say nothing of having to stand in relationship to them.

This point of view has taken on considerably more significance since the events of the last weeks [this refers to the "Kristallnacht" of November 9–10, 1938—Author]. Developments have shown that it has become in supportable for Germans and Jews to live in the same house. Implementation of the tenancy contract is threatened by the person of the tenant, by his membership in the Jewish race. . . .

The plaintiffs' right to termination without notice is in the present instance not affected by the fact that the contract was revoked subject to the contractual period of notice. For if the regular notice served by the plaintiffs on November 1, 1938, was based on the fact that the defendants are Jews, the Jewish murder in Paris on November 7, 1938, and the defense measures of the German people and the Reich government thus engendered have indicated the need for an *immediate* separation in space of German and Jews in all clarity.[107]

Nonetheless, there were also a number of judgments pronounced in conformity with the law, and eviction actions against Jewish tenants on the sole grounds of their descent were overruled for want of a legal basis.

Thus, for example, in October 1938 the Charlottenburg Court of First Instance was still delivering such judgments,[108] which were criticized by the proponents of a hard line as being completely misguided. The court held that recourse to legal regulation for discriminatory action must be upheld in pleas against Jews. This was opposed by lawyers who argued that, notwithstanding the lack of legal regulation, interpretation of the law "according to ideological arguments" was correct.[109]

Other courts, too, came under similar criticism ("a complete misunderstanding" of ideological unity)[110] for passing fair judgments. Examples are the Spandau Court of First Instance in its decision of October 1938[111] and that of the Hindenburg Court of First Instance of September 1937, which also rejected the senseless interpretation of the concept of "nuisance" quoted above; a nuisance presupposed a fault on the part of the tenant, but the fact of Jewish descent was not a fault.[112] Lastly, in a decision of May 1938, the Nuremberg Court of First Instance, still firmly anchored in the liberal tradition, flatly refused the use of political slogans—that is to say the National Socialist community concept—in civil law: "Regulations under public law of a political nature are not applicable in the civil matter of a tenancy agreement."[113]

The coming into effect of the Law on Tenancy Contracts with Jews of April 30, 1939,[114] elevated special law to the rank of legality. Decisions in favor of Jewish tenants were rendered impossible, since protection of the latter was declared inapplicable, and the right to terminate at any time was established for all tenancy contracts (including long-term and fixed-term contracts). Admittedly, in order to prevent the crassest abuse, a certificate from the local authority was required of the landlord showing that the Jewish tenant was assured of alternative accommodation (sec. 9). But even without such a certificate, a landlord was able to lodge a petition to terminate the tenancy under the terms of the Protection of Tenants Law.[115] Of significance, however, as the Prussian Supreme Court in Berlin stated, is the fact the court was not bound to check the accuracy of the certificate, and this could only go against the interests of the Jewish tenant.[116]

Just as discrimination against Jews in all sorts of ways was taken for granted in tenancy law, the special-law principle was never allowed to operate in favor of a Jew; the Prussian Supreme Court in Berlin refused a claim for a rent reduction by a Jewish tenant pleading major commercial losses: the exclusion of Jews from the German economy, on which the claim was based, did not justify a reduction in rent.[117]

d. Labor Law

As in tenancy law, the concept of termination without notice was introduced into labor law for racist reasons.[118] Although the racist legislation concerning Jewish employees engaged in public service was basically not applicable to the private sector until 1938, the right to terminate was frequently invoked on the grounds of freedom of contract. From 1933 on, a wave of dismissal notices swept over employees of Jewish descent, either subject to a period of notice or with immediate effect "for an important reason" (sec. 626, Civil Code). A large number of such rulings were published in 1933 and 1934; they became rarer after 1935, probably because Jews no longer dared seek the protection of the courts.

The differentiated approach adopted by legal practice has already been outlined in detail in part 1, section 1, V. ("Professional and Labor Law"), so a few brief notes will suffice here. Regarding dismissal for the sole reason of race, it was clear following the judgments given by the Reich Labor Court in particular that labor contracts with Jewish employees could be terminated by regular notice.[119] Economic considerations were also admitted, even if they were only a pretext, as grounds for such layoffs of Jewish workers. There was disagreement about whether race was an "important reason" for dismissal without notice within the meaning of section 626 of the Civil Code. The Reich Labor Court, though maintaining the standpoint that the dismissal of non-Aryan personnel without notice was admissible only in the public service domain, not the economic sector, recognized that it was "impossible to ignore the effects that the German people's new attitude toward Jewry, engendered by the national revolution, would have in the field of private law of contract." The question was thus whether it was reasonable to continue a contractual relationship until the expiry of the regular time limit. Whether or not the race question conflicted with the maintenance of an employment contract could, however, only be judged according to the specific circumstances of the case.[120]

The Decree on the Exclusion of Jews from German Economic Life of November 12, 1938,[121] was bad news for executive personnel, since it provided for termination of their employment contracts with a period of notice of six weeks. The right to give notice to such personnel was greatly expanded, in that, for example, legal practice defined executive personnel not only as persons with a supervisory function; the category also included those who "had even only an indirect influence on the running of the undertaking."[122]

In addition to the matter of termination of employment, Jewish workers were subject to a special law regarding social benefits. From 1939 on, the courts had maintained the principle that Jews should be excluded from payment of wages for public holidays and vacations and from other social benefits, that payment should be made only for the actual work performed,[123] a precise anticipation of future legislation excluding Jews from all social benefits.

In doctrinal terms—in line with the National Socialist ideology of community and loyalty—this discrimination against Jews under special law was justified by the existence of an obligation of loyalty and care toward workers set out in laws and wage agreements, an obligation in which only those who shared the identity of race, that is national comrades, could participate. This was tantamount to denying Jews all the benefits of laws "designed exclusively for German workers."[124] The same result was reached by appealing to the "enlightened contemporary views" as a source of judgment.[125]

A new development set in with the implementation of the Decree on Employment of Jews of October 3, 1941,[126] which retroactively legalized the jurisdiction hitherto exercised. This decree effectively removed Jews from the protection of labor law and declared their employment contracts to be "special employment relations." Such legal relations sui generis thereby became subject exclusively to the special regulations of the Reich Labor Administration and the Security Police, a matter that cannot be pursued in more detail in the present context.[127]

Pension rights under company pension plans were also in effect reduced or withdrawn from Jews without basis in the law. The Reich Labor Court drew the fine distinction that although the litigious claims were "in principle" founded, the amounts to be granted ("appropriateness") should be reduced because of the claimants' Jewish descent; justification for this was found in section 242 of the Civil Code, because the present sense of justice gave the race concept priority over purely economic considerations.[128] The "claim to satisfaction" should not be allowed to come into conflict with what the National Socialist convictions of the German people considered right and proper.[129]

Jewish workers who had retired before the Exclusion Decree of November 12, 1938,[130] did not lose their entitlement, but they were subject to cuts in the sums paid.[131] Jews who had left their jobs before January 30, 1933, however, were fully excluded from company pension benefits, since it would be in contradiction to the "sound thinking of the people" to allow a Jewish worker "to partake of the positive development of the committed undertaking when a fair assessment of his pension is made, for such success owes nothing to him but is a result of the upsurge in the economy brought about by the National Socialist leadership."[132]

e. Commercial Law

Prior to 1938, court judgments in commercial law followed the government line that special treatment of Jews was not permissible with respect to their economic activity. The Jewish question, as the Reich minister of justice stated in a decree dated March 14, 1936,[133] was regulated by the state leadership alone. The only exception at that time was in the matter of company names, where the special-law principle of separating Aryans from non-Aryans was enforced in advertising.

Thus, the acquisition of a trading company with retention of the former trade name (sec. 22, Commercial Code) was nullified as an offense against public morality (sec. 138, Civil Code) if it led to "a Jew doing business under an Aryan name," irrespective of whether the vendor was aware of the purchaser's race.[134] It was also a violation of public morality to change a firm's name that indicated a Jewish owner with the intention of concealing the owner's Jewish origins.[135] A Jewish owner who displayed the name of his firm in large letters and his Jewish last name in smaller letters in an attempt to deceive was found guilty of an infringement of both industrial law and the law against unfair competition.[136] The designation *German* in the name of a firm could be prohibited and a change of name justified (sec. 18, par. 2, Commercial Code) if the owners of the firm included "a Jewish-sounding name,"[137] since the word *German* gave the impression that the owners were of Aryan descent and its use was permitted only if this was in fact the case.[138]

The year 1939 saw the appearance in commercial law of discrimination practices that had long been current in other fields. Court rulings became increasingly harsh. "The commitment of an Aryan businessman to a restraint-of-competition clause designed to protect the Jewish party to the agreement" was in contradiction with good faith and common usage if the competitive situation arose solely out of de-Judaization measures in the German economy.[139] The boycott of a "wholesaler of Jewish kin" by a wholesale coal association with a monopoly position, which had "acted without intent to cause injury," was, in the opinion of the Reich Supreme Court, neither in contradiction to the law nor an infringement of the rules of fair dealing.[140] In addition, the regulations promulgated against Jews since 1938 were further tightened up.

In the implementation of the Decree against Conspiring to Camouflage Jewish Businesses of April 22, 1938,[141] the term "Jewish character" of the business (sec. 1) was interpreted broadly by the Reich Supreme Court, which declared a de facto dominating influence of Jews to be sufficient, irrespective of the legal situation,[142] a standpoint anchored in the Third Decree to the Reich Citizenship Law of June 14, 1938.[143] On this basis the Reich Supreme Court declared the acquisition of a Jewish-owned spa by an Aryan for his son from a marriage with a Jewess to be a violation of the Camouflage Decree, since the business continued to be "under Jewish management," whereas the district president had permitted the purchase on condition that it would be managed by Aryans.[144] In interpreting the offense of camouflage of the Jewish character of a business, "ethnic considerations" and the "racial obligations" of the owner were the criteria of whether or not there had been deception.[145] Jewish owners whose company had a non-Jewish name were forced to drop it. This was also the case for the liberal professions, which were not covered by the trade regulations, in defiance of the meaning of the Camouflage Decree.

The terms of the Decree on the Utilization of Jewish Property of December 3, 1938,[146] were of course extensively interpreted to the greatest disadvantage of Jews. Under the terms of the decree, a compulsory sale or liquidation order could be served within a given time limit on Jewish owners of businesses and Jews with agricultural or forestry undertakings or similar landed property or other assets (secs. 1, 6, 8, 16).[147] The acquisition of real estate was forbidden to Jews; dispositions of real estate were subject to official approval, a limitation that was also interpreted very broadly.[148]

In the view of the Prussian Supreme Court in Berlin, Jews were not permitted to acquire such rights even as legal heirs, notwithstanding the fact that this prohibition applied only to legal transactions. Jews were further not permitted to acquire rights or partial rights under the law of obligations to real estate or parts thereof or assimilated rights, whether from living persons, as testamentary heirs, or as acquirers of portions of an inheritance, because the decree of December 3, 1938, applied not only to limitations regarding the disposition of real estate but also to executory agreements.[149] Conversely, in the event of cancellation of the execution, Jews were in principle not debarred from the purchase of an execution lien registered in favor of the creditor (secs. 866, 868, Code of Civil Procedure),[150] whereas the registration of a provisional judicial mortgage on a Jews's land as a guarantee of the execution (secs. 916, 932, Code of Civil Procedure) was basically not forbidden,[151] since this was not a purchase or a disposition qualifying as a legal transaction but an acquisition by force of law or execution.

III. Discriminatory Principles in Procedural Law

1.   Discrimination against Jewish Judges and Lawyers

The principle of discriminatory legislation against Jews was broadly applied in procedural law, which mostly contained strict regulations that were not open to interpretation, because the "spirit of National Socialist development" also applied to civil proceedings.[1] This greatly simplified the rejection of Jewish judges, for example. Although such rejection required a reason "sufficient to justify distrust in a judge's impartiality" (sec. 42, Code of Civil Procedure), that is, objective grounds were presupposed, the judge's race now served as such a reason. Thus, as early as November 1933, the Berlin District Court accepted the challenge of a Jewish judge by a defendant who earlier had insulted "the Jews," since it was "natural that the content and form of the attacks should hurt the feelings of a Jewish judge."[2] Rulings such as this were readily taken as a direct encouragement to petition for such a challenge. For example, in a ruling of February 1934, the court found that there were "objective reasons" for concern over the partiality of a Jewish judge in the matter of testimony by a Jewish witness, since the district court could not imagine that a Jewish colleague was "capable of evaluating this testimony."[3] Similarly, the Hanover District Court reversed a 1933 ruling in which an arbitration tribunal had found the refusal of a Jewish associate judge to be without foundation.[4] Following the passage of the Nuremberg Laws, the question arose whether judgments pronounced by Jewish judges or in which they had been involved were legally effective or whether they could be revoked through proceedings for annulment, on the grounds that since November 15, 1935, Jewish judges had no longer been permitted to serve (secs. 1, 3, 4 of the First Decree to the Reich Citizenship Law). But in this case considerations of legal security took precedence, and the Reich Supreme Court denied the possibility of annulling such decisions, invoking section 5, paragraph 4, of the Second Decree to the Reich Citizenship Law of December 21, 1935.[5]

This totally unfounded legal practice greatly curtailed the rights and thus the livelihood of Jewish lawyers, although their actual disbarment occurred only with the Fifth Decree to the Reich Citizenship Law of September 27, 1938.[6] Jewish lawyers representing Aryan parties were no longer permitted to be assigned to legal aid (Frankfurt Court of Appeal),[7] because according to "the meaning and the spirit of the legal concept that has predominated since the national revolution, based on the principles of the nation and race, German parties can no longer be represented by counsel foreign to the race" (Hamm Court of Appeal and others).[8] This position held even when a relationship of trust existed between the party and the Jewish lawyer; for an Aryan party who chose to have a non-Aryan lawyer "violated the basic tenets of the German community." The German judge should thus not "yield to such requests" (Naumburg Court of Appeal).[9] It was possible for an Aryan lawyer to be assigned to a Jewish party, on account of the fees earned—but this was exceptional (Dresden District Court).[10]

Jewish lawyers who had been axed were refused audience in court as counsel in pursuance of section 157 of the Code of Civil Procedure,[11] even if no costs were involved (Charlottenburg Court of First Instance),[12] and despite the fact that section 157 spoke only of "representation involving payment of a fee" and that section 90 of the Code of Civil Procedure should have applied in such cases.[13] The (double) legal fees incurred through the ban on Jewish counsel were not recoverable, contrary to the law (Prussian Supreme Court in Berlin).[14] There was some disagreement about the appearance of Jewish counsel before the labor court. The *Land* Labor Court of Berlin banned Jewish union representatives from the labor courts as early as mid-1933, assimilating them to Jewish lawyers.[15] It later reversed this ruling, however, following an appeal by the lawyer in question, declaring inadmissible the refusal to admit such people as counsel in labor proceedings (sec. 11 of the Labor Court Law) on grounds of race. This justification makes it clear how easy it was to make use of technicalities to avoid discrimination and that boundless interpretation of the regulations "in the National Socialist spirit" was by no means mandatory. The court found that section 11 of the Labor Court Law did not provide for application of the "Aryan principle." As a result it was not applicable here, since the court could not act in place of the legislator.[16] Other labor courts continued to declare the appearance of such persons inadmissible, however.[17]

2. Discrimination against Jewish Parties (Legal Aid) and Witnesses: The Plan to Renounce from Legal Proceedings

A further opportunity to apply discriminatory legislation was provided by the provisions on the granting of legal aid (secs. 128 ff., Code of Criminal Procedure), which in the main appear to have been correctly applied into the early years of the war. Reports by the Security Service in 1941, as usual quoting opinions allegedly expressed by the people, complained that "politically minded comrades . . . simply fail to understand how Jews are still able to plead under legal aid."[18] The local justice authorities now felt encouraged to practice unlawful discrimination, especially since the Reich Ministry of Justice was beginning to express itself in increasingly harsh terms at that time.

At first the Reich Supreme Court hinted at possibilities of circumventing the authorization of legal aid, albeit in special cases.[19] Legal aid to Jews was subsequently refused in various districts, as is documented at least for that of the Hamburg Court of Appeal.[20] As the president of the Hamburg Court of First Instance explained to the judges of his district, legal aid should not be refused "on principle," in default of a legal basis, but authorization should be granted only in exceptional cases and only on submission to the district court president.[21]

The refusal to grant legal aid was thus in complete accord with the Nazi philosophy of discriminatory legislation, yet the absence of "a relevant legal regulation or directive" still rankled and was felt to be "awkward."[22] But such support was not long in coming. In August 1942 the right of Jews to legal aid was reduced throughout the Reich by administrative guidelines issued by the ministry.[23]

Procedural discrimination against Jews in court was practiced in other ways, too, or at the very least the courts were prodded in this direction by the ministry. In a lecture before the judges of the city in 1942, the presiding judge of the Hamburg Court of Appeal explained the ministry's policy on the legal treatment of Jews. Jews were still permitted to testify as witnesses, but their testimony should be evaluated "with caution."[24] But these were only the first steps in the direction of complete abolition of all the rules of procedure. At the meeting of the court of appeal presiding judges and chief public prosecutors in Berlin on February 10–11, 1943, the representatives of the ministry put forward the planned judicial policy, namely to achieve the severance of the courts from the procedural law regulations by a statutory instrument already in force in the Annexed Eastern

Territories, with respect to all court procedures, including civil law.[25] That this did not come about, in spite of the ministry's efforts, was due only to the facts that the deportation and extermination operations undertaken since 1941 had depleted Germany of Jews and that the institution of civil action by Poles was in any case hardly conceivable and in practice impossible given their dependence on the police statues.

3. Discrimination against Jewish Participants in the Estate Execution/ Administrative Process

The estate administration law was also applied to the disadvantage of non-Aryans. Like Jewish executors, Jewish official receivers could also be dismissed, even if they were war veterans, because—as the Berlin District Court put it as early as May 1933, during the wave of anti-Semitic violence of the National Socialist revolution—the "continuing agitated mood of the people" and "difficulties in dealing with landlords, creditors, etc." constituted an important reason for dismissal in pursuance of section 153 of the Compulsory Auction Law.[26]

Furthermore, Jews did not benefit from the Decree on Exemption form Judicial Execution of May 26, 1933,[27] since its expanded protection of debtors guaranteed by the National Socialist state had not been created for Jews.[28] The Misuse of Execution Law of December 13, 1934,[29] excluded Jewish tenants from protection against eviction in the event of termination actions, including eviction from apartment houses in the large cities, on the grounds that the concept of the "community of occupants" could make the removal of a non-Aryan necessary (Schöneberg Court of First Instance);[30] foreigners permanently resident in Germany, however, enjoyed protection under this law and were thus treated more fairly than German citizens of Jewish descent.[31] In the view of the Schöneberg Court of First Instance, Jews also could not defend themselves against seizure of radio sets by using the otherwise valid claim that they were their personal property and therefore exempt from confiscation (sec. 811, no. 1, Code of Civil Procedure), since possession of such objects by Jews was not considered necessary.[32] The executing court was not authorized to order the utilization of a seized object by transferring it to a Jewish party (sec. 825, Code of Civil Procedure), since business with Jews was "dishonorable" and "the nation could not understand" how a court could make such a transfer of ownership to a Jew.[33]

To summarize, we may note that the discriminatory practices had little effect on civil law in formal terms and that (with the exception of matrimonial law) it was not subject to the "general reassessment," that is, "adaptation of the civil law regulations to political necessities," demanded by the proponents of radical anti-Jewish measures.[34] Such "general reassessment" was, however, basically unnecessary, since the various methods used to interpret the law had the same effect with less trouble and in a less spectacular manner: segregating Jews and other non-Germans from Germans in the basic spheres of human relations (family law, tenancy law, etc.), destroying or preventing family and hereditary bonds, and, not least, giving the principles of state-run robbery the necessary veneer of legality. Whether the law was interpreted according to its meaning and purpose or applied in the light of the "ideologies of the day," or a racist proviso was incorporated into every regulation to the detriment of Jews, the exclusion of an entire section of the population from their basic rights was accomplished by enforcing laws when they worked to the disadvantage of Jews and flouting them when they worked to their advantage. Thus, civil law serves as the prime example of the main technique used in Nazi law, whereby a whole legal fabric could remain largely intact, but the exclusion of Jews from its protection was readily achieved under the cover of an interpretation consonant with the ideology of the period.

Section Two

The Implementation of *Völkisch* Inequality in the Annexed Eastern Territories

INTRODUCTION

The Political Objectives in the Annexed Eastern Territories: Testing the
Ethnic Struggle

With the incorporation of the occupied Polish western territories into the
Reich by a Führer decree on October 8, 1939,[1] all state and Party departments
were faced with completely new tasks. Not only did they have to cope with the
administrative problems resulting from a territorial gain of around ninety-nine
thousand square kilometers and a population increase of almost 9.5 million people;[2] they also had to implement the principle of *völkisch* inequality (special law)
on a large scale, a measure with which they had little experience. Although the
struggle against "alien" nations was one of the tirelessly repeated dogmas of the
National Socialist ideology in the Altreich, there had as yet been no possibility
of actually trying it out in practice, with the exception of the measures instituted
against the Jews. However, these latter being German state subjects, they were
accorded a certain "special status."[3] In contrast, the Annexed Eastern Territories,
with their almost exclusively non-German population (approximately 86%
Poles, 5% Jews, 7% Germans, 2% "others"),[4] and above all with the "model district" of the Wartheland,[5] now provided the first opportunity of realizing the
principle of *völkisch* inequality on a large scale and without any of the "hurdles"
presented by traditional legal principles.

As described in the introduction to part 1, section 2, the basis and justification for this was the concept of the "ethnic struggle," the political version of the
concept of special law, inseparably linked to the National Socialist policies, in
the Annexed Eastern Territories, where it first achieved importance in its own
right, namely the extermination of the leading Polish classes and the Polish
Jews,[6] the deportations and expulsions (the "resettlement" of the "undesirable"
local population),[7] and the "total Germanization" by introduction of new German
settlers. Although there had been no lack of efforts and special laws in the Altreich to implement the "ethnic struggle" against German state subjects of Jewish
descent,[8] legal practice had not swung around to a drastic line against "non-
Germans" to the extent desired by the National Socialist leadership,[9] because

despite all attempts to control them, the courts were still unable to free themselves completely from the principle of equality. But things would be different in this new playground for racial policy. There was a feeling of being part of a conspiracy in a country of pioneers on "Germany's Eastern front," where the local "non-German" population should be "suppressed" as far as possible and work would be performed to "reconstruct" Germany and the "border territories."[10] As explained above, any commitment to the principles of international law (the Hague Convention)[11] and to domestic (Reich) law was therefore rejected, because such legal or bureaucratic principles had proven to be "obstacles" in the realization of racial policy objectives. The only guiding principle of all state activities was thus the political objective of the "ethnic struggle," in other words the Germanization of the Eastern Territories; all means were justified to achieve this goal, and everything was subordinate to the dictates of racial policy.

The judiciary also had to serve this objective, a demand that was implemented almost to the full—in contrast to the situation in the Altreich, where the submission of the judiciary to the policies of the government was repeatedly demanded but never fully achieved, one of the reasons being that the freedom of judges from political interference (except for their duty to obey Führer orders) was never cast into doubt even by the most zealous advocates of the National Socialist judicial model.[12] In the Annexed Eastern Territories, the judiciary was "absolutely National Socialist,"[13] as the Posen (Poznań) chief public prosecutor told a meeting of the League of National Socialist German Jurists.

Right from the start, no doubts were allowed about the goal of degrading the judiciary to a compliant tool of the political leadership. The latter was still circumscribing this task with a certain degree of understanding for the mentality of the judges, with phrases such as the duty of the judiciary being to guarantee the "legal basis" for "racial conflicts," the national leadership needing the "cooperation of the judiciary," as the basis of law was one of the "necessary prerequisites for building a country," and was not economical with praise (the judiciary had performed its duty "to our fullest satisfaction"),[14] but the representatives of the judicial administration were much more direct: according to the Posen chief public prosecutor, the judiciary must become the "powerful instrument of the political leadership."[15] This meant that the public prosecutors must be men who were particularly open-minded as regards "the reality of life," who would give precedence to the "concept of nationhood" in all their decisions[16] and, as "political civil servants," would be, "like soldiers," "devoted and obedient" to their superiors "on their own battlefield."[17] The president of the Posen Court of Appeal claimed that only "politically thinking judges" who could thus fulfill their task of being "comrades-in-arms in the political racial struggle and champions of the realization of the unity of party and state"[18] could be considered as judges. State Secretary Freisler of the Ministry of Justice expressed himself in even clearer terms. The conquered territories were the place where the judge could prove himself as "the Führer's political soldier in the field of the law," "marching in formation in the political struggle."[19] The military principle was therefore perverted completely and elevated to the guiding principle of the administration of justice.[20] The struggle against "non-Germans" was now viewed as "frontline experience," "proving oneself in the ethnic struggle" was the criterion that qualified the official for a career in the judiciary in the East and the principle used for selecting leading judicial officials,[21] and gaining this qualification was the aim of the first wave of judicial officials to reach the Annexed Eastern Territories, most of whom had arrived as volunteers.[22] In addition, a "posting to the East" was designed to become the "top school" for the jurist, both within and without the judiciary, as well as the selection principle for the other districts.[23]

As State Secretary Freisler explained, the entire process of legislation and legislative interpretation was therefore required to conform with the "particular requirements of ethnic policy."[24] The administration of justice in the Annexed Eastern Territories thus centered around the application of an increasingly stricter special law for the "non-German" Polish population to protect the "German development work" against the "dangers posed by the Polish nation."[25] This aim was promoted and supported in every way by the judicial administration and the political leadership, which is likely to have swept aside the bulk of the legal and moral inhibitions of the judicial officials in the Annexed Eastern Territories about the blunt implementation of *völkisch* inequality. The aim was the introduction of a comprehensive statute for Poles ("Polish statute"), not contained in a separate legal code but merely anchored as special law in the individual legal frameworks.[26] However, relevant publications have shown that in the national Ministry of the Interior, there were concrete plans to issue a comprehensive Polish Code at a later date.[27] It was public knowledge that the structuring of this special law was oriented toward "Germany's mission in the East," "determined by the venomous hatred displayed by the Polish nation at all times toward Germany and all Germans."[28] As a result of this exclusively (ethnic) political orientation of the administration of justice, tirelessly repeated or tacitly understood in the literature and in practice, there was no legal foundation whatsoever for the principle of special law.[29] The specified revolutionary goals and the uninhibited totalitarian claims of the National Socialist leadership could not be reconciled with traditional legal and administrative concepts and measures. Despite all attempts, the aims of discrimination and annihilation of the "enemy Polish nation" could not be fitted into any legal framework.

Because of a lack of any substantive arguments, the judicial representatives restricted themselves in their publications to the statement that the "non-Germans" living in the Annexed Eastern Territories, representing 93 percent of the population in 1939,[30] were (in all seriousness) referred to as "alien elements" in the "ethnic [German] fabric,"[31] who under no circumstances should be allowed to enjoy the benefits of German law without restriction. In the published opinion of the majority of leading judicial officials,[32] it was "inexpedient," or "even dangerous and thus wrong," to "apply within the Reich" the law "designed for German compatriots" to "non-German persons," particularly where "settlement areas of racially differing peoples with different cultural levels were interlinked"; "for this reason, the *general* and *consistent* application of German law could not be considered, either at the present or in the future."[33] They were either unwilling or unable to see that the policy of special law was inappropriate, even from a National Socialist viewpoint, because the quickest possible integration of the "newly gained territories" should have demanded the most widespread possible introduction of German law, to establish the consistency and uniformity of the law. But the prevailing practice turned everything upside down by asserting that the requirement of "integrating the Eastern Territories" demanded a deviation from principles applied in the Reich and the subjugation of the Poles to special law.

A. Stages in the Implementation of *Völkisch* Inequality

In line with the governing principles described above, the development of special law in the Annexed Eastern Territories was implemented in a comprehensive fashion in both substantive and procedural law right from the outset.

Three phases are evident in this process; initially, these were not so much planned as decided by the war and practical necessities, but they were subsequently developed with a certain consistency. It was not that undisguised special law was introduced for the Polish population at one fell swoop, as was advocated in particular by the Party and police leadership. This would have run counter to the legal philosophy of the time, in which formal regulations and legal unity were still the determining factors. Despite the justification for recognizing special-law measures in principle, considerable efforts were still being made to introduce these measures only gradually, primarily by the interpretation of existing law.

Since the *direct* application of German law to the Polish population could not be considered because of its inherent principle of equal treatment for all beneficiaries of the community of law, efforts were made to find alternative methods of realizing the determining principle of *völkisch* inequality for the population but without having to abandon German law in its entirety. The magic formula common to and linking all these three phases, and invented to overcome this difficulty, was the formula of the *analogous interpretation* and *application* of German law. It was originally conceived as a temporary legal measure to take account of the legal vacuum arising as a result of the precipitate withdrawal of the military administration from the Eastern Territories at the end of October 1939,[1] but it was also retained in the subsequent period. It allowed all deviations from German law while retaining such law in principle, with the nature and scope of the application of law governed by the "demands of the ethnic struggle." This was phase one. Apart from the analogous application of German law, specific regulations under special law for "non-Germans" within the framework of general law also emerged from mid-1940 on (phase two). From the fall of 1941, there was no longer any scope for even the analogous application of general law, and the final separation of Reich law from special law was formally completed at that time (phase three). This is highlighted by the following overview.

I. The Principle of the Analogous Application of German Law (October 1939–May 1940)

During the first months of civil administration in the Annexed Eastern Territories, there were no legal regulations for the activities of the German administration, apart from a few regulations for the special courts and a number of special provisions regarding unauthorized possession of firearms, and so forth.[2]

The only binding regulation was the Decree by the Führer and Reich Chancellor regarding the Division and Administration of the Eastern Territories of October 8, 1939,[3] under section 7 of which "the current prevailing law [remained] in force until further notice where it did not contradict the assimilation into the German Reich." However, this wording was of little use, since it specified neither what the "current prevailing law" was nor what was supposed to replace this current law. When interpreting the regulation, there was therefore a question of whether the "current law" was the Polish law in force before September 1, 1939, or the law that was applied by the German authorities between September 1, 1939, and the coming into force (October 26, 1939) of the assimilation decree. The further question under discussion in legal circles was, as reported by the SD, whether only the "current law" that contradicted the territorial *changes* (for instance that required the existence of the Polish state) should be suspended, or all law running counter to the National Socialist *ideology*,[4] which would also have included numerous Reich regulations from the period before

1933. However, it soon emerged that these were specious questions being discussed in professional journals primarily for form's sake and that they merely served to confirm the existing legal situation;[5] the courts were making political decisions "unhampered by theoretical reservations"[6] and were interpreting section 7 of the Führer decree of October 8, 1939, not legally but politically, contrary to the actual wording and intentions.[7] Court practice adopted the Führer's dictum "I do not believe in any law in the world that is not shielded by a power" as the dictum of the law and legal policy.[8] The continuance in force of Polish law as the law of the vanquished was rejected unanimously by all courts (in the Reich district of the Wartheland) as "legally and politically impossible."[9]

Polish law was thus replaced by a legal system organized at the individual's discretion.[10] In concrete terms, this meant the effect of German law, even without its formal introduction.[11] "Current law" under the terms of the decree of October 8, 1939, was interpreted to mean the German law applied by the German authorities.

The question of the scope of the (indirect, i.e., analogous) application of German law would result in a further extensive, even nonsensical interpretation of section 7 of the Führer decree of October 8, 1939. Although the decree stated that the current law continued in force where it did *not* "contradict the effect of integration," this was interpreted in practice to mean that the current Reich law applied since September 1, 1939, continued to apply only if it *corresponded* to the "effect of integration." This restricted the Reich law to be applied: Reich law that had previously been applied only with a neutral effect was to be suspended. Any deviation from normative standards of Reich law was thus permitted, even necessary,[12] at any time, if demanded by the effect of assimilation, that is, by political interests. This was the starting point of the "analogous" application of German law.[13]

The principle of the analogous application of Reich law was regarded as an instrument that could be used with ease to bridge the lack of legal regulations. In reality, this saw the judiciary facing insoluble difficulties, since neither the "legal basis" of section 7 of the Führer decree of October 8, 1939, nor any other pointers or criteria provided any details about the scope of the Reich law to be applied. The appeals to the judges for "law-creating activity" and for "awareness of their political mission,"[14] the confidence that judges would always find the right law corresponding to the "special circumstances in the East,"[15] would act as "pioneers of the law" in the "Eastern Territories," and would continue to develop the law "creatively" and free "from all . . . restricting, rigid standards," were basically phrases without substance. Neither were central measures to control events of much help in individual instances. Discussions among judges and the references by the judicial authorities "to the aims of the legal and ethnic struggle" were able, perhaps, to secure the "uniform basic position" of the judges, but whether these, as claimed by the vice president of the Posen Court of Appeal, also guaranteed "uniform adjudication" in the desired sense,[16] must be left open to doubt, because a decision had to be taken in each and every case to be judged whether German law should be applied directly or analogously or the judge should decide entirely at his own discretion.

The consequences of this unclear legal situation were confusion and legal uncertainty in the judicial authorities. It soon emerged that the slim "legal basis" of the Führer decree of October 8, 1939, and the "enthusiastic decisiveness and energy" of legal practice alone were insufficient.[17] The pressure for performing the much extolled "law-creating" activity was more of a burden than a relief to the judges and public prosecutors, most of whom came from the original Reich administration and were bound up in a traditional positivist way of thinking, and reinforced the need for the formal introduction of German law.[18] The Reich Ministry of the Interior, too, which had as early as 1935 emphasized the need for introducing German law in *each single case* of future territorial acquisitions for reasons of certainty of justice,[19] demanded the introduction of German law, but with a heavy slant on special law to the detriment of the "non-Germans."[20] In contrast, the Party leadership, as the major political power in the Annexed Eastern Territories, pursued the line that, as expressed by an official in the Party Chancellery, it would be

> wrong to regard as necessary the unconditional introduction of German law . . . to territories in which the conditions of the original Reich would first have to be established simply to possess a secure legal basis for development. The development and total Germanization of new territories should not start with the introduction of German law, but should rather be preceded by development. Only when acts of political despotism have been eliminated and the conditions in these territories have been harmonized with those in the original Reich can any thought be given to the implementation of the complete concurrence of the law of the original Reich with the law in the new territories.[21]

II. From the Analogous Application of German Law to Special Law (Summer 1940–Fall 1941)

However, both the Party and the Reich (judicial) administration were soon forced to realize that the "conditions were begging for explicit regulation by the law."[22] In view of this need, the second phase of legislative development, which should be placed roughly between summer 1940 and fall 1941, appears in retrospect to be a compromise (discussed in greater detail below) between the two views outlined above. At this point, it is sufficient to point out that the need for a more solid legal basis was met by the formal introduction of numerous Reich laws in the Annexed Eastern Territories, above all in individual areas of administrative law;[23] as will be shown below, key elements of German penal law were also introduced by the Decree on the Implementation of German Penal Law in the Annexed Eastern Territories of June 6, 1940.[24] In practice, this meant that the principle of the analogous application of German law without restriction (without any link per se to the "effect of assimilation") was declared to be in order in cases where a penal law regulation could not be applied "directly." Civil law experienced a similar development, with the Civil Code introduced by a decree of September 25, 1941,[25] but with the stipulation of a mandatory deviation from statutory law if required by "the needs of assimilation" (sec. 4, par. 1). An increasing number of individual special regulations affecting "non-German" Poles (and Jews) were also introduced; these have already been discussed above.[26] However, this did not achieve an improvement in the legal situation to the extent desired. In many instances, the former uncertain legal situation was merely continued, as in cases where no special regulations had been issued, Reich law largely applied; it was possible to deviate from the provisions of Reich law at any time, though, if such a course was dictated by political reasons.

III. The Establishment of Overt Special Law for "Non-Germans" (after Fall 1941)

In the third phase, which started around fall 1941 but overlapped with the second phase in many cases, the transition from a (still) generally applicable legal framework to overt special law for Poles (and Jews), a process initiated in the second phase, was finally concluded. This special law, embodied in particular in the Decree on the Administration of Penal Justice against Poles and Jews of December 4, 1941,[27] withdrew from these "non-Germans" the few legal guarantees still remaining to them under general law (e.g., the right of appeal) and subjected them to a system of special law governed exclusively by political criteria dominated by police requirements. This was accompanied by the dissolution of the concept of legal rules and the statutory definition of offenses, such that "law" for "non-Germans" was restricted to a few vague general provisions. This completed the abolition of the unity of the legal system in favor of political tyranny and a development toward an overt emergency law for "non-Germans." This process of the abolition of traditional principles in favor of political directives governed by police requirements is described below using examples of the development of special law in the field of penal and civil law.

B. Penal Law as a Central Element of the Special Law against "Non-Germans"

Although its general understanding of law meant that the main emphasis of the administration of justice under National Socialism lay in the area of penal law, "to maintain the striking power of the German people in the struggle against the powers hostile to Europe,"[1] the primacy of penal law in the Annexed Eastern Territories was considerably reinforced.[2] It was naturally the most suitable means for the judiciary to "suppress the Polish nation," in line with its task of collaborating in the "ethnic struggle." Penal law and penal law policy in the Annexed Eastern Territories thus did not only follow the general tightening of criminal justice and the criminalization of far-reaching areas of life in the original Reich, but were additionally characterized by the "struggle against the Polish nation."[3] This was, as it were, penal law reinforced by special law. The consequence was that the judiciary was no longer thought of in the sense of *administration of justice*, even one judging by harsher standards, but rather as an "instrument of the struggle" against everything "alien,"[4] and it manifested itself to the local population almost exclusively in the form of penal justice. With the idea of the unity of the legal system already thereby abandoned in principle, the second stage involved committing the courts to implementing the unequal treatment of "non-Germans" by a generally harsher interpretation of offenses and sentencing policy or by ensuring unequal treatment through the "analogous application" of German law where there was no legal basis for punishment. This erosion of the principle of *nulla poena sine lege* was the transitional phase to the decree of overt special law for "non-Germans," which concludes the development of special law in the Annexed Eastern Territories.

I.   Principles of Substantive Special Penal Law

1.   Decrees of the Military Administration

In the early days of the war, special courts were established in the occupied Polish territories; their task was at first merely political, that is, to initiate the punishment of criminal offenses committed against Germans in the first days of the war (the "September crimes").[5] The basis for this was two decrees by the commander in chief of the army dated September 5, 1939, one regarding special courts in occupied Polish territory and the other on the introduction of German penal law.[6] Under the second decree, German penal law (including military penal law) was to be applied *directly* by the special courts, so that "right from the outset," there could be no "doubts about the application of the law" by the special courts.[7] It is doubtful that these decrees were particularly important; neither the literature nor legal practice make any comments on whether these decrees were still valid after the end of the military administration on October 25, 1939. Even if their continuation in force is assumed, since they were never formally abolished,[8] they were not obeyed. This is because after this time, German penal law was merely applied analogously: "the general and consistent application of German law [was] not considered at the time or in the future."[9] These decrees, however, certainly excluded any deviation from German penal law. In reality, this practice, glossed over as the "generous interpretation and appropriate continuation of penal law," meant that there was a *deviation* from German penal law in order to be able to punish crimes by "non-Germans" more harshly than provided for under the law.[10] In contrast, the direct application of German penal law was approved, if it ensured the greatest possible punishment for the individual involved. For instance, the purview of German law was also antedated to the time before the occupation of Poland, with a decree by the commander in chief of the army dated October 1, 1939,[11] specifying that crimes committed before September 1, 1939, in the occupied Polish territories could be judged by German courts using German penal law (although prosecution was not compulsory), with the aim of bringing before the special courts crimes by Poles against ethnic Germans committed before that date. The justification—that the Eastern Territories now annexed were "old German *Kulturland*" that had never been abandoned,[12] and that the Reich had been forced to assume the "moral" protection of the ethnic Germans in 1933 because the Polish state was incapable of doing so[13]—shows clearly the minor role played by traditional legal principles in the Eastern Territories.[14]

2. Führer Decree on the Division and Administration of the Eastern Territories, October 8, 1939

As mentioned above, the legal basis used for the practice of the "analogous application" was the regulation in section 7 of the Führer decree of October 8, 1939, under which "current law" continued in force where it did not contradict the "effect of assimilation." The regulation served to justify the extensive application of penal law to the detriment of the "non-Germans," by rejecting the *direct* continuation of the then current law (German law). The "effect of assimilation" was thus served only by the analogous application of German penal law. As was publicly admitted, this was effective whenever the direct application of German law "allowed no or only insufficient punishment"; in practical terms, this meant that the offenses defined by the law were arbitrarily strained so as to achieve the political goal of the harshest possible punishment of the Poles.

The most extreme example of the practice of analogous application is provided by the special-court trials of crimes committed by Poles against ethnic Germans at the beginning the war ("September crimes"), regarded as the most urgent task of the special courts, indeed of the judicial system itself.[15] To achieve the harshest possible punishment of the Polish defendants, numerous legal constructions were invented to circumvent the law, to allow the courts to prove that they were certainly not thinking "formally" when they passed down the maximum sentence. For instance, the offenses were stretched beyond all bounds by applying to these cases—where it turned out to be difficult to provide sufficient evidence—not the rules governing culpable homicide (homicide, second degree homicide, bodily injury) (secs. 211, 212, 223, et seq., Penal Code), but the rules governing breach of the peace (secs. 125 et seq., Penal Code). The former would have required the demonstration of a criminal offense or participation in one in each individual instance, whereas the rules governing breach of the peace allowed the mere *presence* at the scene of the crime as a crime,[16] in other words emphasized the collective element. Under these terms, it was allowable to punish someone as a criminal if all that were proven were his or her participation in riotous assembly, where an element of premeditation was present, that is, that the culprit was aware that acts of violence had been committed.[17] However, the definition of the offender was extended to the interpretation that the Polish defendants were accused of crimes against ethnic Germans committed at other locations where they were not present and of which they were totally unaware if the crimes "had been committed . . . as part of the bloody overall events," with no detailed examination of whether the culprit had approved of these "overall events" (psychological accessory to a crime).[18]

When deciding on the punishment, extensive use was also made of other regulations, since the possible punishments for breach of the peace (prison or hard labor) were insufficient for the desired atonement for such crimes; only the death penalty was judged suitable. For this reason, acts of violence by Poles against ethnic Germans were essentially regarded as aggravated armed breach of the peace,[19] to allow the application of the Decree on the Protection of the People and the State of February 28, 1933,[20] under which aggravated armed breach of the peace could also be punishable by death (sec. 5, par. 2). The concept of "armed" was interpreted not in the technical sense but by "analogy" to the interpretation of section 223a of the Penal Code (dangerous bodily violence), such that all "dangerous implements" similar to a weapon, "such as cudgels, staves, axes, etc.," were regarded as weapons under section 5, paragraph 2, of the decree of February 28, 1933.[21] Jurists noted with satisfaction that on the basis of this decree, the special courts issued "innumerable judgments" (death sentences) against Poles and that the courts were neither bothered by the extensive interpretation of the definition of a weapon nor by the fact that according the preamble to the decree of February 28, 1933, it had been issued "to prevent Communist acts of violence endangering the state,"[22] although the reinterpretation of the original meaning and objective of this regulation was also contentious according to the view prevailing at that time.[23] Indeed, an interpretation contradicting the purpose of this decree was absolutely vital for the National Socialist jurists, because without further ado, the need for revenge for the "September crimes" was declared to be the "entire objective" of the decree of February 28, 1933. This was the only solution that would allow the prosecution of "many Polish atrocities to be successful in accordance with the purpose and task of the law."[24]

In other fields, the special courts ruled similarly: based on section 7 of the Führer decree of October 8, 1939, they applied German penal law[25] partly directly, partly "analogously" in order to come to punishments as harsh as possible.[26]

For instance, the Decree on Extraordinary Broadcasting Measures of September 1, 1939,[27] which provided for hard labor for listening to foreign broadcasts, or the death penalty for particularly severe cases, and introduced in the Annexed Eastern Territories by a decree of April 29, 1940,[28] was applied even before it had come into force.[29] Without any formal implementation, the Explosives Law of June 9, 1884,[30] the Decree on the Protection of the People and the State of February 28, 1933,[31] mentioned above, the Law on the Prevention of Acts of Political Violence of April 4, 1933,[32] the Law to Guarantee the Public Order of October 13, 1933,[33] the Treachery Law of December 20, 1934,[34] and the Law against Economic Sabotage of December 1, 1936,[35] were all applied directly. Penal regulations already slanted toward a special law for particular groups "of danger to the community" or that were "alien," such as the Decree on Parasites upon the *Volk* of September 5, 1939,[36] the Decree against Violent Criminals of December 5, 1939,[37] and the Blood Protection Law of September 15, 1939[38] (this latter applied only to Germans),[39] were also applied directly, although they were implemented formally only with the decree of May 31, 1941.[40]

German penal law was also applied directly to cases in which "the former Polish penal law provided for a more lenient sentence or even exemption from punishment."[41] Under Polish law, for instance, indecency between men (sec. 174 Penal Code, old version), was punishable only if committed for pecuniary gain (sec. 207 of the Polish Penal Code of July 11, 1932); protection against seduction (sec. 182, Penal Code) was granted only to female minors under the age of 15 (sec. 203 of the Polish Penal Code); abortion on ethical grounds under medical supervision were generally permitted in cases of pregnancy resulting from sexual offenses (sec. 233 of the Polish Penal Code),[42] whereas under German law, the prohibition on abortion under section 218 of the Penal Code applied. In such cases, the harsher provisions of German law were, of course, applied.[43]

In contrast, the deviation from statutory law, that is, merely "analogous" application, was always regarded as imperative if required by the interests of the development of the Eastern Territories.[44] These interests demanded, for instance, that "non-German" defendants should also be punished *contra legem* even if this would have been prohibited under German penal law.

Examples: in the question of aggravation of penalty due to recidivism (theft, receiving stolen goods, fraud) requiring two sentences for the same type of crime "within Germany" (secs. 244, 261, 264, Penal Code), sentences not only within the territory of the German Reich, but also sentences by Polish courts in the recently annexed Annexed Eastern Territories *before* September 1, 1939, indeed even in the General Government, were taken into consideration.[45] Although this practice was implemented in all annexed territories (Austria, the Protectorate),[46] the legal substantiation there was that the former law continued in force in these territories; Poland was a special case, since the total downfall of the Polish legal system was assumed. Occasionally, sentences from part of eastern Poland, occupied by the Soviet Union between 1939 and 1941, were even recognized as domestic German sentences, to procure additional potential for harsher sentences in the "struggle against habitual Polish criminals."[47] In passing sentence on cases of body-snatching that had occurred at the beginning of the war, the courts applied neither the relevant regulation of section 168, Penal Code (removal of the dead: maximum sentence two years of prison), or section 246, Penal Code (misappropriation: maximum sentence five years of prison), to Polish defendants, because this "could not do justice to the extent of wrongdoing of such a deed." The remedy chosen was to use a peculiar solution via the analogous application of section 243, paragraph 1, number 1, Penal Code (aggravated theft in the form of removal of objects serving for religious services from buildings designated for religious services: maximum sentence ten years of hard labor), with the aim of thereby assuming a property offense characterized by the "object of the crime and the nature of its perpetration"[48] and thus achieving a harsher sentence, although there were no elements of such an offense whatsoever.

3. Decree on the Implementation of German Penal Law in the Annexed
    Eastern Territories, June 6, 1940

It was realized gradually that the practice of applying German law to meet
the political considerations of the moment could not be upheld in the long term.
For reasons of certainty of the law, statutory standardization of the law was imperative. This standardization was implemented in early summer 1940 by the
Decree on the Implementation of German Penal Law in the Annexed Eastern
Territories of June 6, 1940[49] (Implementing Decree). With this decree, the Ministry of Justice was able once again to prevail over the Party and the SS and police leadership, which had from the outset urged the decree of overt special law
for the Polish inhabitants of the Annexed Eastern Territories.[50]

In formal terms, the Implementing Decree did away with the previous lawless state and established the administration of justice on a firm basis, by introducing major elements of German substantive and procedural penal law with
clearly defined possibilities of appeal.[51] Although practitioners regarded this decree as merely the legalization of the previous practices in the application of the
law, in other words saw it as merely confirming the existing legal situation,[52] its
very existence embodied a certain security in the law compared with the earlier
situation.

The extent to which the earlier lack of a secure legal basis was perceived as
an uncertainty factor is demonstrated by the provision of section 7 of the Implementing Decree. Under this, the formally implemented substantive German penal law introduced by section 1, number 1, and sections 1–15 of the Juvenile
Court Law of February 16, 1923,[53] was also to be applied to crimes committed in
the Annexed Eastern Territories *before* the coming into force of the decree. Furthermore, all decisions and orders issued by German courts and criminal prosecution authorities after September 1, 1939, were declared valid retroactively, if
they corresponded to the Implementing Decree directly or analogously, an arrangement that would have been unnecessary if the principle of analogous application had in fact been taken seriously and anchored as firmly in practice[54] as
the relevant comments would have one believe.

However, this state of relative security in the law was eroded again by the
provision of section 2 of the Implementing Decree, which formally reaffirmed
the "racial policy" qualification, opening the floodgates to all forms of special
law. Section 2 stated that where a regulation coming into force was not to be applied directly, it should be applied "analogously," without describing the preconditions for this analogous application.

This concealed a host of risks. The principle of analogous application was also contained in section 2 of the Penal Code[55]—in this respect, section 2 of the Implementing Decree was superfluous, because the Penal Code applied in the Annexed Eastern Territories in any case—but relatively little use was made of it in the Altreich, because the idea of punishment without a legal standard was alien to the judiciary, and much more use was made of "extensive interpretation" (of the law).[56] In contrast, there were many fewer reservations in the Annexed Eastern Territories about abandoning the principle of *nulla poena sine lege*. Due to the initial lack of legal standards, the courts and prosecuting authorities were used to making decisions without any formal basis in law. For this reason, section 2 of the Implementing Decree offered an opportunity to apply and extend infinitely all regulations of Reich penal law, irrespective of whether they had been implemented in the Eastern Territories or not, so that the purpose of the Implementing Decree—to enable the conclusive regulation of prevailing penal law provisions, was not achieved.[57]

The following examples illustrate the "analogous," that is, extensive, interpretation of German penal law on the basis of section 2 of the Implementing Decree. The concept of "extraordinary circumstances due to the war" in section 4 of the Decree on Parasites upon the *Volk* of September 5, 1939,[58] under which any crime exploiting these "circumstances" could be punished by limited or lifelong hard labor or the death penalty, was interpreted so widely that practically every crime committed in the Annexed Eastern Territories could be punished under this regulation.[59] In the case of political comments by Poles, for which punishment under the Treachery Law of December 20, 1934,[60] could only be achieved "on thin grounds," the courts "were forced to adopt a far-reaching break from the statutory offenses";[61] the wearing or possession by Poles of German insignia containing National Socialist symbols was also consistently punished by the special courts in the Warthegau (or Wartheland) by the analogous application of the Treachery Law,[62] although these regulations (secs. 3, 5, par. 2) related only to the unauthorized wearing of insignia of the NSDAP, its subdivisions, or affiliated associations.

4. The "Special Penal Provisions for the Annexed Eastern Territories" in the Decree on the Implementation of German Penal Law in the Annexed Eastern Territories, June 6, 1940

The freeing of the administration of justice from the statutory offense demonstrated clear special-law tendencies in the treatment of "non-German" culprits, but the principle of special law was taken still further by explicit legal standardization. "Special Penal Provisions for the Annexed Eastern Territories" were included in the Implementing Decree (secs. 8–16). These special provisions, representing an all-too-obvious alien element in the Implementing Decree and included at the urging of the SS and police leadership,[63] punished all cases of Polish insubordination against the German administration with draconian sentences. These involved eight offenses: acts of violence against members of the Wehrmacht and the police, acts of violence against Germans "due to their membership of the German nation," damage to German facilities, calls for disobedience of German directives, arson, prohibited possession of firearms, and the relevant forms of complicity in such offenses; these offenses were punished by death as the standard penalty, or by prison in "less serious cases." These special provisions also legally abolished the principle of the unity of the legal system for the first time. Those affected were singled out only in the negative sense, since the provisions did not apply "to German state subjects, foreigners of German blood and subjects of the Protectorate of Bohemia and Moravia," or to nationals of neutral countries and privileged ethnic groups[64] (sec. 16 of the Implementing Decree); special law for the remaining groups, that is, Poles and Jews, was thus created de facto.

The further development of penal law in the Annexed Eastern Territories shows that once the concept of the unity of the legal system had been abandoned, principles of law and order no longer played a decisive role. The political situation between the rival power groups in the Reich and the Annexed Eastern Territories, as well as political expediency, that is, the "ethnic struggle" itself, decided the form and extent of the application of special law to "non-Germans" and the extent to which principles of Reich law were observed—if at all. The expedient solution of the analogous application of German law, with which special-law practices had until then been concealed, now lost the importance it had formerly enjoyed. As such, it was replaced by overt special law of a completely new species, completely divorced from general law, having nothing in common with the traditional principles of Reich law, and embodying the very ideal of the National Socialist concepts of the treatment of "non-German" inhabitants of the "Greater German Reich."

5. The Decree on the Administration of Penal Justice against Poles and Jews (Decree on Penal Law for Poles), December 4, 1941

The departure from the twin-track Reich law–special law approach and the trend toward overt special law reflects the decisive political power struggle between the Ministry of Justice and the SS and police leadership, which had never abandoned its goal of taking complete control of the administration of justice for Poles and Jews. There could be no doubt from the outset about the outcome of this power struggle, already described in detail elsewhere,[65] because the Ministry of Justice, under the weak leadership of Gürtner and then Schlegelberger, had few resources to counter the pressure of the *Reichsführer*-SS and chief of the German police and the chief of the SIPO and the SD, supported by the Party Chancellery[66] and, in part, also by the administration heads in the Annexed Eastern Territories. Compared with the rigid, resolutely advocated ideas of Himmler, Heydrich, and Bormann, the arguments of the Ministry of Justice, fixated on issues of jurisdiction and void of any content, against overt special law for Poles and Jews (no cause for this "had emerged to date"; but there were "no reservations about establishing supplementary special regulations on the *basis* of German law directed exclusively against Poles, should such a need arise")[67] necessarily appeared as a tiresome legal dispute that simply could not be taken seriously by the power politicians in Berlin. The result of the contest between the Ministry of Justice and the police and Party leadership, lasting almost a year and half, was the Decree on the Administration of Penal Justice for Poles and Jews,[68] issued on December 4, 1941 (the Decree on Penal Law for Poles), which came into force on January 1, 1942, and corresponded almost identically to the draft elaborated jointly by the Ministry of Justice and the presidents of courts of appeal and chief public prosecutors in the Annexed Eastern Territories.[69]

a. Basic Principles of the Decree on Penal Law for Poles and
    Its Justification

The decree "took substantial account of the suggestions of the Führer's deputy" and created both substantive and procedural "total special law."[70] As stated in the official justification in the Ministry of Justice draft, the special provisions still to be discussed "guaranteed the greatest degree of deterrence" and "clearly expressed the political inequality between Germans on the one hand and Poles on the other."[71] However, the Ministry of Justice had only been able to rescue its jurisdiction at a cost of giving up all constitutional and regulative principles in the face of the pressure by Bormann, Heydrich, and Himmler to seize for themselves the administration of penal justice for "non-Germans": the Decree on Penal Law for Poles rightly enjoyed a reputation as a "shrewd move" in the "dismantling of the legal system in the Third Reich."[72] The overt purpose of the decree was not the maintenance of order, but deterrence and annihilation. There was no precedent that could be compared with the purpose of this decree.[73] As in the case of all special-law provisions in the Annexed Eastern Territories, it blatantly violated not only the principles of international law;[74] its formulations, structure, categorization of offenses, and contents also contravened the internal German penal law of the day, in particular the principle of *nulla poena sine lege*, the principle of penal law based on the requirement of personal guilt, the principles of criminal offenses and range of punishments, and many more.

The decree retained no more than "trace elements" of Reich law, such that dispensing with the specific implementation of German penal law, Poles and Jews could be punished under German penal law directly or analogously (if the crime "deserves punishment according to the fundamental principle of a German penal law," "based on the raisons d'état existing in the Annexed Eastern Territories") (clause 1, no. 2). However, this clause was only subordinate; that is, it applied only to cases where the subsequent special provisions on punishment were insufficient. Because these special provisions were construed without limit and could cover all disapproved acts by "non-Germans," it was therefore a completely superfluous safeguard and should be understood only as a symbolic residue of the unity of the legal system that had been abandoned.

Apart from these traces of Reich law, the Decree on Penal Law for Poles was the first and most intimidating example of overt special law for "non-Germans" (Poles and Jews) and thus an absolute novelty in modern legal history. To a certain extent, this involved *duplicate special law*, because—as was explained above—Poles (and Jews) were already being punished under general Reich law more harshly than Germans, normally with the maximum sentence, as a matter of principle. The Decree on Penal Law for Poles created additional new offenses and opened the way for further discrimination alongside the general, already extremely harsh, punishment practice. The Decree on Penal Law for Poles thus represented not a form of regulation (albeit extraordinarily harsh) of living conditions for the purpose of the maintenance of order, at least in formal terms, but turned out to be an instrument of political struggle to annihilate the racial and political opponent. The Decree on Penal Law for Poles was a law of political expediency that, as lauded by the Kattowitz chief public prosecutor, "[contained] neither a philological nor a judicial, but only a criminal view of the means to the end: intimidation and neutralization."[75] In its formalities, such as the form of its promulgation—it was issued as a decree by the Ministerial Council for the Defense of the Reich and, significantly, did not bear the signature of the responsible minister of justice—its overt description as special law (Decree on the Administration of Penal Justice for Poles and Jews); its superficial form, which did not contain the standard subdivision into paragraphs (legal provisions) but was structured in clauses; the disregard for all formal requirements; and its brutal language,[76] it was evident that all this "law" had in common with the concept of law was the name. This applied all the more to the contents of the decree. Poles and Jews not only had a lower legal status but—as had been demanded by doctrine and practice since 1933—were now actually placed outside any legal system whatsoever (they had completely lost all rights).

The "ethical" justification allowed for punishment was simply a breach of the "general duty of obedience" to the German occupying powers established in clause 1, paragraph 1, of the decree. The purpose of intimidation and neutralization was met by the sentences, which generally provided for the death penalty as the *standard sentence*, permitting a prison sentence only for the exception of "less serious cases," which always required specific justification.[77] A new form of sentence was introduced, specifically aimed at "intimidation" and "the strictest atonement": "statutory prison camp"—replacing a prison sentence—and "strict prison camp"—replacing hard labor,[78] to be enforced in special prison camps.[79] These punishments, too, were subject to the provisions of a general clause, but as a matter of principle, all crimes could be punished by the death penalty, "even where the law does not provide for the death penalty, if the crime is evidence of a particularly base character or is particularly serious for other reasons" (clause 3, par. 2, sentence 2).[80] The intimidatory purpose of the decree was fulfilled further by its geographical and personal purview; in terms of substantive law, it also covered Poles living in the Altreich (e.g., Polish "foreign workers"),[81] and in terms of the individuals it affected, it covered all Poles ("protected nationals and stateless Poles") not entered in the German Ethnic Classification List (clauses 14, 15).[82] This extensive trend was further equaled by a retroactive clause that declared that the decree was also applicable to crimes committed before it had come into force.

The only element of this decree conforming to judicial standards was that the courts (special courts; in less serious cases the district courts) were responsible for sentencing for crimes committed by Poles and Jews. But even their jurisdiction was perforated and cast into doubt by the authorization (discussed later) of the *Reichsstatthalter* (higher presidents) to employ police courts martial (clause 13, Decree on Penal Law for Poles).

The establishment of an exclusively special law was managed by a technical legal process that corresponded in full to the wishes of the SS and police leadership and those of the Party leadership and may be regarded as a model for future special-law provisions concerning the treatment of "non-Germans." The special provisions for Poles and Jews contained in the Penal Law Implementing Decree of June 6, 1940,[83] were still linked to the possibility of appeal in legally defined cases, and definitions of offenses were restricted to a certain degree, but the substance of the Decree on Penal Law for Poles was that all limitations on the definitions of offenses were abolished, and the individual provisions were made subject to vague general clauses, which allowed unlimited extension of application in terms of both substantive and procedural law, as well as in sentencing.[84] The main focus was no longer the individual provisions but rather these general clauses; the purpose of its application was no longer the subsumption of crimes under legal regulations but rather the inclusion of "all punishable behavior" by Poles;[85] it was the "point of crystallization of substantive penal law for Poles."[86] Even the Ministry of Justice had no illusions when it denied penal law for Poles the character of "law" in the traditional sense and described it as "overtly political law,"[87] "a political law" to "suppress" the Poles ("political pacification of the East"), or as serving to "protect the German nation" "against attacks by the Polish people disturbing law and order."[88] In view of this unique case of exclusively "political law," the questions arose whether and how the judicial administration and the political leadership could prepare the courts in the Annexed Eastern Territories for the issuing of this decree and convince them of its justification in the legal sense, given that the Penal Law Implementing Decree of June 6, 1940, issued only one and a half years previously, had been regarded as perfectly satisfactory both by the Ministry of Justice itself[89] and by practitioners.[90] Despite all rudiments of special penal law (in the "Special Penal Provisions") in the Implementing Decree and in legal practice,[91] "only" the principle of unequal treatment had hitherto been practiced, which allocated a lower legal status to Poles and Jews but still treated them in principle as falling within the German legal system.[92]

The justification of the total deprivation of all rights for the "non-Germans" was a thorny issue even for the "hard core" in the Ministry of Justice and the judicial authorities in the Annexed Eastern Territories. The policy was now to abandon the principle of the analogous application of German law, which was a comfortable legal formula allowing deviation from the statutory standards at any time in the interests of (racial) political administration of justice and had relieved the courts of the tricky question of explicit special law for "non-Germans." What reasons could now be given for the replacement of the principle of analogous inequality by the concept of the essential *disfranchisement* of Poles and Jews? Previous theory and practice provided no examples or pointers, nothing that could be used to establish a link to the new concept.

As a result of this, neither theory nor practice was able to deal with this new form of special law in any way whatsoever, far less fit it into any form of jurisprudential framework. With observations on the legal situation applying until the end of 1941 a rare enough event in the literature,[93] once the Decree on Penal Law for Poles had been issued, with the exception of the official explanations penned by State Secretary Freisler,[94] such observations more or less disappeared completely.[95] The purpose of the previous treatments in the literature was to prepare the courts for the future tightening up of penal law,[96] but despite their strict anti-Polish line, they implicitly stuck to the principle of the unity of the legal system and the framework drawn up by the Implementing Decree of June 6, 1940. Even for those jurists who were more than willing to contribute to the realization of the "ethnic struggle" in the East, it must have been as good as impossible to justify with any plausibility the leap from the status of persons with *fewer* rights to the status of *zero* rights for "non-Germans" under the former legal categories. State Secretary Freisler undoubtedly expressed the opinion of all legal practitioners when, at a conference, he observed that "this penal law for Poles" was not suitable "for public scientific discussion for all-too-obvious reasons."[97] His explanations on the penal law for Poles, which in his own words was "only" the consolidation of the political character of the penal law, something that had always been evident in any case and which "did not conflict at all . . . with justice,"[98] dispensed right from the outset with justifying the penal law for Poles using conventional legal arguments; instead, he attempted to tread completely new ground on the basis of exclusively political and racial concepts.

In concrete terms, this involved nothing less than creating a new theory of penal law for "non-Germans." The slogan of the political "requirements of the ethnic struggle," previously serving to justify the arbitrary deviation from Reich law ("analogous" application in *individual cases*), had to be replaced by other slogans and concepts, branding the Poles in general as enemies of the German people and placing them in *general terms* outside the law. In his famous speech "Penal Law and Non-Germans in the Reich," given shortly before the decree was issued, he had hinted at the underlying themes of the new concept,[99] which represented a radical break with all traditional concepts of penal law. The penal law for Poles, according to Freisler in 1942 in a speech to the court of appeal presidents and chief state prosecutors,[100] had nothing in common with traditional penal law. It was a law "that could be pinned to the door of [each] Bürgermeister's office for the Poles." It was not an "internal German penal law," not a "penal law for offenders," but an "authoritarian form of penal law." The principles governing character and personality did not apply here. For this reason, the "interpretation and establishment of individual provisions of the penal law for Poles were not desirable," to allow flexibility to be retained.[101] Indeed, no rigid interpretation was necessary, since clause 1, paragraph 3, contained "the wonderful provision" covering all "behavior hostile to Germany."[102] This allowed the punishment of actions that were essentially exempt from punishment: the very reason for the existence of the clause.[103]

424 *Völkisch* Inequality in the Field of Justice: The Annexed Eastern Territories

But simply establishing a negative divorce of the penal law for Poles from Reich penal law was not enough; a positive definition of the purpose of the decree was now needed. The magic formula invented for this was the slogan of "the threat to the community by the nature of the Polish people," probably coined by Freisler, which became the basis of the new penal law for "non-Germans."[104]

This slogan, based on the concept of the National Socialist community[105] and linked to the established doctrine of the "threat to the community" of particular groups of criminals or crimes,[106] was, however, difficult to justify with regard to the Poles, because the traditional political or ethnic friend-enemy pattern could not be applied to them easily. Attempts at ethnic psychological definitions, deriving the Polish people's "threat to the community" from their national character, which was said to be inherently "treacherous," "cunning," and "inherently pathological,"[107] demonstrate only the helplessness of theory in the face of the phenomenon of overt special law for millions of "non-German" inhabitants of the Annexed Eastern Territories.

The situation was different with the superficially solid political arguments, on which the thesis of the "threat to the community by the nature of the Polish people" was based. These arguments related to the Polish violence against ethnic Germans at the beginning of the war ("September murders," "Polish atrocities"), in which an estimated five thousand to six thousand people had died, but the number was simply multiplied by propaganda that unremittingly fanned the flames of hatred.[108] The courts, bowing to this propaganda of revenge—either under pressure or at their own initiative—were therefore sure of the support not only of the political leadership but also of sections of the population in the Eastern Territories when they raised to the status of their leading principle the fight against this "threat to the community."[109] Not only the direct culprits but also the political leadership, the intelligentsia, indeed the entire Polish people were held responsible for this violence,[110] providing a pretext for "objectifying" the concept of the "threat to the community," that is, extending it to an entire nation. It was no longer individual Poles who were now a "threat to the community" but the Polish people in its entirety, whose character had shown it to be "unworthy of Europe" and thus also "unworthy of protection under the law."[111]

The major consequences of the thesis of the "threat to the community by the nature of the Polish people" were therefore the people's essential disfranchisement and an objectively collective approach to all Polish crimes that excluded any consideration for individual aspects. In short, this meant that any appraisal of Polish crimes was undertaken exclusively under political aspects dominated by police requirements, that is, based on the principle of "protection against ethnic dangers" from an entire people of potential enemies of the state.

As a result, any "unlawful" acts by a member of such a people necessarily appeared as an essentially political crime against the German people. In concrete terms, all principles of German penal law, such as the concepts of guilt, complicity, or assessment of penalty, lost their validity. The "application of the principles of German penal law" to Poles and Jews in the Eastern Territories thus signified rather a dangerous slide toward the "threatened punishments and classifications of fundamental German offenses," which was not only condemned but also regarded as "mistaken," even as "an error in law."[112]

b.   Details of the Decree on Penal Law for Poles

The provisions of the Decree on Penal Law for Poles were more or less identical to the "Special Penal Provisions" already included in the Penal Law Implementing Decree of June 6, 1940,[113] under pressure from the Party and the police; only the offense of premeditated arson was dropped, now being punished by Reich law (clause 1, par. 4, no. 2).[114] The main feature that distinguished the decree was that the individual offenses were now subject to limitless general clauses, through which—totally independent of these individual offenses—each and any behavior, indeed any statement of opinion by the "non-Germans," was declared to be "hostile to Germany" and could treated as a capital offense; these clauses far exceeded the general clauses being used increasingly in Reich law. There were two of these provisions in substantive law: the first part of clause 1, paragraph 1, of the decree established a general duty of obedience for Poles and Jews to all German establishments, by stipulating the following: "Poles and Jews in the Annexed Eastern Territories must behave in accordance with German laws and the directives issued for them by the German authorities. They must refrain from doing anything that would be detrimental to the sovereignty of the German Reich and the standing of the German people."

Of much greater importance was the infamous regulation ("wonderful provision")[115] in clause 1, paragraph 3, which made the application of the individual provisions essentially superfluous and was the best example of a "legal" basis in the new criminal classification of penal law for Poles: "They [Poles and Jews] shall be punished by death, or with imprisonment in less serious cases, if they manifest a hostile attitude to Germany by spiteful acts or agitation, in particular by making remarks hostile to Germany or removing or damaging public notices by German authorities or departments, or if by any other form of behavior, they disparage or damage the reputation or the well-being of the German Reich or the German people."

All sentences of Poles and Jews in the Annexed Eastern Territories under

penal law were essentially based on this type of misconduct by "non-Germans."
It either was used to replace the provisions of Reich law that should basically
have been applied,[116] so as to avoid at least the appearance of a community in
law uniting "non-Germans" and Germans, or else it was listed as an omnibus
offense alongside the relevant individual offenses.[117] The Reich penal laws supposed to be applied to Poles and Jews under clause 2 of the decree were reinterpreted so that they became no more than an expression of the "general duty of
obedience" for Poles under the Decree on Penal Law for Poles; they underwent
"in this respect a special classification, in that not the scope of the *elements of an
offense*, but the degree of failure to comply with the duty of obedience became
the subject . . . of the punishment." In other words, it was not the "crime as such"
that was punished, but the "defiance of the duty of obedience" to the German
sovereign power "expressed in it."[118] On the basis of this "authoritarian classification of offenses," the practice tended increasingly away from subsuming
crimes by Poles under German penal law and toward defining them from the
outset as specific "crimes by Poles" within the meaning of clause 1, paragraph
3,[119] even in the case of minor offenses. The extent of this development becomes
clear only when one remembers that under the Decree on Penal Law for Poles,
the *standard punishment* was the death penalty, with imprisonment for "less serious cases" only. With this development toward a special penal law with its own
classification of offenses, all conventional criteria for the form of perpetration
and guilt of a crime were altered; the division of offenses into the three categories of felonies, misdemeanors, and offenses disappeared for crimes by Poles and
Jews. Now, there was only a single offense of "violation," that was always treated
as a crime from 1943 on and reported as such in the Reich criminal statistics.[120]
The following examples illustrate this transformation of penal law into "objective offense-related penal law."

The statutory periods for crimes by Poles and Jews disappeared, and the
concurrence rules (secs. 73, 74, Penal Code)[121] and complicity provisions were
no longer applied in practice. With the fulfillment of individual elements of an
offense being replaced by the degree of "violation of the duty of obedience" as
the decisive factor, offenses by Poles and Jews that should have been treated as
abetment were punished as an accomplished crime.[122] It was reported from Upper Silesia that preparatory acts exempt from punishment, when carried out by
Poles and Jews, were treated as a breach of the "duty of obedience," thereby abolishing the boundary to punishable attempts; both acts were punished as an accomplished crime.[123] There were prosecutions not only of acts by Poles and Jews
that would have been punishable under German law, but also of any behavior

that did not match the political line of the "ethnic struggle" without being sanctioned under penal law.

In particular, the "crime" of sexual intercourse between Poles and Germans was a thorn in the flesh of those in power and received draconian punishment for "behavior hostile to Germany," because "sexual intercourse [by a Pole] with a German woman represented the "violation of the honor of the entire German people," and the "Pole thereby disparaged the reputation and well-being of the German people."[124] Punishable in practice was also "any form of Polish propaganda," or even "serious and repeated disciplinary offenses by a Polish convict,"[125] indeed any behavior that was allegedly directed against "German interests." The Ministry of Justice proposed legitimizing these attempts by practitioners to "create law" by creating special offense for these infinitely stretchable "crimes,"[126] a suggestion that was not followed up solely because of the war. Further attempts at tightening penal law for Poles not provided for under German penal law were decreed by the Ministry of Justice, such as the prohibition on the application of German penal law for juvenile offenders in the penal law for Poles (because "there is no place for the educational concept in penal law for Poles"),[127] with juvenile Polish offenders being treated under the penal law for adults.

c.   Plans by the Ministry of Justice to Extend the Decree on Penal Law
     for Poles

For the radical "ethnic warriors" in the Ministry of Justice and the Annexed Eastern Territories, however, this total special penal law still did not go far enough. In the Ministry of Justice, plans were hatched with the agreement of the senior administrative officials in the Annexed Eastern Territories to amend the Decree on Penal Law for Poles to extend still further its already very wide purview; although these plans were never realized, they do show the extent to which the bureaucracy had made the principle of "*völkisch* inequality" its own.[128] Of particular significance in this respect was the project for a "decree on the penal liability of complicity in punishable acts by Poles and Jews," the justification for which was that it would provide an "additional political tool in the ethnic struggle."[129]

The proposed decree addressed how the "complicity" of Germans in crimes committed by Poles and Jews, who were subject to the Decree on Penal Law for Poles, could be qualified in legal terms, since the principles of the special "crimes committed by Poles" and punishment categories (prison camp) could not be transferred to forms of complicity of Germans under the principle of "accessoriness."

This involved finding legal arrangements for behavior by Germans that was not in itself punishable but was "undesirable" in terms of racial policy.[130] These arrangements, the lack of which had been termed a "painful, even unbearable gap" by practitioners, were aimed at criminalizing the numerous cases of behavior by Germans that was "friendly toward the Poles" (providing material help for Poles, paying them good wages, etc.)—a situation that caused a good deal of hand-wringing by racially aware "judicial leaders"[131]—as "violations of moral racial conduct."[132]

However, no agreement was reached on the decree drafted by the Ministry of Justice in 1940, because it was impossible to reach a consensus about the principles under which punishment was to be made (under the analogous provision of sec. 2, Penal Code; or clause 1, par. 3, of the Decree on Penal Law for Poles; or under a new offense to be created). A new draft by the ministry dated August 11, 1942, which created a new offense, "the undermining of ethnic work by Germans,"[133] based on the Decree on Penal Law for Poles, met with resistance by the senior administrative officials in the Annexed Eastern Territories, who raised objections to the terms of the draft ("complicity") and to the linking of criminal offenses for Germans with special penal law for Poles; they believed that the new offense should be worded much more widely and cover all ethnically prejudicial behavior.[134] In turn, the *Reichsstatthalter* in the Warthegau raised his objections to this, presenting his own draft decree,[135] maintaining that the version proposed by the appeal court presidents and the Posen (Poznań) chief public prosecutor went much too far.[136] Shortly thereafter, however, he came around to accepting the rejected version,[137] since in the meantime the Gestapo had intervened in the cases of "ethnically prejudicial" behavior by Germans and, because of the lack of sufficient legal grounds, took the "offenders" into protective custody instead of handing them over to the judicial authorities.

Faced with initiatives by the Gestapo to continue this practice,[138] the *Reichsstatthalter* stuck to his position that the "will of the national community would be expressed more visibly in court sentences than in summary sentences imposed by the police."[139] However, neither the Ministry of Justice nor the drafts emanating from Posen were able to prevail over the practices of the Gestapo, which from mid-1942 on not had only usurped prosecutions against "non-Germans" almost completely but had also increasingly extended its grip on Germans.[140] In March 1943, the Ministry of Justice let it be known that none of the drafts would be pursued any further.[141] A counterproposal by Arthur Greiser, seeking to issue a penal regulation at least as a decree by the *Reichsstatthalter* for the Warthegau,[142] was unsuccessful because the Reich minister of the interior refused his consent. Discussions on an amendment to the Treachery Law of December 1, 1934, in which the relevant penal provision on ethnically prejudicial behavior by Germans was to be included,[143] achieved no concrete result, either because of the war or because of obstruction by the SS and police, in the face of which the central administration retreated. The situation thus remained as it was, with all support by Germans for Poles being increasingly regarded as political offenses—unless they were punishable under German law—and dealt with by the Gestapo.

II. The Status of "Non-German" Individuals in Procedural Law

1. Special Courts as an Instrument for Combating "Non-German" Crime

The key element of the special-law system, the abolition of statutory offenses in favor of vague general clauses, is also evident in procedural law, although the erosion of the rigid, formal provisions was more difficult and proceeded at a slower pace than in substantive law, with traditional judicial attitudes also playing a role. But the starting point here, which was the same as with substantive law, namely the dominance of political goals of the "suppression" of the "Polish people" ("ethnic struggle") and the task of the judicial authorities to contribute to this "suppression," excluded from the outset any application *ipso jure* of general Reich German judicatory law and criminal procedure law.[1] The result was that ordinary jurisdiction in the Annexed Eastern Territories was never of more than minor importance.

Special jurisdiction was another matter. With its very name suggesting its role, it reached true fruition in its application against "non-Germans." Designed from the outset to punish all offenses by Poles and Jews against the "German development structure," that is, against German interests in the widest sense, special courts had already been established in the first days of the war and were sitting as the only civil courts long before the regular judicial authorities started working (around summer 1940).[2] Special jurisdiction was of lesser importance in the first months of the German civil administration, with the unleashed terror of the special-operations groups and the flying courts-martial of the Security Police, as well as the drumhead courts of the local "self-defense" corps preventing any form of appreciable administration of penal justice for the local population.[3] But the special courts had been assigned responsibility for the politically explosive field of prosecuting Polish attacks on (ethnic) Germans at the start of the war (the "September crimes"),[4] and in line with the slogan of the "striking power" of special jurisdiction, they had started on this task while the war against Poland was still under way.[5] The status of the special courts was only cemented after the implementation of German penal law in June 1940.[6] As in the German homeland, they became a permanent institution, differing, however, in their large number[7] and in the selection of staff[8] and—as State Secretary Schlegelberger in the Ministry of Justice noted approvingly—in their "particularly quick and effective procedures," such that they developed into the almost exclusive instrument of the "struggle against all Polish and Jewish crime."[9]

a.   Jurisdiction

This development was the result not only of selective penal law and personnel policy but also of the far-reaching jurisdiction of the special courts. Although their jurisdiction in the Altreich was still separate from the jurisdiction of the general courts, despite the substantial increase in responsibilities allocated to them over time,[10] the special courts in the Annexed Eastern Territories received sole jurisdiction.

The decree of September 5, 1939,[11] by the commander in chief of the army on special courts in occupied Polish territory had implemented Reich law jurisdiction in principle,[12] but at the same time it had stipulated that *all* criminal cases could be brought before the special court if the public prosecutors regarded "sentencing by the special court as necessary for particular reasons" (sec. 2).[13] The phrase "for particular reasons" was without significance in the first few months of civil administration, because the special courts were in any case the sole civil courts and therefore enjoyed sole jurisdiction. Appropriate measures by the local military administration also explicitly stipulated the comprehensive jurisdiction of the special courts.[14]

However, the scope of special-law jurisdiction began to become blurred when the regular judicial authorities started working, because their former sole jurisdiction collided with the responsibilities of the regular judicial authorities. This question of the scope of the responsibilities of the special courts, a matter for dispute between the Ministry of Justice and the Reich Ministry of the Interior,[15] was clarified to a certain degree by the introduction of German penal law with the decree of June 6, 1940.[16] Although the decree did not introduce explicitly the responsibilities of the special courts defined under Reich law (the Jurisdiction Decree of February 21, 1940),[17] there was general agreement that with the Reich Code of Criminal Procedure applying in its entirety under this decree, the decree of February 21, 1940, had been implemented concurrently and the original general jurisdiction of the special courts had thus been restricted.[18] In terms of the treatment of "non-Germans" under special law, however, this restriction existed more or less on paper only, since under the Jurisdiction Decree—in a similar way to the military decree of September 5, 1939—*all* offenses could be tried before a special court if they were particularly "serious" or "reprehensible," or if this was demanded by "public outcry" or a "risk to public security and order."[19] That any offense by a "non-German" could be subsumed under one of these categories without further ado, thus providing a starting point for the monopolization of criminal jurisdiction against "non-Germans" in the special courts, is self-evident. Confirmation of this monopolization intention is shown in the Decree on Penal Law for Poles of December 4, 1941,[20] which concentrated jurisdiction for offenses by Poles and Jews almost exclusively in the hands of the special courts. Although offenses by Poles and Jews could still be sentenced by district courts, the public prosecutors could bring indictments before the special courts "in all matters" at their own discretion (clause 5, pars. 1, 2) without having the necessary conditions for this defined in any way whatsoever. The wheel thus turned full circle, restoring the situation that had reigned at the time of the legal vacuum in the Annexed Eastern Territories. The special courts had once again become the most important instrument for the treatment of "non-German criminals" under special law.

b. Proceedings

The same approach of making the special courts the sole instruments of the prosecution of "non-Germans" by abolishing all ties to general penal law is also evidenced by the special-court proceedings.

Although the general Reich law procedure rules of the Decree on Special Courts of March 21, 1933,[21] originally applied under the aforementioned decree of the military governor of September 5, 1939, there was even there a departure, in that the proceedings were not referred to as regular court proceedings.[22] This excluded any appeal in a regular court against the ruling of a special court. There is little evidence that "non-German" offenders made any use whatsoever of the sole remaining possibility of review by reopening the proceedings;[23] the authorities were, in any case, in favor of restricting legal remedies for "non-Germans," because it did not appear "practicable" to allow "Poles to flood the criminal prosecution authorities and courts, overburdened as they are, with usually unsubstantiated appeals and petitions."[24]

A further departure from general procedural law to the detriment of "non-Germans" is represented by the decree by the commander in chief of the army for Polish territory of October 1, 1939,[25] under which the prohibition on retroactive effect was abolished and the compulsory prosecution of criminal offenses (sec. 152, par. 2, Code of Criminal Procedure) set aside,[26] allowing the optional sentencing of all offenses committed before September 1, 1939, in occupied Polish territory. Under this decree, exclusively motivated by political factors (i.e., to serve as the basis for punishing crimes by Poles against Germans shortly before and during the outbreak of the war), crimes by Poles against Germans (the "September crimes") were prosecuted but not crimes by Germans against Poles, because these involved the "protection of the German nation."[27]

The authorities were able to apply this nullification of the compulsory prosecution of criminal offenses all the more, as the subsequent Penal Law Implementing Decree of June 6, 1940, had also explicitly annulled the compulsory prosecution of criminal offenses (art. 1, clause 2, no. 1). The granting of privileges to German offenders was generally considered when crimes were committed against Poles in which it was "expedient" to ignore any punishment "in a properly understood sense of the well-being of the German nation," because punishment "would excite the Poles, cause satisfaction, or even awaken or strengthen their spirit of resistance."[28]

One of the decisive privileges granted to Germans was that politically explosive crimes, such as the numerous acts of violence by Germans against Poles committed during the reign of the military authorities, came under a general amnesty and were thus tacitly sanctioned under an unpublished secret decree by the Führer and Reich Chancellor of October 4, 1939.[29] Under this decree, which was to be seen as an act of revenge for the perceived Polish excesses at the beginning of the war, crimes "committed between September 1 and October 4, 1939, in the Annexed Eastern Territories because of rage at the atrocities committed by the Poles" were not to be prosecuted. Final and absolute sentences were to be remitted, pending criminal proceedings to be discontinued.[30] Hitler, however, had more far-reaching plans: by means of a general amnesty, for instance on April 20, 1940 (Hitler's birthday), *all* crimes committed by Germans "in the former Polish territories" were to receive amnesty. This would have meant the collapse of the regular administration of justice and the official sanctioning of all crimes committed against Poles. The Armed Forces High Command, which was given the task of reviewing this proposal and, together with the Ministry of Justice, providing professional support, came out against a general amnesty, supporting only the "mild treatment" of some types of cases. This would be possible because the opportunity principle applied in general to criminal prosecutions in the Eastern Territories; that is, expediency would be the key factor. This convinced Hitler to scrap the planned amnesty.[31]

The opportunity principle further discriminated against Poles in that the authorities did not recognize any compulsory prosecution of criminal offenses *among* Poles and rejected any intervention if "this would serve only for the protection of the Polish people." As the Posen (Poznań) chief public prosecutor explained, it could not be the "function of the German state prosecutors and judges" "to assume the protection of the Polish people by applying German penal law."[32]

Apart from these special provisions, the relevant provisions of Reich law applied to special-court proceedings,[33] with the period of relative stability that started with the coming into force of the Decree on Penal Law for Poles of December 4, 1941,[34] now coming to an end.

2. Procedural Discrimination against Poles and Jews under the Decree on Penal Law for Poles

With the Decree on Penal Law for Poles bringing "unequal treatment on racial grounds" to perfection, it was no longer necessary to maintain the general law of criminal procedure as a facade for "non-Germans." The complete severance from general law reached its peak in procedural law. As in the Implementing Decree, the abolition of the principle of mandatory prosecution—already the reigning practice of criminal prosecution—was also set out in this decree; under clause 4, the public prosecutor was to prosecute "crimes by Poles and Jews that he believed it would be in the public interest to punish." This provided the decisive starting point for a practice of discriminatory criminal prosecution, since it was clear that for crimes by Poles and Jews (including offenses for which an application for prosecution was required), there was always a public interest in criminal prosecution,[35] whereas crimes committed by Germans against Poles and Jews were to be prosecuted and punished more leniently as a matter of principle.[36]

As was the case in substantive law, clause 12 of the Decree on Penal Law for Poles replaced the previous rules of criminal procedure with a boundless general clause and also appealed for an overt breach of the law: "The court and the public prosecutor shall organize the proceedings on the basis of the German law of criminal procedure in accordance with their own best judgment. They may deviate from the provisions of the Judicature Code and the Reich Law of Criminal Procedure in cases where this would be expedient for the rapid and firm enforcement of the proceedings."

Despite assertions to the contrary, this far-reaching enabling provision, this ability "to enforce quick proceedings . . . unhampered by formalities,"[37] placed great difficulties in the way of the courts, because—as during the time of the legal vacuum—it was now necessary to develop original new forms of court proceedings.[38] Together with the aforenamed general clause, however, the Decree on Penal Law for Poles also contained a number of special provisions aimed at safeguarding the policy of the courts in the general disfranchisement of Poles and Jews. For instance, they lost all guarantees they had previously enjoyed while Reich procedural law still applied (art. 1, no. 2, Penal Law Implementing Decree of June 6, 1940); arrest and temporary detention were now permissible at all times if there was "strong suspicion" (and in committal proceedings, even without an arrest warrant signed by a judge [clause 8, Decree on Penal Law for Poles]), whereas section 112 of the Code of Criminal Procedure required specific reasons for arrest. Sentences in criminal proceedings against Poles and Jews could be enforced without delay. Although this had always been the rule for sentences by the special courts,[39] it was an innovation for the courts of first instance. In contrast, the criminal prosecution authorities retained wide-ranging possibilities of appealing against court rulings (clauses 6, 10).

The remaining rights of Polish and Jewish individuals under the law of criminal procedure were also eliminated in full. The right of private and accessory prosecution, already suspended under the Implementing Decree of June 6, 1940,[40] was fully abolished, as was the right to reject judges on the grounds of partiality. The competence of Poles and Jews to take an oath was also abolished (clauses 7, 9, 11); this was adhered to despite all the resulting difficulties in trials.[41] As with almost all special-law provisions, this was merely a legalization of existing practice. Even before the Decree on Penal Law for Poles had come into force, an internal administrative instruction had established that Poles should not be examined as witnesses in court proceedings wherever possible, "as long as such an examination was not imperative"; at the very least, they should not be put on oath, "to prevent a violation of ethnic policy guidelines."[42] The abolition of the oath for Poles applied—at least in the Warthegau—in civil proceedings as well, because, according to the Posen Court of Appeal, "the arrogance of the Poles, their tendency to exaggerate, and their lack of love for the truth give rise to particular prudence when assessing statements made by Polish witnesses."[43] Furthermore, the appearance of Poles and Jews before the court was to be prevented if at all possible. A supplementary decree of January 31, 1942,[44] to the Decree on Penal Law for Poles empowered the courts to have Poles and Jews examined as witnesses by an authorized representative or by a request to another judge. An attempt was also made to prevent the appearance in court of sworn Polish interpreters ("impossible procedure"), particularly if Germans and Poles were on opposing sides. "Rightly or wrongly," complained the president of the Hohensalza

(Inowrocław) Administrative District to the *Reichsstatthalter* in Posen, Germans would transfer their distrust of the court interpreter to the entire court, "giving rise to the impression that Poles were sitting in judgment over Germans."[45]

The opportunities for Poles and Jews to defend themselves in court, still permitted under general procedural law even in the special courts, were either mostly abolished or completely eliminated. Although the Decree on Penal Law for Poles itself did not contain any provision for this, elimination was equally effective because of pressure from above, with the president of the Königsberg Court of Appeal, for instance, resolutely disapproving of the right of Poles to elect defense by German lawyers in his own district ("impossible situation");[46] in addition, a decree was circulated by the Ministry of Justice on May 21, 1942,[47] stating that any assumption by German lawyers of the elective defense of Poles would contradict the purpose of the Decree on Penal Law for Poles. This should be "prohibited by professional ethics," which was indeed what happened promptly—at least in East Prussia (and probably in other districts as well)—by the local bar association.[48]

The ban on elective defense for Poles, which was a particularly hard blow to lawyers in small towns, was supported to the full by the local judicial leadership on the grounds of absolute separation of Germans and Poles ("it is unworthy of any German to act for a Pole against payment"), and—as reported by the president of the Königsberg Court of Appeal—it was supposedly welcomed "warmly" by the judges and public prosecutors (because, perhaps, it was possible to finish the proceedings more quickly without any legal representation?).

The justification supplied was that it would damage "the standing of the Germans in the eyes of the Poles if one jurist [lawyer] were to plead for a lenient sentence, but the other jurist [judge] were to pass a harsh sentence."[49] German lawyers who still acted as elective defense lawyers for Poles were to be reported to the responsible appeal court presidents and could expect political difficulties.[50] According to a recommendation by the president of the Danzig (Gdańsk) Court of Appeal to his subordinate authorities, the courts "should" generally reject German lawyers' defending Poles as elective counsel,[51] although there was no legal basis for this. The ability of Jews and Poles to allow themselves to be represented by Polish lawyers was also eliminated almost completely, because Polish lawyers ("advocates") enjoyed only an "advisory status" in the Eastern Territories and could be admitted as defense lawyers only in cases of particular political reliability.[52] Finally, the right of court-assigned defense, which section 32 of the Jurisdiction Decree of February 21, 1940, stipulated as mandatory in certain cases ("necessary defense"), was also eliminated substantially; an administrative instruction by the Ministry of Justice in May 1942 had generally prohibited court-assigned defense of Poles and Jews to remove from them any opportunity of defense.[53] This being the case, there could certainly be no legal right for defendants to any defense in the penal law for Poles, especially since "free procedural organization" applied in any case. Under this concept, the appointment of a defense lawyer was at the discretion of the court; it should be obvious that for Polish defendants, most of whom were sentenced to death or long prison sentences, a court-appointed defense lawyer was hardly ever deemed necessary, as was openly admitted by the judicial administration.[54]

The political leadership strove to tighten special law even further, but such efforts were not realized because this would have represented an all-too-blatant violation of the principle of the courts' power to pass sentence, to which the judicial authorities continued to adhere, at least formally. Deserving mention is the attempt by the *Reichsstatthalter* of the Warthegau to transfer in full to the public prosecutors the authority to issue summary punishment orders (a right that had already been exercised by the courts, in part very arbitrarily),[55] because he claimed that it was unfortunate that "differing opinions between the judge and the public prosecutor" "were being voiced in front of Poles on the record, as it were."[56]

The subjection of the Poles to absolute special penal law was finally completed by the authorities' taking care to ensure that a purely territorial justice was developed, on which no Reich instance could have any influence. Because the public prosecutors could bring charges at their own discretion, they always prosecuted punishable actions by Poles and Jews so that the ruling by the last court of appeal was always a court in the Eastern Territories, that is, a special court or a court of first instance, because their rulings were unappealable, or could be reviewed in the final instance only by the court of appeal responsible (sec. 121, Judicature Code).[57] For this reason, no prosecutions at the criminal divisions of the courts of appeal, which would in any event have been possible for political criminal proceedings (secs. 5 and 6 of the decree of February 21, 1940),[58] were recorded (at least in the early stages) because the final instance in this case would have been the Reich Supreme Court.[59] Along the same lines as the creation of territorial justice, the Reich minister of justice delegated the prerogative of mercy for Polish and Jewish cases in the first instance to the *Reichsstatthalter* of the Warthegau in response to his constant urging, and later—under political pressure—to the *Reichsstatthalter* in Danzig–West Prussia as well.[60] This exclusion of Reich courts of appeal completed the alienation of the "non-Germans" from general law, delivered them to the territorial justice of the local administration, and put them at the mercy of the principles of the "ethnic struggle."

III. The Elaboration of Special Law by the Courts: Overview of Sentencing Practice

Because of the lack of relevant regulations or the fact that such regulations as existed were more of the nature of umbrella clauses, court rulings were of supreme importance for the elaboration of special law in the Annexed Eastern Territories. In contrast to the Altreich, where, as described above, there were still clearly defined offenses despite the trend toward weakening the statutes at large, there was still a well-established literature, and court rulings had not lost their significance, in the Annexed Eastern Territories the primacy of the "ethnic struggle" meant that rulings in individual instances were completely dependent in the attitude of the individual public prosecutors and judges—despite a large number of mostly ineffective guidelines and recommendations from above[1]— and were thus, as was expressed at the time, a "question of the personalities of the individuals concerned."[2] This applied in particular during the initial phase of the legal vacuum, in which the courts had taken the place of the legislators and had initiated the special treatment of the "non-German" population, true to the political maxim of the "ethnic struggle."[3] Later on, court rulings continued to retain their dominant position, because even after the implementation of German penal law in the Annexed Eastern Territories, the principle of unequal treatment for ethnic policy reasons, concealed under the concept of "analogous application," remained in force.[4] Finally, the Decree on Penal Law for Poles consisted largely of extremely elastic general clauses requiring concretization from case to case.

However, because of the lack of documentation or the inaccessibility of much of it and the meager statements in the literature,[5] it is not possible to establish with any degree of certainty the use made by the courts of these opportunities that were open to them. It can be shown that there were certain tendencies in court rulings depending on the type of court and the area in which sentence was passed, and to this extent they can be said to produce a fairly accurate picture of the way in which special law was administered in the Annexed Eastern Territories.

By combining these trends, it is possible to establish that court rulings against Poles and Jews were very harsh, at least according to official documents, as had always been demanded and emphasized with acclaim by the political leadership and the judicial administration.[6] However, this should be seen in the light of the fact that court rulings against German state subjects and ethnic Germans were already draconian. In the case of "non-German" defendants, the harshness knew no bounds. This development therefore reflects penal practice in the Alt-reich, but with the harshness of penal practice with respect to both Germans and "non-Germans" many times more severe. The following principles can be identified with regard to "non-Germans": as a rule, Poles and Jews were pun-ished more harshly than Germans, first as revenge for the Polish "atrocities," but primarily because of the "inherent reason" that Poles "were only tolerated in this old land of German civilization" and were thus "required to obey German order particularly strictly."[7] The special courts in particular did their utmost to en-force the "ethnic struggle," that is, the treatment under special law of Poles and Jews. A wide variety of reasons played a role in this—the administrative control of the judicial system and the National Socialist image of the judge as a "vassal of the Führer,"[8] the pressure of the judicial bureaucrats and of the propaganda, the conformity of the judicial officials with the general Polish policy, the ambi-tion of influential judges and public prosecutors, the motivation of the individ-ual "to perform development work in the German East,"[9] and an appropriate personnel policy ("experience in the ethnic struggle" as a qualification for the courts and the top posts in the judicial administration)[10]—all of which ensured the severe administration of justice. The judicial system thus demonstrated that it too was in a position to "resort to drastic measures" to meet the "needs of eth-nic policy," which meant not only the harshest possible sentencing but also the quickest possible (punishment "on the hoof").[11]

These "drastic measures" were possible only because many judges and pub-lic prosecutors were prepared to adopt to a large extent the police-state concepts of the "ethnic struggle," "protection against ethnic dangers" and the legal in-equality of Poles and Jews as a matter of principle. For instance, there was noth-ing preventing them from assuming a less serious case (punishable by imprison-ment) and not a standard case (for which the death sentence was always to be imposed) when applying the Decree on Penal Law for Poles, in order to rescue the accused from execution. Instead of this, however, the special courts recog-nized a rapidly decreasing number of such less serious cases. The heads of the courts of appeal played a key role in this draconian penal practice; even under the standards of the day, they frequently showed far-reaching "sympathy" for the urgings of the leadership, and none of them are known to have raised serious objections to the "legal situation" in the Annexed Eastern Territories, a situation that was a mockery of any concept of law. On the contrary, they did much more than was necessary to secure the favor of the judicial leadership and the Party:[12] the general policy of penal law for Poles was received neither with criticism nor with silence, but rather frequently with effusive praise and approval ("thankful task," "weapon in the struggle" against "the subverters of German defense," etc.);[13] only when it came to details were there some complaints. If the reports by senior officials to the ministry contained complaints, they almost always involved complaints about the *general* situation: the growing difficulties with staff, the lack of loyalty to official policies and the poor quality of the staff,[14] the widespread dissatisfaction in the judicial administration with accommodation and pay,[15] and, from 1942 on, in particular, the intrusion by the police into the jurisdiction of the judicial authorities.[16]

Any attempt to outline the trends in court rulings in the Annexed Eastern Territories will uncover a variety of distinguishing criteria, such as the legal right under attack, the individual branches of the judiciary, the districts or provinces concerned, or the development of special law over time. The greatest distinction is seen in the type and severity of the legal right under attack. Of course, criminal prosecutions concentrated on offenses directed in any way whatsoever against the German occupying powers and their interests, and these received draconian punishments. This applied in particular to acts of violence by Poles against Germans in the first days of the war, for which—as has already been discussed in detail—the death sentence was imposed almost without exception.[17] For offenses that—in the opinion of the day—did not affect German interests, for instance crimes by Poles against Poles, the policy was reversed; no criminal prosecution was pursued, since the bureaucrats at the time believed that it was not the task of the judicial system to "punish" violations of the law among Poles and Jews, that is, not to apply penal law at all, as this would only serve "the protection of the Polish people" or the "safeguarding of Polish interests."[18] For instance, State Secretary Freisler had issued an instruction that proceedings should be quashed in cases where Poles had injured other Poles,[19] the aim of this being to leave the "non-Germans" to their own devices in the area of penal law and thus promote their criminality.

With regard to the sentencing practice of the individual branches of the judiciary, it should be remembered that criminal offenses by "non-Germans" were brought before the regular courts only if these involved cases of a relatively minor nature. As a rule, the regular courts operated more carefully, and compared with the practice of the special courts, they displayed a degree of relative restraint, although one is forced to refer to "leniency" when prison sentences approaching the maximum range of penalties were imposed.[20] The vast majority of criminal offenses committed by "non-Germans" were brought before the special courts, which therefore dominated the sentencing practice to a very large extent. In contrast to the regular courts, these special courts—in particular those in the Warthegau[21] and the Zichenau Special Court (responsible for the former Polish areas incorporated into the province of East Prussia)—exercised right from the outset a previously unknown degree of deterrent and retaliatory justice; the harshness of their sentences and the continuous publicity given to them[22] more than met the intimidatory target demanded by the political leadership and the judicial administration.[23] In particular since the coming into force of the Decree on Penal Law for Poles, their rulings had become "consistently severe" and their proceedings "sufficiently harsh and quick" to satisfy all the demands of the policy of ethnic and racial repression, according to the chief public prosecutor in Kattowitz (Katowice).[24]

The speed with which death sentences were executed also contributed substantially to the deterrent effect; as a rule, there were only six to eight days between the death warrant and the execution itself,[25] and often no more than a couple of days, even—as reported from the Warthegau—frequently no more than twenty-four hours.[26] The shortcomings established by the Ministry of Justice—that the prison officers in the Warthegau could not be expected to carry out hangings because of their advanced age[27]—do not seem to have had much of an affect on the enforcement of death sentences, since the guillotine was also used for executions. Efforts to achieve the *immediate* enforcement of death sentences failed only because of the lack of executioners, a job for which numerous applications were received from all over the Reich.[28] To multiply the deterrent effect, executions were often carried out in public; there must be some doubt, however, as to whether these achieved their desired effect, because such measures either reinforced resistance or the population became "used" to them.[29]

The harsh sentences meant that the special courts could be sure of the undivided approval of the judicial administration[30] and the political leadership, whereas the regular courts often aroused displeasure, particularly in the ranks of the Party, since they "deliberately favored" the Poles.[31]

Reports on sentencing practice from Danzig–West Prussia are typical of the situation at the time. According to these, *Reichsstatthalter* Albert Forster, who had a "positive attitude to all questions of justice," had explicitly noted that the special courts had also won the "unrestricted approval" of the political leadership, whereas the sentences passed by the regular courts (courts of first instance, criminal divisions) had initially been "unsatisfactory" and had therefore been criticized by the political leadership because the standards they had set had been too lenient.[32]

Only after the Decree on Penal Law for Poles had been issued was the president of the Danzig (Gdańsk) Court of Appeal able to report to the Ministry of Justice that "no more complaints" had been voiced about excessively lenient judgements.[33] Similarly severe court rulings were reported from the other areas in the Annexed Eastern Territories.[34]

It is not possible to establish any uniform policy from the trends in court rulings in the individual phases of the development of special law, because both before and after the formal implementation of Reich penal law, all penal provisions were always subject to the proviso of no more than "analogous" application if this was necessary for political reasons; the result was large variations. Nevertheless, the rulings by some of the special courts were still relatively restrained, because of the extremely high sentences for crimes by Poles.[35] The death penalty, as the standard sentence for offenses committed by "non-Germans" against members or facilities of the German administration under the Penal Law Implementing Decree of June 6, 1940, should most certainly not be regarded as "an adequate regulator," as claimed by the literature,[36] because before mid-1941 (with the exception of sentences for crimes of violence against Germans),[37] death sentences, although frequent, were not yet the rule.[38] However, long prison sentences had always been imposed on Poles right from the outset;[39] these can only be regarded as lenient when compared with the situation reigning before the implementation of the Decree on Penal Law for Poles. Occasional attempts were made to redress the situation in the face of particularly harsh special penal law provisions, either by proposing their amendment or by interpretation,[40] but these attempts were inconsistent with the very severe rulings handed down by the Reich Supreme Court against Polish defendants.[41]

However, the courts often pursued a policy of more severe punishments by extensive interpretation of the law even before the Decree on Penal Law for Poles came into force. This applied in particular to the Decree against Violent Criminals of December 5, 1939,[42] which punished serious crimes of violence involving the use of weapons or other dangerous instruments by death, and which served as a "substitute regulation" to punish "acts of violence" by Poles against Germans before the Decree on Penal Law for Poles came into force.[43] There were no reservations about interpreting this decree arbitrarily by regarding the bodily force used by the Polish offenders as a "dangerous instrument," so as to be able to impose the death sentence in all situations. Politically undesirable statements by Poles, "whose nature made them tend toward rumor-mongering" and which would have been punishable under the Treachery Law of December 20, 1934,[44] were prosecuted as an "insult to the German people" by analogy with section 134a of the Penal Code, under which only insults to the Reich or the Wehrmacht were actually punishable. Offenses committed by Poles while under the influence of alcohol were not subject to the mitigating circumstances allowed by section 330 of the Penal Code; to the contrary, drunkenness was regarded as aggravating the offense, since this expressed the "true inner attitude" of the accused.[45]

This trend in court rulings, which had increasingly eliminated the opportunities for interpretation under clearly defined criteria, reached its peak after the Decree on Penal Law for Poles had come into force. The courts were now subject to growing pressure from the political and judicial leadership to take "drastic" and extremely severe action.

The severity of court rulings under the application of the Decree on Penal Law for Poles is shown by the following sentencing practice: whereas a prison sentence was frequent before the Decree on Penal Law for Poles, the courts imposed strict-regime prison camp sentences in many cases once the decree was in force, because such a sentence corresponded roughly to hard labor. Later, however, the criminal prosecution authorities, at least in the Warthegau, were instructed to apply for strict-regime prison camp sentence in exceptional cases only, to prevent mass imprisonment; instead, standard prison camp sentences were to be applied for. In cases in which the maximum sentence (ten years) for standard prison camp would probably be exceeded, "regular" application for the death penalty would be suitable.[46]

Essentially, because the authorities believed that the core of the Decree on Penal Law for Poles was no longer punishment of the "crime as such," but rather of "the disobedience expressed in the crime,"[47] all otherwise unpunishable behavior could be criminalized and subsumed under the general clause of "behavior hostile to Germany" (clause 1, par. 3, Decree on Penal Law for Poles).[48] For instance, statements in private letters written by Poles regarded as "hostile to Germany," in themselves exempt from punishment, resulted in criminal prosecution, but sometimes with the sole intention of rescuing the accused from the Gestapo.[49] "Behavior hostile to Germany" also included all expressions of Polish national sentiment, such as the singing of Polish songs or the national anthem, as well as contact with prisoners of war, which—particularly when women were involved—was punished by long penitentiary sentences.[50] Even the most minor insubordination by the most humble of individuals (farm laborers, messengers, etc.) to their German masters was punished with great severity, by death or long prison sentences;[51] for violations of "wartime penal law," such as black-marketeering,[52] theft of food, illegal slaughter of animals,[53] forging ration cards, and the like, all of which were to be brought before the special courts under an order issued by the minister of justice on September 25, 1940,[54] and which accounted for a substantial number of cases sentenced by these courts,[55] the "most severe punishments" were also imposed;[56] in particular the numerous death sentences for illegal slaughter of animals (crimes against the Decree on the War Economy) were "praised to the skies" by the political leadership, as reported by the Danzig chief public prosecutor.[57]

The draconian punishment practice did not relate only to special penal law alone, but also to all offenses by "non-Germans" against "German interests," even if sentence was passed under Reich law or in conjunction with the Decree on Penal Law for Poles after its issue.[58] Offenses against the provisions of labor law, such as unauthorized absence from the place of work (breach of employment contract) also received harsh punishment (sentences of between nine months' imprisonment and a fine of twenty reichsmarks).[59] However, Germans too were sentenced to death for violations of regulations (e.g., concerning the Winter Relief Fund) aimed at strengthening the National Socialist sense of community.[60]

Whether the aim of deterrence was ever actually achieved must remain doubtful. In the Eastern Territories, the crime rate was high from the outset because of the numerous crimes committed in connection with the "resettlements" ("evacuation thefts").[61] As the war continued, further growth in economic crime was recorded despite increasingly severe punishments, as was reported in East Prussia; there was also a rise in sexual offenses committed by Poles.[62] An increase in crime in the annexed territories of Upper Silesia was also reported,[63] either because offenses such as the illegal slaughter of animals, previously dealt with as administrative penalty offenses, were now brought before the special courts,[64] or because there was a genuine increase in the number of crimes. The crime rate did not start to drop until 1943, perhaps a result of the draconian punishment practice of the judiciary but more likely because the latter was increasingly replaced by the police in the prosecution of crimes by "non-Germans."[65]

Crimes by Germans in the Annexed Eastern Territories grew disproportionately to their percentage of the population, particularly as regards property offenses, economic crimes, and crimes involving bodily harm. According to reports by the judicial authorities, this was put down to the high number of criminal elements coming from the Altreich (because they were unable to earn a living there any more)[66] and to "incitement" by Poles to commit crimes,[67] as well as their behavior as members of the "master race" ("outrageous behavior by Reich Germans to Poles and Jewesses."[68] The loosening of the compulsory prosecution of criminal offenses by Germans, and the acknowledgment of a *right to beat* Poles,[69] regarded as a "charter" to commit all kinds of crimes,[70] must also have contributed to the high crime rates.[71]

Considerable differences can be identified with regard to the severity of court ruling practice in the individual areas of the Annexed Eastern Territories. Although only a few relevant documents still exist that indicate how similar crimes were punished in the case of Polish and German perpetrators,[72] such breakdowns are possible with reasonable accuracy for death sentences, because corresponding execution lists have been preserved. As the death sentence was the standard sentence for crimes by "non-German" criminals after the Decree on

Penal Law for Poles had come into force, it can also be used to draw general conclusions regarding trends in court rulings. The harshest anti-Polish line was pursued by the judicial authorities in the Zichenau Administrative District in East Prussia (Zichenau Special Court), followed by the "model district" of the Wartheland, regarded as the most important area of the Eastern territories because of its size and political significance. According to the execution lists of the Ministry of Justice, the number of death sentences as a proportion of the population of the administrative district was highest at the Zichenau Special Court headed by district court president Dr. Alfred Funk, a favorite of Gauleiter Erich Koch, followed again by the Warthegau.[73] A clear break is evident between the time before and after the Decree on Penal Law for Poles came into force. Even in the Warthegau, "only" 45 death sentences had been carried out by December 1941,[74] and the prisons of Posen (Poznań) held a total of 172 persons condemned to death before February 1942.[75] Once the Decree on Penal Law for Poles came into force, the number of death sentences rose steeply. In the *Reichsgau* Wartheland, 800 death sentences were executed in 1942 (December 24, 1941–December 24, 1942),[76] and 72 in the Zichenau Administrative District in the first half of 1942 (January 1–June 15, 1942), with a sharp rise to 103 in the second half of the year.[77]

The draconian punishment practice of the Zichenau Special Court is particularly clear if compared with that of the Königsberg Special Court. In the first half of 1942, the Königsberg court passed 645 sentences, including 56 death sentences, corresponding to a ratio of around 11.5:1. In the same period, the Zichenau Special Court passed around 310 sentences, including 72 death sentences,[78] a ratio of 4.3:1.

The *Reichsgau* Danzig–West Prussia proved to be relatively "moderate," with "only" 154 executed death sentences passed in 1942;[79] no figures are available for the Kattowitz Appeal Court district for 1942.

After 1942, the figures started to drop, but they were still very high. In the Warthegau, 508 death sentences were carried out in 1943 (December 25, 1942–December 23, 1943), 188 in the Zichenau Administrative District, 70 in Danzig–West Prussia, and around 97 in the Kattowitz Appeal Court district.[80] In 1944 the death sentence was passed in the Warthegau in 291 trials, with 6 of the accused being pardoned; 188 death sentences against Poles and Jews were executed; in the Zichenau Administrative District, at least 69 death sentences were executed; in Danzig–West Prussia (by October 1944), 53; and in the Kattowitz Administrative District, around 14.[81]

Overall, 1,129 death sentences (against Poles and Jews) were therefore documented as having been executed in the Annexed Eastern Territories in 1942. If one remembers that the vast majority of death sentences in the Annexed Eastern Territories were imposed on Poles, and that only a very few sentences in the Annexed Eastern Territories were ever reprieved,[82] a total number of around 1,100–1,200 executed death sentences against Poles (and Jews) would be a realistic figure for 1942.

The official figures from both the Eastern Territories and the Ministry of Justice[83] show considerably lower numbers; furthermore, they relate only to the death sentences *passed* by the courts, not those actually carried out. For this reason, these figures cannot be compared with the number of executions stated above. Any comparison with the Ministry of Justice figures in the *Führerinformationen* is also impossible, because this number relates to the total death sentences passed (on Poles and Germans).[84]

In 1943 and 1944, the number of death sentences fell. For 1943, the execution lists number around 863, and for 1944 around 324 executed death sentences.[85]

The deterrence practiced in the Annexed Eastern Territories becomes all the more clear if it is compared with the overall sentencing practice in the Altreich. According to the (confidential) Reich crime statistics,[86] 63,786 persons (i.e., Poles and Jews) were sentenced under the Decree on Penal Law for Poles, including 930 death sentences, whereas 341,540 unappealable sentences were passed on Germans and foreigners (apart from Poles and Jews in the Eastern Territories), of which 1,061 were sentenced to death. This shows that where the Decree on Penal Law for Poles applied (principally in the Annexed Eastern Territories), the ratio was around 1 death sentence per 68 sentences, but around 1 per 356 in the Reich, so that the rate of death sentences for Poles and Jews solely under the Decree on Penal Law for Poles was about *five times higher* than for Germans, not to speak of the death sentences for Poles and Jews passed on the basis of *other* penal law provisions, these not being stated separately in the crime statistics.

However, it must have been the case that the sentencing practice of the courts frequently still did not fulfill the desires of the political leadership and the local judicial administration for the implementation of the Decree on Penal Law for Poles, because the situation reports of the appeal court presidents and the chief public prosecutors very frequently mention criticism of judgments by political officials and—despite all the assertions about the "penal law for Poles having proven itself"[87]—complaints about the lack of appreciation of many judges for the "ethnic policy situation" in the Annexed Eastern Territories. For instance, the Königsberg Appeal Court president complained in his situation report dated May 4, 1942, that the "young, receptive judges" were at the front, but it was "very difficult" for the older judges "to divorce themselves from traditional views," "despite their good intentions[!]."[88]

The penal law for Poles, originally welcomed with enthusiasm by the senior judicial officials, was still obviously not being applied radically enough for many of them; this shows that even "National Socialist justice" could not be turned into limitless arbitrariness. Whether through their own awareness or for other reasons, many were not at all satisfied with the Decree on Penal Law for Poles or its contents. As early as the beginning of 1941, for instance, the president of the Danzig Court of Appeal demanded further training for judges and public prosecutors so that they could learn the "special duties of the administration of justice in the Annexed Eastern Territories," after Party offices had openly scorned the "incompetent judiciary."[89] The Posen chief public prosecutor, who had always supported a hard line in the penal law for Poles, wrote to the Ministry of Justice in 1942 that public prosecutors were of the opinion that despite the guidelines and instructions of the chief public prosecutor, the Decree on Penal Law for Poles had not met expectations "in full" and that court rulings differed from district to district, a development that could only be redressed in part by uniform control. The success of the Decree on Penal Law for Poles depended on the individual court, it was claimed, and it was evident that attitudes toward "the Polish people and the demands of the administration of penal justice in wartime" differed considerably. The courts had not "exhausted the entire potential of the Decree on Penal Law for Poles."[90]

That differing opinions on the treatment of "non-Germans" under penal law held sway even in the extremely anti-Polish Warthegau (or Wartheland) is also shown by the fact that there were reservations about the decree's minimum prison sentence of three months' prison camp because it was too high for petty offenses; that some local courts of first instance had therefore passed sentences of less than three months was sharply rebuked by the Posen chief public prosecutor.[91]

These differences in sentencing practice became increasingly irrelevant, because since around mid-1942, the police steadily usurped the administration of penal justice against "non-Germans," particular for petty and less serious crimes; by 1943 it had largely eliminated the judiciary from the criminal prosecution of "non-Germans."

EXCURSUS
Encroachment upon the Jurisdiction of the Judiciary: Extension of Police Jurisdiction for Criminal Matters

1.   Efforts by the Police to Create a Police "Penal Law for Alien Peoples"

The preceding examination of the sentencing practice of the courts in the Annexed Eastern Territories could lead the reader to conclude that even the most

minor offense by Poles or Jews was prosecuted by the judicial authorities. However, the activities of the judicial authorities accounted for only a part of the administration of penal law against Poles and Jews; from the outset, major elements
of criminal prosecution had been usurped by the police, and over the years—at
the latest, from 1943 onward—the judicial authorities were increasingly pushed
into a background role, in the end being excluded almost totally. As explained
above, the goal of the SS and police leadership right from the start had been to
enforce a total special law for "non-Germans": the SS and police alone, not the
judicial authorities, were to have total control of its administration. In contrast to
the Reich territory, where the jurisdiction of the courts was still anchored relatively firmly, with the result that there had been no opportunity of enforcing in
the Reich a uniform policy on the criminal prosecution of Poles and Jews in the
sense of the radical course outlined above, the efforts of the police in the Annexed Eastern Territories met with great success for several reasons.

The first of these was that the traditional administration and the traditional
administrative principles, still oriented in the Third Reich to the principle guaranteeing the general liability of the law in the formal sense, either were weak or
had been forced completely into the background: as has been shown, the Annexed Eastern Territories were the domain and testing ground of the "ethnic
struggle," to which the principles of Reich law were not applied.

Secondly, the considerable, indeed dominating influence of the NSDAP
contributed to the weakening and undermining of the traditional administration: embodied in the Gauleiter, the local Gau Office for Ethnic Policy, and the
NSDAP Gau Legal Office, the Party cooperated closely with the SS and police
leadership; the aim of both organizations was to avoid any definition whatsoever
in (penal) law of regulations for "non-Germans." Under the authoritative influence of Bormann (as head of the Office of the Deputy Führer), the central Party
leadership fully supported these efforts by the SS and police leadership in both
the Altreich and the Annexed Eastern Territories. With his appointment as head
of the Party Chancellery and the conferment on him of the powers of a Reich
minister by a Führer decree of August 20, 1942,[1] Bormann's additional status as
member of the Reich government and the Ministerial Council for the Defense
of the Reich gave him a direct influence on government legislation, as he was
now to be included as a "participating Reich minister" in all legislative work.[2]

The third and most important reason why the police were able to assert their
authority in the Annexed Eastern Territories much sooner than in the Reich,
however, was because the police were free from constitutional or administrative
"scruples," regarded legal statutes as no more than a technical means to enforce
their own goals, and knew what they wanted from the outset, whereas the Reich

administration had no concept of its own. What the police had in mind was the creation of a "special penal law" for all "non-Germans" in the East (Jews, Poles, Russians, etc.) under the exclusive jurisdiction of the SS and police, which the regular judicial authorities would be unable to interfere with; in other words, the creation of its own *police jurisdiction* for "non-Germans." Particularly the Annexed Eastern Territories, in which the population was more than 90 percent "non-German" and "inferior," were the ideal testing ground for developing for the first time in the history of the Third Reich a police "penal law for alien peoples," in which statutory regulations were regarded as being of minor importance and the existing legal tradition was perverted, indeed eliminated almost in full.

Given this interpretation of a general claim of police jurisdiction for all offenses committed by "non-Germans," any jurisdiction of the judicial authorities over criminal offenses committed by "non-Germans" would necessarily appear from the beginning as unwarranted interference that demanded vigorous resistance, not only on matters of principle, but also because the application of any judicial standards in the criminal prosecution of "non-Germans" must be avoided at all costs. As the police saw things, exclusively ethnic aspects enforced by the police, judging the subject "non-Germans" as either being useful to the German national community (for labor) or as "antisocial parasites" who should be "eradicated," should apply to such cases. The extent to which the ideas of the police about a "special penal law" for "non-Germans" were governed by the aspect of the "eradication of antisocial parasites" is shown, for example, by the views of Himmler, who told Minister of Justice Franz Gürtner, after the execution by the police of a mentally deficient Polish woman, that the execution was justified because the national community demanded that "antisocial parasites . . . be eliminated . . . irrespective of any legal impossibility of guilt."[3] In the eyes of the police, therefore, any application of German penal legislation to the "non-Germans," even if it had been revised or recreated to meet National Socialist goals, was bound to be viewed as a hindrance. This claimed general jurisdiction provides a clue to the conflicts with the Ministry of Justice, which steered a zigzag course in the face of the resolute demands of the police, as does the fact that all concessions by the judicial authorities resulted only in an increasing number of new demands by the police and the Party. For the police leadership, concessions on any points, however important they might be, right up to the abandonment of all principles of German legal tradition, meant nothing more than a cure for the symptoms, not the elimination of the root of all evil: the independent judiciary. What they really wanted to do was eliminate the judiciary as an institution. And in the Annexed Eastern Territories, they succeeded in doing so to a great extent.

The specific notions of the police and Party leadership about a special penal law for Poles and Jews were diametrically opposed to the efforts of the Ministry of Justice to adhere to Reich penal law, albeit including special regulations for "non-Germans" where this proved necessary.[4] Both agreed that the application of German penal law did not meet "the special conditions in the East" and hampered the freedom of action of the German authorities unnecessarily. As Bormann explained to the head of the Reich Chancellery in this context, the "Führer had recently repeated that the implementation of Reich law in the Annexed Eastern Territories would mean making work difficult, even impossible, for the men charged with the task of reorganization." The Führer expected only one report from his Gauleiters, namely that their district was purely German. It was for him "an irrelevance if at some time in the future it is established that the methods for gaining this territory had been unsightly or legally objectionable."[5]

Therefore, the Party and the police, who had never accepted the introduction of German penal law by the decree of June 6, 1940,[6] believed that a few umbrella clauses, which should cover "all irregular conduct if at all possible," that is, not merely criminal offenses by "non-Germans," plus a vaguely worded code of procedure allowing a "quick and effective trial," would suffice for Poles and Jews.[7] As Bormann continued to the head of the Reich Chancellery, "the regulations created in 1870 to protect the accused or the defendant, which have still not been eliminated today [meaning the Reich Code of Criminal Procedure] should be abandoned as far as possible."[8] Punishments "must be governed clearly by the criteria of intimidation and the political goals applying to the Eastern Territories," whereby the "imperviousness of the Poles to prison sentences" should be taken into account. As punishments for Poles and Jews, the NSDAP demanded not only the death sentence but also the formal introduction of corporal punishment, already firmly established as a custom, as well as "other measures with, perhaps, more of a police-like character," meaning certainly the imposition of protective custody, that is, committal to a concentration camp or a "work training camp."[9] These endeavors were largely realized in the Decree on Penal Law for Poles of December 4, 1941.

2.   Developments before the Coming into Force of the Decree on Penal Law for Poles: Arbitrary Acts and Police Court-Martial Jurisdiction

However, the police did not act in accordance with these principles of an exclusively police jurisdiction only after the effective date of the Decree on Penal Law for Poles. Corresponding to their practice of plunging single-mindedly into legal vacuums or regarding existing regulations as nonexistent, the SS and police were able to do as they pleased in the Annexed Eastern Territories right from the outset, in the same way as they were to do later in other parts of occupied Eastern Europe. The expansion of police power was made considerably easier by the convoluted legal situation described above, especially in the first phase of the legal vacuum when the German civil administration had to be built up at considerable effort. However, the arbitrary measures of the SS and the police, which raged from fall 1939 until spring 1940, had nothing to do at first with "criminal prosecution" in the sense meant by the police at the time.

The acts of "unbridled terror,"[10] characterized by innumerable "blind programs of action" (such as the mass seizures and deportations),[11] but above all by the arbitrary justice of the SS and the police, the special-duty detachments of the Security Police,[12] and the local self-defense groups,[13] consisted not only of raging "spontaneous" actions. To a much larger extent they involved well-planned (blacklist) executions (frequently in public to serve as intimidation) of hostages and politically undesirable individuals, to which some ten thousand Poles and Jews fell victim, not including the victims in camps and prisons.[14] With the effective cooperation of the judicial leadership, ways were found to conceal these murders (e.g., dispensing with the statutory requirement of official publication of notices in daily newspapers for the purpose of announcing the death of "missing" persons).[15]

The first "courtlike" institutions of the police (all they had in common with the concept of a court was their name) appeared in the courts-martial of the Security Police, which came into action as soon as "scheduled" and selective executions took place that did not represent individual acts of terror or revenge. Their first appearance was in the form of "mobile" courts-martial, which assembled at the headquarters of the relevant task forces of the Security Police or police battalions as required and which themselves decided the form of their proceedings. In line with the policy of practicing the "ethnic struggle" by means of violence, murder, and terror, this procedure scorned all legal concepts, as evidenced by the few remaining sources (there was generally no examination of witnesses; death sentences were passed summarily); only the personal details of the accused and the names of the members of the court-martial were recorded, and the facts of the case and the charges were no more than summarized, if they appeared at all.[16] Crimes worthy of the death penalty were sometimes no more than alleged "ill repute," membership in Polish organizations, or simply belonging to the "leading intellectual class."[17] These courts-martial, thus, perceived only the concerns of the Security Police, leaving aside any procedural standard, even in a minimal sense; they were nothing but a mere instrument of a random terror, directed mainly against members of the Polish intelligentsia. In addition, they were already at this early stage assuming the function of the courts to deal with "normal" criminal matters, such as property offenses, "utterances" hostile to Germany,[18] arson, manslaughter,[19] and so forth, evidence that the police had pursued from the outset the goal of eliminating the judicial authorities completely from the criminal punishment of "non-Germans";[20] at the least, the judicial institutions were subjected to massive pressure—even by the lowest-level police authorities—to obtain judgments convenient to the police.[21]

Even on the basis of National Socialist legal opinion, there was no regulatory basis for the establishment and activities of these police courts-martial.

In terms of statutory law, there was only the decree by the commander in chief of the army of September 21, 1939, which also assigned the punishment for illegal possession of weapons (for which the courts-martial of the Wehrmacht had originally been responsible) to the police courts-martial (consisting of members of a police battalion or police regiment or of the Gestapo) but had expressly limited their jurisdiction to these matters.[22] Recourse to the comprehensive powers described above by the courts-martial of the Security Police and the regular police was therefore based not on this decree but rather on the infamous decree of the head of the SIPO and the SD on the Principles of Internal State Security during the War of September 3, 1939,[23] which in turn derived from a verbal order given by Hitler to the *Reichsführer*-SS and chief of the German police to "preserve security in the territory of the Reich by all means,"[24] which also included "cleansing the territory of the Reich of Jews and Poles."[25]

This decree, under which action was to be taken with "ruthless harshness and severity" against not only "subversive endeavors" but also all criminal offenses, which were to be treated as "sabotage of the solidarity and fighting spirit of the German people," was obviously now understood by the police leadership to be authorization for mass executions without trial and for the establishment of special courts; this was tolerated and approved of by Hitler, although he notified the Reich judicial administration officially that he had given no general instruction for mass executions but could not dispense with the need for executions in individual instances.[26]

The extent to which the courts-martial lacked any formal basis is shown in particular by the fact that although the courts-martial of the police battalions punished "normal" offenses (e.g., theft, receiving stolen goods), the bases cited (wrongly) were the aforementioned decree of September 21, 1939,[27] covering the possession of weapons, and in addition a "special instruction" of the *Reichsführer*-SS and chief of the German police that was not defined in greater detail (it is possible that this decree is identical to the decree of September 3, 1939);[28] the courts-martial of the Gestapo dispensed with such formalities.[29] The legal situation in the Annexed Eastern Territories, already tangled enough due to the lack of formally implemented Reich law, was complicated even further by the fact that along with the Wehrmacht and civil courts, the police courts-martial also claimed court jurisdiction in criminal matters. In practical terms, as Reich Minister of Justice Gürtner lamented as early as September 1939, there was a competing jurisdiction between the People's Court of Justice, the Wehrmacht courts, the special courts, and the police courts-martial,[30] which only served to exacerbate the jurisdictional chaos even further.

However, even the activities of the SS and the police could not survive in the long term without a formal basis in law; they required a legal gloss, however threadbare this might be. Himmler therefore intended to introduce a Decree on Acts of Violence in the Annexed Eastern Territories, which was to legalize all "actions" by the SS and police, including also those of the courts-martial and of the special-duty detachments of the SIPO and the police battalions, with retroactive effect to September 1, 1939, and which provided for draconian punishments (the death penalty as the standard sentence) for all cases of Polish insubordination. Under the draft,[31] all cases in which the offense was directed toward the German police, its members, or auxiliary personnel and in which "immediate sentencing was possible and necessary" were to be tried not only by the special courts and the Wehrmacht courts but also by the police courts-martial; the decree was not to apply to Reich and ethnic Germans or to members of neutral countries. In other words, it was to create special law for "non-German" offenders (in particular Poles and Jews) ("The instruments of power of martial law should be directed with full severity against the enemy").[32] This attempt at overtly curtailing the powers of the courts met with criticism not only from the Reich Chancellery and the Ministry of Justice;[33] the chairman of the Ministerial Council for the Defense of the Reich (Göring), in his capacity as plenipotentiary for the Four Year Plan interested in the quickest possible normalization in the Annexed Eastern Territories, could not warm to the view of the *Reichsführer*-SS that "we cannot yet dispense with the martial-law jurisdiction of the police because normal conditions, similar to those in the Altreich, have yet to be achieved and cannot be expected in the near future,"[34] because he believed that the powers that would thereby be vested in the police would go too far.[35] Himmler therefore had to accept the implementation of Reich penal law in the Annexed Eastern Territories, but he was able to record a certain success because (as stated above), his draft was adopted, practically without change in terms of substantive law, as "special penal regulations" in the Decree on the Implementation of Penal Law of June 6, 1940.[36] In return, Himmler consented to halting the activities of the police courts-martial.[37]

However, the decree of June 6, 1940, had no effect on the objectives of the SS and police leadership to obtain full jurisdiction over the Poles and Jews for criminal matters; the police leadership had no intention whatsoever of accepting the legal situation as it stood. This is why the police courts-martial were never formally abolished but merely ceased their activities "until further notice";[38] this was no more than an attempt to reassure the judicial and administrative authorities.[39] In the Warthegau at least, the courts-martial organization was even reinforced shortly before the implementation of German penal law on June 6, 1940, by the establishment of permanent courts-martial to replace the mobile courts-martial;[40] following the previous practice of the mobile courts-martial, these permanent courts-martial claimed comprehensive jurisdiction in criminal matters. Although the court-martial of the regular police was responsible only for punishing illegal possession of weapons under the decree of September 21, 1939,[41] the Gestapo court-martial was declared to be responsible "for all other cases," without any further definition.[42] Such cases included, for example, "homicide," "sabotage," and "arson," but they related especially to the "political" crimes ("treason and high treason") and similar offenses, which fell, of course, under the jurisdiction of the general courts.[43]

A further attempt at reversing the existing legal situation related to the other extralegal actions of the SS and police, which had increased since the implementation of German penal law, in particular the shooting or hanging of Jews for a wide variety of crimes; these were not even tried before the courts-martial, because the Jews were, in any case, no more than fair game for the police.[44] These were measures against which the judicial authorities could not or would not protest, since they "only" involved Jews. In addition, the (Gestapo) courts-martial or simply the "normal" (regular) police always moved into action when the case involved the performance of "atonement measures," that is, retaliatory actions for attacks on Germans or damage to German facilities by the execution of hostages or allegedly "suspicious" persons.[45] Some of those actions were directed by the local *Reichsstatthalter*; others were ordered directly by the Reichsführer-SS and chief of the German police.[46]

In these actions, most of which took place in public with forced attendance by the entire Polish population,[47] the hostages were either singled out from lists carefully drawn up by the police (blacklists)[48] or picked at random from the population of the community where the crime was committed ("from the environment of the criminal").[49]

In addition, of course, the Gestapo made the widest possible use of illegal police "protective custody" or "preventive detention" to punish crimes by "non-Germans."[50]

The reaction of the judicial authorities to this flagrant breach of jurisdiction in criminal matters is not known. Even if they were not informed officially of the operations, they often had no objection in principle to the actions of the police, because such atonement and retaliatory actions were regarded as political measures instituted by the police within the context of "fighting the enemy" or the "ethnic struggle," with which the judiciary had nothing to do. However, the illegality of such measures must have been clear to any knowledgeable individual, since the authorities undertook everything possible to conceal the outcome of the activities or prevent them from finding their way into the records.[51] But there were also authorities that actively supported these murderous activities.

The chief public prosecutor in Posen (Poznań), for instance, who welcomed "all ruthless . . . and severe action against Poles in his area of responsibility" and did not see the "interests of justice affected by such measures," regarded the deterrent quota stipulated by Hitler—twenty Poles to be shot for each act of violence by Poles—as "suitable" and stated his willingness to help by proposing that the judicial authorities be included in the selection of "suitable Poles." His thoughts turned in particular to the "professional criminals sitting in prison"; "irrespective of whether these were convicts or remand prisoners," he could provide them or male members of the environment of the criminal for execution as soon as the execution had been approved by the Führer or the *Reichsführer*-SS and chief of the German police; he believed that "non-delivery [of the prisoners, etc.] would mean that fewer less incriminated persons would be shot, whereas the criminals would only be spared."[52] "In principle," the ministry had no objections to this proposal, but it reserved the right to consent to the delivery in each individual case.[53]

The political leadership at the head of the administration of the Annexed Eastern Territories was thoroughly aware that the circumstances resulting from the activities of the police were untenable, and it tried to redress the situation in its own way. In conjunction with the "retaliatory action" he ordered in May 1941,[54] for instance, the Gauleiter and *Reichsstatthalter* of the Warthegau (Greiser) immediately requested from Hitler the authority to deploy courts-martial, "as he did not possess the inherent legal basis for this" (i.e., for such instructions).[55] The proceedings of these courts-martial deployed by the *Reichsstatthalter* were intended to give the appearance of courtlike proceedings, with the *Reichsstatthalter* acting as the "appellate authority" with oral powers of intervention.

How many courts-martial were established in this way and the scope of their activities is, however, a matter of doubt; it is clear that the judicial authorities were still able to exercise a restraining effect at that time. The chief public prosecutor in Posen, for instance, was able to insist that he had to be approached *before* courts-martial were established. The problem was not seen as one of principle. In line with the practice of settling organizational and procedural questions in criminal cases against "non-German" criminals by "agreements" between the administration (the police) and the judicial authorities, rather than by means of existing regulations,[56] it was a question of "expediency." The chief public prosecutor reported to the minister of justice that courts-martial should always be established if the judicial authorities were "overburdened." In the Warthegau, corresponding "agreements" existed at a relatively high level between the senior public prosecutors and the presidents of the administrative districts.[57]

3. Developments Following the Coming into Force of the Decree on Penal Law for Poles

The efforts of the police to continue the jurisdiction of the police courts-martial were unable to meet with any definitive success as long as German penal law applied in the Annexed Eastern Territories and the sentencing of Jews and Poles lay exclusively in the hands of the judicial authorities. It was therefore a logical step for the police, in pursuing their final goal, to apply heavy pressure on the Ministry of Justice to reverse the implementation of German penal law and introduce overt police special law for Poles and Jews. We have already seen that in the more than eighteen months of dispute between the Ministry of Justice and the Reich Security Main Office (RSHA),[58] the police were able to assert themselves in this matter to a very large extent, since their wishes were largely included in the Decree on Penal Law for Poles of December 4, 1941.[59] However, the major goal of also acquiring jurisdiction over offenses by "non-Germans" was achieved only in part, because any statutory incorporation of the jurisdiction of the police courts-martial was defeated not by the weak Ministry of Justice but rather by the resistance of the *Reichsstatthalter* in the Eastern Territories, who rightly feared that the *Reichsführer*-SS and chief of the German police or the head of the Security Police could "gain control over another area."[60]

So what the judicial authorities viewed as an absolute defeat was regarded by the police as no more than a partial victory; it was more than a "flaw" that the Decree on Penal Law for Poles adhered to the fundamental jurisdiction of the general courts (special courts and courts of first instance) and had transferred the power to reestablish police courts-martial not to the police but to the *Reichsstatthalter* (and only with the consent of the minister of the interior and the minister of justice, and then only for certain types of cases—"serious outrages against Germans" and "crimes posing a serious threat to German development work"). A new feature in the corresponding clause 13 of the Decree on Penal Law for Poles, which the Ministry of Justice had been forced to accept under pressure from the head of the Security Police and the Security Service,[61] was that, for the first time, committal to a concentration camp (transfer to the Gestapo) was legally recognized as a punishment or substitute punishment; paragraph 2 of this clause stated that "the punishment to be imposed by the courts-martial is the death penalty. The courts-martial may also refrain from imposing a punishment, ordering transfer to the Secret State Police as an alternative."

Even this very far-reaching substantive empowerment of the police courts-martial was not sufficient to satisfy the police leadership, because—as Himmler informed Bormann on July 8, 1943—the application of even the most diluted penal "regulations" to "non-Germans" was "thoroughly out of place."[62] It should therefore come as no surprise that legal developments in the Annexed Eastern Territories after the Decree on Penal Law for Poles had become effective were characterized by increasing efforts by the SS and the police to monopolize the criminal prosecution of Poles and Jews. Often with the active support of the local Gauleiters, the police used a number of methods. On the one hand, they intensified their previous illegal practices, and on the other, they undermined the already far-reaching umbrella clauses in the Decree on Penal Law for Poles.

a.   Continuation of Illegal Police Practices

The widespread impact of the "proven" practice of not handing over investigations to the public prosecutors, in defiance of section 163, paragraph 2, of the Code of Criminal Procedure,[63] but rather keeping them in the hands of the police, was of particular importance. In other words, the local heads of the Gestapo decided on a case-by-case basis what was to be handed over to the judicial authorities.[64] It is clear that the judicial authorities were therefore excluded from all important cases, in particular those involving "political" criminal matters. For especially significant cases, there were also special instructions to the subordinate departments reinforcing this principle still further.[65] It was reported from East Prussia, for instance, that the gendarmerie had been instructed to report all crimes committed by Poles *first* to the Gestapo, so that only a very few criminal cases involving Poles ever came before the courts.[66] In particular, all kinds of sexual offenses, viewed as being of equal importance to political crimes, were handled exclusively by the Gestapo on the basis of a corresponding decree by the *Reichsführer*-SS and chief of the German police of March 11, 1942.[67] In addition, the SA took it upon itself to sabotage the judicial authorities' investigations of crimes committed by Poles, as was reported from Bromberg (Bydgoszcz).[68] Moreover, the illegal executions by the police, primarily "retaliatory" actions but partly also sanctions for "normal" crimes, did not come to an end with the implementation of the Decree on Penal Law for Poles.[69] From this point on, the police acted with increasing openness and self-assurance, supported in the Warthegau by the *Reichsstatthalter* himself, who threatened sentencing by the courts-martial in the event of "further insubordinate behavior" by the Poles (with regard to the regulations governing compulsory labor).[70]

In the eyes of the police, however, these actions were more or less sporadic isolated acts that were by no means sufficient to achieve control over the entire administration of penal justice for "non-Germans"; although the executions continued, the situation was regarded as unsatisfactory, since a major occasion or serious resistance by the "non-Germans" (attacks on Germans, etc.) was always needed to be able to carry out "deterrent" or "retaliatory measures."

b.   Legalization of the Jurisdiction of the Police Courts-Martial

This all changed with the establishment of police courts-martial in the Annexed Eastern Territories in 1942 when the *Reichsstatthalter* made use of their authority vested in clause 13 of the Decree on Penal Law for Poles. Although the situation report by the chief public prosecutor in Kattowitz (Katowice) of August 6, 1942, notes that the *Reichsstatthalter* of Danzig–West Prussia and the Warthegau opposed the "reestablishment of police courts-martial" in a meeting at the Ministry of Justice on July 28, 1942,[71] this probably served only to allay the fears of the ministry with regard to further curtailment of the jurisdiction of the courts, rather than to reveal the true intentions of Hitler's "*Gau* kings." The temptation to develop "police justice," controlled only by themselves and independent of the Reich, was simply too great.

As early as August 3 1942,[72] the Decree on the Establishment of Courts-Martial was promulgated for the *Reichsgau* Warthegau, which transferred the sentencing of "serious acts of violence by Poles and Jews against Germans" and other crimes by Poles and Jews (sec. 1) seriously threatening "German development work" to the courts-martial established at the local Gestapo offices and headquarters, under the chairmanship of the local head of the Gestapo office or headquarters.

These crimes were not defined in any greater detail. In cases of doubt, the *Reichsstatthalter* decided whether a crime within the meaning of section 1 was involved. At any rate, the procedure was defined in greater detail than in the Decree on Penal Law for Poles, insofar as the principle of official investigation and the examination of the accused had to be observed. The judgments of the courts-martial were the death penalty, transferal to the Gestapo (concentration camp), or acquittal; the courts-martial could also refrain from a punishment or pass the case on to another court (sec. 2). The *Reichsstatthalter* reserved the right to confirm or reverse the judgments of the courts-martial (clause 3), but this was *delegated* in a decree of August 3, 1942, to the inspector of the Security Police and the Security Service in Posen and thus to the local police leadership.[73] In this way the entire jurisdiction of the courts-martial was concentrated in the hands of the Security Police.

The extent to which these courts-martial started operating in the Warthegau is not certain; in his final statement to the Polish Supreme People's Court of Justice in 1946, Greiser himself claimed that no use was made of the decree of August 3, 1942.[74] Even if such courts-martial had indeed been established, the Gestapo frequently used "simpler" methods; that is to say, it continued its previous practice of execution without trial even after the decree of August 3, 1942.[75]

In Upper Silesia, a decree of June 1, 1942, by the higher district president established Gestapo courts-martial for sentencing "serious crimes" by Poles and Jews.[76] The wording of the decree corresponded in full to the subsequent Posen decree of August 3, 1942.

Here, too, the right of confirmation of court-martial judgments was transferred by the higher district president to the higher SS and police leader (HSSPF) and thus completely to the Security Police. In the Annexed Eastern Territories of Upper Silesia, otherwise regarded as relatively moderate, the list of crimes for which trial by court-martial was stipulated by a instruction of the higher district president of June 1, 1942,[77] was so extensive that it far exceeded the scope of clause 13 of the Decree on Penal Law for Poles; it covered all political crimes, war economy laws, and all minor or less serious offenses directed against Germans; no offense was excluded.[78]

Despite this, the police continued their efforts to retain sole jurisdiction for the sentencing *without trial* of "non-German" offenders, because this list was linked to offenses under Reich penal law and demanded definitions and demarcations, and the higher district president evidently transferred only a small percentage of cases presented by the Gestapo to the courts-martial.[79] However, this did not mean that the other cases were handed over to the judicial authorities; rather, the police, who controlled all investigations, made increasing use of Gestapo "special treatment" (execution or protective custody) without any court-like proceedings,[80] this being much easier to accomplish than court-martial trials.

The legal situation was similar in East Prussia, where the higher district president and Gauleiter E. Koch established a court-martial in the Zichenau Administrative District by a decree of August 15, 1942,[81] but reserved for himself the decision as to which crimes should be sentenced by the court-martial.

Originally, it was intended for cases in which "crimes by members of the Polish resistance movement particularly affected public security," a clause that was obviously construed very extensively, as seen by the fact that Koch deemed it necessary to stipulate in the concluding provision of the decree that crimes "would continue to be sentenced by the general courts." In this case, too, the activities of the courts-martial appear to have been minor, since the police preferred to continue their established practice of public executions without trial.[82]

Only in Danzig–West Prussia were no police courts-martial established; in view of the large mixed Polish-German population in the *Gau*, *Reichsstatthalter* Forster feared for the success of his Germanization policy, which he saw as being put at risk by the surrender of judicial powers to the police.[83]

Finally, the extension of illegal and "legal" police practices resulted in the police controlling most criminal prosecutions against Poles and Jews from mid-1942 onward, whether by means of the courts-martial or by the customary executions without trial, as ascertained in a meeting of the senior presidents in Berlin in September 1942.[84] For this reason, once they were in the hands of the police, "non-German" prisoners rarely saw freedom again. Beginning in 1943, the judicial authorities also delivered their Polish prisoners officially to the police after serving their sentence if they had been sentenced to more than six months' imprisonment (and Poles normally received more than this) or (from 1944 on) more than a year.[85] As was reported from the Warthegau, this practice had the grotesque result that the courts frequently handed out sentences *lower* than the level at which transfer to the Gestapo was the rule (that is, less than six months/one year) or sentenced the defendants to death rather than to long terms of imprisonment, in order to "give the criminals the benefits associated with immediate execution of the death penalty[!]."[86]

c. The Undermining of the Decree on Penal Law for Poles by Police Orders

The establishment and activities of the courts-martial on the basis of clause 13 of the Decree on Penal Law for Poles alone could not have been the cause of the massive rise in police actions from 1942 on; rather, it was due to the general growth in the power of the police, which steadily swamped the civil powers. A substantial contribution to this was made by Minister of Justice Thierack, in office since August 20, 1942, who consistently supported the efforts of the SS and police leadership to gain exclusive jurisdiction over penal matters, and even when these efforts had been broken by the resistance of the *Reichsstatthalter* (higher district presidents) in the Annexed Eastern Territories,[87] Thierack continued to support this policy in recommendations and guidelines to the judicial authorities.[88] A general transfer of jurisdiction for criminal prosecutions of Poles and Jews to the police by way of decree, as planned by Thierack and Himmler in fall 1942 (in breach of the Decree on Penal Law for Poles), would have removed the bulk of all criminal cases from the judicial authorities in the Annexed Eastern Territories; in Danzig–West Prussia, for instance, as the minister of justice noted, the local judicial authorities, who were in any case "strictly trained and monitored" in all cases involving Poles (i.e., were stalwartly anti-Polish), would have lost 50–70 percent of all criminal cases.[89] However, this loss of jurisdiction was implemented via the back door when it proved to be impossible to issue such a decree; the police fell back on the expedient, "proven" in the Reich, of secret directives, or they simply continued their arbitrary interference.

In summer 1942, the situation reports of the presiding judges of the appellate courts and chief public prosecutors in the Annexed Eastern Territories were full of complaints about the growing activities of the police courts-martial, executions by the police without trial by court-martial, and the lack of information provided by the police to the judicial authorities, which practically paralyzed the activities of the judicial authorities.[90] However, it would be a mistake to think that this paralysis had set in only in 1942. From the outset, as shown by the reports of senior judicial officials, arbitrary actions by the police and violations of the jurisdiction of the judicial authorities had been daily occurrences.[91] As early as 1941, a report mentioned the "paralysis of the public prosecutors to the benefit of the police" in Posen.[92]

Redress for this situation, viewed as scandalous even by judges and public prosecutors who essentially approved of the "ethnic struggle," was demanded not, or not only, with arguments about legality, that is, jurisdiction and division of responsibilities, which in a totalitarian state frequently appear to be the sole possibility of appeal and were preferred by the judicial authorities;[93] rather, they took the initiative, in line with the approach of the Reich leadership. To emphasize the efficiency of the judicial authorities, the reports from the appeal court districts are therefore full of praise for the "speed and effectiveness" of the special courts, which were well ahead of the police and could execute death sentences (including by having hangings carried out by the police)[94] much more quickly; therefore, these strong police activities were not at all necessary.[95] They attempted to show that the judiciary could punish just as harshly and could impose the same sanctions on the accused as they would suffer under the police (death or life imprisonment);[96] indeed, the senior officials themselves often urged the courts to impose harsher sentences and made suggestions about how the court-martial trials and the execution of sentences could be accelerated still further.[97] This was all done in the vain hope that they could hold out against the pressure of the Gestapo.

The situation in Upper Silesia was particularly scandalous, with the police having become the "far-reaching master of the administration of penal justice against Poles and Jews."[98] It is significant that the police extended their scope to Germans on the German Ethnic Classification List who had received German state subject status, a practice pursued not only in Upper Silesia but also elsewhere in the Annexed Eastern Territories.[99] The device frequently employed by the police to make things "formally" appear to be "orderly" was to revoke the German state subject status of persons registered in the German Ethnic Classification List and reclassify them as Poles; any protests worthy of being termed as such therefore related primarily to such cases, whereas the jurisdiction the police had usurped was increasingly accepted as part of the "regulatory power of facts"; it was certainly not queried explicitly. The reports restrict themselves to mere statements of findings.[100]

These reactions to the arbitrary conduct of the police were, taken overall, of little consequence, because they remained within the judicial apparatus and no action was taken by the central authorities in Berlin, either with regard to the surrender of "non-Germans" to the police (Minister of Justice Thierack fully supported Himmler's views) or those German state subjects who were never brought before a regular court. These facts were either hushed up, or the ministry refused to believe the reports.[101] When the judicial leadership did rouse itself to lodge a protest, it acted so feebly that nothing ever happened.[102] The very nature of the complaints meant that they could meet with no success. On the one hand, the objections must have appeared equivocating and contradictory, because it was very often the senior officials themselves who had actively supported the illegal practices of the police, for instance by close understandings or agreements, as were frequent in the Altreich, or by transferring persons who could not be prosecuted under penal law because of lack of evidence to the Gestapo with the "suggestion" of "Gestapo measures" (protective custody).[103] On the other hand, despite all the complaints, there were no *material* objections to the police usurpation of criminal prosecutions against Poles and Jews; the reports were silent in particular on the establishment of the jurisdiction of the courts-martial, or else they explicitly refused to make any comment.[104] The objections were principally restricted to formal aspects, that is, to arguments about jurisdiction, which any totalitarian power found it easy to overrule. It is clear that resignation became widespread in the judicial authorities once they saw that all their complaints and objections had borne no fruit. Later situation reports from the appeal court districts were restricted to reporting the complete *abdication* of the judiciary; they no longer contain complaints or pleas for assistance.[105]

The complaints of the judicial authorities were all the more justified, but similarly unsuccessful, because the police not only had increasingly removed from the judicial authorities the power to sentence *less serious* and *serious* offenses (in the extensive meaning applied at the time) by "non-Germans," but also had extended their powers much further.

As in the Reich, for instance, the police themselves handled the punishment of the "crime" of breaches of employment contracts by Poles (and other "non-German" workers), namely, violations of compulsory labor regulations.[106] The labor administration was powerless to intervene;[107] this is shown by the fact that the subordinate police authorities were notified that from 1943 on, the police (Gestapo) had been instructed to "punish" violations of compulsory labor regulations by all foreign workers "with the consent of the plenipotentiary for labor allocation."[108]

In quantitative terms, though, the fact that the police had gained control over everyday crimes by Poles and Jews was much more significant. Although the conclusive Decree on Penal Law for Poles of December 4, 1941, had exhausted the legal possibilities of justifying new areas of jurisdiction for the police once the wishes of the SS and police leadership had been taken into account, the police leadership in Berlin then took the steps common in the Altreich of applying extensive interpretation to the law and making use of actual or alleged loopholes in the law to evade existing regulations and gradually break out of the jurisdiction of the judicial authorities, a procedure that was made particularly easy by the Decree on Penal Law for Poles with its boundless umbrella clauses. If this method proved to be insufficient, it was still always possible to claim jurisdiction over Poles and Jews in criminal matters by overtly opposing the existing legal position.

A prime tool in the realization of these goals was the practice of directives and decrees. For the SS and police leadership, that even proved to be a more effective solution, because it allowed them to avoid being bound to publicly known umbrella clauses such as those in the Decree on Penal Law for Poles, however vague they might be. Rather, they could use unpublished instructions that could be amended at any time to undermine the activities of the government administration and the judicial authorities without becoming entangled in always exhausting and time-wasting jurisdictional disputes with the Reich administration. The solution of undermining jurisdiction from within became even more attractive when the police in the Annexed Eastern Territories were forced to be considerate toward the Gauleiters and *Reichsstatthalter* (higher district presidents). These officials, who were seen as Hitler's governors, formally headed the *Gau* judicial administration and jealously defended their autonomy, including with respect to the police, although they were otherwise friendly toward them.[109] With this gradual approach along the path of least resistance, it was therefore necessary to maneuver carefully and give the impression that the police were only exercising the functions permitted to them by the law. Himmler, who was a master at employing this instrument of silent erosion of jurisdiction, also understood only too well how to use appropriate instructions not made available to the judicial administration (or announced when it was already too late) to keep the judicial authorities in a state of permanent uncertainty about which crimes were handed over by the subordinate police departments to the public prosecutors, with the result that they increasingly lost track of criminal prosecutions and the criminal situation in the Polish population.[110]

The area of police *summary sentences* offered an ideal way of undermining the jurisdiction of the judicial authorities by police directives. Under Reich law, *Land* regulations had always empowered the police to impose their own summary sentences for minor offenses.[111] The legal guarantees provided for those affected, the ability to apply for a court judgment and to appeal against any sentence then imposed,[112] were now turned upside down by Himmler, using a legal trick. In a circular by the *Reichsführer*-SS and chief of the German police on June 15, 1942,[113] the subordinate authorities of the Security Police and the regular police were instructed that in the Annexed Eastern Territories, the Decree on Penal Law for Poles of December 4, 1941 (which had no provision for appeals), would now apply also to police criminal proceedings. Under the circular, there was therefore no right of appeal against police summary sentences (in violation of sec. 413, Code of Criminal Procedure); they were final immediately on notification to the criminal. Prison camps and fines were designated as "police punishments," although the Decree on Penal Law for Poles reserved the imposition of "prison camps" as a punishment exclusively for the courts. Finally, the provisions of the circular applied "analogously," even in the case of "the imposition of police fines for offenses against police ordinances" (arts. 33, 76, Prussian Police Administrative Law).[114]

This circular was probably a replacement for the Decree on Administrative Penalty Procedures already drafted by the Ministry of Justice, which summarized the law on misdemeanors in standardized fashion and also envisaged the extension of police jurisdiction for criminal matters. The draft was successfully sabotaged by the Reich Security Main Office (RSHA), because it would have meant the definition in law of (administrative) police activities, which in the opinion of the Security Police should certainly be "avoided," because it would have opened the floodgates to unrestricted police power over everday crimes. In contrast, a simple directive in the form of a decree was much more suitable for pushing through the intended extension of police jurisdiction for criminal matters to "all offenses" for which the police did not view the "sentences stipulated for summary sentences" as sufficient.[115]

The decree of June 15, 1942, succeeded in excluding Poles and Jews from all legal remedies against police orders (administrative complaints, administrative lawsuits, applications for court rulings) and eliminating the judicial authorities from the entire area of petty crimes involving "non-Germans, police punishments, and police enforcement measures.

The desired side effect of this was that misdemeanors (offenses against police ordinances) were criminalized (offenders could be sent to prison camp) by police summary sentences, and both misdemeanors and offenses against section 413 of the Code of Criminal Procedure were punished by police sentences.

This criminalization was achieved by distancing the sentencing power of the police from conventional offenses and crimes; the decree circulated on June 15, 1942, contained only a vague mention of "minor crimes." Definition of the term *minor crime* was thus completely at the discretion of the police, and it could cover misdemeanors, offenses, and other violations. The police could therefore impose punishments for violations of police ordinances that were essentially *penalties for criminal offenses*, whereas under reigning police law, police ordinances did not involve penalties for criminal offenses, and violations could be punished only by standard police enforcement measures.[116] The increased criminalization of "minor crimes" was additionally achieved by the wide scope of punishments allowed to the police under the decree circulated on June 15, 1942—three to six months' prison camp or fines of 3,000–10,000 reichsmarks—which far exceeded the standard scope of punishments for misdemeanors—up to six weeks' prison, fines of up to 150 reichsmarks (secs. 360 et seq., 18, 27, Code of Criminal Procedure, amended version).[117]

This was a complete departure from the range of conventional punishments and the conventional jurisdiction of the police over criminal matters as defined by section 413 of the Code of Criminal Procedure. In legal terms, the fact that the police had thereby assumed the function of the courts was concealed, because the decree simply stipulated that the principle of "free procedural organization" under clause 12 of the Decree on Penal Law for Poles, which also permitted deviations from the Code of Criminal Procedure, also applied to police summary sentences via section 413 of the Code of Criminal Procedure.

The extension of the principle of "free procedural organization" to police

summary sentences was a clear breach of the law, because this principle was exclusively reserved for the courts and public prosecutors. Nonetheless, Himmler's
directive, which was proclaimed in the period of the "judicial crisis" triggered by
Hitler's Reichstag speech on April 26, 1942, and marked the nadir of the political
and general standing of the judiciary, prevailed right from the outset; the considerable "reservations" of the senior judicial officials in the Ministry of Justice fell
on deaf ears, or at least had no effect.[118] In conjunction with the drafting of the
decree on administrative penalty procedures, the ministry had already shown itself to be culpably passive by declaring that it had "no objections to the extension
of the permissibility of police summary sentences," although it wanted to wait for
the "initiative" of the Reich Security Main Office.[119] This "initiative" now occurred in the form of the decree of June 15, 1942. Since no action had been undertaken in view of the obvious illegality of the efforts of the police, there was no alternative but to accept this new usurpation of jurisdiction; all the ministry could
rouse itself to do was to submit a proposal that the police summary sentences
should be legalized in an amending decree to the Decree on Penal Law for
Poles,[120] that is, to cloak an overt breach of the law in the "proper form"; this did
not happen because it would have diminished the "flexibility" of the police.

With the circular of June 15, 1942, the police came much closer to their goal,
because it allowed them to assume the function of an autonomous criminal
prosecution authority—together with the courts and the public prosecutors—
and gave them their own jurisdiction, thus raising the police to the status of an
independent organ of the administration of justice. However, the implementation of the decree caused considerable difficulties and induced the administrative leadership to issue further elucidations to keep its impact more or less
within the scope of general Reich law.

A directive by the *Reichsstatthalter* of the Wartheland to the president of the
Posen Administrative District on April 24, 1943, stated that the local police authorities could only prosecute criminal acts by Poles and Jews who had committed misdemeanors, as defined by the Code of Criminal Procedure (up to three
weeks' prison or fines of up to 150 reichsmarks); at the same time, the directive
formally rehabilitated the judiciary by decreeing that a strict criterion must be
applied when interpreting the concept of "minor crimes" as specified in the decree circulated on June 15, 1942, and that "suitable cases" should be handed over
to the judicial authorities "because the authority of the state is more clearly expressed in court judgments than in police criminal proceedings."[121] However,
this directive was really more lip service than a serious attempt to rescue the jurisdiction of the judicial authorities, since the administrative leadership in the
Annexed Eastern Territories was at one with the interest of the SS and police in

gaining complete control over the conduct of "non-German" persons. Further decrees tightened this control. In the Warthegau, for instance, the police were instructed to act with "particular severity" in their summary sentences on Poles involving violations of "ethnic principles," which included such "offenses" as the use of railway compartments designed for Germans only or failing to mark an apartment as Jewish.[122]

It should be obvious that in the eyes of the police, the range of punishments contained in the circular of June 15, 1942, was by no means sufficient in the long term for the increased severity with which "non-Germans" were treated. Once it had been usurped by the police, the principle of special law demanded even further extension. What the police really wanted was to link police summary sentence proceedings to general Gestapo proceedings, which provided for only two sanctions, irrespective of whether reasons for arrest existed or not: either sending those in disfavor to a concentration camp or liquidating them for "security" or "criminal investigation" reasons. Whenever possible, everyday crimes were now to be subject to this procedure; to this end, it was necessary to blur the borders between criminal offenses and political offenses, in other words to politicize criminal offenses, in order to allow the inclusion of the political police (Gestapo) and the criminal investigation police, with their unrestricted powers of sanction, to take part in police summary sentence proceedings. This inclusion was implemented by a circular decree by the *Reichsführer*-SS and chief of the German police on September 20, 1943,[123] which represented another classic example of the tactics of the police in undermining existing jurisdiction. This decree used the preferred method of changing the terms of existing regulations while preserving the formal "legal position," in other words treating provisions primarily as organizational and jurisdictional issues and shifting or redefining responsibilities to achieve the desired change in substance.

For "reasons of expediency," the circular decree correspondingly empowered not only the organs of the regular police authorities but also the Gestapo and criminal investigation offices and headquarters, that is, the Security Police, to impose police summary sentences on Poles (Jews are no longer mentioned for obvious reasons—ghettoization, deportation),[124] and assigned them the same punitive powers that the regular police had received on the basis of the decree of June 15, 1942. However, this involved much more than the *coexistence* of the regular and Security Police: the latter clearly gained the upper hand through the provision of clause 3 of the decree, which set out that when an offense "was of prime importance to the criminal investigation police," the case was to be handed over to the criminal investigation police (part of the Security Police); "as before," "cases with a political impact" were to be transferred to the Gestapo.

When doubt existed, the relevant criminal investigation or Gestapo offices, in other words *not* the organs of the regular police (uniformed police, gendarmerie), were to make a *binding decision* about whether such criminal investigation or Security Police "interests" existed.

The potential jurisdiction of the Security Police in the treatment of "non-Germans" was therefore now actually without limit, since there were no misdemeanors by a "non-German" that were not inherently political or criminal crimes in areas where the "ethnic struggle" was being waged.

The monopolization of criminal prosecutions under the control of the Security Police was accompanied by the removal of powers from the local police authorities (regular police), whom the police headquarters mistrusted in principle in any case, because there was always a "risk" that they would not act with sufficient severity. The decree of September 20, 1943, therefore completely removed from the local police authorities the power to impose prison camp sentences on Poles and restricted their power to impose fines for offenses for which fines of 5 to 200 marks (or up to three weeks of prison camp) were sufficient.[125] The district police authority (prefect) was responsible for all punishments exceeding this scope.

In other words, if an offense by a Pole was reported to the police, the following alternatives were possible: if it was a crime of some importance, it was passed on to the public prosecutors or, more often, to the Gestapo on the basis of the usurped jurisdiction for criminal matters. If it involved a minor crime, to which the summary sentence proceedings could be applied, in the best case the miscreant could be fined up to 200 reichsmarks by a police summary sentence imposed by the local police authority, where no criminal investigation or political interest existed. However, a police summary sentence of prison camp or a fine (between 200 and 10,000 reichsmarks), imposed by the district police authority (prefect), could also be considered. For offenses in which there was a prime "criminal investigation" interest, the person was handed over to the criminal investigation police, who in turn passed the case on to the Gestapo "for further investigation" (sentencing by a court-martial) or (although this occurred with decreasing frequency) to the public prosecutor for charges before a court of first instance or a special court. For crimes with a "political impact," the case was always passed on directly to the Gestapo.

This decree brought developments in the Annexed Eastern Territories to a certain conclusion. The police were now in a position to register without exception all offenses by Poles against German regulations of all kinds and to deal with them under their own responsibility. For everyday crimes ("minor crimes" or misdemeanors), the instruments of police summary sentences (fine or prison camp) or criminal investigation or political police "treatment" (protective custody) were available; for more serious or grave offenses (when they affected "German interests"), the police courts-martial were responsible (with the exception of Danzig–West Prussia) or could be declared responsible by the *Reichsstatthalter* (higher district president), if such jurisdiction was not specifically defined. This was compounded by the usurpation of additional "penal jurisdiction" by the police by means of secret decrees, which criminalized conduct by "non-Germans" that was not in itself punishable, such as violations of the principle of "racial separation" (sexual relations with Germans).[126] The relationship between the public prosecutors and the police had been turned on its head; the criminal investigation police filed charges at their own discretion, namely, only if the case did not interest the Security Police "for whatever reason."[127] And the police were essentially interested in all cases of crimes by "non-Germans" in the era of the "ethnic struggle."

The exclusion of the judicial authorities from the administration of penal justice against "non-Germans" was finally complete: as the chief public prosecutors complained, they were not even informed about the activities of the police courts-martial and were forced to rely on ad hoc inquiries or the "courtesy" of the local police authorities.[128] All they could achieve was the abolition of *public* executions of Poles by the police in Upper Silesia (no doubt due to the heavily mixed German-Polish population);[129] in the other areas of the Annexed Eastern Territories, such executions continued (for "reasons of deterrence"), but they had the opposite effect.[130] All protestations by the judicial authorities about the "severity and effectiveness" of the special courts, all draconian convictions and sentences, all efforts to please the political leadership had therefore only reinforced the totalitarian claims of the police.[131] The police simply did not bother with such matters, particularly since the Ministry of Justice had largely surrendered all initiative after the death of Gürtner in 1941 and had let things drift. On the basis of their experience in the Annexed Eastern Territories since 1940, the police could be sure that the judicial administration would either knuckle under or do nothing that seriously threatened any jurisdiction the police had usurped; they could therefore afford to snub the judicial authorities in public, for instance by executing Poles who had been acquitted by the special courts or Polish remand prisoners who had been handed over to the Gestapo for interrogation and whose return was requested by the judicial authorities.[132] An additional factor was that since Thierack had been appointed minister of justice on August 20, 1942, there was close agreement between the Reich judicial administration and the Party and police leadership on the treatment of "non-Germans," in view of which all complaints and warnings from below were bound to peter out.[133]

Nonetheless, the judicial authorities continued to be a thorn in the side of the police leadership, because they continued to apply the last vestiges of regular proceedings, and despite their indoctrination and severity in many cases, they still took account of the individual circumstances of the case—the facts of the case, the character of the accused—in short because, as Himmler once complained to Bormann, they were still trying to "administer justice" instead of implementing the "interests of the German people." What essentially bothered the SS and police leadership was therefore less the judgments of the courts, which they believed were often too lenient, but rather their very existence as a state institution, because their activities could not be controlled and "oriented" so totally as those of the police; they therefore continued to represent a factor of uncertainty and unreliability in the "great task" of the struggle against the "non-Germans." In the view of the Party and the police, the judicial authorities had no business being involved in the "ethnic struggle." That struggle demanded the exclusive jurisdiction of the SS and the police, which ought to replace the judicial authorities as an "organ of the administration of justice" sui generis and achieve the public impression of an independent "administration of justice" for "non-Germans."[134] In the Annexed Eastern Territories, this goal was achieved with near perfection.

C. Civil Law

I. "Analogous Application" of Civil Law

Although the prime judicial and political focus in legal developments in the Annexed Eastern Territories was on penal law, the implementation of special law was not limited to the area of penal law, because such a restriction would have contradicted the totalitarian nature of the regime. Less spectacular, but no less single-minded (and often more far-reaching in their impact), the conditions for the separation of Germans and "non-Germans" and the unequal treatment of the latter in practice had been created right from the outset in the area of civil law. The development of civil law can also be divided into three phases, although these overlapped and were less precisely demarcated than in the case of penal law. The first phase of legal vacuum was followed in around mid-1940 by a phase in which individual provisions of Reich law were implemented and some overt special regulations for Poles and Jews were issued; in the third phase, complete civil law was implemented in the Annexed Eastern Territories but at the same time was made subject to the proviso of "*völkisch* inequality" by an umbrella clause.

In line with the area of penal law, the first phase, from September 1939 to around mid-1940, was distinguished by the basic concept that exclusively German law applied, without its formal implementation in the Annexed Eastern Territories. As described above, the only "legal basis" was section 7 of the Assimilation Decree of October 8, 1939,[1] under which the "existing law" remained in force where it did not contradict the "effect of assimilation." The reader is referred to part 2, section 2, B, I, 2 ("Führer Decree on the Division and Administration of the Eastern Territories, October 8, 1939") with regard to its interpretation and the definition of what was to be regarded as "current law" (i.e., German law as applied by the authorities since the start of the war), as well as the underlying doctrine of the collapse of the Polish state under international law on account of the German occupation.[2] Another justification resulting from court practice expressed the actual reason for the abandonment of Polish law in much clearer terms: since Polish law was a means for combating Germanness, the (ethnic) Germans living in the Eastern Territories could not be expected to continue living under Polish law. In addition, if Polish law had been permitted, the Polish population could have been left in doubt as to the "irrevocable decision" to "merge the Eastern Territories completely with the German Reich for all time."[3] It was therefore not at all a matter for dispute that German law alone would determine civil law. The question of why German law should suddenly apply in a formerly foreign state territory without any formal implementation was answered with the argument that this law more or less flowed into an "area of legal vacuum" by itself "to fill a gap," that is, without any formal implementation.[4]

Nevertheless, the validity of German civil law was merely the starting point for the subsequent considerations, and it was by no means consistently thought out. The complete and direct application of German law was not at all in the interest of the Germans, because then both Poles and Germans would have enjoyed its benefits. This was ruled out by the completely different "ethnic (racial) circumstances," which made discrimination against the local population the duty of all authorities. Following the example of developments in penal law, the principle of "analogous application" was also used for civil law. According to this formula, German law only applied *in principle* and could be amended in individual instances at the discretion of the authorities to meet "ethnic" or "political" interests; in the eyes of the Nazis, of course, there could be no equality of treatment of Poles and Jews.[5] In practice, the analogous application of German law therefore meant that German law was applied directly if this was politically desirable, that is, if it had a detrimental effect on the Poles, and was not considered if it would have favored Polish interests.

This maxim is clearly exemplified in an express letter from the Ministry of the Interior to the supreme Reich authorities of November 16, 1939. Therein the minister of the interior requested that if it proved to be absolutely necessary to introduce Reich law provisions, an examination should be made as to whether foreigners of German blood would be ensured the preferential status due to them and that, if necessary, the Reich law provisions should be revised so that it could be implemented in such a way that "non-German" nationals did not become the beneficiaries of German law.[6]

For the exercise of the administration of justice, however, these formulations did not supply any concrete criteria. The "ethnic" proviso of the application of German law was therefore mostly paraphrased; the rule of thumb was "reasonable discretion" and "greatest possible regard for the requirements of assimilation,"[7] or the vague concept of "flexibility and adaptation" of the administration of justice.[8] However, this only replaced one umbrella clause by another, which did not help much and left many questions unanswered.[9] This was because, as a rule, civil law contained precise definitions of offenses and only a few clauses and concepts requiring interpretation (in the form of umbrella clauses) and was therefore of little use for the analogous application of German law or "conformity" with German law. The authorities were therefore faced with the question of how they could decide whether regulations (for instance, having to do with contract law, commercial, and company law) could be suitably applied to meet Nazi purposes, and if so, which regulations could be applied; they also had to decide in which cases a divergent application was preferred. In turn, such decisions depended on the extent of the "ethnic and racial loyalty" of the regulation in question.[10]

To wade through all provisions of civil law to determine the extent of this "loyalty" was simply impossible for practical reasons. In this respect, Reich German civil law was adopted more or less as it stood—without formal introduction—so that the motto of the corresponding application was more a concession to the guiding political principle than a practical guideline for justice, and did not have the same significance as it had in penal law. As a rule, justice was administered on the basis of the application, "to the widest extent possible,"[11] of German civil law. All associated legal matters, with the courts applying German law directly,[12] were supported by guidelines from the courts of appeal, based partially on recommendations by the minister of justice, in part drafted by the courts themselves.[13]

From 1940 on, however, there was a move toward *overt special law* for "non-Germans." Once efforts had been started to implement formally certain areas of civil law in which there was a particular interest for reasons of security in the law (e.g., liability law, law of bills and checks, commercial law, etc.),[14] the purview of these areas was—in part—restricted explicitly to German state subjects and for-eigners of German blood, or explicit discriminatory provisions were imple-mented to the detriment of "non-Germans," as shown by the provisions on lower wages for Poles and on the exclusion of Poles and Jews from social welfare benefits.[15]

In addition, special law exclusively for "non-Germans" was introduced from 1940 on. Although this involved not civil law but regulations under public law, such as drastic restrictions in real estate law and the law of enforcement,[16] as well as the confiscation regulations dealt with above,[17] these are worthy of mention here because they are representative of the scope with which the disfranchise-ment of the local population was to be implemented under flimsy pretenses.[18]

Apart from these special regulations, civil law as a whole was not regulated, although innumerable questions of legal relations between Germans and Poles were waiting for an answer. As the minister of justice reported to the minister of the interior, the consequence of this unclear legal situation was that the courts were very uncertain about the scope of the analogous application of German law.[19] This applied in particular to areas of the law that demanded that circum-stances be absolutely clear, for instance procedural law, land registry and regis-try law, family law (marriage law), and so forth. It became evident that the prin-ciple of applying in the Annexed Eastern Territories "at least the fundamentals and major elements" of the civil law in force in the Reich without the aid of the legislators could not last in the long term.[20] The inevitable consequence was that disputes arose about which provisions of Reich law were to be applied directly, which "analogously," and which not at all. Despite their emphasis on the princi-ple that the courts had to be flexible because of the needs of "German develop-ment work" in the East, both the courts themselves and the Ministry of Justice[21] were forced to admit that the circumstances "absolutely" demanded explicit reg-ulation by law.

II. Disputes between the Judicial Administration and the Political Powers about the Implementation of Civil Law

Despite this, the administration of civil law in the Annexed Eastern Territo-ries remained without any legal basis for two whole years, because the relevant political powers (Party leadership, the head of the Security Police and the Secu-rity Service), and in particular Himmler in his capacity as Reich Commissar for the Strengthening of German Nationhood, who controlled the entire "ethnic policy" (the expulsion of Poles from the Eastern Territories), rejected any legal stabilization for reasons of the "ethnic struggle" and blocked the implementation of even the most minor formal legal basis for the "non-Germans." In the area of penal law, the judicial authorities had given in to the more severe policy desired by the Nazi leadership,[22] but in the area of civil law, which was much less suitable for such considerations, there were considerable disputes between the judicial authorities and the antilegal considerations of the political leadership. As head of the Deputy Führer's Office, Bormann emerged as a particularly strong hawk. He complained, for instance, that by the application of the German Civil Code, the judges had already "allowed Poles a form of treatment that must be reserved for ethnic German comrades"; he even considered the idea that "perhaps . . . in individual instances, the execution of court rulings would have to be prevented by police measures."[23]

The Ministry of Justice had consented in principle to the Party's desire to discriminate against Poles and, since they (the Poles) were stateless, to treat them as (stateless) foreigners under prevailing international private law,[24] but even this "inferior law" for Poles was too much for Bormann: he would have preferred to have civil law not implemented at all, or only for the German inhabitants of the Annexed Eastern Territories; all the concessions that the Ministry of Justice was prepared to make therefore seemed totally inadequate in Bormann's eyes.[25] The implementation of civil law, he told the minister of justice, in complete agreement with the police leadership, might result in the "unsuitable equal status of Poles and Germans";[26] the legal uncertainty that currently existed was preferable, because the implementation of German law would "only favor the Poles."[27] Security in the law was necessary only for Germans,[28] since only in this way could "economic development," "in which only Germans can participate," be guaranteed.[29] On the one hand, the problem with the proposals by the minister of justice was "that the judges were tied too strongly to the law."[30] On the other hand, Bormann also wanted to avoid any autonomy of the courts.

The only possible solution for him was the ideal of all totalitarian rulers, total control of the courts by the Party. As a result, he also rejected the umbrella clause for the application of the Civil Code proposed by the minister of justice, under which account was always to be taken of "ethnic interests," because a "political decision . . . would be imposed" on the judges who were unable to make it.[31]

Faced with this extreme attitude, the administrative heads in the Annexed Eastern Territories took a variety of stances. Most of them believed that the implementation of civil law was "expedient" in principle but favored very heavy discriminatory measures (exclusion of all rights of action and acquisition of property, prohibition on "mixed marriages" for Poles). Furthermore, implementation should not be a blanket measure but rather successive as required by the circumstances, not by Reich law, but by a decree by the *Reichsstatthalter* with the consent of the minister of justice, in order to emphasize still further their autonomy over Reich authorities.[32] One exception was E. Koch, the higher district president and Gauleiter of East Prussia, responsible for the Zichenau Administrative District, who intended to rule the district solely by administrative directives and regarded the implementation of German law as "totally inappropriate." The *Reichsstatthalter* of the *Reichsgau* Wartheland stated his consent to the implementation of the Civil Code, but he wanted to make its application no more than illusory, by supporting the proposal of the president of the Posen (Poznań) Court of Appeal for the inclusion of a rider to the implementing decree such that German law applied to Poles only where this was commensurate with "German interests." As the vice president of the Posen Court of Appeal expounded during an internal meeting on October 1, 1940, a personnel statute, an "inferior law," a "special law" must be established for and applied to the Poles.[33]

Even such far-reaching proposals did not go far enough for the Party leadership. To eliminate the "unacceptable situation" that a Pole could sue a German or give evidence against a German, Bormann demanded a measure that so far had not been contemplated by the Nazis: the total political control by the *Party* of all proceedings in which Poles were involved. This would be effected by demanding—with the agreement of the Gauleiter of the Warthegau—a preliminary examination by the NSDAP (*Kreisleiter*) of all actions by Poles against Germans.[34] The *Kreisleiter* would then decide if the action could be brought before the courts.[35] What Bormann really wanted—as the Reich Chancellery complained—was to reduce the Polish population to the level of "natives" totally dependent on the goodwill of the Party.[36]

Since both the Party leadership and the Ministry of Justice stuck to their positions, the only solution was to ask for a Führer decision. Before this decision, which would have inevitably been against the judicial authorities, was taken, the Ministry of Justice retreated and hastened to accommodate the wishes of the Party to a large extent ("the differences of opinion are not so fundamental as might at first appear").[37] In contrast to Bormann, the ministry "merely" insisted on the principle that "*some* sort of legal system must apply to the Poles" and that this could only be the German one. In the question of the content and scope of this legal system, however, the ministry made substantial concessions. But even these were still too distant from Bormann's radical ideas. By constantly rejecting and protesting against the proposed reforms emanating from the Ministry of Justice,[38] he was able, with the support of the head of the Security Police and the Security Service, who declared his solidarity with Bormann in all points,[39] and of the *Reichsführer*-SS himself,[40] to delay the implementation of the Civil Code and maintain the lawless situation until the mass expulsion ("resettlement") of Poles and Jews from the Annexed Eastern Territories had been initiated, the settlement of resettled Germans from the Baltic states and Soviet territories had started, and numerous legal issues that were awaiting a solution had become irrelevant.

Only after long negotiations did the minister of justice and the NSDAP (the deputy Führer) finally reach agreement in 1941 on the following basis:

> implementation of Reich law by a statutory order of the minister of justice (not by decrees by the *Reichsstatthalter*);

> consideration of the "special circumstances" in the Eastern Territories in the entire administration of civil law (material political qualification); and

> political preliminary examination of actions by Poles against Germans by the responsible presidents of the courts of appeal, if the court expressed reservations about the proceedings (i.e., no preliminary examination of each action by the *Kreisleiter*).

III. Decree on the Implementation of Civil Law in the Annexed Eastern Territories, September 15, 1941 (Decree on the Civil Law in the East)

The result of this agreement was the Decree on the Implementation of Civil Law in the Annexed Eastern Territories of September 15, 1941 (Decree on the Civil Law in the East), together with the First Implementing Regulation of the same date.[41] This decree implemented the entire civil law in the Annexed Eastern Territories effective October 1, 1941, without distinguishing between Germans and "non-Germans." Because the enumeration of the individual provisions now implemented would have been too voluminous, the decree settled for the enumeration of the relevant subject areas and fields of law whose provisions (in their prevailing versions) automatically applied in the Annexed Eastern Territories. Under section 1 of the Decree on the Civil Law in the East, for instance, the laws and other regulations for which the Ministry of Justice was responsible, including the associated penal regulations, now applied.

The major elements of substantive law included civil law, commercial law,[42] copyright, publishing rights and competition law, and insurance law (from January 1, 1942); explicitly excluded were, among others, rent protection law, hereditary farm law, and homestead law, because these provisions contained particular privileges that, of course, could not be allowed to Poles. Legal transactions and acts undertaken after August 31, 1939, but before October 1, 1941, were declared valid where they corresponded to the implemented civil law at least "analogously" (sec. 1, Implementing Regulation). This legalized the former legal situation with retroactive effect. Practitioners did not view the Decree on the Civil Law in the East as a constitutive act but rather as a clarification needed for reasons of security in the law, as confirmation of the previous administration of justice oriented toward "ethnic interests."

1.   Substantive Law

    a.   The Principle of Political Reservation for the Application of German Law in the Annexed Eastern Territories (Sec. 4)

Despite the fact that the Decree on the Civil Law in the East gave the impression that almost all German civil law now applied irrespective of the person concerned, it was qualified by numerous conditions. In the same way as had been formulated in the Führer decree of October 8, 1939, all these legal regulations were subject to the general condition of the "effect of assimilation," that is, the "ethnic struggle" against the Poles, laid down in section 4 of the political umbrella clause.[43] This regulation, which represented the clearest admission of a totally politicized administration of law, read as follows:

> (1) In the interpretation and application of the law applying in the Annexed Eastern Territories, attention must be paid to the special requirements resulting from assimilation into the German Reich.
>
> (2) In the event that in individual instances, the application of a regulation would give rise to a result incompatible with the effect of assimilation, the regulation shall not be applied and a decision shall be taken that complies with the effect of assimilation.

Of course, this provision was principally intended for all litigation by Poles against Germans. The question the court had to examine first was the extent to which German law applied. The provision did not clarify matters but merely legalized the previous ambiguity, as there was no binding regulation governing occasions when a regulation complied with the "requirements of assimilation"; the consequence was that—as expounded in the literature—the German jurist had to bear within himself the "guiding principle of his activities," namely, the unequal treatment of those seeking the protection of the law in accordance with the "ethnic way of life and legal system."[44] The next question was about how to proceed if German law did not apply. The provision in paragraph 2 provided something novel for this, by calling on judges to breach the law overtly if the application of a regulation was politically undesirable. Here, too, no binding standards were laid down. In the opinion of practitioners, the decision should be "drawn directly from the way of life of the German national community."[45]

The provisions of section 4 can be viewed as an approximate counterpart to the conventional analogy. It differs from the analogy provision of section 2 of the Code of Criminal Procedure of 1935 in that the latter allows for the punishment of an offense under the terms of a penal regulation and on the basis of the "sound thinking of the people" in cases where a legal basis was *nonexistent*, whereas section 4, paragraph 2, of the Decree on the Civil Law in the East instructed the judge not to apply a fundamentally *applicable* regulation if it was incompatible with the "effect of assimilation."

With regard to the general political line in the application of section 4, there was agreement that the German law implemented in the Annexed Eastern Territories should never have a detrimental effect on the Germans living there,[46] which was nothing other than a paraphrasing of the unequal treatment of the "non-Germans." Essentially, everything hinged on the "ethnic struggle," which meant that "non-Germans" could not make use of German courts as a right, but only if this was "compatible . . . with ethnic interests."[47] In the examination of whether *any* legal protection or right to due process of law could be granted, citizenship and nationality therefore played a crucial role.[48] Essentially, section 4, paragraph 2, of the Decree on the Civil Law in the East thus represented a charter for the judges to proceed at their own discretion without being bound to existing law: they were to declare prevailing law inapplicable in individual cases or generally ("on the basis of an interpretation of the law that takes the Nazi ideology into account"),[49] so as to "maintain their freedom of action in the interpretation of the law after the coming into force of the Decree on the Civil Law in the East."[50]

Nonetheless, because the "proven line" of the "ethnic struggle" was decided by the political leadership, only judges "who had made themselves conversant . . . with the aims and wishes of the political leadership" could develop "law-creating activities," as an official of the Ministry of Justice stated.[51] As a judge at the Posen Court of Appeal remarked, this included "carefully following the events of the day (in other words, the practice of routine discrimination)"; they would then see how "regulatory duties and development concepts are put into practice."[52]

However, the provisions of section 4, paragraph 2, of the Decree on the Civil Law in the East achieved general significance beyond their original area of application. They were understood to be a general principle and "authorization" to deviate from all provisions of the law to be applied in the Annexed Eastern Territories, depending on the needs of political expediency, an authority that had never before been granted to German judges.[53] The justification for this, though, was more than banal: the decree of September 15, 1941, was entitled the Decree on the Civil Law in the East, so its fundamental principles applied to all fields of the law.[54]

b.   Areas of Application of Section 4

No generalized assessment of the extent to which the courts made use of the interpretation potential of section 4 in their rulings can be reached using the few published sources available.[55] However, a number of underlying trends are evident.

Not permitted, for instance, was the nonapplication of German regulations to Poles solely because they were Poles. In a December 4, 1942, ruling, the Posen Court of Appeal, for example, declared inadmissible a Wartheland court's refusal to examine by way of juridical assistance a Polish defendant. The case involved a claim for child maintenance; the defense alleged that someone else had fathered the child. The lower court had denied the Pole this *Mehrverkehr* defense simply on the grounds that he was a Pole.[56] However, German law was not to be applied if it would give Poles rights contradicting the "effect of assimilation" (the policy of discrimination). In addition, contradicting its wording, which related only to "individual instances," its general significance meant that section 4, paragraph 2, was extensively interpreted in such a way that the courts could rule the nonapplication of German law to parallel or similar *groups* of individual instances.[57] Moreover, numerous discriminatory regulations under written law in the First Implementing Regulation to the Decree on the Civil Law in the East were viewed in the prevailing opinion as being merely an expression of the concepts contained in section 4 and thus also subjected to extensive interpretation.[58]

One particularly important area where discrimination was practiced on the basis of section 4 was marriage and family law, where Reich law applied, but with substantial variations.

In the law of matrimonial property, the former Polish matrimonial regime was not continued, although under German law for marriages of foreigners (and stateless persons of equivalent status) resident in Germany (in the opinion of the Germans, this applied to the Poles), the law of the native country of the husband was decisive (sec. 15, Introductory Law to the Civil Code), and for all marriages before January 1, 1900, the law prevailing at the time applied (sec. 200, Introductory Law to the Civil Code).[59] According to the literature, an examination must be made of each individual case to determine whether German marriage and family law did not offer "unjustified advantages" to the Polish petitioners.[60] One expression of this ethnically and racially biased examination was that the marriage license (certificate of nonimpediment to marriage under sec. 14 of the Marriage Law) to be supplied by all "non-Germans" was based on Polish, not German law, since the German racial regulations applied only to the German people.[61] The defense of *Mehrverkehr* in child-support actions for illegitimate children was not permitted to Polish defendants (counter to sec. 1717 of the Civil Code), because there was a German interest in establishing a "paying father" as quickly as possible so that the child did not become a burden on the German public relief agencies.[62]

An important role was played by German-Polish marriages ("mixed-nationality marriages"), which were seriously undesirable "from the point of view of ethnic policy," with their divorce receiving special support from the government.[63] In line with the divorce policy for German-Jewish "mixed marriages," not only was a mistake about the nationality of the defending spouse recognized as grounds for nullity within the meaning of section 37 of the Marriage Law of July 6, 1938 (mistake as to a personal characteristic of the spouse), but also a mistake about the "genuine *meaning* of nationality."[64] A further ground for divorce recognized in some instances was the pro-Polish conduct of the defending spouse.[65] Particularly in marriage law, where racial aspects were most strongly affected, the political condition of section 4 of the Decree on the Civil Law in the East was interpreted in the relevant literature as a form of *lex specialis*, to which all "special regulations" of German law had to yield.[66] A result of this was that impediments to marriage "for political aspects, including those to be observed by the courts," such as an increase in the marriageable age for Poles in order to depress the birthrate, were regarded as quite permissible: for the same reason, the grounds for nullification and divorce in the Marriage Law could not be transferred to "non-German marriages" straightforwardly. The argument stated was that these provisions were designed only for German marriages, for instance, nullity on the grounds of infertility or sterility (secs. 37, 53, 55, Marriage Law); Polish divorces on these grounds were therefore out of the question.[67]

Another example of special-law practices differing from Reich law is the treatment of Polish associations, to which the provisions of sections 21 ff. of the Civil Code should have applied. Under section 3, paragraph 1, of the Implementing Regulation, associations with legal status under Polish association law lost their legal status (if they had not already been dissolved)[68] if they had not successfully applied for registration in the register of associations by October 1, 1942. Of course, there was no right of registration, because the freedom to form an association had been abolished in the entire territory of the Reich for the protection of the people and the state by a decree of the Reich president of February 28, 1933.[69] Registration was therefore at the "dutiful discretion" of the authorities. However, this was merely a sham formula: an application by a Polish association was always to be rejected because, as explained in the comments in the First Implementing Regulation, no further cooperative activities by Poles could be tolerated. This would contradict not only the effect of assimilation under section 4 of the Decree on the Civil Law in the East but also the legal situation in the Reich, where any activities by Polish organizations were forbidden (Decree on the Organization of the Polish Ethnic Groups in the German Reich of February 27, 1940);[70] this applied all the more to the Annexed Eastern Territories.[71] The principle of the extinction of all Polish association activities applied to all associations and clubs, not merely political societies, although sections 61 ff. of the Civil Code did not exclude nonpolitical association activities.[72] Of course, these principles applied with even greater force to Jewish associations.[73] The admission of Poles into associations already registered also had to be prevented, since "it was obvious that the admission of Polish protected-status subjects and stateless Poles to an association must be condemned in view of the way of overall life and legal status in the Annexed Eastern Territories of Polish protected-status subjects in a stateless Poland"; if necessary, came the recommendation, the police could do "what was necessary"[74] [arrest those involved—Author]. Further recommendations by judicial practitioners (to the administrative authorities) were that in the case of new associations being formed, a provision should be included in the statutes whereby the association would admit only German members and that the admission of "non-German" members was forbidden.[75]

In conclusion, it can be established that in the Annexed Eastern Territories, the courts applied discriminatory provisions under special law by invoking the political condition of section 4 of the Decree on the Civil Law in the East with relative consistency in those areas dominated by racial ideologies, such as family and marriage law, or in which discrimination was written into the law. Apart from this, the judicial authorities were probably relatively restrained in the application of section 4, because direct release from the constraints of the law was a most unfamiliar situation for modern German law. It should be assumed that in line with their traditions, judges preferred to tread an indirect course, achieving the desired result by the expansive or restrictive *interpretation* of the law, rather than resorting to the provisions of section 4, difficult to grasp in legal terms as they were.

2. Procedural Law

A second category of principles in the Decree on the Civil Law in the East had a crucial effect on increasing the discrimination against "non-Germans." Whereas section 4 related to changes in *substantive* law, once the trial was already pending before the court, these principles hinged around the question of whether Poles were entitled to any protection of law whatsoever in German courts.

a. Rejection of Polish Claims on the Basis of "General Legal Principles"

Because of Poles' fundamental inequality in law, the most important *unwritten* basic concept of procedural law was that Poles ("protected-status subjects" or stateless persons) had no automatic right to due process of law in the courts and were only allowed to bring any action under the strictest conditions. Such permission was not to be granted whenever political reasons did not preclude it but, as the head of the Security Police and the Security Service explained to the head of the Party Chancellery, only if due process of law was necessary in the German interest.[76] In other words, this involved a certain extension—affecting particular persons—to the material political condition of section 4 of the Decree on the Civil Law in the East. This unwritten legal principle was derived in part from general "legal principles" and in part directly from section 4, with the aim of enforcing the slowly emerging "aliens law" for Poles in the field of civil law,[77] as was openly expounded in the literature.[78] This principle was therefore based on an equally unwritten condition: that there was initially a presumption opposing the granting of due process of law to eligible Poles. To clarify the question of whether German interests "demanded" that the proceedings be conducted, two strategies were formulated to provide a preliminary examination—or "filter"— of suits filed by Poles.

In all civil proceedings (including noncontentious proceedings) in which Poles were involved, an examination was first to be made as to whether the granting of a right to due process of law, that is, the admission of the suit, was in accordance with "German interests," as described by the commentaries of the practitioners (judges in the Eastern Territories) on the Decree on the Civil Law in the East. For litigation involving only Poles, it can be assumed that such an interest was normally denied. In such cases, the petitioner or claimant was given verbal notice of rejection.[79] A German interest was to be approved *as an exception* in litigation involving Poles if the granting of the right to due process of law served to "retain the working capacity of the Pole in the interests of the German Reich"[80] or if other German interests were affected. In contrast, a German interest in a lawsuit filed by a Pole was to be denied if Poles enforced claims that were aimed against the legal position of a German. On the basis of section 4 of the Decree on the Civil Law in the East, claims in such cases that were "substantiated under procedural law, but materially [meaning politically] unsubstantiated" should be capable of being rejected "automatically" "in this way."[81]

b.   The Principle of Political Reservation toward Claims by Polish Nationals (Sec. 5)

For those cases whose "conduct" could "*not be prevented*" (my emphasis) solely on the basis of the umbrella clause (sec. 4), the special additional provision of section 5 of the Decree on the Civil Law in the East was created as an omnibus provision to prevent any lawsuits filed by Poles from reaching the courts. This provision represents the procedural counterpart to section 4 and epitomizes the now familiar compromise between the judicial authorities and the Party with regard to the political right of preliminary examination of claims by Poles. In cases in which a suit by a Pole was not inadmissible in any case due to a lack of "German interest," section 5 provided for a general right of control by the responsible appeal court presidents:

(1) In the event that a claim is enforced or any other application is made against a German state subject that contests the legal position of a German state subject or an ethnic German in the course of litigation instigated by a protected-status subject of Polish nationality or a stateless Pole, and in the event that the court has reservations about whether the conduct of the proceedings might be at variance with state or ethnic concerns, the court must obtain an decision from the president of the court of appeal. This decision shall bind the court and cannot be challenged. In the event that the president of the court of appeal declares that the conduct of the proceedings is at variance with state or ethnic concerns, the proceedings shall be discontinued where they are affected by the decision.[82] At the request of the president of the court of appeal, the court shall issue an interim order on the enforcement of any decision ruling already taken. Until the decision is received, the court may take only such measures as permit no stay of proceedings. It may issue orders necessary for the ruling.

(2) Instead of making the decision himself, the president of the court of appeal may obtain from the Gauleiter and *Reichsstatthalter* (or from the Gauleiter and higher district president in those areas where no *Reichsstatthalter* has been ap-

pointed) a statement specifying whether the proceedings are at variance with state or ethnic concerns. Paragraph 1, sentences 3–6, apply correspondingly.[83]

The concept of "state or ethnic concerns" in section 5 was worded in much broader terms here than the concept of "German interests" in the section just before this one (a. "Rejection of Polish Claims on the Basis of 'General Legal Principles' "). Whereas the latter was based on *practical* considerations (e.g., of a financial nature), as described in the examples above, the former related to *political* decisions of all kinds, to bring the judicial authorities in line with the general political policy, which was to be practiced—without consideration for individual cases and the will of those involved—not by the judge but by the responsible senior bureaucrat, who acted in this instance not as an organ of justice but as an organ of the political leadership.

Nothing would have prevented transferring such preliminary examinations to the individual courts, whose "activities in creating law" were praised to the skies so frequently in official statements. But these were mere phrases without any practical effect. When it came to making political decisions, the courts often had no say whatsoever; rather, the decisions were centralized in the hands of the responsible appeal court presidents, who at that time were political civil servants in the real sense of the word.

This centralization was justified with the cynical argument—but one quite appropriate to the situation—that the interpretation of the concepts of "state or ethnic concerns" could not be left to the courts because the question of whether the enforcement of a claim by a Pole was politically "tolerable" or not "regularly exceeded the potential awareness of the individual judge,"[84] who "was not always aware of the political line being followed by the leadership";[85] the "central authorities" were in a better position to have a clear view of the "political requirements."[86] In other words, whereas the courts (either on the basis of general principles or on the basis of section 4 of the Decree on the Civil Law in the East) could decide independently whether the lawsuit of a Pole was at all in "German interests," section 5 of the decree covered cases in which such interests could be established but where such a lawsuit would offend "state or ethnic concerns," taking account of the legal concept (already contained in the Law on the Participation of the Public Prosecutor in Civil Law Matters of July 15, 1941)[87] that "the political leadership must be assured a possibility to influence court rulings in individual cases . . . notwithstanding the fundamental position of the judge."[88] Proceedings were regulated as follows.

If the court was convinced from the outset that the pursuance of a claim by a Pole against a German would offend "state or ethnic concerns," the suit was to be rejected at that time as inadmissible on the basis of the general political condition explained above.[89] Section 5 was applied only if the court had reservations about the conduct of the proceedings but considered them generally admissible. In such cases, the matter was to be submitted for a decision. If the appeal court president established no violation of "state or ethnic concerns," the proceedings were continued.[90] If he established such a violation, the proceedings were regarded as suspended (secs. 293 ff., Code of Civil Procedure) in terms of procedural law but de facto as unfounded, that is, as "settled."[91] The matter was simpler if a Pole was enforcing a claim by way of defense (setoff, contestation) or objection (e.g., right of retention); where they violated "ethnic concerns," defenses or objections were not considered in the ruling of the court (sec. 43, First Implementing Regulation).

c.   The Principle of Political Reservation for the Recognition of Decisions by Polish Courts and for Their Enforcement

Although as regards individual claims, it had now been "expressed in law for the first time that Poles are not equal to Germans in the field of civil law," thus preparing the way for the "emergence of aliens law for Poles,"[92] this inequality corresponded to the provisions for the recognition of rulings by *Polish courts* contained in sections 42 ff. of the First Implementing Regulation to the Decree on the Civil Law in the East. The fundamental principle involved was that on the one hand, proceedings that had ended in a final and conclusive ruling should be left as they were, but on the other, ethnic Germans should be protected "from litigation based on unjust Polish judgements."[93]

The extent to which the courts in the Annexed Eastern Territories made use of the possibility of political preliminary examination of suits by Polish claimants or of former decisions by Polish courts (if they did so at all) can only be surmised, since no relevant decisions were published in the general literature. This is no doubt because under section 5 of the Decree on the Civil Law in the East, neither relevant submissions at the appeal court presidents' offices nor the decision of the appeal court president were announced publicly. The question of the treatment of Polish rulings was probably also of little interest to the wider judicial public.

To sum up, it may be assumed with some certainty that in the field of civil law, judges were allowed numerous facilities for ensuring inequality and arbitrary decisions but that this probably had a less detrimental effect on the Poles than in the field of penal law. The administration of penal justice was subject to stricter controls by the judicial administration than was the administration of civil law. In addition, the boundless special umbrella clauses of the Decree on Penal Law for Poles were almost exclusively decisive in the "penal law for alien peoples," with the provisions of Reich law having only a subsidiary relevance,[94] whereas under the Decree on the Civil Law in the East, all provisions of civil law were essentially implemented, and in formal terms, special-law elements were introduced only in part. Despite the political clauses of the Decree on the Civil Law in the East, the need for the judge to examine each civil law regulation of Reich law for its compatibility with the "effect of assimilation" (sec. 4, par. 1) must have had a certain restraining or inhibitory effect. This did not, of course, eliminate arbitrary and unjust decisions, but it did prevent *universal* special-law practices by the courts, controlled from above. The fact that the right of political preliminary examination under section 5 did not provide for a examination of the compatibility of lawsuits by Polish claimants with "ethnic concerns," which was generalized by categories of cases, but instead—formally—a separate examination of each individual case, kept the *direct* influence of central political agencies at a distance and allowed the courts substantial freedom of choice. It was up to them to grant or deny Polish claimants the due process of law. In contrast to penal law, the invoking of "recommendations" or "principles" of the judicial administration to avoid taking responsibility for decisions was not possible here, or certainly not to the same extent. The same applied for the provision of section 4, paragraph 2, of the Decree on the Civil Law in the East, under which the application of a civil law regulation could only be departed from "in individual instances"; even if this provision opened up numerous possibilities for practicing special law, it can be assumed that in overall terms court rulings did not reflect the *centrally* controlled, universally anti-Polish line in every single decision.

Section Three

The Implementation of *Völkisch* Inequality in the General Government

INTRODUCTION

Main Contours of the Legal Policy: Continuation of Domestic Law and Primacy of the German Supervisory Authority

The conditions in the General Government contrast strongly in several respects with the extreme form of discriminatory legislation as practiced in the Annexed Eastern Territories. Although the principle of *völkisch* inequality remained the unquestioned maxim of the judicial administration in the General Government, as elsewhere, the political aims underlying its implementation were fundamentally different. In the Annexed Eastern Territories, discriminatory legislation was used both to segregate "non-Germans" from the German population and to bring about their total disfranchisement; in the General Government, the major aim of the legal policy, as set out in the official report on development in the General Government, was the segregation and encapsulation of Germans and "non-Germans,"[1] in line with the idea of a minority German ruling class in the colonial *Ostraum*.[2] Accordingly, in this first attempt at German judicial administration "in alien territory,"[3] the most important principle was to ensure that German law and German jurisdiction should benefit the Germans living there. No German should have to come before a "non-German court"; Germans were entitled to German justice.[4] The segregation concept not only served technical ends, but of course it was also used for propaganda purposes: the German courts became the platform from which the privileged position of the German master class could be proclaimed. The privileges were not limited to jurisdiction but extended also to procedure and the execution of sentences.[5]

As in the Annexed Eastern Territories, the question arose whether or not German law should be made to apply to "non-Germans." The decision made was not to introduce German law on a general basis. In contrast to the blind, radically ethnic activism in the Annexed Eastern Territories, economic considerations were the main motive force here. The General Government was perceived as a territory to be exploited for the benefit of the Reich. In order to keep the economic machine rolling (and as the office of the governor general made no bones about proclaiming), there was no question of displacement, repression, or

Germanization campaigns, the declared aims of administrative policy in the Annexed Eastern Territories. Thus, exclusively economic rather than political considerations motivated the decision to refrain from imposing a legal system on the Poles from outside; it was expedient to cause as little unrest and change among the local population as possible.[6]

Given that the German statutes were not to apply directly to Poles, three possibilities existed. The first, which was the line of the Party leadership, the SS, and the police, was not to give the country any legal system at all, to rule purely on the basis of police constraints. The second possibility was to apply German law "analogously" whenever the political situation required and to practice discriminatory law against "non-Germans" at the discretion of the judges or on the basis of secret directives, as was the administrative practice in the Annexed Eastern Territories. Third, there was the possibility of maintaining the established territorial law and limiting administrative intervention to its supervision. This last alternative best suited the German desire to maintain the economic activity of the region with as little disruption as possible. The official line was that extending the benefits of German law to the 12.5 million Poles, Jews, and other "non-Germans" of the General Government was neither desirable nor possible.[7] The maintenance of the domestic legal system also fitted most closely into the political concept of a "protected area" under German sovereignty populated by helots subservient to the German Reich. Governor General Hans Frank reveled in the dream of a colonial imperial legal system borne by the consciousness of German probity. The Poles, too, should have this consciousness, which should "spread its flavor to the whole community": "I put my confidence in these German judges." In a speech marking the inauguration of German jurisdiction, he spoke explicitly ("let us now say it out loud") of a primacy of German judicial practice over "native" practice, which logically therefore must be placed under German supervision.[8]

This form of "supervisory administration"[9] was thus defensive in character, allowing the domestic judicial administration to persist in principle[10] and limiting itself to taking care of the interests of the Reich and of German citizens and German nationals.[11] The organization and procedures of the judiciary thus had two facets: a system of legal protection available exclusively to Germans and a supervisory and control apparatus over the Polish judicature. Unlike the judicial administration in the Annexed Eastern Territories, the function of the supervisory authority was in principle not to include "non-Germans" in the German legal system and then to subject them to discriminatory law; it remained, so to speak, one step ahead, imposing supervisory regulations on the "non-German" judiciary in individual cases. All the while, care was taken to keep the supervisory activity of the German administration as discreet as possible in order to maintain the appearance of an independent Polish judiciary. The continued existence of Polish jurisdiction was the occasion for a great propaganda effort stressing the autonomy of the Poles in their own affairs.[12] In his press releases to the Polish people, Governor General Frank in particular took great pleasure in "showing that the Germans do not interfere in internal Polish affairs" and that "the Polish people can live with the law that is right for them."[13] But there was no question of two legal systems coexisting side by side, and certainly not two systems with equal status. For the political leadership it was clear that the domestic legal system, now subject to the political condition of the "security and grandeur of the German Reich," could not have the same scope as before. Polish jurisdiction was thus allowed to operate only insofar as it did not conflict with German interests; in the event of a conflict of interests, it had to yield, in the same way as "anything prejudicial to the fabric of German power in the region."[14] At the same time, this style of unequal treatment of "non-Germans" still left a certain legal status intact, even if of a lesser quality, in stark contrast to the complete lawlessness of the "rationalized totalitarian organization" in the Annexed Eastern Territories.[15]

The legal foundation of these political objectives was constituted by the Decree of the Führer and Reich Chancellor on the Administration of the Occupied Polish Territories of October 12, 1939,[16] which provided the sole basis of all subsequent special regulations: its section 5 empowered the governor general to decree autonomous regulations without being bound to the approval or the administrative rules of the Reich administration.

The continuance of Polish law was provided for in section 4 of the decree, under the terms of which the former law remained in force, "provided it did not conflict with administration by the German Reich." The purview of German interests was narrower here than in the Annexed Eastern Territories, where the out-and-out ethnic struggle lent political significance to "even the small and insignificant affairs of everyday life."[17] It went without saying that German interests included the politically most important areas[18] and everything touching on German concerns, both general and individual; first and foremost among these was the administration of justice, which relegated Polish jurisdiction to a secondary role.[19]

The particular style of judicial administration in the General Government,[20] which for the first time anywhere fully implemented the National Socialist principle of segregating Germans and "non-Germans," was something of a novelty, for no model existed for such a combination of a special administration concerned with German interests and a supervisory administration over the local jurisdiction. The governor general's autonomy made the judicial administration of the General Government completely independent of the Reich. The head of the Department of Justice at the governor general's office and the president of the German Superior Court did not participate in the regular meetings of the highest justice officials of the Reich at the Ministry of Justice, nor were they on the mailing list for the directives, recommendations, and other control measures issued by the ministry, apart from personal connections and avenues of information through the earlier relations of the senior law officers and the ministry.[21] The judicial administration of the General Government was under no obligation to send the central Reich administration business reports or situation reports. The absolute highest authority for the judicial authorities of the General Government was the (Central) Department of Justice. Thus, a self-contained judicial organization came into being, which, though it had many features in common with its counterpart in the Reich, possessed its own characteristic stamp in the form of even greater centralization based on the principle of "unity of the administration."

A. The Function and Structure of the German Judiciary

I. Supervision of the Polish Judiciary

The supervision of the Polish judiciary, which essentially maintained its domestic staff,[1] paralleled the structure that had been set up in the colonial territories to oversee the native judiciary. Its purpose was to ensure the absolute priority of the interests of the "German community" (whatever served the community was right)[2] and to eliminate from Polish procedural or substantive law all elements that in any way conflicted with "the grandeur of the German Reich."[3] There was, however, no need for detailed discriminatory or control regulations governing Polish jurisdiction, since this came about automatically with the priority of the German legal system. Polish jurisdiction was stripped of all important responsibilities and subordinated to the German system, thus ensuring adequate control at all times.

Although Polish law and Polish jurisdiction remained intact (after a brief interruption at the beginning of the war), their role was only subsidiary. Section 1 of the Decree on Polish Jurisdiction of February 19, 1940,[4] laid down the principle that Polish courts were competent for a case only if it did not fall within the jurisdiction of a German court. A similar provision held later for the domestic jurisdiction of Galicia.[5]

The judicial organization in Poland remained basically unchanged:[6] the courts were organized around a three-tiered structure: the *Burggericht*, which was generally composed of a single judge and corresponded approximately to the *Amtsgericht* (court of first instance); the *Bezirksgericht* (district court), which acted as court of appeal and court of last resort for the *Burggerichte*, corresponding approximately to the *Landgericht*; and one *Appelationsgericht* (court of appeal) for each district, corresponding approximately to the *Oberlandesgericht* (court of appeal).[7] The Supreme Court in Warsaw (as a court of cassation) ceased to function. The reconstruction of the Polish judicial apparatus was undertaken from the bottom up: already in October 1939, following the removal of "anti-German" persons and Jews, the military commanders once again permitted the *Burggerichte* and *Bezirksgerichte* to operate, and these remained active during the period of civil administration.[8] These courts regained their former importance relatively quickly, and according to the official reports were back to their prewar position by 1942.[9]

The procedure of the Polish courts remained based on Polish law but underwent a number of changes that eliminated certain constitutional elements; thus, the activity of the labor courts and lay judges was curtailed, as was that of the administrative jurisdiction.[10] Pending procedures were discontinued and declared null and void, and judgments under appeal were rendered final.[11] A special feature that very clearly brought out the principle of the segregation of Germans and "non-Germans" was the provision that Germans should not appear before a Polish court as witnesses; they could be examined only by way of judicial assistance through the German court.[12]

In line with the political aims of the German authorities, the jurisdiction of the Polish courts was restricted most heavily in criminal cases, which were generally handled by the German courts. Following the issue of the Decree on the Transfer of Judicial Matters in German and Polish Jurisdiction of February 19, 1940,[13] criminal cases pending as of that date were transferred *ipso jure* to the competent German prosecution; rulings of the Polish authorities were ineffective where German jurisdiction was operative. The German public prosecutor could at his discretion hand over a criminal case to the Polish judiciary, however, retaining the right to reclaim it at any time without explanation.[14] The intention was doubtless to get rid of insignificant cases that were of no interest to the German judiciary; at least, this may be deduced from a circular instruction[15] issued by the Central Department of Justice in the office of the governor general dated October 14, 1941, according to which no transfer could be effected if the accused had a criminal record, and especially if he was a habitual offender within the meaning of section 20a of the Penal Code. The decision to transfer was therefore always contingent on previous convictions. In the later years of the war, an increasing number of minor penal cases were passed over to the Polish judiciary in order to relieve the caseload of the German authorities.

Polish jurisdiction remained effective for all civil litigation between Poles and Jews among themselves. The German courts took over the case if either of the parties was a German citizen or a German national.[16] Civil cases subject to German jurisdiction that were pending before the Polish courts were therefore passed *ipso jure* to the competent German courts. Any doubts as to the appropriate jurisdiction were settled by the German court in the first instance and the German Superior Court in the second instance, and this decision was binding. There was no transfer in the reverse situation, that is to say when a case subject to Polish jurisdiction was pending before a German court. Rather, the case was dropped with the observation that it did not come under German jurisdiction.[17]

These restrictions on the Polish judicial administration were supplemented by wide-ranging controls over the German judiciary at both the personal and technical levels.[18] Newly instated Polish law officers were obliged to take an oath of loyalty and became subject to the immediate supervision of the district governor (justice department). The regular business of the courts and the personal reliability of the law officers were also supervised, but not the actual administration of justice or the impartiality of rulings.[19] A certain extraordinary remedy was instituted, however, in that every decision passed by a Polish court, even when unappealable, could be reviewed by the German superior court at the instigation of the head of the justice department in the office of the district governor, if the case touched upon "the greater public good." The superior court either brought the case before German jurisdiction or judged it itself without being bound to rules of procedure.[20] The range of rulings that could be reviewed in this way was extremely broad. In "particularly important cases affecting the interests of the German people," unappealable rulings by Polish courts dating even from before July 31, 1938, could be reviewed.[21] Nevertheless, there was a certain limitation of the right of review, in that the application for review had to be submitted within six months of the date the ruling became final (with the exception of those that had become final before July 31, 1938, which were not subject to a time limit).[22]

On the whole, however, supervision of the Polish judiciary was not highly efficient. Political control of the system depended on specific spot checks, and the effect could never be as sweeping as the incorporation of all "non-Germans" into the German legal system. Nor was the German judiciary without its technical problems: the chronic overload of the justice authorities, shortage of staff, and language difficulties made it impossible to implement the right to review Polish rulings in any significant measure.[23]

II. The Adoption of the Principles of Reich Law

The second task of the judicial administration in the General Government, that of developing a German judicial administration, was a very difficult one in view of the inefficient supervision of the domestic judiciary. Given the administrative autonomy of the General Government, there was no obligatory plan to carry over the Reich system of organization and jurisdiction across the board, but the creation of a completely new judicial system was felt to be too burdensome. The compromise that was reached was to apply the basic principles of the Reich judicial administration and to use that of the General Government to fill in the details.

1.   Supervisory and Control Powers

The foremost principle taken over from the Reich was that of authoritarian leadership, expressed in the form of vast supervisory and control measures. These involved questions of interpretation above all, to ensure that individual court rulings were consistent with the current policy. The personality of the individual in charge of the Justice Department in the office of the Governor General, greatly aided by his experience at the Reich Ministry of Justice,[24] ensured the conditions for a strict control policy and a hard line against the Poles. Since the control measures of the Reich Ministry of Justice were not applicable in the General Government, the Central Department of Justice opted to erect its own system of instructions and directives on the model of the Reich administration. These enactments served to clarify and the individual provisions to provide commentaries, but they also introduced completely new regulations, in which capacity they were doubtless intended to more or less replace the commentaries issued by the Reich, especially regarding the so-called War Penal Code.[25]

This intense regulatory activity was due not only to the basic doctrine of the need for supervision of the judiciary, but also to the confusion occasioned by the numerous penal provisions of the governor general's decrees (regulations against Jews, for example),[26] by the volume of Reich criminal law to be applied directly in the General Government,[27] and in relation to the procedural law practiced by the courts,[28] and there was a strong need for centralized regulation. The relative clarity of the situation in the General Government doubtless allowed these administrative measures to be complemented by oral instructions at meetings within the individual courts and with the supervisory authorities and through informal exchanges of information between the judges themselves. Such informal control was probably more effective than the control measures in the Reich, since the limited number of German judges and lawyers—barely one hundred in 1940[29]—working at a considerable distance from one another with very poor communications, probably gave rise to a greater closeness among law officers than in other Reich territories and a greater need for a unified control.

2. Review of Unappealable Decisions

The supervisory authorities also reserved for themselves the right to intervene directly in the administration of justice, however. In accordance with the basic Reich principles on the right to an extraordinary appeal by the Reich attorney general against a final and absolute decision,[30] any such ruling by a German court in the General Government could be reviewed within six months of its becoming legally effective if there were "serious doubts as to the soundness of the decision" (sec. 32, Decree on German Jurisdiction in the General Government of February 19, 1940).[31] The right to appeal was vested not in the chief of the prosecuting authority at the German superior court, as the Reich regulations provided, but (reflecting the control powers of the judicial administration) in the central authority itself, that is to say the head of the justice department in the office of the district governor. Whereas, however, in the Reich the court defined by the law was guaranteed insofar as the Reich Supreme Court decided on the basis of an extraordinary appeal, in the General Government the control exerted over the judiciary was total, for a special court decided on the exceptional opposition in penal cases and a German superior court in civil cases, designated each time by the Central Department of Justice in the office of the governor general, with a view to ensuring that the decision would go in the right direction. Nevertheless, for reasons of staff shortages or because the decisions by German courts were in any case harsh enough, little use was made of this exceptional remedy.

One such rare case was the use of an exceptional opposition by the German Superior Court in Kraków on June 18, 1943, when it condemned a Polish physician to death for practicing an abortion on a German woman (sec. 218, Penal Code), after the lower court had sentenced him to two years' imprisonment.[32]

The principles imported from the Reich were also applied to settle the prerogative of mercy, in order to bring home the strong position of the governor general as the Führer's representative. As early as 1940 Hitler granted Governor General Frank the prerogative of mercy, although the act was not made public.[33]

On the strength of this delegation, the governor general issued a decree on March 16, 1940, requiring that all death sentences passed by the German courts and the summary police courts of the General Government be submitted to him.[34] From mid-1940 on, however, the police were less and less willing to comply with this order on account of the differences between Governor General Frank and Higher SS and Police Leader (HSSPF) Friedrich Wilhelm Krüger (see below), for they executed the death sentences pronounced by the summary police courts in the concentration camps, which were totally under the control of the SS, and in police prisons, controlled by the Security Police. A pardons commission composed of the deputy governor general (the head of the Governor General's Office, State Secretary Joseph Bühler), the higher SS and police leader (HSSPF) (Krüger), the head of the Justice Department in the office of the governor general (Kurt Wille), and the head of the Burg Chancellery (Franz Keith), as reporter, acted as an advisory body in court decisions to grant a reprieve.[35] Execution of a judgment was possible only after the governor general had declared that he would not exercise his prerogative of mercy.[36] Otherwise the appropriate Reich regulations governing mercy applied.[37]

The political leadership, that is, the governor general, further claimed the right to review all judgments passed by the Wehrmacht courts, in his capacity of sole representative of the Führer.[38] Frank was unable to have his way here, since the Wehrmacht remained adamant about retaining sole jurisdiction and such a prerogative on Frank's part would have conflicted with the prevailing regulations under which Hitler as Führer and Reich Chancellor alone possessed such a prerogative (which he could delegate).[39]

3.   The Structure and Organization of the German Judiciary

As we have mentioned, the judicial organization in the General Government was structured fundamentally on principles taken over from the Reich. A number of simplifications were introduced, however, and the structuring of the supervisory apparatus went its own way in an attempt to bring the traditional forms of justice into line with the principle of administrative uniformity.

Whereas in the Reich a three- or four-tiered structure was the rule (court of first instance, district court, court of appeal, supreme court), the General Government made do with a two-tiered court organization. On the basis of the relevant Decree on German Jurisdiction in the General Government of February 19, 1940,[40] which produced a regular judicial structure in as little as a month,[41] the lower echelon of German jurisdiction consisted of the German courts (in Kraków, Rzeszów, Lublin, Chelm, Radom, Petrikau [Piotrków Trybunalski],

Warsaw, and Żyrardów),[42] which with their single judge corresponded approximately to the courts of first instance. The higher level consisted of four German superior courts established at the official seat of the district governor (Warsaw, Lublin, Radom, Kraków, and from 1941 on, Lemberg [L'vov]).[43] These courts, each of which had a panel of three judges, corresponded approximately to the district courts. The subordinate position of these German courts in relation to the special courts is illustrated by the fact that, unlike the regular judiciary in the Reich, they did not have their own prosecuting authority, and the business of the public prosecutor was accomplished by the prosecution authority attached to the special courts.

The special courts, which were established on the Reich model, took over the major part of the administration of justice with respect to the local population, as was common in "alien territory." These courts were among the first to be set up. Their chambers were composed of three judges, or one judge in simple cases.[44] As in the Annexed Eastern Territories, special courts were set up from the very start of the military occupation, in September 1939, in the region that was to become the General Government (Kraków, Radom, Czenstochau [Częstochowa], Kielce, Petrikau, Warsaw),[45] subject to all the pertinent Reich regulations on special courts.[46] With the end of the military occupation, a decree on special courts issued by the governor general and dated November 15, 1939, replacing that on the military administration of September 5, 1939,[47] maintained the application of the Reich special-court regulations. The special courts were now a part of the judicial system of the General Government. In parallel with the Reich, where a special court was set up in each court of appeal district, a special court was established at the official seat of each district governor (Warsaw, Radom, Kraków, Lublin, and in 1941, Lemberg). The special courts created in September 1939 that were not situated in the district capitals of Kraków and Radom continued as independent divisions of the local special court;[48] further divisions were established in Rzeszów (for Kraków), Zamość (for Lublin),[49] Ternopol', and Ivano-Frankivs'k (for Lemberg).[50]

The direct supervision of the judicial authorities was conducted by the district governor (department of justice); the highest supervising authority was the government of the General Government itself.[51] The principle of authoritarian leadership, embodied by the district governor as head of all the administrative authorities of the district, was breached once again, however, because the two-tiered structure of the supervisory authority was too complex for the small number of German law officers;[52] all important questions, including personnel matters, were in any case dealt with at the Central Department of Justice in the office of the governor general.[53] At the end of 1940, in line with the general trend toward centralization, the German judicial authorities, except for the public prosecutor, were subordinated directly to the office of the governor general (Central Department of Justice),[54] where they functioned as independent outposts of the General Government authority in the outlying districts.[55]

Some remnant of the principle of administrative uniformity remained for the justice departments of the districts by virtue of their function as relay and information centers for all the judicial authorities of the district. They served as collection points for correspondence between the Central Department of Justice and the courts, so that all decrees, instructions, and directives issued by the Central Department of Justice passed through these departments on their way to the lowest judicial authorities—a tight organization, which precluded all direct communication between the central office and the courts, and which the justice departments guarded jealously. This was even truer for communications traveling upward; in that case the justice department intervened as central agency for all reports, proposals, and complaints from the courts to the Central Department of Justice.[56]

An example of the significance of the judicial administrations of the districts as information centers is provided by the obligation to send in reports. Unlike the court of appeal presidents and chief public prosecutors in the Reich territory, the heads of the judicial authorities of the General Government were under no obligation to report directly to the central office. Rather, the justice departments of the district offices had to send monthly "district reports" on the number of meetings, incoming complaints, matters dealt with, personnel questions, and so on to the Central Department of Justice of the General Government. These reports were compiled from the progress reports of the various local justice authorities.[57] Certain differences existed as regards the public prosecutors' obligation to report.[58]

B.   Criminal Law as the Principal Tool of Discriminatory Law (Special Law) against "Non-Germans"

I.   The Basis of the Substantive Penal Law

Substantive criminal law in the General Government was also based on the Reich model, since in spite of its constitutional status[1] the General Government was considered politically as home territory,[2] being, in the words of a circular issued by the Central Department of Justice, "attached for eternity to the zone of power of Greater Germany."[3] As a result of this close connection with Reich law, which hindered, to say the least, the enactment of explicit discriminatory regulations, the development of penal law in the General Government was relatively straightforward, and it was possible to avoid many of the difficulties encountered by the judiciary of the Annexed Eastern Territories.

In the first months of the occupation, a legal vacuum existed in the General Government. But the region was spared the problems of analogous application of German law to "non-Germans," which dominated practice in the Annexed Eastern Territories,[4] since as early as fall 1939 the governor general had issued a number of decrees that avoided the use of vague umbrella clauses and legalization of the principle of analogous application. The crucial Decree on Administration of Justice in the General Government of October 26, 1939,[5] issued the very day the civil administration was established, fixed the principle of separation of the German and the Polish legal systems by placing Germans (German citizens and German nationals, later also called *deutschstämmige*, or persons of German descent)[6] under German law in all their legal relations (the "principle of ethnic affiliation," *Personalprinzip*).[7]

"Non-Germans" (Poles, Jews, Ukrainians, etc.) were liable to German jurisdiction whenever German interests were affected. They thus came before a German court for any criminal action that in any way affected German concerns and for other serious offenses,[8] or indeed in principle for any criminal offense whatsoever.[9] By order of the Central Department of Justice, Jews were always tried by German courts in penal matters; otherwise they came before Polish courts.[10] Except for the reservations just mentioned, other "non-Germans" were left to the mercies of the local justice system.

"Non-Germans" prosecuted before the German civil courts of the General Government did not have to fear the harsh discriminatory measures of the Decree on Penal Law for Poles, however, since this discriminatory law applied only to Poles with protected status in the Eastern Territories and the territory of the Reich,[11] and the General Government came under neither head. Similarly, Poles from the Annexed Eastern Territories who became liable to punishment in the General Government were not subject to this decree.[12]

General German penal law was to be directly applied by the civil courts of the General Government. The relevant Decree on the Administration of Justice in the General Government of October 26, 1939, spoke only of "German jurisdiction" and did not authorize the analogous application of German law. Similarly, the terms of the Decree on Special Courts in the General Government of October 15, 1939,[13] and the subsequent Decree on German Jurisdiction in the General Government of February 19, 1940,[14] expressly established the validity of the German general criminal code, which intrinsically applied to "other persons" than German citizens and German nationals.

The special criminal law regulations of the Reich, too, were applied directly throughout, although their formal adoption was not total. Certainly in the early days, the political leadership still proclaimed the principle that whatever benefited the community was right; the governor general made it known that over and above all "formulated texts," the judges were always to decide as the Führer would decide: they were not to abide by "the formal letter of a previously formulated system" but by the "strong eternal law being created on the path of national destiny."[15] But as we shall see, the courts hung on to these "formulated systems," that is, to Reich penal law, because they were happy to have clear regulations and hesitated to venture onto the slippery slope of analogous application with all its political and ethnic ramifications, and for which the excesses of the discriminatory legislation in the Eastern Territories served as a horrific example. Thus, basically the entire substantive penal code of the Reich was applied in the General Government, including the Juvenile Court Law,[16] discriminatory legislation such as the Treachery Law of December 20, 1934, the Decree on Parasites upon the *Volk* of September 5, 1939, and the whole section of the penal code dealing with commercial offenses. The race laws were formally introduced, on account of the alleged high frequency of racial offenses between (ethnic) Germans and Jews,[17] as were the Reich regulations on habitual offenders.[18] Further special penal law regulations were promulgated in the governor general's decrees, above all with respect to commercial offenses.

This broad application of the general penal law nevertheless did not preclude the enactment of regulations discriminating against "non-Germans." A number of regulations issued overtly under special law existed, but they were few in number and limited to a small number of offenses. An example was the infamous Third Decree on Residence Restrictions in the General Government of October 15, 1941,[19] under the terms of which Jews who left the assigned "residential area" (i.e., the ghetto) without permission, and any who afforded them a hiding place, were liable to the death penalty.[20] What is more, this decree was interpreted extensively by the Central Department of Justice to the effect that "on account of the political, criminal, and hygienic risks occasioned by Jews," anyone helping Jews who had not "left" the ghetto was analogously punishable by death (sec. 2 of the Penal Code),[21] because according to the "sound thinking of the people," this was no more than their just deserts. An extensive interpretation was similarly called for when young children below the age of criminal responsibility left the ghetto, this being interpreted as incitation by the parents to "leave without authorization" and punished by death.[22] The judiciary, which preferred to leave such "offenses" to the police and sometimes refused to enforce the decree,[23] was constantly admonished to adopt a harsher attitude.[24]

It is doubtful that the courts saw many of these cases, however, for the officials of the internal administration responsible for Jewish questions maintained that the procedure "to the point of liquidation" was too slow and burdened by too many formalities:[25] "rapid and uncomplicated shooting" of Jews was possible only by way of the police courts, a necessary recourse because "the Führer has charged the police with the final solution of the Jewish question."[26] In such cases the police intervened more and more frequently, shooting fleeing Jews without further ado on the strength of a secret order (not preserved) issued by the commander of the regular police in Kraków.

Further elements of discriminatory legislation in the penal code of the General Government are to be found in the procedural regulations. Here the attentions of special discriminatory law were shifted from the level of substantive law to that of jurisdiction and procedure. There was a reluctance to enact substantive regulations under special law for political and economic reasons, since the German administration depended on the cooperation of the Poles and wanted to avoid too blatant discrimination in law. Discrimination could be practiced more discreetly and easily through matters of organization and jurisdiction than through the public promulgation of special law. The special courts serve as striking examples of such covert discriminatory legislation.

II. The Situation of "Non-Germans" under Procedural Law

1.   The Special Courts as Instruments in the Struggle against "Non-German" Offenses

The idea of the Reich administration that jurisdiction through the special courts, which it understood to be "the mainstay of criminal law,"[27] was the major and ideally the sole instrument of penal prosecution against "non-German" and other offenders was not fully realized in the Reich, since as the youngest branch of the general administration of justice, such discriminatory jurisdiction existed only side by side with, and not over, the jurisdiction as a whole.

In the General Government, where it was possible to build up an administrative system more or less from scratch and the principles of the Reich held less sway, these ideas were able to flourish much more freely from the start. The population of approximately 10.5 million people living in the General Government (as of 1940) was 90 percent "non-German."[28] It was primarily for those "non-

Germans" that special-court jurisdiction was created, to demonstrate the severity and power of German justice, and it thus served as the major instrument in the realization of *völkisch* inequality before the law.

a. The Competence of Courts

The virtually exclusive responsibility of the special courts for dealing with criminal acts by "non-Germans" was originally guaranteed by the introduction of the opportunity principle. Since their institution in mid-September 1939, the special courts had operated side by side with the Wehrmacht courts and the summary courts of the SS and police;[29] they adjudicated in all offenses that the public prosecutor deemed it "necessary" to punish by a special court (sec. 2 of the Special Courts Decree of September 5, 1939).[30] That this was understood to refer primarily to offenses by "non-Germans" goes without saying. The special courts remained the chief instrument in the implementation of discriminatory law against "non-Germans" in the regulations later issued by the civil administration. Great care was taken to avoid promulgating special law openly, and the governor general's Decree on Special Courts in the General Government of November 15, 1939,[31] was universally valid and contained no special substantive provisions for particular groups, in contrast, say, to the Decree on the Implementation of German Penal Law in the Annexed Eastern Territories of June 6, 1940,[32] or the Decree on Penal Law for Poles of December 4, 1941.[33] Special regulations were introduced, rather, by way of abstract provisions. Under section 2 of the decree of November 15, 1939, the special courts were responsible for all offenses whose adjudication required special-court jurisdiction "by virtue of the seriousness or reprehensibility of the offense or the public outrage prompted by it," a provision that reproduced almost word for word section 14 of the Jurisdiction Decree enacted under Reich law on February 21, 1940.[34] Since the treatment of particularly serious or reprehensible cases by a special court was intended above all to intimidate the general population, it is logical that it should be aimed at "non-Germans," so that they would learn what German justice was all about. The head of the Central Department of Justice openly stated that the general clause referring to particularly serious or reprehensible acts was intended to put "non-German" offenders in the hands of the special courts, which were to "intervene energetically in the spirit of the German sense of order without soft sentiments toward criminals."[35] Where "non-German" offenders were concerned, the range of such acts was not limited to so-called serious criminality but included moderate crimes and economic offenses, in order to bring as many charges as possible before the special court. The special court further handled all criminal activity that the governor general's decrees put within its jurisdiction.[36] Since the majority of the governor general's decrees contained discriminatory provisions relating to Poles, Jews, and other "non-German inhabitants" of the General Government,[37] it is clear that the very great majority of prosecutions before the special court involved "non-Germans."

b. Procedure

The procedure of the special courts was also based mainly on the model of the Reich,[38] that is, the Code of Criminal Procedure and the specific provisions in the Special Courts Decree of March 21, 1933,[39] and the Jurisdiction Decree of February 21, 1940);[40] unlike substantive penal law, however, Reich legal procedural law was not to be instituted directly, but in principle only by analogy, unless the decree of November 15, 1939, provided otherwise.[41] The purpose of these arrangements was to endow the special courts with considerably broader responsibilities than the regular courts and thus implicitly to broaden their jurisdiction over "non-German" offenders. They also provided for a rationalization of procedure, which could thus be implemented from the start, much earlier than in the Reich judiciary.[42] In accordance with the principle of introducing a simpler court organization and procedure in the annexed and occupied territories than in the motherland,[43] the organization was tightened up, the procedure simplified, and the position of the sole judge strengthened.

Thus, in contrast to the Reich regulations,[44] the retrial procedure was not employed to transfer special-court proceedings to a regular court.[45] A motion for retrial was decided upon not by the criminal division of the regular court, as was the case in the Reich,[46] but by the special court itself,[47] that is to say by the very court whose decision was contested.

The main difference between the special courts of the General Government and those of the Reich resided in the position of the sole judge. The relevant General Government regulations contained no explicit provisions on this point. Since the analogous application of procedural law offered great freedom to decide whether or not to apply the Reich norms, the sole judge, a legal entity designed for the court of first instance, was simply pasted onto special-court procedure. This was done not by way of the legislation but by the easier route of internal administrative regulations. The original implementing regulations issued by the Central Department of Justice provided for the jurisdiction of a single judge when the maximum sentence to be expected was six months' imprisonment. With the coming into force of the Reich Jurisdiction Decree of February 21, 1940, which greatly enhanced the punitive power of district court judges, this change was carried over to the sole judge at the special court, whose position was "comparable to that of the district court judge." This was manifestly false, however, since the right of appeal was available against judgments by the court of first instance but not against those of the special court. In the same way, the summary procedure before the district court judge (secs. 28 ff. of the Jurisdiction Decree of February 21, 1940) not only was carried over analogously to the special court procedure, but also was transferred to the special court judge,[48] so that henceforth a single judge before a special court could pass sentences of up to two years' hard labor and up to five years' imprisonment in a summary trial.

Regulations on the issue of orders imposing punishment were a further move toward cost-saving and "technical rationalization" (O. Kirchheimer). Whereas under Reich law prison sentences of up to three months could be imposed by punishment order (and from September 1, 1939, up to six months),[49] in the General Government the authority of the sole judge at the special court was extended to the issue of punishment orders for up to one year's imprisonment or collection of a fine (secs. 8, 9 of the Decree on Special Courts of November 15, 1939).[50] The year 1942 saw an amendment unique in the history of German law, when the Decree on the Simplification of Criminal Jurisdiction in the General Government of October 24, 1942,[51] passed the authority to issue orders imposing punishment (sec. 5) to the chief German public prosecutor at the seat of the corresponding German court. Even in the Reich itself, public prosecutors had never been invested with such power, however much their authority had been extended. Only toward the end of the war, in December 1944, were they awarded this right in order to take pressure off the courts.[52] The decree of October 24, 1942, was part of the policy of strengthening the position of the public prosecutor, as had also been attempted in the Eastern Territories, where the Reich governor of the Wartheland, Greiser, had pressed for such an arrangement ("The Poles don"t make any difference between a judge and a public prosecutor in any case"), but this demand was refused by the Ministry of Justice, which insisted on maintaining the authority of the judges. No such scruples existed in the independently administered General Government, and indeed the position of the public prosecutor was also enhanced in other respects. Thus, he was authorized to make an arrest in the course of preliminary proceedings even without an arrest warrant issued by a judge, and he had the right to pass penal matters "of lesser importance" to the Polish authorities (sec. 1, par. 1, and sec. 2, decree of October 24, 1942).

The other procedural provisions also diverged from Reich law. The defendant had the right to (court-appointed) counsel only insofar as this was "feasible" (sec. 6 of the Decree on Special Courts of November 15, 1939), whereas under Reich law such cases were clearly enumerated and defense counsel was always appointed if justified by the "seriousness of the act or the difficulty of the technical and legal situation" (compulsory representation, sec. 32 of the Jurisdiction Decree of February 21, 1940).

None of these procedural rules contained special provisions discriminating against "non-Germans," in order to preserve the appearance of fair treatment of all suspects. It was nevertheless clear that the extensions of the special-court powers referred to were directed primarily against "non-Germans," who constituted the great majority of arrests. Discriminatory law was also practiced by way of the established directives, as illustrated by the example of the defense of "non-Germans" before German courts given below.[53] But the Special Courts Decree of November 15, 1939, nevertheless still provided "non-Germans" with a more or less orderly trial and certain legal rights. The procedure of the special courts in the General Government thus appear a model of moderation in contrast to the conditions reigning in the Annexed Eastern Territories. At the same time, it must not be forgotten that the most important field of criminal law, namely resistance against the occupying powers, had been taken out of the hands of the special courts and transferred to the military courts or the summary drumhead police courts. The basic Decree on Combating Acts of Violence in the General Government of October 31, 1939 (death sentence for all violent acts against "the German Reich," German individuals, or German property [see below]),[54] provided for transfer of a case to the public prosecutor at the competent special court only if its complexity or difficulties of obtaining evidence made it unsuited for judication by a summary police court (sec. 11, par. 2). The decision in this regard was at the discretion of the police court, and the extensive interpretation of the term *violent offense* by the SS and the police ensured that the special courts dealt only with cases of passing interest.

The jurisdiction of the special courts was thus limited to criminal cases passed over from the police courts or less serious offenses not covered by the Acts of Violence Decree of October 31, 1939 (for example anti-German remarks).[55] Until 1942 political crimes that did not involve violence, such as high treason or espionage, fell within the purview of the Reich court-martial, not the special courts.[56] The authorities of the General Government were not willing to accept this reduced competence, and in their desire for autonomy they made efforts to establish their own people's court for such cases and to recruit a former assistant judge there as adviser. The justification given was the excessive caseload of the Reich court-martial. The plan was of course attacked by the justice administration of the Reich, and State Secretary Freisler above all spoke out against the proposal to establish a branch of the People's Court in the General Government.[57]

The legal situation changed in 1942, however, and the Wehrmacht used its new-found authority to transfer more and more of these offenses to the special courts;[58] finally they were dealt with centrally by the Special Court of Kraków.[59]

To summarize, the effective jurisdiction of the special courts was such that all nonpolitical offenses having a bearing on German interests, such as economic crimes (smuggling, black-market dealing, unauthorized sale of ration cards) and violations of the governor general's decrees, were transferred to them;[60] further purely criminal acts directed in any way against Germans or German institutions (e.g., blackmail, impersonation of an official) and moderate and serious criminal offenses came under the general clauses mentioned above.

2.   Jurisdiction and Procedure of the "German Courts"

The German courts also existed for dealing with "non-German" crimes. Their jurisdiction was very limited and their role doubly subordinate, however, for the governor general's crucial Decree on German Jurisdiction in the General Government of February 19, 1940,[61] explicitly maintained the powers of both the summary police courts and the special courts (sec. 2, pars. 2, 3). The named responsibilities of the German courts were offenses committed "in a building, room, or installation serving the purposes of an official German agency" or "in the service of the German administration" (sec. 7, par. 2, subpars. 3, 4). The other competences were summarized in a general clause in sec. 7, par. 2, subpars. 1, 2):

> This jurisdiction applies to other persons not already subject to German criminal jurisdiction under the terms of section 2 of the Decree on Special Courts in the General Government of November 15, 1939 (*VoBl. GGP*, p. 34), and who have committed offenses that
>
> (1) are directed against the security and reputation of the German Reich and German people, its interests, and the life, health, honor, and property of German citizens and German nationals;
>
> (2) are punishable under decrees issued by the governor general or under his authority.

The implications of these broad formulations are even greater than they appear, for in effect the German courts were competent to deal only with offenses of minor importance with no political impact and without interest for special-court proceedings, such as crimes by Poles and Jews among themselves or minor offenses such as violations of statutory closing hours, refusal to work, refusal to wear the yellow star, and so on.[62] This was an omnibus clause intended to cover all offenses by "non-Germans" that could in some way harm German interests.

Given the wide-ranging jurisdiction of the summary police courts and the special courts, however, the number of those offenses was inconsequential. Thus, few cases were dealt with by the German courts,[63] which had a correspondingly simple structure and procedure.

Although in penal matters the special courts were to implement Reich procedural law analogously, provided no other provisions applied,[64] the special rules set out in sections 10–15 and 26–28 of the decree of February 19, 1940, contained so many derogations that essential Reich principles were lost in the process. The exceptions referred to simplifications of procedure and a strengthening of the position of the sole judge. (The same exceptions applied to special-court procedure.) Thus, it was not obligatory for a representative of the public prosecutor to be present in criminal cases tried before the German court. In accordance with a decree issued by the Central Department of Justice on December 4, 1941, the Reich regulations on the summary procedure before the court of first instance were to be applied analogously by the German courts (as well as by the special courts).[65] A decision by the German lower court could be contested only by an appeal against sentence or an interlocutory appeal to the German Superior Court (with a time limit of two weeks), which gave a final ruling. Recourse to an appeal on points of law was done away with "for the sake of simplicity."[66] Further simplifications were the inadmissibility of private prosecution, the abolition of the right to court-assigned defense, which was permitted "only insofar as feasible," and finally the aforementioned extension of the authority of the public prosecutor, who as a result of the Simplification Decree of October 24, 1942, was also authorized to issue a summary punishment order of up to one year's imprisonment by way of the regular procedure.[67]

The Simplification Decree of October 24, 1942, the advent of which coincided approximately with the first deportations of Jews from the ghettos of the General Government to the extermination camps, further introduced special procedural provisions that explicitly discriminated against "non-Germans," valid also in the special courts. Thus, the swearing in of Jews as witnesses in criminal proceedings was proclaimed generally inadmissible earlier than in the Reich,[68] so as to render their statements valueless. Notwithstanding sections 59 and 60 of the Code of Criminal Procedure, the German courts were further empowered to refuse to swear in a witness even if the defendant and the defense counsel (sec. 4) were not averse to it, a regulation that of course was also aimed at "non-Germans." Particular simplifications were introduced for criminal proceedings against Jews who had been resettled by a decree from the Central Department of Justice dated August 21, 1942,[69] promulgated precisely at the time of the first Jewish resettlements from Warsaw. Thus, an indictment could be waived in accordance with section 153a, paragraph 3, Code of Criminal Procedure,[70] or subsequently dropped (it no longer being necessary in view of the imminent extermination of the accused). A Jew who was already in custody was to be handed over to the "competent authority," the Security Police. Judgments were not to be executed, except for the death sentence.

III. The Elaboration of Discriminatory Law by the Courts: A Review of Sentencing Practice

Despite the elements of discriminatory legislation introduced into the criminal law system of the General Government by the regulations governing jurisdiction and procedure mentioned above, the very structure of the system still benefited "non-Germans" in some ways. The absence of overt discriminatory regulations and the relatively orderly system of criminal law had the effect of consolidating judicial practice in a way that never came about in the Annexed Eastern Territories. The legal structure in the General Government largely prevented the implementation of discriminatory practices by boundless interpretation of the regulations. Whereas in the Reich and the Eastern Territories, völkisch inequality was developed as an exception to the general legislation applicable to Germans, such an approach was not possible in the General Government with its largely "non-German" population, since by definition all statutory provisions were applied virtually exclusively to "non-Germans." The purviews of the different branches of the law were also clearly distinguished. The decrees on special courts and German courts of November 15, 1939, and February 19, 1940,[71] explicitly established the direct application of the Reich Penal Code and the subsidiary continuance of Polish law, so that there was little room for controversy over the type and scope of the analogous application of German law such as had caused legal confusion in the Eastern Territories. These clear demarcations also had the advantage of avoiding conflicts of jurisdiction, so common in the Annexed Eastern Territories. Accordingly, the sentencing practice of the General Government followed a relatively moderate and consistent line, leaning heavily on the penal tenets of the Reich.

This is not to say that the general principle of treating Germans more leniently than "non-Germans" was not followed in the General Government, except when a deterrent effect was desired, such as economic crimes in wartime, bribery, and so on, and also in cases of race defilement. Here the rule was (long-term) imprisonment;[72] death sentences were rare.[73]

In any case, Germans came before the courts very infrequently, since criminal proceedings against Reich Germans working in the German administration had always been referred back to the Reich (following approval by the governor general).[74] Offenses committed by members of other German agencies (self-defense groups, SS and the police, *Sonderdienst*, etc.) were largely immune from the law, since they came under the appropriate special jurisdiction of the SS and the police.[75] Excesses by German officials against "non-Germans" were judged leniently, if indeed they got as far as a charge, and a subtle difference was made between excesses against Jews and against Poles.[76] This erosion of general criminal justice was naturally aimed at privileging German offenders and keeping them out of the "non-German" public eye. In a similar vein, the execution of judgments against Reich Germans did not take place in the General Government but exclusively in the Reich,[77] since the presence of members of the German "master race" in General Government prisons could only be detrimental to the German image.

The other side of the coin was the principle of tightening up the treatment of "non-Germans." The judicial administration played an important part in this practice, calling for harsh treatment in a great number of recommendations and exhortations. A circular from the Central Department of Justice to all the judicial authorities dated March 31, 1941,[78] for example, called for severe action against economic crimes, especially illegal slaughtering; another, dated March 13, 1942,[79] demanded the deterrent measure of punishing all serious cases of transport theft (on the *Ostbahn* railway) "at the place [of the crime] before the full special court" by the immediate imposition of the death sentence ("the very harshest measures") in pursuance of section 4 of the Decree on Parasites upon the *Volk*. A similarly hard line was pursued by the police leadership, claiming that mild punishment, even imprisonment, had no effect at all on the Poles: Higher SS and Police Leader (HSSPF) Krüger demanded the infliction of heavy punishment, including execution, as a matter of principle.[80] Such recommendations did not fall on deaf ears. The heaviest penalties were imposed for even relatively mild offenses, such as the death sentence for nine farmers in Lublin who had not delivered their agricultural produce,[81] the sentencing of a Pole who had evaded the obligatory construction service in Radom to six years' imprisonment,[82] or the death sentence passed on a Polish physician who had undertaken an abortion on a German woman in Kraków.[83] Some courts had no hesitation in flouting the established law in individual cases and imposing severer penalties than were provided for by the statutes or illegally awarding such high court costs that they hurt the defendant more than any punishment.[84]

Despite such harsh practices in individual cases, the existing records of the special courts and German courts in the General Government and reports in the German newspaper of the territory, the *Krakauer Zeitung*, on the whole indicate a certain restraint that contrasts strongly with the deterrent and exterminatory justice of the Annexed Eastern Territories;[85] press reports, it should be noted, contained only death sentences and the heaviest prison sentences, probably for their deterrent effect.[86] There were still other reasons for this restraint, apart from the alignment of the justice system with Reich law. For although there were no direct organizational connections between the judiciaries of the General Government and of the Reich, so that the Reich Ministry of Justice was unable to exert political pressure and administrative controls, the General Government judiciary played a relatively minor role compared with the widespread police courts (about which more below), because the jurisdiction of the judiciary was confined and kept it out of the political firing line to some extent. In addition, the criminal courts were less subject to the pressures of the judicial administration and the NSDAP than were their counterparts in the Reich, since Governor General Frank, jealous of his autonomy and doubtless aided by his Reich experience, was at pains to keep out the influence of the Party on the administration of justice and also denied the Party a say in personnel policy.[87] Lastly, politico-legal considerations were also operative in the relative lenience of sentencing practice in the General Government: unlike in the Annexed Eastern Territories, there was no push for the out-and-out extermination of "non-German criminals," and the deterrent effect was balanced against the value to the Reich of maintaining manpower. The repressive policy of the political leadership in the Annexed Eastern Territories was characterized by the motto "hard but fair"; the propaganda slogan of Governor General Frank's brand of justice was "hard but human."[88]

This statement about relatively lenient judicial practice is true especially of the German courts, which adjudicated on more minor offenses and almost never passed sentences of hard labor and rarely of imprisonment; their sentences were mainly detention or a fine. Nor did the jurisdiction of the special courts against "non-Germans" ever equal the harshness of the special courts of the Annexed Eastern Territories. Although no criminal statistics or lists of judgments enforced in the General Government are available, a sample of the judgments of the special courts and press notices of the period suggests that the administration of justice of the special courts was relatively lenient in comparison with the totalitarian terrorizing justice of the Annexed Eastern Territories.[89] This does not hold for the severity of the penalties in absolute terms, but only for the number of death sentences passed. Conclusions about the sentencing practice of the other special courts can only be drawn on the basis of the general political circumstances, with which court practice probably ran largely parallel. Thus, we may presume that the special court of the Lublin district, for example, which had always taken the strongest anti-Polish measures under its governor, Ernst Zörner, pursued a very harsh judicial line, and this is doubtless also true of the Special Court of the Warsaw district, whose governor, Dr. Ludwig Fischer, also took a very strong line. Kraków was something of an exception, also as regards the administration as a whole, since in general more moderate conditions prevailed in the administrative capital than in the other districts. The official press reported "only" seventy-three death sentences between 1939 and 1941. According to internal reports, however, the actual number was very much higher, since only those sentences were published that would serve as a deterrent and an example.[90]

Regarding punitive practice in the Warsaw district, on March 1, 1940, a total of 33,000 criminal proceedings were pending before the German and Polish courts,[91] including 15,000 at the Warsaw Special Court in April 1940. Up to this time, as the head of the Justice Department in the Office of the Governor General stated, "only" 15 death sentences had been passed, "for murder, theft, and pickpocketing."[92] The Warsaw Special Court was reported to have imposed 36 death sentences in 1939 and 1940,[93] whereas in 1941 their number was at least 20. According to reports by the Warsaw district governor, as many as 498 trials were brought before the special court in 1942, 329 of which resulted in convictions, including 192 death sentences. Of these last, 187 were passed on Jews.[94] The death sentence statistics for the other special courts in 1940/1941 respectively are as follows: Radom, 3/7; Kielce, 7 (1940); Czenstochau (Częstochowa), 7/5; Zamość, 6/9; Rzeszów (Kraków district), 28/4; Kraków, 17/20 (including 1/6 for illegal possession of firearms).[95]

A review of all the rulings of these special courts indicates that a death sentence was generally passed on all serious crimes involving violence, such as murder, manslaughter, armed robbery, resistance against the state authority, and major theft, e.g., mail robberies. Economic offenses, especially illegal slaughtering, were, with few exceptions, punished by heavy prison sentences (a minimum of two years as a rule), and in the severest cases by death, when black marketeering (e.g., sale of the slaughtered animals) was also involved. Cases of theft received between three months' and eight years' imprisonment, mail and train theft up to fifteen years; poaching and other forestry offenses generally carried up to one year's imprisonment, whereas failure of Jews to wear the yellow star attracted penalties ranging from a 150 złoty fine to three years' imprisonment or even penitentiary. Currency offenses, forgery, fraud, receiving of stolen goods, and embezzlement generally attracted fines or several months' imprisonment, or one or two years' penal servitude in serious cases. Sexual offenders generally received a penitentiary term. As in the Reich and the Annexed Eastern Territories, sentencing became markedly harsher from 1942 on, probably related to the re-settlement of Jews that began in that year.

In 1940 and 1941 in Warsaw, for example, Jews arrested for not wearing the yellow star were sentenced to a fine or a maximum prison sentence of one year. On June 13, 1942 a Jew was condemned to five years in the penitentiary by the Warsaw Special Court. On March 27, 1943, in contrast, three Jews were fined only 150 złoty each.[96] A similar story can be told for Jews found in the Aryan quarter of the city without authorization, on which count the Warsaw Special Court sentenced a Jew to three years' imprisonment on March 15, 1942, and two others to two years' imprisonment on March 17 and June 8, 1942, respectively.[97]

The relatively lenient sentencing practice in the General Government clearly also had practical and personal motivations. Following the initial phase of deterrence, during which jail sentences were the rule, it was soon clear that such a policy was putting excessive pressure on the prisons of the General Government.[98] Accordingly, sentencing became milder between 1940 and 1942, with fewer jail sentences and more fines.[99] The choice of the judges and public prosecutors in the General Government may also have contributed to this development. Not all the law officers of the General Government had been active in the ethnic struggle, and the enthusiasm expected of them by the political leadership was often wanting. This can be seen in the very fact that whereas a large number of justice officials initially signed up voluntarily for service in the Annexed Eastern Territories (*Osteinsatz*),[100] in the General Government there was very little voluntary recruitment; the Reich administration was loath to send personnel out east, where it had no direct control of them, and the supply was already short on account of the draft. Hardly anyone was keen to serve in the General Government, where living conditions were reputed to be very much inferior to those in the Reich and many other disadvantages were to be feared.

Various horrific reports on the poor living and working conditions in the General Government circulated in the Reich, and their effect was exacerbated by the fact that promises to promote and repatriate judges posted there had not been honored. Justice officials were already dissatisfied enough and had given up hope of better days after the war. The judges and public prosecutors took particular umbrage to the fact that conditions were much better in the other branches of the judiciary, that is, the courts of the Wehrmacht and the SS and police courts, with plentiful manpower and even translation,[101] while the judiciary was unable to cope with the growing volume of work. The best heads were clearly not going to volunteer for service in the General Government under such conditions.

As a result, the Ministry of Justice had to accept the employment of lawyers as judges or public prosecutors and transfer them to the General Government. Most of the law officers posted to the General Government in this way probably viewed their missions without any great personal or political ambition. Another reason for the judiciary's failure to attract ambitious individuals was the enormous caseload, many times greater than that in the Reich; the judicial authorities did nothing to relieve the situation, although transferring the prosecution of Poles for offenses among themselves to the Polish courts (sec. 1, par. 2, of the Decree on Polish Jurisdiction of February 19, 1940)[102] would have eased the workload considerably. The mentality of the top echelons of the administration appears, however, to have precluded all possibility of transferring "sovereign rights" to the Polish courts.

EXCURSUS
The Criminal Jurisdiction of the Police

In addition to the legal and personal aspects discussed above, a major criterion for the German courts in the General Government was the fact that they were not exposed to the many burdens experienced by their counterparts in the Eastern Territories: a wide-ranging summary police court system designed to counter all forms of active resistance against the German occupying power relieved the courts from having to demonstrate whether they could exert the rigorous deterrent justice expected by the political leadership.

The police courts, for their part, did not have to fight the established judiciary or be set up illegally, as was the case in the Annexed Eastern Territories; they were incorporated into the legal system of the General Government from the start.

1. Summary Police Jurisdiction Following the Decree on Combating Acts of Violence in the General Government, October 31, 1939

The basis of the jurisdiction of the police courts was the Decree on Combating Acts of Violence in the General Government of October 31, 1939 (the Acts of Violence Decree).[1] The drumhead courts of the SS and the police had been set up in the very first days of the occupation, and through this decree they were now elevated to the rank of independent administrators of justice;[2] thus, the police realized their aim of taking complete charge of all criminal offenses by "non-Germans" in the major branches of the law.

The legalization of police jurisdiction came about as the result of Security

Police arguments that dominated the political scene. That Frank never intended these courts to become a permanent institution is clear from section 14 of the Acts of Violence Decree, which gave the governor general the right to repeal the instrument at any time. Himmler, however, as *Reichsführer*-SS and police leader, could not be expected to relinquish such powers once he had obtained them. He and Higher SS and Police Leader (HSSPF) Krüger did not dream of relaxing their grip, and at the beginning there was little pressure on them to do so. The administrative leadership was intent on maintaining good relations with the SS and the police (the subsequent differences emerged only after mid-1940)[3] and from the outset approved the idea of breaking all resistance, real or imagined, by the conquered Poles through police action rather than the courts. Governor General Frank's Decree on Security and Public Order in the General Government of October 26, 1939,[4] which authorized the higher SS and police leader to promulgate police decrees without any limitation of their object or scope, was a testimony to this desire for good relations. And after the establishment of the civil administration in the new district of Galicia, the governor general himself pressed for implementation of summary police jurisdiction in this region too.[5]

Consequently, the SS and the police were spared interminable struggles with the civil administration in order to achieve the position they desired. Attempts by subordinate offices to include the civil authority in the summary court system were blocked by the administration itself, which insisted on maintaining the jurisdiction of the police courts. For example, the judicial authority of the Kraków district proposed extending such jurisdiction to the *Kreishauptmann*, and with the support of the head of the Warsaw district, Fischer, submitted a draft amendment to the Acts of Violence Decree in February 1940.[6] The initiative had no success, however, since the judicial administration, in accord with the district governor of Lublin[7] and Radom, claimed the existing jurisdiction in the General Government to be "completely satisfactory."[8] Thus, the power of the summary police courts persisted through the end of German control in the General Government, with no desire on the part of either the administration or the police to change it. The sole concession the Justice Department obtained was to have the name "summary police court" (*Polizeistandgericht*), replaced by "police special court" (*Polizeiausnahmegericht*),[9] doubtless so as at least to put on record the exceptional nature of the arbitrary justice meted out by the SS and the police. By that time, however, the power of the police was so firmly established that no amending decree was ever issued.

The desire of the police to give their courts a veneer of official justice can be seen in their proposal to grant them the right to confiscate a condemned prisoner's property "as punishment" in addition to the death penalty. The administration was at first able to thwart this plan, but such a provision was later included in the Decree on the Possession of Firearms in the General Government of November 26, 1941.[10]

The Decree on Combating Acts of Violence in the General Government of October 31, 1939,[11] threatened every single offense against the German occupying force, however minor, with the death penalty exclusively and as such was virtually identical with the Decree on Penal Law for Poles,[12] except that it made no provision for a mitigation of the penalty in less serious cases as did the latter. The offenses covered were

> acts of violence directed against the Reich or German sovereign power exercised in the General Government (sec. 1);

> malicious damage to German establishments or public facilities (sec. 2) (all Jewish dwellings being classed as "German establishments");[13]

> incitement to disobedience of decrees and instructions issued by the German authorities (sec. 3);

> acts of violence toward a German on account of his German nationality (sec. 4);

> arson causing damage to the property of a German (sec. 5);

> complicity in such acts, including attempted acts and failure to report one of the aforementioned offenses (secs. 6, 8, 9).

Possession of firearms and failure to report such possession were also liable to the death penalty, provided the offense did not come under the jurisdiction of the military courts-martial.[14]

The summary police courts were composed of a regiment commander or a battalion commander of the regular police or (from 1941 on), of a highly placed officer reporting to the commander of the Security Police and SD with a minimum rank of *Hauptsturmführer* and two members of the unit concerned.[15] As regards procedure, the rule was unlimited discretion. No statements by the accused or witnesses were recorded, merely the name of the accused, the name of the judge, the offense, and the date of conviction and execution of the sentence. Complex cases or those in which it was difficult to obtain evidence could be referred to the public prosecutor of the special court, although this was not mandatory.[16] But however deficient these regulations were in even the minimum procedural requirements, they did contain rudiments of a certain order such as was completely lacking in the summary court procedure of the Annexed Eastern

Territories. There, as we have seen, it was sufficient to belong to the Polish intelligentsia or to be classed as anti-German to receive the death penalty; in the General Government at least some recognized "offense" needed to have been committed. Certainly the court records contained no more than the bare minimum of information mentioned, whereas those of the military courts-martial indicated the offense, the motives, and the evidence, albeit in telegraphic form.[17]

2. The Extension of Police Summary Jurisdiction

Beginning in 1942, which was a turning point in the political and administrative development of the General Government toward a radically anti-Polish line, the already broad competence of the police courts was constantly expanded.

The first step was the enactment of the Decree on Protection of the Harvest of July 11, 1942,[18] under which all acts committed with an intent to damage or destroy the harvest were prosecuted, apparently in the belief that the General Government could supply enough food to make up the greatly increased requirements of the Reich. The decree also covered unlawful slaughtering.[19] Such offenses had hitherto been dealt with through administrative penal proceedings or the special courts.[20] Now they became subject exclusively to the death penalty and were passed over to the police courts, which made ruthless use of this prerogative, particularly in agricultural areas.[21] Such rough justice (combined with massive police engagement in bringing in the harvest) was still not enough for the police, and despite the strained relations between the governor general and the police chief (Krüger),[22] Frank granted them even more sweeping powers with respect to general administrative policy. For no apparent reason, given that the existing jurisdiction of the police courts was sufficient to satisfy even the most extreme ambitions of the SS and police leadership, Frank yielded to the pressures of the Security Police and, "setting aside all formal reservations,"[23] on October 2, 1943, enacted the Decree on Combating Attacks on the German Development Effort in the General Government.[24] This granted the police absolutely unlimited and uncontrollable powers, including jurisdiction over political offenses in the narrow sense of the term. The decree recognized only one single offense, expressed in the form of a vague general clause, which of course applied only to "non-Germans": "Non-Germans who violate laws, decrees, and official orders and instructions with intent to prevent or hinder the German development effort in the General Government shall be punished by death" (sec. 1, par. 1), a formulation that by comparison with the Acts of Violence Decree of October 31, 1939, must really have appeared to be based on case law. Such a formula constituted a quite unparalleled extension of police powers.[25] It gave the police unlimited authority to use their courts against acts of any type and degree that could in any way be interpreted as detrimental to German development (the secret implementing provisions included economic offenses such as black marketeering, illegal slaughtering of animals, profiteering, etc.).[26] To increase the effect of intimidation, the only detail made known to the public was that all disturbance of German development would be punished by death.[27] The already weak judiciary was now pushed completely into the background, and the triumph of brute force over at least a semblance of justice was firmly instated. The few rulings that have been preserved illustrate the casual manner in which the decree was implemented, death sentences being passed using preprinted forms, in contempt of all the recognized rules of procedure.[28]

The decree of October 2, 1943, also tightened up the type and composition of the summary police courts as compared with the original Acts of Violence Decree. The only courts authorized to prosecute were those of the Security Police (to the exclusion of those of the regular police force), and it was no longer obligatory for their sessions to be conducted by a high-ranking SS chief; they could now be headed by any SS chief from the office of the commander of the Security Police and the SD (sec. 4). The provision concerning the transfer of cases to the special court (sec. 11, par. 3, of the decree of October 31, 1939) was dropped. The immediate execution of judgments was stated explicitly, without any provision concerning the submission of a petition for mercy (so that the police often did not submit cases), whereas under the Acts of Violence Decree, execution was expressly contingent on the governor general's decision regarding mercy.[29]

Such heavy-handed implementation of the decree finally brought about a change of mind at the governor general's office, for the practices of the police presented the administration with an insoluble dilemma. If ever a pardon was granted to the recipient of a death sentence, he was immediately sent to concentration camp, despite the fact that the pardon prescribed a specific period of imprisonment. Governor General Frank, who expressed his strong disapproval of the police executions and deportations in private, considered repealing the "Sabotage Decree" (that is, the decree of October 2, 1943); the head of the judicial administration, Kurt Wille, opposed Frank's plan on account of the "security situation.[30] But apart from expressing his unease to his colleagues, Frank took no steps against the arbitrary police practices,[31] and the head of the justice administration also saw no possibility of bringing any influence to bear.[32]

The evident reluctance of the judicial administration to change the boundless jurisdiction of the summary police courts was probably due to this "security situation." For police jurisdiction was directed above all against acts committed by actual or alleged members of Polish resistance organizations,[33] and the judiciary in any case could not claim that those individuals fell within its purview. In the process, however, it cut itself off from major fields of criminal law and acknowledged the political hegemony of the Security Police, just as it bowed to pressure in individual proceedings.[34] For in the present circumstances the terms *hostile element* and *member of the resistance* were used to denote not only those who had actually committed an act of resistance but anyone who in the judgment of the police might possibly be expected to commit such an act. Thus, the pretext of opposing the resistance movement opened the floodgates to arbitrary police action. Some examples will illustrate this point.

Following the senseless acts of violence perpetrated during the "battle of production" (*Erzeugungsschlacht*) of summer and fall 1942, the Polish resistance considerably increased its operations in rural areas that had hitherto cooperated with the German authorities. In retaliation, the police courts turned to a well-tried method of political blackmail, that of taking hostages (a method that had also been used by the administration) and shooting them in large numbers.[35] Depending on the opportunity and "need," a number of "persons suspected of resistance" ("criminals" or "bandits") were rounded up and first sentenced to death for some offense, initially under the Acts of Violence Decree of October 31, 1939, and later under the Sabotage Decree of October 2, 1943. It was then announced publicly that the condemned prisoners were eligible for mercy but that the granting of mercy depended on the conduct of the population. Should further attacks on Germans or German property occur, the sentences would be executed in a ratio of 1:10, 1:20 or even 1:50, depending on the number and rank of the Germans affected.[36] This practice claimed thousands of victims.[37]

The majority of these executions took place in the city of Warsaw, where between October 1943 and July 1944 alone, on the authority of the decree of October 2, 1943, 2,705 people who had been rounded up on the streets and taken as hostages were publicly shot by the Security Police courts as reprisals against attacks on the occupying power or for alleged violations of the decree. A further 4,000 people were secretly executed on the site of the destroyed Jewish ghetto. In the district of Warsaw, at least 4,000 people were executed on the authority of the said decree alone,[38] a practice surpassed only by the excesses of the SS and police in the Occupied Eastern Territories and the Białystok district.[39] In the Lublin district at least 573 people were shot by "court-martial" between November 1942 and December 1944, in Radom at least 380 between November 1943 and December 1944, in Kraków at least 198 between November 1943 and January 1945, to which the executions of "a certain number" or "several" Poles must be added.[40]

If originally such police actions were carried out under the guise of punishing actual or alleged acts of resistance, very soon the summary police jurisdiction gave up using a formal pretext for the completely arbitrary terror they exercised against innocent people and every suspected hostile element, whether or not there was the slightest evidence of an act of resistance. For example, secret instructions issued by the commander of the *regular* police force ordered that Jews found outside the walls of the ghetto should be liquidated immediately.[41] The day-to-day reports of the gendarmerie include hundreds of such cases with the remark, "proceeded according to current instructions."[42] The main focus of police terror was, however, the so-called political arena. Early on, without any basis in "law," the police began a campaign to eliminate ethnic opponents through what they called preventive operations, directed particularly at the intelligentsia, who were then liquidated through the summary police courts. Such operations began with the roundups that were to become a regular feature in Warsaw,[43] subsequently spreading elsewhere, as for example the arrests of the university professors of Kraków and Lemberg (L'vov) in November 1939 and fall 1941. The victims were either liquidated on the spot or sent to the concentration camps, where the majority of them perished.[44] Neither the authorities of the General Government nor the judicial administration generally made any protests against such operations, except when they provoked too much public notice, as in the case of the Kraków professors, when the governor general intervened personally. Protests on the part of the judiciary in any case had very little clout, for following the establishment of jurisdiction of the summary police courts, it had relinquished any say in the whole enormously expanded field of political offenses and had even supported the broadening of arbitrary police measures by a tightening up of the Acts of Violence Decree as early as spring 1940.[45] Nor did the judiciary change its attitude when it came to light that the police had considerably overstepped their already extensive powers from the very start.

The best-known example of an operation against "hostile elements"[46] is the infamous "exceptional peacemaking action" (AB operation), which the governor general authorized the commander of the Security Police and SD to carry out on pretext of the "serious security situation."[47] Between the end of May and early July 1940, some 3,500 Polish political and intellectual leaders "suspected of resistance" were summarily tried in Warsaw and subsequently executed by the Security Police in the forest of Palmiry nearby.[48] Advantage was taken of this shooting to get rid of a further 3,000 "professional criminals" who were "unnecessarily" filling the prisons, without even the semblance of a summary trial.[49] Here, too, the judicial administration raised no objection, since such operations ranked as purely political measures and thus did not fall within its jurisdiction. The illegality of the situation was obvious to all concerned, however. Before the operation, the governor general expressly warned the judicial authorities not to initiate criminal investigations against members of the police and SS in connection with police operations;[50] the warning carried no threat of material consequences, and given the known predilection of the governor general for pithy turns of phrase, it made little impression. The warning referred to the misgivings of a number of judges who were "somewhat disquieted about the imminence of the AB operation."[51] The head of the Justice Department responded that he had been unconcerned by the police operation from the outset, since it did not fall within the purview of his activity. For him the problem was less the operation itself than the fact that "the cases had been treated very differently," and he accepted the governor general's assurance that although "severe measures" had been necessary, it would now be possible to go back to a "normal situation."[52] Nonetheless, Frank and his colleagues were not fooled into imagining that the police would relinquish the powers they had usurped and change their ways.

The "normal situation" thus reinstated was that not only did the summary police court procedures continue as before, but the police stepped up their illegal mass arrest operations on the pretext of "preventive actions against suspected resistance elements." Such operations were no longer even purely politically motivated, for the high mortality of the concentration camps brought about an increasing need to "recruit labor,"[53] for which the General Government was the major source. Thus, in 1943 alone, some 20,000 Poles were indiscriminately herded together by order of Himmler and transferred directly to the concentration camps by way of a "collective preventive custody order."[54]

3. Cooperation and Conflict between the Judiciary and the Police in the Criminal Prosecution of "Non-German" Offenders

Regarding such mass deportations of "non-Germans" to the concentration camps, there was even less concern than in the Reich whether or not the victims had been condemned and sentenced for a crime. For in the matter of "state police measures," and indeed throughout the criminal justice system, the judiciary and the police were working hand in hand to ensure that the police had access to all "non-Germans" remanded in custody, as in the Reich and the Annexed Eastern Territories. In October 1940 all the judicial authorities of the General Government were instructed to inform the commander of the Security Police and the SD of the number and type of all criminal proceedings conducted, the sentence passed, and the names of accused and convicted persons.[55] The police were further to be informed whenever a convicted person had served his or her sentence.[56] Requirements such as these, which gave the local police headquarters a full picture of judicial activity, went far beyond the standard practice of the Reich. The principal victims of police interventions were the Jews, whose "re-settlement" to the extermination camps began in August 1942.

A circular directive dated August 21, 1942, from the Central Department of Justice empowered the judicial authorities to stay proceedings against Jews in pursuance of section 154a, par. 3, of the Code of Criminal Procedure and to re-frain from executing a sentence except for the death penalty under section 456a of the Code,[57] so as to release Jews committed to criminal or executory proceed-ings for deportation to the camps. In order to include Jews who had already been "resettled," a further directive was issued on October 7, 1942, to the effect that criminal proceedings or execution of the sentence should be suspended in such cases. The Polish judiciary was also to dispense with a record of proceedings con-cerning resettled Jews, since in view of the present circumstances and the heavy workload of the police authorities, "determination of the new place of residence of a resettled individual" would give rise to "insurmountable difficulties."[58]

These directives clearly indicate the contribution of the justice authorities to their present insignificant and weak position vis-à-vis the power of the police. Far too late, the governor general and his officials discovered the extent to which they had set the seal on illegal practices. Only in 1944 did the governor general insist that the judiciary assert itself more actively against police detention prac-tices.[59] By that time there was no hope for anything other than a makeshift solu-tion. Regarding people who had been convicted by the police courts and subse-quently granted a pardon so that they could be transferred to a concentration camp after their release, the governor general appealed only for a transmutation to a prison sentence, in a bid to preserve at least the executory prerogative of the courts.[60] But police arbitrariness continued unabated.

The justice authorities had, however, already earlier made a number of at-tempts to maintain their punitive and executory prerogatives with respect to concentration camp inmates. According to the current doctrine, preventive de-tention was clearly distinguished from criminal proceedings and execution, and committal to a concentration camp did not affect the course of criminal pro-ceedings. When, as often happened in such cases, the judiciary hesitated to go through with the penal procedure, they were reminded—in the last instance by the directive of February 12, 1943—that preventive detention was not a ground for a temporary stay of proceedings, since the "absence" of the accused under the terms of section 205 of the Code of Criminal Procedure was not applicable, nor was an offense under section 154a, paragraph 2, of this Code, since "accom-modation in a concentration camp" was "neither a punishment nor a preventive detention and correction measure." In the case of minor offenses, at most a stay of proceedings was possible under section 154a, paragraph 2, of the Code of Criminal Procedure, but apart from this the prosecution of criminal offenses was to be conducted against all suspects in a concentration camp. The Security Police were to request that the prisoner be handed over; and in the event of difficulties, a report was to be sent to the Central Department of Justice.[61] A directive of August 13, 1941, had earlier established that penalties recognized by the Polish or German courts were in principle also to be carried out when the prisoner had been committed to a concentration camp and that the sentence was to be served in a General Government prison,[62] not in concentration camp. In such cases, too, the Security Police was to request that the prisoner be handed over.[63] On the basis of a later directive dated February 12, 1943, however, prisoners were only to be brought out of a concentration camp to serve a prison sentence when a sentence of six months or more was to be expected. If a shorter sentence was anticipated, proceedings were to be suspended and the prisoner was to remain in protective detention.[64]

The police did not, of course, take kindly to measures designed to restore the judiciary's authority. The higher SS and police leader (HSSPF), SS-*Obergruppenführer* Krüger, had always held the imprisonment of Jews and Poles to be completely misguided, considering forced labor in a concentration camp the only suitable activity for "non-Germans," and the SS and police authorities frequently refused to hand over prisoners to the judiciary. The judiciary, having no support in political circles, attempted to safeguard its interests by dint of compromise. A circular from the Central Department of Justice dated March 15, 1941, reported an "agreement" between the Central Department and the higher SS and police leader (HSSPF) to the effect that prisoners were to be released to the justice authorities only at the request of the Security Police after they had served their sentence or if an arrest warrant was refused or canceled. The justice authorities had strict instructions to return them to the Security Police only when there was an individual request to do so.[65] We may thus conclude that until this time such transfer to the police was effected automatically on release from imprisonment.

Any other "agreements" existing at the local level were superseded by the directive of March 15, 1941. Thus, in contrast to the situation in the Reich, the judicial authorities were explicitly bound to hand over discharged prisoners who had served a sentence or were on remand, nobody of interest to the police was released.[66] They nevertheless tried, with some success, to avoid returning people who had been in preventive detention before the institution of criminal proceedings: an order dated May 22, 1943, from the Central Department of Justice instructed that requests by the Security Police to return prisoners after release from custody should not be "indulged."[67] For their part, the Security Police complied less and less with requests from the judiciary to release detainees for the purpose of serving a sentence. The judicial administration reported that the police refused to release prisoners detained in concentration camp because their political record was such that they would constitute a danger to the people and the state.[68] The commanders of the Security Police and the SD in the various districts later even spread the rumor that the release of prisoners in preventive custody had been agreed upon only for the purpose of executing the death penalty (intending to dissuade the judiciary from making further requests for their release), a contention that was sharply refuted by the Central Department of Justice. Such actions by the police nevertheless had some success in shaking the confidence of the judiciary, who were instructed to continue to comply with the directives of August 13, 1941,[69] and February 12, 1943,[70] requiring that all prisoners in preventive custody against whom proceedings were pending or who had received a penalty exceeding six months were to be claimed by the Security Police.[71]

Once a "non-German" was in the hands of the police, there was thus little chance that he would ever see freedom again. If he was already in custody in a police prison or a concentration camp, he was often not released to the judiciary for his case to be pursued. If this did happen, however, he was rearrested and handed over to the police immediately after his release from pretrial confinement or imprisonment, since, as we have seen, the police were kept informed of the outcome of all criminal proceedings and the discharge of prisoners. This interplay between the judiciary and the police undermined the already weak position of the judiciary in the General Government still further. Yet, in spite of its lack of authority compared with the rest of the Reich and its subservience to police demands, the very existence of the judiciary remained a thorn in the side of the SS and the police, thwarting as it did Himmler's idea of sole police jurisdiction over all "non-Germans." Himmler voiced his complaints against the judiciary of the General Government, like that of the Annexed Eastern Territories, claiming that "the Poles are much too interested in the idea of expiation, rather than in defense against real threats."[72] In his view, the police were entitled to sole criminal jurisdiction over "non-Germans," which had already been largely granted by the decrees of October 31, 1939, and October 2, 1943, without "interference" by the judiciary. It was in the General Government that the police came closest to achieving this ambition.

C. Civil Law

I. Discriminatory Elements in Substantive Law

In a far greater measure than in criminal law, the civil law system of the General Government was structured along the lines of strict separation of Germans and "non-Germans" (*Personalprinzip*): German jurisdiction and German law for German citizens and German nationals, Polish law and Polish jurisdiction for everyone else.[1] German law was thus a discriminatory law privileging Germans, based on the notion of nationality.[2] It was not enacted afresh, but with the Decree on German Jurisdiction in the General Government of February 19, 1940,[3] Reich civil law exclusively held sway over the territory.

For civil litigations, cases of execution of civil sentences, bankruptcy and settlement matters, noncontentious proceedings, and matters concerning the register of commerce, Reich law alone was applicable when German citizens and German nationals were involved among themselves. But in order to privilege Germans, the same rule was also applied in cases in which only one of the parties was German, irrespective of whether he was the plaintiff or the accused.[4] In execution proceedings and in bankruptcy and settlement matters, Reich law held when the proceedings were directed against German citizens and German nationals. This "homeland law" also applied in matters of civil status[5] and in personal, family, and inheritance questions, and it applied to the form of the marriage when one of the partners was a German citizen or a German national.[6] In company law, German jurisdiction was applicable for companies established under that regime, for other corporate bodies in private and public law, and for management of the register of commerce. Associations established under Polish law were to be dealt with under German law only if the personally liable associate of a trading association was a German citizen or a German national, or where at least half of the board was composed of German nationals.[7]

This enumerative treatment precluded analogous application of other Reich laws to both Germans and "non-Germans." Important fields of Reich civil law were thus not applicable in the General Government, for example tenancy, labor, insurance, and so forth; a considerable number of branches were dealt with under the former Polish law, as the practice of keeping land register and mortgage records within Polish jurisdiction illustrates.[8]

Regarding all civil matters concerning Poles and Jews among themselves, the principle of enumeration ensured that Polish law continued to be valid except when it ran counter to the "objectives of the German administration" or in situations covered by special regulations issued by the governor general.[9] Little use appears to have been made of this blanket proviso—if only on account of ignorance of the Polish law—so that the territorial civil law remained almost completely intact.[10]

II. Discriminatory Elements in Jurisdiction and in Procedural Law

In matters of jurisdiction and procedure, the civil courts also followed the prevalent principle of separating Germans and "non-Germans." The German courts, as we have already seen, were available solely for the protection of German citizens and German nationals, covering civil litigations of natural persons and corporate bodies with respect to execution of civil sentences, bankruptcy and settlement matters, and noncontentious proceedings, so long as German citizens and German nationals were involved. As in criminal law, the courts of first instance were the German courts, of second instance the German superior courts, which for their part also acted as review bodies for the Polish courts of second instance whenever German citizens or German nationals were attacked by way of a special right of rescission,[11] since no German could be obliged to submit to the decision of a non-German court. Civil procedure was based on the Prussian regulations by virtue of sections 22 and 25 of the Decree on German Jurisdiction in the General Government of February 19, 1940, but only when not determined otherwise. Thus, in litigations involving Germans, the Code of Civil Procedure was to be applied together with the special regulations arising out of sections 26–28 of the decree of February 19, 1940. These special regulations included the limitation of the right to appeal to a single appeal court (the German superior courts), abolition of compulsory representation by counsel, and an equivalence of the General Government with the Reich in matters of execution, in that judgments made by Reich courts could automatically be executed in the General Government. The political hold of German jurisdiction over the Polish civil courts was expressed in the regulation establishing that for reasons of the "greater public good," the right of review of the German superior courts also extended to unappealable rulings of the Polish civil court (at the request of the head of the justice department in the office of the competent district governor),[12] an arrangement that was doubtless never of great significance.

III. Summary

A comparison of the discriminatory laws and practices in the General Government and the Annexed Eastern Territories shows that the formal legality existing in the General Government provided, on the whole, a certain degree of legal security, whereas in the Annexed Eastern Territories, all formal and substantive principles and definitions were in a constant process of disruption. This is true first for civil law. Until 1941 the judiciary of the Annexed Eastern Territories was only able to apply Reich civil law analogously, and even following implementation of the Decree on the Implementation of Civil Law in the Annexed Eastern Territories of September 15, 1941, the jurisdiction was still subject to the political proviso of assimilation and conformity with "state or ethnic concerns" (secs. 4, 5 of the decree). In the General Government, the most important elements of Reich civil law had been introduced enumeratively from the start on the basis of the ethnic affiliation of the individual, with Polish law remaining intact providing German interests were not at stake (sec. 19, Decree on German Jurisdiction in the General Government of February 19, 1940). The courts of the General Government were thus in a far more favorable position than those of the Annexed Eastern Territories, which were obliged to check every regulation and every procedure involving "non-Germans" for their compatibility with the principle of assimilation, that is, with principles of racial hatred and the inferiority of other peoples (the ethnic struggle). In the realm of civil law, these umbrella clauses rendered the application of Reich law to "non-Germans" subject to political considerations almost as much as did the boundless umbrella clauses covering Poles and Jews in criminal law. The difference between these two laws was merely that with the Decree on the Implementation of Civil Law in the Annexed Eastern Territories, the Reich Ministry of Justice once again managed to retain legal relations between Germans and "non-Germans," at least in formal terms, whereas in the Decree on Penal Law for Poles, these bonds were definitively severed.

The differences between the Annexed Eastern Territories and the General Government with respect to their legislation and legal practice are more apparent in the field of criminal than in civil law. Before the enactment of the Decree on Penal Law for Poles on December 4, 1941, in fact, tolerable security existed in the Annexed Eastern Territories, too, since until then "non-Germans" were governed by Reich law (Decree on the Implementation of Reich Penal Law of June 6, 1940). As we have shown, the principle of analogous application paved the way for replacement of the Reich statutes by a jurisdiction based on the ethnic struggle and their circumvention at any time as the political situation required. This process of disintegration culminated in the Decree on Penal Law for Poles of December 4, 1941, which abolished all formal definitions of criminal offenses and replaced them by the umbrella phrase "anti-German behavior" (clause 1, par. 3), thus setting a legal seal on the deprivation of the rights of "non-Germans" under the law. Compared with this situation of insecurity and the absence of formal criteria, the criminal law of the General Government presented a model of clarity. Though the drafting of criminal law was extensive and vague, the jurisdiction of the special courts at least was more or less firmly laid down. The direct application of German criminal law excluded the possibility of deviating from substantive Reich law. The principle of analogous application was found only in procedural law, so as to tighten up and simplify proceedings. Therefore, whereas in the Annexed Eastern Territories the abandonment of the statutes and legal principles of the Reich led to insecurity and lawless areas, wide open to arbitrary political actions, the form and content of criminal law in the General Government remained largely intact and shielded the administration of justice against excessive abuse by the political authorities.

This difference between the legal insecurity and confusion in the Annexed Eastern Territories and relative clarity in the General Government is also found expressed in the jurisdiction. The concept of deterrence, which under National Socialist criminal law underlay all decisions in the courts, served of course as leitmotiv in all the occupied Polish territories. But whereas in the Annexed Eastern Territories, this meant annihilation and extermination—as so many examples show—in the General Government, where the accent was on preserving manpower in the German interest, such a course was generally undesirable. In the realm of purely criminal offenses, we see a sharp contrast between the relatively lenient practice of the special courts and German courts of the General Government—notwithstanding the sometimes very harsh punishment of economic and certain other offenses—and the increasingly arbitrary justice in the Annexed Eastern Territories, which can only be described as relentless vindictive jurisdiction against "non-German" offenders, at least in the latter years of the war.

It should not be forgotten, however, that the function and field of activity of the judiciary in the two regions were conceived completely differently, and this naturally affected the composition of the courts and the attitude of the judges. In the Annexed Eastern Territories, the judiciary saw itself as belonging to a dominant political apparatus designed to keep the population down and gain ascendancy in the ethnic struggle. In the General Government, the judiciary was in a weak position from the start in the face of the summary police courts, but it was not without political ambition. It saw its role less as the instrument of a far-reaching new ethnic order than as prosecutor of individual criminal acts—its traditional role. The different arrangements regarding the responsibilities of the courts also contributed strongly to the differences in jurisdiction in the two territories. In the Annexed Eastern Territories, common criminality was usurped by the police, de facto at first and later officially (by the circular decree by the

Reichsführer-SS and police leader of June 15, 1942), so that no comparison is possible at this level. Similar regulations indeed existed in the General Government, empowering the administrative authorities (government, district governor, *Kreishauptmann*) to issue orders imposing punishment (Decree on the Administrative Criminal Procedure in the General Government of September 13, 1940). But the scope of police power in the Annexed Eastern Territories was vastly greater, covering infringements of both the Reich Penal Code and police orders and directives; the administrative penalty procedures of the General Government were limited to infringements of the orders and directives of the local authorities. This jurisdiction in the General Government was merely subsidiary, operative only if no court penalty was imposed, whereas in the Annexed Eastern Territories the judiciary was completely bypassed in this regard. In the Annexed Eastern Territories, too, police penalties were immediately final and absolute, with no possibility of subsequent review by the courts; in the General Government it was possible to bring an appeal against decisions of the *Kreishauptmann*. And despite the great harshness and harassment experienced by individuals in the General Government, enforcement of the fines and custodial penalties imposed through the administrative penalty procedures was probably exercised more leniently than the execution of police custody in the "work training camps" run by the police in the Annexed Eastern Territories, which were reminiscent of concentration camps, for in the General Government so-called administrative prison camps, which were under the control not of the police but of the general administration authority (*Kreishauptmann*), existed for this purpose.[13]

Another difference was in the jurisdiction over politically significant criminality, that is, acts of resistance against the occupying power (acts against German citizens and nationals and German installations). Whereas in the General Government the Acts of Violence Decree of October 31, 1939, brought such offenses—and later all violations of German regulations—under the jurisdiction of the summary police courts, in the Annexed Eastern Territories they continued to be dealt with by the special courts (secs. 8–16 of the Decree on the Implementation of Penal Law of June 6, 1940; clause 1, par. 4, of the Decree on Penal Law for Poles). Thus, in the General Government the judiciary was excluded from the major areas of the criminal prosecution of "non-Germans." The result of these differences in jurisdiction was that many of the (death) sentences passed by the special courts in the Annexed Eastern Territories were for offenses tried by the summary police courts in the General Government, where the justice system itself was limited to general criminality and minor political offenses (anti-German remarks, for example). But even here great differences in sentencing practice emerge. In particular, as the numerous examples given above have shown, the broad powers of the special courts in the Annexed Eastern Territories were such that they often dealt with extremely minor offenses normally handled by the German courts of first instance in the General Government, which, with their much more limited range of punishment, imposed very much milder penalties.

Taking all these differences in function, responsibilities, and sentencing practice into account, we may therefore note that the comparison only holds with respect to criminal acts in the narrow sense. Here, the jurisdiction against "non-Germans" in the Annexed Eastern Territories was dominated by the whims of the special courts, which, having largely shaken off the shackles of the Reich statutes, exercised draconian justice in even the most minor cases; the special courts of the General Government, oriented as they were toward the principles of Reich law, retained a relatively orderly procedure and relatively moderate sentencing.

This review of legal practice in the Annexed Eastern Territories and the General Government would not be complete without mention of the gradual spread of police power outside the regulated limits of jurisdiction. In the latter years of the war, at least, in real terms it was less significant who was formally responsible for the prosecution of a crime or a misdemeanor than who had the right to the first step against the accused. In the Annexed Eastern Territories, "non-Germans" could, at the discretion of the (regular) police authorities (*Schutzpolizei*, gendarmerie), be handed over to the judiciary; but also (even for a simple misdemeanor), they could be referred to the Security Police, that is, to the criminal police or the Gestapo, who had a wide range of sanctions (fines, custody, prison camps, concentration camps) at their disposal. The situation was similar in the General Government. Even in the event of a misdemeanor, it was largely a matter of chance whether the police or the administrative authorities stepped in first or the offender was handed over to the judiciary, whatever the formal jurisdiction. But the evolution of the relations between the police and the judiciary was such that a long-term period of detention was the rule for all "non-Germans" in German custody, including those convicted by the courts of justice. It is worth remembering that before early 1943 the Poles of the Annexed Eastern Territories still had a chance of being set free after a term of imprisonment. From then on, however, any Poles sentenced to more than six months' imprisonment were automatically committed to a concentration camp "for the duration of the war." On account of the labor shortage, this arrangement was limited in early 1944 to sentences of a year or more. Still harsher was the practice in the General Government. The judiciary dealt with "non-Germans" only insofar as the summary police courts did not get in first. But even then the police were so well informed of all judicial proceedings that it was never a problem for them to ensure that anybody who interested them for any reason would be sent to concentration camp after having served his sentence. The right of the police to impose "protective" or preventive detention at will remained intact, so that anybody under trial could be removed from the power of the court if he was not actually serving a sentence. Once in the clutches of the police or the judiciary, innumerable "non-German" individuals or groups could never hope to see freedom again. The major question was whether they would be sent to a regular prison or a police prison, prison camp, work training camp, or concentration camp, for on this their chances of survival depended.

Conclusion

In attempting to draw conclusions from the present work, four focal points present themselves under which the principle of special law in the Third Reich can ultimately be considered:

1. Technical efficiency.
2. Limitless area of personal and substantive applicability.
3. Unlimited judicial authority and the escalation of special law from west to east.
4. Distribution of jurisdiction and the struggle for authority between the regular service and the exceptional powers of the Third Reich.

1. The process involved in implementing the idea of special law in the areas of general inner civil service and the judicial system confirms the thesis proposed in the introduction to this volume that the leadership of the National Socialist state was, within a relatively short time, in a position to indoctrinate the entire judicial and administrative apparatus in the new political policy, although the previous set of legal standards (with the exception of the basic liberal values of the Weimar Constitution) was adopted unchanged and preserved in most essentials. This transition from traditional administrative thinking to the new state ideology of National Socialism occurred almost without a hitch, since, the better to uphold the appearance of legality, National Socialism's entire thinking and mode of expression—as demonstrated by the quotations cited herein—was aimed at depicting itself as guardian and conservator of German legal tradition. This in turn led to the tactic, so typical for the Nazi regime, of obscuring normative and ethical questions or excluding them altogether from the domains of justice and the Civil Service; or, more precisely, reformulating them as questions of administrative technique.

This method of replacing political goals by an obsession with technique met, to an extraordinary degree, the needs of a Civil Service that for some time past had been oriented toward principles of efficiency and procedural functionalism. These principles took on ever more importance; indeed, they increasingly came to be valued for themselves, since owing to the considerable loss of moral fiber and religious teaching that followed on the heels of World War I, they were no longer shored up by generally accepted standards and values. One consequence of this loss of moral substance was that, although the old values were still formally recognized, they were largely robbed of content and meaning; thus, as empty "conceptual husks," they provided to some extent an alibi for the values of the ruling powers. This development played a decisive role in permitting the National Socialist leadership to take over not only the normative apparatus but also and simultaneously the traditional values (duty, order, authority, honor, fidelity, etc.), removing them from context, giving them different meanings, and carrying them forward with no reference to moral and ethical standards.

In this way the old values were put directly into the service of National Socialist ideas, just as members of the old oligarchy, who, clinging to "tradition" and "order" (although without values clearly anchored in formal legal acts), offered the regime their services. Into this vacuum, then, the ideology of the NSDAP—whether adopted directly or indirectly admitted under cover of traditional values and ideas of order—was able to pour its fundamental values ("race," "blood and soil," "community," etc.) virtually without hindrance. The result for the bureaucracy and the judiciary was that the introduction of National Socialist ideology into the traditional set of values and standards presented itself not as a *fundamental* question but merely as one of (administrative) *technique* and political opportunity. That is to say, we are talking about processes of adaptation that, from a formal juristic perspective, could be undertaken relatively smoothly but which implicated both legislation and jurisprudence, imperceptibly at first, then to an ever greater extent, in the methodical implementation of injustice and despotism. Of this influx of totalitarian ideas into traditional standards and values emptied of meaning, of this transformation of political goals into technical efficiency, the principle of special law presents the prime example. It shows that, as a result of this smooth transition, only relatively insignificant (by the standards of the time) changes in the legal system (such as, for instance, the racial codes) were necessary to recast the practice of law to fit, explicitly and for all to see, the fundamental values of the National Socialist "ethnic community."

2. This formally smooth transition from the administrative thinking of the Weimar period to the ideas of National Socialism meant that in principle there

were no *legal* restrictions, either substantively or in regard to persons, upon the idea of racial hatred.

a. The examples cited in this study confirm the thesis that in its very approach, the concept of special law was designed to allow for unlimited interpretation. Although at first only the Jews, as the incarnation of the "racially foreign" element within the German nation, were the objects of special legal provisions, other peoples or ethnic groups judged undesirable "foreign racial" elements within the population (some for racial, some for political reasons) soon followed. In accordance with the National Socialist concept of a "racially" organized and hierarchized society, these models of special jurisprudence were ultimately applied to all "non-German" inhabitants of the Reich, including those groups deemed for racial or political reasons to be "of kindred blood" or "racially related"—which in itself ought to have precluded racial discrimination. Not only the "undesirable" populations of the occupied Eastern European regions were subject to discrimination, but also foreign workers in Germany from Western and Northern Europe and other "non-German" groups considered for reasons of racial politics to be "undesirable" (such as White Russians, Goralians, or Ukrainians) were put under special statutes, as described in the sections on labor and police law. And although these statutes were generally milder in nature than those in effect for the first groups, they could at any time be tightened or relaxed according to the political needs of the moment.

Application of the special-law concept, however, was by no means limited to "non-German" persons or groups. As shown in particular for the area of criminal law, albeit not in great detail, judgments under special law were in fact imposed on *all* unpopular persons and groups (political and clerical opponents, criminals, work dodgers, etc.), all of whom were lumped together under the catchword *asocial*. The term *asocial* here means those who were expelled from the community and thus from the realm of law, a condition that was, at least for public consumption, euphemized under the National Socialist expression "alien to the community." As mentioned in the introduction, this suggests points of departure for further studies that might extend the investigation into particular aspects of discrimination in the Third Reich. In the present context, it will suffice to recall the Law on Aliens to the Community frequently cited above; meant to take effect on January 1, 1945, it provided for the mandatory imprisonment of all "aliens to the community" in "police camps" (concentration camps) or "reformatories" (work camps).

Empirical evidence thus confirms the premise that the principle of special law became progressively detached from its racist origins, becoming instead the *general legal and administrative principle* of National Socialism. Although most starkly applied against "non-German" individuals and groups, it claimed validity for all "undesirable" persons regardless of racial origin. The principle of special law (originally motivated by racism) thus becomes inseparably intertwined with the idea of oppression. It is an expression of the contempt for the individual peculiar to any totalitarian system: the compulsion to absolute sacrifice of the individual to the state as embodied in the "ethnic community," segregation of all those who, in the opinion of state leadership, are unwilling or unable to subjugate themselves and are therefore worthless to the state, that is, asocial, hence "inferior."

b. Such exclusion of undesired elements, however, did not (as official usage and propaganda would have had one believe) mean merely *separation* from the "ethnic community." This would not have kept the persons in question from retaining some sort of legal status, if only an inferior one. Rather, the concept of special law in the National Socialist sense, as illustrated in numerous examples, resulted in the affected persons being excluded, *expelled*, from the community of law; they lost all legal standing, indeed all status in the legal sense. In other words, they became outlaws. Not for nothing did National Socialism develop a predilection for the word *Ächtung* (outlawry, ostracism), a term adopted from Teutonic law; not for nothing was this term to be enshrined, as a new criminal sanction in specific cases, in the new Penal Code of the Third Reich. Thus, the principle of special law under National Socialism not only meant the abolition of individual rights and the introduction of an inferior legal status for "non-Germans" and other undesirables; it became itself an expression of the absence of rights, of nonlegality, of injustice. In a *substantive* sense, then, the principle of special law was nowhere more restricted than in regard to persons. From the outset every act of "non-German" individuals potentially fell under special legal regulation. As a result, every legal protection, every personal or economic activity, was deemed a "privilege" necessitating special permission and having to be first "earned" by dint of exceptional achievements (work performance, good behavior).

It was not possible, within the present context, to pursue in detail the question of whether the National Socialist principle of special law *necessarily* led to the physical extermination of persons, groups, or population elements deemed undesirable on racial or political grounds. To round out the picture of the significance and scope of the concept of special law would require further studies of whether, as can be surmised, special legal practices were ultimately predestined to end in the raging tide of annihilation of which Auschwitz is the symbol. For instance, it would be necessary to examine whether, for the purpose of methodical annihilation of undesirable minorities, a straight line can be drawn from the

Führer Decree for the Strengthening of the German Nation dated October 7, 1939, to the decree of the chief of the SIPO and the SD dated September 21, 1939, on the Deployment of Special Operations Squads (*Einsatzgruppen*), to the unwritten police authorization allowing the imposition of protective custody and preventive detention and the expulsion and ghettoization of entire population groups; or whether, taken on a case-by-case basis, the idea of special legal treatment of undesirables could have been brought to a halt at a status of inferior rights or of a fundamental lack of legal rights that would have retained a guarantee of due process. If the present study can contribute anything at all to answering this question, it is the conclusion that, at least in respect to their consequences, numerous plans and actions of the Nazi leadership aimed at *discriminating* against "non-Germans" closely approximated their *physical annihilation* as well, since they were based on the totalitarian idea of the worthlessness and the fundamental lack of legal rights of the individual. Forcing "non-German" persons or groups to live at or below subsistence level, inhumane expulsion and resettlement, the planned or intentional death by starvation (as long as enough other laborers were available) of countless persons and groups were *just as much* a fundamental component of the National Socialist idea as the plans and schemes for the methodical annihilation of particular groups (e.g., of the Jews or the leadership circles of the conquered nations of Eastern Europe) that have occupied most of the previously published literature.

3. The third conclusion resulting from this study can be summarized as follows: The realization of National Socialist goals, especially as regards the treatment of the "non-Germans," permitted the legislative and civil service branches almost unlimited latitude for designing their own rules. Since these same goals were only loosely defined ("racial struggle," "suppression," "separation" of Germans and "non-Germans," etc.), the resulting interpretive latitude was first of all to the advantage of the departmental bureaucrats who carried out the preparatory *legislative* work. They themselves were able to flesh it out with numerous blanket clauses ("significance of annexation," "ethnic interests," "anti-German activity," "interference with the work of German reconstruction," "German interests," etc.). At the same time, they hardly ever set legal definitions, in order to keep developments perpetually "flexible." Accordingly, the central recommendations and *guidelines* for managing administrative and judicial procedure described only vaguely what was intended by the leadership and thus were of little or no help in interpreting legal standards. The result was not only a general sense of legal uncertainty; more importantly, the decision as to when the facts of a particular case met the conditions of the above-mentioned blanket clauses was shifted to ever lower levels, so that, ultimately, discriminatory practices were

largely dependent on the whim and discretion of whichever department was involved.

Civil servants and judicial authorities made widely differing use of this virtually limitless discretionary latitude. The portrait that emerges within the framework of the regional jurisdictions herein studied confirms the premise that, indeed, one can only speak of a progressive *escalation*, from west to east, in the intensity with which special law was applied, something that the following summary will serve to demonstrate.

In the region of the Altreich, the formal transition from liberal to National Socialist ideology was relatively smooth. Many civil servants and authorities who had all professed allegiance to liberal and constitutional principles before the Nazi seizure of power were now perfectly happy to put into practice the exact opposite, namely inequality, open discrimination, and despotism. However, the fact that the established administrative and judicial apparatus was principally responsible for enforcing the system of special law in itself exerted a certain moderating and inhibitory effect—that is, when actual practices are measured against the extreme ideas of the National Socialist leadership, in particular as expressed in Hitler's remarks to his inner circle. In addition, special-law practices in the region of the Altreich, as far as domestic administration (excluding the police) and the judicial system were concerned, were at first tested "only" against German Jewish citizens; and since they were directed against *German citizens*, these practices were generally kept within the bounds of procedural legality. The formalization of discriminatory practices by means of laws and decrees guaranteed, on the one hand, the even-handed enforcement of despotic National Socialist concepts, while at the same time effecting a certain containment of said ideas, since they had to be integrated into the existing framework of judicial reasoning and legal standards. Finally, it must be remembered that in individual cases, that is, cases in which standards of special law had to be interpreted by administrative officials and the courts, the established principles of order, legal guarantees, and (to some extent) constitutionality as well were, despite all attempted influences to the contrary, still robust enough that despotic National Socialist concepts, much to the displeasure of the political leadership, could not be carried out as completely as was originally intended. Therefore, the domain of special-law practices was to be the conquered territories of Eastern Europe, where the political leadership was free to disregard established legal principles as it saw fit.

The virtually inescapable conclusion is that special law was applied with far greater intensity in the Annexed Eastern Territories than was the case in the Altreich. The concept of the National Socialist leadership whereby these regions were, politically and administratively, new "ethnic" territory wherein the author-ities were to have a free hand without constitutional "impediments" was largely put into practice. Since in this instance an entire "non-German" population was at their disposal, one that was to be treated according to the principles of "ethnic warfare" (according to the principles of expulsion, "repression," "intimidation," and "annihilation"), a true *annexation* of the Eastern Territories to the Reich was not attempted. Rather, they were administered according to *colonial* precepts. Thus, in addition to the special-law model largely adopted from the Reich, there now appeared the new, radical policy of "ethnic warfare." As shown in numerous examples, this meant not only a radicalization of the practical application of special law but also an escalation in the procedural sense, which in turn served to increase the intensity of special-law practices.

In the Annexed Eastern Territories, where the "elite" of the party bureau-cracy (who were frequently ignorant of administrative procedure) and the spe-cial branches of the police were in constant competition and conflict with the traditional administrative authorities, the basic structures of special-law policy (in contrast with those of the Altreich) were characterized by an almost total lack of formal legality. The determining principles of special law were no longer set in place by means of the usual legislative process (adoption of Reich laws, decrees by the responsible Reich ministers or the local *Reichsstatthalter* with the approval of the Reich minister of the interior), but often merely by means of in-ternal administrative instructions or ad hoc regulations by the responsible au-thorities (*Reichsstatthalter*, district president, *Landrat*). As in the Reich itself, such regulations were largely defined by limitless general clauses and vague guidelines that opened the floodgates to considerations of "ethnic interests," that is, to despotism by individual ruling. This included reliance on "analogous" ap-plication of German law as well as the reluctance on the part of the authorities to fix normative definitions, particularly when these were to be officially pro-mulgated. Moreover, the practice, in decrees, circulars, or individual directives, was frequently to sketch the "grand design" and leave all else to the discretion of whichever authorities were responsible for a particular case. This lack of norma-tive definitions created a vacuum into which arbitrary totalitarian power (of *Reichsstatthalter*, Party, police) could flow unhindered, and which, at least as it affected politically important areas of the civil service and the justice system (criminal law), generally could not be curbed by individual judges or legally minded department heads, since the orientation of the departments was, by dint of a deliberate personnel policy and other measures of control, "National Social-ist through and through."

A peculiarity in this escalation of the intensity of special law must be noted in the case of the General Government. The specific purpose of the General Government as an object of economic exploitation and a labor pool necessitated that the situation be made as orderly as possible. At least, this was the case in the area of general administration and the judicial system, if not for the terrorist actions of the organs of the Security Police and the SS, which were largely unfettered by administrative constraints. Administratively speaking, this region was largely modeled on the situation in the Altreich.

This includes the structuring of the administration after the pattern of the Reich, as well as the complete dependence upon the Reich for financing and staff[1] and the adoption of Reich laws or the imitation of its legislative procedures and techniques. Thus, deviations from Reich law were not as far-reaching as in the Annexed Eastern Territories but were more moderate in character. One example of such borrowing from the legal system of the Reich is that the special-law provisions in the General Government—though perhaps in simplified form—were often still promulgated *in conformance with* legal procedure (decrees of the governor general), including complicated rules of publication,[2] not by means of secret guidelines, and that their scope and range of application were relatively distinct and clearly regulated. What is more, paradoxically, the war itself preserved a certain order in the General Government. Quotas and the requisition of laborers forced a kind of regulated administration at the expense of "ethnic" or ideological considerations, whereas in the Annexed Eastern Territories, which were less affected by the war, total "ethnic warfare" raged on regardless of the legal and economic consequences, its heedless mass persecutions setting a horrific example of "ethnic" discrimination policy.[3] To this extent, the General Government showed far more legal clarity (in the procedural sense) than could be discovered in the absolutely totalitarian administration of the Annexed Eastern Territories. This contrast, by the way, was clearly perceived even at the time. There was constant tension and friction between the two regions (particularly between the General Government and the "model *Gau*" of Wartheland), because each side claimed to represent the only correct special-law policy for dealing with "non-Germans."[4] Where the escalation of special law in the administrative sector is concerned, therefore, the General Government must be ranked between, not after, the Altreich and the Annexed Eastern Territories.

This escalation of special law from west to east (allowing for the exception just mentioned) would be even plainer if measured against the discriminatory policies in the Occupied Soviet Territories (the Occupied Eastern Territories). Here, too, there are numerous points of departure for further studies whose outlines can only be hinted at in the present work. However, to round out the discussion of the escalation of rule by special law, and to stake out the terrain for future work, it should be noted that further studies would have to show that oppression of "non-Germans" under the Third Reich reached its zenith in the Occupied Soviet Territories (Occupied Eastern Territories. In particular, they would demonstrate that (whereas the economic and human substance of the General Government was to be largely preserved) the Occupied Eastern Territories were the object of exploitation and annihilation pure and simple, in which not even the barest allowances were to be made,[5] politically,[6] legally, or economically, and where a senseless, unimaginative, and crude policy of violent domination was unleashed, not only against "non-Germans" ("if we can't use them, let them perish"), but against *every* member of the population (including ethnic Germans).[7] Thus, unlike the inhabitants of the Polish territories, the people of these regions were no longer permitted to subsist for the sake of preserving the labor force, but rather they were denied everything, "any sense of life," and thus, in principle, the right to life itself.

In the Occupied Eastern Territories, the dominant ideas,[8] common practices (depopulation by means of epidemics,[9] starvation of "superfluous" population elements, etc.), and current expressions and attitudes would have been unthinkable in the other parts of the Reich even by contemporary standards.[10] However, all this can only be hinted at in this study. It was here that principles of special law and discrimination, the totalitarian idea of the worthlessness of the individual, reached their high-water mark. Since the Nazi leadership's simpleminded policy of violence rested on the assumption that there would always be an unlimited amount of new "human material" at its disposal in the East, the policy was not to secure the minimum standards needed to preserve the economy and the labor force; rather, there arose a spendthrift exploitation of existing recourses, starvation and annihilation of the work force after its labor had been exhausted.

Hence the National Socialist leadership not only planned but also put into practice a policy whose principles, it was hoped, could also be applied to the native peoples of still-to-be-conquered overseas territories,[11] and whose rudiments were already in place in the occupied Polish territories.

4. The fourth and final aspect under which the problem of special law in the Nazi state must be considered concerns the division of responsibility, the question to what *degree* the traditional administrative and normative apparatus allowed itself to be employed for the purposes of the despotic regime of National Socialism.

a. The basic idea of the present work can be set forth as follows, namely, that the readiness of civil service and judiciary to be used in the implementation of what was (in all respects) a limitlessly expandable concept of special law was very great indeed. Nor did they balk at technical, economic, or bureaucratic difficulties in their oppression of and discrimination against "non-German" persons and groups. Thus, for example, the expulsion of tens of thousands of Poles from the Annexed Eastern Territories to the General Government was carried out within the shortest possible time despite all technical, climatic, and economic difficulties and in the face of all objections from responsible authorities, simply because the resettlement quota had to be met at all hazards. The expropriation of Jewish property put an extraordinary burden on the authorities. From an economic standpoint, this operation led to significant losses and, particularly in the East, to senseless squandering, indeed even to economic ruin. Not only was this predictable, but, as we have demonstrated, it actually turned out to be the case. There is another factor whose significance can hardly be overestimated: even the most important measures of "ethnic" and racial discrimination were deliberately carried out by the leadership *during the war* and were railroaded through without regard to "objective" or economic considerations, something that the authorities who were oriented to such considerations could never bring themselves to understand. Yet this had its deeper reason, since, as Himmler once put it to the president of the Central Department of the Internal Administration in the General Government, such operations were much easier to manage during the war, in times of general privation and insecurity, "when everything is at sixes and sevens," than they would be in orderly circumstances.[12]

For the administrative authorities, however, the limits of discriminatory practices were to be found where the economic *substance* of their respective objects of exploitation was attacked or where economic considerations were entirely disregarded. In this connection let us recall, for instance, that the authorities in the Annexed Eastern Territories protested the all-too-stiff fines imposed as summary sentences by the police against Polish peasants, since the fines were exhausting the Poles' holdings. After the radical expulsion and compulsory resettlement operations of 1939–40 had subsided, they also objected to the deportation of Poles (or at least of those who belonged to the workforce) to the General Government or their transfer to the Reich. Instead, every attempt was made to keep them in the region. The authorities in the General Government may have expressed no objection to maintaining the native "non-German" population on the lowest possible wages and provisions and literally exposing the Jewish laborers to death by starvation ("starvation status"); however, they came out against the *annihilation* of the Jewish workforce, since this deprived the manufacturing sector of a large number of qualified specialists. In many cases, such objections on the part of the administrative authorities were able to delay annihilation operations already planned; of course they could not be altogether prevented, since according to the ideas of the Nazi leadership, fanaticism was mightier than expertise, and rational economic or political considerations were always obliged to give way before the postulates of ideology. All of the senseless acts of oppression, terror, expulsion, and annihilation in the occupied Polish territories can be traced to this "primacy" of political considerations, or, more precisely, to the primacy of the irrational—an essential feature of the National Socialist system of government, which reveals its incapability of following the dictates of (political, military, economic) reason even when these sprang directly from its own interests. Humanitarian considerations, of course, never even entered the picture.

The limited readiness of the traditional apparatus of legal standards and administration to be manipulated for the purposes of the regime meant, in turn, that functional aspects took on ever greater significance. Hand in hand with the increasingly discriminatory practices in the Reich and the occupied Polish territories, therefore, went a shift in jurisdictions, as numerous examples have shown. As long as it was somehow possible to locate the discriminatory special laws within the framework of traditional administrative thinking and traditional administrative technique, jurisdiction generally remained within the purview of the *administrative and judicial authorities*. But where naked acts of violence such as expulsions, kidnappings, and annihilation were concerned, the *exceptional powers* of the National Socialist regime came into play; that is, the Party headquarters, the police under the command of Himmler in his role as *Reichsführer-SS*, the SS itself, and the special authorities of the Reich Commissar for the Strengthening of German Nationhood, which were also concentrated in the person of Himmler. Thus, for instance, the total political, economic, and cultural disfranchisement of Jews in the Reich took place for the most part under the aegis of the authorities of the *general and inner administration* as well as of the finance and labor departments; whereas those responsible for the immediate preparation and all questions pertaining to their deportation, as well as for all expulsions from the occupied Polish territories, were the Security Police (whether by virtue of their original brief or by dint of jurisdictional usurpation) and the special authorities vested in the Reich Commissar for the Strengthening of German Nationhood. The more extreme the tasks expected of discriminatory special law, therefore, the more likely they were to be discharged by the extraordinary powers within the Nazi regime and not by the traditional administration.

This "division of responsibilities" between administration and judiciary, on the one hand, and the extraordinary powers of the Third Reich on the other, was intended from the beginning by the political leadership. Hitler himself, significantly enough, saw Himmler's preeminent importance not in his capacity as *Reichsführer*-SS and police leader, but rather in his capacity as Reich Commissar for the Strengthening of German Nationhood (RKF), since this invested him with the entire responsibility for expelling "non-Germans" in the East and settling their lands with Germans and included the necessary *authority to issue directives* to the functionaries of the general and inner administration.[13]

In this "division of responsibilities," too, one can discern an east-west gradation; that is, the further east the occupied territories lay, the greater the use of special authorities to the detriment of the traditional administration. The great extermination and concentration camps lay in the East, the great resettlement operations were directed thence or took place there. Even in the Annexed Eastern Territories, as we have seen, the Party apparatus and the special authorities of the Reich Commissar for the Strengthening of German Nationhood (in the form of the centers for migration and immigration, etc.) had established themselves beside the traditional administration as powers of equal or superior standing; and, whereas the administrative authorities in the autonomous General Government were able with some success to defend themselves against such interference, they ultimately proved largely powerless against the terror of the police and the SS and their operations aimed at expulsion and annihilation.

Here, too, further investigation of the situation in the Occupied Eastern Territories would be profitable; it would show that in the National Socialist system of government, questions of jurisdiction, which are the basis of any administration, steadily decreased in significance and that the balance of power shifted in favor of whichever power was most ruthless in sweeping aside such questions. Detailed studies would simultaneously provide insight about the degree to which the policy of disfranchisement and discrimination was capable of *intensification* once the extraordinary powers of National Socialism came into play, with their previously unthinkable reign of terror perpetrated against all unpopular "non-Germans" by the offices of the SS and the police as well as the Reich commissars (who answered solely to Hitler)—a process against which the responsible administrators (of the ministry for the Occupied Eastern Territories) were condemned to fight a losing battle.[14]

b.   The function of the extraordinary powers within the Third Reich, however, was by no means limited to direct execution of acts of violence, expulsion, and extermination. Rather, to an ever increasing extent and with the full approval or toleration of the political leadership, they appeared as *organs of correction* against the administrative and judicial authorities. Whenever it was perceived that discriminatory policy was not being pursued expeditiously or thoroughly enough by means of legislation, administrative fiat, or judicial decision, "corrective measures" on the part of Party and police offices came into play. This is particularly apparent in the practice of police "protective custody" or "preventive detention" as carried out in the concentration camps; such detention became ever more common both for "non-German" offenders and for any other suspicious or unpopular persons and represented a serious infringement upon the jurisdiction of the administrative and judicial authorities. To be sure, such violations of administrative jurisdiction first made themselves felt only as concrete intervention in individual cases and were to a large extent accepted by the authorities. The belief that these instances were nothing more than individual acts of arbitrariness or political caprice that were in any case immune from administrative or judicial scrutiny prevented the recognition that such encroachments, far from being mere eruptions of individual power politics on the part of local Party bosses or police officers, were in fact part of a long-term and successful strategy to supplant the traditional administration to the greatest possible extent.

These encroachments upon administrative and judicial jurisdiction finally reached the point where entire territories and groups within the Reich were detached from the responsibility of the administrative and judicial authorities and transferred—by means of special act, "understanding," internal guidelines/decrees, and legal empowerment—to that of the police. Recall, for instance, that the police in the Altreich had usurped responsibility for regulating *each and every* aspect of the living conditions of the foreign labor force and that they had also—after 1942 with the decisive support of the Party and the Reich Ministry of Justice—taken charge of the administration of criminal justice against "non-Germans." Criminal prosecution of Jews was even transferred to the police by legislative act (the Thirteenth Decree to the Reich Citizenship Law), since in this area there were no judicial reservations about openly declaring, by means of formal legislation, the power shift in favor of the police.

In the Annexed Eastern Territories, the police took over the prosecution of all types of everyday crime; likewise, they largely usurped the prosecution of all crimes of insubordination against the occupying forces by means of (illegal) drumhead courts-martial, which were later legalized de facto by the Decree on Penal Law for Poles.

The general lack of legal standards specifically promulgated for the Eastern Territories and the failure to adopt regulations in effect in the Reich (e.g., the futile attempts to introduce the Prussian police administrative law) resulted in a vacuum in the remaining areas of law as well, one in which a kind of generalized police jurisdiction over anything and everything having to do with "non-German" populations could take root. Conditions in the General Government were even more extreme; there, the prosecution of Polish insubordination against the occupying forces was entrusted to police drumhead courts-martial from the first. Later on, their brief was expanded beyond all bounds by the so-called Sabotage Decree of October 2, 1943, so that, ultimately, any kind of misdemeanor or violation of German statutes whatsoever was susceptible to capital punishment by the drumhead courts-martial. Of course, police power encroached upon other areas as well; examples include the illegal operations carried out against actual or suspected members of the Polish resistance movement, which took place to the total exclusion of the judiciary, or the prosecution of Jews who had escaped from the ghetto, something that originally came under the jurisdiction of the special courts but was usurped by the police.

Fundamental to all such proceedings, as the present research has shown, was the idea of the police and Party leadership that, at bottom, criminal prosecution of "non-German" persons, for which the judiciary was entirely unsuited, was to be exclusively the responsibility of the police. However, as demonstrated by the usurpation of *administrative responsibilities*, this principle of exclusive police jurisdiction was to have been expanded into every other area, since from the National Socialist point of view, complete subordination to police statutes, that is, forced labor and incarceration (and, if necessary, extermination in police-run camps), or at the very least constant police surveillance, was seen as the only appropriate way of life for "non-Germans." The treatment of the individual under the totalitarian state—constant supervision, required labor for everyone, forced labor for undesirables, eradication of actual or suspected opponents (in short, the principle of injustice)—here reaches its apogee: the concentration camp as the permanent home and workplace for all dissidents, for all those persons or groups who for racial, political, or any other reasons were expelled from the community of law.

The conclusions to be drawn from this rise in National Socialist extraordinary powers may be summarized as follows: the traditional administration could be used for the revolutionary goals of National Socialism to the extent that the principles and aims of oppression were, by contemporary standards, justifiable either in terms of administrative procedure or jurisprudence or were otherwise in some way rationally comprehensible.

Because of the impossibility of integrating them into the thought processes and procedures of the administration, actions that went beyond such limits, measures that were *patently* arbitrary or unjust, as for example the annihilation of the Jews or the expulsion and eradication of the Polish intelligentsia, could not be executed without calling into question the administration's very existence. Thus, the usefulness of the administration ended at such borderline cases; this was where the practice of using the traditional instruments of order and the arguments of the judiciary to prop up, directly or indirectly, the revolutionary goals of totalitarian power was bound to fail. This explains how the above-mentioned "division of responsibilities" was, as demonstrated by the numerous examples cited, accepted and supported by the administration at least as far as concrete results were concerned—because they could then feel absolved of responsibility for all such actions. But when it became a question of areas that originally belonged under the jurisdiction of the administrative or judicial authorities, there were only two alternatives for confronting crude "corrective measures" on the part of police and Party headquarters: either the administration carried the day with typically administrative arguments (e.g., questions of jurisdiction or of technical or economic efficiency), thus curbing the use of arbitrary political violence; or else they relinquished their jurisdictions, thus (of course) also giving up all rights of participation.

The examples discussed in the present study show that administration and judiciary attempted to follow both courses. In cases in which their jurisdictions were formally *uncontested*, they clung to those jurisdictions to the last, even at the cost of forgoing fundamental legal principles—a state of affairs particularly evident in the controversy over the introduction of the Decree on Penal Law for Poles. However, where the original jurisdictions were undermined by constant intervention and "corrections" on the part of the police, or else had become *questionable* even by contemporary legal standards—and in the later years of the war this was increasingly the case with regard to the treatment of Jews and "non-Germans"—they were not stubbornly defended; rather, they were often recklessly abandoned, perhaps in part from the consideration that this simultaneously permitted the avoidance of difficult situations that could have led to tensions with the forces in control of police and Party.

Thus, if empirical evidence confirms the premise that the revolutionary goals of National Socialism could not be completely carried out with the old administrative apparatus, but only up to what could be termed inherent administrative limits, we come full circle to the starting point of this study: namely, to the dominant role played by the bureaucracy, whose compliance, on the one hand, lent the political system of National Socialism its great stability and efficiency while, on the other hand, its inertia and the inherent characteristics of the system prevented the complete success of the National Socialist ideology within its domain, or at least acted in manifold ways as a restraint and check.

In studies of this type, finally, it seems reasonable to ask what inferences or conclusions might be drawn from the development of law under the Third Reich. As in all studies of a historical subject, this question must be met with skepticism. If any conclusions may be drawn, it can only be done in the form of a few guidelines that, abstracting from the concrete historical situation, must be formulated generally enough that they may also be applied to other kinds of political systems.

One such guideline could well be the conclusion that the introduction, by means of *law* and the *legal system*, of discriminatory practices that exceed the bare minimum of special regulations necessary for the survival of the state results not only in general *inequality*, but brings with it, as its necessary corollary, the *relinquishment* of law itself. For in doing so, opportunities are created for the subordination of *any* group and *any* field of law to entirely arbitrary special sanctions and legal proceedings that are not subject to legal or ethical limitations—thus, in a manner of speaking, employing the law to open the floodgates of despotism. Discrimination has been and is common in many states; however, only its elevation to the status of law endows it with state authority and normative validity. In Germany, the tradition of legal positivism gave discrimination under special statute the color of binding law in the traditional sense, whereas in other systems such extraordinary law is simply not recognized as law at all.[15] By the same token, as this study makes plain, such a legal system also ensures continuity, that is, the perpetuation of discriminatory practices into the indefinite future. For inherent in any legislation is the tendency to cleave to existing regulations and, if anything, to expand them, rather than mitigating their effects or abolishing them entirely.

As a further conclusion from the example of the smoothly implemented surrender of general equality, it may be asserted that a highly organized administrative and civil service apparatus oriented to the doctrine of efficiency can be utilized to a high degree, indeed almost without restriction, to further the (totalitarian) goals of a revolutionary regime, even when that apparatus was formerly committed to entirely different basic concepts and standards, provided that the forms of traditional legality, procedures, and nomenclature are at least nominally preserved. The loss of or indifference to moral values and the principles of an ordered state, their want of support in the normative and organizational structure of society, the resulting dissolution of traditional jurisdictional boundaries, and their infiltration by the extraordinary powers of totalitarianism, all lead to a systemic breakdown and arbitrariness in the legislature's treatment of central concepts, to unlimited discretionary latitude on the part of the authorities and the political powers that control them, and ultimately to the subversion of the traditional administrative apparatus itself. The continuity of law, the preservation of a formal facade by a revolutionary regime, serves to secure the alliance of the old leadership classes with modern practitioners of discrimination and mass persecution and leads to an inseparable bond, even identification, with the practices of injustice, as long as the position of those leadership groups (army, bureaucracy, industry) remains unquestioned or is even, as the Nazi regime was particularly astute at doing, strengthened and expanded. Thus, the consciousness of what is just shrinks in favor of a now merely procedural concept of legality; the law is robbed of its substantive content, loses its independence, and takes on an *exclusively* instrumental or technical character. "Legal problems" can henceforth arise only in regard to the manner in which the policies of the leadership can best be justified and carried out most efficiently. The law thus becomes a *quantité négligéable*, that is, a mere *means* by which all designs of so-called political or administrative expediency can be realized. This development can be traced back to the recognition that the formulation of law can always be managed in advance by political fiat. This applies not only to subsumptions of a juristic nature, that is, to the interpretation of legal standards, but also to rulings in individual cases through control of the political images, information, and knowledge available to those who are called upon to implement the law. In order to preserve and promote the law, therefore, it is always necessary to have in place sufficient legal checks (in the form, for instance, of a constitutional court),[16] which in turn require the support and institutional guarantees provided by constitution and law—a problem confronted by every political system. The example of the Nazi period merely makes this particularly plain.

Appendixes

Appendix 1: The Reich Structure (State and Party)

This chart has been reproduced with the kind permission of Professor Dr. Hubert Rottleuthner, Institute for the Sociology of Law, Free University of Berlin.

For abbreviations used in the chart, see the list of abbreviations. For definitions of Nazi terminology, see the glossary.

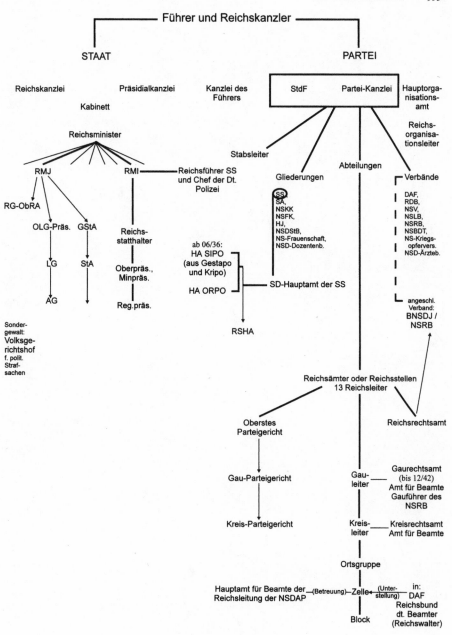

Appendix 2: The Wannsee Protocol of January 20, 1942 (English Version and Original German Version)

This protocol is one of the most important documents of the Holocaust. It outlines the bureaucratic organization of the murder of the European Jews. The protocol is composed in a "neutral" language, in which the term *killing, extermination,* or *Final Solution* never appears; it is therefore one of the best-known examples of Nazi bureaucratic language, which did not explain but concealed its aims. The protocol is reproduced in the German original and in an English-language version.

The English text is based on the official U.S. government translation prepared for evidence in trials held by the International Tribunal for War Criminals at Nuremberg (Doc. N6-25866), as reproduced in John Mendelsohn, ed., *The Holocaust: Selected Documents in Eighteen Volumes*, vol. 11, *The Wannsee Protocol*, and a 1944 "Report on Auschwitz" by the Office of Strategic Services (New York: Garland, 1982), 18–32. Revisions to the Nuremberg text, for clarification and correction, were made by Dan Rogers of the University of South Alabama.

The "Wannsee Conference" was named for an SS-owned villa on the shores of a Berlin lake called the Wannsee; that is where the conference took place. Assembled there were high officials of all Reich ministries; they were convened at the request of Reinhard Heydrich, the chief of the Reich Security Main Office (RSHA) and head of the German Secret Police apparatus (Gestapo). Heydrich and his superior, Heinrich Himmler, head of the SS, were in the process of assuming leadership in the "Final Solution of the Jewish Question," that is, the murder of Europe's Jews. According to documents recently found in Moscow, the decision for the "Final Solution" was made not earlier than autumn 1941 (presumably October 1941). The meeting was a part of that process, as bureaucratic coordination would be required for the massive efforts to be undertaken throughout Europe to kill 11,000,000 Jews described in the document. The Nazis ultimately succeeded in killing between 5 and 6 million of Europe's Jews. The following protocol of this conference was stamped Top Secret.

Stamp: Top Secret

30 copies

16th copy

Minutes of discussion.

I. The following persons took part in the discussion about the final solution of the Jewish question which took place in Berlin, am Grossen Wannsee No. 56/58 on 20 January 1942.

Gauleiter Dr. Meyer and Reichsamtleiter Dr. Leibbrandt	Reich Ministry for the Occupied Eastern territories
Secretary of State Dr. Stuckart	Reich Ministry for the Interior
Secretary of State Neumann	Plenipotentiary for the Four Year Plan
Secretary of State Dr. Freisler	Reich Ministry of Justice
Secretary of State Dr. Bühler	Office of the Government General
Under Secretary of State Dr. Luther	Foreign Office
SS-Oberführer Klopfer	Party Chancellery
Ministerialdirektor Kritzinger	Reich Chancellery
SS-Gruppenführer Hofmann	Race and Settlement Main Office
SS-Gruppenführer Müller	Reich Main Security Office
SS-Obersturmbannführer Eichmann	
SS-Oberführer Dr. Schöngarth Commander of the Security Police and the SD in the Government General	Security Police and SD
SS-Sturmbannführer Dr. Lange Commander of the Security Police and the SD for the General-District Latvia, as deputy of the Commander of the Security Police and the SD for the Reich Commissariat "Eastland."	Security Police and SD

II. At the beginning of the discussion Chief of the Security Police and of the SD, SS-Obergruppenführer Heydrich, reported that the Reich Marshal had appointed him delegate for the preparations for the final solution of the Jewish question in Europe and pointed out that this discussion had been called for the purpose of clarifying fundamental questions. The wish of the Reich Marshal to have a draft sent to him concerning organizational, factual and material interests in relation to the final solution of the Jewish question in Europe makes necessary an initial common action of all central offices immediately concerned with these questions in order to bring their general activities into line. The Reichsführer-SS and the Chief of the German Police (Chief of the Security Police and the SD) was entrusted with the official central handling of the final solution of the Jewish question without regard to geographic borders. The Chief of the Security Police and the SD then gave a short report of the struggle which has been carried on thus far against this enemy, the essential points being the following:

a)   the expulsion of the Jews from every sphere of life of the German people,
b)   the expulsion of the Jews from the living space of the German people. In carrying out these efforts, an increased and planned acceleration of the emigration of the Jews from Reich territory was started, as the only possible present solution.

By order of the Reich Marshal, a Reich Central Office for Jewish Emigration was set up in January 1939 and the Chief of the Security Police and SD was entrusted with the management. Its most important tasks were

a)   to make all necessary arrangements for the preparation for an increased emigration of the Jews,
b)   to direct the flow of emigration,
c)   to speed the procedure of emigration in each individual case.

The aim of all this was to cleanse German living space of Jews in a legal manner.

All the offices realized the drawbacks of such enforced accelerated emigration. For the time being they had, however, tolerated it on account of the lack of other possible solutions of the problem.

The work concerned with emigration was, later on, not only a German problem, but also a problem with which the authorities of the countries to which the flow of emigrants was being directed would have to deal. Financial difficulties, such as the demand by various foreign governments for increasing sums of money to be presented at the time of the landing, the lack of shipping space, increasing restriction of entry permits, or the cancelling of such, increased extraordinarily the difficulties of emigration. In spite of these difficulties, 537,000 Jews were sent out of the country between the takeover of power and the deadline of 31 October 1941. Of these

approximately 360,000 were in Germany proper on 30 January 1933
approximately 147,000 were in Austria (Ostmark) on 15 March 1939
approximately 30,000 were in the Protectorate of Bohemia and Moravia on 15 March 1939.

The Jews themselves, or their Jewish political organizations, financed the emigration. In order to avoid impoverished Jews' remaining behind, the principle was followed that wealthy Jews have to finance the emigration of poor Jews; this was arranged by imposing a suitable tax, i.e., an emigration tax, which was used for financial arrangements in connection with the emigration of poor Jews and was imposed according to income.

Apart from the necessary Reichsmark exchange, foreign currency had to presented at the time of landing. In order to save foreign exchange held by Germany, the foreign Jewish financial organizations were—with the help of Jewish organizations in Germany—made responsible for arranging an adequate amount of foreign currency. Up to 30 October 1941, these foreign Jews donated a total of around 9,500,000 dollars.

In the meantime the Reichsführer-SS and Chief of the German Police had prohibited emigration of Jews due to the dangers of an emigration in wartime and due to the possibilities of the East.

III. Another possible solution of the problem has now taken the place of emigration, i.e. the evacuation of the Jews to the East, provided that the Führer gives the appropriate approval in advance.

These actions are, however, only to be considered provisional, but practical experience is already being collected which is of the greatest importance in relation to the future final solution of the Jewish question.

Approximately 11 million Jews will be involved in the final solution of the European Jewish question, distributed as follows among the individual countries:

	Country	Number
A.	Germany proper	131,800
	Austria	43,700
	Eastern territories	420,000
	General Government	2,284,000
	Bialystok	400,000
	Protectorate Bohemia and Moravia	74,200
	Estonia	–free of Jews–
	Latvia	3,500
	Lithuania	34,000
	Belgium	43,000
	Denmark	5,600
	France/occupied territory	165,000
	unoccupied territory	700,000
	Greece	69,600
	Netherlands	160,800
	Norway	1,300
B.	Bulgaria	48,000
	England	330,000
	Finland	2,300
	Ireland	4,000
	Italy including Sardinia	58,000
	Albania	200
	Croatia	40,000
	Portugal	3,000
	Rumania including Bessarabia	342,000
	Sweden	8,000
	Switzerland	18,000

Country	Number
Serbia	10,000
Slovakia	88,000
Spain	6,000
Turkey (European portion)	55,500
Hungary	742,800
USSR	5,000,000
Ukraine	2,994,684
White Russia, excluding Bialystok	446,484
Total	over 11,000,000

The number of Jews given here for foreign countries includes, however, only those Jews who still adhere to the Jewish faith, since some countries still do not have a definition of the term "Jew" according to racial principles.

The handling of the problem in the individual countries will meet with difficulties due to the attitude and outlook of the people there, especially in Hungary and Rumania. Thus, for example, even today the Jew can buy documents in Rumania that will officially prove his foreign citizenship.

The influence of the Jews in all walks of life in the USSR is well known. Approximately five million Jews live in the European part of the USSR, in the Asian part scarcely ¼ million.

The breakdown of Jews residing in the European part of the USSR according to trades was approximately as follows:

Agriculture	9.1%
Urban workers	14.8%
In trade	20.0%
Employed by the state	23.4%
In private occupations such as medical profession, press, theater, etc.	32.7%

Under proper guidance, in the course of the final solution the Jews are to be allocated for appropriate labor in the East. Able-bodied Jews, separated according to sex, will be taken in large work columns to these areas for work on roads, in the course of which action doubtless a large portion will be eliminated by natural causes.

The possible final remnant will, since it will undoubtedly consist of the most resistant portion, have to be treated accordingly, because it is the product of natural selection and would, if released, act as the seed of a new Jewish revival (see the experience of history.)

In the course of the practical execution of the final solution, Europe will be combed through from west to east. Germany proper, including the Protectorate of Bohemia and Moravia, will have to be handled first due to the housing problem and additional social and political necessities.

The evacuated Jews will first be sent, group by group, to so-called transit ghettos, from which they will be transported to the East.

SS-Obergruppenführer Heydrich went on to say that an important prerequisite for the evacuation as such is the exact definition of the persons involved.

It is not intended to evacuate Jews over 65 years old, but to send them to an old-age ghetto—Theresienstadt is being considered for this purpose.

In addition to these age groups—of the approximately 280,000 Jews in Germany proper and Austria on 31 October 1941, approximately 30% are over 65 years old—severely wounded veterans and Jews with war decorations (Iron Cross I) will be accepted in the old-age ghettos. With this expedient solution, in one fell swoop many interventions will be prevented.

The beginning of the individual larger evacuation actions will largely depend on military developments. Regarding the handling of the final solution in those European countries occupied and influenced by us, it was proposed that the appropriate expert of the Foreign Office discuss the matter with the responsible official of the Security Police and SD.

In Slovakia and Croatia the matter is no longer so difficult, since the most substantial problems in this respect have already been brought near a solution. In Rumania the government has in the meantime also appointed a commissioner for Jewish affairs. In order to settle the question in Hungary, it will soon be necessary to force an adviser for Jewish questions onto the Hungarian government.

With regard to taking up preparations for dealing with the problem in Italy, SS-Obergruppenführer Heydrich considers it opportune to contact the chief of police with a view to these problems.

In occupied and unoccupied France, the registration of Jews for evacuation will in all probability proceed without great difficulty.

Under Secretary of State Luther calls attention in this matter to the fact that in some countries, such as the Scandinavian states, difficulties will arise if this problem is dealt with thoroughly and that it will therefore be advisable to defer actions in these countries. Besides, in view of the small numbers of Jews affected, this deferral will not cause any substantial limitation.

The Foreign Office sees no great difficulties for southeast and western Europe.

SS-Gruppenführer Hofmann plans to send an expert to Hungary from the Race and Settlement Main Office for general orientation at the time when the Chief of the Security Police and SD takes up the matter there. It was decided to assign this expert from the Race and Settlement Main Office, who will not work actively, as an assistant to the police attaché.

IV. In the course of the final solution plans, the Nuremberg Laws should provide a certain foundation, in which a prerequisite for the absolute solution of the problem is also the solution to the problem of mixed marriages and persons of mixed blood.

The Chief of the Security Police and the SD discusses the following points, at first theoretically, in regard to a letter from the chief of the Reich chancellery:

1)   Treatment of Persons of Mixed Blood of the First Degree

Persons of mixed blood of the first degree will, as regards the final solution of the Jewish question, be treated as Jews.

From this treatment the following exceptions will be made:

a)   Persons of mixed blood of the first degree married to persons of German blood if their marriage has resulted in children (persons of mixed blood of the second degree). These persons of mixed blood of the second degree are to be treated essentially as Germans.

b)   Persons of mixed blood of the first degree, for whom the highest offices of the Party and State have already issued exemption permits in any sphere of life. Each individual case must be examined, and it is not ruled out that the decision may be made to the detriment of the person of mixed blood.

The prerequisite for any exemption must always be the personal merit of the person of mixed blood. (Not the merit of the parent or spouse of German blood.)

Persons of mixed blood of the first degree who are exempted from evacuation will be sterilized in order to prevent any offspring and to eliminate the problem of persons of mixed blood once and for all. Such sterilization will be voluntary. But it is required to remain in the Reich. The sterilized "person of mixed blood" is thereafter free of all restrictions to which he was previously subjected.

2)   Treatment of Persons of Mixed Blood of the Second Degree

Persons of mixed blood of the second degree will be treated fundamentally as persons of German blood, with the exception of the following cases, in which the persons of mixed blood of the second degree will be considered as Jews:

a)   The person of mixed blood of the second degree was born of a marriage in which both parents are persons of mixed blood.

b)   The person of mixed blood of the second degree has a racially especially undesirable appearance that marks him outwardly as a Jew.

c)   The person of mixed blood of the second degree has a particularly bad police and political record that shows that he feels and behaves like a Jew.

Also in these cases exemptions should not be made if the person of mixed blood of the second degree has married a person of German blood.

3)   Marriages between Full Jews and Persons of German Blood.

Here it must be decided from case to case whether the Jewish partner will be evacuated or whether, with regard to the effects of such a step on the German relatives, [this mixed marriage] should be sent to an old-age ghetto.

4)   Marriages between Persons of Mixed Blood of the First Degree and Persons of German Blood.

   a)   Without Children.
          If no children have resulted from the marriage, the person of mixed blood of the first degree will be evacuated or sent to an old-age ghetto (same treatment as in the case of marriages between full Jews and persons of German blood, point 3.)
   b)   With Children.
          If children have resulted from the marriage (persons of mixed blood of the second degree), they will, if they are to be treated as Jews, be evacuated or sent to a ghetto along with the parent of mixed blood of the first degree. If these children are to be treated as Germans (regular cases), they are exempted from evacuation as is therefore the parent of mixed blood of the first degree.

5)   Marriages between Persons of Mixed Blood of the First Degree and Persons of Mixed Blood of the First Degree or Jews.

In these marriages (including the children) all members of the family will be treated as Jews and therefore be evacuated or sent to an old-age ghetto.

6)   Marriages between Persons of Mixed Blood of the First Degree and Persons of Mixed Blood of the Second Degree.

In these marriages both partners will be evacuated or sent to an old-age ghetto without consideration of whether the marriage has produced children, since possible children will as a rule have stronger Jewish blood than the Jewish person of mixed blood of the second degree.

SS-Gruppenführer Hofmann advocates the opinion that sterilization will have to be widely used, since the person of mixed blood who is given the choice whether he will be evacuated or sterilized would rather undergo sterilization.

State Secretary Dr. Stuckart maintains that carrying out in practice of the just mentioned possibilities for solving the problem of mixed marriages and persons of mixed blood will create endless administrative work. In the second place, as the biological facts cannot be disregarded in any case, State Secretary Dr. Stuckart proposed proceeding to forced sterilization.

Furthermore, to simplify the problem of mixed marriages possibilities must be considered with the goal of the legislator saying something like: "These marriages have been dissolved."

With regard to the issue of the effect of the evacuation of Jews on the economy, State Secretary Neumann stated that Jews who are working in industries vital to the war effort, provided that no replacements are available, cannot be evacuated.

SS-Obergruppenführer Heydrich indicated that these Jews would not be evacuated according to the rules he had approved for carrying out the evacuations then underway.

State Secretary Dr. Bühler stated that the General Government would welcome it if the final solution of this problem could be begun in the General Government, since on the one hand transportation does not play such a large role here nor would problems of labor supply hamper this action. Jews must be removed from the territory of the General Government as quickly as possible, since it is especially here that the Jew as an epidemic carrier represents an extreme danger and on the other hand he is causing permanent chaos in the economic structure of the country through continued black market dealings. Moreover, of the approximately 2½ million Jews concerned, the majority is unfit for work.

State Secretary Dr. Bühler stated further that the solution to the Jewish question in the General Government is the responsibility of the Chief of the Security Police and the SD and that his efforts would be supported by the officials of the General Government. He had only one request, to solve the Jewish question in this area as quickly as possible.

In conclusion the different types of possible solutions were discussed, during which discussion both Gauleiter Dr. Meyer and State Secretary Dr. Bühler took the position that certain preparatory activities for the final solution should be carried out immediately in the territories in question, in which process alarming the populace must be avoided.

The meeting was closed with the request of the Chief of the Security Police and the SD to the participants that they afford him appropriate support during the carrying out of the tasks involved in the solution.

Abschrift des sogenannten *Wannseeprotokolls*
aus dem Staatsarchiv Nürnberg.

Document NO. NG-2586 G Office of Chief of Counsel for War Crimes.

(Stempel): Geheime Reichssache;

30 Ausfertigungen
16.Ausfertigung

Besprechungsprotokoll.

I. An der am 20.1.1942 in Berlin, Am Großen Wannsee Nr. 56/58, stattgefundenen Besprechung über die Endlösung der Judenfrage nahmen teil:

Gauleiter Dr. Meyer und	Reichsministerium
Reichsamtsleiter Dr. Leibbrandt	für die besetzten Ostgebiete
Staatssekretär Dr. Stuckart	Reichsministerium des Inneren
Staatssekretär Neumann	Beauftragter für den Vierjahresplan
Staatssekretär Dr. Freisler	Reichsjustizministerium
Staatssekretär Dr. Bühler	Amt des General-gouverneurs
Unterstaatssekretär Luther	Auswärtiges Amt
SS-Oberführer Klopfer	Partei-Kanzlei
Ministerialdirektor Kritzinger (Handschriftliche Notiz):	Reichskanzlei D III. 29 G.Rs.
SS-Gruppenführer Hofmann	Rasse- und Siedlungshauptamt
SS-Gruppenführer Müller, SS-Obersturmbannführer Eichmann	Reichssicherheitshauptamt
SS-Oberführer Dr. Schöngarth, Befehlshaber der Sicherheitspolizei und des SD im Generalgouvernement	Sicherheitspolizei und SD
SS-Sturmbannführer Dr. Lange Kommandeur der Sicherheitspolizei und des SD für den Generalbezirk Lettland, als Vertreter des Befehlshabers der Sicherheitspolizei und des SD für das Reichskommissariat Ostland.	Sicherheitspolizei und SD

II. Chef der Sicherheitspolizei und des SD, SS-Obergruppenführer Heydrich, teilte eingangs seine Bestellung zum Beauftragten für die Vorbereitung der Endlösung der europäischen Judenfrage durch den Reichsmarschall mit und wies darauf hin, daß zu dieser Besprechung geladen wurde, um Klarheit in grundsätzlichen Fragen zu schaffen. Der Wunsch des Reichsmarschalls, ihm einen Entwurf über die organisatorischen, sachlichen und materiellen Belange im Hinblick auf die Endlösung der europäischen Judenfrage zu übersenden, erfordert die vorherige gemeinsame Behandlung aller an diesen Fragen unmittelbar beteiligten Zentralinstanzen im Hinblick auf die Parallelisierung der Linienführung.

Die Federführung bei der Bearbeitung der Endlösung der Judenfrage liege ohne Rücksicht auf geographische Grenzen zentral beim Reichsführer-SS und Chef der Deutschen Polizei (Chef der Sicherheitspolizei und des SD).

Der Chef der Sicherheitspolizei und des SD gab sodann einen kurzen Rückblick über den bisher geführten Kampf gegen diesen Gegner. Die wesentlichsten Momente bilden

a/   die Zurückdrängung der Juden aus den einzelnen Lebensgebieten des deutschen Volkes,

b/   die Zurückdrängung der Juden aus dem Lebensraum des deutschen Volkes

Im Vollzug dieser Bestrebungen wurde als einzige vorläufige Lösungsmöglichkeit die Beschleunigung der Auswanderung der Juden aus dem Reichsgebiet verstärkt und planmäßig in Angriff genommen.

Auf Anordnung des Reichsmarschalls wurde im Januar 1939 eine Reichszentrale für jüdische Auswanderung errichtet, mit deren Leitung der Chef der Sicherheitspolizei und des SD betraut wurde. Sie hatte insbesondere die Aufgabe

a/   alle Maßnahmen zur *Vorbereitung* einer verstärkten Auswanderung der Juden zu treffen

b/   den Auswanderungsstrom zu *lenken,*

c/   die Durchführung der Auswanderung im *Einzelfall* zu beschleunigen.

Das Aufgabenziel war, auf legale Weise den deutschen Lebensraum von Juden zu säubern.

Über die Nachteile, die eine solche Aus-wanderungsforcierung mit sich brachte, waren sich alle Stellen im klaren. Sie mußten jedoch angesichts des Fehlens anderer Lösungsmöglichkeiten vorerst in Kauf genommen werden.

Die Auswanderungsarbeiten waren in der Folgezeit nicht nur ein deutsches Problem, sondern auch ein Problem, mit dem sich die Behörden der Ziel- bzw. Einwandererländer zu befassen hatten. Die finanziellen Schwierigkeiten, wie Erhöhung der Vorzeige- und Landungsgelder seitens der verschiedenen ausländischen Regierungen, fehlende Schiffsplätze, laufend verschärfte Einwanderungsbeschränkungen oder - Sperren, erschwerten die Auswanderungsbestrebungen außerordentlich. Trotz dieser Schwierigkeiten wurden seit der Machtübernahme bis zum Stichtag 31.10.1941 insgesamt rund 573.000 Juden zur Auswanderung gebracht. Davon

vom 30.1.1933 aus dem Altreich	rd. 360.000
vom 15.3.1938 aus der Ostmark	rd. 147.000
vom 15.3.1939 aus dem Protektorat	rd. 30.000
Böhmen und Mähren	

Die Finanzierung der Auswanderung erfolgte durch die Juden bzw. jüdisch-politischen Organisationen selbst. Um den Verbleib der verproletarisierten Juden zu vermeiden, wurde nach dem Grundsatz verfahren, daß die vermögenden Juden die Abwanderung der vermögenslosen Juden zu finanzieren haben; hier wurde, je nach Vermögen gestaffelt, eine entsprechende Umlage bzw. Auswandererabgabe vorgeschrieben, die zur Bestreitung der finanziellen Obliegenheiten im Zuge der Abwanderung vermögensloser Juden verwandt wurde.

Neben dem Reichsmark-Aufkommen sind Devisen für Vorzeige- und Landungs-gelder erforderlich gewesen. Um den deutschen Devisenschatz zu schonen, wurden die jüdischen Finanzinstitutionen des Auslandes durch die jüdischen Organisationen des Inlandes verhalten, für die Beitreibung entsprechender Devisenaufkommen Sorge zu tragen. Hier wurden durch diese ausländischen Juden im Schenkungswege bis zum 30.10.1941 insgesamt rund 9.500.000 Dollar zur Verfügung gestellt.

Inzwischen hat der Reichsführer-SS und Chef der Deutschen Polizei im Hinblick auf die Gefahren einer Auswanderung im Kriege und im Hinblick auf die Möglichkeiten des Ostens die Auswanderung von Juden verboten.

III. Anstelle der Auswanderung ist nunmehr als weitere Lösungsmöglichkeit nach entsprechender vorheriger Genehmigung durch den Führer die Evakuierung der Juden nach dem Osten getreten.

Diese Aktionen sind jedoch lediglich als Aus-weichmöglichkeiten anzusprechen, doch werden hier bereits jene praktischen Erfahrungen gesammelt, die im Hinblick auf die kommende Endlösung der Judenfrage von wichtiger Bedeutung sind.

Im Zuge dieser Endlösung der europäischen Judenfrage kommen rund 11 Millionen Juden in Betracht, die sich wie folgt auf die einzelnen Länder verteilen:

	Land		Zahl
A.	Altreich		131.800
	Ostmark		43.700
	Ostgebiete		420.000
	Generalgouvernement		2.284.000
	Bialystok		400.000
	Protektorat Böhmen und Mären		74.200
	Estland	–judenfrei–	
	Lettland		3.500
	Litauen		34.000
	Belgien		43.000

Land	Zahl
Dänemark	5.600
Frankreich/Besetztes Gebiet	165.000
Unbesetztes Gebiet	700.000
Griechenland	69.600
Niederlande	160.800
Norwegen	1.300
B. Bulgarien	48.000
England	330.000
Finnland	2.300
Irland	4.000
Italien einschl. Sardinien	58.000
Albanien	200
Kroatien	40.000
Portugal	3.000
Rumänien einschl. Bessarabien	342.000
Schweden	8.000
Schweiz	18.000
Serbien	10.000
Slowakei	88.000
Spanien	6.000
Türkei (europ. Teil)	55.500
Ungarn	742.800
UdSSR	5.000.000
Ukraine	2.994.684
Weißrussland auschl.	
Bialystok	446.484
Zusammen:	über 11.000.000

Bei den angegebenen Judenzahlen der verscheidenen ausländischen Staaten handelt es sich jedoch nur um Glaubensjuden, da die Begriffsbestimmungen der Juden nach rassischen Grundsätzen teilweise dort noch fehlen. Die Behandlung des Problems in den einzelnen Ländern wird im Hinblick auf die allgemeine Haltung und Auffassung auf gewisse Schwierigkeiten stoßen, besonders in Ungarn und Rumänien. So kann sich z.B. heute noch in Rumänien der Jude gegen Geld entsprechende Dokumente, die ihm eine fremde Staatsangehörigkeit amtlich bescheinigen, beschaffen.

Der Einfluß der Juden auf alle Gebiete in der UdSSR ist bekannt. Im europäischen Gebiet leben etwa 5 Millionen, im asiatischen Raum knapp ¼ Million Juden.

Die berufsständische Aufgliederung der im europäischen Gebiet der UdSSR ansässigen Juden war etwa folgende:

In der Landwirtschaft	9.1%
als städtischer Arbeiter	14.8%
im Handel	20.0%
als Staatsarbeiter angestellt	23.4%
in den privaten Berufen -	
Heilkunde, Presse, Theater, usw.	32.7%

Unter entsprechender Leitung sollen im Zuge der Endlösung die Juden in geeigneter Weise im Osten zum Arbeitseinsatz kommen. In großen Arbeitskolonnen, unter Trennung der Geschlechter, werden die arbeitsfähigen Juden straßenbauend in diese Gebiete geführt, wobei zweifellos ein Groß teil durch natürliche Verminderung ausfallen wird.

Der allfällig endlich verbliebende Restbestand wird, da es sich bei diesem zweifellos um den widerstandsfähigsten Teil handelt, entsprechend behandelt werden müssen, da dieser, eine natürliche Auslese darstellend, bei Freilassung als Keimzelle eines neuen jüdischen Aufbaues anzusprechen ist. (Siehe die Erfahrung der Geschichte.)

Im Zuge der praktischen Durchführung der Endlösung wird Europa vom Westen nach Osten durchgekämmt. Das Reichsgebiet einschließlich Protektorat Böhmen und Mähren wird, allein schon aus Gründen der Wohnungsfrage und sonstigen sozial-politischen Notwendigkeiten, vorweggenommen werden müssen.

Die evakuierten Juden werden zunächst Zug um Zug in sogenannte Durchgangsghettos verbracht, um von dort aus weiter nach dem Osten transportiert zu werden.

Wichtige Voraussetzung, so führte SS-Obergruppenführer H e y d r i c h weiter aus, für die Durchführung der Evakuierung überhaupt, ist die genaue Festlegung des in Betracht kommenden Personenkreises.

Es ist beabsichtigt, Juden im Alter von über 65 Jahren nicht zu evakuieren, sondern sie einem Altersghetto - vorgesehen ist Theresienstadt - zu überstellen.

Neben diesen Altersklassen - von den am 31.10.1941 sich im Altreich und der Ostmark befindlichen etwa 280.000 Juden sind etwa 30% über 65 Jahre alt - finden in den jüdischen Altersghettos weiterhin die schwerkriegsbeschädigten Juden und Juden mit Kriegsauszeichnungen (EK I) Aufnahme. Mit dieser zweckmäßigen Lösung werden mit einem Schlag die vielen Interventionen ausgeschaltet.

Der Beginn der einzelnen größeren Evakuierungsaktionen wird weitgehend von der militärischen Entwicklung abhängig sein. Bezüglich der Behandlung der Endlösung in den von uns besetzten und beeinflußten europäischen Gebieten wurde vorgeschlagen, daß die in Betracht kommenden Sachbearbeiter des Auswärtigen Amtes sich mit dem zuständigen Referenten der Sicherheitspolizei und des SD besprechen.

In der Slowakei und Kroatien ist die Angelegenheit nicht mehr allzu schwer, da die wesentlichsten Kernfragen in dieser Hinsicht dort bereits einer Lösung zugeführt wurden. In Rumänien hat die Regierung inzwischen ebenfalls einen Judenbeauftragten eingesetzt. Zur Regelung der Frage in Ungarn ist erforderlich, in Zeitkürze einen Berater für Judenfragen der Ungarischen Regierung aufzuoktroyieren.

Hinsichtlich der Aufnahme der Vorbereitungen zur Regelung des Problems in Italien hält SS-Obergruppenführer H e y d r i c h eine Verbindung mit Polizei-Chef in diesen Belangen für angebracht.

Im besetzten und unbesetzten Frankreich wird die Erfassung der Juden zur Evakuierung aller Wahrscheinlichkeit nach ohne große Schwierigkeiten vor sich gehen können.

Unterstaatssekretär L u t h e r teilte hierzu mit, daß bei tiefgehender Behandlung dieses Problems in einigen Ländern, so in den nordischen Staaten, Schwierigkeiten auftauchen werden, und es sich daher empfiehlt, diese Länder vorerst noch zurückzustellen. In Anbetracht der hier in Frage kommenden geringen Judenzahlen bildet diese Zurückstellung ohnedies keine wesentliche Einschränkung.

Dafür sieht das Auswärtige Amt für den Südosten und Westen Europas keine großen Schwierigkeiten.

SS-Gruppenführer H o f m a n n beabsichtigt, einen Sachbearbeiter des Rasse- und Siedlungshauptamtes zur allgemeinen Orientierung dann nach Ungarn mitsenden zu wollen, wenn seitens des Chefs der Sicherheitspolizei und des SD die Angelegenheit dort in Angriff genommen wird. Es wurde festgelegt, diesen Sachbearbeiter des Rasse- und Siedlungshauptamtes, der nicht aktiv werden soll, vorübergehend offiziell als Gehilfen zum Polizei-Attaché abzustellen.

IV. Im Zuge der Endlösungsvorhaben sollen die Nürnberger Gesetze gewissermaßen die Grundlage bilden, wobei Voraussetzung für die restlose Bereinigung des Problems auch die Lösung der Mischehen- und Mischlingsfragen ist.

Chef der Sicherheitspolizei und des SD erörtert im Hinblick auf ein Schreiben des Chefs der Reichskanzlei zunächst theoretisch die nachstehenden Punkte:

1)   *Behandlung der Mischlinge 1. Grades.*

Mischlinge 1. Grades sind im Hinblick auf die Endlösung der Judenfrage den Juden gleichgestellt.

Von dieser Regelung werden ausgenommen:

a)   Mischlinge 1. Grades verheiratet mit Deutschblütigen, aus deren Ehe Kinder (Mischlinge 2. Grades) hervorgegangen sind. Diese Mischlinge 2. Grades sind im wesentlichen den Deutschen gleichgestellt.

b)   Mischlinge 1. Grades, für die von den höchsten Instanzen der Partei und des Staates bisher auf irgendwelchen Lebensgebieten Ausnahmegenehmigungen erteilt worden sind.

Jeder Einzelfall muß überprüft werden, wobei nicht ausgeschlossen wird, daß die Entscheidung nochmals zu Ungunsten des Mischlings ausfällt.

Voraussetzungen einer Ausnahmebewilligung müssen stets grundsätzliche Verdienste des in Frage stehenden Mischlings *selbst* sein. (Nicht Verdienste des deutschblütigen Eltern- oder Eheteiles.)

Der von der Evakuierung auszunehmende Mischling 1. Grades wird - um jede Nachkommenschaft zu verhindern und das Mischlingsproblem endgültig zu bereinigen - sterilisiert. Die Sterilisierung erfolgt freiwillig. Sie ist aber Voraussetzung des Verbleibens im Reich. Der sterilisierte "Mischling" ist in der Folgezeit von allen einengenden Bestimmungen, denen er bislang unterworfen ist, befreit.

2)   *Behandlung der Mischlinge 2. Grades*

Die Mischlinge 2. Grades werden grundsätzlich den Deutschblütigen zugeschlagen, *mit Ausnahme folgender Fälle*, in denen die Mischlinge 2. Grades den Juden gleichgestellt werden:

a)   Herkunft der Mischlinge 2. Grades aus einer Bastardehe (beide Teile Mischlinge).

b)   Rassisch besonders ungünstiges Erscheinungsbild des Mischlings 2. Grades, daß ihn schon äußerlich zu den Juden rechnet.

c)   Besonders schlechte polizeiliche und politische Beurteilung des Mischlings 2. Grades, die erkenne läßt, daß er sich wie ein Jude fühlt und benimmt.

Auch in diesen Fällen sollen aber dann Ausnahmen nicht gemacht werden, wenn der Michling 2. Grades deutschblütig verheiratet ist.

3)   *Ehen zwischen Volljuden und Deutschblütigen.*

Von Einzelfall zu Einzelfall muß hier entschieden werden, ob der jüdische Teil evakuiert wird, oder ob er unter Berücksichtigung auf die Auswirkungen einer solchen Maßnahme auf die deutschen Verwandten dieser Mischehe einem Altersghetto überstellt wird.

4)   *Ehen zwischen Mischlingen 1. Grades und Deutschblütigen*

a)   Ohne Kinder.
     Sind aus der Ehe keine Kinder hervorgegangen, wird der Mischling 1. Grades evakuiert bzw. einem Altersghetto überstellt (Gleiche Behandlung wie bei Ehen zwischen Volljuden und Deutschblütigen. Punkt 3.)

b)   Mit Kindern.
     Sind Kinder aus der Ehe hervorgegangen (Mischlinge 2. Grades), werden sie, *wenn sie den Juden gleichgestellt werden*, zusammen mit dem Mischling 1. Grades evakuiert bzw. einem Ghetto überstellt. Soweit diese Kinder *Deutschen gleichgestellt werden* (Regelfälle), sind sie von der Evakuierung auszunehmen und damit auch der Mischling 1. Grades.

5)   *Ehen zwischen Mischlingen 1. Grades und Mischlingen 1. Grades oder Juden.*

Bei diesen Ehen (einschließlich der Kinder) werden alle Teile wie Juden behandelt und daher evakuiert bzw. einem Altersghetto überstellt.

6)   *Ehen zwischen Mischlingen 1. Grades und Mischlingen 2. Grades.*

Beide Eheteile werden ohne Rücksicht darauf, ob Kinder vorhanden sind oder nicht, evakuiert bzw. einem Altersghetto überstellt, da etwaige Kinder rassenmäßig in der Regel einen stärkeren jüdischen Bluteinschlag aufweisen, als die jüdischen Mischlinge 2. Grade.

SS-Gruppenführer H o f m a n n steht auf dem Standpunkt, daß von der Sterilisierung weitgehend Gebrauch gemacht werden muß; zumal der Mischling, vor die Wahl gestellt, ob er evakuiert oder sterilisiert werden soll, sich lieber der Sterilisierung unterziehen würde.

Staatssekretär Dr. S t u c k a r t stellt fest, daß die praktische Durchführung der eben mitgeteilten Lösungsmöglichkeiten zur Bereinigung der Mischehen- und Mischlingsfragen in dieser Form eine unendliche Verwaltungsarbeit mit sich bringen würde. Um zum anderen auf alle Fälle auch den biologischen Tatsachen Rechnung zu tragen, schlug Staatssekretär Dr. S t u c k a r t vor, zur Zwangssterilisierung zu schreiten.

Zur Vereinfachung des Mischehenproblems müßten ferner Möglichkeiten überlegt werden mit dem Ziel, daß der Gesetzgeber etwa sagt: "Diese Ehen *sind* geschieden".

Bezüglich der Frage der Auswirkung der Judenevakuierung auf das Wirtschaftsleben erklärte Staatssekretär N e u m a n n, daß die in kriegswichtigen Betrieben im Arbeitseinsatz stehenden Juden derzeit, solange noch kein Ersatz zur Verfügung steht, nicht evakuiert werden könnten.

SS-Obergruppenführer H e y d r i c h wies darauf hin, daß diese Juden nach den von ihm genehmigten Richtlinien zur Durchführung der derzeit laufenden Evakuierungsaktionen ohnedies nicht evakuiert würden.

Staatssekretär Dr. B ü h l e r stellte fest, daß das Generalgouvernement es begrüßen würde, wenn mit der Endlösung dieser Frage *im Generalgouvernement begonnen würde*, weil einmal hier das Transportproblem keine übergeordnete Rolle spielt und arbeitseinsatzmäßige Gründe den Lauf dieser Aktion nicht behindern würden. Juden müßten so schnell wie möglich aus dem Gebiet des Generalgouvernements entfernt werden, weil gerade hier der Jude als Seuchenträger eine eminente Gefahr bedeutet und er zum anderen durch fortgesetzten Schleichhandel die wirtschaftliche Struktur des Landes dauernd in Unordnung bringt. Von den in Frage kommenden etwa 2½ Millionen Juden sei überdies die Mehrzahl der Fälle *arbeitsunfähig*.

Staatssekretär Dr. B ü h l e r stellt weiterhin fest, daß die Lösung der Judenfrage im Generalgouvernement federführend beim Chef der Sicherheitspolizei und des SD liegt und seine Arbeiten durch die Behörden des Generalgouvernements unterstützt würden. Er hätte nur eine Bitte, die Judenfrage in diesem Gebiet so schnell wie möglich zu lösen.

Abschließend wurden die verschiedenen Arten der Lösungsmöglichkeiten besprochen, wobei sowohl seitens des Gauleiters Dr. M e y e r als auch seitens des Staatssekretärs Dr. B ü h l e r der Standpunkt vertreten wurde, gewisse vorbereitende Arbeiten im Zuge der Endlösung gleich in den betreffenden Gebieten selbst durchzuführen, wobei jedoch eine Beunruhigung der Bevölkerung vermieden werden müsse.

Mit der Bitte des Chefs der Sicherheitspolizei und des SD an die Besprechungsteilnehmer, ihm bei der Durchführung der Lösungsarbeiten entsprechende Unterstützung zu gewähren, wurde die Besprechung geschlossen.

"A CERTIFIED TRUE COPY"

END

Appendix 3: Area and Population of the Eastern Regions and the General Government

TABLE A

Area and Population, including Population Density
The Eastern Regions of the German Reich in Reichsgau Provinces and Government Districts

Reichsgau-Province Government Districts	Area in Square Kilometers	Population Total	Per SquareKilometer
Province Ostpreußen	53 038,53	3 191 688	60,18
Reich Territory Prior to 22. 3. 1939	*34 065,82*	*2 055 961*	*60,35*
Memel	*2 828,93*	*141 645*	*50,07*
Former Polish State Territory	*16 143,73*	*994 082*	*61,58*
1. Government District Königsberg	13 146,61	957 363	72,82
Reich Territory Prior to 26. 10. 1939	*13 146,61*	*957 363*	*72,82*
2. Government District Gumbinnen	15 033,54	812 773	54,06
Reich Territory Prior to 22. 3. 1939	*9 399,36*	*546 057*	*58,10*
Memel	*2 828,98*	*141 645*	*50,01*
Former Polish State Territory	*2 805,20*	*125 071*	*44,59*
3. Government District Allenstein	12 011,08	578 733	48,18
Reich Territory Prior to 26. 10. 1939	*11 519,85*	*552 541*	*47,96*
Former Polish State Territory	*491,23*	· *26 192*	*53,32*
4. Government District Zichenau	12 847,30	842 819	65,60
Former Polish State Territory	*12 847,30*	*842 819*	*65,60*
Reichsgau Danzig-Westpreußen	26 055,85	2 179 134	83,60
Reich Territory Prior to 19.1939	*2 925,93*	*277 310*	*94,79*
Former Free City of Danzig	*1 892,90*	*407 517*	*215,29*
Former Polish State Territory	*21 237,02*	*1 494 277*	*70,36*
1. Government District Marienwerder	8 715,94	644 771	73,98
Reich Territory Prior to 26. 10. 1939	*2 412,27*	*178 729*	*74 09*
Former Polish State Territory	*6 30367*	*466 042*	*73,93*
2. Government District Danzig	9 914,29	963 611	97,19
Reich Territory Prior to 1.9.1939	*513,66*	*93 611*	*191,98*
Former Free City of Danzig	*9 914,29*	*963 611*	*97,19*
Former Free City of Danzig	*1 892,90*	*407 517*	*215,29*
Former Polish State Territory	*7 507,73*	*457 483*	*60,93*
3. Government District Bromberg	7 425,62	570 752	76,86
Former Polish State Territory	*7 425,62*	*570 752*	*76,86*

574 Appendix 3

TABLE A
(continued)

Reichsgau-Province Government Districts	Area in Square Kilometers	Population Total	Per SquareKilometer
Reichsgau Wartheland	43 942,99	4 546 408	103,46
Former Polish State Territory	*43 942,99*	*4 546 408*	*103,46*
1. Government District Hohensalza	14 460,84	1 188 405	82,18
2. Government District Kalisch	14 062,62	2 083 274	148,14
3. Government District Posen	15 419,53	1 274 729	82,67
Province Silesia	47 591,04	7 359 728	154,65
Reich Territory Prior to 1. 10. 1938	*36 696,38*	*4 710 372*	*128,36*
Hultschin	*316,76*	*54 734*	*172,80*
Former Polish State Territory	*10 577,90*	*2 594 622*	*245,29*
1. Government District Liegnitz	14 023,41	1 273 772	90,83
Reich Territory Prior to 26. 10. 1939	*14 023,41*	*1 273 772*	*90,83*
2. Government District Breslau	12 957,92	1 953 829	150,78
Reich Territory Prior to 26. 10. 1939	*12 957,93*	*1 053 829*	*150,78*
3. Government District Oppeln	11 712,33	1 320 266	112,72
Reich Territory Priot to 1. 10. 1938	*8 626,93*	*960 957*	*111,39*
Hultschin	*316,76*	*54 734*	*172,79*
Former Polish State Territory	*2 768,64*	*304 575*	*110,01*
4. Government District Kattowitz	8 897,38	2 811 861	316,03
Reich Territory Prior to 26. 10. 1939	*1 086,12*	*521 814*	*479,56*
Former Polish State Territory	*7 809,26*	*2 290 047*	*293,24*

From: *Die Ostgebiete des Deutschen Reiches und des Generalgouvernements der besetzten polnischen Gebiete in statistischen Angaben* (for official use only), Berlin: Publikationsstelle Berlin-Dahlem, Selbstverlag, 1940.

TABLE B
The General Government of the Occupied Polish Territories by Districts

Districts	Area in Square Kilometers	Population Total	Per SquareKilometer
General Government total	95 742,61	10569 039	110,39
1. District Cracow	26 912,43	3 194 059	118,68
2. District Lublin	26 848,28	2 144 658	79,88
3. District Radom	25 259,80	2 505 647	99,20
4. District Warsaw	16 722,10	2 724 675	162,94

From: *Die Ostgebiete des Deutschen Reiches und des Generalgouvernements der besetzten polnischen Gebiete in statistischen Angaben* (for official use only), Berlin: Publikationsstelle Berlin-Dahlem, Selbstverlag, 1940.

Appendix 4: Poster Showing the Execution of Polish Defendants on June 4 and 9, 1942, in Poznań (Poland)

Bekanntmachung.

Das Sondergericht in Posen hat zum Tode verurteilt:

am 4. Juni 1942

Johann W a w r z y n i a k aus Posen

wegen hetzerischer Betätigung deutschfeindlicher Gesinnung und wegen unerlaubten Waffenbesitzes,

am 9. Juni 1942

Adam Z e b r o w s k i aus Posen

wegen Kriegswirtschaftsverbrechens (Schleichhandel),

am 9. Juni 1942

Sigismund v o n J o r d a n aus Posen,

Salomea K o l o d z i e j c z a k aus Posen

wegen gewerbsmässiger Hehlerei, Kriegswirtschaftsverbrechens und Nichtanzeige von Waffenbesitz, Jordan ausserdem wegen fortgesetzten Einbruchsdiebstahls.

Die Urteile sind heute vollstreckt worden.

(Übersetzung): Przez Sondergericht w Posen skazani zostali na śmierć: dnia 4 czerwca 1942 roku Jan Wawrzyniak z Posen z powodu podburzania do wrogiego usposobienia przeciwniemieckiego i z powodu niedozwolonego posiadania broni, dnia 9 czerwca 1942 roku Adam Zebrowski z Posen z powodu wykroczeń przeciw ustawom wojenno-gospodarczym (handel pokątny), dnia 9czerwca 1942 r. Zygmunt Jordan z Posen, Saloma Kolodziejczak z Posen z powodu procederowego paserstwa, wykroczeń przeciw ustawom wojemo-gospodarczym i niezgłoszenia posiadania broni, Jordan oprócz tego z powodu ciągłych kradzeży z włamaniem. Wyrok został dzisiaj vykonany.

Posen, den1. Juli 1942.

Der Oberstaatsanwalt.

Source: Archiwum Pañstwowe Poznań, al. 23 lutego 41/43, 60-967 Poznań 9, Poland; file Gendarmerie des Kreises Posen 6, p. 176.

Appendix 5: The Command and Administrative Structure of Police Forces in the General Government

The following chart shows the organizational structure of the various police forces and their integration into the hierarchy of the General Government. It shows that the police structure was very complicated, confusing, and overlapping in the assigned competences. This confusion was purposely created by the police command, which was united in 1936 with the SS in the person of Heinrich Himmler, who was *Reichsfürer*-SS and chief of the German police. Because the SS and police forces were the most powerful institutions in the National Socialist state, they eventually succeeded in virtually removing the police from the whole system of the regular administrative controls, submitting them instead to the system of political and random control of the SS. This complex structure, which hardly could be disentangled, provided a measure of camouflage while serving even higher political strategy. Endless quarrels between the various police branches were the consequence of the inevitable confusion about the hierarchy and competences, a result that accorded with Hitler's policy *divide et impera*. This chart is based on one in the Central Office of the Administrations of Justice of the *Länder*, Ludwigsburg, Germany, file Varia, vol. 103.

Command and Administrative Structure of Police Forces in the General Government
(October26,1939 – 1944)

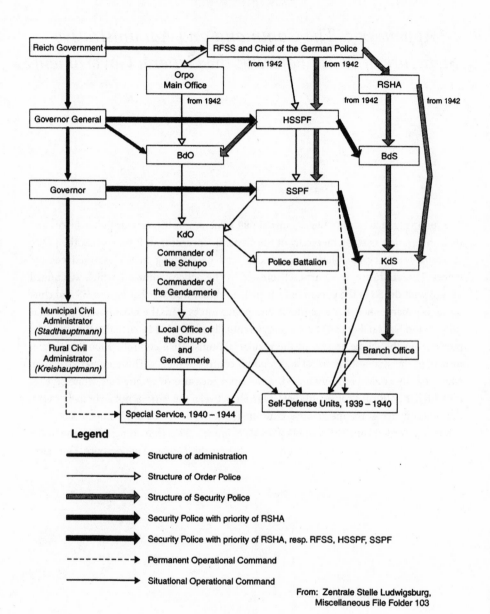

Legend

➡	Structure of administration
➩	Structure of Order Police
➡	Structure of Security Police
➡	Security Police with priority of RSHA
➡	Security Police with priority of RSHA, resp. RFSS, HSSPF, SSPF
- - - ➤	Permanent Operational Command
──➤	Situational Operational Command

From: Zentrale Stelle Ludwigsburg,
Miscellaneous File Folder 103

Appendix 6: Maps

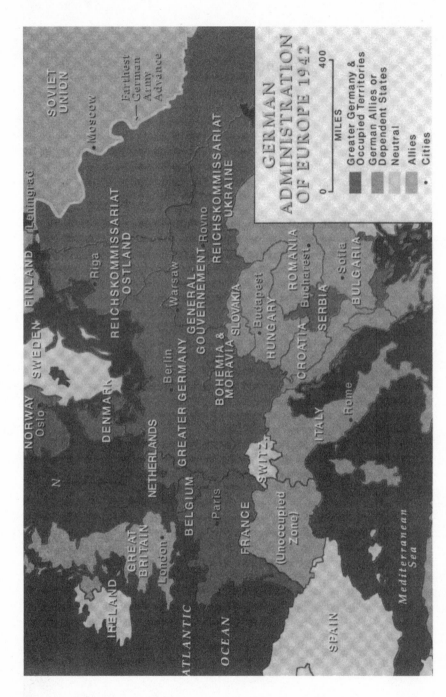

Source: United States Holocaust Memorial Museum

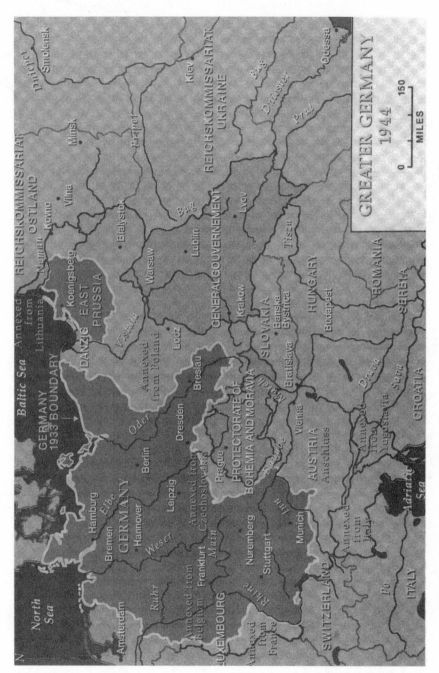

Source: United States Holocaust Memorial Museum

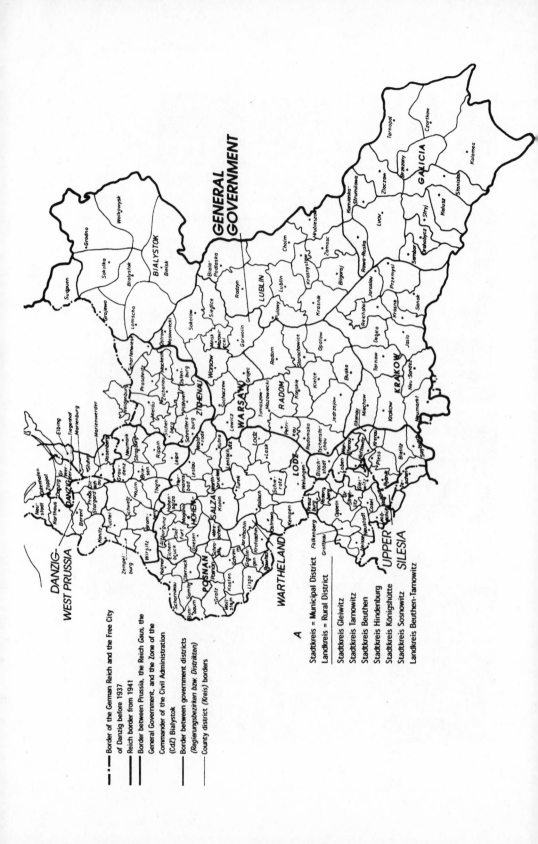

DANZIG-
WEST PRUSSIA

GENERAL
GOVERNMENT

BIALYSTOK

DANZIG

ZICHENAU

WARSAW

LUBLIN

POSNAN

WARTHELAND

LODZ

RADOM

KRAKOW

GALICIA

HOHEN-
SALZA

UPPER
SILESIA

A

--- Border of the German Reich and the Free City
    of Danzig before 1937

— Reich border from 1941

━ Border between Prussia, the Reich Gaus, the
    General Government, and the Zone of the
    Commander of the Civil Administration
    (CdZ) Bialystok

— Border between government districts
    (Regierungsbezirken bzw. Distrikten)

— County district (Kreis) borders

A = Stadtkreis = Municipal District
    Landkreis = Rural District

Stadtkreis Gleiwitz
Stadtkreis Tarnowitz
Stadtkreis Beuthen
Stadtkreis Hindenburg
Stadtkreis Königshütte
Stadtkreis Sosnowitz
Landkreis Beuthen-Tarnowitz

Notes

Full reference information for the sources cited briefly here may be found in the bibliography.

Preface to the First German Edition

1. See, for example, F. Siebert in his report "Hauptabteilung Innere Verwaltung der Regierung des Generalgouvernements," November 11, 1959 (BA Ostdok. 13, General Government I b/5).

2. Cf. guidelines for the editorial staff of the journal *Deutsches Recht (DR)*, the organ of the League of National Socialist German Jurists (in which above all proposals for reform affecting future legislation were discussed), according to which only contributions from Aryan persons were published and discussed, and "as a matter of course" only those authors were printed who stood "unequivocally behind the government of national revolution" (*DR* [1933]: 200).

Deutsche Justiz (DJ) (before 1933 *Preussisches Justizministerialblatt*), the official organ of the Reich Ministry of Justice, with numerous supplementary sections, was dedicated to the "guidance and enlightenment" of the judicial system; everything that was printed there appeared "on official orders and with official approval" and was "an important means ... of promoting consensus on [the] goals of legislation" (Sauer, *Das Reichsjustizministerium* [1939], 24 f.). Publications in this journal were in the hands of the judicial press offices, under the central control of the Ministry of Justice (cf. A. Klütz, "Die Aufgaben der Justizpressestellen," *DJ* [1933]: 405 ff.; secs. 6, 8, par. 3, of the administrative instructions of the minister of justice dated June 1, 1938, special edition of *Deutsche Justiz*, no. 17 [1938]: 23, reprinted in *DJ* [1938]: 546); for further details on the guiding role of *DJ*, see H. Hattenhauer in Federal Ministry of Justice, ed., *Vom Reichsjustizamt zum Bundesministerium der Justiz* (1977), 1 ff., 78.

Another example that could be mentioned is *Juristische Wochenschrift (JW)*, the journal of the German Bar Association, which mainly published contributions on the law in force. From 1933 it appeared with the addition "in the League of National Socialist German Jurists." The editor was Hans Frank, leader of the League of National Socialist German Jurists, and thus a strict National Socialist orientation was ensured. With issue 43 (October 28, 1933) the *JW* became the *Zeitschrift der Fachgruppe Rechtsanwälte im BNSDJ e. V.* (BNSDJ is the abbreviation for League of National Socialist German Jurists). On April 1, 1939, *JW* merged with *Deutsches Recht*, the organ of the NSRB (formerly the League of National Socialist German Jurists), becoming *Deutsches Recht vereint mit JW*. From 1941 *Juristische Wochenschrift* disappeared completely from the official nomenclature.

3. Cf. Fraenkel, *Der Doppelstaat* (1974), 15.

4. For the purposes of this English translation, place names in the former Annexed Eastern

Territories and the General Government are generally given in German with the Polish name supplied, at intervals throughout the text, in parentheses, except where standard English equivalents exist.

5. For example, to designate all persons who were subject to racial persecution measures, the then current designations *nichtarisch* (non-Aryan) and *nichtdeutsch* (non-German) are used. These are combined in the designation *Fremdvölkische* (persons of foreign race or non-Germans), the main term used by the SS and police, which later became current in administrative and judicial circles.

6. Literature appearing after that time is taken into account in the notes.

Introduction. I. The Tense Relations between State Leadership and State Administration

1. Picker, *Hitlers Tischgespräche* (1951), 195.
2. Table talk on the evening of March 29, 1942, quoted from ibid. (1968), 65 ff., which contains the familiar invective against the legal profession, particularly lawyers (*Advokaten*). There was a similar discussion at dinner on the evening of July 22, 1942 (ibid., 244).
3. Conversation at table on the evening of March 29, 1942, quoted in ibid. (1951), 236.
4. Conversation at table on the evening of June 24, 1942, quoted in ibid. (1968), 191.
5. Cf. Jacoby, *Die Bürokratisierung der Welt* (1969), 210 ff., which draws on examples from Russian history and central bureaucracy; Bracher, *Die Auflösung der Weimarer Republik* (1960), 174 ff.
6. Loewenthal, "Totalitäre und demokratische Revolution" (1960–61), 29 ff.
7. Bracher, *Zeitgeschichtliche Kontroversen* (1976), 41.
8. Ibid.

Introduction. II. Law and Administration as Party Autonomous Powers

1. Cf. the relevant chapters in Neumann, *Behemoth* (1963); and in Bracher, Sauer, and Schulz, *Die nationalsozialistische Machtergreifung* (1962).
2. Mommsen, *Beamtentum im Dritten Reich* (1966); Matzerath, *Nationalsozialismus und kommunale Selbstverwaltung* (1970); Staff, *Justiz im Dritten Reich* (1978); Tessin, *Zur Geschichte der Ordnungspolizei 1936–1945* (1957); Diehl-Thiele, *Partei und Staat im Dritten Reich* (1969); Broszat, *Der Staat Hitlers* (1971); Bollmus, *Das Amt Rosenberg und seine Gegner* (1970); J. Klenner, *Verhältnis von Partei und Staat 1933–1945, dargestellt am Beispiel Bayerns* (1974); Echterhölter, *Das öffentliche Recht im Nationalsozialismus* (1970); Ostler, *Die deutschen Rechtsanwälte* (1971); Schorn, *Der Richter im Dritten Reich* (1959); Schorn, *Die Gesetzgebung des Nationalsozialismus als Mittel der Machtpolitik* (1963); Weinkauff and Wagner, *Die deutsche Justiz* (1968).
3. The fact that many of those already active in the Nazi period also influenced judicial life in the Federal Republic, with all the personal culpability and deference to colleagues that implies; the mediocrity that passed for the Nazi weltanschauung, which was taken over virtually lock, stock, and barrel; and finally the concern that was felt about the unforeseeable consequences of a system whose advantages were initially so lauded by theoreticians and practitioners alike—all of this must have contributed to the failure of jurisprudence to address this question.
4. Rüthers, *Die unbegrenzte Auslegung* (1973); Stolleis, "Gemeinschaft und Volksgemeinschaft" (1972), 16 ff.; Stolleis, *Gemeinwohlformeln im nationalsozialistischen Recht* (1974).
5. Ramm, "Nationalsozialismus und Arbeitsrecht" (1968); F. K. Kaul, *Geschichte des Reichsgerichts* (1971); Kolbe, *Reichsgerichtspräsident Dr Erwin Bumke* (1975). For a critical appreciation of the development of the judicial system, see Kübler, "Der deutsche Richter und das demokratische Gesetz" (1963).

6. Descriptive and reportorial works include Ostler, *Die deutschen Rechtsanwälte* (1971); H. Schorn, *Der Richter im Dritten Reich*; Schorn, *Die Gesetzgebung des Nationalsozialismus als Mittel der Machtpolitik*; Echterhölter, *Das öffentliche Recht im Nationalsozialismus*. Early apologetic studies were Weinkauff and Wagner, *Die deutsche Justiz*; Schorn, *Der Richter im Dritten Reich*. More recently, H. Kessler, "25 Jahre Bundesgerichtshof," *Deutsche Richterzeitung* (1975): 294 ff., writes of the good judicial tradition of the Reich Supreme Court, which by and large also held up during the Nazi period; cf. also the essay by Martin, "Die Bundesanwaltschaft beim Bundesgerichtshof" (1975), in which the author draws on his six months as a scientific assistant at the Reich Attorney General's Office to give his impressions of the Reich attorneys of the day (by no means an "assortment of committed Nazi lawyers"; no "protagonists of the Nazi ideology"; "notable reticence toward if not downright opposition to the party line"), without "wishing to play down the subsequent fateful entanglement of the Attorney General's Office and the Supreme Court's administration of justice, which undermined the traditional principles of judicial interpretation."

7. Cf. Weinkauff and Wagner, *Die deutsche Justiz*, with R. Schmid, "Je m'excuse," *KJ* (1969): 102 ff.

8. For the best analysis of the system of administration in the Reich, see Lassar, "Reichseigene Verwaltung unter der Weimarer Verfassung" (1926); Arndt, *Kommentar zum Reichsbeamtengesetz* (1923); H. Nawiasky, "Die Stellung des Berufsbeamtentums im parlamentarischen Staat," *Recht und Staat* 37 (1925).

9. Cf. in particular the speech by R. Naumann at the Congress of German Constitutional Law Teachers on October 14–15, 1954, *VVdStRL*, no. 13 (1955): 88 ff., in which he comes to the conclusion that, in the legal sense, the permanent Civil Service had survived the crisis of 1945, though there was evidently historical and political discontinuity (118). The only contribution at the conference to support the thesis of the demise of the permanent civil service in 1945 was that of E. Friesenhahn (see *VVdStRL*, no. 13 [1955]).

10. See Hitler's comments on the cities' arts policies in a conversation at table on the evening of May 3, 1942, quoted from Picker, *Hitlers Tischgespräche* (1951), 236: "Berlin's central administration is confusing the responsibility of the central power, which should set the general line and only intervene when things go wrong, with that of unitarianism, which stifles all life around it. One should therefore endeavor to train as many effective administrators as possible in the country at large and use them to implement the powers of the ministerial bureaucracy."

11. Cf. Schmitt, who ascertained that the laws approved or decreed by Hitler were usually limited to general clauses that left all possible scope to the departmental legislative powers ("Der Zugang zum Machthaber," in *Verfassungsrechtliche Aufsätze* [1958], 430 ff.).

12. Medicus, "Das Reichsministerium des Innern—Geschichte und Aufbau" (1940).

13. Cf. Fraenkel, *Der Doppelstaat* (1974), 101, with reference to the finding of Justice Brandeis: "The doctrine of the separation of powers was taken over in 1787 by the [Federal] Convention, not in order to increase efficiency but to prevent the exercise of arbitrary powers" (U.S. Supreme Court, *Meyers v. United States* 272 US 52, 293).

14. Cf. BVerfGE 6, 133 (162).

15. See secs. 1, 3, par. 1, of the German Civil Service Code dated January 26, 1937 (*RGBl.* I 39), according to which a civil servant had a "duty of service and loyalty" to the "Führer and Reich," having to remain "loyal to the Führer beyond the grave." Cf. Schmitt, "Der Zugang zum Machthaber," in *Verfassungsrechtliche Aufsätze*, 430 ff.; Diehl-Thiele, *Partei und Staat im Dritten Reich*, 24. He asserted that the "problem of access to the Führer was less—or not only—an organizational expression of power being concentrated in Hitler's hands" than a result of the fact that the ultimate *power of decision* resided with him and him alone, but that analysis can be applied only to major political decisions, since the above-cited executive powers of the administration left considerable scope for decision making.

16. The discussion about the administration of justice in Boberach, ed., *Richterbriefe* (1975), contains much instructive material.

17. Rüthers, *Die unbegrenzte Auslegung*, 111 ff., 133 ff.

18. The "concrete philosophy of order" (C. Schmitt, *Über die drei Arten rechtswissenschaftlichen Denkens* [1934]) was the contemporary expression of the so-called institutional approach to the law, whose basis is to formulate the consititution of a political system only in its statutory law [denying natural law or ethical principles]. Though it was not possible before 1933 to put the value system of the Weimar Republic into practice in the framework of statutory law, because there was too much resistance to the fundamental democratic-republican decisions (for evidence of that, see Kirn, *Verfassungsumsturz oder Rechtskontinuität* [1972], 67 n. 190), this "philosophy" of law became the leading thinking after 1933, with the effect that the positions of power inherited or usurped by the Nazis were transferred into statutory law, legitimated, and resolutely defended (66 f.).

19. More details in Rüthers, *Die unbegrenzte Auslegung*, 270 ff.

20. Cf. Kirn, *Verfassungsumsturz oder Rechtskontinuität*, 67.

21. Ibid.

22. See as an example E. Ebermeyer, *Denn heute gehört uns Deutschland* (1959), 76 f.; and Grunberger, *Das zwölfjährige Reich* (1973), 125 f. Cf. Hillgruber, "Die 'Endlösung' und das deutsche Ostimperium" (1972), 143.

23. Picker, *Hitlers Tischgespräche* (1968), 27; but very few lawyers were acknowledged by Hitler—for example, Frick, Pöhner, and the head of the Reich Chancellery, H. H. Lammers (evening table talk on March 29, May 10, and July 22, 1942 (65 ff., 125, 127, 243). Of Lammers, Hitler said he was so industrious because he knew he was there to give the necessities of the state a legal underpinning (H. Picker and H. Hoffmann, *Hitlers Tischgespräche im Bild* [1969], 163).

24. Similarly in the more recent *Polish Society under German Occupation*, by Jan T. Gross (1979), 31 f.

25. With hindsight, an example of the identification of the state apparatus with the political program of the Nazis is the exact objective harmonization and synchronicity of the various Reich departments in the question of the persecution and economic exploitation of the Jews, so vividly described by Adler (*Der verwaltete Mensch* [1974]), part of the growing realization of how the implementation of the racial-political extermination program was characterized by a thoroughgoing methodicalness (Hillgruber, "Die 'Endlösung' und das deutsche Ostimperium"). However, it is evident that the Nazi leadership was unable to prevail in every instance in which the civil service was uncooperative. Examples include (1) the unsuccessful attempt of the leading circles in the judiciary and the police to remove "non-Germans" *generally* from the ambit of the judiciary and place them under the jurisdiction of the (summary) police courts and (2) the fact that, though the administration of justice paid lip service to the binding force of the Nazi philosophy as the basis for the interpretation of all written law, it remained intrinsic to the system that the judge's obligation was to the law (this being the expression of the Führer's will); cf. OVGE (Decisions of the Prussian Administrative Supreme Court), 91, 215; 92, 217; more details in Stolleis, *Gemeinwohlformeln im nationalsozialistischen Recht*, 240, with further examples. This hindered legal interpretation at deviance with the law and had a systematic delaying and braking effect.

26. More details in Kirn, *Verfassungsumsturz oder Rechtskontinuität*, 19 ff.

27. Buchheim, *SS und Polizei im NS-Staat* (1964), 16 f.

28. See also the summaries by Friedrich, "The German and the Prussian Civil Service" (1930), 283–453; A. Brecht, "Democracy and Administration," in M. Ascoli and F. Lehmann, *Political and Economic Democracy* (1937), 217 ff. (no. 13); Brecht, "How Bureaucracies Develop and Function" (1954), 292:1 ff.; Brecht, "Bureaucratic Sabotage" (1937), 48 ff.; Brecht, "Civil Service" (1936), 202 ff.; Brecht and Glemstock, *Administration in German Ministries* (1940) (Brecht was the head of a gov-

ernment department and from 1921 to 1927 head of the Department for Constitutional and Civil Service Law in the Reich Ministry of the Interior, later [1927–33] working in the Prussian State and Finance Ministry. In 1933 he emigrated to the USA); Salomon, "Leadership in Democracy," 243 ff. (no. 15).

29. Regarding this method, see Nolte, *Die Krise des liberalen Systems* (1968).

30. BVerfGE 3, 58 (98 ff.); 6, 133 (166, 197).

31. This is especially true of the publications of the Academy of German Law (*Akademie für deutsches Recht*) and its committees, the key legal institution of the NSDAP. It counted among its members not only National Socialist lawyers but—when one considers the composition of its committees—virtually all the teachers of jurisprudence of rank and reputation, who among them produced a wealth of articles, commentaries, and lectures on the reform of the penal and civil codes and other areas of the law. For further examples, see the *Nationalsozialistisches Handbuch für Recht und Gesetzgebung*, edited by Hans Frank in 1934, whose authors were prominent law teachers. This work was widely used by students, lecturers, and judges; it was in a way a lexicon of National Socialism. Similarly well-known works included Dietze, *Nationalsozialistisches Naturrecht,* whose scientific substance was as thin as its distribution was wide, and the popular series *"Schäffers" Grundrissen*, one volume of which—*Staatsrecht* (Constitutional Law)—contained an exposition of scientifically indefensible, even *völkisch*, legal thinking (H. Nicolai), which found an eager readership among young lawyers since it contained the gist of what they needed to know for their examinations; see also Nicolai, *Die rassengesetzliche Rechtslehre* (1933).

32. This is true, for example, of the "five basic principles of legal practice" defined by Carl Schmitt ("Neue Leitsätze für die Rechtspraxis" [1933]) and for the observations of other prominent legal scholars.

33. The best example of this superficial equivalence of parlance is the authoritarian penal law (*autoritäres Strafrecht*), which was propounded using the same terms by National Socialist and non–National Socialist teachers alike. In a similar way, the terms *Volk* (people, nation), *völkisch* (racial, national), *Volksgemeinschaft* (national community), *Rasse* (race), *Volksschädling* (antisocial parasite), *Unschädlichmachen* (neutralization), etc. were constantly used in non-Nazi writing (cf. for example, H. K. Filbinger, "Nationalsozialistisches Strafrecht—Kritische Würdigung des geltenden Strafgesetzbuches und Ausblick auf die kommende Strafrechtsreform," in *Werkblätter*, published on behalf of *Bund Neudeutschland (ND)-Älternbund*, nos. 5–6 [1935]: 265 ff.; H. Puvogel, "Die leitenden Grundgedanken bei der Entmannung von Sittlichkeitsverbrechern" [1937], pt. 2, sec. D). After 1945 this identity of parlance and terminology led to the problem of continuity in legal thinking after 1933 (for a fuller account, see Kirn, *Verfassungsumsturz oder Rechtskontinuität,* 69 ff.).

34. Were the investigations into the Nazi state to be pursued using the deductive methods described, it would become apparent that these elements were an integral part of the fundamental structures of the Nazi hegemony in every sphere: the latest research findings come to the same or similar conclusions; cf. S. Neumann, *Permanente Revolution* (1965), where the key elements are identified as terror, the authoritarian principle, fascism, a totalitarian elite (in leadership circles), and a totalitarian party with its own administration. According to Hayes, *Fascism* (1973), structural elements of National Socialism were the racial, elitist, and authoritarian principles and fascism and fascist economic theory. See also, more recently, Kirn, *Verfassungsumsturz oder Rechtskontinuität,* 23 ff., 25 f., 29 ff., who sees three "poles" in the Nazi constitution: party, state, and the authoritarian principle. And see J. Winter, *Die Wissenschaft vom Staatskirchenrecht im Dritten Reich* (1979), pt. 1, chap. 6, A–D; and Bracher, *Zeitgeschichtliche Kontroversen* (1976), 27, 37, 53 ff., 66. This method could be used to make an empirical-comparative analysis of all totalitarian systems, the importance of which is repeatedly underscored by Bracher.

35. Cf. for example, Scheuner, "Die nationale Revolution" (1933–34), 265, 325 ff.

Introduction. III. 1. The Führer Principle

1. Hitler, *Mein Kampf* (1939), 436 ff., 444.

2. Freyer, *Der Staat* (1925), 113 f.

3. Cf. also Weber, "Der Reichspräsident" (1918); Weber, "Parlament und Regierung" (1918), 294 ff.

4. Bracher, Sauer, and Schulz, *Die nationalsozialistische Machtergreifung* (1962) 24.

5. Lerner, *The Nazi Elite* (1951), 53 ff.; H. Winkler, *Demokratie und Nationalsozialismus* (1972); Winkler, "Extremismus der Mitte?" (1972).

6. In point 24 of the NSDAP program of February 24, 1920, it says merely: "In order to carry out all this [i.e., this program], we demand the creation of a strong central power of the Reich." That was a demand that echoed many similar demands made around this time. Nazi *law* allowed indirect conclusions about the Führer's absolute power, which are explained by the following examples. The position of the chancellor was defined in arts. 55 and 56 of the WRV, according to which he held the chairmanship of the Reich government and determined the broad lines of policy; the so-called Enabling Act of March 24, 1933 (*RGBl*. I 141), contained the empowerment of the Reich government to pass laws at divergence with the processes laid down in the constitution. Secs. 1, 8 of the Law to Secure the Unity of Party and State of December 1, 1933 (*RGBl*. I 1016), stipulated that the NSDAP as "the bearer of the ideal of the German state [was] inseparably bound up with the state" and that the chancellor as leader of the NSDAP decreed the detailed executive orders. The Law on the Head of State of the German Reich of August 1, 1934 (*RGBl*. I 747), united the office of the Reich president with that of the chancellor, handing over its powers "to the Führer and Reich Chancellor Adolf Hitler."

7. Bracher, *Zeitgeschichtliche Kontroversen* (1976), 28, 39, 53 f.

8. Goldhagen, "Weltanschauung und Erlösung" (1976), 381.

9. The new Führer idea, for example, promised not a solution to, but "deliverance" from, all the "evils" of democracy, in particular the squabbling of the parties. In place of the political will there was the "unshakable" will or "unshakable determination." One no longer spoke of Germany's importance but of its "greatness," no more of long-term but of "eternal" goals. Political opponents became "enemies" or "traitors"; those out of favor were not excluded but "eliminated"; in this way the political was replaced by the "heroic," social development by "destiny"; instead of the traditional concepts of state, justice, and politics, there were mystic surrogates such as Führer, national community, greatness, and so forth. For more details, cf. Kirn, *Verfassungsumsturz oder Rechtskontinuität* (1972), 34 ff.; Fraenkel, *Der Doppelstaat* (1974), 153 ff., 201 f.; Goldhagen, "Weltanschauung und Erlösung," 379 ff.

10. Cf. von Bayer-Katte, "Das Verlockende im nationalsozialistischen Führerprinzip" (1963).

11. The attitude of nationalist circles toward Versailles, Weimar, and the NSDAP is exemplified by the speech of then parliamentary deputy Fritz Schäffer of the Bavarian People's Party to the 150th session of the Bavarian Provincial Diet (*Landtag*) on November 21, 1922 (*Stenographischer Bericht über die Verhandlungen des Bayerischen Landtages*, 7:175 ff., 177, 180 f.), in which he said:

> We stand today dishonored by the Versailles peace treaty . . . Bavaria is the only German *Land* that shows that it can manage without socialists. . . . The government could win the favor [also of those circles;] it is a question of the language used: "the wicked, wicked National Socialists!" . . . We have no cause to feel particularly pleased about the National Socialist Party. That we admit. Nor do we enjoy the favor of the National Socialist Party . . . [a shout from the seats of the Unified Social Democratic Party]. My dear Mr. Heckler, even if you think I enjoy the particular favor of the National Socialists, I can tell you that that isn't nearly as vexacious as would be the favor of the other side [laugher in the center and on the right]. We certainly

also have our doubts about the National Socialist Movement. . . . Perhaps many of the goals of this Movement are unclear—like the juice of the grape when it is fermenting. . . . But therein lies a certain danger; for this Movement also appeals to the warm patriotic feelings of our young people, to the longing of our youth for liberating action. And that awakens . . . a good feeling that attracts many thousands . . . who are striving for what is good and honorable. Yet, precisely because the objectives are so unclear . . . there is also the danger that, in certain circumstances, sections of our youth will be led toward goals that, were they to stop and think, they would not want. Of the objectives set out in the party program as it stands there are many we cannot condone, as we cannot condone the Social Democrats' Erfurt program, from which—by the way—they have been lifted. . . . But for all that we must endeavor to judge such a movement calmly and fairly. That is why we wish the National Socialist Movement would place more emphasis on that which alone can preserve and keep alive the spirit of duty, also duty toward the Fatherland. That is the moral weltanschauung, the moral idea.

12. See, for example, the description of the Führer in Freyer, *Der Staat*, sec. 8, "Der Führer und sein Volk," 113 f.: "But as with all creative people, when the work in hand demands, the Führer seems to have at his command—as though by a miracle, without teaching or practice—all the ideas and tricks, all the skills and arts, an unwavering certainty about the way ahead, an irresistible effect on people, inexhaustible powers of resistance, and a prophetic eye for the essential."

13. Herrfahrdt, "Politische Verfassungslehre," 107 n. 2; cf. also A. Koettgen, "Die Gesetzmässigkeit der Verwaltung im Führerstaat," *RVerwBl.* (1936): 457 ff.

14. For more details, see Fest, *Hitler* (1973), 582 f.

15. Cf. Hitler's observations about the judiciary at table on March 22 and 29, May 5 and 10, and July 22, 1942, in Picker, *Hitlers Tischgespräche* (1951), 211, 359 f.; and Picker and Hoffmann, *Hitlers Tischgespräche im Bild* (1969), 122, 171. Cf. Hitler's observation about the education of young National Socialists in the elite Party schools (*Ordensburgen*): "Knowledge spoils" (Rauschning, *Gespräche mit Hitler* [1950], 237 ff.).

16. Cf. Nicolai, *Grundlagen der kommenden Verfassung* (1933), 13 f., 23 ff.

17. "*Völkisch*" science tried to explain this by maintaining that the legitimation of the Führer's power resided in the "existential racial identity" (*Artgleichheit*) between leader and led. But the very concept of *Artgleichheit*—as will have to be shown—was so vague as to be merely a case of replacing one slogan with another.

18. Cf. Freyer, *Der Staat*, 113 f.

19. According to Hitler; for more details see Bracher, Sauer, and Schulz, *Die nationalsozialistische Machtergreifung*, 23 f.

20. Cf. Fraenkel, *Der Doppelstaat*, 235.

21. Hitler, *Mein Kampf* (1939), 371 f.; cf. also Freyer, *Der Staat*, 113 f.; H. H. Lammers, *Der Führerstaat* (1935), 21 ff.

22. The form of this acclamation was the institution of the popular referendum, which explains the National Socialists' glorification of the popular referendum as an expression of the "will of the people." Cf. Lammers, *Der Führerstaat*, 21 ff. (the "Führer 'does not ask first but afterward' ").

23. "Führung als Rechtsprinzip" (1934).

24. Cf. Frank, *Nationalsozialistisches Handbuch für Recht und Gesetzgebung* (1934), xvi. Cf. H. Frank, "Recht und Verwaltung," *DVerw* (1938): 739: "The Führer cannot . . . be held back by any legal restrictions placed on him." W. Frick, "Der Führer als Schöpfer Grossdeutschlands, Innere Ordnung—äussere Stärke," *DVerw* (1936): 364, 366. H. Frank, *Verwaltungsrecht* (1938), 739. Hitler, *Mein Kampf* (1939), 444 f.; Nicolai, *Grundlagen der kommenden Verfassung*, 23 ff. "The Führer, Adolf Hitler, as bearer of the highest sovereignty of the greater German Reich, is the sole font of all justice" (Lammers, "Zum 30. Januar 1943" [1943], 43).

25. Hitler himself speaks only vaguely of the "absolute responsibility . . . of the Führer" to a

higher power (*absolute Verantwortlichkeit . . . des Führers nach oben*); he speaks more clearly later of "absolute authority" (*absolute Autorität*) (*Mein Kampf*, 444).

26. Arendt, *Ursprünge und Elemente totaler Herrschaft* (1958), 134; Maunz, *Gestalt und Recht der Polizei* (1943), 10: "In place of the old law [is] the will of the Führer."

27. Küchenhoff, "Der Umbruch 1933–36, Die Rechtsentwicklung der Jahre 1933–35–36" (1937), 207. Maunz, *Gestalt und Recht der Polizei*, 10; also Hildebrandt, "Rechtsquellen" (1937), 564; Best, *Die deutsche Polizei* (1941), 15: "The will of the Führer—whatever the form of its expression: law, decree, individual or general order, ruling on organization and responsibility, etc.—is law and changes previously existing law."

28. E. R. Huber, "Das deutsche Staatsoberhaupt," *ZStW* (1935): 210 ff.; Kühn, "Der Führergedanke in der neuen Arbeitsverfassung" (1970); Frank, "Die Zeit des Rechts" (1936), 1 ff., 3. W. Frick, "Neubau des Reichs," *DVerw* (1939): 228.

29. The binding nature of the "will of the Führer" gave Hitler's inner circle unlimited power. The main interpreter of the "will of the Führer" in the party sphere was the chief of staff of the deputy Führer's office and later head of the Party Chancellery, Martin Bormann; in the administrative sphere it was the Reich minister and head of the Reich Party Chancellery, Hans Heinrich Lammers.

30. Cf. Rothenberger, "Die Rechtsquellen im neuen Staat" (1936).

31. This was how the special treatment under the criminal law of the "alien peoples" of the Annexed Eastern Territories was pushed through under pressure from the Party Chancellery, which itself invoked the apparent "will of the Führer"; for more details, see part 2, section 2.

32. Hitler, in Rauschning, *Gespräche mit Hitler*, 232 f.

33. Cf. von Bayer-Katte, "Das Verlockende im nationalsozialistischen Führerprinzip," 69.

34. Cf., among many others, Scheuner, "Die nationale Revolution" (1933–34).

35. Hamel, "Die Aufgabe der Polizei im nationalsozialistischen Staat" (1936).

36. Cf., for example, Koellreuter, *Zur Entwicklung der deutschen Rechtseinheit* (1935); Koellreuter, *Vom Sinn und Wesen der nationalen Revolution* (1933); C. Schmitt, *Das Reichsstatthaltergesetz* (1933); Schmitt, *Staat, Bewegung, Volk* (1935), 32 ff.; Krüger, *Die Verfassung der nationalsozialistischen Revolution* (1933).

37. Cf., for example, Krüger, *Führer und Führung* (1935), foreword, 5; Hamel, "Die Aufgabe der Polizei im nationalsozialistischen Staat"; in Schmitt, *Staat, Bewegung, Volk*, the Führer concept "could in no way be understood using the concepts and forms of the Weimar system," let alone "be justified. . . . It is significant that any image is inadequate" (41 f.). Frequently, allusions and comparisons were made to the Teutonic era; cf., for example, observations of the former presiding judge of the Hamburg Court of Appeal, Curt Rothenberger, in Steiniger and Leszczyński, *Das Urteil im Juristenprozeß* (1969), 158.

38. Schmitt, *Staat, Bewegung, Volk*, 33, 39 f.; cf. also Freyer, *Der Staat*, 113 f.

39. Krüger, *Führer und Führung*, foreword, 5.

40. Fest, *Hitler*, 582 ff.

41. On that point and generally on the National Socialist justice system, see von Hippel, *Die nationalsozialistische Herrschaftsordnung* (1947); von Hippel, *Die Perversion von Rechtsordnungen* (1955); G. Radbruch, *Gesetzliches Unrecht und übergesetzliches Recht* (1947); Püschel, *Der Niedergang des Rechts im Dritten Reich* (1947); Broszat, *Der Staat Hitlers* (1971), 403 ff.; Marcuse, *Vernunft und Revolution* (1968), 360 ff.; Ramm, "Nationalsozialismus und Arbeitsrecht," (1968), 108 ff.; Kirchheimer, "Staatsgefüge und Recht des Dritten Reiches" (1976), 33 ff., 50 ff.; Ridder, "Zur Verfassungsdoktrin des nationalsozialistischen Staates" (1969), 221 ff.

42. Kluge and Krüger, *Verfassung und Verwaltung* (1941), 18.

43. Cf. Koellreuter, *Zur Entwicklung der deutschen Rechtseinheit*; Koellreuter, *Vom Sinn und Wesen der nationalen Revolution*; Schmitt, *Staat, Bewegung, Volk*, 32 ff.

44. Cf. Herrfahrdt, *Die Verfassungsgesetze des nationalsozialistischen Staates* (1935); Kruger, *Die Verfassung der nationalsozialistischen Revolution.*

45. Sauer, *Das Reichsjustizministerium* (1939), 23.

46. Kluge and Krüger, *Verfassung und Verwaltung.*

47. Huber, *Vom Sinn der Verfassung* (1935); the basic concepts of democracy (the common people, equality of civil rights) are alien concepts without substance and the democratic constitution is not a "living order" (10 f.). The *völkisch* constitution is the "overall order of our common political life," characterized by the principles of "unity," "wholeness," "movement" (20 ff.); cf. also Krüger, "Der Wille des Gesetzgebers" (1943), 108 ff.

48. For example, they were called a "mixture of pacifism, humanitarianism, entrepreneurial spirit, self-abasement, brotherhood of nations, infamy, enlightenment, democratic vulgarity . . ." (Nicolai, *Grundlagen der kommenden Verfassung*, 13); in these comments by Nicolai—who in 1933 became *Ministerialdirektor* (head of department) in the Ministry of the Interior—it is apparent that the National Socialists also equated Jewry with the structures and values of parliamentary democracy, since all the slogans used here to condemn the German republic crop up again in anti-Semitic propaganda.

49. For Hitler, all cultural and moral values were synonymous with the "Jewish entity" (*das jüdische Wesen*—i.e., everything deemed Jewish), with that which had to be extinguished and rendered completely "devoid of value" in the present day. He contrasted these values with the "dignity" of power and terror as the most effective political instrument (Rauschning, *Gespräche mit Hitler*, 79, 81, 95, 211, 249, 254 ff.). Regarding the role of terror in the totalitarian system, see further Arendt, *Ursprünge und Elemente totaler Herrschaft*, 133 f., 171 ff.

50. F. Jerusalem, *Das Verwaltungsrecht und der neue Staat* (1935), 10; Kluge and Krüger, *Verfassung und Verwaltung*, 16; on ranking in the *völkisch* constitution in general, see Fraenkel, *Der Doppelstaat*, 148 ff.; on the influence of the Führer constitution on the civil service, cf. BVerfGE 3, 94 ff.; 6, 152 ff.; by contrast BGHZ 13, 295 ff.; cf. also the contributions to the discussion in VVdStRL 13 (1955): 154 ff.

51. Schmitt, "Neue Leitsätze für die Rechtspraxis" (1933) (fifth principle: "The National Socialist state is a just state"); Frank, "Leitsätze des Reichsjuristenführers zur richterlichen Unabhängigkeit" (1936). Göring, *Die Rechtssicherheit als Grundlage der Volksgemeinschaft* (1935); Hildebrandt, *Rechtsfindung im neuen deutschen Staate* (1935), 32. "Everything that is beneficial to the nation is just, everything harmful is unjust" was the constant refrain (first used in 1926) of the chief lawyer of the Reich (*Reichsjuristenführer*), H. Frank, quoted in Frank, *Nationalsozialistisches Handbuch für Recht und Gesetzgebung*, introduction, xiv; summary, Kirschenmann, *Gesetz im Staatsrecht* (1971), 72 ff., 77.; Echterhölter, *Das öffentliche Recht im Nationalsozialismus* (1970), 46 ff., 85 ff., 227 ff., with many examples.

52. Cf. Huber, *Neue Grundbegriffe des hoheitlichen Rechts* (1935): "It is not therefore possible to gauge the Führer's laws against a higher legal authority, since every law promulgated by the Führer is itself a direct expression of this '*völkisch*' legal authority" (40); K. Larenz, "Deutsche Rechtserneuerung und Rechtsphilosophie," *Recht und Staat*, no. 109 (1934): "No one other than the Führer can make the final decision on the validity of a particular ruling. No guarantee of the upholding of justice is necessary from him since, by virtue of his *Führertum* [leadership], he is the 'guardian of the constitution,' i.e., the unwritten *Rechtsidee* [lit. conception of justice] of his people" (34). In this context see also Maunz, "Neue Grundlagen des Verwaltungsrechts" (1934). Cf. also Schmitt, "Richter und Gesetz" (1934). Krüger, *Führer und Führung*; E. R. Huber, "Das deutsche Staatsoberhaupt," *ZStW* (1935): 210 ff.; Walz, "Der Führerstaat." Frank, "Der Führer und das Recht" (1936); H. Frank, "Rechtsgrundlegung der nat. soz. Führerstaates," *DVerw* (1938): 639 ff.; Poetzsch-Heffter, Ule, and Dernedde, "Autoritäres volksverbundenes Führertum," "Volksverbundenheit des Führertums und ihre organisatorische Sicherung," and "Der völkische Staat" (1935); Köttgen, "Der Führer" (1937), 1

ff., and sec. C, "Der Staat des deutschen Volkes," 63 ff.; Kühn, "Der Führergedanke in der neuen Arbeitsverfassung" (1936); Höhn, "Das Führerprinzip in der Verwaltung" (1936); Küchenhoff, "Führung und Verwaltung im Dritten Reich" (1936).

53. Cf. Hueber, "Justiz im Führerstaat" (1942).

54. Huber, *Vom Sinn der Verfassung*, 19.

55. There is a more detailed discussion in Best, *Die deutsche Polizei* (1941), 15; Seel, "Die Gestaltung des Deutschen Beamtentums seit dem 30. Januar 1933," 154 ff. (164).

56. Cf. Kirschenmann, *Gesetz im Staatsrecht*. Jerusalem, *Das Verwaltungsrecht und der neue Staat*, 10 (the legality of the administration is no longer bound to an "abstract legal provision" but to an "intrinsic legality," which is to be developed from the actual operation of the administration in question—so-called *Ordnungsrecht* [a Nazi concept: law unto itself, i.e., devoid of ethical values—Trans.]). Cf. a similar statement in Maunz, *Gestalt und Recht der Polizei*, 10: "It is both necessary and logical that this system replace the old principle of legality, given that the old law has been superseded by the will of the Führer."

57. Cf. K. Larenz, "Deutsche Rechtserneuerung und Rechtsphilosophie,"[34].

58. Thierack, *DJ* (1942): 550.

59. For a more detailed account, see W. Stuckart, "Zentralgewalt, Dezentralisation und Verwaltungseinheit," in *Festgabe für H. Himmler* (1941), 1 ff.; Jarmer, "Die Einräumigkeit" (1940).

60. "Führerprinzip als Rechtsprinzip," *DR* (1934): 327.

61. Cf. Hitler, in Picker, *Hitlers Tischgespräche* (1951), 251.

62. Further details in von Stutterheim, *Die Reichskanzlei* (1940); Just, "65 Jahre Reichskanzlei" (1943).

63. For more details, see Matzerath, *Nazionalsozialismus und kommunale Selbstverwaltung* (1970); for discussion of the Führer principle in local government, see Weidemann, "Gemeinde und Staat" (1936), 310 f., 318 f.

64. In this sense, see BVerfGE 6, 133 (162).

65. In the realm of justice, for example, there was the *Reichsjuristenführer* (chief lawyer of the Reich—Frank). In internal administration there was a *Reichssportsführer* (chief health officer) as well as a *Reichssportsführer* (chief sports officer) and a *Reichsarbeitsführer* (chief labor officer). (Cf. Reich Labor Service Law in the draft of September 9, 1939, *RGBl.* I 1947). In the realm of labor law, there was a *Betriebsführer* (works leader) in place of the industrialist.

66. Cf. a letter from the minister of the Reich and chief of the Reich Chancellery to the Party Chancellery of May 6, 1941, and notes from the Reich Ministry of the Interior (no date, no author) in which the demise of the administration and the standing of civil servants are described in detail (BA R 43 II/425).

67. According to Goebbels's diaries of 1942–43 (*Tagebücher 1942–43* [1948]), 243, an entry dated March 2, 1943: following his appointment as Reich interior minister in 1943, Himmler tried (in vain) to scale down the "top-heavy bureaucracy" and to keep the apparatus flexible; see also the illuminating remarks made by Himmler (no date) in BA R 18/3523 and his ideas about the principle of rotation for *Landräte*, which he developed at a conference of Reichsleiter and Gauleiter in Posen (Poznań). He proposed that *Landräte* should not work in the same place for longer than ten years to prevent sedentarism and "loss of drive." In contrast, see letters from the head of the Party Chancellery to the Reich Ministry of the Interior, dated December 8, 1943, in which Martin Bormann expresses his opposition to this idea (BA R 18/3369), maintaining that a longer period of service has various advantages, including better contact with the population and supervision of the local authority. The principle of rotation was firmly rejected by the local government bureaucracy itself (a submission of the state secretary in the Reich Ministry of the Interior to the Reich Ministry of the Interior, dated February 19, 1944, ibid.); Himmler continued to insist on the ten-year period of service but promised flexibility in settling the question (Reich Ministry of the Interior to the head of the Party Chancellery, March 29, 1944, ibid.).

68. An example from the area of administrative torts or offenses: breaches of discipline at the place of work could lead to fines imposed by the Labor Offices, criminal proceedings, or use of "state police powers" ("protective custody"); infringements of rationing regulations could, depending on the seriousness of the offense, lead to fines imposed by the Food Offices, criminal proceedings, penal orders, court sentences, or action by the Gestapo.

69. Cf. BVerfGE 3, 58 ff.; 6, 133; *BGHZ7*, 76 ff. (94 ff.); Redeker, "Bewältigung der Vergangenheit als Aufgabe der Justiz" (1964); Welzel, "Gesetzmäßige Judentötungen?" (1964); Lewald, "Schlußbetrachtungen der Schriftleitung zu den Beamtenurteilen des BVerfG" (1954), 1274 ff.; Ridder, "Zur Verfassungsdoktrin des nationalsozialistischen Staates" (1969); Ramm, "Nationalsozialismus und Arbeitsrecht."

70. On the relationship between justice and the Führer principle, see Steinlechner, "Der Richter im Dritten Reich" (1974), 27 ff., 52 ff., with examples.

71. According to Kordt, *Wahn und Wirklichkeit* (1947), 30, this assurance vis-à-vis the centrist politicians Dr. Kaas and Dr. Brüning was given verbally but never in writing.

72. For an overview, see Wagner, "Die Umgestaltung der Gerichtsverfassung" (1968), 229 f.

73. (Reich) Supreme Court of June 6, 1934, Supreme Court for Civil Cases, 144, 306 ff., 311: "Still valid is the principle guaranteeing general liability of the law—which is the leading principle of the Procedural Law for the Courts—that the judge is subordinate to the law. Similarly, sec. 336, Penal Code, is still valid, according to which the punishment for 'bending' (*Beugung*) the law is up to five years' prison."

74. In this way the terms *Rechtsfindung* (interpreting the law) and *Rechtswahrung* (preserving the law), which often describe the work of a judge more accurately than the traditional terms, were usurped and brought into discredit by the National Socialists.

75. Opening address by Minister of Justice Thierack to a conference of presiding judges of State Superior Court (OLG) and chief public prosecutors in the Reich Ministry of Justice on September 29, 1942 (BA R 22/4199; also in Weinkauff and Wagner, *Die deutsche Justiz* [1968], 153). Thierack continued: Judges ought to enjoy an elevated status, but must be led as well. The worthy, industrious judges with narrow horizons must be removed. The crisis between leadership and judiciary stems from the fact that the men at the top are "Old Campaigners" whose experience of the Weimar justice system has been negative. After the National Socialist reforms, the justice system will be transformed. For a fuller account of the control of the judiciary, see part 2, section 1; also, Steinlechner, "Der Richter im Dritten Reich," 67 ff.

76. "Guiding Principles" of the NSRB are in Frank, "Leitsätze des Reichsjuristenführers zur richterlichen Unabhängigkeit," 176 f.; according to these (*Leitsätze*), the National Socialist weltanschauung was the basis for the interpretation of the law; laws from the period before 1933 were not applicable where this was in contradiction with the sound sentiment of the people (*Volksempfinden*).

77. Schmitt, "Neue Leitsätze für die Rechtspraxis":

(1) The independence of the judge is based on subjection to justice and the legal code of the state, whose justice it is the judge's duty to dispense. Without this subjection to the law, judicial independence is arbitrary, politically arbitrary. (2) The decision as to whether a matter is unpolitical is itself always a political decision. (3) The so-called general clauses that are being implemented today in all areas of the judicial system do not affect the obligation of the judge. (4) For the application and handling of the general clauses by judges, lawyers, judicial administrators, or law teachers, the principles of National Socialism are the direct and exclusive authority. (5) The National Socialist state is a just state.

After 1945 Schmitt corrected his earlier statements; cf. his interrogation at the so-called Wilhelmstrasse trial in Nuremberg, in Kempner, *Das Dritte Reich im Kreuzverhör* (1969), 239 ff., 296 ff.

78. R. Freisler, *DR* (1942): 145 ff., "As the supreme judicial authority, the Führer is also the highest-ranking German judge, *the* German judge as it were. A judiciary that fails to take account of this fundamental principle is unthinkable under National Socialist law" (149).

79. Frank, "Leitsätze des Reichsjuristenführers zur richterlichen Unabhängigkeit," 176 f.; Schmitt, "Neue Leitsätze für die Rechtspraxis"; C. Schmitt, "Zur Frage der Unabhängigkeit des Richters," *DJ* (1935): 181; R. Freisler, *Etwas über Führertum in der Rechtspflege, Schriften der Akademie für Deutsches Recht*, reprint no. 1 (Berlin, 1935); R. Freisler, "Reich, Richter und Recht," *DR* (1942): 145, 149.

80. Cf. Supreme Court for Civil Cases, 152, 88; for more details, see Freisler, "Recht, Richter, Gesetz"; communication of Reich Ministry of Justice (Freisler) to Reich Ministry of the Interior on April 12, 1934 (BA R 43 II/424; also reproduced in Mommsen, *Beamtentum im Dritten Reich* [1966], 180 f., where the right of judicial review is vehemently rejected). In a similar sense also see Frank, "Leitsätze des Reichsjuristenführers zur richterlichen Unabhängigkeit," 179 ff.; Huber, "Das richterliche Prüfungsrechts und seine künftige Gestaltung" (1940), 262; on formal retention of the judicial right of scrutiny except in the case of "political acts," cf. Ipsen, *Das Problem der justizlosen Hoheitsakte* (1937); Scheuner, "Die nationale Revolution," 166 ff., 344; Scheuner, "Die Gerichte und die Prüfung politische Staatshandlungen" (1936); Grundmann, "Die richterliche Nachprüfung von politischem Führungsaktsen" (1940); (Reich) Supreme Court, *DR* (1939): 1785; Nobe, "Das richterliche Prüfungsrecht und die Entwicklung der gesetzgebenden Gewalt im neuen Reich," *AöR*, NF, 28 (1937): 194 f.

81. Scheuner, "Die nationale Revolution," 344.

82. Scheuner, "Die Gerichte und die Prüfung politische Staatshandlungen"; Scheuner—after Smend (*Festgabe für Kahl*, 3:16 [1923])—refers to as "political" "any act that serves the preservation and governance of the state as a whole"; he proposes as a practical solution that the decision on whether or not an act is political be referred by legislation to a central authority (439 f.).

83. According to sec. 7, par. 1, of the so-called Professional Civil Service Code of April 7, 1933 (*RGBl.* I 175), the supreme Reich or *Land* authority had the "final" decision, without recourse to the law, thereby excluding any judicial challenge to dismissal on political or racial grounds; cf. also Reich Supreme Court (RG) of May 6, 1936, *DJ* (1936): 1165.

84. Sec. 7 of the Prussian Law on the Secret State Police of February 10, 1936 (*Preuß. Gesetzesammlung* 21); for more details, see Frick, "Probleme des neuen Verwaltungsrechts" (1936); Frick, "Über grundsätzliche Verwaltungsaufgaben" (1939); Echterhölter, *Das öffentliche Recht im Nationalsozialismus*, 100 ff.; cf. also Higher Administrative Court (Prussian Administrative Supreme Court), Hamburg, *RVerwBl.* (1935): 1045; rights of recourse for wrongful imprisonment or persecution were also refused. On January 25, 1934, for example, the district court (LG) in Tübingen refused legal aid for an applicant who had demanded compensation rights because of wrongful imprisonment in a concentration camp. The court's position was "that the judicial system could not adopt a different standpoint and disavow what the state has undertaken as a political act" (*JW* [1934]: 627). The Reich Supreme Court (RG) rejected the right to compensation from the state claimed by a lawyer who had been excluded from practicing his profession because of Communist activities; the grounds given were that formal legal procedures were inappropriate as a means of reviewing decisions of a political nature ([Reich] Supreme Court of May 6, 1936, *JW* [1936]: 2982).

85. Frick, "Probleme des neuen Verwaltungsrechts," 334: moreover, control by the administrative court should be dropped in cases where, although[!] the courts have jurisdiction, a judicial review would not be desirable "on grounds of state interest."

86. OVG (Prussian Administrative Supreme Court) law of October 25, 1934; OVGE (Decisions of the Prussian Administrative Supreme Court), 94, 134 ff., 138 f. (same decision in *RVerwBl.* [1935]: 458).

87. In a decision of October 2, 1935, the court, invoking the principle of enumeration, declared Gestapo files beyond the reach of judicial review (nonjusticiable), since the Gestapo was a special police authority and no law had declared its files to be liable to judicial scrutiny (*RVerwBl.* [1935]: 577; for further details see OVG; *JW* [1935]: 2670; and OVGE, 97, 117 ff., 120).

88. *JW* (1936): 2189.

89. PrGS 21.

90. *JW* (1939): 282.

91. *DVerw* (1936): 318; *RVerwBl.* (1936): 549.

92. See introduction, III, 3, "The Principle of Racial Inequality (Special Law)," note 266.

93. Cf. Ostler, *Die deutschen Rechtsanwälte* (1971), 280 f., 291.

94. *RGBl.* I 1535; the complaints authority decided on a case-by-case basis whether or not proceedings in the administrative court were admissible. See Fauser, "Verwaltungsverfahren und verwaltungsgerichtliches Verfahren" (1940).

95. Rößiger, *Führertum und Verwaltungsgerichtsbarkeit* (1936), 22, 35.

96. Kluge and Krüger, *Verfassung und Verwaltung,* 350; Rößiger, *Führertum und Verwaltungsgerichtsbarkeit,* 35 f.

97. For more details, see Stolleis, *Gemeinwohlformeln im nationalsozialistischen Recht* (1974), 244, with many examples.

98. Fraenkel, *Der Doppelstaat,* 69.

99. Freisler, "Deutscher Osten" (1941); R. Freisler, *DJ* (1936): 50 ff., 90 ff.; 433 ff.

100. H. Frank, quoted in W. Raeke, "Der national-sozialistische Rechtskampf des BNSDJ," *JW* (1935): 2857 f.

101. Wolf, "Das Rechtsideal des nationalsozialistischen Staates" (1934–35), 348 ff., 352.

102. A good example is given in H. Frank, *Nationalsozialistische Monatshefte* (1930), quoted in Raeke, "Der national-sozialistische Rechtskampf des BNSDJ"; further in Dahm, "Richtermacht und Gerichtsverfassung im Strafrecht" (1941), 287 ff.; Malz, "Richtertum im nationalsozialistischen Staat" (1941), 2217 ff. (2218); Sauer, "Rechtsprechung und Regierung," lecture delivered by Curt Rothenberger, presiding judge of Hamburg State Superior Court, on August 19, 1941, at a conference in the Reich Ministry of Justice, quoted in Johe, *Die gleichgeschaltete Justiz* (1967), 234: "direct supporting role between the Führer . . . and the individual judges." For more about the National Socialist model for the judiciary, see ibid., 202 n. 7, 236 f.; Weinkauff and Wagner, *Die deutsche Justiz,* 129.

103. Cf. the devastating critique by R. Freisler in *DJ* (1941): 998 ff. to a district court justice, Rozycki-von Hoewel, who had raised such demands in a document entitled "Justiz am Scheidewege."

104. Kriek, "Der Weg zum politisch-völkischen Richter" (1936).

105. Freisler, "Justiz und Politik" (1938).

106. Sattelmacher, "Richter und Rechtsfindung" (1942), 93 f.

107. Rothenberger, "Der Richter im nationalsozialistischen Staat" (1943), 260, with reference to Plato ("The law does not apply to whomsoever is best but to the man who is wise and kingly"); Rothenberger, *Der deutsche Richter* (1943), 20 ff., 40 ff., 60 ff.; on the National Socialist concept of the judiciary, see also the comments of Reich Minister of Justice Thierack on the occasion of the inauguration of Chief Public Prosecutor Steinberg in Posen:

> In view of the highly responsible tasks of leadership that the judiciary must assume . . . particular importance must be attached to the selection of the leading figures: besides professional competence . . . requirements of mental aptitude and character must also be met. Above all, in the daily duties of a leading judge, his guiding principle must be the soldierly manner of thought and action, in other words the concepts that National Socialism has restored to their rightful place in our nation: the sentiments of loyalty, honor, courage, the readiness to give of oneself at any time for the greater good, and the belief in German values and the future of Germany. (*Ostdeutscher Beobachter,* January 13, 1944)

A detailed account is also given in Freisler, "Die Ausbildung des Juristen" (1933); C. Rothenberger, "Denkschrift zur Justizreform 1943," BA R 22/4173; Sattelmacher, "Richter und Rechtsfindung";

"Recht und Richter im Führerstaat," memorandum from the Reich Ministry of Justice office *Richter und Rechtspflege*, dated February 18, 1944, BA R 22/240 (the author of the memorandum was a certain Stegmann, head of the Chamber of the Court of Appeal); draft of a new law on the judiciary, dated June 15, 1944, from the Reich Ministry of Justice, BA R 22/240; in a speech to the Fourth German Lawyers' Conference, State Secretary R. Freisler clearly differentiated between "National Socialist" and the "Marxist" or "bourgeois" lawyers; of the latter he said a "fundamental change in their mental attitude was not be expected." National Socialist judges differed from this type in their "heroic" qualities (BA R 22/240).

108. According to Hitler's view, judges should in future be selected solely from those who had "proved" themselves in office and in the Party and were at least thirty-five years old (cf. comments by Hitler at the dinner table on May 31, 1942, quoted in Picker, *Hitlers Tischgespräche* [1968], 173).

109. Memorandum (BA R 22/240); communication from the presiding judge of the People's Court (Thierack) to the Reich minister and the head of the Reich Chancellery, BA All. Proz. XVII B 2, Bl. 212 to 214; for more details, see Thierack, "Gedanken zum Neuaufbau der deutschen Rechtspflege" (1942); Sattelmacher, "Richter und Rechtsfindung"; Rothenberger, "Die ersten Gedanken" (1942), 365 ff.; and Rothenberger, "Die ersten fachlichen Maßnahmen" (1943) (during his time as state secretary in the Reich Ministry of Justice in 1942–43, Rothenberger was the leading advocate of sweeping judicial reform [*Grobe Justizreform*]). By way of preparation for this great transformation, various offices were created in the Reich Ministry of Justice effective January 1, 1943: Judges and Judicial Administators (*Richter und Rechtspfleger*) (for details of its ambit and activities, see the organizational plan, BA R 22/204, Bl. 5, 29 ff., 165 ff.; further in the implementing order of the Reich Ministry of Justice of July 3, 1943, *DJ* [1943]: 339), Administration of Justice by the People (*Rechtsprechung durch das Volk*) (its responsibilities: the creation of the office of Arbitrator [*Friedensrichter*]), and Reform of Procedural Law for the German Courts (*Neuordnung der deutschen Gerichtsverfassung*). In the course of this reorganization, it was planned to abolish the dual leadership of the district judiciary State Superior Court presiding judge–chief public prosecutor. The chief public prosecutor was to take on the functions of the State Superior Court presiding judge; see also the Reich Ministry of Justice draft of a corresponding decree and an ordinance in BA R 22/244; further, a note from the Reich Ministry of Justice dated October 1944 (BA R 22/243). For details of the distribution of tasks of the judicial reform process between the Reich Ministry of Justice and the Academy of German Law, see the minutes of a meeting of the *Richter und Rechtspflege* committee of the Academy of German Law on March 23, 1943, in Berlin (BA R 22/3764).

110. Amlacher, "Über die Richterreform zur Rechtsreform" (1943).

111. See also a speech by O. Ohlendorf, head of domestic intelligence in the SD, "Über Recht, Sicherheit und richterliche Unabhängigkeit vom Oktober 1942," Nuremberg doc. NO-4638, quoted in *VjhZ* (1956): 408 ff.; cf. also Weinkauff and Wagner, *Die deutsche Justiz*, 161.

112. Order from Reich Ministry of Justice dated October 12, 1942, Nuremberg doc. NG-631; further, memorandum from Reich Ministry of Justice, "Recht und Richter im Führerstaat" (BA R 22/240).

113. BA R 22/240.

Introduction. III. 2. The Primacy of Party over State

1. Because the term *administration* is applied to the polity and is therefore by its very nature political, the term *politicized administration* has been used here to characterize the monopolist party and the alignment of the administration exclusively behind its political maxims.

2. *RGBl.* I 1016.

3. For the development and position of the NSDAP generally, see Bayle, *Psychologie et ethique du National-Socialisme* (1953); Horn, *Führerideologie und Parteiorganisation* (1969); Schäfer, *NSDAP*

(1956); more recently, Schulz, *Aufstieg des Nationalsozialismus* (1975), in particular pt. 1, chap. 6, and pt. 2.

4. Nicolai, *Grundlagen der kommenden Verfassung* (1933), 23.

5. In a speech at the Brown House in Munich at the end of 1930, Hitler said, "In so doing I assert for myself and my successors in the leadership of the NSDAP the claim to political infallibility. . . . I trust that the world will get used to it as quickly as it got used to the claim of the Holy Father" (quoted in Krebs, *Tendenzen und Gestalten der NSDAP* [1959], 138 f.); cf. also Hitler in Rauschning, *Gespräche mit Hitler* (1950), 184 ff., and in *Mein Kampf* (1939), 571 ff.

6. See also Hitler in Rauschning, *Gespräche mit Hitler*, 257; further, Nicolai, *Grundlagen der kommenden Verfassung*, 23, who sees the party as a mystical "order" that claims lordship over the souls of the people. For more on the power of monopoly parties in the totalitarian state, see Neumann, *Permanent Revolution* (1942), 126 ff.

7. More in Broszat, *Der Staat Hitlers* (1971), 328 ff.

8. For example, the Reich minister for food and agriculture was also the head of the Reich Food Supply Administration (*Reichsnährstand*) as well as chairman of the farming industry's own Court of Entail (*Reichserbhofgericht*) (cf. C. Schmitt, "Nationalsozialistisches Rechtsdenken," *DR* [1934]: 225 ff., 228 f.).

9. The merging in one person of the offices of *Reichsstatthalter* (Reich Governor) and Gauleiter was accomplished only in certain areas of the Altreich, but in the Annexed Eastern Territories it was comprehensive. In the Prussian provinces, Gauleiter also held the office of *Oberpräsident* (the senior administrative official of the province)—cf. Bracher, Sauer, and Schulz, *Die nationalsozialistische Machtergreifung* (1962), 506.

10. Mommsen, *Beamtentum im Dritten Reich* (1966), 110 ff.; in 1937 the merging of offices at district level was abandoned because saturation with state functions was threatening to blunt the revolutionary impetus of the Movement. For a fuller account, see Diehl-Thiele, *Partei und Staat im Dritten Reich* (1969), 113 ff., 135 ff., 190 ff.

11. For more on the recruitment of "Old Campaigners," see Merkl, "Die alten Kämpfer der NSDAP" (1971), 495. The study is based on an evaluation of 582 autobiographical statements made in 1934 by NSDAP members.

12. Hitler, proclamation of September 11, 1935, in *Die Reden Hitlers am Parteitag der Freiheit 1935* (1936).

13. Law against the Reestablishment of Parties of 14 July 1933 (*RGBl.* I 479).

14. Sec. 1, par. 2, of the law of December 1, 1933 (*RGBl.* I 1016), rescinded by Führer's decree of December 12, 1933 (*RGBl.* I 733), with the justification that the NSDAP had a sui generis status and should not be subject to the legal oversight of the state. For an account of the legal status of the NSDAP, see Frank, *Deutsches Verwaltungsrecht* (1937); Köttgen, "Der Führer" (1937), 58; Neese, "Die Rechtsnatur der NSDAP" (1935); Neese, "Die Verfassungsrechtliche Stellung der Einheitspartei" (1938), 692; Huber, "Die Rechtsgestalt der NSDAP" (1939), 314 ff.

15. For more details, see Neumann, *Behemoth* (1963), 73 ff.; Fraenkel, *The Dual State* (1941), 34 ff.; Lingg, *Die Verwaltung der NSDAP* (1940), 113 ff., all with numerous examples, including specific cases; Buch, "Parteigerichtsbarkeit" (1934), 4; for details of the party apparatus, see Bracher, Sauer, and Schulz, *Die nationalsozialistische Machtergreifung*, 381 ff., with further examples.

16. The Law Guaranteeing the Unity of Party and State of December 1, 1933, sec. 6 (*RGBl.* I 1016).

17. Ibid., sec. 2.

18. Decree issued by the Führer and Reich chancellor on May 29, 1941 (*RGBl.* I 295), in connection with sec. 2 of the implementing order of January 26, 1942 (*RGBl.* I 35).

19. Schmitt, *Staat, Bewegung, Volk*, with review by Reuß, *JW* (1935): 2254 f.; Reuß, "Partei und Staat," *DVerw* (1934): 289 ff.; (1937): 321 ff. (speech to the 1937 German Civil Servants' Conference in

Munich); Stuckart, "Partei und Staat" (1936); Köttgen, "Die Nationalsozialistische Deutsche Arbeiterpartei" (1937), 1 ff., 49 ff.

20. According to sec. 1 of the German Civil Service Code of 1937, the civil servant was the executor of the will of the state embodied by the NSDAP. According to sec. 3, par. 1, subpar. 2, he had a duty of loyalty to the Führer until his dying day. According to sec. 3, par. 2, his entire conduct "had to be guided by the fact that the NSDAP, in indissoluble solidarity with the people, was the bearer of the idea of the German state."

21. Reich Supreme Court, dated February 17, 1939, HRR no. 845/1939: "The Party is not a state organization. It exists beside the state; it has grown out of the people and derives its supreme rights from the people, not the state. It is not the state that is the decisive entity, but the people. State and people are not one and the same, no more than the state and the Party are one and the same. . . . There can be no doubt about the political precedence [of the party] over the 'state.' "

22. Cf. also the statement of the state secretary in the Reich Ministry of Finance, Fritz Reinhardt, that "the real basis of unity is not the state but the NSDAP" (*Münchener Neueste Nachrichten*, November 1938, no. 319/20, quoted in Neumann, *Behemoth*, 73 f.).

23. Hitler at the 1935 Reich Party Conference in Nuremberg on September 16, 1935 (*Reden Hitlers*, 2d ed., 1935, 283 f.), and on July 6, 1933, speaking to the Reich governors. The Reich governors had to ensure that the Party offices did not accumulate government powers (note BA R 43 II/995).

24. Hitler, *Mein Kampf* (1939), 382, 384 ff.

25. Hitler at the 1933 Reich Party Conference, March 1–3, 1933 (in *Der Kongreb des Sieges* [1934], 8).

26. Cf. Hitler at the Reich Party Conference of the NSDAP in 1933 (ibid.): the polarity of party and state is essential so that the development "is protected from rash experiments, on the one hand, and from the paralysis of bureaucratic anxieties about competences."

27. Thus, on July 14, 1933, at an NSDAP conference, he explained that "it needs perhaps a year" for the process of clarification of the relationship between state and Party to run its course (BA R 43 II/995); at the Party Conference in Munich on September 1, 1933: "Die NSDAP ist die einzige Trägerin der Staatsgewalt" (an overview of the contradictory statements from Hitler may be found in Diehl-Thiele, *Partei und Staat im Dritten Reich*, 17 ff.).

28. Hitler, *Mein Kampf* (1939), 445.

29. Diehl-Thiele, *Partei und Staat im Dritten Reich*, 28.

30. Ibid., 27 ff.; Buchheim, *Totalitäre Herrschaft* (1962), 109 ff.; Buchheim, "Die Struktur der nationalsozialistischen Herrschaft" (1965), 13 ff. The key question is, according to these authors, whether totalitarian power, the essence of which is expressed in the absolute power of the Führer and authority of the Party, represents an excess of state power or whether it is an element that stands *in opposition to* the essence of the state (order, rules). The opposition of these elements may be useful as an ideotypical construct for reaching an understanding of Nazi power, but in reality it appears to be an artificially constructed opposite.

31. Huber, *Vom Sinn der Verfassung* (1935), 231.

32. For more details, see Kirn, *Verfassungsumsturz oder Rechtskontinuität* (1972), 25 ff.; Bollmus, *Das Amt Rosenberg und seine Gegner* (1970), 242.

33. Examples of judgments that expressly gave recognition to the supreme function of the NSDAP include State Superior Court. Karlsruhe, *JW* (1936): 3268; State Superior Court, Hamburg, *DJZ* (1936), col. 772; *Land* Labor Court, Berlin, *DJ* (1935): 73.

34. For more, see Fraenkel, *The Dual State*, 30 ff.

35. This area underwent a profound transformation. In May 1933 alone, seventy major cities lost their Oberbürgermeister; twelve major cities (including Cologne, Düsseldorf, Magdeburg, Altona, Gelsenkirchen, Hagen, Darmstadt, and Würzburg) lost their entire municipal leadership (for

more details, see Bracher, Sauer, and Schulz, *Die nationalsozialistische Machtergreifung*, 66, 446 f., [506]). The "legal grounds" for this was the so-called enabling act of March 24, 1933 (*RGBl.* I 153), according to which the *Land* governments were empowered to intervene in municipal administrative matters in contravention of the *Land* constitution and the properly constituted laws and regulations in force; for example, the Prussian law of December 15, 1933 (*GS* 427), according to which the appointment or dismissal of leading municipal officers could be carried out only after consultation with the responsible Gauleiter. For an example of the step-by-step approach of the National Socialists, see Allen, *Das haben wir nicht gewollt!* (1966), 169 ff.

36. Cf. Reich Ministry of the Interior to RMuChdRkzlei, urgent communication (BA R 43 II/421, 421a).

37. German Civil Service Code of January 26, 1937, sec. 26, par. 1, subpar. 2 (*RGBl.* I 39), in connection with subpar. 8 of the Principles Governing the Appointment, Employment, and Promotion of Civil Servants (Reichsgrundsätze über die Einstellung, Anstellung und Beförderung von Beamten) of October 14, 1936 (*RGBl.* I 893). In accordance with these principles, the political *attitudes* of candidates were tested prior to appointment, and on promotion, their political attitudes and activities. A civil servant could be dismissed for the same reasons that he was appointed (sec. 71, German Civil Service Code). However, judges could not be dismissed for reasons connected with their work in the judiciary. Nonetheless, the Reich minister and head of the Reich Chancellery, Lammers, announced on July 12, 1938, that judges could face dismissal because of specific *decisions*. Later, even this criterion was dropped (see Weinkauff and Wagner, *Die deutsche Justiz* [1968], 122). Judges who had fallen from favor were usually removed from office by early retirement on the grounds of unfitness for service, invoking sec. 73 of the German Civil Service Code, or by citing political grounds for their removal; cf. correspondence between the Party Chancellery and the head of Department 1 of the Reich Ministry of Justice, December 15, 1942, in which it is "suggested" that certain judges at the district court of Paderborn be removed for passing light sentences. In its reply of December 18, 1942, the Reich Ministry of Justice says that the removal of a municipal court judge *Landgerichtsdirektor* because of "strong religious ties" is approved, but the other dismissals should be left in abeyance (BA R 22/4202).

38. BVerfGE 6, 133 (180).

39. Reich Disciplinary Court, May 3, 1939, *Amtliche Entscheidungssammlung* 3, 1 (3).

40. Cf. subpar. 5 of the decree of the *Oberpräsident* of the Rhine Province (Rhenish-Prussia) to the Reich and state authorities and the Party, SA, SS, and Hitler Youth offices, dated August 12, 1935, quoted in Brandt, *Die politische Treuepflicht* [1976], 123 ff.):

In accordance with the directives of the Party, political appraisal of civil servants at state and local level will not be undertaken by the Reich Association of German Civil Servants, nor by any professional body, but by the responsible *Hoheitsträger* (the Party official in whom authority is vested), and such appraisal will be passed on to the relevant authority by him alone. Whether or not the authority within the Party contacts the Office for the Civil Service (of the NSDAP) or the civil servants' association with a request for information, and in particular whether or not the high Party official asks the Civil Service Office to open dossiers on the attitude and reliability of civil servants, is entirely up to him. The implementation of this order must not impair the functioning of the Civil Service nor cause disquiet among officials.

41. For low-, middle- and high-ranking officials, the relevant Gauleitung; for top civil servants, the Office of the Deputy Führer (Party Chancellery) (decree of the Führer and Reich Chancellor of March 26, 1937; July 10, 1937; and March 26, 1942, *RGBl.* 1937 I 153, 769; *RGBl.* 1942 I 298, with executive orders from the Reich Ministry of the Interior, dated December 1, 1942, *RGBl.* I 670); more details in Wagner, "Die Umgestaltung der Gerichtsverfassung" (1968), 232 ff. The main informants for the political evaluations produced by the deputy Führer's Office were the Gauleitungen and local Party offices, so it was open season for denunciations. For the political evaluation of

higher-ranking officials, cf. directive no. 52/36 of the deputy Führer, dated March 30, 1936, quoted in Diehl-Thiele, *Partei und Staat im Dritten Reich*, 235 n. 77; for more details and further examples, see ibid., 235; Sommer, "Partei und Staat" (1936), 596.

42. Führer's decree of September 24, 1935 (*RGBl.* I 1203), with amending decrees dated March 26, 1937 (*RGBl.* I 153), July 10, 1937 (*RGBl.* I 769), and March 16, 1942 (*RGBl.* I 153); the hearing (*Anhörung*) of Party members was of course general practice before September 24, 1935 (Mommsen, *Beamtentum im Dritten Reich*, 75).

43. Ordinance of the head of the Party Chancellery of August 29, 1941 (*Verfügungen*, 2:288 ff.).

44. Implementing regulations issued by the Reich Ministry of Justice on December 1, 1942 (*RGBl.* I 679), to the Führer decree of July 10, 1937 (*RGBl.* I 769).

45. Cf. directive of the head of the Party Chancellery of August 29, 1941 (*Verfügungen*, 2:289). The Party's approval was considered to have been given when no response was made within one month. The requirement of approval was of course a practical reality before 1941.

46. Membership in the NSDAP was not, however, a formal requirement for appointment; "only" for "important posts"—according to a note appended by the Reich Chancellery to the draft law of April 6, 1939—was such a requirement "considered desirable" in accordance with instructions from the Führer (quoted in Mommsen, *Beamtentum im Dritten Reich*, 190 ff.). But in practice, membership was *generally* "desirable," at least membership in one of the organizations (SA, SS, National Socialist Motor Corps, NSV) or one of the associations affiliated with the NSDAP (NSRB, RDB, etc.), which as a rule meant the same as "obligatory"; this applied to appointments and promotions alike—cf. a note from the Reich Ministry of Justice to the Reich Ministry of the Interior in July 1940 (BA R 22/4466; statement of presiding judge of State Superior Court, Munich, at a discussion of Bavarian State Superior Court presiding judges on June 23–24, 1943, notes BA R 22/4278). In fact, as a circular from the Reich Ministry of Justice of December 19, 1937, specified, what was demanded was *active* involvement, since formal membership was already *requisite (geboten)* on the basis of "the loyalty of every official to the Führer" (quoted in Weinkauff and Wagner, *Die deutsche Justiz*, 121). For the training of officials, this was already formally specified: every candidate had to belong to the NSDAP or one of its organizations, according to a decree of February 28, 1939 (*RGBl.* I 371); virtually the same applied for the training of candidates for the judiciary; cf. also a note from the presiding judge of State Superior Court, Kassel, to the Reich Ministry of Justice on July 30, 1943 (BA R 22/4467); a note from the Party Chancellery to the Reich Ministry of Justice on June 2, 1942 (BA R 22/4467) (involvement of the Party in the appointment of junior barristers), and the corresponding Reich Ministry of Justice circular of June 30, 1943, to all State Superior Court presiding judges; letter from NSRB to the Reich Ministry of Justice of January 7, 1937, and the reply of the Reich Ministry of Justice of January 23, 1937 (BA R 22/4533). Membership in the NSDAP was to be noted in the personal files, with the date of joining and the offices held (circular of the Reich Ministry of Justice of August 22, 1938, quoted in Weinkauff and Wagner, *Die deutsche Justiz*, 121). Earlier the opposite had been the norm: membership in one of the so-called center or left-wing parties of the Weimar Republic (but not in one of the so-called right-wing parties) was considered "politically untenable" and led to rejection of the candidate as unsuitable. In the case of officials appointed before January 30, 1933 this led to dismissal on political grounds in accordance with sec. 4 of the Law for the Restoration of the Professional Civil Service of April 7, 1933 (*RGBl.* I 175) (without pension rights), and with sec. 71 DRG 1937 (this applied particularly to membership in the KPD, the SPD, and in some cases also in the DVP [cf. Diehl-Thiele, *Partei und Staat im Dritten Reich*, 55 ff.; Mommsen, *Beamtentum im Dritten Reich*, 60; for an account of the purging of the Prussian administration, see Bracher, Sauer, and Schulz, *Die nationalsozialistische Machtergreifung*, 599 ff., with examples]). At the very least, those concerned were not promoted. In practice, Party members were *automatically* preferred (cf. the corresponding instruction circulated by the Reich Ministry of Justice of December 18, 1936 [Erlaßsammlung (collection of instructions), BA], and of May 8, 1936 [BA

R 22/20597]; the implementing orders of November 14 and December 17, 1935 [*DJ* (1935): 1656, 1860], and of May 15, 1943 [*DJ* (1943): 284]). For these reasons the influx of new members to the Party—whether voluntary or under pressure from the authorities—was considerable (further in Diehl-Thiele, *Partei und Staat im Dritten Reich*, 55 ff.). According to a communication from the state secretary in the Reich Ministry of Justice, R. Freisler, by 1938 54.8% of all judges were in the NSDAP or one of its affiliated organizations; the majority of these also engaged actively in political work (taken from a note in *DR* [1938]: 111). For more on the promotion of NSDAP members, see also note 85 below.

47. Positive attributes included "political tact"; "approval of the National Socialists"; being "held in particular esteem in leading and National Socialist circles"; for a judge, being keen "to inculcate subordinate officials with the spirit of National Socialism"; and "political attitude beyond reproach; also showed commitment to the party early on." Particular importance was also attached to the so-called leadership qualities, for example, a "resolute and energetic approach." Negative attributes included a "questionable attitude toward the Party," a "dubious attitude to the wartime penal code," "opposition to . . . 'the move toward the death penalty,' " a chief public prosecutor's allowing mainly "pleas for preventive detention rather than the death penalty," "no active commitment" (to the Party), "weltanschauung dubious," etc.

48. Directive of the deputy Führer of March 30, 1936, in Diehl-Thiele, *Partei und Staat im Dritten Reich*, 234 n. 77.

49. RArbG, *JW* (1937): 2311. A negative value judgment by the NSDAP with regard to an employee did not relieve the court of the duty to reach its own judgment. However, the question of the legal authority of decisions reached by a Party body must be clearly separated from the question of the de facto importance that must attach to the view taken by the district leader. In the administration of justice, it had to be recognized "that unjustified reproaches, even unfounded suspicion on the part of the proper authorities, were of such gravity that by themselves they could give grounds for dismissal" (cf. also *Land* Labor Court, Munich, July 31, 1937, *DJ* [1937]: 1159).

50. Regarding the character of the head of Department 1 (H. Nicolai) and other leading officials in the Reich Ministry of Justice, see Bracher, Sauer, and Schulz, *Die nationalsozialistische Machtergreifung*, 409 f., 412; and Diehl-Thiele, *Partei und Staat im Dritten Reich*, 57 n. 70; Mommsen, *Beamtentum im Dritten Reich*, 171 n. 1; regarding the character of the Reich minister and head of the Reich Chancellery, H. H. Lammers, the only lawyer on Hitler's staff of whom the Führer spoke approvingly, see Bracher, Sauer, and Schulz, *Die nationalsozialistische Machtergreifung*, 409 ff., 583; Diehl-Thiele, *Partei und Staat im Dritten Reich*, 242 n. 96. For an account of the appointments to leading posts in the Reich Ministry of Justice, see a note from the Reich Ministry of Justice to the Reich propaganda minister of December 17, 1942 (BA R 22/20337), a note from the Reich Ministry of Justice on a discussion with RFSSuChddtPol on September 18, 1942 (BA R 22/4062); further details are in Nuremberg doc., NG-587; and Heiber, "Zur Justiz im Dritten Reich" (1955), 283, 296; a sworn affidavit by Dr. Joël of March 6, 1947 (Nuremberg doc., NG-915); Johe, *Die gleichgeschaltete Justiz* (1967), 233; notification of the Reich Ministry of Justice in *DJ* (1942): 551 and *DJ* (1943): 157 (also in Nuremberg doc., NG-643); Nuremberg docs., NG-413 and 525; letter from the head of SIPO and the SD to the Reich Ministry of Justice (BA R 22/1462, sheet 98); Bracher, Sauer, and Schulz, *Die nationalsozialistische Machtergreifung*, 526; Heiber, "Zur Justiz im Dritten Reich," 275 ff.

51. With a marginal comment from the Reich Cabinet councillor Leo Killy of the Reich Chancellery: "Where did he get them all from?" (BA R 43 II/421); the deployment of fellow Party members proved particularly problematic when—as was largely the case in the East of the Reich—they had no administrative experience; cf. also a note from the Reich Ministry of the Interior to RMuChdRkzlei of May 26, 1941 (BA R 43 II/1136 b), which says, inter alia: "of the Prussian *Landrat* offices, 62.75% [are] occupied by trained administrative officers, 5.75% by lawyers without training in administration, and 31.5% by unqualified persons. . . . In the non-Prussian *Länder*, 93.75% are

trained administrative officers and only 6.25% are persons without training. . . . The results [of the initial restaffing of the *Landrat* offices in the Annexed Eastern Territories] is shocking. . . . Of the 63 *Landrat* offices, 40 [were] filled by unqualified persons, some of them young Party members. . . . Almost half the staff had failed within 1½ years."

52. Up to January 30, 1933, only 30 of the approximately 7,000 Prussian judges were active members of the NSDAP (0.4%). For an account of the situation in the Cologne district State Superior Court, where most judges joined the Party under political duress at the end of April, see Wolfram and Klein, *Recht und Rechtspflege in den Rheinlanden* (1969), 218; Schorn, *Der Richter im Dritten Reich* (1959), 36 f.; for Hamburg, see Johe, *Die gleichgeschaltete Justiz*, 58 ff.

53. A particularly good example is the Frankfurt district, where the Gauleiter, Jacob Sprenger, demanded that a judicial officer marry as a precondition for promotion (personal files, Chief Public Prosecutor, Frankfurt, Federal Ministry of Justice). Of course, the NSDAP influence was exerted above all on the leading posts, which were occupied exclusively by Party-approved candidates. For the appointment of the presiding judge of the State Superior Court and chief public prosecutor, it was necessary to have the approval of the Reich leadership of the NSDAP as well as that of the responsible Gauleitung (letter from State Secretary Freisler–Reich Ministry of Justice to Gauleiter Bracht [Upper Silesia] of March 22, 1941, with reply from Bracht on March 29, 1941 [personal files, presiding judge of State Superior Court Kattowitz (Katowice), Federal Justice Ministry]). Moreover— as is clear from the corresponding personal files—*all* personnel matters regarding judicial officers in the *Länder* were apparently discussed with the responsible Gauleiter, whose suggestions and complaints were largely taken into account. See also the next note.

54. Cf., for example, a letter from the chief public prosecutor of Düsseldorf to the Reich Ministry of Justice dated September 18, 1937; also a memorandum from Reich Minister of Justice Thierack of December 10, 1942, about a visit by Gauleiter Grohé, Cologne (BA 22/4062), who wanted to have the presiding judge of State Superior Court, Cologne, and the chief public prosecutor and presiding judge of the State Court of Appeals in Aachen replaced; memorandum from Reich Minister of Justice Thierack of November 1942 regarding requests and complaints from the Gauleiter of the *Gaue* Franconia, Vienna, Hamburg, and Saxony about the replacement of members of the judiciary (BA 22/4062). In Frankfurt the Gauleiter campaigned for the removal of the chief public prosecutor, who had been appointed before 1932, with the result that he volunteered for retirement in 1944. (Where no source is given, see the sources detailed in note 79.) The removal of the presiding judge of State Superior Court, Nuremberg, Döbig, in 1943 was the result of pressure exerted by the Party. It was said that he was steeped in "stagnant ideas" and pursued an anti-NSDAP personnel policy (letter from the NSDAP's legal adviser in Franconia to the deputy Gauleiter of Franconia on December 18, 1943, accompanied by a twenty-two-page "indictment" against Döbig [Nuremberg doc., NG-2167]; letter from the deputy Gauleiter of Franconia to the Reich Ministry of Justice on January 11, 1943, with postscript [Nuremberg doc., NG-2125]; memorandum from the State Superior Court presiding judge, Emmert [successor to Döbig], dated June 1, 1943 [Nuremberg doc., NG-2167]). For an account of the tension between the presiding judge of State Superior Court Rostock and the Gau leadership of Mecklenburg, see a note from Reich Minister of Justice Thierack dated November 6, 1942, according to which the Gauleiter had asked for the removal of the State Superior Court presiding judge. The arrangement made was that the candidate for the post put forward by the ministry should "present himself [!] to the Gauleiter" (BA R 22/4062). Regarding the pressure applied by the NSDAP on the chief public prosecutor of Frankfurt/Main, who had been in office since 1932, see the personal files of the chief public prosecutor of Frankfurt (Federal Ministry of Justice). For an account of the tensions between the Party and the judiciary in the Cologne district State Superior Court, see Wolfram and Klein, *Recht und Rechtspflege in den Rheinlanden*, 219 ff., 223, 236 f.

55. Letter from the Moselland Gauleiter (G. Simon) to the Reich Ministry of Justice, dated December 9, 1942, concerning the Cologne district State Superior Court of which it was said that

"an active and heartfelt National-Socialist personnel policy could not be expected" (BA R 22/281); reply from Reich Ministry of Justice of December 9, 1942, to the effect that for the time being all matters not essential to the war effort should be deferred (ibid.). A corresponding circular was sent out on June 16, 1943 (ibid.); cf. also Wolfram and Klein, *Recht und Rechtspflege in den Rheinlanden*, 219 ff., 223, 236 f.

56. This was the home district of the Prussian minister of justice, H. Kerrl, a former *Justizobermeister* (ranking above *Justizmeister*, the lowest rank in the administration of the judiciary), who thoroughly purged the top echelons of all the courts. On July 25, 1933, the presiding judges of the *Länder* Courts (State Courts of Appeals) in Koblenz, Trier, Bonn, and Cologne were removed from their posts; the presiding judge of the State Superior Court–Court of Appeal (*Oberlandesgericht*) was transferred to the Prussian Supreme Court (*Kammergericht*) in Berlin. In principle, the top posts were reserved for "Old Campaigners," though they were few in number. The new district court presiding judge in Bonn was a drunkard who lasted only a few days in the job; his successor was a Frankfurt lawyer. Several municipal court judges were promoted to presiding judge positions for political reasons (Wolfram and Klein, *Recht und Rechtspflege in den Rheinlanden*, 219 ff., 223).

57. Cf. Reich Ministry of the Interior to RMuChdRkzlei, urgent communication (BA R 43 II/421, 421a).

58. This is also underlined by the following overview of the religious affiliations of the State Superior Court presiding judges and chief public prosecutors.

Affiliation	25 presiding judges of appeal courts	19 chief public prosecutors
Protestant	12	12
Catholic	5	2
Belief in God	4	1
No data	4	4
(data from sources given in note 79)		

59. For more details, see Zunker, "Institutionengeschichte und Regierungslehre" (1975), 62; Köhler, *Lebenserinnerungen* (1964), 197. For example, the State Superior Court presiding judges and chief public prosecutors—as detailed in the sources given in note 79—had mostly been alumni of student fraternities (*Altherrenbünden*) or members of student (dueling) corps or societies, in some cases also of other groups on the right or extreme right of the political spectrum (of the State Superior Court presiding judges, 2 were members of the Pan-German League [Alldeutscher Verband], 1 of the Stahlhelm, 1 of the Deutschbund [the oldest *völkisch* association in Germany], 1 of the Deutschvölkischer Schutz- und Trutzbund, and 1 of the Nationalverband deutscher Offiziere [of which 1 chief state prosecutor was also a member]). Many top civil servants in the Reich Ministry of Justice and the Reich Ministry of the Interior had been members of the Deutschnationale Volkspartei (*DNVP*) before 1933; see notes 65 and 68 below.

60. Statement of the former head of Hitler's Presidential Chancellery, Secretary of State Otto Meißner, at his interrogation at the Nuremberg trial of lawyers, in Kempner, *Das Dritte Reich im Kreuzverhör* (1969), 166.

61. Kübler, "Der deutsche Richter und das demokratische Gesetz" (1963), in particular 109 ff.

62. Cf. Federal Supreme Court of April 30, 1968 (*NJW* [1968]: 1339, Rehse judgment), according to which the (independent) position of a career judge in the Third Reich could not be changed by any actual circumstances to the extent that the Court of General Sessions (which had condemned Rehse as associate judge of the former People's Court [*Volksgerichtshof*]) assumes.

63. Circular from the Reich Ministry of Justice dated November 14, 1935 (*DJ* [1935]: 1656).

64. Kolbe, *Reichsgerichtspräsident Dr. Erwin Bumke* (1975), 221.

65. For details of Reich Minister of Justice Franz Gürnter, who had been a member of the Deutschnationale Volkspartei and held office from 1932 to 1941, see Reitter, *Franz Gürtner* (1976); cf. also Kolbe, *Reichsgerichtspräsident Dr. Erwin Bumke*, 219; in 1933 some of the Reich Ministry of Justice departmental heads were also taken over (*Handbuch der Justizverwaltung* [1942], 23). According to Schneller, the former head of the Budget Department of the Reich Ministry of Justice, the following were dismissed from the Reich Ministry of Justice after 1933 on political grounds: 15 senior civil servants (*höhere Beamte*), 7 principal administrative officers (*Amtsräte*), 2 senior clerks (*Amtmänner*), and 2 inspectors (Nuremberg doc., NG-560).

66. Reich Minister of Justice Thierack, who took up his office on August 20, 1942, as successor to Dr. Franz Gürnter (who died in January 1941), conducted wide-ranging purges. There are lists of staff changes with much accompanying detail in BA R 22/4378; numerous leading officials (State Superior Court presiding judges or chief public prosecutors) in top positions in the districts left the Reich Ministry of Justice through temporary retirement and pensioning off or transfer to the Reich Supreme Court. For biographies and further details on this subject and on the new appointees in the Reich Ministry of Justice, see Nuremberg doc., NG-413 (BA All. Proz. 1 XVII B 1, 24), 525, 587, 643, 915; *Handbuch der Justizverwaltung*, 166 (BA A VI R 9); letter from head of SIPO and SD to Reich Ministry of Justice (BA R 22/1462); note in *DJ* (1942): 551; Johe, *Die gleichgeschaltete Justiz*, 233; Heiber, "Zur Justiz im Dritten Reich," 283, 296. Cf. also notes 76 and 77 below.

67. Thus, Dr. Franz Gürtner, who became Reich minister of justice in 1932, remained in office because Hitler—as he said in 1942—had not found "anyone better"; Freisler was "a Bolshevik in his whole manner, and as far as the other one [meaning Secretary of State Schlegelberger] is concerned: he is just what he appears, and to look at him once is enough" (table talk on evening of March 29, 1942, quoted in Picker, *Hitlers Tischgespräche* [1968], 67).

68. Bumke was not thought to be vulnerable with regard to Party-political affiliations. It was not known that he was a member of the Deutschnationale Volkspartei from 1919 until at least 1929, and he was therefore able to prevail against the candidates of the "dominant parties," Radbruch (SPD), Landsberg (SPD), Marx (Center) and Koch-Weser (DVP). The right-wing press in particular had stirred up public opinion against these candidates and demanded that all "Party-political influences" be eliminated (cf. *Das Deutsche Tageblatt*, January 30, 1929; *Kreuzzeitung*, January 31, 1929), sources and quotes from Kolbe, *Reichsgerichtspräsident Dr. Erwin Bumke*, 57 ff.

69. Of the State Superior Court presiding judges and chief public prosecutors in office on November 1, 1931, only the chief public prosecutors in Marienwerder and Naumberg and the presiding judge of State Superior Court, Celle, were still in office by the end of 1933 (*Taschenkalender für Verwaltungsbeamte* [1932], 521, 92 and 1934, 766 ff.), but no grounds are given for their leaving; cf. also *Handbuch der Justizverwaltung* (status on January 1, 1942) and lists of State Superior Court presiding judges and chief public prosecutors in BA R 22/1462 (status in 1938) and 4402 (status in 1942), which show that immediately after the seizure of power in 1933, the following were removed from their posts either by pensioning off or temporary retirement: the *Kammergericht* (Prussian Supreme Court [KG]) presiding judge of Berlin; the State Superior Court presiding judges of Naumburg, Kassel, Kiel, Cologne, Düsseldorf, Stettin, and Hamm; and the chief public prosecutors at the Prussian Supreme Court and State Courts of Appeals of Berlin, Breslau, Königsberg, Kassel, Cologne, and Hamm. In Prussia, too, State Superior Court presiding judges, chief public prosecutors, and departmental civil servants were transferred to other departments (in some cases to lower-ranking posts); cf. statistics in *Handbuch der Justizverwaltung*.

70. *Handbuch der Justizverwaltung*.

71. Although the *Handbuch der Justizverwaltung* states that, of the State Superior Court presiding judges and chief public prosecutors in office on January 1, 1942, only two judges and four prosecutors were pre-1933 appointees, this does not carry much weight since there are no details about the officials who were replaced in 1933 or later or about the reasons for their replacement (such as political grounds, death, retirement age). Nor do the personnel files contain details of the

reasons for retirement (other than the attainment of the age limit). With the exception of Prussia, reference books for the judiciary or the administration covering the period up to 1933 giving information about personnel in the *Land* Justice Administration (cf. note 69 above) have not been tracked down.

72. Johe, *Die gleichgeschaltete Justiz*, 65.

73. *Handbuch der Justizverwaltung*; personnel lists for 1938 and 1942 (BA R 22/1462, 4402).

74. Already before 1933, Oldenburg, Thuringia, Brunswick, Anhalt, Lippe, Mecklenburg-Schwerin, and Mecklenburg-Strelitz had Nazi-led governments (Diehl-Thiele, *Partei und Staat im Dritten Reich*, 37 f.).

75. Apart from the purges following the so-called Professional Civil Service Code of April 7, 1933. Similar intolerance was apparently shown toward civil servants who had business connections with Jews (circular from Reich Ministry of Justice of January 7, 1936, Allgemeine Erlaßsammlung, BA, with the instruction to indicate which officials had business connections with Jews and when such ties could be broken). As a rule women were excluded from the judiciary from 1936 onward (circulars from the Reich Ministry of Justice on January 10 and 16, 1936 [ibid.]).

76. Kolbe, *Reichsgerichtspräsident Dr. Erwin Bumke*, 219 ff.; news item in *DJ* (1943): 127, 157, with detailed report about the new officials. For more about the changes in personnel in the State Superior Court district of Cologne, see Wolfram and Klein, *Recht und Rechtspflege in den Rheinlanden*, 231 ff., 243 f.; see also above, note 66.

77. According to the statement by Schlegelberger to American Military Court no. 3 in Nuremberg on June 27, 1947 (protocol d, 4315 ff., 4355, in BA All. Proz. 1, XVII A 58), after Thierack's appointment the whole top echelon of the ministry, with the exception of the Budget Department, was replaced. Of 22 State Superior Court presiding judges, 11 were replaced, along with 4 chief public prosecutors; also dismissed were all judges and public prosecutors who were not totally Aryan, as well as all non-Party members who worked in the ministry. According to a list sent by Thierack to the Reich minister and head of the Reich Chancellery in a letter dated October 20, 1942, 75 judges and public prosecutors were to be pensioned off because of non-Aryan descent, mixed marriages, lack of cooperation with the Party, failure to join the party, or "pro-Jewish or pro-Polish" behavior. Bormann and Lammers assented in a letter of November 3, 1942 (quoted in Steiniger and Leszczyński, *Das Urteil im Juristenprozeß* [1969], 164).

78. Johe, *Die gleichgeschaltete Justiz*, 65 ff.

79. Details from personnel files and documents on 25 State Superior Court presiding judges and 19 chief public prosecutors held in 35 State Superior Court districts, Federal Ministry of Justice.

80. *RGBl.* I 529.

81. An official Party publication of the NSDAP on the verdict of the Reich Supreme Court of December 23, 1933, *DR* (1934): 19; *JW* (1934): 24; reproduced also in Schorn, *Der Richter im Dritten Reich*, 868.

82. On this and the foregoing, see Kolbe, *Reichsgerichtspräsident Dr. Erwin Bumke*, 212 ff., 219 ff., with examples.

83. More details in Johe, *Die gleichgeschaltete Justiz*, 68 ff., especially 70 n. 35, regarding the presiding judge of State Superior Court Dr. A. Engel, who took up his office on September 16, 1933; he was regarded as a "representative of the older generation of lawyers" and precisely for this reason appeared to be the right man for the job, since he conveyed the impression that the program of the NSDAP "was more a return to national tradition than a revolution" (69); cf. also Kolbe, *Reichsgerichtspräsident Dr. Erwin Bumke*, 222, with regard to the behavior of members of the Reich Supreme Court and its presiding judge Dr. E. Bumke.

84. Kübler, *"Der deutsche Richter und das demokratische Gesetz,"* 104 ff.; Schorn, *Der Richter im Dritten Reich*, 6 ff.; cf. also Federal Supreme Court of April 30, 1968, *NJW* (1968): 1339 (Rehse verdict).

85. Cf. a decree issued November 10, 1934, by the Baden Ministry of Justice on the conditions

of employment of judicial officials, according to which the minister was to get information through the Party on the political attitudes of judicial officials. Key posts, particularly those dealing with personnel matters, could be filled only by the politically reliable, who were members of the NSDAP (see Weinkauff and Wagner, *Die deutsche Justiz*, 99). He would deal ruthlessly with civil servants who tried to disrupt the "work of construction . . . while hiding behind a pretence of cooperation" and, if necessary, remove them from office (99). According to a decree of the Reich Ministry of the Interior issued on August 1, 1940, the higher Reich legal authorities were instructed to promote in particular the careers of those who held the highest decorations for service in the war and to the Movement and also holders of rescue medals (cf. Secretary of State Freisler at a discussion in Berlin, minutes, undated—probably May 1942—BA R 22/4162, sheet 91). But to gain promotion to higher-ranking posts, mere membership in the Party was sufficient. Cf. the list of promotion candidates sent by the Reich Ministry of Justice to the Reich Ministry of the Interior on February 7, 1939, which proposed the elevation of 4 chief public prosecutors, 2 *Kammergericht* officials, 1 *Oberregierungsrat* (senior executive officer) and 2 *Landgericht* directors—all of them working in the Reich Ministry of Justice—to *Ministerialräte* (departmental principals) in violation of the regulations, because they were old Party members (usually since 1932) or high-ranking officers in the SA or Freikorps volunteers (BA All. Proz. 1, XVII B 6, 147 ff.). For more details on the reform of personnel policy, see Freisler, "Personalpolitik im höheren Justizdienst" (1939), who fulminates against promotion for reasons of religious affiliation, against the "unpolitical attitude" of the officials, against "parochialism" and the "cult of seniority"; see also Kennert, "Der Einsatz deutscher Verwaltungspersonals in den eingegliederten und besetzten Gebieten und seine zentrale Lenkung," *DVerW* (1940): 113 ff. For an account of the disciplining of antagonistic judges, see *Führerinformationen* no. 116, September 2, 1942 (BA R 22/4089); Schorn, *Der Richter im Dritten Reich*, documentary section.

86. See, for example, the corresponding appeal of the Prussian Judicial Association of April 21, 1933, and the appeal of the Law Association of Württemberg of April 27, 1933, to those "who sensed a deeply felt affinity with the new 'Germany and its Führer' " (quoted in Weinkauff and Wagner, *Die deutsche Justiz*, 109). Cf. circular from Reich Ministry of Justice of December 19, 1937 (121), with the demand to all officials to commit themselves to the Movement and its goals; also, decrees of February 14, 1935 (the introduction of the Hitler salute "by raising the right arm" and simultaneously clearly uttering the words "Heil Hitler"), of March 28, 1936 (the creation of personal files recording the racial origins and past and present political affiliations and membership in groups and associations of higher judicial officials), and of August 22, 1938 (120 f.); cf. also Schorn, *Der Richter im Dritten Reich*, 23 and 37.

87. Weinkauff and Wagner, *Die deutsche Justiz*, 112, with examples.

88. Speech by Thierack on August 29, 1942, in Berlin (notes in BA R 22/4199).

89. Cf. H. Boberach, ed., *Richterbriefe, Dokumente zur Beinflussung der deutschen Rechtsprechung 1942–1944* (1975) (reviewed by Majer, *ZRP* [1977]: 115 ff.).

90. For details, see Johe, *Die gleichgeschaltete Justiz*, 119 ff.

91. Letters from the Reich Ministry of Justice to the head of the SIPO and the SD on August 10 and 17, 1943; report by Dr. Drescher to the Reich Ministry of Justice on August 10, 1943 (BA R 22/4204), report of the presiding judge of State Superior Court, Hamburg, to the Reich Ministry of Justice on April 12, 1944 (BA R 22/3366).

92. The State Superior Court presiding judges and chief public prosecutors (like most of the judges and public prosecutors) were all members or officials of the Nationalsozialistischer Rechtswahrerbund (NSRB) (e.g., *Gauführer, Gaugruppenwalter, Gaurechtsamtsleiter*) and of other National Socialist organizations (e.g., Reichsbund Deutscher Beamter [RDB]) and in some cases held high office in the Party jurisdiction (SA judges, etc.) (details from sources cited in note 79); for more about the leading judicial officials of the State Superior Court districts of Danzig, Leitmeritz, and Hamburg, see also Johe, *Die gleichgeschaltete Justiz*, 230.

93. Details from sources cited in note 79.

94. Cf. Weinkauff and Wagner, *Die deutsche Justiz*, 109.

Introduction. III. 3. The Principle of *Völkisch* Inequality

1. For an account of the origins and nature of the term *Volksgemeinschaft* (national community) in the National Socialist doctrine, see Stolleis, "Gemeinschaft und Volksgemeinschaft" (1972); Stolleis, *Gemeinwohlformeln im nationalsozialistischen Recht* (1974) (in each case with detailed examples); Stolleis emphasizes particularly that behind the idea of the community lay the belief in a supposed prehistoric harmony and the will to reestablish this harmony in history (*Gemeinwohlformeln im nationalsozialistischen Recht*, 27 f.).

2. Schmitt, *Staat, Bewegung, Volk* (1939), 42; summarized in Stolleis, *Gemeinwohlformeln im nationalsozialistischen Recht*, 229 ff.

3. Scheuner, "Der Gleichheitsgedanke" (1939), 255 f.

4. "Führung als Rechtsprinzip" (1934).

5. For further details see Fraenkel, *Der Doppelstaat* (1974), 221 ff., with examples; cf. Tönnies, *Gemeinschaft und Gesellschaft* (1926); H. Marr, *Die Massenwelt im Kampf um ihre Reform* (1934), 549 ff.

6. Bracher, *Zeitgeschichtliche Kontroversen* (1976), 28.

7. According to him, a person's outward appearance, in terms of color and morphology, is also indicative of *value* differences. The Aryan was the most valuable, the only creative human being (Hitler, *Mein Kampf*[1939], 285), and therefore—as was appropriate to the relationship between the strong and clever and the weak and stupid—had greater rights vis-à-vis all other races and a higher duty of self-preservation; this consisted in the rejection of interbreeding with other races in the struggle for supremacy, that is, against all inferior beings (*Minderwertige* [the weaker]) for the purpose of higher breeding (*Höherzüchtung des Lebens*). This exemplified the "iron logic of nature" (281 f.). The close ties between the racial principle and the principle of the Movement (the Party) are evinced by the tenet that the rights of higher races can be won only through movement, through struggle; struggle was therefore not only a means but also an end, as well as the wellspring of the further development of the race. For a fuller account of Hitler's racial ideas, see A. Bullock, *Hitler, Eine Studie über Tyrannei* (Düsseldorf, 1960), 35 ff.; Bracher, Sauer, and Schulz, *Die nationalsozialistische Machtergreifung* (1962), 274 ff.; Hill, *Artgleichheit und Gleichartigkeit* (1966); Phelps, "Hitlers 'grundlegende' Rede"; von zur Mühlen, *Rassenideologien* (1977), 237 ff.

8. Von zur Mühlen, *Rassenideologien* (1977), 235 f.

9. Hitler, *Mein Kampf* (1939), 373.

10. An attempt was made to define race as "a community of common origin with common mental and physical characteristics" or as "hereditary equality" (*Erbgleichheit*), as "physical traits *and* mental characteristics," a group that "perpetually generates its own kind" (F. K. Günther, quoted in Kluge and Krüger, *Verfassung und Verwaltung* [1941], 162); see also Nicolai, "Grundsätzliches über den Zusammenhang von Rasse und Recht" (1934), 76. But no concrete definition was arrived at because the racial mixture in Germany did not fit into the National Socialist concept of pure race; similarly, Hitler only *describes* races—he never defines them (*Mein Kampf*, 238 ff.).

11. Cf. in particular Feder, *Das Programm der NSDAP* (1932); Rosenberg, *Der Mythos des 20. Jahrhunderts* (1930); Rosenberg, *Die Protokolle der Weisen* (1923). Cf., for example, Hill, *Artgleichheit und Gleichartigkeit* (1966), 255 ff.; Saller, *Die Rassenlehre des Nationalsozialismus* (1961); T. Toblanski, *Die Entwicklung zum Menschen* (1948); Tenenbaum, *Race and Reich* (1956); Breitling, *Die nationalsozialistische Rassenlehre* (1971).

12. Hitler on the "day of culture" at the 1933 Party rally (quoted in Kluge and Krüger, *Verfassung und Verwaltung*, 161). Also, Hitler at the 1935 Reich Party rally in Nuremberg: The political

idea is the National Socialist weltanschauung as the "recognition of racial and hereditary contingencies of the German people" (18).

13. Nicolai, "Grundsätzliches über den Zusammenhang von Rasse und Recht," 76; in this sense see also Nicolai, *Die Rassengesetzliche Rechtslehre* (1934); Nicolai, *Rasse und Recht* (1934); Meyer, *Rasse und Recht* (1937).

14. For further details, see von zur Mühlen, *Rassenideologien*, 235 f.

15. The determining factor for him was not race but "destiny," with which he justified the legitimacy of his own claim to power. Already in a speech on May 1, 1937, he had said that, although the foundation of the national community (*Volksgemeinschaft*) was certainly "blood," "language," "history," and "manners and customs," there was "something else . . . something that not only leads but actually drives us to this community: it is our common destiny, this ineluctable common destiny that none of us can escape" (quoted in Koellreuter, *Deutsches Verfassungsrecht* [1938], 70 f.). Cf. also Hitler's remarks at table on June 2, 1942: following a flight to Poltava (today part of the Ukraine), he had doubts about his own ideas on race, which had been "somewhat shaken" by the previous day's trip. In Poltava he had seen "so many blue-eyed, blond women that—thinking of the photographs of Norwegian or even Dutch women submitted to me with applications for permission to marry—I would speak of the need to 'southify' (*Aufsüden*) rather than 'Nordicize' (*Aufnorden*—an official term of Nazi ideology) our northern European states" (Picker, *Hitlers Tischgespräche* [1968], 174).

16. In this sense see also Rauschning, *Die Revolution des Nihilismus* (1938), 435; he saw the key element of National Socialism as its *dynamism* rather than as the Party program. Similarly in foreign policy, National Socialism was "in the middle of the second phase of the nihilist revolution, in which the *völkisch* element has already largely been cast aside."

17. Cf. Hitler's remarks in Rauschning, *Gespräche mit Hitler* (1950): "But we . . . are burning with the desire for power and we are in no way shy of admitting it. . . . For us this is . . . nothing less than the meaning of life" (219, 255).

18. Cf., for example, Hitler's remarks in ibid.; for further details, see Hill, *Artgleichheit und Gleichartigkeit*, 244 ff., with examples.

19. Rauschning, *Gespräche mit Hitler*, 216 ff.; cf. also Hitler's speech to the 1935 Party rally in Nuremberg (quoted in Kluge and Krüger, *Verfassung und Verwaltung*, 16).

20. Hitler, *Mein Kampf* (1939), 384; Nicolai, "Grundsätzliches über den Zusammenhang von Rasse und Recht"; for further details, see Bracher, *Zeitgeschichtliche Kontroversen* (1976), 89 f., 93 f.

21. Hitler in speech on the first anniversary of the seizure of power on January 30, 1934: "The new state itself can acknowledge no other task than the creation of the conditions necessary for the preservation of the *Volk*" (quoted in Nicolai, *Der Neuaufbau des Reiches* [1934]). For greater detail, see also Hitler, *Mein Kampf*, 165, 291 ff., 389, 394.

22. Hitler to the 1935 Party rally in Nuremberg (quoted in Kluge and Krüger, *Verfassung und Verwaltung*, 16): "The starting point for the National Socialist doctrine is not in the state but in the *Volk*," which "teaches the primacy of the people instead of the primacy of individual freedom. The nation alone is an end in itself . . . the state is but an organization, though the highest of the life of the *Volk*."

23. Huber, *Vom Sinn der Verfassung* (1935), 10 f.

24. Scheuner, "Der Gleichheitsgedanke," 256 f.; in this sense see also Held, *Volk, Recht und Staat* (1935), 15; Frank, introduction to *Nationalsozialistisches Handbuch für Recht und Gesetzgebung* (1934), xvii.

25. For further details, see Freisler, "Schutz von Rasse und Erbgut" (1936), 141 ff.; Stuckart, *Nationalsozialistische Rechtserziehung* (1935), 5: "Identity of race (*Artgleichheit*) is the biological basis for a 'racially appropriate' (*artgemäss*) German law"; Nicolai, "Grundsätzliches über den Zusammenhang von Rasse und Recht," 76 n. 21; For example, the future penal code in its entirety was to

be an expression of racial values and racial preservation; cf. *Preußische Denkschrift für ein neues Strafgesetzbuch* (Berlin, 1933).

26. Nicolai, "Grundsätzliches über den Zusammenhang von Rasse und Recht," 76.

27. H. Frank, "Nationalsozialistische Rechtpolitik," *DR* (1936): 389: "Power is the life of the law"; for further details, see Fraenkel, *Der Doppelstaat*, 136 ff., with examples.

28. Cf. article entitled "Rechtsstaat" in *Handwörterbuch der Rechtswissenschaft*, ed. Erich Volkmar, Alexander Elster, and Günther Küchenhoff (Berlin, 1937), 8:567 ff., 572, which says: "For this task [safeguarding the rights of the people] there is only the concerted power of the people, just as a tank threatening the frontline can only be stopped by a concentrated explosive charge; this concerted deployment of a concentrated charge of popular power for the protection of national life is how we see the constitutional state." Freisler had written the article for the *Völkischer Beobachter* of December 21, 1931 (for further details see Fraenkel, *Der Doppelstaat*, 231).

29. Forsthoff, *Der totale Staat* (1933), 13, 29 ff.

30. Wolf, "Das Rechtsideal des nationalsozialistischen Staates" (1934–35), 352. For more on the concept of the National Socialist "constitutional state," see R. Höhn, *Staat und Rechtsgemeinschaft* (1935), 676. Schmitt, "Nationalsozialismus und Rechsstaat" (1934) ("We do not define the constitutional state on the basis of outmoded concepts but on the basis of National Socialism"—i.e., the basis for a just state); for more details, see Scheuner, "Die nationale Revolution" (1933–34), 161 ff.; Koellreuter, *Volk und Staat* (1935), sees the legitimacy of every concept in the notion of the *Völkisch*; thus, the "Bolshevik state" is a "nonconstitutional state" because it is "a-*völkisch*" (23); Frank, introduction to *Nationalsozialistisches Handbuch für Recht und Gesetzgebung*, xii; Göring, *Die Rechtssicherheit als Grundlage der Volksgemeinschaft* (1935) (letters of the German Law Academy). Scholz, "Die Rechtssicherheit" (1944): "National Socialist law in its substance and drafting has opened the way to supreme justice" (32). (The author was *Senatspräsident* at the Administrative Court.)

31. A. Rosenberg, "Lebensrecht, nicht Formelrecht," *DR* (1934): 233 f.; for more details, see Rosenberg, *Der Mythos des 20. Jahrhunderts* (1933), 571 f.

32. For an account of the disintegration of judicial and legal norms under National Socialism, see Püschel, *Der Niedergang des Rechts im Dritten Reich* (1947); von Hippel, *Die Perversion von Rechtsordnungen* (1955), 52 ff.; von Hippel, *Die nationalsozialistische Herrschaftsordunung* (1947); Kirschenmann, *Gesetz im Staatsrecht* (1971).

33. Schraut, "Blutgebundenes Recht" (1934).

34. Wolf, "Das Rechtsideal des nationalsozialistischen Staates," 352.

35. Directive of the deputy Führer of December 11, 1937:

We have to hammer these fundamental principles into the German people, until the essence and thinking of our nation, for so long buried, are set free. . . . The party must keep these . . . principles pure and clear for centuries. That is its great task. Nothing would please our opponents more than if the Nazis were to be sidetracked from these core principles of National Socialism into the uncertain field of scientific side issues and controversies, which might be of significance in terms of the history of human thought but politically are bound to become a burden of intolerable proportions. Science is subordinate to ongoing developments and experience; it is constantly expanded and complemented by new insights and observations. The Nazis proclaim the eternal truths of our *völkisch* existence, which were as valid a thousand years ago as they will be in a thousand years' time. (*Verfügungen*, 1:478 f., directive no. 152/37) See also a similar directive in ibid., 474 f., no. 7/409 of December 2, 1940.

36. Examples: already in 1933 the Reich Ministry of the Interior had an Advisory Board on Population and Racial Affairs with the following departments: National Health (Volksgesundheit), headed by Gütt; Reich Health Board; Reich Committee for the National Health Service; and Reich Central Office for Health Management; from 1933 on, there was also an "Adviser on Racial

Research"—Dr. Achim Gercke (Bracher, Sauer, and Schulz, *Die nationalsozialistische Machtergreifung*, 285 n. 119); the German Medical Association (Deutsche Ärzteschaft) had an Office for Population Policy and Racial Affairs; the Reich leadership of the NSDAP had a Department for National Welfare and Health (Abteilung für Volkswohlfahrt und Volksgesundheit), and even the district courts had so-called Hereditary Health Courts (Erbgesundheitsgerichte). In 1935 an Institute for the History of the New Germany (Reichsinstitut für die Geschichte des neuen Deutschland) was established—which from April 1936 had a research department for the "Jewish question" under the aegis of H. Frank, though this ranked far behind Rosenberg's Institute for Research into the Jewish Question (Institut zur Erforschung der Judenfrage) in Frankfurt. The latter was to be the nucleus of a central Nazi university to be set up after the war in which it was intended to house the confiscated Jewish libraries and archives (Bracher, Sauer, and Schulz, *Die nationalsozialistische Machtergreifung*, 312 n. 244). For an overview of the institutions devoted to "Racial Affairs," see Frick, "Die Rassenpolitik" (1936); Bracher, Sauer, and Schulz, *Die nationalsozialistische Machtergreifung*, 285.

37. "[As a result] the German people lack a true herd instinct that resides in the homogeneity of the blood" (Hitler, *Mein Kampf* [1939], 387).

38. "Vertrauliche Information der Parteikanzlei," no. 34/355 of August 9, 1941, in *Verfügungen*, 2:48 f. Similarly, the designation "white" or "European race" was not permitted.

39. Gütt and Linden, *Kommentar zum Erbgesundheitsgesetz* (1936), 20 f., for example, wanted to rescue the notion of the homogeneous race by ascertaining that this can be understood in relation to the German people only in the sense of the *Systemrasse* (system race), as a scientific classification, not in the sense of the *Vitalrasse* (vital race), i.e., having the same genotype. Similarly, Kluge and Krüger, *Verfassung und Verwaltung*, 162, consider that *Volk* is not synonymous with race but is made up of several races.

40. Gütt and Linden, *Kommentar zum Erbgesundheitsgesetz*, 21.

41. Hitler, quoted in Rauschning, *Gespräche mit Hitler*, 232 ff.

42. Held, *Volk, Recht und Staat*, 25 ff.

43. However, the term *non-Aryan* was kept; cf. sec. 3 of the so-called Professional Civil Service Code of April 7, 1933. Regarding the etymology of the terms *deutschen oder artverwandten Blutes* (German or related blood) and *deutschblütig* (of German blood), cf. Berning, *Vom Abstammungsnachweis zum Zuchtwert* (1964), 54.

44. Kluge and Krüger, *Verfassung und Verwaltung*, 18; cf. also sec. 13, par. 2, Reich Entailment Law: "Not included among those of German or kindred (*stammesgleich*) blood is anyone who has ancestors on either side of the family with Jewish or colored blood."

45. Palandt, *Bürgerliches Gesetzbuch* (1942), appendix 1 to the Marriage Law, first decree to sec. 1, "Blood Protection Law," according to which *artverwandtes Blut* was "the blood of peoples racially related to the German people, that is peoples settled in Europe," and the blood of their descendants in other parts of the world, insofar as this has been kept pure.

46. Hitler, *Mein Kampf*, 368 ff., 372 ff.

47. For more details, see Scheuner, "Die nationale Revolution," 271.

48. An excellent example is given in the comprehensive account in ibid., in particular 266 ff., where he expressly refers to Herder and German Romanticism.

49. Cf. Held, *Volk, Recht und Staat—Volk* as *Naturgemeinschaft* (natural community), *Geschichts- und Kulturgemeinschaft* (historical and cultural community) (19). According to Huber, "the *Volk* [was] . . . a political community determined by the homogeneity of the race, characterized by its common history" (*Idee und Ordnung des Reiches* [1941], 25); cf. also Huber, *Verfassungsrecht des Großdeutschen Reiches* (1939), 150; Gerber, *Staatsrechtliche Grundlinien des neuen Reiches* (1933), 19.

50. Gerber, *Staatsrechtliche Grundlinien des neuen Reiches*, 19.

51. Cf., for example, Koellreuter, *Volk und Staat*; Höhn, "Rechtsgemeinschaft und Volksge-

meinschaft"; Nicolai, *Die rassengesetzliche Rechtslehre;* the *völkisch* political theory of the state was also championed by Poetzsch-Heffter, Ule, and Dernedde, "Der völkische Staat" (1935), 30 ff.; Walz, "Neue Grundlagen des Volksgruppenrechts" (1940); Kluge and Krüger, *Verfassung und Verwaltung,* 16 ff., and many more.

52. See, among many others, Scheuner, "Die nationale Revolution," 261 ff., although he uses the concept of race as well as that of *völkisch.*

53. Gerber, *Staatsrechtliche Grundlinien des neuen Reiches,* 19, according to which the state was "the *Volk* in its historical reality." In the *Volk* "the state embodies the idea of the guarantor who allows the will of creation to be fulfilled in history." Huber, *Vom Sinn der Verfassung,* 19 ff. Koellreuter, *Staat und Rechtsgemeinschaft,* 16, 22, 23. Frank, "Die staatsrechliche Bedeutung" (1934), 25 f.: "Blood and soil are the foundations of the state. The new state should be built on customs, race and soil."

54. Cf. in particular Schmitt, *Staat, Bewegung, Volk* (1933); Huber, *Vom Sinn der Verfassung;* Huber, *Verfassung des Großdeutschen Reiches* (1935); Scheuner, "Die nationale Revolution."

55. A striking description is given in Scheuner, "Die nationale Revolution":

Volk does not mean the outward union of a nation state, formed of rights of citizenship: the sum of its citizens. *Volk* is the living community, born of the natural affinity of blood ties and shaped by its historical destiny, in which a particular primordial law of creative development unfolds. Liberalism had gone too far in turning the concept of the *Volk* into a question of mere mentality and therefore a matter of individual belief. By contrast, this new concept— here as elsewhere reaching down into the depths of the irrational forces underlying human life—places a decisive emphasis on the natural fundament of the *Volk,* the racial element. However, we should not be misled by the stress on the influence of the basic nature into assuming that this view of the phenomenon of nationality (*Volkstum*) focuses exclusively on the biological element. No less weight is given to the mental element; only the two together—the natural and spiritual traits—form the basis of the individuality of the *Volkstum,* form that entirety . . . that whole which—bound by a particular law—gives rise to the divine . . . that constitutes a special human essence whose living form imbues its every member. (261 ff.)

Cf. furthermore:

Moreover, for National Socialism, *Volk* is not merely a number of people, rather it is a social structure, a unity, springing from the diversity of the groups formed by nature and history . . . This emphasis on the significance of the racial basis of the *Volk* gives rise to the National Socialist demand for protection of these blood-related forces through the state. It is the basis for legislation in the interests and for the health of the *Volk,* to maintain and strengthen the perpetuation of the racial substance by preventing the admixture of foreign blood and fostering the sound elements of the German *Volk,* above all those constituent parts which stem from the countryfolk. (244)

In similar vein is Koellreuter, *Deutsches Verfassungsrecht* (1936), 67; Wolf, "Das Rechtsideal des nationalsozialistischen Staates," 352.

56. See Gerber, "Der politische Begriff des Volkes" (1940); he places the *völkisch* idea to the fore, while rejecting other national ideas (e.g., that of the French, which demands an avowal of *la civilisation française,* "thereby opening wide the door to the assimilation of foreign races"). Spirit and nature are inseparable. The "natural" ("racially determined") *Volk* is at the same time a political *Volk* ("In our historical situation the racial identity of the *Volk* has at last taken up a dominant position in the political sphere") (133 ff., 139 ff., 146 ff., 153).

57. Cf. Höhn, "Rechtsgemeinschaft und Volksgemeinschaft" (1935); Höhn, "Volk und Verfassung" (1937); Koellreuter, *Grundriß der allgemeinen Staatslehre* (1933); Koellreuter, *Deutsches Verfassungsrecht;* Koellreuter, *Deutsches Verwaltungsrecht* (1938); Walz, *Artgleichheit gegen Gleichartigkeit* (1938); Walz, *Der Begriff der Verfassung* (1942); Gerber, *Staatsrechtliche Grundlinien des neuen Reiches,* 6 ff., 14, 19.

58. For a fuller account, see Walz, *Artgleichheit gegen Gleichartigkeit*, in particular 14 f.

59. Höhn, "Volk und Verfassung," 107.

60. Stolleis, *Gemeinwohlformeln im nationalsozialstischen Recht* (1974), 255.

61. Ibid.

62. Scheuner, "Die nationale Revolution," 269, 272.

63. Huber, *Verfassungsrecht des Großdeutschen Reiches* (1939), 141 f. Schmitt, *Staat, Bewegung, Volk* (1933), 46.

64. Rauschning, *Gespräche mit Hitler,* 44.

65. Scheuner, "Der Gleichheitsgedanke," 243 ff., 260, 267; H. H. Lammers, "Staatsführung im Dritten Reich," *Reich und Ostmark* (1938): 9 ff., 13.

66. A. Mohler, *Die Konservative Revolution* (1950), 94, states that there were 430 such organizations.

67. Mohrmann, *Antisemitismus, Ideologie und Geschichte* (1972), 111, 136 ff., 149 ff.; Pulzer, *Die Entstehung des politischen Antisemitismus* (1966), 235 ff., 245 ff., 251 ff., 264 ff.

68. For further details, see Pulzer, *Die Entstehung des politischen Antisemitismus*, 264 ff.

69. Scheuner, "Der Gleichheitsgedanke," 245 ff.

70. For an account of the basic principles of the National Socialist concept of equality, see Walz, *Artgleichheit gegen Gleichartigkeit.*

71. See also U. Scheuner's essay "Der Gleichheitsgedanke," 245 ff.

72. Ibid., 259. The *völkisch* constitution no longer embodies the idea of the citizen, but instead of the "productive and devoted *Volksgenosse* (national comrade)," a concept that takes into account the natural differences between people and the "differences between Führer and followers."

73. For further details, see Fraenkel, *Der Doppelstaat*, 175; Schmitt had taken over from Hegel the tendency—inherent in Liberalism—to use the concrete as a weapon against the abstract.

74. C. Schmitt, *Die drei Arten des rechtswissenschaftlichen Denkens* (1934), 13, 52.

75. Wolf, "Das Rechtsideal des nationalsozialistischen Staates," 352.

76. I refer here to a series of essays, all of which polemicize against the "formalization of rights" in the liberal epoch. The series opened with an essay by the Nazi ideologue Höhn, "Form und Formalismus im Rechtsleben" (1934). This was followed by Forsthoff, "Der Formalismus im öffentlichen Recht" (1934); Schaffstein, "Formalismus im Strafrecht" (1934), 249 ff.; Hildebrandt, "Formalismus im bürgerlichen Recht" (1934); Noack (*Gauführer* of the League of National Socialist German Jurists), "Formalismus im Strafprozeß" (1934), 357 f.; Wagner, "Formalismus in der bürgerlichen Rechtspraxis" (1934); see also Fraenkel, *Der Doppelstaat*, 172 f.

77. For an overview, see Anschütz, *Die Verfassung des Deutschen Reiches* (1933), 521 ff. (This commentary was published before the Nazi seizure of power.)

78. Stuckart and Globke, *Reichsbürgergesetz* (1936), introduction, 3, 13, 24 f.: "The doctrine of the equality of all men and of the basic, unrestricted freedom of the individual vis-à-vis the state is countered in the National Socialist philosophy by the harsh but essential acknowledgment of the natural inequality and diversity of man." Cf. also Scheuner, "Der Gleichheitsgedanke," 249 f., with examples.

79. Schmitt, *Die drei Arten des rechtswissenschaftlichen Denkens*, 13, 52.

80. Stuckart and Globke, *Reichsbürgergesetz*; cf. also Scheuner, "Der Gleichheitsgedanke."

81. The Reich Supreme Court expressed the view that the Weimar Constitution had "lost its validity through the upheaval of 1933" (judgment of February 17, 1939 [*DR* (1939): 1785]).

82. *RGBl.* I 83; according to the preamble, the order was to serve the protection against "acts of Communist violence," but de facto it constituted a *general* waiver of the reservations of basic legal rights; cf. Supreme Court for Criminal Cases, 69, 342 f.; OVG (Prussian Administrative Supreme Court) 98, 93; 96, 99; Administrative Court, Hamburg, *RVerwBl.* (1935): 1045; Supreme Court, Berlin, *RVerwBl.* (1936): 61 (extension of the scope of the order to other parties when "this

serves the defense against Communism in the broadest sense"); Reich Administrative Court, *DVerw* (1943): 288; for a summary of the "unrestricted interpretation" of the order in legal theory, see Reich Administrative Court, *DVerw* (1943): 288.

83. Huber, "Bedeutungswandel der Grundrechte" (1932), 1 ff., 30 ff.; Huber, "Die Rechtsstellung des Volksgenossen" (1936), illustrated by the example of property rights. Maunz, "Das Ende des subjektiven öffentlichen Rechts" (1935), 71 ff. (92 ff.); cf. also Löwenstein, "Law in the Third Reich" (1936). For a detailed account of the dismantling of basic rights, see Echterhölter, *Das öffentliche Recht im Nationalsozialismus* (1970), 15 ff., with numerous examples.

84. Cf., for example, Law on the Revocation of Naturalization and the Deprivation of German Citizenship of July 14, 1933 (*RGBl.* I 480), which provided for the seizure of assets in cases of forfeiture of citizenship. Emigrants always had their assets confiscated (cf. statement of the *Oberfinanzdirektionspräsident* [head of finance authority], Berlin, February 2, 1942, quoted in Schorn, *Der Richter im Dritten Reich* [1959], 456 ff.). See also sec. 2 of the order of July 26, 1933 (*RGBl.* I 538), which threatened anyone making antigovernment statements abroad with deprival of citizenship and confiscation of assets.

85. *DJ* (1934): 64.

86. E. R. Huber, "Anm. zur Entscheidung des Sondergerichts Darmstadt," *JW* (1934): 1747.

87. Cf. Hoche, "Grundsätze, Aufbau und Verwaltung des nationalsozialistischen Staates" (1934), 3: "Even though—as was unavoidable with a measure decreed on the basis of art. 48, par. 2 of the Reich constitution—this order only invalidated basic rights 'until further notice,' in actual fact it has invalidated these basic rights for good. For basic rights that automatically afford the individual firm areas of freedom from state influence are incompatible with the totalitarian principle of the National Socialist state"; see also OVG of October 10, 1940, *RVerwBl.* (1941): 56. For further details, see Stolleis, *Gemeinwohlformeln im nationalsozialstischen Recht*, 242 ff.: "Seen from the point of view of the weltanschauung of the Third Reich, the individual rights of the subject, with all that is inherent in this concept of liberal science, will not be recognized, since National Socialism takes the view that the individual is a member of the state organism, with no position other than within the state, and therefore has no right to make a legal claim against the state based on such a position."

88. For an account of the tacit abolition of basic rights, see Kluge and Krüger, *Verfassung und Verwaltung*, 165; for further details, see Echterhölter, *Das öffentliche Recht im Nationalsozialismus*, 26 ff.

89. Cf. Poetzsch-Heffter, Ule, and Dernedde, *Jahrbuch des öffentlichen Rechts*, 1 ff., 265.

90. Special Court (SG), Hamburg, *DRiZ* (1935), no. 553, regarding the religious liberty of Jehovah's Witnesses.

91. Schmitt, "Ein Jahr nationalsozialistischer Verfassungsstaat" (1934), 27; Poetzsch-Heffter, Ule, and Dernedde, *Jahrbuch des öffentlichen Rechts*, 1 ff., 265; initially, judicial proceedings were quite correctly based on the assumption of the continuing validity of the Weimar Constitution, insofar as this was not formally invalidated (Supreme Court for Civil Cases, 1939, 396; 143, 107, 145, 373 f.; 147, 253; Supreme Court for Criminal Cases, 67, 130, 221; Reich Supreme Court, *JW* [1934]: 767; *DR* [1939]: 1785; OVG 91, 136; Württemberg State [Superior] Administrative Court, May 16, 1933, *RVerwBl.* [1934]: 979; Thüringen Administrative Supreme Court, January 16, 1935, *DVerw* [1935]: 148); increasingly, however, the courts represented the view that even those articles not expressly abrogated were to be considered as "effectively" invalid (Supreme Court for Civil Cases [Reichsgericht], 142, 393; Special Court, Hamburg, of March 15, 1935, *RVerwBl.* [1935]: 700; and Special Court, Schwerin, verdict of March 15, 1935, *JW* [1935]: 2082; Special Court, Breslau, of April 27, 1935, *DRiZ* [1935]: 440). To a certain extent, the question of the continuing validity of the Weimar Constitution was left open (Supreme Court for Civil Cases, 69, 345; Prussian Administrative Supreme Court, Hamburg, *RVerwBl.* [1938]: 253) or it was interpreted from the "standpoint of the . . .

political goals of the National Socialist state" (Württemberg VGH [State Superior Administrative Court], *DVerw* [1938]: 126; State Superior Court, Jena, *ZAKfDtRecht* [1938]: 712; OVG, *DVerw* [1936]: 128; OVG, 100, 325; Sächsen Administrative Supreme Court, *Jahrbuch* [1939], 7); thereby the courts tacitly nullified its continued validity on both grounds (cf. Reich Administrative Court, September 3, 1942, *DR* [1943]: 660). For more details on the position of the administration of justice, see Echterhölter, *Das öffentliche Recht im Nationalsozialismus*, 164 f.

92. State Court of Appeals, Dresden, *JW* (1935): 1949.

93. Special Court, Hamburg, *RVerwBl* (1935): 700; BadVGH, *DVerw* (1938): 503.

94. Schmitt, "Ein Jahr nationalsozialistischer Verfassungsstaat," 27: "It therefore goes without saying that any exploration of the question of the creation of the [new] constitution must begin with the simple phrase: the Weimar Constitution is no longer valid."

95. In any case, the basic rights of the Weimar Constitution not specified in the order of February 28, 1933, were later rendered de facto null and void by a series of regulations. For more on the nullification of a guaranteed legal authority (art. 105) see the Law on the Establishment of the People's Court of April 24, 1934 (*RGBl.* I 340), the July 3, 1934 (*RGBl.* I 529), Law on the Suppression of Treasonable Attacks of June 30 and July 1–2, 1934 (Röhm putsch), and the so-called Decree on the Competence of the Courts (*Zuständigkeitsverordnung*) of February 21, 1940 (*RGBl*, I 405). For more on the nullification of the principle *nulla poena sine lege* (art. 116), cf. sec. 2 of the Penal Code following the Penal Code Amendment Law of 1935, see, further, Gürtner and Freisler, *Das Neue Strafrecht* (1936), 77; for more on the nullification of professional and commercial freedom (art. 151), see Echterhölter, *Das öffentliche Recht im Nationalsozialismus*, 37 ff., with details of all the individual regulations. Employee participation was de facto annulled by secs. 2 and 5, par. 1, of the Law for the Regulation of National Labor of January 20, 1934 (*RGBl.* I 45) since it stipulated that "the works leader . . . was responsible for all decisions concerning the running of the enterprise" and only a shop steward acting in an advisory capacity would be allowed in the place of the works commission. For an account of the abrogation of the freedom of religious association (art. 137), see Special Court, Darmstadt, of March 26, 1934 (*JW* [1934]: 1747), which had still affirmed the validity of art. 137 WRV for the Jehovah's Witnesses. Contrast with the State Court of Appeals, Dresden, *JW* (1935): 1949. The Reich Supreme Court declared art. 137 WRV still valid but justified a ban on religious communities "where these were irreconcilable with the order of the state" (*JW* [1935]: 3378).

96. For further details, see Fraenkel, *Der Doppelstaat*, 40 ff., with numerous examples from judicial proceedings.

97. For an account of the concept of equality in the Weimar period, see Anschütz, *Die Verfassung des deutschen Reiches*, 14th ed., 521 ff.; Triepel, *Goldbilanzenverordnung und Vorzugsaktien* (1924); Leibholz, *Die Gleichheit vor dem Gesetz* (1925); Aldag, *Die Gleichheit vor dem Gesetz in der Reichsverfassung* (1924); Kaufmann, "Die Gleichheit vor dem Gesetz" (1926); Rümelin, *Die Gleichheit vor dem Gesetz* (1928); Bindewald, *Der Gleichheitsgedanke im Rechtsstaat der Gegenwart* (1931), with numerous examples; Huber, "Bedeutungswandel der Grundrechte" (1932), 1 ff. (30 ff.); Nef, *Gleichheit und Gerechtigkeit* (1941).

98. Reuß, "Partei und Staat im Dritten Reich" (1935); H. O. Ziegler, "Autoritärer und totaler Staat," *AöR*, NF, 24, 122 ff.; W. Frick, *Jahrbuch des öffentlichen Rechts*, vol. 22, 25 ("authority of the total state"); Lammers, "Die Staatsführung im Dritten Reich" (1934); Gerber, *Staatsrechtliche Grundlinien des neuen Reiches*, 26 f.; Schmitt, *Staat, Bewegung, Volk*, 33 f., 46; E. R. Huber, *AöR*, NF, 24, 250 (discussed in Leibholz, *Die Auflösung der liberalen Demokratie in Deutschland* [1933]). For an account of the total incorporation of the individual in the Nazi, see Kirchheimer, "Die Rechtsordnung des Nationalsozialismus" (1971), 356 ff.; Fraenkel, *Der Doppelstaat*, 82 ff., with examples.

99. Reuß, "Partei und Staat im Dritten Reich," with a discussion of the book by Meißner and Kaisenberg, *Staats- und Verfassungsrecht im Dritten Reich*, in which he explains: "The total state

also contains . . . *in nuce* the demand for a total domination of the mind" and "affects the entire content of social existence" (Scheuner, "Die nationale Revolution," 203–4); in this respect see also Ziegler, "Autoritärer und totaler Staat," *AöR*, NF, 24, 122 ff.

100. AG, Berlin-Lichterfelde, *Das Recht* (1935), no. 8015; AG, Hamburg, *Das Recht* (1935), no. 8016; AG, Wilster, *JW* (1938): 1264; *Sondergericht* Breslau, *DRiz* (1935), no. 554; AG, Frankfurt/M.-Höchst, *DR* (1937): 466.

101. Krüger, "Volksgemeinschaft statt subjektiver Rechte" (1935), 57 ff.; Kirchheimer, "Die Rechtsordnung des Nationalsozialismus," 356 ff. (370).

102. O. Dietrich: "The individual, according to today's teaching, has neither the right nor the duty to exist, for all rights and duties derive initially from the community" (*Völkischer Beobachter*, December 11, 1937).

103. Hitler, *Mein Kampf* (1939), 436 ff.

104. Siebert, "Gemeinschaft und bürgerliches Recht" (1934) ("Rather than killing off the individual, the community raises him to a higher level"); in this respect see also von Scheurl, "Grundsätze deutscher Verwaltung" (1934).

105. Huber, "Bedeutungswandel der Grundrechte" (1932); Dennewitz, *Das nationale Deutschland, ein Rechtsstaat* (1933), 28 f.; Kluge and Krüger, *Verfassung und Verwaltung*, 159 ff.; no. 1.4: "National Socialism safeguards property, equality, religious freedom, but always in relation to the community. . . . Justice ends with the protection of the national community; injustice begins with the infringement of its interests."

106. Kluge and Krüger, *Verfassung und Verwaltung*, 356.

107. Vogel, *Vom Wesen des ständischen Rechts* (1937), 3 ff.

108. Lammers, "Staatsführung im Dritten Reich," 9 ff., 13.

109. Scheuner, "Der Gleichheitsgedanke," 253, 255; Huber, "Bedeutungswandel der Grundrechte," 1 ff., 30 ff., 34 ff.; Dennewitz, *Das nationale Deutschland, ein Rechtsstaat*, 26 ff.; Krüger, "Verfassungsrecht und Verfassungswirklichkeit" (1943).

110. Scheuner, "Der Gleichheitsgedanke," 253; Lammers, "Staatsführung im Dritten Reich," 9 ff.; Schmitt, *Staat, Bewegung, Volk* (1933), 46; Koellreuter, *Volk und Staat*, in particular 9, 16 ff.; Höhn, "Form und Formalismus im Rechtsleben."

111. Huber, "Bedeutungswandel der Grundrechte," 30, 32 ff., 79 ff., 89 ff., 93 ff.

112. Cf. instead of many others Hegel, *Grundlinien der Philosophie des Rechts* (1955), 207 f., 212 f. (secs. 257 ff.); Hegel, *Vorlesungen über die Philosophie der Geschichte* (1961), 87 f.

113. Krüger, "Verfassungsrecht und Verfassungswirklichkeit," 228; and the sources mentioned in introduction, III, 1, of this volume ("The Führer Principle"). The same view was expressed by the Reich Supreme Court in its judgment of September 8 and 22, 1938 (*JW* [1938]: 2955 ff.), which stated that even though many measures (taken by the state) gave "the impression" that "the state does not act in accordance with justice and legality, but arbitrarily," this could be ruled out for the simple reason that "the state . . . is the arbiter of its own justice"; cf. Fraenkel, *Der Doppelstaat*, 89, 93.

114. Best, *Jahrbuch der Akademie für Deutsches Recht* (1937), 132 ff., 132.

115. Huber, "Bedeutungswandel der Grundrechte," 30, 32 f., 91 ff.

116. "One side of the triangle is formed by the 'Labor Front.' This is the social community, where there are no classes, where everyone helps everyone else. Here, everyone feels safe, receiving the community's support and advice, engaging in its leisure activities. Here, everyone is valued equally highly. Here, equality prevails. . . . The second side is that of the professional organization. Here, the individual is ranked separately and called upon to work for the community according to his abilities and qualities. Here, skill is the deciding factor. Here, people are valued according to their skills. . . . The third side is formed by the Party, which through one or other of its many organizations embraces every German who is not in some way unworthy. In the Party, everyone is called upon to take part in the leadership of the nation. Here, devotion and strength of will are

decisive. Here, every Party comrade is equal, but he must accept the rank accorded him, which is immutable" (Rauschning, *Gespräche mit Hitler*, 178 ff.).

117. For further details see Scheuner, "Der Gleichheitsgedanke," 250, 253, 255, 259 f.

118. Ibid., 275 f.

119. Speech by Hitler to the congress of the German Workers' Front on May 10, 1933, quoted in Scheuner, "Die nationale Revolution," 261 ff., 270 n. 23.

120. Ibid., 270.

121. Kluge and Krüger, *Verfassung und Verwaltung:* "To be a national comrade (*Volksgenosse*) does not mean one has inalienable rights"; rather it is "a responsibility and a duty"; rights derive from this only as an "assertion of equality of duty" of all other national comrades (164). For an account of the individual as the bearer of duties ("special tasks"), see Vogel, *Vom Wesen des ständischen Rechts*, 16 ff., 19 ff.

122. The duties in question were military service (sec. 1, WehrG of May 21, 1935), personal duty of commitment (Reich Requisition Law of July 13, 1938, *RGBl.* I 887; in the version of September 1, 1939, *RGBl.* I 1639, 1645), duty of service for tasks of special national importance (order of February 13, 1939, *RGBl.* I 206), labor service duty, air raid protection (Law on Air Raid Precautions of 26 June 1935, *RGBl.* I 827), duty to provide assistance in accidents (sec. 330c *Penal Code*), fire protection duty (law of November 23, 1938, *RGBl.* I 1662), "preferential charges" (contributions for special services), and "community levies" (taxes and charges). In addition there was the "moral" obligation to deliver, to collect funds, to donate, etc. (Kluge and Krüger, *Verfassung und Verwaltung*, 357 f.).

123. Cf. the decision of the Reich Disciplinary Court of June 15, 1937 (*Zeitschrift für Beamtenrecht* 1937–38, 105), which found a civil servant—who for years had been at the forefront of the struggle for the *völkisch* idea—guilty of breach of duty because he had refused to give a donation to the Winter Relief Appeal, claiming that he had regularly given a considerable proportion of his income to private charities. The official had emphasized that his refusal to donate could not have any legal consequences in view of the constant official assurances that such donations were "voluntary." The Disciplinary Court countered: "The accused still holds onto a notion of . . . freedom in its crassest liberalistic form . . . for him freedom means the discretion to shirk any duties not expressly written down in the law. He has declined to contribute to a common cause because he wants to show that no one can compel him—a free man—to do something against his will." He had to recognize that he had "acted in abominable fashion, abusing the freedom granted him by the Führer as an expression of his trust in the German soul." W. Weimar, "Kann durch Polizeiverfügungen dem einzelnen Volksgenossen eine Pflicht zur Beflaggung auferlegt werden?" *RVerwBl.* (1937): 479 ff., asks whether hoisting the swastika flag at celebrations could be enforced by the police and comes to the conclusion that raising the flag, though not a legal obligation, was a manifestation of loyalty to the Führer. Not raising the flag could be a sign of shortcomings in Nazi training. He proposes a stay in a concentration camp to make up for this lacuna in the offender's education.

124. Lammers, "Staatsführung im Dritten Reich," 9 ff., 13: "In conscious and diametrical opposition to liberalism, National Socialism takes as its starting point a firm belief in the inequality of man . . . because nothing can be perfect, National Socialism prefers a—perhaps—just inequality over the unjust inequality of unrealistic Liberalism. . . . The *Volk* is primary . . . not the individual. . . . For the *Volk* life only makes sense when it has an eternal foundation in . . . the community of the *Volk*."

125. "It is not a question of doing away with the inequality of man but on the contrary of deepening it and—as in all great cultures—of making it law through insurmountable barriers. There are no equal rights for all. . . . I will, therefore, never accord other peoples the same rights as those I grant the Germans. Our mission is to subjugate other peoples. The vocation of the German nation is to provide the world with a new ruling elite" (Rauschning, *Gespräche mit Hitler*, 44).

126. Gütt, Linden, and Maßfeller, *Blutschutz und Ehegesundheitsgesetz* (1936), 226.

127. Lösener, "Die Hauptprobleme der Nürnberger Grundgesetze" (1935), 929 (931) (also BA R 58/243).

128. Cf. A. de Toqueville to Gobineau: "The theory of the perpetual inequality of races begets arrogance, tyrrany and depravity" (Schemann, *Briefwechsel Toqueville an Gobineau 1843–1859* [1908], 187).

129. Rousseau, "De l'inégalité parmi les hommes," in Rousseau, *Du contrat social* (1962), 90; similarly, Bracher, *Zeitgeschichtliche Kontroversen*, 99 f.; regarding the efficiency of National Socialist despotism, see also Kirchheimer, "Die Rechtsordnung des Nationalsozialismus," 356 ff. (358 ff.).

130. Forsthoff, *Der totale Staat*, 41.

131. Wolf, "Das Rechtsideal des nationalsozialistischen Staates," 352; he continues: "For our sense of justice would be more profoundly offended by insisting on the fiction of equality—whose falseness is commonly accepted—than any act of open and therefore resistible despotism"; cf. also Lösener, "Die Hauptprobleme der Nürnberger Grundgesetze," 929 (931).

132. Cf. Hegel, *Grundlinien der Philosophie des Rechts*, 270.

133. Reich Supreme Court of June 27, 1936, *Az. I* 297/35, *JW* (1936): 2529 ff., 2530. In this respect see also Lösener, "Die Hauptprobleme der Nürnberger Grundgesetze," 929 (931).

134. Mayer, *Deutsches Verwaltungsrecht* (1924), 9 f.

135. For further details, see Fraenkel, *Der Doppelstaat*, 96 ff., with numerous examples.

136. Ibid., 231 ff., 235.

137. Schmitt, *Staat, Bewegung, Volk*, 5 f.; Forsthoff, *Der totale Staat*, 38.

138. Forsthoff, *Der totale Staat*, 40.

139. Koellreuter, *Verfassungsrecht* (1938), 91 f.

140. Koellreuter, *Volk und Staat:* In the Führer state, the political elite is drawn from the "Movement" (16 f.).

141. Ipsen, *Das Problem der justizlosen Hoheitsakte* (1937), foreword.

142. Walz, *Artgleichheit gegen Gleichartigkeit*, 40; Poetzsch-Heffter, Ule, and Dernedde, *Vom deutschen Staatsleben, Jahrbuch für öffentliches Recht* 22 (1935): 1 ff., 265; clearly expressed in Lammers, "Staatsführung im Dritten Reich," *Reich und Ostmark* (1938): 9 ff., 13, according to which National Socialism strives for a "just inequality."

143. Vogel, *Von dem Wesen des ständischen Rechts* (1937) (every professional body has rights characteristic of its type [*arteigenes Recht*], 16 f.); similarly, Best, " 'Die Weimarer Verfassung' " (1939), 759 f.

144. Maunz, *Die Staatsaufsicht* (1938), 83 f.; he gives, by way of example, the exclusion of "people of alien race" (*Artfremde*) from "municipal swimming baths." The "equality of the racially identical" (*Artgleiche*), he says, shows that if equal treatment were not accorded exclusively to the racially identical, there would be no equality in this country.

145. Cf. Scheuner, "Die nationale Revolution," 261 ff., 267, 273, on equality between those of the same species and "aliens."

146. Ibid.; Forsthoff, *Der totale Staat*, 39 ff.; Walz, in his essay "Gleichheit und Rangordnung im Recht" (1941), expounds the necessity of "dissimilation" of "aliens" and the "racially appropriate representation of the gradual development of the nation as a whole" (2214). In a later essay, "Neue Grundlagen des Volksgruppenrechts," he demanded the "absolute dissimilation" of the racially dissimilar (Jews, Gypsies). *Völkisch* groups had to be treated according to their racial difference. Where "the line has to be drawn" cannot be decided in general terms but depends in part on the concrete political situation; at any rate it is necessary to preserve the cultural way of life of the *Volksgruppe* (school, language, church, welfare, education) (97). (Precisely these areas were the only ones left to the Jews after their exclusion from administration and business.) According to Klein, "Zur Stellung des Generalgouvernements" (1941), 227 ff., 262, the idea of *völkisch* inequality could also be applied to the way of life of ethnic groups (*Volksgruppen*) and states.

618 Notes to Pages 52–54

147. In particular Walz, "Gleichheit und Rangordnung im Recht," 2214 f.: "The dissimilation of the alien type can, among other things, lead to limitation of his legal status in certain areas of common law, to his exclusion from certain areas of communal life that serve the fundamental order of the *Volk*. The legal proceeding is not yet complete. . . . Having overcome . . . an abstract form of individual equality, we have only now created the space for genuine, rational equality in the sense of *suum cuique*." Walz puts forward the same view in his book *Artgleichheit gegen Gleichartigkeit*, 40, according to which the Reich Citizenship Law shows the "new legal approach to framing people's origins, also vis-à-vis a politically unsatisfactory transitional status." For a similar view, see Forsthoff, *Der totale Staat*, 39 ff., who welcomes the "great purge" that followed the arrival in office of the "national government," as well as the expatriation of political opponents ("renegades"); see also von Massow, "Die Tragweite der bisherigen Begriffe" (1936), 31: "Should the worthless (*Nichtwertige*) be deprived of rights? The development of the law has already shown the way to discover such enemies of the people (*Volksschädlinge*). One has only to think of the expatriation of numerous former Germans whose behavior led to loss of citizenship. Their exclusion from the national community occurred because they did not want to serve the nation, the state. It is inconceivable that such outcasts (*Volksfremde*) should enjoy the same legal rights as other national comrades (*Volksgenossen*)."

148. Poetzsch-Heffter, Ule, and Dernedde, *Vom deutschen Staatsleben, Jahrbuch für öffentliches Recht* 22 (1935): 265.

149. This is exemplified by Stuckart and Globke, *Reichsbürgergesetz*, 135: These principles of racial and population studies "consciously refrain from judging the question of the superiority of one race over another. They take as their basis merely physical and spiritual diversity of the races and peoples made of different racial types. The danger inherent in racial mixture does not stem from the difference of value, but the different characteristics of the races. There is no absolute ranking of the races; but there are mixtures of related races that can be accepted without hesitation as Reich citizens, and there are crossbreeds of alien races who are a pernicious racial influence and destructive of the *Volk*."

150. Scheuner, "Die nationale Revolution," 272.

151. Gütt and Linden, *Kommentar zum Ehegesundheitsgesetz* (1936), 226.

152. Cf. Forsthoff, *Der totale Staat*, 37.

153. Franzen, *Gesetz und Richter* (1935), 19 f.

154. "The National Socialist racial theory and its underlying racial principle do not lead to contempt or undervaluation of other peoples but rather to an acknowledgment of the tasks we must accomplish with respect to the appropriate maintenance and development of our own people" (Stuckart and Globke, *Reichsbürgergesetz*, 6).

155. Forsthoff, *Der totale Staat*, 37; cf. also Frank, *Nationalsozialistisches Handbuch für Recht und Gesetzgebung*, introduction, xviii: The only reason for this exclusion of the "influence of alien races" from public life is "to protect and . . . preserve the vigor of the German people"; similarly, Lösener, "Die Hauptprobleme der Nürnberger Grundgesetze."

156. Lösener, "Die Hauptprobleme der Nürnberger Grundgesetze."

157. See also Stuckart and Globke, *Reichsbürgergesetz*, comments on sec. 1 of the law; see further Gütt and Linden, *Kommentar zum Ehegesundheitsgesetz*, 225; foreign criticism of the law was "incomprehensible": after all, in the USA there were thirty states where to some extent the regulations prohibiting marriage between Negroes and whites went much further (17 ff.).

158. Lösener, "Die Hauptprobleme der Nürnberger Grundgesetze."

159. Fraenkel, *Der Doppelstaat*, 136.

160. Lorenzen, "Judentum und Judenfrage" (1939); in this sense see also Groß, *DR* (1939): 2 ff., 9.

161. Forsthoff, *Der totale Staat*, 31 ff., explains that racial differences should not automatically

mean enmity but that this would arise if the "racially different" impinge on the "territorial . . . or . . . spiritual Lebensraum of another people. That is why the Jew, without regard for good or bad faith and good or ill will, became an enemy and as such had to be removed as a threat." (Apparently, who played the role of enemy or aggressor was determined by the supposed victim.)

162. Best, *Jahrbuch der Akademie für Deutsches Recht* (1937), 132 ff., 132.

163. Ibid.

164. For further details, see Fraenkel, *Der Doppelstaat*, 93.

165. Cf., for example, compulsory military and labor service for Poles from the Annexed Eastern Territories who were "capable of Germanization" and who had attained German citizenship until revoked.

166. The order of September 20, 1941 (*MinbliV* [1941]: 1788), imposed on Jews (and Poles) a special "social compensation tax" in the form of a nondeductible 50% increase in income tax. By way of justification it was pointed out that Jews enjoyed the "protection of the Reich" without being German (Walk, *Als Jude in Breslau* [1975], 2). Membership in this "protective community" came at a high price. Incidentally, financial burdens were imposed on others in disfavor who came into conflict with the authorities; see also the judgment by the Reich Supreme Court in Supreme Court for Civil Cases, 155, 297, in the case of the mayor of Eutin, who was removed from his post after the seizure of power and taken into protective custody. Negotiations between his lawyer and the president of the higher administrative authority of the district (*Regierungspräsidium*) ended with a written declaration in which the mayor relinquished all claims with respect to salary and so forth and pledged to pay the government three thousand reichsmarks by way of compensation for the (supposed) damage to the reputation of the town of Eutin (despite the fact that the Civil Code does not recognize compensation for *dommage morale*). After this goal had been reached, the president of the district administration and the newly appointed mayor of Eutin showed magnanimity: both declared that the "affair was closed and further steps that might hinder the plaintiff in his career would not be undertaken. The government declared the protective custody order null and void with immediate effect" (Reich Supreme Court, ibid.). To rule out any further doubt, they requested a statement in which the plaintiff and his lawyer swore "that the declarations were given of their own free will and that no pressure was brought to bear." There was an epilogue to this trial when the plaintiff later contested his declaration, renouncing all claims because of coercion. In view of the decree issued by the minister of the interior accepting jurisdiction in the matter on the basis of the *Ausgleichsgesetz* (Law relating to Compensation of Social Benefits—a Nazi law comparable to the *Schutzgelder* levies paid by Jews in the Middle Ages) of December 13, 1934 (*RGBl.* I 1235), the courts refused to hear the case. The Reich Supreme Court confirmed the earlier judgments.

167. Too narrow in that sense is the view of Arendt, *Ursprünge und Elemente totaler Herrschaft* (1958), 39, who sees the chief characteristic of the totalitarian state in the problem of refugees and stateless persons and equates deprivation of rights with deprivation of citizenship. The Jews in Germany, as long as they remained there, were not stateless, but they were without rights.

168. The direction was indicated by sec. 1 of the Tax Adjustment Law; see also Prussian Supreme Court, Berlin, judgment of October 26, 1934, *Deutsches Strafrecht* (1935): 50.

169. State Labor Court of Appeals, Düsseldorf, of July 7, 1939, *Deutsches Gemein- und Wirtschaftsrecht* (1939): 194, quoted in Rüthers, *Die unbegrenzte Auslegung* (1973), 170; cf. also 188.

170. Reich Supreme Court, *JW* (1937): 99 f.

171. In the judgment of the State Court of Appeals, Halle, of September 12, 1941 (*DR* [1941] [A]: 2662), the private libel action brought by a Jew against a convict was turned down. The plaintiff—who was seriously disabled as a result of wounds sustained fighting on the front in World War I—had brought his action because the convicted prisoner had asserted that, like the rest of his race, he was "all lies and deceit." However, the protection of the honor of the plaintiff was considered secondary to that of the accused. The criminal court came to the conclusion that a Jew had no

honor: "the general personal honor of the German *Volksgenosse* must also be respected in someone who is temporarily deprived of the citizen's rights of honor, whereas the Jew stands outside the German national community with regard to protection of honor."

172. Weinkauff and Wagner, *Die deutsche Justiz*, 133, with reference to an article in the SS organ *Das Schwarze Korps*, ser. 50 (1938): 14, which had applauded such a judgment.

173. Weinkauff and Wagner, *Die deutsche Justiz*, 133, with reference to an article in *Das Schwarze Korps*, ser. 44 (1938): 11, in which various verdicts were attacked or applauded, depending on whether the evictions carried out by Aryan landlords against Jewish tenants had succeeded or failed.

174. Sächsen Administrative Supreme Court, November 20, 1937 (*DVerw* [1938]: 125).

175. Cf. Rosenberg, *Der Mythos des 20. Jahrhunderts* (1933), 558: "If a German woman voluntarily becomes involved with Negroes or Jews, she has no recourse to any form of legal protection for herself or her children, illegitimate or legitimate, who are excluded a priori from the rights of German citizenship"; implemented through sec. 4 of the Twelfth Decree to the Reich Citizenship Law of April 25, 1943 [*RGBl.* I 268]: "Jews and Gypsies cannot become nationals."

176. *RVerwBl.* 136, 360 f. (also in OVGE [Decisions of the Prussian Administrative Supreme Court], 97, 117 ff., 120); similarly, OVG 100, 141: "As German nationals, Gypsies do not enjoy special rights. In the sense that they are subject to general statutory duties, they are both without and within the protection of the law."

177. Eleventh Decree to the Reich Citizenship Law of November 25, 1941 (*RGBl.* I 722).

178. Regarding the different forms of anti-Semitism at that time, see G. Mann, *Der Antisemitismus* (1960), 11 ff., 18 ff., 22 ff.; Massing, *Vorgeschichte des politischen Antisemitismus* (1959); Mieses, *Der Ursprung des Judenhasses* (1923); Mohrmann, *Antisemitismus. Ideologie und Geschichte;* Pulzer, *Die Entstehung des politischen Antisemitismus;* Coudenhove and Kalergi, *Das Wesen des Antisemitismus* (1932); cf. also Löwenstein, *Psychoanalyse des Antisemitismus* (1968); Silbermann, "Exkurs über die Aufgaben der Soziologie zur Bekämpfung des Antisemitismus" (1967), 736 ff.

179. Sec. 5 of the First Implementing Decree to the Reich Citizenship Law of November 14, 1935 (*RGBl.* I, 1333); for further details, see Adler, *Der verwaltete Mensch*, 278; Groß, "Die rassenpolitischen Voraussetzungen zur Lösung der Judenfrage," 2 ff., 7, 9.

180. Cf. Coudenhove-Kalergi, *Das Wesen des Antisemitismus*, 243 ff., Mieses, *Der Ursprung des Judenhasses*, 21 ff., 222 ff., 305 ff., 308 ff., 312 ff., 318 ff., 346 ff. They point out that the most extreme racialists were also fierce opponents of Christianity. The Pan-Germans, for example, wanted to reestablish the Wotan cult; E. Dühring, *Der Ersatz der Religion durch Vollkommeneres* (Leipzig, 1926), calls for the abolition of Christianity. According to Günther, *Rassenkunde*, 428, Christianity had rendered the nation "totally helpless in the face of the alien Indian mentality." For similar comments, see 398 f. The abolition of Christianity was also a long-term goal of the NSDAP leadership.

181. Circular from the Reich Ministry of the Interior dated November 26, 1935 (*MinbliV* [1935]: 1430).

182. Günther, *Rassenkunde* (1930), 13; Groß, "Die rassenpolitischen Voraussetzungen zur Lösung der Judenfrage," 2 ff., 4 f.

183. Cf., for example, W. Groß (head of the NSDAP's Office of Racial Affairs), "Die rassenpolitischen Voraussetzungen zur Lösung der Judenfrage," 2, 5, 9; according to him, non-European races were—as a general principle—inferior to European races. The non-European nature of the Jews stemmed from the form of racial mixture found in their "Near Eastern" and "Oriental" branches; the negative characteristics of the Jews did not derive from these two racial types as such but from the "singular racial mixture that has become established . . . over a period of centuries." Whereas the Semitic peoples of the Arabian world doubtlessly had "estimable" and "likable" qualities, the Jews were an "inharmonious racial mixture"; given that the Arabs were similar to the Jews, it would be better not to speak of "anti-Semitism." The struggle was exclusively directed against "Near-Eastern/Oriental/Mediterranean" Jewry.

184. Gütt and Linden, *Kommentar zum Ehegesundheitsgesetz*, 22.

185. Günther, *Rassenkunde* (1930), 398 f., 415 ff., 417, 419 f.

186. Cf. among many others Günther, *Rassenkunde* (1922), which can be regarded as a classic of so-called scientific anti-Semitism. The description of the characteristics of the Jewish *Volkstum* (367 ff., 420 f.) consistently implies negative traits in facial form, odor, skin, hair, and expression of the eyes; it also specifies lisping, "slovenly gait," tendency to flat feet, and a marked propensity for certain mental and nervous diseases and for all criminal acts relating to money and commerce, such as theft, fraud, falsification of documents; a "calculating," "cunning" mentality; flexibility, "Jewish haste," and a particular prevalance of *sexuelle Applanation* (translates roughly as "sexual approximation"—meaning "effeminate males and masculine females"). It also asserts that a high proportion of Jews work in the intellectual professions, where success "depends largely on exerting influence over others" (373 ff., 379, 381 f., 426 ff.); the hypothesis of the "international Jewish conspiracy" is already recognizable (cf. 423 ff.).

187. See, for example, ibid., 385, 395 ff., 400; cf. also Gauch, *Neue Grundlagen der Rassenforschung* (1933), for whom only the Nordic race counted as a human race; all other races were (together with the animal world) "non-Nordic"; this was equated with the "subhuman," that is, a transitional stage from animal to man (17, 77 ff., 84 ff., 155, 175).

188. Günther, *Rassenkunde* (1922), 369 f.

189. W. Groß, "Die rassenpolitischen Voraussetzungen zur Lösung der Judenfrage," 2, 5, 9; Gütt and Linden, *Kommentar zum Ehegesundheitsgesetz*, 22.

190. For further details, see Phelps, "Hitlers 'grundlegende' Rede," 395, reprint of the speech on 400 ff.

191. Hitler, *Mein Kampf* (1939), 297 ff.; for more details, see table talk of May 29, 1942: "The manner in which the Jewish police beat their coreligionists in the ghettos—worse than the German police during the period of 'struggle' against National Socialism—shows 'the whole crudeness of the Jewish nature.' " So-called highly cultivated Jews, doctors and lawyers from European countries, were totally ghettoized within two weeks, running around in kaftans. What clearer proof could there be "that the Jews . . . are Asians and not Europeans. They should not be sent to Siberia—that would only harden them. They should be sent to Africa to an unhealthy climate" (Picker, *Hitlers Tischgespräche* [1968], 172).

192. Remarkably, it was a Jewish contemporary, no less, who called for the book to be taken seriously (Walk, *Als Jude in Breslau*, 34).

193. Hitler, *Mein Kampf* (1939), 310 f.

194. Regarding the anti-Semitism of the NSDAP, see the recent illuminating essay by Goldhagen, "Weltanschauung und Erlösung" (1976); he puts forward the view that the anti-Semitism of the Nazis was not only a political instrument but sprang from the most deeply held convictions (392 f.).

195. Hitler, *Mein Kampf* (1939), 160, 295 ff. (297 ff.), 302 ff.; the most important characteristics of the Aryan was his idealism, that is, "capacity for sacrifice" and the "readiness to do his duty" (293 f.).

196. Cf. Schmitt, "Die deutsche Rechtswissenschaft" (1936), 1194 ff., which says among other things, "The relationship of Jewish thinking to the German intellect is as follows: the Jew has a parasitic, mercantile attitude toward our intellectual work. By virtue of his talents as a trader, he often has a strong sense of what is genuine. That is his instinct as a parasite, a true merchant."

197. Von Schwerin-Krosigk, *Freiheit und Gebundenheit im germanischen Staat* (1933).

198. Cf. Stuckart and Schiedermair, *Rasse- und Erbpflege in der Gesetzgebung des Reiches* (1942), 12: "This [Jewish] race—as the Führer stressed in his speech to the Party labor rally—is neither intellectually nor morally superior; on the contrary, it is by both criteria a thoroughly inferior race. Therefore, the extermination of the Jews is justified not only by the different nature but the different value of Jewry."

199. Hitler, *Mein Kampf* (1939), 302 ff. For more on the period of assimilation, see G. A. Walz,

DR (1942) (A): 2 ff.: "It appears to us today that this whole period of assimilation was a comprehensive attempt at mimicry. The blame can also be placed at the door of the French revolution with its notions of equality."

200. Cf. the remarks of R. Freisler: "Those with Jewish blood are lost to the community. Jewish blood makes Judases"; for more details, see the outcome of congresses of the League of National Socialist German Jurists of October 3–4, 1936, on the theme "The Jews in Jurisprudence" and November 19–21, 1936, on "German Science and the Jews." For example, a speech by Joh. von Leers, supervisor of the Berlin Academy of Administrative Studies (later a professor in Jena), contained the following "insights": that "in Antiquity—the Jews were considered the embodiment of criminality"; the "Jewish heroes of the Old Testament" were convicts and criminals. "Jewishness is genetic criminality. . . . Every people has the right to weed out genetic criminals" (all quotations in Göppinger, *Die Verfolgung der Juristen jüdischer Abstammung* [1963], 72 ff.).

201. For more details, see Goldhagen, "Weltanschauung und Erlösung," 385 f., 400.

202. For further details, see Fraenkel, *Der Doppelstaat*, 231.

203. Hitler, in Rauschning, *Gespräche mit Hitler*, 220, 223, 227; "The Jew remains our worldwide enemy"; "The Jew is the antihuman." Replying to Rauschning's question whether the Jews should be destroyed, Hitler said: "No," for "then we would have to invent him. One needs a visible enemy, not an invisible one." The Germans, not the Jews, should be God's "chosen people." In the mideighties, however, the source cited here was revealed to be a fake (cf. F. J. Schoeps, *Frankfurter Allgemeine Zeitung*, no. 183, August 10, 1985, 8; K. Janßen, *Die Zeit*, no. 30, July 19, 1985, 16).

204. Hitler, *Mein Kampf* (1939), 547 ff., 616 ff., 692 ff.

205. Cf. an excerpt from the "propaganda speech" by the Reich minister for education of the people and propaganda in confidential information no. 25/318 of May 21, 1943: "The Jews are to blame for this war. And with that they are also to blame for what this war has brought the German people in terms of grief, sorrow, discomfort, privations, oppression, and adversity. . . . We must always keep sight of the fact that the end of the war must be followed by an anti-Jewish world revolution that will destroy the influence of the Jews everywhere in the world" (*Verfügungen*, 4:461 f.). See also Goldhagen, "Weltanschauung und Erlösung," 389, 392.

206. For more about the racial character of the war in the East, see Hillgruber, "Die 'Endlösung' und das deutsche Ostimperium" (1970), 137 ff.

207. Cf. Feldscher, "Rassenpflege und Erbpflege im deutschen Recht" (Feldscher was an *Oberregierungsrat* in the Reich Ministry of the Interior), in *Reichsrechtspflege und Verwaltung, 1943. Die Juden und die Justiz*, written at the request of the Reich Ministry of the Interior by Dr. S. Lorenzen, *Amtsgerichtsrat* in the Reich Ministry of the Interior; Streicher, *Die Judengesetze Großdeutschlands* (1939); Breusing, "Die Juden" (1936); Meyer, "Das jüdische Hehlerrecht" (1937); Ruth, "Wucherund Wucherrecht der Juden im Mittelalter" (1937); Franz, "Der Jude im katholischen Kirchenrecht" (1937); Claßen, "Der Judeneid" (1937); Köhler, "Die Juden in Deutschland" (1937); Lorenzen, "Judentum und Judenfrage" (a report on a series of evening lectures at the University of Berlin, January 12–28, 1939, on the theme of "Jewry and the Jewish Question"); Lorenzen, "Das Eindringen der Juden in die Justiz vor 1933" (1939), 731 ff., 768 ff., 958 ff.; Lorenzen, "Die Rechtsstellung der Juden vor der Emanzipation" (1939), 1949 ff.; Menzel, *Minderheitenrecht und Judenfrage* (two lectures given to the League of National Socialist German Jurists, Hamburg, on February 17 and April 28, 1933); von Medeazza, "Judenfrage und Judengesetzgebung in Europa" (1941); for more details, see NSRB, ed., "Das Judentum in der Rechtswissenschaft" (undated), which contained the discussions of a scientific meeting of the NSRB in 1936. It includes the following titles: (1) "Die Deutsche Rechtswissenschaft im Kampf gegen den jüdischen Geist," (2) "Das Judentum in der Wirtschaftswissenschaft," (3) "Judentum und Verbrecher," (4) "Judentum und Strafrecht," (5) "Der Einfluß des Judentums in Staatsrecht und Staatslehre," (6) "Der Einfluß jüdischer Theoretiker auf die deutsche Völkerrechtslehre," (7) "Das Judentum im Handels- und Rechtsverkehrsrecht," (8) "Rechtsquellen-

lehre und Judentum," and (9) "Judentum und Wettbewerb." For an account of the conceptual world of anti-Semitism, see Bein, "Der jüdische Parasit" (1965).

208. Cf., for example, the remarks of Schmitt in his lecture "Die deutsche Rechtswissenschaft im Kampf gegen den jüdischen Geist" at the conference of the Reich Group of High School Teachers in the *NS-Rechtswahrerbund* (Nazi Association of Law Officers), October 3–4, 1936, *DJZ* (1936): 1194 ff.: "An exact list must be drawn up if we are to continue the work of librarianship that is necessary to cleanse our libraries and save our students from confusion." Cf. also a speech by the *Reichsrechtsführer* H. Frank to the Reich Group of High School Teachers of the NSRB in Berlin on the theme of "Das Judentum in der Rechtswissenschaft," October 3, 1936 (BA All. Proz. 1 ZVII B 1, 60 f.; also as Nuremberg doc., NG-778); according to this, (1) Jews could never represent German law; (2) German jurisprudence was reserved for "men as specified in the racial legislation of the Third Reich"; (3) there were to be no new editions of works by Jewish authors; (4) all Jewish works were to be removed from public libraries; these works were "merely the views of foreign observers of German juridical ideas" and had "nothing whatsoever to do with German jurisprudence"; and (5) quotations from Jewish works could be understood only as illustrations of "a typical Jewish mentality."

209. Cf. the declaration of the League of National Socialist German Jurists of March 14, 1933, which demanded the "purging of all German courts of judges and officials of foreign races" (quoted in Schorn, *Die Gesetzgebung des Nationalsozialismus als Mittel der Machtpolitik* [1963], 84); for more details, see the directive of the NSDAP leadership of March 28, 1933, on the formation of an "Action Committee for the *Preplanned Implementation of the Boycott* [author's emphasis] of Jewish businesses, Jewish goods, Jewish doctors, and Jewish lawyers" on April 1, 1933 (quoted in Göppinger, review of Schorn, *Die Gesetzgebung des Nationalsozialismus als Mittel der Machtpolitik*, 783).

210. Cf. Hitler's remarks as reported in Hillgruber, "Die 'Endlösung' und das deutsche Ostimperium," 137: "When our best soldiers fell at the front [in the World War], at least the vermin could be exterminated at home. . . . If twelve or fifteen thousand of these Hebrew corrupters of the nation had been given a whiff of the poison gas that hundreds of thousands of the very best of our German soldiers from all classes and professions had to suffer in the field, the sacrifice of millions at the front would not have been in vain. On the contrary: the timely elimination of twelve thousand of these scoundrels would have saved a million promising young German lives." As early as summer 1933, Hitler told Rauschning that the "Jews were Germany's best protection, its security. For if the foreign powers did not desist from their boycott, he would take from the Jews in the same measure as Germany was being damaged by the boycott. When there was nothing more to take away, there would still be precious Jewish lives"; "Streicher . . . has suggested to me that, in the next war, we should send them out ahead of our skirmish lines. That would be the best way of shielding our soldiers. I'll give it some thought. . . . Everything we undertake to do, will be done. I will not make compromises" (Rauschning, *Gespräche mit Hitler*, 86 f.). Concerning the authenticity of Rauschning's book, see note 203 above.

211. Goldhagen, "Weltanschauung und Erlösung," 381.

212. For further details, see ibid., 388 f.

213. Hillgruber, "Die 'Endlösung' und das deutsche Ostimperium," 135 ff.; Hillgruber emphasizes the unbreakable link between politics and anti-Semitism in the East and the purely power-motivated politics in the West.

214. For further details, see Jan T. Gross, *Polish Society under German Occupation* (1979), 39, 49.

215. Cf. Gütt and Linden, *Kommentar zum Ehegesundheitsgesetz* (concerning sec. 6 of the First Implementing Order to the Blood Protection Law of November 14, 1935 [*RGBl.* I 1334]): " 'Alien blood' within the meaning of sec. 6 refers mainly to the Negro bastards left over from the period of French occupation and Gypsies currently in Germany" (226). For a fuller account of discrimination against the Gypsies, see H. J. Döring, *Die Zigeuner im nationalsozialistischen Staat* (1964).

216. Circular of the Reich and Prussian ministers of the interior of June 5, 1936, concerning the establishment of an "international central office for the campaign against the Gypsies" in Vienna (*MinbliV* [1936], no. 27, 783); and of June 6, 1936, concerning "fighting the Gypsy pestilence" (785). The decree of June 6, 1936, said among other things: "The Gypsies, with their restless wanderings across the countryside, living mainly from theft, swindle, and begging, still constitute a plague. It is difficult to get the Gypsy people, who are alien to the German *Volkstum*, to accept an ordered, civilized way of life based on honest work. . . . I would ask that the following be taken into consideration: . . . ruthless action in response to all crimes committed by wandering Gypsies."

217. Cf. OVG of December 5, 1935, OVGE, 97, 117 ff., 120.

218. *DJ* (1942): 25 ff. (30).

219. Scheuner, "Die nationale Revolution," 245 f.

220. Von zur Mühlen, *Rassenideologien*, 243 f.; a different view is expressed by Gross, *Polish Society under German Occupation*, 39, 49, who supports the theory of the racial motivation of Nazi administrative policy.

221. Decree on the Regulation of Nationality Questions of January 20, 1942 (*RGBl.* I 40), which also empowered the minister of the interior to award so-called collective naturalization.

222. This decree was drafted in a secret Reich Ministry of the Interior document (signed by Dr. Globke) addressed to the head of the Party Chancellery, dated September 19, 1944 (Main Commission Warsaw, Archive, Government of General Government, Central Department of Internal Administration II/140; transcript). This regulation concerned primarily those "persons of foreign race" who were fighting in the Wehrmacht and the Waffen-SS and was intended as a reward for services rendered. This plan must not be confused with the awarding of German citizenship on entry into the Wehrmacht and the Waffen-SS (Führer decree of May 19, 1943, *RGBl.* I 315), which applied solely to foreigners "of German origin."

223. Günther, *Rassenkunde* (1930), 6: "There are Germanic, Romance, and Slavonic languages but not a Germanic, Romance, and Slavonic race."

224. As early as the spring of 1934, Hitler made the following remarks to H. Rauschning on the subject of the Slav national character (Rauschning, *Gespräche mit Hitler*, 128 f.): "Anyway, we've already got far too much Slav blood in our veins." In this area,

an asocial, inferior section of the population is gradually edging its way into the position of a leading social class. . . . This is a source of great danger for the German people. . . . I admit that the danger will not be reduced by the forthcoming occupation of mixed Slav areas, where there will be no quick way of ridding ourselves of the Slav population. . . . We have a duty to depopulate such areas, just as we have a corresponding duty to take care of the German population. A systematic method of depopulation will have to be developed. What, you may ask, does depopulation mean? Do I propose to eliminate whole population groups? Yes, indeed, something like that will have to be done. . . . Nature is cruel; that is why we can permit ourselves to be cruel, as well. If I am to send the flower of German manhood into the pitiless storm of the coming war, should I not have the right to eliminate millions of members of an inferior race who multiply like vermin, not by exterminating them but by systematically preventing their marked natural fertility from taking its course. For example, by ensuring that the men are separated from the women for years. . . . We declare our faith in such a methodical control of population movement.

Regarding the destruction of, in particular, the Polish population through resettlement, labor, and slaughter, see also the account by Gross, *Polish Society under German Occupation*, 47 ff., 49.

225. Hitler, table talk of January 22, 1942 (Picker, *Hitlers Tischgespräche* [1968], 45).

226. Cf. directive of the Reich minister for education of the people and propaganda of January 1942, which stipulated that the designation *Slavs* or *Slavic* should be dropped from all official declarations since the main representatives of the states of eastern and southeastern Europe reject

this epithet and there is accordingly no cause to coin a common term to cover these peoples (communicated through Confidential Information from the Party Chancellery, no. 3/39 of January 26, 1942 [*Verfügungen*, 2:64 f.]).

227. Hitler, talking at table on January 22, 1942 (Picker, *Hitlers Tischgespräche* [1968], 45).

228. The extent to which this hatred of the Russians was racially founded cannot be determined conclusively. There are strong arguments for the equal importance of political motivations: for example, the fact that the non-Communist White Russians received better treatment than the Soviet Russians and that, in 1939, Hitler united with the Soviet Russians in the nonaggression pact and spoke in praise of Stalin and his policy (quoted in Picker, *Hitlers Tischgespräche*, 133, 242: "Behind Stalin there are the Jews"; 245: "In front of Stalin one should have unconditional respect . . . he knows his role models such as Ghengis Khan intimately").

229. Stuckart and Globke, *Reichsbürgergesetz*, introduction, 6; Gütt and Linden, *Kommentar zum Ehegesundheitsgesetz*, 22: "Qualitatively there is no racial difference between the European peoples"; "Reich citizens can therefore become the minorities in Germany, for example, Poles, Danes, . . ." However, this was the subject of controversy. As early as 1933, H. Nicolai had described the Poles as a "social group of alien people," which should be "subject to a special status" (*Grundlagen der kommenden Verfassung* [1933], 17 ff., 23).

230. Cf. Hitler, table talk of April 5, 1942, in which he warned about large-scale Germanization of—for example—Czechs and Poles since the Poles, as the partitions of their country showed, were "adept at tolerating foreign domination." Himmler put forward the view that, "historically, the Poles were the toughest of nations." They would therefore need to be gripped in the "iron tongs" of the German *Volkstum* (Picker, *Hitlers Tischgespräche*, 90 ff., 96 f.).

231. Thus also "Diensttagebuch" (1975), introduction, 8.

232. Freisler, "Das deutsche Polenstrafrecht," *DJ* (1942): 25 ff.

233. For more details, see H. A. Jacobsen, quoted in Picker, *Hitlers Tischgespräche*, 45; Jacobsen, "Vom Wandel des Polenbildes in Deutschland" (1973).

234. Memorandum on racial policy of November 25, 1939, reproduced in *Doc. Occ.* 5:3 ff. For further details see Broszat, *200 Jahre deutsche Polenpolitik* (1972), 26.

235. Instruction of the Reich head of propaganda of the NSDAP to all heads of propaganda in the *Reichsgaue*, dated February 15, 1943 (Nuremberg doc., PS-634, IfZ, Munich).

236. *RGBl.* I 1334: "No marriage should be contracted if the progeny of that marriage could be expected to endanger the purity of German blood."

237. Gütt and Linden, *Kommentar zum Ehegesundheitsgesetz*, 226 f.: "Marriage will also be prohibited when the alien blood" is of particular potency, for example, "Negroes and their blood relations among the primitive peoples of Africa, as well as the Australian aborigines and to some extent those of eastern India." Every case would have to be carefully investigated. The investigating physician had to pay particular attention to "brown or yellow skin color, broad, low nose, distended nose [the German word *Nüster* refers to the nose of an animal;] slanting, triangular nostrils are clear indications of an alien racial strain. The root of the nose is often broad and low. Further suspicious signs include protruding, thick lips. . . . Other features are a prominent lower face or prominent jaw [prognathism], broadening of the cheek bone area and flatness of the nose and eye area."

238. Cf. draft Law on Acquisition and Loss of German Citizenship, RuPreußMdI, February 1938. The Reich Ministry of Justice was concerned that the law should also apply to non-Jewish "aliens" (*Fremdvölkische*) and recommended avoiding, wherever possible, "the words Jew and Jewish half-caste" (*Jude und jüdische Mischling*) and instead speaking of "people of alien blood" or "people of non-German or non-related blood" (*nichtdeutsches oder nicht artverwandtes Blut*) (official statement of July 19, 1939; for further details see *Abschnitt Innere Verwaltung/Reich*, vol. 3).

239. Political by definition were activities that were "destined to serve the protection of the state internally and externally" (Prussian Supreme Court, Berlin, *DJ* [1935]: 1831).

240. *Ministerialdirektor* Crohne of the Reich Ministry of Justice wrote in an essay: "Among the . . . significant political cases we must also count criminal proceedings against church members, which can be divided into three main categories: currency offenses, sexual offenses, and fraud . . . since August 1936, the Führer has commanded that—on political grounds—such criminal cases are no longer to proceed to trial" ("Die Strafrechtspflege 1936," 9).

241. The decision of January 27, 1937, is inconspicuously recorded in *Jahrbuch für Entscheidungen für freiwillige Gerichtsbarkeit*, 15:58 ff.

242. Reich Supreme Court, *JW* (1935): 3377.

243. See, for example, the decree of the Reich minister of finance on "special treatment in fiscal matters" for Jews of February 10, 1940 (*RStBl.* 265); directive no. 4 of the commissioner general for allocation of labor on the procurement, welfare, accommodation, feeding, and treatment of foreign workers, dated May 7, 1942, 5: "Sonderbehandlung einzelner Gruppen von ausländischen Arbeitskräften" (quoted in *Handbuch für die Dienststellen des Generalbevollmächtigten* [1944], 79 ff.); for more details see Harry von Rosen–von Hoevel, "Das Polenstatut," (1942), 109 ff. (The author was *Oberregierungsrat* [ORR] in the Reich Ministry of the Interior).

244. Cf., for example, circulars of the RFSSuChddtPol, in Nuremberg doc., NO-1532, 1542, 5132, 5126, 1389, 4634, 5277. For a full account of the use of the term *special treatment* to mean execution, see Auerbach, "Der Begriff 'Sonderbehandlung' im Sprachgebrauch der SS," *Gutachten des IfZ*, München, 2 (1960): 182 ff.

245. Cf. Hitler, conversation with Rauschning, spring 1933, Rauschning, *Gespräche mit Hitler*, 52 f.: The Catholic Church has received only a stay of execution; its time is up. If Rome wants "to get into a fight," he would not make "martyrs out of priests" "but criminals," "plain criminals." If that isn't enough, "I will make them into figures of ridicule, of scorn . . . and if that makes the good citizens' hair stand on end, so much the better. . . . The young people will accept it—the young and the *Volk*. I can happily do without the rest of them."

246. W. Hamel, in Hans Frank, *Deutsches Verwaltungsrecht* (1937), 387.

247. Forsthoff, *Der totale Staat*, 39 ff.

248. Sondergericht, Hamburg, *DRiZ* (1935), no. 553.

249. *RGBl.* I 83.

250. Hamel, in Frank, *Deutsches Verwaltungsrecht*, 386 f.

251. Ibid., 387.

252. *MinbliV* (1933): 233.

253. The OVG ascertained in 1935 that, following the issue of the order of February 28, 1933, the police had been restricted to simply responding in the event of danger to themselves within the meaning of sec. 14, and that a police instruction that went beyond this—in the absence of any specific legal justification—would be in contravention of sec. 15, Law of Police Administration, and therefore invalid (*RVerwBl.* [1935]: 923).

254. Württemberg State (Superior) Administrative Court, *DVBl.* (1936): 385.

255. Reich Supreme Labor Court, *JW* (1935): 379.

256. Prussian Supreme Court, Berlin, "Rechtsprechung," supplement to *Deutsche Richterzeitung* (1935), no. 624; similarly, Reich Supreme Court, *JW* (1934): 76; see, further, Fraenkel, *Der Doppelstaat*, 43 ff.

257. For further details, see Fraenkel, *Der Doppelstaat*, 43 ff., with numerous examples.

258. *DJ* (1934): 64.

259. State Superior Court, Munich, November 4, 1937, quoted in Fraenkel, *Der Doppelstaat*, 60, my emphasis.

260. Judgment of March 15, 1935, quoted in *JW* (1935): 2989.

261. Baden State (Superior) Administrative Court, *Badische Verwaltungs Zeitschrift* (1938): 96 ff.

262. State Superior Court, Brunswick, HRR (1936), no. 98.

263. Prussian Supreme Court, Berlin, *RVerwBl.* (1936): 62, my emphasis.

264. *DJ* (1935): 1831 f., emphasis mine. The pastor, a member of the Confessing Church (*Bekennende Kirche*), had given his confirmation class a letter for their parents that spoke out against the German Christians (*Deutsche Christen*). As a result, he had been prosecuted for contravening an order of the responsible *Oberpräsident* on the conducting of "immaterial arguments in ecclesiastical controversy" but had been found not guilty by the Court of Lay Assessors. The Prussian Supreme Court, Berlin, quashed this verdict and pronounced a sentence.

265. Reich Supreme Court, *Deutsches Strafrecht* (1936): 429.

266. Verdict of the State Superior Court, Munich, January 27, 1937, *Jahrbuch für Entscheidungen der freiwilligen Gerichtsbarkeit*, 15:58 ff.; the verdict confirms that the name of a committee member of the Cab Owners' Cooperative could be deleted from the association's register at the behest of the police: "The constitutional rulings listed in the order [of February 28, 1933] and the statutory regulations specified by sec. 1, subpar. 2, of same have effectively been stripped of their legal significance in favor of the police, affecting everybody concerned. . . . In that sense, legal rights . . . in dealings with the police have been abolished. . . . It is of no relevance whether it is an economic association, particularly a commercially registered one, for example a limited company or similar . . ."

267. For further details, see part 2, section 1, A, excursus.

268. Hamel, "Die Polizei im neuen Reich" (1935), 414; Hamel, in Frank, *Deutsches Verwaltungsrecht*, 394, 395 n. 25.

269. See, for example, the July 14, 1933, Law on the Revocation of Naturalization and Forfeiture of Citizenship, *RGBl.* I 480.

270. Decree of March 21, 1933 (*RGBl.* I 134), on the Granting of Impunity, which granted same on the basis of art. 48, par. 2, WRV, for all criminal acts that predated the order and that were committed "in the struggle for the national awakening of the German people, its preparation, or in the struggle for the native soil."

271. Bühler and Frank, "Nationalsozialistische Strafrechtspolitik" (1939).

272. Schmitt, *Politische Theologie* (1922), 13.

273. Cf. Fraenkel, *Der Doppelstaat*, 51, 187 f.; aptly citing the judgment of the Supreme Court, he points out that it was not really a question of martial law but rather of a state of emergency owing to the lack of binding legal rules.

274. Wolf, "Das Rechtsideal des nationalsozialistischen Staates," 360 f. Although everybody with a "human countenance" who lives within the scope of German law has the right to legal protection, the "allocation and exercise of rights" must depend on the person's "legal status, which is exclusively endowed by membership in the *Volksgemeinschaft* [national community] and its essential elements . . . legal status cannot therefore be enjoyed by those of another race. . . . The guest residents (*Volksgäste*) who do not enjoy legal status include those of alien racial origin and foreigners . . . their legal position . . . in contrast to that of the legal status of the *Volksgenosse*—can be termed a *Rechtsschutzgenossenschaft* [community of those who enjoy the benefits of the law]. [It] is accorded as long as the *Volksgast* complies with the rules, customs, and manners of the host nation and in no way acts against the vital interests of the host nation"; cf. also sec. 1, *AuslPolVO* (Police Decree on Foreigners) of August 22, 1938 (*RGBl.* I 1053): "Residence in the territory of the Reich is permitted to foreigners whose demeanor and purpose of stay . . . give some surety that they are worthy of the hospitality accorded to them."

275. Reich Supreme Court of June 27, 1936, *JW* (1936): 2529 ff.

276. Reich Ministry of the Interior draft of the Law on Aliens to the Community (BA R 22/4428), which failed to become law only because of the outbreak of war.

277. Nicolai, *Grundlagen der kommenden Verfassung*, 87 f. The new constitution must be free of the sort of "mendacious phrases" that characterize the basic constitutional rights (*Grundrechte*).

"Even the earlier one was no more than a set of *guidelines* for legislation." The constitution had to be "honest." "There is only one basic right: that of right itself."

278. Cf., among many others, ibid; Nicolai was a head of department in the Reich Ministry of the Interior from 1933 to 1936. In the book, which appeared before the seizure of power, he says among other things: In the *völkisch* state there could only be rights for those who have done their duty; the status of *Staatsbürger* = *Reichsbürger* (citizen) should be reserved for those who have served in the forces or done labor service. Accordingly, those who could not be citizens included minors, invalids, "non-Germans." Women too would be excluded from citizenship—the grounds given revealing the author's complete lack of historical knowledge: "The fact that, as a rule, women cannot acquire citizenship comes about of its own accord because of the link with military service . . . and the Germanic character of our *Volk* . . . the feminism that is apparent in recent legislation, the morbid clamor for 'the emancipation of women' is a phenomenon of degeneracy of the most disquieting sort and contradicts the high esteem that, in the Nordic way of thinking, men should accord to women. For this is expressed in the principle that women should not be misused in professional or public life or enter into unbridled competition with men. The 'Amazon' is no German ideal but—significantly—one that is at home in Asia."

279. Ibid., 20–22; Nicolai clearly delineates the process: Reich citizenship is more than simple nationality (60 f.). Only Germans could be Reich citizens. Being a German is something that is determined by race, by origin, independently of language, nationality, religion: decisive is only the "German origin." The new constitution should have a corresponding provision (Nuremberg laws). There are other "aliens" (*Fremde*) who are also not of German nationality. They will have to reckon with the "law of the future." This group of "aliens" has "nothing to do with us legally." "Aliens who for the time being hold German citizenship will keep it but will not enjoy the rights of citizenship, though they are subject to the state's authority. The state would only act on their behalf where this did not conflict with German interests." The legislation (on Reich citizenship) must be followed by "legislation on aliens." This clearly foreshadows the future Jewish legislation, beginning with the classification and registration of "alien people" (*Artfremden*). ("In practice we will differentiate three groups: the Jews, the Poles, and the other aliens"), through the decree of "racial protection legislation," to "protect the German people from further bastardization."

280. For further details, see "Diensttagebuch," ed. Präg and Jacobmeyer, introduction, 7.

281. BA R 22/4219; R 18/11 and 12.

282. BA R 22/204 (also reproduced in Sauer, *Das Reichsjustizministerium* [1939], 7, 54 ff.). According to this account, the Reich Ministry of Justice had three departments in 1933 and six in 1938. The departments—to give them their brief titles—were (1) Organization, Administration, and Personnel, (2) Criminal Legislation and Execution of Sentence, (3) Implementation of Criminal Law, (4) Civil Law including Involvement in Racial Law, (5) Commercial, Economic, and Public Law, (6) Budget. In 1939 one department was added. A new distribution of activities was published through an announcement of the Reich Ministry of Justice of May 8, 1942 (*DJ* [1942]: 328). For an account of the structure of the Reich Ministry of Justice and the organization of its activities, see also the general documentation plan of the Reich Ministry of Justice, 1935, in Kluge and Krüger, *Verfassung und Verwaltung*, 425.

Part One. Section 1. I. General Outlines

1. Fraenkel, in *The Dual State* (1941) (esp. 89 ff.), was the first to draw a conceptual distinction between *prerogative state* and *normative state*, in which the former served to resolve all political issues, including that of the treatment of Jews. It is difficult to situate emergency laws against Jews within this distinction, however, insofar as they had the quality of normative laws: for though formally they belonged to the sphere of the *normative state*, materially they have to be attributed to

that of the *prerogative state* since they diverge from the principle of public law. For our discussion the concept of the emergency state as proposed by Franciszek Ryszka in *Państwo i stanu wyjątkowego* (1964) is more appropriate.

2. See, in particular, Krausnick, "Judenverfolgung" (1965), 310 ff., 312; Adam, *Judenpolitik im Dritten Reich* (1972), 46 ff.; Bracher, Sauer, and Schulz, *Die nationalsozialistische Machtergreifung* (1962), 172; Ostler, *Deutsche Rechtsanwälte* (1971), 248, which describes in detail the beginning of concerted actions against the "practice of the law corrupted by the Jews," especially the actions of March 11, 1933, against Jewish judges and public prosecutors in Breslau (Wrocław) and other events in Breslau; an attack on Jewish law offices planned for March 16, 1933, was canceled following an appeal to Hitler by the *Reichskommissar* for Prussia, Papen (see Neumann, "Vom Kaiserhoch zur Austreibung," 6).

3. A considerable number of Polish citizens were also molested in Leipzig in April 1933 (Krausnick, "Judenverfolgung" [1965], 312); see also the report of the American consul in Leipzig of April 1993, Nuremberg doc. PS-2709.

4. Directive of March 28, 1933, quoted in Scheffler, *Judenverfolgung im Dritten Reich 1933–1945* (1960), 109 ff.

5. Neumann, "Vom Kaiserhoch zur Austreibung," 6 f.

6. See Krausnick, "Judenverfolgung," 311–14.

7. Cf. Stuckart and Globke, *Reichsbürgergesetz* (1936), 15: "The two Nuremberg Laws with their implementing provisions contain the fundamental solution to this racial problem. They make a clear distinction, based on blood, between Germandom and Jewry and thus create the legal basis for a modus vivendi that satisfies all requirements. . . . The Nuremberg Laws [guarantee Jewry] its own existence within the limits of the law."

8. Krausnick, "Judenverfolgung," 316.

9. As stated by Göring, head of the Four Year Plan, at a discussion on the Jewish question in the Reich Air Ministry on November 12, 1938, shorthand transcription, Nuremberg doc. PS-1816; quoted from Poliakov and Wulf, *Das Dritte Reich und die Juden* (1961), 75 ff., 76 (excerpts).

10. Reich Finance Minister Count Schwerin von Krosigk, discussion of November 12, 1938, at the Reich Air Ministry, shorthand transcription, Poliakov and Wulf, *Das Dritte Reich und die Juden*, 75 ff., 79.

11. As set out in the plans of the Nazi leadership at the Reich Air Ministry discussion of November 12, 1938, and especially those of the Security Police (Heydrich), which were endorsed by the Reich minister of finance, who wanted to be free of the whole "social proletariat as rapidly as possible," and the Reich minister of the interior, shorthand transcription from ibid. Regarding the phases of the preparation, implementation, and modalities of the emigration and the deportations, see Adler, *Der verwaltete Mensch* (1974), 3 ff., with exhaustive references and documentation section (645 ff.)

12. Cf. Adam, *Judenpolitik im Dritten Reich* (1972), 357, who speaks of "a process of disfranchisement carried out with almost methodical consistency" and refers to the corresponding "stage theory" (16).

13. Even before the seizure of power, detailed plans existed for depriving "alien" German inhabitants of their rights (cf. Nicolai, *Grundlagen der kommenden Verfassung* [1933]), which apart from the wording were substantially identical with the subsequent measures. In *Mein Kampf* Hitler himself left no doubt as to the role of the Jews, though avoiding certain explicit conclusions. But both he and his acolytes continually stressed the need to eliminate the Jewish influence from public life and the economy. Hitler also speaks at length of dealing with the "alien" inhabitants of the "Greater German Reich" (Jews, Poles, Russians, etc.) by expulsion and decimation in his discussions with Rauschning in 1933 and 1934. The physical annihilation of the Jews was already discussed at that time (Rauschning, *Gespräche mit Hitler*). A. Hillgruber, *VjhZ* (1972): 133 ff., particularly, has

pointed out the consistency of anti-Semitism in National Socialist policy, in apparent contrast to Adam, *Judenpolitik im Dritten Reich*, 17 and 357 ff., who attempts to demonstrate that no master plan detailing the type, content, and extent of persecution of the Jews ever existed, because the "structural anarchy" of the National Socialists had triumphed over the former forces of order.

14. Cf. Mommsen, "Der nationalsozialistische Polizeistaat" (1962); Krausnick, "Judenverfolgung," 283 ff.; Blau, *Das Ausnahmerecht für Juden in Deutschland* (1965); Bracher, Sauer, and Schulz, *Die nationalsozialistische Machtergreifung;* Adam, *Judenpolitik im Dritten Reich;* Göppinger, *Die Verfolgung der Juristen jüdischer Abstammung* (1963); Mommsen, *Beamtentum im Dritten Reich* (1966); Matzerath, *Nationalsozialismus und kommunale Selbstverwaltung* (1970); Echterhölter, *Das öffentliche Recht im Nationalsozialismus* (1970). Further references may be found in Adam, *Judenpolitik im Dritten Reich*, 17 nn. 8, 9. For contemporary references, see Huber, *Verfassungsrecht des Großdeutschen Reiches* (1939), 181 ff.; further, see the list of special anti-Jewish legislation in the public and vocational domains in Kluge and Krüger, *Verfassung und Verwaltung* (1941), 215 ff., 222 ff.; a compilation of all the special provisions relating to Jews up to 1938 may be found in Streicher, *Die Judengesetze Großdeutschlands* (1939). See also the anti-Jewish regulations in the collection by Sartorius, *Verfassungs- und Verwaltungsrecht* (1944) (nos. 23, 74a, 89 f., 95a, 97, 97a, 97c, 98–98n, 136b, 147, 150c, 172b, 183; annex I, 4).

15. According to the organization charts of the Reich Ministry of the Interior dated January 15, 1937 (BA R 22/4219), and April 4, 1940 (BA R 18/11 and 12), the Ministry of the Interior consisted of the following departments: Department 1 (headed by Dr. Stuckart), Constitution and Legislation (in 1940 it dealt with matters pertaining to the constitution, legislation, administration, and civil defense of the Reich); Department 2 (headed by Ministry Director Schütze), Personnel, with a subdivision for the Civil Service; Department 3, Veterinary; Department 4, Public Health (including population policy, heredity and racial affairs, the Marital Hygiene Law, and the Law for the Prevention of Progeny with Hereditary Diseases); Department 5, Municipal Administration; Department 6, German Nationhood and Surveying (colonial affairs); Department 7, Labor Administration; Department 8, Sport.

16. According to the organization chart of January 15, 1937 (BA R 22/4219), Department 1 comprised the following sections (as of 1937): Group 1, Movement and State; Group 2, Constitution and Organization (including constitutional law of the Reich and *Länder*, Reich reform, administrative reform, administrative structure of the Reich and *Länder*, and special Reich administrations); Group 3, Administrative Law and Legislation; Group 4 (from 1940 on), Reorganization of the Eastern Territories and Affairs of the Occupied Polish Territories; Group 5, Reich Civil Law and Reich and State Citizenship; Group 6 (headed by Dr. Bernd Lösener), Racial Law and Racial Policy (Jewish questions, general and particular; the situation in the state; the economy; acquisition of real estate; cultural activity; people of mixed race [*Mischlinge*], non-Jewish aliens; the Blood Protection Law, general and specific questions; determination of racial lineage; the Reich Family Research Office). This group did not cover the whole field of racial law; some aspects of racial law were dealt with by Department 4 (see the previous note). Various regroupings were carried out in the course of the war. The most important was the inclusion of all racial, particularly Jewish, questions under Department 1 (see the organization charts of September 14, 1939 [AZ 283/39/5231], and July 1, 1943 [Z 6616/43/5231]). According to a later organization chart of January 15, 1945 (ZHB 1001/15.1.1945), Jewish matters falling within the realm of racial questions and still dealt with by Department 1B in 1943 were no longer included, since in September 1943 the responsibility for Jewish affairs had passed to the chief of the SIPO and the SD after Himmler had become Reich minister of the interior.

17. For details see Adler, *Der verwaltete Mensch;* Genschel, *Die Verdrängung der Juden* (1966); Müllerheim, *Die gesetzlichen und außergesetzlichen Maßnahmen* (1962); Seeber, *Zwangsarbeiter in der faschistischen Kriegswirtschaft* (1964); with regard to the cultural sphere, see Bresser, *Die Kunstpolitik des Nationalsozialismus* (1963); and the following documentation: Wulf, *Theater und Film im Dritten Reich* (1966); Wulf, *Die bildenden Künste im Dritten Reich* (1966); Wulf, *Literatur und Dich-*

tung im Dritten Reich (1966); Wulf, *Presse und Funk im Dritten Reich* (1966); Wulf, *Musik im Dritten Reich* (1966); von Olenhusen, "Die 'nichtarischen' Studenten" (1966).

18. *RGBl.* I 1988, 823.

19. Secs. 41, 58 of the Reich Ministries joint standing orders, general section (Combined Rules of Procedure for the Reich Ministries I), in Reich Ministry of the Interior, ed., *Gemeinsame Geschäftsordnung der Reichsministerien, Allgemeiner Teil (GGO I)* (1927), 21, 28; sec. 27 of the joint standing orders, special section (Combined Rules of Procedure for the Reich Ministries II), in Reich Ministry of the Interior, ed., *Gemeinsame Geschäftsordnung der Reichsministerien, Allgemeiner Teil (GGO II)*, 2d, rev. ed. (1929), 14.

20. *RGBl.* I 627, 372.

21. *RGBl.* I 414.

22. *RGBl.* I 1580.

23. *RGBl.* I 887; the preamble to the Decree on the Implementation of the Four Year Plan, announced at the 1936 Reich Party Rally, gave Göring full powers over the next four years to issue decrees, regulations, and instructions to the authorities. The decree was extended for a further four years by decree of the Führer and *Reichskanzler* of October 18, 1940 (*RGBl.* I 1395), when Göring was again invested with all the previous powers.

24. *RGBl.* I 1709.

25. The decree dated December 3, 1941, was based on sec. 1 of the second directive of the plenipotentiary for the Four Year Plan dated November 24, 1938 (*RGBl.* I 1668). The directive was based on the Decree on the Registration of Jewish Property of April 26, 1938 (*RGBl.* I 414).

26. *RGBl.* I 675.

27. *RGBl.* I 887.

28. *RGBl.* I 681.

29. Cf. Scheuner, "Die Gerichte und die Prüfung politischer Staatshandlungen" (1936); further references in the introduction, III, 1. ("The Führer Principle"), note 80.

30. An example can be found in Adler, *Der verwaltete Mensch*; Adler investigates the Würzburg archives, among others.

Part One. Section 1. II. Civil Service Law

1. Prussian Minister of Justice H. Kerrl, in *Der Völkische Beobachter*, no. 88 of March 29, 1933.

2. BVerfGE 3, 58 ff.

3. Sec. 3, par. 1, subpar. 2, German Civil Service Code, 1937.

4. As emphatically stated by E. Friesenhahn at the meeting of the Association of German Constitutional Law Teachers, 1954. The instrumental factor, as he put it, was the official's constitutional situation, not his individual sentiments. In his opinion this situation could be achieved only through positive law and the historical-political facts (*VVdStRL* 13 [1955]: 169). It is noteworthy that the subsequent discussion barely touched on Friesenhahn's statements (171 ff.).

5. A typical example was E. R. Huber in his paper "Rechtliche Gestaltung des öffentlichen Amtes und rechtliche Gestaltung des privaten Angestelltenverhältnisses" (1939), quoted by Friesenhahn, ibid., 169 f.: "The civil servant has become the bearer of the common obligations and the operative organ of the Führer's will. . . . An inner commitment to the National Socialist philosophy should overcome the merely mechanical functioning of an apparatus without a soul. . . . The bond with the nation as a whole and unswerving obedience to the Führer's will, which underpins the civil servant's political oath of loyalty, are the core of public office. . . . By virtue of his official status, the civil servant is duty bound to the Führer to pledge unreserved loyalty and unconditional obedience; this particular political obligation of loyalty toward the Führer, reinforced as it is by the oath, is fundamental to public office."

6. BVerfGE in the so-called Gestapo decision, BVerfGE 6, 133 (180).

7. Bracher, Sauer, and Schulz, *Die nationalsozialistische Machtergreifung* (1962), 171.

8. Gerber, *Politische Erziehung* (1933).

9. Cf. Bracher, Sauer, and Schulz, *Die nationalsozialistische Machtergreifung* (1962), 171: National Socialism was able to achieve the "antiparliamentary," "antidemocratic revolution" without external scission, "through the official channels."

10. Ibid., 172; Krausnick, "Judenverfolgung" (1965), 312; Adam, *Judenpolitik im Dritten Reich* (1972), 36 ff., with examples.

11. For more details, see Bracher, Sauer, and Schulz, *Die nationalsozialistische Machtergreifung* (1962), 174, where further references will be found.

12. Wolfram and Klein, *Recht und Rechtspflege in den Rheinlanden* (1969), 219 ff.

13. Bracher, Sauer, and Schulz, *Die nationalsozialistische Machtergreifung* (1962), 519.

14. *RGBl.* I 175. The validity of the law was originally limited to September 30, 1933, but the limit was extended several times: acts of March 22, 1934 (*RGBl.* I 203), and September 26, 1934 (*RGBl.* I 845). The Professional Civil Service Code was accompanied by a total of seven implementing orders (Sartorius, *Verfassungs- und Verwaltungsrecht* [1944], annex II, 7, 5 n. 1). For details of the law, see Bracher, Sauer, and Schulz, *Die nationalsozialistische Machtergreifung* (1962), 498 ff.

15. Bracher, Sauer, and Schulz, *Die nationalsozialistische Machtergreifung* (1962), 497, speak rather loosely of "parallels."

16. For a detailed history of its development, see Adam, *Judenpolitik im Dritten Reich*, 51 ff.; and Mommsen, *Beamtentum im Dritten Reich* (1966), 39 ff., 151 ff.

17. A compilation of all the relevant Civil Service laws, orders, and decrees may be found in Brandt, *Die politische Treuepflicht* (1976), 110 ff.

18. First Implementing Order of April 11, 1933 (*RGBl.* I 195). All officials were to declare their affiliation with political parties when called upon to do so, including affiliation with the Reichsbanner Schwarz-Rot-Gold, the Association of Republican Judges, and the League for Human Rights.

19. With regard to the term *aptitude* (*Eignung*), see no. 1 of the First Implementing Order to the BBG (Professional Civil Service Code) and BBG, sec. 2a, in pursuance of the supplementary law of July 29, 1933 (*RGBl.* I 518), according to which all officials who were members of the Communist Party or "Communist support or front organizations" were not "apt" under the terms of the law.

20. According to no. 2 of the Implementing Order (to sec. 3 of the Professional Civil Service Code) of April 11, 1933 (*RGBl.* I 195), the term *non-Aryan* was defined as follows: "(1) A person is non-Aryan if he is descended from non-Aryan, especially Jewish, parents or grandparents. It is sufficient for one parent or one grandparent to be non-Aryan. This may be presumed to be the case in particular when a parent or grandparent has belonged to the Jewish religion. (2). . . . (3) If Aryan descent is doubtful, a report is to be obtained from an expert in race research designated by the Reich minister of the interior." Identical in wording with par. 1 is point 1, par. 1 of the Directives of the Reich minister of the interior of August 8, 1933 (*RGBl.* I 575), relating to sec. 1a, par. 3, of the Reich Civil Service Code in its version of June 30, 1933 (*RGBl.* I 433). With respect to the term *non-Aryan* (*nichtarisch*), see also Bracher, Sauer, and Schulz, *Die nationalsozialistische Machtergreifung* (1962), 503. The term *non-Aryan*, which was broader in meaning than the term *Jewish* (Jewish descent required two Jewish grandparents), was rendered inoperative by sec. 5 of the First Decree to the Reich Citizenship Law of November 14, 1935 (*RGBl.* I 1333).

21. Frick, "Wiedergeburt des deutschen Beamten" (1934).

22. Seel, in H. Frank, ed., *Deutsches Verwaltungsrecht* (1937), 151, 159.

23. A note in the files of April 27, 1933, by Reich Minister of the Interior W. Frick on this discussion, quoted in Mommsen, *Beamtentum im Dritten Reich*, 159 f.

24. The Professional Civil Service Code was amended or extended several times (cf. laws of June 23, July 20, September 22, 1933 [*RGBl.* I 389, 518, 655]; laws of March 22, July 11, and Septem-

ber 26, 1934 [*RGBl.* I 203, 604, 845]); in accordance with its sec. 18, it was repealed after the time limits set by the law itself (sec. 7), or at the latest when the new German Civil Service Code (1937) came into force on January 26 (*RGBl.* 39 I 186) (cf. sec. 184, par. 2, German Civil Service Code).

25. A note in the files by Reich Minister of the Interior W. Frick of April 27, 1933, quoted in Mommsen, *Beamtentum im Dritten Reich*, 159 f.

26. Cf. administrative instructions of April 1, 1935, from Reich Ministry of Justice, *DJ* (1935): 546, no. 4c, sec. 2.

27. Mommsen, *Beamtentum im Dritten Reich*, 54 ff., with further references.

28. See, for example, the letter of April 5, 1935, from the Reich minister of justice to the *Kammergericht* presiding judge, Berlin (BA R 22/10953), where it is requested that Prof. Fritz Schulz no longer be employed for state law examinations, his examination authority having been withdrawn by the Reich minister for science on account of his non-Aryan descent. The authority to conduct examinations was also rescinded in the case of examiners in political disfavor, such as members of freemason lodges (cf. letter of February 24, 1937, from the Reich Ministry of Justice to the presiding judge of the Prussian Supreme Court, Berlin, regarding dismissal of *Kammergerichtsrat* Dr. Hartung [ibid.]). See also the letter of March 1, 1937, from the Reich Ministry of Justice (Freisler) to the presiding judge of the *Kammergericht*, Berlin, in which Freisler refuses the request by the presiding judge to use former assistant judge of the *Kammergericht* Weber (first name not given) as examiner once again, on the grounds of "a reduction in the number of examinations" (ibid.). Weber had no longer been used as examiner after failing three SA members in the first law examination; a further attempt to be reinstated in 1938 was unsuccessful (exchange of correspondence [ibid.]) Carl Schmitt proposed Werner Weber, *Oberregierungsrat* in the Prussian Ministry of Culture and professor at the Berlin Business School, a highly qualified Party member who had been with the SA since 1933, as successor to Weber (letter to Freisler of January 10, 1936 [ibid.]). Freisler also rejected this proposal on grounds of "a reduction in the number of examinations" (letter to C. Schmitt of March 1, 1937 [ibid.]). Whether there really was a reduction in the number of examinations appears doubtful. The application by Prof. Siebert (Berlin) to the post of examiner on account of an increase in the number of examinations is also worthy of note (letter of November 30, 1938, from the president of the Legal Examination Office, Palandt, to the Reich Ministry of Justice regarding the appointment of Prof. Siebert and of December 1938 regarding that of Prof. Koschaker [ibid.]).

29. Dismissals were prompt in the municipal administrations; at least eighty-seven *kreisfreie* towns (towns constituting a *Kreis* of their own) were affected. At the beginning of May 1933, seventy Oberbürgermeister were relieved of their duties; twelve of these towns (including Cologne, Düsseldorf, Magdeburg, Darmstadt, and Würzburg) lost their entire governing authority. By the summer of 1933, only four of the Oberbürgermeister elected before January 30 were still in office (Bracher, Sauer, and Schulz, *Die nationalsozialistische Machtergreifung* [1962], 446 f., including further references and numerous examples). For full information on the usurping of local positions of power by way of numerous unlawful actions against leading municipal officers on the part of the NSDAP (suspensions, dismissals, arrest, murder, suicide), which far exceeded those against members of the department of justice, see Matzerath, *Nationalsozialismus und kommunale Selbstverwaltung* (1970), 61 ff., and for personnel changes, 74 ff.; and Bracher, Sauer, and Schulz, *Die nationalsozialistische Machtergreifung* (1962), 447 ff.

30. Official report of December 4, 1950, from State Superior Court presiding judge Hamm to the North Rhine–Westphalia minister of justice (quoted in Weinkauff and Wagner, *Die deutsche Justiz* [1968], 102).

31. According to Mommsen, *Beamtentum im Dritten Reich*, 55, who bases his information on the Hamburg archives (see note 58 below, which can be taken as an example of the Reich's policy in general). If the cases based on sec. 4 (54) are added to those of sec. 6 (286), which may be regarded as a variant of removal from office for political reasons, and given a total number of statutory posts

of 2,666, close to 12.75% cases of removal from office for political reasons results. Three officials were dismissed on the grounds of sec. 2, and 10 on the basis of the Aryan Paragraphs in the Professional Civil Service Code, sec. 3; further, two Jewish functionaries were superannuated on the grounds of sec. 4 of the First Decree to the Reich Citizenship Law. For the justice department, see Johe, *Die gleichgeschaltete Justiz* (1967), 68 ff.; and notes 55 and 64 below.

32. Figures from Prussian Ministry of Justice statistics, quoted in Schorn, *Der Richter im Dritten Reich* (1959), 730 f.; see note 64 below for further details.

33. *RGBl.* I 195; membership in the Communist Party or a Communist organization as a reason for dismissal was introduced into the Professional Civil Service Code by the supplementary law of July 20, 1933 (*RGBl.* I 518), as sec. 2a.

34. Implementing Order to Professional Civil Service Code dated May 6, 1933 (*RGBl.* I 245).

35. See, for example, the official report of December 4, 1950, from State Superior Court presiding judge Hamm to the minister of justice of North Rhine–Westphalia, according to which thirteen non-Jewish judges were disciplined (promotion freeze, forced retirement, dismissal, transfer) on political grounds, including membership in one of the Weimar parties (quoted in Weinkauff and Wagner, *Die deutsche Justiz*).

36. See the letter of April 25, 1938, from the Reich minister of the interior to the deputy Führer, containing proposals for the promotion of various officials from the position of *Oberregierungssrat* (ORR) to that of *Ministerialrat*. In paragraphs a–c the Reich Ministry of the Interior pointed to the excellent technical work of ORR Ritter von Lex, stating that it would not be appropriate to reproach him now with remarks made against the NSDAP during an election campaign years earlier. ORR Krug von Nidda, for his part, had never been politically *active* and had "proved himself highly capable," and ORR Globke was among the "most competent and diligent officials [of the] ministry," and had not stood out politically. In spite of their former political affiliations, therefore, these officials could exceptionally be promoted "by the Führer's will" (BA R 18); Diehl-Thiele, *Partei und Staat im Dritten Reich* (1969), 55 ff., similarly reports that members of the Center Party, the German People's Party, or the Bavarian People's Party were generally suspect. Mommsen, *Beamtentum im Dritten Reich*, 60, gives evidence that membership in the SPD and the KPD were put on an equal footing when the political reliability of officials was evaluated, at least in the realm of the Reich financial administration. Subsequently, however, members of the Center Party were also removed from office; the only distinction that can be made is whether dismissal or retirement was imposed.

37. Circular of July 14, 1933, issued in the name of all Reich ministers (*RMinbliV* [1993]: 887).

38. Cf. Mommsen, *Beamtentum im Dritten Reich*, 59, who stresses that the cleansing of the Civil Service apparatus "had little impact on its internal cohesion, apart from the dismissal of Communists and Jews."

39. Nos. 1 and 2 of the First Implementing Order to the Professional Civil Service Code of April 11, 1933 (*RGBl.* I 195); either Aryan descent or qualification for service on the front had to be proved in accordance with the emergency regulations, sec. 3, par. 2, of the law. Only officials who had been in service since August 1, 1914, were exempt from this requirement.

40. Third Implementing Order to the Professional Civil Service Code of May 6, 1933 (*RGBl.* I 245); application of the rules was strict in the Ministries of the Economy, Food, and Justice; more lenient (no checking of information, for example) in Transport, Labor, and Finance, and initially also in the Ministry of the Interior (Bracher, Sauer, and Schulz, *Die nationalsozialistische Machtergreifung* [1962], 500).

41. Cf. RuPrMdI circular of January 26, 1935, regarding the "ancestry certificate," *MinbliV* no. 6; the decree was modified by order from the commissioner-general for administration of the Reich (Frick) of August 1, 1940 (*RGBl.* I 1063 f.). With regard to the judiciary, see the relevant provisions in the administrative instructions issued by the Reich minister of justice of April 1, 1935 (*DJ* [1935]: 546, no. 4c, par. 2), and of July 6, 1936 (quoted in the decree of the Reich minister of justice

to the State Superior Court presiding judge of Breslau [Wrocław] of September 16, 1936 [BA R 22/4430]). The obligation to prove Aryan descent was extended to officials of the Reich Ministry of Justice and their wives by the circulars of April 15, 1936, and December 7, 1936 (BA R 22/4433).

42. Cf. *Ministerialdirigent* H. Seel, "Die Gestaltung des deutschen Beamtenrechtes seit dem 30. Januar 1933" (1937), 164.

43. Erwin Schütze, *Ministerialdirektor* (a high-ranking official post) in the Reich Ministry of the Interior, "Beamtenpolitik im Dritten Reich," in Pfundtner, *Dr. Wilhelm Frick und sein Ministerium* (1937), 59 ff., quoted in Mommsen, *Beamtentum im Dritten Reich*, 57 n. 68.

44. *RGBl.* I 1063; cf. also the draft of this decree, which was sent with a covering letter of February 19, 1940, by the Reich Ministry of the Interior to the highest authorities of the Reich for their comments (BA R 22/4430).

45. Note from the Reich Ministry of Justice of August 3, 1942 (BA R 22/4433); the officials involved were *Ministerialdirektor* Schäfer, *Ministerialräte* Koffka and Anders, and *Oberregierungsrat* Dr. Hans von Dohnanyi.

46. Handwritten (unsigned) addition to the note of August 3, 1942: "The same [i.e. lack of proof of Aryan descent—Author] is true of *Oberregierungsrat* Dr. v. Dohnanyi; the outcome of his case is transferred to an outpost" (ibid.). Schäfer was pensioned off as part of the major personnel reshuffle of fall 1942; it is not known how other cases were dealt with.

47. Similar sanctions were imposed even *before* the revision of the disciplinary provisions in the German Civil Service Code of 1937. Thus the pension of a middle-ranking Jewish official was reduced "only" to 70% by the Justice Disciplinary Court on account of his long irreproachable service and advanced age; a post office official who had mixed with Jews since 1933 and continued relations into the summer of 1933 had her pension reduced to 75% for six years; a tax inspector who had received a loan of RM 500 from a Jew was transferred on disciplinary grounds and sentenced to a fine of RM 50, taking into account the mitigating circumstance that he had been wounded in the war and decorated (all examples quoted from Schulze, Simons, and Förster, *Die Rechtsprechung des Reichsdisziplinarhofes* [1935], 28, 70, 116).

48. H. Huber, *Der Aufbau des deutschen Hochschulwesens* (1933), 17, according to whom 45% of the official posts were already occupied in 1933. Non-Aryan lecturers had been suspended even before the Professional Civil Service Code was promulgated (Bracher, Sauer, and Schulz, *Die nationalsozialistische Machtergreifung* [1962], 280). The number of university lecturers fell from 8, 515 to 7, 881, by 7.5%, between the winter term 1932–33 and the summer term 1933. A total of 1,664 scientists were dismissed (Hartshorne, *The German Universities and National Socialism* [1937], 87 ff., 92 f.). According to Bracher, Sauer, and Schulz, *Die nationalsozialistische Machtergreifung* (1962), 321 or 14.34% of the official teaching staff and 11% of the regular professors were removed from office in the winter term 1932–33, an estimated third of them on racial grounds, 56% on racial *and* political grounds, and some 6.5% by "voluntary" resignation. In the law faculties, departures on racial grounds are said to have been as high as 78.5%.

49. According to Schütze, "Beamtenpolitik im Dritten Reich," 59 ff., quoted by Mommsen, *Beamtentum im Dritten Reich*, 56 nn. 62–64. Bracher, Sauer, and Schulz, *Die nationalsozialistische Machtergreifung* (1962), 507, report that by 1937, 369 of the 1,663 senior officials in Prussia (established posts) had been dismissed or pensioned off, and a total of 349 senior officials in the other *Länder*. The disparity between these and the Ministry of the Interior figures given in Mommsen, *Beamtentum im Dritten Reich*, 56, is presumably due to the fact that the latter do not include the period up to 1937. According to Bracher, Sauer, and Schulz, *Die nationalsozialistische Machtergreifung*, only three of the 34 Prussian district presidents and only one of the 13 other than Prussian officials of the same rank remained in office. All 31 Prussian district vice presidents were dismissed; of the 14 deputy officials of the same rank, 6 remained in office (507). Only 101 of the 361 Prussian *Landräte* remained in office, and 178 of the 326 non-Prussian *Landräte*. By the beginning of 1937,

81% of the political positions of the general and interior administration in Prussia were occupied by Party members, as were 63% in all the other *Länder* (508). Detailed figures are available for Prussia. In the police force the following numbers were dismissed or superannuated by December 31, 1933, under the law of April 7: administrative police, 60 officials (1.3%); criminal police, 103 officials (1.5%); Security Police, 200 officers (7.3%), 326 *Wachtmeister* (1.7%); *Landjägerei*, 12 officers (13.5%), 73 officials (0.9%); municipal police, 45 officials and officers (15%), 131 *Wachtmeister* (1.3%); medical staff, 3 officials (2.5%); veterinary staff, 0 officials; training staff, 16 officials (42.1%); newly admitted personnel: 627 officials, 1,163 employees, and 879 wage-earners from the "national movement," of whom 1,898 belonged to the SA, 1,086 to the SS, 368 to the Steel Helmets, and 317 were Party members (report of February 1, 1934, from Daluege to Hitler, BA R 43 I/2290; Bracher, Sauer, and Schulz, *Die nationalsozialistische Machtergreifung* [1962], 504 n. 161).

50. More details in Mommsen, *Beamtentum im Dritten Reich*, 56, 56 nn. 62–64, with reference to Schütze, "Beamtenpolitik im Dritten Reich."

51. Cf. Seel, in Frank, *Deutsches Verwaltungsrecht*, 151, 158 f.

52. For a definition of "ex-combatant" (*Frontkämpfer*), see no. 3 of the Third Implementing Order to the Professional Civil Service Code of May 6, 1933 (*RGBl*. I 245): "(1) An ex-combatant as defined by the law is anybody who took part in a battle, engagement, trench warfare, or siege in the World War (between August 1, 1914, and December 31, 1918), according to the entries in the war roll. . . . (2) An ex-combatant is anyone, in particular, who has received the war-wounded decoration. (3) Participation in the battles in the Baltic, Upper Silesia, against Spartacists and separatists, and against the enemies of the national revolution is equivalent to participation in World War battles."

53. Compilation from the Reich Ministry of the Interior, undated (presumably end of 1933), quoted in Mommsen, *Beamtentum im Dritten Reich*, 57 n. 65.

54. Lorenzen, "Das Eindringen der Juden in die Justiz vor 1933" (1939), with extensive statistics on Jewish judges and lawyers. According to these figures (765 f.), the following numbers of Jewish judges and public prosecutors employed in the Reich judiciary between November 9, 1918, and December 31, 1935, had been dismissed: 928 by January 30, 1933; 574 officials by April 30, 1934, on the basis of Professional Civil Service Code sec. 3; 239 officials on the basis of the Reich Citizenship Law, sec. 3 ("only citizens of the Reich may hold . . . an official office"); a total of 1,741 non-Aryan officials by December 31, 1935. (Lorenzen was *Amtsgerichtsrat* in the Reich Ministry of Justice) The statement by Blau, *Das Ausnahmerecht für Juden in Deutschland* (1965), 18, according to which 381 of 717 non-Aryan judges and public prosecutors lost their jobs and 336 stayed in office, has not been confirmed, since the source quoted in *DJ* (1934): 950 f. refers only to the lawyers and notaries leaving the service.

55. Prussian Ministry of Justice circular of June 27, 1933, cited by Bracher, Sauer, and Schulz, *Die nationalsozialistische Machtergreifung* (1962). Of the 1,704 non-Aryan judiciary officials in Prussia (out of a total of 45,181 officials), 214 high-ranking officials, 35 assistant judges, 65 junior barristers, and 17 others remained in office (19.4%) (Schorn, *Der Richter im Dritten Reich*, 730 f.).

56. Lorenzen, "Das Eindringen der Juden in die Justiz vor 1933," 765 f.

57. Statistics quoted by Schorn, *Der Richter im Dritten Reich*, 730 f., who gives an overview of the conditions in the individual State Superior Court districts.

58. The 8 Jewish assistant judges were dismissed immediately (total 17 dismissals, i.e., approx. 3% of senior officials); (of 70 Jewish junior barristers, 7 were allowed to continue their training for the time being and 63 were dismissed). Of the 6 judges referred to in the text who remained in office, 2 *Oberlandesgerichtsräte*, both qualified judges who had been proposed for promotion to the *Reichsgerichtsrat*, were forcibly retired in the course of the year. One (Hess) emigrated to the USA and was apppointed honorary *Reichsgerichtsrat* after the war; another (Prof. Goldschmidt) was killed when the ship he was traveling in was torpedoed. The two others, *Oberlandesgerichtsräte* and excombatants, resumed their duties after "forced leave" but were definitively pensioned off in 1935

on the grounds of the First Decree to the Reich Citizenship Law of November 14, 1935 (*RGBl.* I 1933). One (Dr. Wolff) died in Auschwitz, and the other (Ikenberg) emigrated and returned after the war (details from Wolfram and Klein, *Recht und Rechtspflege in den Rheinlanden*, 217, 233).

59. Johe, *Die gleichgeschaltete Justiz*, 65 ff., based on material from Hamburg; he states that even before the Professional Civil Service Code was promulgated, three public prosecutors (including the prosecutor general) asked to be freed from their duties. The presiding judge of the *Landgericht* was superannuated at his own request. The irremovable Jewish judges were excluded from penal justice by a reorganization of duties, so arranged that Jewish judges no longer sat together in the disciplinary courts. Five further judges were dismissed on the basis of the Reich Citizenship Law of September 15, 1935 (*RGBl.* I 1146). In fall 1936 five Jewish judges and public prosecutors (most in the civil law field) were still active (Johe, *Die gleichgeschaltete Justiz*, 67), as were those judges with Jewish wives working in civil law (circular of October 4, 1937, from the Reich Minister of Justice, quoted in Johe, *Die gleichgeschaltete Justiz*, 67 n. 29). On April 13, 1933, the president of the *Land* Justice Administration (Rothenberger) ordered that "the convocation of Jewish and Marxist jurors and commercial court judges should cease in the Hamburg courts" with immediate effect (67 n. 30).

60. Data on overall figures from a speech by Hamburg justice senator Rothenberger, quoted in Johe, *Die gleichgeschaltete Justiz*, 70 nn. 36, 37.

61. Data from the official report of December 4, 1950, by State Superior Court presiding judge of Hamm to the minister of justice of North Rhine–Westphalia, in Weinkauff and Wagner, *Die deutsche Justiz*, 102. The official figures given by Schorn, *Der Richter im Dritten Reich*, 730 f., are not the same, however.

62. Mommsen, *Beamtentum im Dritten Reich*, 56; regarding Gürtner, see von Krosigk, *Es geschah in Deutschland* (1961), 319 f.

63. Cf. the official report by State Superior Court presiding judge of Hamm (Weinkauff and Wagner, *Die deutsche Justiz*, 102), according to which grounds for disciplinary measures (promotion freeze, demotion, forced retirement, dismissal) included membership in one of the Weimar parties or a freemason lodge; denunciations and actions from Party offices, e.g., on account of mistreatment or condemnation of SA members on trial before 1933; being on friendly terms with a Jewish lawyer; not giving the German salute; not making donations to the NSDAP; and having a "defeatist attitude." In addition, a judge was attacked by the press following a decision not approved of by the Party and subsequently taken away by the SA and mistreated. It is not stated which of these grounds gave rise to which sanctions.

64. According to the statistics of the Prussian Ministry of Justice quoted by Schorn, *Der Richter im Dritten Reich* (the number of non-Aryan cases is given in parentheses), among higher-ranking officials 2 cases were dealt with on the basis of Professional Civil Service Code sec. 2, 2 (1) cases based on Professional Civil Service Code sec. 2a, 100 (36) on Professional Civil Service Code sec. 4, 290 (95) on Professional Civil Service Code sec. 5, and 192 (64) on Professional Civil Service Code secs. 5 and 6, a total of 586 cases.

65. Cf. sec 5, pars. 1 and 2, of the First Decree to the Reich Citizenship Law of November 14, 1935 (*RGBl.* I 1333).

66. The law providing for changes in the general Civil Service regulations (*RGBl.* I 433), designed to clarify the new position created by the Professional Civil Service Code of April 7, 1933, was enacted as early as June 30, 1933. No clarification, not to speak of finalization, of the changes was achieved, however, as the subsequent amendments show.

67. *RGBl.* I 39 f.

68. *RGBl.* I 1146.

69. See, for example, the introduction of the Nuremberg Laws in Austria by the decree of May 31, 1938 (*RGBl.* I 607).

70. *RGBl.* I 1333; cf. in this regard the circular of December 21, 1935, from the Reich and

Prussian minister of the interior, issued also in the name of all Reich ministers (*MinbliV* [1935], no. 52, 1506), according to which Jewish holders of an official post (civil servants and all persons called upon to fulfill important duties such as, for example, "arbitrators, meat inspectors, stamping officers") were excluded as early as November 15, 1935, by virtue of the law. A previous circular of December 9, 1935, from the Reich and Prussian minister of the interior (*MinbliV* [1935], no. 51, 1467) ruled that all Jewish officials remaining in office should be pensioned off in accordance with sec. 4, par. 2, of the First Decree, effective *December 31, 1935*. For the corresponding pension entitlement arrangements, see Reich Supreme Court III 12/39 of December 8, 1939 (HRR 1940, 864). (Sec. 4, par. 2, of the First Decree to the Reich Citizenship Law was repealed by sec. 2 of the Seventh Decree to the Reich Citizenship Law of December 5, 1938 [*RGBl.* I 1751]).

71. Lorenzen, "Das Eindringen der Juden in die Justiz vor 1933," 956 f.

72. Although art. 129, par. 1, sentence 3, of the Weimar Reich Constitution spoke of the "inviolability" of the well-earned rights of officials, the arrangements for retirement benefits (par. 2) were subject to simple legal reservation.

73. Cf. memorandum of January 17, 1939, from the deputy Führer to the head of the Four Year Plan, quoted in Blau, *Das Ausnahmerecht für Juden in Deutschland*, no. 212 (Nuremberg doc. PS-069). *RGBl.* 1938 I 1751.

74. Reich Labor Tribunal, decision of February 6, 1937, Reich Supreme Labor Court 222/36, Cologne, *JW* (1937): 2070 f.

75. Sec. 2, par. 1 of the Second Decree to the Reich Citizenship Law, dated December 21, 1935 (*RGBl.* I 1524).

76. *RGBl.* I 39 ff., with implementing orders of June 29, 1937 (*RGBl.* I 669), October 13, 1936 (*RGBl.* I 1421), November 12, 1941 (*RGBl.* I 715), June 29, 1942 (*RGBl.* I 416), July 29, 1942 (*RGBl.* I 483), October 13, 1942 (*RGBl.* I 624), June 22 1943 (*RGBl.* I 367).

77. Cf German Civil Service Code, sec. 184, par. 2. Deviations from the old Reich Civil Service Code are found in the provisions on race (secs. 25 ff.) and political trustworthiness (sec. 26, par. 1, no. 3; sec. 71) and the provision in sec. 148 on important duties to be fulfilled only by officials.

78. Cf. Huber, "Die verfassungsrechtliche Stellung des Beamtentums" (1941/43); Maunz, "Die Auslese in der deutschen Beamtengesetzgebung seit 1933" (1942); Muth, "Die verfassungsrechtliche Stellung des Beamtentums" (1942); regarding the validity of officials' terms of employment in the Third Reich, cf. BVerfGE, 6, 32 ff., which declared all terms of employment established between 1933 and 1945 to be null and void.

79. In connection with such breaches of the established principles of the Civil Service and general equality, which also reigned in the Third Reich, is the fact that women in public service were considerably disadvantaged, although art. 128, par. 2, of the Weimar Constitution had removed all exceptional provisions discriminating against female officials. Thus women could become officials only at the age of 35 years (men 27), and those who married were dismissed if their economic maintenance was "permanently assured," i.e., if the husband was a civil servant for life (DBG [German Civil Service Code], sec. 28, par. 2., subpars. 1, 63). On account of the manpower shortage resulting from conscription to the Wehrmacht, this rule was relaxed again by the decree of October 9, 1942 (*RGBl.* I 580). The Reich Ministry of Justice was in the forefront of the restrictions, a circular of January 10, 1936, having already ordered that women could no longer be admitted as judges and public prosecutors, except in cases in which dismissal would cause economic distress. Serving female judges could be employed only in matters of voluntary jurisdiction. A circular of January 16, 1936, stated that nonemployment of women as judges was "an order of the Führer" and that women could henceforth be employed only in the judiciary administration (Reich Ministry of Justice decree collection, Federal Ministry of Justice). A circular of July 4, 1944, ordered that on account of the poor employment situation, women could now be called upon as judges at any time, but only in voluntary jurisdiction (BA R 22/provis. no. 20510).

80. Sec. 6 of the law of June 30, 1933, amending regulations in the field of general Civil Ser-

vice, salary, and pensions law (*RGBl.* I 433) in conjunction with no. 3 of the directives of August 8, 1933 (*RGBl.* I 575), under sec. 1a, par. 3, of the law (of June 30, 1933).

81. Reich Civil Service Code, sec. 1a, par. 3, in the version of June 30, 1933 (*RGBl.* I 433), and no. 10 of the second amending order to the second implementing order to the Professional Civil Service Code of September 28, 1933 (*RGBl.* I 678).

82. Reich Ministry of the Interior directives of August 8, 1933, no. 2, par. 1 (*RGBl.* I 575).

83. First Law on the Transfer of the Judiciary to the Reich, February 16, 1934 (*RGBl.* I 91).

84. Procedural Regulation for the Education of Jurists, sec. 10, par. 1, of July 22, 1934 (*RGBl.* I 727), in conjunction with sec. 25 of the First Implementing Order of September 13, 1934 (*RGBl.* I 831). According to the First Decree to the Reich Civil Service Code of November 14, 1935 (*RGBl.* I 1333), descent from three Aryan grandparents was in principle sufficient to be considered of German blood.

85. As early as 1933 the amendment to the Reich Civil Service Code (RGB sec. 1a, par. 3, in the version of the law of June 30, 1933, *RGBl.* I 433) laid down imperatively that no person married to a non-Aryan could hold an official post. The proof of Aryan descent that had been required of each applicant to the Civil Service since mid-1933 included proof of descent of the spouse or fiancé (no. 2, par. 1, of the directives of the Reich Ministry of the Interior of August 8, 1933 [*RGBl.* I 575], relating to sec. 1a, par. 3 of the Reich Civil Service Code in the version of the law of June 30, 1933 [*RGBl.* I 433]). In the Reich justice administration, the same also applied to applicants for the post of judge and public prosecutor, in line with the general decree of the Reich Ministry of the Interior of April 1, 1935 (*DJ* [1935]: 546, no. 4c, sec. II). Cf. also Reich Ministry of Justice circulars of April 15, 1936, and December 7, 1936, in accordance with which the obligation to prove Aryan descent could be extended to officials of the Reich Ministry of Justice and their wives (BA R 22/4433); see in addition secs. 3, 4, 14 of the implementing orders to the Career Code for judges and public prosecutors of June 26, 1935 (*RGBl.* I 312). Under the terms of the Reich Ministry of Justice decree of October 4, 1937, judges married to Jewish women could henceforth be employed only in land register, administrative, and registry matters—on no account in personnel matters (BA R 22/20597).

86. The wording of the regulation was "The official is to be dismissed if after his appointment it is established that he or his wife are not of German or related blood or if after his appointment he marries a person of non-German or related blood without the authorization required in accordance with sec. 25, par. 2, subpar. 2, or par. 3 [conditional authorization of the Reich Ministry of the Interior for marriage with persons of "non-German or related blood"]. This rule does not apply if at the time of the appointment or the marriage it was presumed through no fault of his own that he or his wife was of German or related blood."

87. Cf. Professional Civil Service Code, sec. 8; Reich Supreme Labor Court of February 6, 1937, *JW* (1937): 2070 f. Cf. Reich Labor Tribunal decision of November 3, 1937, Reich Supreme Labor Court 186/37, Breslau, *JW* (1938): 977 f.

88. German Civil Service Code, sec. 72, read, "(1) If in cases covered by sec. 59, par. 1, it is assumed through no fault of the official that he or his wife are of German or related blood, he should be superannuated; if he is an official until revoked, he should be dismissed; sec. 62, pars. 1 and 2, apply. (2) Sec. 15, pars. 2 and 3, apply analogously."

89. The official was an "executor" of the state borne by the NDSAP (German Civil Service Code, sec. 1, par. 2), and "his whole behavior had to be guided by the fact" that the NDSAP was the "vehicle of German state thinking" (German Civil Service Code, sec. 3, par. 2).

90. Decision of the Reich Disciplinary Court of June 12, 1940 (RDHE 3, 55, *DVerw.* [German Administration] [1941]: 21); grounds for dismissal were intimate relations on the part of the official with a Jewish woman before the coming into effect of the Nuremberg Laws, which he subsequently continued on a platonic basis. The Reich Disciplinary Court stated, among other things, that the accused "ought to have conformed more to the position of the state toward Judaism."

91. Subsequently the Reich Ministry of Justice investigated three notaries in accordance with

sec. 71 of the German Civil Service Code in conjunction with the Reich Notary Code of February 3, 1937, sec. 38, par. 3 (*RGBl.* I 191), with the aim of pensioning them off on grounds of political untrustworthiness (preliminary instructions of May 19, 1938, and December 6, 1938, respectively, Nuremberg doc. NG-901). The result of the proceedings is not known.

92. According to an (undated) account by the Reich Ministry of Justice, the procedure provided for in German Civil Service Code sec. 71 was resorted to 11 times between 1938 and 1941:7 times against judges and 4 times against notaries. The grounds for forced retirement or dismissal were affiliation with the church, buying from Jews, "a friendly attitude toward Poles," etc. In addition, proceedings were instituted (on January 20, 1944) against a half-Jewish justice official on grounds of *Rassenschande* (racial defilement) (BA R 22/4469), which in the absence of a provision in the German Civil Service Code corresponding to the Aryan Paragraphs of BBG, sec. 3, were carried out on the basis of German Civil Service Code sec. 71.

93. See, for example, the secret notification from the Reichsgericht presiding judge of December 21, 1942, in which he conveys to the Reich minister of justice that "according to your instructions" two *Reichtsgerichtsräte* have been transferred to other senates (higher court divisions). The document bears the handwritten note by Reich Minister of Justice Thierack, "Copy to Party Chancellery" (BA R 22/20325). The basis for the transfer was the German Civil Service Code, sec. 35, replaced by sec. 1 of the Second Decree on Measures concerning the Rights of Officials of October 9, 1942 (*RGBl.* I 580) (see also note 94).

94. According to the decree of October 9, 1942, any official could be transferred "when required by the service" to a position with a similar career status—even to one with a lower salary (though maintaining the same pension benefits). A Reich Ministry of Justice decree dated October 1942 (Nuremberg doc. NG-199) created a similar situation for officials of the justice administration. The Reich Chancellery had approved this decree on condition that it be used only when other legal measures were not adequate (letter of November 11, 1942, from the RMuChdRkzlei to the Reich Ministry of Justice [ibid.]).

95. *RGBl.* I 71.

96. Sec. 3 of the German Civil Service Code stated: "(1) Appointment to the Civil Service is a mark of trust by the state leadership, which the official must justify by remaining constantly aware of the high duties with which his office entrusts him. Führer and Reich demand true love of the Fatherland, a willingness to make sacrifices, complete dedication, obedience to superiors, and comradeship toward colleagues. The civil servant should be a model of loyal fulfilment of duty to all his fellow citizens. Toward the Führer, who assures him of his special protection, he must remain loyal unto death. (2). . . . (3) The official is responsible for the conscientious execution of his duties."

97. Reich Disciplinary Court, May 3, 1939, RDHE 3, 1 (3).

98. Seel, in Frank, *Deutsches Verwaltungsrecht*, 151 ff., 164.

99. RuPrMdI circular of February 27, 1936, Sp. 275–78: In the event of the resignation of an official from the NSDAP, the deputy Führer was required to inform his highest superior. A thorough investigation had to be carried out in every case as to the official's reasons for leaving the Party. If it was because he refuted the Party's program or political position, he could no longer remain in official service. But even if this was not the case, the withdrawal of an official from the Party, given the close relations between Party and state, could lead to the conclusion that he lacked a sincere commitment to the National Socialist State, or that he lacked the necessary spirit of sacrifice. He could then expect at least to be excluded from preferential promotions and to be demoted in the case of normal promotions.

100. Decision of the Reich Disciplinary Court, August 16, 1939, RDHE, vol. 3, 14. This was a primary-school teacher who had left the NSDAP because he felt let down in a matter of maintenance and had made insulting remarks toward his superiors. The Reich Disciplinary Court sentenced him to a one-tenth reduction in salary for three years. For a similar case—resignation from the Party not necessarily a cause for dismissal—see also Prussian Administrative Supreme Court,

June 23, 1937, *RVerwBl.* (1937): 385; OVGE, 100, 285; decision of the Reich Disciplinary Court of May 20, 1938, *RVerwBl.* (1938): 865.

101. Cf. Seel (Seel was *Ministerialdirigent* [a high official post] in the Reich Ministry of the Interior), in Frank, *Deutsches Verwaltungsrecht*, 164. "Thorough investigation" was necessary to decide whether an official could remain in office.

102. Prussian OVG, *RVerwBl.* (1937): 762.

103. Bracher, Sauer, and Schulz, *Die nationalsozialistische Machtergreifung* (1962), 172.

104. Cf. Seel, in Frank, *Deutsches Verwaltungsrecht*, 164: "in the circumstances reigning today, not all the present generation can be considered for membership in the NS." Certainly only part of the Civil Service corps had joined the Party by May 1, 1933, when the ban on new members was instituted (see Schäfer, *NSDAP*, 35 f.). According to Diehl-Thiele, *Partei und Staat im Dritten Reich*, 56, based on NSDAP statistics (NSDAP, *Parteistatistik der NSDAP*, vol. 1 [1935], notes 65, 67), some 250,000 officials joined the Party between January 30 and April 30, 1933. By January 1, 1935, approximately 20% of all officials (307,205 out of a total of 1,483,768) were members of the NSDAP; only 18.6% of these had been Party members before January 30, 1933; 81.4% were the so-called March intake, who joined the Party between January 30 and April 30, 1933. Teachers were represented particularly strongly in the NSDAP; already by the end of April 1933, almost one in three teachers was a member (84,993 out of a total of 271,184 teachers) (Diehl-Thiele, *Partei und Staat im Dritten Reich*, 56 n. 67). Although the principle of voluntary membership was constantly emphasized, strong pressure was often exerted on officials to join (60 n. 80); see also the decree of the deputy Führer no. 101/39 of May 8, 1939, in which Bormann asks for an investigation of why a number of *Gemeinderäte* (honorary officials) in various *Gaue* had not joined the Party and demands that they be dismissed should their failure to join be out of "lack of interest in Party duties" (quoted in Diehl-Thiele, *Partei und Staat im Dritten Reich*, 60 n. 80).

105. Seel, in Frank, *Deutsches Verwaltungsrecht*, 164, who speaks of a circular from the Reich and Prussian minister of the interior according to which applicants for official positions whose sixteenth birthday was after December 31, 1935, had to be successful graduates of the Hitlerjugend. Thus it was ensured that all officials would be National Socialists "in the not too distant future."

106. Decision of the Berlin Disciplinary Court of May 3, 1939, cited at the Federal Disciplinary Court proceedings of July 21, 1955 (*Entscheidungssammlung* [1955]: 174 ff.). The applicant had been dismissed for failing to join the NSV and negligent execution of the Hitler salute as an expression of his lack of respect for a superior. The Federal Disciplinary Court acknowledged that the sanction for the applicant's nonmembership in the NSV had a political basis. This was, however, not the case for his lack of respect toward a superior: this action had been rightly punished, since a negligent salute to a superior—even if the prescribed form was the Hitler salute—was a dereliction of duty in any regime. In this connection see the annotation "Der rechtsstaatliche Kern im Hitlergruß," in Kirn, *Verfassungsumsturz oder Rechtskontinuität* (1972) (digression).

107. Seel, in Frank, *Deutsches Verwaltungsrecht*, 164.

108. The Reich Disciplinary Court fined a police captain a 5% reduction in wages for a year for buying goods from Jews (*Amtliche Entscheidungssammlung*, 2:69). As late as 1937, the Baden Administrative Court reduced by 20% the retirement pay of a Baden Bürgermeister who had sold a cow to a Jewish cattle dealer, claiming, "In accord with the representative of the state interests, the Disciplinary Court holds the fundamental view that the obligations of an official preclude business relations with members of the Jewish race, even in his personal affairs" (*DVerw.* [1937]: 286); in a similar vein the Reich Disciplinary Court reduced an official's salary in a judgment of March 21, 1939, stating that "if in the National Socialist state in 1935, 1936, and 1937, an official still buys goods from a Jew, whether directly or through a third party, he thereby damages not only his reputation and that of the whole Civil Service, but he also betrays the trust placed in him in the crudest fashion" (*DVerw.* [1940]: 13).

109. A Jewish official who had been in retirement since 1925 and possessed an undeclared

fortune abroad (approx. 120,000 Swiss francs) was sentenced to two and a half years' hard labor and the forfeit of his entire pension by the Reich Disciplinary Court (*Reichsverwaltungsgericht* E 2, 2213).

110. Reich Ministry of the Interior circular of July 11, 1933 (*MinbliV* [1933]: Sp. 807–10).

111. See, for example, the decree by the *Oberpräsident* of the Rhine Province to the Reich and state authorities and all Party offices, *Geheimes Staatsarchiv*, Rep. 90, no. 2326, sheets 307–9 (also quoted in Brandt, *Die politische Treuepflicht*, 123 ff.).

112. Reich Ministry of the Interior circular of June 22, 1933, on "Combating defeatism (*Miesmachertum*)," *MinbliV* (1933): Sp. 731–32, which reveals particularly clearly the prevailing mores in Civil Service law:

It has frequently been observed of late that officials, employees, and workers express opinions in conversations with other persons that are apt to foment discontent about the measures taken by the national government and sow the seeds of mistrust. Such people can be rightly described as defeatists. I wish to make it clear to all officials, employees, and workers that in future such methods will be looked upon as a perpetuation of Marxist agitation, and the perpetrators will be regarded as crypto-Marxists still pursuing Marxist goals. I also request all officials, employees, and workers who have supervisory duties to take note of such cases and to let me know the names of the people involved immediately. I shall have to regard failure to do so as a clear declaration of solidarity with such agitators and trouble-makers.

113. This was particularly true of the jurisdiction of the Reich Disciplinary Court (*Reichsdisziplinarhof*, later renamed *Reichsdienststrafhof*); see BVerfGE, 3, 107 ff., for details.

114. *RGBl.* I 1333; the text of the provision was "(2) Defined as a Jew is also a citizen descending from two fully Jewish grandparents, a *Mischling* who (a) belonged to the Jewish religious community at the time of promulgation of this law or was later received into it; (b) was at the time of promulgation of this law married to a Jew or later married one such; (c) descends from a marriage with a Jew as defined by par. 1, contracted after the coming into effect of the Law for the Protection of German Blood and German Honor of September 15, 1935 [*RGBl.* I 1146]; (d) was born from extramarital intercourse with a Jew as defined by par. 1 and born out of wedlock later than July 31, 1936."

115. See Stuckart and Globke, *Reichsbürgergesetz* (1936), 17 ff.; H. Graml, "Zur Stellung der Mischlinge 1. Grades," *Gutachten des IfZ* 2:31 f.; Fauck, "Verfolgung von Mischlingen."

116. *RGBl.* I 433; under the terms of sec. 1a, par. 3, non-Aryans were denied a career in the Civil Service. The directives of August 8, 1933 (*RGBl.* I 575), under sec. 1, par. 3, of this law defined a person as non-Aryan if even only one parent or one grandparent was non-Aryan.

117. Circular of November 16, 1934, ZS, file 257, sheet 75.

118. See Fauck, "Verfolgung von Mischlingen," report 2, 29 ff.

119. For the general legal status of *Mischlinge*, see the memorandum prepared by the office of the *Reichsführer*-SS in 1944, which contains proposals with much detail in this regard (IfZ, Personal Staff archives, RFSS, microfilm).

120. See, for example, the record of a discussion on March 6, 1942, at the Reich Security Main Office (RSHA) on the "final solution to the Jewish question" with reference to the forced sterilization of all *Mischlinge* (Nuremberg doc. NG-2586; excerpts in Poliakov and Wulf, *Das Dritte Reich und die Juden* [1961], 385 f.).

121. Decree of the head of the Four Year Plan of October 13, 1943, quoted in Fauck, "Verfolgung von Mischlingen," 29.

122. Reich Ministry of the Interior decree (signed by Stuckart), 1944, undated (ZS, file 257, sheet 76), which contains the request "Please do not publish or discuss publicly" (to keep the planned discriminatory measures secret).

123. Ibid.

124. See the record of the discussion of March 6, 1942, at the RSHA (note 120, above).

Part One. Section 1. III. Race Legislation in the Narrower Sense

1. See von zur Mühlen, *Rassenideologien* (1977), 244.

2. *RGBl.* I 529 (with amending laws of June 26, 1935 [*RGBl.* I 773], and of February 4, 1935 [*RGBl.* I 119]). See also the implementing order of August 31, 1939 (*RGBl.* I 1560).

3. Detailed references and examples will be found in K. Nowak, *"Euthanasie" und Sterilisierung im "Dritten Reich" Die Konfrontation der evangelischen und katholischen Kirche mit dem "Gesetz zur Verhütung erbkranken Nachwuchses" und der "Euthanasie"-Aktion* (1978), 42 f.

4. Hereditary diseases listed in sec. 1, par. 2, of the law were congenital mental retardation, schizophrenia, cyclic (manic-depressive) psychosis, hereditary epilepsy, Huntington's chorea, inherited blindness, hereditary deafness, and severe malformation; in addition, people suffering from severe alcoholism could be sterilized.

5. Nowak, *"Euthanasie" und Sterilisierung im "Dritten Reich,"* 40 ff., 41 f.

6. See Reich Ministry of Interior circular of February 27, 1934, Az. IIIa II 713/34 (*MinbliV* [1934], no. 10, 455), which states:

> First and foremost it should be made clear that appropriate measures must be taken to prevent reproduction. Persons with congenital diseases as defined by the law of July 14, 1933, must ... be removed to an institution with or without their consent or that of their relatives. ... It is particularly stressed that for the purposes of the law a "closed institution" ... must be such that the prevention of reproduction is fully guaranteed. ... Special arrangements may be necessary for guarding persons ... who by virtue of the type of their disease or infirmity do not endanger or disturb those around them, such as the physically weak, congenitally blind, and deaf-mute. The measures necessary to ensure prevention of reproduction ... must always be taken notwithstanding.

7. Hereditary Disease Court, decision of April 19, 1934 (Az. 261 XIII 163/34), *DJ* (1934): 948.

8. Circular from the Reich and Prussian Minister of the Interior dated December 2, 1936, regarding the leaflet entitled "Congenitally Diseased Offspring Means Death of the Nation" (*MinbliV* [1936], no. 52, 1621), which states that "the readily understandable form in which the leaflet is written will be extremely valuable for explaining the law. It should therefore be widely used."

9. Details in Weinkauff and Wagner, *Die deutsche Justiz* (1968), 198; M. Barella, "Die Tötung Geisteskranker im Dritten Reich," *DRiZ* (1960): 144 ff.; L. Martin, "Die Tötung Geisteskranker im Dritten Reich," *DRiZ* (1960): 218 f.; Henkys, *Die nationalsozialistischen Gewaltverbrechen* (1964), 62, 65.

10. *Völkischer Beobachter*, August 7, 1929. Examples in Reich Supreme Court of January 17, 1941 (*DR* [A] [1941]: 1458), and April 1, 1942 (*DR* [A] [1942]: 1163); see also the Hereditary Disease Court, Jena, of January 25, 1939 (*DR* [1939]: 731), and Hereditary Disease Superior Court, Jena (733).

11. See more recently Nowak, *"Euthanasie" und Sterilisierung im "Dritten Reich."*

12. See ibid., 71.

13. See von zur Mühlen, *Rassenideologien*, 224; also K. Dörner, "Nationalsozialismus und Lebensvernichtung," *VjhZ* 15 (1967): 121 ff.; Nowak, *"Euthanasie" und Sterilisierung im "Dritten Reich,"* 71 ff.

14. H. Puvogel, "Die leitenden Grundgedanken bei der Entmannung von Sittlichkeitsverbrechern," legal thesis (Göttingen, 1937), pt. 2, sec. D.

15. See Nowak, *"Euthanasie" und Sterilisierung im "Dritten Reich,"* 78 ff.

16. For more details, see A. Rückerl, ed., *NS-Vernichtungslager im Spiegel deutscher Strafprozesse, Belzec, Sobibor, Treblinka, Chelmno* (1977), 66 ff.

17. Weinkauff and Wagner, *Die deutsche Justiz*, 198; Barella, "Die Tötung Geisteskranker im

Dritten Reich," 144 ff.; Martin, "Die Tötung Geisteskranker im Dritten Reich," 218 f.; Nowak, *"Euthanasie" und Sterilisierung im "Dritten Reich,"* 119 ff., 129 ff.

18. According to the Implementing Order on the Granting of Marriage Loans of June 20, 1933, sec. 1 (*RGBl.* I 377), loans were not granted if it was likely that one of the partners was not "unreservedly devoted to the national state at all times." This was interpreted such that loans were not granted if one of the partners was non-Aryan (RFM Directive of July 5, 1933, cited in Krausnick, "Judenverfolgung" [1965], 263).

19. For terminology, see Bein, "Der jüdische Parasit" (1965).

20. See, for example, the series published by the Deutscher Rechtsverlag, Berlin, *Das Judentum in der Rechtswissenschaft.* In particular see the monograph by Menzel, *Minderheitenrecht und Judenfrage* (1934), which reproduces two papers read at the Association of National Socialist German Jurists, Hamburg, on February 17 and March 28, 1933. The author was an *Amtsgericht* judge in Altona. See also Breusing, "Die Juden" (1936), 149 f.; Meyer, "Das jüdische Hehlerrecht" (1937); Ruth, "Wucher- und Wucherrecht der Juden im Mittelalter" (1937); Franz, "Der Jude im katholischen Kirchenrecht" (1937); H.-K. Klaußen, "Der Judeneid," *Dt. Rechtswiss.* (1937): 190 ff.; Göppinger, *Die Verfolgung der Juristen jüdischer Abstammung* (1963), 72 ff., reports two seminars of October 3–4,1936, on "Jews in Jurisprudence" and November 19–21, 1936, on "German Jurisprudence and Jews," in which "findings" relating "Jewry" to "[hereditary] criminality" were broadcast. See also Lorenzen, "Die Rechtstellung der Juden vor der Emanzipation" (1938); Lorenzen, "Judentum und Judenfrage" (report on a series of lecture evenings at Berlin University, January 12–28, 1939); Lorenzen, "Das Eindringen der Juden in die Justiz vor 1933" (1939) (Lorenzen was an *Amtsgerichtsrat* in the Reich Ministry of Justice). Von Medeazza, "Judenfrage und Judengesetzgebung in Europa" (1941); Feldscher, "Rassenpflege und Erbpflege im deutschen Recht" (1943) (Feldscher was an *Oberregierungsrat* in the Reich Ministry of the Interior).

21. See Reich Ministry of Interior circular of March 5, 1934 (*MinbliV* [1934], no. 11, 455), regarding training of teachers in racial studies, hereditary science, etc., which contains the following points: "(1) It is eminently desirable that teachers at all schools should take courses and workshops to gain information on the fundamentals of hereditary science, racial studies, racial hygiene, family studies, and population policy and their application to the various fields of education and teaching. Nevertheless, great care should be taken in the selection of lecturers and school principals so that only those . . . who are willing and able to draw the philosophical conclusions in the spirit of the National Socialist movement are chosen. (2) For this reason, teachers who have proved their National Socialist loyalty can be considered as leaders." See Lorenzen, "Judentum und Judenfrage," 235 ("the Jews are not only foreign to us, they are also our enemies").

22. *RGBl.* I 1146, with the first, second, and third implementing orders of November 14, 1935 (*RGBl.* I 384). For details, see Maßfeller, "Das Reichsbürgerrecht" (1935) (*RGBl.* I 3417 ff.) (Maßfeller was an official in the Reich Ministry of Justice); detailed information is also to be found in the "Confidential Information from the Party Chancellery," no. 51/680, July 17, 1942, in *Verfügungen*, 2:169 ff., 176. See also Frick, "Das Reichsbürgergesetz" (1940); Frick, "Die Rassenfrage" (1939); Gütt, "Gesundheits- und Rassenpflege im Dritten Reich" (1940).

23. See for example Gütt, Linden, and Maßfeller, *Blutschutz und Ehegesundheitsgesetz* (1937), 16 f.; Stuckart and Globke, *Reichsbürgergesetz* (1936), 14 ff. (16) ("Since only Jewry posed an acute threat to the German nation, the first aim of the law was to prevent mixing of blood with Jews").

24. See RuPrMdI circular of November 26, 1935 (*MinbliV* [1935], no. 49, 1436).

25. The term *Jew* was defined in the First Decree to the Reich Citizenship Law of November 14, 1935, sec. 5, par. 2 (*RGBl.* I 1333). The prohibition also applied to marriages between Jews and "Jewish *Mischlinge* with Reich subject status" having only one Jewish grandparent (First Implementing Order of November 15, 1935, sec. 2 [*RGBl.* I 1334]); marriages between Jewish *Mischlinge* and people of "German blood" (*Deutschblütige*), that is to say marriages between "*Mischlinge* of the

first degree" were also fundamentally forbidden; in exceptional cases a special authorization from the Reich minister of the interior or the deputy Führer could, however, be issued (First Implementing Order of November 14, 1935, sec. 3, [*RGBl.* I 1333]). Reich Ministry of the Interior decree of December 4, 1935 (*MinbliV* [1935]: 1455). There was no right of appeal against refusal of the authorization (Vienna Administrative Court, decision of January 30, 1940, *DVerw.* [1940]: 158). Marriages were also forbidden between Jewish *Mischlinge* with Reich subject status with one fully Jewish grandparent ("*Mischlinge* of the second degree") (pars. 2a and 3a and b of the Reich and Prussian Ministry of the Interior circular concerning the Blood Protection Law of November 26, 1935 [*MinbliV* (1935): 1436]).

26. According to Reich Ministry of the Interior circular, December 7, 1936 (*MinbliV* [1936], no. 53, 1631), in pursuance of the Blood Protection Law, sec. 6, with the agreement of the deputy Führer and the Reich minister of justice, it was forbidden for even a person "of German-blood" married to a Jew to "raise the Reich and national flag and display the Reich colors." The prohibition applied analogously in all cases in which Jews lived in a household with people "of German blood."

27. See the Führer's decree of October 8, 1939 (*RGBl.* I 2042), and the Decree on the Establishment of a German Ethnic Classification List of March 4, 1941 (*RGBl.* I 118).

28. Decree on the Establishment of a German Ethnic Classification List of March 4, 1941, sec. 7, par. 2 (*RGBl.* I 118), in conjunction with the Twelfth Decree to the Reich Citizenship Law of April 25, 1943, sec. 3 (*RGBl.* I 268).

29. Gütt, Linden, and Maßfeller, *Blutschutz und Ehegesundheitsgesetz*, 16.

30. Pars. 3 A and B of the RuPrMdI circular concerning the Blood Protection Law of November 26, 1935, I B 3/324 II, *MinbliV* (1935): 1429 f.

31. Sec. 6 of the First Implementing Decree to the Blood Protection Law dated November 14, 1935 (*RGBl.* I 1334); RuPrMdI circular of November 26, 1935, par. 4 (I B 3/324 II, *MinbliV* [1935]: 1429 f.).

32. See par. 5c of the RuPrMdI circular of November 26, 1935 (I B 3/324 II, *MinbliV* [1935]: 1429 f.), according to which evidence that "no offspring endangering the preservation of the purity of German blood were to be expected" had to be submitted in the form of a "certificate of fitness for marriage." Until such time, to be determined by the Reich minister of the interior, that the "certificate of fitness for marriage" would serve as evidence in a general way, the registry official had to require the certificate from partners of different races, for example, "in the case of marriage between people of German blood with Gypsies, Negroes, or their bastards."

33. Confidential information from the Party Chancellery dated July 17, 1942, no. 51/680, *Verfügungen*, 2:169 ff., 176.

34. First Decree on Protective Citizenship of April 25, 1943 (*RGBl.* I 271).

35. Memorandum of August 21, 1940, from the RFSS to the Reich Ministry of the Interior, in which he—unlike the Reich Ministry of the Interior—further wanted to prevent intermarriage between Poles and Jews (Nuremberg doc. NG-1916).

36. *RGBl.* I 1246, with First and Second Implementing Orders of November 29, 1935 (*RGBl.* I 1419), and October 22, 1941 (*RGBl.* I 650).

37. *RGBl.* I 529.

38. See note 32.

39. First Implementing Order to the Marital Hygiene Law of November 29, 1935, sec. 3 (*RGBl.* I 1419).

40. According to sec. 8, par. 2, of the law, the Reich minister of the interior determined the moment at which sec. 2 would come into effect. Until then a certificate of fitness for marriage needed to be produced in doubtful cases only.

41. Second Implementing Order to the Marital Hygiene Law of October 22, 1941, sec. 1 (*RGBl.* I 650).

42. See Claudio Schwarzenberg, *Diritto e giustizia nell'Italia fascista* (Milan, 1977), 147 f.

43. See memorandum of December 27, 1938, from the Reich minister and head of the Reich Chancellery (RMuChdRkzlei) to the Reich minister of justice and notes from the RMuChdRkzlei of January 7, 1939, and March 14, 1939 (BA R 22/465).

44. The decision is quoted in Schwarzenberg, *Diritto e giustizia nell'Italia fascista*, 147 ff.; this programmatic declaration was in part codified, a law of January 5, 1939, forbidding so-called mixed marriages (*matrimoni misti*), a term that presumably included marriages between Italians and non-Aryans (see also 150 f.).

45. Party Chancellery circular of January 13, 1941, *Verfügungen*, 2:58.

46. Defense Law of May 21, 1935 (*RGBl.* I 609), sec. 15, par. 1; Jewish *Mischlinge* (half Jews) were liable to conscription but could serve only in the reserve force (Decree on the Admittance of Non-Aryans to Active Armed Service of July 25, 1935, sec. 2, par. 2, sec. 3, *RGBl.* I 1047); they were not permitted to become officers in the Wehrmacht (Defense Law of May 21, 1935, sec. 15).

47. Subpar. 3 of the Decree on Marriage of Members of the Wehrmacht (Marriage Decree) of April 1, 1936; *HeeresVOBl.* 121, quoted in Gütt, Linden, and Maßfeller, *Blutschutz und Ehegesundheitsgesetz*, 315 f.

48. Subpar. 2, no. 3a, of the implementing regulations to the Marriage Decree, *HeeresVOBl.* 123, quoted in Gütt, Linden, and Maßfeller, *Blutschutz und Ehegesundheitsgesetz*, 316. Even if the fiancé had only one grandparent who was non-Aryan, i.e., was only a so-called quarter Jew, it was sufficient grounds for refusal of permission to marry.

49. Secret decree cited in *Verfügungen*, 2:58 ff.

50. Secret decree by the OKW chief of January 26, 1942 (ibid.). The applicant had to submit a photograph, a political and racial-political assessment of the bride, a "certificate of fitness for marriage" for both parties, and proof of the Aryan descent of both. Later Hitler ordered that two full-length photographs of the bride (front and side views) in postcard format should be provided *in addition* (confidential information from the Party Chancellery 61/820, September 11, 1942, ibid., 60 f.)

51. Party Chancellery instruction no. V/10/40 of November 23, 1940, *Verfügungen*, 2:56 f.

52. Palandt, *Bürgerliches Gesetzbuch* (1942), note 2 on sec. 13 of the Marriage Law.

53. Confidential information 36/362 from the Party Chancellery of August 21, 1941, *Verfügungen*, 2:56 ff.

54. See Olczewski, "Rassengebundene Rechtsprechung" (1941), with examples from inheritance and marriage law; Mössmer, "Rassenmischehe und geltendes Recht" (1934); Maßfeller, "Grundsätze der Erb- und Rassenpflege" (1935). For details of mixed German-Jewish marriages, cf. H. Graml, "Zur Stellung der Mischlinge 1. Grades," *Gutachten des IfZ*, 2:31 f.

55. Wöhrmann, "Die Auflösung der Ehe zwischen Juden und Ariern" (1933).

56. More details in ibid.

57. Reichsgericht of August 22, 1935, IV 128/35, quoted in Gütt, Linden, and Maßfeller, *Blutschutz und Ehegesundheitsgesetz*, 210.

58. The attitude of the time is best illustrated by a passage from Rosenberg, *Der Mythos des 20. Jahrhunderts* (1933), bk. 3, IV 5, 558: "If a German woman voluntarily has relations with Negroes or Jews, she will in no event be protected by the law, nor will her illegitimate or legitimate children, who at no time are granted the rights of the German citizen."

59. *RGBl.* I 807.

60. For the preparatory work, see Mössmer, *Neugestaltung des deutschen Ehescheidungsgesetzes* (1936).

61. Palandt, *Bürgerliches Gesetzbuch*, introduction 2 to the Marriage Law.

62. Gütt, Linden, and Maßfeller, *Blutschutz und Ehegesundheitsgesetz*, 16. The Blood Protection Law, sec. 1, had forbidden only marriages between Germans and Jews; the Marriage Law, sec. 4, now forbade marriages between Germans and all "alien" persons and thus offered unlimited possibilities of extension.

63. Marriage Law, sec. 28, according to which the public prosecutor alone was authorized to prosecute in cases of annulment of marriage on the grounds of the Blood Protection Law and the Marital Hygiene Law, and in addition to the husband in all other cases of annulment (adultery, related partners, etc.).

64. According to the official statistics (Nuremberg doc. NG-2982) quoted by Adler, *Der verwaltete Mensch* (1974), 281, the number of mixed German-Jewish marriages in "Greater Germany" at the end of 1942 was 27, 774 (16, 760 in the Altreich, 4, 803 in Austria, 6, 211 in the Protectorate); as of April 1, 1943, 16, 668 German-Jewish marriages were reported in the Altreich, 12,117 of which were "privileged" mixed marriages (e.g., mixed marriages whose offspring did not count as Jews). The then *Rassenreferent* (expert in charge of the Race Desk) in the Reich Ministry of the Interior, Lösener, estimated the number of "privileged mixed marriages" in the German territories (including Holland) at about 20,000 (Nuremberg doc. NG-2982; cited by Adler, *Der verwaltete Mensch*, 281).

65. Minutes of the discussion of March 6, 1942, at the Reich Security Main Office (RSHA) on the Final Solution to the Jewish Question (Nuremberg doc. NG-2586; excerpts in Poliakov and Wulf, *Das Dritte Reich und seine Diener* [1956], 383 f.).

Part One. Section 1. IV. Citizenship Law

1. Report by the Chief of Referat I/50 (Bureau for Nationality Questions) of the office of the Reich governor of Posen (Poznaω) to the Reich governor himself, July 30, 1941. An enormous bureaucracy had developed in the Reich. In 1933 "only" 90 offices dealt with nationality questions. Now there were already 146 (Institute for Western Studies, Poznań, doc. I-145).

2. *RGBl.* I 582.

3. Thus the right to nationality was already changed de facto by the Law on Revocation of Naturalization and the Deprivation of German Citizenship of July 14, 1933 (*RGBl.* I 480), and fundamentally transformed by the Decree on German Citizenship of February 5, 1934 (*RGBl.* I 85). *Technically* the Reich and State Citizenship Law was changed in only one place by the decree of February 5, 1934 (cf. RuStAG, sec. 13), but it was then largely annulled by the Law to Amend Reich and State Citizenship of May 15, 1935, sec. 2 (*RGBl.* I 595). Further amendments through the Decree on Withdrawal of Citizenship of September 1, 1939 (*RGBl.* I 1656), and the Decree on Regulation of Nationality Questions of January 20, 1942 (*RGBl.* I 40; naturalization of foreigners permitted even without residence in the country).

4. *RGBl.* I 480, with the First Implementing Order of July 26, 1933 (*RGBl.* I 538), and the Second Implementing Order of January 16, 1941 (*RGBl.* I 40).

5. In accordance with sec. 1, par. 2, this regulation ceased to have effect two years after its promulgation but was extended by the law of July 10, 1935 (*RGBl.* I 1015), until December 31, 1935.

6. This is shown especially by the deprivation of citizenship of famous scholars, artists, and so forth.

7. First Implementing Order of July 26, 1933, no. 1a, *RGBl.* I 538.

8. Lichter, *Das Staatsangehörigkeitsrecht* (1943), sec. 1, note 1.

9. First Implementing Order of July 26, 1933, no. 1a, *RGBl.* I 538. Lichter, *Das Staatsangehörigkeitsrecht*, sec. 1, note 1.

10. Lichter, *Das Staatsangehörigkeitsrecht*, sec. 1, notes 5 and 6. Though the Reich and State Citizenship Law of 1913 also recognized withdrawal of nationality, including that of the family of the person involved, such withdrawal was limited to extremely narrowly defined cases (secs. 27 and 28).

11. First Implementing Order of July 26, 1933, no. 5, *RGBl.* I 538.

12. Lorenzen, "Das Eindringen der Juden in die Justiz vor 1933" (1939), 965 f.; Lichter, *Das Staatsangehörigkeitsrecht*, sec. 2, note 11 (57).

13. First Implementing Order, no. 1, *RGBl.* I 538.

14. For details see Lichter, *Das Staatsangehörigkeitsrecht*, 53.

15. Sec. 1 of Law on Limitation of the Right of Inheritance on Grounds of Antisocial Behavior of November 5, 1937, *RGBl*. I 1161; cf. also Lichter, *Das Staatsangehörigkeitsrecht*, note 6 to sec. 2 (56).

16. Stuckart and Globke, *Reichsbürgergesetz* (1936), introduction, 30; and Reich Citizenship Law, sec. 1, note 3: "In certain cases, however, nationality may be either acquired or lost under the current legislation without the control of the state (marriage, legitimation, etc.). Such an arrangement is difficult to reconcile with the current legislative philosophy. The state can never be denied a say in any case in which a person comes under its protection or wishes to leave it. This standpoint must be accommodated in a future new regulation of the right to nationality" (52).

17. *RGBl*. I 593, by virtue of which secs. 10–12, 26, par. 3, subpar. 2; 31; and 32, par. 3, of the Reich and State Citizenship Law were revoked, as were sec. 15, para 2, and sec. 34, insofar as they allowed a claim to naturalization. German nationality was granted at the discretion of the naturalization authorities. Claims to naturalization were generally excluded (secs. 1, 2); Lichter, *Das Staatsangehörigkeitsrecht*, 49; Kluge and Krüger, *Verfassung und Verwaltung* (1941), 167.

18. *RGBl*. I 1146.

19. Program of the National Socialist German Worker's Party (NSDAP) of February 24, 1920, quoted in Sartorius, *Verfassungs- und Verwaltungsrecht* (1944), appendix 1. See in particular Stuckart and Globke, *Reichsbürgergesetz*, 1 ff., 47 f.; Maßfeller, "Das Reichsbürgerrecht" (1935) (a reproduction of the text of the law with detailed annotations); Gütt, Linden, and Maßfeller, *Blutschutz und Ehegesundheitsgesetz* (1937), 16 ff.; Frick, "Das Reichsbürgergesetz" (1940); Stuckart, "Staaatsangehörigkeit und Reichsgestaltung" (1943); Huber, "Das Reichsbürgerrecht" (1941).

20. See Frick, "Die Rassenfrage" (1939).

21. Lösener, "Die Hauptprobleme der Nürnberger Grundgesetze" (1935); similarly, Stuckart and Globke, *Reichsbürgergesetz*, introduction, 3, 13.

22. Stuckart and Globke, *Reichsbürgergesetz*, introduction, 15, 16; see, further, 24 f.

23. Huber, "Das Reichsbürgerrecht."

24. Stuckart and Globke, *Reichsbürgergesetz*, introduction, 22 ff., 3.

25. Ibid., introduction, 1.

26. More details in Huber, "Das Reichsbürgerrecht," 16 f., 27 ff.: "A Reich citizen is a citizen who possesses nationality in the Reich and has proved his readiness to serve the German people and the Reich loyally."

27. Stuckart and Globke, *Reichsbürgergesetz*, 55.

28. *RGBl*. I 1333; sec. 4, par. 1; cf. Stuckart and Globke, *Reichsbürgergesetz*, 53, 55; nonetheless, so-called privileged Jewish *Mischlinge* (that is persons with one or two Jewish grandparents), who did not count as Jews, could be citizens of the Reich.

29. Huber, "Das Reichsbürgerrecht," 17, 27.

30. See Lösener, "Als Rassenreferent im Reichsinnenministerium" (1961); demands were made, however, for the Reich Citizenship Law to be introduced (only) for citizens of equivalent race even before the seizure of power (Nicolai, *Grundlagen der kommenden Verfassung* [1933]). It may therefore be presumed that the idea of the Reich Citizenship Law originated before 1935.

31. Conditions for acquiring citizenship in the Reich were thus possession of German nationality, being of "German or related blood," and "the will and ability of the citizen to serve the German people" (Stuckart and Globke, *Reichsbürgergesetz*, 54).

32. See Huber, "Das Reichsbürgerrecht," 25 f., 32.

33. Stuckart and Globke, *Reichsbürgergesetz*, 25, 29.

34. First Decree to Reich Citizenship Law of November 14, 1935, sec. 1, par. 1 (*RGBl*. I 1333); see Gütt, Linden, and Maßfeller, *Blutschutz und Ehegesundheitsgesetz*, 196, for more details.

35. Stuckart and Globke, *Reichsbürgergesetz*, suggest a variety of "objective characteristics" as criteria for the aptitude to "serve the German people," such as a "blameless leadership record" and

"proven professional competence," but also "fulfillment of military and labor service conscription" (54). Grounds for forfeiture of citizenship rights were thus "serious crimes, activities hostile to the state, neglect of citizen's duties, such as not serving in the Wehrmacht, unworthiness to serve, unsuitability for an official post, and professional unworthiness" (26 f.).

36. RuPrMdI circular of November 26, 1935, par. 2S, *MinbliV* no. 49, 1430.

37. In practice, persons "of German blood" were members of the races or race mixtures as represented by the National Socialist race theory in Germany (Günther, *Rassenkunde* [1930], 13 f.: Stuckart and Globke, *Reichsbürgergesetz*, introduction, 6 f.). Persons of "related blood" were primarily members of European nations or races (6 f.), with the exception of Jews and Gypsies.

38. RuPrMdI circular of November 26, 1935, *MinbliV* no. 49, 1430.

39. See Stuckart and Globke, *Reichsbürgergesetz*, introduction 6, 15, who state that "strictly speaking there is no more a Jewish race" than a German one. Cf. Adler, *Der verwaltete Mensch*, 278, for more details.

40. RuPrMdI circular of November 26, 1935, *MinbliV* no. 49, 1430, where it is stated, "The criterion whether someone is or is not Jewish is not whether he is a member of the Jewish religious community, but whether he belongs to the Jewish race. To avoid difficulties in bringing proof, it is, however, expressly stipulated [in the First Decree to the Reich Citizenship Law] that a grandparent who belonged to the Jewish religious community is automatically considered a member of the Jewish race; no evidence to the contrary is admissible." The official Party justification for associating race with religious affiliation was that at that time neither confession nor descent indicated anything about the quality of being Jewish, because the Jews had become emancipated and assimilated since the mid-nineteenth century. In the centuries preceding that time, the Jews had been a unit in terms of their faith. For that reason the religious affiliation of the ancestors had to be pursued beyond the point at which extensive assimilation occurred, that is back to about 1800 [for which reason the religious affiliation of the *grandparents* was significant—Author]. If the ancestors were Christian until 1800, the person involved was not classed as Jewish, and vice versa (Groß, "Die rassenpolitischen Voraussetzungen zur Lösung der Judenfrage" [1942], 2 ff., 6 ff.). (Groß was head of the NSDAP's Race Policy Office.)

41. OVG (Administrative Supreme Court), Hamburg, of October 6, 1939, *DVerw* (German Administration) (1940): 362 f.

42. After the Wannsee Conference, the Reich Ministry for the Occupied Eastern Territories negotiated a new definition of the term *Jew*. The agreed formulation opened the door to arbitrariness in the extreme: "(1) The term *Jew* will be defined as follows for persons who have their residence or who usually live in the Occupied Eastern Territories: (2) A Jew is a person who professes to belong to the Jewish community or has otherwise declared or acknowledged himself as a Jew or whose association with Jewry comes out of some other circumstances. (3) A person who has a parent who is Jewish according to the definition of par. 1 is considered equivalent to a Jew. In doubtful cases the *Generalkommissar* [commander of the Security Police and the SD] or the agency commissioned by him will decide with generally binding effect"; these prescriptions were also to include Jews *from* the General Government, the Protectorate, from Romania, and from Slovakia (Nuremberg doc. NG-5035; quoted by Adler, *Der verwaltete Mensch*, 283 ff.). Himmler as RFSS, however, wanted no definition of the term *Jew* (RFSS memorandum of July 27, 1942, to Gruppenführer Berger, his liaison officer with the Reich Ministry for the Occupied Eastern Territories, cited by H. Heiber, ed., *Reichsführer, Briefe an und von Himmler* [1970], 167 f.).

43. First Decree to the Reich Citizenship Law of November 14, 1935, sec. 7; for more details, see H. Graml, "Zur Stellung der Mischlinge 1. Grades," *Gutachten des IfZ* 2:31 f. The provision in sec. 7 signified that in accordance with sec. 5, par. 1, of the First Decree to the Reich Citizenship Law, so-called equivalent Jews (*Geltungsjuden* [persons counting as Jews under the law]) could apply for equivalence with *Mischlinge* of the first degree, and *Mischlinge* of the first or second degree

for equivalence with those of "German blood." According to notes made by Bernd Lösener, then *Rassenreferent* in the Reich Ministry of the Interior, on September 10, 1941 (cited by Graml, "Zur Stellung der Mischlinge," 32; and Adler, *Der verwaltete Mensch*, 293), before fall 1941 Hitler granted 339 *Geltungsjuden* equivalence with "*Mischlinge* of the first degree," 238 "*Mischlinge* of the first degree" were promoted in the Wehrmacht, and 394 *Mischlinge* were granted equivalence to "German blood"; see Lösener, "Als Rassenreferent im Reichsinnenministerium," for more details.

44. Reich Ministry of the Interior circular, *MinbliV* (1942): 1711, quoted in *Verfügungen*, 146 f., where it is stated: "Until further notice, applications from Jews and Jewish *Mischlinge* will not be dealt with. . . . Processing of current applications shall cease immediately."

45. According to Adler, *Der verwaltete Mensch*, 281, there were 72,738 half Jews living in Germany and Austria at the May 1939 census. Lösener estimates their number at 64,000 in 1939, the number of quarter Jews at 43,000, and half Jews in Bohemia and Moravia at 30,000 (Nuremberg doc. NG-2982). For the legal status and the fate of Jewish *Mischlinge* in particular, see Fauck, "Verfolgung von Mischlingen"; Graml, "Zur Stellung der Mischlinge," 31 f.; Adler, *Der verwaltete Mensch*, 284 ff.

46. See the memorandum from the Race Policy Office of the NSDAP (Hecht and Wetzel, authors) of November 1939 (Nuremberg doc. NG-3732, quoted by Adler, *Der verwaltete Mensch*, 283 f.), where it is stated: "With regard to the German-Jewish *Mischlinge* of hitherto Polish nationality, the . . . *Mischlinge* of the first degree are to be deported forthwith to the Polish *Restgebiet* (rump state). In the case of German-Jewish *Mischlinge* of the first degree, exceptions can be made in very special circumstances, if the persons involved have shown complete loyalty to Germanness and if the *Mischling* involved is married to a person of German blood. German-Jewish *Mischlinge* of the second degree may remain in the territory of the Reich if their previous political or *völkisch* behavior has given no cause for concern." No flexibility, however, is to be found in the statement, "Polish-Jewish *Mischlinge* of any degree are without exception considered equivalent to Jews and Poles and are to be deported in any circumstances."

47. Report of the Wannsee Conference of January 20, 1942 (Nuremberg doc. NG-2586), according to which exceptions were foreseen for *Mischlinge* if children ("*Mischlinge* of the second degree") considered "of German blood" were forthcoming from the marriage, also for *Mischlinge* for whom an exceptional authorization (in the event of special services) had been granted. Persons exempted from "evacuation" should be sterilized "voluntarily"; sterilization was, however, a precondition for remaining in the Reich. The sterilized *Mischling* should then be freed of "all restrictive regulations." Mass sterilization of all Jewish *Mischlinge*, proposed by the Reich Ministry of the Interior (to ensure their remaining in the Reich), was not carried out on account of the great administrative expense involved (report on a discussion in the RSHA on March 6, 1942, Nuremberg doc. NG-2586); on this and on the deportation of Jewish *Mischlinge*, see Adler, *Der verwaltete Mensch*, 285 ff., 289.

48. Huber, "Das Reichsbürgerrecht," 22 f., 27.

49. Stuckart and Globke, *Reichsbürgergesetz*, introduction, 15.

50. Kluge and Krüger, *Verfassung und Verwaltung* (1941), 167.

51. Nuremberg doc. NG-894, in BA, All. Proz. 1 XVII B 30, 3 ff. (substantiation of the draft, BA, 42–87). As the basis for the intended new nationality regulations, Mommsen, *Beamtentum im Dritten Reich* (1966), 369, names the decree by the RFSS/Reich Commissar for the Strengthening of German Nationhood of September 12, 1940, "regarding revision and segregation of the population in the incorporated territories," which provided for four levels of nationality for the inhabitants of the Annexed Eastern Territories (BA R 43 II/137). See also Broszat, *Nationalsozialistische Polenpolitik* (1961), 124 ff.

52. Thus was the summarizing note of the Reich Chancellery to the draft of February 23, 1936 (Nuremberg doc. NG-894).

53. The draft had the approval of the Reich and Prussian minister for ecclesiastical affairs; see his note of March 8, 1938, to the Reich Ministry of the Interior (Nuremberg doc. NG-894).

54. BA R 43 II/137.

55. See the decree of the RFSS/Reich Commissar for the Strengthening of German Nationhood, September 12, 1940, "regarding revision and segregration of the population in the annexed territories" (BA R 43 II/137), according to which the following people should in future live in the Annexed Eastern Territories: Germans with or without the right to Reich citizenship, "persons reinstated as Germans," "persons of German descent," Poles with simple German nationality, "valuable aliens . . . [Ukrainians, Great Russians, White Russians, Czechs and Lithuanians]," "German renegades" with German nationality unless countermanded, and "members of foreign nations" who were "protected members of the German Reich with limited indigenous rights." A German Ethnic Classification List with four sections should be set up to establish nationality. See also Broszat, *Nationalsozialistische Polenpolitik*, 124.

56. Note of June 19, 1941, BA R 43 II/137.

57. BA R 43 II/137; the draft concerned the loss of nationality on leaving the Reich territory during resettlement.

58. See note of December 6, 1942, on a meeting in the Reich Ministry of the Interior of November 21, 1942, in which the three levels of nationality (normal, conditional, and protected state subject status) were discussed (BA R 43 II/137, Bl. 1).

59. Reich Chancellery note of June 19, 1941, BA R 43 II/137. Introduction of the groups "protected nationals" and "conditional nationals" should be delayed on account of too short a testing time for the Altreich.

60. Twelfth Decree to the Reich Citizenship Law of April 25, 1943 (*RGBl.* I 268); Decree on Citizenship unless Countermanded of April 25, 1943 (*RGBl.* I 269); First Decree on Protective Citizenship of the Reich of April 25, 1943 (*RGBl.* I 271). For more details see section 1, IV, 5, "The Constitutional Status of 'Non-German' Inhabitants of the Reich and the Occupied Territories," below.

61. See the preceding note.

62. For the declaration of statelessness, see RFSS/RKF decree of September 12, 1940, BA R 43 II/137 (quoted in *Doc. Occ.* 5:144 ff.), and Decree on Protective Citizenship of the Reich of April 25, 1943 (*RGBl.* I 271). Also RGZ (Supreme Court for Civil Cases) 167, 274. Draft, December 1940, with notes from the Reich minister of the interior to the highest authorities of the Reich (Nuremberg doc. NG-2610), and Reich Ministry of the Interior communication (Stuckart), January 12, 1941, to the Reich minister and head of the Reich Chancellery (Nuremberg doc. NG-2610): it was impossible "to treat Jews, who are of alien blood, better than non-Germans of related blood."

63. See file note of December 17, 1939, from the Reich Chancellery (Kritzinger). See also Reich Ministry of the Interior letter of April 7, 1941, to the highest competent authorities of the Reich, in which the recipient is informed that the Führer considered it sufficient to strip Jews living abroad of their nationality and to confiscate their assets. Similarly, the RMuCHdRkzlei memorandum of late December 1941 to the Reich minister of the interior (all three documents in Nuremberg doc. NG-2610). On the role of the Reich Chancellery in the drafting of the Eleventh Decree to the Reich Citizenship Law, see Mommsen, "Aufgabenkreis und Verantwortlichkeit," 369 ff., 387 ff.

64. Transcript of this discussion between representatives of the Reich Ministries of the Interior, Economy, Justice, Finance, and Foreign Affairs, the Security Head Office, and others on the "regulation of nationality in the Greater German Reich," January 25, 1941, Nuremberg doc. NG-300.

65. Ibid.

66. Personal note from the Reich minister of the interior of April 22, 1941 (Nuremberg doc. NG-299); the disadvantages connected with statelessness were, however, to be regulated by a decision of the Reich Ministry of the Interior in consultation with the RFSS only in individual cases; see also note 85 below.

67. Memorandum of April 8, 1941, from the Reich Ministry of the Interior (Pfundtner) to the RMuChdRkzlei, Bl. 17 (Nuremberg doc. NG-299, also quoted in Mommsen, "Aufgabenkreis und Verantwortlichkeit," 385 n. 54), in which the Reich minister of the interior states that if German nationality is withdrawn from indigenous Jews, they "would then be stateless and subject to the law for foreigners. This obviates the politically awkward situation in which measures to be taken against the Jews, such as deportation, etc., have to be taken against state subjects." The situation must not be allowed to arise whereby, as a result of statelessness, Jews "were to be in a better position . . . [than German nationals—Author] under certain aspects of the law."

68. *RGBl*. I 1053, 1067; by virtue of sec. 7, par. 5, deportation was permitted when, among other things, a prohibition of residence had been decided against foreigners, including stateless persons, or their residence permit had expired.

69. Though in his letter of April 8, 1941, to the RMuChdRkzlei (Nuremberg doc. NG-299), the Reich Ministry of the Interior quotes the July 14, 1933, Law on Forfeiture of Citizenship (*RGBl* I 480) as the basis for the seizure of assets, the relevant sec. 2 referred only to Reich nationals living abroad. Since the Reich Ministry of the Interior supported the withdrawal of nationality from indigenous Jews, the law of July 14, 1933, on the Seizure of Assets of Enemies of the People and State (*RGBl*. I 479) was the determining factor for confiscation of the assets of indigenous nationals. The Reich Security Main Office (RSHA) and the Party leadership from 1942 on in particular supported treating all Jewish assets generally as "assets of enemies of the people and state" without proof in individual cases; see section 1, VII, "Commercial and Property Law," for more details.

70. Note of April 22, 1941, from *Ministerialdirigent* Kritzinger to the Reich Chancellery (Nuremberg doc. NG-299, Bl. 5 f.), which, however, expressly approved the withdrawal of nationality in the case of foreign Jews; for details of the different points of view, see Mommsen, "Aufgabenkreis und Verantwortlichkeit," 386.

71. Content of the "Führer's decision" communicated by the RMuChdRkzlei to the Reich Ministry of the Interior in a letter of June 7, 1941 (Nuremberg doc. NG-1123).

72. Nuremberg doc. NG-2499; this document superseded earlier drafts by the Reich Ministry of the Interior and was completely rewritten compared with the original version of December 1940 on account of the contentious question of mixed marriages (Nuremberg doc. NG-2610). The latest text was sent to the Reich Chancellery with a covering letter from the Reich Ministry of the Interior of October 22, 1941 (Nuremberg doc. NG-2499). See interministerial discussion of July 7, 1941, in the Reich Ministry of the Interior, note by Ficker, Reich Chancellery, of July 15, 1941 (Nuremberg doc. NG-2499). *RGBl*. I 722; the contents of the decree are discussed in detail by Mommsen, "Aufgabenkreis und Verantwortlichkeit," 381 ff.

73. Law on the Revocation of Naturalization and the Deprivation of German Citizenship of July 14, 1933 (*RGBl*. I 480); see section 1, IV, 1, "The Law on the Revocation of Naturalization and the Deprivation of German Citizenship," above; cf. also Kaul, *Geschichte des Reichsgerichts* (1971), 77.

74. *RGBl*. I 83.

75. Lichter, *Das Staatsangehörigkeitsrecht*, notes 5 and 6 to sec. 2 of the Eleventh Decree.

76. The term *Aufenthaltsort* (literally, the place where one is staying or residing) had a broader interpretation than *Wohnsitz* (domicile) (Civil Code, sec. 7) or *Niederlassung* (intention to settle permanently at a given place).

77. Implementing decree of December 12, 1941, from the Reich minister of the interior (*MinbliV* [1941]: 2179). Being "normally domiciled abroad" applied under sec. 11 of the decree of November 25, 1941, when a Jew resided abroad in circumstances "that indicate that his stay there is not merely temporary"; for more details, see Lichter, *Das Staatsangehörigkeitsrecht*, 146 ff., esp. notes 1–3 to sec. 1.

78. Official grounds for the drafting of an eleventh decree (Nuremberg doc. NG-2499).

79. The Annexed Eastern Territories and the Protectorate of Bohemia and Moravia were not

considered foreign countries (sec. 12), the latter being an integral part of the Greater German Reich; according to the Decree on the Loss of Protectorate Citizenship of November 2, 1942 (*RGBl.* I 637), however, the Eleventh Decree applied also to Jews of the Protectorate.

80. See letter of October 22, 1941, from the Reich Ministry of the Interior (Stuckart) to the RMuChdRkzlei (Nuremberg doc. NG-2499), according to which assimilation of the General Government to a foreign country should not be included in the Eleventh Decree, "since it does not appear appropriate to treat the General Government as a foreign country in a decree." This contrasts with the letter of January 7, 1942, from the government of the General Government, which states that "Jews evacuated from the Reich to the General Government do not automatically lose their German nationality. This is possible only on deportation from the German state or on deprivation of German nationality. The evacuated German Reich Jews are subject to the special regulations on Jews, which are generally applicable in the General Government" (ZS, Poland, binder 257, Bl. 62, and Poland 317, Bl. 6).

81. Unpublished decree of December 3, 1941, from the Reich minister of the interior (Nuremberg doc. NG-5336); see Lichter, *Das Staatsangehörigkeitsrecht*, 147 ff., note 4 to sec. 1 of the Eleventh Decree.

82. According to the decree of November 25, 1941, sec. 3, subpar. 2, the assets of Jews who were stateless when the decree came into force and had last possessed German nationality were also forfeited if they normally lived abroad. This applied to Jews who had fled or emigrated before the decree came into force. Jewish assets in the Łódź ghetto, which was within the borders of the Reich, were confiscated by a secret decree of June 25, 1942 (Reich Ministry of the Interior), in accordance with the Law on the Seizure of Assets of Enemies of the People and State of July 14, 1933 (*RGBl.* I 479).

83. The principal case was a wife of "German blood" and the child common to both (cf. Lichter, *Das Staatsangehörigkeitsrecht*, note to sec. 6).

84. Ibid., 147, note 1 to sec. 1 of the Eleventh Decree.

85. The representatives of the RFSS/RKF and the Party Chancellery had presented their points of view at the meeting of state secretaries of January 15, 1941, at the Reich Ministry of the Interior (Nuremberg doc. NG-300). After prolonged interministerial discussions, the Reich minister of the interior proposed a new draft of a decree with implementing order on April 8, 1941 (Nuremberg doc. NG-299, Bl. 11 ff.), which did not provide for any *general* exceptions to the loss of nationality for *Mischlinge* but did contain *individual* exceptions through a decision of the Reich minister of the interior in consultation with the Reich Chancellery. Jews in privileged mixed marriages would be excluded from the regulation if the children issuing from the marriage were not considered Jews (draft implementing order, Nuremberg doc. NG-299, Bl. 20). For further details, see Mommsen, "Aufgabenkreis und Verantwortlichkeit," 383 f.

86. Eleventh Decree to the Reich Citizenship Law, sec. 8.

87. The only detailed discussion is to be found in the commentary by Lichter, *Das Staatsangehörigkeitsrecht*.

88. Mommsen, "Aufgabenkreis und Verantwortlichkeit," 388 f.

89. Reich Chancellery note of June 19, 1941 (BA R 22/137).

90. RGZ 167, 274.

91. Institute for Western Studies, Poznań, doc. I-53, quoted in *Doc. Occ.* 5:114 ff.

92. *RGBl.* I 118. Details in section 2, "The Implementation of *Völkisch* Inequality in the Annexed Eastern Territories."

93. *RGBl.* I 268 f. (quoted in *Doc. Occ.* 5:165 f.).

94. See transcript of February 6, 1943, of the meeting of January 21, 1943, at the Reich Ministry of the Interior, in which nationality questions were discussed (Bl. 1, nos. 2, 5, 6, BA R 43 II/137).

95. Both decrees of April 25, 1943, *RGBl.* I 269 and 271.

96. See note from the Reich Chancellery regarding the draft of a new law on nationality of February 23, 1938, from the Reich Ministry of the Interior, according to which an "oath of allegiance" was to be taken on being received into the "protection of the German Reich" (BA, All. Proz. 1 YVII B 30, 39 ff.).

97. *RGBl.* I 315, quoted in *Doc. Occ.* 5:172 f.

98. According to a decree of the Reich minister of the interior of May 23, 1944 (quoted in *Doc. Occ.* 5:173 n. 39), "foreigners" were people "who [possess] foreign nationality or are stateless." Not considered as foreigners were Germans with "conditional nationality" (Poles in Category 3 of the German Ethnic Classification List), "protected nationals" (Poles in Category 4 of the same list), and "Protectorate nationals."

99. For the history of the decree, see *Doc. Occ.* 5:173 n. 39.

100. Decree on Protective Citizenship of March 25, 1943 (*RGBl.* I 271), sec. 11: "The Reich minister of the interior in consultation with the *Reichsführer*-SS/RKF and the head of the Party Chancellery can also regulate the legal situation of protected nationals through the administrative channels as appropriate. Such administrative regulation is binding for courts and administrative authorities." According to sec. 10 of the decree, the higher administrative authorities in consultation with the office determined by the RKF were to decide on the exclusion of the provisions contained in the decree.

101. BA R 18/468. Himmler's powers extended to effecting the return of Reich Germans and ethnic Germans from abroad, "elimination of the harmful influence of foreign sections of the population," the creation of new German settlement areas, and "the designation of living areas for the sections of the population in question."

102. Decree on the German Ethnic Classification List of March 4, 1941 (*RGBl.* I 118), sec. 10; Twelfth Decree to the Reich Citizenship Law of March 25, 1943 (*RGBl.* I 268), sec. 5; Decree on Citizenship unless Countermanded of April 25, 1943 (*RGBl.* I 269; *Doc. Occ.* 5:166 ff.), sec. 1: "The Reich minister of the interior in consultation with the *Reichsführer*-SS/RKF for the Strengthening of German Nationhood is responsible for the granting of nationality unless countermanded."

103. *RGBl.* I 118.

104. Reich Ministry of the Interior circular of November 25, 1939 (*MinbliV* [1939]: 2385).

105. RFSS/RKF directives of September 12, 1940, quoted in *Doc. Occ.* 5:114 ff.

106. Decree on the German Ethnic Classification List of March 4, 1941 (*RGBl.* I 118), secs. 5 and 6.

107. Confidential information from the Party Chancellery, no. 51/680 of July 17, 1942, quoted in *Verfügungen*, 2:169 ff., 174, 176.

108. *RGBl.* I 271.

109. General instruction no. 12/C of February 9, 1942 (BA R 22/20994; also quoted in *Doc. Occ.* 5:150 ff.), a good summary of the overall status of this group of people.

110. Confidential information from the Party Chancellery, no. 51/680, quoted in *Verfügungen*, 2:169 ff., 174, 176.

111. Administrative instruction no. 12/C of February 9, 1942 (BA R 22/20994).

112. Confidential information from the Party Chancellery, no. 51/680, quoted in *Verfügungen*, 2:169 ff., 174, 176.

113. For more details, see ibid.

114. RFSS/RKF decree no. 420 of February 16, 1942, to the highest authorities of the Reich and the governments of the *Länder*, the higher SS and police authorities, Gauleiter, *Oberpräsidenten*, and presidents of district administrations in Prussia (ZS, Versch. 29, Bl. 236–243; quoted in *Doc. Occ.* 5:156 ff.).

115. For comprehensive details of the legal status of these Poles, see the RFSS/RKF decree of February 16, 1942, ibid.

116. According to confidential information from the Party Chancellery, no. 51/680 of July 17, 1942 (quoted in *Verfügungen*, 2:176), "asocial and otherwise genetically inferior persons" and "persons of highly suspect political views" were to be "transferred to a concentration camp." "The wives and children from the latter group [were to be] resettled in the old Reich and given German nationality."

117. Ibid., 176 f.

118. Ibid., 177 f., from which the following information is also derived.

119. For the "Germanization" of Polish children, see Łuczak, *Dyskryminacja Polaków* (Discrimination against Poles) (1966), 223 ff.

120. Quoted in *Doc. Occ.* 5:168 f.

121. For more details, see Broszat, *Nationalsozialistische Polenpolitik*, 84 ff., 89 ff.

122. Confidential information from the Party Chancellery No. 51/680 (quoted in *Verfügungen*, 2:169 ff., 176).

Part One. Section 1. V. Professional and Labor Law

1. Cf. the extensive compilation of anti-Jewish measures in the public and professional domains in Kluge and Krüger, *Verfassung und Verwaltung* (1941), 215 ff. Regarding professional and commercial freedom under National Socialism generally, see Echthölter, *Das öffentliche Recht im nationalsozialismus* (1970), 208 ff.

2. Ostler, *Die deutschen Rechtsanwälte* (1971), 248 f., with numerous examples from Breslau (Wrocław), Cologne, and Munich; also Weinkauff and Wagner, *Die deutsche Justiz* (1968), 113, with references. In Breslau only a small number of Jewish lawyers were allowed to practice by order of the local police president on account of an alleged danger to public security and order—see Ostler, *Die deutschen Rechtsanwälte*, 248 f., for details.

3. Ostler, *Die deutschen Rechtsanwälte*, 249, with examples.

4. The decree of February 28, 1933 (*RGBl.* I, 83), also, did not suspend these rights.

5. Law to Relieve Distress in the Nation and Reich of March 24, 1933 (*RGBl.* I, 141).

6. Art. 2 of the Enabling Act (ibid.); replaced by art. 4 of the Law on the Reconstruction of the Reich, January 30, 1934 (*RGBl.* I, 75): "The Reich government can create new constitutional law."

7. For example, the decrees under the Reich Citizenship Law contained numerous provisions limiting the choice of profession, although according to sec. 3 of the Reich Citizenship Law the Reich minister of the interior was empowered only to issue regulations on the "execution and amendment" of the law, i.e., implementing regulations in the domain of nationality law.

8. For the situation of attorneys in general, see Noack, "Der freie Anwalt im Dritten Reich" (1936); Noack, "Die Stellung des Rechtsanwalts" (1934); see also Ulrich, "Das Recht der Patentanwälte" (1934), 1535 ff.; Wolgers, "Das Notariatsrecht" (1934), 1440 ff.; an overview is found in Ostler, *Die deutschen Rechtsanwälte*, 229 ff., 267 ff.

9. In this respect see also Ostler, *Die deutschen Rechtsanwälte*, 266.

10. See the official figures from the Reich Ministry of the Interior in *JW* (1934): 2956 and (1935): 758, according to which a total of 19,500 lawyers were accredited as of April 1, 1933; the proportion of non-Aryans at this time is not stated. The situation in Prussia is clearer: see data from the Reich Ministry of Justice in Lorenzen, "Das Eindringen der Juden in die Justiz vor 1933"; according to the data in *DJ* (1939): 966, a total of 11,814 lawyers (6,226 notaries) were accredited as of April 7, 1933, 3,370 of whom were non-Aryan lawyers (1,210 non-Aryan notaries). Similar figures are given by Frank in the *Nationalsozialistisches Handbuch für Recht und Gesetzgebung* (1934), introduction, xxviii f.: he reports a total of 11,814 lawyers admitted in Prussia as of April 1933, including 3,387 non-Aryans (28.5%) (*Kammergericht* district, Berlin, 3,890 accredited, including 1,879 non-Aryans [48%]; State Superior Court District, Frankfurt, 607 lawyers accredited, including 275 non-Aryans [45%];

State Superior Court District, Breslau, a total of 1,056 lawyers accredited, including 376 non-Aryans [35%]); the proportion of non-Aryan lawyers was particularly high in Austria (in Vienna out of a total of 2,200 lawyers, 1,750 were non-Aryan, cf. *DRiZ* [1934]: 61), where anti-Jewish regulations were introduced after the *Anschluss* by the decree of March 31, 1938 (*RGBl.* I, 383).

11. The representative body of lawyers attempted to counter such defamations; see Raeke, "Gemeinsame Mitteilung" (1934), which, referring to remarks of Göring's in this vein, declared, "The German lawyer has long created his ideal picture and feels himself to be the guardian and mediator of the law" (3049).

12. See Noack, "Die Entjudung der deutschen Anwaltschaft" (1938): "From the position of confidentiality of a doctor, a lawyer, he [the Jew] tries to infiltrate the spiritual life of his host people and to destroy their nature so as to make them always more ready to accept the Jewish culture and the Jewish poison parasite."

13. *DRiZ* (1933): 122.

14. It is presumably to this that the report by Wulf, *Theater und Film im Dritten Reich* (1966), 431, refers when stating that limited numbers only of Jewish lawyers were permitted to practice at the bar in early 1933. As a result of these measures, lists of Jewish lawyers still practicing were published.

15. Lorenzen, *Die Juden und die Justiz* (1943), 175 ff. For the legal situation after promulgation of the Law on Admission to the Legal Profession of April 7, 1933 (*RGBl.* I, 188), with respect to these prohibitions, see Ostler, *Die deutschen Rechtsanwälte*, 474 n. 14.

16. Neumann, "Vom Kaiserhoch zur Austreibung," 7.

17. Quoted from the Reich Supreme Court, *Leipziger Zeitschrift*, 1933, 1030, and from RArbG, ibid., 1149.

18. For example, the commentaries by Stein and Jonas and by Rosenberg on the ZPO and by Staub, Düringer, and Hachenburg on the Commercial Code, and in part the commentary by Staudinger; for the main specialist literature under the Nazi ban, see Göppinger, *Verfolgung der Juristen jüdischer Abstammung* (1963), 90 ff.; Ostler, *Die deutschen Rechtsanwälte*, 250. The major commentaries by A. and F. Friedländer on the Attorneys' Code and the Lawyer's Fees Code are examples of suppressed writings by Jewish attorneys (250).

19. *RGBl.* I, 109, 119; chap. XIII. By the March 28, 1934, Law on Amendment of the Regulations concerning the Legal Profession Disciplinary Code (*RGBl.* I, 252), the court of honor of the second instance, which hitherto had been conducted in the Supreme Court of the Reich, was transferred to the Reich Chamber of Attorneys; for this and the further development of the disciplinary code, see Ostler, *Die deutschen Rechtsanwälte*, 251, 261 ff.

20. Directives of the Reich Chamber of Attorneys of July 2, 1934 (*Anwaltsbl.* no. 62, 106); Neubert, "Neue Richtlinien für die Ausübung des Anwaltsberufes" (1934) (Neubert was president of the Reich Chamber of Attorneys).

21. *RGBl.* I, 186.

22. Circular issued by the Prussian minister of justice, November 20 (*DJ* [1933]: 729 ff.); the State Superior Court president was to undertake investigations of his own with regard to the accuracy of the information. See also Neumann, "Vom Kaiserhoch zur Austreibung," 8.

23. Law of April 22, 1933, *RGBl.* I, 217.

24. The Law on the Admission of Tax Advisors of May 6, 1933 (*RGBl.* I, 257), withdrew all licenses of Jewish tax advisors without exception and prohibited new admissions in general.

25. Neumann, "Vom Kaiserhoch zur Austreibung," 8 ff., from whom the following information is taken.

26. Ibid., 10; Neumann had been a member of the German Democratic Party and took his appeal to be readmitted in the capacity of notary as far as the *Reichsgericht*. Since no lawyer was prepared to take on the case before the *Reichsgericht*, he applied for ex officio counsel. The *Reichsgericht* refused, since the appeal was hopeless.

27. Weniger, "Die zahlenmäßige Entwicklung der Anwaltschaft seit 1933" (1937); according to H. Frank, based on data from the Reich Ministry of Justice in *DJ* (1934): 950, and in his *Nationalsozialistisches Handbuch für Recht und Gesetzgebung*, introduction, xviii f., the following departures occurred between promulgation of the law on April 7, 1933, and May 1, 1934. In Prussia 1,084 non-Aryan lawyers and 280 lawyers "for other reasons" (death, voluntary departure, political reasons, etc.) departed, a total of 1364. Of the 6,226 notaries practicing in Prussia on April 7, 1933, 2,051 (33%) of whom were non-Aryans, 1,199 had left the profession by May 1, 1934, 1,055 of them through revocation of their license or dismissal by virtue of the Professional Civil Service Code and 144 for "other [i.e., political] reasons." See also the statistics, which are sometimes contradictory, of the Reich Ministry of Justice for Prussia, in Lorenzen, "Das Eindringen der Juden in die Justiz vor 1933," with full tables categorized by State Superior Court district. According to details in *DJ* (1939): 966, a total of 11,814 lawyers (6,226 notaries) were registered as of April 7, 1933, including 3,370 non-Aryan lawyers (1,210 non-Aryan notaries); 1,364 non-Aryan lawyers (1,199 non-Aryan notaries) left the profession between April 7, 1933, and April 30, 1934; on May 1, 1934, a total of 10,885 lawyers (5,216 notaries), including 2,009 non-Aryan lawyers (825 non-Aryan notaries) were registered, who had also left the profession by November 30, 1938. At the end of 1933, a total of 18,053 lawyers, 2,900 (16%) of whom were non-Aryan, were still registered in Germany. On January 1, 1938, a total of 17,360 lawyers, including 1,753 non-Aryans, were registered (*Mitteilungen der Reichsrechtsanwaltskammer* [1938]: 134). Thus between 1934 and 1936 some 1,150 Jewish lawyers must have left the profession.

For the Reich see also data from the Reich Ministry of Justice in *JW* (1934): 2967, according to which a total of 19,500 lawyers were registered in the Reich on April 1, 1933. The licenses of 1,494 of them were revoked by virtue of the law of April 7, 1933, and 774 departures occurred as a result of death, voluntary resignations, etc. There were still 18,053 lawyers, including 2,900 non-Aryans, registered by the end of 1933 (number of new admissions, 794). According to information from the Reich Ministry of Justice in *JW* (1935): 758, there were a total of 18,432 lawyers on January 1, 1934, whereas 1,016 had left the profession (because they were non-Aryans or for other reasons); as of January 1, 1935, there were a total of 18,780 lawyers, 2,736 of whom were non-Aryan (approx. 15%).

28. *RGBl.* I, 522.

29. *RGBl.* I, 1258, with official explanatory notes from the Reich Ministry of Justice, *DJ* (1935): 6.

30. *DJ* (1933): 142 (*DJZ* [1933]: 130).

31. Second Implementing Order under the Law on Admission to the Legal Profession of October 1, 1933 (*RGBl.* I, 699), under the terms of which every lawyer and patent agent who remained in the profession not only "maintained full enjoyment of his professional rights" but also had "a claim to the respect due to his professional status. No lawyer or patent agent may be hindered or restricted in the exercise of his profession in conformity with the law."

32. Circular of May 26, 1933, from the *Gauobmann* (the official responsible for a *Gau*) of the League of National Socialist German Jurists in the *Gau* of Greater Berlin (transcript BA P 135, 6334, fol. 153) to the Reich and *Land* director of the League of National Socialist German Jurists, all League of National Socialist German Jurists members, the Berlin Lawyers Association, the Prussian Ministry of Justice, the president of the Prussian Supreme Court and State Court of Appeals, Berlin, and the directors of the Amtsgericht, Berlin.

33. H. Frank at the Party rally on September 14, 1934: the "unswerving aim" would remain the "removal" of Jews from legal practice (cited in Steiniger and Leszczyński, *Das Urteil im Juristenprozeß* [1969], 203).

34. Decision of the Prussian Ministry of Justice in a special issue of *DJ* (1933): 127, according to which the State Superior Court presidents had until May 5, 1933, to report and to request information on the reliability of the applicant, from the courts and chamber directors, the Police, the *Gauobmänner* of the League of National Socialist German Jurists, and "other . . . organizations that appear appropriate."

35. See the ruling of the Reich Chamber of Attorneys in EGHE (Decisions of the Disciplinary Court of the Lawyers' Chamber) 28, 166: "In the overall judgment it should furthermore not be lost to sight that as a Jew the accused had to be particularly conscious of his acceptance by the German judiciary and that this gave him particular responsibility not only to behave impeccably but also to respect the standpoint of the German people as expressed in the race legislation." A Jewish lawyer who got excited about a remiss debtor and made "remarks hostile to the state" on the record was struck off; no allowance was made for the fact that his irritability resulted from a previous illness (EGHE 29, 88). A Jewish lawyer who had mocked various National Socialist leaders was also banned. The Disciplinary Court of the Reich Chamber of Attorneys furthermore stated, "Evaluation of the accused's conduct must be based upon the fact that he is a Jew. Permission to practice his profession of lawyer in the National Socialist state carried with it an obligation to exercise the greatest discretion, especially in political matters. It was incumbent on him to avoid all remarks that could be seen as a criticism of existing conditions or which might hurt the feelings of German citizens" (EGHE 28, 166). A lawyer was also suspended for not having disclosed that his grandfather was a Jew, although he had known this to be the case since 1933 (EGHE 31, 122), as was one who in 1935 had married a Jewess who had supported him financially for years and in 1930 had saved his life (EGHE 30, 65). A later cause for dismissal was simply that a woman lawyer had eaten and walked together with a Jewish doctor who lived in the same boarding house as herself (EGHE 33, 123), and that a Jewish lawyer had written letters to a prominent emigrant (EGHE 28, 233 ff.).

36. Breaches of professional discipline included, for example, the sale of the practice through a Jewish lawyer, who was given a warning; a lawyer was reprimanded whose father had represented him on the board of the local Chamber of Attorneys in his absence and had kept quiet about the fact that the lawyer's mother was a Jewess (EGHE 29, 83). Acquiring a Jewish lawyer's practice and taking over the clientele, on the other hand, did not yet constitute an offense in 1933 (EGHE 28, 176); in 1934, however, such action was considered highly dubious (EGHE 28, 125). A lawyer who had had intimate relations and since 1935 only friendly relations with his Jewish secretary was fined 300 Reichsmark and reprimanded (EGHE 31, 62).

37. General instruction of the Reich minister of justice of December 19, 1935 (*DJ* [1935]: 1858); Neumann, "Vom Kaiserhoch zur Austreibung," 11.

38. Cf. the exclusion on May 24, 1934 (*JW* [1934]: 1509), of Jewish lawyers as advocates for the poor at the Oberlandesgericht, Frankfurt; Kammergericht, January 25, 1935 (*JW* [1935]: 1039); State Superior Court, Hamm, March 23, 1935 (*JW* [1935]: 1446); State Superior Court, Naumburg, July 5, 1935 (*JW* [1935]: 2216 f.); the refusal to admit Jewish lawyers as official defense, State Court of Appeals, Berlin, June 20, 1935 (*JW* [1935]: 2393). The State Labor Court of Appeals, Berlin, banned all non-Aryan persons from practicing law and rejected both Jewish lawyers and Association representatives as a matter of principle (decision of July 27, 1933 [*JW* (1933): 2788]); similarly, the Labor Court, Berlin, June 20, 1933 (*JW* [1933]: 1794); Labor Court, Magdeburg, May 25, 1935 (*JW* [1935]: 1895), and August 1, 1935 (*JW* [1937]: 275).

39. Circular from the Reich minister of the interior of October 17, 1938 (*MinbliV* [1938]: 1722), according to which youth agencies were forbidden to "propose" Jews as guardians, trustees, counselors, or advocates in a clearly defined domain.

40. Neumann, "Vom Kaiserhoch zur Austreibung," 14, with examples.

41. Ibid., 12, 11 f.

42. Reich Ministry of Justice general instruction of December 19, 1935 (*DJ* [1935]: 1858).

43. Grimm, "Das Reichsgesetz über die Zulassung zur Rechtsanwaltschaft" (1933): These were "not everyday laws . . . involving the organization of our legal profession in some way, but laws that constitute a central element of a completely new order, which penetrate to the very depths of our jurisdiction" (651).

44. Law of July 20, 1933 (*RGBl.* I 522) (Measures in Favor of the Overcrowded Legal Profes-

sion), which amended the rules for admission in the Attorneys' Code (secs. 5, no. 7; 6, no. 4; 5, 14a, 21a); a further law of December 20, 1934, amending the Attorneys' Code (*RGBl.* I, 1258), extended the grounds for refusing admission by way of a boundless general clause; see Ostler, *Die deutschen Rechtsanwälte*, 253 ff., for more details.

45. *RGBl.* I, 107; for the early history and content of the Attorneys' Code, see Ostler, *Die deutschen Rechtsanwälte*, 257 ff.; the relevant commission of the Reich Ministry of Justice agreed that admission should be brought into line with the judicial qualification system. But a number of quite bizarre demands were also made, such as the dismissal of all unmarried lawyers on attaining the age of forty years, those who had not fought at the front, etc. (257). The admission requirements of the new Attorneys' Code of 1936 (*RGBl.* I, 107) did not provide for formal refusal of claims, but admission was to be based on a "selection principle," for which above all evidence of National Socialist attitude and thinking was instrumental (see Ostler, *Die deutschen Rechtsanwälte*, 258, 260). This was expressed in a bland provision of the Attorneys' Code, new series, sec. 15, par. 2, whereby no more lawyers "should" be authorized than was "appropriate for orderly jurisdiction" (whereas according to sec. 2 of the old series, admission of those qualified to be judges was obligatory); thus an appraisal of need replaced the free practice of law. "No claim to admission can any longer be made. Admission is rather based on a free decision of the state. A plea against refusal is not receivable" (Noack, *Kommentar zur Rechtsanwaltschaftsordnung* [1937], sec. 15, note 17).

46. In addition to the regulations cited in the next note, see the Law on the Directors of the Chambers of Attorneys, January 6, 1934 (*RGBl.* I, 21); the Law on Amendment of the Regulations concerning the Legal Profession Disciplinary Code, March 28, 1934 (*RGBl.* I, 252); the Law Supplementing the Attorneys' Code, June 20, 1935 (*RGBl.* I, 749); the Law on the Payment of Attorney's Fees in Matters of the Poor, December 13, 1935 (*RGBl.* I, 1469); the second Law Amending the Attorneys' Code, December 13, 1935 (*RGBl.* I, 1470); and the Law on Prevention of Abuse in the Field of Legal Counseling, December 13, 1935 (*RGBl.* I, 1478).

47. *RGBl.* I, 1403; implementing regulations quoted in *JW* (1938): 2797 ff.

48. On the decree of September 27, 1938, see Noack, "Die Entjudung der deutschen Anwaltschaft"; for the effects of the decree in detail, see Ostler, *Die deutschen Rechtsanwälte*, 265 ff.

49. Ostler, *Die deutschen Rechtsanwälte*, 266.

50. *RGBl.* I, 1478.

51. Noack, "Die Entjudung der deutschen Anwaltschaft," 2796 ff.

52. Schlegelberger's testimony before American Military Court 3 on June 27, 1947, Nuremberg Trials 3, Prot. d), 4315 ff., 4347 ff., in *BA All. Proz.* 1, XVII, A 58.

53. Instruction of the Reich Ministry of Justice, *DJ* (1938): 1670.

54. Ostler, *Die deutschen Rechtsanwälte*, 266.

55. Instruction of the Reich Ministry of Justice, *DJ* (1938): 1974 (*JW* [1939]: 24).

56. Ostler, *Die deutschen Rechtsanwälte*, 266 ff., with examples.

57. See ibid., 292, with examples, based on the statements of former legal advisers; but Ostler also claims that only a few legal advisers survived.

58. Noack, "Die Entjudung der deutschen Anwaltschaft."

59. In this connection see the detailed article by the director of the *Gau* Legal Office of the NSDAP, Berlin, H. Steffens, "Die rechtliche Vertretung der Juden im Reich" (1942).

60. Gürtner, "Richter und Rechtsanwalt im neuen Staat" (1934), 372. See T. Kelfisch, "Die Stellung des Strafverteidigers im Licht der heutigen Rechtsanschauung," *JW* (1935): 3350 ff.; the author deplores the lack of the "necessary understanding and trust" on the part of the justice apparatus toward the defense counsel and the restriction of his rights (surveillance of conversations with prisoners, no access to archives in the preparatory procedure).

61. Ostler, *Die deutschen Rechtsanwälte*, 277; see also the case of the protection of the interests of the widow of the president of Katholische Aktion, Dr. Klausener, murdered by the Gestapo on

June 30, 1934, by the attorney Pünder before the State Court of Appeals, Berlin (288). Pünder was taken into protective custody, threatened several times with death, and finally released only through the intervention of the Reich minister of justice, Gürtner; for more on Pünder, see also *NJW* (1970): 1764.

62. See the example given in Fritsche, "Was ist ein Eingriff in die Berufsaufgaben eines Rechtsanwalts?" (1937): at a small civil court a local attorney was commissioned to represent the claims of a Jewish businessman from the Weimar period against the municipality. The Bürgermeister and the local section head demanded that the attorney drop the case, threatening that otherwise he "was finished in society and as a man." Complaints by the attorney to the NSRB were unsuccessful: he had "acted with complete disregard to his duty"; the rule from the system period, that "whatever is not explicitly forbidden, is permitted," no longer obtained.

63. Steffens, "Die rechtliche Vertretung der Juden im Reich."

64. By a decision of the Reich Disciplinary Court of June 6, 1944 (FD 9/44), *DR* 1945, 25), an attorney was punished for having accepted the request from a non-Jew to represent the interests of Jews who were to be "evacuated." It was held that this was permissible only with the authorization of the Chamber of Attorneys or the Gestapo.

65. Disciplinary senate at the Reich Supreme Court of June 25–26, 1943 (FD/71/43), January 27, 1944 (FD/112/43), and October 20, 1943 (FD/85/43) ("*Mischlinge* have a duty to be especially prudent in racial policy proceedings"), quoted in Neubert, "Anwaltliche Ehrenrechtsprechung in der Spruchpraxis des Dienststrafsenats" (1944), 426. By the decree of March 1, 1943 (*RGBl.* I, 123), the disciplinary code was suspended for the duration of the war and the disciplinary courts transferred to the *Oberlandesgericht* and the disciplinary senate to the Reich Supreme Court; from the adjudications of the disciplinary senate cf. also *DR* (A) (1944): 523 f., 525, 653 f., overview in Neubert, "Anwaltliche Ehrenrechtsprechung in der Spruchpraxis des Dienststrafsenats."

66. Reich Minister of Justice Gürtner, League of National Socialist German Jurists, and *Reichsfachgruppe Rechtsanwälte*, "Aus der Arbeit für das neue deutsche Volksrecht," *JW* (1934): 823 f.

67. For the attorneys' position, see Noack, "Die Stellung des Anwalts sowie der freien Berufe im Staat" (1933).

68. Quoted in Ostler, *Die deutschen Rechtsanwälte*, 279.

69. For the suspension of attorneys by the court of honor for political reasons and the difficulties of defense in political criminal actions in general, see ibid., 278 f.

70. EGHE 32, 160.

71. Steffens, "Die rechtliche Vertretung der Juden im Reich," 10.

72. Instructions of August 16 and October 8, 1934, by the deputy Führer and of November 8, 1934, by the Reichsrechtsamt (Reich Legal Office) of the NSDAP, quoted by Steffens, ibid.

73. Instructions of September 2, 1935, by the *Reichsrechtsführer*, quoted in ibid., 9; see also *JW* (1934): 2961 and (1935): 2544, 2707; Sülwald, "Grundsätzliches Verbot der Vertretung von Juden" (1939).

74. *RGBl.* I, 1403.

75. Steffens, "Die rechtliche Vertretung der Juden im Reich," 10.

76. Instruction 204/38 in *Verfügungen*, 2:405, also quoted by Sülwald, "Grundsätzliches Verbot der Vertretung von Juden." Instruction XXI-1/39, quoted by Sülwald on p. 85.

77. Announcement of December 31, 1938, by the president of the Reich Chamber of Attorneys, *JW* (1939): 274; see also Echthölter, "Das öffentliche Recht im Nationalsozialismus," 224. For attorneys who were members of the Party, sections of it, and associated organizations, authorization was granted by the NSDAP Reich Legal Office, which had basically passed its authority to the Gauleiter (*Gau* legislation office), and in district court cases to the *Kreisleiter* (Steffens, "Die rechtliche Vertretung der Juden im Reich," 12), and for all other attorneys by the president of the local Chamber of Attorneys. An authorization was also always required for representation of underage

Mischlinge of the first degree or of the Aryan wives of Jews, since in such cases the interests of the client's Jewish relatives were generally also affected. Representation of Jewish *Mischlinge* was not expressly forbidden, but attorneys who were members of the Party were expected to refuse such cases since this was "not generally compatible with the honor of Party members." In the event of infringement, there was the threat of legal action in the Party court or the court of honor. In such cases "particular discretion" was also expected of attorneys who were not Party members (11).

78. Steffens, "Die rechtliche Vertretung der Juden im Reich," 13.

79. Instructions of the deputy Führer, December 19, 1938, and of the head of the NSDAP Reich Legal Office, January 2, 1939, quoted by Sülwald, "Grundsätzliches Verbot der Vertretung von Juden," 84 ff.

80. Steffens, "Die rechtliche Vertretung der Juden im Reich," 11.

81. For the individual conditions of authorization, see ibid., 10 ff.

82. Ibid., 12.

83. Ibid., 10, with examples (including "activity on behalf of an authority": administration of assets of absentees, trusteeships, liquidations, administration of Jewish real estate—particularly their homes—since "Jewish wealth is but a part of the wealth of the German people").

84. Here too, authorization needed careful consideration, since a successful defense would lead to the incorporation of *Judenstämmlinge* (people of Jewish descent). Representation should immediately be dropped if a positive outcome no longer seemed likely (ibid.).

85. Ibid., with examples.

86. For the concept of political reliability, see ibid., 12.

87. Ibid.

88. Ibid., for the *Gauleitung* Berlin, which "always acted without clemency" in such cases.

89. Ibid.

90. "Depending on the circumstances . . . the support of the Gestapo will be called upon . . . in particularly serious cases" (ibid.).

91. Ibid., 13, without further details of the relevant instruction.

92. *RGBl.* I, 222.

93. Decree on the Activity of Dentists and Dental Technicians in Health Insurance, June 2, 1933 (*RGBl.* I, 350).

94. Decree on the Admission of Doctors, Dentists, and Dental Technicians to Health Insurance Activity, November 20, 1933 (*RGBl.* I, 983). Decree on the Admission of Doctors to Health Insurance Activity, May 17, 1934 (*RGBl.* I, 399). Third Decree on the Admission of Dentists and Dental Technicians to Health Insurance Activity, February 13, 1935 (*RGBl.* I, 192), brought into line with the arrangement for doctors (decree of May 17, 1934 [*RGBl.* I 399]) by the decree of May 9, 1935 (*RGBl.* I, 594).

95. Decree of February 13, 1935 (*RGBl.* I, 192); in the event of marriage to a non-Aryan, the license was withdrawn.

96. For dentists and dental technicians, see the decree of February 13, 1935 (*RGBl.* I, 192); ex-combatants had to have worked with the health fund for at least one year. For doctors, see the decree of May 17, 1934 (*RGBl.* I, 399), according to which doctors who were non-Aryan or whose wives were non-Aryan were admitted if they were ex-combatants (with at least one year's service on the front or severe war injury).

97. *RGBl.* I, 1524.

98. How such cases were dealt with is illustrated by that of the dismissal of Dr. K., the deputy chief physician of the Municipal Hospital in Rastatt, which in 1975 gave rise to an administrative lawsuit for compensation payments (VG Karlsruhe, AZ VII 93/75). On the basis of his contract with the city of September 15, 1929, Dr. K. was head of the Department of Internal Medicine and appointed deputy chief physician. Notice was six months in advance, at six month intervals; after

three years, notice could be given only on serious grounds. The existence of such grounds was a matter for a court of arbitration, to which each party nominated two jurors, the chairman being chosen from among the judges by the presiding judge of the *Landgericht* Karlsruhe. Dr. K. was dismissed on April 1, 1933—apparently without formal written notice—with maintenance of his salary until July 1, 1933. The dismissal was undertaken at the insistence of the NSDAP, whereas the Bürgermeister proposed submitting the matter to the court of arbitration. This proposal was rejected by the NSDAP at the request of Dr. K.'s former attorney, since "no legal measures" were necessary. In May 1933 discussions took place between Dr. K. and an attorney of the Rastatt town council, who was a notary and *simultaneously* an NSDAP representative, culminating in Dr. K.'s statement of May 23. The attorney had submitted this prepared statement to Dr. K. with the demand that he either sign it or "go to the concentration camp." Dr. K. signed the statement ("considering the acute economic situation of the town and in the spirit of the patriotic movement of our time, I renounce all claims to my service contract . . . of September 15, 1929, specifically to my monthly salary as of July 1"). After his dismissal he worked as a private physician in Rastatt. In 1934 he emigrated to the USA, where he died in 1965. [A decision to grant Dr. K. compensation payments in 1952 was opposed by the municipality of Rastatt on the grounds that his claim was not justified because he had explicitly renounced his salary—Author.]

99. RArbG, in Dersch, Hueck, Mansfeld, Mende, Nipperdey, and Volkmar, eds., *Entscheidungen des Reichsarbeitsgerichts und des Reichsehrengerichtshofs der Landesarbeitsgerichte, Arbeitsgerichte und Ehrengerichte* (ARS) (1935–36), 33:3.

100. Schäfer, "Anspruch auf Ruhegeld im Arbeitsrecht" (1939), 37.

101. Decree of September 8, 1937 (*RGBl.* I, 973). Fifth Decree on Admission of Dentists, January 12, 1938 (*RGBl.* I, 29).

102. Fourth Decree to the Reich Citizenship Law, July 25, 1938, secs. 1, 3 (*RGBl.* I, 969), and Eighth Decree to the Reich Citizenship Law, January 17, 1939, sec. 1 (*RGBl.* I, 47).

103. Fourth Decree to the Reich Citizenship Law, July 25, 1938, sec. 5 (*RGBl.* I, 969).

104. Jews were permitted only to treat other Jews or work in Jewish institutions, as were Jewish paramedical staff (Eighth Decree to the Reich Citizenship Law, January 17, 1939, sec. 2, par. 2, *RGBl.* I, 47).

105. First Decree on Professional Practice of Medicine, September 28, 1938 (*RGBl.* I, 1310).

106. *RGBl.* I, 1391.

107. *RGBl.* I, 1855.

108. Reich Ministry of the Interior decree of October 15, 1936, *MinbliV* (1936): 1330, announced in the Reich Ministry of the Interior General Decree of October 30, 1936 (*DJ* [1936]: 167 ff.). The decree also applied to all former administrative employees and the survivors of administrative employees, but not to Jewish officials in retirement.

109. *RGBl.* I, 1433, and announcement of the new version of sec. 3, par. 2, no. 5, of the Reich Physicians Decree of June 12, 1939 (*RGBl.* I, 1014). *RGBl.* I, 347.

110. Fourth Decree to the Reich Citizenship Law, July 25, 1938, sec. 3, par. 1; sec. 4 (*RGBl.* I, 969—Jewish physicians); Eighth Decree to the Reich Citizenship Law, January 17, 1939, sec. 2, pars. 1, 3; sec. 3, par. 2 (*RGBl.* I, 47—Jewish dentists, dental technicians, veterinary surgeons).

111. Regulations for the Conduct of Examinations for Pharmacists, December 8, 1934, quoted in Blau, *Das Ausnahmerecht für die Juden in Deutschland*, no. 59.

112. First Decree to the Law on the Leasing and Administration of Public Pharmacies, March 26, 1936 (*RGBl.* I, 317).

113. Eighth Decree to the Reich Citizenship Law, January 17, 1939 (*RGBl.* I, 1567).

114. Appointment Statute for Pharmacists of October 8, 1937 (*RGBl.* I, 1118).

115. Decree of September 1, 1939 (*RGBl.* I, 1567).

116. Göring, head of the Four Year Plan and chairman at a discussion on the Jewish question

at the Reich Air Ministry on November 12, 1938, shorthand transcription (Nuremberg doc. PS-1816; excerpts in Poliakov and Wulf, *Das Dritte Reich und die Juden* [1961], 75 ff).

117. *RGBl.* I, 1580.

118. *RGBl.* I, 45.

119. *RGBl.* I, 823.

120. *RGBl.* I, 713; according to sec. 5, editors-in-chief of newspapers and political journals listed in the Reich German Press Association had to be "citizens of the Reich," in possession of their civil rights, of Aryan descent, not married to a person of non-Aryan descent, over twenty-one years of age, and qualified to act and contract, as well as possessing the appropriate technical qualifications. They further had to have "the qualities" demanded by a position exerting a moral influence on the public. According to sec. 6, the requirement of Aryan descent was based on the Reich Civil Service Law and its implementing regulations.

121. See the Film Chamber Law of July 14, 1933, *RGBl.* I, 483 (uniting the German film industry in the "provisional Reich Film Chamber," which had the status of a corporation in public law with obligatory membership for all filmmakers and distributors and for *all* involved in production, including so-called film creators [secs. 1, 3]); Chamber of Culture Law of September 22, 1933, *RGBl.* I, 661 (creation of the Reich Chamber of Literature, the Reich Press Chamber, the Reich Radio Chamber, the Reich Theater Chamber, the Reich Chamber of Music, and the Reich Chamber of Fine Arts, all of which were brought together with the Reich Film Chamber under the umbrella of the Reich Chamber of Culture [the Reich minister for education of the people and propaganda was empowered to issue regulations] with obligatory membership for everybody active in these fields); Cinema Law of February 16, 1934, *RGBl.* I, 95; Theater Law of May 15, 1934, *RGBl.* I, 411.

122. *RGBl.* I, 179. Second Implementing Order to the Law for the Restoration of the Professional Civil Service, May 4, 1933 (*RGBl.* I, 233—possibility of terminating civil law contracts of service with non-Aryan workers and employees at one month's notice, with the exception of excombatants). Prohibition against recruiting non-Aryans as workers or employees in the public service (decree of September 28, 1933, *RGBl.* I, 678).

123. For details see Rohlfing, "Rechtsfragen aus der Zugehörigkeit zur jüdischen Rasse" (1933), 2098 ff.

124. Law on the Regulation of National Labor, January 24, 1934 (*RGBl.* I, 45): Non-Aryans were not permitted to hold a confidential position or be a works manager or a member of the German Workers' Front; see also the Law on the Reich Labor Service of June 26, 1935 (*RGBl.* I, 769), with amending law of March 19, 1937 (*RGBl.* I, 327) (no admission of non-Aryans). The Reich Labor Service came under the remit of the Reich Ministry of the Interior (decree of January 30, 1937, *RGBl.* I, 95).

125. According to the Decree on the Public Welfare of Jews, November 19, 1938 (*RGBl.* I, 1649), Jews were barred from public welfare and directed to Jewish welfare organizations; if these were unable to provide support, the state stepped in.

126. Law on the Regulation of Employment, May 15, 1934 (*RGBl.* I, 381); see also Siebert, "Die Entwicklung der staatlichen Arbeitsverwaltung" (1942); Siebert, *Die deutsche Arbeitsverfassung* (1942); Syrup, "Gegenwartsaufgaben im Arbeitseinsatz" (1940).

127. Instruction of the deputy Führer of February 4, 1939, in which Bormann, as chief of staff of the deputy Führer's office, requested all Party agencies to support the Reich Labor Exchange in this endeavor (Nuremberg doc. PS-1720).

128. Nuremberg doc. PS-1720.

129. Decree of March 4, 1939, quoted by Adler, *Der verwaltete Mensch*, 209; see also Reich Criminal Police Department Decree, September 7, 1939 (ibid.), according to which all Jews "granted leave of absence" for the purpose of emigration from the KL (concentration camps) and not passed over were to be "integrated into the work process without delay."

130. See ibid., 210 f., for examples.

131. See decree of March 14, 1941, by the Reich minister of labor (president of the Reich Labor Exchange and Unemployment Insurance) to the presidents of the *Land* Labor Offices, revoked by decree of the Reich minister of labor of April 7, 1941 (Nuremberg doc. NG-363).

132. Reich Supreme Labor Court, *JW* (1934): 122.

133. See Noam and Kropat, *Juden vor Gericht* (1975), 81, with numerous examples.

134. RArbG, *Arbeitsrechtliche Entscheidungen*, 30, 153.

135. RArbG, *JW* (1937): 2310.

136. Sec. 103, par. 2, of a draft law on labor relations, drawn up by the Labor Law Committee of the German Law Academy, 1938.

137. Noam and Kropat, *Juden vor Gericht*, 82.

138. Ibid., with references; see also 90 ff.

139. RArbG of November 25, 1933, *DJ* (1934): 229 f. ("Investigation of the importance of the reason for dismissal must always address whether, not only in the mind of the party serving notice, but also in *reality* [original italics], conditions obtain and are confirmed that, in the view of the employee, make continued employment of the individual involved so damaging or threatening to his interests that it cannot reasonably be expected of him; it must thus seek to determine whether the subjective point of view that gives rise to the notice in fact has a substantial objective basis."

140. Schäfer, "Anspruch auf Ruhegeld im Arbeitsrecht," 38; Palandt, *Bürgerliches Gesetzbuch* (1939), sec. 626, explanatory note 3.

141. Decision of February 28, 1934 (Reich Supreme Labor Court 304/33), *DJ* (1934): 802 ff. (The judgment was not recorded in the official archives of the Reich Labor Court).

142. Schäfer, "Anspruch auf Ruhegeld im Arbeitsrecht," 37.

143. Ibid., referring to the jurisdiction of the *Land* Labor Court, Duisburg, in Dersch, Hueck, Mansfeld, Mende, Nipperdey and Volkmar, *Entscheidungen des Reichsarbeitsgerichts, Arbeitsgerichte und Ehrengerichte* (ARS), 31:104.

144. Reich Labor Court of March 20, 1937, ARS 29, 291.

145. Reich Labor Court of February 6, 1937, ARS 29, 298.

146. The decision of the RArbG referred to above, which still constituted correct application of the law (note 145), was made very early on; the jurisdiction is likely to have become harsher from year to year; points of reference are the decisions cited in notes 145 and 151.

147. Neumann, "Vom Kaiserhoch zur Austreibung," 1 ff., 16 ff.

148. See Noam and Kropat, *Juden vor Gericht*, 83, with many references.

149. *RGBl.* I, 45.

150. Palandt, *Bürgerliches Gesetzbuch* (1939), introductory note to sec. 620, 3 f.

151. Leipzig Labor Court, December 21, 1937, *DJ* (1938): 1244. The company sued, a printing firm, had given notice to the Jewish plaintiff, a compositor employed there since 1919, effective October 29, 1937. The reason for serving notice was the imminent participation of the firm in the "Reich industry competition" plus the fear of getting into trouble with the NSDAP and the DAF, which provided most of the orders. The tribunal admitted these factors as justifiable grounds for dismissal but rested its case primarily on the first-named reason.

152. Schäfer, "Anspruch auf Ruhegeld im Arbeitsrecht," 38.

153. For the direct application of these principles, see von der Goltz, *Das arbeitsrechtliche Ruhegehaltsverhältnis als Teil des Arbeitsvertrages*, Festschrift for F. Schlegelberger (*Beiträge zum Recht des neuen Deutschland*) (1936), 312 ff.; for analogous application, see Hauck, ARS 22, 16, and 10, 24; see also Siebert in the discussion of the judgment of September 6, 1935, State Labor Court of Appeals, Hamburg (*JW* [1936]: 751), in *JW* (1936): 752. For a possibility of withholding pension payments, see also Rauchfuß, "Studien zur außerordentlichen Kündigung" (1936), 47 f. n. 3, which draws a distinction according to whether the agreement to pay the pension was made while the work contract was valid or only after its termination.

154. State Labor Court of Appeals, Königsberg, ARS 4, 113; Reich Labor Court, ARS 22, 5 ff., 13 ff.; 23, 21 ff., 25.

155. For details see Schäfer, "Anspruch auf Ruhegeld im Arbeitsrecht," 47 ff.

156. Decision of September 4, 1940, quoted by Noam and Kropat, *Juden vor Gericht*, 99 f. Vacations "flowed from the employer's welfare obligations" based on "a relationship of loyalty and welfare" between employer and employee. No such relationship could ever obtain between Aryans and non-Aryans.

157. *Meldungen aus dem Reich* of July 17, 1941, BA R 58/162.

158. Decision of August 4, 1939, quoted by Noam and Kropat, *Juden vor Gericht*, 98 f.; in the substantiation it was stated that the legislator would doubtless have excluded Jews from continued payment of wages if "the necessity of such a decision had occurred to him." The law of April 26, 1934 (*RGBl.* I, 337), in fact guaranteed continued payment of salary to all employees, "but since the solution to the Jewish question [had] progressed further, this law too [could] only be interpreted on the basis of current legal thinking."

159. *RGBl.* I, 675.

160. *RGBl.* I, 681 f. (also quoted in Adler, *Der verwaltete Mensch*, 213 ff.). Regarding implementation of the decree, see Walk, *Als Jude in Breslau* (1975), 77 f.: "All men of 16 to 60 years of age and all women of 16 to 55 must register. They are examined by officially designated [Jewish] doctors and generally made to do heavy work for long hours, often of the most menial type . . . usually in the suburbs or on the edge of town. Wage: RM 1, from which tram fares, 30 Pf., still have to be deducted. . . . The treatment of Jewish workers by the owners of the business or other high-ranking personnel . . . by supervisors, foremen, and other colleagues is almost always irreproachable. They all acknowledge the Jews' willingness to work and the quality of their work and take into account their lack of dexterity and physical ability").

161. Walk, *Als Jude in Breslau*, 15, 24.

162. *RGBl.* I, 2403; details in Frode, "Die Verordnung über den Arbeitsschutz" (1940).

163. *DJ* (1941): 1143.

164. Regarding the camps, see Auerbach, "Arbeitserziehungslager 1940–1944."

165. For details, see Seeber, *Zwangsarbeiter in der faschistischen Kriegswirtschaft* (1964); Adam, "Beschäftigung ausländischer Arbeitskräfte" (1941).

166. Vol. 9 of *Documenta Occupationis*, "Położenie polskich robotników przymusowych w Rzeszy 1939–1945" (The situation of Polish forced laborers in the Reich, 1939–1945), Poznań, 1975; and vol. 10, "Praca przymusowa polaków pod panowaniem hitlerowskim" (Enforced Labor of the Poles under Hitlerian domination), Posnań, 1976, appeared just as the present work [the German first edition—Trans.] was completed (summer 1975). These volumes contained previously unpublished regulations and instructions by local police authorities, as well as publications dealing with the treatment of the Polish workforce, internal memoranda between authorities, etc., which it was too late to take into consideration in the German edition of this book.

167. See Sauckel, "Manifest des Generalbevollmächtigten für den Arbeitseinsatz vom 20.4.1943" (1944), 49; Sauckel, "Totaler Arbeitseinsatz für den Sieg," 227 ff. (1944) ("We shall cast off the last shackles of humanitarian nonsense"); for more details, see Seeber, *Zwangsarbeiter in der faschistischen Kriegswirtschaft*, 20 ff., 30 ff., with more references.

168. As early as 1934, Hitler stated: "There are many methods of getting rid of an undesirable race systematically and quite painlessly, at least without bloodshed, . . . not that I root them out, but that I systematically prevent their natural high fertility from being effective. For example, by keeping the men separated from the women for many years . . ." (from Rauschning, *Gespräche mit Hitler* [1950], 129).

169. Sauckel, "Das Wesen des Großdeutschen Arbeitseinsatzes" (1944), 53. See the Plenipotentiary General for Labor Allocation Program for April 20, 1942; see also Sauckel, "Programm des Generalbevollmächtigten" [1944], 27 ff., 38: "Anything that might make the presence and work of

foreign workers in Germany more difficult or unnecessarily unpleasant over and above the restrictions and rigors imposed by the war should be avoided. We are ... dependent on their goodwill and their labor"; similarly, the Plenipotentiary General for Labor Allocation Manifesto of April 20, 1943 (Sauckel, "Manifest des Generalbevollmächtigten für den Arbeitseinsatz vom 20.4.1943" [1944], 41 ff., 48); cf. also Sauckel, "Das Wesen des Großdeutschen Arbeitseinsatzes," 53 ff., 55: "Every worker ... [must] be regarded as an irreplaceable asset and maintained as such"; Sauckel, "Totaler Arbeitseinsatz für den Sieg" (1944), 227 ff., 233; plenipotentiary general for labor allocation's circular of March 15, 1943, to all NSDAP Gauleiter (Sauckel, *Handbuch*, 63 ff.; also in ZS, file 246 g, G.J. no. 79).

170. An example is the generally acknowledged right of supervisors or the German employer to punish Polish agricultural workers, should "admonitions and exhortations be ineffective." The works manager was in no event to be held to account; any right of appeal was of course ruled out for Poles (circular of March 6, 1941, from the Baden *Landbauernschaft* [farmers' association] to all district *Bauernschaften*, Nuremberg doc. El-168).

171. See the review of the situation with regard to the Forced Labor Service (*Arbeitseinsatz*), November 30, 1942 (Nuremberg doc. PS-1739); also the BGA secret report in J. Hohlfeld, ed., *Dokumente der Deutschen Politik und Geschichte von 1848 bis zur Gegenwart* (1953), no. 161, 5:392 ff.; statistics can also be found in Seeber, *Zwangsarbeiter in der faschistischen Kriegswirtschaft*, 89 ff.

172. Regarding the program and organization of the plenipotentiary general for labor allocation's office, i.e., the Allocation of Labor Administration, see the Plenipotentiary General for Labor Allocation Program of April 20, 1942 (Sauckel, *Handbuch* [1944], 27 ff.); Plenipotentiary General for Labor Allocation Manifesto of April 20, 1943 (41 ff.); organization of Plenipotentiary General for Labor Allocation Offices (251 f.); organizational plan of Central Departments 1, 1a, 3, 3e, 5–5c, 6–7, 9 of the Reich Ministry of Labor (267 ff.); Seeber, *Zwangsarbeiter in der faschistischen Kriegswirtschaft*, 65 ff.

173. Decree of the Führer and chancellor of March 21, 1942 (*RGBl.* I, 179), on a plenipotentiary for the Forced Labor Service. Departments 3 (wages) and 5 (labor) of the Reich Ministry of Labor and their subordinate offices were available to the plenipotentiary for the Forced Labor Service. The decree was apparently prepared by way of an urgent memorandum dated January 29, 1942, from the Reich Ministry of Labor to the competent authorities in the occupied territories, in which the directive was given to prepare orders for the introduction of "compulsory use of labor" "up to readiness for publication" (Nuremberg doc. PS-1183). Implementing regulations subsequent to the decree: First and Second Implementing Orders of September 30, 1942, and March 4, 1943, respectively (Sauckel, *Handbuch*, 23 f.); instructions from the head of the Four Year Plan of March 27, 1942 (22), and decree of March 25, 1942, issued by the head of the Four Year Plan on legislation created by the plenipotentiary for the Forced Labor Service (25).

174. According to the Führer's decree of September 30, 1942 (Sauckel, *Handbuch*, 23) on the implementation of the Führer's decree of March 21, 1942, the plenipotentiary for the Forced Labor Service was empowered "to take at his discretion all measures in the Greater German Reich, including the Protectorate, and in the occupied territories to ensure an adequate labor force for the war economy under all circumstances." To this end he could nominate labor commissioners in the military and civil administration who for their part were empowered to give instructions to all the relevant departments.

175. Decree of October 25, 1942, from the plenipotentiary for the Forced Labor Service on the situation of labor commissioners (ibid., 25; also Nuremberg doc. PS-3352; PS-016; EC-1913).

176. Instruction no. 1 of March 6, 1942, from the plenipotentiary general for labor allocation (Sauckel, *Handbuch*, 69).

177. Ibid., 25.

178. See Plenipotentiary General for Labor Allocation Program of April 20, 1942, section titled

"Erkenntnisse und Grundsätze des optimalen Arbeitseinsatzes" (ibid., 27 ff., 45, 46 f.), where under letter *I* it is stated: "In particular the performance principle must be applied under all circumstances, in the Eastern Territories as elsewhere, and when prisoners of war and civilian workers are employed, the usual occurrence that only one of a group works badly while seven others stand around watching and doing nothing must be eradicated" (47).

179. Ibid., 117 ff.

180. For more details, see H. Kneppers-Bannier, *Arbeitsrecht der Polen im Deutschen Reich* (1942) (*BA* E II C 33); RFSS circulars of September 3, 1940, July 5, 1941, and March 10, 1942, ZS, Versch. 9, 2345–97); summary of the current special regulations in the deputy Führer's announcement of January 4, 1940 (Notice B 42/40 with annexes I and II), which reproduces the relevant instructions of the *Reichsführer*-SS (*Verordnungsblatt der Reichsleitung der NSDAP*, 1940, ser. 210, IV). Plenipotentiary General for Labor Allocation Instruction no. 4 of May 7, 1942, on the recruitment, care, accommodation, feeding, and treatment of foreign workers (Sauckel, *Handbuch*, 79 ff.), par. 2 of the preamble, which states: "Recruitment of foreign workers is on a voluntary basis. Where in occupied territories, however, a call for volunteers does not suffice, compulsory labor and conscription will necessarily be imposed. This is an indisputable requirement in the light of our labor market situation." According to details given by the president of the Reich Labor Exchange and Unemployment Insurance, Syrup, in *DVerw.* (1940): 81 ff., 140,000 Polish workers were employed in the territory of the Altreich as of February 1940, plus 300,000 Polish prisoners of war; it was planned to put a million and a half Poles to work in the Reich territory (transcript of a discussion on preparing the economy for "total war" with the head of the Four Year Plan on July 16, 1938, Nuremberg doc. NG-1162).

181. See Reich Collective Wage Ruling, January 8, 1940 (*Reichsarbeitsblatt*, 1940, IV, 38); breaches of the wage agreement were punished with prison sentences and/or fines at the instigation of the *Reichstreuhänder* (Labor Executor) (sec. 2 of the Reich Collective Wage Ruling, June 25, 1938, *RGBl.* I, 691).

182. Report of July 30, 1941, by the Department of *Volkstumspolitik* (nationality policy) of the office of the Reich governor of Posen (Poznań) to the Reich governor of Posen (West Institute Poznań, Doc. I 145).

183. *Reichsarbeitsblatt*, 1941, I, 442, 448.

184. *RGBl.* I, 45, 220, 2145, 337, 763; *Reichsanzeiger*, 1937, no. 280.

185. Decree of October 5, 1941, by the Reich labor executor on the treatment of Polish workers in conformity with the labor legislation, cited by Seeber, *Zwangsarbeiter in der faschistischen Kriegswirtschaft*, 182 f. A small separation and accommodation allowance (up to RM 1 per day) was paid. See also the Reich Collective Wage Ruling, January 8, 1940 (*Reichsarbeitsblatt*, 1940, IV, 38 [7]; additional information in Seeber, *Zwangsarbeiter in der faschistischen Kriegswirtschaft*, 170 f.).

186. Reich Collective Wage Ruling of January 8, 1940, for Polish agricultural workers, *Reichsarbeitsblatt*, 1940, IV, 38, 727; 1339.

187. See summary in Fröde, "Das Urlaubsrecht im Kriege" (1940). At the outbreak of war, all vacation regulations were annulled (sec. 19 of the War Economy Decree of September 4, 1939, *RGBl.* I, 1609), but they were reinstated by instruction of the Reich minister of labor of November 17, 1939 (*Reichsarbeitsblatt*, 1939, 545), effective January 15, 1940; see also explanatory circular of February 16, 1940, by the Reich minister of labor (*Reichsarbeitsblatt*, February 25, 1940).

188. Decree of March 31, 1941, issued by the Reich minister of labor on holidays of civilian workers of Polish nationality working in the Reich (*Reichsarbeitsblatt*, 1941, I, 195) (also in *Vertraul. Mitteilungsblatt des Gauschulungsamts Posen*, 13, 1). Rusiński, *Położenie robotników* (1948–49), 229 n. 170.

189. Decree of the Reich minister of labor IIIa, no. 12/501/41; cited under report ref. I/50 of July 7, 1941, office of the Reich governor of Posen, to the Reich governor of Posen (Institute for Western Studies, Poznań, doc. I-145).

190. Cf. Plenipotentiary General for Labor Allocation Program of April 20, 1942 (Sauckel, *Handbuch*, 27 ff., 32); for further details see Seeber, *Zwangsarbeiter in der faschistischen Kriegswirtschaft*, 55.

191. Plenipotentiary General for Labor Allocation Program of April 20, 1942 (Sauckel, *Handbuch*): "It is therefore absolutely necessary to take full advantage of the human resources in the Occupied Soviet Territories. If it is not possible to achieve the workforce required on a voluntary basis, conscription or compulsory labor must be instituted immediately.... It is thus important above all to mobilize civilian and specialist workers aged fifteen and over into the German workforce" (32); "As long as the German armaments economy did not render it absolutely necessary, recruitment of Soviet prisoners of war and civilian workers ... from the Soviet territories had to be avoided at all costs. But now this is no longer possible. The working capacity of these people must be exploited to the fullest possible extent" (37). See the Decree on Recruitment Conditions for Eastern workers of June 30, 1942 (*RGBl.* I, 419); implementing and amending order of April 5, 1943 (*RGBl.* I, 1181).

192. Implementing and amending order on Recruitment Conditions for Eastern Workers of March 26, 1944 (Sauckel, *Handbuch*, 210 ff.).

193. Decree on Recruitment Conditions for Eastern Workers of March 25, 1944 (*RGBl.* I, 68), which superseded the decree of June 30, 1942 (*RGBl.* I, 419).

194. Plenipotentiary General for Labor Allocation Instruction no. 11 of July 23, 1943, on home leave and vacations for foreign workers (Sauckel, *Handbuch*, 103 f.) and implementing order of March 26, 1944 (*RGBl.* I, 70; Sauckel, *Handbuch*, 210 ff.), under the Decree on Recruitment Conditions for Eastern Workers of June 30, 1942 (*RGBl.* I, 419).

195. Plenipotentiary General for Labor Allocation Instruction no. 12 of October 2, 1943 (Sauckel, *Handbuch*, 105).

196. The breaches included "vagrancy, refusal to work, slacking, and other disciplinary offenses [for example, fighting at work]," explanatory notes to Plenipotentiary General for Labor Allocation Instruction no. 13 of November 1, 1943 (ibid., 110 ff.).

197. Unauthorized change of workplace was punished by prison sentences and/or fines at the instigation of the head of the relevant Labor Office (Change of Workplace Decree of September 1, 1939, *RGBl.* I, 1685).

198. Cf. Plenipotentiary General for Labor Allocation Instruction of July 20, 1942 (*RArbBl.* I, 341), and of October 1, 1942 (*RArbBl.* I, 443); Instruction no. 13 of November 1, 1943 (Sauckel, *Handbuch*, 107 ff.), with official explanatory notes (110 ff.). For more details, see Adam, "Die rechtlichen Handhaben" (1940). For the punishment of disciplinary offenses by Polish workers, see Seeber, *Zwangsarbeiter in der faschistischen Kriegswirtschaft*, 158.

199. See report by the prosecutor general for Posen of April 10, 1942 (BA R 22/851), in which the prosecutor general lodges a complaint against "unwarranted interference" by the police in the regular legal process [a breach of work contract by Polish workers could have been punished as anti-German behavior on the strength of the Decree on Penal Law for Poles—Author].

200. "Work training camps" were set up in May 1943 at the latest by instruction of the *Reichsführer*-SS (memorandum of July 27, 1943, from head of SIPO and SD to the Higher SS and Police Chiefs [HSSPF], Nuremberg doc. PS-1063 a-b, quoted by Seeber, *Zwangsarbeiter in der faschistischen Kriegswirtschaft*, 199); see also Auerbach, "Arbeitserziehungslager 1940–1944."

201. Decree of the *Reichsführer*-SS of January 19, 1942, quoted in the Chief Public Prosecutor Posen Report of April 10, 1942 (BA R 22/851).

202. See, for example, the decree of December 12, 1939 (*RGBl.* I, 2403), and the implementing order of the same date issued by the Reich Ministry of Labor (*RArbBl.* III, 380), which established a working day of eight hours, with a maximum of twelve. For more details, see Fröde, "Die Verordnung über den Arbeitsschutz." For Polish agricultural workers, by contrast, there was no limitation

on working hours, at least locally. Circular of March 6, 1941, from the Baden farmers' association to all district farmers' associations (Nuremberg doc. EL-068, quoted by Seeber, *Zwangsarbeiter in der faschistischen Kriegswirtschaft*, 163).

203. Plenipotentiary General for Labor Allocation Program of April 20, 1942 (Sauckel, *Handbuch*, 37).

204. Statement made by the head of the German Workers' Front, Robert Ley, early in 1940 (Nuremberg doc., IMT doc. [USSR] 93, quoted by Seeber, *Zwangsarbeiter in der faschistischen Kriegswirtschaft*, 154).

205. Plenipotentiary General for Labor Allocation Program of April 20, 1942, section titled "Erkenntnisse und Grundsätze des optimalen Arbeitseinsatzes," b and k (Sauckel, *Handbuch*, 27 ff., 45, 47 f.).

206. Plenipotentiary General for Labor Allocation Instruction no. 7 of November 18, 1942, on accommodation of foreign workers according to nationality (ibid., 93 ff.); for more details on the accommodation see Seeber, *Zwangsarbeiter in der faschistischen Kriegswirtschaft*, 157.

207. Plenipotentiary General for Labor Allocation Instruction no. 4, point I 2 b and IV, of May 7, 1942 (Sauckel, *Handbuch*, 79 ff.), and agreement of June 2, 1943, between the plenipotentiary general for labor allocation and the German Workers' Front on the care of foreign workers (174). The central office of the German Workers' Front for this purpose was the Central Inspectorate for Care of Foreign Workers.

208. See Seeber, *Zwangsarbeiter in der faschistischen Kriegswirtschaft*, 174 f., with further references.

209. According to E. Seeber, ibid., the nutrition of foreign workers in 1942–44 was similar to that of Germans.

Part One. Section 1. VI. The Cultural and Social Sector

1. Riefersauer, "Die Juden in der deutschen Grundstücks- und Wohnungswirtschaft" (1939), 1270.

2. The Reich Chamber of Culture Law of September 22, 1933 (*RGBl.* I, 661), and First Implementing Order of November 1, 1933 (*RGBl.* I 797); the Theater Law of May 15, 1934, with First Implementing Order of May 18, 1934 (*RGBl.* I 411), and Second Implementing Order of June 28, 1935 (*RGBl.* I 829); the Cinema Law of February 16, 1934 (*RGBl.* I 95) (the introduction of censorship); other regulations and texts may be found in Wulf, *Theater und Film im Dritten Reich* (1964); on cultural discrimination in detail, see Wulf, *Literatur und Dichtung im Dritten Reich* (1964); Wulf, *Presse und Funk im Dritten Reich* (1966); Wulf, *Musik im Dritten Reich* (1966); H. Seier, "Der Rektor als Führer," *VjhZ* (1964): 105 ff.; from the contemporary literature, see W. Schnetz, *Grundgedanken nationalsozialistischer Kulturpolitik*, 2d ed. (1943).

3. According to sec. 5 of the Law on Editors of October 4, 1933 (*RGBl.* I, 713), Aryan descent was explicitly required for the profession of editor-in-chief. Substantiation of this was subject to sec. 1 of the Reich Citizenship Law and its implementing regulations.

4. See the regulations referred to in note 2 and the Reich Chamber of Film Law of July 27, 1933 (*RGBl.* I, 531). (This law replaced the Law on the Provisional Reich Chamber of Film of July 14, 1933 [*RGBl.* I, 483].)

5. Official notifications of the Stage Guild of October 10, 1935, quoted in Wulf, *Theater und Film im Dritten Reich* (1964), 261. These required Aryan descent on the part of the applicant for membership in the guild and his wife, evidence of which was to be provided by the so-called Aryan certificate (262). The legal basis was sec. 25 of the First Implementing Order to the Reich Chamber of Culture Law, which regulated the conditions for the operation, opening, and closing of Reich Chambers of Culture and individual chambers.

6. Sec. 4 of the First Implementing Order of November 1, 1933, to the Reich Chamber of Culture Law (*RGBl.* I, 797).

7. Sec. 10 of the First Implementing Order of November 1, 1933, to the Reich Chamber of Culture Law (ibid.); the Reich Film Chamber Law of July 22, 1933 (*RGBl.* I, 531), and the Theater Law of May 15, 1934 (*RGBl.* I, 411), contained similar provisions. See the memorandum of March 5, 1934, from the Reich minister for education of the people and propaganda to all *Land* governments (quoted by Wulf, *Theater und Film im Dritten Reich* [1964], 261), according to which non-Aryans were refused admission to the individual chambers on the strength of sec. 10 of the First Implementing Order of November 1, 1933, to the Reich Chamber of Culture Law, (*RGBl.* I, 797).

8. For individual treatments, see Hollstein, *Antisemitische Filmpropaganda* (1971); and Dammeyer, "Nationalsozialistische Filme im historisch-politischen Unterricht," with numerous references.

9. *Berliner Lokalanzeiger*, May 9, 1933, quoted by Wulf, *Theater und Film im Dritten Reich* [1964], 255.

10. Wulf, *Theater und Film im Dritten Reich* [1964], 41, regarding non-Aryan staff employed in theaters.

11. Reich Supreme Court of June 27, 1936, *JW* (1936): 2529 ff. The decision of the Prussian Supreme Court, Berlin, is also reproduced there; see also J. W. Gerlach, "Radikalenfrage und Privatrecht," *Recht und Staat* 482–83 (1978): 53 n. 131.

12. Law against the Overcrowding of German Schools and Universities of April 25, 1933 (*RGBl.* I, 22), according to which the proportion of non-Aryans in relation to the total number of new students should not be higher than the proportion of non-Aryans in the German population; exceptions were made for *Mischlinge* and the children of ex-combatants. See also the directives of July 2, 1937, by the Reich minister of education on the legal status of Jews in German schools (*MinbliV* [1937]: 346); Blau, *Das Ausnahmerecht für die Juden in Deutschland* (1965), 346; directive of November 15, 1938, by the Reich minister for science, education, and culture (*RMinBl. der Deutschen Wissenschaft* [1938]: 520, quoted in Main Commission Warsaw, Archiv, Reg. des General Government, Hauptabteilung Innere VW, II/374; transcript; also quoted in *Dokumente der Deutschen Politik und Geschichte*, vol. 503) (Jews forbidden to attend all German schools; Jewish schoolchildren to be suspended immediately; Jews allowed to attend only Jewish schools, since after the "disgraceful assassination in Paris . . . no German teacher [can] be expected to give lessons . . . to Jewish children"). Jews were also excluded from the universities by the decree of December 8, 1938, of the Reich minister for science, education, and culture (*RMinBl.* [1938]: 555).

13. Regarding the treatment at school of the other "alien peoples" (foreign workers), see the instruction of September 1943 issued by the Reich minister for science, education, and culture (made known by way of confidential information from the Party Chancellery 40/510 of September 14, 1943, *Verfügungen*, 4:512 f. [1943]), according to which "for reasons of allocation" the "undesirable allocation of foreign families" had to be permitted in some degree, whereas "children of equivalent race" could be admitted to the *Volksschule* without restriction. Children of Polish civilian workers and of workers from the Eastern Territories were not admitted. At school children of "alien parents" had to sit apart from the "German children." At harvest time they were to be "generously excused from classes." In the larger towns special classes were set up in which lay helpers were to give short lessons "in the basic principles of the German language and arithmetic."

Attendance at colleges and universities was granted—through a secret instruction of the Reich minister for science, education, and popular instruction to the universities and the boards of education of January 20, 1942—only for *Ukrainians* who had already matriculated or who had come to Germany before September 1, 1939. All other applicants had to be rejected. By a further secret instruction of February 18, 1942, the same ministry interdicted enrollment in German universities by *Russians* from the occupied Polish and Soviet territories. By "urgent instruction" of April 17, 1942, the minister reminded the universities that also *Poles* and *Czechs* were not to be enrolled, as already ordered by the circular instructions of November 10 and 13 and December 28, 1939, and October 21, 1940. A further secret instruction of March 13, 1943, interdicted the matriculation of students from the occupied Ukrainian territories. Students from Lithuania, Latvia, and Estonia were admitted only on particular decision of a central office in the Reich Ministry of Science, Education, and Popular Instruction. Another secret instruction of November 6, 1943, interdicted the enrollment of Slovenian students; of interest here is also the secret "urgent order" of the Reich minister of science of May 12, 1943, by which the minister gave instructions to inaugurate "Copernicus celebrations" on May 24, 1943, at all universities of the Reich, in order to show that Copernicus (born in ToruΩ , Poland) was a "*German astronomer*" (University Archives, University of Innsbruck, Austria).

14. This included the *jüdische Kulturbund*, which organized concerts and theatrical and film performances that only Jews could attend (Walk, *Als Jude in Breslau* [1975], 80).

15. According to the Tenth Decree to the Reich Citizenship Law of July 4, 1939 (*RGBl.* I, 1097), the Reich Association of Jews was also responsible for Jewish schooling; cf. the decrees issued by the Reich minister for science, education, and culture of November 15, 1938, and of April 26, 1941, on Jewish schools (Blau, *Das Ausnahmerecht für die Juden in Deutschland*, no. 313); Reich Ministry of the Interior decree of June 20, 1942, on the Closure of Jewish Schools (unpublished, quoted in a letter dated July 7, 1942, from the Reich minister for science, education, and culture to the district president, reproduced in ibid., no. 293).

16. Walk, *Als Jude in Breslau.*

17. Jews were forbidden access to theaters, cinemas, concerts, and all other cultural events under the instruction of November 12, 1938, issued by the president of the Reich Chamber of Culture, Dr. Goebbels (Hohlfeld, *Dokumente der Deutschen Politik und Geschichte* [1951], 5:502).

18. According to the Decree on the Public Welfare of Jews of November 19, 1938 (*RGBl.* I, 1649), Jews were barred from public welfare and directed to Jewish welfare organizations. The Decree on Compensation of War Damage in the Reich of July 20, 1941 (*RGBl.* I, 437), excluded Jews from compensation for damage to property occurring as a result of the war.

19. The Jewish community lost its status as a corporation in public law (decree of March 28, 1938, *RGBl.* I, 338) and was amalgamated with all other Jewish foundations and institutions into the Reich Association of Jews, which was under the supervision of the Security Police (Gestapo). The financial situation of the Reich Association was catastrophic: the increasing number of welfare beneficiaries contrasted with the rapidly diminishing tax income from Jews. See Walk, *Als Jude in Breslau*, 78, for more details.

20. Walk, *Als Jude in Breslau*, 79.

21. See, for example, ibid., 31, 78 f., regarding Aryan hairdressers.

22. Neumann, "Vom Kaiserhoch zur Austreibung," 14 f., 30.

23. Walk, *Als Jude in Breslau*, 2, 8, 78.

Part One. Section 1. VII. Commercial and Property Law

1. In this connection see Hitler, quoted in Rauschning, *Gespräche mit Hitler* (1950), 86 f.

2. According to Rauschning, ibid., what was passed off in 1938 as an "enraged knee-jerk reaction to an unfortunate assassination" had long been planned and mulled over.

3. Shorthand transcription of a discussion chaired by Göring at the Reich Air Ministry in Berlin, PS-1816; the most important part is reproduced in Poliakov and Wulf, *Das Dritte Reich und die Juden* (1955), 75 ff. Göring was in favor of swift, centralized action: the surest targets were Jewish businesses; shutting these down should be the first step. The Jews had to be thrown out of economic life, "made to pay up, and pensioned off" (75 f.). The chief of the Security Police and the SD, Heydrich, supported by the Reich minister of finance and Göring, demanded the speediest possible emigration of the Jews (79).

4. See the list in Kluge and Krüger, *Verfassung and Verwaltung* (1941), 222 ff.; and Rilk,

"Judentum und Wirtschaft" (1938); Höver, "Entjudungsfragen" (1941) (referring particularly to economic and property law); Riefersauer, "Die Juden in der deutschen Grundstücks- und Wohnungswirtschaft" (1939).

5. Decree of November 12, 1938, on an Expiatory Action of Jews of German Nationality (*RGBl.*
I, 1579), based on the Decree of October 18, 1936, on Execution of the Four Year Plan (*RGBl.* I, 88).

6. Decree of November 12, 1938, on the Restoration of the Streetscape in the Matter of Jewish
Businesses (*RGBl.* I, 1581).

7. *RGBl.* I, 414; for more on the decree, see Adler, *Der verwaltete Mensch* (1974), 547 ff.

8. For more details, see Fauck, "Vermögensbeschlagnahmen an jüdischem Eigentum"; Arndt,
"Entziehung und Verbringung jüdischen Vermögens," (1966), 92 ff. See Adler, *Der verwaltete
Mensch;* Adler includes the text of the comprehensive declaration of assets required by the decree
of April 26, 1938. Seizure came under Penal Code sec. 42 in association with Penal Code sec. 430 ff.
(seizure of objects used or intended for use in criminal acts). In the event of later declaration, indemnity could not be guaranteed under the Reich Tax Code, sec. 410; in this case the provision did
not apply either indirectly or directly (Reich Supreme Court of January 25, 1940, 3 D 833–39, *DR*
[1940] [A]: 497 ff.; *DJ* [1940]: 298).

9. Decree of April 26, 1938, issued by the plenipotentiary for the Four Year Plan (*RGBl.* I, 415).

10. *RGBl.* I, 1709. It was based on the Decree of the Führer and Reich chancellor of October
18, 1936, on the Execution of the Four Year Plan (*RGBl.* I, 887) (according to which Göring as plenipotentiary for the Four Year Plan was empowered to issue decrees and administrative regulations),
in conjunction with the Second Decree of November 24, 1938, by the plenipotentiary for the Four
Year Plan (*RGBl.* I, 1668) and the Decree of April 26, 1938, on Registration of Jewish Property
(*RGBl.* I, 414). For more details on the decree, see Adler, *Der verwaltete Mensch,* 495.

11. *RGBl.* I, 627; see also the circular of July 14, 1938, from the Reich minister of the interior
(*MinbliV*, 1152); under the terms of secs. 1 and 3 of the decree, a business was defined as Jewish if
the owner was a Jew (sec 5 of the First Decree to the Reich Citizenship Law). The business of a
public trading company or a limited company was considered Jewish if one or several personally
responsible members of the company were Jews. A business also passed for Jewish "if it was effectively under the controlling influence of Jews."

12. See Scholl, *Die Entjudung des deutschen Grundbesitzes* (1940). Adler, *Der verwaltete
Mensch,* 638 ff., is of the opinion that properties remained in Jewish hands until 1945 without being
"Aryanized" even though they may have been formally declared forfeited on the strength of the
Eleventh Decree. According to confidential information from the Party Chancellery of October 2,
1942 (*Verfügungen*, 2:143 ff.), however, no Jewish property had remained in Jewish hands since 1941.

13. Decree of October 22, 1938, against Collusion in Misrepresenting Jewish Businesses (*RGBl.*
I, 404), which was directed against Jewish nationals who "for selfish reasons wilfully help to conceal the Jewish character of a business with a view to deceiving the public or the authorities."

14. Göring at the ministerial meeting on the "Jewish question," November 12, 1938 (Nuremberg Doc. PS-1816, quoted in Poliakov and Wulf, *Das Dritte Reich und die Juden*, 75 ff.).

15. Judgment of May 17, 1940, Vienna Administrative Court, *DVerw* (German Administration) (1940): 269 f.: a third party (competitor) had no right of appeal against the sale of Jewish
property to another applicant.

16. At the meeting of November 12, 1938, Göring demanded that the Aryan taking over the
business must absolutely be qualified to do so. Regarding the problems of Aryanization of Jewish
businesses, see also the report of January 11, 1940, by the presiding judge, State Superior Court,
Nuremberg, BA R 22/3381.

17. Full details in Neumann, "Vom Kaiserhoch zur Austreibung," 27 ff.

18. Decision of the Reichsgericht of December 10, 1942 (RGSt. 76, 316 ff.), without further
explanation.

19. Fauck, "Vermögensbeschlagnahmen an jüdischem Eigentum," 24, speaks of the surrender

of goods in January 1939, referring to several urgent memoranda from the Reich Ministry of Economics. Cf. the Third Decree on the Registration of Jewish Property of February 21, 1939 (*RGBl.* I, 282), which required all objects of gold, platinum, silver, and precious stones or pearls to be handed over within two weeks.

20. See the instructions for implementation of art. 3, sec. 14, of the Fourth Implementing Order to the Currency Regulations of June 12, 1933 (*Deutscher Rechtsanzeiger* no. 137, June 15, 1933). More details in Adler, *Der verwaltete Mensch*, 495. No one classed as a national with respect to currency regulations was allowed to export more than RM 10. Jewelry was not mentioned explicitly at first, but in sec. 4 of the Fifth Implementing Order of May 25, 1936 (*RGBl.* I, 467), to the Currency Regulation Law of February 4, 1935 (*RGBl.* I, 105) (prohibition of export of gold, securities, money, etc.), included in the terms *gold* and *precious metal* were other artifacts "not normally made of gold and other precious metals." The penalty was seizure of the goods in all cases. New Currency Law of December 12, 1938 (*RGBl.* I, 1733).

21. See also Fauck, "Mitnahme von Devisen und Schmuckstücken"; cf. State Superior Court, Karlsruhe, of August 19, 1937, Ss 56/37, *DJ* (1938): 1394. In a 1941 judgment, the *Reichsgericht* confirmed the sentence of a Jew (and other accused persons) who had relinquished a future claim in foreign currency against a foreigner to imprisonment and fines, because this was deemed not an attempted but an actual negotiation of currency as set out in the Currency Law of 1938 (Reich Supreme Court of September 30, 1941, 4 D 423/41, *DR* [1942] [A]: 129).

22. Walk, *Als Jude in Breslau* (1975), 78.

23. According to ibid., Hitler claimed that in a few years there would only be Jewish cemeteries and beggars.

24. Neumann, "Vom Kaiserhoch zur Austreibung," 31; among these was the authorization to pack, which was issued by the Currency Office to Jews willing to emigrate after presentation of an inventory of all the objects to be taken on the journey, however trivial, classified separately according to whether they were acquired before or after 1933. For more details, see ibid., 31 f. Neumann, who until 1939 had been a laywer in the Berlin area, describes the tortuous path leading to his departure in March of that year. The only way he could obtain the money to replace personal effects destroyed in the *Reichskristallnacht* was by the sale of securities in compulsory deposit. However, the bonds could be disposed of only with the authorization of the Securities Office, which for its part required the applicant to first submit the receipts for the purchase of goods needed for emigration; only after this could the papers be sold and the bank transfer the money to the suppliers, who would then hand over the goods to the purchaser. Now that gold and silver objects had to be surrendered without compensation, the Currency Office passed the list required for the authorization to pack (see previous note) on to the Customs Surveillance Office, which was to report back to the Currency Office. This report was not issued until the Jewish owner had personally delivered the goods in question. After delivery the individual was informed that he had to pay a gold discount charge equal to 100% of the value of the goods delivered. These sums for their part could be obtained only by way of the same complicated system of sale of securities or the realization (sale) of other capital goods. Payment for travel tickets by Jews emigrating abroad was subject to a similar labyrinthine process: before authorizing release of the documents, the Currency Office required a certificate of approval from the Department of Finance. Until this certificate was available, it was impossible to pay for the documents, but this payment had to be made within a time limit, after which the documents would be invalid (on account of the great demand for tickets). The Department of Finance issued a certificate of approval only when the so-called Jewish tax, i.e., the Reich abandonment tax and all other taxes due had been paid; the certificate then had to be submitted to the bank where the securities were on compulsory deposit, which passed it on to the Securities Office. The Securities Office then authorized the sale of the securities, so that finally the bank was able to transfer payment for the travel document to the travel agency concerned.

25. For more details on the realization of Jewish assets, see Adler, *Der verwaltete Mensch*,

541 ff., with numerous references. The main beneficiary of the Jewish fortunes was, however, the fiscal administration, and this constituted a victory for the Reich minister of finance over the efforts of the Reich Security Main Office (RSHA), which had wanted to get its hands on the fortunes of the deported Jews too. Cf. sec. 8, par. 2, of the Eleventh Decree of November 25, 1941, to the Reich Citizenship Law (*RGBl.* I, 722), according to which the management and utilization of assets of deported Jews expropriated by the Reich fell within the remit of the chief president of financial affairs, Berlin. A similar legal situation obtained even before the issue of the Eleventh Decree, with the difference that the chief presidents of financial management of the districts in which the properties were situated were responsible for their administration and seizure (Reich Ministry of Finance decree of November 4, 1941, Nuremberg Doc. NG-4905; and of February 27, 1942, Nuremberg Doc. NG-4903).

According to the Reich Ministry of Finance decree of April 22, 1942 (*Verfügungen*, 2:144 [1942]), the sale of Jewish real estate from expropriated Jewish assets was held in abeyance "in order to give soldiers returning from the front sufficient opportunity to acquire such property." As far as the movable assets were concerned, "gilt-edged" securities in Jewish hands were to be delivered to the *Reichshauptkasse* (Central Cashier's Office) in Berlin (Reich Ministry of Finance decree of November 4, 1941, Nuremberg Doc. NG-4905; see Adler, *Der verwaltete Mensch*, 621 ff., for more details and references). With regard to jewelry, cf. the Reich Ministry of Economics directives of October 16, 1944 (Nuremberg Doc. NG-5248, reproduced in Adler, *Der verwaltete Mensch*, 636 f.; Adler also refers to earlier directives of April 29 and May 12, 1941); for the disposal of other Jewish property in favor of the Reich, see the decree of March 21, 1942, from the Reich Minister of Finance to the chief president of financial management (Nuremberg Doc. NG-5340). Works of literature were put at the disposal of the Reich minister for the occupied territories, Rosenberg, "for research on the Jewish question"; "records and record-playing equipment" passed to the Reich Ministry of Propaganda; printing machines to the Printers Trade Group, Berlin; "sewing machines and other artisanal equipment" to the Łódź Ghetto Administration; the latter acted for the Warthegau to administer and benefit from the Jewish assets as a whole by order of the Reich governor (communication from the Łódź Ghetto Administration to the offices in the Warthegau, quoted in Adler, *Der verwaltete Mensch*, 539 f.).

26. See letter of August 27, 1942, from the finance section (Vialon) of the *Reichkommissar* to the general commissariats in Riga, Kaunas (Kowno), and Minsk on "administration of the Jewish ghetto," the directives on administration of the Jewish ghetto and of the asset accruing there (IfZ, Akz. 3322/63, Bestand Fb 85, 185/8; quoted in Adler, *Der verwaltete Mensch*, 540 f.). Par. 2 states: "The principal object of asset management is movable assets. To this must be added the exploitation of Jewish labor, which in this respect may be considered accrued assets."

27. *RGBl.* I, 772.

28. For more details, see Adler, *Der verwaltete Mensch*, 106 ff., 168 ff., 205 ff., 303 ff., Göppinger, *Die Verfolgung jüdischer Juristen Abstammung* (1963), 40 f.; statistics of Jewish refugee movements in Bracher, Sauer, and Schulz, *Die nationalsozialistische Machtergreifung* (1962), 1283.

29. The assets of people deported to the Auschwitz Concentration Camp also fell to the Reich, although Auschwitz was still part of the Reich territory (Reich Ministry of the Interior decree of December 3, 1941, Nuremberg Doc, NG-5336). See, for example, Adler, *Der verwaltete Mensch*, 577f., who uses the case of Jews deported from Würzburg to show that though the usual "travel money" was collected from the Jewish, the transports were not given money as was usually the case, because "there could be no more expenses."

30. The form is reproduced in Adler, *Derverwaltete Mensch*, 553 ff.

31. The basis for the seizure order was the Reich Ministry of Finance decree of November 4, 1941, to the chief presidents of financial management, according to which the Gestapo was to submit the inventories of assets and seizure orders to them. Under the Reich Ministry of Finance de-

cree of December 9, 1941, the chief presidents of financial management were to receive only the inventories, while the seizure orders were served by the Gestapo (Nuremberg Doc. NG-4905). See also the Reich Ministry of Finance directives of February 27, 1942 (Nuremberg Doc. NG-4903); and April 4, 1942 (Nuremberg Doc. NG-4982); and the RSHA directives, Dept. IV B 4, on the treatment of Jews to be deported to the General Government that winter, under the terms of which the seizure order was to be issued by the Gestapo (undated, quoted in Adler, *Der verwaltete Mensch*, 518 ff.); for the seizure orders, see ibid., 510 ff., 518 ff., 553 ff., 577.

32. In this connection see the confidential information from the Party Chancellery 65/869 of October 2, 1942 (*Verfügungen*, 2:143 ff., 147), and the Reich Ministry of Finance decree of December 9, 1941, to the chief presidents of financial management (Nuremberg Doc. NG-4905).

33. Communication from the head of the Reich Security Main Office (RSHA) to the Foreign Office of October 29, 1940, quoted in Fauck, "Vermögensbeschlagnahmen an jüdischem Eigentum," 25.

34. See also ibid., with reference to deportations from Stettin (Szczecin), Schneidemühl (Piᵃa), Königsberg, and other north German towns and from Baden and the Saar. Similarly, see Adler, *Der verwaltete Mensch*, 417 f.; according to him the earliest victims of deportation (from Vienna, Baden, and Stettin) lost almost their whole assets.

35. Fauck, "Vermögensbeschlagnahmen an jüdischem Eigentum," 25; see the communication of January 15, 1944, from the head of the Central Economic and Administrative Office of the SS to the *Reichsführer*-SS, where the writer states that although he had been entrusted with management of these assets by the *Reichsführer*-SS, the banks would not deliver the funds and securities since it was not clear who had to order their release (Nuremberg Doc. NO- 5368).

36. See the instruction of July 4, 1944, by the head of the Central Economic and Administrative Office of the SS (Pohl): "The chief presidents of financial management are responsible for the management of immovable and movable Jewish property in the Reich territory and the government of General Government in its own territory" (Nuremberg Doc. NO-3161).

37. *RGBl.* I, 479, with the first and second amending orders of August 5, 1933 (*RGBl.* I, 572), and September 26, 1933 (*RGBl.* I, 668). The law was applied frequently in conjunction with the Law on Seizure of Communist Assets of May 26, 1933 (*RGBl.* I, 293).

38. Decrees of November 18, 1933 (*RGBl.* I, 1620), May 12, 1939 (*RGBl.* I, 911), and October 4, 1939 (*RGBl.* I, 1998).

39. *RGBl.* I, 480.

40. *RGBl.* I, 303; if necessary, objects seized could be transferred to the district and municipal authorities without charge (sec. 1, par. 2). Details are contained in the Reich Ministry of the Interior Decree on the Assets of Enemies of the Reich of April 15, 1942 (*MinbliV*, 687). The form issued with the Eleventh Decree to the Reich Citizenship Law (ZS, file 247) contains the various grounds for seizure of assets, which are then checked off according to the individual case. It reads: "1. On the basis of the Law on Seizure of Communist Assets of May 26, 1933, sec. 1 [*RGBl.* I, 293], in conjunction with the Law on Seizure of the Assets of Enemies of the People and State of July 14, 1933 [*RGBl.* I, 479]; 2. Of the Decree on Seizure of the Assets of Enemies of the People and State in the *Land* Austria of November 18, 1938 [*RGBl.* I, 1620]."

41. Directive by the chief of the Security Police and the SD, of July 16, 1943, quoted in Adler, *Der verwaltete Mensch*, 511.

42. Communication from the head of the Central Economic and Administrative Office of the SS to the director of the SS Headquarters Administration, Lublin, and the administration of Auschwitz Concentration Camp of September 26, 1942 (Nuremberg Doc. NO-724).

43. See the Party Chancellery instruction in *Verfügungen*, 2:135 ff., according to which the assets of the Jewish cultural communities and the Reich Association of Jews were not in fact "to be regarded as Jewish assets" "but only as furthering the aims of the Reich."

44. More details in Walk, *Als Jude in Breslau*, 62 f., 77 f.

45. Reich Security Main Office (RSHA) instruction of April 22, 1942 (Dept. IV B 4, b4, B no. 305/42), to the State Police Directorate, Berlin, according to which the assets of all Jews evacuated from the administrative district Stettin in 1940 were surrendered to the Reich within the terms of the Eleventh Decree (quoted in Fauck, "Vermögensbeschlagnahmen an jüdischem Eigentum," 25). The situation was similar for the Jews from Baden and the Saar (26). The directives of winter 1942 by the Reich Security Main Office (RSHA) (Dept. IV B 4) on the Treatment of Assets of Jews to be Deported to the General Government took account of the new situation as brought about by the Eleventh Decree (quoted in Adler, *Der verwaltete Mensch*, 518 ff.).

46. *RGBl.* I, 479.

47. RSHA directive of March 2, 1942, Sign. PolS, IV A 5–192/42, quoted in Fauck, "Vermögensbeschlagnahmen an jüdischem Eigentum," 25.

48. Cf. the urgent memorandum of July 30, 1942, from the Foreign Office to the plenipotentiary for the Four Year Plan, the Reich Ministry of the Interior, the minister of economics, the foreign minister, the minister of finance, the minister of justice, the forestry commissioner, and the Party Chancellery, which summarizes a discussion at the Foreign Office held the day before. The practical difficulty of working together with the authorities abroad made it impossible to lay hands on foreign Jewish assets that accrued to the Reich under the terms of the Eleventh Decree of November 25, 1941, to the Reich Citizenship Law. It had also been found, however, that when foreign Jews were evacuated from the Reich and the Annexed Eastern Territories, it was impossible to establish the value of the assets and secure them for the foreign state. The Foreign Office, in agreement with the Reich Security Main Office (RSHA), thus proposed to negotiate with the governments concerned on the basis of the territorial principle, "in order not to endanger the continued solution of the Jewish question in Europe."

49. Third ordinance of February 21, 1939, relating to the Decree on the Registration of Jewish Property (*RGBl.* I, 282). Jewelry and all articles made of gold, platinum, silver, and pearls were to be handed in within fourteen days.

50. RSHA decree of November 27, 1941, contained in a confidential information bulletin from the Party Chancellery, 1/13, of January 3, 1942, in *Verfügungen*, 2:135 ff., 137 ff.

51. Göring as plenipotentiary for the Four Year Plan instructed Heydrich to act accordingly on July 31, 1941 (ZS, G.J. no. 95/294; copy).

52. Quoted in Adler, *Der verwaltete Mensch*, 612. Radios had been taken away from Jews already at the beginning of the war.

53. Letter of April 24, 1942, from the Nuremberg Gestapo to outstations, which contains instructions for the confiscation of the objects mentioned, in ibid.; instructions of January 12, 1942, from the Düsseldorf Gestapo regarding "action to seize wool and fur objects in the hands of Jews, as well as skis and ski boots for shipment to the Eastern front," in ibid., 613. Reich minister of finance circular of August 31, 1942, to the chief presidents of financial affairs (Nuremberg doc. NG-5312), stating that objects seized under the RSHA decree of November 13, 1941, as equipment for the Gestapo should be used "in the newly acquired and occupied territories."

54. Made known in a confidential information bulletin from the Party Chancellery of January 3, 1942 (*Verfügungen*, 2:135 ff.); the decree was valid only in the territory of the Altreich; in the Annexed Eastern Territories all Jewish assets were confiscated and put under the control of the Main Trustee Office East.

55. The form to be filled in on application is reproduced in Adler, *Der verwaltete Mensch*, 527 f.

56. Circular to the Jewish cultural associations in Germany, in *Verfügungen*, 2:140 ff., containing the text of the RSHA decree of January 27, 1941, with the following addition: "The prohibition order covers the disposal (sale, pawning, donation, management) of all movable assets [e.g., furniture, household goods, fittings], bank balances, and securities." Authorization was given only "in

particularly deserving cases" (137). Disposition of assets was forbidden with the exception of RM 150 per month from bank accounts and payment of taxes. The circular of November 13, 1941 (ordered by the RSHA decree of November 13, 1941), announcing the seizure of all typewriters, bicycles, cameras, binoculars, etc., belonging to Jews, was not affected.

57. See Adler, *Der verwaltete Mensch*, 491 ff., 517 ff., and other references.

58. Sec. 17 of the decree of December 3, 1938 (*RGBl.* I, 1709).

59. See note 51 above.

60. Instruction concerning the Surrender of Clothing. Instruction concerning the Surrender of Optical Appliances, etc. (*Jüdisches Nachrichtenblatt* of June 9 1942, in Blau, *Das Ausnahmerecht für die Juden in Deutschland* [1965], no. 386). Items to be handed over included stoves and heaters, infrared lamps, electric blankets, saucepans, cooking rings, vacuum cleaners, hairdryers, irons, etc., phonographs and records, typewriters, mimeograph machines, bicycles and accessories, cameras, photo enlargers and projection apparatus, exposure meters, and binoculars; exceptions were made only for Jews of foreign nationality who were not citizens of an annexed and occupied area and Jews in "privileged mixed marriages." This instruction is presumably a more concrete or rigorous follow-up to the RSHA decree of November 13, 1941 (in Adler, *Der verwaltete Mensch*, 612).

61. Decree by the Reich minister of economics, published in the *Jüdisches Nachrichtenblatt* of February 6, 1940 (BVerfGE 6, 132 ff, 190). According to Walk, *Als Jude in Breslau*, 78 f., Jews could obtain sewing material only to the value of 20 pfennig, and they received only 50 kg. of coal per month. Under the decree by the Reich minister for food and agriculture of June 12, 1942 (*Deutscher Rechtsanzeiger und Preuß. Staatsanzeiger* [1942], no. 43), Jews no longer received an egg-ration card; according to the decree of June 11, 1943, Jews received a ration card for tobacco only "if a clothing card was authorized" (no. 135). Since in principle they did not receive a clothing card, they were unable to obtain tobacco. See also the Reich minister of food's decree of September 18, 1942 (Nuremberg doc. PS-1347; also in "Vertrauliche Informationen der Parteikanzlei 70/924" of October 23, 1942, *Verfügungen*, 2:147 ff.). According to this decree, Jews were no longer able to obtain meat or meat products after October 19, 1942. Priority distribution to the sick, infirm, pregnant and nursing mothers, and children no longer applied to Jews. Ration cards for Jews had to have the word *Jew* stamped on them. According to Walk, *Als Jude in Breslau*, Jews also no longer received any pulse, fish, biscuits, etc.

62. Foreign food parcels were counted in full against the food ration. From 1941 the customs posts were instructed by the Reich Ministry of Finance decree of April 29, 1941 (*Verfügungen*, 2:140), to report to the food authorities each week all food parcels from abroad of which the "recipients were Jews" (known or suspected). Once the Gestapo was informed of foreign food parcels mailed to Jews, the parcels were intercepted and passed on to the food authorities to be counted against the food ration; they were then distributed at will to other recipients, such as the NSV, military hospitals, etc. Parcels containing rationed goods such as coffee, cocoa, or tea were confiscated in all cases. The only exceptions were Jewish war veterans with war injuries: parcels for them had to be passed by the Gestapo.

63. The decree by the Reich minister for food and agriculture of September 18, 1942 (reproduced in *Verfügungen*, 2:147 ff.), recommends setting special shopping hours for Jews. Long before this, however, in grocery stores in Berlin the shopping hours for Jews were restricted to between 4 and 5 P.M. (instruction of the president of police, Berlin, of July 4, 1940, *Amtsblatt für den Landespolizeibezirk Berlin*, nos. 202 and 230, quoted in Blau, *Das Ausnahmerecht für die Juden in Deutschland*, 282). In Breslau shopping hours were limited to 11 A.M. to 1 P.M. Other towns also practiced such restrictions, and an instruction printed in the *Jüdisches Nachrichtenblatt* of June 26, 1942, orders the times to be strictly adhered to (quoted from Walk, *Als Jude in Breslau*, 46, 74).

64. Decree dated November 19, 1938 (*RGBl.* I 1649). Until the issue of this decree, needy Jews received benefits according to the general principles of the *Reichsgrundsätze über Voraussetzung,*

Art und Maß der öffentlichen Fürsorge (Principles on public welfare), August 1, 1931 (*RGBl.* I 439). The decree excluded Jews from the state welfare system and referred them to Jewish charities (to be financed exclusively by the Jews themselves), which were sponsored by Jewish cultural associations (cf. Law on the Legal Status of Jewish Associations, March 28, 1938 [*RGBl.* I 383]); state welfare was to be available only in cases in which Jewish charities were unable to provide support; the exceptions for the seriously disabled specified in the decree were rescinded in the administrative degree issued by the Reich Ministry of the Interior December 21, 1942 (*MinbliV* [1942]: 2377); from that point on, all Jews were excluded from the state welfare system.

65. The Jews had to fall back on "Jewish Free Welfare" run by the Reich Association of Jews; this was financed out of donations from the Jewish community and was only provided subject to the means being available (sec. 2, par. 1, subpar. 2, and sec. 12 of the Tenth Decree to the Reich Citizenship Law of July 4, 1939, *RGBl.* I 1097).

66. *RGBl.* I 1270.

67. For further details, see Brohl, "Polenvermögen im Altreich" (1942).

68. Decree of the Reich minister of finance, July 18, 1941, quoted in Steffens, "Die rechtliche Vertretung der Juden im Reich," 10.

69. *RGBl.* I 191.

70. *RGBl.* I 2026; for more details, see Möhring, "Die Behandlung feindlichen Vermögens im Inland" (1940).

Part One. Section 1. Excursus: Tax Law

1. For more details, see Echterhölter, *Das öffentliche Recht im Nationalsozialismus* (1970), 283 ff.

2. For a more detailed account, see ibid., 191 ff., with examples.

3. Cf. Thüringisches Oberverwaltungsgericht (Supreme Administrative Court of Thuringia), judgment of December 19, 1934, *DVerw* (German Administration) (1936): 163.

4. See, for example, the decision of the Reich Finance Court in *RStBl.* (1943): 263, in which the Catholic Church parishes in Sudetengau were deprived of their status as public law bodies, despite the Reich Concordat of July 20, 1933 (*RGBl.* II 679), which guaranteed Catholic parishes this status (sec. 13). Tax exemption under revenue laws on grounds of public good or non-profit-making activities was withheld for activities that benefited Jews, even in cases where the tax status was no longer subject to revision by the fiscal authorities. It was argued by the court that the principle of equal taxation would make necessary such a corrective measure (Reich Finance Court, *RStBl.* [1938]: 476 ff.).

5. Reich Finance Court, 1936, 950 f.

6. Reich Finance Court, *RStBl.* (1937): 1 ff.

7. Emergency order of December 8, 1931 (*RGBl.* I [699] 731 ff.).

8. Cf. Reich Finance Court, *RStBl.* (1934): 794 ff. The compatibility of this tax with the principle of equality under the law and the guarantee of freedom of emigration according to art. 112 of the Weimar Reich Constitution was ascertained by the Reich Finance Court in a ruling of December 15, 1932 (*RStBl.* [1933]: 92 ff.).

9. Uffelmann, "Die Rechtsprechung des Reichsfinanzhofes unter nationalsozialistischem Einfluß in den Jahren 1933–1943" (legal diss., 1943), 103; from a figure of RM 0.1 million in 1932, revenue increased to RM 17.6 million in 1933, reaching RM 81.3 million in 1937.

10. Reich Finance Court, *RStBl.* (1934): 565 f., 590 ff.; (1937): 949.

11. Ibid., *RStBl.* (1934): 794.

12. Ibid., 1225.

13. *RGBl.* I 338, with First Implementing Decree of January 30, 1939 (*RGBl.* I 153), and Second Real Estate Tax Implementing Decree of March 29, 1938 (*RGBl.* I 360).

14. *RStBl.* (1941): 372.

15. BayVGHE 58, 77 (freedom from house tax for synagogues); Thür. Prussian Administrative Supreme Court, *Jahrbuch der Entscheidungen des Thür. Oberverwaltungsgerichts*, 17, 81.

16. Reich Finance Court of April 7, 1936, *DVerw* (1936): 291: "According to the National Socialist weltanschauung, an object that only serves the interests of non-Aryan citizens cannot be considered of public benefit in the sense of sec. 9, par. 1, subpar. 7, of the Corporation Tax Law of 1925." In this sense also see the verdict of the Reich Finance Court of March 18, 1937 (*RStBl.* [1937]: 436).

17. Reich Finance Court of March 17, 1938, *JW* (1938): 1545 ("The activities of Jewish sports associations cannot be considered of public benefit"); more in Reich Finance Court, *RStBl.* (1937): 21; (1938): 393; (1937): 476 (rejection of charitable status for an institute for the preservation, furtherance, and dissemination of the study of Jewry); (1941): 553; and Reich Finance Court decision 50, 273: no tax exemption for Jewish hospitals, despite earlier recognition of their status. Sächs. Prussian Administrative Supreme Court of June 9, 1938, *RVerwBl* (1939): 666; and *Fischers Zeitschrift* 76, 240, of June 30, 1938, *JW* (1930): 2504: no tax exemption for a Jewish association that served to foster "Jewish studies and nurture Jewish religious services" on the grounds that the promotion of such purposes does not serve the "community."

18. Circular of June 11, 1937, *MinbliV* (1937), no. 27, 1050 ("The same applies to exemption from court costs hitherto granted to Jewish charitable foundations"); similarly, circular from Reich Ministry of Justice of June 1, 1938 (*MinbliV* [1938]: 971).

19. For further details, see Stolleis, *Gemeinwohlformeln im nationalsozialstischen Recht* (1974), 289, with examples.

20. *RGBl.* I 1936, 961, 977, no. 4; Reich Finance Court of February 10, 1936, *RStBl.* (1937): 21; of March 18, 1937, *RStBl.* (1937): 476.

21. Reich Finance Court, *RStBl.* (1941): 806.

22. *RStBl.* (1933): 590.

23. Reich Finance Court, *RStBl.* (1941): 881.

24. Ibid., *RStBl.* (1939): 258.

25. Ibid., *RStBl.* (1937): 501.

26. Ibid., *RStBl.* (1941): 774.

27. Ibid., 168.

28. Cf. Decree of Reich Ministry of Finance on Special Treatment for Jews in regard to Fiscal Matters, February 10, 1940 (*RStBl.* 265), which sets out the basic principles of taxation for Jews.

29. *RGBl.* I 99; sec. 32, par. 3; sec. 27, par. 3, of Second Implementing Order of Income Tax Law of February 6, 1938 (*RGBl.* I 1943); sec. 8, par. 3, subpar. 2, on "pay as you earn" income tax of February 6, 1938 (*RGBl.* I 149); sec. 1, par. 5, First Law on Changes in Citizen Tax Law [*Bürgersteuergesetz:* a Nazi law discriminating against Jews, which was a kind of poll tax—Trans.] of October 31, 1938 (*RGBl.* I 1543); regulations implementing wage tax, March 10, 1939 (*RGBl.* I 449, art. 2, sec. 7, par. 8).

30. Sec. 21, par. 3, Implementing Regulations to Income Tax Law of March 17, 1939 (*RGBl.* I 503). The regulation is worded as follows: "Because of the extraordinary burden posed by children and other Jewish dependents, no tax reduction is granted."

31. Decree of Reich minister of the interior of June 1, 1938 (*MinbliV* 971).

32. Decree of Reich minister of finance of April 17, 1939, quoted in Blau, *Das Ausnahmerecht für die Juden in Deutschland* (1965), no. 232.

33. Decree of Reich minister of the interior of August 19, 1940 (*RStBl.* 786), and August 1941 (*RStBl.* [1941]: 281).

34. *RGBl.* I 338.

35. *MinbliV* (1941): 1788 (also BA R 22/20994), with numerous exemptions for "Poles *capable of Germanization,*" as well as for Poles in "racially mixed" marriages (*völkischen Mischehen*); Jews were liable for social welfare contributions irrespective of their citizenship status; exceptions were

Jews in mixed marriages, who were exempt from income tax when the husband was Aryan and from wage tax when the Jewish husband had no income from work as an employee (i.e., not from self-employment).

Part One. Section 1. VIII. Discrimination against "Non-Germans" in Public Life

1. Sec. 3 of Third Decree to the Reich Citizenship Law of June 14, 1938 (*RGBl.* I 627).

2. *RGBl.* I 627.

3. Notification from Reich minister of the interior to the governments of the *Länder*, in which the Reich minister of the interior forbade public offices to display stickers with the words "No Jews served here" (ZS, Ordner 103, 120).

4. *MinbliV* (1934), no. 988.

5. Third Proclamation on Compulsory Identification Cards, July 23, 1938 (*RGBl.* I 922).

6. Second Implementing Order of August 18, 1938 (*RGBl.* I 1044), on the Law on Changes to Surnames and Forenames of January 5, 1938 (*RGBl.* I 9).

7. Letter from State Secretary Bang to the head of the Reich Chancellery, March 6, 1933, and letter from head of the Reich Chancellery to Reich minister of the interior, March 9, 1933 (hand-written; not official business), Nuremberg doc., PS-902, quoted in Bracher, Sauer, and Schulz, *Die nationalsozialistische Machtergreifung* (1962), 280 n. 96.

8. These guidelines (*MinbliV* 1345) contained barely 270 exclusively Hebraic forenames (re-produced in Blau, *Das Ausnahmerecht für die Juden in Deutschland* [1965], no. 174, 50 f.).

9. Prussian Supreme Court, Berlin, decision of November 18, 1938, Az. 1 b Wx 180/38, *JW* (1939): 108 f.: "Children of German citizens who belong to a non-German people—unless covered by the special ruling for Jews—may be given forenames in their traditional native tongue, also in cases where there is a German equivalent of the name."

10. Decree on Jewish Passports, October 5, 1938 (*RGBl.* I 1342).

11. Unpublished circular of Reich minister of the interior on the passport status of Jews, No-vember 16, 1937 (Az. Pol. S V/6.2252 [37], quoted in Blau, *Das Ausnahmerecht für die Juden in Deutschland*, no. 135). Passports were issued exclusively for the purpose of emigration, for journeys of benefit to German economic interests, in the event of serious illness or a death in the family, se-rious illness of the person in question, or visits to children in educational establishments abroad.

12. Sec. 10 of First Implementing Order of the Law on Air Raid Precautions of May 4, 1937 (*RGBl.* I 559); circular decree of the *Reichsführer*-SS and chief of the German police, October 17, 1938 (*MinbliV* [1938]: 1749).

13. Third Implementing Order to the Law on the Fire-Fighting Services of October 24, 1939 (*RGBl.* I 2096); a further discrimination was that stipulated in sec. 24 of the Administrative Regula-tion to the Reich Hunting Law of March 27, 1935 (*RGBl.* I 431), forbidding Jews to hold hunting permits.

14. *RGBl.* I 547.

15. *Jüdisches Nachrichtenblatt*, June 12, 1942, quoted in Blau, *Das Ausnahmerecht für die Juden in Deutschland*, no. 388.

16. According to secret SD reports, the privileged status of these people had given rise to "dis-may and anger," there being no justification in the framework of racial policy and its being an "in-tolerable" instance of legalized *Rassenschande [racial defilement*, the term used for sexual relations between a German and an "alien," i.e., a non-German—Trans.]. There was an expectation that these privileges should be removed (quoted in Boberach, *Meldungen aus dem Reich* [1965], 228 ff.); the supposed public reaction was more probably a reflection of the view of the Party and the police, who used "public opinion" as a pretext.

17. Cf. Walk, *Als Jude in Breslau* (1975), 59 f. ("Then, wearing the 'ornament' of the Star of David, [I] went to the Storch synagogue; I wanted to go at all costs on that day, so that no one could

say I had stayed away out of cowardice; I walked the whole way, and people's behavior generally was beyond reproach; no one bothered me; rather, one got the impression that people felt awkward. . . . With regard to our insignia, people on the street—and there was quite a crowd out that day—behaved absolutely correctly. The insignia had the opposite effect to that intended by the government").

18. Notification concerning the Identification of Jewish Dwellings of March 26, 1942 (*Jüdisches Nachrichtenblatt* of April 3, 1942, quoted in Blau, *Das Ausnahmerecht für die Juden in Deutschland*, no. 375).

19. Walk, *Als Jude in Breslau*, 10.

20. Ibid., 78 f.; see also part 1, section 1, VII ("Commercial and Property Law"), note 63.

21. Instruction of the president of the Reich Chamber of Culture of January 14, 1938, which prohibited Jews from attending all cultural events, quoted in Ostler, *Die deutschen Rechtsanwälte* (1971), 245. Decree circulated by Reich minister of the interior on Jews in public baths and spas, June 16, 1939 (*MinbliV* [1939]: 129 ff.).

22. Instruction of the *Reichsführer*-SS of fall 1939, quoted in Party Chancellery circular 206/39 of October 30, 1939 (no exact date given), in *Verfügungen*, 2:130 f.; according to Walk, *Als Jude In Breslau*, 62, the curfew began at 8 P.M.

23. Temporary instruction of the *Reichsführer*-SS and chief of the German police, December 3, 1938, quoted in Kluge and Krüger, *Verfassung und Verwaltung* (1941), 221.

24. *RGBl.* I 1676, 1704.

25. In Berlin the authority responsible—the chief of police—had brought in the "Jew ban" for (a) all theaters, cinemas, cabarets, fairgrounds, exhibition centers, the *Deutschlandhalle*, the *Reichssportsfeld*, all sports stadia, and railways; (b) public and private bathing facilities and openair swimming pools; (c) Wilhelmstraße from Leipziger Straße to Unter den Linden and Wilhelms-Platz; (d) Voßstraße from Hermann-Göring-Straße to Wilhelmstraße; (e) the Reich War Memorial with the northern sidewalk of Unter den Linden, from the university to the Zeughaus (quoted in Kluge and Krüger, *Verfassung und Verwaltung*, 221; the date of the corresponding instructions is not given).

26. Walk, *Als Jude in Breslau*, 19, 52, 54, describes in great detail how Jewish apartments were viewed daily by "the curious." Those Jews with less attractive apartments were the fortunate ones, for if anyone took a liking to an apartment, he or she would be allocated it by the authorities (44).

27. Ibid., 50.

28. Letter from *Reichsführer*-SS and chief of the German police to Reich ministers and head of the Reich Chancellery of February 3, 1939 (BA R 43 II/1482 b).

29. Cf. handwritten letter from Reich Minister and Head of the Reich Chancellery H. H. Lammers to the Reich minister of the interior, March 9, 1933; Lammers advocated among other things a ban on immigration of Eastern Jews (*Ostjuden*), "which could perhaps be justified on grounds of demographic policy and hygiene laws," as well as the expulsion of some of the nonnaturalized Eastern Jews; for the latter administrative measures would suffice (Nuremberg doc., PS-901, quoted in Bracher, Sauer, and Schulz, *Die nationalsozialistische Machtergreifung*, 280 n. 96).

30. Sächs. Prussian Administrative Supreme Court of November 20, 1937, *JW* (1938): 704. (Guiding principle: "Arts. 2 and 9 of the Law on Expulsions from the Reich. In view of the threat to the purity of the German race, foreigners of alien races can be expelled from the Reich.")

31. Letter from *Reichsführer*-SS and chief of the German police to Reich minister and head of the Reich Chancellery, October 20, 1938; memorandum of Reich minister and head of the Reich Chancellery, December 10, 1938 (BA R 43 II/1482 b).

32. Letter from *Reichsführer*-SS and chief of the German police to Reich minister and head of the Reich Chancellery, February 3, 1939, and memorandum of Reich minister and head of the Reich Chancellery, February 8, 1939 (BA R 43 II/1482 b).

33. *RGBl.* I 547.

34. Secret decree circulated by the Reich minister of the interior, February 16, 1942, quoted in *Verfügungen*, 2:132 f.

35. Sec. 2 of the decree of September 1, 1941 (*RGBl.* I 547), and guidelines of October 10, 1941 (quoted in Blau, *Das Ausnahmerecht für die Juden in Deutschland*, no. 339, 91 ff.); cf. also instructions of the Reich minister of traffic of September 18, 1941, that regulate use of the *Reichsbahn* and *Reichspost* (railroad and postal services) in the event that permission is granted (no. 336).

36. Secret decree circulated by the Reich minister of the interior, February 16, 1942 (Blau, *Das Ausnahmerecht für die Juden in Deutschland*, no. 336).

37. No. 23 of the Guidelines on the Implementation of the Decree on the Identification of Jews, *Jüdisches Nachrichtenblatt* of October 10, 1941, quoted in BVerfGE, 6, 132 ff., 191.

38. *Jüdisches Nachrichtenblatt* of July 10, 1942, quoted in BVerfGE, 6, 132 ff., 191; the decree in question must be that issued by the Reich minister of traffic, disclosed in confidential information 48/648 dated July 7, 1942 (*Verfügungen*, 2:135; date of actual decree not specified). According to the letter from the *Reichsstatthalter* of Posen to the *Regierungspräsidenten* (district presidents) of July 14, 1942, the decree dates from July 6, 1942 (State Archive Poznań, *Reichsstatthalter* 1218, Bl. 79).

39. Guidelines issued by the Reich minister of the interior on October 10, 1941, quoted in Blau, *Das Ausnahmerecht für die Juden in Deutschland*, no. 339, 91 ff.

40. See also administrative decree of Reich minister of traffic, July 13, 1942 (*RVerwBl./B* [1942]: 119), requiring "the most stringent checks" when issuing insignias for the blind to Jews and supervising their use.

41. Express letter of the Reich Ministry of the Interior (signed Heydrich) of October 16, 1941, Az. Pol. S IV B 4 b, 940/41, 37 (quoted after Blau, *Das Ausnahmerecht für die Juden in Deutschland*, 91 ff.). According to the administrative decree of July 13, 1942, overland postal bus services "should carry only Jews with permits when seating is available. If necessary, Jews will be obliged to leave buses at intermediate stops to allow other passengers to travel. Tickets already paid for should be refunded proportionally, without retaining the special administrative costs" (no. 4). "Jews may occupy only seats not required by other passengers." (no. 5) (*RVerwBl./B* [1942]: 119).

42. Cf. administrative decree of March 24, 1942 (reproduced in *Verfügungen*, 2:133 f.; publicized by *Jüdisches Nachrichtenblatt* of April 24, 1942, quoted in Blau, *Das Ausnahmerecht für die Juden in Deutschland*, no. 337).

43. Supplement (no date), published in *Jüdisches Nachrichtenblatt* of May 8, 1942, quoted in Blau, *Das Ausnahmerecht für die Juden in Deutschland*, no. 379.

44. Cf. discussion on November 12, 1938, among various Reich departments in the Reich Air Ministry (Nuremberg doc., PS-1816 [ZS, Versch. 6/1783 ff., copy]); letter from the chairman of the Ministerial Council for the Defense of the Reich (Göring) to the chief of the Security Police and the SD, July 31, 1941, which repeats the order already issued in the decree of January 24, 1939 (ibid., copy), "to prepare for . . . an overall solution of the Jewish question" (Nuremberg doc., PS-710 [ZS, G.J. no. 95/294; copy]). Instruction issued in September 1941 by Hitler regarding the earliest possible date for deportation of Jews to the East, recorded in the letter from the *Reichsführer*-SS to the *Reichsstatthalter* Posen of September 18, 1941 (IfZ, Himmler Files 94); minutes of the so-called Wannsee Conference on January 20, 1942 (Nuremberg doc., NG-2686; also in ZS, Versch. 460, Bl. 2267 ff., copy) and of a conference held on September 26 and 28, 1942, in Berlin, whose subject was the "evacuation of the Jews" to and from the General Government (ZS, Versch. 9, Bl. 2256, copy). For details see Adler, *Der verwaltete Mensch* (1974), 106 ff., 158 ff., 205 ff., 234 ff., 255 ff., 323 ff.; Poliakov and Wulf, *Das Dritte Reich und die Juden* (1956), 111 ff.

45. Walk, *Als Jude in Breslau*, 46. Walk also reports these comments about the deportations: "The plans for the evacuation of the Breslau Jews to the General Government are said to be ready and waiting at the office of the Gauleiter." "At this time of the year, when the weather has turned so bitterly cold, it is doubly cruel, but it just has to be gone through with" (42); "If one thinks through

our present situation . . . one cannot help but conclude that the Germans seem to be directing their war effort exclusively toward our *annihilation* [my emphasis]" (51 ff., 64); "Thousands of Jews have been taken away, especially from Berlin . . . they came to Jewish apartments in the evening and gave the occupants no more than three hours to get ready before transporting them. . . . We [have] heard a lot about the big campaign currently being conducted against Berlin Jews . . . they are being brought to Łódź. Apparently they were removed from their homes amid terrible scenes; it is said that many were driven to suicide!" (66, 68 f.).

46. Neumann, "Vom Kaiserhoch zur Austreibung" (1936), 422; (1937), 476.
47. Cf. Reich Finance Court, *RStBl.* (1936): 442; (1937): 476.
48. *RGBl.* I 338.
49. *RGBl.* I 1097.
50. Minutes of the meeting (BA R 2/11872).
51. *RGBl.* I 479.
52. At the suggestion of the Reich minister of the interior, minutes (BA R 2/11872).
53. *RGBl.* I 444.
54. For further details, see Menard, "Rechtsfragen zur Abwicklung der Organisationen der polnischen Volksgruppen im Reich" (1941).

Part One. Section 1. Excursus: Police Law

1. For a discussion of the new concept for the police, cf. Lauer, "Die Polizei im nationalsozialistischen Staat" (1935), 16 ff.; Liepelt, *Über den Umfang und die Bedeutung der Polizeigewalt im nationalsozialistischen Staat* (1938), 36 ff.; Best, "Volksordnung und Polizei" (1939); W. Best, "Die deutsche Polizei im Reichsgefüge," *DVerw* (1941): 93 ff.; E. R. Huber, "Die Deutsche Polizei, Bem. zum Schrifttum des Polizeirechts," Zeitschrift für gesamte Staatswissenschaft 101 (1941): 723 ff.; Scheerbarth, "Polizeirecht"; Maunz, *Gestalt und Recht der Polizei* (1943), 23 ff., 54 ff.

According to Himmler, *Dr. Welhelm Frick und sein Ministerium* (1937), the only obligation of the police was to carry out the orders of the Führer; their only limits were those of "self-discipline" (128); according to Hamel, "Die Polizei im neuen Reich" (1935), 415, "to want to contain the police within the liberal boundaries was sabotage of the new Reich." The monograph by Drews, *Preußisches Polizeirecht* (1936), vol. 1, *Allgemeiner Teil*, is written in exactly the same style as the classic textbook on the police code. The new concept for the police is nowhere mentioned or explained; it is only touched upon indirectly in a few pages (9 ff.) in connection with the concept of disturbing public order, which was extended after 1933, under the terms of sec. 14 of the Prussian Police Administrative Law: "According to today's interpretation of the law, anything that objectively has the effect of undermining, inhibiting, or disturbing the state, or merely giving rise to disaffection, can be construed as disturbance of public order. Also negative, nagging criticism of the existing institutions of the state, which in the individualistic-liberalistic age were considered the basic right of every citizen vis-à-vis the 'adversary' of the state, must today be regarded as a disturbance of the peace" (13 f.); for more about the interpretation of the traditional criminal law in jurisprudence, see Just, "Das Ende des Paragraf 14 Polizeiverwaltungsgesetz" (1943), 339 ff.

For an explanation of the new criminal law in jurisprudence, cf. Württ. State Administrative Court, June 17, 1936, *DVerw* (1940): 221; Prussian Administrative Supreme Court, Hamburg, November 19, 1937, *RVerwBl.* (1938): 147 (JW [1937]: 3335 f.); Prussian Administrative Supreme Court in OVGE, 91, 140. From the literature after 1945, see Buchheim, *SS und Polizei im NS-Staat* (1964); Plum, "Staatspolizei und Innere Verwaltung" (1965); Rasch, "Die Organisation der Polizei" (1960); Weinkauff and Wagner, *Die deutsche Justiz* (1968), 63; Echterhölter, *Das öffentliche Recht im nationalsozialismus* (1970), 69.

2. For further details, see Maunz, *Gestalt und Recht der Polizei*, 8 ff., 28. (The prohibition of

secret powers does not refer to the "sweeping institutionalized powers" of the police, which—both theoretically and practically—had become clear and "unequivocal" in substance, despite the absence of any formally worded definition. But not every organ of the police could consider itself as being empowered by the Führer; this was the exclusive right of the head of the police—the *Reichsführer*-SS and chief of the German police—and his general staff; his actions alone were *normfrei* (not bound by the code of law) but not *justizfrei* (outside the law).

3. This was the ineluctable consequence of the train of thought outlined in the preceding passage, for a police force whose actions are outside the code of law was in a position to give subordinate offices powers not bound by the code of law. See also Maunz, *Gestalt und Recht der Polizei*, 53: "The restructuring was procedural in nature rather than affecting the substance of the law. What is currently necessary and appropriate outweighed the desire for a legal system that determines police jurisdiction. In a rapidly changing political situation, it seemed more important to adopt an approach that is systematically oriented toward local circumstances and requirements than scrupulously hanging onto carefully worded legal principles. In this endeavor, the principles of the police code were initially of secondary importance."

4. Ibid. (there is a need to "secure a widely extended state by means of a powerful inner police corps [*Schutzkorps*] operating under central direction. Concerns about protection of [individual] rights play no part whatsoever in this"). Furthermore,

disapproval and mistrust were also directed toward the courts that had spared no pains over the decades in carefully nurturing the principles of police jurisdiction. Jurisdiction in police matters was seen from the point of view of interference in political decisions and weakening of police authority, as well as a cause of delay in obtaining results. . . . The number of writs contesting police orders diminished after 1933 anyway; apparently, in many cases plaintiffs did not expect anything to come of their pleas. . . . In this way the so-called prevailing legal practice in published verdicts, which had made a crucial contribution to the development of legislation concerning the police, waned or lost its earlier prominent position in police practice. (53)

5. Cf. Law on the Establishment of a Secret State Police Bureau, April 26, 1933, and the Law on the Secret State Police of November 30, 1933 (PrGS 1933, 122), with implementing order of March 8, 1934 (*RGBl.* I 143), replaced by the Prussian Law on the Secret State Police of February 10, 1936, with implementing order of the same date (PrGS 21 ff.); circular decrees of the Reich Ministry of the Interior of September 20, 1936 (commissioning the State Secret Police Bureau in Berlin to act as political police commanders of the *Länder*), of November 11, 1938 (commitment of the authorities of the general and internal Civil Service to judicial and administrative cooperation with the SD) (*MinbliV* [1936]: 1343; [1938]: 1906), and of October 15, 1941 (*MinbliV* [1941]: 1828), as well as circular decrees of the *Reichsführer*-SS and chief of the German police of August 28, 1936; April 22, 1937; February 15, 1938; November 7–8, 1939; October 28, 1942; and October 9, 1943 (*MinbliV* [1936]: 1344; [1937]: 661; [1938]: 825; [1939]: 22, 91 ff.; [1942]: 2087 ff.; [1943]: 1595); service instruction of chief of the Security Police and the SD of May 15, 1940 (*MinbliV* [1940]: 1938; also BA R 58/2043). Decree issued by *Reichsführer*-SS and chief of the German police of September 27, 1939 (IMT Nuremberg 38:102; also in BVerfGE 6, 132 ff., 207) (the introduction of the new rank of higher SS and police leader [HSSPF]). See also H. Buchheim, *Die Höheren SS- und Polizeiführer* (1953) (4), 362 ff. For a detailed account of police organization, see Maunz, *Gestalt un Recht der Polizei*, 38 ff.; Maunz, "Die Polizei im Reichsgefüge" (1941), 95; Haenich, "Der organisierte Weg zur einheitlichen Reichspolizei seit 1933" (1939), 48 ff.; W. Best, "Die Geheime Staatspolizei," *DR* (1936): 125 ff., 257 ff.; Best, "Die Schutzstaffel der NSDAP und die Deutsche Polizei" (1939); Best, *Die Deutsche Polizei* (1941), 28 ff., 41 ff., 50 ff., 62; Malz, "Der Weg der deutschen Polizei" (1936), 461; Schmidt, "Polizeiverwaltungsrecht" (1937); Sievers, "Maßnahmen der Polizei außerhalb ihrer sonstigen Grenzen" (1940); A. Schweder, *Politische Polizei* (1937); Heydrich, "Die Bekämpfung der Staatsfeinde" (1936),

121; Wagner, "Die Umgestaltung der Gerichtsverfassung" (1968), 293 ff. The diagram in Best, *Die Deutsche Polizei*, shows the intricate system of new police branches (*Ordnungspolizei*—uniformed police, Security Police) and their impenetrable intermeshing with the police authorities of the *Länder, Regierungspräsidien* and *Kreise* (summer 1941).

On the responsibilities of the Security Police and the regular police, in particular the duties and responsibilities of the Gestapo, cf. "Geheime Erlaßsammlung des Chefs SIPO und des SD-RSHA Berlin" (no date); BA RD 19/3 (in Allgemeine Erlaßsammlung des RSHA); for more details, see Kluge and Krüger, *Verfassung und Verwaltung* (1941), 393 ff.; on the tug of war between the Security Police and the regular police for increased powers, particularly the arguments over powers because of the intention of the chief of the SIPO and the SD to take over the passport office, which was really the purview of the regular police, cf. a letter from the chief of the main office of the regular police (Daluege) to the chief of SIPO and SD (Heydrich), October 1, 1941 (IfZ, MA 325, 8591–8615).

6. In a decree issued by the Führer and Reich chancellor concerning the appointment of a chief of the German police of June 17, 1936 (*RGBl.* I 487), the police leadership was subordinated to Heydrich in his capacity as RFSS, a merger of functions that created the office of *Reichsführer*-SS and chief of the German police in the Reich Ministry of the Interior (for further details see Maunz, *Gestalt und Recht der Polizei*, 6 ff.). At this time the police were effectively detached from the internal administration and made into an independent apparatus; cf. decree of Reich Ministry of the Interior on the creation of a Central Office of the Security Police and a Central Office of the regular police, June 26, 1936 (*MinbliV* [1936]: 947). The focus of police powers and activities was of course in the area of the SIPO, as their organizational plan of July 31, 1936, shows (BA R 22/4219). Of the four offices Administration and Justice, Political Police, Criminal Police, and Security Police, that of the Political Police was the most important: in 1939 the Central Office of the Security Police was merged with the SS's own Security Service, the SD to create the Reich Security Main Office (decree of the RFSSuChddtPol of September 27, 1939, International Military Tribunal, Nuremberg, 38:102 ff.); the Gestapo was run from Office 4, the Criminal Police from Office 5 (crime prevention) (Organizational plan of the RHSA of October 1, 1943, ZS, Ordner 103, Bl. 125; also in BVerfGE 6, 132 ff. 208).

7. In this sense see also Maunz, *Gestalt und Recht der Polizei:* "Thus, one direction continues working with the old basic concepts . . . with the notion, express or tacit, that it is in the Führer's power to eradicate old concepts by means of a change in the law; not getting rid of them was tantamount to a decision that they should continue. . . . The other direction advocated change, proposing a blanket clause for police responsibilities and police actions, the gist of which was that every value held by the *völkisch* order and the leadership of the Reich should be protected by use of police powers. In practical terms, though, the two directions were not far removed from one another" (56). Very clearly also, "the concepts of security, order, and danger proved so elastic they could be used to justify any action whatsoever by the police which 'furthered the interests of the community', protected *völkisch* values, supported the order of social life. This gives them a tactical superiority over their opponents. . . . Hardly does a new example of such usage appear, coined by the vanguard in their struggle against the old concepts, than the old legal practices, now become too restrictive, are discarded and official powers of defense of the state are extended to include the new case." (57).

8. The starting point was sec. 7 of the Prussian Law on the Gestapo, February 10, 1936 (Preußische Gesetzessammlung, 21). See also the decree circulated by the chief of the Prussian Gestapo on March 9, 1936 (Allgemeine Erlaßsammlung des RSHA, 2 F 1); guidelines on consistent conduct of protective custody in an unpublished decree of the Reich Ministry of the Interior, April 12, 26, 1934 (quoted in Broszat, "Nationalsozialistische Konzentrationslager" [1965], 35); for further details, see Tesmer, "Die Schutzhaft und ihre rechtlichen Grundlagen" (1936), 137; Scheerbarth, "Polizeirecht" (1942), 52.

9. Already before the cessation of judicial review of Gestapo measures under the terms of sec. 7 of the law promulgated on February 10, 1936 (PrGS, 21), the administrative court had refused its

reviewing responsibilities (Prussian Administrative Supreme Court, May 2, 1935, *RVerwBl.* [1935]: 577; Bavarian Administrative Court, October 17, 1934, *DJ* [1935]: 300); regarding affirmation of the fundamental legality of protective custody by the criminal courts, cf. German Supreme Court, September 30, October 28, 1935 (*JW* [1935]: 3380; [1936]: 388; State Superior Court, Kassel, October 7, 1934, *DJ* [1934]: 1647).

10. Sec. 7 of the law of February 10, 1936 (Preußische Gesetzessammlung 21), which was implemented uniformly throughout the Reich.

11. *RGBl.* I 1582; by a Führer's directive of June 7, 1939 (*RGBl.* I 1039), the decree of November 14, 1938, was to some extent also introduced in the Protectorate of Bohemia and Moravia. For more details on this decree, see Maunz, *Gestalt und Recht der Polizei*, 13 ff., 16 (with examples).

12. Prime examples of this practice of boundless discretion are the administrative decrees of the *Reichsführer*-SS and chief of the German police.

13. For a detailed account, see Echterhölter, *Das öffentliche Recht im Nationalsozialismus*, 207 ff.; cf. for example OVGE, 101, 206; *DVerw* (1936): 319; Thür. Prussian Administrative Supreme Court, *Jahrbuch der Entscheidungen des Thür. Prussian Administrative Supreme Court*, 17, 74; and Sächs. Prussian Administrative Supreme Court, *Jahrbuch des Sächs. Prussian Administrative Supreme Court*, 90, 180; Bad. State Administrative Court, Reger 58:147; and *DVerw* (1939): 286; "Verwaltungsgerichtshof Wien," *DVerw* (1939): 313 ff., concerning the withdrawal of a dental technician's credentials for the same reasons: because this did not accord with "sound national sentiment" (*gesundes Volksempfinden*). The withdrawal of an innkeeper's license was condoned; he had tolerated the presence of "adherents of Communism" in his restaurant (Prussian Administrative Supreme Court, *DVerw* [1936]: 319).

14. Decree no. V 15653/35 II, August 15, 1935, quoted in Bay. Decisions of the State Administrative Court, VGHE 56, 213 ff., 215.

15. Bay. State Administrative Court, VGHE, 56, 213; in the same sense also Bad. State Administrative Court, Reger 55:191.

16. Bavarian Higher Administrative Court, February 4, 1938 (VGHE 59, 76 ff.) (Priniciples: "(1). . . . (2) The ban on employing female Aryan personnel under forty-five years of age to wait in public houses and bars where most of the customers are German and very few are Jews is substantiated neither by the Law on Public Houses nor by the Reich Law on the Protection of German Blood and German Honor of September 15, 1935—nor by appropriate application of sec. 3 thereof.")

17. Fraenkel, *Der Doppelstaat* (1974), 105, 121, with examples.

18. *JW* (1937): 1032. The court emphasized the dangers that would arise as a result of rescinding the right to trade: "The repeal and modification of laws is not the responsibility of the judge, even those he personally considers out of line with Nazi thinking. . . . The right to make the law is alone that of the Führer."

19. The decision was rescinded on the strength of a judgment by the Prussian Administrative Supreme Court on November 21, 1935 (*RVerwBl.* [1936]: 353).

20. Decision of June 17, 1936 (*DVerw* [1937]: 305): "Whether or to what extent . . . individuals can be restricted in their freedom of action must be decided by the police authorities in accordance with their statutory . . . discretionary powers." The court could only check whether the discretion had been properly exercised. This was the case.

21. Bay. State Administrative Court of April 17, 1936 (Reger 56:329 ff.).

22. Bay. State Administrative Court of July 5, 1938 (*DVerw* [1939]: 94):
According to a specific directive of the Bavarian Ministry of State for Economics of August 10, 1938—the scope of which was then extended to the whole territory of the Reich through a decree issued by the Reich and Prussian minister of economics—a license to run a public house exclusively for Jewish customers could be granted only with certain provisos: (1) that this restriction be made known by means of clearly legible notices; (2) that no female personnel

of German origin be employed. . . . This is the view of the Reich ministry responsible regarding the requirements that ought to apply to the running of exclusively Jewish public houses, from the standpoint of the German people, staunchly faithful to the National Socialist worldview, as its perception of what constitutes public morals and customary practice. According to the principles of the Führer state, this judgment is binding on the authorities and spares the judge from having to make any more decisions along these lines.

23. Bay. State Administrative Court (VGHE 1938, 17).

24. *Sächs. Oberverwaltungsgericht* (Prussian Administrative Supreme Court [Supreme Administrative Court of Saxony]), September 23, 1937 (*DVerw* [1938]: 95 [*JW* (1939): 79 ff.]), where among other things it was stated that "in the case in point, the position of the premises—which had been closed by order of the police—actually favored the secret liaison between the Jewish manager and the Aryan daughter of the landlord who lived in the same house. . . . The closure of the premises—whose position had favored the crime—by public demand was an appropriate action to take to end the liaison."

25. Prussian Administrative Supreme Court, Oldenburg, *Oldenburger Zeitung*, 1938, 35 (quoted in Echterhölter, *Das öffentliche Recht im Nationalsozialismus*, 220). The court left open the question as to whether the plea should not have been granted "also on legal grounds."

26. Bay. State Administrative Court, verdict of February 26, 1937 (*DVerw* [1937]: 354).

27. *RGBl.* I 1053.

28. *RGBl.* I 1667.

29. In a decree circulated to the supreme *Land* police authorities of March 8, 1940, Himmler—in his capacity as chief of the German police—declared that Polish workers were to be subject to regulations applying to resident aliens until such time as their nationality status had been clarified (ZS, Versch. 26, Bl, 15 ff.). Just such a clarification was forthcoming with the Order on the Establishment of the German Ethnic Classification List (*Deutsche Volksliste*) and German Citizenship in the Annexed Eastern Territories, issued on March 4, 1941 (*RGBl.* I 118); from this point onward, the Resident Aliens Decree was no longer applicable to Polish seasonal workers and later other "guest workers." The statement in the circular decree issued by the RFSSuChddtPol on September 10, 1943 (Erlaßsammlung RSHA, 150 ff.), to the effect that the Resident Aliens Decree was not applicable to Poles was therefore merely a confirmation of the existing legal situation. The fact that the Poles were not subject to the Resident Alien laws is shown by the administrative instruction of the *Reichsführer*-SS and chief of the German police that has already been mentioned, RFSS no. 12/c of February 9, 1942 (BA R 22/20994, reproduced in *Doc. Occ.* 5:150 ff.), and the decree issued by the RFSS/RKF no. 420 of February 16, 1942 (reproduced in *Doc. Occ.* 5:156 ff., reproduced in "Vertraul: Information der Parteikanzlei 51/680," July 17, 1942, in *Verfügungen*, 2:169 ff., 176). This instruction concerns the treatment of Poles listed in category 3 or 4 of the German Ethnic Classification List. It is self-evident that the Resident Aliens Decree, which in spite of everything afforded some degree of constitutional protection to foreigners, would not be applied to other workers from Eastern Europe.

30. BA, Schumacher Collection, 271.

31. See also the decrees circulated by the Reich Criminal Police Department on September 7, 1939 (Erlaßsammlung Vorbeugende Verbrechensbekämpfung, 147, quoted in Broszat, "Nationalsozialistische Konzentrationslager," 110); September 9, 1939 (BA R 58/1027); September 12, 1939 (Erlaßsammlung Vorbeugende Verbrechensbekämpfung, 147); and October 18, 1939 (157). For further details, see Broszat, "Nationalsozialistische Konzentrationslager," 110 ff.

32. Authorization quoted from the statement by the Reich minister of justice at the conference of State Superior Court presiding judges and chief public prosecutors held February 10–11, 1943, in Berlin (minutes in BA R 22/4200). It is not known whether this was merely an oral authorization or given in writing.

33. Letter from RFSSuChddtPol to the deputy Führer dated March 8, 1940 (ZS, Versch. 26, Bl. 96 ff.); decree circulated by RFSSuChddtPol to the supreme *Land* police authorities of March 8, 1940, with supplements on September 3, 1940 (Bl. 15 ff., now also in *Doc. Occ.* 10:11, 29 ff.); all regulations concerning the treatment of Polish workers are summarized in a decree circulated by RFS-SuChddtPol of September 10, 1943 (*Doc. Occ.* 10:57 ff.).

34. *RGBl.* I 555.

35. For further details, see Seeber, *Zwangsarbeiter in der faschistischen Kriegswirtschaft* (1964), 69.

36. Cf. minutes of a discussion between Hitler and Sauckel, the plenipotentiary for the Forced Labor Service, January 4, 1944 (Nuremberg doc., PS-1292).

37. ZS, G.J. no. 168, Bl. 2357–64.

38. With reference to the sphere of judicial administration, cf. summing up by the Reich minister of justice at the conference of State Superior Court presiding judges and chief public prosecutors held February 10–11, 1943, in Berlin (minutes, BA R 22/4200).

39. Letter from RFSSuChddtPol to deputy Führer, March 8, 1940 (ZS, Versch. 26, Bl. 96–98; also *Doc. Occ.* 10:25 ff.).

40. Guidelines issued by RFSSuChddtPol on September 3, 1940, and July 5, 1941, quoted in *Doc. Occ.* 10:108 ff.

41. Seeber, *Zwangsarbeiter in der faschistischen Kriegswirtschaft*, 157.

42. A case that resulted in implementation of the quoted directive of the RFSSuChddtPol of March 8, 1940, was reported to the RSHA by the Gestapo Potsdam on December 17, 1940:

During October 1940, in Neumecklenburg, in the District of Friedeberg, the above-named repeatedly had sexual intercourse with a *Volkspole* (ethnic Pole), although she was aware of the relevant ban and of the fact that the man in question was an ethnic Pole. . . . After the incident became public knowledge in Nauen, the local population—with the aid of the district leadership of the NSDAP—decided to take direct action against R. On the afternoon of November 12, 1940, she was paraded through the streets, shaven-headed and clothed in sacks. She carried a placard bearing the message: "I am a dissolute individual, because I have gone with a Pole. That is why I am leaving this town in disgrace and going to prison." (quoted in *Doc. Occ.* 10:117)

However, such instances of public censure were later prohibited on Hitler's orders; cf. express letter from RFSSuChddtPol to all Gestapo offices, November 4, 1941, according to which "public pillorying of German women of questionable honor . . . [had to] cease" (quoted from *Doc. Occ.* 10:122 ff.).

43. Express letter from the chief of the Security Police and the SD to all local Gestapo HQs (*Staatspolizeileitstellen*) and all commanders of the Security Police and the SD, August 5, 1940 (B. no. 3642/40 g-IV A 1 c) (BA Koblenz). Though formally the decree applied only to prisoners of war from countries of the Western Alliance (France, Britain, Belgium), they were used as forced labor (though officers were exempt). It was not possible to establish whether the scope of the decree also extended to the volunteers from France and Belgium—few though they were—who were allocated to work within the boundaries of the Reich.

44. ZS, G.J. No. 168, Bl. 2357–64.

45. Regarding the details of the instruction and the implementation of the "special treatment," cf. minutes of a meeting of leading officials in the RSHA on September 26, 1939 (ZS, Versch. 26, Bl. 44; copy); guidelines issued by the RFSSuChddtPol on January 6, 1943 (ZS, G.J. no. 117, Bl. 259 ff.; copy).

46. Administrative decrees circulated by the RFSSuChddtPol on September 3, 1940; July 5, 1941; March 10, 1942 (ZS, Versch. 9, Bl. 2345 ff.; copy); and circular from the Party Chancellery dated March 5, 1943 (ZS, G.J. No. 195, Bl. 2365 ff.). In a confidential administrative decree circulated on May 4, 1943, the chief of the Security Police and the SD impressed once more upon all Gestapo offices and commanders of the Security Police and the SD that Polish civilian workers having sex-

ual intercourse with German women were to be sent either to a special SS camp or to a concentration camp (depending on racial origin and aptitude for Germanization). The decree reiterated the strictly binding nature of the circulars of the Reich minister of the interior of January 25, 1938 (concerning the directive on protective custody), and of October 4, 1939 (concerning prolongation of protective custody), and the decree of the chief of the Security Police and the SD of January 14, 1941 (concerning interrogation of those held in protective custody). Protective custody was also appropriate in cases where execution was a possible outcome. Because of the need for secrecy, the instruction was *not* to be passed on to district and local police authorities (Allgemeine Erlaßsammlung des RSHA, 2 F VIIIa; also as Nuremberg doc. NO-1532). In addition, the imposition of protective custody on Polish forced laborers was greatly facilitated by the fact that Himmler, as *Reichsführer*-SS and chief of the German police, had transferred the responsibility for ordering protective custody—hitherto a central responsibility of the RSHA—to the chief of the Security Police and the SD, Kaltenbrunner (and he, in turn, had transferred it to the local Gestapo offices and headquarters and the commanders of the Security Police and the SD in a decree circulated on May 4, 1943 [ibid.], with the directive not to release Polish detainees during the war).

47. Decree circulated by the chief of the Security Police and the SD, January 8, 1940 (Nuremberg doc., NO-2430).

48. Date unknown, ZS, Versch. 26, Bl. 99–100.

49. See part 2, section 1, excursus, 3b ("Usurpation of Sentencing Powers in Specific Domains").

50. Decree circulated by RFSSuChddtPol to the supreme *Land* police authorities on March 8, 1940 (ZS, Versch. 26, Bl. 15 ff.; copy; also in *Doc. Occ.* 10:11 ff.); see also decrees circulated—but not received—on March 20, April 8, July 10, September 3, 1940; December 10, 1941; July 26, 1942, rescinded by the decree circulated on September 10, 1943 (Allgemeine Erlaßsammlung des RSHA 2 A III f., BA R 19/3, which lists the decrees not received). For further details, see Seeber, *Zwangsarbeiter in der faschistischen Kriegswirtschaft*, 125.

51. For further details, see Seeber, *Zwangsarbeiter in der faschistischen Kriegswirtschaft*, 169 ff., with further examples.

52. Decree circulated by RFSSuChddtPol on September 27, 1943 (Allgemeine Erlaßsammlung RSHA 2 A III ff.).

53. Letter from RFSSuChddtPol to district president of Potsdam, May 6, 1940, quoted in *Doc. Occ.* 10:27 ff.

54. Unpublished administrative decrees circulated by the RFSSuChddtPol regarding the treatment of forced laborers of Polish nationality, June 30 and September 10, 1943 (Erlaßsammlung, Allgemeine Erlaßsammlung RSHA 2 A III ff., 123 ff., 150 ff. [Cf. also *Doc. Occ.* 10:57 ff.]). The regulations were probably only of a confirmatory nature; that is, the prohibitions had already been in force earlier, since regulations concerning discriminatory regulations against persons of "foreign race" were usually only confirmation of long-standing practices.

55. Seeber, *Zwangsarbeiter in der faschistischen Kriegswirtschaft*, 176.

56. Guidelines issued by the RFSSuChddtPol of March 8, 1940; and decree circulated by the RFSSuChddtPol of September 10, 1943, quoted in *Doc. Occ.* 10:82 ff., 57 ff. (also in Seeber, *Zwangsarbeiter in der faschistischen Kriegswirtschaft*, 150 ff.).

57. Implementing Order of Reich Minister for Ecclesiastical Affairs, June 13, 1940, quoted in Seeber, *Zwangsarbeiter in der faschistischen Kriegswirtschaft*, 168; also in *Doc. Occ.* 10:84 ff.

58. Quoted from "Rundschreiben der Landesbauernschaft Baden," Nuremberg doc., EL-068.

59. Cf. a leaflet dated April 15, 1943 (quoted in *Doc. Occ.* 10:312 ff.), and a letter from the Gauleiter of Wartheland to the *Kreisleiter* of the NSDAP, Scharnikau, July 20, 1943, quoted in *Doc. Occ.* 10:229 f.

60. Conditions in "work training camps" are described in the report of SS-*Sturms 2/8 Muskau*

to the 8th SS-*Standarte Hirschberg* (Silesia) concerning the deployment of the SS for supervision of prisoners, July 6, 1940 (quoted in *Doc. Occ.* 10:38 ff.); see also the regulations issued by the chief of the Security Police and the SD for labor camps, December 12, 1941 (quoted in *Doc. Occ.* 10:163); these expressly forbade (surely not in accordance with actual practices) any "physical acts" (*körperliche Einwirkung*) against prisoners. Decree circulated by RFSSuChddtPol on September 27, 1943 (Allgemeine Erlaßsammlung RSHA, 2 A III f.). Cf. the RSHA statistics on the arrest of Poles for leaving their places of work between May 1942 and March 1943, quoted from *Doc. Occ.* 10:199 f.

61. Unpublished circular decree of the chief of the Security Police and the SD dated September 10, 1943 (Allgemeine Erlaßsammlung des RSHA, 2 A III ff., 150 ff., with implementing orders, 159 ff.).

62. Circular decree of September 27, 1943, ibid.

63. Secret decree circulated by the RFSSuChddtPol on June 30, 1943 (Allgemeine Erlaßsammlung des RSHA, 2 A III f., 123 ff.).

64. Circular decree of RFSSuChddtPol of September 10, 1943, ibid., with regard to the Poles; for major work projects they were accommodated in camps. For the so-called "Eastern workers," who were accorded the same status as prisoners of war, "accommodation in camps subject to strict discipline" was obligatory (circular decree of RFSSuChddtPol of February 20, 1942, ibid.).

65. Police order of Reich Ministry of the Interior dated March 8, 1940 (*RGBl.* I 555), and administrative decree circulated by the RFSSuChddtPol on the same date (ZS, Versch. 26, Bl. 15; copy; also in *Doc. Occ.* 10:11 ff.) Unpublished circular decree of RSHA dated August 4, 1942 (Allgemeine Erlaßsammlung 2 A III f.). For more details on identification of the "Eastern workers," see decree circulated by the chief of the Security Police and the SD to the Reich governors on July 17, 1944 (State Archive Poznań, *Reichsstatthalter* 1218, Bl. 182).

66. See, for example, a complaint, submitted by letter, about the management of the Jaworzno coalfield (Upper Silesia) to the Upper Silesia district group of the mining employers' organization Steinkohlenbergbau, June 11, 1942; report by the Warthenau District Gendarmerie to the prefect of the district of Warthenau dated December 21, 1943 (quoted from *Doc. Occ.* 10:272 ff., 274 ff.); letter from Governor General Hans Frank to the plenipotentiary for the Forced Labor Service (Sauckel), dated November 21, 1943 (Nuremberg doc., PS-908; also *Doc. Occ.* 10:306 ff.).

67. Unpublished decree of the RFSSuChddtPol of February 12, 1943 (ZS, Polen Film 64, Bl. 337).

68. Secret decree circulated by the RFSSuChddtPol of June 30, 1943 (Allgemeine Erlaßsammlung des RSHA, 2 A III ff., 123 ff.)

69. Cf. program of the plenipotentiary for the Forced Labor Service, April 20, 1942, in Sauckel, *Handbuch* (1944), 27 ff., 38; manifesto of the plenipotentiary for the Forced Labor Service, April 20, 1943 (41 ff.); Sauckel, "Das Wesen des Großdeutschen Arbeitseinsatzes" (1944), 51 ff., 54.

70. "News from the Reich" issued by the chief of the Security Police and the SD, September 26, 1940 (24 ff.), BA R 58/154.

71. See summary of the modified "Principles for the Treatment of Foreign Workers in the Reich" in the leaflet dated April 15, 1943 (quoted from *Doc. Occ.* 10:312 ff.), which among other things says:

Everything must be subordinated to the goal of ending the war victoriously. Foreign laborers working in the Reich should therefore be treated in such a way as to maintain and encourage their reliability . . . so that, in the long term, their manpower will remain fully at the service of the German war effort, or even a further increase in efficiency will be achieved. In this connection the following points should be seen as crucial: (1) Every human being, even primitive man, has a well-developed sense of justice. Accordingly, every instance of unjust treatment has grave consequences. Injustices, insults, oppressive measures, mistreatment, etc. must therefore cease. Beatings as a form of punishment are forbidden. . . . (2) It is impossible to get someone actively involved in a new idea if, at the same time, his self-esteem is being undermined. One can hardly ask people who are insulted as beasts, barbarians, and subhumans to give of their best efforts. In contrast, every opportunity should be taken to stimulate and foster positive characteristics, such as the will to fight against Bolshevism, the desire to safeguard one's existence and home, readiness for service, and working morale. (3). . . . (d) Foreign workers receive the rations stipulated by the Reich minister for food and agriculture, based on the rationing quotas for comparable German workers. . . . (e) Every foreign worker has a right to receive effective healthcare. . . . (f) The pastoral care of foreign workers is very important for the maintenance of their capacity and appetite for work. Entertainments, leisure activities, sports, etc. should be conducted in the camp itself by camp inmates. . . . (g) All foreign workers should have access to pastoral care, insofar as this is desired. . . . (h) Political persuasion should concentrate on strengthening feelings against Bolshevism and should be organized accordingly.

Part One. Section 2. Introduction. I. Objectives and Outlines of the Implementation of National Socialist Policy

Nazi laws in the occupied territories often had no sections, only "numbers." This was done on purpose, to show that these territories were of juridically minor status and not worthy of the "gift" of normal German rules. It is therefore important to show this disdain in the quoting of the regulations. Sections and paragraphs indicate normal leegal status; numbers indicate something much more inferior. The reader not familiar with details will see, in the manner of quoting the German original exactly, the trace of discriminatory law.

1. For details see Gruchmann, "Nationalsozialistische Großraumpolitik" (1962), 20 ff., 71 ff.

2. Hitler, *Mein Kampf* (1934), 739, 742 f.; Hitler, *Hitlers Zweites Buch* (1961), 217 f.

3. Cf. Hitler's proclamation at the Reich Party Rally of September 7, 1937, in Nuremberg, in Hohlfeld, *Dokumente der Deutschen Politik und Geschichte* (1951), 5:360; more details in Gruchmann, "Nationalsozialistische Großraumpolitik" (1962), 71 ff., 93 ff.

4. Cf. the statement of Hitler's chief interpreter of the time, Paul Schmidt, after the war: "The general aims of the Nazi leadership, that is to say, domination of the European continent, were obvious from the start. . . . The implementation of these basic objectives was, however, so designed as to give an impression of improvision. Each step appeared to follow as the response to a new situation; but each of them was in line with the ultimate aim mentioned above" (Nuremberg doc. PS-3308).

5. Hitler, *Mein Kampf* (1934), 704, 710 f., 728 ff., 739, 741 f., 754 ff., 766 f. The same train of thought is repeated with stronger emphasis on the "struggle for Lebensraum" in Hitler, *Hitlers Zweites Buch*, 217 f.

6. Walz, *Das britische Kolonialreich* (1935); Seeley, *Die Ausbreitung Englands* (1954); Bennet, *The Concept of Empire* (1953); Lufft, *Das britische Weltreich* (1930).

7. As early as 1940 Hitler had decided that questions of "recovering the German colonies [were] to be dealt with by the Foreign Office and that the Colonial-Political Office of the NSDAP should prepare for the administration of the colonies in accord with the relevant Party and state agencies" (quoted from Party Chancellery Order 3/409 of January 23, 1940, in *Verfügungen*, 3:254); it is clear from a Party Chancellery communication following the order that the Party was designed to play the leading role in the colonies: "The Foreign Section of the NSDAP is the sole competent agency for taking care of people in the colonies."

8. Draft of a colonial law (signed Dr. Hahl) of March 28, 1940, with amendments and corrections dated April 12, 1940; cf. the amendments to the draft and finally the (eleventh) draft of a Reich colonial law of January 17, 1941, further the draft of a Führer's decree on the German colonies, un-

dated (presumably 1940) (BA R 22/20977). See a draft order (signed Winkelmann) on jurisdiction for "nonnatives" and an order on jurisdiction for "natives" that was submitted on April 12, 1940, by the Reich Ministry of Justice; cf. also a draft order by the governors of "the colonies Cameroun and New Guinea regarding jurisdiction for natives," undated (presumably from 1940), and the draft of an implementing order by the governors "of German east and southwest Africa regarding jurisdiction for natives of the German colonies." A draft order of March 29, 1940, regulated land rights in the German colonies—authorization required before natives can issue injunctions, etc. (BA R 22/20997).

9. These regions had been German colonies since 1884–85 and ("except for German East Africa," which was held by the German Defense Force under von Lettow–Vorbeck until the 1918 armistice) were occupied by Allied troops (British, South African, Australian) during World War I. The German Reich renounced all claims to its overseas territories in section 4 of the Versailles Peace Treaty of June 28, 1919.

10. See the sources quoted in notes 5 and 6, as well as the colonial legislation of the period before 1914 (Protected Territories Law of September 10, 1900, sec. 1) (*RGBl.* I 813); Representation Law of March 17, 1878; Kaiser's decree of July 3, 1908; *Reichskanzler's* directive of February 21, 1913 (*Kolonialblatt* [1913]: 213); Kaiser's decree of July 14, 1905 (Zorn and Sassen, *Deutsche Kolonialgesetzgebung,* 147). For full details, see Sachweh, "Die Verwaltung der deutschen afrikanischen Kolonien" (1941).

11. Reich Ministry of Justice circular of April 4, 1939 (Erlaßsammlung Reich Ministry of Justice, BA Koblenz), which obliged all subordinate authorities to report on applications by officals for vacations "in the German colonies." The Reich Ministry of Justice reserved the right of decision for itself. A career in colonial administration was suggested to the Colonial-Political Office of the NSDAP by the Colonial Institute of Hamburg University on February 13, 1942. See also a letter of July 6, 1942, from the Colonial-Political Office of the NSDAP to the Reich minister for science (BA R 22/4440).

12. The main content of a speech on agricultural and land settlement policy at the Brown House in Munich to a select circle of Party members in the summer of 1932, quoted in Rauschning, *Gespräche mit Hitler* (1950), 37 ff., from which the following details are taken. Confirmation of the authenticity of Rauschning's statements as a historical source will be found in T. Schieder, *Rauschnings "Gespräche mit Hitler"* (1972) (Rheinisch-Westfälische Akademie der Wissenschaften Vorträge, G 178). With regard to the concept of a Greater German Reich, see also Fest, *Hitler* (1973), 927 ff.; Gruchmann, "Nationalsozialistische Großraumpolitik," 71 ff. Hitler, *Mein Kampf* (1934), 704, 710 f., 728 ff., 739, 741 f., 754 ff., 766 f. For Hitler's Eastern policy, see also H. Krausnick, "Zu Hitlers Ostpolitik im Sommer 1943," *VjhZ* (1954): 305 ff.

13. Hitler, quoted by Rauschning, *Gespräche mit Hitler,* 39 f.; Hitler was of the opinion that "a core of eighty or a hundred million Germans determined to settle" was necessary. Austria would "of course" be part of this core, as well as Bohemia and Moravia, the western regions of Poland, and the Baltic states.

14. Quoted in ibid., 85 f.; Hitler also indicated that all was ready for a Putsch attempt in Austria.

15. Ibid., 37; also Hitler, *Mein Kampf* (1934), 115 ff.

16. Specifically it was planned to annex Alsace-Lorraine and Luxembourg, as well as Belgium and part of northern France, to subdue France definitively, to annex Denmark and Norway to the Reich in the form of satellite states or German provinces (full details in Gruchmann, "Nationalsozialistische Großraumpolitik," 76–93, with references), and to transform Holland into "a part of the Reich" (Hitler, discussion at table, November 8–10, 1941, quoted by Picker, *Hitlers Tischgespräche* [1951], 45). Plans for the East included annexation of western Poland; transformation of the Baltic states into a protectorate; complete Germanization of the General Government and large parts of

the Ukraine; annexation of the Crimea as a Reich territory; creation of the Reich commissariats Caucasus and Moscow; and making Finland, Slovakia, and the Balkan states satellites (Gruchmann, "Nationalsozialistische Großraumpolitik," 93–109, with numerous references). For the status of the neutral states (Sweden, Switzerland, Portugal, Spain) from the National Socialist point of view, see ibid., 111 ff.

17. See the memorandum of October 13, 1941, by Italian foreign minister Count Ciano (quoted by Jacobsen, 1939–1945 [1961], 270): "The conquered states will to all intents and purposes be colonies; Germany's allies will be allied provinces, with Italy as the most important. We must come to terms with this situation."

18. Fest, Hitler, 938 ff.

19. As expressed by Hitler to Rauschning (fall 1933), in Rauschning, Gespräche mit Hitler, 115 f.

20. Ibid., 113, 115.

21. Broszat, "Soziale Motivation und Führerbindung des Nationalsozialismus" (1970), 392 ff., 407, 408.

22. Gruchmann, "Nationalsozialistische Großraumpolitik," 74 f., 98 ff.

23. Rauschning, Die Revolution des Nihilismus (1938), 465 f.; see also Krausnick, "Zu Hitlers Ostpolitik im Sommer 1943" (1954); and an excerpt from the Führer's speech to the military group leaders on the evening of July 1, 1943 (309 ff.).

24. Broszat, "Soziale Motivation und Führerbindung des Nationalsozialismus," 406.

25. See also Rauschning, Die Revolution des Nihilismus, 466 f.

26. For details, see ibid., 473 f., 468 f.: Germany "had an adventurous youth," just waiting "for the doors to a hard but colorful and exciting colonial life to open for them."

27. For more details, see ibid., 468 ff.; Rauschning states that National Socialism had itself not recognized its "long-term aims" and intentions, which certainly extended beyond Europe; they "might include a colonial empire as easily as the great Vlissingen-Vladivostok Line, a colonial empire in South America as easily as a South Sea–Oceania empire."

28. See ibid., 467, 473.

29. The theory put forward by Broszat, "Soziale Motivation und Führerbindung des Nationalsozialismus," 407, that there was no planned discussion and preparation for the conquest of the Eastern Territories, including the fate of Poland, must be doubted in the light of the extremely precise statements by Hitler on Poland quoted in Rauschning, Gespräche mit Hitler. More likely is the thesis that the plan to conquer Poland was basically irrational but was carried out in a rational and determined manner.

30. In particular see Fest, Hitler, 375 ff., 582 ff.

31. An example of such shrewdness will be found in Rauschning, Gespräche mit Hitler, 465 ff.

32. Ibid.; Rauschning already in 1938 drew the "logical conclusion" that if "Germany's brother Austria" were treated in this manner, how much more severe would be the occupation of the Slav countries.

33. Ibid., 473.

34. Thus titles such as Chef der Zivilverwaltung (head of the civil administration) or Generalgouverneur (governor general) used at the time of the military administration or the civil administration of occupied Poland dated from World War I (for more details see Geiss, Der polnische Grenzstreifen [1960], 160 ff.). The concept of "protective nationality" originating in the colonial administration was introduced in the Annexed Eastern Territories (Decree on the German Ethnic Classification List of March 4, 1941, RGBl. I, 118; more details in Ludwig, "Ethische Grundzüge" [1937], 503; Decree on Protective Citizenship of the German Reich of April 25, 1943, RGBl. I, 271). During discussions on the introduction of civil rights in the Annexed Eastern Territories, the cautious Reich Chancellery noted that the political leadership (the Party Chancellery) wanted to treat the Poles like "natives of a colony" (Reich Chancellery note of September 11, 1940, BA R 43 II/1520).

Administrative regulations and emergency legislation for "alien peoples" in the Annexed Eastern Territories, but also in the General Government and the Occupied Eastern Territories, were similar in many respects to the colonial legislation, down to the use of the same terms, prepared at the Foreign Office for future occupations overseas (see the references cited in notes 8 and 9).

35. Cf. Höhn and Seydel, "Der Kampf um die Wiedergewinnung des Deutschen Ostens" (1941), 61 ff., 64: Poles had "always been incapable of creating and maintaining a state"; similarly, Lasch, "Die deutsche Aufgabe im Osten" (1940).

36. Full details also in Ludwig, "Ethische Grundzüge," 499 ff.

37. Cf. Hitler at a discussion on July 17, 1941 (Nuremberg doc. L-221); a note dated October 25, 1942, on statements by E. Koch, the *Reichskommissar* for the Ukraine (Nuremberg doc. PS-294). Hitler in conversation at table on February 3, 1942, quoted by Picker, *Hitlers Tischgespräche,* 72; with regard to the occupied Soviet Russian territory, cf. for example the Führer's decree of June 29, 1941 (Nuremberg doc. NG-1280); see also the RSHA communication (in *Mitteilungsblatt des RSHA,* no. 6, July 10, 1942, BA R 58/225, 75 f.), according to which the Occupied Eastern Territories were "exploited along colonial principles and with colonial methods"; the requirements of the war economy were regarded as the first law of economic action. See too the interesting description of the Eastern administrative policy by Fritz Markull (who in his time was active in the Rosenberg administration). Here he took a position with respect to a letter of July 23, 1942, from Bormann to Rosenberg regarding the treatment of the Ukrainians (both to be found in Ilnytzkyj, *Deutschland und die Ukraine,* 2:293 ff.). For example, Markull quotes such everyday statements in the Ukraine civil administration as "When it comes to it, we are among niggers here" (discussion in the Cultural Department of the Reich Commissariat for the Ukraine, April 1942 [297 ff.]).

38. See the letter from the head of the Four Year Plan, Göring, of October 19, 1939: "Factories not absolutely necessary to maintain the bare necessities of the population must be transferred to Germany" (Nuremberg doc. EC-410, quoted by Seeber, *Zwangsarbeiter in der faschistischen Kriegswirtschaft,* 104).

39. In this connection belong the general obligation to work (forced labor), extremely long working hours, etc., as well as conscription to defend the country without military service, justified on "moral grounds," since the natives shared in the "successful cultural effort of the white people," with the result that it was "immoral" for them not to participate (Ludwig, "Ethische Grundzüge," 503).

40. As Reich minister for the Occupied Eastern Territories, Rosenberg, for example, was in favor of autonomy for the Ukraine in order to guarantee the supply of food and raw materials (Nuremberg doc. PS-1028) but was unable to prevail against Hitler and the *Reichskommissar* for the Ukraine, Erich Koch.

41. From a discussion at table on April 11, 1942, quoted by Picker, *Hitlers Tischgespräche,* 72; with regard to the occupied Polish territories, see the proclamation by the governor general, Hans Frank, of October 26, 1939 (*VBl. GG* [1939]: 1), and his speech in Kraków on August 15, 1940, according to which autonomous statehood for Poland was forever ruled out (Six, ed., *Dokumente der deutschen Politik und Geschichte,* 8 II, 598); at best "a form of self-administration at the lowest levels" would be granted (H. Frank at the Reich Defense Commission, March 2, 1940 [Nuremberg doc. PS-2233]).

42. Discussion between Hitler, Koch, and Rosenberg on May 19, 1943, transcribed by Bormann (BA R 58/1005, 3 ff.); regarding the harsh administrative regime in the Ukraine, see, variously, the record of Hitler's discussion with Koch and others on July 17, 1941 (Nuremberg doc. L-221), the note of October 25, 1942, of Koch's statements on the Reich Commissariat for the Ukraine (Nuremberg doc. PS-294), and Koch's memorandum to Rosenberg of March 16, 1943 (Nuremberg doc. PS-192).

43. Cf., for example, Hitler's statement at the working supper on July 22, 1942: agreeing with

Jodl, who had objected to a notice in the Occupied Eastern Territories whereby it was forbidden to cross the railway lines, "What does it matter to us if one more native gets himself knocked down?" (quoted in Picker, *Hitlers Tischgespräche*, 146 ff., 248).

44. Cf. Hitler's statement at the working supper on July 9, 1942: "By leaving the natives completely to their own devices, we would not antagonize them unnecessarily in their way of life. . . . The easiest way to stop fraternization with the indigenous population would be to prevent them from taking over our way of life and thus looking like part of us" (ibid., 233). Elsewhere in *Hitlers Tischgespräche*, Hitler names the Romans as a model for racial segregation, quoting them as a precedent; discussion at table, evening of July 22, 1942 (246 ff.).

45. Rauschning, *Gespräche mit Hitler*, 38, who quotes the statements from Darré's staff, expressly approved by Hitler, about a "planned population and depopulation policy" in the East. "Slav fertility" was the "great menace to the Nordic race," since "Alpine-Slavic [*ostisch-slawisch*] people . . . like everything inferior, replace the quality they lack by quantity; the import of the struggle was thus to push back the Slav smallholder, make a landless worker of him, and thus reduce his fertility."

46. In a romantic glorification of the eastern colonization of the Middle Ages, the whole of the East should be settled by Germans who were "secondary heirs" under the terms of law of entail (according to the Reich Law of Entail of September 29, 1933, secs. 19 and 24, farming property passed *integrally* to the principal heir) and would therefore be forced to go east to become important landowners (Rauschning, *Gespräche mit Hitler*, 39). In the mind of Hitler and his settlement policy advisers, ethnic Germans, soldiers, the war wounded, and deserving functionaries should be given priority to settle. Details were set out in relevant administrative instructions (RFSS Order no. 14/IV, dated August 10, 1942, with implementing regulations, reproduced in *Verfügungen*, 2:206, 209 ff.). The native population, insofar as it was regarded as racially inferior, should be pushed back eastward "to Siberia or the Volhynian regions," whereas such expulsion was not necessary for that part of the population which was "close" to the German race, for example in the Baltic states (Hitler, quoted by Rauschning, *Gespräche mit Hitler*, 42 f.). For a summary of the policy of Germanization, see the memorandum by the Race Policy Office of the NSDAP of November 15, 1939 (Nuremberg doc. NO-3732); the secret report of January 1940 from the German Law Academy on the "establishment of German Polish policy according to racial-political principles" (Nuremberg doc. PS-661); the general plan for the Eastern Territories drawn up by the RSHA in April 1942 (see *VjhZ* [1958]: 281 ff.). Regarding the settlement of the General Government and the Ukraine, see the confidential settlement plans of March 27, 1942, and the confidential report on the plans developed by Himmler in Kraków (Nuremberg doc. PS-910); Hitler spoke of the Ukraine as the "new German Austria (*Ostmark*)" (working lunch of May 8, 1942, quoted by Picker, *Hitlers Tischgespräche*, 8). With regard to the settlement plans for the Ukraine, see further the note by SS-Obergruppenführer Berger on a discussion between Hitler and the *Reichskommissar* for the Ukraine, Erich Koch, and others at the Führer's headquarters in the summer of 1942 (Nuremberg doc. NO-2703). See also Hitler's remarks at table on April 5, 1942 (quoted by Picker, *Hitlers Tischgespräche*, 69).

47. Rauschning, *Gespräche mit Hitler*, 39.

48. Full details on this in Fest, *Hitler*, 933 ff.

49. Hitler, quoted by Rauschning, *Gespräche mit Hitler*, 39: "Without the establishment of a certain modern form of subordination, or slavery if you like, the culture of man cannot be further developed. . . . The German agricultural worker would simply become a peasant or find a job in industry as a qualified worker."

50. More details and references in Ludwig, "Ethische Grundzüge," 502, with further references.

51. Cf. the considerations developed in the early work of O. R. Tannenberg (nom de plume of H. Riesler), who described himself as a Pan-German; see his *Großdeutschland*, concerning the

construction of an "alien" school system for the Baltic states once they were occupied by Germany. For the period dealt with here, see the letter of November 26, 1942, from the Reich minister for the occupied territories (Rosenberg) to the Reich commissars for Ostland and the Ukraine, in which he proposes removal of Poles from all high posts, the reduction of Polish schooling to elementary school only, etc., claiming that the Poles were the most dangerous enemies of Germanness. It was unnecessary for them to learn German (Nuremberg doc. EC-336). In line with Himmler's ideas about "the treatment of aliens in the East" (*VjhZ* [1957]: 197 ff.), it was enough if the Poles understood German orders; see also Hitler, quoted by Picker, *Hitlers Tischgespräche*, 248.

52. Statements by Darré, expressly approved by Hitler, quoted by Rauschning, *Gespräche mit Hitler*, 40.

53. F. Markull describes the National Socialist education policy as follows: "Education is dangerous; it is enough if they can count up to a hundred. At most an education that gives us usable manual workers is permitted. Every educated person is a potential enemy" (quoted in Ilnytzkyj, *Deutschland und die Ukraine*, 2:297). See also Hitler's comments at table on the evening of July 22, 1942: unfortunately German work automatically created a higher standard of living, i.e., "excessive welfare"; such a rise in the standard of living should be avoided (Picker, *Hitlers Tischgespräche*, 246 ff.).

54. Cf. Hitler's comments at supper on July 9, 1942: For the "newly acquired Eastern Territories, it is not a matter of wanting to groom the subject population or raise them to the German level of hygiene. Whether or not they sweep out . . . their houses every day is of no concern to us. For our function is not to act as a supervisory organ but exclusively to secure our interests" (Picker, *Hitlers Tischgespräche*, 233); see also F. Markull, in Ilnytzkyj, *Deutschland und die Ukraine*, 2:297 ff., who describes the hygiene policy of the NS leadership in the Occupied Eastern Territories in the following terms: "As long as we don't need them, they might as well die. . . . Compulsory vaccinations and German medical care are therefore superfluous. . . . In any case the people are just dirty and lazy." A typical everyday statement among the civil administration of the Occupied Eastern Territories was "The best thing the superfluous sections of the population can do is starve to death."

55. Bormann at the working supper of July 22, 1942; Hitler at the working supper of July 22, 1942, both quoted by Picker, *Hitlers Tischgespräche*, 246 f.

56. Hitler, quoted in ibid., 233, 246 f., 248.

57. Ludwig, "Ethische Grundzüge," 502 f.

58. Ibid.; cf. also statements by Darré, quoted by Rauschning, *Gespräche mit Hitler*, 38 f.

59. H. Frank at the Reich Defense Commission, March 2, 1940 (Nuremberg doc. PS-2233); full details of the autonomy movement in the Ukraine and further references will be found in Ilnytzkyj, *Deutschland und die Ukraine* (1956), esp. 386 ff.

60. For more details see Ilnytzkyj, *Deutschland und die Ukraine*, 159 ff., with numerous references; Ilnytzkyj describes Germany's delaying tactics with regard to the Ukraine: "Work and wait," as well as admonitions to combat Bolshevism and not "upset" the German authorities through their memoranda.

61. In the General Government the Polish administration was replaced by the "Government of the General Government," with its district administrations, district prefectures, and commissars. Only at the municipal level was there "a sort of self-management . . . , completely detached from the local situation and closely controlled by the German authorities" (Governor General Frank at a meeting at the Reich Defense Commission on March 2, 1940, Nuremberg doc. PS-2233); more details in Klein, "Zur Stellung des Generalgouvernements" (1941), 248; Lasch, "Die deutsche Aufgabe im Osten." For the administrative structure of the Occupied Eastern Territories, see the Führer's decree of July 17, 1941 (Nuremberg doc. NG-1280) (division of the regions into Reich commissariats, each subdivided into general and regional commissariats); under the regional commissariats the Ukrainian auxiliary administration functioned in the form of department heads (*Rayonchefs*), who had no powers to issue orders of their own (F. Markull, in Ilnytzkyj, *Deutschland und die*

Ukraine, 2:297 ff.); for details see Wuttke, "Der Deutsche Verwaltungsaufbau in der Ukraine" (1942) (Wuttke was a *Landrat* entrusted with directing the administration department under the Reich commissar for the Ukraine); Mommsen, "Die Rechtsstellung des Reichskommissariats Ukraine" (1966); Wilhelmi, "Die Rechtspflege in den besetzten Ostgebieten" (1942) (Wilhelmi was in charge of the legal department of the RM for the occupied territories). A similar procedure was followed in the "Reichskommissariat Ostland," comprising Lithuania, Latvia, Estonia, and the region inhabited by the "White Ruthenians" (Directive of the Führer and *Reichskanzler* of July 17, 1941, Nuremberg doc. NG-1280).

62. For more details on the Ukraine, see Mommsen, "Die Rechtsstellung des Reichskommissariats Ukraine."

63. Speech by Rosenberg on June 20, 1941 (Nuremberg doc. PS-1058); see also Nuremberg docs. PS-1056 and EC-347.

64. According to the Directive of the Führer and Reichskanzler of July 17, 1941, the Reich minister for the occupied territories was invested with wide administrative powers—as specified in the official communication of November 17, 1941 (Hohlfeld, *Dokumente der deutschen Politik und Geschichte*, 5:346). The powers of the Wehrmacht (which was the supreme military authority [Führer's directive of June 25, 1941]), the head of the Four Year Plan (who was in charge of the economic exploitation of the factories [Führer's directive of June 29, 1941]), the railways and the postal administration, which were initially under the authority of the chief of the OKW, were all unaffected by this, however. In the field of security, Himmler had received broad powers by virtue of the Führer's directive of July 17, 1941, and was thus authorized to issue instructions to the civil administration. The further order contained in the Führer's decree, that all instructions of a general or politically important nature should be transmitted via the Reich minister for the occupied territories, was of no concern to Himmler, since he was able to act at will by way of the HSSPF, attached to the Reich commissars, or the SSPF. More details of the power struggle between these offices will be found in Ilnytzkyj, *Deutschland und die Ukraine*, 63. With regard to the individual conditions in the Ukraine, see the Führer's directive of August 15, 1941 (Nuremberg doc. NG-3480). In addition to its actual policing duties, the RFSSuChddtPol had other, broadly embracing powers that put all internal political authority into his hands ("resulting out of the struggle, yet to be finally decided, between two rival political systems"), including the liquidation by the SIPO task forces of all undesirable groups such as Jews, the intelligentsia, the politically suspect, etc. (cf. the directives "Richtlinien auf Sondergebieten zur Weisung 21—Fall Barbarossa," Nuremberg doc. PS-447, 2 f., issued by the OKW chief on the basis of an order of the Führer). Over and above this, the police demanded direct priority access and answerability to the Reich authorities, that is to say, *supreme powers*, and strove to anchor them in a corresponding legal document (a Führer's directive or an ordinary decree), a move countered only with difficulty by the Reich Chancellery (see also the following note). With regard to the conditions in the district of Bialystock, where Hitler's vassals reigned supreme without obeisance to any Reich authority, see the Führer's decrees of July 17 and August 15, 1941. For all the Führer's decrees in this note not otherwise identified, see Nuremberg doc. NG-1280.

65. The *complete authority* of the police with *priority* over all offices of the civil administration was intended to get rid of the whole annoying dependence on the administrative and legal principles of the Reich in "foreign territories." In a letter to the RMuChdRkzlei dated September 18, 1941, a few months after the war with Russia began (BA R 43/396), in which he pursued *total* internal political hegemony—under the camouflage, of course, of "internal security"—the SIPO and SD head, R. Heydrich, had already attempted a move toward this totalitarian position. These demands were discussed by Lammers and Himmler on October 6, 1941 (cf. the note of October 7, 1941, from the Reich Chancellery and the letter of the same date from the RMuChdRkzlei to the SIPO and SD head [BA R 43 II/396]).

66. These directives were based on the Führer's decree of May 13, 1941, regarding

"implementation of martial law in the Barbarossa region and special measures by the troop" (IMT Nuremberg 0150 C, quoted by Ilnytzkyj, *Deutschland und die Ukraine*, 66–68). They put the population of the occupied territories outside the prevailing law, sanctioned reprisals in the event of attacks on the Wehrmacht, ordered the execution of political leaders without legal action, and flouted the Geneva Convention regarding the treatment of Soviet Russian prisoners of war on the grounds that the Soviet Union had not been a party to The Hague Land Warfare Convention of 1907 and the Geneva Convention and had thus distanced itself from international law. With regard to the liquidation of political functionaries by the SIPO task forces, see the so-called Commissar's Decree of May 6, 1941 (Nuremberg doc. PS-884), the so-called Hostage Decree of October 1, 1941 (Ilnytzkyj, *Deutschland und die Ukraine*, 70) (seizure of hostages from civilian and Communist circles in the event of attacks on the Wehrmacht); the "Communist Decree" of September 16, 1941 (69), according to which 50–100 "Communists" were to be shot in the area for every German soldier killed by partisans, and the "Night and Fog" (*Nacht und Nebel*) Decree of December 7, 1941 (70). With regard to the treatment of the population, see Ilnytzkyj, *Deutschland und die Ukraine*, 64.

67. Fest, *Hitler*, 28.

68. See the statements made by Darré, quoted in Rauschning, *Gespräche mit Hitler*, 39 f., according to which the new social order should no longer apply only in a small country such as Germany but for the whole continent as well, "the whole universe." More details in Fest, *Hitler*, 928 f.

69. Hitler, quoted by Rauschning, *Gespräche mit Hitler*, 43 f.: "Our considerations are not primarily economic." The economic wealth of these countries was of course needed, but "our idea is to establish our dominance and to anchor it so firmly that it remains secure for a thousand years." "To this end no political or economic treaties are of any use . . . they are just liberalistic trifles. . . . We are today faced with the dire necessity of creating a *new social order*" (emphasis in the original).

70. Hitler, in ibid.

71. Rauschning, *Gespräche mit Hitler*, 36 f., 41; Rauschning reproduces an agrarian-political speech by the agricultural and land-settlement expert of the NSDAP, Darré, at the Brown House in Munich in the summer of 1932.

72. Hitler, in ibid., 46 ("The racial-biological aspect is always only one side of the whole problem. We will very soon reach out beyond the limits of today's narrow nationalism").

73. Ibid., 39, 45 f.

74. About which Hitler himself said that it was urgent to put a stop once and for all to what was known as general education. General education "is the corrosive poison that liberalism has found for its own destruction." Full freedom of education is the privilege of the elite and of those who are allowed in. "Knowledge is useful in life but is not the main point as far as I am concerned. Let us therefore be consistent and give the masses of the lower classes the benefit of illiteracy" (ibid., 37 ff.).

75. Ibid., 46.

76. Poland was divided up into the Annexed Eastern Territories and the General Government; the Baltic states were renamed Ostland; a confidential note from the Party Chancellery (25/349 of March 28, 1942) made it known that the Reich press office of the NSDAP had requested that the editors of the whole German press speak rather of "Ostland" than "the Baltic" when writing about Lithuania, Estonia, and Latvia and similarly not to speak of German colonization but of the hundreds of years of German pioneer work (*Verfügungen*, 1:217). Geographic names such as Galicia or Ukraine were not affected.

77. See, for example, Esch, *Polen kreuz und quer* (1939); von Zeska, *Der großdeutsche Freiheitskrieg* (1940); Scheuermann, *Der Deutsche Osten ruft* (1942); Reimers, *Der Kampf um den deutschen Osten* (1943).

78. Rauschning, *Gespräche mit Hitler*, 33; cf. also the discussion of January 27, 1940, between Hitler and Rosenberg: "The Führer speaks of Poland. He says a small ruling class regarded the coun-

try as a plantation but themselves preferred to live in Paris than in the country. I maintained . . . that control had been left in the hands of a class with a veneer of culture, capable of the occasional brave act but incapable of anything constructive" (quoted in Seraphim, *Das politische Tagebuch Alfred Rosenbergs* [1964], 119). Against such an opponent there was no need—indeed it was disadvantageous—to keep to one's word, and all agreements were merely tactical (Hitler, in Rauschning, *Gespräche mit Hitler*, 33, 106 ff., 109, 113 [these were statements made in 1932 and 1933—Author]).

79. Thus even before 1939, for example, records were kept of Polish anti-German activities, such as judgments against members of German organizations on account of "conspiratory activity": see a Foreign Office letter of March 19, 1938, to the RMuChdRkzlei; the Foreign Office note of November 26, 1938, on the "de-Germanization" of the Olsa region through provocative behavior of the Germans settled there; a telegraphic report of March 29, 1939, from a German correspondent on attacks on Germans in Poland and anti-German promulgations (BA R 43 II 1482 b).

80. Originally it was intended that Poland should be a rump state without access to the sea (Hitler, quoted by Rauschning, *Gespräche mit Hitler*, 113). In his Reichstag speech of October 6, 1939, however, he announced that the Polish state had ceased to exist (quoted in *Der großdeutsche Freiheitskampf, Reden Adolf Hitlers* [1942]).

81. See also Gruchmann, *Der Zweite Weltkrieg* (dtv no. 4010), introduction.

82. Hitler's speech at the end of August 1939 to the military commanders (quoted by Püschel, *Der Niedergang des Rechts im Dritten Reich* [1947], 68).

83. *RGBl.* I, 2042.

84. Cf. Supreme Court for Civil Cases 167, 274; cf. also Pungs, Buchholz, and Wolany, *Ostrechtspflegeverordnung* (1943); in their opinion, all regulations of the former state (general and particular) were annulled with the dissolution of the Polish state. The occasional application of the previous legislation by the yielding state occurred only on the strength of the legislation of the state taking over. The yielding state can regulate all legal relations with its own laws, and thus basically establish the internal juridical order in the acquired territories.

85. Pungs, Buchholz, and Wolany, *Ostrechtspflegeverordnung*.

86. With regard to the annexation of these areas in contravention of international law, see Strupp and Schlochauer, *Wörterbuch des Völkerrechts* (1960–61), 1:69 f.; 2:776; see also BVerfG I, 322; Dahm, *Völkerrecht* (1958), 1:90 n. 3, 605; H. Lauterpacht, *Recognition in International Law* (1948), 99, 124, 125; Oppenheim and Lauterpacht, *International Law* (1952), 2:252; K. Marek, *Identity and Continuity of States* (1954), 564 f.; Verdross, *Völkerrecht*, 5th ed. (1964), 251 f.

87. With regard to Greiser, who had previously been president of the Senate in Danzig (Gdańsk), as a person, see the official communication in the *Gauamtsblatt der NSDAP Posen*, no. 1, of May 1, 1940; see also the description by C. J. Burckhardt, who described Greiser as "soft by nature": "But when circumstances forced him to be hard, and that they did regularly, he overdid the hard side." "No price was too high" for him to pay to be in Hitler's good graces (*Meine Danziger Mission* [1960], 75 ff., 78). For information on Greiser as a person from the Polish viewpoint, see Wietrzykowski, *Powrót Artura Greisera* (1946), an unofficial German translation of which will be found in ZS, AZ I 110 AR 655/73, 6–8. Greiser was taken prisoner by the British in 1945, extradited to Poland, condemned, and executed on July 9, 1946, in Posen (Poznań), where he had been active.

88. See the speech of November 5, 1939, by the Gauleiter in Schroda (ZS, Poland, film 14, sheet 731 ff.).

89. Best, "Neue Gliederung und Verwaltung des ehemaligen polnischen Staatsgebiets" (1939), according to which the administration structure in the Annexed Eastern Territories had created "a maximum of collective spirit and unity," which was the "model for the future administrative reform of the entire Reich."

90. For more details on the liquidation, see Broszat, *Nationalsozialistische Polenpolitik* (1961), 41 ff.; regarding extermination of the Jews, see T. Berenstein, A. Eisenbach, and A. Rutkowski,

700 Notes to Page 195

Eksterminacja hitlerowskiej (1957). With regard to evacuation, see the summary in Broszat, *Nationalsozialistische Polenpolitik*, 84 ff.; Łuczak, *Wysziedlenia Ludności Polskiej* (1969) (*Doc. Occ.* 8); also Datner, Gumbowski, and Leszczyński, "Wysiedlenia Ludności ziem polskich wcielonych do Rzeszy" (1960); Stach, "Polenreservate im Warthegau" (1967), 153 ff.; Szulc, *Wysziedlenia Ludności Polskiej*, W. Tzw. Kraju Warty I Na Zamoczyźnie Oraz Popełnione Przy Tym, *Bulletin of the Main Commission Warsaw* 12 (1971) (all sources contain numerous references and documents); with regard to migration of the German population 1939–45, see the synthesis by Sobczak, *Hitlerowskie przedsiedlenia ludności niemieckiej w dobie II wojny s'wiatowej* (1966).

91. Memorandum of November 25, 1939, from the Race Policy Office of the NSDAP, quoted in *Doc. Occ.* 5:2 ff., 16. See the letter of March 16, 1943, from the Reich governor of Wartheland to the RFSS on the principles of the "racial investigation of the Poles" and the answer from the RFSS of April (BA R 43 II/333); full details in Broszat, *Nationalsozialistische Polenpolitik*, 112 ff.

92. Full details of this Polish policy will be found in Greiser, *Der Aufbau im Osten* (1942), Jena, 1942. Kiel speeches, no. 68, Institute for Western Studies, Poznań, Bibl. Sign. II 40903/68. A good description of the Polish policy will also be found in the unsigned note from the office of the Reich governor of Posen dated November 24, 1939 (State Archive Poznań, *Reichsstatthalter* 835, p. 4), which contains the following: "Regarding political principles of welfare legislation. *Secret:* Following a discussion with SS-Oberführer Mehlhorn, head of Abt. I, the following is noted: (1) Welfare legislation must be completely in the service of the principles of National Socialist policy in the former Poland. There is thus an interest in the Polish population only insofar as the working classes are concerned. The intelligentsia, particularly the leaders of officialdom, should all be deported to the area of the General Government. Those remaining here, who will be treated more or less as work slaves, should, however, be adequately remunerated and supported."

93. Full details in Greiser, *Der Aufbau im Osten;* see also Greiser's speech at a meeting of the *Gau* Bureau for Nationhood Affairs, Wartheland, on March 20–21, 1943, in Posen, for the installation of the new *Gauamtsleiter* (Institute for Western Studies, Poznań); report on a celebration in Posen on "Freedom Day" 1943 with speeches by Himmler and Greiser, *Ostdeutscher Beobachter*, February 25, 1943; Greiser's speech before NSDAP *Kreisleiter* on January 3, 1944, *Ostdeutscher Beobachter*, January 4, 1944.

94. Greiser, *Der Aufbau im Osten*, 9: "The German is the master of the land, and the Pole who works loyally and diligently is under the protection of the Reich . . . and indeed the great mass of the Poles feels absolutely fine with this" (see also Łuczak, *Diskriminierung der Polen* [1966], 57).

95. See, for example, progress report, district director of Hermannsbad (Ciechocinek)/ Regierungsbezirk Hohensalza (Inowrocław), for June 1941 (State Archive Poznań, NSDAP Gauleitung Wartheland 13, sheet 12), which contains the following passage: "The behavior of the Poles has greatly deteriorated of late. They take much less pleasure in their work. . . . In order to be sure to catch every work-shy Polish layabout we intend to clamp down on the Polish churches one after the other and check all the Poles for their papers, work allocation, and so on." Regarding the raids, see also the report of the Order Police, Kalisch (Kalisz), of November 15, 1939 (State Archive Poznań, *Reichsstatthalter* 1831, sheet 11).

96. Reich Governor Greiser at a speech in Kiel on June 10, 1942 (*Der Aufbau im Osten*, 9 f.): "We have come to grips with the problem of the labor force among the Jews, and I think that we have solved the Jewish question in a way that neither the Jews themselves, nor probably the German people, imagined in the past. The conclusion is that it is possible to make foreign labor useful to the German people if you approach things in an uncomplicated and unbureaucratic way. Certainly, however, I must note (and this is not a criticism, only an observation), if we had put good Prussian officials in to carry out these tasks, the Jews would probably still not be working today. We put in National Socialists, however, who have attacked the problem completely unbureaucratically."

97. For a summary, see von Rosen–von Hoevel, "Das Polenstatut" (1942).

98. Report of July 8, 1941, by the district president of Hohensalza (State Archive Poznań, *Reichsstatthalter* 856, sheet 30) and secret reports nos. 7 and 8 by the economic directorate of the Reich governor of Posen to the head of the Four Year Plan, December 12, 1941, and January 13, 1942 (State Archive Poznań, *Reichsstatthalter* 855, sheet 19, 48).

99. H. von Rosen–von Hoevel, *Deutsche Verwaltung* (1941), 114.

100. For more details, see notes 48–61 above.

101. See, for example, the general report of October 3, 1939, on the activity of the administration department to the head of the civil administration, Posen (State Archive Poznań, head of the civil administration 53, sheet 45); letter dated June 10, 1940, from the district president of Posen to the chief of police in Posen and the district *Landräte* (State Archive Poznań, Gendarmerie Schrimm 103, sheet 26).

102 Telex from the chief of police of Łódź, no. 229, to the Reich governor of Posen, dated June 18, 1940 (State Archive Poznań, *Reichsstatthalter* 1232, sheet 68), and his answer of October 1, 1943 (sheet 46); letter from the *Landrat*, Łódź, to the Reich governor of Posen (sheet 50).

103. For more details, see Broszat, *Nationalsozialistische Polenpolitik*, 50 f.; K. M. Pospieszalski, *Sprawa 58,000 Volksdeutschów* (c. 1985); cf. also A. Scheuermann, "Festigung deutschen Volkstums in den eingegliederten Ostgebieten," in *Reich-Volksordnung-Lebensraum*, vol. 6, 475 ff.: "The Polish arbitrariness . . . makes particular consideration unnecessary."

104. Progress report of September 11, 1943, from the district president of Łódź for "Freedom Day" 1943 (State Archive Poznań, *Reichsstatthalter* 65, 19): "It has generally been possible to repress the occasional attempts to revolt associated with the development of the overall political situation; unfortunately, certain elements of the local German population have not shown as strong a character as four years of German control of the area would lead one to expect. The educational work of the NSDAP has been brought into play in this connection to counter the difficulties."

105. All reports from the *Landkreis* authorities were to be transmitted via the *Landrat*, who passed them on to the district president with his own comments (decree of July 29, 1940, from the district president of Posen to the district *Landräte*, State Archive Poznań, Landrat Schrimm, sheet 104). The district presidents for their part were required to report to the Reich governor. Only fragments of these reports are extant. The *only* complete reports from the Wartheland are those by the district president of Hohensalza from 1942 (Posen University Library), which were found by chance in Czech territory. The State Superior Court presidents and prosecutors general of the Annexed Eastern Territories, as in the Reich itself, regularly had to send, in addition to the usual business reports, so-called reports to the Reich Ministry of Justice, giving details not only of the legal practice but also of important individual cases, questions of interpretation, the activity of the police courtsmartial, etc., as well as the general political and economic situation, the mood of the population, and so on. Cf. Reich Ministry of Justice circulars of November 25, 1935 (Az. III 196, quoted in the report of August 11, 1942, by the chief state prosecutor of Königsberg [BA R 22/3375]); Reich Ministry of Justice decrees of April 29, 1940 (Az. 313 I a, 1015, quoted in the report of August 14, 1942, by the chief state prosecutor of Posen [BA R 22/3383]), and of October 29, 1942 (Az. 3130 I A 0, 1746, quoted in the report of November 31, 1943, by the chief state prosecutor of Königsberg [BA R 22/3375]). The collected reports of the State Superior Court presidents and chief state prosecutors from the Annexed Eastern Territories will be found in BA R 22/850, 3360, 3372, 3375, 3383.

With regard to Security Service reports, cf., for example, the general report on the activity of the Administrative Department of the head of the civil administration for Posen, dated March 10, 1939 (State Archive Poznań, head of the civil administration 53, sheet 45); reports by the SD Posen of October 31 and November 7 and 24, 1941 (Institute for Western Studies, Poznań). The main source of information was the reports of the SIPO and SD chiefs (*Meldungen aus dem Reich* [News from the Reich], BA R 58/151 ff.).

106. Greiser in his Kiel speech of June 10, 1942 (*Der Aufbau im Osten*, 8): "The Pole will remain

tractable only as long as we treat him firmly and fairly. He will immediately become intractable, and bring out his cunning, underhand manner if he notices that we become soft and weak. The Pole also has a completely different approach to the things of daily life and European culture." See also the report of October 10, 1941, on the meeting of the Reich Labor Executors for the Eastern Territories in Posen, October 9, 1941 (quoted in *Doc. Occ.* 5:274 ff.), containing statements by state and Party officers (Reich Governor of Posen Greiser: "He . . . sees the Poland question as a real one. The Polish people should never again succeed in resurging here in the East, for here the battle between German and Polish nationhood would be a battle for existence. The nationhood policy is made here on the front, not in Berlin. We had to win the nationhood battle for existence and would have begun this by pushing the Poles up to the German standard of living, something they could never have achieved in the Polish period. . . . [The Pole] may never be in the right" [275 ff.]).

107. See the Reich Ministry of Justice draft of an implementing order issued by the governors of "German East and Southwest Africa regarding legislation on natives in the German colonies," in which (sec. 3) corporal punishment was stipulated for adults and youths (BA R 22/20977).

108. See also agenda no. 21 of the BdO Posen, dated December 19, 1939, wherein a complaint is lodged that members of the SS and the police carried riding whips and publicly beat Poles with them. The BdO decreed the "strictest prohibition" against carrying riding whips (Institute for Western Studies, Poznań). Cf. the transcript of an official discussion of September 26, 1941, with the gendarmerie chief of the Schrimm district, which contains the following text: "1. *Measures against Poles.* It is often necessary to intervene against Poles in matters for which no laws exist. In such cases action must be according to individual discretion. In the case of minor offenses, the Poles should be warned energetically. The Pole must, however, be aware why he has been warned" (State Archive Poznań, Gendarmerie Schrimm 100, sheet 249). Further, the report of October 10, 1941, on the meeting of the Reich Labor Executors held in Posen on October 9, 1941 (sheet 280—see note 106), with reports on beatings in the different districts, and the circular of the commander of the Gendarmerie Posen of February 2, 1942, in which reprimands to "effectively teach" the Poles are prescribed at identity checks (Institute for Western Studies, Poznań). A letter dated July 20, 1944, from the Wartheland Gauleiter (Greiser) to the NSDAP *Kreisleiter* in Scharnikau (quoted in *Doc. Occ.* 10:229) shows that this practice was approved of at the highest level: "Since, however, my name has been falsely called upon to justify a basic prohibition of beating of Poles, perhaps even with reference to an alleged Führer's order, . . . I feel it necessary to make the following clarification: 1. My previous Polish policy has not changed. Poles will be treated *firmly* and *fairly* as before. If a Pole is rebellious and insolent, he must receive an appropriate answer in an immediate reaction. . . . My *Kreisleiter* are responsible for the application of these principles. This letter is intended for you and you alone. I forbid written duplication of it."

109. Report of February 21, 1941, from the district president of Posen for the period January 16 to February 15 (State Archive Poznań, *Reichsstatthalter* 854, sheets 30–31).

110. Report of February 10, 1942, from the NSDAP district director of Hohensalza for the month of January (State Archive Poznań, NSDAP Gauleitung Wartheland 14, 78–79).

111. Cf. report of July 8, 1941, by the district president of Hohensalza (State Archive Poznań, *Reichsstatthalter* 856, 8); progress report by the district director of Hermannsbad (administrative district Hohensalza) for the month of June 1941 (State Archive Poznań, NSDAP Gauleitung Wartheland 13, 12); report dated February 21, 1941, by the district president of Posen (State Archive Poznań, *Reichsstatthalter* 854, sheet 1); Reich Propaganda Office Lissa (Leszno), September 20, 1942 (State Archive Poznań, NSDAP district director for Lissa 46, 43); brief propaganda report of October 8, 1943, by the District Propaganda Office, Lissa (27). Cf. report dated June 19, 1941, on the behavior of Polish workers, the general situation in Poland, the state of nutrition, etc. (ZS, Poland, film 63, sheets 79 ff.); letter of April 25, 1941, from *Landrat* vom Zempelburg to the Gestapo Bromberg, according to which the mood of the Polish population was constantly getting worse (Institute for Western Studies, Poznań); review of the present status of Polish policy in the letter of July 30,

1941, from the Gau Bureau for Nationhood Affairs of the NSDAP in the Warthegau, Dr. Coulon, to the *Reichsstatthalter* on the general mood and work and welfare conditions, with very negative results (Institute for Western Studies, Poznań).

112. *Reichsstatthalter* Greiser in the *Gauamtsblatt of the NSDAP Gau Wartheland*, no. 11/43 of June 1, 1943, p. 1 (State Archive Poznań): "I set particular store by consistency and consistent application of the principles I represent regarding the treatment of the Polish people in all walks of life." Łuczak, *Diskriminierung der Polen*, 53 f.

113. Position paper of October 1944 from the RSHA/Abt. III, BA R 58/1002, 157 ff.

114. Directives of September 29, 1939, from the head of the Civil Administration Posen on the administrative structure (ZS, Poland, film 14, sheet 764 ff.; copy).

115. The ultimate aim according to the directives of the RFSS/RKF was a new order of the whole settlement such that so-called central villages, each with six villages grouped around it, constituted a focal point for the settlement and administration (RFSS/RKF general order II/7 of November 26, 1940, quoted in the Reich Ministry of the Interior directives on the Redesign of the Rural Settlement Structure, I Ost 623/41/4150, undated [presumably end of 1940], BA R 18/1205).

116. Cf. Noack, "Das deutsche Kriegsrecht-Kriegsgesetzgebung" (1940); K. Lemigi, "Die Rechtsentwicklung auf dem Gebiet des Verwaltungsrechts," DR (1943) (A): 127 ff.

117. This included the obligation for Germans to wear a badge making them recognizable as such (circular of May 6, 1940, from the Gauleiter and Reich governor of Warthegau to all Party and state offices, State Archive Poznań, *Reichsstatthalter* 3, sheet 39). All uniformed members of the Wehrmacht and the Party were to demonstrate German unity to the "foreign population" by saluting one another (circular of May 23, 1940, from the *Gauleitung* of the NSDAP, Posen, sheet 53). Convictions of Germans were not published, in order not to endanger the "authority of Germanness" in the East (information sheet—strictly confidential—of the *Gau* press office, Wartheland, dated February 20, 1942, State Archive Poznań, *Reichsstatthalter* 468, sheet 4).

118. Greiser, *Der Aufbau im Osten*, 19.

119. On the "German Restructuring Effort," see, for example, Holtz, "Zur Volksgeschichte der Ostgebiete" (1940); Höhn and Seydel, "Der Kampf um die Wiedergewinnung des deutschen Ostens" (1941); Schürmann, "Festigung deutschen Volkstums in den eingegliederten Ostgebieten" (1943); Reich Governor A. Greiser: The "greatest reforestation program" in the world is planned in the Warthegau, reforestation of 400,000 hectares; a reservoir with a capacity of over a thousand million square km. is planned for the Wartheland, etc. (*Der Aufbau im Osten*, 18). A total of 500,000 Germans (from Bessarabia, Wolhynia, Bukovina, Galicia, the Baltic, etc.) were said to have immigrated to the Reich, 300,000 of them to the Warthegau; this was "double" what the Prussian Settlement Commissions managed over a period of peace of thirty years in two provinces; but it was only a beginning (14). In the Wartheland all state-owned property as well as that of the monasteries and churches was confiscated. The local *Gau* administration thus became "the largest landowner in the *Gau*" (10).

120. "Thousands of German businesses, thousands of official and teaching posts will in the very first instance be occupied by German soldiers; not only technically qualified officials are needed in the German East: anybody who has his heart in the right place . . . good common sense," can become an employee or an official in the East, too. Thus the Fatherland thanks its soldiers (Greiser, *Der Aufbau im Osten*, 14).

Part One. Section 2. Introduction. II. The New Type of Administration in the Annexed Eastern Territories

1. Greiser, *Der Aufbau im Osten* (1942), 14.

2. Cf. Hitler at the working supper of June 24, 1942 (quoted by Picker, *Hitlers Tischgespräche* [1951], 190): "If, in a manner of speaking, he had made *Gaukönige* ('*Gau* Kings') of the Gauleiter,

who received only major orders from above, he is now giving the individual Reich governors a large measure of freedom—even if this does not meet with the approval of the minister of the interior. Only when you give Reich governors and Gauleiter sufficient scope to act on their own initiative do you get to know who has the talent. Otherwise all you get is a stupid bureaucracy."

3. More details in Broszat, *Der Staat Hitlers* (1969), 162 ff.

4. Cf. Hubrich, "Gliederung und Verwaltung der Ostgebiete" (1939) (Hubrich was *Ministerialrat* in the Reich Ministry of the Interior and head of the New Order Division in the Incorporated and Occupied Territories, Foreign Administration); Best, "Die bisherige polnische Verwaltung" (1939).

5. For the development of the NSDAP in the *Reichsgau* Wartheland, see the circular of December 9, 1939, from the Reich governor of Posen (Poznań) to all state agencies, which contained an appeal to further the development of the Party organization by all available means (State Archive Poznań, *Reichsstatthalter* 2, Bl. 70). The most important agencies were (1) the *Gau* Personnel Office, which had to report whenever a member of the Civil Service, but also a private individual, was to take up an important position in the Party, the administration, or the economy (see the statements by the head of the *Gau* Personnel Office for the *Reichsgau* Wartheland, *Gauamtsblatt der NSDAP Gau Wartheland*, May 1, 1940, Bl. 1, State Archive Poznań); (2) the *Gau* Civil Service Office, which was responsible for the clearance of all officials at their recruitment and transfer to other positions and also participated in Civil Service legislation (ibid.); with regard to the work of officials in the Party, see the letter of April 30, 1941, from the Reich governor of Posen to the *Gau* Personnel Office; minutes of the head of Dept. I of the office of *Reichstatthalter* Posen of August 4, 1941; see also the directive of August 30, 1941, issued by the Reich governor of Posen to the district presidents, requiring them to commit all officials to work harder within the Party and its sections and affiliated organizations (State Archive Poznań, *Reichsstatthalter* 924, Bl. 21, 2, 1); (3) the *Gau* Legislation Office, which was responsible for the political alignment of the administration in assimilating the law to that of the "Old Reich," participation in the legislation, recruitment of all law officers to Party service, and the legal charge of the German settlers (*Gauamtsblatt der NSDAP Gau Wartheland*, May 1, 1940, Bl. 1, State Archive Poznań); (4) the *Gau* Office for Community Policy, which had the task of nominating Bürgermeister and official commissioners for office and investigating their credentials, overseeing the municipal structure, etc. (ibid.); (5) the Race Policy Office, which was entrusted with the "uniform alignment of the ethnic German group" toward "correct race-political thinking," information on "Polish nationality problems," and participation in dealing with the "asocial question" and the "solution of the Jewish question" (ibid.); (6) the Party jurisdiction (*Gau* court), which was responsible for the supervision and discipline of Party members (ibid.); (7) the Gau Bureau of Nationhood Affairs, which took care of the "right" political treatment of "non-Germans" and worked closely with the Nationhood Policy Division in the office of the Reich governor (merging of top posts; see note 11).

6. All orders of a fundamental nature from Party and state services dealing with the treatment of Poles and Jews were to be submitted before publication to the head of the *Gau* Bureau of Nationhood Affairs of the NSDAP for comments and approval (decree of June 3, 1943, by the Reich governor of Posen, State Archive Poznań, *Reichsstatthalter* 11, Bl. 93/94, repeated in fundamental order no. 13/44 of June 17, 1944, from the Reich governor of Posen, State Archive Poznań, *Reichsstatthalter* 1174, Bl. 276). Proclamations to the population of the Warthegau, whatever form they took, were to be submitted to the *Gau* Press Office of the NSDAP, which passed them on to the press (instruction by the head of the *Gau* Press Office, January 5, 1940, State Archive Poznań, NSDAP Gauleitung 41). As the brief biographies in the NSDAP official *Gau* bulletins showed, the heads of the Party offices mentioned were all deserving "old soldiers," some of them with high SA or SS positions, who had many years of experience in the "nationhood struggle"; most of them were from Danzig (Gdańsk). But the influence of the Party stretched far beyond the field of administration:

landed property was assigned (at least in the Warthegau) to ethnic German settlers at the insistence of the Party (progress report, *Landrat* Alexandro for the period July 15, 1942, to March 1, 1943, State Archive Poznań, *Reichsstatthalter* 857, Bl. 110); distribution of food ration cards was sometimes also undertaken by NSDAP block leaders (report by the district president of Posen for the period January 16 to February 15, 1941, State Archive Poznań, *Reichsstatthalter* 854, Bl. 34). The influence of the NSDAP was also strongly felt in the field of justice: the Party endeavored to prevent publication of convictions of its members whenever possible, as this was felt to be detrimental to the reputation of the Party among the Poles (political report of the NSDAP district director, Hohensalza [Inowrocław], for February-March 1944, State Archive Poznań, NSDAP Gauleitung Wartheland 14, Bl. 132). In the event of private acts of vengeance ("self-aid") on the part of Germans against Poles, caused by the "state of war and the attacks and atrocity acts of the Poles," the Party attempted to obtain indemnity for the culprit if he had supported Germanness during the Polish period (statements by the *Gau* inspector in the *Gauamtsblatt der NSDAP Gau Wartheland*, May 1, 1940, Bl. 4).

7. From a review of Party careers prepared by the author comprising 29 *Landräte*, vice-*Landräte* and Bürgermeister of the Warthegau in 1939 and 1940 based on documents in the State Archive Poznań (*Reichsstatthalter* 1024 [1939–40], Bl. 2, 5, 7, 8, 17, 19, 34, 45, 63, 66, 69, 114, 138; 1066 [1939], Bl. 38–40, 43, 58; 1066 [1940], Bl. 112, 113, 232), at least 9 of them (31%) were "old soldiers" (that is, Party members before the seizure of power), 5 had been Party members since April 1 or May 1, 1933 (17%), 6 since May 1, 1937 (removal of the limitation of Party membership) (20.7%), 3 were applicants for Party membership (10.3%); in the case of 4 of them, only the fact of Party membership and the Party number is indicated (13.7%); 2 were not members of the Party but did belong to various associated organizations (National Socialist Motor Corps, NSRB, Reich Air Defense League, NSV, Reichsbund deutscher Beamter [RDB]); the Party members for the most part were also at the same time members of such associations or Party sections (SS, SA), where they held quite high positions (storm-troop leaders, SA *Oberführer*, political leaders).

8. Regarding the position of the Reich governor and the *Oberpräsident*, see Hasche, *Der Reichsstatthalter* (1938); Broszat, *Der Staat Hitlers*, 140 ff.; Diehl-Thiele, *Partei und Staat im Dritten Reich* (1969), 49, 53.

9. The Polish population should not learn that "there are conflicts of authority between the various ministries" or that "undeniable tensions exist between Party and state"; letter of October 11, 1939, from the staff of the deputy Führer (signed Sommer) to State Secretary Stuckart/Reich Ministry of the Interior, quoted by Diehl-Thiele, *Partei und Staat im Dritten Reich*, 125 f. n. 41.

10. RFSSuChddtPol circular of November 7, 1939, on the organization of the Secret State Police in the Eastern Territories (*Minbliv* [1939]: 2291).

11. Thus the officer for nationhood policy (SS-*Sturmbannführer* Höppner in Department 1 of the office of the Reich governor of Posen, I/50) was at the same time head of the Bureau of Nationhood Affairs of the *Gauleitung* of the NSDAP (decree of June 3, 1943, by the Reich governor of Posen, State Archive Poznań, *Reichsstatthalter* 11, Bl. 193–94) (he was also head of the SD-*Leitabschnitt*, Posen). The head of Department 1, Internal Administration (SS-*Oberführer* Mehlhorn), was also head of the *Gau* Legislation Office of the NSDAP (note in *Gauamtsblatt der NSDAP Gau Wartheland*, May 1, 1940, Bl. 1).

12. RFSSuChddtPol decree, November 7, 1939 (*MinbliV* [1939]: 2291).

13. For full details, see Broszat, *Nationalsozialistische Polenpolitik* (1961), 52 ff.; Mommsen, *Beamtentum im Dritten Reich* (1966), 110 ff., and the material contained in BA R 22/2234 and 2241 on the appointment of the *Landrat* offices in the administrative district of Zichenau. In 1940–41, 17 of the *Landräte* of the administrative district of Posen were also *Kreisleiter*; in the administrative district of Hohensalza, 2 of the 3 Oberbürgermeister of the municipal districts (Hohensalza, Gnesen, Leslau), and 7 of the 11 *Landräte* were probably also *Kreisleiter*. In the administrative district of Łódź, 8 of the 9 *Landräte* were also *Kreisleiter* ("Verwaltungsaufbau des Warthegaues 1940–1941,"

State Archive Poznań, *Reichsstatthalter* 1067, Bl. 85–87). With regard to the conflicts between the minister of the interior and the Reich governor of Posen and Danzig, the deputy Führer's office, and the Reich Chancellery, see the exhaustive material in BA R 43 II/643 and 1136b.

14. Order of the deputy Führer of February 19, 1937, quoted by Diehl-Thiele, *Partei und Staat im Dritten Reich*, 182, requiring that all official links between *Kreisleitung* and the offices of *Landrat*, Oberbürgermeister, and Bürgermeister should be removed by October 1, 1937, since NSDAP officers tended all to often to heed only the requirements of the state administration. Similarly the circulars of August 7, 1942, from the head of the Party Chancellery to all *Reichsleiter* and Gauleiter, etc. (in *Verfügungen* 2 [1943]: 223 ff.; also in Mommsen, *Beamtentum im Dritten Reich*, 239 f.). Regarding the development of the merging of posts between *Kreisleiter* and *Landrat*, see Diehl-Thiele, *Partei und Staat im Dritten Reich*, 176 ff.

15. Decree of the Reich minister of the interior of December 1, 1939 (State Archive Poznań, *Landgericht* Posen 19, Bl. 34–35); order of the Reich minister of the interior of December 2, 1939 (*RGBl.* 1940 I 8), repeated in the urgent memorandum of June 24, 1941, from the commissioner-general for administration of the Reich (Frick) to the Reich defense commissioners (BA R 43 II/703 a). See also the letter of July 18, 1941, from the RMuChdRkzlei to the commissioner-general for administration of the Reich (ibid.).

16. See the decree of November 16, 1939, from the Reich governor of the Warthegau to all *Landräte* of the district and others: "So long as the merging of posts between *Landrat* and *Kreisleiter* or Oberbürgermeister proposed by me to the deputy Führer does not exist, the *Landrat* remains my political delegate in his field" (State Archive Poznań, *Reichsstatthalter* 4, Bl. 27).

17. Transcript of a paper by *Hauptamtleiter* Friedrich of the staff of the deputy Führer's office in early 1940, reproduced in Diehl-Thiele, *Partei und Staat im Dritten Reich*, 182 f. n. 23; Mommsen, *Beamtentum im Dritten Reich*, 228 ff.

18. As many as 40 of the 63 *Landrat* offices in the *Reichsgaue* Danzig, West Prussia, and the Wartheland were held by nonspecialists, i.e., Party functionaries; Danzig and West Prussia in fact had the highest rate of Party functionaries as *Landräte* (88%), whereas in the Wartheland the proportions appeared somewhat more balanced (52.6% pure administrative officials, who of course had to belong to the Party, and 47.4% Party functionaries [personal letter of May 26, 1941, from the Reich Ministry of the Interior to the RMuChdRkzlei, BA R 43 II/647]). But there too, at least initially, there was a heavy bias toward the Party. Of the 23 *Landräte* for the *Reichsgau* Wartheland championed by the Reich governor of Posen at the end of 1939, 16 were also to be installed as *Kreisleiter*, the other 7 only as *Landräte* (letter of January 2, 1940, from the Reich Ministry of the Interior to the RMuChdRkzlei, BA R 43 II/647; quoted in Mommsen, *Beamtentum im Dritten Reich*, 227). The rest, some 14 *Landräte*, consisted of pure Party functionaries without any specialized training. Thus, out of the 37 *Landräte* of the Warthegau, 30 were also active as *Kreisleiter*, while in the administrative district of Łódź the merging of posts of *Kreisleiter* and *Landrat* was realized almost 100%. (According to the review "Verwaltungsaufbau des Warthegaus, 1940–41," no author, State Archive Poznań, *Reichsstatthalter* 1067, Bl. 85–87, the number was 31 *Kreisleiter*).

Toward the end of the war the proportion changed in favor of separate incumbents of the offices of *Kreisleiter* and *Landrat*: on May 1, 1944, there was a merging of posts in "only" 25 of the 37 districts of the Warthegau (67.6%) (register of *Landräte* and *Kreisleiter* as of May 1, 1944, State Archive Poznań, *Reichsstatthalter* 1067, Bl. 351–53). Of the 31 *Landkreise* still existing on January 1, 1945, in the Warthegau, there was a merging of posts (*Kreisleiter* and *Landrat*) in 16 (51.6%) (register of *Landräte* and *Kreisleiter* as of May 1, 1945, Institute for Western Studies, Poznań, doc. I, 258, Bl. 7). The merging of posts between Party and state offices is also found in other branches of the administration. For the justice department, see personnel files, State Archive Poznań, State Superior Court Posen 1311; "Tautphaeus," *DR* (1941) (A): 2466 ff. (2467) ("merging of posts in the Warthegau has been achieved as far as possible"). "Law officers primarily hold Party positions in the legal field in addition to other political offices. . . . Refusal to cooperate in the NSDAP and its organizations would give rise to discharge and dismissal from the Warthegau"; Public Prosecutor Drendel, Posen, *Ostdeutscher Beobachter*, June 24, 1940: "[There is] not a single one of my staff foreseen for work in the Wartheland who is not active in the NSDAP or its sections." Reich Ministry of Justice report on a visit of Reich Ministry of Justice representatives to the public prosecutor's offices in East Upper Silesia, October 22–25, 1940 (the attorney general in Ratibor [Racibórz], head of the local branch of the SD, has been "brought to state" that it is desirable for justice officers—especially high-ranking ones—to hold Party positions).

19. Note by *Ministerialrat* Dellbrügge, Reich Ministry of the Interior, of December 1939, BA R 32 II/647 (excerpts in Mommsen, *Beamtentum im Dritten Reich*, 224 f.)

20. See Broszat, *Nationalsozialistische Polenpolitik*, 52 ff.; Mommsen, *Beamtentum im Dritten Reich*, 110 ff.; note by *Ministerialrat* Dellbrügge, Reich Ministry of the Interior, of December 1939 (224 f.); urgent memorandum of December 23, 1939, from the Reich Ministry of the Interior to the president of the Council of Ministers for Defense of the Reich and to the RMuChdRkzlei (BA R 32 II/647; quoted in Mommsen, *Beamtentum im Dritten Reich*, 223 f.). Letter dated January 2, 1940, from the Reich Ministry of the Interior to the RMuChdRkzlei (BA R 32 II/647; quoted in Mommsen, *Beamtentum im Dritten Reich*, 227 f.). Personal letter from *Reichsleiter* Bormann to Reich minister Lammers, March 1, 1941 (BA R 43 II/1136 b).

21. Personal letter from Reich Ministry of the Interior to RMuChdRkzlei, May 26, 1941 (BA R 43 II/1136 b; quoted in Mommsen, *Beamtentum im Dritten Reich*, 233 ff.).

22. Though at the level of the district presidents there was the Party office of the *Gau* inspector, which was run as a merged office with the district presidency, this was not an intermediate office between the Gauleiter and the *Kreisleiter* but dealt with the various special tasks of the Party (statements of the district president and *Gau* inspector of Posen, May 1, 1940, *Gauamtsblatt der NSDAP Gau Wartheland*, 1/40, Bl. 5).

23. According to the Second Implementing Order of November 2, 1939, sec. 7 (*RGBl.* I 2133), to the decree of the Führer and *Reichskanzler* of October 8, 1939 (*RGBl.* I 2042), the office of the district president comprised the following departments only: General and Internal Affairs (Dept. 1), Education and Mass Education (Dept. 2), Economic Affairs (Dept. 3), Agriculture and Estates (Dept. 4). In the Altreich the Gestapo and the Forestry Administration had been withdrawn from the district presidents since 1933.

24. More details in Diehl-Thiele, *Partei und Staat im Dritten Reich*, 120, 123 ff., where the tendency to elbow out the district presidents is traced to the dualism between Party and state. Letter of December 7, 1940, from the chief of the head office of the *Ordnungspolizei*, which reports on a discussion between the Reich governor and other departments in which the Reich minister of the interior presented plans to dissolve the offices of the district president and to transfer their duties to the *Landräte* (BA R 19/395).

25. Frick, "Der Oberpräsident als Organ des Zentralgewalt des Reiches" (1941). Frick contests the "superfluous and damaging centralism" and argues in favor of maintaining the intermediate offices.

26. Twelfth Decree of April 25, 1943, to the Reich Citizenship Law, sec. 5 (*RGBl.* I 268); Decree on Citizenship unless Countermanded of April 25, 1943, sec. 1 (*RGBl.* I 269); and Decree on Protective Citizenship of April 25, 1943, sec. 11 (*RGBl.* I 271).

27. See Greifelt, "Festigung deutschen Volkstums in den Ostgebieten" (1940), for more details.

28. Führer directive on the Eastern territories of October 8, 1939, sec. 3 (*RGBl.* I, 2042), in conjunction with the so-called Sudetengau Law of April 14, 1939 (*RGBl.* I, 780).

29. Führer directive on the Organization and Administration of the Eastern Territories of October 8, 1939, sec. 3 (*RGBl.* I 2042), in conjunction with the Law on the Administrative Structure in the *Reichsgau* Sudetenland of April 14, 1939, sec. 3 (RGBl. I 780).

30. For more details on the autonomy of the Reich governors, see Broszat, *Der Staat Hitlers*, 162 ff., 167 ff.

31. The four-tiered administration structure included the Reich administration, the Reich governor, the district president, and the *Landrat*. The situation of the office of the Reich governor was never made completely clear. It was inserted between the Reich ministries and the middle- and lower-level authorities, but it not only served as an intermediary between the central and middle-level authorities, as had the *Land* governments or lord lieutenancies in the "Old Reich" but had numerous independent powers. See the order of November 2, 1939 (*RGBl.* I, 2133); organization chart of the office of the Reich governor of Posen (ZS, Polen film 55/773). An example of a regulation is the one dealing with the duty to report. The rule was for reports by the district president in Berlin, for example, to be transmitted via the office of the Reich governor. Since, however, there was no guarantee that the reports would be passed on to Berlin, some district presidents continued to send in their reports directly to the central office, with resulting continuous annoyance to the office of the Reich governor.

32. Law on the Administrative Structure in Austria of April 14, 1939 (*RGBl.* I, 777). Law on the Administrative Structure in the *Reichsgau* Sudetenland of April 14, 1939 (RGBl. I, 780).

33. Regarding the question of the *Gauräte*, see full details in Teppe, "NSDAP und Ministerial-bürokratie" (1976), esp. 372 ff.

34. Broszat, *Der Staat Hitlers* (1969), 171.

35. In fact, orders from above were that only qualified personnel should be sent to the Eastern Territories; a possibility considered was to commit all young officials who wanted promotion to go to the Annexed Eastern Territories for a few years once peace had been achieved (letter of July 21, 1939, from the Reich minister of the interior to the highest authorities of the Reich; letter from the chief of staff of the deputy Führer's office of November 2, 1940, to the RMuChdRkzlei; memorandum of November 13, 1941, from the Reich Chancellery, and draft of a letter to the Reich Ministry of the Interior of November 14, 1940; letters of January 4 and February 13, 1941, from the Reich Ministry of the Interior to the RMuChdRkzlei [all in BA R 43 II/423]).

Actual practice was in complete contradiction with this official version. The home authorities, which released their staff only with extreme reluctance, in the first instance ordered those who appeared to be the least capable to the Eastern Territories. For this reason, and on account of the unfavorable living conditions, transfer to the Eastern Territories was regarded as a punishment, except by those who had voluntarily committed themselves to service there. Reports from the SD and administrative authorities are filled with descriptions and complaints about these difficulties and the employment of "inferior" officials, misdeeds and criminal acts of all types on the part of German officials, the general dissatisfaction in the Civil Service, and their poor living conditions; cf. *Meldungen aus dem Reich* of April 3, June 24, October 10, September 12, November 21, 1940; February 24, June 9, and December 10, 1941 (BA R 58/149, 151, 154, 155, 156, 157, 161); reports of the district presidents of Posen of January 29, 1940, for the period December 16, 1939, to January 15, 1940; and of February 21, 1941, for the period January 16 to February 15, 1941 (State Archive Poznań, Reichsstatthalter, hereafter R-sta 922, Bl. 15–16, and 854, Bl. 8); report from the district president of Kalisch (Kalisz) for the period February 16 to March 15, 1940 (R-sta 1830, Bl. 10–14; and R-sta 922, Bl. 26); report from the district president of Łódź (previously Kalisch) for the period March 21 to June 20, 1941 (R-sta 1830, Bl. 45–46); reports from the district president of Hohensalza of February 21, 1940 (R-sta 922, Bl. 17), of July 8, 1941 (R-sta 856, Bl. 10), and of September 10, 1943 (R-sta 65, Bl. 1); letter of May 9, 1940, from the RFSS/RKF to the Reich minister for science, education, and culture (R-sta 992, Bl. 29); secret report, no. 6, of November 15, 1941, from the Reich governor of Posen—economic directorate to the head of the Four Year Plan (R-sta 855, Bl. 12); letter of January 13, 1942, from the Reich governor of Posen—food office—to Dept. 5 (internal) (ibid., Bl. 41).

Regarding the technical and personal inadequacies of the members of the German administration and of Party members in the Annexed Eastern Territories, see also the correspondence between the Reich minister of the interior and the Reich governor of Posen dated January 29, May 4, and May 20, 1940 (BA R 18/462), regarding the Oberbürgermeister of Łódź; memorandum of the deputy Reich governor of Posen (District President Jäger) of May 14, 1940 (State Archive Poznań, R-sta 1023, Bl. 6), regarding the private sale of the jewelry of executed Poles by the *Landrat* of Schrimm; the result of a disciplinary action against the *Landrat* was thought to be questionable because the sale of such goods often occurred among officials and the sale "did not occur while the impression of the . . . execution was still fresh"; report from the district president of Hohensalza of September 18, 1940 (Bl. 8–9) (Posen University Library). Letter from the chief of the SIPO and SD to HSSPF, Posen, on "unprofessional behavior of senior officials in Posen" (Institute for Western Studies, Poznań). For criminal acts on the part of police officials (attacks against Poles, acts while drunk), see the letter of September 18, 1941, from the *Kreisleiter* of Loben to the Kattowitz (Katowice) *Gauleitung* (ZS, Poland, film 63, 76–78); report of January 8, 1940, from the State Superior Court president, Hamburg (BA R 22/3366): "The officials of my office stationed in Poland express reservations both by word of mouth and in writing about the too 'rigorous' methods of our police force. I pass this on."

36. Cf. Hitler's working supper of June 24, 1942, in Picker, *Hitlers Tischgespräche*, 190 (see note 2 above).

37. Letter from the chief of the SIPO and SD of September 18, 1941, to the RMuChdRkzlei regarding the status of the head of the civil administration in the East. Heydrich declared therein that the heads of the civil administration in the "German sphere of influence" were freed by Führer's decree from their obligation to take orders from the Reich central authorities and were subject only to the authority of the Führer (exceptions were the postal administration and the head of the Four Year Plan). For this reason the "position of the *Reichsführer*-SS in this regard toward the head of the civil administration must be 'cleared up' on account of the 'unity of police measures' "; answer of the RMuChdRkzlei of October 7, 1941: the planned presentation to the Führer was postponed in agreement with the *Reichsführer*-SS (BA R 43 II/96).

38. Teppe, "NSDAP und Ministerialbürokratie," 367.

39. Examples: the development of the *Gauräte* referred to above and the conflicts over the introduction of the Prussian Law of Police Administration in the Annexed Eastern Territories described below.

40. Cf., for example, the note in the files by the head of Referat I/50, office of the Reich governor of Posen, dated July 14, 1943 (State Archive Poznań, Reichsstatthalter 1174, Bl. 39).

41. File note of July 14, 1943: "I do not consider it appropriate to draft a notice on the treatment of Polish workers: these are things that can be discussed only by word of mouth. It cannot be put down in writing, for example, when a Pole may or may not be beaten" (ibid.); and of July 17, 1943: "I spoke today with Fräulein Thröh (head of the NS women's association and *Gau* women's association) about work rules for domestic staff. Frl. Thröh agrees that . . . no detailed regulations whatsoever for Poles are desirable but that very general guidelines should be set up so as to avoid at all costs the possibility that the Poles could make reference to them" (ibid., Bl. 41).

42. Overview of the entire administrative structure in the *Reichsgau* Wartheland, undated, Institute for Western Studies, Poznań; H. Faust, "Neuordnung und Aufbau der Verwaltung in Oberschlesien," *DVerw* (1940): 433 ff.; (1941): 433 ff. See also Hubrich, "Gliederung und Verwaltung der Ostgebiete."

Part One. Section 2. Introduction. III. Results

1. Roesner, "Der neue Ostraum Großdeutschlands," *DJ* 2 (1940): 857 f.
2. With regard to the administrative practices, see the descriptions of the conditions in two

districts of the Wartheland, Sieradz and Łódź, by M. Cygański, "Powiat Sieradzki w latach okupacji hitlerowskiej 1939–1945," *Rocznik Łódzki* 14 (17) (1970): 79 ff.; Cygański, "Powiat Łódzki w latach okupacji hitlerowskiej 1939–1945 r." (1970–72).

3. Thus the report of July 30, 1941, by the nationhood-political officer in the office of the Reich governor of Posen (Poznań) (Institute for Western Studies, Poznań, doc. I-145). For the policy in Danzig (Gdańsk)–West Prussia, see also the report of May 21, 1941, by the district president of Hohensalza (Inowrocław) (Posen University Library).

4. See full details in "Die Aufgaben des Gauamtes für Volkstumsfragen im Reichsgau Wartheland," undated, no author, 36 (Institute for Western Studies, Poznań, doc. I-4); further references in part 1, section 2, Introduction, II ("The New Type of Administration in the Annexed Eastern Territories"), note 35.

5. Report of August 18, 1940, by the district president of Hohensalza (Posen University Library).

6. Report of September 18, 1940, by the district president of Hohensalza, ibid.

7. Institute for Western Studies, Poznań, doc. I-145 (also circular of February 23, 1943, from the Reich governor of Posen, Institute for Western Studies, Poznań); examples of "Pole-friendly" or "unpatriotic" behavior were to prepare a recommendation for a Pole, to drink together with Poles or visit their homes, etc.

8. Reports of August 18, September 18, November 21, 1940; March 18, May 25, 1941, from the district president of Hohensalza (Posen University Library); reports of November 27, 1943; September 20, November 30, December 18, 1944, from the SD, Posen, containing numerous details; report of April 10, 1943, from the SD, Danzig. See also the letter of March 10, 1943, from the NSDAP, Alt-Bergund, to a German woman in Wappin, reproaching her for having friendly relations with Poles; a complaint (undated) "on the friendly relations" of members of the Wehrmacht with Poles; letter of April 2, 1941, from the *Landrat* of Kosten (Kościan) to the headquarters of the Gestapo, Posen, on relations of members of the Wehrmacht with Poles (all Institute for Western Studies, Poznań); see the complaints in *Meldungen aus dem Reich* of July 4, 1940, that members of the Wehrmacht went to Polish restaurants with Polish women (BA R 58/152). Also the report from the Gendarmerie chief of the Grätz district for the period April 1 to March 24, 1942 (State Archive Poznań, *Landratsamt* Grätz 36, Bl. 55).

9. Report of July 30, 1941, from district president, Hohensalza: "Anybody who associates with Poles goes to the concentration camp." Report of November 21, 1940, from district president, Hohensalza (Posen University Library).

10. See, for example, report no. 270 of September 31, 1940, by the Security Police, Rawitsch (Rawicz) (Institute for Western Studies, Poznań).

11. Transcript of a discussion with the commander of the Security Police, Posen, on September 29, 1941 (State Archive Poznań).

12. Note from the *Gau* Bureau of Nationhood Affairs of the NSDAP, Posen, of April 23, 1943, regarding statments by a Reich railway official, with a letter of April 30, 1943, sent to the SD-*Mittelabschnitt*, Posen, "for further consideration"; the Poles, who included a large number of the intelligentsia (professors, etc.), were said to be operating in a very sophisticated manner, apparently directed from a central headquarters (see also the report of July 30, 1941) (Institute for Western Studies, Poznań, doc. I-214).

13. Report of July 30, 1941, Institute for Western Studies, Poznań, doc. I-145.

Part One. Section 2. A. The Principal Features of the National Socialist Policy of Special Law

1. It is not possible to go into greater detail here about the privileges accorded German citizens and German nationals in the Annexed Eastern Territories. They occurred above all in the

business and tax domains, so as to compensate German residents for the disadvantages that had accrued during the Polish period, to facilitate new settlement by Germans, and to stimulate economic investment from the Altreich. Cf. the Decree on Damage to the Nationhood of February 7, 1941 (*RGBl.* I 85). As in all the Annexed Eastern Territories (Austria, Sudetengau, Memel, Danzig [Gdańsk]), the Reich tax legislation (and Prussian fiscal law), including the emergency tax laws applying to Poles, Gypsies, and Jews (Decree on Social Compensatory Taxes of August 5, 1940, *RGBl.* I, 1077, with its first, second, and third implementing orders, *RGBl.* 1940 I 1666, 1942 I 149), was also promulgated in the Eastern Territories (decrees of November 18, 1939, *RGBl.* I, 2258; January 7, 1940, *RGBl.* I, 149; January 10, 1940, *RGBl.* I, 211; February 24, 1940, *RGBl.* I, 418; September 24, 1940, *RGBl.* I, 1288; December 8, 1940, *RGBl.* I, 1587) but with considerable fiscal advantages in favor of "Germanness"; see the list of regulations in Kluge and Krüger, *Verfassung und Verwaltung* (1941), 126 ff.; the most significant was the Decree on Tax Remissions in Favor of the Annexed Eastern Territories (Eastern Aid Decree) of December 9, 1940 (*RGBl.* I 1565; *RStBl.* 1013), which accorded considerable preferential conditions to German nationals but not to naturalized Poles (cf. the so-called Poland Administrative Decree of May 8, 1941, by Reich Minister of Finance Schulz and Brachmann, *Oststeuerhilfe* [1941], 67 f.); full details in ibid., 131 ff., with further references and implementation orders from the Reich minister of finance (42 ff.).

2. Police decree of April 15, 1941 (*ABl. des Regierungspräsidenten Kattowitz* [1941]: 77 f.; Institute for Western Studies, Poznań, Library, Sign. C III/266).

3. Instruction of November 1, 1941, Reich governor of Wartheland, on first names permitted for Polish children (Az. I/52–141–1–13; Institute for Western Studies, Poznań, doc I-842; quoted in Łuczak, *Diskriminierung der Polen* [1966], 365 ff.); see also the letter of May 1941 from the Reich governor of Posen (Poznań) to the Reich minister of the interior (362 ff.), in which Greiser proposes some of the measures that he later implemented. Thus Poles were not allowed to bear German first names or surnames, and vice versa.

4. Police decree of July 7, 1943, by district president, Kattowitz (Katowice), Stück 30, no. 137, university library, Warsaw, Sign. O34693): "Male and female Eastern workers shall wear a square badge in blue and white on the right chest of all outer garments, bearing the sign *Ost.*"

5. Transcript of a discussion on June 25, 1942, between Gauleiter Bracht (Upper Silesia) and the head of the Race and Settlement Office (SS-*Gruppenführer* Greifelt), in which the latter made a suggestion to this effect (Institute for Western Studies, Poznań).

6. Presumably there was a corresponding central instruction from the Reich governor of Posen. Cf. the activity report of the *Kreisleitung* Hermannsbad (Ciechocinek) for June 1941 (State Archive Poznań, NSDAP Gauleitung Wartheland 13, Bl. 13): "In all localities, but especially in the larger ones of the district, the greatest care shall be taken that every German is recognizable as such by his external appearance. Any German not wearing a sign will be treated like a Pole and will just have to accept being turned out of shops during shopping hours reserved for Germans."

7. Letter of March 30, 1943, from the District Propaganda Office of the NSDAP Lissa (Leszno) to the *Gau* Propaganda Office of Posen (State Archive Poznań, NSDAP *Kreisleitung* Lissa 46, Bl. 34).

8. Police decree of September 4, 1940, by the district president of Posen (*Abl. Regierung Posen*, no. 10, of September 5, 1940, 47 f.; also in State Archive Poznań, Gendarmerie Schrimm, 103, Bl. 62).

9. Decree of October 22, 1940, communicated by way of Posen Gestapo circular of October 24, quoted in an administrative decree by the Reich governor of Posen of April 21, 1941 (State Archive Poznań, Gendarmerie Schrimm, 104, Bl. 50).

10. Instruction of the *Gau* Bureau of Nationhood Affairs of the NSDAP of November 3, 1943 (Institute for Western Studies, Poznań).

11. Fines were imposed of up to RM 150; in nonprosecuting cases prison sentences of up to three weeks could be imposed (police decree of September 4, 1940, issued by the district president of Posen, *Abl. Regierung Posen*, no. 10, of September 5, 1940, 47 f.). Under the terms of the administrative decree of April 21, 1941, by the district president of Posen (State Archive Poznań, Gendarmerie

Schrimm, 104, Bl. 50), Poles found wearing German or Austrian medals or decorations were to have these taken away from them and were expressly forbidden to continue wearing them. It was always presumed that there was an intention to deceive. Any Pole who continued to wear medals or decorations after being warned was to be taken to the Secret State Police. In some cases the Pole could also be brought before the Gestapo immediately. Cf. p. 2 of the report of August 18, 1940, by the district president of Hohensalza (Posen University Library).

12. Instruction (undated) by the *Landrat* of the Konin District on the obligation of all male Poles to salute uniformed Germans, reproduced in a letter dated October 1, 1942, from the SD Posen to the deputy Gauleiter of Posen (*Doc. Occ.* 5:301 ff.); directives of September 29, 1939, by the head of the Civil Administration Posen (ZS, Poland, film 14, 764 ff.) (prohibition of standing around with hands in pockets when Wehrmacht vehicles are passing by); instruction of October 17, 1939, from the Bürgermeister of Strzelno to the Strzelno police (Łuczak, *Diskriminierung der Polen*, 143 f.), forbidding Poles from "standing around on the street and in doorways, and having their hands in their pockets": in the event of nonobservance, twenty strokes of the whip were threatened in punishment.

13. K. M. Pospieszalski, in *Doc. Occ.* 5:301 f. n. 44.

14. Instruction of November 4, 1939 (quoted in Łuczak, *Diskriminierung der Polen*, 343 ff.); repeated in the decree of November 25, 1939, quoted in the letter of October 1, 1942, from the SD-*Leitabschnitt* Posen to the deputy Gauleiter of Posen (printed in *Doc. Occ.* 5:301 ff.): the obligation to salute should be introduced "for reasons of discipline" and relates to leaders of the Party, state, and Wehrmacht.

15. Letter of October 6, 1941, from the District Propaganda Office of the NSDAP, Lissa, to the Gauleitung Wartheland (State Archive Poznań, NSDAP *Kreisleitung*, Lissa, 46, Bl. 51): "Regarding the obligation of Poles to salute, I have issued an appropriate instruction and request the *Kreisleiter* from now on not to impose fines in the event of nonobservance and to order forced labor during the Pole's free time. This will enable us to keep our streets clean, particularly in winter, and many other things." Cf. also the report of November 21, 1940, from the district president of Hohensalza (Posen University Library). Administrative decree of July 28, 1941, issued by the Reich governor of Wartheland (State Archive Poznań, Gendarmerie Schrimm, 108, Bl. 388):

> The discipline of the Poles in public places has worsened considerably. The Gauleiter and Reich governor have noted to their concern when traveling in the *Gau* that the majority of Poles not only do not salute but confront the Gauleiter's car with a neglectful and sometimes provocative attitude, although the vehicle and its occupants are clearly distinguished by the territorial flag and uniforms. . . . I request that the discipline demanded be enforced with all severity. Poles are to obey the obligation to salute Germans in all cases in the countryside, especially if the German is in uniform or is exhibiting the service flag. In towns this rule will have to be relaxed somewhat, although here too it is essential that the Gauleiter and Reich governor be saluted.

See too daily instruction no. 79 of the HSSPF Posen of July 18, 1942 (State Archive Poznań, Befehlshaber der Ordnungspolizei 5, Bl. 29): "It has been noted on several occasions that the obligation of Poles to salute has come under strong criticism. I request the subordinate police agencies to apply the rule without exception, using force if necessary. . . . I will make spot checks in the future. If a German service issues such an order in an area at present primarily inhabited by Poles, it is a matter of prestige for the whole of Germandom in this respect that the above order be strictly carried out. Signed, Koppe"; see also the report of the NSDAP *Kreisleitung* Hohensalza to the *Gauleitung* Wartheland for August 1941 (State Archive Poznań, NSDAP *Gauleitung* Wartheland 14, 27): "Since of late the Poles are neglecting a respectful attitude toward Germans and virtually never any longer observe the obligation to salute, I have laid down a general instruction for the Hohensalza district in this regard. I trust that with this I will teach the Poles the necessary respect for Germans."

16. Cf. the decree of July 28, 1941, issued by the Reich governor of Wartheland (State Archive

Poznań, Gendarmerie Schrimm, 108, Bl. 388); instruction of July 18, 1942, by the HSSPF Posen; reports of August 18, September 18, and November 21, 1940; and October 20, 1941, by the district president of Hohensalza: Poles complied with mandatory saluting only "very reluctantly" (Posen University Library).

17. Letter of October 1, 1942, from the SD-*Leitabschnitt* Posen to the deputy Gauleiter of Posen, in *Doc. Occ.* 5:301 ff.; in the Gostingen district, for example, force was used.

18. Ibid.; examples quoted are Samter (Poles rarely salute), Wreschen (Wrzesnia) (no insistence), Schrimm (no obligation to salute).

19. Ibid., 304

20. Letter of February 3, 1943, from the Party Chancellery to the NSDAP *Gauleitung* Wartheland (*Doc. Occ.* 5:304 f.): "Experience tells that it would be extremely difficult to enforce the obligation to salute in the larger towns on account of insufficient police and surveillance forces, and thus the reputation of the Germans could only be damaged."

21. Cf. letter of November 27, 1939, from the Bürgermeister of Strzelno, in Łuczak, *Grabież polskiego mienia* (1969), 14; letter of June 10, 1940, from the *Landrat* of Wollstein (Wolsztyn) (21). See also the instruction from the curator of the University of Posen dated December 4, 1941, to drop the "Mr." when talking to Poles (diary no. H 6656/41, Institute for Western Studies, Poznań, doc. I-675).

22. The changing of Polish place names was begun spontaneously very early by local administrative and Party agencies; some of the changes were later reversed by the Reich Ministry of the Interior, a move that, the Party accused, "damaged the German reputation" (*Vertrauliche Information der Parteikanzlei* 4/40 of January 14, 1942, *Verfügungen*, 2:255). In the Warthegau the Germanization of place names began with the Reich governor's instruction that the original German name should be researched for each place, an enterprise that was often impossible on account of a shortage of staff (report of August 18, 1940, from the district president of Hohensalza, p. 6, regarding districts that had once belonged to Russia, Posen University Library). Under a decree of May 18, 1943, all place names were to be given in the German *and* Polish languages (*VOBl. Reichsstatthalter Wartheland*, 1943).

23. Decree of September 23, 1939, issued by the head of the civil administration, Posen, regarding removal of Polish signs (*VOBl. Posen*, p. 9; *Doc. Occ.* 5:64), and instruction of the same date by the municipal commissar of Posen, according to which all notices and signs on the street side of buildings had to be in German (*VOBl. Posen*, p. 12; *Doc. Occ.* 5:64). Proclamation of April 17, 1940, by the Oberbürgermeister of Posen that in order to "restore the German appearance of the streets," all property owners, commissary administrators, and lessees of Polish and Jewish houses, businesses, and workshops should remove all Polish signs, names of firms, etc. by May 15, 1940 (High Commission Archives Warsaw, poster collection XIV 103 t/1, photocopy).

24. Letters of July 27 and September 4, 1940, from the district president of Posen to Reich governor Greiser, reproduced in Łuczak, *Dyskryminacja Polaków*, 311 ff., 331 ff.; a circular of February 23, 1943, issued by the Reich governor of Posen protested the practice of individual firms of punishing Poles if they spoke Polish. This was not the right thing to do: the Polish language should not be forbidden, and nobody should be forced to speak German; the Poles should not be Germanized (Institute for Western Studies, Poznań). The use of the Polish language by Germans, on the other hand, was strongly opposed; cf. a report of the chief public prosecutor of Kattowitz dated May 3, 1942 (BA R 22/3372).

25. Circular of February 23, 1943, by the Reich governor of Posen (Institute for Western Studies, Poznań). SD reports, *Meldungen aus dem Reich*, of March 27, 1940 (BA R 58/149).

26. Cf. the announcement of April 2, 1940, in the district gazette for Plozk (Płock) dated January 5, 1940, on language courses for ethnic Germans (Institute for Western Studies, Poznań, doc. I-706); Plozk came under the control of the Zichenau District, which was incorporated into the province of East Prussia as so-called Southeast Prussia.

27. Circular of December 7, 1943, to all *Kreisleiter* (Institute for Western Studies, Poznań).

28. A typical poster was that of the People's Association for Germandom Abroad (VDA), *Gau* association, East Prussia, undated (Institute for Western Studies, Poznań, doc. I-631).

29. Cf. H. G. Koehling, *Die Behandlung der Polenfrage* (undated), and the broadsheet "Die Aufgaben des Gauamtes für Volkstumsfragen im Reichsgau Wartheland" (undated, no author; Institute for Western Studies, Poznań).

30. As late as January 10, 1940, a week before Posen was occupied, the *Gau* Bureau of Nationhood Affairs of the NSDAP found time to prepare information notices and draft circulars by the Gauleiter to prevent relations of "alien" associations of the Wehrmacht with Germans and Poles and members of the same "nation" (note of January 10, 1945, with draft of secret circular from the Gauleiter to all local section heads, undated; draft of a "Wartheland notice on the behavior of members of the military of friendly or allied states toward Poledom," undated) (Institute for Western Studies, Poznań, doc. I-231).

31. Reproduced in Łuczak, *Dyskryminacja Polaków*, 238 ff.

32. Letter of November 11, 1940, from the Gestapo Posen to the Criminal Police Posen: "Re: Maria K., Pole, born . . . , domiciled in . . . : K. was re-arrested on October 26, 1940, for continuing to consort with a soldier. She is being held in holding camp Fort VII for further action. I now request that she be admitted to a brothel and that I be informed of the decision there by November 25, 1940. (Signed) Bischoff." Cf. further the record of the Gestapo Posen of November 23, 1940: "Unemployed worker Maria K. appeared . . . and made the following statement: It has been communicated to me today that as of today's date I have been put under moral supervision and am to take up residence in the brothel Fischerei 19. . . . I have been given an information sheet on prostitutes. I am to observe the rules of conduct contained therein; otherwise I shall be taken into preventive custody or transferred to a concentration camp." See also the action report by the Criminal Police Office Posen, journal nos. 14414/40 and 13536/40: "Maria K . . . was today brought to the municipal health office for examination. Since she was found to be free from venereal disease, she was transferred today to brothel Fischerei 19" (Institute for Western Studies, Poznań, doc. I-17).

33. See letter from the Gestapo Posen of June 2, 1942, AZ II H, B. no. 1431–42—"to the District *Landräte*" requesting that in the future such procedures be not passed to the justice authorities but directly to the Gestapo (Institute for Western Studies, Poznań).

34. Decree issued by the Reich governor, November 14, 1940 (Institute for Western Studies, Poznań, doc. I-131). General instruction of September 25, 1940, by the Reich governor of Posen to the HSSPF Posen; decree of April 25, 1941, by the HSSPF Posen, reproduced in *Doc. Occ.* 5:306 (original in archives VIII K 607/48, District Court Posen; copy in Institute for Western Studies, Poznań, doc I-422): "Any unauthorized relation with Polish women is dishonorable for SS men and members of the police force and is therefore most strictly forbidden. Sexual intercourse with a Polish woman is shameful for any German, since blood and honor are the basic fundaments of the national socialist weltanschauung. Maintaining the purity of the German blood is thus the primary dictate of honor. Any who are wanting here brand themselves as traitors to the national struggle and thus place themselves outside our community." The threatened sanction was to be tried before SS and military courts for military insubordination, with a minimum punishment of four months in prison, demotion and exclusion from the SS, and in serious cases expulsion. See also the decree of February 27, 1941, by the district president of Posen to the police authorities under him (State Archive Poznań, Gendarmerie Schrimm 104, Bl. 12). More importantly, in addition to disciplinary measures, offenders were sent to concentration camps; cf. order of the day, January 10, 1942, issued by the commander of the Gendarmerie Łódź regarding punishment of Gendarmerie officers for sexual intercourse with Polish women and other offenses (Institute for Western Studies, Poznań). Instruction of January 22, 1941, by the *Kreisleiter* of Posen, forbidding entry to Polish bars to all members of the NSDAP, SS and police, and all employees of state offices (Institute for Western Studies, Poznań).

35. Circular of June 1, 1940, by the police president, Posen, reproduced in Łuczak, *Diskriminierung der Polen*, 237. The prohibition on visiting bars was perhaps also imposed later by a decree of the Reich governor, since a note dated February 18, 1942, by the head of Referat I/50 (Bureau of Nationhood Affairs) of the office of the Reich governor to Referat I/23 of that office indicated that he had no objection to the decree prohibiting entering public houses.

36. *Meldungen aus dem Reich*, July 4, 1940 (BA R 58/152).

37. Cf. for example the note dated December 18, 1943, from SS-*Sturmbannführer* Höppner of Referat I/50 at the office of the Reich governor of Posen, I/50 (State Archive Poznań, *Reichsstatthalter* 1174, 218), in which he refused a request from his office that Polish truck drivers working for German services might eat in German public houses, in order not to create a precedent: exceptions were to be made "only in very special cases."

38. But see police decree of June 1, 1941, by the district president of Łódź (Litzmannstadt) (*Amtsblatt Regierungspräsident Litzmannstadt*, in *Doc. Occ.* 5:307), which forbade "other persons" to enter specific Polish public houses.

39. See the SD reports, *Meldungen aus dem Reich*, July 4, 1940 (BA R 58/152): "Interested circles" were of the opinion that these instructions were the ruin of the "German public houses."

40. See, for example, the police decree (by the district president of Posen) of June 16, 1941, on opening hours for restaurants and public houses, admission of Poles to German bars, etc. (*Amtsbl. der Regierung zu Posen*, 1941, no. 9, p. 41); letter of September 16, 1940, from the district president of Posen to the police president of Posen and the district *Landräte* (State Archive Poznań, Gendarmerie Schrimm 104, Bl. 68); order of the day, January 20, 1940, by the HSSPF, Posen, no. 34 (Institute for Western Studies, Poznań); letter of September 16, 1940, from the district president of Posen to the police president of Posen and the district *Landräte* (State Archive Poznań, Gendarmerie Schrimm 103, Bl. 163); police decree of June 16, 1941, by the district president of Posen (*Amtsbl. der Regierung zu Posen*, 1941, no. 9, p. 41). For Upper Silesia, see the police decree by the *Oberpräsident* of Upper Silesia of September 28, 1941 (*Amtsblatt Regierungspräsident Kattowitz*, 1940, Stück 26, no. 296, Warsaw University Library, Sign. 034693).

41. Police decree of June 17, 1941, by the district president of Posen, which forbade the purchase of spirits over the counter by Poles (*Amtsblatt der Regierung zu Posen* 1941, no. 9, 41).

42. Inquiry dated January 23, 1941, by the police president, Sosnowitz (Sosnowiec), to the police president of Posen, who planned film shows for Poles in his district (Aktenzeichen IV 1, 6100, Institute for Western Studies, Poznań, doc. I-54), and answer of February 11, 1941, to the effect that visits to afternoon showings were permitted to Poles on working days only (Aktenzeichen II, 1, Institute for Western Studies, Poznań, doc. I 4/29).

43. Letter of January 18, 1944, from the Reich governor of Posen, Referat I/50, to the *Gau* Propaganda Office, Posen (State Archive Poznań, *Reichsstatthalter* 1174, Bl. 246).

44. Letter of June 17, 1943, from Referat I/50 of the office of the Reich governor of Posen to Abt. II 2 D: such construction was out of the question "for political reasons" (State Archive Poznań, *Reichsstatthalter* 1174, Bl. 110).

45. Letter of August 1943 (day of the month not indicated) from the Reich governor of Posen, Referat I/50, to Referat I/40, ibid., Bl. 207. Note dated June 12, 1944, from the head of Referat I/50 to the office of the Reich governor (Höppner) (Bl. 31).

46. Letter of September 22, 1943, from the *Kreisleitung* of the NSDAP Hohensalza to *Gauleitung* NSDAP Posen, in Łuczak, *Dyskryminacja Polaków*, 351.

47. In Polish law the districts (*Kreise*), towns, and rural communities (*Landgemeinden*) were autonomous corporations. Cf. Best, *Die Verwaltung in Polen* (1940) (Institute for Western Studies, Poznań, library, Sign. II, 929).

48. Explanations of the legal situation in a note from the Reich Ministry of the Interior toward the end of 1939 (undated, no author) (BA R 81/461) and RMI circular dated June 8, 1940, with

implementing instructions to the decree of December 21, 1939 (*RGBl.* I 2467, reproduced in *Amtsblatt Regierungspräsident Kattowitz*, 1940, Stück 30, no. 256, Warsaw University Library, Sign. 034693).

49. *RGBl.* I, 2467. In Danzig–West Prussia and the Wartheland these were the municipal districts of Danzig, Bromberg (Bydgoszcz), Gnesen (Gniezno), Posen, and Hohensalza (Reich Ministry of the Interior note dated October 31, 1939, BA R 18/1205).

50. Reich Ministry of the Interior circular of June 8, 1940, with implementing instructions to the decree on the introduction of the German Municipal Code (DGO) in the Annexed Eastern Territories (*RGBl.* I 2467, reproduced in *Amtsblatt Regierungspräsident Kattowitz*, 1940, Stück 30, no. 256, Warsaw University Library, Sign. 034693); see also letter of January 7, 1941, from the Reich Ministry of the Interior to the *Oberpräsident* of East Prussia (BA R 18/1205).

51. Decree of December 21, 1939, sec. 3 (*RGBl.* I, 2467); letter of December 8, 1943, from the *Reichsführer*-SS/RKF to the Reich Ministry of the Interior, and answer from the Reich Ministry of the Interior of December 22, 1943 (BA R 18/1208).

52. This was the express policy of the Reich Ministry of the Interior. See the transcript of a discussion in the Reich Ministry of the Interior of December 31, 1939, on the preparation and introduction of the German municipal regulations in the Annexed Eastern Territories (BA R 18/1205) and a letter of October 13, 1941, from the Reich Ministry of the Interior to the *Oberpräsident* of Upper Silesia (BA R 18/1205).

53. On this point the Reich Ministry of the Interior and the offices of the RFSS/RKF were in agreement; letter of December 8, 1943, from the RFSS/RKF to the Reich Ministry of the Interior and answer from the Reich Ministry of the Interior of December 22, 1943 (BA R 18/1208).

54. Letter of November 18, 1940, from the Reich Ministry of the Interior to the Reich governor of Danzig and Posen; negative report of December 4, 1940, from the Reich governor of Danzig and of December 11, 1940, from the Reich governor of Posen. Note by the responsible official at the Reich Ministry of the Interior; the report of November 19. 1940, by the *Oberpräsident* of Breslau (Wrocław), announced granting of the right to the German municipal regulations (BA R 18/1205).

55. Report by the *Oberpräsident* of Breslau (ibid.); see variously the announcement by the *Oberpräsident* of Breslau, September 1, 1940 (*Amtsblatt Regierungspräsident Kattowitz*, 1940, no. 260, Warsaw University Library, Sign. 034693), on the granting of the right to the German municipal regulations to several municipalities in the districts of Bendzin (Będzin) (3 municipalities), Bielitz (Bielsko-Biała) (5 municipalities), Chrzanów (4 municipalities), Kattowitz (3 municipalities), Rybnik (81 municipalities), and Teschen (11 municipalities); also the letter of September 1, 1941, from the Reich Ministry of the Interior on the granting of the right to the German Municipal Code to the towns of Saybusch (8.5% German inhabitants), Sucha (3.9% German inhabitants), Ilken (9.2% German inhabitants) and Warthen (1.9% German inhabitants) (BA R 18/1205); see too the letter of July 21, 1941, from the *Oberpräsident* of Upper Silesia to the Reich Ministry of the Interior (BA R 18/1205), and the decision of March 28, 1943, by the *Oberpräsident* of Upper Silesia on granting German Municipal Code status to the municipality of Auschwitz, which had a common border to the north with the Concentration Camp District (*Amtsbezirk Konzentrationslager*) (as of January 1, 1945: District of Birkenau [Brzezinka]) (*Amtsblatt Regierungspräsident Kattowitz*, 1943, Stück 43, no. 163, Warsaw University Library, Sign. 034693).

56. Letter of March 14, 1941, from the *Oberpräsident* of Königsberg to the Reich Ministry of the Interior regarding granting German Municipal Code status to the municipality of Pułtusk (6.3% German inhabitants), and letter of April 1, 1941, from the district president of Zichenau to the *Oberpräsident* of Königsberg with the request to grant the right to the German Municipal Code to the municipality of Ostrolenka (Ostrołęka), since as a result of the settling of three thousand Lithuanians almost half of the inhabitants were German; letters of January 17 and September 16, 1941, from the *Oberpräsident* of Königsberg to the Reich Ministry of the Interior regarding granting German Municipal Code status to the municipalities of Plozk and Mlawa and that of Praschnitz (justification: existence of an airfield and army training camp); letter of April 1, 1941, from the district presi-

dent of Zichenau to the *Oberpräsident* of Königsberg with the request to grant the right to the German Municipal Code to the municipality of Płonsk on account of the settlement of a number of German agencies (central customs office, post office, finance office, Reichsbank, etc.) (BA R 18/1205).

57. Letters of July 31, 1941, from the Reich governor of Danzig to the Reich Ministry of the Interior on granting German Municipal Code status to the municipalities of Dirschau (Tczew) (33%), Stargard Szczeciński and Konitz (Chojnice) (27.7% each), and Neustadt (Prudnik) (20%); of September 30, 1941, on granting German Municipal Code status to the municipalities of Leipe (17%), Neumarkt (Nowy Targ) (16%), Rippin (25%) and Strasburg (31%); and of December 15, 1941, on granting German Municipal Code status to the municipality of Briesen (20%) (BA R 18/1205).

58. Letter of March 17, 1941, from the Reich governor of Posen to the Reich Ministry of the Interior regarding granting German Municipal Code status to the towns of Kolmar (Colmar), Ostrowo (Ostrów Wielkopolski), Łódź, Kempen, and Lask (BA R 18/1205). After January 1, 1942, all towns were granted German Municipal Code status (letter of January 9, 1942, from the Reich governor to the Reich Ministry of the Interior, BA R 18/1205).

59. Cf. German Municipal Code, sec. 32; with regard to the (advisory) function of the *Gemeinderäte*, see circular G 26/1941 from the Central Office for Community Policy, to which a circular of September 22, 1941, from the NSDAP Office for Community Policy, Kempen (State Archive Poznań, Landratsamt Kempen 14/86), is attached. Under the terms of German Municipal Code sec. 118, the office of an "NSDAP delegate" was created (in municipalities, *Ortsgruppenleiter*; in districts, *Kreisleiter*) (more details in *Verfügungen*, 2:255 ff., and Bracher, Sauer, and Schulz, *Die nationalsozialistische Machtergreifung* [1962], 621), which gave rise to considerable friction between *Landrat/Bürgermeister* and *Kreisleiter/Ortsgruppenleiter*. Exceptionally, in the Wartheland it was not the *Kreisleiter* but the Gauleiter who represented the NSDAP (letter of February 17, 1941, from the district president of Łódź to the *Landrat* of Kempen, State Archive Poznań, Landratsamt Kempen 14, sheet 75).

60. Diehl-Thiele, *Partei und Staat im Dritten Reich* (1969), 140 ff., 161 ff., 173 f. At the municipality and district levels, the Party constantly desired participatory powers over and above German Municipal Code sec. 118, notwithstanding the fact that *Kreisleiter* were forbidden the assumption of state functions (deputy Führer's decree of February 29, 1937 [141 n. 116]). A Reich Ministry of the Interior decree was issued on December 28, 1939, to delimit the competencies between *Landrat* and *Kreisleiter*, under the terms of which "leadership of people" was the business of the Party, whereas all administrative matters came under the responsibility of the *Landrat* (announced in deputy Führer's instruction of January 23, 1940, *Verfügungen*, 2:252); it is clear that nothing was achieved by this, as since 1935 the municipal authorities had at the request of the deputy Führer been instructed to consult the *Kreisleiter* or the NSDAP delegate in matters "of general significance" (Reich Ministry of the Interior instruction of May 8, 1935, reproduced in *Verfügungen*, 2:251), an instruction that was expressly repeated for the Annexed Eastern Territories (activity report of March 1943 by the *Landrat* of Alexandrowo for the period July 15, 1942, to March 1, 1943, State Archive Poznań, *Reichsstatthalter* 857, Bl. 108).

61. German Municipal Code sec. 19; implementing decree of December 21, 1939, art. 2, sec. 6; part 5 of the Reich Ministry of the Interior decree of June 8, 1940 (*Amtsblatt Regierungspräsident Kattowitz*, 1940, Stück 30, no. 256). Reich Ministry of the Interior circular of June 8, 1940 (*RGBl.* I 2467).

62. A Reich Ministry of the Interior note at the end of 1939 (BA R 18/461) states that an instruction for the commissars (*Amtskommissare*) was being prepared. For details of the duties and problems of commissars, see von Hohenstein (pseud.), *Wartheländisches Tagebuch* (1963), dtv vol. 99.

63. The correspondingly difficult position of the commissars is best illustrated by the circular of February 15, 1941, sent by the district president of Łódź to the *Landräte* and Gendarmerie heads

of the district, which purports to "clarify" the relations between commissars and the police (State Archive Poznań, Gendarmerie Kreis Schrimm, 6, Bl. 190 f.):

(1) The Gendarmerie stations are not subordinate to the head of the local police authority (local police administrator) either in matters of supervision of the service or in the technical performance of their duties. The Gendarmerie does, however, . . . have the obligation to respond punctually and conscientiously to requests from the local police authority that relate to the execution of police decrees or instructions or other measures instituted by the local police authority. Apart from issuing warnings that are subject to a charge, Gendarmes have no powers to fine. Should a station chief have serious and well-founded doubts about the legality or appropriateness of a request, he must *immediately* attempt to achieve agreement [with the commissar—Author]. If no agreement is reached, he must immediately call for a decision from the *Landrat* (Gendarmerie-*Kreisführer*) . . . and inform the local police administrator of the provisional nonexecution of the request. A similar procedure is to be followed if the station chief feels it necessary to refuse a request on the grounds that it is not a policing matter. . . . (5) The Gendarme shall cooperate with the local police authority with understanding and consult regularly with it.

A decree of June 27, 1942, from the RFSSuChddtPol to the district president again refers to complaints by the municipal authorities and instructs "the Gendarmerie to carry out local police duties without question" (State Archive Poznań, Gendarmerie Schrimm, 136, Bl. 4–5).

64. Letter of August 10, 1940, from the Reich governor of Posen to the district president of Hohensalza (district archives, Lissa, Akten Stadt Kosten, 1086, 5).

65. von Hohenstein, *Warthländisches Tagebuch* (1963), 208 ff. (in this book the author, a former commissar in the Warthegau, describes his administratiive experience). But also, without the introduction of the German Municipal Code, the controlling body insisted on the closest cooperation between commissars and *Kreisleiter/Ortsgruppenleiter*. Apparently as technical personnel, the commissars were not able to satisfy this requirement to the extent demanded; cf. activity report of March 1943 by the *Landrat* of Alexandrowo for the period July 15, 1942, to March 1, 1943, according to which it was "almost always impossible" to reconcile the interests of both parties (State Archive Poznań, *Reichsstatthalter* 857, Bl. 108).

66. Letter of May 23, 1934, from the autonomous *Gau* administration, Posen, to the Reich governor of Wartheland (State Archive Poznań, *Reichsstatthalter* 1174, Bl. 196 f.).

67. Letter of May 31, 1943, to the *Landräte* of the district and the police president, Posen (State Archive Poznań, *Landrat* Schrimm, 105, Bl. 156): "There are a growing number of complaints lately of visits by Reich Germans . . . to Polish relatives. . . . That such visits are totally undesirable for nationhood and general political reasons needs no further explanation . . . given that departure can only be enforced by a prohibition order by the Secret State Police."

68. Letter of February 2, 1942, from the *Landrat* to the Bürgermeister of Schrimm (Institute for Western Studies, Poznań).

69. Letter of May 23, 1944, from Abt. III of the autonomous *Gau* administration in the *Reichsgau* Wartheland to the Reich governor in the Wartheland, Referat I/50 (State Archive Poznań, *Reichsstatthalter* 1174, Bl. 196–97).

70. Secret note of June 10, 1944, from the head of Referat I/50 at the office of the Reich governor of Wartheland (ibid., Bl. 273), the text of which constitutes a masterpiece of totalitarian thinking.

Part One. Section 2. B. The Manifestations of Special Measures

1. Report of July 30, 1941, by the Department of National Policy (Referat I/50) at the office of the Reich governor of Posen to the Reich governor of Posen on the practice and aims of the Polish policy (Institute for Western Studies, Poznań, doc. I-145).

2. Ibid.: "Any show of consideration would be a sign of weakness."

3. For more on this, see von Rozycki, "Über den Geltungsbereich des Reichsrechts im Großdeutschen Reich" (1941); Kobelt, "Einzelfragen der Rechtseinführung in den eingegliederten Ostgebieten" (1940); Marder, "Verwaltungsprobleme in den eingegliederten Ostgebieten," *DVerw* (1940): 198 ff.

4. Von Rozycki, "Über den Geltungsbereich des Reichsrechts im Großdeutschen Reich," 57.

5. This arrangement was either to have been set out in a special Polish legal code (Polish Statute) (von Rosen-von Hoevel, "Das Polenstatut" [1942]) or, as was the intention of the Reich Ministry of the Interior, to be promulgated in the form of a special Decree on the Legal Status of Protected Nationals and Stateless Illegitimate Children of Polish Nationality; cf. travel report of January 18, 1944, from the office of the Reich governor of Posen (Poznań) on a discussion at the Reich Ministry of the Interior on January 14 on the draft of such an order (State Archive Poznań, *Reichsstatthalter* 909).

6. Cf. the status report of August 18, 1940, by the district president of Hohensalza (Inowrocław), 7 f., according to which there were lacking basic elements in police order law, police criminal law, firearms law, registration regulations, police regulations on foreign nationals, residence law, and identity card and passport regulations. The report stated that this was most disagreeable for both the Polish and the German population since matters were dealt with at the discretion of the individual district or local police authorities, with the result that "often highly doubtful principles" were applied. The status reports of March 18 (pp. 8–9) and October 8, 1941 (p. 9), urge strongly in favor of uniform registration and residence regulations for the Eastern Territories. That of October 1940 (p. 14) contests the arbitrary payment of Poles in German offices in a number of municipal administrations; that of January 18, 1941 (p. 31), reports on the awkward situation arising out of the fact that the Reich decree was not valid in the Annexed Eastern Territories (Posen University Library).

7. See Nawrocki, *Policja hitlerowska w kraju warty* (1970), 56 ff.

8. The Reich Ministry of the Interior had made use of this authority in the Decree of March 6, 1940, on the Establishment of a State Police Authority in the *Reichsgaue* Danzig (Gdańsk)–West Prussia and Wartheland (*RGBl.* I 495); cf. the other decrees issued on the basis of sec. 12, par. 2, of the Führer's decree, in Sartorius, *Verfassungs- und Verwaltungsrecht*, note 3 to no. 172. With regard to the organization of the police force, see also M. Wrzosek, "Deutsche Polizei in Oberschlesien" (with documentation), *Bulletin of the Main Commission Warsaw*, vol. 15, 101 ff.

9. Institute for Western Studies, Poznań. *RGBl.* I, 1582; introduced into the Eastern Territories by the order of July 31, 1940 (*RGBl.* I 1063).

10. See report by Dr. Lavaux, office of the Reich governor of Wartheland, on an official trip to Danzig on November 21, 1940 (State Archive Poznań, *Reichsstatthalter* 802, sheet 101).

11. According to sec. 3, par. I, of this decree (*RGBl.* I 2042), the Law on the Administrative Structure in the *Reichsgau* Sudetenland of April 14, 1939 (*RGBl.* I 780), was applicable as appropriate. Sec. 9 gave the *Landrat* at district level control of the whole state administration within the limits of previous competence. This included the authority to issue police orders. Regarding the authority of the police, see details in Nawrocki, *Policja hitlerowska w kraju warty*, 69 ff.

12. Letter of March 4, 1940, from district president Kalisch (Kalisz) to the Reich governor of Posen (State Archive Poznań, *Reichsstatthalter* 802, sheet 2). For Upper Silesia, in contrast, formal regulations in police order law were issued by way of a decree of October 24, 1939, by the head of the Civil Administration (CdZ) Kattowitz (Katowice) (official gazette of the *CdZ Kattowitz*, no. 21, of the same date).

13. The Decree on the Introduction of the German Municipal Code in the Annexed Eastern Territories of December 21, 1939 (*RGBl.* I 2467), art. 3, sec. 1 ff., in conjunction with the circular of November 25, 1939 (I W 133), par. 3 (circular quoted in a letter of March 1, 1940, from the district president of Posen to the Reich Ministry of the Interior and the Reich governor of Wartheland,

State Archive Poznań, *Reichsstatthalter* 802, sheet 18). See also the decree of June 28, 1940, by the district president of Posen (Gendarmerie Schrimm, 103, sheets 27–28), according to which the police order law was the exclusive domain of the district police authorities and the higher police authorities (the *Landratsamt* or the district president's office); letters of March 31, 1941, from the Reich governor of Wartheland to the district president of Łódź (*Reichsstatthalter* 1216, sheet 77), and of April 5, 1941, to the *Gau* legislation office of the NSDAP (*Reichsstatthalter* 802, sheet 123).

14. Decree of July 31, 1940, by the Reich governor of Posen (State Archive Poznań, *Reichsstatthalter* 1218, sheet 386) regarding the obligation of the district presidents and *Landräte* to obtain authorization to issue police orders. The circular of September 25, 1940, by the district president of Posen stated the authorization requirement for police orders by the *Landrat* offices; since the authorization was an internal matter, no mention of it was allowed to be made in the title of the police order (State Archive Poznań, Landratsamt Kosten 7, sheet 6). The obligation to submit the document, which was totally in line with the disempowerment of the district presidents and *Landräte*, applied to quite minute details. Cf. the letter of October 10, 1941, from the district president of Łódź to the district president of Posen requesting the latter's permission to issue a police order "on the collection of forestry by-products" (State Archive Poznań, *Reichsstatthalter* 1218, sheet 161). Furthermore, police orders issued by *Landräte* had to be authorized by the district president's office (Posen district president circulars of September 25, 1940 [State Archive Poznań, *Reichsstatthalter* 1218, sheet 161], and June 28, 1940 [State Archive Poznań, Gendarmerie Schrimm 103, sheets 27–28]).

15. Letter of March 4, 1940, from the district president of Kalisch (State Archive Poznań, *Reichsstatthalter* 802, sheet 2); letters of March 1, 1940, from the district president of Posen to the Reich governor of Posen (sheet 18) and of June 28, 1940, to the *Landräte* and commissars of the district (State Archive Poznań, Gendarmerie Schrimm 103, sheets 27 f.); letters of March 14, 19, and 20, 1940, from the higher SS and police chief to the Reich governor of Posen (sheets 8, 9, ll); letter of April 4, 1940, from the police president of Posen to the Reich governor of Posen (sheet 14).

16. Führer's decree of October 8, 1939, sec. 3 (*RGBl.* I 2042), in conjunction with the Sudetengau law of April 14, 1939, sec. 4, par. 1 (*RGBl.* I 780).

17. Note dated December 6, 1940, from the office of the Reich governor, Referat I 7, on the important discussion of December 4, 1940, which contained the following passage: "Many points of the police authority law run contrary to the basic principle of National Socialist legislative thought, particularly since the principle of strict separation of the legal treatment of Germans and Poles can be enforced only with difficulty under it. The issue of a very brief decree establishing the right of the Reich governor to issue police orders and instructions and to transmit them to the subordinate police authorities is therefore proposed, and Dezernat I/7 charged with requesting the Reich minister of the interior for its authorization."

18. The draft was submitted to the Reich Ministry of the Interior by urgent memorandum on December 19, 1940. In the event that authorization was refused, the Reich governor would be "obliged to follow the route, hitherto avoided, of a decree on the corresponding application of the Prussian police authority law." Should the Reich Ministry of the Interior have any reservations, he requested that his own order [i.e., not the Prussian police authority law—Author] be published as an Reich Ministry of the Interior order on the strength of the Führer's decree of October 8, 1939, sec. 8 (State Archive Poznań, *Reichsstatthalter* 802, sheets 109–10).

19. The Posen draft apparently crossed a corresponding request by the Reich Ministry of the Interior to the Reich governor of Posen (ibid., sheet 120).

20. Report of October 21, 1940, on a trip to Danzig by the office of the Reich governor of Posen: "In answer to my question on what basis the police order law was implemented in Danzig–West Prussia, *Regierungsrat* Löhr expressed the opinion that a formal legal basis was quite unnecessary, also for the *Reichsstatthalter*, and that police orders could be issued as sovereign administrative

acts. He further advises that the subordinate services be instructed by decree to apply the Prussian police authority law as applicable, as he has done" (ibid., sheet 101).

21. Sent with covering letter of July 1940 by the Reich governor of Posen (ibid., sheets 55 f.).

22. Ibid., sheet 100.

23. See (in chronological order), the urgent memorandum of January 28, 1941, from the Brown House, Munich, to the NSDAP *Gauleitungen* of the Annexed Eastern Territories (State Archive Poznań, *Reichsstatthalter* 802, sheet 117); letters from the Reich governor of Posen to the *Gau* legislation office of the NSDAP, Posen (for the attention of *Oberlandesgericht* president Froböß of February 5 [sheet 118] and of April 5, 1941 [sheet 123]). Letter of March 14, 1941, from the RFS-SuChddtPol to the Reich governor of Posen (sheet 122).

24. Urgent memorandum of March 14, 1941, from the Reich Ministry of the Interior (ibid., sheet 116).

25. Ibid., sheet 126.

26. Letter of December 15, 1941, from the Reich governor of Posen, Referat I/40 to Referat I/23 (ibid., sheet 129).

27. Urgent memorandum of January 14, 1942, from the Reich Ministry of the Interior: "It would be completely unacceptable to concede a right of complaint to Poles. . . . The penal justice order of December 4, 1941, against Poles and Jews [*RGBl.* I 769] takes the requirements of the national struggle into account in many particulars. It allows the justice authorities efficient action without being tied down by restrictive provisions. In a similar way it is unthinkable not to have an equivalent overriding freedom of action against Poles in the police sector too" (State Archive Poznań, *Reichsstatthalter* 802, sheet 138).

28. Report by Dr. Körth from the office of the Reich governor of Posen on an official trip to Berlin on March 27–28, 1942: "According to a communication from *Regierungsrat* von Rosen, the introduction of the police authority law is still hampered by differences between order police and Security Police. . . . Abteilung 1 East now intends to send a decree signed by State Secretary Stuckart to the chief of the German police indicating the urgency of its introduction, which has now been pending for two years" (State Archive Poznań, *Reichsstatthalter* 802, sheet 139).

29. "I shall propose to the Reich minister of the interior that we include appropriate provisions in the introductory order, or otherwise that these questions be settled in a decree to be issued by myself in accordance with sec. 8 of the draft text" (ibid., sheet 128; circular also to be found in ZSt, Poland, film 14, 772 ff., copy; IfZ, MA-708/2, 772–73).

30. The ultimate aim of the police leadership was to preclude *all* legal action against *any* political measure. The exclusion by law of legal recourse against ordinances by the Gestapo (Secret State Police Law of February 10, 1936, sec. 7, *Preußische Gesetzessammlung* 21) was only the first step in broad plans to brand all "offenses not covered by the justice system" as criminal, i.e., all offenses under the economic legislation and all the rest of the administrative penal law (exclusion of *administrative* sanctions, introduction of *penal* provisions), and to derogate the judicial verification of police ordinances. The Ministry of the Interior (Abteilung 1), in accord with the regular police headquarters and the Reich Security Main Office (RSHA), therefore planned to abolish requests for judicial verification (Code of Criminal Procedure, secs. 413 ff.) against penal decisions by the police (note dated February 2, 1943, by the Reich Ministry of the Interior, Pol. O-VuR. Org. Ost 133/41, State Archive Poznań, *Reichsstatthalter* 802, sheet 144, in which suspension of the Code of Criminal Procedure, secs. 413 ff., is declared necessary "for reasons pertaining to the police not defined in more detail"), a situation that did not in fact materialize. The police were, however, able to chalk up a certain success in that they introduced the *reformatio in peius* clause in the event of a complaint against penal action by the police, so as to deter people from taking legal action (RFSSuChddtPol decree of December 2, 1942, *MinbliV* [1942]: 2245).

31. The draft envisaged a separation, on the Austrian model, of judicial and administrative

offenses (no judicial appeal against punishment possible), communication by *Ministerialrat* Rietzsch of the Reich Ministry of Justice at the meeting of chief presidents and prosecutors-general, Berlin, February 10–11, 1943 (record BA R 22/4200, Ref. Rietzsch, sheet 48 ff.).

32. See Reich Ministry of the Interior note of February 1943, Pol. O-VuR. Org. Ost 133/41: "It is felt necessary to preclude the possibility of an appeal for a judicial decision on police grounds, and efforts are being made to include the territory of the Altreich. . . . In the opinion of the chief of the Party Chancellery, a special arrangement is required for the Polish and Jewish populations, as is the case in penal law. The following is in line with this standpoint" (State Archive Poznań, *Reichsstatthalter* 802).

33. Letter of March 25, 1943, from the *Gau* staff office of the NSDAP *Gauleitung* Wartheland to the Reich governor of Posen:

It is far more important to counter all legal action against decisions of the secret police and the criminal police, as provided for in sec. 1, par. 1, of the draft. This proposal goes too far. . . . To exclude legal recourse in such serious decisions necessarily gives the individual the impression that he is at the mercy of the judgment of relatively subordinate offices of the police in matters that are of vital importance to him, and that he has lost his rights. . . . And the absence of legal recourse could even have a deleterious effect on the police officer himself. Experience shows that when there is an overload of work, our police officers, like those of other departments, have a tendency to use the harshest means only because they achieve the desired aim more rapidly and conveniently. Such a tendency will doubtless be enhanced if no appeal is possible. It is dangerous because it is likely to produce or strengthen a very problematic contrast between the police and the citizen. Appeals to the Reich governor against police decisions and the imposition of coercive measures by offices of the secret state police are legitimate. The decision of the Reich governor is final. (ibid., sheet 7)

34. Ibid., sheet 142.

35. Communications of June 28, 1940, from the district president of Posen to the *Landräte* and commissars of the district (State Archive Poznań, Gendarmerie Schrimm, 10, sheets 27 f.), and of March 31, 1941, from the Reich governor of Posen to the district president of Łódź (State Archive Poznań, *Reichsstatthalter* 1216, sheet 17); circular of July 31, 1941, by the Reich governor of Posen (*Reichsstatthalter* 1218, sheet 386).

36. State Archive Poznań, *Reichsstatthalter* 802, sheet 128.

37. *MinbliV* (1942): 1309; see also the circular of December 28, 1942, by the RFSSuChddtPol on the creation of punishment camps, issued by way of a *police order* against Poles and Jews (S II C 3 no. 55 20/42, 273, 2 allg., State Archive Poznań).

38. Letter of August 1, 1942, from the *Landrat*, Kempen, to the Bürgermeister and commissars of his district (State Archive Poznań, Landratsamt Kempen 16, sheet 81): "Now that the above-mentioned circular has given the police the possibility of combating Polish disobedience by substantial fines and restriction of freedom, I request that such fines and compulsory payments be established against Poles." Cf., in contrast, the RFSSuChddtPol circular of December 21, 1942 (Institute for Western Studies, Poznań): fines against Polish farmers should be kept low, as otherwise the working capital would be completely lost.

39. State Archive Poznań, *Reichsstatthalter* 802, sheet 142.

40. Decree of August 23, 1941, Reich governor of Posen (ibid., sheet 128), repeated in the RFS-SuChddtPol circular of June 15, 1942, relating to Gestapo and criminal police decisions (*MinbliV* [1942]: 1309).

41. Führer's directive of October 8, 1939, sec. 3, par. 2 (*RGBl.* I 2042); under the terms of sec. 1 of the Second Implementing Order of November 2, 1939, from the Reich Ministry of the Interior (*RGBl.* I 2133), the office of the Reich governor was organized as follows: Dept. 1, General Internal and Financial Affairs; Dept. 2, Health and Nationhood; Dept. 3, Education, Culture, and Commu-

nity; Dept. 4, Agriculture, Settlement, Relocation, and Water; Dept. 5, Economy and Labor; Dept. 6, Forestry, Timber, and Hunting; Dept. 7, Construction.

Part One. Section 2. C. I. The Social. Political. and Cultural Sector

1. Note in the files of the office of the Reich governor, Referat I/50, dated April 2, 1943 (State Archive Poznań, *Reichsstatthalter* 1174, sheets 139 f.). See also letter of January 10, 1944, from the *Gau* Bureau of Nationhood Affairs (sheets 162 f.).

2. Sick pay was included in the payment. For Poles employed in the armament and mining industries, sick pay was increased to RM 1.50 per day in the Annexed Eastern Territories as of 1943, on the proposal of the district president of Kattowitz (Katowice) (NSDAP *Gauleitung* Wartheland to the Party Chancellery, December 23, 1943 [no objection to the proposal], with letter of January 4, 1943, to the Reich governor of Posen [both in State Archive Poznań, *Reichsstatthalter* 828, sheet 38]).

3. Secret (unsigned) note dated November 24, 1939, from the office of the Reich governor (State Archive Poznań, *Reichsstatthalter* 835, sheet 4), which clearly indicates the profit-seeking policy of the government:

(1) The welfare legislation must be completely aligned with the national policy principles in the former Poland. An interest in the Polish population exists only insofar as working people are concerned. The intelligentsia, especially former officials, should be deported to the Government district without exception. The portion of the population remaining, which will be used as work slaves, so to speak, should, however, be paid and compensated adequately. (2) For this reason . . . it follows that pensions previously paid by the Polish state are out of the question for Polish officials. If they are capable of working, they should be sent to the labor exchange, otherwise to public welfare. . . . (6) *Development of the legislation:* The welfare carrier must be the same for Poles and Germans. Autonomy of Polish welfare, as, for example, for Jews in the Reich, is out of the question. A distinction must be made, however, between Germans and Poles with respect to the type and quantity of payments—perhaps for Germans a higher, and for Poles a more general, welfare system. The technical difference between the treatment of Germans and Poles should not be anchored in the legislation but regulated through internal instructions. To the exterior we might present a higher welfare system for special cases, without expressly stating, however, that it applies only to Germans.

As was the case with the Jews, the welfare funds were to be obtained from the wealthy classes and taken over by the public authorities after their deportation to the General Government; see report by the district president of Posen dated December 23, 1939, for the period December 1–15 (State Archive Poznań, *Reichsstatthalter* 853, p. 6). Thus the conditions for support and the amount paid depended solely upon the discretion of the authorities: the support amounted to only half of the basic tariffs for Germans (circular of December 5, 1939, from the head of the Main Trustee Office East [HTO], quoted in a Main Trustee Office East decision of May 4, 1940, *Mitteilungsblatt HTO* 1940, no. 6, p. 215; *Doc. Occ.* 5:237 f.). The conditions were tightened still further later, in that Poles and Jews received support only if their fortunes had been confiscated and the support was covered by their active assets (decision by the head of the Main Trustee Office East of May 4, 1940 [*Mitteilungsblatt HTO* 1940, no. 6, p. 215; *Doc. Occ.* 5:237 f.]). *Poles incapable of working,* however, did not obtain support from the revenue of their confiscated assets (Main Trustee Office East decision of December 17, 1940, *Mitteilungsblatt HTO* 1941, no. 2, p. 113, quoted in *Doc. Occ.* 5:237).

4. See the notification of September 11, 1939, by the Schenkendorff group, forbidding the printing and sale of all press products on pain of prison or death (State Archive Poznań, Abt. Plakate 15); the assets of publishing houses and printing works "hostile to Germans" were confiscated (head of the Civil Administration Posen decree of October 1, 1939, with Implementing Decree of October 10, 1939 [*VOBl. Posen* 1939, p. 30, in *Doc. Occ.* 5:66]); see also the decree by the

head of the Civil Administration Kattowitz of September 15, 1939, regarding newspapers and periodicals (*VOBl. Grenzschutz* 39, p. 63, in *Doc. Occ.* 5:69 f.).

5. See the communication of June 18, 1942, from the SD-*Leitabschnitt*, Posen, to the district president of Posen (State Archive Poznań, *Reichsstatthalter* 2335, Bl. 148); decree of September 10, 1939, issued by the head of the Civil Administration Danzig (Gdańsk) (*VOBl. Reichsstatthalter Danzig–West Prussia*, p. 11, HK Warschau, Plakatsammlung II, doc. t 12/6; in German and Polish); decree of October 2, 1939, from the head of the Civil Administration Kattowitz (*VOBl. Head of the Civil Administration* 12/39, p. 67, in *Doc. Occ.* 5:74); also the dissolution orders by the Kattowitz Gestapo office of July 4, 1940, regarding the meeting of Jehovah's Witnesses and July 7 regarding the "unified evangelical Seventh Day Christians" (*Amtsblatt Regierung Kattowitz*, 1940, Stück 24, no. 221, and Stück 37, no. 309, Warsaw University Library, Sign. 034693); the legal basis was the decree of February 28, 1933, sec. 1 (*RGBl.* I, 83), which declared restrictions on the right of assembly to be admissible.

6. Decree of October 8, 1940, by the State Archive Poznań, Gendarmerie Kreis Schrimm 143, p. 14: "It has come to my notice that the Polish population frequently use funerals as a welcome opportunity for private meetings. To prevent such cases in the future, it appears desirable to prohibit Polish funerals from starting at the home (where normally people drink and talk politics) and to have them start at the funeral parlor and to limit participation to close relatives only."

7. See the activity report of the *Kreisleitung* of Hermannsbad (Ciechocinek) for June 1941 (State Archive Poznań NSDAP, Gauleitung Wartheland 13, 12–13): "The clerics are even showing themselves in their skirts on the streets and in the culture centers once again. This has now been forbidden by the commissar and *Ortsgruppenleiter*."

8. Regarding the persecution of the church in Poland, see the detailed report by Madajczyck, *Polityka* II, sec. "Religious Life," 176 ff., 195 ff.; Broszat, *Verfolgung polnischer katholischer Geistlicher 1939–1945* (1959) (BA IV d 70); Broszat, *Nationalsozialistische Polenpolitik* (1961), 143 ff.; with respect to the individual measures, see, for example, the letter of February 6, 1941, from the Reich governor of Posen to the then Episcopal Council of Posen (Nuremberg doc. NG-3914) (prohibition of religious assembly); confiscation order of January 20, 1941, by the Main Trustee Office East–Danzig>N>West Prussia regarding the assets of the Catholic Church and Catholic foundations and orders in Danzig–West Prussia (Institute for Western Studies, Poznań, doc. I-140); a summary will be found in the Main Trustee Office East activity report for 1939–42, reproduced in Łuczak, *Diskriminierung der Polen* (1966), 172 ff., 192 (real estate and cattle belonging to the Catholic Church went to the district heads of agriculture; see letter of October 16, 1941, from the Gestapo, Posen, to the district *Landräte*, ZS); see also the report of July 8, 1941, from the district president of Hohensalza (State Archive Poznań, *Reichsstatthalter* 856, Bl. 9) (surveillance of church services); circular of May 17, 1940, from the Apostolate Nuntius Culm and the bishop of Danzig (Gesch. no. 635/40; Institute for Western Studies, Poznań, I-40) (removal of Polish inscriptions in churches; prohibition of processions and the use of the Polish language in confessions). Decree of July 31, 1940, no. 115/40, quoted in the report of September 18, 1940, by the district president of Hohensalza (Inowrocław) (Posen University Library) (dispersion of Polish clerics all over the country); reports of September 18, 1940, and of March 8, 1942, from the district president of Hohensalza, Posen University Library (arrest and deportation of the Polish clergy); reports of February 18, 1941, and March 8, 1942 (Posen University Library, 8) (prohibition of reduction of Catholic services); letter of October 16, 1941, from the Gestapo Posen to the *Landräte* of the district (ZS) (closure of Polish churches in Posen); decree of April 24, 1941, by the Reich governor of Wartheland, issued as order of the day by BdO Posen of May 8, 1941 (Institute for Western Studies, Poznań, doc. 635) (prohibition of attendance at Polish services by Germans).

9. *RGBl.* I 679.

10. Cf. Hitler's statements at table in June 1942:

He was, however, in no way affable with regard to the Vatican's efforts to extend the concordat to the new Reich territories. The Saar, Sudetenland, Bohemia and Moravia, the *Reichsgau* Danzig–West Prussia, the Warthegau, and a large part of Silesia and Alsace-Lorraine had no official relationship whatsoever with the Roman Catholic church. . . . Organization of ecclesiastical affairs in these regions was exclusively a matter for the governor and the highest local head of the religious association of the region. . . . If the clerics had no legal recourse to state funds, they would have to earn them by behavior agreeable to the state. . . . Funds would then have to be stopped for the individual priests . . . , so as to provoke petty squabbling between them, to our own great enjoyment. (Picker, *Hitlers Tischgespräche* [1951], 215 ff.)

11. Ibid.; Hitler then said that it was "only because of the war that he had not yet put into practice his intention to declare the so-called relations with the Vatican superfluous."

12. See note 10 above; also Hitler at the working supper of July 4, 1942 (ibid., 218): "The behavior of this Bishop von Galen [von Galen was the bishop of Münster] will also be an opportunity to dissolve the concordat immediately after the war, to replace it by regional arrangements, and immediately to confiscate the contractually assured financial assets of the church."

13. Report of October 8, 1941, by the district president of Hohensalza (Posen University Library, 4 f.): "The measures . . . are also being hotly discussed in Evangelical circles in the Altreich . . . there is a certain bitterness, and people are asking whether the National Socialist State needs to set itself up against the Evangelical church too."

14. Decree of September 13, 1941, issued by the Reich governor of Wartheland (*VOBl. Reichsstatthalter Wartheland* 1941, 463, in *Doc. Occ.* 5:319 ff.); these associations were "the Posen Evangelical Church of German Nationality in the Wartheland, the Evangelical Lutheran Church of German Nationality in the West Wartheland, the Roman Catholic Church of German Nationality in the *Reichsgau* of Wartheland." The church tax under public law ceased to exist. The German churches in the Wartheland and in the regions incorporated into the provinces of Upper Silesia and East Prussia were, however, empowered to levy contributions through the decree on the collection of contributions dated March 14, 1940 (*Verordnungsblatt Reichsstatthalter Wartheland* 1940, 299), or the Reich Ministry of the Interior decree of December 22, 1941 (*RGBl.* I, 794).

15. Cf. the activity reports of July 8, 1941, by the district president of Hohensalza (State Archive Poznań, *Reichsstatthalter* 856, Bl. 9) and October 8, 1941 ("It is recommended that the church problem continue to be watched closely in the future") (Posen University Library).

16. Commissar of Wollstein (Wolsztyn) to the *Landrat* there, July 3, 1941 (Diary no. Verw/He; Institute for Western Studies, Poznań, doc. I-727).

17. With regard to cultural life in the Annexed Eastern Territories in general, see the decree of July 16, 1940, issued by the Reich Ministry for Science, Education, and Culture (Az. E II a no. 889, Institute for Western Studies, Poznań, doc. I-2); Łuczak, *Dyskryminacja Polaków*, 311 ff.; Nawrocki, *Hitlerowska okupacja* (1966), pt. 3, p. 5, Buchst. I-n; regarding the appropriation of Polish cultural property, quoted in the Main Trustee Office East note dated June 21, 1940 (Nuremberg doc. NO-5112), according to which the decree had to date been implemented only in part. See also the letter of August 5, 1940, from the Reich Security Main Office (RSHA) to the *Reichsführer*-SS regarding art treasures in Lettow-Vorbeck Castle (Nuremberg doc. PS-2535). See also the *Bulletin of the Main Commission Warsaw* 4 (1952): 175 ff.

18. Law on Editors of October 4, 1933 (*RGBl.* I 713). Law of September 22, 1933 (*RGBl.* I 661).

19. Hitler at the working supper of June 30, 1942, quoted in Picker, *Hitlers Tischgespräche*, 201.

20. With regard to the situation in the education sector, see a report published by the Inter-Allied Information Committee, London (Nuremberg doc. L-36).

21. The University of Posen was later reopened for German students and called the Reich University of Posen. Regarding conditions there, see "Z pamiętka profesora," Reich University of Posen, *Przegląd Zachodni*, vol. 11, 275 ff.; and K. M. Pospieszalski, K. Tymieniecki, and Z. Wojciechowski,

"Uniwersytet Poznańskina na początku Hitlerowskiej okupacji," *Przegląd Zachodni*, vols. 7–8 (1955). See, for example, the report by the Office of the Chief of the Counsel for War Crimes, "The Germanization of Poland," Nuremberg doc. D-956, where it is stated that on December 13, 1939, the Reich governor of Wartheland ordered the registration of all public and private libraries and collections, which were then seized, brought to a central place, and sorted. The volumes were sent either to Berlin or to the newly created State Library of Posen. Books of no interest to either were sold or destroyed (p. 11). See also the letter of April 5, 1941, from a local branch of the Emigration Center, Posen, to the Emigration Center (pp. 28 f.), which contained a list of the libraries confiscated. "In the Hohensalza district the libraries have been collected either by the Gestapo or by the local SD office, or, as in other districts, burned" (Hauptkommission Warschau, archive no. 1058, typed original). For more details see Łuczak, *Grabież mienia polskiego* (1969), 28 f.

22. Note dated November 23, 1943, from the district president of Kattowitz, Institute for Western Studies, Poznań, doc. I-38.

23. Quoted in *Doc. Occ.* 5:312 n. 50.

24. K. M. Pospieszalski in ibid.

25. Note dated November 23, 1943, from the district president of Kattowitz (Institute for Western Studies, Poznań, doc. I-38).

26. Decree on Schools dated September 22, 1939 (*VOBl. Militärbefehlshaber Danzig–Westpreußen*, 25), and directives by the head of the Civil Administration Danzig–West Prussia (Institute for Western Studies, Poznań, doc. I-107).

27. It was intended to extend the practice to Upper Silesia, but this was opposed by the district president of Kattowitz: see his note of November 23, 1943 (Institute for Western Studies, Poznań, doc. I-38).

28. Decree of September 20, 1939, by the head of the civil administration, Posen (*VOBl. Posen*, 1939, 9 V, 63 f.), which permitted dismissal without notice if "no need" existed. That there was no such need was of course confirmed in the circular by the district president of Posen (February 28, 1940) (Łuczak, *Dyskryminacja Polaków*, 335 f.).

29. At table on the evening of June 8, 1942, Hitler agreed with Bormann's remark that it had been necessary to cut teaching in the Warthegau even more than in Austria. Hitler felt that primary school teachers should not be "made stupid by . . . excessive training." Those among the Warthegau teachers who felt called to higher things, "who took continuing education upon themselves, who showed that they were suited to grade school and secondary school, would be promoted, with or without studies" (quoted by Picker, *Hitlers Tischgespräche*, 188 ff.). This remark apparently referred to teaching at German schools; how much more was it true for the teaching of "alien" children! See also note 32.

30. Letter dated July 22, 1940, from the district president of Posen to the Reich governor of Posen (Łuczak, *Dyskryminacja Polaków*, 331 f.).

31. According to the report of the Inter-Allied Information Committee, London, already quoted, Nuremberg doc. L-36 (hardly two hours of classes daily, destruction of books, which it was forbidden to replace, no heating in classrooms, frequent requisition of schools for the military, etc.).

32. Circular of March 26, 1940 (Łuczak, *Dyskryminacja Polaków*, 333 ff.), and decree of June 27, 1942, by the district president of Hohensalza (Institute for Western Studies, Poznań, doc. I-1213) ("education in cleanliness and orderliness, decent behavior and obedience to Germans").

33. Circular of March 26, 1940, and decree of June 27, 1942, by the district president of Posen (Institute for Western Studies, Poznań, doc. I-1213).

34. Decree dated September 20, 1939, by the head of the civil administration of Posen on the introduction of the German language in all schools (*VOBl. Posen*, p. 9; in *Doc. Occ.* 5:62 f.).

35. ". . . and so that brief printed or written instructions on work processes, operation of ma-

chines, etc. can be read. Teaching of German should be limited to the simple ability to make oneself understood. No effort should be wasted . . . in attempting to teach error-free German"; education project of December 16, 1943, issued by the district president of Hohensalza (Institute for Western Studies, Poznań, doc. I-12).

36. Teaching schedule dated December 16, 1943 (ibid.); such collections (therapeutic plants) were common in Upper Silesia too (note of November 23, 1943, from the district president of Kattowitz, Institute for Western Studies, Poznań, doc. I-38).

37. Circular dated March 26, 1940, from the district president of Posen (Institute for Western Studies, Poznań, doc. I-1213).

38. Letter of July 22, 1940, from the district president of Posen to the Reich governor of Wartheland (Łuczak, *Dyskryminacja Polaków*, 331 ff.); see too the comment of the same date by the district president of Posen on the decree of July 16, 1940, issued by the Reich Ministry for Science and Education (Institute for Western Studies, Poznań, doc. I-2). Decree of June 27, 1942, issued by the district president of Hohensalza (doc. I-1213), sec. 4: "It is not acceptable to have Polish children in a school building where German children are taught, unless the classrooms, playgrounds, and toilets can be so completely separated that the Polish children in no way come into contact with the German children."

39. In the administrative district of Posen, schooling of Polish children began in 1940 (circular of March 26, 1940, by the district president of Posen), and in the administrative district of Hohensalza probably not until 1942 (decree of June 27, 1942, by the district president of Hohensalza): ". . . gives rise to the need for Polish children in general to go to school" (Institute for Western Studies, Poznań, doc. I-1213).

40. Report for October 1940 by the district president of Hohensalza, p. 32 (children already at school were sent voluntarily; no pressure was exerted on the parents), and that of October 20, 1941, pp. 4–5: "The neglect of Polish children is increasing." More schools needed to be built, but care should be taken that "the Poles could not become competitors to Germans." The report claimed that there were five schools for Poles, with 7,700 children and 30 German volunteer staff; only children who went voluntarily were still taught. The effect of schooling was said to be unmistakable: the children were "hard-working and attentive," more polite, etc.

41. Note dated November 1, 1940, from the industrial department of the Wartheland Chamber of Commerce, no. 6 (Łuczak, *Dyskryminacja Polaków*, 336 ff.).

Part One. Section 2. C. II. The Economic and Commercial Sector

1. For full details, see the collection of documents published by Łuczak, *Grabież polskiego mienia na ziemiach zachodnich rzeczypospolitiej "wcielonych" do rzeszy 1939–1945* (The seizure of Polish property in the Polish western territories "incorporated" into the Reich in 1939–1945) (1969), containing numerous previously unpublished sources from Polish archives, which confirm the arguments set out here in every particular; also the sources quoted in *Doc. Occ.* 5:174 ff.; see also the comprehensive introduction by K. M. Pospieszalski, with further references. With regard to the general National Socialist economic policy in Poland, see Madajczyk, *Polityka*, 1:509–36, 596 ff.; Nawrocki, *Hitlerowska okupacja wielkopolski* (1966), 242 ff.; Łuczak, *Dyskryminacja Polaków*, (1966), 204 f., 271 ff., 372 f.; as to the difference in economic policy between the Annexed Eastern Territories and the General Government, see the letter of October 19, 1939, from the head of the Four Year Plan to Governor General Frank and the Reich governor of Danzig (Gdańsk) (Nuremberg doc. EC-410) (in the General Government, exploitation for the benefit of the Reich; in the Eastern Territories, development of the economy, seizure of Polish and Jewish assets for the Reich); a list of the various special economic provisions can be found in Kluge and Krüger, *Verfassung und Verwaltung* (1941), 128 ff. No complete overview of the National Socialist economic policy in the Annexed Eastern Territories and

the General Government yet exists. Polish archives contain comprehensive material from the Main Trustee Office East.

2. Decree of March 3, 1942 (*RGBl.* I 166); the property of Jews previously of Polish nationality was confiscated under the so-called Polish Assets Decree of September 17, 1940 (*RGBl.* I 1270).

3. Decrees of the chief of the Army Command dated September 29, 1939, on the use of commissionary administrators for businesses, factories, and real estate (*VOBl.Posen*, 21; reproduced in *Doc. Occ.* 5:54 f.) and on the acquisition of real estate, commercial business, etc. (*VOBl. Posen*, 23; reproduced in *Doc. Occ.* 5:55 ff.). For Upper Silesia, decrees issued by the head of the Civil Administration Kattowitz (Katowice) of September 5, 1939 (property of people who had fled, *VOBl. Grenzschutz*, no. I/39, reproduced in *Doc. Occ.* 5:68), September 16, 1939 (retail shops and artisanal workshops, *VOBl. Grenzschutz*, no. 6/39, reproduced in *Doc. Occ.* 5:70 f.), September 20, 1939 (administration of the property of people who had fled, *VOBl. Grenzschutz*, no. 8/39, reproduced in *Doc. Occ.* 5:72 ff.); and decree by the commander of the Frontier Defense Commando Unit regarding seizure (*VOBl. Grenzschutz*, no. 9/39, reproduced in *Doc. Occ.* 5:71 f.). For Danzig–West Prussia, see decrees issued by the military commander for Danzig–West Prussia of September 27, 1939 (seizure of Polish assets, *VOBl. Militärbefehlshaber* 1939, 61, reproduced in *Doc. Occ.* 5:57 f.), with supplementary decree of the same date (*VOBl. Militärbefehlshaber* 1939, 133, reproduced in *Doc. Occ.* 5:58 f.); third decree, dated October 22, 1939, by the head of the Civil Administration Danzig–West Prussia (seizure of Polish property, *VOBl. Militärbefehlshaber* 1939, 162, reproduced in *Doc. Occ.* 5:59). For the Warthegau, see the decree of September 28, 1939, issued by the head of the civil administration of Posen (Poznań) (trade in real estate and real rights, *VOBl. Posen*, 12, reproduced in *Doc. Occ.* 5:65).

4. Full details in Arndt, "Entziehung und Verbringung jüdischen Vermögens" (1960), 92 ff.; with regard to the situation in the Annexed Eastern Territories, 104 ff.

5. See, for example, the Directive on the Safekeeping of Jewish Assets of January 8, 1940, in the Ostrowo District (*Kreisblatt Ostrowo* of January 22, 1940; Institute for Western Studies, Poznań).

6. The report by Arndt, "Entziehung und Verbringung jüdischen Vermögens," gives no details of unofficial confiscations, since the German Federal Republic archives contain no relevant documents (92). The following Polish sources are extremely valuable: reports of the Security Police, Rawitsch (Rawicz) (Wartheland) dated September 25; October 5, 7, 10; November 6, 10, 11, 12, 20, 22, 29; December 20, 1939 (State Archive Poznań, Schutzpolizei, Dienstabteilung Rawitsch 16, Bl. 9, 27, 32, 48, 51, 53, 54, 63, 66, 71, 83). Letter dated November 27, 1939 (presumably from the Bürgermeister office, Strzelno) to a Pole in Strzelno (State Archives Bromberg, Dept. Inowrocław, Hohensalza—Magistrat Strzelno no. 832, Bl. 205, quoted by Łuczak, *Grabież polskiego mienia*, 14 f.) and a letter of January 29, 1940, from the Bürgermeister office, Strzelno, to the Ostmark Hotel in Strzelno (Bl. 241, quoted on 15); report of October 8, 1939, by the SIPO, Posen (State Archives Bromberg, Dept. Inowrocław, Hohensalza—Magistrat Strzelno no. 832, "Der Chef der Zivilverwaltung," 54, Bl. 86, quoted on 12), regarding the seizure of goods of all kinds for German offices and private individuals (settlers, company directors, etc.), including bicycles, typewriters, knitwear, cattle, living accommodations and furniture, sewing machines, coal, bed linen, records of political organizations, savings bank books, cars, cutlery, alcoholic drinks, works of art, records of Polish trade unions, etc. See also the letter of November 13, 1939, from the district president of Posen to *Generaljustitiar* Leibrock (internal) (State Archive Poznań, *Reichsstatthalter* 4, 21) regarding seizure of the libraries of Polish and Jewish lawyers and notaries for use in the office of the Reich governor of Posen, with explicit approval of the Posen Chamber of Lawyers. Report of November 6, 1939, by the Bürgermeister of Hohensalza (private collection, reproduced in Łuczak, *Grabież polskiego mienia*, 12 f.):

> The behavior of the army in Hohensalza is no different from that in the other three *kreisfreie* cities and rural districts of the *Gau*. Pretentiousness and arrogance have sometimes been close to bearable limits. Above all, the troops believe they can requisition whatever they want. I

have had to intervene most severely. . . . Furs, clothes, bedclothes, and so on have all been taken in the name of requisitioning. This goes for officers too. Particularly the behavior of the younger officers was not consonant with the principles of the National Socialist upbringing. Men who in their private lives were primary school teachers or assistant teachers at secondary school stood out in this respect.

See also the secret correspondence from the head of the Central Trustee Office of the Eastern Territories to the head of the Four Year Plan, dated February 5, 1941 (DZA Potsdam, Reich Ministry of Finance no. 6176, 35, excerpts in Łuczak, *Grabież polskiego mienia*, 196).

7. Cf. *Meldungen aus dem Reich* of May 16, 1940, BA R 85/184 (where it is reported that many Reich Germans used the term *confiscation* for stealing valuable objects; the need for such measures could no longer be examined and indeed never had been examined). It was also reported that actions had been instituted for minor thefts committed by ethnic Germans during hostilities or shortly after the occupation (of Łódź). There was thus a movement among law officers for an amnesty, given the bitterness on the part of the ethnic Germans.

8. See the excerpt from the transcript of a meeting of the heads of the trustee offices on July 23–24, 1940, in Berlin, the report by the head of the trustee office in Łódź (State Archive Poznań, Treuhandstelle Posen, 10654), which states, "In addition, the evacuation of Poles and Jews was often accompanied by measures to secure the personal assets of those involved, and all these measures considerably increased the reigning confusion. The first thing to concentrate on, therefore, was everything that concerned the administration. . . . Thus a search was carried on in virtually every house, including the landings, and finally every flat was looked through to see whether it did not contain some articles of value or business that concerned our administration."

9. Letter dated February 5, 1941, from the head of the Main Trustee Office East (HTO) to the head of the Four Year Plan, quoted by Łuczak, *Grabież polskiego mienia*, 196: "Up to the beginning of 1940, tens of thousands of measures have been taken by all sorts of incompetent and officious offices and the Party, none of which have been recorded. In very many of these cases, goods have been embezzled, in others they have ended up in the hands of Landräte, Bürgermeister, police, and military stations, without their origin being discernible. Enormous quantities of furniture, clothes, and other everyday objects disappeared during that period."

10. Administrative decree of October 19, 1939; all individuals enriching themselves in this manner were to be prosecuted by law. Violations would be punished "without discrimination" and reported to the RSHA (*Mitteilungsblatt HTO* 1940, no. 4, 15, reproduced in *Doc. Occ.* 5:212 f.).

11. See also the report dated January 10, 1940, from the municipal administration of Łódź (State Archive Poznań, Stadverwaltung Litzmannstadt, 81a): "Acts of aggression, unofficial confiscation of goods, and so on, formerly commonplace in the circumstances of the war . . . have diminished considerably as a result of the control measures taken in cooperation with the army command." In an instruction dated June 7, 1940, Himmler as RKF was still urging inclusion of Göring's instruction in his decree of October 19, 1939 (*Doc. Occ.* 5:212 f.).

12. Decree of January 15, 1940, by the head of the Four Year Plan on the Protection of the Assets of the Former Polish State (*RGBl.* I 174).

13. *RGBl.* I, 270.

14. Decree of July 18, 1940, by the Reich minister of finance; details in Steffens, "Die rechtliche Vertretung der Juden im Reich" (1942). See also the status report of November 15, 1939, for the Kalisch (Kalisz) District (State Archive Poznań, *Reichsstatthalter* 1831, Bl. 3): "Business and industry was virtually exclusively in the hands of the approximately 32,000 Jews who had established themselves here in Kalisch. The Jews have been excluded from all occupations, and a large number of businesses have been taken over by ethnic Germans and sometimes also Reich Germans as trustees."

15. Instruction of August 26, 1941, by the *Reichsführer-SS/RKF* (*Mitteilungsblatt HTO* 1942, no. 1, 30 f.; reproduced in *Doc. Occ.* 5:245 f.).

16. Some 3.5 million reichsmarks from the sale of Polish and Jewish household goods (in the

Warthegau alone?), circular of October 18, 1941, from the Main Trustee Office East, quoted in Łuczak, *Grabież polskiego mienia*, 204.

17. Sec. 2, par. 1b, of the decree of September 17, 1940 (*RGBl.* I 1270). For the Warthegau, see the secret decree of November 12, 1939, by the HSSPF Posen (ZS, Polen, film 62, Bl. 0547–0551); confidential information sheet from the head of the Emigration Center, Łódź, Zamos branch, dated November 21, 1942, on the desettlement of Polish farmers (Institute for Western Studies, Poznań, doc. 1–53).

18. Decree of November 24, 1939, by the HSSPF Posen (ZS Polen, film 62, Bl. 0544 f.), which supplemented the secret decree of November 12 (Bl. 0547–0551); the Jews to be evacuated to the General Government were to be thoroughly searched: "Before the search . . . the Jews [were] invited to hand over [unauthorized objects] on pain of the severest punishment." See also the instructions of November 24, 1939, and February 24, 1940, by the police president of Posen (Institute for Western Studies, Poznań). Regarding deportation to the Łódź ghetto, see the instruction of April 20, 1942, by the Łódź Oberbürgermeister (Ghetto Administration) (ZS Polen, film 257, Bl. 179), according to which the following articles "were to be put at the general disposal of the Ghetto Administration": machines of all types, German reichsmarks, foreign currencies, coins of all types, precious stones, raw materials of all types; "utilization of household goods—used furniture, beds, crockery and other equipment, foodstuffs"—was "left to" the relevant commissioners.

19. See Main Trustee Office East notice dated July 20, 1941, on the occupation of former Polish owners (*Mitteilungsblatt HTO* 1940, 169, reproduced in *Doc. Occ.* 5:195, no. 5): "It is fundamentally out of the question to refrain from confiscating property from the Poles, as this would prejudice later arrangements for the Polish question."

20. ". . . in order to permit Poles and Jews . . . so long as they remain economically active, to accumulate new assets" (an exception was the "new assets" of persons who had fled or had been deported), decree of November 13, 1940, by the head of the Main Trustee Office East (*Mitteilungsblatt HTO* 1941, 70, excerpts in *Doc. Occ.* 5:228 ff. n. 50).

21. *RGBl.* I, 355, with first and second implementing orders of January 24 and February 1, 1941 (*RGBl.* I 67 and 68).

22. Decree of February 28, 1940, by the Reich minister for food and agriculture on the appointment of the Ostdeutsche Landbewirtschaftungsgesellschaft mbH as general administrator under the terms of the decree of February 28, 1940, IV B 5, 126 (*Mitteilungsblatt HTO* 1940, no. 1, 13), with implementing provisions of February 26, 1941 (all the provisions referred to are also reproduced in *Doc. Occ.* 5:215 ff.).

23. Statement under oath by Kurt Kleindienst of August 6, 1947 (Nuremberg doc. NO-5246).

24. Decree of September 29, 1939, by the head of the civil administration of Posen (*VOBl. für die besetzten Gebiete Polen*, no. 7/39).

25. Statement under oath by Kurt Kleindienst of August 6, 1947 (Nuremberg doc. NO-5246); the sale of real estate began in 1942.

26. Decree of March 27, 1940 (*RGBl.* I 549, also Nuremberg doc. NG-4612, reprint).

27. See, for example, the report in the *Frankfurter Zeitung* of February 22, 1941, that of the more than four thousand textile factories in Łódź and Bielitz (Bielsko-Biała), only the "most competitive" were still in existence (Nuremberg doc. NO-3742). The machines were destroyed because no technicians were available to dismantle the equipment (protocol of a discussion in the Reich Ministry of Finance with representatives of the Main Trustee Office East on July 3, 1942, quoted by Łuczak, *Grabież polskiego mienia*, 197 f.).

28. Decree of January 21, 1940 (*RGBl.* I 255), in the version of the law of December 23, 1940 (*RGBl.* I 1533). Decree of September 28, 1939, by the head of the civil administration of Posen (*VOBl. Polen*, 12, reproduced in *Doc. Occ.* 5:65).

29. Cf. the Foreign Office draft of March 29, 1940 (BA R 22/20977).

30. Support contributions up to the value of the welfare rate from the confiscated assets for Poles and Jews were permitted without reference to the tax-free limit of RM 1,000, in order to relieve the public purse of this burden; cf. Main Trustee Office East decree of May 4, 1940 (*Mitteilungsblatt* 1941, no. 6, 194 ff., 215; reproduced in *Doc. Occ.* 5:237).

31. Decree on the Utilization of Jewish Assets of December 3, 1939 (*RGBl.* I 1709).

32. Unpublished decree by the *Reichsführer-SS* dated November 10, 1939 (Nuremberg doc. PS-17075; *Doc. Occ.* 5:205 ff.), and instruction of November 10, 1939, by the head of the Main Trustee Office East (reproduced in *Doc. Occ.* 5:207); unpublished urgent circular of December 16, 1939, by the RFSSuChddtPol (207 ff.); instruction by the RFSS/RKF dated June 7, 1940 (212 ff.).

33. Göring in his capacity of head of the Four Year Plan established the Main Trustee Office East, with headquarters in Berlin and Kraków and branches in Danzig, Posen, Zichenau, Kattowitz, and Warsaw, for the "administration" of the confiscated private and public Polish property (instruction of June 12, 1940, reproduced in *Doc. Occ.* 5:190 ff.), later followed by the creation of further branches. In some cases these branches came into being before the promulgation of the material seizure regulations, and in others at the same time. The Real Estate Company of the Main Trustee Office East, with headquarters in Berlin, was established for the management and exploitation of the houses and land that had been seized (Main Trustee Office East instruction of May 27, 1940, *Rechtsanzeiger* 1940, no. 122, reproduced in *Doc. Occ.* 5:199); details will be found in the Main Trustee Office East decree of May 30, 1940 (*Doc. Occ.* 5:200 ff.); a separate limited real estate company was set up in 1942 for each trustee office district (corresponding to the structure of the Annexed Eastern Territories) (second Main Trustee Office East instruction of September 24, 1942, *Rechtsanzeiger* 1942, no. 227, reproduced in *Doc. Occ.* 5:203 f.). The Main Trustee Office East was also authorized to make any further administrative rules relating to the confiscated property and had a say in all arrangements made by the technical ministries relating to the administration of Polish and Jewish assets, "in the interest of uniform interpretation" (letter dated January 5, 1940, from the Reich minister of the interior [Stuckart] to the supreme Reich authorities, BA R 43/II/694). Full details concerning the Main Trustee Office East will be found in Broszat, "Kompetenzen und Befugnisse der Hauptreuhandstelle Ost"; statement under oath by lawyer Edgar Hoffmann (Nuremberg doc. NO-5125).

34. See the sources given in *Doc. Occ.* 5:188 ff.; the Main Trustee Office East issued numerous instructions relating to the treatment of confiscated real estate in particular; see, for example, the letter of December 6, 1943, from the Reich governor (head of the Trustee Office) to the district delegates of the NSDAP, Posen, regarding inventory of the real estate confiscated in the Posen district (Institute for Western Studies, Poznań, doc. I-729).

35. The respective Reich governors or *Oberpräsidenten* acted as heads of the trustee offices in the Annexed Eastern Territories (second instruction on the Main Trustee Office East of February 17, 1941, par. 1, *Rechtsanzeiger* 1941, 151; reproduced in *Doc. Occ.* 5:197 f.). Initially the Main Trustee Office East *alone* was authorized to manage confiscated property and to designate trustees (Main Trustee Office East instruction of June 12, 1940, sec. 3, *Rechtsanzeiger* 1940, no. 139, reproduced in *Doc. Occ.* 5:190 ff.), but following the urgent circular of December 16, 1939, issued by the RFSSuChddtPol (207 ff.), the offices of the *Reichsführer-SS* as head of the German police and as Reich Commissar for the Strengthening of German Nationhood were empowered to effect seizures of property (sec. 1 of the decree). The Main Trustee Office East for its part had empowered the offices of the Reich Forestry Administration (regarding forest land), the staff of *Generalmajor* Bührmann (armaments headquarters of the Wehrmacht) (regarding raw materials and semifinished and finished goods), and the Oberbürgermeister and *Landräte* (regarding house contents of Poles who had fled or had been deported) to declare seizures on its behalf but had reserved further individual powers for itself (sec. 2 of the decree). In addition there remained the power of the Gestapo to confiscate "property of enemies of the people and state," although in the Annexed Eastern Territories

this power was in no way anchored in the law (RSHA circular of January 21, 1941, *Befehlsblatt des RSHA* 1941, no. 4, 14; quoted in *Doc. Occ.* 5:226 f. n. 48). The whole procedure was further complicated by the fact that although the Main Trustee Office East ordered seizures, the *execution* of the orders devolved exclusively on the Gestapo (see the regulations referred to in note 44).

36. See the instruction of June 7, 1940, issued by the *Reichsführer-SS/RKF* (*Mitteilungsblatt HTO* 1940, no. 4, 15, reproduced in *Doc. Occ.* 5:212 f.), in which Himmler once again sets out all the instructions important for the work of the trustee offices, with the emphatic request to avoid duplication among the authorities and organizations involved and to mutually inform and support one another on an ongoing basis. In order to obtain "uniform cooperation," the liaison chief of the Main Trustee Office East with the RFSSuChddtPol was designated *Generalreferent* for the Strengthening of German Nationhood (second instruction of the Main Trustee Office East of February 17, 1941, reproduced in *Doc. Occ.* 5:197 f.); instruction of April 4, 1941, by the *Reichsführer-SS/RKF* (reproduced in *Doc. Occ.* 5:214 f.). In spite of this, one office often did not know what the other was doing. See, for example, the RFSS/RKF decree of April 10, 1940 (Nuremberg doc. NG-1833, microfilm), which instructed the offices of the SIPO and SD to report objects from the former Polish state or from private Polish collections that it had confiscated or made secure only to the Main Trustee Office East Berlin and not to the subordinate trustee offices.

37. Instruction of June 7, 1940, by the *Reichsführer-SS/RKF*, sec. 5 (*Mitteilungsblatt HTO* 1940, no. 4, 15, reproduced in *Doc. Occ.* 5:212 f.).

38. Decree of February 12, 1940, secs. 3 and 4 (*RGBl.* I 355); so-called Polish Assets Decree of September 17, 1940, sec. 4 (*RGBl.* I 1270).

39. Decree of August 26, 1941, on the correct treatment of the rights entered in the land registers of the German Reich for the former Polish state, sec. 1 (*RGBl.* I 533).

40. Instruction of June 12, 1940, on the Main Trustee Office East, sec. 2, Buchst. a and b (*Rechtsanzeiger* 1940, no. 319, reproduced in *Doc. Occ.* 5:190 ff.).

41. Statement under oath by lawyer Edgar Hoffmann on the activity of the Main Trustee Office East (Nuremberg doc. NO-5125).

42. Main Trustee Office East instruction of May 27, 1940, on the handling of land in the Annexed Eastern Territories (instruction no. 4) (*Rechtsanzeiger* 1940, no. 122, reproduced in *Doc. Occ.* 5:199 f.).

43. Testimony of an official of the Reich Ministry of Finance, April 25, 1941 (quoted by Łuczak, *Dyskryminacja Polaków*, 199 f.).

44. Unpublished decree by the *Reichsführer-SS* dated November 10, 1939 (Nuremberg doc. PS-17075; *Doc. Occ.* 5:205 ff.), sec. 2, and unpublished urgent circular of December 16, 1939, by the RFSSuChddtPol (reproduced in *Doc. Occ.* 5:207 f.). Unpublished decree by the *Reichsführer-SS* of November 10, 1939, regarding cooperation of the offices of the *Reichsführer-SS* with the Main Trustee Office East, sec. 4 (reproduced in *Doc. Occ.* 5:205).

45. Nuremberg doc. NG-1911.

Part One. Section 2. C. III. Civil Service Law

1. Note (undated and unsigned) from the offices of the Reich governor of Posen (Poznań) (State Archive Poznań, *Reichsstatthalter* 835, Bl. 4).

2. See the letter of April 7, 1941, from the district president of Posen to the *Landräte* of the district and to the Oberbürgermeister of Posen, reproduced in Łuczak, *Dyskryminacja Polaków* (1966), 303 ff. For example, the head of the Civil Administration Posen, Greiser, ordered as early as October 25, 1939, that Poles in the administration should be replaced as soon as possible by ethnic Germans; if this was not possible, they should be left with only 60% of their salaries after taxes, the

rest being used "to reconstruct the province" (quoted on 284 f.). In 1942 the basic maximum wage for Poles was set at 80% of that of Germans.

3. See transcription of a special committee meeting in Posen on December 11, 1942 (ZS, file 47, 253), in which the guidelines for public office issued on December 7, 1942, by the Reich trustee for the Warthegau were announced.

4. Letter of April 7, 1941, from the district president of Posen to the *Landräte* of the district (reproduced in Łuczak, *Diskriminierung der Polen*, 303 ff.).

5. Published in a circular dated March 21, 1941, from the district president of Hohensalza (Inowrocław) to all school directors and inspectors (II, 2 B: 135/41/II 4/II 104; State Archive Poznań, 1939–44, 106).

6. Decree of November 10, 1941 (BA R 22/4466).

7. Decree of June 27, 1941, to the *Oberlandesgerichtspräsidenten* and prosecutors-general in Danzig (Gdańsk) and Posen; quoted in a letter from the prosecutor-general of Kattowitz (Katowice) to the Reich Ministry of the Interior (BA R 22/4466).

8. Decree of August 30, 1941, by the Reich governor of Posen to the district presidents in Posen, Hohensalza, Łódź, etc. (State Archive Poznań, *Reichsstatthalter* 742, Bl. 3 and 4): "The Supreme Authorities of the Reich were requested to take the necessary action in their respective provinces."

9. Decree of November 10, 1941 (BA R 22/4466).

10. Decree of August 30, 1941, by the Reich governor of Posen, in which all department chiefs were requested to obtain statements to this effect from the officials and other employees under their authority (State Archive Poznań, *Reichsstatthalter* 742, Bl. 3 and 4).

11. See the letter of July 27, 1941, from the prosecutor-general of Kattowitz to the Reich minister of justice, suggesting that the Reich minister of justice's decree of June 27 be extended to officials who had *hitherto* worked in Upper Silesia. The Reich minister of justice expressed his agreement in a letter dated August 9, 1941, "if this were necessary" (BA R 22/4466).

Part One. Section 2. C. IV. Professional and Labor Law

1. See the Directive of July 15, 1941, on Jewish Camps in the *Landkreis* Posen (Poznań) (ZS Posen, film 5/753–755; working day anything up to fourteen hours). Notification dated August 13, 1940, by the *Landrat* of Plozk (Płock) (administrative district Zichenau) on the erection of a Jewish camp for the purpose of "complete separation" from the Poles (Institute for Western Studies, Poznań).

2. See decision of July 20, 1940, by the Main Trustee Office East (HTO) (*Mitteilungsblatt HTO 1940, no. 5, 169; Doc. Occ.* 5:195 ff.) on the employment of former Polish proprietors and managers. Under it they were forbidden delegation of fundamental authority and to share common living quarters with the German trustees. The trustees were required to keep Polish employees away from business and private correspondence as far as possible, since "the Polish intelligentsia and semiintelligentsia and the land-owning middle class particularly had been the vectors of the chauvinistic hatred of all Germans during the Polish period"; see also the circular of November 19, 1940, from the head of the Main Trustee Office East (*Mitteilungsblatt HTO 1941, no. 1, 73;* reproduced in *Doc. Occ.* 5:197), forbidding the employment of auditors of Polish nationality; letter of November 25, 1942, from the HSSPF of Posen and inspector of the SIPO and SD to the deputy Reich governor of Posen (Institute for Western Studies, Poznań).

3. Letter of April 3, 1940, from the State Superior Court president, Danzig, to the *Landgerichtspräsidenten* and the invigilators of the *Amtsgerichte* (BA R 22/20993).

4. Letter of November 25, 1940, from the State Superior Court president, Danzig, to the *Landgerichtspräsidenten* and the invigilators of the *Amtsgerichte* (BA R 22/20993).

5. For example, see the letter of April 28, 1944, from the Reich governor of Posen to the head of the *Land* Labor Office, Posen (quoted by Łuczak, *Dyskryminacja Polaków*, 169 f.).

6. Report on a meeting of the labor trustees of the Eastern Territories held in Posen on October 9, 1941 (reproduced in *Doc. Occ.* 5:274 ff.). Statements by SS-*Oberführer* Mehlhorn, head of Dept. 1 of the offices of the Reich governor of Posen.

7. Regarding the allocation of labor and the conditions of work and pay for the Poles, see details in Seeber, *Zwangsarbeiter in der faschistischen Kriegswirtschaft* (1964); Madajczyk, *Polityka*, 2:7 ff., 34 ff. (with statistics); Łuczak, *Dyskryminacja Polaków*, 284 ff., with numerous references; Rusiński, *Położenie robotników* (1949, 1955); *Doc. Occ.* 9:1975. See note 166 to part 1, section 1, V ("Professional and Labor Law"), regarding a more recent study on Polish labor and working conditions.

8. See, for example, the letter of August 1943 (precise date not given) from the Reich governor of Wartheland, Referat I/50 to Referat I/40 (State Archive Poznań, *Reichsstatthalter* 1174, Bl. 207), regarding drivers in the voluntary fire services in the Wartheland. Poles could be used as drivers when no Germans were available; situations in which they could give orders to Germans should, however, be avoided. Similar training for Germans and Poles was "impossible." Letter of March 27, 1943, from the head of the Security Police and the *Sicherheitsdienst* to the Reich governor of Wartheland (Bl. 216) regarding Polish drivers, who should "not exercise any functions that in practice make them the superiors of German nationals."

9. Directives (1940) of the *Reichsführer*-SS/RKF regarding training of young Poles for industry, in *Verfügungen*, 2:577.

10. Report on a meeting of the labor trustees, reproduced in *Doc. Occ.* 5:275 ff.

11. Order of July 27, 1940, by the Reich governor of Posen, quoted in a letter of June 18, 1941, from the *Landrat* of Kempen to the Kempen Bürgermeister and the commissioners of the district (AZ KA VI, Institute for Western Studies, Poznań, App. 11).

12. Report of July 30, 1941, from Referat I/50 of the Reich governor of Posen to the Reich governor of Posen (Institute for Western Studies, Poznań, doc. I-145), which refers to emergency regulations of June 1, 1941, from the Reich trustee (no further detail given).

13. Order of October 5, 1941, from the Reich minister of labor (*RArBl.* 1941, I, 448, preamble); also H. von Rosen—von Hoevel, "Das Polenstatut," *DVerw* (1942): 109 ff.

14. Order by the Reich minister of labor of October 5, 1941 (*RArBl.* 1941, I, 448, preamble), secs. 2–7, 9, 10, 14.

15. Order of March 31, 1941, on vacations for civilian workers of Polish nationality (*RArBl.* 1941, I, 194) (sec. 2).

16. Report of a meeting of the Reich labor trustees for the Eastern Territories on October 9, 1941, in Posen (*Doc. Occ.* 5:274 ff.).

17. Report of October 9, 1941, ibid., 275 ff., 279; list of sanctions for poor work production in the notice *Streng aber gerecht* for Polish workers in German factories, who had to sign it when taking on work (Institute for Western Studies, Poznań, doc. I-873), and order by the inspector of the SIPO and SD, Danzing, on the punishment of violations of work discipline, communicated in the directives of December 9, 1941, by the State Police Directorate, Graudenz (Grudziądz) (State Archives Bromberg [Bydgoszcz], Akten Gestapo Graudenz, reproduced in *Doc. Occ.* 5:265 ff.).

18. See the various statements contained in the report of October 9, 1941 (*Doc. Occ.* 5:275 f., 278 f.), by the representative of Pomerania (very positive), Upper and Lower Silesia (Poles preferred among all workers), the Gnesen (Gniezno) labor office (70% were "modest and hardworking"), and the Samter labor office (90% "willing to work").

19. Report of October 9, 1941 (*Doc. Occ.* 5:279): "A way out of the dilemma is apparently being discussed in private . . . the struggle between the German and the Polish nations is a matter of very existence."

20. Report of July 30, 1941, by the *Referent* for nationhood questions of the Reich governor of Posen to the Reich governor of Posen (Institute for Western Studies, Poznań, doc. I-145). Probably as a result of this suggestion, an order was drafted, the contents of which are still not known (quoted in the report of October 9, 1941, *Doc. Occ.* 5:275).

21. Letter dated June 22, 1944, V A, 580/212, from the Reich governor of Wartheland to the *Gau* Chamber of Commerce, Wartheland (State Archive Poznań, *Reichsstatthalter* 924, Bl. 196):

Regarding maternity arrangements for Polish women . . . The general political line should of course be respected in the application of these protective provisions set out in sec. 9 of the Implementing Order to the Maternity Protection Law of May 17, 1942 (*RGBl.* I 324). From these general principles for the treatment of Poles it emerges that Polish mothers-to-be are never justified in refusing to work. Furthermore, past experience has shown that maternity leave before and after the confinement of Polish women is not always necessary. For this reason pregnant women should as a rule no longer be employed if they are likely to be delivered within two weeks. Women who have given birth should not be employed less than two weeks after confinement. They should resume work six weeks at the latest after confinement. . . Deputy Head Jäger.

22. Report of July 30, 1941 (Institute for Western Studies, Poznań, doc. I-145); letter of September 15, 1941, from the management of the Elektronische Werke Zychllin to the armaments inspector in Posen, quoted by Łuczak, *Diskriminierung der Polen*, 295 ff. See also the report of October 9, 1941 (*Doc. Occ.* 5:275). In the administrative district of Zichenau and in Danzig–West Prussia, vacations were awarded only as a bonus for increased work performance (report of October 9, 1941[275 ff.]).

23. Report of October 9, 1941 (*Doc. Occ.* 5:275), according to which the Poles' wages were reduced by a further 15% beyond the 15% deducted for social compensation tax in order to cover bonuses for good workers. *Wirtschaft* (organ of the Chamber of Economics), no. 9 (September 1941): 17.

24. See the announcement to his employees by W. Kaes, master house-painter, of Wreschen (Wrzesnia), in *Streng aber gerecht* (Institute for Western Studies, Poznań, doc. I-873).

25. Report of October 9, 1941 (*Doc. Occ.* 5:276).

26. Ibid.; see the statements by the deputy Gauleiter of Posen, Dr. Derichsweiler, from the office of the Reich governor of Posen: "If Poles make up the majority in a factory, or indeed 100% of the manpower, they work little or badly. If they work properly, they should be properly paid. The piecework system is to be preferred as an inducement. A Posen construction company increased the output of Polish bricklayers from 300 to 1,200 bricks a day by the introduction of piecework" (*Doc. Occ.* 5:277); and Gauleiter Greiser: "The Pole has to achieve a minimum output, and he should be paid for this. The time he needs to achieve this performance is not relevant. We may regard him as nothing but a laborer whom we are to look upon without feeling . . . he should never have any rights. He prefers a hundred selfish bosses who treat Poles badly to a regular legal system for Poland. . . . He doesn't want a minimum wage for Poles but only a wage corresponding to his work performance. How this principle is achieved is a matter of form, for which he has his employees" (277 ff., 280).

27. *VOBl. CdZ Posen*, October 27, 1939. *VOBl. Reichsstatthalter Wartheland*, February 2, 1940; May 28, 1941; and May 24, 1943; report of October 9, 1941 (*Doc. Occ.* 5:279).

28. Report for the period January 16 to February 15, 1941 (State Archive Poznań, *Reichsstatthalter* 854, Bl. 49 f.).

29. Report of October 9, 1941 (*Doc. Occ.* 5:276).

30. Ibid., 279; statements by the *Gau* economic adviser Batzer, Wartheland. See also the letter of January 5, 1942, from Zellgarn AG, Posen, to the Reich governor of Posen (ZS Posen, film 14, 603 ff.).

31. See the report by the commissioner of the Opalenitza District of March 1942 (State Archive Poznań, Landratsamt Grätz 36, pp. 16, 22): "Recruitment will be pursued with the greatest energy this spring. At present lists of all Polish youths between 12 and 18 years of age are being prepared for the labor office." Confidential circular of May 5, 1944, by the Reich minister of labor, according to which children over 10 years could also be used for suitable light work within their capacities (if necessary also for more than four hours a day (Łuczak, *Diskriminierung der Polen*, 306).

32. For example, the note of June 25, 1941, by the Security Police, Posen, regarding preparation of a raid (especially in places where long queues of Poles were to be found), and secret directives of April 22, 1941, by the commander of the Security Police regarding rounding up of unemployed Poles, with supplement of June 11 regarding rounding up of "vagrant" Poles; report on manpower recruitment in the *Ostdeutscher Beobachter*, March 12, 1941; activity report for June 1941 by the *Kreisleitung* Hermannsbad (Ciechocinek) (administrative district Hohensalza [Inowrocław]): "In order to be sure to catch every work-shy Polish layabout, we intend to clamp down on the Polish churches one after the other and check all the Poles for their papers, work allocation, and so on. In this way we hope to teach them some respect once again" (Institute for Western Studies, Poznań).

33. Regarding compulsory dispatch to the Reich, see full details in Seeber, *Zwangsarbeiter in der faschistischen Kriegswirtschaft*; Łuczak, *Diskriminierung der Polen*, 220 ff.; by mid-1943, 400,000 Polish workers had been sent to the Reich from the Warthegau alone (statement by an official of the *Land* Economic Office, Posen, July 21, 1943 [222]); see also circular of March 1, 1944, by the *Gau* Bureau of Nationhood Affairs (State Archive Poznań, *Reichsstatthalter* 1174, Bl. 55).

34. Note for Referat I/50 of the office of the Reich governor of Posen dated June 17, 1944, on a meeting of the armaments commission in Posen (State Archive Poznań, *Reichsstatthalter* 1174, Bl. 53), stating, "It will not be possible to maintain the seventy-two-hour week indefinitely, especially since the proportion of workers with tuberculosis is extremely high. State Official Schneider informs us that he loses some 20 men each week to tuberculosis at the DMW [Deutsche Munitions-Werke]. Since a further 40 were taken away last month by the State Police, and further such removals can be expected, the long-term running of the factory is at risk. He intended to speak to *Oberregierungsrat* Stoßberg [head of the State Police bureau], since the people taken away by the Stapo are the most intelligent and most able workers."

35. Letter of March 4, 1944, from the *Gau* Bureau of Nationhood Affairs of the NSDAP to the Wartheland *Gau* Chamber of Labor: the working conditions were far worse than in the "Old Reich" (Institute for Western Studies, Poznań). See the letter of January 5, 1942, from Zellgarn AG, Posen, to the Reich governor of Posen (ZS Posen, film 14, 603 ff.); report for June 1941 by the *Kreisleitung* Hermannsbad (Institute for Western Studies, Poznań); order of July 23, 1940, by the *Landrat* of Plozk, administrative district Zichenau (poor work performance by Poles); letter of July 15, 1940, from the district president of Zichenau to the *Landräte* of the district (Institute for Western Studies, Poznań).

36. Confidential note dated July 27, 1944, from the office of the Reich governor of Posen for Referat I/50: "Malnutrition and physical overexertion do in fact constitute a danger" (State Archive Poznań, *Reichsstatthalter* 1174, Bl. 281).

37. According to the confidential note of July 27, 1944 (ibid.), the chairman of the armaments commission stated that it was time "to recognize the mistakes we made in the early years and to remedy them"; this passage was underlined by the head of the Referat for Nationhood Questions (I/50) of the Reich governor of Posen, and a question mark was added in the margin.

38. Note dated May 9, 1944, from the office of the Reich governor of Posen, according to which Poles would be permitted a right to complain against the abuse of disciplinary measures by managers; but any complaint would be rejected "in order not to disturb discipline at work," and "influence [would be] exerted" on the manager in private if it was justified (quoted by Łuczak, *Dyskryminacja Polaków*, 301).

Part One. Section 2. C. V. Citizenship Law for Poles and Other "Non-Germans"

1. For more details, see Stuckart, "Die Staatsangehörigkeit in den eingegliederten Ostgebieten" (1941); Berger, "Die Deutsche Volksliste in den eingegliederten Ostgebieten" (1941).

2. Full details in Huber, *Idee und Ordnung des Reiches* (1941).

3. Dahm, *Völkerrecht* (1958), 1:471 ff.; Verdross, *Völkerrecht* (1964), 307 ff.; BVerfG I, 322; according to this, the collective naturalizations did not change the earlier nationality in the eyes of international law, since the acquisition of the territory was in itself illegal. In terms of international law, the new nationality did not exist. An exception was when—as in the case of the German inhabitants of Czechoslovakia—naturalization corresponded to the desire of the persons involved. In this case collective naturalization contrary to international law is interpreted as informal naturalization on the basis of an option (Dahm, *Völkerrecht*, 1:474; BVerfG I, 322).

4. Law of March 13, 1938, on the Reunification of Austria with the German Reich (*RGBl.* I 237; decree of July 3, 1938).

5. Law of November 21, 1938, on the Reunification of the Sudeten Territories with the German Reich (*RGBl.* I 1641). Under the agreement with Czechoslovakia of November 30, 1939 (*RGBl.* I 895), Czechs who had emigrated since 1920 were excluded from the acquisition of German nationality.

6. It was in this context that the term *ethnic Germans (Volksdeutsche)* was first defined with any precision. In a circular dated March 29, 1939 (*MinbliV* 783), the Reich minister of the interior defined "German ethnic nationals" as persons who recognized themselves as belonging to the German people, provided this was confirmed by certain facts such as language, culture, and education (Nuremberg doc. NG-295). Persons of foreign blood, especially Jews, could never be German ethnic nationals. See too the term *Volksdeutsche* described in the letter of January 25, 1938, from the RMuChdRkzlei to the Supreme Authorities of the Reich (RK 1355 D) as those persons "who are of German extraction in their language and culture but do not belong to the German Reich as citizens" (quoted in the decree of May 6, 1940, by the Reich minister of the interior—*Staatssekretär* Pfundtner, BA R 43 II/135a; reproduced in *Verfügungen*, 2:167).

7. Law of March 23, 1939, on the Reunification of Memelgebiet with the German Reich (*RGBl.* I 559), according to which people of Jewish descent also acquired German nationality.

8. Decree of the Führer and Reich chancellor of May 23 1940 (*RGBl.* I 803); only persons of "German or related blood" acquired German nationality, however.

9. Decree of August 23, 1942 (*RGBl.* I 553). German nationality was acquired by persons "of German descent" (*deutschstämmig*) who had served in the Wehrmacht or the Waffen-SS or had been recognized as "worthy Germans."

10. For more details, see Huber, "Das Reichsbürgerrecht" (1941), 15 ff., 20 ff.; Huber gives the children of Swedes, Danes, the French, Italians, and Hungarians as examples of related groups, but he also includes children of Polish nationality in Upper Silesia who became Reich citizens when their parents acquired German nationality (17 f.).

11. *RGBl.* I, 2042, 2077.

12. Dahm, *Völkerrecht*, 1:472: even when the acquisition of territory was *effective* under the terms of the law, the occupant was obliged to allow protection under public law (naturalization), in order to preclude mass statelessness and thus deprivation of rights, since abode in the home country would thereby also be endangered. The deportations from the Eastern Territories that did in fact occur confirm the legal consequences of statelessness.

13. Decisions of the Supreme Court for Civil Cases, 167, 274.

14. According to the Law of September 1, 1939, on the Reunification of the Free State of Danzig with the German Reich (*RGBl.* I 1547), all nationals of the former Free State of Danzig became German nationals.

15. More details in Broszat, *Nationalsozialistische Polenpolitik* (1961), 113.

16. Draft decree of August 23, 1940, by the Reich minister of the interior, which was never implemented, to clarify the Führer's decree of October 8, 1939 (Secret State Archives, Berlin-Dahlem, StS Pfundtner, Rep. 320/127, part of BA R 18).

17. *Minbliv* (1939): 2385 (also BA R 18/461); also reproduced in *Doc. Occ.* 5:108 ff. The decree was rescinded by the Decree of March 4, 1941, on the German Ethnic Classification List and German Nationality in the Annexed Eastern Territories in the version of the decree of January 31, 1942 (*RGBl.* I 1941, 118; 1942, 51).

18. These included German ethnic nationals who had possessed Danziger nationality before September 1, 1939, or had possessed Polish nationality before October 26, 1939, and were residents of the German Reich (including the Annexed Eastern Territories) until that time, or who following the loss of Polish nationality were stateless until October 26, 1939, and at that time were resident in the German Reich (including the Annexed Eastern Territories). To determine "German ethnic nationality," including in the protectorate, the Reich Ministry of the Interior decree of March 29, 1939, referred to in note 6 above (*MinbliV* 783) was instrumental. With the acquisition of German nationality, such persons were officially designated German nationals (Reich Ministry of the Interior decree of May 6, 1940, reproduced in *Verfügungen*, 2:167), even though the term *ethnic German* remained in wide everyday use.

19. In the latter years the Reich Ministry of the Interior had in fact prepared a draft of a Decree on the Legal Status of Protected Citizens and Stateless Illegitimate Children of Polish Nationality, which, however, was not passed. See the travel report of an official of the office of the Reich governor of Posen on a discussion in the Reich Ministry of the Interior on January 14, 1944 (State Archive Poznań, *Reichsstatthalter* 909).

20. At the demand of the Reich minister for education of the people and propaganda for uniform treatment of ethnic Germans in the Annexed Eastern Territories (letter of December 5, 1939, BA R 43 II/135a), State Secretary Stuckart declared that the acceptance of ethnic Germans as German nationals should be done "in as generous a manner as possible in the German interest . . . so as to include a large proportion of the nationally indifferent intermediate classes" (letter of January 4, 1940, Nuremberg doc. NG-295, also BA R 2/1172).

21. ZS, Versch. 26/112 ff. (copy): Himmler was empowered to eliminate "pernicious sections of the population" and to establish the new German settlement areas.

22. In the Reich Ministry of the Interior decree of November 25, 1939 (*MinbliV* [1939]: 2385), the *Kreisleiter* had a say only in cases in which German nationality was in doubt (details in the Reich Ministry of the Interior circular of June 22, 1939, *Minbliv* [1939]: 1337).

23. For further details, see Broszat, *Nationalsozialistische Polenpolitik*, 114 ff., with numerous references.

24. See no. 2 of the Reich minister of the interior's administrative decree of March 13, 1941 (quoted in *Doc. Occ.* 5:122 ff.: "No German blood may be lost or be put to use by foreign nations").

25. More details in Broszat, *Nationalsozialistische Polenpolitik*, 114 ff.

26. Administrative Decree on the Scrutiny and Segregation of the Population in the Annexed Eastern Territories (BA R 43 II/137; also reproduced in Lichter, *Das Staatsangehörigkeitsrecht* (1943), 116 ff.; and *Doc. Occ.* 5:114 ff.).

27. As stated in the Reich Ministry of the Interior circular of October 31, 1940 (Secret State Archives, Berlin-Dahlem, StS Pfundtner, Rep. 320/127, part of BA R 18).

28. More details in Broszat, *Nationalsozialistische Polenpolitik*, 115 ff.

29. In its memorandum of November 25, 1939, on the treatment of the population of the former Polish territories according to politico-racial standpoints (Nuremberg doc. NO-3732; also reproduced in *Doc. Occ.* 5:1 ff.), the Race Policy Office had proposed that the procedure of the German

Ethnic Classification List employed in the Warthegau should be used in the Annexed Eastern Territories generally.

30. *RGBl.* 1941 I, 118; 1942 I, 51; also reproduced in Lichter, *Das Staatsangehörigkeitsrecht*, 116 ff.; and *Doc. Occ.* 5:119 ff.; full details in Berger, "Die Deutsche Volksliste in den eingegliederten Ostgebieten" (1941).

31. Von Rosen—von Hoevel, "Das Polenstatut" (1942), 109 ff.: "In the spirit of the early Germanic era, National Socialism has made a clear analysis of the blood-determined differences between peoples and individuals. It is thus not a matter of equality among men, as the liberals would have it, but indeed of inequality, based on their natural racial, mental, and physical characteristics. Accordingly, they must have different rights and obligations depending on their value for the future existence of the people." (The author was *Regierungsrat* in the Reich Ministry of the Interior).

32. Decree of March 4, 1941 (*RGBl.* I 1941, 118; 1942, 51), sec. 3.

33. Ibid., secs. 5 and 6, in conjunction with the implementing decree of March 13, 1941, issued by the Reich Ministry of the Interior, no. 2, pars. 6 and 7 (BA R 18/3746, reproduced in *Doc. Occ.* 5:122 ff.).

34. Decree of March 4, 1941 (*RGBl.* I 1941, 118; 1942, 51), sec. 4, par. 2, and sec. 7, par. 2, and explicitly once again the Twelfth Decree of April 25 1943, to the Reich Citizenship Law (*RGBl.* I 268), sec. 4, according to which Jews and Gypsies could neither *become* nationals of the state nor *be* citizens unless the decree was countermanded. In this respect Huber errs in *Idee und Ordnung des Reiches*, 21 f., when he claims that Jews resident in the Annexed Eastern Territories were protected citizens of the Reich.

35. BA R 18/3746.

36. Decree of September 12, 1940, by the *Reichsführer*-SS/RKF (BA R 43 II/137), according to which the population of the Annexed Eastern Territories should in the future be composed of Germans with or without the right to Reich citizenship, "valuable alien renegades," and "foreign nationals."

37. Administrative decree of October 30, 1940, by the *Reichsführer*-SS/RKF, ZS Posen, film 2, Bl. 502.

38. Administrative decree of May 6, 1940, by the Reich Ministry of the Interior to the Reich protector in the Protectorate of Bohemia and Moravia, the Reich governor in Danzig and Posen, the *Oberpräsidenten* in Königsberg and Breslau (Wrocław), the district presidents in the Annexed Eastern Territories, and the Supreme Authorities of the Reich (BA R 43 II/1359).

39. See, for example, the implementing provisions of May 21, 1941, to the Decree on the German Ethnic Classification List issued by the Reich governor of Danzig–West Prussia (BA R 22/20994).

40. Reich Ministry of the Interior circulars of March 13, 1941 (BA R 18/3746), and of July 28, 1943 (*Doc. Occ.* 5:148 ff.). Reich Ministry of the Interior instruction of March 15, 1944 (ibid.).

41. Instruction no. 66 I of February 10, 1942, issued by the *Reichsführer*-SS/RKF (BA R 18/468), according to which Germans were to have made their application by March 31, 1942, at the latest; the Decision Committee for the German population was composed of the Bürgermeister and the local section heads of the municipality in which the applicant was resident, a delegate of the Security Police and the SD, and two "reliable ethnic Germans" (BA R 18/468).

42. Decree of January 1, 1942, by the Reich governor of Posen to all subordinate offices, setting out a broad equivalence of these persons with Germans (Institute for Western Studies, Poznań, doc. I-166). Letter of August 7, 1941, from the RFSS to the RSHA on how to deal with Poles living in the Reich and qualifying for naturalization (ZS, Versch. 29/242 f.); general instruction of February 9, 1942, by the *Reichsführer*-SS/RKF, no. 12/C, BA R 2220994, also reproduced in *Doc. Occ.* 5:150 ff.; circular of February 16, 1942, from the *Reichsführer*-SS/RKF (ZS, Versch. 29/236 ff.), communicated

to the Wartheland authorities by the Reich governor of Posen with covering letter of May 26, 1942 (Institute for Western Studies, Poznań); regarding the position of persons subject to military service registered under the DVL (German Ethnic Classification List), group 3, see OKW decree of October 2, 1942 (Az: 1 K 2036 AWA, BWSiwd./AWA AHA/Ag./E/[Ia] no. 3358/42, reproduced in *Doc. Occ.* 5:161 ff.).

43. Circular of October 31, 1941, from the RFSS/RKF, announced in the circular of May 30, 1942 (BA R 18/466, also reproduced in *Doc. Occ.* 5:150). The Reich governor of Posen, Greiser, resisted the interference of the Supreme Examining Court—as that of all central authorities—in cases concerning the people's register that might undermine the autonomy of his administration; cf. letter to the RFSS/RKF of April 2, 1943 (Institute for Western Studies, Poznań).

44. Reich Ministry of the Interior decree of March 13, 1941, sec. 2, par. 2c (*Doc. Occ.* 5:124); instruction of the SS/RKF no. 50/I of September 30, 1941 (reproduced in *Doc. Occ.* 5:144). The investigation was carried out by the Race and Settlement Office of the *Reichsführer*-SS. The authority for the instruction was vested—an indication of the broad powers claimed by the RKF—not in a Reich Ministry of the Interior circular but in the secret decree of October 7, 1939, issued by Hitler, who had given Himmler full powers in all nationhood questions (ZS, Versch. 26, Bl. 112 ff.).

45. Letter of November 11, 1941, from the representative of the Reich governor in the Wartheland (A. Jäger) to the *Reichsführer*-SS/RKF: "The association between the German Ethnic Classification List as a racial-political measure and racial investigation . . . is in contradiction to fundamental nationhood policy . . . The investigations undertaken so far have only been able to prove descent in a superficial manner. People who are indicated as being of German descent by this procedure cannot be forced into becoming Polish without considerable anxiety being caused among the general population as a result of this racist investigation procedure" (Institute for Western Studies, Poznań, doc. I-236, K. 4).

46. More details in Broszat, *Nationalsozialistische Polenpolitik*, 120 ff.

47. Reproduced in *Doc. Occ.* 5:122 ff.

48. Institute for Western Studies, Poznań, doc. I-53; also reproduced in *Doc. Occ.* 5:114 ff.

49. The decree of March 29, 1939, from the Reich Ministry of the Interior to the district president (Nuremberg doc. NG-295), defined "of German descent" as meaning "descending from ancestors of German origin," without specifying who was "of German origin." See also the letter of June 19, 1942, from the district president of Łódź to the Reich governor of Wartheland (State Archive Poznań, *Reichsstatthalter* 1174, Bl 37) and that of November 16, 1942, from the head of the SD-*Leitabschnitt*, Posen, to the Reich governor of Wartheland (Bl. 100).

50. Because there was a broad German-Polish middle class, the procedure was applied relatively generously in Danzig–West Prussia and Upper Silesia and was based primarily on political considerations, so that often all "undesirable" persons were included in the German Ethnic Classification List virtually en bloc. In Danzig–West Prussia, where in any case great tensions existed between the Reich governor, the SS, and the RKF, racial investigation was either refused or not considered binding (Broszat, *Nationalsozialistische Polenpolitik*, 121 ff., with references). In Upper Silesia the additional racial investigations demanded by Himmler had been completely suspended since 1943. The idea held by the RFSS/RKF that every single person included under group 3 of the German Ethnic Classification List—for whom "German descent" was not fully demonstrable—should be subjected to strict politico-racial investigation, was put into effect with any degree of completeness only in the Warthegau (123 f., with examples), where the rules of the German Ethnic Classification List had always been strictly applied. Only people who were of 50% German descent were included (report of the Wartheland Gauleiter dated June 16, 1942, to the *Reichsführer*-SS/RK, Nuremberg doc. NO-3993). Greiser's "great concern" was that the original Germanization policy would be watered down in the General Government, where 12.5% German descent was sufficient; a total of 3–4 million Germanizations were to be expected (reports from the Wartheland Gauleiter to

the *Reichsführer*-SS/RKF of June 16, 1943 [Nuremberg doc. NO-3992], and April 15, 1943 [Nuremberg doc. NO-2418]). The extremely extensive Germanization policy pursued (in areas other than the Warthegau) had thus had a considerable impact. By January 1944 a total of some 2.75 million people had been included in the German Ethnic Classification List in the Annexed Eastern Territories, including 1.7 million alone under group 3 and only 83,000 under group 1. In addition 370,000 Reich Germans, 353,000 ethnic German settlers possessing full German nationality, and approx. 6.01 million "protected" "aliens" lived in the Annexed Eastern Territories (figures from data from the RFK/staff headquarters, January 1944, Nuremberg doc. NO-3568, reproduced in Broszat, *Nationalsozialistische Polenpolitik*, 125).

51. More details in Adler, *Der verwaltete Mensch* (1974), 310 ff., esp. the moving description (313 ff.) of the tragic case of the "half Jew" Ernst Brüll from Nickelsdorf near Bielitz (Bielsko-Biała) (Upper Silesia); Brüll, the co-owner of a textile factory, was married to a "full Aryan" woman, with whom he had two children. In spite of a credible connection with Germandom, Brüll was refused registration in the German Ethnic Classification List and continued to fight for inclusion in it. Finally the *Reichsführer*-SS/RKF decided on December 10, 1942, that one daughter should be included under group 2 in the list and that a decision on the acceptance or classification of the parents should be held in abeyance until either the marriage was annulled or proof of Brüll's sterilization had been provided. The wife would then be admitted under group 2, whereas Brüll had first to be investigated with respect to a purported espionage business. Brüll was sent to Auschwitz on July 22, 1943, on the grounds that he had circulated atrocity stories and was strongly suspected of having obtained passports from Switzerland. He was transferred to Buchenwald on January 3, 1944. He and his wife refused a divorce, and he also refused sterilization. The last document is dated January 21, 1945, and contains the following: "Since Brüll is in the concentration camp and will probably not be released before the end of the war, no further undesirable offspring are to be expected. I therefore do not consider it necessary at the present time to pursue the question of divorce or sterilization and suggest that no further action be taken with regard to this family." The further fate of the Brüll family remains unknown.

52. Status report of April 8, 1942 (p.3). On account of the lack of this information and coordination, the motivation of all the officials dealing with the German Ethnic Classification List had considerably declined (Posen University Library).

53. Letter dated July 10, 1942, from the Reich Ministry of the Interior to the Reich Ministry of Justice (BA R 22/851). The delimitation was particularly difficult in areas with a large mixed German-Polish population such as Danzig–West Prussia (status report of March 10, 1942, by the State Superior Court president of Bromberg [Bydgoszcz] to the State Superior Court president of Danzig [BA R 22/3360] or Upper Silesia). See, for example, the report of July 18, 1944, from the State Superior Court president of Bromberg to the State Superior Court president of Danzig, in which the author complains of the "unwise" attitude of the police toward people on the German Ethnic Classification List, which was likely to alienate them with regard to Germandom. When DVL-3 Poles made civil charges against Reich Germans for the return of gardens that had been confiscated before Germanization, the Gestapo representative had wanted to undertake "police measures" in order to make these "Poles" think twice about pursuing their claims, and the police president wanted to prevent this "Polish action." The State Court of Appeals president pointed out that these people were Germans with full rights. The response was that though this objection was "formally correct," they still had to prove themselves and until then should be treated as Poles (BA R 22/3360).

54. Reich Ministry of the Interior circular dated November 14, 1940 (*MinbliV* 2111; *DJ* [1940]: 1433), according to which the "members of other foreign peoples" living in the Annexed Eastern Territories, "in particular Lithuanians, Great Russians, Belorussians, Ukrainians, and Czechs" were not regarded as Poles, nor the members of the mixed German-Polish population in the administrative districts of Oppeln (Opole) and Kattowitz (Katowice) or the "Kashubs" or Masurs living in the

Gau of Danzig–West Prussia; members of these "other non-Polish foreign peoples and stock" were to be given a certificate on request testifying to their "nonmembership in the Polish nation." If they claimed to be Poles, however, they were treated as Poles.

55. The question was whether such people were subject to the Polish penal code—as was the opinion of the RFSS/RFK—or were to be dealt with on the basis of German law—as thought the judicial administration. In Upper Silesia the police and the judiciary agreed to treat as Germans all those who had applied for inclusion in the German Ethnic Classification List or were already included in it but against whom the RFK had instituted an objection procedure on account of an alleged criminal offense (cf. the Reich Ministry of the Interior general instruction of June 5, 1943, *DJ* [1943]:320), since their inclusion was proof of their "biological German descent" (status report of September 3, 1942, BA R 22/850, 10), as a means of circumventing the unpredictable difficulties of the "political concept" of "the Pole" (pro-Polish activity) until the German Ethnic Classification List was complete (status report by the chief public prosecutor Kattowitz of March 2, 1942, BA R 22/850).

56. Von Rosen—von Hoevel, "Das Polenstatut" (1942).

57. Quotation in Huber, *Idee und Ordnung des Reiches*, 21. The Twelfth Decree of April 25, 1943, to the Reich Citizenship Law (*RGBl.* I 268) circumvented the definition by the following provision (sec. 3): "Protected citizens of the German Reich are such inhabitants of the German Reich as do not belong to the German nation, whose protected status is or will . . . be recognized by virtue of a general instruction or decision in the individual case." The Decree on Protective Citizenship of the same date (*RGBl.* I 271) contained no definition whatsoever of protected citizenship.

58. Klee, *Die Bürgerliches Recht* (1942).

59. General instruction of February 9, 1942 (BA R 22/20994), and circular of February 16, 1942 (ZS, Versch. 29, 236 ff.).

60. Status reports of May 21, 1941, and April 8, 1942 (p. 2), by the district president of Hohensalza (Inowrocław) (University Library of Posen).

61. Cf. the circular of January 1, 1942, by the Reich governor of Posen (Institute for Western Studies, Poznań, doc. I-166).

62. Report of February 28, 1943, from the district director of Lentschütz, Wartheland (Institute for Western Studies, Poznań).

63. See the report of October 8, 1939, by a *Landrat* of the Wartheland to the head of the civil administration, Posen (State Archive Poznań, CdZ 20, Bl. 20): "It has been reported on numerous occasions that they [the ethnic Germans] have repeatedly been involved in pilfering and looting and that even important landowners have helped themselves not only to livestock but also to items of furniture. There is a noticeable tendency to use the unclear situation to the greatest possible personal advantage. In addition they are often reluctant to manage their property correctly and especially to take care of the harvest. These facts force me to act rigorously against ethnic Germans too."

64. Report of August 31, 1943, by the Security Police, Schroda (Institute for Western Studies, Poznań), with details of individual cases (e.g., denunciation of family members).

65. Report of September 1943 (unsigned) with examples (ibid.).

66. Situation report of August 18, 1940, by the district president of Hohensalza (p. 4), "Wongrawitz [Wągrowiec] district . . . When it was recently pointed out to someone that his application came very late, he answered quite naively: 'But we couldn't know which way the war was going until now.' "

67. See the general instruction of February 9, 1942, by the RFSS/RFK 12/C (Nuremberg doc. NO-4851; *Doc. Occ.* 5:150 ff.). Cf. the memorandum of January 16, 1940, by SS-*Untersturmführer* Dr. Strickner from Minsk (Masovia) (Institute for Western Studies, Poznań, doc. I 5–18).

68. According to A. Greiser, *Der Tag der Freiheit* 1943 (*Der große Rechnschaftsbericht*, December 1943, Institute for Western Studies, Poznań, Sign. III 757778), by October 14, 1943, 400,000

persons had received their registration cards 1 and 2 (German nationality), 60,000 group 3 cards, and 20,000 group 4 (German nationality until revoked).

69. Instruction A 39/40 of March 2, 1940 (Institute for Western Studies, Poznań, doc. I–332).

70. RFSS/RFK instruction 66/1 regarding the implementation of the preliminary version of the German Ethnic Classification List (Institute for Western Studies, Poznań, doc. I–253, reproduced in *Doc. Occ.* 5:145 f.).

71. Broszat, *Nationalsozialistische Polenpolitik*, 126, with examples from Upper Silesia and Danzig–West Prussia.

72. Thus, people of "German stock" who had not applied for inclusion were to be reported to the appropriate Gestapo headquarters, which required that they provide evidence of registration within one week; those who did not provide such evidence were taken into protective custody or sent to a concentration camp (decree of February 16, 1942, by the *Reichsführer*-SS/RKF; *Doc. Occ.* 5:147), "with a view to preventing them from continuing their flirtation with Poland." Poles "of German stock" who had returned or refused to accept their registration cards in order to avoid serving in the Wehrmacht were also arrested (given "protective custody") and asked after two weeks at the earliest whether they wished to undertake their military service. In the event of refusal, they too were sent to concentration camp for an "appropriate period of imprisonment" (RSHA decree of May 12, 1942, Institute for Western Studies, Poznań, doc. I-253, reproduced in *Doc. Occ.* 5:147 f.; also printed in *Vertrauliche Information der Parteikanzlei* no. 51/680 of July 17, 1942; *Verfügungen*, 2:169 ff., 178 f.).

73. As stated in a secret communication dated November 6, 1944, from the head of the SD in Posen to the Reich governor of Posen; the *Reichsführer*-SS had ordered "vigorous measures" in such cases and had already had a person in group 3 of the German Ethnic Classification List executed. If in spite of such examples people on the register refused to accept their registration cards, a "recommendation for special treatment" (i.e., execution) should be submitted to the appropriate quarters (*Kommandeur* of the Security Police IV) for transmission to the RSHA "on instructions of the head of the SIPO and the SD" (State Archive Poznań, *Reichsstatthalter* 1174, Bl. 8).

74. Manuscript (undated) submitted by the NSDAP *Gauleitung* of Wartheland in 1944 (Institute for Western Studies, Poznań).

75. More details in Broszat, *Nationalsozialistische Polenpolitik*, 127.

Part One. Section 2. C. VI. Marriage Law

1. Decree of May 31, 1941, on the Introduction of the Nuremberg Race Laws in the Annexed Eastern Territories and Second Implementing Order (*RGBl.* I 297).

2. Regarding restrictions among members of the Party on permission to marry "aliens" (Poles, Czechs, and Hungarians), see the deputy Führer's instruction of November 23, 1940 (*Verfügungen*, 2:56 f.); with regard to top-ranking officials of the Party, public service, or the Wehrmacht, see the confidential information from the deputy Führer of August 21, 1941 (56 ff.); with regard to SS members, see the deputy Führer's circular of January 13, 1941 (58); regarding members of the Wehrmacht, see the secret OKW decree of January 26, 1942 (58 ff.), and the Party Chancellery circular of November 26, 1942 (60).

3. As noted in the letter of April 14, 1943, from the Reich Ministry of the Interior to the Reich governor in Danzig–West Prussia and the Warthegau (ZS, Posen, film 14, Bl. 610–15).

4. If thereby racial questions were involved, the matter also concerned the Reich Ministry of the Interior (Abt. IV, Ref. I) (Sauer, *Das Reichsjustizministerium* [1939], 58 f.).

5. Transcript of meeting at Reich Interior Ministry on January 21, 1943, on marriage questions in the Annexed Eastern Territories (reproduced in Łuczak, *Dyskryminacja Polaków* [1966], 360 f.)

6. Report of September 19, 1940, from the district president of Hohensalza (Inowrocław), p. 2

(University Library Posen). Cf. also Hitler, quoted in Picker, *Hitlers Tischgespräche* (1951), 247: "Given the Poles' fecundity, the more abortions performed the better. Consistent use of contraceptives must therefore not only be permitted, but even encouraged."

7. Order of the day no. 28, quoted in Łuczak, *Diskriminierung der Polen*, 359 f.

8. AZ I/6, 113/5; State Archive Poznań 1941–43, 11.

9. Polish Civil Code of 1928, sec. 1303.

10. Decree of September 10, 1941, by the Reich governor of the Wartheland to the district presidents (State Archive Poznań, Polizeipräsidium Posen 11, Bl. 6).

11. More in Greifelt, "Festigung Deutschen Volkstums in den Ostgebieten" (1940).

12. Reich Ministry of the Interior instruction of December 8, 1939, I. Ost 1012/39/4107, in which the Reich governors (*Oberpräsidenten*) were ordered to follow the instructions of the RFK insofar as these instructions were not issued on the basis of RKF directives by way of the Supreme Reich Authorities (Greifelt, "Festigung Deutschen Volkstums in den Ostgebieten," 18).

13. Transcript (reproduced in Łuczak, *Diskriminierung der Polen*, 360 f.).

14. Letter of April 14, 1943, to the Reich governors in Danzig–West Prussia and the Wartheland (ZS, Poland, film 1, Bl. 610–15).

15. Nuremberg doc. NO-3592.

16. RGBl. I 271.

17. See the directives of September 22, 1944, by the head of the Central Race and Settlement Office of the SS regarding the Reich Ministry of the Interior/RKF decree of January 10, 1944 (Nuremberg doc. NO-3592), according to which all marriages of Polish "protected nationals," including among themselves, were forbidden pending the proclamation of the implementing provisions.

18. Report of October 20, 1941, from district president Hohensalza (p. 7–8): "Since for the Poles marriage is not a condition for having children, and indeed the Polish Catholic priests not only encourage Polish couples to have a lot of children, but even approach Polish girls to put children into the world (see my comments in my previous race policy report), while this decree [i.e., of September 10, 1941, Az. I/52, 113/3–4, by the Reich governor of Posen on raising the age of consent], may not have the effects its form might lead us to expect, it may be presumed that it will help to prevent the birthrate from increasing further among the Poles." Also, in a report of April 8, 1942 (p. 8), he states: "The number of illegitimate Polish children has constantly increased these past months, so that we have to presume that it is systematic. Under these circumstances I do not believe that reducing the age of consent for Polish men and women will have a practical impact in the long run. We should therefore study what measures to take in order to put an end to the constant rise in the number of illegitimate births (higher maintenance costs for the father of the child, exclusion of unmarried Polish mothers from welfare through the official guardianship)."

19. Note by the SS brigade chief, Danzig-Posen, of October 7, 1944 (Institute for Western Studies, Poznań doc. I-729).

Part One. Section 2. C. VII. Freedom of Movement and Personal Liberty

1. Police decree of April 30, 1942, by the district president of Kattowitz (Katowice) (*Amtsblatt Regierung Kattowitz* of April 30, 1942, Stück 19, no. 129, University Library, Warsaw, Sign. 034693).

2. Decree of July 16, 1943, by the district president (*Amtsblatt* 1943, Stück 31, no. 143, University Library, Warsaw, Sign. 034693).

3. These included Ukrainians, Russians, White Ruthenians, Masurians, Kashubs, etc.

4. Police decree of April 25, 1942 (*Amtsblatt* of April 30, 1942, no. 129, University Library, Warsaw, Sign. 034693).

5. Police decree of February 12, 1940, by the district president of Łódź, printed in the *Litzmannstädter Zeitung* of November 22, 1941.

6. Preliminary result in the *Ostdeutscher Beobachter* no. 15 of November 15, 1939, reproduced in the circular of December 11, 1939, by the district Gendarmerie chief of Posen (Poznań), no. 19 (reproduced in Łuczak, *Diskriminierung der Polen* [1966], 269 f.); ban on new arrivals repeated in a decree of January 1943 by the Reich governor of Posen, printed in the *Hohensalzaer Zeitung* of January 15, 1943.

7. State Archive Poznań 1940–41, 28.

8. Report of February 21, 1941, for the period January 16 to February 15 by the district president of Posen (State Archive Poznań, *Reichsstatthalter* 854, Bl. 5).

9. Instruction of November 11, 1939, by the chief of police of Posen (*Ostdeutscher Beobachter*, November 14, 1939).

10. Instruction by the Reich Railways director, Posen, in *Amtsblatt der Reichsbahndirektion Posen*, Folge 40, of September 6, 1944, 281.

11. Instruction of April 5, 1940, by the Bürgermeister of Plozk (Płock), *Kreisblatt für Płock* of the same date (Institute for Western Studies, Poznań).

12. Police instruction of July 26, 1940, by the Bürgermeister of Plozk, *Kreisblatt für Płock* of July 27, 1940. Instruction of February 10, 1940, by the *Landrat* of Plozk, *Kreisblatt für Płock* of the same date (Institute for Western Studies, Poznań).

13. Report by Dept. 2 of the office of the Reich governor of Posen for the last quarter of 1941 (State Archive Poznań, *Reichsstatthalter* 855, Bl. 24).

14. See the report of July 8, 1941, by the district president of Hohensalza (Inowrocław) (State Archive Poznań, *Reichsstatthalter* 856, Bl. 16), demanding "centralized sanatoriums for tuberculous Poles" and concentration of all Jews in one place, on account of the "epidemic risk" they entail; report by Dept. 2 of the office of the Reich governor of Posen for the last quarter of 1941 (*Reichsstatthalter* 855, Bl. 24), according to which the possibility of isolating 3,000–5,000 sick Poles in the first instance was being investigated. That report indicated that 7,122 Germans and 17,592 Poles suffering from tuberculosis had been reported in the Warthegau as of October 1, 1940.

15. Reich governor of Posen to *Reichsführer*-SS, May 1, 1942 (Nuremberg doc. NO-246).

16. Letter of June 27, 1942, from the *Reichsführer*-SS to the Reich governor of Posen (Nuremberg doc. NO-244).

17. Letter from Dr. Blome to Reich governor Greiser of November 18, 1942 (Nuremberg doc. NO-250).

18. Letter of December 3, 1942, from the *Reichsführer*-SS to Reich governor Greiser (Nuremberg doc. NO-251).

19. See the letter of May 27, 1941, from the *Landrat* of the Schrimm district to the *Amtskommissar* of Schrimm (Institute for Western Studies, Poznań). See also the police decree of August 24, 1940, by the *Landrat* of the Bendzin (Będzin) district, administrative district Kattowitz, on permission to be out at night for Jews, on whom a curfew was imposed between 9 P.M. and 5 A.M. (*Amtsblatt Regierungspräsident Kattowitz* 1940, no. 270, University Library, Warsaw, Sign. 034693).

20. See, for example, the report of February 21, 1941, by the district president of Posen for the period January 16 to February 15 (State Archive Poznań, *Reichsstatthalter* 854, Bl. 5): "As we have been informed, the curfew for Poles has been extended to 11 P.M. because of the presence of the Krone Circus in Hohensalza. This was decided in consultation with the district president. The circus is making this permission known by means of a poster entitled 'Attention, Poles!' The Germans of the town were understandably appalled, whereas the Poles were extremely happy and presume that they will soon be given more freedom." Note from Referat I/50 of the office of the Reich governor (Bl. 18): "The men then went into action and in one evening twenty Poles were arrested for violation of the curfew. In Łódź stronger measures were immediately instituted following the experience in Hohensalza and Posen. (signed) Dr. Coulon."

21. Letter of July 12, 1941, from the head of the Department of Nationhood Policy in the

NS-DAP *Gauleitung*, Wartheland, to the Reich governor (Abt. I/50) (State Archive Poznań, *Reichsstatthalter* 1174, Bl. 17).

22. Letter, March 25, 1943, from RSHA to the inspector of the SIPO and the SD in Posen (State Archive Poznań, *Reichsstatthalter* 1215, Bl. 2): "At present it is not feasible to establish uniform regulations for the use of public transport by Poles. The inspectors of the Security Police and the SD in Breslau (Wrocław) and Danzig (Gdańsk) are also against such an arrangement at this time. . . . The question of uniform regulations for the use of public transport throughout the Annexed Eastern Territories must therefore be deferred to a later date. I therefore request that the internal regulations established for the *Gau* by the Reich governor in the Warthegau on February 1, 1943, be maintained."

23. Reich Ministry of the Interior decree of October 16, 1941, to all Gestapo directorates, district presidents, etc. (Az. Pol. S. IV B 4 b, 940, 41, 37) (Institute for Western Studies, Poznań). The prohibition was explicitly repeated by the local agencies. Police decree of February 12, 1940, by the district presidents of Łódź (*Litzmannstädter Zeitung*, November 22, 1941).

24. Decree of July 6, 1942, by the Reich minister of transport, communicated to the district presidents of the Warthegau by the Reich governor of the Warthegau on July 14, 1942 (State Archive Poznań, *Reichsstatthalter* 1218, Bl. 79).

25. Letter of February 2, 1942, from the *Landrat* of Schrimm to the Bürgermeister of Schrimm (Institute for Western Studies, Poznań).

26. Letter from the district president of Posen to the *Landräte* of the district (State Archive Poznań, Gendarmerie Kreis Schrimm 143, Bl. 95): "As before, I consider it urgent to stop the constant vacationing of Poles as far as possible. For this purpose strict police surveillance must be exercised over all Poles who have come here."

27. Decree of January 14, 1943, by the Reich governor of the Warthegau to the district presidents (reproduced in Łuczak, *Dyskryminacja Polaków*, 251 f.); see also note 34.

28. Instruction of June 15, 1940, by the Reich governor of Posen (Institute for Western Studies, Poznań, doc. I-424). See also directives of January 20, 1944, by the Reich governor of Posen (Az. I/41, 161/1, 5/36) (Institute for Western Studies, Poznań).

29. Police decree of July 1, 1940, by the district president of Łódź; see also the police decree of April 7, 1942, by the district president of Posen (*Amtsblatt der Regierung zu Posen* 1942, no. 5, p. 45, also quoted in Łuczak, *Dyskryminacja Polaków*, 243 ff.), sec. 1: "Former Polish nationals who are ethnic Poles may use public transport only if authorized to do so by the proper police authority. The use of trams does not require authorization."

30. RGBl. I 2133; second Reich Ministry of the Interior decree of November 2, 1939, implementing the Führer's Decree on the Organization and Administration of the Annexed Eastern Territories, sec. 6.

31. Thus the internal regulations for the *Gau* issued on February 1, 1943, by the Reich governor were reiterated several times: They were quoted in the letter from the Reich Security Main Office (RSHA) IV D 2a of March 25, 1943 (State Archive Poznań, *Reichsstatthalter* 1215, Bl. 2). See also the circular of May 20, 1941, from the district president of Posen to the *Landräte* of his district and the chiefs of police of Posen (Gendarmerie Schrimm 104, Bl. 92); also the instruction of March 4, 1941, by the district president of Posen to the subordinate offices (Bl. 8).

32. See the "Addendum to Basic Instruction No. 21/44" of December 14, 1944, by the Reich governor of Wartheland (State Archive Poznań, Gendarmerie Kreis Schrimm 143, Bl. 152; also reproduced in Łuczak, *Dyskryminacja Polaków*, 248 f.):

Regarding Travel! The proceedings before the German People's Court in Kalisch [Kalisz] from December 6 to 8, 1944, with respect to high treason, at which I was present, illustrated the sad fact that it is still possible for Polish agents to make journeys of any length or duration from all stations of the Reich *Gau* of Wartheland without hindrance. The travel permits necessary for the purchase of tickets were not only obtained by means of forged identity cards, but above all they had been quite carelessly issued by state and commercial agencies. I remind all those with responsibility for issuing travel permits of their obligation to exercise the greatest vigilance when doing so. Travel permits issued for long periods are to be considered particularly carefully.

33. *Ostdeutscher Beobachter*, August 4, 1944; see also the police decree of October 20, 1944, on the use of public transport by Poles in the *Reichsgau* Wartheland (Institute for Western Studies, Poznań, doc. I-250).

34. Letter of October 20, 1944, from the Reich governor of Posen to the district presidents, containing directives regarding travel permits for Polish nationals (Az. I/41, 161, 1, 5/36, Institute for Western Studies, Poznań).

35. Letter of January 14, 1943, from the Reich governor of the Warthegau to the district presidents in Posen, Hohensalza, and Łódź (reproduced in Łuczak, *Dyskryminacja Polaków*, 251 f.), in which Greiser states: "A large number of Poles apply for travel permits on grounds that they wish to marry Poles working in the Reich. Since it is never or only rarely possible to verify the facts, and on account of the difficult transport situation of the *Reichsbahn*, no permits whatsoever are to be issued in such cases." See also the circular of April 28, 1942, by the Gestapo in Posen, requiring under the decree of April 21, 1942, that all requests to travel on the part of Poles be refused on account of the situation of the *Reichsbahn* (251).

36. Letter of July 2, 1942, from the Railways director of Posen to the Reich governor of the Warthegau, reproduced in Łuczak, *Dyskryminacja Polaków*, 246 f.; see also the *Amtliche Nachrichten des Polizeipräsidenten Posen* (internal circulation only) of July 29, 1943 (Institute for Western Studies, Poznań, doc. I-639). Police decree of March 1, 1943, by the district president of Posen (*Amtsblatt der Regierung zu Posen*, June 1, 1943).

37. Letter of February 24, 1943, from the *Gau* Chamber of Commerce, Warthegau, to the Reich governor of the Warthegau, reproduced in Łuczak, *Dyskryminacja Polaków*, 252 f.

38. Police decree, October 21, 1940, by Reich governor of Posen on use of the waterways between the Oder and Vistula Rivers (Tgb. no. 5772.7, Institute for Western Studies, Poznań). Police decree of November 21, 1940, by the district president of Posen (*Amtsblatt der Regierung zu Posen* 1940, 65, Institute for Western Studies, Poznań).

39. Instruction of June 15, 1940, by the Reich governor of Posen (Az. I/11, 16575; Institute for Western Studies, Poznań, doc. I-424).

40. See the instruction by Posener Straßenbahn AG, *Ostdeutscher Beobachter* no. 332 of November 29, 1940 (reproduced in Łuczak, *Dyskryminacja Polaków*, 257), forbidding Poles to use trams at the beginning of the working day (7:15 to 8:15 A.M.); Poles were to leave all tramcars at 7:15 A.M.; on certain lines Poles were allowed to use only the trailer, but the measures were considerably tightened later (see instruction of January 21, 1941, by the *Kommandeur* of the Posen Security Police, Az. S 1b 7161/22.1, Institute for Western Studies, Poznań). Poles could no longer use Posen trams between April 1 and 30, 1941, from 6:30 to 7:30 A.M.; travel in the front carriage was forbidden *all* days of the week (including Sunday) after 7:30 A.M.; smoking was forbidden in the cars and on the platforms (instruction of Posener Straßenbahn AG, *Ostdeutscher Beobachter* no. 91 of April 1, 1941; reproduced in Łuczak, *Diskriminierung der Polen*, 256). Later instructions of December 1941 were particularly humiliating, requiring that certain locomotives carry the notice "For Germans only" (*Kommandeur* of the Security Police, Posen, December 8, 1941, Az. S 1a 5140/6.12, Institute for Western Studies, Poznań) and that if all seats were taken in a car, Poles were to make room for Germans (instruction of December 1, 1941, by Posener Straßenbahn AG, reproduced in Łuczak, *Dyskryminacja Polaków*, 257 f.).

41. See the report from a government department, State Archive Poznań, *Reichsstatthalter* 853, p. 2: "The *Landkommissar* of Kosten (with a view to suppressing the illegal exchange of information) has had all bicycles confiscated and has returned them only against passes on which the routes taken each day are marked."

42. Police decree of June 25, 1941 (Institute for Western Studies, Poznań, doc. I-423; *Amtsblatt*

der Regierung zu Posen 1941, pp. 52 f.), with implementing instructions of September 20, 1941, regarding the marking of bicycles, in the communication of October 10, 1941, from the district president of Posen to the chief of police of Posen and the *Landräte* of the district (State Archive Poznań, Gendarmerie Schrimm 104, Bl. 177). Police decree of July 1, 1940, by the district president of Łódź, in which it was specified in addition that the bicycles used should be marked with white stripes (*Litzmannstädter Zeitung* of November 22, 1941). See also order of the day no. 8 of September 22, 1944, by the HSSPF Posen (reproduced in Łuczak, *Diskriminierung der Polen*, 258).

43. See the application of March 12, 1942, by a Pole for permission to use his bicycle to visit his parents, who lived 20 km away, reproduced in Łuczak, *Diskriminierung der Polen*, 254 f.; the *Amtskommissar* and the *Landrat* had no objection, but the Gestapo refused the application on "political grounds in the interest of the state."

44. See the summary propaganda report of September 4, 1943, by the District Propaganda Office, Lissa (Leszno), for August 1943 (State Archive Poznań, NDSAP District Directorate, Lissa, 46, Bl. 29).

45. For example, reference by the Oberbürgermeister of Posen on the severe punishments imposed for misuse of bicycles, *Ostdeutscher Beobachter* of June 6, 1943. Order of the day no. 8 of September 22, 1944, by the HSSPF Warthegau (reproduced in Łuczak, *Diskriminierung der Polen*, 258).

46. Sec. 4 of the police decree of June 25, 1941, by the district president of Posen (*Amtsblatt der Regierung zu Posen* 1941, no. 10, p. 52 f.).

47. See urgent memo of November 18, 1941, from the district president of Posen to the chief of police of Posen and the district *Landräte* (State Archive Poznań, Landratsamt Grätz, 22, 56 f.): "Subject to final regulation of the ownership of the bicycles seized, the Reich governor has agreed to the proposal by the deputy Gauleiter that the bicycles seized from Poles should be made available for the following purposes of public interest: official visits to settler farmers, which is particularly difficult on account of the long distances involved, the care of settlers by the NS women's association, care of the NSV, League of German Girls [Bund Deutscher Mädel] allocation camps, and for those looking after students."

48. In this context see the transcript of a discussion between Heydrich, Goebbels, Göring, and others on November 12, 1938, regarding the continued treatment of Jews after the so-called *Kristallnacht* (ZS, Ordner Versch. 6/1783 ff.; copy); regarding the fate of the Jews of Greater Poland, see Nawrocki, *Hitlerowska Okupacja Wielkopolski* (1966), no. 3, 5 g.

49. Circular of September 21, 1939, from the head of the SIPO and the SD to the head of the task forces of the Security Police, with detailed instructions on the concentration of rural Jews in the towns as part of the "final solution" (ZS, Ordner Versch. 6/1783 ff.; copy).

50. Regarding the catastrophic conditions in the Łódź ghetto (some eight hundred deaths daily as a result of disease and killings by the police), see the report by the Council of Jewish Elders of the Łódź ghetto dated June 16, 1940 (State Archive Poznań, 1940–42, Befehlshaber der Ordnungspolizei, 7). The immediate use of firearms against Jews at the slightest provocation is chronicled in the report of November 15, 1942, by the inspector of the SIPO and the SD (State Archive Poznań, *Reichsstatthalter* 1174, Bl. 131 and 133). Raids were a popular means of extorting every last penny from Jews, or of selecting victims for deportation: see the report for the period February 16 to March 15, 1940, by the district president of Kalisch, who was still responsible for Łódź at that time (State Archive Poznań, *Reichsstatthalter* 1830, Bl. 8), describing an "unplanned evacuation": "Since the Jews often did not obey the ban on leaving the Łódź ghetto, the police undertook an extensive raid in which 2,951 Jews were taken into custody. A number of them were released into the ghetto again after payment of the official police fine of RM 150 [the maximum fine—Author]; (this whole operation brought in a total of RM 71,400) the majority were evacuated." The plundering of the Jews by the ghetto administration and the police is documented in the report of November 15, 1942 (ibid.), by the district president of Kalisch and the letter of December 1940 by the Oberbürgermeister

of Łódź (ZS, Versch. 25 [2], Bl. 480 ff.). For the conditions in the Łódź ghetto, see Wulf, "Lodz: Das letzte Ghetto auf polnischem Boden" (1962).

51. Gestapo Posen to the *Landrat* of Lissa, August 27, 1943, regarding evacuation of the Jews from Lissa (Institute for Western Studies, Poznań).

52. Even before their isolation in the ghetto (and to an even greater extent than in the Reich), the majority of Jews were already physically and emotionally devastated by the absolutely intolerable conditions imposed by the civil administration: the barest requirements for living were not even satisfied, and they had been stripped of every possibility of support. On July 1, 1941, Reich governor Greiser had already ordered that no further correspondence with Jewish and especially American aid committees supporting Jews in need was to be permitted, thus making the aid efforts themselves impossible (Reich governor, Wartheland, to the district presidents of Posen, Hohensalza, and Kalisch, July 1, 1941, I/50, Akten der Geheimen Staatspolizeileitstelle Posen II B-Wi, Institute for Western Studies, Poznań). There was of course no question of support from public funds. Some local authorities ran their own Jewish camps to cover their labor requirements (letter of August 17, 1943, from the *Landratsamt*, Lissa, to the District Construction Office, in which the *Landrat* demanded abolition of the Jewish work camp at Buchendorf maintained by the latter, where the Jews were kept in a "state of starvation" [cf. the camp kitchen note dated April 13, 1943, which indicated that the food costs for April 1943 amounted to less than RM 0.50 per inmate], State Archive Poznań 1943–44, Landrat Kreis Lissa, 19). Further details of the Jews' living conditions in the Warthegau will be found in von Hohenstein, *Wartheländisches Tagebuch* (1963); under the administrative decree issued by the *Reichsführer*-SS on August 2, 1943, quoted in the letter of August 17 from the *Landratsamt* of Lissa to the District Construction Office of Lissa (State Archive Poznań 1943–44, Landrat Kreis Lissa, 19), all Jews who were still living outside the ghetto were to be sent there by August 1943 at the latest.

53. Walk, *Als Jude in Breslau* (1975), entry of August 15, 1941, 50.

54. Cf. Hitler's *Reichstag* speech of October 6, 1939, according to which "ethnic resettlement" (*völkische Umsiedlung*) would help bring about a new order in Europe, "so that at the end of this development, better borders would result than those existing at present"; Führer's decree of October 7, 1939, which appointed Himmler to the position of *Reichskommissar* for the Strengthening of German Nationhood (RKF).

55. The HSSPF of Posen, Danzig, Königsberg, and Breslau (later Kattowitz) were named as delegates of the RKF (second Reich Ministry of the Interior decree of November 2, 1939, implementing the Führer's Decree on the Organization and Administration of the Eastern Territories, sec. 2, par. 1, subpar. 2, RGBl. I 2133). There was still a lack of clarity, however, with regard to the powers of the RFSS/RFK over the government authorities. With a view to "establishing a clear order of command," it was therefore established by way of the Reich Ministry of the Interior decree of December 8, 1939, that the RKF had authority over the Reich governor in the Eastern Territories so long as the orders were not issued by the Supreme Reich Authorities (according to the RKF directives). A very short time later, however, an instruction issued on December 19, 1939, by the *Reichsführer*-SS/RKF (Institute for Western Studies, Poznań, doc. I-373) established that only the HSSPF in Danzig–West Prussia and Posen were delegates *ipso jure* of the RKF, whereas the HSSPF of Königsberg, Breslau (later Kattowitz), and Kraków were delegates of the RKF on the strength of a special order of the RFSS/RFK. See also the letter (undated) from the Reich governor of Posen to the RKF, quoted in *Doc. Occ.* 5:90 n. 16 (further details in Greifelt, "Festigung deutschen Volkstums in den Ostgebieten" [1940]).

56. Regarding the resettlement of Poles in the General Government, coordinated by the relevant HSSPF and the HSSPF Kraków, see the letter of May 21, 1940, from the inspector of the SIPO and the SD of Posen (Danzig) to the Reich governor in the Warthegau, regarding the institution of a "resettlement center" in Posen "to implement evacuation of foreigners in the Warthegau"; also the

confidential communications of May 5, 7, and 27 and June 6, 10, 14, and 24, 1940 (Institute for West-ern Studies, Poznań); notification, February 24, 1940, by the *Kommandeur* of the Security Police, Posen, setting out principles for the evacuation (Institute for Western Studies, Poznań, doc. I-419). Letter of January 17, 1940, from the chief of police of Posen (Institute for Western Studies, Poznań); instruction of January 22, 1940, from the HSSPF Posen to the chief of police of Posen (Institute for Western Studies, Poznań, doc. I-419). Letter of November 30, 1942, from the R-sta, Posen, to the district president of the Warthegau (State Archive Poznań, R-sta 1174, Bl. 106); for more informa-tion on the "resettlement," see Datner, Gumbowski, and Leszczyński, "Wysiedlanie ludności pol-skiej z żiem polskich wcielonych do Rzeszy" (1960); Stach, "Polenreservate im Warthegau" (1967); and the documents printed in the *Bulletin of the Main Commission Warsaw*, vol. 21, 11 ff.; also the sources given in Łuczak, *Diskriminierung der Polen*, 154 ff.; report on organizing the transport of Poles (ZS, Poland, film 60, Bl. 418 ff.); notice by the Resettlement Center, Łódź, on the apprehen-sion of persons to be evacuated for actions on May 15 and 17, 1940 (Institute for Western Studies, Poznań); see also RSHA directives IV B 4 a (Eichmann) on "the technical execution of the evacua-tion of Jews to the East," dated June 4, 1942 (ZS, Polen 243, Bl. 181–87, 257–73). HSSPF decree of November 24, 1939 (ZS, Polen, film 62, Bl. 0544 f.); report of January 26, 1940, by the HSSPF Posen (first short-term plan) (Institute for Western Studies, Poznań, doc. I-198; also in ZS, Poland, film 14, 634 ff.); closing report of December 31, 1942, by the Resettlement Center on the work of the center under the third extended short-term plan (ZS, Poland, film 57/221 ff.). Closing report of December 31, 1943, on the work of the Resettlement Center in the Wartheland and the General Government for 1943 (IfZ, MA-708/2, 712). Statement under oath of September 30, 1947, by the former head of the Resettlement Center, Łódź, Alois Krumey (Nuremberg doc. NO-5364).

Generally the Poles feared that they would suffer the same fate as the Jews, since despite all efforts to maintain secrecy, rumors were rife of mass executions in the East (SD report, Posen, of November 16, 1942, in *Meldungen des SD aus dem Reichsgau Wartheland*, November 8, 1942 [Insti-tute for Western Studies, Poznań]). See the reports for the period January 16 to February 15, 1941, by the district president of Posen (State Archive Poznań, R-sta 854, Bl. 33–34) regarding the eco-nomic consequences of the resettlement and for December 1 to 15, 1939 (R-sta 853, Bl. 3 f.). For the "settlement" of Germans in the "liberated" areas, see Sobczak, *Hitlerowskie przedsiedlenia Ludności niemieckiej w dobie II wojny s'wiatowej* (1966).

57. Cf. the basic instructions no. 1/II of October 30, 1939, by the RFSS/RFK (ZS, Poland, film 62, Bl. 0546) and the implementing provisions of November 12, 1939, by the HSSPF Posen (Bl. 0547–0551); RSHA directives IV B 4 a (Eichmann) and secret circular of the HSSPF Posen dated November 12, 1939 (ZS, Poland, 243, Bl. 181–87, 257–73), according to which all Jews, "the whole Polish intelligentsia or Poles whose nationalistic attitude *might* make them a danger to the consoli-dation of German nationhood" [my emphasis], and "criminals" were to be deported from the War-theland. A further circular of November 16, 1939, extended this to include members of politically and economically important professions, above all "teachers, important landowners, and factory owners," but also craftsmen and small shopkeepers, and all people of asocial appearance(!) (repro-duced in Łuczak, *Diskriminierung der Polen*, 154 ff.); see also report, December 23, 1939, district president of Posen for the period December 1 to 15 (State Archive Poznań, R-sta 853, Bl. 26). Re-garding the administrative confusion and duplication of powers in the settlements, see the letter of November 30, 1942, from the R-sta Posen to the district president (R-sta 1174, Bl. 106). According to a decree dated November 29, 1939, by the RFSS/RFK, anybody returning from the General Govern-ment was to be "immediately shot under martial law" (report of January 17, 1940, by the district president of Posen, Institute for Western Studies, Poznań, doc. I-419); in this respect see also the instruction dated October 30, 1940, by the Gendarmerie chief, Posen (reproduced in Łuczak, *Dys-kryminacja Polaków*, 166).

With regard to the extent of the resettlement, see the secret circular of November 12, 1939, from the HSSPF Posen to the governor general of Poland; report by the HSSPF Posen dated January 26, 1940 (ZS, Poland, film 62, Bl. 0547–0551); report of December 18, 1939, from the HSSPF Posen to the RSHA (film 14/634 ff.). Closing report of the Resettlement Center, Posen, on the evacuations in the framework of the transfer of Germans from Wolhynia-Galicia and Cholm ("second short-term plan") in the *Reichsgau* Wartheland between December 1, 1939, and January 20, 1941 (film 14, Bl. 650 ff.); closing report on the evacuations in the framework of the transfer of Germans from Bessarabia ("third short-term plan") in the *Reichsgau* Wartheland between January 20, 1941, and January 20, 1942 (IfZ, MA-708/2, 663–68; also ZS, Poland, film 62, Bl. 663); further see the closing report under the third extended short-term plan of December 31, 1942 (IfZ, MA708/2, Bl. 701–5; also ZS, Poland, film 57, Bl. 221 ff.); closing report for 1943 (film 14, Bl. 701 ff.; and IfZ, MA708/2, Bl. 701–5); letter of January 6, 1941, from the head of the SIPO and the SD/Resettlement Center, Posen, to the RSHA (Eichmann) (ZS, Versch. 84/398); regarding the "catastrophic consequences" of the resettlement, see the letter of June 25, 1940, from the governor general to the RMuChdRkzlei (Nuremberg doc. NG-1627, 2); urgent memorandum of March 1940 from the president of the Council of Ministers for Defense of the Reich and the head of the Four Year Plan (Hauptkommission Warschau, Archiv Regierung des GG, Hauptabteilung Innere Verwaltung, II/374). Report by Dr. Siebert, "Zur Polenpolitik im GG," May 4, 1959, BA Ostdok. 1 General Government 1 b/3.

Part One. Section 2. C. VIII. Restrictions on Communication Information Exchange and the Confiscation of Cultural Goods

1. Decree by the head of the Civil Administration (CdZ) Kattowitz (Katowice) (*VOBl. Militärbefehlshaber Oberschlesien* 39, no. 16). Secret directives from the head of the Civil Administration Danzig (Gdań sk)—West Prussia (Institute for Western Studies, Poznań, doc. I-107; reproduced in *Doc. Occ.* 5:65 n. 30). However, no central decree on seizures was issued under the terms of the directives. Seizures did occur at the local level; cf. letter of October 18, 1939, from the *Stadtkommissar* Gnesen (Gniezno) to the head of the Civil Administration Posen (State Archive Poznań, CdZ 43).

2. *VOBl. Posen* 39, 21 (in *Doc. Occ.* 5:65); see also the letter of October 12, 1939, from the head of the Civil Administration Posen (CdZ) to the police president of Posen (State Archive Poznań, CdZ 43, 6); cf. protocol of a meeting at Armeeoberkommando 8 on September 22, 1939, in Posen: "Since it has been established that English radio stations have considerably increased their anti-German propaganda, all radio receivers should be confiscated and recalled" (State Archive Poznań, CdZ 47, 23); cf. also the corresponding pronouncements of October 7 and 31, 1939, in Polish by the Bürgermeister of Klodawa (Kolo-Warthbrücken district) (Kreisarchiv [district archive] Konin, Akten Stadt Klodawa 21). The head of the civil administration was established until October 12, 1939, under Wehrmacht rule. After that date the territories were annexed formally and a Reich governor established.

3. Letter of September 27, 1939, from the *Landrat* of Posen to the Schenckendorff group in Posen (State Archive Poznań, CdZ 43, 1): "I had had radio sets seized from Poles and Jews even before the order was received." See also the proclamation from the police president of Posen (undated) to the population of the town of Posen (State Archive Poznań, CDZ 43, 2).

4. Letter of October 18, 1939, from the *Stadtkommissar* Gnesen to the head of the civil administration (CdZ) (State Archive Poznań, CdZ 43, 15).

5. Quoted in a letter of October 7, 1939, from the *Landrat* of Ostrowo (Ostrów Wielkopolski) to the head of the Civil Administration Posen (CdZ) (ibid.):

Regarding radio instruction of October 2. Shortly after the takeover by the civil administration, the radio sets were confiscated by the head of the civil administration and delivered to A.O.K. [*Armeeoberkommando*] 8. After the operation the head of the civil administration ordered them to be released again, since in the meantime all the Polish radio stations were in

German hands, and it appeared desirable from now on to influence the Polish population in favor of the German viewpoint via the air waves. As a result the majority of the radio sets have been returned to their owners. To confiscate them once again in the Ostrowo district would mean another extremely time-consuming operation for the Bürgermeister and the municipal authorities and might perhaps give the impression among the Polish population that the German authorities were acting haphazardly. I therefore request you to agree tacitly that no further seizures will be undertaken.

6. State Archive Poznań, BdO 2; the Führer had instructed "that all radio sets are to be taken in from the Polish population . . . as rapidly as possible."

7. Letter of October 12, 1939, from the head of the civil administration to all *Landräte* and the police president of Posen, according to which the Reich Propaganda Office should receive two thousand sets from the Posen stock for distribution (State Archive Poznań, Cdz 43, Bl. 6).

8. Letter of April 11, 1942, from the Reich Propaganda Office, Posen, to all state and Party agencies (State Archive Poznań, R-sta 1174, Bl. 75). Cf. the examples given in *Doc. Occ.* 5:352, 385 f. Decree of September 1, 1939, on Exceptional Radio Measures; in this context see the documentation, "Goebbels außerordentliche Rundfunkmaßnahmen 1939–1945," *VjhZ* no. 4 (1963): 418 ff.

9. Cf. the announcement of September 21, 1939, by the *Landrat* of Rawitsch (Rawicz) (Warthegau), reproduced in Łuczak, *Diskriminierung der Polen* (1966), 260 f. In the district of Plozk (Płock) (administrative district Zichenau), the *Landrat* had in 1940 already set up separate service hours at post offices for Poles and Jews (see the instructions of February 10, 1940, *Kreisblatt Płock* of that date, Institute for Western Studies, Poznań).

10. Decree of April 2, 1943, by the Reich governor of Wartheland, reproduced in Łuczak, *Dyskryminacja Polaków*, 264 f.

11. Ibid., 265 f.; but order of the day no. 95 of July 23, 1943, speaks of "an extremely urgent reason" (e.g., a death or very severe disease) (State Archive Poznań, BdO 6, 11).

12. Letter of August 6, 1943, from the inspector of the SIPO and the SD to the Reich governor, Wartheland, where he nevertheless demands strict surveillance measures for Polish doctors (installation of the telephone line by the police post; daily journal to be kept) (State Archive Poznań, Reichsstatthalter 1174, Bl. 22), and the answer from the Reich governor, Referat I/50, dated August 26, 1943, according to which such surveillance measures would not be very effective (Bl. 24).

13. Administrative decree of March 5, 1943, from the Reich governor in the Warthegau, reproduced in Łuczak, *Dyskryminacja Polaków*, 267.

14. Administrative decree of May 6, 1943, from the Reich governor in the Warthegau (Az. GS I/40, 160/1, 94; Institute for Western Studies, Poznań).

15. Administrative decree of August 6, 1943, from the Reich governor in the Warthegau, reproduced in Łuczak, *Dyskryminacja Polaków*, 266.

16. Letter of July 14, 1942, from the local SD office, Schrimm, to the Gendarmerie Schrimm (with reference to an instruction by the head of the *Leitabschnitt* Posen), with the request to contact the police in order to intercept Polish correspondence and to hand over any letters found during house searches to the SD (State Archive Poznań).

17. Nuremberg doc. NO-1614.

18. See, for example, instruction no. 51 of September 11, 1939, by the Reich Rubber Office regarding delivery and confiscation of tires (*Amtsblatt der Regierung zu Posen* 1940, 30 f.).

19. Letter of November 25, 1941, from the district president of Posen to the *Gau* Chamber of Commerce of Posen; the district president asked the district presidents of Hohensalza (Inowrocław) and Łódź to issue identical instructions (State Archive Poznań, Gendarmerie Kreis Schrimm 143, Bl. 50).

20. Police decree of December 6, 1941 (*Verordnungsblatt des R-sta Warthegau* no. 43 of December 19, 1941, pp. 608–9; reproduced in Łuczak, *Dyskryminacja Polaków*, 209 ff.). In addition to

the usual fine of RM 150 or three weeks' detention, violations carried the penalty of forced labor for Poles; see also the letter of November 25, 1941, from the district president of Posen to the *Gau* Chamber of Commerce of Posen (State Archive Poznań, Gendarmerie Kreis Schrimm 143, Bl. 50).

21. Letter of June 28, 1941, from the district president of Posen to the *Landräte* of the district and the police president of Posen, which refers to a police decree published in the *Ostdeutscher Beobachter* and instructs its implementation (State Archive Poznań, Gendarmerie Kreis Schrimm 143, Bl. 43). It is not clear whether the police decree was issued by the supreme SS and police chief or the district president of Posen. The decree is perhaps identical with that of July 5, 1941, issued by the district president of Posen on seizure and surrender of cameras and binoculars in Polish hands (Institute for Western Studies, Poznań). See also the letter of August 13, 1941, from the *Landrat* Grätz (Graz) to the district president of Posen (State Archive Poznań, Landratsamt Grätz 22, Bl. 49; also reproduced in Łuczak, *Grabież polskiego mienia* [1969], 31 f.): "Sixty-three cameras and binoculars have been surrendered by Poles or confiscated in this district."

22. Police decree of January 21, 1942, by the district president of Kattowitz (*Amtsblatt des Regierungspräsidenten Kattowitz* of January 31, 1942, Stück 5, University Library, Warsaw, Sign. 034693).

23. Confidential radio message from the district president of Łódź to all police offices, January 5, 1942 (Az. P 1, 120/11/1; State Archive Poznań, Landratsamt Kempen 16, Bl. 22–23).

Part One. Section 2. IX. Food Supply

1. The police decree (*Amtsblatt Regierung Kattowitz* 1940, University Library, Warsaw, Sign. 034693) was issued "to the decree of October 24, 1939, by the head of the civil administration, Kattowitz [Katowice], on dealing with police violence" (*Verordnungsblatt* no. 21, October 24, 1939).

2. *Amtsblatt Regierung Kattowitz* 1943, Stück 1, Ausgabe B, University Library, Warsaw, Sign. 034693.

3. Notification by the Chamber of Commerce and Industry of Posen (Poznań) dated February 20, 1940, published in the *Ostdeutscher Beobachter*, March 4, 1940 (reproduced in the directives of September 11, 1940, by the Security Police, Posen, on shopping hours for Poles, Institute for Western Studies, Poznań, doc. I-640, Bl. 2), according to which Germans were permitted to shop throughout the day, including the morning hours between 8:00 and 12:00, whereas Poles were restricted to the afternoon. A police decree by the Oberbürgermeister and the police president of Posen dated November 8, 1940, was appended to the notification (Bl. 5, also in *Amtsblatt der Regierung zu Posen* 1940, no. 7, 64, Institute for Western Studies, Poznań, doc. I-421). The decree applied to the food shops designated as German businesses and to all market stalls, whoever owned them. Only Germans identifying themselves as such were permitted to purchase food at the latter between 6:00 and 9:30 A.M. from April to September, inclusive, and between 7:00 and 10:00 A.M. from October to January. Notification of March 15, 1940, by the Oberbürgermeister of Posen, contained in the directives of September 11, 1940, by the Security Police, Posen (Institute for Western Studies, Poznań, doc. I-640, Bl. 2), forbidding sales to "aliens" between 6:30 and 10:00 A.M. from April to September, inclusive, and between 7:00 and 11:00 A.M. from October to March. Order of the day no. 43 of July 25, 1940, by the BdO, Posen, calling for strict surveillance of shopping hours on account of "repeated complaints" (State Archive Poznań, Befehlshaber der Ordnungspolizei 3).

4. See the decree of November 8, 1940, sec. 2, by the Oberbürgermeister of Posen (Institute for Western Studies, Poznań, doc. I-640, Bl. 5; also in *Amtsblatt der Regierung zu Posen* 1940, no. 7, 64, Institute for Western Studies, Poznań, doc. I-421): "It is forbidden to hold back goods during the hours reserved for the German population; goods in short supply delivered in the afternoon may not be offered for sale before the following morning."

5. Under sec. 7 fines *and* police custody were threatened in the event of violations for everyone

concerned (the shop owner and assistants as well as the shopper) (ibid.). See directives of November 18, 1940, by the Security Police, Posen, attached to the police decree of November 8, 1940 (point 5b) (Institute for Western Studies, Poznań, doc. I-640, Bl. 3).

6. Instruction of November 12, 1940, by the police president of Posen; quoted in the directives of November 18, 1940, by the Security Police, Posen, (Institute for Western Studies, Poznań, doc. I-640, Bl. 3, points 3, 4b); in areas with a high proportion of Poles in the population, shopping was also permitted in the morning; only where German customers filled the shop all morning was it required to follow the police decree strictly.

7. A police decree dated July 29, 1942, by the Landrat of Kempen (administrative district Łódź) may be mentioned here (Amtsblatt des Regierungspräsidenten Litzmannstadt 1942, no. 15, Ausgabe A, University Library, Warsaw, Sign. 011368); it extended the limitations for Poles from German businesses to all businesses and compressed the shopping hours allotted to them to 10:30–12:00 A.M. and 3:30–5:00 p.m.; the rest of the time was reserved for Germans. In the weekly street markets and hairdressers' shops, Polish customers were to be served only after 10:00 A.M. The decree also contained the same principles as that of November 8, 1940, from the police president of Posen (Institute for Western Studies, Poznań, doc. I-640, Bl. 3) (preferential treatment for Germans, etc.).

8. Reproduced in Łuczak, Diskriminierung der Polen (1966), 281.

9. Further details in ibid., 204 f., 271 ff., 372 ff.

10. Report of February 18, 1941, by the district president of Hohensalza (Inowrocław) (p. 7) (University Library of Posen).

11. Report of October 1940 by the district president of Hohensalza (p. 1) (University Library of Posen).

12. Reports of October 1940 by the district president of Hohensalza (pp. 50–51) and February 18, 1941 (University Library of Posen).

13. Report of July 30, 1941, by the R-sta Posen, Referat I/50, to the R-sta Posen (Institute for Western Studies, Poznań, doc. I-145) (Poles obtained only working clothes with their clothing coupons). Letter dated March 6, 1943, from the Landrat to the Bürgermeister—local police authority—of Schrimm (State Archive Poznań, Gendarmerie Kreis Schrimm 143, p. 90). Letter from the District Propaganda Office, Lissa (Leszno), to the Gau Propaganda Office, Posen—summary propaganda report for the month of January 1944 (State Archive Poznań, NSDAP-Kreisleitung Lissa, 46, Bl. 21): "Many Polish women have been seen wearing brand new boots of late. Since I have heard similar reports from other districts, it is to be recommended that stricter surveillance be exercised over the shoemakers. (signed) Kolberg, district head of propaganda." Letter from the R-sta, Posen, Abt. V/LWA, to Abt. I/50 (State Archive Poznań, R-sta 1174, Bl. 251): "The regulation that Poles of the kreisfreie towns be supplied with German Reich soap coupons is now over two years old. It was made on hygienic grounds, since Germans and Poles lived in close proximity. In this respect I note merely that male Poles are allowed only one piece of shaving soap instead of two pieces per allocation period." Instruction dated April 1, 1942, by the Reich Chamber of Pharmacists and the Warthegau Chamber of Pharmacists (reproduced in Łuczak, Dyskryminacja Polaków, 279 f.): the sale of drugs to Poles was forbidden between 5:00 and 6:00 P.M., except in emergency cases and to Polish physicians and midwives.

14. Report of July 30, 1941 (Institute for Western Studies, Poznań, doc. I-145).

15. Report of May 21, 1941 (p. 30), by the district president of Hohensalza, demanding adequate supplies for working Poles, especially bread, in the interests of production (University Library of Posen).

16. Report of 30 July 1941; Polish children were said to be treated too well, since those under six years received 1,000 g of white bread or 750 g of wheat flour every four weeks. Report of March 18, 1941 (p. 4), by the district president of Hohensalza, which, responding to a report by the Oberbürgermeister of Leslau states, "The milk supply regulation brought with it an undesirable and in-

tolerable boost to their [the Poles'] confidence. The fact that Polish children receive half a liter of milk up to the age of six years, while Germans [adults—Author] receive only skim milk, brings about a situation in which German housewives are supplied with skim milk while the Poles next to them get large jugs of whole milk, all the while laughing up their sleeves. In my opinion this regulation should be revised posthaste on political grounds" (both reports in Institute for Western Studies, Poznań, doc. I-145).

17. Report of February 18, 1941, by the district president of Hohensalza, p. 7 (University Library of Posen). This report concerns the sale of wheat to Poles. For the sale of cakes and other such items, see the decree in *Verordnungsblatt R-sta Wartheland* no. 40, November 26, 1941, 583 (reproduced in Łuczak, *Dyskryminacja Polaków*, 227 f.); this decree is very probably the result of the objection contained in the report of July 30, 1941, mentioned above, and a complaint by the district president of Posen of October 8, 1941 (State Archive Poznań, R-sta, 835, 132), that "instead of buying white bread for their children, the Poles use these markets to obtain cakes and tarts. Given the limited supply of these goods, Germans often go without."

18. Instruction by the *Land* Food Office of the R-sta Wartheland Posen of August 9, 1941 (reproduced in Łuczak, *Dyskryminacja Polaków*, 276 f.), and of March 16, 1942 (278 f.). Notification of November 8, 1940, by the Oberbürgermeister of Posen (Dr. Gerhard Scheffler) (Main Commission Warsaw, Plakatsammlung XIV, 103t/3c; photocopy): "As of this time fruit will be given only to German children and adolescents up to 18 years."

19. Instruction of March 16, 1942, by the *Land* Food Office, Posen; reproduced in Łuczak, *Dyskryminacja Polaków*, 278 f.

20. Instruction of May 1, 1942, by the *Landrat* of Kempen (reproduced in ibid., 280) forbidding Poles to buy fish and crustaceans.

21. Circular of August 29, 1941, from the district president of Posen regarding the specific case of a mailing of butter, on the basis of which an action was initiated against the Polish recipient on a charge of violation of the decree on consumption regulations of April 6, 1940 (State Archive Poznań, Gendarmerie Schrimm 104, Bl. 155).

22. Walk, *Als Jude in Breslau* (1975), entry of April 1, 1941, 21.

23. Report of October 1940 by the district president of Hohensalza (University Library, Warsaw); export controls also existed in Danzig (Gdań sk)—West Prussia (report of May 21, 1941, by the district president of Hohensalza, p. 30, ibid.). Report of October 1940 by the district president of Hohensalza (p. 50 f., ibid.). Report of 18 September 1940 by the district president of Hohensalza (p. 6, ibid.), according to which the prices for everyday goods were much higher than in the Altreich. Rice, semolina, barley, and legumes were not to be had for weeks, to say nothing of fruit. The food shortage was attributed to massive purchases by the Wehrmacht.

24. *Meldungen aus dem Reich*, November 26, 1942, BA R 58/176 (wheat harvest almost totally "confiscated" by the Germans).

25. See report no. 8 by the economic directorate of the office of the Reich governor of Posen to the head of the Four Year Plan, dated January 13, 1942 (State Archive Poznań, R-sta 855, 51–52): "It was discovered that half of the Polish saleswomen had up to ten clothing cards that did not belong to them. A large number of loose coupons from Polish and German cards as well as German and Polish meat and fat coupons were also found. Foods such as sausage, butter, flour, and apples were also taken from the Polish saleswomen; they claimed to have received them for good service to German and Polish customers." See also the circular of December 17, 1941, from the district president of Posen (State Archive Poznań, Gendarmerie Kreis Schrimm 143, Bl. 52); activity report for July 1941 by the *Kreisleitung* of Hohensalza *Land* (State Archive Poznań, NSDAP Gauleitung Wartheland 14, Bl. 19): "Regarding the decree on the purchase of specific goods by Poles, such as bakery goods and fruit: though the decree is correct, it is rendered illusory by the behavior of the police. . . . For Poles are still being abundantly served by the Polish sales staff. The German owner of

the shop is often not in a position to supervise these things. The population is rightly asking itself why [such] decrees are published at all, if they are not rigorously implemented" (*Meldungen aus dem Reich*, October 26, 1942, BA R 58/176). Extortionate prices were charged on the black market: for example, RM 50 for 1 kg of potatoes; RM 5 for 1 kg of bread; RM 12 for 1 kg of flour; RM 12 for 1 kg of peas; RM 2 for 1 liter of milk; RM 20–24 for 15 eggs; RM 26 for 1 kg of sausage; RM 70 for 1 kg of bacon; for details, see order of the day no. 77 of May 28, 1942, by the BdO Posen (State Archive Poznań, BdO 5, p. 19) and the reports by the Security Police of Rawitsch (Rawicz) dated November 7 and 21, 1939 (State Archive Poznań, Schutzpolizei 16, Bl. 49, 64), on searches of houses and apartment houses and seizure of hoarded food and other goods.

26. This is reflected again in the reports by the district president of Hohensalza; see reports of February 18, 1941 (p. 7), and October 20, 1941 (p. 2) (University Library of Warsaw).

Part One. Section 3. Introduction. I. Immediate Aims

1. Hitler in a discussion with Wilhelm Keitel on October 17, 1939 (reproduced in *Doc. Occ.* 6:27 ff., 30); cf. also Hitler's discussion with Hans Frank and Baldur von Schirach on October 2, 1940 (minutes, ZS, Ordner 325 a, G.J. no. 83, copy).

2. Discussion between Hitler and Keitel on October 7, 1939 (*Doc. Occ.* 6:27 ff., 30); for more details see Jan T. Gross, *Polish Society under German Occupation* (1979), 43 ff., 47 ff.

3. See comments by Frank at a meeting on December 14, 1942 ("Diensttagebuch 1942," III, 482 ff., 484; ZS, Versch. 104, 484 ff., copy), in which he complains of contradictory directions in the Polish policy: "One could say that all Poles engaged in work here should be kept, but those who are not should be exterminated. . . . The extermination of millions of human beings [, however, is] bound up with certain conditions we cannot currently fulfill." Frank wanted to "extract what can still be extracted"; cf. also Frank's comments to leading Party members in the General Government on February 11, 1944:

It will be not help if I kill 100,000 Poles; this is of no use to the Führer. It will only be of use if I put 100,000 Poles to work. . . . It should not be regarded as a sign of softness toward the Poles if one tries to ensure that they remain capable of working and willing to work. It should not be regarded as a sign of weakness if we do all that without recourse to the utmost brutality. I am not so stupid that I don't know that someone who has a revolver can shoot someone else. . . . We must get to a point where 14 million Poles are working for Germany. . . . That, and that alone, is now the order of the day.

The policy of "keeping everyone happy" . . . with all the means at our disposal . . . has certain consequences that we National Socialists do not find to our liking at present. We should not apply the principles that are valid for Posen [Poznań], Danzig [Gdańsk], and Upper Silesia to our own area. The Führer has said expressly that the first task is to return the territories incorporated into the Reich to German nationhood, but that the General Government is the official Reich protectorate of Polish nationhood. This must be repeated, over and over again, especially in Party circles, because one frequently encounters the misapprehension that the General Government is a sort of extension of Warthegau. [There is an] enormous difference between the two. . . . In Warthegau the Pole is a subject, who in due course will be deported or removed in some other fashion. . . . We must ensure that the Poles and other non-Germans are kept quiet. You know as well as I how the security situation develops when compulsory settlement such as that in Lublin is undertaken. ("Diensttagebuch 1944," I, February 11, 1944, 304 ff.; BA R 52 II/213)

Cf. also a speech by Reich Minister of Justice Franz Gürtner, December 15, 1940, in Kraków ("Diensttagebuch 1940," III, 1132 ff.; BA R 52 II/179).

4. Accordingly, there were plans to issue food ration cards only to those Poles who worked in the service of Germans; they would be withheld from all other Poles, along with accommodation, power, and heating. As far as is known, it was the SS and police leader (SSPF) of Lublin who first put forward this suggestion at a police conference on June 18, 1942. Frank proposed to this same meeting that from September 1, 1942, onward, ration cards and dwellings would be provided only to Poles who could produce an endorsement from an agency of the German authorities. This would also help track down work-shy elements ("Diensttagebuch 1942," III 325 ff., 329 ff.; quoted from copy, IfZ). The same proposal was put forward by *Generalleutnant* Max Schindler of the Wehrmacht's armaments inspectorate on the grounds that workers were constantly leaving their places of work and engaging in stockpiling. Frank countered that such regulations had already been tried in certain districts and an extension to the rest of the General Government was planned (367 f.).

5. "Diensttagebuch," November 21, 1941, 1075 f. (quoted from copy in IfZ, Sign. FB-105).

6. "Diensttagebuch," February 11, 1944, BA R 52 II/213; for a detailed account of the wholly negative policy of the Nazis in the General Government, see Gross, *Polish Society under German Occupation*, 47 ff.

7. "Diensttagebuch," ed. Präg and Jacobmeyer, introduction, 9.

8. Nuremberg doc., EC-344. Though it is true that Frank later spoke out against the use of the term *colony* to refer to the General Government, saying it was neither a colony nor an occupied territory (winding up speech at an economic conference held on August 3, 1943; "Diensttagebuch 1943," III, 703 ff.; 707 f.), this statement was something of a tactical ploy.

9. "Diensttagebuch 1939," I, 10; quoted from copy in IfZ.

10. "Diensttagebuch 1940" I, 280 ff., BA R 52 II/176.

11. Report by SS-*Sturmbannführer* Dr. Herbert Strickner, "The Polish Policy to Date and Proposals for Its Relaxation or Reorientation," October 19, 1944, which was requested by the chief of the Security Police and the SD on October 16, 1944 (IfZ, MA-641, 2094 ff.).

12. Reproduced in *Dokumente der deutschen Politik 1942–1944*, vol. 7, II, 673; in this sense see also Governor General H. Frank, March 15, 1940, in Kattowitz (Katowice), quoted from F. Klein, "Zur Stellung des Generalgouvernements" (1941), 234; for more details, cf. H. Frank speaking to Party leaders from the General Government on February 11 1944 ("Diensttagebuch 1944," I, February 11, 1944, BA R 52/213).

13. Report of July 1, 1940, Bd. I (BA R 52 II/247).

14. Frank in a speech April 9, 1940 ("Diensttagebuch 1940," I, 280 ff.; BA R 52 II/170); also, "It is self-evident that we must compare this judiciary for the natives of Poland to that of native peoples in other parts of the world" ("Diensttagebuch," May 25, 1940, 525–28; BA R 52 II/177; also reproduced in *Doc. Occ.* 6:108 n).

15. Thus *Ministerialdirigent* Emmerich, head of the (Central) Department of Economics in the General Government, stated at a meeting on 12 July 1940: "If one imagined that Poland is, so to speak, a colony, then one would arrive at a trade balance that would resemble that of a colonial structure. In the business that is Poland we must start by investing something" ("Diensttagebuch 1940," III, 657; BA R 52 II/178).

16. This is apparent from a telegram sent on August 19, 1941, by the Department of Internal Administration of the General Government to the president of the department, Eberhard Westerkamp, at that time in Berlin, in which State Secretary Joseph Bühler grants permission to hold a lecture and the setting of a date is requested (Main Commission Warsaw, Archive, Regierung des GG, HA Innere Verwaltung II/45); the lecture was probably held in early or mid-October 1941.

17. Speech in Kraków on December 15, 1940, in which it was also said: "That which has been debated for years, for a lifetime even, is here being put into practice" ("Diensttagebuch 1940," IV, 1132 ff., BA R 52 II/179).

18. Frank at a working conference of political leaders responsible for the question of the

General Government within the NSDAP on December 14, 1942 ("Diensttagebuch 1942," 1311; quoted from copy in IfZ). Conversation between Frank and officials of the Reich Ministry of the Interior, January 20, 1943 ("Diensttagebuch 1943," 37; quoted from copy in IfZ).

Part One. Section 3. Introduction. II. Ultimate Aims

1. For further details see "Diensttagebuch," ed. Präg and Jacobmeyer, introduction, 7 f.

2. Cf. statement issued by RSHA Abteilung 3 in October 1944 on the question of changing the Polish policy in the Annexed Eastern Territories and the General Government; a change of policy in the General Government was made dependent on whether the General Government would be designated a German settlement (in which case there would be no change) or not (in which case a change was possible) (BA R 58/1002, 157 ff.).

3. Discussion between Hitler and Governor General Frank on February 6, 1944 ("Diensttagebuch 1944," February 6, 1944).

4. Frank speaking to Party leaders of the General Government on February 11, 1944 ("Diensttagebuch 1944," I, BA R 52 II/213), and at a meeting of departmental heads on April 12 1940 ("Diensttagebuch 1940," I, 134 ff., 136; quoted from copy in IfZ).

5. Cf. statement of the Central Office of the Reich Commissar for the Strengthening of German Nationhood, in "Himmler zu den Aufgaben des Ostens," from the periodical *Deutsche Arbeit*, quoted from the *Krakauer Zeitung*, August 7, 1942.

6. For further details, see Broszat, *Nationalsozialistische Polenpolitik* (1961), 164 ff.

7. Cf. diary entries 1939–45 of Dr. Troschke, the former head of the Department of Economics in the office of the *Kreishauptmann* in Rzeszów, who was later active in the district administration of Galicia (Bl. 190 ff., 192). According to these notes (produced after 1945), a meeting took place in spring 1944 in Lemberg (L'viv) between representatives of the SD from Berlin and the district administration, at which the resettlement and economic integration of *Volksdeutsche* streaming back from Russia were discussed. The representative of the district administration turned down integration on the grounds that the immigrants were farmers, not workers; the manpower already available was entirely sufficient; and most of the immigrants in question were old and frail. The SD representative is reported to have said: "Regarding what has just been said about the particularly high proportion of frail and elderly people, may I inform you in strict confidence of the attitude of SS Central Office. . . . That we will make short work of these people" (BA Ostdok. 13 GG 1 a/10). (The actual words used were "Mit denen verfahren wir kurz." This is the only known written evidence of plans for mass murder of sections of the German population deemed "useless").

8. Cf. minutes of a discussion held on February 4, 1942, in the Reich Ministry for the Occupied Eastern Territories "on the question of Germanization" (Nuremberg doc., NO-2525). The term *Ostraum* [which stood for the Eastern lands claimed by the Nazis—Trans.] can be construed here as including the General Government. For more details, see the "General Plan for the East" of the RFSS (reproduced in *VjhZ* [1958]: 281 ff.; [1960]: 119) and the stated position and reflections (*Geheime Reichssache*—secret Reich document) of Wetzel, the *Referent* in the Race Policy Office of the NSDAP, April 27, 1942 (Institute for Western Studies, Poznań, doc. I-777); letter from RFSS to the chief of the Central Office of Racial Affairs and Settlement of the SS (Greifelt), June 12, 1942 (doc. I-325); according to this, 80–85% of the Poles were to be resettled and no more than 3–4.8 million were to remain in the "German settlement area."

9. Cf. speech by Frank on July 23, 1940, in Kraków (reproduced in Poliakov and Wulf, *Das Dritte Reich und die Juden* [1955], 178 ff), according to which he initially rejected outright any thought of Germanizing the General Government. Cf. working meeting February 25, 1940, quoted from *Doc. Occ.* 6:159 n. 3. The Germanization plan was originally drawn up for the time *after* the Germanization of the Annexed Eastern Territories (Frank to the meeting of departmental heads of

April 12, 1940 [160 n. 6]) though later affirmed unreservedly as the goal of German policy after the war (Frank to a meeting of police officers, May 30, 1940 [160 n. 7]: "I speak quite openly of Germanization"). In contrast to this, cf. Frank's statement to a meeting on October 9, 1940 (160 n. 8: "It is clear that we will neither denationalize nor Germanize"). Cf. also Frank's statement on March 25, 1941 ("Tagebuch 1941," I; *Doc. Occ.* 6:160 n. 9: "The Führer is resolved to make this area an all-German country in the course of the next 15–20 years. . . . This gives a complete transformation of the purpose of our work in this area"), on December 16, 1941 (161 n. 11: "For it has become quite clear that in the near future this area, the General Government, is destined to become part of the settlement program of our people, part of the progress of German ethnic groups in the East"), and on March 11, 1942 (reproduced on 161 n. 12: "The national problem in the General Government must be seen exclusively in light of the area's ultimate destiny as a German resettlement zone. . . . That of course is only possible because . . . [the] Poles and Ukrainians . . . are being removed from the area. If we already had peace. . . we would have a free hand, also in matters of ethnic policy"). For an account of the concept of Germanization, see Madajczyk, *Polityka*, 1:287 ff., 453 ff.

10. W. Hallbauer, in *Das Generalgouvernement*, no. 1 (1944): 12 ff., 17 (University Library, Warsaw, Sign. 011248).

11. "Creation of a regular network of local centers throughout the area," whose role was to be "the direct expression of German hegemony" (Schepers, head of the Central Department for Urban Planning in the General Government, in *Krakauer Zeitung*, March 6, 1942). These local centers were to be strictly divided into German and non-German residential districts. According to the very advanced development plans, the church was no longer to be the center of the new districts; the center would be the headquarters of the *Kreishauptmann*, with a parade ground and public buildings (cf. Gollert, *Warschau unter deutscher Herrschaft* [1942], 236). In this connection see the instruction of the district leader of Warsaw in October 1940 about the formation of a German and a closed Jewish district (ghetto) (*Warschauer Zeitung*, October 16, 1942). Cf. also a letter from the RFSS to Governor General Frank in November 1939, according to which Lublin was earmarked to become a German town by 1944, with 20–25% of the population German by 1944, rising to 30–40% in later years, compared with 10–15% in the present day (1939). In Himmler's view, the resettlement of the indigenous population (Operation Werewolf) should be started before the end of the war (Nuremberg doc., NO-2444). Lemberg was planned as a future Eastern European center (for further details, see Hallbauer, in *Das Generalgouvernement*, no. 1 [1944]: 10 ff., 17, University Library, Warsaw, Sign. 011248).

12. Cf. discussion held on February 4, 1942, in the Reich Ministry for the Occupied Eastern Territories (i.e., the large tracts of the western Soviet Union occupied by the Nazis) with representatives of the ministry, the offices of the RKF, the RSHA, etc., "concerning Germanization, in particular in the Baltic countries" (Nuremberg doc., NO-2525). Drawing on ancient Sparta as a model, it had the Germans as the Spartans (the ruling elite), and the Latvians, Estonians, etc., as the "perioecians" (the middle class); the Russians were allocated the role of "helots" (the serfs)—the same model is readily applicable to the relationship between Germans and Poles.

Part One. Section 3. Introduction. III. Legal Status

1. Cf. Albert Weh, in *Übersicht über das Recht des Generalgouvernements* (1943) (loose-leaf collection), A 120 n. 2.

2. A. Weh, in *Das GG, seine Verwaltung und seine Wirtschaft* (Kraków, 1943), 64 ff.; Kundt, "Entstehung, Probleme, Grundsätze und Form der Gestaltung des Generalgouvernements," *Die Burg*, no. 2 (1944): 47 (University Library, Warsaw); cf. also Klein, "Zur Stellung des Generalgouvernements" (1941), 253.

3. By decree of the governor general, August 15, 1940 (Weh, *Übersicht über das Recht des*

Generalgouvernements, A 102), the addendum ". . . for the occupied Polish territories" was dropped and the areas renamed General Government.

4. Klein, "Zur Stellung des Generalgouvernements" (1941), 254, 252, 255; in this sense see also von Medeazza, "Ein Jahr Generalgouvernement" (1940).

5. RGZ 167, 274.

6. International law recognizes three ways in which a subject with status under international law can cease to exist: loss of national territory, dissolution of the legal system, and so-called *debellatio*. The latter occurs when a state relinquishes its functions as the result of defeat in war (Anzilotti, *Lehrbuch des Völkerrechts* [1929], 137). For Poland the requirements were not fulfilled, since the Polish government in exile in London was recognized as the legitimate government of Poland by numerous states, and certain state functions (including the organization of armed forces) were exercised.

7. Pungs, Buchholz, and Wolany, *Ostrechtspflegeverordnung* (1943), 4.

8. Klein, "Zur Stellung des Generalgouvernements," 228 f., 252 f.

9. Cf. Guggenheim, *Lehrbuch des Völkerrechts* (1948), 403 ff.; P. Guggenheim, *Die völkerrechtliche Lehre vom Staatenwechsel* (1925), 27 ff.; Kelsen, *Théorie générale du droit international public* (1932), 316; Oppenheim and Lauterpacht, *International Law*, 7th ed. (1952), 2:252; Dahm, *Völkerrecht* (1958), 1:91; Verdross, *Völkerrecht* (1964), 250 f.; Strupp and Schlochauer, *Wörterbuch des Völkerrechts* (1960–61), 2:776; Department of State, Bulletin, November 4, 1939, 458 (quoted from Steiniger and Leszczyński, *Das Urteil im Juristenprozeß* [1969], 170); judgment of the Polish Supreme People's Court, July 9, 1946, against Arthur Greiser, quoted from *Arbeitsübersetzung*, ZS, AZ I, 110 AR 655/73.

10. Speech to the Reichstag, October 6, 1939 (*Der großdeutsche Freiheitskampf. Reden Adolf Hitlers*, vols. 1 and 2 in a single edition [1942], 94).

11. Klein, "Zur Stellung des Generalgouvernements," 252 f.; cf. also Walz, *Völkerrechtsordnung und Nationalsozialismus* (1942); Schmitt, "Raum und Großraum im Völkerrecht" (1941).

12. Cf. letter from Reich minister and head of the Reich Chancellery to the Supreme Reich Authorities, June 22, 1942 (Nuremberg doc., NG-3454). The Górales were people from the region of the mountain Góralen in southern Poland.

13. State Secretary Ernst Freiherr von Weizäcker, Foreign Office, at a meeting of state secretaries of the Reich authorities (Nuremberg doc., NG-4330).

14. This was directed, generally speaking, against the theory of international law prevalent in the West, which was considered "liberalistic" and weak. This gave rise to provocative comments about the dwindling significance of neutrality, the tendency toward regional organization, and the "surfeit" of international agreements. Cf. Nußbaum, *Geschichte des Völkerrechts* (1960), 313 ff.; Gott, "The National Socialist Theory of International Law" (1938), 704; Walz, "Die Inflation im Völkerrecht der Nachkriegszeit" (1939).

15. The concept of *Großraum* (sphere of imperial expansion) is used above all by Carl Schmitt. On this subject and also on the theory of the *Großraum*, cf. Schmitt, "Völkerrechtliche Großraumordnung" (1941), 145; Schmitt, "Großraum gegen 'Universalismus' " (1939); Schmitt, "Reich und Raum" (1940); Schmitt, "Raum und Großraum im Völkerrecht" (1941); Schmitt, "Die Raumrevolution" (1940). In this sense see also Maunz, "Verfassung und Organisation im Großraum" (1941), which refers to the "leading and equilibrating role" of the Reich "toward the subject peoples." For more details, see Freisler, "Die Idee des Reiches" (1940), 253; Grewe, "Der Reichsbegriff im Völkerrecht" (1939); Daitz, "Echte und unechte Großräume" (1942); Höhn, "Reich—Großraum—Großmacht" (1942); R. Diener, "Das Reich und Europa," *Reich-Volksordnung-Lebensraum* 2 (1942): 360 ff.; R. Diener, "Reichsverfassung und Großraumverwaltung im Altertum," *Reich-Volksordnung-Lebensraum* 2 (1942): 177 ff.; Stuckart, "Die Neuordnung der Kontinente" (1941); H. Friedl, "Der Raum als Gestalter der Innen- und Außenpolitik," *Reich-Volksordnung-Lebensraum* 1 (1941): 349 ff.; H. Krüger, "Der Raum als Innen- und Außenpolitik," *Reich-Volksordnung-Lebensraum* 1 (1941):

77 ff.; R. Höhn, "Großraumordnung und völkisches Rechtsdenken," *Reich-Volksordnung-Lebensraum* 1 (1941): 256 ff.; Suthof and Groß, "Deutsche Großraumlehre und Großraumpolitik" (1943); Best, "Nochmals" (1941); Dietze, "Die Entwicklung des Sonderrechts im Kriege" (1944) (Lebensraum as the central concept of the new National Socialist Großreich). The right of the "leading power" to expand could justify every future annexation policy in a purported (though misleading) analogy to the American Monroe Doctrine and also to the administration of occupied Eastern European (for further details, see L. Gruchmann, "Nationalsozialistische Großraumordnung" [1962]).

16. Klein, "Zur Stellung des Generalgouvernements," 229.

17. Speech by Frank on August 3, 1943, reproduced in *Dokumente der deutschen Politik* (1943), 597 ff., 598; Klein, "Zur Stellung des Generalgouvernements," 233.

18. "Ordnung der Gesetze und Gebräuche des Landkrieges zum Haager Abkommen, betreffend die Gesetze und Gebräuche des Landkrieges," October 18, 1907 (*RGBl.* 1910, 107). "Abkommen über die Behandlung von Kriegsgefangenen," July 27, 1929 (*RGBl.* I 1934, II 207).

19. Freisler, "Grundsätzliches zur Ministerratsverordnung" (1941).

20. *RGBl.* I 2077.

21. Kundt, "Entstehung, Probleme, Grundsätze und Form der Verwaltung des GG," in Bühler, *Das GG, seine Verwaltung und seine Wirtschaft* (1943). Klein, "Zur Stellung des Generalgouvernements," 262.

22. The governor general was independent of the Reich administration and combined all authority in his person (sec. 5 of the Führer decree on the administration of the occupied Polish territories, issued on October 12, 1939, *RGBl.* I 2077). The General Government had foreign exchange, currency, customs, and economic borders, and in that respect was a foreign country (instruction no. 3 issued by the head of the Foreign Exchange Control Office in the office of the governor general, November 20, 1939, *VBl. GG* [1939]: 55; decree on customs legislation, November 7, 1939 [92]); it had its own police borders with the Reich and its own postal and rail administration; in other ways, too, it was discrete from the Reich (decree of October 26, 1939 [7], amended by decree of October 29, 1941, *VBl. GG* [1941]: 619); decree of September 4, 1941 (511 ff.). Numerous regulations were modeled on those of a foreign state (decree of September 13, 1940, *VBl. GG* 1 [1940]: 289); for more details, see instruction of the district president of Kattowitz (Katowice), August 5, 1940 (*Amtsblatt Reg./Präs. Kattowitz 1940*, 27, no. 237, University Library, Warsaw, Sign. 034693), on the granting of judicial and administrative assistance to the courts of the German Reich; the governor general was represented by a "plenipotentiary" in Berlin. However, the General Government had no non-derivative powers, as all its sovereign authority was obtained from the Reich (sec. 3 of the Führer decree of October 12, 1939, *RGBl.* I 2077), and it remained wholly dependent on the Reich for allocation of personnel and resources. Its large measure of administrative autonomy and the many examples of the leadership's high-handed attitudes had no effect on this (cf. report by RMuChdRkzlei, April 12, 1943, listing the failures of the German administration in the General Government, sent to the *Reichsführer*-SS on April 17, 1943. Among other things, this accused the governor general of having wanted to make the General Government completely independent from the Reich. He is said to have referred to himself as "head of state" [IfZ, Bestand Pers. Stab/RFSS, MA 300, 4008 ff.]).

23. Kundt, "Entstehung, Probleme, Grundsätze und Form der Verwaltung des GG."

24. Speech on December 15, 1940, in Kraków ("Diensttagebuch 1940," 3:1141 ff.; BA R 52 II/247).

25. Speech on August 3, 1943 ("Diensttagebuch," 3:703 ff.; 707 f.; *Dokumente der deutschen Politik* [Berlin, 1943], 597 ff., 598). See also recommendation of Rosenberg's office, confidential memo 36/481 of the Party Chancellery, May 19, 1942 (*Verfügungen*, 1:214 f.), according to which the General Government should no longer be referred to in official parlance as "belonging to the East" but as "a country adjoining the German Reich whose sovereignty was already established." Also see

Dr. F. Siebert's report on the establishment and status of the General Government, April 14, 1959 (BA Ostdok. 13 GGI a/9). Greetings telegram sent by Hitler on the second anniversary of the founding of the General Government on October 26, 1941 (quoted from Weh, *Übersicht über das Recht des Generalgouvernements* [1943], A 120 n. 2).

26. Frank, "Der Aufbau der Verwaltung im GG" (1940). Report by Dr. Siebert, April 14, 1959 (BA Ostdok. 13 GG I a/9). Speech by Frank on August 3, 1943 (*Dokumente der deutschen Politik* [1943], 597 ff., 598). Klein, "Zur Stellung des Generalgouvernements," 255 ("the National Socialist idea of the state is an unprecedented, sovereign, independent, autonomous entity that is secular and in full accordance with the fundamentally *völkisch* spirit," a "legislative and organizational creation of the first order," comparable with the concept of the Protectorate of Bohemia and Moravia), with reference to Klein's essay, "Die staats- und völkerrechtliche Stellung des Protektorats Böhmen und Mähren" (1940), 258; in this sense see also Frank, "Der Aufbau der Verwaltung im GG," 97.

27. Pungs, Buchholz, and Wolany, *OstrechtspflegeVO* (1943), 3; OLG (State Superior Court) Posen (Poznań), *DR* (1942): 858; KG (Prussian Supreme Court) Berlin, *DR* (1941): 2199; OLG Danzig (Gdańsk), March 26, 1941, III W 48/41, quoted from Pungs, Buchholz, and Wolany, *OstrechtspflegeVO*, 3. Partly different: OLG Danzig, *DR* (1941): 395, which did not follow the line that the GG was automatically part of the Reich.

28. Klein, "Die staats- und völkerrechtliche Stellung des Protektorats Böhmen und Mähren," 255 ff.; in this sense see also Weh, "Das Recht des GG" (1940).

29. See note 15 above.

30. Klein, "Zur Stellung des Generalgouvernements," 259 n. 126 (the difference was, according to him, not of a quantitative but a qualitative nature; compared with the concept of "Gebiet" [area], "Raum" [space] was an *Aliud*, an "expression of imperial vision").

31. Speech by H. Frank on October 26, 1940, at the official ceremony to mark the anniversary of the General Government, *Warschauer Zeitung*, October 27 and 28, 1940.

32. Klein, "Zur Stellung des Generalgouvernements," 265.

33. For a detailed account, see Best, "Grundfragen einer deutschen Großraumverwaltung" (1941); and the essays of Stuckart, Höhn, and Diener cited in note 15; regarding the Monroe Doctrine, cf. Scheuner, "Die Machtstellung der Vereinigten Staaten in Zentralamerika" (1940), 309 ff.

34. Frank, "Der Aufbau der Verwaltung im GG," 99. A "land of the future" is from the big Party rally on October 5, 1940, in Warsaw (*Deutsche Allgemeine Zeitung*, October 7, 1940).

35. Klein, "Zur Stellung des Generalgouvernements," 262.

36. Best, "Grundfragen einer deutschen Großraumverwaltung."

37. State Secretary Ganzenmüller from the Reich Ministry of Traffic, November 25, 1942, "Diensttagebuch," 3:465 ff.

38. Decree of February 19, 1942 (*DJ* [1942]: 214).

39. Instruction on exchange of judicial assistance with foreign countries, May 10 and August 1, 1940, was implemented through diplomatic channels with the involvement of the Reich Ministry of Justice and the Foreign Ministry (instruction of September 7, 1940; all instructions in Weh, *Übersicht über das Recht des Generalgouvernements*, C 180, 184, 190; II-665 a).

40. Sec. 27 of the Decree on German Jurisdiction in the General Government of February 19, 1940 (*VBl. GG* 1 [1940]: 57).

41. It had no budget of its own; the funding requirements were authorized by the Reich. The department staffing schedules were issued by the relevant Reich department. The civil servants and staff in the General Government were transferred or detailed by the Reich authorities; the governor general's right of appointment was confined to the lower, clerical ancillary and clerical grades and excluded executive grades (Führer Decree on the Appointment and Termination of Service of Civil Servants in the General Government, May 20, 1942, *RGBl.* I 341).

42. *Krakauer Zeitung*, January 1, 1943.

43. Frank at the meeting of department heads held on July 12, 1940 ("Diensttagebuch 1940").

44. Renaming of the Generalgouvernement für die besetzten polnischen Gebiete (General Government for the occupied Polish territories) to Generalgouvernement, Führer decree of July 8, 1940, and decree of the governor general of July 31, 1940 (Weh, *Übersicht über das Recht des Generalgouvernements* [1943], 102). The postal administration of the General Government issued 1941 stamps with the legend *Deutsches Reich—Generalgouvernement (Krakauer Zeitung,* September 6, 1941).

45. Instruction issued by Frank during a discussion with Press Secretary Gassner on December 17, 1940; instead it should be referred to as *östlicher Machtbereich Deutschland* (Germany's Eastern sphere of influence) or *östliches Vorfeld* (Eastern glacis) ("Diensttagebuch 1940," 1144).

46. H. Frank at the working meeting of September 20, 1940 ("Diensttagebuch 1940," 2:130), and the conference of department heads April 12, 1940 ("Diensttagebuch," 1:134 ff., 136); for more details, see *Die nationalsozialistische Gemeinde* (1940), 97.

47. Letter from Reich Ministry of the Interior (signed by State Secretary Hans Stuckart) to RMuChdRkzlei, February 13, 1941 (BA R 43 II/423). The Führer's understanding of "Eastern Territories" encompasses the Annexed Eastern Territories, all Reich territories east of the Oder, and the General Government. See also minutes of a conference of department heads, July 12, 1940, in Kraków, at which, among other things, Frank declared: "The Führer says the new designation (for the General Government) should express the fact that the General Government is and will remain an essential component of the German Reich and . . ." ("Diensttagebuch 1940," 2:80).

48. Discussion in the Führer HQ on July 16, 1941, with Lammers, Rosenberg, Keitel, and Göring (Nuremberg doc., L-221).

49. Decree issued by the Reich Ministry of the Interior on February 19, 1942, concerning administrative assistance for the authorities of the General Government and the Reich (*DJ* [1942]: 214).

50. Freisler, "Grundsätzliches zur Ministerratsverordnung über das Stafrecht gegen Polen und Juden," 2631. Klein, "Zur Stellung des Generalgouvernements," 257. H. P. Ipsen, "Reichsaußenverwaltung," *Monatshefte für Auswärtige Politik* 10 (1943): 521.

51. For example, in the Eleventh Decree to the Reich Citizenship Law of November 25, 1941 (*RGBl.* I 722), which governed the loss of citizenship and forfeiture of assets of Jews moving abroad, the General Government was classified as a foreign country (decree of Reich Ministry of the Interior, December 12, 1941, *MinbliV* [1970]); Lichter, *Das Staatsangehörigkeitsrecht* (1943), 147 ff. n. 4. However, the General Government was classified as home territory in the case of "alien" criminals who had committed crimes outside the boundaries of the Reich, which were to be punished under German law; cf. verdict of the People's Court, June 25, 1940 (*DJ* [1940]: 1062); see also Lämmle, "Ausder Rechtsprechung des Volksgerichtshofs" (1944), 507.

52. A letter dated June 25, 1940, said, among other things: "In the near future it will be necessary to issue a Führer decree that will effect absorption of the General Government into the German Reich, while preserving its entire legal structure" (Nuremberg doc., NG-1227). Discussion between Frank and Reich Ministry of the Interior State Secretary Stuckart on October 13, 1941, in Berlin ("Diensttagebuch," October 13, 1941).

53. At a meeting of political leaders from the NSDAP's General Government working party on December 14, 1942, Frank further declared ("Diensttagebuch," 1310 ff.) that the Reich administrative apparatus "is unhappy about the fact that the thousands upon thousands of regulations, ordinances, and decrees it enacts are not automatically applied in the General Government."

54. Discussion between Frank and State Secretary Bühler on August 27, 1942 ("Diensttagebuch," 3:416 f.).

55. Notes taken by Frank on the development of the last quarter year, August 29–31, 1941 ("Diensttagebuch 1942," 3:419 ff., 432).

Part One. Section 3. Introduction. IV. Principles of Administrative Policy and Their Results

1. For further details, see "Diensttagebuch," ed. Präg and Jacobmeyer, introduction, 7 f.

2. Interview with Keitel, October 17, 1939 (minutes, quoted from *Doc. Occ.* 6:27 ff.). See also a report by Dr. Siebert, "Zur Polenpolitik im GG," May 4, 1959 (BA Ostdok. 13 GG I b/3).

3. "Report on the Development of the General Government," July 1, 1940, 1:67 ff. (BA R 52 II/247).

4. *RGBl.* I 2077.

5. Report dated July 1, 1940 (1:67; BA R 52 II/247).

6. For full details on the policy of segregation, see report of the chief of the President's Office of the Reich protector in Bohemia and Moravia, Dr. Blaschek, concerning his official journey to Kraków on August 21–26, 1942 (reproduced by J. Gumbowski and K. Lesczyński, "Generalne Gubernatorstwo w oczach niemca," *Bulletin of the Main Commission Warsaw* 15 [1965]: 129 ff., 135 ff., which gives a very good overview of the general policy of segregation in the General Government [Appendix 13]). On the exclusion of the Jews, see the "Report on the Development of the General Government," July 1, 1940 (BA R 52 II/247); it said about 1.6 million Jews lived in the General Government (14.5% of the population), above all in the cities (approx. 25% of the urban population); 34% of these worked in commerce, 32% in crafts; there were scarcely any Jewish industrial or agricultural workers; however, there were as yet no reliable statistics.

7. Best, "Grundfragen einer deutschen Großraumverwaltung" (1941), 43; Maunz, "Verfassung und Organisation im Großraum" (1941), 457, with further examples.

8. Stuckart, "Die Neuordnung der Kontinente" (1941), 5, 7.

9. Maunz, "Verfassung und Organisation im Großraum"; the emphasis is on the *völkisch* core and goals of the German Großraum theory. Maunz says that his emphasis has helped the foreign states to understand the Großraum theory, because they misunderstood(!) it as a means of mere conquest.

10. Höhn, "Großraumordnung und völkisches Rechtsdenken" (1941), 276.

11. Maunz, "Verfassung und Organisation im Großraum," 459.

12. Report by Dr. F. Annexed Eastern Territories (then head of the Central Department of Internal Administration in the General Government) "Zur Polenpolitik im GG," May 4, 1959, 15 (BA Ostdok 13 GG I b/3). Cf. discussion between Governor General H. Frank and State Secretary J. Bühler, head of the Central Departments, and the higher SS and police leader (HSSPF), Krüger, March 25, 1941, in Kraków: in this discussion, Frank said that it would be necessary to keep some of the General Government civil servants in readiness to "bring order to other areas," should this be necessary. He and Keitel agreed on 500 officials ("Diensttagebuch 1941," vol. 2).

13. Cf. discussion in Lemberg (L'viv) on July 31, 1942, in which the serving district governor, Ludwig Losacker, explained the principles of the German administration in Galicia. Among other things, the Soviets had achieved "results in the administrative sphere . . . albeit in the name of an objective that is a mockery of German concepts of legality . . . which on face value had to be seen as extraordinary." For the German administration, "the conclusion to be drawn was that, when implementing its own administrative goals in the Galicia District, it should apply a degree of harshness that did not fall short of that applied by the Soviets. . . . Otherwise, the population would be inclined to doubt the earnestness of the instructions emanating from the district administration" ("Diensttagebuch 1942," 717).

14. Cf. minutes of a discussion between Hitler, Frank, and von Schirach on October 2, 1940 (ZS, Ordner 325, G.J. no. 83; copy).

15. F. Siebert, "Zur Polenpolitik im Generalgouvernement" (BA Ostdok 13 GG I b/3, 17).

16. Hitler, Frank, and von Schirach discussion, October 2, 1940 (ZS, Ordner 325, G.J. no. 83;

copy), in which Hitler declared that the Germans were the masters, the Poles the slaves. The Polish ruling classes should be killed. "AB Operation" was the codename for the Extraordinary Pacification Operation.

17. Hitler, Frank, and von Schirach discussion (ibid.): Living standards should, in Hitler's view, be kept as low as possible; the Poles should be kept as ignorant as possible. For more details, see "Bericht über den Aufbau im GG bis zum 1 July 1940," vol. 1 (BA R 52 II/247), which among other things says: the planned further development of the General Government was not "misconstrued humanitarianism" toward the Polish people but rather was informed by "pragmatic considerations"; the task of planning was not to "introduce the principles of settlement policy appertaining in the German Reich" but to guarantee "harmony and security," as well as to "relieve the economic and ethnic burden" (on the Reich). In this sense see also Kundt, "Entstehung, Probleme, Grundsätze und Formen der Verwaltung des Generalgouvernements" (1944), *Die Burg*, 51, 53 (University Library, Warsaw, Sign. 011249). A different view is given by Siebert, "Zur Polenpolitik im Generalgouvernement" (BA Ostdok 13 GG I b/3, 19), who maintains that the treatment of the Poles reflected the presence of "feelings of regret, as well as political intentions" [though in the kindest of interpretations it can only have been the reverse: political considerations first and regret, in the best of cases, second—Author].

18. Siebert, "Zur Polenpolitik im Generalgouvernement" (BA Ostdok 13 GG I b/3, 19); concerning the activity of the Central Polish Aid Committee, cf. the report of H. Heinrich, former adviser on "free welfare for non-Germans" in the Department of Population and Welfare in the Central Department of Internal Administration, August 27, 1958; memo of the Department of Population and Welfare, September 15, 1943 (BA Ostdok 13 GG I k 1). See also the order on the Provisional Regulation of Benefit Payments to pensioners of the former Polish states and the Polish self-management associations, December 9, 1939 (*VBl.GG* [1939]: 206 ff.), and the so-called War Victims Decree of December 20, 1939 (*VBl.GG* 1 [1940]: 1 ff.).

19. See, for example, the letter from Supreme Command East to OKW, March 8, 1940, reporting a meeting of the Reich Defense Council held on March 2, 1940, in Warsaw; at the meeting it was agreed to adopt the general line that the Polish people had to be maintained at the bare subsistence level (Nuremberg doc., NO-EC-300; English summary). Also see Frank's statement at a meeting held on December 14, 1942 in Warsaw: "The situation here is one of absolute starvation" ("Diensttagebuch 1942," 3:482 f., 487). Kundt, "Entstehung, Probleme, Grundsätze und Formen der Verwaltung des Generalgouvernements," *Die Burg*, 51, 53 (University Library, Warsaw, Sign. 011249).

20. Although the fundamental direction of the policy—like that toward the Jews and the exploitation of the General Government for the benefit of the Reich—was established in Berlin, one cannot go along with Siebert's view ("Zur Polenpolitik im Generalgouvernement" [BA Ostdok 13 GG I b/3, 27]) that the administration had acted under pressure from on high (the basics of the policy on Poland had been accepted virtually without debate. "That which had been commanded could not be changed. Attempts at resistance met with no success!") In fact, because the basic policies were so general, the administration had plenty of flexibility in their implementation and in all matters not determined by Berlin. An energetic exercise of official powers (bureaucratic sabotage) could have prevented much harm or alleviated some of the suffering, all the more so as it was very difficult for Reich officials to gain an insight into the almost autonomous General Government. In Siebert's opinion, the central administration of the General Government "did everything in its power" to make use of their scope of action (27).

21. For more details see Broszat, *Nationalsozialistische Polenpolitik* (1961), 168 ff.; G. Eisenblätter, "Grundlinien der Politik des Reiches gegenüber dem Generalgouvernement" (1969), 361 ff.

22. For further details, see Frank's memos dated June 19, 1943 (BA R 52 II/12 a), and May 25, 1943 (ZS, Ordner 439, 419 ff., copy). Corresponding proposals were put forward by Frank in a letter to the chief of the Security Police and the SD, Ernst Kaltenbrunner, July 5, 1944 (BA R 52 II/12 a).

See also the speech by Frank on December 9, 1942, in which he complained about the mistreatment of Polish workers in the Reich ("If you want to milk a cow, you don't slaughter it"); details of Frank's proposals are given in Eisenblätter, "Grundlinien der Politik des Reiches gegenüber dem General-gouvernement." Cf. Siebert, "Zur Polenpolitik im GG," BA Ostdok. 13 GG I b/3, Bl. 12/13.

23. Cf. letter from Reich Ministry of the Interior to State Secretary Bühler of the government of the General Government, October 19, 1944, in which a secret agreement with the Poles, based on the principle of *legal* cooperation, was considered (BA R 58/1002). Three further options for a change in the Polish policy were weighed: reassertion of "German authority with sweeping pow-ers"; no mention of the "long-term goal" of German settlement of the General Government, but only "short-term policies"; and acceptance of the Poles as partners in the "struggle against Bolshe-vism." For further details, see an internal memo from the Reich Ministry of the Interior to Ref. III A 6, October 17, 1944 (BA R 58/1002).

24. In a meeting on February 12, 1944, Frank asked Himmler to back his new line. Himmler agreed ("Diensttagebuch," February 12, 1944). In a letter from the chief of the SIPO and the SD to the RFSS of October 1944 (BA R 52 II/12 a), Kaltenbrunner explained that two things were impor-tant for the realignment of the policy toward the Poles: first, the decision whether or not to desig-nate the General Government an area for future German settlement; second, a change of direction on three fronts: an end to all statements discriminating against Poles (including propaganda mate-rial); the abolition of harassment measures; and cooperation with the Polish *Heimatarmee* (through the commander of the Security Police and SD, BdS Kraków—without legalization).

25. Reich Ministry of the Interior to State Secretary Bühler, government of the General Gov-ernment (BA R 58/1002).

26. Ibid.

27. Broszat, *Nationalsozialistische Polenpolitik*, 81.

28. Ibid., 171 f.

Part One. Section 3. Introduction. V. Principles of Administrative Organization

1. Best, "Die deutsche Militärverwaltung in Frankreich" (1941), 29; Schröder, "Die Heeresver-waltung" (1943), with a detailed overview of the historical development of the administration in areas defined as occupied under international law; Maunz, "Verfassung und Organisation im Großraum" (1941), 457 f.; Spanner, "Fragen der Verwaltung besetzter Gebiete" (1944).

2. Krüger, "Der Raum als Aufgabe der inneren Verwaltung" (1941); Stuckart, "Die europäische Neuordnung" (1942); Stuckart, "Die Neuordnung der Kontinente" (1941); Ernst, "Erlebnis und Ge-staltung deutscher Großraumverwaltung" (1943) (with a useful overview of the administration—mostly military administration—of all occupied territories in Europe); Best, "Grundfragen einer deutschen Großraumverwaltung" (1941); Maunz, "Verfassung und Organisation im Großraum," 456 ff.

3. Spanner, "Fragen der Verwaltung besetzter Gebiete."

4. Labs, "Die Verwaltung der besetzten Ostgebiete" (1943); Runte, "Die Verwaltung der be-setzten Ostgebiete" (1942).

5. Best, "Grundfragen einer deutschen Großraumverwaltung."

6. Maunz, "Verfassung und Organisation im Großraum," 456.

7. Best, "Grundfragen einer deutschen Großraumverwaltung": German rule is included here only in the form of "wishes" (54 f.); German rule is to be implemented through instructions (56 f.); implementation of German rule is to be by directives (57).

8. Ibid., 57 f.

9. Although Polish local government, which was de facto subject to loose German control, remained largely autonomous, in the Occupied Eastern Territories local self-government remained

intact though under strict German supervision only in the *Rayons* (districts in the Ukraine) and in the districts of the former Baltic states (for further details, see Runte, "Die Verwaltung der besetzten Ostgebiete," 227).

10. Letter from the chief administrator of the Military District of Kraków to the head of the civil administration (CdZ) of the commander-in-chief East, October 1939 (IfZ, Bestand MiG, MA-682, Bl. 0226 ff.).

11. Dr. F. Siebert, president of the Central Department of Internal Administration, at a meeting in Lemberg (L'viv) on July 31, 1942 ("Diensttagebuch 1942," July 31, 1942). Report by Siebert, May 4, 1959, on the Polish policy in the General Government (BA Ostdok. 13 GG I b/3), 21; Lasch, "Die deutsche Aufgabe im Osten" (1940), with detailed descriptions of the "neglect" in Poland, the "political incompetence" of the Poles, and the German "work of construction."

12. Report by Siebert, "Die Hauptabteilung Innere Verwaltung im Generalgouvernement," November 11, 1959 (BA Ostdok. 13 GG I b/5).

13. Report by Siebert, November 11, 1959, on the development and position of the General Government (BA Ostdok. 13 GG I a/9), in which he puts forward the view that cooperation with the Polish intelligentsia was out of the question anyway.

14. Report by Siebert, ibid.; Broszat, *Nationalsozialistische Polenpolitik* (1961), 159 f.

15. "Report on the Development of the General Government," July 1, 1940 (BA R 52 II/247). Hitler in a discussion with the cief of the Armed Forces High Command on the future shape of Polish affairs, October 17, 1939 (quoted from *Doc. Occ.* 6:27 f.). Frank, "Der Aufbau der Verwaltung im Generalgouvernement" (1940), 98.

16. Every aspect of the system of administration was regulated down to the last detail in accordance with the criteria of the Reich administration; the ponderous legislative machinery remained intact—untouched by the events—almost until the end of the German administration. The last decrees issued in the General Government were the Decree on Supplements to the Law of Civil Status, November 25, 1944, and the Decree on the Increase of Telephone Charges, December 4, 1944.

17. This is underestimated by Präg and Jacobmeyer in their introduction to "Diensttagebuch," 23: they explain that "the beginnings of a model administration" were nipped in the bud by the designation of the General Government as an object for exploitation.

18. For more details, see Broszat, *Nationalsozialistische Polenpolitik*, 75 ff., 80 ff.; Eisenblätter, "Grundlinien der Politik des Reiches gegenüber dem Generalgouvernement" (1969), 235 ff.; report by Siebert, May 4, 1959 (Ostdok. 13 GG I b/3).

19. The secretary of state of the General Government, Joseph Bühler, had been a public prosecutor (Frank, *Nationalsozialistisches Handbuch für Recht und Gesetzgebung* [1934], xxix–xxxii). The head of the Department of Legislation in the office of the governor general, Albert Weh—a "straight A" law graduate—came originally from the Austrain administration; the head of the Department of Education and Science, Watzke, had a similar background. The head of the Central Department of Justice, Wille, originally worked in the Reich Judicial Administration of the Weimar period and was responsible for political crimes ("Personalliste des RMJ," BA R 22/4378; and "Geschäftsverteilungsplan des RMJ" [Organizational Plan of the RMJ (Reich Ministry of Justice)], April 1938, BA R 22/4223). The governor of the Warsaw District, Fischer, was *Regierungsrat*. The heads of the offices of the district governor were also specialists from the Interior Administration of the Reich or the Austrian administration.

20. Quoted from "Diensttagebuch," ed. Präg and Jacobmeyer, 10.

21. Cf. Goebbels, *Tagebücher 1942–43* (1948), 243, 279 ff., 362; letter from RMuChdRkzlei to the head of the Party Chancellery, January 1, 1945, which clearly shows the resignation of the administration toward the political powers that be (IMT, Nuremberg, Bd. 34, 494; doc. 753 D; reproduced by Diehl-Thiele, *Partei und Staat im Dritten Reich* [1969], 257). Cf. also Schmitt: "Der Zugang

zum Machthaber, ein zentrales verfassungsrechtliches Problem," reproduced in Schmitt, *Verfassungsrechtliche Aufsätze* (1958), 430 ff.

22. Speech by Frank to leading Party functionaries of the Department for the General Government of the NSDAP, January 11, 1941 ("Diensttagebuch 1941," 22 ff.).

23. For a detailed account, see von Medeazza, "Ein Jahr Verwaltung im GG" (1940); Westerkamp (head of the Department of Internal Administration in the General Government), "Die Einheit der Verwaltung" (1941); Westerkamp, "Ein Jahr Einheit der Verwaltung im GG" (1941); Frank, "Der deutsche Aufbau im GG" (1941); Weh, "Galizien, Bestandteil des GG" (1941).

24. Lammers had wide-ranging responsibilities in his office of chief administrator, dealing with all matters centrally, submitting them to Hitler when necessary. He was also responsible for the business of the Ministerial Council for the Defense of the Reich (Führer decree, August 30, 1939, *RGBl.* I 1539); the departments no longer had direct "access to the ruler," as Carl Schmitt would say. For details see von Stutterheim, *Die Reichskanzlei* (1940); Just, "65 Jahre Reichskanzlei" (1943).

25. Cf. Stuckart, "Zentralgewalt, Dezentralisation und Verwaltungseinheit" (1941), 1 ff. The "Unified Administration" centralizes the power of the state once more in the hands of the general state administration and counteracts department splintering and the "hopeless splintering of the administration" on all levels. It is the most complete embodiment of the Führer principle developed by National Socialism and the "necessary consequence" of the "*völkisch* idea of the state" and the "holistic organizational concept that stems from it" (21). Stuckart was the most zealous advocate of the idea of the Unified Administration. See also Jarmer, "Die Einräumigkeit" (1940); Maunz, "Verfassung und Organisation im Großraum," 457.

26. Cf. the basic principles of the administrative structure of the General Government: First Decree on the Development of the Administration in the Occupied Polish Territories, October 26, 1939 (*VBl.GG* [1939]: 3); Second Decree on the Development of the Administration in the General Government (Decree on the Unified Administration), December 1, 1940 (*VBl.GG* 1 [1940]: 357), with administrative instructions nos. 1 and 2 issued on March 31, 1941; no. 3 of April 7, 1941; no. 4 of April 18, 1941; no. 5 of March 17, 1943 (Weh, *Übersicht über das Recht des Generalgouvernements* [1943], A 121–A 121 e); Third Decree on the Development of the Administration in the General Government, March 16, 1941 (*VBl.GG* [1941]: 99), with administrative instruction no. 1 of April 7, 1941; no. 2 of March 17, 1943 (Weh, *Übersicht über das Recht des Generalgouvernements*, A 122 e, 122 b); Fourth Decree on the Development of the Administration in the General Government, September 25, 1941 (*VBl.GG* [1941]: 561); for more on the development of the administration and copious statistics, see Franke, "Allgemeine Staatsverwaltung," *Das Generalgouvernement*, ser. 13–14 (November 1941): 7 ff. (Franke worked in the Central Department of Internal Administration in the General Government); F. Siebert, "Die Hauptabteilung Innere Verwaltung der Regierung des GG," report dated November 11, 1959 (BA Ostdok. 13 GG I b/5; ZS, Versch. 104, 769 ff., copy). Pfundtner and Warnak, *Taschenbuch für Verwaltungsbeamte*, 603 ff. (ZS, Versch. 103; 197 ff.).

27. Secs. 3, 5 of the Führer directive of October 12, 1939 (*RGBl.* I 2077). The district governors ran the *entire* administration of the district in accordance with the instructions of the government of the General Government and were also responsible for supervising the *Kreishauptleute* (heads of regional [county] administration) (sec. 5 of the order of October 26, 1939, *VBl.GG* [1939]: 1, in conjunction with secs. 4, 5 of the order issued on December 1, 1940, *VBl.GG* 1 [1940]: 357). They were the "sole political representatives" of the supreme administration of the Reich and had the right to appoint and dismiss certain groups of employees and officials as well as exercising supervisory and leadership functions in various bodies (housing and settlement associations). At the same time they were representatives of the power of the NSDAP in their district. Their position cannot therefore be compared with that of the *Regierungspräsident* in the Reich, whose competence was equivalent only to that of the Department of Internal Administration in the Office of the District Governor. Secs. 4 to 6 of the First Decree on the Development of the Administration in the Occupied Polish Territories, October 26, 1939 (*VBl.GG* [1939]: 3). The function of a *Kreishauptmann*

(*Stadthauptmann*) was roughly equivalent to that of a *Landrat* (prefect of a *Land*), though with the difference that he was the central authority of all branches of the administration at district level (exceptions being railways, postal services, and the police).

28. Order on the Unified Administration, December 1, 1940 (*VBl.GG* 1 [1940]: 397).

29. Kundt, "Entstehung, Probleme, Grundsätze und Form der Verwaltung des GG" (1944), *Die Burg* (University Library, Warsaw, Sign. 011249).

30. Cabinet meeting, December 9, 1942 ("Diensttagebuch 1942"). Frank spoke more candidly at the meeting held on October 15, 1941, expressly welcoming the fact that the lower echelons (*Kreishauptleute*) were disregarding the instructions of the middle echelons and the government. This, he said, was the "illegal approach typical of the East," which worked counter to "the previous bureaucratic approach" ("Diensttagebuch," October 15, 1941). A deliberate move to strengthen the district administration was the governor general's request to have reports from the *Kreishauptleute* sent directly to the central administration and only duplicates circulated to the district governors (Frank's speech to a conference of *Kreis-* and *Stadthauptleute* from the Lublin district held on March 4, 1940, "Diensttagebuch," March 4, 1940), although the proper channels required direct delivery to the district governor. The corresponding instruction from the Central Department of Internal Administration—Department of Municipal Administration dates from October 30, 1940; in it, *Kreishauptleute* are instructed to forward their reports directly to the head of the office for the government of the General Government by the 10th of the following month (Main Commission Warsaw, Archives, Reg. des GG, Hauptabteilung Innere Verwaltung II/125).

31. Frank to a meeting of department heads on December 2, 1939, in Kraków ("Diensttagebuch," 1:10).

32. Thus, for example, subdivisions of the Party—with the exception of the Hitler Youth—were not tolerated (order of April 22, 1942, *VBl.GG* [1942]: 217). Regarding the position of the Party, cf. von Medeazza, "Die Partei im GG" (1941); for an account of the tense relationship with the Party, cf. Frank's contribution to the meeting of department heads on April 12, 1940 ("Diensttagebuch 1940," 1:134 ff.) and at a meeting of officials from the NSDAP's work group on the General Government held on December 14, 1942 ("Diensttagebuch 1942," 1312–16, 1335 ff.); report by Party judge Brodmann to the meeting of the NSDAP's work group on the General Government on May 13, 1944 ("Diensttagebuch 1944," vol. 4); letter from SSPF Lublin to RFSS, December 10, 1942 (IfZ, Bestand Parteikanzlei, FB-50, Bl. 269); discussion between the *Hauptabschnittleiter* der NSDAP, Stahl, and Ministerial Councillor Weh of the government of the General Government, August 16, 1943 ("Diensttagebuch 1943," 3:714 ff.); H. Frank, in "Diensttagebuch," August 16, 1943, Bl. 716. Letter from the deputy head of the NSDAP's work group on the General Government to the head of the Party Chancellery, September 28, 1944 (Bl. 109 f.); letter from the Cracow District Govenor to RFSS, 27 June 1944 (IfZ, Bestand RFSS/Persönl. Stab [GG], in Ma 300, 3664).

33. See also excerpt from the protocol of the government meeting of November 18, 1943, which contains comments by Frank ("Diensttagebuch," November 18, 1943).

34. Cf. Frank's interview with the *Völkischer Beobachter* on February 6, 1940, in which among other things he says: "I will send anyone packing who is not worth his salt, every weakling, every ne'er-do-well; rotten, corrupt examination candidates, etc., are no use to us. The personality is all-important here. I don't give a damn whether someone has passed their exams. As far as I'm concerned, anyone who has the necessary abilities [for the job] can become a district governor straightaway. Hysterics and bureaucrats need not apply" ("Diensttagebuch," 1:86 ff., 90).

35. The designation *Kreishauptleute* had existed since 1772 when Galicia was subsumed by Austria as part of the first division of Poland; cf. memorandum concerning a reform of the administration in Galicia sent by Joseph II to Maria Theresia on May 18, 1780 (quoted from J. Sommerfeld, "Galizien bei der Besitznahme durch Osterreich," *Das GG*, no. 3 [1942]: 4 ff., 9, 12). Frank at a discussion in Łódź on October 29 and December 2, 1939 ("Diensttagebuch," 1:10); F. Siebert, "Der Verwaltungswirrwarr im GG" (BA Ostdok. 13 GG I a/1).

36. The *Kreishauptleute*, who had much larger territories to administer than a *Landrat*, were usually considerably younger than *Landräte* in the Altreich, some of them less than 30 years of age (*Krakauer Zeitung*, February 20, 1942). Already in the period of military administration, the majority had been active as *Landkommissar* or *Stadtkommissar* in the 27 districts of the occupied territories (later to become the General Government). (Overview of the previously engaged *Landkommissare*, October 5, 1939, and with other dates, IfZ Bestand MiG, Ma-682, Bl. 0837 f.). In political terms, the *Kreishauptleute* were naturally orthodox National Socialists (cf. anonymous report, June 1940, "Der Kreishauptmann," BA). "Report on the Development of the General Government," July 1, 1940, BA R 52 II/247, 42 f.; these unqualified officials were recruited largely in spring 1941 and brought with them "a breath of fresh air into the administrative apparatus" (diary notes, Dr. Troschke, BA Ostdok. 13 GG 1a/10, Bl. 110).

37. Cf. report by an anonymous Party comrade: "The government of the General Government has stuck, with a determination bordering on stubborness, to the principle that important leadership tasks can be entrusted only to lawyers, who are still held in esteem today, preferably to administrative lawyers with the rank of *Oberregierungsrat* [senior executive officer] and higher. There has been almost 100% adherence to this principle" (quoted from "Einzelstimmen aus der Parteigenossenschaft: Die Krise im GG," April 12, 1942, IfZ, Bestand RSHA Ma-641, 2130 ff.); F. Siebert, "Der Verwaltungswirrwarr im GG," BA Ostdok. 13 GG I a/1.

38. An overview of appointments to leading positions is given in Du Prel, *Das Generalgouvernement* (1942), 375 ff.; cf. also Frank, *Nationalsozialistisches Handbuch für Recht und Gesetzgebung* (1934), introduction, xxix–xxxii and the list of collaborators in the publication. For more details, see F. Siebert, "Der Verwaltungswirrwarr im GG," BA Ostdok. 13 GG I a/1, which gives numerous names, showing that the higher ranks were predominantly made up of "veterans" of the early struggles of the Party, high-ranking SS and SA officers, the head of the Party Reich office, etc. See also a report by F. Siebert, "Hauptabteilung Innere Verwaltung im GG," November 11, 1959 (ZS, Versch. 104, 769 ff.).

39. Sec. 3 of the Decree on the Development of the Administration in the Occupied Polish Territories, October 26, 1939 (*VBl.GG* [1939]: 3); decree of the Führer on the setting up of a State Secretariat for Security Matters, June 3, 1942 (*VBl.GG* [1942]: 321). The line of command went from the RSHA or the Central Office of the regular police (*Ordnungspolizei*) to the HSSPF East (the higher SS and police chiefs East), from there to the head of the SIPO or the head of the regular police, then down to the SS- and police chiefs at the level of the district governor's office, then the commanders of the SIPO and normal police, and finally to the Gendarmerie or Security Police (*Schutzpolizei*) on the local level. For an account of relations between the police and the administration, cf. Broszat, *Nationalsozialistische Polenpolitik*, 75 ff.; Eisenblätter, "Grundlinien der Politik des Reiches gegenüber dem Generalgouvernement," 130 ff., 235 ff.

40. Führer decree of June 3, 1942 (*VBl.GG* [1942]: 321).

41. Secs. 3, 5, par. 2, of the Decree on the Development of the Administration in the Occupied Polish Territories, October 26, 1939 (*VBl.GG* [1939]: 3).

42. This applied not only to Poles and Jews but also to Germans, against whom the police were able to proceed without the knowledge or permission of the authorities. Cf. the account of a case in Max Frauendorfer's report, "Die Arbeitsverwaltung im GG," July 20, 1951, p. 11, in which police surrounded a branch of the Kraków Labor Office and arrested its manager, Szepessy, for alleged "friendliness to Jews"; he was subsequently sent to a concentration camp; the branch office itself was closed down; Frank vainly pleaded for his release (BA Ostdok. 13 GG IV b/3).

43. For example: monthly report, *Kreishauptmann Dębica*, November 1940 (IfZ Ma-158/1, Fasz. 19, Bl. 4).

44. Although postal and rail services were under the authority of the governor general, they had their own administrative structures (sec. 1, par. 2, of the Third Decree on the Development of the Administration in the General Government, March 16, 1941, *VBl.GG* [1941]: 99). At district

level, labor, finances, and forestry were not *incorporated* in the general administration but rather *affiliated* with it (there were finance inspectors, the Labor Office, the Forestry Service, and the *Wehramt* [military office]). (Section C of administrative instruction no. 4 of April 18, 1941, Weh, *Übersicht über das Recht des Generalgouvernements* [1943], A 121 d).

45. The supervisory authority was the district governor; nor did *Kreishauptleute* have any authority over the special administration; the only provisions were for a reciprocal *duty of notification* on all matters "politically or otherwise significant," with authority vested in the *Kreishauptmann* "in order to maintain a uniform political line or reconcile conflicting points of view held by various branches of the administration," clauses that are open to any interpretation (subpar. 1, 3 of administrative instruction no. 2, March 31, 1941, to the Decree on the Unified Administration of December 1, 1940, which contains a list of the authorities to be incorporated or affiliated; in Weh, *Übersicht über das Recht des Generalgouvernements*, A 121 b).

46. Monthly report, *Kreishauptmann* Hrubieszów, November 6, 1940 (IfZ Ma-158/1, Fasz. 17, Bl. 2 ff.). Special authorities operating without knowledge of the *Kreishauptmann* included the SIPO, the *Schutzpolizei*, the Gendarmerie, the Labor Office, the Financial Inspectorate, the Roads Department, the Forestry Service, the district farms inspector, the Water Board, and the Land Registry Office. It was "always galling" for the *Kreishauptmann* to learn from Poles or Ukrainians of measures being implemented in his own district.

47. Monthly report, *Kreishauptmann* Jedrzejow, January 4, 1940 (IfZ Ma-158/1, Fasz. 16, Bl. 4); monthly report, *Kreishauptmann* Ilza, August 1940 (Fasz. 6, Bl. 4), in which the *Kreishauptmann* of Ilza complains that the agricultural administration sees itself as a special department. Accordingly, five offices were established to oversee food provision: the district farms inspector, the agricultural expert in the office of the *Kreishauptmann*, the District Agricultural Cooperative, a consumer cooperative, and the *Kreishauptmann* himself.

48. Cf. meeting of district governors and Governor General Frank on June 7, 1940, in which the district governors complained that the *Kreishauptleute* received directives directly from the central administration and not via the office of the district governor. This altered situation was also apparent in the tone of the department heads ("Diensttagebuch 1940"). At a meeting with the governor general on May 30, 1942, the governors complained, among other things, that the various Central Departments of the government demanded reports directly from the departments of the district administration ("Diensttagebuch 1942," vol. 3).

49. One example of this is the duty of notification. Normally, the reports of the specialist departments were produced by the *Kreishauptleute* or the district chiefs as situation reports and forwarded to the government of the General Government. But on occasion Kraków demanded direct reports and the district chief issued instructions countermanding this request (monthly progress reports of the Office of the Warsaw District Chief, School Board, November 4, 1940, IfZ, Ma-158/1, Fasz. 14, Bl. 2 f.).

50. See F. Siebert, "Der Verwaltungswirrwarr im Generalgouvernement" (BA Ostdok. 13 GG I a/1; ZS, Versch. 104, 695 ff., copy); for the Kraków and Warsaw districts, cf. in particular sheets 700, 702.

51. One can sense a "distressing loss of authority" on the part of the German leadership. The government is not governing but merely administering, in many cases bypassing the district administration (meeting of the governors, May 30, 1942, "Diensttagebuch 1942," vol. 3).

52. Concerning the exclusion of the district chief, cf. complaints voiced at the meeting of the district governors on June 7, 1940 ("Diensttagebuch 1940," vol. 2).

53. For full details see F. Siebert, "Der Verwaltungswirrwarr im Generalgouvernement" (BA Ostdok. 13 GG I a/1; ZS, Versch. 104, 695 ff., copy).

54. According to the Office of the Governor of Galicia at a meeting with police representatives on June 18, 1942 ("Diensttagebuch," 3:331).

55. Many measures taken by *Kreishauptleute* were later introduced generally by means of an

order. For example, the creation of the first *all-Jewish districts* in May 1940 in a *Kreishaupt-mannschaft* of the Warsaw District; it was only later that Jewish enclaves were created throughout the General Government (cf. the brochure by Gollert entitled *Warschau unter deutscher Herrschaft* [1942], 87 f.).

56. Monthly report, *Kreishauptmann* Ostrowo (Ostrów Wielkopolski), May 1940 (ZS, Polen 257, 644 f.); monthly reports, *Kreishauptmann* Łowicz, May 1940 (629 f.), and January 1941 (Polen 347 ff.); monthly report, *Kreishauptmann* Petrikau (Piotrków Trybunalski), May 1940 (607); monthly reports, *Kreishauptmann* Krakau-Land, May 1940 (553) and August 1940 (155 ff.); monthly report, *Kreishauptmann* Tomaschow (Tomaszów Mazowiecki), July 1941 (458); monthly report, *Kreishauptmann* Siedlce, January 1942 (Polen 348, 796 ff.).

57. Report from the General Government, February 1942 (no author, BA Ostdok. 13 GG 19/10); monthly report, *Kreishauptmann* Hrubieszów, November 6, 1940 (IfZ, Ma-158/1, Fasz. 17, 1 f.).

58. A deluge of decrees and directives impossible to carry out flooded over the *Kreishauptleute* (cf. complaints of the *Kreis-* and *Stadthauptleute* of the Lublin District at an official meeting, March 4, 1940, "Diensttagebuch 1940," March 4, 1940) and district chiefs; as early as mid-1940, only nine months after the setting up of the civil administration, it was demanded that the flow of decrees from the office of the governor general should cease (meeting of department heads, June 1940, "Diensttagebuch 1940," 2:65).

59. Monthly report, *Kreishauptmann* Hrubieszów, November 6, 1940 (IfZ, Ma-158/1, Fasz. 17, 1 f.); monthly report, *Kreishauptmann* Siedlce, February 1942 (ZS, Polen 348, 813 ff.).

60. The objections of the *Kreishauptleute* to centralization should not therefore be seen in absolute terms but against the background of the presumption of almost unlimited freedom by National Socialist "administrative heads." According to a report by the economist Dr. Troschke on his activities in the General Government (Bl. 10), the central authority allowed a certain latitude— "The Czar is far away" (BA Ostdok. 13 GG no. 1 a/10). (See also note 65, below.)

61. Diary notes, Dr. Troschke: "One can but offer assistance and try to make good the injustices perpetrated by the powers that be" (ibid., Bl. 59, 61).

62. Proposal by Frank to the cabinet meeting of March 11, 1942 ("Diensttagebuch 1942"): a majority of the younger employees and officials in the Kraków central office should spend three to six months working in a *Landkreis*, "so that these gentlemen get to know from the bottom up what life is really like in this country."

63. From late 1941 the administration started shifting responsibility not only for supervision but also for implementation of administrative matters to German officials, further reducing Polish involvement and increasing the workload without any increase in staff levels (cf. complaints voiced by the district chiefs at the meeting of May 30, 1942, with a detailed representation of the arguments, "Diensttagebuch," May 30, 1942, Bl. 1–23).

64. At their meeting on May 30, 1942 (ibid.), the governors complained that they were frequently overruled by the specialist departments of the central authorities, whereupon Frank— rejecting the blinkered view of departmental bureaucracy—emphasized the pivotal position of the governors as the central administrative authority in their districts. But in a conversation with State Secretary Ernst Boepple on November 24, 1942, he also complained about the increasing tendency of the governors to assert their independence: Fischer (governor of the Warsaw District) "clearly [wants] to make Warsaw the center, as it were, of the General Government. I'm not standing for it. I will also take action in the case of Globocnik [HSSPF of Lublin]." The general governor said that by January 1, 1943, he wanted to see Kraków taken out of the district administration and made the Federal capital; the district chief of Warsaw should be transferred to Kraków, the district chief of Radom should be transferred to Warsaw, and the district chief of Kraków sent to Radom ("Diensttagebuch 1942," vol. 3).

65. Diary entry, Dr. Troschke, dealing with his activity in the General Government, Bl. 44 f.

(BA Ostdok. 13 GG No. 1a/10); (the diaries were written *after* 1945, based on notes made between 1940 and 1945). Dr. Troschke was head of the Department of Economics in the office of the *Kreishauptmann* in Reichshof (Rzeszów), moving later to Lemberg (L'vov), where he headed the economic administration of Galicia. Troschke was an economist, not a professional civil servant.

Part One. Section 3. Introduction. VI. Actual Development

1. Speech by the governor general during a visit to the head of the German Labor Front, Dr. R. Ley, on November 7, 1940, quoted from "Diensttagebuch," ed. Präg and Jacobmeyer, 18 n. 41.

2. "Report on the Development of the Administration in the General Government," July 1, 1940 (Bd. I, BA R 51 II/247; also: IfZ, Sign. 1442/54, Bestand ED 6); for the judicial sphere see the summary in a letter from the president of the German Supreme Court Kraków to the head of the Central Department of Justice—personal—December 8, 1944 (Main Commission Warsaw, Archive, Reg. des GG, Hauptabteilung Justiz V, 81, Bl. 898 ff.); also "News from the Reich," no. 193, June 12, 1941 (IfZ, Ma-441/4, Bl. 4039–42).

3. Letter sent by Reich Ministry of the Interior to Interior Minister of Württemberg, February 9, 1940, saying there was no need for *Stadthauptleute* (heads of city administration) (quoted from Seeber, *Zwangsarbeiter in der faschistischen Kriegswirtschaft* [1964], 111). According to a statement by Frank, 1,100 applications for administrative posts in the General Government had been received by October 18 1939 ("Diensttagebuch 1939," 1:5 f.).

4. In the spring of 1941, the Department of Food and Agriculture of the Warsaw district administration alone had 88 employees; counting the field offices, the staff totaled 848 (138 Germans, 710 Poles); report by the head of Subsection 1 of this department on April 3, 1941 ("Diensttagebuch 1941," 224 ff.). On July 1, 1941, there were 1,100 Reich German civil servants and three to four times that number of German employees and auxiliary staff (not counting the police); (Gstöttenbauer, in Du Prel, *Das Generalgouvernement* [1942], 200). Moreover, in August 1941 the numbers were further swollen by the personnel of the Galicia District. In early 1943 the government of the General Government felt obliged (in its own words) "to limit the administrative apparatus to a minimum of properly qualified officials" and take on more Poles to fill the gap left by 800 civil servants who had been called up for military service. The personnel of the special authorities, like those of the offices of the RFSS/RKF, increased dramatically (note in the files on a discussion of February 24, 1943, between representatives of the government of the General Government and representatives of the Reich Chancellery, IfZ, Bestand HSSPF [Ost], FB-59, Bl. 44 ff., according to which the State Secretariat for the Security Services alone had 86 new *Referate* [policy desks] in the Bureau for the Strengthening of German Nationhood).

5. At the end of 1941 each *Landkreis* had an average of 10 to 15 German officials and between 15 and 30 other staff (statement by Governor General Frank to members of the Berlin Civil Service Academy, November 18, 1941, "Diensttagebuch 1941," 1030). At first, various offices tried to remedy the situation on their own initiative by "luring" new recruits from the Reich. For the judiciary, see the decree issued on February 28, 1941, by the head of the Justice Department in the office of the governor general to the districts, which strictly forbade such recruiting intiatives. Requests for postings were to be his exclusive preserve (Main Commission Warsaw, Archive, Reg. des GG, Hauptabteilung Justiz V 6); cf. also decree issued by the government of the General Government to the Central Department of Internal Administration on June 24, 1941, with instructions to set up personnel control bureaus to prevent employees sacked from the public services from gaining employment with other offices (ZS, Polen 256, Bl. 185 f.).

6. It was less the scarcity of food and material goods than the poor traffic conditions, the confined living space, the alienation from political and cultural life, the unfamiliar surroundings and unaccustomed administration practices, the high workload, the failure to honor assurances

with regard to promotion, etc., that made an assignment in the General Government and the Occupied Eastern Territories singularly unattractive for established civil servants; indeed, it was often perceived as a "transfer for disciplinary reasons." There were also conflicting loyalties with the Reich authorities (this sometimes led to a double game, which the governor general was all too willing to play along with; in Berlin, the official concerned declared himself in agreement with the point of view of the central administration, but in Kraków he did the opposite [Frank at a meeting of the Department of Internal Administration on January 19, 1941, "Diensttagebuch 1941," Bl. 83]). Forbidding stories about life in the General Government were circulating in the Reich (*News from the Reich*, no. 217, November 4, 1941, IfZ, Ma-441/4, 4727 ff.; also BA R 22/243).

7. Decree circulated by the RFSSuChddtPol on the deployment of the Gendarmerie as a special service within the General Government, November 11, 1940 (BA R 19/304). Letter from RFSS to HSSPF Ost, July 19, 1941 (ZS, USA doc., film no. 2, 860–64). At a meeting of the government on December 16, 1941, however, Governor General Frank declared that, in view of the acute scarcity of manpower, "the most recent and stringent selection criteria . . . are not paramount; anyone who is more or less acceptable should be retained" ("Diensttagebuch," December 16, 1941, Bl. 317). See, for example, monthly report of *Kreishauptmann* Łowicz, January 1941 (ZS, Polen 347 ff.), as well as the sources cited in note 9, below. Report, F. Siebert, "Der Verwaltungswirrwarr im Generalgouvernement" (BA Ostdok. 13 GG I a/1; ZS, Versch. 104, Bl. 695 ff., 699, copy). Regarding the miserable conditions in the Galicia District, cf. RSHA reports of events in the USSR, no. 50 of August 12, 1941 (BA R 58/216, Bl. 12, 51, 76, 72). Report of the commander of the SIPO Radom from spring 1943 (half the *Kreishauptleute* "fell far short of the accepted moral standards") (IfZ, Ma-641, 2217 ff.). [The word "moral" referred mainly to economic performance, relationship to Poles and Jews, and sexual morality—Author.]

8. Report, Dr. F. Siebert, "Hauptabteilung Innere Verwaltung" (BA Ostdok. 13 GG I b/5).

9. Excerpt from the situation reports of *Kreis*- and *Stadthauptleute* of the General Government for February 1941 (Institute for Western Studies, Poznań). The president of the Central Department of Internal Administration in a discussion on November 21, 1941, in Kraków ("Diensttagebuch 1941"); Governor General Frank at a government meeting of July 13, 1942, in Kraków ("Diensttagebuch 1942," 3:361 ff., 362). Summary of charges relating to a total of 11 cases against the *Stadthauptmann* Kraków, September 9, 1944 (ZS, USA doc., film no. 4, Bl. 130 ff.). Material about professional and personal misconduct of members of the police, including a lack of "toughness" in dealing with Poles, in BA R 19/115. See also report of the commander of the SIPO and the SD Radom about the "undignified" conduct of the Germans in the General Government, spring 1943 (IfZ, Ma-641, 2271 f.).

10. Report, F. Siebert, "Der Verwaltungswirrwarr im GG" (BA Ostdok. 13 GG I a/1), especially with regard to the presidents and officials of the Eastern railway: "A thousand and more kilometers from home the most trustworthy of officials [turned] to women and alcohol . . . and went to the bad." Cf. also diary notes by Dr. Troschke (BA Ostdok. 13 GG No. 1a/10): "There are some . . . who believe that, once in Poland, they may indulge in vodka and other temptations until the cup is drained to the last drop" (46 f.). Many have succumbed to vodka and "loose living," which makes a "shameful impression" on the Poles. "Many behaved sensibly in the Reich, but once across the border, they think anything goes" (78, 94).

11. See, for example, the description of alcoholic excess and corruption among members of the local Gestapo unit in Przemyśl (a branch office of the Security Police Commander [KdS] in Radom) given in a judgment of the LG (State Court of Appeals) Hamburg against Karl F. Reisener et al., January 14, 1969 (AZ. Sign. 50–38/67, Bl. 64 ff.).

12. Cf. a report by the military commander of Kraków for the first week of October 1939, dated October 9, 1939, which related the positive reception given to the course of the war and the occupation by country people and industrial workers (because they hoped for improved economic

conditions and believed the war was directed only against government and "international Jewry") and the hostile attitude of the intelligentsia (IfZ, Bestand MiG, Ma-682, Bl. 486 ff.). The thesis of relatively tolerable conditions in the General Government is also supported by H. Roos, "Polen in der Besatzungszeit" (1959), 179, who put the anti-German resistance of the Poles down to the police terror rather than the acts of the administration. [This thesis was probably close to the truth until 1942, when the mood turned irrevocably against German rule—Author.]

13. The final turning point came in 1942, the year of the so-called *Ernteschlacht* (harvest battle), in which the delivery quotas imposed on Polish farmers, the round-ups of workers, and the police terror reached a high point. A summary of the causes is given in a report by the chief of the General Staff of the District Military Command of the General Government to the chief of Army General Staff, April 7, 1943 (IfZ, Ma-1017, Bl. 0715 f.): "growing hardship," "increasing burden of the war," "emotional oppression," "restriction of civil liberties," "psychological mistreatment," "misplaced severity," and "complete contempt coupled with lack of welfare" had robbed "the Poles of the last shreds of belief in the goodwill of the Germans." Report, Dr. F. Siebert, Central Department of Internal Administration, November 11, 1959 (BA Ostdok. 13 GG I b/5), with numerous illuminating examples. Cf. also diary notes by Dr. Troschke (BA Ostdok. 13 GG no. 1a/10), 45 ff., according to which the *Kreishauptmann* of Reichshof (Rzeszów), a *Regierungsrat* in the Reich Ministry of the Interior, tried, with "grim determination," to prevail but proved incompetent in every way. The Poles hated him, because he played the *Herrenmensch* (member of a superior race) wherever he went. He had Poles and Jews whipped, something that would never be forgotten. For him, Poles were human beings of a lower rank. In his monthly report of February 1941, the *Kreishauptmann* of Łowicz proposed cutting off the ears of Polish hostages as a reprisal for attacks on German soldiers (ZS, Polen 347, Bl. 408 f.).

14. Report, Dr. F. Siebert (BA Ostdok. 13 GG I b/5), according to which there were many rackets involving supplies of food from the so-called district stocks to the offices of the *Kreishauptleute* and district governors; many were certainly involved in small-time swindles (the Central Department of Internal Administration was—Siebert said—by and large free from corruption). *Herrentum* (lordship) had been misunderstood: taking into consideration "certain transgressions of wartime regulations and the special situation prevailing in the occupied territories," in which "not all the fundamental principles of the homeland could be upheld," it was "not correct to say that the majority of civil servants" had behaved in a "morally reprehensible manner."

15. Secret report from the commander of the Security Police and the SD for the Galicia District in Lemberg (L'viv) to RSHA Amt III (III A) (III D) and to the commander-in-chief of the Security Police and the SD in the General Government concerning "the conduct of the Reich Germans in the occupied areas," May 14, 1943 (Reich security matter; 5 copies), AZ III A 4 SA: 23 (ZS, Versch. 48, Bl. 49 ff.). The report has 142 pages. It has been proved—according to the report—"that the Germans posted here have failed right down the line" and that the "Propaganda Offices and press of the General Government . . . have given a deliberately distorted picture of the situation . . . banking on the Reich administration's ignorance of the real conditions in the General Government" (Bl. 133 f.). Further details are supplied by another 100-page report from the same source in June 1943 (ZS, Ordner 36, Bl. 49 ff.). Cf. report of the commander of the Security Police in Radom in spring 1943 about the "undignified behavior" of the Germans in the General Government (IfZ, Ma-641, 2271 f.). On the basis of this account, the Reich Chancellery produced a report, "The Conditions in the General Government," dated April 12, 1943, which was sent to Himmler on April 13, 1943, with the intention that it should be used as the basis for a verbal report to Hitler on conditions in the General Government to be given by the RMuChdRkzlei and the RFSSuChddtPol. Himmler replied on May 8, 1943, saying he had nothing to add to the report (Nuremberg doc. no. 3321).

16. Report by F. Siebert (BA Ostdok. 13 GG I b/5). A catalog of accusations, put together by the Reich Chancellery on April 12, 1943 (Nuremberg doc. no. 3321), included the following reproaches

directed toward Frank: "Mistaken perception of the General Government as a state in itself, independent of the Reich," by means of which Frank was able to display "all the trappings of power";
toward the Reich and within the General Government: numerous "ill-considered instructions," as
well as "arbitrary acts" and "emotional impulses"; the effect was to undermine the confidence of
both the local population and the Civil Service in the stability of governmental and administrative
leadership, with the consequence that decrees and laws were frequently ignored, sidestepped, or
sabotaged. Moreover, there had been a "conspicuous absence of a sense of propriety in personal
conduct"; Frank, it was said, was predisposed by his "great vanity" to "surround himself with largely
incompetent yes-men . . . who, by painting a rosy picture of the real conditions in the General Government, had created a false impression of success in the political and administrative spheres . . . to
pander to the smugness of the governor general" and further their own careers; the result was a
regime based on "favoritism and nepotism." In the economic sphere, the bad example given—in
some cases by close relatives of the governor general—had led to a prevalence of "ruthless wheeler-
dealers and brutal war profiteers," resulting in "signs of corruption" permeating the Civil Service,
with "hundreds of cases" of graft and racketeering by petty officials and employees.

17. Memorandum of the commander-in-chief East, February 6, 1940 (inhuman and barba-
rous behavior by the SS, the Security Police, and the SD) (ZS, Versch. 12, Bl. 3423 ff.). Anonymous
report, February 1942, detailing the actions of SS members in the General Government (BA Ostdok. 13 GG 19/10). Unsigned letter from a German living in Kraków to Hitler, March 25, 1943, in
which the sender reported police manhunts against Poles, the starvation conditions suffered by the
Polish population while the Germans had plentiful food supplies, and acts of cruelty perpetrated by
the Gestapo against Jews in the Ghetto. The Führer should know about such acts; if he—the letter-
writer—were given safe conduct, he would report on them in person (ZS, Eichmann, no. 1567).
Concerning the general conduct of the SS in the East, cf. parallel report by the chief of the general
Wehrmacht Bureau in the Oberkommando der Wehrmacht (high command of the Wehrmacht) to
the RSHA (*Obergruppenführer* Wolff) of August 2, 1943, which dealt with the excesses of the SS in
Russia (including killings, theft, molestation, beating and rape of women; ZS, no sources given). To
some extent the Wehrmacht also gave grounds for complaint: cf. letter from the garrison headquarters Warsaw to the police regiment Warsaw, November 13, 1939 (with numerous accusations of dishonorable conduct by soldiers, such as consorting with prostitutes and Jewish women, maltreatment of Jews, etc.).

18. Report by SS-*Sturmbannführer* Dr. Herbert Strickner, October 19, 1944, which refers to
the statement on the Polish policy requested from the chief of the Security Police and the SD on
October 16, 1944, IfZ, Ma 641–2094 ff.; a more recent account of Polish resistance is given in W. Jacobmeyer, "Polnischer Widerstand im deutschen Urteil," *VjhZ* 4 (1977): 658 ff., with numerous examples. See also report by F. Siebert (BA Ostdok. 13 GG I b/5); the chief blame lay with the Reich
authorities who had seen the General Government as "a place of refuge for unwanted elements of
society" (Siebert was the head of the Central Department of Internal Administration in the General Government).

19. Cf. detailed report of the Security Police Command in Radom produced in spring 1943
(IfZ, Ma-641, Bl. 2271); unsigned report, February 1943, on the leadership of the administration in
the General Government (BA Ostdok. 13 GG 19/10). Cf. also report by Dr. Siebert on November 11,
1959 (BA Ostdok. 13 GG I b/5), according to which complaints were rarely followed up with criminal proceedings but usually led to nothing more than transfer and withdrawal of their "reserved
occupation" status [i.e., not liable for call-up—Trans.].

20. For a personal portrait of Frank, see Fest, *Das Gesicht des Dritten Reiches* (1964), 286 ff.;
cf. also a report by Max Frauendorfer, "Arbeitsverwaltung im GG," July 20, 1961, BA Ostdok. 13 GG
IV b/3, Bl. 9. On his leadership of the administration and friction with the SS and police, cf. Broszat, *Nationalsozialistische Polenpolitik* (1961), 75 ff., 80 ff. Concerning his contradictory policy on

the Jews, cf. Frank's statements in a speech given on December 9, 1942 (ZS, Eichmann, no. 1383). Regarding his loss of power vis-à-vis the Berlin authorities, cf. events detailed in the telex sent by the RFSS to HSSPF Kraków on March 29, 1943, and to the governor general on October 21, 1943; telex from State Secretary Stuckart to Reich Ministry of the Interior (Himmler) on October 22, 1943 (IfZ, Bestand RFSS Persönl. Stab, GG, Ma-300, 58–3072). Regarding the "sensational" restoration of the governor general's tarnished prestige through Hitler's intervention, cf. summary of discussion between Hitler and Frank on February 6, 1944, in "Diensttagebuch," February 6, 1944, Bl. 4) and Himmler's meeting with Frank on February 12, 1944, recorded in "Diensttagebuch," February 12, 1944, vol. 4. For more details, see "Diensttagebuch," ed. Präg and Jacobmeyer, introduction, 14 f.

21. For more details on Frank's management style, see report by F. Siebert, "Verwaltungs-swirrwarr im Generalgouvernement" (BA Ostdok. 13 GG I a/1; ZS, Versch. 104, 695 ff.; copy). See also the interesting list made by Siebert of various personalities in the administration of the General Government, August 1958 (ZS, Versch. 47, 442 ff.; copy).

22. More recently also "Diensttagebuch," ed. Präg and Jacobmeyer, introduction, 29, in which it is said that Governor General Frank had no "real power of decision" and was a mere "executor." But as head of the administration, Frank had *unlimited* powers (sec. 5 of the Führer decree of October 12, 1939, *RGBl.* I 2077) and also a certain scope for action with regard to the implementation of the Reich's political demands. He exercised this discretion by trying to "overfulfill" the exigencies of the Reich.

23. Report, F. Siebert, "Verwaltungswirrwarr im GG" (BA Ostdok. 13 GG I a/1; ZS, Versch. 104, 695 ff.; copy).

24. A conflicting view is held by Präg and Jacobmeyer, "Diensttagebuch," introduction, 11, who ascribe the failure of the administration primarily to external factors: interference by the Reich department and the fact that the SS and police were a law unto themselves; however, the authors overestimate the impact of these factors on the everyday operations of the administration.

25. Cf. also "Diensttagebuch," ed. Präg and Jacobmeyer, introduction, 23 ("Raubbau an Menschen und Wirtschaftskraft des GG"—plundering of human and economic resources in the General Government).

Part One. Section 3. A. Fundamentals

1. According to the report on development in the General Government (GG) (July 1, 1940), at this time there were about 1.6 million Jews in the General Government; according to earlier official estimates, there were 200,000 Jews in the Kraków District (5.3% of the population), 310,000 Jews in the Radom District (10.4% of the population), 250,000 in the Lublin District (9.6% of the population) and 540,000 in the Warsaw District (17.4% of the population)—a total of 1.3 million (BA R 52 II/247). See also diary notes by Dr. Troschke (BA Ostdok. 13 GG no. 1a/10, Bl. 37), according to which the vast majority of business and trades were in Jewish hands; statistics in the report of July 1, 1940 (BA R 52 II/247); cf. also report "Das Judenproblem" issued in mid-1942 (no author) on the influence of the Jews on the Polish economy and their elimination (BA Ostdok. 13 GG IX a/5).

2. Decree on the definition of the term *Jew* in the General Government, June 24, 1940, *VBl. GG* 1 (1940) (ZS, Ordner 94, Bl. 314–16; copy).

3. OLG-Rat Weh (head of the Legislative Office) in a discussion on June 6, 1942 ("Diensttagebuch," 3:319).

4. Decree on the identification of Jews in the General Government, November 23, 1939 (*VBl. GG* [1939]: 61); cf. also the decree circulated by the Central Department of Justice on July 21, 1941, to the district Departments of Justice, according to which, in the event of violations of the decree by Jewish subjects of allied or neutral states, the procedure set out in sec. 153, par. 2, of the Code of Criminal Procedure (StPO) was to be instituted (Main Commission Warsaw, Archive, government

of the General Government, Central Department of Justice V/6). Cf. also circular decree of the government of the General Government (Central Department of Internal Administration), April 23, 1941: ban on carrying additional armbands, to "avoid disguise" (ZS, Polen 257, Bl. 64). Police order on the appearance of Jews in public in the Reich, September 1, 1941, *RGBl.* I 547.

5. The government of the General Government notified the district chiefs on November 23, 1940, that the RSHA, in a decree of October 25, 1940, had described the emigration of Jews, also from the General Government, as "undesirable," since it only strengthened "world Jewry"; at the same time they were empowered to reject requests for emigration by Jews without further examination. Only applications from foreign Jewish subjects should be processed; quoted from Berenstein, Eisenbach, and Rutkowski, *Eksterminacja żydów* (1973), S. 55 f.

6. Diary notes by Dr. Troschke (BA Ostdok. 13 GG no. 1a/10, Bl. 93).

7. Decree of the Department of Internal Administration in the office of the governor general, December 11, 1939, ZS, Polen 257/5; according to this, Poles were to pay the German authorities onehalf złoty (0.25 RM) per application, and Jews were to pay twice as much.

8. See, for example, Steiner, "Verändertes Tarnow," Press Service of the General Government, June 9, 1942, ZS. Cf. pictures of the ghetto and Jewish markets in Warsaw and of the insurrection in the Warsaw ghetto in *Berliner Illustrierte Zeitung*, Institute for Western Studies, Poznań. Cf. diary notes by Dr. Troschke (BA Ostdok. 13 GG no. 1a/10, Bl. 40).

9. "Richtlinien für die Durchführung der antijüdischen Ausstellung 'Jüdische Weltpest' in den Gemeinden" (no date), Institute for Western Studies, Poznań.

10. Just how much anti-Jewish propaganda and how many anti-Jewish measures found favor with the Polish population is a matter of controversy. According to the reports of the German administrative authorities, the attitude of the population was predominantly positive; cf. diary notes, Dr. Troschke (BA Ostdok. 13 GG no. 1a/10), according to which the Poles hailed the "pushing back of Jewish influence"; cf. monthly report from the *Kreishauptmann* of Jasło on June 2, 1940 (ZS, Polen 347, Bl. 539): reprisals against work-shy Jews met with an "enthusiastic response"; monthly report by the *Kreishauptmann* of Końskie, August 1940 (Bl. 187, also IfZ, Ma-158/2, Bl. 15): "particular satisfaction" about the transportation of Jews to forced labor; previously the Jews had "triumphed," since the Poles had been obliged to go to the Reich as seasonal workers; monthly report, *Kreishauptmann* of Jasło, Kraków District, August 1940 (ZS, Polen 347, Bl. 101 ff.): The Poles seem to be disturbed by the treatment of the Jews; the prospect of an "overall solution of the Jewish problem" was no compensation for the fact that the "population has to put up with the invasion of the Jews from Kraków." The population did not understand why Kraków had to be completely "Jew-free" when it would be far simpler to carry out the necessary controls in Kraków itself. Monthly report, *Kreishauptmann* of Siedlce, February 1942 (ZS, Polen 348, 813 ff.): The anti-Jewish measures were—it was said—"supported and understood by the cities"; but the farmers were against the resettlement of the Jews because they were involved in smuggling operations with them and needed their craftsmen's products. But see also Bartoszewski and Lewin, *Righteous among Nations* (1969), which gives numerous examples of Poles helping Jews.

11. This included all Jewish questions, except matters of economic and industrial law, for which the various departments of the administration were responsible. Unlike the Reich, the General Government did not set up special Jewish bureaus. Jewish matters were dealt with in the Department of Population and Welfare or the Department of Health (from 1943 they were called Central Departments): administrative instruction no. 1 of April 7, 1941, and of March 16, 1941, on the organization of the government of the General Government (Weh, *Übersicht über das Recht des Generalgouvernements* [1943], A 122 a); and Decree on the Establishment of the Central Department of Health, January 20, 1943 (B 500). For more details, cf. part 1, section 3, C, VIII ("Freedom of Movement and Personal Liberty"), note 24.

12. Cf. situation report from the military commander Kraków, October 9, 1939 (IfZ, Bestand

MiG, Ma-682, Bl. 486 ff.), according to which the Jews believed themselves indispensable (because of their influence on the economy and commerce): "They are hoping for merciful treatment or a more or less advantageous solution of the Jewish question." The Jews in eastern Poland showed an even greater degree of naïveté: SS offices expressed amazement that in 1939, after the Soviet take-over of eastern Poland, when commissions were established to oversee reciprocal repatriation of refugees (so-called Resettlement Offices, run by the SS), many Jews as well as a large number of Poles applied for return to the General Government; "gentle hints" from the SS offices fell on deaf ears. Regarding general living conditions, and in particular the availability of food to Jews in the General Government, cf. Madajczyk, *Polityka*, 2:225 ff.

13. Decree on Forced Labor for Jews, October 26, 1939, *VBl.GG* (1939): 1. As early as May 1940, a Jewish ghetto was established on a trial basis in the Warsaw District. By the end of 1940, the ghetto was firmly established.

14. The first three phases are clearly discernible in the "Report on the Development of the General Government" of July 1, 1940 (BA R 52 II/247).

15. The first phase comprised (in chronological order): the introduction of forced labor, a ban on kosher butchering, the abolition of tax exemption for Jewish organizations, and compulsory identification badges and insignia for Jews and Jewish businesses; Jewish Councils were also instituted (decree of November 28, 1939, *VBl.GG* [1939]: 7, with implementing regulation issued on June 7, 1940, *VBl.GG* 2 [1940]: 45; all quoted from "Bericht über den Aufbau im GG," BA R 52 II/247), which effectively cut individual Jews off from any contact with German officialdom, since all decrees and directives were channeled exclusively through the Jewish Council, which was responsible for everything that happened in the Jewish community. An example of the scope of the responsibilities vested in the Jewish Council is the decree issued by the *Stadthauptmann* (head of town or city administration) of Warsaw to the commissioner for the Warsaw ghetto on February 27, 1941, which declared the Jewish Council responsible for any damage caused during clearance of apartments by Jews being resettled in the ghetto (ZS, Polen 352, 1127); as for the rest, the Jews were left to fend for themselves ("self-government"). Cf. also Decree on the Identification of Jews and Jewesses in the General Government of November 23, 1939 (*VBl.GG* [1939]: 61). From the age of 10, Jews were required to wear the Jewish star, on the *outer* sleeve. Any violation of the compulsory identification regulations carried the threat of prison and/or an unlimited fine as stipulated by the Second Decree on the Identification of Jews and Jewesses in the General Government, February 19, 1940 (*VBl.GG* [1940]: I 79). With regard to Jewish subjects of a neutral or allied country, cf. the instruction circulated by the head of the Central Department of Justice on July 21, 1941 (Main Commission Warsaw, Archive, government of the General Government, Central Department of Justice V/6) (see note 4, above).

16. For further details, see "Bericht über den Aufbau im GG," BA R 52 II/247, Bl. 190 f. This included compulsory registration for the purposes of "official records," the obligation to notify the authorities of assets on the part of Jews, limitations on residence—reservation of permission to leave the commune (First Implementing Order to the Decree of October 26, 1939, on Forced Labor for Jews), and proscriptions on the use of public roads and squares, public transport, private vehicles, etc.

17. For this phase, the authority to issue regulations governing conditions within the ghetto was disputed, since the SS and the police claimed sole regulatory powers (such matters being the concern of the Security Police), whereas the administration (*Kreishauptmann*) had the authority to set up ghettos (Decree on Residence Restrictions in the General Government, September 13, 1940, *VBl.GG* 1 [1940]: 288) and, deriving from this, also authority in all regulatory matters concerning the ghetto.

18. See, for example, the concluding report of the SSPF in the Galicia District regarding the solution of the Jewish question, sent to the HSSPF Kraków with a letter dated June 30, 1943 (Institute

for Western Studies, Poznań); report on the dissolution of the ghetto in Lemburg (L'viv), no date (probably 1942), no author (Institute for Western Studies, Poznań); the so-called Stroop Report on the destruction of the Warsaw ghetto, May 1943 (Nuremberg doc. PS-1061; published as J. Stroop, *Es gibt keinen jüdischen Wohnbezirk mehr* [1976]); Szender, "Der letzte Jude aus Polen," 1945 (BA D IV d 226 a).

19. The basis for the change in jurisdiction was the decree sent on September 21, 1939, by the chief of the Security Police and the SD to the chief of the *Einsatzgruppen* (Special Operations Squads), which concerned the secrecy of the Final Solution and the ghettoization of the Jews as a preliminarty step (Nuremberg doc. EC-307–1). See concluding report of the SSPF Galicia (Institute for Western Studies, Poznań).

20. Cf. memorandum from the Armed Forces High Command about a discussion with Hitler on October 20, 1939, item 3: "We must prevent a Polish intelligentsia from forming a ruling class. A lower standard of living should be maintained in the country; we need it only as a manpower reservoir" (Nuremberg doc. PS-864).

21. Decree of December 20, 1940, *VBl.GG*1 (1940): 378. Decree of March 8, 1940 (98). Decree issued by the government of the General Government on May 14, 1941 (ZS, Polen 256, 147), concerning "removal from public buildings of all artifacts that keep the memory of Pilsudski alive"; for more details, see directive ("request") from the Central Department of Internal Administration, Department of Ecclesiastic Affairs, to the archepiscopal diocesan authorities in Kraków, June 28, 1941, to remove all Polish statuary, pictures, and memorial plaques from Polish churches, for example, busts of Koszciuszko or Pilsudski, on the grounds that "their further retention . . . is not in keeping with the real conditions in the General Government" (Main Commission Warsaw, Archive, Reg. des GG Hauptabteilung Innere Verwaltung II/270).

22. The center for such research was the Institut für Deutsche Ostarbeit (Institute for German Development in the East) in Kraków, which was intended as the core of a future German university of the East, whose establishment under the presidency of the governor general was the subject of a decree dated April 19, 1940 (*VBl.GG*1 [1940]: 149 f.).

23. The plans were developed as early as 1940, above all in relation to Kraków, Warsaw, and particularly Lemberg (L'vov); for further details, see Urban, "Krakauer gegenwärtige und zukünftige Neubauten" (1940).

24. Decree on the Identification of Businesses in the General Government, November 23, 1939, *VBl.GG* (1939): 61. Guidelines issued by the head of the Governor General's Office (Bühler) concerning the behavior of Germans in Poland, April 24, 1940, no.1 (court records from the Bühler trial), vol. 16, K. 198, in *Doc. Occ.* 6:381 f. Decree circulated by the government of the General Government on March 23, 1941, ZS, Polen 256/1969.

25. Decree issued by the Central Department of Internal Administration on January 15, 1941 (Main Commission Warsaw, Archive, government of the General Government, Central Department of Internal Administration, II/374; also ZS, Polen 257, Bl. 42; copy); the district chiefs were instructed to have any contradictory directives removed step by step, without this appearing to be a "climb down" on the German side. At a meeting of *Kreis-*and *Stadthauptleute* of the Lublin District on January 17, 1941, it was agreed to abolish the "onerous compulsory Hitler-*Gruß* by Jews," in accordance with the decree of January 15, 1941 (minutes, ZS, Polen 347, 293 ff.).

26. Guidelines issued on April 24, 1940, by the head of the Governor General's Office concerning the behavior of Germans in Poland (*Doc. Occ.* 6:381 f.), which stated, among other things, "Service in Poland is service in an enemy country and demands that we Germans adopt an especially responsible attitude . . . a constant awareness that each and every one of us represents the honor and dignity of the German Reich toward the enemy. . . . No. 3: . . . Social intercourse with Poles or Jews of either sex will be shunned by every German as a matter of course. In particular, intimate relations with enemy subjects are undignified and a danger to health. . . . No. 4: . . . Similarly

in religious matters, this separateness is to be rigorously observed. . . . It is not commensurate with the proper conduct of any German who holds his sense of honor dear to attend . . . church services involving Polish clerics." These guiding principles were handed out to all officials and employees in the office of the governor general; cf. letter from the head of the Governor General's Office to all departments and district chiefs, October 11, 1940, quoted from *Doc. Occ.* 6:380 f.

27. Decree of October 26, 1939, on the Introduction of Identification Cards in the General Government (*VBl.GG* [1939]: 8) and First and Second Implementing Regulations of June 13, 1941 (*VBl.GG* [1941]: 55), and April 17, 1943 (*VBl.GG* [1943]: 31). The identity cards were issued by the *Kreishauptamt* (*Stadthauptamt*) and were valid for five years (secs. 8, 10, par. 1, of the First Implementing Regulation of June 13, 1941). Identification cards were obligatory for Jews and Gypsies, even for those who were German citizens (First Implementing Regulation of June 13, 1941, *VBl.GG* [1941]: 55).

28. Sec. 4 of the First Implementing Regulation of June 13, 1941 (*VBl.GG* [1941]: 55).

29. Distribution was held up until 1941, apparently on technical grounds (for example, lack of photographic material), according to Governor Ernst Zörner of the Lublin District, speaking at a government meeting held on October 15, 1941, and *Landrat* Dr. Schönhals at the government meeting of October 17, 1941 ("Diensttagebuch 1941").

Part One. Section 3. B. The Nature of the System of Special Law

1. Cf. record, dated October 20, 1939, from the Armed Forces High Command (OKW) of a "discussion between the Führer and the chief of the OKW on the nature of future relations between Poland and Germany," held on October 17, 1939 (Nuremberg doc., PS-864), in which Hitler's concept was set out; no. 2: Poland "will become neither a part of the German Reich nor an administrative territory of the Reich"; no. 4: "The Civil Service . . . should not be dependent on Berlin. . . . Responsibility is not borne by the Berlin ministries, because it is not a German administrative unit."

2. Statements by Hitler, in minutes from the OKW, October 20, 1939, ibid., no. 4.

3. Cf. observations made by Frank, "Diensttagebuch 1943," vol. 2, May 26, 1943: "To begin with we treated this country as a mere object of plunder. . . . The first success was . . . the dismantling of all economic functions in the territory within a matter of months. But a short time [later] . . . we had to recognize that this course of action would lead to a complete impasse; the German Reich would suffer most as a consequence. . . . Thus, in January—February 1940, what I should like to call the Governor General's Plan was launched, a plan whose object is to harness the area economically to the greatest possible benefit of the German Reich."

4. Memorandum from the OKW, October 20, 1939 (Nuremberg doc., PS-864), no. 6, in which is added: "The 'Polish economy' must be made to flourish."

5. Ibid., no. 3.

6. Concerning legislative work up to 1940, cf. the very detailed synopsis in Adami, "Die Gesetzgebungsarbeit im GG" (1940), 604–17; for more details, see Weh, "Das Recht des GG," *DR* (1940) (A): 1393 ff., 1601 ff.; a complete collection of the laws is given in A. Weh, *Übersicht über das Recht des Generalgouvernements* (loose-leaf collection), 1940 ff., with additional material.

7. Roesner, "Der neue Ostraum Großdeutschlands," *DJ* 2 (1940): 857 f.; according to this, the population totaled 10.565 million (not counting Galicia). See also *Die Ostgebiete des Deutschen Reiches und des Generalgouvernements* (Berlin-Dahlem, 1940) (ZS), Bl. 9.

8. "Legal security" (*Rechtssicherheit*) in the sense of legal clarity but without elements of justice, i.e., ethical elements.

9. *RGBl.* I 2077.

10. Exceptions: Legislative competence was vested in the Führer and Reichskanzler; morever, in addition to the governor general, the Ministerial Council for the Defense of the Reich and the

plenipotentiary for the Four Year Plan also had the right to make law by decree (sec. 5 of the Führer decree of October 12, 1939, (*RGBl.* I 2077); list of Führer decrees and ordinances—concerning less important areas—of the cited authorities in *Doc. Occ.* 6:51 f.

11. All decrees issued by the governor general were published in the Official Gazette, the *Verordnungsblatt für das Generalgouvernement (VBl.GG)*; similarly, police orders for the whole territory of the General Government (sec. 3 of the Decree on Security and Public Order in the General Government [GG] of October 26, 1939, *VBl.GG* [1939]: 5). See also the Decree on the Publication of Proclamations in the General Government of July 23, 1940 (*VBl.GG* [1940]: 223), according to which all proclamations required by law or agreement were to be published in the *Krakauer (Warschauer) Zeitung* in German and Polish, insofar as this was not at divergence with the decrees of the governor general. Instructions, proclamations, appeals, etc., issued by the local authorities at district (*Kreis*) level were usually made public by means of bilingual posters.

12. By means of a Decree Governing the Provisional Regulation of Administrative Jurisdiction in the General Government of July 23, 1940 (*VBl.GG* [1940]: 222); contestation of decisions of the administrative authorities was, with retroactive effect from October 16, 1939, declared inadmissible "until further notice."

13. The governor general alone had the authority to make law by decree; the heads of the (main) departments in his office merely issued implementing orders; also, like other authorities, they could issue administrative instructions when expressly authorized to do so by the government of the General Government. Apart from the governor general, then, no authority had the right to issue decrees; attempts by district governors to make laws by decree were energetically rejected by Frank; cf. letter from the Reich Ministry of Justice to the Reich Minister and Head of the Reich Chancellery, February 13, 1941, and further correspondence (Nuremberg doc., NG-342). The HSSPF of the General Government issued instructions to implement decrees when empowered to do so in decrees issued by the governor general. The right to issue police orders had been granted to the HSSPF by the governor general in sec. 3 of the Decree on Security and Public Order in the General Government of October 26, 1939 (*VBl.GG* [1939]: 5); list of relevant decrees in *Doc. Occ.* 6:87 n. 3). Even without the necessary authority, the HSPPF delegated the right, in certain cases, to issue decrees to the SSPF or the commander of the Security Police (BdS).

14. Cf. report, Dr. F. Siebert, "Zur Frage der Gesetzgebung," of April 22, 1959 (BA Ostdok. 13 GG VII a/1), which reflected the view of many former administrators in the General Government, namely that the legislative process, though tailored to conditions in the Reich, was too unwieldy and time-consuming for the General Government (out of touch, an avalanche of paper from the top). It is said to have taken months to get the administration in Kraków up and running. With the establishment of the government, "legislative fecundity" had grown. This had led to the formation of a top-heavy bureaucracy; more and more departments were spawned. A "Legislature" Department was established within the office of the governor general in January 1940 to initiate, supervise, and centralize the legislative process in the different administrative areas. The department was headed by the "straight A" law graduate OLG-*Rat* (Councillor of the State Superior Court) Albert Weh. It also published the *Gazette of Decrees* and the government section of the *Official Gazette for the General Government*. In keeping with the Reich Statute Book, Weh was also editor of the complete loose-leaf Statute Book of the General Government, "Das Recht des GG," *DR* (1940) with supplements in 1940 and subsequent years. According to the statistics in Weh, "2 Jahre Gesetzgebungsarbeit," 30, the office of the governor general was responsible for a total of 99 acts of legislation in 1939, 446 in 1940, and 289 in 1941, as of September 30; up to October 10, 1941, the government of the General Government alone had promulgated 1,115 draft laws, of which 834 had been put into force. Cf. letter from Governor General Frank to the Reich Minister of Finance, July 9, 1942, which contains Frank's staffing schedule for the Legislature Department, BA R 2/5049, 133 ff. For further details, see Du Prel, *Das GG* (1942), 155; a particular feature of the plan was the circulation and hearing procedure, which was very time-consuming. A further delaying factor was—as F.

Siebert ("Zur Frage der Gesetzgebung," April 22, 1959, BA Ostdok. 13 GG VII a/1) says—the way draft legislation was not discussed in depth centrally in cabinet meetings but only at meetings between Frank the relevant departmental head.

15. The position of the Party in the General Government (for a contemporary view, see von Medeazza, "Die Partei im GG" [1941], who gives an overview, though naturally this skirts round the tensions between Party and Civil Service) was always weak, because Frank would not tolerate Party organizations, with the exception of the Hitler Youth, founded as late as 1942 by special decree (Decree on the Hitler Youth in the General Government of April 22, 1942, *VBl.GG* [1942]: 217; cf. Euller, "Die Hitler-Jugend im GG" [1940], University Library, Warsaw, 011248, no. 2, 24). Frank, the fanatical proponent of the Unified Administration, underlined that the Party in the General Government was a unit and needed no secondary organizations (meeting of department heads on April 12, 1940, "Diensttagebuch," 1:134 ff., 136). The unity would be best preserved in the form of social gatherings.

16. For example, the Decree on Administration of Criminal Justice Affecting Poles and Jews, December 4, 1941 (*RGBl.* I 759); secs. 4, 5 of the Decree on Administration of Civil Law in the Annexed Eastern Territories, September 25, 1941 ("Ostrechtspflegeverordnung"), *RGBl.* I 597 ff.

Part One. Section 3. C. I. The Cultural Sector

1. Sec. 3, the Führer decree of October 12, 1939 (*RGBl.* I 2077), in conjunction with secs. 5, 6 of the Decree on the Occupied Polish Territories, October 26, 1939 (*VBl.GG* [1939]: 3).

2. For details on the cultural administration, see the sources cited in *Doc. Occ.* 6:406 ff. and the introduction of K. M. Pospieszalski (ibid., 391 ff.); Madajczyk, *Polityka*, 2:120 ff.; *Nazi Culture in Poland* (1970) (no author); for an account of cultural policy in the General Government (GG), see Clemen, "Kunstdenkmäler und Denkmalsschutz im Generalgouvernement," BA Br. II/46, and the "Report on the Development of the Administration in the General Government," July 1, 1940, Bl. 113 ff., BA R 52/247. For details on the economic administration, see *Doc. Occ.* 6:243 ff.; and the regulations reproduced in Weh, *Übersicht über das Recht des Generalgouvernements*, sec. E. Regarding the labor administration, see also *Doc. Occ.* 6:306 ff.; Weh, *Übersicht über das Recht des Generalgouvernements*, 2:F; and Melies, *Das Arbeitsrecht des GG* (1943).

3. For a detailed account, see C. Kleßmann, *Die Selbstbehauptung einer Nation, Nationalsozialistische Kulturpolitik und polnische Widerstandsbewegung im GG 1939–1945* (1971); Stamati, "Zur 'Kulturpolitik' des Ostministeriums" (1958), 78 ff.

4. In the office of the governor general, all areas of importance for propaganda purposes (propaganda, the press, radio, film, print, music, theater, visual arts, the Department for Tourism, and trade fairs and exhibitions) were subordinated to the (Central) Department of Propaganda, in keeping with the arrangements in the Reich. The head of the Press Department was simultaneously the chief press spokesman for the government of the General Government; in view of his desire to build up an independent press office, this led (as also in the Reich between the Reich Press Office and the Ministry of Propaganda) to a running feud with the head of the Central Department of Propaganda (press conference, April 14, 1942, "Diensttagebuch 1942," 1:297; also in *Doc. Occ.* 6:437 ff.; also discussion between the latter and Frank on January 10, 1941). This Central Department, which was chiefly concerned with the underpinning of the Geman hegemony claims in the Weichsel (Wisła) area (*Krakauer Zeitung*, October 26, 1940), appears to have been largely incompetent in terms of personnel and conduct of business. The president, Nebing, was accused of "unparalleled economic corruption"; moral standards were said to be such that, "under this leadership, no decent man" would be able to work in the department (report by the *Referent* for Education of the People and Propaganda to Governor General Frank at the meeting of January 10, 1941). Frank responded by setting up an inquiry ("Diensttagebuch 1941"); the outcome was the replacement of the president of the department.

5. The Central Department of Propaganda was very active: already by the spring of 1940 it

had built up an "ethnic German cultural organization" with 34 local groups, its own German publishing companies (three up to December 1941), turned Polish theaters into German-language theaters and provided subsidies for them (in Kraków, Warsaw, and Lublin); up to the end of 1941 it had arranged more than 20 state ceremonial occasions and 170 concerts by visiting musicians from the Reich (cf. "Diary of Events of the General Government for the period from May 16 to 31, 1942," ZS, Versch. 341, 449); it produced its own weekly newsreels and film reports for showing in Polish cinemas; a Tourist Board was set up in Kraków, with its own branch office in Berlin to advertise the General Government as a "holiday destination" (Jaenicke, "Propaganda und Kulturarbeit" [1941], 3 ff., 5 ff.). In 1943, at Frank's instigation, a *Baedeker* for the General Government was published (IfZ). The confiscated Polish sports fields and tennis courts, water sports centers, swimming pools, athletic stadia, and arts facilities were reserved solely for the use of Germans; German bookstores were established, German restaurants, NSDAP adult education centers, and in every town a *Deutsches Haus* ("German House") where social events were held for the German population. October—November 1940 saw the first Warsaw Cultural Festival (Grundmann, "Deutsches Kulturleben in Warsaw" [1941]).

6. Already in 1940 the governor general appointed a special commissioner to oversee sporting activities for Germans; under him were four district commissioners and 30 *Kreis* sports leaders. As early as June of that year, the Warsaw District held its own athletic championships; in 1940 the first tennis championships were held in the General Government. By 1940 Warsaw already had 25 sports clubs with 6,000 members and two SS-*Führerheime* (social clubs for SS leaders) (Grundmann, "Deutsches Kulturleben in Warsaw"; University Library, Warsaw, Sign. 011248). In 1940 8 *Land* championships were held in a range of sports, and 200 sports centers, gymnasiums, etc. were reestablished; in Kraków the Deutsche Kampfbahn sports and leisure center (athletic stadium, football field, swimming pool, open-air theater, tennis courts) was opened in 1941; by 1941 there were 99 German gymnastics and sports clubs in the General Government; for further details see G. Niffka, *Das Generalgouvernement* (March 1941), Folge 6, 15 ff. (University Library, Warsaw, Sign. 011248). (The author was the governor general's special commissioner for sports).

7. Cf. Du Prel, *Das Generalgouvernement* (1942), 186 ff. One result of these efforts was the establishment of the Institut für Deutsche Ostarbeit (Institute for German Development in the East) in Kraków (decree issued on April 19, 1940, VBl.GG 1 [1940]: 149 f.), which was conceived as a replacement for the closed University of Kraków, having "in a certain sense" sections that corresponded to faculties (Prehistory; History; History of Art; Ethnology, including Jewish studies; Slavonic Philology; Law; Economy; Geography; Agriculture; Horticulture; Forestry). According to sec. 3 of the decree, the institute's objective was "fundamental scientific research into all aspects of the Eastern lands"; in other words, to prove that the General Government had been an area of German settlement since time immemorial; for further details, see Du Prel, *Das Generalgouvernement*; according to a report in the *Krakauer Zeitung*, April 21, 1942, the institute had—by 1942—become the largest institute of Eastern studies with branches in Warsaw and Lemberg (L'vov), in which 100 staff were employed. Along the same lines, the office of the commissioner appointed by Frank in 1942 to oversee the security of art treasures was changed into an Office for the Preservation of Historical Art Treasures (decree, July 27, 1942, VBl.GG [1942]: 419); however, the office was closed a year later because of mismanagement by the head, Kajetan Mühlmann (discussion on July 13, 1943, between Mühlmann and the head of the Legislative Office, Weh ["Diensttagebuch," 3:678]).

8. Cf. the implementing regulation of January 15, 1940 (*VBl. GG* 2 [1940]: 61), under the terms of which a special commissioner was appointed by the governor general to check these actions ("Diensttagebuch," March 4, 1940; report, June 30, 1942, on the actions of the special commissioner, Nuremberg doc., PS-1709); the *Ahnenerbe* (Heritage) Bureau of the *Reichsführer*-SS claimed responsibility for cataloging art treasures in the General Government and, as early as October 1939, had undertaken expropriations on their own initiative—for example the Veit-Stoß altar from Kraków

(cf. letter from the special commissioner, October 24, 1939, to the chief of the Heritage Bureau [Wolfram Sievers], Nuremberg doc., NO-572); thereupon, Peter Paulsen made an agreement with Mühlmann, according to which the Heritage Bureau would be responsible for cataloging prehistoric artifacts and collections, and everything else would be left to Mühlmann (memorandum by Mühlmann, October 31, 1939, and letter from Paulsen to Sievers, Heritage Bureau, October 24, 1939, Nuremberg doc., NO-572). But the confusion over competences remained: Himmler entered the fray with his own directive on the expropriation of art treasures, issued on December 1, 1939, as well as internal instructions (for example the decree of December 16, 1939, to the commander of the Security Police and the SD in the General Government, ZS Polen, film 60, 501 ff.) to expropriate all historic and prehistoric treasures, jewelry of artistic value, etc., where these were not owned by Germans. On the basis of the instruction of December 1, 1939, the chairman of the Ministerial Council for the Defense of the Reich appointed a general trustee to administer the confiscated treasures (under the aegis of the Heritage Bureau), which action was meant to establish Himmler's remit as RKF to exercise responsibility for all art treasures in the Annexed Eastern Territories and the General Government (details from "Diensttagebuch 1940," 1:93 ff.). Mühlmann resigned in July 1943 after receiving heavy criticism about—among other things—a "chaotic state of affairs" ("Diensttagebuch," July 13, 1943).

9. Cf. Nuremberg doc., NO-965 (confiscation of books, paintings, archives, libraries; enrichment of top officials); for more details, see K. M. Pospieszalski, *Doc. Occ.* 6:391 ff.; concerning theft of Polish art treasures, see Piotrowski, *Hans Franks Tagebuch*, 159 ff.; *Bulletin of the High Commission Warsaw*, 4:175 ff.; Madajczyk, *Polityka*, 2:120 ff.; comments of the former special commissioner for the cataloging of art and cultural treasures in the General Government, Mühlmann, November 6, 1945 (Nuremberg doc., PS-3042), on plans to take all important works of art to Germany after the war, as well as the report on Mühlmann's activities, June 30, 1942, Nuremberg doc., PS 1709; the basis for the expropriation of Polish cultural treasures was a decree of the governor general, December 16, 1939 (*VBl.GG* [1939]: 209), declaring the confiscation of publicly owned art collections (of which confiscated private collections were considered a part).

10. Draft and final version (no exact date) Institute for Western Studies, Poznań, doc. I-674, according to which Germans could not appear in front of Polish audiences, though Polish artists were allowed to appear in German shows (though not together with Germans); Polish musical performances, but not concerts, were allowed; Polish music—marches, folk and national songs, all classical pieces—was banned; also prohibited were theatrical performances and opera; maps and atlases showing the former Poland were to be withdrawn from circulation, as well as English and French works of literature and Polish flags and insignia; Poles were to be prevented from gaining access to German books.

11. Cf. discussion between the governor general and the minister of propaganda, Goebbels, et al., on October 31, 1939, on the future cultural policy in the General Government ("Diensttagebuch 1939," 21—excerpts in *Doc. Occ.* 6:406 ff.). Among other things, Goebbels remarked that the Poles were to have newspapers containing only news, no opinion pieces. "In principle, they should also be deprived of theater and cinema to avoid having what they've lost paraded constantly before their eyes. . . . The Führer said only yesterday that we should not come along with a bee in our bonnets about helping the Poles rebuild their culture; the Poles should rebuild it themselves."

12. Cf. press conference held on April 14, 1942, "Diensttagebuch 1942," 1:297 (reproduced in *Doc. Occ.* 6:437 ff.), at which representatives of the Press Office, backed by Frank, endeavored to strengthen Polish *trust* in German authority; they would have to be given more than just the Wehrmacht report and a few statistics. The Central Propaganda Office had made many mistakes (441 ff.). Frank concluded: "We are clear in our minds that this population of 1 million needs a press that provides more than just straight news. This is not for the sake of the Poles themselves but is in our own vital interests. At the very least we must act as though the General Government were

a protectorate in the Greater German sphere. . . . As long as the Poles live, they must work for us."
He wanted to stick to the "present course" of providing the Poles with "more attractive newspapers." He sensed that the Berlin headquarters showed "a complete lack of understanding" for the
situation (442):

> The Poles should feel they are being treated not like swine but like Europeans and human be-
> ings. We devote so much attention to the Poles that we can say with some justification that
> despite the miserable conditions they must endure, the Poles live better in the General Gov-
> ernment than the Italians in Italy. . . . Indeed, we are dependent on the Poles: if Polacks don't
> drive the trains, who will? The responsibility is so great that we must put up with a few choice
> words about Christianity and Catholicism in the Polish press. . . . If I want to win the war, I
> must think clinically like a technician. . . . The Poles must [therefore] . . . be given more in
> [the]) press than just orders. (443)

13. The concept of the police had no place in cultural life, because its political horizons did
not reach beyond the exercise of power and "holding down" the foreign population. In *Meldungen
aus dem Reich* (News from the Reich), no. 257, February 5, 1942, from the chief of the Security Police and the SD (IfZ, Ma-441/5, 5800–5904), the CSSD complained about a revival of Polish cultural
life that was in no way in keeping with the political line, namely "to curb home-grown cultural activities and prevent their achieving anything more than the shallowest level." One example was the
so-called coffee-house meetings, said to be common in all larger towns and at which permission
had even been given for an orchestral performance of music by Chopin; the limit—the report
said—was the Philharmonic Orchestra of the General Government whose German director had
been confirmed in his post by Hitler himself and which was made up of 90 Polish musicians; German opinion that Poland had never possessed a high culture of its own was thereby turned on its
head. The report demanded the creation of a German central orchestra under Polish direction,
though this "should not be allowed to attain a level of performance above the mediocre." This principle was to be applied to all Polish cultural performances. Furthermore, the Polish theater in Warsaw was described as "excellent"; Polish theater performances were helping to break down the barriers between Germans and Poles and establish the claim to equal treatment for the Poles. The new
line must adhere to the principle of a ban on the appearance of Polish artists in front of German
audiences and on Germans attending Polish performances. These latter were not to be "of a high
caliber culturally or of a morally uplifting nature." However, the governor general stuck to his line
that the Poles should be permitted a measure of cultural "autonomy."

14. Report, F. Siebert: "Hauptabteilung Innere Verwaltung," November 11, 1959, BA Ostdok. 13
GG Ib/5.

15. Monthly report, *Kreishauptmann* Reichshof (Rzeszów), May 1940 (ZS, Polen 347, Bl. 564,
566); monthly report, *Kreishauptmann* Jasło, August 1940 (Bl. 101 ff.). According to the report, the
raids by the Security Police—with their *summary proceedings*—gave rise to unnecessary upheaval,
also in loyalist Polish circles (e.g., the working class).

16. Cf., in general, the sources cited above in note 2.

17. Guidelines issued by the head of the Department of Cultural Affairs on January 10, 1940
(Institute for Western Studies, Poznań, doc. I-127); for further details, see Madajczyk, *Polityka*,
2:142 ff. The Polish grammar schools (*Gymnasien*) were not reestablished. Comments by Central
Department of Science and Education (meeting on July 4, 1944, "Diensttagebuch") to the effect that
they were to be permitted again from September 1944, as a concession to the Poles, were not to be
taken at face value. Himmler, alerted by the governor of the Lublin District (Richard Wendler),
considered it "good that, for Polish public opinion, the matter was being treated with all seriousness. Steps have been taken to ensure that no harm will come of it" (telex from the personal staff of
the *Reichsführer*-SS, Rudolf Brandt, to Wendler on May 27, 1944, IfZ, Bestand Reichsführer-SS/Pers.
Stab, FB-50, Bl. 286, copy). These Polish *Gymnasien* were in any case considered nothing more

than a prize for good behavior, i.e., for pupils and parents who "had proved their worth in the service of Germany," and a way of countering the spread of illegal Polish schools (meeting on July 4, 1944, "Diensttagebuch"). For Ukrainians, in contrast, high schools were permitted (guidelines of January 10, 1940, Institute for Western Studies, Poznań, doc. I-127).

Discussion between Frank and Goebbels on October 31, 1939, and other dates, "Diensttagebuch 1939," 21 (quoted from *Doc. Occ.* 6:406 ff.). The Polish universities continued only on an administrative level, under the supervision of university commissioners (Decree on the Appointment of University Commissioners in the General Government, October 29, 1940, *VBl.GG* 1 [1940]: 327, with decree issued by the Department of Science, Education, and Public Enlightenment to the district chiefs on December 19, 1940, *Amtsblatt der Abteilung Wissenschaft, Erziehung und Volksbildung in der Regierung des GG*, March 1941, quoted from *Doc. Occ.* 6:417 f.). In this sense see also the first guidelines issued by Mühlmann, head of the Department of Cultural Affairs (forerunner of the Department of Science and Education), on January 10, 1940 (Institute for Western Studies, Poznań, doc. I-727 3 f.). Polish students who had finished their studies were not permitted to take exams—the only exceptions being medical students and graduates of the polytechnic school and the higher school of commerce, who were needed as qualified workers (*Gazeta Illustrowana*, April 18, 1940); however, they did not receive degrees, only certificates saying they had taken part in the examinations (decree issued by the Department of Science, Education, and Public Enlightenment to the district chief, Warsaw, on August 29, 1940, Institute for Western Studies, Poznań, doc. I-668, quoted from: *Doc. Occ.* 6:418 f.). The Ukrainians in Galicia enjoyed certain privileges to the extent that there were university standard courses in Lemberg for doctors, veterinary surgeons, engineers, agronomists, etc.; for more details, see K. M. Pospieszalski, *Doc. Occ.* 6:392 f. nn. 6–9, with further examples.

Guidelines issued by the head of the Department of Cultural Affairs on January 10, 1940 (Institute for Western Studies, Poznań, doc. I-727 3 f.); a priests' seminary remained in existence as a "university-like institution"; the others were closed down.

18. Warsaw University was carried on by the Poles in the underground, as were similarly the higher schools; cf. also diary notes by Dr. Troschke, Bl. 36 f. (BA Ostdok. 13 GG 1a/10); concerning Polish science 1939–45, cf. Madajczyk, *Polityka*, 2:142 ff.

19. Report by *Amtsleiter* Gauweiler, February 28, 1940 ("Diensttagebuch 1940," 121 ff., 124 f.); Decree on Schools in the General Government, October 31, 1939 (*VBl.GG* [1939]: 18); guidelines issued by the head of the Department of Cultural Affairs on January 10, 1940 (Institute for Western Studies, Poznań, doc. I-727 3 f.), according to which authorization was given to reestablish vocational and technical schools "in small numbers" and "teacher training colleges in limited numbers"; Decree on Vocational Schools in the General Government, April 29, 1941 (*VBl.GG* [1941]: 265 ff.), with an implementing order issued on November 26, 1941 (*VBl.GG* [1941]: 679 f.), which authorized attendance at technical schools; in April 1942 a state technical college was established in Warsaw that also accepted Polish undergraduates (*Krakauer Zeitung*, February 28, 1942). Sec. 5 of the Decree on Schools in the General Government, October 31, 1939 (*VBl.GG* [1939]: 18); Decree on Private Schools in the General Government, April 12, 1940 (*VBl.GG* 1 [1940]: 134); Decree on Private Schools in the General Government, April 23, 1940 (*VBl.GG* 1 [1940]: 160).

20. Decree on Schools in the General Government, October 31, 1939 (*VBl.GG* [1939]: 18). In Warsaw in February 1940 there were already as many as 29 German schools with approximately 4,000 German pupils (Report by *Amtsleiter* Gauweiler, February 28, 1940, "Diensttagebuch 1940," 121 ff., 124 f.). In 1941 there was a total of 300 German schools in the General Government, with *volksdeutsche* teachers working alongside 46 teachers of Reich German origin. There was an "almost complete" lack of recruits (because of the lowering of public esteem for the teaching profession), according to the head of the Central Department of Science, Adolf Watzke, at a cabinet meeting on October 15, 1941 ("Diensttagebuch 1941," 213 ff.). In 1944 there were 2 million Polish *Volksschüler*,

22,000 Polish teachers, and 4,000 teachers of religious education. Numerous illegal schools, particularly *Gymnasien*, were active (Secretary Schmelzer of the Central Department of Science and Art in a working discussion on July 4, 1944, "Diensttagebuch 1944," vol. 4). Jewish children were banned from attending schools until the Decree on Jewish Schools of August 31, 1940 (*VBl.GG* 1 [1940]: 258); after that, the Jewish schools (*Volksschulen*) were run under the aegis of the Jewish Councils, which had been formed in every municipality, though they had only the status of private schools. Higher schools for Jews were closed in December 1939 and all teachers peremptorily dismissed. For a detailed account, see the "Report on the Development of the General Government" of July 1, 1940, BA R 52 II/247, 113 f. (138). Decree on the Development of the School Administration of March 16, 1940, *VBl.GG* 1 (1940): 106; for an account of the school policy and the issue of curricula guidelines, cf. minutes of a meeting of the school commissioners of the district chief, January 1, 1940, in Kraków (Institute for Western Studies, Poznań).

21. Up to 1942 there were no textbooks whatsoever. Report from the governor of the Warsaw District for February 1942 of March 17, 1942 (Institute for Western Studies, Poznań, doc. I, 10, 203). The Polish textbooks were not usable because they were "full of anti-German sentiments." Thereupon, the Central Department of Science commissioned a math book, a reading book, and a *Fibel* (primary school textbook); but these could not be printed owing to the paper shortage (250 tons of paper would have been needed). As a result, the Polish *Volksschulen* mostly made very slow progress because of the lack of teaching material and schoolrooms; the Polish technical and vocational schools (over 150 in Warsaw) clearly suffered less from the shortages (discussion of district chiefs on January 14, 1941, "Diensttagebuch 1941," vol. 2). Frank issued a decree on April 13, 1940, which reduced the numbers of Polish teachers by getting rid of those who were "politically unreliable" and "bad characters," those earning two salaries, and *Vertragslehrer* (teachers who operated as *privatdozents*) (Du Prel, *Das Generalgouvernement*, 135). Polish teachers at former higher schools were not reemployed at Polish *Volksschulen* as a matter of principle—a further measure to eliminate the Polish intelligentsia ("Report on the Development of the General Government," July 1, 1940, BA R 52 II/247, 113 f.). Schools for Poles were founded only in places where, in five successive years, there were at least 40 pupils. Class numbers were around 70 (Du Prel, *Das GG*, 172, 135). By contrast, German schools were to be established in all localities with more than 10 school-age children (secs. 1, 2 of the Decree on Schools of October 31, 1939, *VBl.GG* [1939]: 18).

22. Frank at a working meeting on February 25, 1940, in Radom ("Diensttagebuch 1940" 1:107 ff., 114): "If school has to be suspended in Germany, then it can also be suspended here. You can always use the lack of coal or shortage of rooms as an excuse. It is perfectly clear that we should safeguard the Polish *Volksschulen* for them. But if they don't want to make use of them, we shouldn't force them. It is certainly not in our interest to encourage raising the level of education of the Poles" (*Doc. Occ.* 6:393 n. 10); cf. also "Diensttagebuch II" of May 27, 1940, 541: "In regard to the school system, it must be emphasized that the number of teachers is still too large. We must get to the point where there are about 70–80 pupils to one teacher [as in the Annexed Eastern Territories—Author]. We have to remove the younger teachers and give the older ones classes so large that the level of education falls all by itself." The curriculum in Polish *Volksschulen* included nature studies, six hours of "practical activities" ("school fields to be used for experiments"), in some cases with "great success." German language lessons were planned (report by Schmelzer, July 4, 1944, "Diensttagebuch").

23. Decree on Associations in the General Government of July 23, 1940 (*VBl.GG* 1 [1940]: 225); charities concerned with free welfare were also affected by the dissolution. The assets of disbanded associations were expropriated; those of charitable organizations were placed at the disposal of the Department of Population Affairs, Central Department of Internal Administration, which *could* use them to support Polish welfare associations (memorandum, Central Department of Internal Administration, September 18, 1940, BA R 52 III/4, 17 ff., 39 f.). For more on the disbanding of associations, cf. Frank, "Staatsverwaltung," *Das Generalgouvernement* (1941), ser. 13, 14, 7 ff., 13).

24. Decree on the Rights of Foundations in the General Government, August 1, 1940, *VBl.GG* 1 [1940]: 244). Religious sects were dissolved as of March 31, 1941 (*VBl.GG* [1941]: 197).

25. Cf. Nuremberg doc., D-965. Amongs other, the University Library in Warsaw and the Polish parliamentary library were expropriated, the latter transported to Berlin and Breslau (Wrocław), on November 15 and 16, 1939; the Hebrew Library and the library of the Polish Foreign Ministry were dealt with similarly; 14,000 volumes are said to have been lost (Nuremberg doc., D-965).

26. Discussion involving Frank, Geobbels, and others on October 31, 1939, in Łódź (reproduced in *Doc. Occ.* 6:406 ff.); more than half of the approximately 300 cinemas in the General Government were closed down; the remaining cinemas showed German films and prewar Polish films (*Nazi Culture in Poland*, 214). In October 1941 there were 17 German, 62 German-Polish, and 44 Polish cinemas operating (Jaenicke, "Propaganda und Kulturarbeit" [1941], 8)—in other words, 106 cinemas for a population of 10.5 million.

27. The following newspapers and magazines (initially carrying only news) were permitted: *Goniec Krakówski, Nowy Kurier Warszawski, Dziennik Radomski, Kurier Kielecki, Kurier Częstochowski*, and *Nowy Głos Lubelski;* these were later joined by *Gazeta Lwówska* (for Galicia); an illustrated magazine, *Illustrowany Kurier Polski* (Du Prel, *Das Generalgouvernement*, 301 f.); a weekly, *7 Dni;* and a monthly, *O Miesiąć Powieść* (Story of the month). A pornographic magazine, *Fala* (The wave) appeared later. Polish special-interest magazines allowed to appear included *Ster* (Tax), *Zawod y życie* (Work and life), a monthly for vocational schools; *Rolnik* (The farmer), a monthly; *Sieco* (The seed); *Wzorowa Gospordaka* (The model business), a monthly; *Las i Drzewno* (Forest and wood); *Zdrowie y życie* (Health and life), a periodical of the Medical Association; in all, nine dailies, four weeklies, one bimonthly, two monthlies and about 20 special-interest periodicals (some fortnightly, some monthly) (Gassner, "Die Presse" [1941], 14). For the Ukrainian population there were two dailies, two weeklies, and various monthly magazines; there was a newssheet for the Jewish population, *Gazeta żydowska* (15). The German newspapers in the General Government were *Krakauer Zeitung*, with a Warsaw edition, *Warschauer Zeitung*, and from October 26, 1941, a Lemberg edition; *Lemberger Zeitung* (12 ff.); there was also a very expensively produced magazine dealing with cultural history, *Das Generalgouvernement* (15,000 circulation, according to comments by the publisher of the *Krakauer Zeitung*, Strotzig, during a discussion with Frank on January 14, 1941, "Diensttagebuch 1941"); the organ of the Institute for Eastern Studies, *Die Burg* (which published research findings from the General Government); *Das Vorfeld*, the organ of the NSDAP; and *Pressedienst des GG*, which was a press agency supplying news from the General Government for the press in the Reich.

28. "News from the Reich," February 4, 1941, BA R 58/157.

29. For further details, see Du Prel, *Das GG*, 150.

30. Decree on Cultural Activities in the General Government, March 8, 1940 (*VBl.GG* 1 [1940]: 103), with First, Second, and Third Implementing Regulations issued on July 5, 1940 (*VBl. GG* 2 [1940]: 399); August 18, 1940 (424) (official authorization was compulsory for all cultural activities, in particular musicians, composers, painters, sculptors, graphic artists, art dealers, actors, singers, directors, artistes, writers, journalists, publishers, booksellers, and photographers); and November 4, 1942 (*VBl.GG* [1942]: 699; authorizations valid for one year only).

31. A decree of March 31, 1941 (*VBl.GG* [1941]: 171), covered public music performances. Decree on the Publishing Industry in the General Government, October 31, 1939 (*VBl.GG* [1939]: 19); and Second Decree of March 21, 1940 (*VBl.GG* 1 [1940]: 19). Decree on the Publishing of Printed Matter, October 26, 1939 (*VBl.GG* [1939]: 7), with First and Second Implementing Regulations issued on March 20, 1940 (*VBl.GG* 2 [1940]: 186—making it compulsory to obtain official authorization for the operation of printing shops); and September 5, 1940 (*VBl.GG* 2 [1940]: 487—making it compulsory to obtain official authorization for *planning* to publish printed matter). Third Implementing

Regulation of October 24, 1940 (*VBl.GG* 2 [1940]: 514) to the Decree on the Publishing of Printed Matter of October 26, 1939 (*VBl.GG* [1939]: 7). First Implementing Regulation of October 24, 1940 (*VBl.GG* 2 [1940]: 513), to the Decree on the Publishing Industry of October 31, 1939 (*VBl.GG* [1939]: 19); this was intended above all to prevent the growth of a Polish underground press. Introduction of paper rationing through a decree issued on July 23, 1942 (*VBl.GG* [1942]: 415 ff.); introduction of compulsory authorization for the production of printed matter by directive no. 2 of the Rationing Office issued on October 24, 1942 (*VBl.GG* [1942]: 688), for the Poles effectively a ban; ban on the manufacture of all paper products (cardboard, paperboard, packaging, cards, exercise books, etc.) by means of directive no. 3 issued by the Rationing Office on April 1, 1943 (*VBl.GG* [1943]: 168 f.). Fourth Implementing Regulation of October 24, 1940 (*VBl.GG* 2 [1940]: 515), to the Decree on the Publishing of Printed Matter of October 26, 1939 (*VBl.GG* [1939]: 7).

32. Responsibility for supervising cultural activities was vested in the district chief, in accordance with instructions from the head of the Department for Education of the People and Propaganda (sec. 1 of the Decree on Cultural Activity in the General Government, March 8, 1940, *VBl. GG* 1 [1940]: 103).

33. Cf., for example, sec. 2 of the Decree on the Publishing of Printed Matter of October 26, 1939 (*VBl.GG* [1939]: 8).

34. Guidelines issued by the head of the Department of Cultural Affairs in the office of the governor general, January 10, 1940 (Institute for Western Studies, Poznań, doc. I-727).

35. Decree on the Division along Ethnic Lines of the Membership of the Evangelical Church in the General Government, issued on March 16, 1941 (*VBl.GG* [1941]: 100).

Part One. Section 3. C. II. The Economic and Commercial Sector

1. Cf. "Report on the Development of the General Government" of July 1, 1940, BA R 52 II/249, 145 ff., according to which, from the outset, the General Government was a *Land* with insufficient energy resources and raw materials and an inadequate transport infrastructure; it did not produce enough consumer goods, nor could it produce enough to feed itself by its own efforts. According to Frank's Four Year Plan for the General Government of January 25, 1940, agricultural production was to be intensified, "superfluous industrial plants" shut down, and the mineral resources and some 700,000 farm workers were to be transported to the Reich (Nuremberg doc., NO-EC-1). According to a report on the armaments industry for the period from March 27 to May 14, 1940 (by Lieutenant General von Backhausen, IfZ, Ma-679/1, 1000), the General Government was a subsidy zone, both agriculturally and industrially. In 1940 the ratio of exports to imports was 1:4; in 1941 the subsidies from the Reich were very low. However, according to figures quoted by the president of the Central Department of Finance, Spindler, at a meeting of department heads on March 25, 1941 ("Diensttagebuch") the General Government must have almost balanced its budget in 1941 (spending and income totaled some 1 billion złoty, the deficit approx. 60 million złoty). But it is unclear whether this takes into account the exports to the Reich. The *Land* had only one significant asset: cheap labor; the economic policy was therefore "colonial in character"—see also the following note.

2. Meeting of department heads on January 19, 1940, "Diensttagebuch 1940," 1:60 ff. Among other comments, Frank said the General Government had so far been seen as a country "ripe for plunder." The task now was to rebuild production "in the service of the Reich"; it was necessary "to extract whatever could be extracted from the country." See also the report on the armaments industry for the period from March 27 to May 14, 1940 (IfZ, Ma-679/1, 1000); from 1941 on, everything possible had been squeezed out of the General Government; and to cap it all, it was expected to be in a position to feed itself.

3. A communication from the deputy Führer dated November 1939 reports—among other things—that Hitler had approved Frank's decision that neither Warsaw nor Polish industry was to

be rebuilt (Nuremberg doc., EC-411). [The comments by Frank quoted in the previous note evidently refer to an industry given over entirely to war production—Author.]

4. A decree issued by Frank on July 31, 1940 (*VBl.GG* 1 [1940]: 233 f.; Weh, *Übersicht über das Recht des Generalgouvernements* [1943], A 140), established the Economic Council for the General Government as the supreme organ of economic policy. It was made up of the heads of department in the office of the governor general and worked under his chairmanship, though he had only advisory status. At Frank's insistence, this Economic Council superseded the existing Office for the Four Year Plan in the General Government (decree of July 31, 1940; Weh, *Übersicht über das Recht des Generalgouvernements*, E 100); in other words, it supplanted the competent Reich offices, thereby widening the governor general's scope of responsibility and allowing him a free hand to pursue his own plans. A notable development was that, in the face of objections by Frank, the Reich-controlled trust company for the "management" of assets seized from Poles and Jews was never established (cf. meeting on November 1, 1939, "Diensttagebuch," and Frank's comments at a meeting with *Kreishauptleute* and *Stadthauptleute* in Lublin on March 4, 1940, and with department heads on March 8, 1940, in Kraków, ibid., 1940); instead the General Government's own trustee administration was established as part of the Department of Economics (cf. Frank in conference with Göring on December 4, 1939, in Berlin, ibid.). It should be noted that the General Government had its own unwieldy, centralized economic structure, which brought together all branches of the economy in a single chamber (the Central Chamber of Industry and Commerce; at district level, the District Chamber of Industry and Commerce) in the form of corporations under public law (decree of March 3, 1941, *VBl.GG* [1941]: 87 ff.; the personnel were largely synonymous with the specialist officials of the state authorities and combined both offices in one person), whose object was to "consolidate" the "economic self-management" of "non-Germans" (Kundt, "Entstehung, Probleme, Grundsätze und Form der Verwaltung des Generalgouvernements" [1944], 65 f., University Library Warsaw, Sign. 011249). These chambers—unlike their equivalents in the Reich—had no sovereign powers but were merely executive organs of the corresponding (Central) Departments of the state administration (*Krakauer Zeitung*, December 5, 1941). They did not, therefore, serve as agencies of self-management; rather, they acted as intermediaries between the state and businesses (*Krakauer Zeitung*, February 4, 1942; Governor Kundt, at a meeting on May 30, 1942, "Diensttagebuch"). "For the purpose of eliminating Jewish commerce," the authorities did not apply sectoral categories but worked on a regional principle, establishing a trading company for each of the 40 *Kreis* districts of the General Government (consolidated in a single GmbH—stock corporation; it was the task of these companies to supply Polish wholesalers and the public, as well as to purchase farm produce (*Warschauer Zeitung*, November 12, 1940, IfZ). For more on the economic and administrative rules, see Bühler, "Das GG und seine Wirtschaft" (BA D IV c/102); "Report on the Development of the General Government," July 1, 1940, 2:167 (BA R 22/249).

5. On the one hand, the desire was for an "administration with wide-ranging powers"; on the other, all vestiges of Polish autonomy had been destroyed (report 39/45 from the Warsaw District, spring 1945, Ostdok. 13 GG IX a/5, 25). As a result, there was much activity by Poles—particularly members of the Polish resistance movement—on the lower echelons (cooperatives), beyond the control of the German authorities (monthly report, February 1941, *Kreishauptmann* Sochaczew-Blonie, March 4, 1941, IfZ, microfilm Ma-158/3, Fasz. 27/52).

6. The economic was administered by the Central Department of Economics in the office of the governor general, with subordinate authorities on district and *Kreis* level. Of the numerous special administrative departments, it was above all the economic and agricultural administration that expanded at the cost of the general Civil Service, with a proliferation of new central and district offices and suboffices, etc.

7. This applied above all to the numerous monopolies operating in the General Government. Before 1939 the monopolies (tobacco, brandy, salt, matches, and the lottery) brought in about 30%

of public revenue. The German administration added mineral oil and sugar monopolies. The proportion of state revenues subsequently rose to about 60% of the income of the financial administration (*Warschauer Zeitung*, November 5, 1940); cf. also "Report on the Monopolies in the General
Government," *Frankfurter Zeitung*, February 27, 1940, quoted from BA R 2/5076.

8. According to the Decree on the Elimination of Bolshevist Economic Systems of July 27,
1942 (*VBl.GG* [1942]: 418), private companies were permitted in Galicia, though not in the General
Government; cf. Dresler, "Die Reprivatisierung in Galizien" (1942), 347 ff.; Losacker, "Aufbau der
Verwaltung im neuen Distrikt Galizien" (1942). An earlier decree, issued on August 1, 1941 (*VBl.GG*
[1941]: 447), had already specified that the Decree on the Seizure of Private Property in the General
Government (*VBl.GG* 1 [1940]: 27 f.) also applied in Galicia. The Decree on the Elimination of Bolshevist Economic Systems of July 27, 1942 (*VBl.GG* [1942]: 418), ordered the reprivatization of craft
businesses and retail stores, albeit "only in cases where their continuance was in the national economic interest"; under the terms of a further decree issued on July 27, 1942 (*VBl.GG* [1942]: 418), it
did not extend to the reprivatization of land in public ownership, and any "cession" (*Überlassung*)
of land to farmers was for the purpose of "management and exploitation only," whereas the first
decree mentioned above spoke of "transfer of title" (*Übertragung*). Farmland thus remained the
property of the German administration. The SS also opposed reprivatization, arguing that this
would place "tremendous obstacles in the way of our [i.e., SS] settlement efforts in the area and the
Eastern lands as a whole" (telegram from SS-*Gruppenführer* Gottlob Berger, Central Settlement Office of the SS to *Reichsführer*-SS, August 7, 1942; Nuremberg doc., NO-5943). For his part, Himmler
planned to restrict transfer of property rights to those farmers who had fulfilled their harvest quotas "faultlessly and in exemplary fashion" since 1941 (letter from Himmler to the Lemberg District
governor, Otto Gustav Wächter, March 28, 1943; IfZ, Bestand RFSS/Pers. Stab, MA-305, 2484 f.).
Wächter and the HSSPF in the General Government, in contrast, were in favor of unconditional
reprivatization. Himmler remained firm (correspondence [2494–2512]). Nor was there a *general*
reprivatization of business enterprises, since this would also have meant restoring to Poles property
placed in public ownership by the Soviet administration—something that neither the German administration nor the SS wanted.

9. Frank at a meeting of department heads, January 19, 1940, quoted from "Report 1939–45"
by the deputy head of the Department of Economics in the Warsaw District, spring 1945 (BA Ostdok. 13 GG, IX a/5, 35).

10. According to the "Report 1939–45" (ibid., 25), the war economy in the General Government foundered on conflicting goals of economic policy, supply shortages, red tape (lack of "the
open-handedness necessary for warfare"), and a lack of self-discipline on the part of personnel.
Concerning the economic policy in the General Government, see the highly critical report by Justus Schmitt, head of the Chamber of Industry and Commerce in Czenstochau (Częstochowa) (Institute for Western Studies, Poznań, reproduced in *Doc. Occ.* 6:350 ff.), who attributed the failures
to the tearing apart of the economic area, a flawed food and price policy, bad working conditions,
and the general misery to which the population had been reduced. See the quarterly reports of the
Armaments Commando (*Rüstungskommando*), Kraków, of July 1 and September 30, 1942, and October 1 and December 31, 1942, which include details of the woeful supply, energy, and transport
situation and the undernourishment of the population (ZS, Versch. 3, 504, 577 ff., 594, 601 ff.); cf.
also situation report of the Office for Price Control in the Warsaw District for March 1941, April 4,
1942, ZS, Akte Auerswald 365e; and the moving report "Erfahrungsbericht 1939–45" (BA Ostdok. 13
GG, IX a/5, 35).

11. Decree on Seizure of the Assets of the Former Polish State within the General Government, November 15, 1939 (*VBl.GG* [1939]: 37). The expropriated asset had to be reported to the the the
trustee company offices (First Administrative Regulation of March 16, 1940, *VBl.GG* 2 [1940]: no.

21/40; also Nuremberg doc., NG-2043); in accordance with his wish to place the entire assets of the state, in particular real estate, under the control of the administration of the General Government (conference of August 4, 1940, "Diensttagebuch 1940 II"), Frank issued a decree on September 24, 1940 (*VBl.GG* 1 [1940]: 313 f.), that stipulated that all confiscated assets of the Polish state were the *property* of the General Government (by contrast, in the Eastern Territories the formal transfer of title of confiscated Polish assets was never pronounced, although in practice these assets were treated as property of the Reich). A decree issued by the Reich Ministry of the Interior on May 8, 1942, declared that the German municipalities of the General Government were the rightful owners of Polish municipal assets (Nuremberg doc., NG-2043). Cf. also decree of August 31, 1940 (*VBl.GG* 1 [1940]: 265 ff.), which coupled a pronouncement that the assets of the enemy states had to be registered with a restraining order.

12. *VBl.GG* 1 (1940): 27 f.; a trustee was appointed for the confiscated assets.

13. Cf. administrative act of the General Government of February 8, 1941, regarding the setting up of two commissions: one to work out legal guidelines for the seizures in the General Government and the other to establish basic principles for compensation (ZS, Polen 256, 19).

14. German Superior Court (*Deutsches Obergericht*) Kraków, *DR* (1942) (A): 1463 f.

15. Decree on Real Estate Transactions in the General Government, March 27, 1940 (*VBl.GG* 1 [1940]: 115). Franke, "Staatsverwaltung," *Das GG* (1941), November 1941, Folge 13/14, 7 ff. Decree on the Acquisition of Commercial Enterprises in the General Government, April 23, 1940 (*VBl.GG* 1 [1940]: 171 ff.).

16. Decree of January 20, 1943 (*VBl.GG* [1943]: 45). Concerning the dissolution of Polish enterprises and industries, cf. Madajczyk, *Polityka*, 1:560 ff.

17. *Reichsführer*-SS/RKF to chief of the Security Police, October 11, 1939 (Nuremberg doc., NO-5026).

18. Cf. administrative act of the General Government of February 8, 1941 (ZS, Polen, 256, 9). The formulation of the draft was relatively constitutional, since it followed an ordered process; he planned temporary or permanent expropriation "in the public interest" as a rule for "appropriate compensation." The person affected had a right of appeal (draft with exchange of letters between Krüger and Pers. Stab RFSS [Brandt], October 1942 to January 1943, IfZ, Ma 300, 3965–4004).

19. Sec. 1 of the draft contains the following terse formulation: "Assets can be expropriated for the benefit of the General Government." In the justification it was stated that the seizure order of January 24, 1940, was of little use, since the title of the previous owner did not lapse; no compensation should be paid except in cases of "extreme economic hardship." And even in such cases the redress should consist only in providing a more advantageous workplace. The new expropriation order was intended to be as "comprehensive as possible," in the sense of "uniform control" (by which Krüger meant the police, for authority in the matter lay with the RFSS/RKF, the expropriations being "planning instruments of economic and settlement policy"; IfZ).

20. German Superior Court (*Deutsches Obergericht*) Kraków, *DR* (1942) (A): 1463 f.

21. Agreement between the Main Trustee Office East (HTO) and the government of the General Government, October 10, 1942 (BA R 2/5100).

22. Cf. Seizure Order for Real Estate for the Benefit of the General Government (*Anordnungsblatt für die Stadt Kielce*, December 21, 1943; Institute for Western Studies, Poznań).

23. "Report on the Development of the General Government" of July 1, 1940, 2:75 ff. (BA R 52 II/249).

24. According to the "Report 1939–45" (BA Ostdok. 13 GG IX a/5), seizures were made only where "German interests demanded . . . a dictatorial intervention in the power of control." Instructions had been given to "spare Polish assets . . . and these had been followed to the letter" (p. 135).

25. For a detailed account of the confiscation of Jewish property in the General Government, see Arndt, "Entziehung und Verbringung jüdischen Vermögens (Ausland und Deutschland)" (1963), expert report, 92 ff. (104 ff., 108 ff., 111–13).

26. "Report on the Development of the General Government," July 1, 1940, 2:116 ff. (BA R 52 II/249).

27. Decree on Compulsory Registration of Jewish Assets, January 24, 1940 (*VBl.GG* 1 [1940]: 28); the decree of August 1, 1940 (*VBl.GG* 1 [1940]: 246 f.), introduced general controls on gold and precious metals in the General Government (prohibition of transfer abroad) and compulsory registration of such assets held abroad. It stipulated that Jews were obliged to place all their assets on deposit at a single bank by December 31, 1939. Cash amounts in excess of 2,000 złoty had to be paid into an account immediately on receipt. A maximum of 250 złoty per week could be withdrawn from frozen accounts. Permission had to be obtained for transactions involving frozen accounts. The decree of September 12, 1940 (*VBl.GG* 1 [1940]: 539; for Galicia, the decree of August 28, 1941, *VBl.GG* [1941]: 514), introduced compulsory registration for precious metals—a de facto trading ban for Jews. According to a directive issued by the head of the Foreign Exchange Control Department in the office of the governor general on March 1, 1940 (*VBl.GG* 1 [1940]: 141), Jews had to obtain permission from the Foreign Exchange Control Office in Kraków to purchase gold and other precious metals; a foreign exchange decree for the General Government issued on November 15, 1939 (*VBl.GG* [1939]: 51), introduced—among other things—exchange controls (compulsory authorization for purchase and disposal of foreign currency and for import and export of means of payment, etc.). The Second Foreign Exchange Decree of February 28, 1940 (*VBl.GG* 1 [1940]: 88 ff.), included penalty clauses; cf. also Decree on the Granting of Immunity for Violations of Foreign Exchange Regulations of April 23, 1940 (*VBl.GG* 1 [1940]: 151 f.), which aimed to prevent hoarding of foreign currency and other assets as a result of the general erosion of the currency; details of foreign exchange controls are given in instructions 1, 2, and 3, issued on November 20, 1939, by the head of the Foreign Exchange Control Department (*VBl.GG* [1939]: 53 ff., 55). In view of the general anti-Jewish policy, it was taken as read that authorization to purchase gold, precious metals, and foreign currency would not be granted to Jews.

28. Jews' accounts were blocked by instructions 4 and 5, issued by the head of the Foreign Exchange Control Department in the office of the governor general on November 20, 1939 (*VBl.GG* [1939]: 57 f.); cf. also Arndt, "Entziehung und Verbringung jüdischen Vermögens." Sec. 8 of the Decree on the Seizure of Private Property in the General Government, issued on January 24, 1940 (*VBl.GG* 1 [1940]: 27 f.); seizures were the responsibility of the *Kreishauptleute* (or, as the case may be, the *Stadthauptleute*); cf. also a decree issued by the governor general on September 2, 1941 (ZS, Polen 256, 186); cf. also a corresponding proclamation of the *Stadthauptmann* in Kraków, February 15, 1940 (Main Commission Warsaw, Plakatsammlung III, 24/t, doc. 24/t/34).

29. "Report on the Development of the General Government," July 1, 1940, 2:222 f. (BA R 22/249).

30. Real estate was also confiscated if it was managed by Jews; they were treated as the owners—cf. the seizure by the Central Office of the *Haupttreuhandstelle* Ost (Main Trustee Office East) of a property whose Swedish owner had appointed a Jewish woman as manager (Mitteilungsblatt HTO, December 12, 1942, no. 5, Nuremberg doc., NO-5937).

31. "Report 4/62" of the deputy head of the Department of Economics in the Warsaw District, spring 1945 (BA Ostdok. 13 GG IX a/5, 49 ff.). According to this report, 1,000 firms in the Warsaw District and 14,000 properties with annual rental incomes of approx. 88 million złoty were seized and used for the purposes mentioned. The Poles are said to have welcomed the seizures.

32. *VBl.GG* 1 (1940): 27 f.

33. Budget discussion on January 26, 1943, in Warsaw; comments in Frank, "Diary."

34. See also "Die Treuhandverwaltung des Grundbesitzes im General Government," no date

(probably 1942), Institute for Western Studies, Poznań. On November 15, 1939, Treuhandstelle für das GG was opened as a main trustee office in Kraków (Arndt, "Entziehung und Verbringung jüdischen Vermögens," 104).

35. At a meeting held on May 31, 1940, the chief executive of the Central Department of Finance—supported by Frank—demanded immediate measures to bring about the "elimination" (*Ausschaltung*) of the trustees, against whom the following criticisms were leveled: most of them had already been called in by the CdZ (head of the civil administration) and earned vast sums, and they administered up to 25 businesses, often employing their wives on high salaries (Frank, "Diary," 1940). Economic conference held on 6 and 7 June 1940 (Frank, "Diary," 1940, vol. 2); the "rapaciousness" of the trustees was apparent above all in their practice of founding companies (to avoid personal liability). According to details given at a session of the Economic Council on October 31, 1940, at that time there were 2,500 firms under the management of 1,200 trustees (Frank, "Diary," 1940).

36. "Report 1939–45," spring 1945, vol. 133, BA Ostdok. 13 GG IX a/5 (see note 31), which also explains that the trustee administration of the Warsaw District desists "from all arbitrary acts" and neither "could nor would mitigate the effects on those concerned . . . of actions taken in the fulfillment of the task entrusted to them." However, the actions taken were strictly "in accordance with the law." The final decision about Jewish assets lay with those who had the political say about the fate of the Jews.

37. Already under the Military Administration, the head of the civil administration (CdZ) had arbitrarily ordered the seizure of Jewish firms whose owners had fled; the inventories were sold and the proceeds "placed in safekeeping" at the disposal of the Reich—letter from *Landrat* Sanok to head of the Civil Administration Kraków, October 5, 1939 (IfZ, Bestand Milbf., Ma-682, Bl. 0770). Regarding Jewish movable property, cf. letter from the government of the General Government, according to which the SS was to place at the disposal of the government the totality of Jewish movable property—whatever was in storage—as well as assets accruing from (police) seizures (Nuremberg doc., PS-2819).

38. Value in January 1944, 180 million reichsmarks (quoted from Arndt, expert report, "Entziehung und Verbringung Jüdischen Vermögens"). Much higher values are mentioned in the next note.

39. See Emmerich, chief executive of the Central Department of Economics, July 13, 1942 (Frank, "Diary," 1942, 3:365). According to this account, there were 50,000 Jewish properties, of which 42,000 were donated to the municipalities in the manner described. The value of the properties (in January 1943) was 1.5 million złoty (equivalent to about 750 million reichsmarks) (budget discussion on January 23, 1943, Frank, "Diary," 3:522 ff., 527).

40. Cf. directive of the state secretary of the government of the General Government of May 16, 1941, in which the chief officers of the lower administrative authorities were made responsible for the orderly conduct of renovation work (ZS, Polen 256, 111 f.).

41. General instruction no. 18/6 of December 15, 1942 (Nuremberg doc., NO-1943).

42. For more details, see Arndt, "Entziehung und Verbringung jüdischen Vermögens," expert report, 111 f., with numerous examples (e.g., Nuremberg doc., NO-724; PS-4024).

43. Budget discussion on January 26, 1943, in Warsaw (Frank, "Diary," 1943, 3:522 ff., 527), which betrays considerable uncertainty as to the legal position—the governors had no idea what to do with the seized real estate. Nevertheless, they reported that they had already issued administrative regulations in pursuance of the directive issued on December 15, 1942, by the *Reichsführer*-SS.

44. Letter from SS-*Obergruppenführer* Oswald Pohl, head of the Central Department of Economic Administration (WVHA), to Frank, January 15, 1944 (Nuremberg doc., NO-5368), which includes the following comment: "I have not been informed about the outcome of the negotiations; however, it is clear that there has been no clarification of the competences."

45. Letter from Pohl to Frank, January 15, 1944, ibid.

46. Frank, "Diary," February 12, 1944, vol. 3).

47. Decree on Fiscal Law and Fiscal Administration of November 17, 1939 (*VBl.GG* [1939]: 60). According to this, German "tax inspectors" working for the district administrations had supervisory powers. According to a statement made by the chief executive of the Department of Finance in the office of the governor general during a meeting of departmental heads on December 1, 1939 (Frank, "Diary") there was one fiscal inspector for every 5–6 of the total of 125 Polish tax offices, which continued to function to the "complete satisfaction of the fiscal administration." Only the customs offices were entirely staffed by Germans.

48. Cf. letter from the Reich minister of finance to the Reich minister and head of the Reich Chancellery, May 7, 1942 (Nuremberg doc., NG-1328).

49. Decree on the Increase in Real Property Tax of March 16, 1940 (*VBl.GG* 1 [1940]: 109).

50. Decree on the Levying of a Residence Tax of January 27, 1940 (*VBl.GG* 1 [1940]: 211 f.).

51. Decree on the Raising of a War Levy in Addition to the Residence Tax, April 16, 1942 (*VBl. GG* [1942]: 202).

52. Amending decree of October 29, 1941 (*VBl.GG* [1941]: 617 f.). The rate was reduced through the revised version of the Decree on the Levying of a Residence Tax of December 6, 1941 (*VBl.GG* [1941]: 721 ff.); the lowest rate dropped to 12 złoty per annum.

53. Decree of October 29, 1941 (*VBl.GG* [1941]: 617 f.).

54. Decree on the Raising of a War Levy in Addition to the Residence Tax, April 16, 1942 (*VBl.GG* [1942]: 202).

55. At least in Warsaw; cf. *Mitteilungsblatt der Stadt Warschau*, January 28, 1941 (Institute for Western Studies, Poznań).

56. Decree on the Withdrawal of Tax Exemption and Tax Privilege for Jewish Associations, issued on November 23, 1939 (*VBl.GG* [1939]: 60).

Part One. Section 3. C. III. Civil Service Law

1. In this respect, see the "Principles for the Conduct of Germans in Poland," published by the head of the Governor General's Office on April 24, 1940 (*Doc. Occ.* 6:381 ff.), which applied in particular to all members of the administration. In addition, the explicit warning to public servants to avoid all contact with Poles and Czechs was reiterated in a letter from the head of the Governor General's Office to all departments in-house and all district chiefs, October 11, 1940, Bühler trial XVI, K. 198 (reproduced in *Doc. Occ.* 6:380 ff.). Cf. "Diensttagebuch," April 30, 1941, 372, IfZ: "The governor general requests State Secretary Bühler to ascertain once more whether the ban on personal contacts between German officials and employees of the administration and Poles has been breached in any way serious enough to warrant punishment. The occasion of this inquiry should be used to reiterate the ban with the utmost vigor." Civil servants were also forbidden to learn the Polish language—indictment brought by the Polish government in the Nuremberg process, charge no. 12, sheet 10 (Nuremberg doc., PS-3226, in English).

2. "The Governor General has repeatedly impressed upon officials, employees, and workers in the General Government that it is their bounden duty strictly to avoid intercourse of any kind with Poles and Czechs. He based this injunction on the consideration that *Deutschtum* in the General Government, as a self-contained entity in all its expressions, was subject . . . to the law of the National Socialist weltanschauung" (letter, October 11, 1941, "Diensttagebuch").

3. Letter from the office of the governor general (Bühler) to all departments and district chiefs, October 11, 1940 (*Doc. Occ.* 6:380 ff.); also employees in public service "who had personal contacts with Poles and Czechs . . . [would be subject] to the severest official sanctions."

4. Ibid., referring to a corresponding directive from the Führer.

5. See also the decree of January 17, 1940 (*VBl.GG* 1 [1940]: 13 f.).

6. First Decree on the Payment of Emoluments to Reappointed Polish Officials and Employees of November 3, 1939 (*VBl.GG* [1939]: 28). However, the government of the General Government was empowered to make exceptions for certain groups or pay categories (decree of February 20, 1940, (*VBl.GG* 1[1940]: 375). Report by F. Siebert, "Hauptabteilung Innere Verwaltung der Regierung des GG," November 11, 1959 (BA Ostkok. 13 GG, no. 1 b/5). The inadequate remuneration of the Polish police, who had worked to the complete satisfaction of the administration, had contributed "very significantly" to the nonfunctioning of the administration.

7. Decree issued by the government of the General Government on January 31, 1941 (ZS, Polen 256 Bl. 3).

8. Decree on the Dismissal . . . of Reappointed Officials of the Former Polish State, July 31, 1942 (*VBl.GG* [1942]: 427 ff.); under the terms of the decree, all reappointed officials who "no longer give an assurance to the German administration that they will exercise their official duties conscientiously, in a spirit of unconditional obedience" were to be dismissed (sec. 1, par. 1). Nor would anyone dismissed in such circumstances be entitled to a pension. Economies were also foreseen: married women who had been reappointed were to be dismissed "if the level of family income was sufficient for their continuing needs" (sec. 4, par. 1), i.e., if the husband's salary was sufficient.

9. Report, F. Siebert, "Hauptabteilung Innere Verwaltung der Regierung des GG."

Part One. Section 3. C. IV. 1. Professions Requiring State Licensing

1. The right of accreditation of lawyers belongs in principle to the realm of judicial administration, the topic of part 2 of this volume. However, because the discriminatory practices of the authorities under special law had a particular impact on the legal code pertaining to attorneys, the subject is dealt with here.

2. See, for example, a circular from the Central Department of Finance dated December 5, 1942 (BA R 22/5074), according to which tax consultants received accreditation in the General Government only if the services were carried out personally and entirely within the General Government. This meant that the prerequisite for gaining accreditation was to give up practicing in the Reich and that the license to practice there had to be withdrawn by the appropriate judicial authorities.

3. See Decree on German Lawyers in the General Government, September 13, 1940 (*VBl.GG* 1 [1940]: 297; Weh, *Übersicht über das Recht des Generalgouvernements* [loose-leaf collection] [1943], C 135), which stated that there was no right to accreditation. A clause forbidding German lawyers from continuing to practice in the Reich was written in for ethnic-political reasons: those practicing in the General Government were "ambassadors of *Deutschtum* in the outpost of the Eastern lands" (circular from the Central Department of Justice, February 17, 1942, and Main Commission Warsaw, Archive, Regierung des General Government/Hauptabteilung Justiz V/7) and therefore were not subordinate to the Chamber of Lawyers in their birthplace, but—like notaries—(Decree on German Notaries in the General Government of December 17, 1941, *VBl.GG* [1941]: 731; and Weh, *Übersicht über das Recht des Generalgouvernements*, C 138; Reich German and ethnic German (*volksdeutsche*) lawyers were entitled to appointment as notary publics in the General Government) they were subject to the authority of the *judicial administration* (sec. 3 of the decree of September 13, 1940, *VBl.GG* 1 [1940]: 297; Weh, *Übersicht über das Recht des Generalgouvernements*, C 135).

4. Circular from Central Department of Justice, February 17, 1942 (Main Commission Warsaw, Archive, Regierung des General Government/Hauptabteilung Justiz V/7); Wolfgramm, "Deutsche Rechtsanwälte" (1942), 1429.

5. Wolfgramm, "Deutsche Rechtsanwälte," 1428, referring to the circular from the Central Department of Justice of February 17, 1942 (Main Commission Warsaw, Archive, Regierung des General

Government/Hauptabteilung Justiz V/7); according to this, German officials had complained that German lawyers were representing the interests of "non-Germans" who "were not even within the scope of jurisdiction," for example in connection with confiscation of assets. In one case, it was reported, there had even been an attempt to exempt property owned by a "non-German" from incorporation in the Jewish quarter. This led to the cited ban on representing Polish interests.

6. Wolfgramm, "Deutsche Rechtsanwälte," 1429: "We need have no qualms about German lawyers representing Poles; indeed, it is even desirable, since they are duty bound to serve the establishment of truth."

7. Ibid.

8. Accreditation was granted by the district chief with prior approval from the head of the Department of Justice in the district administration—or so was the practice in the Warsaw District; all other "noncertified" Jewish lawyers (practically all of them) had to close their offices (*Krakauer Zeitung* May 1–2, 1940). The names of accredited "advocates" were made public by means of notices posted on all law courts (*Krakauer Zeitung*, April 9, 1940). Strict standards were necessary because "among the Polish advocates . . . are to be found the strongest opponents of *Deutschtum*" (report of the Department of Justice in the Warsaw District, March 1940, Main Commission Warsaw, Archive, Regierung des General Government/Hauptabteilung Justiz V/87).

9. Cf. the item in the *Krakauer Zeitung* on the "purge" among lawyers in the Warsaw District, May 1–2, 1940. According to the *News from the Reich*, May 16, 1940, 1,400 Polish lawyers applied (*after* the purge) for reaccreditation; 718 of the applications were granted (BA R 58/184).

10. Instruction from the Central Department of Justice issued on August 8, 1941; they were also to be referred to as advocates on letterheads, nameplates, etc. (Main Commission Warsaw, Archive, government of the General Government/Central Department of Justice V/6).

11. *Krakauer Zeitung*, May 1–2, 1940. "Of 2,237 lawyers in Warsaw, more than 1,000 were Jews" (*Krakauer Zeitung*, April 9, 1940).

12. Discussion on September 5, 1940 ("Diensttagebuch," 1940, vol. 3; BA R 52 II/178).

13. In a progress report of the head of the Department of Justice in the office of the Warsaw district chief (signed Brehm) for March 1940, it is stated that "the former *Anwaltsbeirat* (Lawyer's Advisory Board) used an application by the Jewish community for accreditation of Jewish lawyers to present a lengthy 'expertise' that maintains that the . . . exclusion of Jewish lawyers is legally inadmissible. This attack on the measures of the German administration prompted the immediate and necessary response: a number of lawyers were arrested in the recent round-up of members of the Polish intelligentsia ordered by the Security Service" (Main Commission Warsaw, Archive, government of the General Government/Central Department of Justice V/6).

14. *News from the Reich*, March 16, 1940. An advisory board set up to look into the problem of the accreditation of Jewish lawyers reportedly maintains the view—on behalf of all Polish lawyers—that Jewish lawyers should also receive accreditation. In fact the situation is quite different: the views of the 718 Polish lawyers (among 1,400 applicants) granted accreditation by the German authorities—expressed subsequent to receiving their certificates (in other words, effectively ruling out "the exertion of pressure to declare one way or the other beforehand ")—were as follows: 10 were for unconditional and 83 for conditional accreditation, whereas 625 advocated the exclusion of Jewish lawyers, expressing "their gratitude for the nonaccreditation of Jews" (BA R 58/184). [This result was inevitable since the Nazi authorities had given credentials only to politically reliable lawyers—Author.]

15. Expert evidence given by Dr. Josef Owsiński, Kraków, in the case of Dr. Josef Walbaum, January 17, 1948 (ZS, Ordner 21). (Walbaum was head of the Office of Health). For further details on the healthcare system in the General Government, see K. M. Pospieszalski, Służba zdrowia, *Doc. Occ.* 6:299 ff., with numerous examples.

16. Hagen thereby made a bitter enemy in HSSPF Friedrich Wilhelm Krüger (letter HSSPF

Kraków to SS-*Standartenführer* Max Sollmann, Munich, December 30, 1942; Nuremberg doc., NO-943); the case went as far as to receive the Führer's personal attention, following a letter to Hitler from Dr. Wilhelm Hagen on December 7, 1942 protesting the planned slaughter of 70,000 Polish people—elderly and children—as part of the "resettlement in the East" on the grounds that, in racial terms, the Poles were "closely associated" with *Deutschtum* (letter from NSDAP-*Reichsleitung* to HSSPF Kraków on January 28, 1943; Institute for Western Studies, Poznań, doc. I-773). Called upon to state their position, the responsible Department of Population Affairs and Welfare demanded the strongest possible action against Hagen; it was merely a question of Poles infected with tuberculosis, for whom no "special welfare measures" were necessary, unless such measures were in Germany's interest (correspondence, ibid.). Hagen was dismissed as a result of pressure from the Department (letter from Weyrauch, head of the department, to HSSPF Kraków, February 4, 1943, and letter from HSSPF Kraków to *Reichsführer*-SS with enclosed details of all proceedings against Dr. Hagen of February 17, 1943, ibid.).

17. According to a letter from the *Reichsführer*-SS to the Reich Chief Health Officer, Dr. Leonardo Conti, dated March 29, 1943, Dr. Hagen was to be committed to a concentration camp; however, Dr. Conti was able to prevent this by means of an emergency order committing Dr. Hagen to compulsory service (letter from the Reich Chief Health Officer to RFSS on March 31, 1943); both letters in Institute for Western Studies, Poznań, doc. I-773.

18. Decree on the Deployment of Doctors and Other Healthcare Workers, July 24, 1943 (*VBl. GG* [1943]: 395 ff.), which superseded a corresponding decree on the deployment of doctors issued on September 24, 1942 (*VBl.GG* [1942]: 550).

19. Of the 8,527 doctors practicing in 1942 in the General Government (4,368 general practitioners and 4,959 specialists), 2,400 (approx. 28%) were Jews (*Gesundheit und Leben* [the official organ of the Chamber of Health in the General Government], 1942, no. 37, 552; University Library, Warsaw, Sign. 032991).

20. "Report on the Development of the General Government," July 1, 1940, 2:222 f. (BA R 52 II/249).

21. Expert evidence given by Dr. Nüssenfeld on January 22, 1948, and statement by Dr. Alexander Biberstein concerning the Walbaum case on January 20, 1948 (ZS, Ordner 21).

22. "Report on the Development of the General Government" (BA R 52 II/247).

23. Monthly report, *Kreishauptmann* Sochaczew (Warsaw District), for January 1941 (ZS, Polen 347, 356 ff.); monthly report, Warsaw District, for June 1941 (442 f.); monthly report, *Kreishauptmann* Siedlce, for January 1942 (348, 796 ff.).

Part One. Section 3. C. IV. 2. Labor Law

1. Confidential note by Bormann on a conversation with Hitler about the character of the General Government, October 2, 1940 (reproduced in *Doc. Occ.* 6:31 ff.). Among Hitler's comments referred to in this note was the following: "The General Government is our reservoir of unskilled labor . . . one cannot expect more of the Slavs . . . than is in their nature."

Vol. 10 of *Doc. Occ.*, titled *Praca przymusowa pod panowaniem hitlerowskim 1939–1945* (Posen, 1976), appeared after completion of the original German edition of the present work. It contains numerous documents detailing labor regulations and conditions for Polish workers.

2. The Labor Administration was already active in the General Government in fall 1939, and it was fully established as early as the beginning of 1940. The offices of the Labor Administration had already begun work under the Military Administration. A decree issued by the Reich minister of labor on October 30, 1939 (BA R 2/5066, 18), ordered the *Land* Labor Office to take over temporary management of projects involving forced labor. Quotation in Melies, *Das Arbeitsrecht des GG* (1943), introduction, 9.

3. Quoted from Melies, *Das Arbeitsrecht des GG*, 13.

4. For further details, see Madajczyk, *Polityka*, 1:629–60, 2:23–24.

5. Decree of October 26, 1939 (*VBl.GG* [1939]: 5), with implementing order of December 14, 1939 (224), which empowered district chiefs to extend the scope of compulsory labor to include youths aged 14 years and over. Public labor service covered work on farms, the building and maintenance of public buildings, and road construction. This first implementing order stipulated that anyone capable of work was subject to conscription (sec. 1). With the assignment to a workplace, a *de lege* employment relationship was entered into. This relationship could be ended only with the agreement of the appropriate Labor Office (sec. 3). Infringements of labor service regulations, particularly absenteeism, refusal to work, or "wanton slacking on the job," were threatened with heavy punishment. However, offenders were prosecuted only if this was demanded by the head of the Labor Office; he also had the power to assign punishment. For more details on labor service, see the comments of the chief executive of the (Central) Department of Labor, Max Frauendorfer, "Arbeits- und Sozialpolitik im GG" (1941); according to this account, up to November 1941, 1.75 million people were "assigned to work in the German war economy." Cf. also report of the former head of the Abteilung Arbeitseinsatz (Department of Forced Labor), Dr. L. Gschließer, June 30, 1960, concerning questions relating to the Forced Labor Service (BA Ostdok. 13 GG IV b/2), which states that compulsory service affected only those Poles who were *not* gainfully employed.

6. At a meeting on October 30, 1939, in Łódź ("Diensttagebuch," 1:12).

7. The view expressed by Gschließer in his report (BA Ostdok, 13 GG IV b/2), that the Labor Service Decree of October 26, 1939, was "essentially something that existed only on paper" is probably wide of the mark, since the decree was the foundation for the whole program whereby Poles were conscripted, sometimes compelled by use of police powers, for forced labor in the General Government and the Reich.

8. The so-called *Baudienst* (the Reconstruction Service, which was incorporated into the Central Department of Internal Administration) had been set up to "carry out significant public works in the national interest" (Decree on the Reconstruction Service in the General Government of December 1, 1940, *VBl.GG* 1 [1940]: 359; reproduced in *Doc. Occ.* 6:336 f.; superseded by a stronger decree on April 22, 1942, *VBl.GG* [1942]: 218; reproduced in *Doc. Occ.* 6:341 ff., according to which all "non-German" males in the General Government between ages 18 and 60 [with the exception of foreigners, Jews, and Gypsies] were subject to conscription into the Reconstruction Service). Those called up were drawn from the younger age groups of "non-Germans" (Poles, though not Jews), according to needs; but the planned Reconstruction Service for the Ukrainians and Górales was apparently not established (according to remarks by Frauendorfer, the former head of the Central Department of Labor, July 20, 1961, BA Ostdok. 13 GG IV 1 b/3). The Reconstruction Service roughly corresponded to the Labor Service in the Reich. Its effectiveness is open to doubt, in spite of the welter of official statistics (according to the situation report for the year 1941 submitted by the head of liaison for the *Reichsarbeitsführer* to the governor general, March 19, 1942, "Diensttagebuch," 1942, 1:214, excerpts in *Doc. Occ.* 6:338 ff., its strength was 11,500 men; according to a report by the Reich minister of finance on April 1, 1944, BA R 2/5053, there were 1,000 Reconstruction Service branches each with 150–80 conscripts), because wages were 50–60% below industry levels, and a very high percentage of those called-up never turned up or later "went on the run" (situation report from the head of liaison for the *Reichsarbeitsführer* to the governor general, March 19, 1942, "Diensttagebuch," 1942, 1:214). The Reich Administration appears to have had a low opinion of this institution anyway (cf. telex from HSSPF/state secretary for the Security Services in the General Government to the Reich minister of finance, August 13, 1942, BA R 2/5049, 123; and his reply of August 29, 1942 [124]). Regarding the Civil Service ranking of German leaders of the Reconstruction Service, cf. situation report from the head of liaison for the *Reichsarbeitsführer* to the governor general, March 19, 1942 ("Diensttagebuch," 1942, 1:214) and report by the Reich minister

of finance of April 1, 1944 (BA R 2/5053). Nevertheless, the Reconstruction Service did play a certain role in major projects (forestry, building of the *Ostbahn*—Eastern railroad—and so on; situation report, March 19, 1942 ["Diensttagebuch," 1942, 1:214]). With the deterioration of the war situation and the strenghtening of the Polish resistance movement, the manpower and effectiveness of the Reconstruction Service was further depleted; because of "attacks by gangs" and the "crumbling of German authority," manpower fell in some parts by 30 to 40%; in Galicia it dropped from 10,000 to 2,000. In the General Government as a whole, desertions from the service led to a reduction in manpower from about 45,000 in January 1944 to 33,000 in May 1944 (situation report on the Reconstruction Service in the General Government, May 10, 1944, Institute for Western Studies, Poznań, doc. I-151, Mappe 25; reproduced in *Doc. Occ.* 6:438 f.).

9. Decree on Compulsory Reconstruction Service for German Citizens, December 15, 1942 (*VBl.GG* [1942]: 761), though there were no *general* regulations on compulsory service for Germans. According to the report by Dr. Gschließer (BA Ostdok. 13 GG IV b/2), there was compulsory service for Germans already as early as 1940. The Decree concerning Restrictions on Changing Workplaces of February 22, 1940 (*VBl.GG* 1 [1940]: 80), which stipulated that giving notice and changing jobs were not permitted without prior approval from the Labor Office (except notice of termination of employment by offices of the Civil Service; cf. instruction of April 24, 1941, *VBl.GG* [1941]: 259), was valid for *all* employees in the General Government. The possibility of withdrawing manpower from existing employment for projects of "particular national importance" had already been introduced in relation to Poles by a decree issued on May 13, 1942 (*VBl.GG* [1942]: 255). According to Dr. Gschließer's report (BA Ostdok. 13 GG IV b/2), this ruling also applied to Germans from January 18, 1943, on. However, the only hard evidence is the Decree on Registration of Men and Women for Service in the Defense of the Reich of February 2, 1943 (*VBl.GG* [1943]: 65 ff.), with supplementary decree of June 30, 1942 (305).

10. For a summary of rulings in the field of labor law in the General Government, see Melies, *Das Arbeitsrecht des Generalgouvernements*, 21 ff., though it does not contain the basic decrees of October 26, 1939 on compulsory labor service and forced labor for Jews (*VBl.GG* [1939]: 6) and for Poles (5). Concerning the situation of Polish workers, cf. S. Datner, "Wywóz ludności polskiej na roboty niewolnicze do niemiec," *Bulletin of the High Commission Warsaw*, vol. 16, 17 ff.; for more details, see Seeber, *Zwangsarbeiter in der faschistischen Kriegswirtschaft* (1964), 116 ff. (with numerous examples); see also note 2 above.

11. As stated in the highly critical report of the head of the Chamber of Industry and Commerce in Czenstochau (Częstochowa), *Justitiar* Schmitt, "Die wirtschaftspolitischen Maßnahmen im GG" (no date, Institute for Western Studies, Poznań, doc. I-13, reproduced in *Doc. Occ.* 6:350 ff., 352).

12. Sec. 4 of the decree of October 26, 1939 (*VBl.GG* [1939]: 5).

13. Ibid.

14. Secs. 1, 2 of the Decree on the Organization of Working Conditions and Industrial Safety in the General Government of October 31, 1939 (*VBl.GG* [1939]: 12), with a total of twelve implementing orders (in *Doc. Occ.* 6:309 f. n. 4; and Melies, *Das Arbeitsrecht des Generalgouvernements*).

15. Sec. 3 of the decree issued on October 31, 1939 (*VBl.GG* [1939]: 12); sec. 1, Third Implementing Order of March 12, 1940 (*VBl.GG* 2 [1940]: 185).

16. Cf. Fifth Implementing Order of December 14, 1940 (*VBl.GG* 2 [1940]: 560), to the Decree on the Organization of Working Conditions and Industrial Safety of October 31, 1939 (*VBl.GG* [1939]: 12). More than one hundred rulings on pay were decreed for the different districts, regulating the pay of "non-German" workers in the various branches of industry; German workers' pay was regulated in accordance with Reich wage agreements (Melies, *Das Arbeitsrecht des Generalgouvernements*, introduction, 9). These pay rulings were applicable to the private sector (*Amtl. Anz.* 1942, nos. 69, 71, 73, 90, 94; 1943, nos. 25, 69) but became more and more obsolete as the system

was geared in practice to creating a uniform wage system modeled on a projected skeleton wage agreement for the private sector and trades (Melies, *Das Arbeitsrecht des Generalgouvernements*, 230 ff.), roughly corresponding to the skeleton wage agreement for the public services. Cf. the skeleton wage agreement for "non-German" workers and employees in the Civil Service (*VBl.GG* [1943]: 9, 14, 23); Wage Agreement Regulating Traveling Expenses for Workers . . . in the Private Sector of March 25, 1942 (*VBl.GG* [1942]: 182); Wage Agreement for Pharmacists of March 8, 1941 (*VBl.GG* [1941]: 296); Wage Agreement for Forestry Workers of October 28, 1942 (*VBl.GG* [1942]: 724; [1943]: 72, 212); Wage Agreement for Oil and Natural Gas Drilling Installations . . . and Oil Refining Plants . . . of April 13, 1943 (*Amtl. Anzeiger* 1943, 1381); Instruction on the Regulation of Working Conditions . . . in the Sugar Industry of October 20, 1943 (quoted from Melies, *Das Arbeitsrecht des Generalgouvernements*, 228 ff.).

17. Frank at a meeting on October 30, 1939, "Diensttagebuch," 1939.

18. Melies, *Das Arbeitsrecht des Generalgouvernements*, 182 f.

19. Law of May 16, 1922 (*Gesetzbl. der Republik Polen*, no. 40, Pos. 334).

20. Fourth and Seventh Implementing Orders, issued respectively on July 20, 1940 (*VBl.GG* 2 [1940]: 404), and March 29, 1941 (*VBl.GG* [1941]: 174), to the Decree on Working Conditions in the General Government of October 26, 1939; Instruction on Regulation of Vacations for "Non-German" Employees in the General Government of March 31, 1943 (*Amt. Anzeiger* 1943, 718; Melies, *Das Arbeitsrecht des Generalgouvernements*, 35 f.). Sixth Implementing Order to the Decree on Working Conditions of March 29, 1941 (*VBl.GG* [1941]: 172), and skeleton wage agreement for "non-German" employees and workers of December 28, 1942 (*VBl.GG* [1943]: 9; Melies, *Das Arbeitsrecht des Generalgouvernements*, 186); this stipulated a four-week period of notice for Polish employees in the private sector. Decree on Modification of Industrial Safety Regulations of June 13, 1940 (*VBl.GG* 1 [1940]: 200), empowering works managers to extend the working hours from eight to ten hours a day, insofar as existing regulations did not allow working days of ten hours or more. In addition, prolonging working hours to ten hours a day was permitted under the terms of wage agreements (secs. 1, 2). A corresponding ruling is to be found in sec. 5 of the skeleton wage agreement for "non-German" workers and employees in the Civil Service of the General Government (*Rahmentarifordnung* or RTO) of December 28, 1942 (*VBl.GG* [1943]: 9; Melies, *Das Arbeitsrecht des Generalgouvernements*, 186). Sec. 1, Decree on Protection of the Working Mother of May 1, 1943 (*VBl.GG* [1943]: 187 ff.in conjunction with sec. 1 of the instruction of May 1, 1943, to the Decree on Protection of the Working Mother, Melies, *Das Arbeitsrecht des Generalgouvernements*, 170), according to which protection of the working mother applied only to German citizens and nationals and persons of German descent, not to Poles and Jews. sec. 6 of Twelfth Implementing Order of March 15, 1943 (*VBl.GG* [1943]: 9, 150), to the Decree on the Organization of Working Conditions . . . in the General Government of October 31, 1944 (*VBl.GG* [1939]: 13). Cf. also the so-called *Arbeitsstrafverordnung* (lit. work discipline decree) of February 16, 1944 (Decree on the Punishment of Violations of Forced Labor Regulations, *VBl.GG* [1944]: 57 f.), which made violations against industrial relations regulations (e.g., those concerning compulsory labor, "work cards," duty of service, etc.), punishable by prison sentences and/or unlimited fines, and in serious cases by penitentiary. Criminal proceedings could be started only at the behest of the *Kreishauptmann* (or *Stadthauptmann*) (sec. 2), maintaining a degree of flexibility. This did not rule out the use of "other appropriate measures" [such as police action—Author], so that dereliction of duty by Poles could be punished by measures such as protective custody.

21. Decree on the Provision of Manpower Requirements for Tasks of Particular National Importance (*Dienstverpflichtungsverordnung* [conscription for essential service]) of May 13, 1942 (*VBl. GG* [1942]: 255). Decree on Conscription for Essential Service for German Citizens in the General Government, December 15, 1942 (*VBl.GG* [1942]: 761).

22. Cf. sec. 1, par. 2, of Decree on Compulsory Labor for the Polish Population of October 26, 1939 (*VBl.GG* [1939]:5): "Special regulations are being issued for Jews."

23. Decree on the Introduction of Forced Labor for the Jewish Population of the General Government, October 26, 1939 (*VBl.GG* [1939]: 6; reproduced in *Doc. Occ.* 6:560 ff.). According to the guidelines issued by the head of the Labor Department in the office of the governor general of July 5, 1940 (reproduced in *Doc. Occ.* 6:568 ff.), Jews were inducted for forced labor from the age of twelve years. Decree issued by the Labor Department in the office of the governor general to the district chiefs (Labor Dept.) and the heads of the Labor Department, July 23, 1940 (ZS, Polen 257, 22 f.). Guidelines of the Labor Department in the office of the governor general of July 5, 1940 (reproduced in *Doc. Occ.* 6:568 ff.; original in the Jewish Historical Institute, Warsaw; copy in ZS, Ordner 103, 161 ff.).

24. Decree issued by the Labor Department in the office of the governor general to the district chiefs, July 23, 1940 (ZS, Polen 257, 22 f.).

25. Cf. monthly report, *Kreishauptmann* of Neumarkt (Nowy Targ) and Dunajec, for August 1940; because Jews achieved only 40–50% of the usual performance in road construction work, a so-called *Zeitakkord* (piece-work schedule) was introduced, according to which every Jew was allocated a stretch of road, and the time required to complete it was left up to him (ZS, Polen 347, Bl. 124 f.). Only single Jews could be recruited for work in the Reich, to avoid making their dependents a burden on state welfare (monthly report, *Kreishauptmann* Seza-Starachowice, Radom District, for August 1940, with objections about the recruitment of married Jews by the Labor Office, Bl. 182 f.; also IfZ, Ma-158/2, Bl. 16); monthly report, *Kreishauptmann* Reichshof (Rzeszów), Kraków District, for January 1941, with report on "idleness in the performance of work" by Jews clearing snow and the demand for harsher measures—where necessary, the hanging of Jews (ZS, Polen 347, Bl. 274 ff.).

26. Reproduced in *Doc. Occ.* 6:568 ff. (original in Jewish Historical Institute, Warsaw; copy in ZS, Ordner 103, 161 ff.).

27. Implementing order issued on December 15, 1941 (*VBl.GG* [1942]: 3), to the Decree on Working Conditions of October 31, 1939 (*VBl.GG* [1939]: 13).

28. Decree issued by the government of the General Government, October 5, 1940 (ZS, Polen 257, 37).

29. Decree issued by the government of the General Government, Central Department of Internal Administration (Population Affairs and Welfare) to the district governors, Department of Internal Administration, March 9, 1942, which stipulated that training and specialist education in handicrafts and farming was to be given to Jews and that the existing courses run by the Jewish Councils were no longer to be approved (ZS, Polen 257, 67; 316, 8, 194).

Because of the authorization to issue implementing orders to the Decree on Forced Labor for Jews of October 26, 1939 (*VBl.GG* [1939]: 6), the HSSPF demanded the authority for both registration and oversight of Jewish forced labor; the Labor Administration, for its part, also claimed authority. In the guidelines of the Labor Department in the office of the governor general, issued to subordinate offices on July 5, 1940 (reproduced in *Doc. Occ.* 6:568 ff.; original in the Jewish Historical Institute, Warsaw; copy in ZS, Ordner 103, 161 ff.), the head of the department stated that, by agreement with the HSSPF, responsibility for implementation of the Decree on Forced Labor for the Jewish Population had now been "transferred to the Labor Department." They also stipulated that the registration of Jews was still fundamentally the responsibility of the police, whereas the deployment of Jews should be determined by the Labor Department in consultation with the police.

Cf. monthly report, *Kreishauptmann* Siedlce, Warsaw District, for February 1942; according to this, Jews were happy to get work at all; they were very poorly provided for; many were dying of malnutrition, and it would be opportune to increase provisions for Jews working in German interests. Polish farmers demanded Jewish workers because they cost less and worked harder (ZS, Polen 348, 813 ff.).

30. Decree on the Provision of Unemployment Benefits of November 9, 1940 (*VBl.GG* 1 [1940]: 329 ff.).

31. Circular from the Central Department of Labor to the District Labor Departments, June 25, 1941 (ZS, Polen Film 64, 167).

32. Cf. report, dating from 1942 (ZS, Akten Auerswald 365 d), of a former employee of the *Lagerschutz* (lit.camp warders) of a labor camp, describing the inadequate food and clothing provided for inmates and the beatings and use of firearms by the *Wachmannschaften* (SS guard units). See, for example, a note in the files of the head of the SS Economic and Administrative Office of September 7, 1943 (ZS, Polen 347/964 f.), to the effect that the ten labor camps in the Lublin District were reclassified as "branch camps" of the concentration camp Lublin, making the inmates concentration camp prisoners. The Jews barracked in labor camps received no pay (the wages were paid by the enterprise employing them to the district SS and police commanders) but were employed as R, W, or Z workers (the initials stood for *Rüstungs-Wirtschafts-Zubringerarbeiter*—armaments/industry/auxiliary workers), with insignia identifying them as such, and worked under the maxim "Rapid removal from the production process and replacement with Polish manpower, then straight to the extermination camps" (agreement between HSSPF Kraków and the *Wehrkreisbefehlshaber* [commander of the Military District] in the General Government, October 15, 1942; Nuremberg doc., NOKW-134, notified by letter from HSSPF Kraków to all authorities on November 27, 1942; ZS, Ordner 104, 480 ff.).

33. Information given by Frauendorfer, head of the Labor Department, on September 20, 1941, "Diensttagebuch," quoted from Seeber, *Zwangsarbeiter in der faschistischen Kriegswirtschaft*, 124.

34. According to information given in a cabinet meeting on December 16, 1941 (quoted from Seeber, *Zwangsarbeiter in der faschistischen Kriegswirtschaft*, 125).

35. Note in the files, *Ministerialdirektor* Kritzinger/Reich Chancellery, February 24, 1943 (Nuremberg doc., NG-1428, S. 1); it states that the obstacles to recruitment of volunteers in the General Government were undernourishment and poor health, the commitment of large numbers of workers to farmwork, the anxiety caused by the "resettlement of Poles" being undertaken by the RKF, and the "defamation of Polish workers in the Reich."

Minutes of a meeting of representatives of the Labor Department in the office of the governor general on March 7, 1940, which discussed the demand by the Reich for a million workers ("Diensttagebuch"); the same source tells us that, up to March 7, 1940, 81,477 Polish civilian workers had already been sent to the Reich; a total of 130,000 Polish workers were working in the Reich. It was planned to send 225,000 to the Reich by April 23, 1940, with approx. 8,000 being transported every day; cf. also Frauendorfer, "Arbeits- und Sozialpolitik im General Government" (University Library, Warsaw, Sign. 011248), according to which, by November 1941, 500,000 workers had been sent to the Reich and a total of 1.25 million persons had been recruited through the Labor Offices of the General Government. In a letter dated August 18, 1942, to Sauckel, the commissioner general for *Arbeitseinsatz*, Himmler complained about the poor organization of the Labor Offices; Galicia had sent 265,000 workers but could provide another 100,000 if it were better organized (Nuremberg doc., NO-3194). The *Arbeitseinsatz* report for December 1943 from the Central Department of Labor provides a good overview with figures (BA R 52 IV, 13 c, 93 ff.): in 1942 approx. 400,000, and in 1943 approx. 175,000 Polish workers were sent to the Reich: since 1939 a total of 1.1 million (7.67% of the population). The drop in the figures for 1943 is explained by the fact that Jews were no longer being recruited and that recruitment by force was virtually the only way. According to a list in *Doc. Occ.* 6:282, which is a compilation of figures give in the governor general's diary, in July 1944 (the last date for which there are statistics) there were 1,214,000 Poles from the General Government working in the Reich (for details, see *Doc. Occ.* 6:282 nn. 30–66).

Cf. the material reproduced in *Doc. Occ.* 6:326 ff. and the introduction by K. M. Pospieszalski (281 ff.); for more details, see letter from Central Department of Labor to BdO Kraków, January 24, 1941, requesting police assistance to recruit Polish farmworkers for the Reich (BA R 70 Polen/180; copy in ZS, Polen 238, 636–44), and decree circulated by BdO Kraków, February 7, 1941, concerning police assistance of this kind (BA R 70 Polen/180). Although attempts were made after 1940 to recruit volunteers through disguised private agencies, with some occasional success (report of the armaments inspector for the General Government for November 1941, December 13, 1941, IfZ, Bestand MiG, Ma-682, 0059), the longer the war continued, the more police raids were used as the only way of securing the supply of labor—report by HSSPF Eastern Territories (Kraków) to the *Reichsführer*-SS on January 14, 1943, on labor supplies for the Reich (Nuremberg doc., NO-3208).

36. Frank and his officials initially resisted the use of coercive police powers and insisted on voluntary recruitment (cf., e.g., discussion on March 7, 1940, with representatives of the Labor Department, "Diensttagebuch," 1940, 1:176 ff., excerpts in *Doc. Occ.* 6:326 ff.). But the Labor Administration, backed by the HSSPF, saw this as the only possibility of ensuring the supply of labor, since the recruiting campaign was having little success. The chief executive of the Central Department of Labor, Frauendorfer, at 32 the youngest head of a main department, wanted to make all 16- to 25-year-olds subject to drafting (meeting of April 23, 1940, in Kraków) ("Diensttagebuch," 1940, 1:273, 295 f.; excerpts, *Doc. Occ.* 6:328 ff.). However, because of the lack of volunteers and under pressure from the Reich, police round-ups of workers began as early as mid-1940; cf. meeting of departmental heads on May 10, 1940 ("Diensttagebuch," 1940, 1:273, 295 f.), at which Frank announced that "under pressure from the Reich," coercion was to be used. In a report compiled after 1945 on the administration of labor in the General Government (July 20, 1961), Frauendorfer laid the blame for the nonfulfillment of recruitment quotas at the door of Frank. According to Frauendorfer, Frank had tried to place most of the blame on the inadequacies of the police (BA Ostdok. 13 GG IV b/3); Frauendorfer volunteered for the Wehrmacht at the end of 1942.

37. In a series of "counteractions," Labor Administration documents were destroyed, transports to Germany held up, "numerous Poles" who worked for outstations of the Labor Administration shot, and remote suboffices destroyed (report of the chairman of the Armaments Commission in the General Government to the Reich minister for armament and munition, May 24, 1943, IfZ, Ma-1017, 0668); cf. the subsequent monthly reports of the *Kreishauptleute*, which describe all the above-mentioned difficulties and the brutality of the police: *Kreishauptmann* Seza-Starachowice (Radom District) for August 1940 (ZS, Polen 347, Bl. 182 f.); *Kreishauptmann* Busko for May 1940 (Polen 348, Bl. 587 ff.); *Kreishauptmann* Neumarkt (Nowy Targ) (Kraków District) for May 1940 (Bl. 555); *Kreishauptmann* Puławy (Kraków District) for May 1940 (Bl. 583); *Kreishauptmann* Jasło (Kraków District) for June 1940 (Bl. 677 ff.) and for June 1941 (Polen 347, 260 ff.); *Kreishauptmann* Petrikau (Piotrków Trybunalski) for May 1940 (Bl. 607); *Kreishauptmann* Jaroslau (Jarosław) for June 1940 (Bl. 672); monthly report, Kraków District chief for January 1941 (Polen 347, 221 ff.); *Kreishauptmann* Dśbica (Kraków District, Bl. 250 ff.); *Kreishauptmann* Lublin region for February 1941 (Bl. 389 f.); *Kreishauptmann* Krasnystaw (Lublin District) for February 1940 (387 f.) ("the Polish resistance is not confining its efforts to passive resistance").

38. Monthly report, Warsaw District chief for January 1941; monthly report, *Kreishauptmann* Jasło (Kraków District) for June 1941 (ZS, Polen 347, 260 ff.).

39. Monthly report, *Kreishauptmann* Jasło (Kraków District) for June 1941, ibid.

40. Concerning the excessive demands of the Reich for harvest contingents and the resulting cancelation or reduction of food rations for Poles, cf. cabinet meeting of August 24, 1942 ("Diensttagebuch"), and Frank's remarks at the cabinet meeting of December 14, 1942 ("Diensttagebuch").

On the role of the General Government as a "food basket" of the Reich (second only to France) and the merciless plundering thereof, see the final report of the plenipotentiary for the Four Year Plan, containing detailed tables and statistics (no date [probably end of 1943 or 1944], BA R 26 IV/Vorl. 12, Bl. 2 ff.), as well as a secret directive of the plenipotentiary for the Four Year Plan of June 28, 1944, on fulfillment of supply targets for 1944 and catching up on the backlog (Vorl. 13); cf. also secret memorandum of the Food Agency (*Geschäftsgruppe Ernährung*) about a meeting with representatives of the OKW and the Reich Food Ministry held on June 29, 1944 (BA R 26 IV/Vorl. 13).

For a detailed account of food supplies for Poles up to 1941, cf. the official report of the *Stadthauptmann* Kraków (Kraków, October 26, 1939–41 [IfZ, Dd 56.09]), and Schulte-Wissermann, in Bühler, *Das Generalgouvernement, seine Verwaltung und seine Wirtschaft* (1943), 218 ff.; see also remarks by Governor General Frank at the cabinet meeting of December 14, 1942 ("absolute starvation level"), "Diensttagebuch." The monthly report by the *Stadthauptmann* Lublin for January 1941 has a detailed list of food rations for Germans, Poles, and Jews (ZS, Polen 347, 308 ff.); see also monthly report, *Kreishauptmann* Czenstochau for December 1940–January 1941 (317 ff.): Poles received only 100 g of bread a day and nothing else; monthly report, *Kreishauptmann* Tomaschow (Tomaszów Mazowiecki) for March 1942 (Polen, film 5, Bl. 468): Germans had adequate provisions, those for Poles were poor; the Jews were starving. Situation report, *Kreishauptmann* Petrikau for May 1940 (Polen 347, Bl. 607): "intolerable conditions." Monthly report, *Kreishauptmann* Cholm for June 1940 (Bl. 578 ff.): "extortionate price inflation." Cf. also *News from the Reich*, June 20, 1940 (BA R 58/151), with precise details on daily rations for Germans, Poles, and Ukrainians. A comprehensive summary is given in the confidential report of the head of the *Hauptgruppe gewerbliche Wirtschaft* (lit. main group trade and industry), November 14, 1941 (ZS, Polen 347), with numerous statistics and calorie tables for Poles (usual allocation, 515; with "A" supplements [for the heaviest manual work], 906; with "B" supplements [for heavy work], 747 calories); however, the minimum daily requirement was said to be 800 calories, for manual work 3,000 calories, and for heavy work 3,500 calories. The agricultural workforce frequently received no food at all (ZS, Polen 359). Cf. also report of the Polish Aid Committee for the City of Warsaw for 1942–43 (daily ration for adults in May 1942, 382.9 calories; for children, 321.3; in March 1943, 447 and 390 calories, respectively; BA R 52 III/8.9). Cf. also report, F. Siebert "Hauptabteilung Innere Verwaltung," November 11, 1959 (BA Ostdok. 13 GG Nr. 1 b/5).

41. In the General Government, therefore, the ration card system was not introduced; a "simpler system" was used. Entitled to provisions were above all the population of the main cities and those working for German interests or where there was some other form of "public interest" (Gollert, *Warschau unter deutscher Herrschaft* [1942], 202 f.). Those not entitled to receive rations included workers from the countryside who were expected to be self-reliant; these were close to starvation because farmers had been reduced to subsistence level by quota requirements.

42. Meeting on April 23, 1940: "The second category comprises the Poles, insofar as I have no use for them. I will feed these Poles by giving them whatever is left over. Otherwise I can only exort them to help themselves and say to them: we are not to blame for the war" ("Diensttagebuch"). "Whether the Jews . . . have food or not is the least of my concerns" ("Diensttagebuch," 1940). The prevailing view was that it would be best to give no food at all to the Jews, though initially a minimum had to be provided to maintain their work potential; cf., e.g., *News from the Reich*, June 20, 1940 (BA R 58/151, Radom District; Jews receive half the rations provided for Poles, but "only when food is left over"). An overview of food rations provided in 1941 is given in Nuremberg doc., NG-618. As the supply situation worsened (at the latest from 1942 on), the German authorities stopped food rations for Jews altogether—with the exception of 300,000 armament workers (Frank at a cabinet meeting on April 24, 1942: "The fact that 'we thereby'—i.e., by fulfilling the quotas for the Reich at any price—condemn 1.2 million Jews to death, is only mentioned in passing"; "Diensttagebuch"). Cf. also situation report, *Kreishauptmann* Tomaschow for March 1942 (ZS, Polen, film 5, Bl.

468; according to this, starving Jews tried to live outside the ghetto but were shot by the police as soon as they were apprehended). For more on the situation of the Jews, cf. *Die jüdische Nährmittellage* (London, 1942) (Nuremberg doc., L-165; also IfZ).

43. Cf. monthly report, *Kreishauptmann* Cholm for June 1940 (ZS, Polen 347, Bl. 578 ff.): "extortionate price inflation." In propaganda material, the black market was blamed on the Jews (cf. report of *Schutzpolizei* lieutenant Alfred Finke, "Die Unverbesserlichen" [The incorrigibles], *Pressedienst des GG*, May 22, 1942, Folge 169; the black market was "of course the work of Jewish elements—diseased, slimy elements"; quoted from ZS, Versch. 108, 402 ff.). However, it was clear to the German administration that supplies could be maintained only through the black market, so the authorities turned a blind eye or even welcomed it. Cf. report, *Stadthauptmann* Kraków, September 12, 1940, IfZ, Ma 158/1–3. Instructions on vigorous action against black marketeers (cf., e.g., decree, government of the General Government, July 10, 1943, ZS, Polen 349, 166 ff.) existed on paper only; for a description of the black market and inflation, cf. the following monthly reports: *Kreishauptmann* Tomaschow (Radom District) for July 1941 (Polen 347, Bl. 448 ff.); *Kreishauptmann* Kraków District for August 1940 (IfZ, Ma-158/2, Bl. 15); *Stadthaptmann* Kraków for September 12, 1940 (IfZ, Ma-158/2, Bl. 15; also ZS, Polen 347, 104 ff.). *Kreishauptmann* Siedlce (Warsaw District) for January 1942 (ZS, Polen 348, 796 ff.); *Kreishauptmann*Tomaschow for March 1942 (826 ff.); *Kreishauptmann* Sochaczew (Warsaw District) (Polen 347, 356 ff.). Regarding the price system (highest prices and price controls), cf. report by the head of the Price Control Office given on July 1942 to the Civil Service Academy of the General Government (quoted from *Krakauer Zeitung*, July 9, 1943). The situation was worsened by the fact that, from mid-1941, the goal of price policy was to ensure supplies to the Wehrmacht and the needs of other Germans became secondary (Gollert, *Warschau unter deutscher Herrschaft*, 180 ff.). The governor general had issued numerous decrees to combat profiteering, which proved totally ineffective; cf. Decree on Measures against Profiteering of January 21, 1940 (*VBl.GG* 1 [1940]: 8 f.), replaced by the Decree on Pricing of April 12, 1940 (131 ff.); final draft, July 1, 1944 (*VBl.GG* [1944]: 211 ff.).

According to the confidential report by the head of the Central Group for Commercial Economy in the Central Chamber for the Whole Economy in the General Government of November 14, 1941 (Institute for Western Studies, Poznań, doc. I-6; reproduced in *Doc. Occ.* 6:356 ff.), some wages remained at prewar levels; some were raised slightly; at best (in the steel and engineering industries), they were brought into line with rates of pay for Germans. In contrast, by November 1941 prices on the black market (Radom District)—which was the one and only means of procuring food—had risen in comparison with prewar levels by about 2,500% for bread, 940% for milk, 1,100% for butter, 2,600% for bacon, 1,200% for potatoes, 1,200% for beef. On increasing food rations to industry, cf. report by the head of the Central Group for Commercial Economy (Institute for Western Studies, Poznań, doc. I-6; reproduced in *Doc. Occ.* 6:359).

44. Frauendorfer, "Arbeits- und Sozialpolitik im GG" (1941); for further details, see Stamm, "Sozialversicherung im General Government und ihre Einordnung in die Arbeits- und Gesundheitsverwaltung" (1942). Cf. report by retired state secretary D. J. Krohn, August 24, 1960, on the beginnings of the Labor Administration in the General Government (BA Ostdok. 13 GG IV b/1).

45. Decree on the Provisional Regulation of Benefit Payments to Pensioners of the Former Polish State, December 9, 1939 (*VBl.GG* [1939]: 206 ff.); reduction of pensions by 50 to 100% by means of the Second Decree of March 20, 1942 (*VBl.GG* [1942]: 142); and First, Second, and Third Implementing Orders (*VBl.GG* 2 [1940]: 209; 510; 1942, 210); so-called War Victims Decree of December 20, 1939 (*VBl.GG*1 [1940]: 1 ff.).

46. Decree, December 16, 1939 (*VBl.GG* [1939]: 226 f.: the highest rate of weekly unemployment benefit was 9 złoty, the family supplement for the first dependent 4.20 złoty, for each further dependent a maximum of 2.40 złoty), superseded by the decree of November 9, 1940 (*VBl.GG* 1 [1940]: 329 ff.). Details in comments by *Oberregierungsrat* Leutert at a discussion with the governor

general on September 30, 1939 ("Diensttagebuch"). The Labor Department in the office of the governor general explained in a letter to the district chiefs, Labor Department, on January 4, 1940 (BA R 2/5066, 27 ff.), that assistance would not be given in the spirit of the law in force but only to maintain their capacity to work in the interests of the Reich—and only in cases where self-help was not possible. As a rule, 7 złoty per week should be sufficient. Cf. also report, Dr. J. Krohn, August 24, 1960 [Krohn was state secretary prior to 1939 and was delegated to the General Government in September 1939, though he quit as early as November 1939 because of differences with Frank—Author].

47. Decree of the governor general, February 7, 1940, quoted from "Report on the Development of the General Government" (BA R 52 II/247, 196 ff.).

48. Ibid., 193.

49. Cf. ibid., 192; decree issued by the government of the General Government, December 17, 1940 (ZS, Polen 257, Bl. 41 f.; directive about stricter supervision of the committees); annual report of the Central Polish Aid Committee 1941–42 (BA R 52 III/7 and 7a); and progress report for March 1943 (7b), as well as report by its chairman on the occasion of a meeting with the governor general on June 19, 1942, and discussions between the chairman and the governor general on July 23 and October 23, 1943 (dissolution and reconstitution of the committee) ("Diensttagebuch"). A detailed account of the viewpoint of the administration is given in the report of Dr. Heinrich, former *Referent* (expert) in charge of the Non-German Free Welfare desk in the Department of Population Affairs and Welfare in the office of the governor general, on August 27, 1958 (BA Ostdok. 13 GG I k/1); overview of the work of the committee, compiled by the Department of Population Affairs and Welfare, September 15, 1943 (k/3).

50. Cf. "Report on the Development of the General Government" (BA R 52 II/247) (with detailed statistical material); progress report of the Jewish Social Self-Help for August 1942 (ZS, Ordner 62, 7–9) (financial hardship suffered by the Self-Help committee due to "incalculable loss of assets"). Letter from the Jewish Social Self-Help, Warsaw, to the commissar for the Jewish quarter, September 6, 1942 (ZS, Polen 349, 205 ff.) (financial resources are exhausted, 94% of the applicants sent away). The Jewish Social Self-Help was dissolved in October 1942 at the behest of the Security Police; it was replaced by the Jewish Aid Office for the General Government, which came under the Central Department of Internal Administration (Department of Population Affairs and Welfare); this body oversaw the remaining aid committees, carried out provisioning measures, and distributed charitable donations (Berenstein, Eisenbach, and Rutkowski, *Eksterminacja Żydów* [1957], 317 f.); however, its dissolution was ordered by the police as early as December 1942, on the grounds that "all Jews would soon have disappeared from the General Government" (letter from commander of the Security Police, Kraków, to the government of the General Government, November 18, 1942, ZS, Versch. 104, Bl. 475 f.); letter, government of the General Government, Department of Population Affairs and Welfare, to the commissioner of the Foreign Office in Kraków, December 5, 1942 (Bl. 485).

Part One. Section 3. C. V. The Legal Status of "Non-Germans"

1. For the office of the governor general, cf. administrative instruction no. 1 of April 7, 1941 (Weh, *Übersicht über das Recht des Generalgouvernements* [loose-leaf collection] [1943], A 122 a), Third Decree on the Development of the Administration in the General Government, March 16, 1941 (*VBl.GG* [1941]: 99). According to this, the ambit of the Central Department of Internal Administration comprised the General Public Administration (subdepartments of Ecclesiastic Affairs and Surveying), the Municipal Administration, the Civil Service Code and Organization, Population Affairs and Welfare (including Jewish policy), Road Traffic, Health, Veterinary Medicine, and Public Works Service. In 1943 a separate Central Department of Health was established. For the district level organization, cf. administrative instruction no. 3, April 7 1941 (Weh, *Übersicht über das*

Recht des Generalgouvernements [1943], A 121 c), to the Decree on the Unified Administration of December 1, 1940 (*VBl.GG* 1 [1940]: 357); this had almost the same structure (except that the Public Works Service was a department in its own right). For the *Kreishauptmann* level, cf. administrative instruction no. 4, April 18, 1941 (Weh, *Übersicht über das Recht des Generalgouvernements* [1943], A 121 d), to the Decree on the Unified Administration of December 1, 1940; the organization is similar, except for the district police services (Commercial Inspectorate, Building Inspectorate, Traffic Police, River Police); for further details, see note 5.

2. Concerning the resettlement of *Poles* within the General Government, in particular the so-called "Zamość action" (grouping of Poles not fit for work in so-called "pensioners' villages"; deportation of able-bodied Poles to the Altreich), cf. memorandum from SS-*Standartenführer* Herbert Böttcher, February 12, 1943, and further correspondence with the UWZ Łódź (*Umwandererzentralstelle*— the Central Resettlement Office) concerning "pensioners villages" (Institute for Western Studies, Poznań); memorandum from the head of the UWZ Łódź (Alois Krumey) about a discussion with the SS and police leader (SSPF) Warsaw on February 24, 1943; report of SSPF Warsaw to UWZ Łódź of March 27, 1943, on the return of evacuated Poles from Zamość to their homeland; letter from *Kreishauptmann* Garwolin to SSPF Warsaw, March 23, 1943; reports to SSPF Warsaw from Zamość on the resettlement of the remaining Polish families from Zamość in Siedlce, February 26, 1943; report (no date, probably end of 1943) about the catastrophic effects of the Zamość action in the Warsaw District (Institute for Western Studies, Poznań). For details see Madajczyk, *Polityka*, 1:280 ff.; Broszat, *NS-Polenpolitik* (1961), 164 ff.

3. Secret decree issued by the Führer and Reich Commissar for the Strengthening of German Nationhood, October 7, 1939 (ZS, Versch. 26/112–13 a); the higher SS and police leaders (HSSPF) under the *Reichsstatthaltern* of Posen (Poznań) and Danzing (Gdańsk) were appointed *by law* (sec. 2, second decree, Reich minister of the interior, November 2, 1939, concerning the implementation of the Führer decree of October 8, 1939) as the representatives of the RKF (Reich Commissar for the Strengthening of German Nationhood) for their sectors; HSSPF Kraków and HSSPF under the *Oberpräsidenten* of Breslau (Wrocław) and Königsberg were appointed by special RKF instruction (instruction RKF no. 13/1, December 19, 1939, BA R 58/243; ZS, Polen, film 35/627). Resettlement was the responsibility of Dept. 4, Population Affairs and Welfare, in the Central Department of Internal Administration of the General Government; the department comprised 12 *Referate* (desks); *Referat* 5, Resettlement (of Poles, Jews, Ukrainians, Gypsies), Evacuation, Welfare, and Prisoners of War, dealt with the resettlement of Jews (organizational structure of Dept. 4, no date, ZS, Versch. 104, 558 ff.).

4. Comments to the president of the Central Department of Internal Administration, Siebert; cf. his report "Zur Polenpolitik im General Government," May 4, 1959 (BA Ostdok. 13 GG Ib/3); cf. also letter from Governor General Frank to the Central Security Department of the Reich IV/B (Eichmann), November 6, 1940 (ZS, Versch. 84/395); this tactic was least transparent to the experts, who continued to believe that pragmatism outweighed ideological goals; see, e.g., memorandum from the head of the Central Department of Food and Agriculture (Naumann), February 23, 1943 (BA, Ostdok. 13 GG, 17), according to which all farm inspectors at *Kreis* and *Bezirk* level in the General Government declared that the entire 1943 harvest was threatened if the resettlements did not cease *immediately*, because (according to a memo from Baumann on April 24, 1942, ibid., 46 ff.) this had resulted in an enormous strengthening of the Polish resistance. On March 18, 1943, the Geschäftsgruppe Ernährung im GG (Working party on food in the General Government) addressed a bitter complaint to Göring in his capacity as plenipotentiary for the Four Year Plan, detailing the economic drawbacks of resettlement in the General Government. Referring back to the RKF was pointless since he was pursuing the resettlement program without consulting the Settlement Committee (comprising representatives of the Reich minister in the occupied Polish territories and the RKF); agricultural production had been significantly disrupted (BA R 26 IV vorl. 33,

9 ff.). In this sense see also a memorandum from the Reich minister for the Occupied Eastern Territories, *Ref.* III, March 17, 1943 (10): in it he complains that the RKF had even personally instigated resettlement measures without consulting his (the minister's) office. And even if agreement were to be reached with these offices, it was to be feared that the resettlements would simply go ahead anyway on the personal orders of the RKF—as had already happened in the Crimea.

5. A comprehensive account of the Reich organization is given in Greifelt, "Festigung deutschen Volkstums in den Ostgebieten" (1940). Police powers were in the hands of the HSSPF, formally "subordinate" to the governor general (Führer Decree on the Administration of the Occupied Territories, October 12, 1939, *RGBl.* I 2077); in practice, though, because the HSSPF had no disciplinary powers, they received their instructions exclusively from the police leadership in Berlin (RFSSuChddtPol by way of RSHA or the *Hauptamt der Ordnungspolizei*).

In the Reich, the *Ordnungspolizei* (the regular police) and the SIPO (Security Police) were formally still part of the Reich Ministry of the Interior. In the General Government, the *Ordnungspolizei* was detached from the Internal Administration and—unlike in the Reich—placed under the HSSPF. Whereas in the Reich the regular police remained an integral part of the general administrative apparatus (the Reich Ministry of the Interior, the Ministry of the *Länder*, the district administration, and the regional administration), in the General Government it was completely detached from the Internal Administration, which retained only the powers of legislation and administration. On the organization of the *Ordnungspolizei* (subordination to the HSSPF, at district level to the SSPF), cf. administrative decree of RFSSuChddtPol of June 5, 1940 (BA R 70 Polen/180). The *Kreis* authorities themselves had no police powers of their own; the gendarmerie forces assigned to them, though in all practical matters subject to the authority of the *Kreishauptleute/ Stadthauptleute*, answered in disciplinary matters not to them but to the commander of the *Ordnungspolizei*, which led to constant quarreling (cf. police discussion on October 17, 1940, "Diensttagebuch" 1940, vol. 2). This organizational structure guaranteed the crucial influence of police headquarters in Berlin—by way of the HSSPF—and thereby that of the SIPO (RSHA) right down to the *Kreis* level. For further details, see Sehn, "Zur Organisation der Polizei im Reich und im GG" (1947). The high point of police autonomy was the Führer directive of May 27, 1942 (*VBl.GG* [1942], no. 41), which removed *all* police matters (including police administration and the police code) and transferred them to the newly created office of state secretary for security in the General Government (decree of the Governor General on June 3, 1942, *VBl.GG* [1942], no. 50), which was run by the HSSPF as a combined office in one person. The police apparatus in the General Government was numerically very strong. In November 1942, police manpower was as follows: 12,000 German police, 12,000 Polish police, 1,500–1,800 Ukrainian militia, 2,000 SIPO officers plus an additional force of 3,000, and 3,000 men in the special forces; at the same time an auxiliary police service of 10,000 Reich Germans was set up (police meeting on November 21, 1942, "Diensttagebuch"). In 1941 the police budget was 347 million złoty, more than a quarter of the total budget of the General Government (*Finanzpräsident* Spindler in a discussion with Frank, July 17, 1941, "Diensttagebuch").

6. Cf. organizational plan of the government of the General Government, March 10, 1940 (ZS, Order 0180, 29–210, copy). According to this, Department 3, Police Matters, came under the Central Department of Internal Administration until 1942 and was integrated into the newly established State Secretariat for Security; see the preceding note). Concerning the status of the *Verwaltungspolizei* (Administrative Police) in the major cities (Kraków, Lublin, Radom, Czenstochau [Czśstochowa], Kielce; *Polizeidirektionen*—the HQs of the municipal police), cf. decree issued by Central Department of Internal Administration on May 12, 1941 (Main Commission Warsaw, Archive, government of the General Government, Central Department of Internal Administration—III/388); for further details, see Schönhals, "Abt. III Polizeiangelegenheiten," *Das Generalgouvernement*, Folge 13–14 (November 1941): 13 ff., University Library, Warsaw, Sign. 011248. Concerning the controversy over the appointment of the *Polizeidirektoren* (who were appointed by the HSSPF *without*

consultation with the administration, cf. cabinet meeting on the security situation of May 4, 1943, at which State Secretary Bühler in particular lodged a strong protest against this practice, but without success ["Diensttagebuch," 1943, 597 ff., 599 f.]). The response of the administration was a decree from the governor general issued the same day, disbanding the *Polizeidirektionen* ("Diensttagebuch" 1943). As a result, only a few months later—in a deal between Frank and the police—the district chiefs were appointed as police authorities (administrative instruction of July 8, 1943, *VBl. GG* [1943]: 306 f.; also, ZS, Versch. 104, Bl. 526 f.); with that, conditions similar to those prevailing in the Reich were formally reestablished after "two years' struggle" (comments by Frank, "Diensttagebuch," 1943, 689 ff., 694). The president of the Central Department of Internal Administration, Siebert, expressed on September 13, 1943, in Kraków, that the police regretted the "admission this decree incarnates" (720). The responsibilities of the administrative police at *Kreis* level were taken over by the Office of Internal Administration (no.1, subpar. B, of administrative instruction no.4 to the Decree on the Unified Administration of December 1, 1940), but were then made the personal responsibility of the *Kreishauptleute* by a decree from Frank on May 4, 1943 ("Diensttagebuch," 1943). For details of matters concerning the administrative police, cf. "Report on the Development of the General Government," July 1, 1940, Bl. 39 (BA R 52 III/247; also IfZ, 1442/54; Bestand ED 6), though this does not take into account the changes described above.

7. The position of the police authorities in the General Government—ignoring for the moment "extralegal" powers (resettlement, protective custody, etc.)—was therefore somewhere between that appertaining in the Reich, which (at least formally) was in line with the traditional legal status of the police as *one* of several central authorities and their de facto status of *Immediatstellung* (direct access and resonsibility to the Führer) in the Occupied Eastern Territories, which gave them the right to issue instructions to all civil authorities (cf. letters from CSSD to RMuChdRkzlei of September 18, 1941, BA R 43 II/396). The dominant position of the police, at least from 1941–42, was further strengthened by the very strained personal relationship between the governor general and HSSPF Krüger (for further details, see the report by F. Siebert, "Das Verhältnis zwischen Innerer Verwaltung und Polizei im ehemaligen GG," BA Ostdok. 13 GG Nr. I b/4; also copy in ZS, Ordner 104, 753 ff. of the report from the district governor of Galicia to Frank, February 24, 1942, concerning the "barely tolerable" tension between administration and police, the effects of which were felt right down to the lowliest *Landkommisar* and local police chief. The conditions on the ground in Galicia were out of all proportion to the difficulties caused by these strains, IfZ, Bestand RFSS/Pers. Stab, Ma-289, Bl. 9796 ff.; Broszat, *NS-Polenpolitik* [1961], 75 ff.). A more important factor was the independent line pursued by the HSSPF (more in ibid.), who countenanced senseless acts of violence in conflict with the policy of the governor general. This was made possible by the fact that legal principles concerning the nature and form of police powers (e.g., procedure based on legal principle) that were valid in the Reich did not apply in the General Government; here, routine police procedure was dominated by the system of directives or ad hoc measures, and records show a relatively small number of police orders or decrees, which the HSSPF was expressly authorized to issue (sec. 3 of the Decree on Security and Order in the General Government, October 26, 1939, *VBl.GG* [1939]: 5).

8. Klein, "Zur Stellung des GG" (1941); Giese, "Die gegenwärtige Staatsangehörigkeit."

9. Decree issued by the government of the General Government, Central Department of Internal Administration, on January 7, 1942 (ZS, Polen 257, Bl. 62).

10. Telex message from the RSHA of March 12, 1942, to the CSSD in Kraków, regarding a discussion on the introduction of the *Deutsche Volksliste* (the German Ethnic Classification List) with representatives of the *Stabshauptamt* (the Central Office of the *Reichsführer*-SS/RKF) and the *Volksdeutsche Mittelstelle* (the Racial German Assistance Office), quoted from *Doc. Occ.* 6:192 ff.

11. Madajczyk, *Polityka*, 1:287 ff., 453 ff. Cf. Frank's comments at meetings held on March 2 and February 25, 1940 (both quoted from *Doc. Occ.* 6:159 n.3), as well as a meeting of departmental

heads on April 12, 1940 (160 n. 6), and at meetings on May 30, 1940 (n. 7), October 9, 1940 (n. 8), December 16, 1941 (161 n. 11), and March 11, 1942 (n. 12).

12. Decree on the Introduction of an Identity Card for German Nationals in the General Government, January 26, 1940 (*VBl.GG* 1 [1940]: 36), with First Implementing Regulation of February 2, 1940 (*VBl.GG* 2 [1940]: 73). This group included those persons who fulfilled the criteria for inclusion in DVL 1–3 (groups 1–3 of the German Ethnic Classification List)—in the Annexed Eastern Territories, DVL-3 Germans (as they were known) were *not* classed as ethnic Germans. Statistics in Gollert, *Warschau unter deutscher Herrschaft* (1942), 129.

13. Decree on the Introduction of an Identity Card for Persons of German Extraction in the General Government, October 29, 1941 (*VBl.GG* [1941]: 622).

14. Report on the activities of the Racial German Assistance Office under the authority of the district SS and police leader of Lublin, in the area of *völkisch* recuperation of Polonicized former German settlements in the Lublin District, May 21, 1942 (Doc. Occ. 6:208 ff.).

15. Announcement by State Secretary Bühler on behalf of the government of the General Government in *Krakauer Zeitung*, October 28, 1943. Circular decree of Reich Ministry of the Interior, November 12, 1942 (MinBliV [1942]: 2143).

16. Decree of Reich Ministry of the Interior, May 22, 1944 (Nuremberg doc., NO-4850).

17. For further details, see Broszat, "Erfassung und Rechtsstellung von Volksdeutschen und Deutschstämmigen im GG," expertise, in IfZ, 2:259 f.

18. As explained above in section 2, the administration considered political and cultural elements, as well as the question of descent ("Bekenntis zum deutschen Volkstum"), whereas the district SS and police leaders held a more racially oriented view of what constituted an ethnic German (*Volksdeutsche*) or a person of German extraction (*Deutschstämmige*). According to the draft by the CSSD of May 14, 1942, *Deutschstämmige* were "Polonicised or Slavicized persons, wholly or partly of German descent" (reproduced in *Doc. Occ.* 6:194 ff.). Concerning the classification by the SS of "*Deutschstämmige* in the General Government in so-called 'value groups,' " see decree of the RFSS/RKF to all representatives of the RKF, May 26, 1944 (reproduced in *Doc. Occ.* 6:207); cf. also Broszat, "Erfassung und Rechtsstellung von Volksdeutschen und Deutschstämmigen im GG," 255; "Diensttagebuch," October 23, 1941. According to Broszat, "Erfassung und Rechtsstellung von Volksdeutschen und Deutschstämmigen im GG," 253, of the total of 73,532 registered *Volksdeutsche*, only 40,144 had "retained their *Deutschtum*" and had declared their loyalty; a further 30,318 were registered as so-called A category (i.e., strongly "Polonicized" but ready for naturalization), 2,622 as G category (*fremdrassig*—of foreign race), and 448 as persons of German blood not ready for naturalization.

19. Instruction of *Reichsführer*-SS/RKF, June 13, 1944, quoted from *Doc. Occ.* 6:204 ff.

20. According to confidential guidelines to the Decree on the Introduction of Identity Cards for Persons of German Extraction in the General Government, October 29, 1941 (Institute for Western Studies, Poznań, doc. I-452; also *Doc. Occ.* 6:187 ff.), the following criteria were to be applied when assessing German extraction: race, health, genetics, performance, *Volkstum*, and security.

21. Instruction of *Reichsführer*-SS/RKF, June 13, 1944 (*Doc. Occ.* 6:204 ff.). Comments by SS-*Sturmbannführer* Hans Weibgen to the Party leadership of the General Government, May 15, 1944 ("Diensttagebuch" 1944).

22. Decree on the Rights of Persons of German Extraction, November 30, 1942 (*VBl.GG* [1942]: 739). For a detailed account of the *Volksdeutsche* and *Deutschstämmige* in the General Government, cf. Broszat, "Erfassung und Rechtsstellung von Volksdeutschen und Deutschstämmigen im GG," 243–60.

23. Monthly report of the district governor of Warsaw, December 10, 1942 (Institute for Western Studies, Poznań, doc. I-10, 94; excerpts in *Doc. Occ.* 6:199 ff.); insofar as they were resettled in

the Reich, they were treated in accordance with the regulations applying to persons "capable of re-Germanization" (Reich minister of the interior RFSS/RKF, May 26, 1944, reproduced in *Doc. Occ.* 6:202 ff.).

Part One. Section 3. C. VI. Marriage Law

1. Cf. "Diensttagebuch," 1940, vol. 2, May 31, 1940 (551): "In the governor general's view, central to settling this question is whether there are objections to such marriages (between Germans and Ukrainians) from the racial standpoint. Where this is not the case, he would not be opposed. The same would of course apply to the marriage of Germans to Polish women. It goes without saying that any German marrying a Polish woman would not be allowed to stay in the General Government."

2. Letter from the head of the Governor General's Office (Bühler) and the department heads and district chiefs, October 11, 1940 (quoted from *Doc. Occ.* 6:380 f.).

3. Nuremberg doc., NO-3592.

4. Cf. decree issued by the chief of the SS Central Office for Race and Settlement, with headquarters in Prague, August 6, 1944 (Nuremberg doc., NO-3295).

Part One. Section 3. C. VII. Public Health

1. Sec. 3, par. 3, Third Decree on the Development of the Administration in the Government General, March 16, 1941 (*VBl.GG* [1941]: 99), administrative instruction no. 1, April 7, 1941, no. I B (Weh, *Übersicht über das Recht des Generalgouvernements* [1943], A 122 a), and decree of January 20, 1943 (*VBl.GG* [1943]: 43; Weh, *Übersicht über das Recht des Generalgouvernements* [1943], B 500). On the health service in the General Government, see detailed account in K. M. Pospieszalski, "Służba zdrowia," *Doc. Occ.* 6:99, with numerous examples; on the organization of the health service, cf. Decree on the Establishment of the Chamber of Health in the General Government, February 28, 1940 (*VBl.GG* 1 [1940]: 89).

2. For example, the hunting down of people with venereal diseases, of whom there were supposed to be many in the General Government. According to details given by the head of the Health Department on January 11, 1940, 6% of the adult population in the General Government were not fit for work as a result of venereal disease, a rate that was ten times higher than in the Reich. For Poles, in the first months, the disease did not have to be reported ("Diensttagebuch," 1:54). Compulsory reporting, however, was introduced by means of a decree issued on January 22, 1940 (*VBl. GG* 1 [1940]: 81 f.), and the medical officers were empowered to enforce treatment where necessary; the decree prohibited any "activities capable of causing infection" until such time as the patient was healed, in particular "engaging in coitus," under penalty of penitential sentence; if a German became infected through coitus, there was the additional threat of the death penalty. As early as November 18, 1939, *Kreis* medical officers were asked, as representatives of the Medical Association, to report such people (instruction, Department of Health, November 18, 1939, ZS, Versch. 104, Bl. 534).

3. However, according to Governor General Frank: "Taking a long perspective, it is impossible that medical training should cease" ("Diensttagebuch," February 26, 1940). See also his notes on a discussion with Hitler: "I . . . emphasized the necessity of developing a minimal training program . . . [the Führer] replied, with the witty observation that he would like to recommend his own physcian, Dr. Brandt, to head the training program for these Polish doctors" ("Diensttagebuch," February 6, 1944, quoted from *Doc. Occ.* 6:299 n. 129).

4. According to the details given in "Diensttagebuch," 1940, vol. 3, September 6, 1940, in

September 1940 there were 8,000 Polish and Ukrainian physicians and only about 50 German doctors working in the General Government (quoted from *Doc. Occ.* 6:299, 299 n. 128). For further details, see *Doc. Occ.* 6:300 n. 132.

5. Expert report, Dr. J. Owsiński, January 17, 1948, in the Bühler trial (ZS, Ordner 21).

6. Said to have been carried out by the head of the Department of Health in person (expert report, ibid.).

7. Statement, Dr. Biberstein, January 20, 1948 (ibid.). According to this statement, they were plundered of everything, right down to bedsheets; cf. also Dr. Olbrycht (ZS, Versch. 17, 310 ff.) and statement, Dr. Nüssenfeld, January 20, 1948 (ibid.). Nüssenfeld was senior physician in the Jewish hospital in the Kraków Ghetto; cf. also remark by Dr. Olbrycht (ibid.).

8. Report, F. Siebert, Central Department of Internal Administration, November 11, 1959 (BA Ostdok. 13 GG No. 1b/5; ZS, Versch. 104, 769 ff.).

9. Cf. the collection of anti-Semitic posters in Institute for Western Studies, Poznań.

10. Statement, Dr. Biberstein, January 20, 1948 (ZS, Ordner 21).

11. Remarks at a meeting of department heads on April 12, 1940 ("Diensttagebuch," 1:142), to the effect that only 1,000 typhus cases were recorded between January 1 and April 1, 1940. Although the number of cases increased subsequently, especially in the Jewish population, this was specifically due to food shortages, which had pushed the Jews to the brink of starvation (cf. "Diensttagebuch," vol. 1, September 6, October 16, 1940; September 9 and 12, June 17, July 21, 1941), so there can be no question of epidemic typhus being spread by Jews. In this context, see also expert report by Prof. Jan Olbrycht presented to the Bühler trial in 1948 (ZS, Versch. 17, Bl. 310–13).

12. For details cf. expert report by Dr. Biberstein (ZS, Ordner 21).

13. Minutes of the proceedings and results of the conference, in ZS, Ordner Versch. 19, Bl. 54–265. At this point, the minutes record "applause."

Part One. Section 3. C. VIII. Freedom of Movement and Personal Liberty

1. Government decrees issued January 7, 1941, and June 1, 1941 (establishment of ghettos) (ZS, Polen 256, Bl. 205 ff., 250); decree issued by Governor General Frank to all district chiefs, May 25, 1940, concerning resettlement of all Jews from Kraków; see letter from Department of Internal Administration in the Governor General's Office to the Warsaw District chief, July 26, 1940 (Institute for Western Studies, Poznań); instruction issued by RFSS to HSSPF Kraków, July 19, 1942, according to which the "evacuation" of all Jews (i.e., their deportation to death camps) had to be completed by December 31, 1942 (Institute for Western Studies, Poznań, doc. I-744). Concerning the deportations from Warsaw, see directives issued by the head of the Department of Resettlement in the Warsaw District, July 22, 1942 (ZS, Ordner 365 c, 58–61), according to which the victims were given no time to prepare themselves; the deportations began the day the directives were issued (11 A.M.). The Jewish Council was responsible, on pain of death, for rounding up a daily "contingent" of 6,000 Jews for deportation. If the orders of the administration were not carried out "one hundred percent," the threat was to shoot a corresponding number of hostages. Any "disturbance" of the smooth running of the deportations or transgression of any kind was punishable by death by shooting. As a result, the use of firearms was part of the daily routine of "resettlement"; cf. report by the chairman of the Jewish Council to the "commissar for the Jewish Quarter," January 1, 1942–March 18, 1943 (ZS, Ordner 305 e/0544 f.), which—though not directly criticizing the actions of the German authorities—gave clear indications of the real conditions (e.g., "fatal accident on the street"; "90 accidents due to bullet wounds," etc.); fatalities were given as "gunshot wounds." Regarding the economic side of "resettlement" (known as Aktion Reinhardt), from which the German administration made huge profits, see report, HSSPF Kraków to RFSS, November 4, 1943, describing how, on completion of the action on October 19, 1943, all Jewish assets (machines, raw materials) to a

value of 6.3 million reichsmarks—with further assets worth 7–8 million reichsmarks still outstanding—were transferred to "Aryan ownership"; Jews were forced to sign over accounts at home and abroad to the German trustee company "Ost" (which in reality was a form of state plundering of Jewish property). Real estate was transferred to the state *Liegenschaftsverwaltung* (property management) (ZS, Ordner 246, 114 ff.).

2. First Implementing Regulation of December 11, 1939 (*VBl.GG* [1939]: 231; *Doc. Occ.* 6 (S): 560 ff.), to the Decree on Forced Labor for Jews of October 26, 1939 (*VBl.GG* [1939]: 6).

3. Sec. 4 of the First Implementing Regulation of December 11, 1939 (*VBl.GG* [1939]: 231; *Doc. Occ.* 6 [S]: 560 ff.).

4. Sec. 2 of the First Decree on Residence Restrictions in the General Government, September 13, 1940 (*VBl.GG* 1 [1940]: 288).

5. The fact that the decree of September 13, 1940 (*VBl.GG*1 [1940]: 288), had this purpose is underlined by the editor of the official collection, A. Weh, *Übersicht über das Recht des Generalgouvernements* (1943) (note 3 to sec. 2 of the decree of September 13, 1940, B 430). Concerning the term *Wohnbezirk* (residential district), see letter of the Radom district governor to the government of the General Government, December 19, 1941 (ZS, Polen 257, 95).

6. Corresponding instructions had existed since February 1940, evidently varying from one *Kreis* district to another; cf. monthly report, *Kreishauptmann* of Krasnystaw, Lublin District, for August 1940 (ZS, Polen 347, Bl. 174 f.); from November 1940 such measures were allowed only with the permission of the appropriate district chief "because of the repercussions on general plans for resettlement" (of the Jews) (letter from the government of the General Government, Central Department of Internal Administration, to the district chiefs, *Kreishauptleute*, and *Stadthauptleute*, November 21, 1940 [Polen film 64, Bl. 138–41]); cf. public notice issued by the mayor of Kielce on April 7, 1941 (poster calling for dwellings vacated by Jews after the establishment of the ghetto to be registered with the authorities; Institute for Western Studies, Poznań, doc. I-519); cf. letter from the Radom district governor to all *Kreishauptleute* and *Stadthauptleute* of the district, December 11, 1941, with the recommendation to set up ghettos and instructions, where necessary, to provide appropriate markings and warn Jews that the penalty for leaving the ghetto was death. However, mass "resettlements" should not be undertaken (ZS, Polen 257, 99 f.).

7. For Warsaw, cf. proclamation by the district chief's commissioner about the setting up of a Jewish district, October 16, 1940 (reproduced in *Doc. Occ.* 6:544). An announcement to this effect had already been made on August 9, 1940 (*Mitteilungsblatt der Stadt Warschau*, August 9, 1940). The decisive instructions were not issued by the Warsaw District chief until October 20 and 31, 1940 (*Amstblatt Distrikt Warschau*, 1940, 145); a corresponding instruction was issued by the Kraków District chief on March 3, 1941. For Lublin, cf. proclamation of the district governor, March 24, 1941, quoted from instruction of the governor, December 9, 1941 (Main Commission Warsaw, Government of the GG, Central Department of Internal Administration II/347, copy). For the Radom District, cf. instruction of district governor, July 1941 (*Amstblatt des Distrikt*, July 15, 1941 [not preserved], Bl. 132 ff., quoted from transcript, ibid.). For a Nazi view of the conditions in the ghetto, cf. von Medeazza, "Die jüdischen Wohnbezirke im GG" (1941), 1441: "It can be stated that Jewish life in the *Wohnbezirk* is proceeding in orderly fashion. . . . How the Jews organize themselves economically . . . within their own *Wohnbezirke*, now that they are prevented from playing their usual trade of exploiting the non-Jewish population, is entirely their own business." Concerning the dire living conditions, even in the smaller ghettos, cf. monthly report, *Kreishauptmann* of Busko, Radom District, for February 1941 (ZS, Polen 347, Bl. 394): "In the Jewish district there are about '20 people' to a room." Conditions in the Warsaw Ghetto were even worse—see note 8. In connection with the creation of Jewish districts and control of Jewish businesses inside and outside the ghetto, further regulations were issued, in particular for the Warsaw ghetto; see, for example, instructions of the Warsaw District chief, January 1 and December 6, 1940 (Institute for Western Studies, Poznań);

cf. also lecture by the head of the Department of Resettlement (*Reichsamtsleiter* Schön) on January 20, 1941, in Warsaw (ZS, Polen, film 14/792–816) and letter from the Central Department of Internal Administration to Dr. Brandl, a *Regierungsrat* in the Governor General's Office, August 6, 1941, on the plan to move only the worst Jewish businesses (those "we must sift out for liquidation") into the ghetto (with note from State Secretary Bühler, "Proposal agreed, August 11—B."). For details of the borders between the Warsaw ghetto and the Aryan district, movement of goods into the ghetto (license requirement, prohibition on providing Jews with goods outside the ghetto), and pass regulations, cf. *Mitteilungsblatt der Stadt Warschau*, January 28, November 3, February 25, and March 28, 1941.

8. Concerning conditions generally, cf. weekly report of the Central Department of Propaganda, April 7, 1942 (ZS, Ordner 62, 84 f., 86–89); Hirzfeld, "Die Stadt des Todes," excerpts in Poliakov and Wulf, *Das Dritte Reich und die Juden* (1956), 273 ff.; and the detailed diary entries of Landau, *Kronika lat wojny i okupacji* (1962). A detailed account is given in the expert report by Dr. H. von Crannhals, with a chronology of the most significant events and instructions (ZS, 211 AR-Z 373/59); see also the material in ZS, Ordner 365 ff., Auerswald files; on the catastrophic economic situation in the Warsaw ghetto (which was completely cut off from the outside world—for example, all telephone, traffic, and other communications were cut and all business and movement of goods were conducted through a so-called transfer office [which worked completely uneconomically]), cf. report on the economic situation (no date, ZS, Polen, film 62, 16–22) and remarks by the Central Department of Industry head, Emmerich, at a meeting in Kraków on April 19, 1941 ("Diensttage-buch"), and minutes of a meeting of tax inspectors of the General Government, held in Krynica on March 14, 1941 (BA R 2/5071, Bl. 122); also progress report 39/45 of the deputy head of the Department of Industry in the Warsaw District, February 1945 (no date, BA Ostdok. 13 GG IX a/5). Regarding internal matters in the ghetto, cf. the illuminating report (also without date) in ZS, Polen, film 62, Bl. 55–62.

9. Gollert, *Warschau unter deutscher Herrschaft* (1942), 134.

10. The district chiefs issued corresponding central regulations, which went far beyond pure "residence restrictions"; cf., for example, directive issued by the Lublin District governor on September 22, 1941 (*Amtsbl. des Distrikt Lublin*, 1941, nos. 8–9, transcript in the Main Commission Warsaw, Archive, Government of the GG, Central Department of Internal Administration, II/347), which banned Jews from even temporarily leaving their locality or using any public or private transport; it also prohibited anyone from providing any kind of support for Jews who violated this ban (*News from the Reich*, June 20, 1940, BA R 58/151); but when it was proved that such rash measures were impossible to carry out, a closed ghetto was set up; cf. directive of the *Stadthauptmann* of October 22, 1940, banning Jews from moving outside the town boundaries (except where such journeys were compulsory, i.e., deportation, forced labor) (*Amtl. Anzeiger* 1940, October 26, 1940, quoted from *Doc. Occ.* 6:543). For the Radom District, cf. corresponding directives issued in July 1941 (543 n. 7), which banned Jews generally from using all main streets and thoroughfares in the district. A further directive of the governor (Department of Internal Administration), December 11, 1941 (ZS, Polen 257, Bl. 96–98; copy), followed the example of Lublin in that all Jews were banned from even temporarily leaving the town (except for labor service, for reasons of public interest, or to carry out instructions of the German authorities) or from using vehicles outside their localities and even then—*without* any basis in formal law—the directive carried the threat that anyone leaving the ghetto would be shot. In Warsaw Jews were banned from entering public places from August 1940; from September of that year, only limited access was allowed to trams; in October 1940 a general ban on entering public streets was imposed; there were also strict regulations concerning the curfew (*Mitteilungsbl. der Stadt Warschau*, August 1, September 26, November 30, and October 10, 1940; *Amtsbl.* of the Warsaw District chief, November 11, 1940, no. 10; Institute for Western Studies, Poznań).

11. Sec. 4a of the Decree on Residence Restrictions in the General Government, April 29, 1941 (*VBl.GG* 1941, 74), in conjunction with the Decree on Administrative Penalty Procedures, September 13, 1940 (*VBl.GG* 1 [1940]: 300 f.). Where such penalties were insufficient, the case could be sent to the Special Court, which had powers to impose prison sentences and/or fines up to 10,000 złoty, and in serious cases even penitential sentences.

12. *VBl.GG* (1941): 595 (also ZS, Ordner 94, Bl. 359 f.; copy); concerning the preparation, drafting, and interpretation of the decree, cf. correspondence between the relevant departments in the government of the General Government (ZS, Polen 257, Bl. 85–87, 118–25, 136–38, 155, 157; Polen, film 63, 169 ff. [correspondence 1940–42]; Ordner 103 and 104).

13. Cf. the numerous examples of such punishments, in Bartoszewski and Lewin, *Righteous among Nations* (1969). These regulations were the result of an internal agreement within the government of the General Government; cf. correspondence quoted in note 12.

14. For Lublin, cf. "Anordnung über Aufenthaltsbeschränkungen im Bereich der Stadt Lublin," December 9, 1941 (*Amtblatt* of the Lublin District chief, 1941, no. 12, quoted from transcript, Main Commission Warsaw, Archive, Government of the GG, Central Department of Internal Administration, II/347). For Radom, cf. directive of the Radom District governor, December 11, 1941 (ZS, Polen 257, Bl. 96–98; copy).

15. The Special Courts had pronounced against the imposition of the death penalty, since the actual facts often justified a milder sentence. Basically, such cases should have been the responsibility of the Security Police. Efforts were also made to give the decree of October 15, 1941, a strict interpretation; cf. monthly report of the *Kreishauptmann* of Tomaschow (Tomaszów Mazowiecki) for March 1941, April 8, 1942 (ZS, Polen, 348, 826 ff.; also Polen, film 5, Bl. 468).

16. According to the report by the SIPO commander, October 7, 1943, about Galicia (Institute for Western Studies, Poznań, doc. I-7; excerpts in *Doc. Occ.* 6:542 n. 10), following an order issued by the chief of the uniformed police in Kraków, the police took matters into their own hands. Cf. also monthly report from the *Kreishauptmann* of Tomaszow (ZS, Polen 348, 826 ff.; also Polen, film 5, Bl. 468), according to which 50 Jews who had left the ghetto had been shot by the police; for more details see his monthly report for March 1942 (468).

17. *VBl.GG* 1 [1940]: 288.

18. *VBl.GG* [1939]: 5.

19. Police meeting on May 30, 1940, in Kraków ("Diensttagebuch").

20. Police orders on the creation of Jewish *Wohnbezirke* in Warsaw and Lublin, October 28, 1942 (*VBl.GG* [1942]: 665 f.; also ZS, Versch. 94, 407 f.), and November 10, 1942, for the Radom, Kraków, and Galicia Districts (*VBl.GG* [1942]: 683 f.).

21. But not the Warsaw ghetto, for which legislative powers were vested in the district chiefs only "within the framework of the general directives of the government of the General Government"; sec. 1 of the Decree on Commerce in the Warsaw Ghetto, April 19, 1941 (quoted from "Diensttagebuch," 1941, 11:1, 301 ff., 312).

22. Police powers for the Jewish *Wohnbezirke* ("quarters") were vested in the *Ordnungspolizei* (commander of the *Schutzpolizei*), who was also responsible for the boundaries of the ghetto. However, since May 1941 there had also been a commissar for the Jewish Quarter in the Warsaw ghetto; this was the executive organ of the district chief, as well as having certain police powers (control of the wearing of armbands, residence regulations, etc.); for further details, see ZS, Polen 349, 247 ff. Concerning the activities of this commissar (Heinz Auerswald), who worked conscientiously as the administrative organ of the extermination policy, cf. the material collected in ZS, Ordner 365 ff.; for more details, see also his report, "Zwei Jahre Aufbauarbeit im Distrikt Warschau—Die Juden im Distrikt Warschau," November 1941, in which he affirms how necessary and useful the establishment of the ghetto was (ZS, Polen 349, 275 ff.); concerning the division of political responsibilities in the ghetto, cf. also the following note.

23. Initially, the administration (district governors) prevailed; the civil administration knew local conditions best and was therefore in the best position—working through the *Kreishauptleute* and *Stadthauptleute*—to organize Jewish labor (meeting on police matters between CSSD Bruno Streckenbach and the district governors held in Kraków, May 30, 1940, "Diensttagebuch," 1940). In Warsaw, however, as in all other ghettos, the Security Police (SIPO) were in the ascendance; as early as fall 1941, there was talk of placing the Jewish *Ordnungsdienst* (responsible for public order) under the authority of the SIPO (letter from district SS and police leader, Warsaw, to the commissar for the Jewish Quarter, November 18, 1941, ZS, Polen 346, 1057). Entry to the ghetto was overseen by the SS guard posts. From 1942, even members of the administration of the General Government needed permission from the Security Service of the SS to gain entry to the ghetto (report, H. Heinrich: "Bevölkerungswesen und Fürsorge im GG," August 27, 1958, BA Ostdok. 13 GG I/K 1, with appendixes). Complete usurpation of control of the Jewish ghettos, beginning with the takeover of guard duties, was finalized in 1942 when the police assumed responsibility for *all* regulations concerning Jewish labor, ostensibly on the grounds of security. A decree of the General Government, June 25, 1942, stipulated that the Jewish *Arbeitseinsatz* (forced labor) had, in all cases, to be organized *in consultation* with the police (ZS, UdSSR, Bd. 431, copy). This initiative corresponded exactly to the plans of the district SS and police leaders, realized at a later stage, which saw the ghettos as vast production plants, run formally along the same lines as concentration camps, in which the Jews worked under the exclusive control of the police or were placed by them at the disposal of German factories.

24. Organizational plan of the government of the General Government, March 10, 1940 (ZS), in conjunction with the organizational plan of Dept. 4, Population Affairs and Welfare (no date); cf. also "Report on the Development of the General Government," July 1, 1940, Bl. 191, BA R 52 II/247. Corresponding to the regulations issued by the central administration, "Jewish Desks" (*Judenreferate*) were also established in the district offices (cf. for example the half-yearly report of the Jewish Desk of the Warsaw District, May 14, 1940; ZS, Polen, film 62, 391 ff.).

25. Decree of January 26, 1940 (*VBl.GG* 1 [1940]: 45); limited usage was not allowed until the decree of February 20, 1941 (*VBl.GG* [1941]: 69), which gave the police the authority to issue special permits in exceptional cases; cf. also circular decree of Central Department of Internal Administration, March 17, 1941 (Main Commission Warsaw, Archive, Government of the GG, Central Department of Internal Administration, II/374). Restrictions for Jews also applied to travel between the district of Galicia and the rest of the General Government (decree of September 4, 1941, *VBl.GG* [1941]: 511 f.).

26. Jews granted such permits were allowed to travel by rail only in the lowest-class accommodation and were not permitted to use fast and express services (sec. 1 of the decree dated February 20, 1941, *VBl.GG* [1941]: 69), nor any other public transport; but see letter from Warsaw District chief, Department of Internal Administration, to the office of the governor general, Department of Internal Administration, March 4, 1940, which said, among other things: "Because certain Jews have evaded compulsory labor, we should consider whether or not to issue a general ban on Jews' using postal bus services" (ZS, Polen 257, Bl. 9 f.). The purpose of suppressing applications and travel was already stipulated in the directives in the circular decree of the Central Department of Internal Administration, March 17, 1941 (Main Commission Warsaw, Archive, Government of the GG, Central Department of Internal Administration, II/374), issued before the decree of the Central Department of Finances on April 30, 1941 (see the next note).

27. Decree of the Central Department of Finances, April 30, 1941 (BA R 2/5071, 108).

28. See note 10 above.

29. Decree circulated by Central Department of Internal Administration, March 17, 1941 (Main Commission Warsaw, Archive, Government of the GG, Central Department of Internal Administration, II/374).

30. At least this was the case in Warsaw; instruction of the Warsaw District chief, November 25, 1940 (ZS).

31. Letter from the Warsaw District chief, Department of Internal Administration, to the government of the General Government, Legislative Office, March 14, 1942 (ZS, Ordner 69, Bl. 313; copy). Decree of the government of the General Government, March 29, 1941 (ZS, Polen 256, Bl. 98–105, 192). Decree of the government of the General Government, July 9, 1941 (Bl. 154).

32. Report, Dr. von Jordan, November 1956 (ZS, Ordner 47, Bl. 378 ff., 399). Dr. von Jordan worked at one time in the Central Department of Internal Administration of the office of the governor general.

33. Decree on the Licensing of Motor Vehicles in the General Government, November 23, 1939 (*VBl.GG* [1939]: 205 f.), with the First and Second Implementing Orders, December 8, 1939, and February 5, 1940, respectively (*VBl.GG* [1939]: 213; 2 [1940]: 81) (termination of the licenses of all vehicles in use in the General Government; new licenses issued by *Kreishauptleute/ Stadthauptleute*). Decree on Licensing of Vehicles for Road Traffic, August 8, 1942 (*VBl.GG* [1942]: 577 ff.), which canceled the decree issued on November 23, 1939, and set out comprehensive prerequisites for licensing, based on the road traffic licensing requirements in force in the Reich; it made permits for the purchase of vehicles compulsory. For details, see Decree on Sales of Vehicles in the General Government, March 27, 1940 (*VBl.GG* 1 [1940]: 153 f., with implementing order of March 28, 1940, *VBl.GG* 2 [1940]: 227), replaced by decree of September 4, 1942 (*VBl.GG* [1942]: 499), with first directive of September 5, 1942 (*VBl.GG* [1942]: 501 f.). Decree of the government of the General Government, April 8, 1941 (ZS, Polen 256, Bl. 125–27); fifth directive of the Central Department of Internal Administration, August 20, 1943 (*VBl.GG* [1943]: 544 f.), to the decree of September 4, 1942 (ban on the use of vehicles for private purposes). Later, "non-Germans" were forbidden from driving vehicles licensed in Warsaw (i.e., including those for Polish employees of German administrative offices) under threat of the *death penalty* (police order on the use of private cars and motorcycles of February 2, 1944, *VBl.GG* [1944]: 45), probably a response to actions of the Polish resistance movement in Warsaw. German officials and employees also found it more difficult—or even impossible—to purchase and use vehicles (decree of the government of the General Government on the "winkling out" of all private cars belonging to officials and employees of the General Government, June 26, 1941, ZS, Polen 256, Bl. 187, 188). An auto lacking an official "*Winkel*" (angular-shaped) permit was not authorized to be driven.

34. Police order on the use of public transport by "non-Germans" in the General Government, October 18, 1943 (*VBl.GG* [1943]: 613); exceptions included journeys to and from work, as well as persons employed in German public offices with appropriate documentation (sec. 1, par. 2).

35. Decree of November 17, 1941 (ZS, Polen 256, Bl. 93 and 210); cf. also police order on the transporting of "non-Germans" and goods on trucks, October 18, 1943 (*VBl.GG* [1943]: 613).

36. Proclamation by the representative of the district chief for the City of Warsaw, September 24, 1940 (*Krakauer Zeitung*, September 25, 1940, quoted from *Doc. Occ.* 6:380). This stipulated that the front platform and the front section of the bus were reserved for Reich Germans and *Volksdeutsche*; the rear section and the second car were for the use of Poles. Jews could be accommodated only in cars specially designated "Jews Only."

37. *VBl.GG* (1942): 421 f.

38. Sec. 3 of the decree of August 3, 1942 (ibid.), in conjunction with the decree on use in road traffic, February 20, 1941 (*VBl.GG* [1941]: 36).

Part One. Section 3. C. IX. Restrictions on Communication and Information Exchange

1. There was a general ban on postal and news communications with enemy countries (decree of April 22, 1942, *VBl.GG* [1942]: 225).

2. Decree on News Communications of April 22, 1942 (ibid.), with amendment of October 20, 1943 (*VBl.GG* [1943]: 621).

3. Decree of April 22, 1942 (*VBl.GG* [1942]: 225); it is impossible to establish whether such restrictions were imposed.

4. A decree issued on March 3, 1943 (*VBl.GG* [1943]: 115), concerning "punishment of postal fraud," provided for penalties "commensurate with the scale of the particular offense," without reference to the basis of computation for penalties set out in sec. 27 of the Postal Services Law of October 28, 1931 (*RGBl.* I 347).

5. SD report on domestic matters (previously *News from the Reich*), November 8, 1943 (BA R 58/190).

6. Letter from the government of the General Government to its plenipotentiary in Berlin, August 16, 1940 (ZS, Polen 257, Bl. 26, 30 b; copy). The German administration thwarted attempts by an American telegraphic agency to establish a branch in the General Government for Jews who wished to emigrate (ibid., correspondence).

7. Directive on Termination of Delivery Services for Small Parcels and Packages Sent by Jews, November 21, 1941 (ZS, Ordner "Verschiedenes" 94, Bl. 369), my emphasis.

8. Order issued by *Armeeoberkommando* 14 (Army HQ 14), October 5, 1939 (IfZ, MA-682, Bl. 0395).

9. Proclamation issued by the *Stadthauptmann* of Kraków, January 11, 1940 (Main Commission Warsaw, Plakatsammlung III t 24—doc. 24 t/22); at the same time, the removal of all "unnecessary aerials" was ordered.

10. Decree on the Confiscation of Radio Transmitters, December 15, 1939 (*VBl.GG* [1939]: 225 f.).

11. Sec. 4 of the Decree on the Confiscation of Radio Transmitters, ibid.

12. "Diensttagebuch," 1:128 ff.

13. Decree on the Registration of Film Equipment, October 18, 1940 (*VBl.GG* 1 [1940]: 318). Cf. Decree on the Surrender of Skis and Ski-boots in the General Government, December 31, 1941, with first directive dated December 31, 1941 (*VBl.GG* [1941]: 749 f.; *VBl.GG* [1942]: 2); failure to comply was punishable by a penitentiary sentence—statement by Dr. Biberstein, January 20, 1948 (ZS, Ordner 21).

14. In this sense, see also H. Roos, *Polen in der Besatzungszeit*, 179; concerning the initial optimism of the rural population and industrial workers, see situation report by the military governor, Kraków, October 9, 1939 (IfZ, Bestand MiG, MA-682, Bl. 486 ff.).

15. Summary by the chief of the General Staff of the District Military Command (*Wehrkreiskommando*) in the General Government to the chief of the General Staff, Army, January 7, 1943 (IfZ, Ma-1017, Bl. 0715 ff.).

16. For a detailed account, see the survey of conditions in the General Government, prepared in the Reich Chancellery (based on material supplied by HSSPF Kraków), which was sent to the *Reichsführer*-SS on April 17, 1943 (Nuremberg doc., NG-3321; IfZ, Ma-300, 4008 ff.).

17. This emerges indirectly from the report by F. Siebert, "Hauptabteilung Innere Verwaltung," November 11, 1939 (BA Ostdok. 13 GG, no. I b/5).

18. Report dated January 7, 1943 (IfZ, Ma-1017, Bl. 0715 ff.).

19. *VBl.GG* (1939): 5.

20. Discussion between Governor General Frank and the head of the Central Department of Internal Administration on November 21, 1941 ("Diensttagebuch" 1941).

21. Cf. report dated April 7, 1943 (IfZ, "Diensttagebuch," Ma-1017, Bl. 0718).

22. Minutes of a meeting about the security situation, October 19, 1943 ("Diensttagebuch" 1943). He (Frank) was determined "to give the security services *every power* appropriate to the task of guaranteeing security" (cabinet meeting, October 26, 1943; "Diensttagebuch," Bl. 757). See also

comments by the commander of the Security Police and SD at a meeting on the security situation in the General Government, September 27, 1943 ("Diensttagebuch" 1943). For an account of the police raids and other reprisals that followed the granting of these powers, see Bartoszewski, *Der Todesring um Warschau* (1968), 196 ff.

23. *VBl.GG* (1943): 589.

24. On the activities of the resistance movement, cf. information given by the commander of the Security Police and SD at a police meeting on October 19, 1943, "Diensttagebuch": at the beginning of January 1942, only six robberies a day were reported; by September 1943 this had risen to an average of 223 daily, and by the first third of October 1943 it was as high as 250 a day.

25. The decree served above all as a basis for shooting hostages and members of the resistance. Such shootings were often carried out summarily—without even a drumhead court-martial. However, on October 23, 1943, the commander of the Security Police and SD ordered that prisoners should in future be sentenced at a court-martial; this was probably the result of protests by Bühler, state secretary in the government of the General Government, who was concerned about the foreign policy implications and advocated avoiding the term *hostage* to describe detainees (discussion, October 23, 1943, "Diensttagebuch" 1943).

26. In a discussion with the president of the Central Department of Justice (Kurt Wille) on May 31, 1944, the governor general expressed strong reservations about the "exceptional executions" carried out by the Security Police. He thought that "perhaps the time had come to nullify the provisions of the Decree on Acts of Violence." Wille counseled against this on the grounds that the security situation had deteriorated ("Diensttagebuch," May 31, 1944). According to remarks by the governor general at a meeting of district governors on October 27, 1943, the national resistance movement (the *Armija Krajowa*) became less active, but not the Communists, who continued their actions in spite of the severity of the reprisals. In a meeting between Frank and police representatives on November 8, 1943, it was stated that the Decree on Acts of Violence had "to some degree calmed" the situation, even brought a "significant improvement" ("Diensttagebuch," October 27 and November 8, 1943). At a cabinet meeting on April 19, 1944, the commander of the Security Police and SD gave the number of murdered Germans as 220 in October 1943, 79 in November 1943, 78 in December 1943, 61 in January 1944, 120 in February 1944, 130 in March 1944 ("Diensttagebuch," April 19, 1944).

27. See Wolfgang Jacobmeyer, "Polnischer Widerstand im deutschen Urteil," *VjhZ* 4 (1977): 658 ff., with detailed examples.

Part Two. Section 1. A. I. The General Thrust of National Socialist Policy in Penal Law

1. For a summary, see Leppin, "Der Schutz des deutschen Blutes und der deutschen Ehre" (1937).

2. Originally sec. 3, par. 1, of the Penal Code, old version, limited liability under German law to the national territory (territorial principle). The Decree on the Scope of the Penal Code of May 6, 1940 (*RGBl.* I 754), broadened the application of German criminal law to offenses committed by Germans on foreign soil.

3. See full details in Schäfer, "Zehn Jahre nationalsozialistische Strafgesetzgebung" (1943). L. Schäfer was *Ministerialdirigent, Geheimer Regierungsrat*, and head of Dept. 3 (criminal legislation in the Reich Ministry of Justice).

4. For amendment of the content of the Penal Code, see also the Reich president's Decree on the Defense of the People and the State of February 28, 1933 (*RGBl.* I 83); the Reich president's Decree on Treason against the German People and Treasonable Activities of March 21, 1933 (*RGBl.* I 85); Decree on Measures to Counter Subversive Activities against the Government of the National Revolution of March 21, 1933 (*RGBl.* I 135), which was superseded by the Law against Treacheous

Attacks on the Party and the State and Protection of the Party Uniform (the Treachery Law) of December 20, 1934 (*RGBl.* I 1269); Law on the Reintroduction of the Death Penalty of March 29, 1933 (*RGBl.* I 151); Law on Defense against Political Crimes of April 4, 1933 (*RGBl.* I 162); Law to Guarantee the Public Order of October 13, 1933 (*RGBl.* I 723); the so-called Police Trap Law of June 22, 1938 (*RGBl.* I 651); see also the so-called Wartime Penal Code: Decree on Exceptional Radio Measures of September 1, 1939 (*RGBl.* I 1883); also Müller-Payer, *Die deutsche Sünde wider das Recht* (1946), 42; Decree on Parasites upon the *Volk* of September 5, 1939 (*RGBl.* I 1679); Decree on Special Wartime Criminal Code of August 17, 1938; Wartime Criminal Proceedings Code of August 17, 1938 (*RGBl.* I 1939, 1455 ff.); Decree on Supplementing the Penal Provisions for the Protection of the Defense of the German People of November 25, 1939 (*RGBl.* I 2319); Penal Code Amendment Law of September 4, 1941 (*RGBl.* I 549); Decree on Violent Criminality of December 5, 1939 (*RGBl.* I 2378); War Economy Code: War Economy Decree of September 4, 1939 (*RGBl.* I 1609); Decree on Penalties and Criminal Proceedings in the Event of Violations of the Price Regulations of June 3, 1936 (*RGBl.* I 999); Penal Decree on Consumption Regulations of November 26, 1941 (*RGBl.* I 734).

For amendment of the form of the Penal Code, see Penal Code Amendment Laws of May 26, 1933 (*RGBl.* I 295); April 24, 1934 (*RGBl.* I 341) (with supplementary laws of September 16, 1939 [*RGBl.* I 1841], and November 29, 1942 [*RGBl.* I 668]); June 28, 1935 (*RGBl.* I 839); and September 4, 1941 (*RGBl.* I 549); the Law against Dangerous Habitual Criminals of November 24, 1933 (*RGBl.* I 995); the Law against Kidnapping of Children with Intent to Ransom of June 22, 1936 (*RGBl.* I 493); law of July 2, 1936 (*RGBl.* I 532).

5. An example of tightening existing legislation is the Law on Prevention of Acts of Political Violence of April 4, 1933 (*RGBl.* I 162), which threatened a sentence of death or penal servitude for bomb attacks, arson, and other offenses such as carrying of poisons, flooding, and damaging railway installations. The death penalty was extended by a law of November 24, 1933 (*RGBl.* I 994). According to the documents available, reproduced in Wagner, *Der Volksgerichtshof* (1974), 943 f. (appendixes 30, 31), the number of death sentences rose from 78 in 1933 to 250 in 1940 and then very much more steeply, but the number of executions did not increase at the same rate. The Reich criminal statistics for 1942 (Nuremberg doc. NG-787) indicated 1,085 death sentences in 1941 and 2,199 in 1942. According to the *Führerinformationen* (BA R 22/4089), 3,643 death sentences were passed within the boundaries of the Reich in 1942 (including the Eastern Territories and the Protectorate). A report by Reich Minister of Justice Thierack in the information sheet *Die Lage* of August 1944 (Nuremberg doc. NG-252) gave the number of death sentences in the Reich (including the Eastern Territories and the Protectorate) as 99 in 1939, 929 in 1940, 1,292 in 1941, 3,360 in 1942, and 5,336 in 1943. In 1943 the majority of death sentences (1,745) were for high treason; 894 sentences were passed in the Annexed Eastern Territories.

6. Law of March 29, 1933 (*RGBl.* I 151).

7. Decree of March 21, 1933, on the Establishment of Special Courts, issued by the Reich government (*RGBl.* I 136), superseded by the so-called Jurisdiction Decree of February 21, 1940 (*RGBl.* I 405). Penal Code Amendment Law of April 24, 1933 (*RGBl.* I 341), and Law on the People's Court of April 18, 1936 (*RGBl.* I 369). For more details of the decisions of the People's Court, see the statistics in Wagner, *Der Volksgerichtshof,* 944 (appendixes 32 and 33).

8. For example, the abandonment of remand proceedings, the abolition of the prohibition of worsening of a sentence on appeal, the greater freedom of the courts to consider evidence, the freer status of the Reich Supreme Court (which was not bound by precedents predating 1933), the curtailment of preliminary investigations, the extension of the grounds for arrest, the facilitation of proceedings against people who had fled the country, and the limitation of swearing in for criminal proceedings. See also the abolition of the Courts of Lay Assessors and the Courts of General Sessions by the Simplification Decree of September 1, 1939, and other provisions of the Simplification

Decree of August 13 1942; further details will be found in Schäfer, "Zehn Jahre nationalsozialist-ische Strafgesetzgebung."

9. Freisler was in charge of *Referat I* (General Affairs) within Dept. 1, as well as that of the Departments of Penal Legislation (2), Administration and Execution of Criminal Justice (3), Reich Legal Examination Office (7), and the Hanns Kerrl Community Camp; State Secretary Schlegel-berger headed the Departments of Organization and Administration (1) (with the exception of *Referat I*), Civil Code (4), Commercial and Economic Law (5) and Budget (6) (Sauer, *Das Reichs-justizministerium* [1939], 23 ff.). See also Kluge and Krüger, *Verfassung und Verwaltung* (1941), 425.

10. See memorandum from the Prussian Ministry of Justice, *Nationalsozialistisches Strafrecht* (1933); Frank, *Nationalsozialistisches Handbuch für Recht und Gesetzgebung* (1934), introduction, which explicitly called the Law against Dangerous Habitual Criminals of November 24, 1933 (*RGBl.* I 995), and the law of April 24, 1934 (*RGBl.* I 341) (Establishment of a People's Court), the "begin-nings of National Socialist penal reform"; Frank, *Nationalsozialistische Strafrechtspolitik* (1938); Frank, *Nationalsozialistische Leitsätze* (1935), pt. 1, 1st–3d ed.; H. Welzel, "Tradition und Neubau in der Strafrechtswissenschaft," *Dt. Rechtswiss.* 1938, 113 ff.; Bühler and Frank, "Nationalsozialistische Strafrechtspolitik" (1939); Schwarz, "Der nationalsozialistische Strafprozeß" (1934); O. Kirchheimer, "Criminal Law in National Socialist Germany," *Studies in Philosophy and Social Science* 8 (1939–40): 444 ff.

11. For more details on penal reform, see Bracher, Sauer, and Schulz, *Die nationalsozialistische Machtergreifung* (1962), 530 ff.; Johe, *Die gleichgeschaltete Justiz* (1967), 41 ff.; Broszat, "Zur Perver-sion der Strafjustiz" (1958), 391 ff. The main thrust of National Socialist penal reform was ostensibly to revive the so-called Germanic principles of justice, such as honor, loyalty, community, and so forth. But this signified nothing other than establishing the primacy of the state, the political ap-paratus, and the interests of the "*Volk* community" and thus anchoring the racial principle in penal law. The memorandum by the Prussian Ministry of Justice, *Nationalsozialistisches Strafrecht*, 60 f., for example, envisaged the introduction of a new comprehensive crime of "offenses to national honor," including "intentional lies detrimental to the German people, insults to the memory of the historical achievements of the German people" ("falsification of history with offensive intent"). Rosenberg, *Der Mythos des 20. Jahrhunderts* (1933), 565 f., proposed the offense of "abuse of the German people," which "according to the seriousness of the case should be punished by imprison-ment, penal servitude, or execution."

For full details on general legal reform, see A. Wagner, "Die Umgestaltung der Gerichtsverfas-sung" (1968), 348 ff.; in the contemporary literature before 1945, a good overview will be found in E. Schäfer, "Der Stand der Strafrechtserneuerung: Der Bericht der amtlichen Straftrechtskommis-sion über den 'Besonderen Teil' des kommenden Deutschen Strafrechts," *DJ* (1935): 773 ff., 952 ff.; E. Schäfer, "Der 'Allgemeine Teil' des kommenden Deutschen Strafrechts," *DJ* (1935): 1515 ff. (Schäfer was *Ministerialdirektor* in the Reich Ministry of Justice). *Grundzüge eines Allgemeinen Deutschen Strafrechts, Denkschrift des Zentralausschusses der Strafrechtsabteilung der Akademie für Deutsches Recht*, in *Schriften der Akademie für Deutsches Recht*, no. 1 (1934).

12. See H. Hattenhauer, "Zur Gründung des Reichsjustizamts," in Bundesministerium der Justiz, ed., *Vom Reichsjustizamt zum Bundesministerium der Justiz* (1977), 9 ff., 80.

13. See Frank, *Nationalsozialistisches Handbuch für Recht und Gesetzgebung*, introduction and "Guiding Principles."

14. *Official* draft of a General Penal Code (*Allgemeines Strafgesetzbuch*), including preamble. Published by order of the Reich Ministry of Justice, in two parts, Berlin, 1925.

15. See, for example, Hueber, "Justiz im Führerstaat" (1942).

16. Memorandum from the Prussian Ministry of Justice, *Nationalsozialistisches Strafrecht* (1933); see further the official draft by the Reich Ministry of Justice penal law committee of a new

penal code with preamble, two parts in one volume, 1936. Parallel with this, the Reich Legal Desk of the Party published the *Nationalsozialistische Leitsätze für ein neues Deutsches Strafrecht* (pt. 1, 1935; pt. 2, 1936); see also full details in Oetker, "Grundprobleme der nationalsozialistischen Strafrechtsreform" (1934), 1317 f.; numerous actions and correspondence regarding the reform of penal procedure by the Official Reich Ministry of Justice Commission may be found in BA R 22/1039, 1083.

17. For a fundamental treatment, see Dahm and Schaffstein, *Liberales oder autoritäres Strafrecht* (1933).

18. Oetker, "Grundprobleme der nationalsozialistischen Strafrechtsreform," 1318. Frank, *Nationalsozialistisches Handbuch für Recht und Gesetzgebung*, introduction, xxi.

19. Sec. 2 of the new version of the Penal Code contained in the amending law of June 28, 1935 (*RGBl.* I 839), was worded as follows: "Any who commit an act punishable under the terms of the law or which deserves punishment according to the basic premise of penal law and the 'sound sentiment of the people,' shall be punished. If the law contains no directly corresponding provision, the act shall be punished under the terms of the law that applies most closely to it." Regarding the question of analogy, see, for example, *Supreme Court for Criminal Cases* (RGSt 74, 45); Becker, *DJ* (1937): 457 ff.; Mezger, *Deutsche Rechtswissenschaft* (1939): 259 ff.; Graehl, *Deutsches Strafrecht* (1940): 49 ff.; Peters, *Deutsches Strafrecht* (1938): 337; Klee, *Deutsches Strafrecht* (1941): 71 ff.; Siegert, *DR* (1943) (A): 739 ff.; G. Küchenhoff, *Nationalsozialistischer Gemeinschaftsstaat* (1934); Frank, *Nationalsozialistische Strafrechtspolitik*, 26; Lämmle, "Aus der Rechtsprechung des Volksgerichtshofs" (1944); Schmelzeisen, *DR* (1938): 261; see also Johe, *Die gleichgeschaltete Justiz*, 45; Thieme, "Führerprinzip in der Arbeitsverfassung" (1935), further demanded that the analogy based on the "sound sentiment of the people" be extended to other types of proceeding.

20. Frank, *Nationalsozialistische Strafrechtspolitik*, 28 f.

21. Dahm, "Verrat und Verbrechen" (1935): 283 ff., 288; G. Dahm, *JW* (1934): 904; Freisler, "Volksverrat im Lichte des Nationalsozialismus" (1935): 907.

22. Diener, "Das System der Staatsverbrechen" (1934), 329 ff.

23. Franzen, *Gesetz und Richter* (1935), 19 f.

24. H. Frank, *Nationalsozialistische Strafrechtspolitik*, 28 f.

25. F. W. Adami, *JW* (1935): 2348; Oetker, "Grundprobleme der nationalsozialistischen Strafrechtsreform," 1318 f.

26. Draft of the law (purely police law) and the implementing regulations in BA R 22/4428. Very few sanctions were proposed for "persons foreign to the community"—imposition of sentences of unspecified duration and subsequent custody in "police camps" (concentration camps) and "welfare institutions" (workhouses)—that would have constituted definitive legalization of the protective custody hitherto illicitly practiced by the police. The concept of "persons foreign to the community" was extended beyond all imaginable limits; it included not only all criminals (especially so-called habitual offenders) but also all who were "constitutionally incapable of being integrated into the community," who "consistently violated the obligation toward the community incumbent on them," such as, for example, by not making a living "in an orderly manner" or "through their own earnings," in spite of work opportunities, as well as alcoholics, beggars, former offenders who had not been reintegrated, people with a "disorderly" way of life, etc. It was clear to all who had eyes to see that this law would have transformed the whole of Germany—in the words of H. Frank—"into a single concentration camp." Furthermore, all *racially undesirable* persons could be included under the definition, and in fact the practice of the police against "alien" criminals, as will be demonstrated, was directed toward putting the intentions of the "Law on Aliens to the Community" into effect to the broadest extent possible.

27. Regarding the equivalence of these terms, see *Vertrauliche Information der Parteikanzlei*, no. 45/597, of June 25, 1942, in *Verfügungen, Anordnungen, Bekanntmachungen*, vol. 2, 49 f. See also

statements made by Hitler in his speech at the Reichstag on January 30, 1937, in which he demanded the severest punishment for those "antisocial elements who were determined to shirk their common obligations or who wronged the common interest" (*Dok. der deütschen Politik* 5: 33).

Part Two. Section 1. A. II. "Non-German" Offenders

1. *RGBl.* I 1146.

2. Sec. 6 of the First Executive Decree of November 14, 1935, to the Blood Protection Law (*RGBl.* I 1334); for more details, see Gütt, Linden, and Maßfeller, *Blutschutz und Ehegesundheitsgesetz* (1937), 225, 227 f.; marriage "would not be permitted" if "foreign blood was particularly dominant."

3. Amending decree of February 16, 1940 (*RGBl.* I 394); regarding the First Implementing Regulation of November 14, 1935, to the Blood Protection Law (*RGBl.* I 1334), see also the Reich Ministry of Justice directives issued by the senior public prosecutor, Hamburg, at a meeting of presiding judges in Hamburg on December 1, 1939 (report in Nuremberg doc. NG-629). The non-prosecution of the German woman was reportedly based on a directive by the Führer, "since as a rule the woman was the victim."

4. Gütt, Linden, and Maßfeller, *Blutschutz und Ehegesundheitsgesetz*, 15.

5. According to the article by G. Mauz, "Unaufgefordert vollkommen entkleidet," in *Der Spiegel* of August 4, 1975, between 1936 and 1943 legal proceedings were brought against 1,580 persons, 429 of whom were convicted. A recent full treatment of the judicial practice in "racial defilement" (*Rassenschande*) cases in Hamburg will be found in Hans Robinsohn, *Justiz als politische Verfolgung* (1977). According to Freisler, "Ein Jahr Blutschutzsprechung in Deutschland" (1936), 385 ff., 299 cases leading to conviction were tried under the law between September 15, 1935, and October 15, 1936; 125 further cases were pending. See also Leppin, "Der Schutz des deutschen Blutes und der deutschen Ehre" (1937); Sandrock, *DR* (1940) (B): 261 ff.

6. See the circular instruction of April 2, 1936, from the Reich Ministry of Justice to all chief public prosecutors and senior public prosecutors (quoted by Robinsohn, *Justiz als politische Verfolgung*, 124 ff.) (penal servitude to be the standard penalty; Jews to be treated particularly harshly); circular instruction of September 1, 1936, from the Reich Ministry of Justice to all presiding judges of the courts of appeal (quoted in ibid., 125 f.), with a further reminder to pass severe sentences and instructions to create special criminal courts. See also R. Freisler, "Rasse als Träger und Ziel des deutschen Volksrechts unter besonderer Berücksichtigung des Strafrechts," *DJ* (1936): 803 ff.; Freisler, "Ein Jahr Blutschutzsprechung in Deutschland"; also Kuhn, "Das Blutschutzgesetz in der strafrechlichen Praxis," *DJ* (1936): 1005 ff. Kuhn worked in the Reich Ministry of Justice.

7. See the ministerial commentary by Gütt, Linden, and Maßfeller, *Blutschutz und Ehegesundheitsgesetz*; Gütt, "Gesundheits- und Rassenpflege im Dritten Reich" (Gütt and Linden were senior officials in the Health Department of the Reich Ministry of Justice). See also the series "Rasse und Volk" in *DJ* (1936): 801 ff.

8. More in Crohne, "Die Strafrechtspflege 1936" (1936), 7 ff.; R. Freisler, "Ein Jahr Blutschutzsprechung in Deutschland"; summaries in Leppin, "Der Schutz des deutschen Blutes und der deutschen Ehre"; Sandrock, *DR* (1940) (B): 261 ff.

9. Sec. 5 of the First Decree to the Reich Citizenship Law, November 24, 1935 (*RGBl.* I 1333).

10. Reich Supreme Court, June 5, 1941, *DR* (1941) (A): 2413 f.

11. Reich Supreme Court, September 2, 1936, *DJ* (1936): 1470 f.; December 23, 1940, *DR* (1941) (A): 772 f.; April 11, 1938, *JW* (1938): 1583; November 21, 1938, *DJ* (1939): 431; July 15, 1940, *DR* (1940) (A): 1668.

12. For more on the definition, see A. Schönke, Penal Code, 1944, sec. 172, note 1.

13. Reich Supreme Court, Großer Senat, December 9, 1936, RGSt 70, 375 (*DJ* [1937]: 122 f.).

See also Augsburg *Landgericht* (district court), December 19, 1935, *JW* (1936): 750 f. (punishment for racial defilement in cases of unnatural sexual intercourse).

14. Reich Supreme Court, April 24, 1939, 1326; the Jewish defendant had made a prostitute walk backward and forward in front of him, naked or dressed, and carry out different body movements. The Supreme Court reversed the acquittal by the criminal court.

15. Reich Supreme Court, March 8, 1940, *DJ* (1940): 597: "If the behavior of the accused toward women is considered as part of a single act," cases would also be included in which there was no contact with the woman's body; thus, "in such cases too it is proved that the woman's body was used for sexual intercourse"(!).

16. Reich Supreme Court, September 8, 1937, HRR 1938, 267; December 9, 1937, *DJ* (1938): 154; November 21, 1939, HRR 1940, 475; October 26, 1939, HRR 1940, 272.

17. Reich Supreme Court, September 5, 1938, *DJ* (1938): 1698; similarly, Reich Supreme Court, January 7, 1937, *JW* (1937): 468 (RGSt 71, 4), and *DJ* (1937): 283 f. (RGSt 71, 7); and January 5, 1939, *JW* (1939): 340 (RGSt 73, 76).

18. Reich Supreme Court, March 28, 1938, RGSt 72, 148 (a "man of German blood" had relations with a Jewish woman who took care of his household. The Supreme Court imposed a more severe punishment because the lower court had been excessively lenient). The refusal to admit mitigating circumstances was based on an instruction of the Reich Ministry of Justice to the chief public prosecutors and senior public prosecutors not to make the long duration of a relationship grounds for leniency (quoted in H. Robinsohn, *Justiz als politische Verfolgung*, 124 f.).

19. Reich Supreme Court, April 17, 1939, 924 f.

20. RGSt 70, 291; Reich Supreme Court, November 28, 1938 (2 D 731/38), *JW* (1939): 227 f., no. 14; December 5, 1940 (2 D 498/40), *DJ* (1941): 225 ff.; March 6, 1936 (6 D 52/36), 517; Reich Supreme Court, June 21, 1937 (3 D 273/37), *Deutsches Strafrecht* (1937): 259 f. (an error regarding membership in the Jewish community is a minor error on the significance of a particular fact of the case); for the contemporary rulings of the Supreme Court on errors, see A. Schönke, Penal Code, 1944, sec. 59, Erl. 6, with references on the Blood Protection Law.

21. Reich Supreme Court, October 14, 1938, *DJ* (1939): 102; February 23, 1938, RGSt 72, 91; May 2, 1938, *DJ* (1938): 1033; February 9, 1940, *DJ* (1940): 486.

22. Reich Supreme Court, October 12, 1937, *JW* (1937): 3083.

23. Reich Supreme Court, December 14, 1937, *JW* (1938): 447: "It is not necessary for a particularly serious case to be proven for a sentence of penal servitude to be passed" (guiding principle).

24. Quoted in Robinsohn, *Justiz als politische Verfolgung*, 124 f.; see also 76, 126 ff., 140, 78. For confirmation of the figures: ibid., 76–79, 94 ff., 103. The duration of the sentence was between 1½ and 2½ years of penal servitude; see, e.g., Dortmund District Court, May 8, 1939 (BA R 22/4425); Berlin District Court, March 23, July 3, 6, 1939 (all BA R 22/4426); Reich Supreme Court, in RGSt 72/161; 70/109; 70/218, and *DJ* (1939): 102, 480, 618, 870, 924, 1283, 1303; *DJ* (1940): 404, 486.

25. Nuremberg doc. NG-2286.

26. Special Court, Kassel, S 3 Js 107/42 (VII 6–43 S). After the war the judges and public prosecutors were accused of perversion of justice but were acquitted on March 28, 1952, by the Kassel Court of General Sessions (3a KS 3/50—Schw. 3/50) (quoted by Noam and Kropat, *Juden vor Gericht* [1975], 173, who describe the interesting background to this case [Holländer had also had sexual relations with the daughter of the presiding judge of the district court, whose husband was serving in the field]).

27. Special Court 3, Berlin PKL s 35/42—2 C 12/43.

28. Walk, *Als Jude in Breslau* (1975), 47.

29. Quoted in Robinsohn, *Justiz als politische Verfolgung*, 106 f.

30. Quoted in ibid.; Robinsohn relates the case in full on the basis of the archives of the public prosecutor's office.

31. Nuremberg-Fürth District Court, Reg. f. H. Sg. 351/41; Hitler refused a reprieve for

Katzen-berger in spite of support by State Secretary Schlegelberger and although Freisler had also expressed legal doubts about this decision. Katzenberger was executed on June 3, 1942 (archives of the Nuremberg-Fürth District Court, regarding a case against the judges Ferber and Hoffmann, 7/28 Ks 1/68 a-b); See also Staff, *Justiz im Dritten Reich* (1964), 194 ff. After the war the American military court sentenced the president of the special court, Rothaug, to life imprisonment on account of Katzenberger's trial, inter alia; the sentence was later commuted to twenty years, but he was released in 1967 after eleven years' imprisonment. Ferber and Dr. Hoffmann were tried for murder in conjunction with perversion of justice at the Court of General Sessions of Nuremberg-Fürth. They were initially sentenced on April 5, 1968, to three and two years' imprisonment, respectively, for manslaughter. The German Federal Court reversed this decision on July 21, 1970 (1 StR 119/69), since the Court of General Sessions had not sufficiently considered certain points of view that could have led to a verdict of murder. In the meantime Ferber's trial has been suspended on account of the defendant's unfitness to plead. The case against Dr. Hoffmann, against whom a new trial was instituted, was provisionally suspended by a decision of April 7, 1974 (Az. Nuremberg-Fürth District Court, Ks 1/68 a-b).

32. *RGBl.* I 759.

33. For the illegality of the Decree on Penal Law for Poles, see BVerfGE 6, 132 ff., 186; Steiniger and Leszczyński, *Das Urteil im Juristenprozeß* (1969), 201 ff., 209.

34. *Richterbrief* no. 4 of January 1, 1943, Ziff. 16; *Richterbrief* no. 9 of June 1, 1943, Ziff. 24, BA R 22/4002. These were death sentences pronounced for extremely minor acts, above all damage to material property. See also the reports of the presiding judges of the courts of appeal and chief public prosecutors, Berlin, of February 10–11, 1943, with negative statements by Reich Minister of Justice Thierack regarding this practice, that it was of course wrong to impose a death sentence and then to recommend clemency (BA R 22/4200).

35. Regarding the question whether, in the case of particularly serious acts committed by Poles and Jews, it was possible to pronounce a death sentence that was not provided for under the general criminal code—as was permitted by the Polish Penal Code Decree, clause 3, par. 2, subpar. 2—the judicial practice of the Reich Supreme Court did not require investigation of whether the act was particularly serious in relation to comparable acts (the principle of equality under the law) but was based on the question whether the act was "particularly serious" compared with "any *conceivable* act by a Pole" (RGSt 76, 151; also *DR* [1942] (A): 1157). In the opinion of the Reich Supreme Court, it was essential to clarify whether a criminal act by a Pole was a *repeated* or an *isolated* act, since in any case the decree only provided for a standard penalty (prison camp) (*DR* [1943] [A]: 80). The court also had no objection to *retroactive* application of the decree, as introduced in the decree of January 31, 1942 (*RGBl.* I 52) (*DR* [1943] [A]: 80).

36. Reich Supreme Court, July 7, 1941, *DJ* (1942): 75.

37. See Schönke, Penal Code, 1944, 156, 473.

38. Charge against the former president of the Stuttgart Special Court, Cuhorst, quoted in Steiniger and Leszczyński, *Das Urteil im Juristenprozeß*, Ziff. 1, 63 (emphasis mine).

39. *Führerinformationen* no. 66 of July 3, 1942 (Nuremberg doc. PS-632). Charge against Cuhorst, in Steiniger and Leszczyński, *Das Urteil im Juristenprozeß*, Ziff. 1, 69 (Pitra case); this case may be identical with the one spoken of in *Führerinformationen* no. 66.

40. Thus, on October 29, 1943, the Nuremberg Special Court condemned a Polish woman to death for sexual intercourse with an "alien" on the strength of the Polish Penal Code Decree, clause 1, par. 3, where clearly the only ground for punishment was the nationality of the "culprit" (charge against the former associate judge of the Nuremberg Special Court, Oeschey, quoted in Steiniger and Leszczyński, *Das Urteil im Juristenprozeß*, 71, Kamińska case: "The German people, engaged in a difficult defensive struggle, rightly expect the most rigorous action against such foreign elements. . . . The special significance resides in the fact that the culprit is a Pole").

41. Situation report of March 18, 1942, by the presiding judge of the Königsberg Court of

Appeal to the Reich Ministry of Justice (BA R 22/850), who wished to exempt the woman from punishment by analogy with the "racial defilement" cases. The Posen (Poznań) chief public prosecutor opposed this with the argument that according to the Blood Protection Law, the acquittal of the woman was "not the criterion in the national struggle against the Poles." It was, however, necessary to punish the German man, for whom penal provisions still had to be established (situation report by the chief public prosecutor, Posen, May 12, 1942, BA R 22/850).

42. Prussian Supreme Court, Berlin, *Deutsches Strafrecht* (1935): 50.

43. See, e.g., the ruling by the People's Court of March 18, 1942, DR (1942) (A): 721 (no deprivation of civil rights under sec. 33 of the Penal Code in the case of Jews, who "in the conviction of the entire people had absolutely no rights"); Reich Supreme Court, February 18, 1941, DR (1942) (A): 429 ff. (two Poles who had desisted from an attempted rape in response to appeals by the victim were not granted indemnity in accordance with sec. 46 of the Penal Code); indeed, the death penalty was not ruled out "on account of willful exploitation of the war situation" under sec. 4 of the Decree on Parasites upon the *Volk* of September 5, 1939 (*RGBl.* I 1679); Reich Supreme Court, July 20, 1939, DJ (1939): 1532 (extension of the provisions on measures for prevention of crime and reform of offenders—in this case castration in accordance with sec. 42k of the Penal Code—to criminal acts committed in foreign countries, in spite of the fact that penalization of such acts was limited to specifically named cases [Penal Code, sec. 4, pars. 2, 3]); Reich Supreme Court, January 8, 1940, DJ (1940): 298 (admissibility of the additional penalty of independent confiscation of property in accordance with sec. 40 of the Penal Code when the offender was Jewish, even after his death, although sec. 40 of the Penal Code dealt only with confiscation of the tools used for the crime or objects produced by the crime and stipulated the *ownership* of the objects by the offender as a necessary condition; see Schönke, Penal Code, 1944, sec. 40, Erl. III 2).

44. For more details, see H. J. R. Bepler, "Übersicht über die Rechtsprechung der deutschen Gerichte zur entsprechenden Anwendung von Strafgesetzen," JW (1938): 1553–70.

45. RGSt 74, 45; similarly, see RGSt 70, 175, 362.

46. See Danzig Special Court, June 20, 1941, DJ (1941): 945.

47. *RGBl.* I 2319.

48. RGSt 74, 45.

49. See Reich Supreme Court, May 28, 1937, RGSt 71, 221; Special Court, Berlin, November 20, 1941, *Deutsches Strafrecht* (1942): 55 f.

50. Halle District Court, September 12, 1941, DR (1941) (A): 2662.

51. Danzig Special Court, July 8, 1941, DJ (1941): 945.

52. Reich Supreme Court, JW (1938): 167.

53. Reich Supreme Court, DR (1943) (A): 581.

54. Itzehoe District Court, January 2, 1942, *Deutsches Strafrecht* (1942): 59 (a Polish worker had stolen clothes from her employer's wife).

55. Quoted from the situation report of December 10, 1940, by the chief public prosecutor of Nuremberg (BA R 22/3381).

56. The Reich minister of justice reproached a municipal court (*Amtsgericht*) ruling of April 24, 1942, e.g., with not having taken "typically Jewish" behavior into account in the case of a Jewish pensioner sentenced to a fine of RM 30 or ten days' imprisonment for not having added her Jewish first name Sara in the telephone book entry. The decision showed "incomprehensible lenience." The idea that legal practice was not yet uniform in such cases, i.e., that the accused could not be sure to be convicted, did not justify the lenient punishment. This was clearly a case of "Jewish subterfuge," which "amazingly" had only been understood bit by bit late in the day (*Richterbrief* of October 1, 1942, Ziff. 5, BA R 22/4002). The conviction of two Polish women for theft was designated an "outrageous mistake" (*Richterbrief* no. 5 of February 1, 1943, BA R 22/4002).

57. *Richterbrief* of October 1, 1942, Ziff. 4 (BA R 22/4002).

58. Noam and Kropat, *Juden vor Gericht,* 129 ff.

59. Ibid., 136 ff.

60. And further:

The people are discerning and convinced that it is unjust to treat an Aryan who has molested a German woman in a really objectionable way more harshly than a Jew who has committed the same act. In addition, it is very doubtful that the Jew will not be punished for an attempted crime, that is for attempted racial defilement. . . . Faced with the suspicion of such a serious criminal act on the part of a Jew, who nevertheless enjoys his freedom, the Court of Lay Assessors finds it unjustifiable to keep in custody an Aryan prosecuted for a much less serious act, especially since there is now less reason to believe that he will abscond. For in all his rulings, the judge must consider the natural sense of justice of the German people. The release of the accused, a family father who has acted most reprehensibly, would cause a public stir. But this would be as nothing compared with the inevitable indignation were he to remain in custody while a Jew guilty of racial defilement is allowed to go scot-free—a Jew who, in the same place as the Aryan, has sullied the honor of German women and thus of the German people. For this reason the Court of Lay Assessors, applying the law conscientiously and in the spirit of popular sentiment, has also withdrawn the arrest order against the Aryan. (Noam and Kropat, *Juden vor Gericht,* 136 ff.)

61. For an overview of the legal practice in martial law, see Brettle, *DJ* (1942): 431 ff.; see also Fölsche, *DR* (1943) (A): 1117 ff.; and Steinert, in Frank, *Nationalsozialistisches Handbuch für Recht und Gesetzgebung,* 1425 ff.

62. Reich Ministry of Justice circular decree (Schlegelberger) of July 24, 1941 (Nuremberg doc. NG-505).

63. Reich Ministry of Justice circular instruction of July 20, 1935 (Nuremberg doc. NG-630); similarly also *Richterbrief* no. 4 of January 1, 1943 (BA R 22/4002).

64. For details, see Engert, "Stellung und Aufgaben des Volksgerichtshofs" (1939); Schauwecker, "Der Volksgerichtshof für das Deutsche Reich" (1936). Examples will be found in Gribbohm, "Der Volksgerichtshof" (1969), 55, 109; and, more recently, Wagner, *Der Volksgerichtshof im nationalsozialistischen Staat* (1974).

65. Decree on the Special War Penal Code of January 17, 1938 (KSStVO) (*RGBl.* I 1939, 1455).

66. Military Installations Defense Decree of November 25, 1939 (*RGBl.* I 2319); the legal basis of indictment to disaffection in the narrow sense was sec. 5 of the Decree on the Special War Penal Code (*RGBl.* I 1939, 1455).

67. Letter of February 19, 1944, from the Reich Ministry of Justice to all presiding judges of the courts of appeal and chief public prosecutors (Nuremberg doc. NG-674).

68. *Richterbrief* of October 1, 1942, Ziff. 3 and 5, and of February 1, 1943, Ziff. 5 (BA R 22/4002). Details of the judicial practice will also be found in the Reich Ministry of Justice circular decree of January 14, 1943 (BA R 22/66; sexual intercourse with prisoners of war was punishable by "substantial imprisonment," i.e., hard labor); overview of rulings from August 1943 to June 25, 1944 (a total of 1,360 cases, in which a sentence of death was pronounced in 297), in BA R 22/20069.

69. Reich Ministry of Justice instruction of May 29, 1940, cited in letter of June 13, 1941, from the presiding judge of the Hamburg Court of Appeal (Nuremberg doc. NG-2215).

70. Report on the meeting of the presiding judges of the courts of appeal and chief public prosecutors of March 31, 1942, in Berlin, *DJ* (1942): 247. Circular instruction of October 28, 1941, from the Reich Ministry of Justice to all chief public prosecutors (BA R 22/20068); in this and a subsequent circular decree of August 7, 1942, the ministry was nevertheless obliged to warn against "unduly rigorous action" (State Archive Poznań, *Landgericht* Posen 17, Bl. 144); see also note 68.

71. Reich Minister of Justice Thierack in *Richterbrief* no. 16 of January 1 and February 1, 1944, Ziff. 39, regarding unlawful slaughtering with examples of court decisions (BA R 22/4002);

explanations of the assertions of the Reich Ministry of Justice in *Vertrauliche Information der Parteikanzlei* 8/69 of March 24, 1944, *Verfügungen,* 6:140 ff.

72. *RGBl.* I 1679; more in R. Freisler, *DJ* (1939): 1452.

73. Every "overly lenient punishment carries the risk of an epidemic [of such acts]" (*Richterbrief* of June 1, 1943 [BA R 22/4002]); full details will be found in the *Richterbriefe* of April 1 and May 1, 1943 (BA R 22/4002), and the Reich Ministry of Justice decree of June 16, 1942, cited in Nuremberg Trial III Prot. d, 4373 (Schlegelberger hearing), in BA Rep 501, XVII A 58; Schlegelberger maintained that the "entire German nation" had stood behind the decree.

74. Nuremberg doc. NG-505; the decree apparently constitutes a clarification of a circular instruction of January 22, 1941, approving the application of sec. 4 of the Decree on Parasites upon the *Volk* to Poles; see situation report of January 29, 1941, by the chief public prosecutor, Hamm (Nuremberg doc. NG-685), which called for intervention of the Reich Ministry of Justice with a view to stricter application of sec. 4 of the Decree on Parasites upon the *Volk* "by way of circulars, articles, and discussions."

75. In his testimony at the Nuremberg Trial, Schlegelberger confirmed that the decree of July 24, 1941, was intended to be applied primarily to Poles, especially for sexual offenses (Protocol 4366, d, BA Rep 501, XVII A 58).

76. Reich Supreme Court, October 23, 1941 (*DJ* [1942]: 19).

77. See the corresponding list in *Führerinformationen* no. 140 of November 4, 1942 (BA R 22/4089).

78. Thiemann, "Anwendung und Fortbildung" (1941).

79. *RGBl.* I 2378.

80. *RGBl.* I 549.

81. Reich Minister of Justice Thierack in *Richterbrief* of January 1, 1943, Ziff. 15, BA R 22/4002; "purging of the nation" required destruction of the wrongdoer.

82. Hitler in Picker, *Hitlers Tischgespräche* (1951), 203, adding that after ten years' hard labor "a person was done for," and "you either stuck him in the concentration camp or you killed him."

83. In the case of multiple offenses, the death sentence was generally applied as "standard penalty" (Reich Supreme Court, February 19, 1942, quoted in Brettle, *DJ* [1942]: 434). Individual circumstances, including the guilt of the accused, were not taken into consideration. The deterrent effect alone dictated the verdict. More details in H. Schickert, *DR* (1943) (A): 116 ff.; H. Schmidt-Leichner, *DR* (1941) (A): 2145 ff.; G. Dahm, *DR* (1942) (A): 401 ff. The Reich Supreme Court did not hesitate to pass the death sentence without basis in law. References on the practice of the courts will be found in Thiemann, *DR* (1941) (A): 2651; Meissner, *Deutsches Strafrecht* (1943): 85 ff.; Schwarz, *ZAkfDtRecht* (1941): 308 (Schwarz was a Supreme Court councillor); Bruns, *ZAkfDtRecht* (1943): 53; H. Schmidt-Leichner, *DR* (1943) (A): 882 ff.; see also the Special Court, Hamburg (quoted in Robinsohn, *Justiz als politische Verfolgung,* 115), which in a ruling of April 29, 1941, condemned a Jewish inland navigator to death for rape in coincidence with racial defilement in (retroactive) application of the Decree against Violent Criminals.

84. Klagenfurt Special Court, *DR* (1941): 579; the use of the unarmed body could not be considered equivalent to the use of a weapon.

85. Reich Supreme Court, *DJ* (1940): 1169; and RGSt 76, 91: The criterion was not the "external appearance [the act itself], but the internal tendency, the raw being, the dangerous state of mind." Under the law of September 4, 1941, even the fist was a "dangerous weapon" (death penalty for a handbag-snatcher who punched his victim).

86. Reich Supreme Court, September 14, 1943, *DJ* (1943): 527. Also RGSt 76, 91; and Reich Supreme Court, *DJ* (1942): 265.

87. Reich Supreme Court (special High Criminal Court), November 20, 1941, *DJ* (1942): 265; a number of Polish agricultural workers were condemned to death for sexual assault of a child.

88. Reich Supreme Court, December 4, 1942, *DR* (1943) (A): 236.

89. Ibid.

90. Publication was subject to strict control, of course, since the judiciary press offices were responsible to the ministry (Bracher, Sauer, and Schulz, *Die nationalsozialistische Machtergreifung* [1962], 564) and rigorous instructions were issued regarding preparation of reports (summary: *Richtlinien für die Tätigkeit der Justizpressestellen vom* 1.6.1938, Berlin, 1938, 20 ff., reprinted in *DJ* [1938]: 846). On account of the generally severe mood against "aliens," it may nevertheless be presumed that the published judgments were more or less representative.

91. State Secretary Freisler to the presiding judges of the courts of appeal and chief public prosecutors, Berlin, March 31, 1941, Johe, *Die gleichgeschaltete Justiz* (1967), 129. According to a report by the SD in *Meldungen aus dem Reich* of November 6, 1941, the Essen Special Court condemned a Polish exhibitionist, who had exposed himself in "indecent attire" to women and children, to six years' penal servitude and castration (SD: "fair" judgment), after the public prosecutor had demanded the death penalty (BA R 22/166).

92. See the situation report of January 5, 1942, by the presiding judge of the Nuremberg Court of Appeal (BA R 22/3381), according to which the majority of the forty death sentences pronounced by the end of 1941 were against Poles, and most of the accused were Poles, Czechs, Belgians, and French.

93. According to *Meldungen aus dem Reich*, no. 235 of November 6, 1941 (BA R 58/166), the Nuremberg Municipal Court sentenced a Pole to three years' imprisonment for bodily harm, whereas a Pole who had first been slapped by the victim was sentenced by the Bonn Municipal Court to two months' imprisonment for grievous bodily harm; the Münster Municipal Court condemned a Pole to ten months' imprisonment for a sexual offense against two children; the Rosenheim Municipal Court condemned a Polish agricultural worker who injured the wife of his employer to three years' imprisonment (SD: a "misjudgment" which was also discussed in legal circles).

94. *Meldungen aus dem Reich* of November 6, 1941 (BA R 58/166).

95. Letters of July 5, 1944, from the Reich Ministry of Justice (signed by Klemm) to the presiding judge of the Stuttgart Court of Appeal (the verdicts of the courts of appeal in matters of incitement to subversion were in "intolerable disproportion in relation to the sentences of the People's Court and other courts of appeal") (Nuremberg doc. NG-676), and of March 1, 1945, to the presiding judge of the Hamburg Court of Appeal ("regrettably lenient" demands and sentences in matters of incitement to subversion; the death sentence should be passed even in cases of moderate fault) (Nuremberg doc. NG-627). As early as September 1, 1936, the Reich Ministry of Justice had published a circular instruction denouncing overly lenient verdicts and calling upon the presiding judges of the courts of appeal to "bring strong pressure to bear" on the judges in racial defilement cases in order to counter "a racial decadence of the German people" (Erlaßsammlung des RMJ, BA); see also Reich Ministry of Justice decree (Freisler) of June 12, 1940, to the presiding judge of the Vienna Court of Appeal (criticism of fifteen verdicts with the "expectation" of greater severity in the future; attempts to achieve "an understanding in 'appropriate penalties' by way of instructions to the public prosecutor" were "not highly successful") (BA R 22/51).

96. The personnel records of the presiding judges of the courts of appeal and chief public prosecutors (Federal Justice Ministry) certainly contain no such references.

97. *Richterbrief* no. 18 of August 1, 1944, Ziff. 14 ff., discussed the case of a 74-year-old widow who had been fined RM 50 for stealing a rose from a cemetery. For having clinked her glass of beer with a French prisoner of war, a 30-year-old innkeeper was fined RM 20, and an innkeeper and his wife (monthly income RM 400) were fined RM 500 for having sold six liters of cider to a French prisoner of war (BA R 22/4002).

98. *Richterbrief* of October 1, 1942, Ziff. 4 (BA R 22/4002).

99. *Meldungen aus dem Reich* of November 6, 1941 (BA R 58/166) (SD reports on domestic matters, November 1941 to December 1943, Bl. 188 ff.)

100. Since 1939 the presiding judges of the courts of appeal and chief public prosecutors were

obliged to submit regular so-called situation reports (circular instructions of November 25 1935, III, 196, and of December 9, 1935, Ia, 11012) with details of important events, the political situation, and the mood of the population. The justice apparatus used these reports to steal a march on the police, who were always well informed on what was going on. Uncoded from the jargon of the time, the situation reports provide a clear picture of the distaste of the population for the arbitrariness of the police, the manipulation of the judicial system, and the mass arrests and executions of "aliens" by the police (more details in Weinkauff, *Die deutsche Justiz* [1968], 167 ff.). With the exception of the chief public prosecutor of Hamburg, who generally stated that nothing of importance was happening in the region concerned, all the senior judiciary officials reported on events in great detail. Situation report collection, BA Koblenz.

The control of the judiciary apparatus in the individual districts fell to the presiding judges of the courts of appeal by way of regular discussions with the presiding judges of the district courts, or it was delegated to the latter, who were to meet regularly with the judges before and after trials (see Reich Ministry of Justice circular instruction of October 13, 1942, State Archive Poznań *Landgericht Posen*, 17, Bl. 170-71; confidential letter of November 4, 1942, from the presiding judge of the Posen Court of Appeal to the presiding judge of the Posen District Court, Bl. 170; situation report of July 3, 1942, by the chief public prosecutor, Kattowitz [Katowice], describing the virtually total surveillance of the judiciary [BA R 22/3372]). Such management meetings occasionally took place before 1942; after 1942 they commonly took the form of "previews and reviews." Regarding the reluctance of certain presiding judges of the courts of appeal to accept these discussions, see the minutes of the meeting of senior presiding judges and chief public prosecutors of September 29, 1942; situation report of December 3, 1942, by the chief public prosecutor of Karlsruhe ("heavy load," offense directed against "the legal establishment itself"), quoted by Wagner, "Die Umgestaltung der Gerichtsverfassung" (1968), 362; also Johe, *Die gleichgeschaltete Justiz*, 184 ff.

Measures of control included the establishment of a central public prosecutor's office for political criminal affairs in the Reich Ministry of Justice (administrative instructions of July 24, 1933, *JMBlatt* 235; administrative instructions of October 6, 1937, BA R 22/1143, 1462, Bl. 119a). To ensure uniformity of application of the law, recording and assessment of decisions, and coordination with the Party, a general political desk was created in the Reich Ministry of Justice under the direction of senior public prosecutor Klemm (Reich Ministry of Justice organization structure, April 1938, BA R 22/4223, 1462, 119b). In "exceptional cases," the court authorities were authorized to change the allocation of duties without the support of the law, "if urgently required in the interests of judicial practice" (Reich Ministry of Justice circular instruction of March 15, 1943, Erlaßsammlung BA). With the exception of the right to issue instructions to the public prosecutor's office ("influence on investigations and arraignments"), control of the judiciary was always disguised in the form of "references," "recommendations," or "suggestions" to the courts, issued by way of circular instructions, administrative instructions, or decrees. This included the *Richterbriefe* (BA R 22/4002) published by the ministry, in which individual judgments were discussed and the desirable general policy for the courts made known. See also the internal Reich Ministry of Justice instruction of June 8, 1944, containing the request for the appropriate material (BA R 22/4275). A later addition were the *Sonderbriefe* dealing with individual cases, and so-called *Rechtsanwaltsbriefe* (from 1944 on) (see BA R 22/4275). In specific cases, the ministry intervened directly (e.g., by instructions to the relevant presiding judges of the courts of appeal to take "appropriate measures," i.e., transfer, against judges who did not toe the line; see Wolfram and Klein, *Recht und Rechtspflege in den Rheinlanden* [1969], 226 f.), and from 1941 onward, centralized meetings of the senior presiding judges and chief public prosecutors in the Reich Ministry of Justice, in which the basic principles of judicial policy were presented (see BA R 22/246, 4163; regarding controls prior to 1939, see Sauer, *Das Reichsjustizministerium* [1939], 24 ff., who complains of the limited possibilities of influencing the judges, and Weinkauff and Wagner, *Die deutsche Justiz* [1968], 146 ff., 156 ff., 211 ff., with numerous references). Legislative instruments of control included pardons and pleas of nullity by the public prosecutors (more in Vollmer, *DJ* [1943]: 78 ff.).

101. *Meldungen aus dem Reich* of September 3, 1942, quoted in M. Broszat, *VjhZ* (1958): 440, 442.

102. For the reception of this speech among judges, see the situation report of June 8 by the chief public prosecutor of Posen, 1942 ("depressed mood," "desire to emigrate") (BA R 22/3383). See also the SD reports, *Meldungen aus dem Reich* no. 50 of February 7, 1940; no. 181 of April 25, 1941; no. 271 of March 26, 1942; and no. 381 of May 1943, quoted in Boberach, *Meldungen aus dem Reich* (1968), 64, 224, 317; also *Meldung* no. 235 of November 6, 1941, and of September 3, 1942 (BA R 58/166). See F. Besselmann, "Die politische Aufgabe des deutschen Richters," *DR*(1942) (A): 1762 ff.; W. Bergmann, "Über das Verhältnis von Rechtsprechung und Gesetzgebung," *DR* (1942) (A): 1768 ff.; for the plea for a new type of judge as "vassal" of the Führer, see Rothenberger, *Der deutsche Richter* (1943); similarly, Dahm, "Richtermacht und Gerichtsverfassung im Strafrecht" (1941).

103. Speech before the presiding judges of the courts of appeal and chief public prosecutors, Berlin, early May 1942 (minutes of meeting, BA R 22/4162).

104. Speech by Schlegelberger in early May 1942 (ibid.), in which he claimed that the judgments on Jews pronounced by the Party Chancellery were too lenient: for example, the conviction to six weeks' imprisonment of a Jewish shopkeeper who had sold three bottles of brandy in 1940, for "opening a Jewish business," would now be dealt with much more severely. Possession of other identity papers than a Jewish identity card was a "serious case of identity card fraud." Speaking of three Jewish women who had received four weeks' imprisonment in Breslau for greeting one another with "Heil Moscow," he said that such an act would today be punished as treachery or high treason (ibid., Bl. 55).

105. Hitler in his Reichstag speech of January 30, 1937 (*Dok. der dt. Politik*, 5:33); in the Reichstag speech of December 11, 1941, he demanded that all elements "who had forgotten their duty" be "mercilessly" expelled from the "*Volk* community" (*Der Großdeutsche Freiheitskampf, Reden A. Hitlers* [1943], 147 f.). Similar statements will be found in the conversations at table (Picker, *Hitlers Tischgespräche* [1951], 203).

106. BA R 22/851.

107. The *Richterbriefe* (BA R 22/4002) were published from October 1, 1942, until the end of 1944 (see note 100 above). See the collection in Boberach, *Richterbriefe* (1975).

108. For more details on Thierack's personnel policy, see the introduction to this volume, III, 2 ("The Principle of the Primacy of Party over State"). Formally, the will of the political leadership was embodied in the basic principle that only the Führer or the office authorized by him (the judiciary) was empowered to decree laws (Reich Minister of Justice Gürtner at the Eleventh International Congress on Criminal Justice and Prisons, Berlin, on August 20, 1935, *Dok. der dt. Politik*, vol. 307). Thierack contended that the Führer ought also to decide in *individual cases;* he strove after direct subordination of the Reich Ministry of Justice to Hitler, in line with the Italian model.

Examples of the consistent persecution of "non-Germans" include the report by the presiding judge of the Düsseldorf Court of Appeal at the meeting of the senior presiding judges and chief public prosecutors in Berlin, February 10–11, 1943, that after sentencing to death a Pole who had damaged a cable in a factory, a special court had recommended a pardon on the ground that no anti-German intention was proven (protocol, BA R 22/4200). The *Richterbrief* of January 1, 1943 (BA R 22/4002), mentions a 1942 special-court decision in which a Pole was sentenced to death for unauthorized possession of a weapon and activity in a secret organization up to the beginning of 1940, but expresses itself in favor of an act of pardon. See also the verdict of the Special Court, Frankfurt, sentencing to 5 years' hard labor and a fine of RM 5,000 a Jewish shopkeeper who had served food to customers without ration tickets (*Berliner Morgenpost*, January 9, 1943, excerpts in ZS, Polen Film 58, Bl. 272).

109. See *Richterbrief* no. 6 of March 1, 1943, and no. 9 of June 1, 1943 (BA R 22/4002). See also Brettle, *DJ* (1942): 431 ff.

110. See *Richterbrief* no. 7 of July 1, 1943 (BA R 22/4002).

111. See note 100.

112. *Richterbrief* no. 17 of March 1–April 1, 1944, 40 (BA R 22/4002).

Part Two. Section 1. A. III. The Situation of "Non-Germans" in Procedural Law

1. Legal foundation: decrees of March 21, 1933 (*RGBl.* I 136); November 20, 1938 (*RGBl.* I 1632); September 1, 1939 (*RGBl.* I 1658); and February 21, 1940 (*RGBl.* I 405).

2. More details in Johe, *Die gleichgeschaltete Justiz* (1967), 92; *Ministerialrat* Rietzsch and *Ministerialdirektor* Crohne (both of the Reich Ministry of Justice), "Die Arbeit der Sondergerichte im Kriege."

3. Reich Supreme Court, October 6, 1939, quoted in Redeker, "Bewältigung der Vergangenheit als Aufgabe der Justiz" (1964), 1100 n. 97.

4. Malz, "Richtertum im nationalsozialistischen Staat" (1941), 2220.

5. Hagemann, *DJ* (1941): 769 ff.

6. Statements by Thierack at the meeting of the presiding judges of the courts of appeal and chief public prosecutors, Berlin, February 10–11, 1943 (BA R 22/4200).

7. Ibid.

8. Cited in the situation report of September 3, 1942, by the senior public prosecutor, Kattowitz (Katowice) (BA R 22/850). Since, however, the directives issued by the ministry generally lagged behind the prevailing situation, it may be presumed that it was already regarded as "undesirable" for Germans to defend Poles and Jews before the courts; in professional tribunals it was forbidden de facto; see part 1, section 1, V, 1, a, "Attorneys and Related Professions," notes 53–58.

9. Situation report by the senior public prosecutor, Kattowitz (ibid.).

10. These ideas were presented by the presiding judge of the Hamburg Court of Appeal in a speech to Hamburg judges. Though Jews were still permitted to appear before the court as witnesses, their testimony was to be evaluated "with caution." The practice of the district of Hamburg, whereby no judgment was passed on the basis of evidence by a Jew, should become standard practice in all courts on the basis of an instruction (quoted by Steiniger and Leszczyński, *Das Urteil im Juristenprozeß* [1969], 237). For the circular, see Nuremberg doc. NG-744. Every opportunity should be taken to manage without such witnesses. If it was not possible to avoid questioning a witness, this should not take place in the main trial itself but before a specially commissioned judge, and statements made by Poles and Jews in cases against Germans should always be considered with the "greatest reservation." Charges against Germans by Jews were to be pursued only if they were "clearly" justified. Furthermore, the person pressing charges should not be informed of the outcome of the investigation.

11. For more details, see Dünnebier, *DR* (1942) (A): 1445: it was the obligation of the court to hear Polish witnesses apart from the main trial proceedings.

12. The project was communicated by way of an urgent memorandum from the Reich Ministry of the Interior to the Reich Ministry of Justice, RFSSuChddtPol, Reich Ministry for Education of the People and Propaganda, the Party Chancellery, and RMuChdRkzlei on the same day (BA R 43 II/15080; also Nuremberg doc. NG-151).

13. Response of the Reich Ministry of the Interior in an urgent memorandum to the Reich Ministry of Justice dated August 13, 1942 (ibid.). Urgent memorandum of August 12, 1942, from the Reich Ministry for Education of the People and Propaganda to the Reich Ministry of Justice (ibid.). Regarding the usurping of penal powers over Jews by the police, see the report by the IfZ, Munich, vol. 2, 391 ff.

14. Letter dated November 16, 1942, from the Reich Ministry of Justice to the head of the

Party Chancellery (BA R 32/1512). See also the Reich Ministry of Justice memorandum of September 18, 1942 (BA R 22/4062); RSHA instruction of September 5, 1942, to the higher SS and police leader, that all "alien" persons, especially Poles, Jews, and Gypsies, should be taken into police custody (Nuremberg Doc. I-316); speech by the Reich minister of justice before the senior presiding judges and chief public prosecutors, Berlin, September 28, 1942 (BA R 22/4199a).

15. *RGBl.* I 372; executive decree of September 1, 1944, *RGBl.* I 201.

16. The police authorities had already anticipated the decree—cf. the RSHA directive of March 11, 1943—regarding the transfer of Jews who had been released from custody and of all Jews to be released from custody in the future, for life, to the Auschwitz and Lublin concentration camps; quoted in a secret circular letter of April 21, 1943, from the Reich Ministry of Justice to the chief public prosecutors (BA R 22/4053); for the Annexed Eastern Territories, see the RFSS circular decree of December 28, 1942, *MinbliV* (1943); 45, whereby the criminal prosecution of Jews was to be carried out by dispatching them to the nearest police station "for further action." According to guidelines subsequently issued by the RFSSuChddtPol on January 3, 1943, the police authorities were instructed to pass on all current criminal charges and all ex officio criminal and preliminary investigative proceedings to the Gestapo post responsible for the domicile or current place of residence of the Jew involved "for further action," from a RFSSuChddtPol circular dated July 3, 1943, *MinbliV* (1943): 1085 (Nuremberg doc. NG-326). The justice department itself had for years prepared the way to giving the police a free hand with Jewish criminals by regularly passing information to the Gestapo; see the Reich Ministry of Justice instruction dated January 20, 1939, to the head of the public prosecutor's office in Leitmeritz (Litoměřice), ordering that the Gestapo was to be informed of the conclusion of a trial for *Rassenschande* by sending a copy of the judgment with, if applicable, the day of release, six weeks in advance, ex officio. A corresponding general instruction doubtless existed in the Reich, too; the instruction referred to was required on account of the introduction of the Nuremberg Laws in the Sudetengau by the decree of December 27, 1938 (*RGBl.* I 1997).

17. Minutes of meeting (BA R 22/4200), Thierack's speech, Bl. 33 f.

18. Ibid., 54.

19. Statements by *Ministerialrat* Grau, Reich Ministry of Justice, minutes of meeting (ibid.).

Part Two. Section 1. Excursus. 1. The Influence of the Party

1. Once under the orders of the *Reichsführer*-SS (Führer's decree of June 17, 1936, RGBl. I 487), the police force became directly answerable to the Party, since the SS was a subdivision of the latter (sec. 2 of the Executive Decree of March 29, 1935, to the Law to Secure the Unity of Party and State, RGBl. I 502, in the version of January 12, 1938, RGBl. I 36); since, however, with respect to their organization, the Party and the police force remained independent, they are treated separately here.

2. Law to Secure the Unity of Party and State of December 1, 1933 (RGBl. I 1016), sec. 2, in conjunction with art. 1 of the Law to Relieve Distress in the Nation and Reich of March 24, 1933 (RGBl. I 141). With the renaming of the office of the deputy of the Führer to "Party Chancellery," the head of the Party Chancellery further became a member of the Ministerial Council for the Defense of the Reich (Führer Decree on the Position of the Head of the Party Chancellery, March 29, 1941, RGBl. I 295) and thus was automatically associated with all legislative work concerning Reich laws, Führer decrees, Ministerial Council decrees for the defense of the Reich, and decrees by the supreme Reich authorities, as well as with all laws promulgated with the approval of the so-called Reich Council (sec. 2 of the executive decree of January 16, 1942, under the Führer decree, RGBl. I 35).

3. Under the Führer decree of February 2, 1935 (RGBl. I 18), the power of clemency rested with the Führer himself; through the decree of September 3, 1939, he had passed this power to the Reich Ministry of Justice "for the duration of [his] absence from Berlin"; Hitler nevertheless reserved the right to make the decision himself in individual cases (Nuremberg doc. NG-700). Thus, on the basis

of this decree, the Reich minister of justice was empowered to order execution of the sentence; if he wished to grant a pardon, Hitler had to be consulted via the head of the *Presidialkanzlei* (Hitler's chancellery as president) (letter of August 17, 1943, from the RMuChdRkzlei, Nuremberg doc. NG-302). In the latter years of the war, the cases to be submitted to Hitler each month were limited to the most important ones in which there was some doubt (letter of November 15, 1944, from the head of the Presidial Chancellery, Meissner, to the RMJ [Nuremberg doc. NG-302]), since in the great majority of cases over the past two years the Führer had gone along with the suggestions of the Reich minister of justice (the letter of November 11, 1944, to the head of the Presidial Chancellery [ibid.] states that of the more than 290 proposals for a reprieve put forward by the Reich Ministry of Justice in the previous two years, the Führer had refused only one [see also the following note])

4. Reich Ministry of Justice circular decree dated April 7, 1936 (RGBl. I 1462), with instructions to the chief public prosecutors also to consult the competent Gestapo bureau in the investigation of petitions for pardon. A confidential circular instruction from the Reich Ministry of Justice dated March 8, 1943 (Nuremberg doc. NG-302), ordered that death sentences should be carried out with the greatest haste, without involvement of other agencies (such as the Gestapo or the police).

5. Administrative instructions of June 10, 1938, from the RMJ, *DJ* (1938): 925.

6. Communication of October 23, 1942, from the RMuChdRkzlei to the Reich Ministry of Justice (BA R 22/vorl. 20087) and corresponding internal Reich Ministry of Justice directive of November 1942 (Nuremberg doc. NG-327); the directive applied only to cases in which the Reich Ministry of Justice itself recommended leniency; see also the affidavit of April 23, 1947, by the former Reich Ministry of Justice official responsible for pardons in so-called nonpolitical death sentences (Nuremberg doc. NG-1307), according to whom all petitions for a reprieve were normally rejected by Reich Minister of Justice Thierack.

7. Details will be found in Weinkauff and Wagner, *Die deutsche Justiz* (1968), 1:119 ff.

8. Secs. 1, 3 of the Law to Secure the Unity of Party and State of December 1, 1933 (RGBl. I 1016).

9. The Nationalsozialistische Reichsjustizamt (Reich Judicial Bureau of the NSDAP) was set up at NSDAP headquarters with the objective of "organized training and education of the German judiciary." For details, see Johe, *Die gleichgeschaltete Justiz* (1967), 197 ff.; Weinkauff and Wagner, *Die deutsche Justiz*, 237 ff.; W. Steinlechner, "Der Richter im Dritten Reich" (diss., Mainz: 1974), 119 ff.

10. For the detailed structure of the League of National Socialist German Jurists (NSRB), see BA R 22/4462; statistics in Becker, "Gaurechtsamt und NS-Rechtswahrerbund" (1939); see also Bracher, Sauer, and Schulz, *Die nationalsozialistische Machtergreifung* (1962), 518 (1,614 members in April 1933, 80,000 by the end of that year); Schraut, "Ein Jahr Reichsjustizkommissariat" (1943), 269 ff. Regarding the smashing of the law student organizations, their incorporation in the League of National Socialist German Jurists, and their structure and development, see Weinkauff and Wagner, *Die deutsche Justiz*, 105 ff.; Ostler, *Die deutschen Rechtsanwälte* (1971), 233 ff., 240; Bracher, Sauer, and Schulz, *Die nationalsozialistische Machtergreifung*; for the contemporary literature, see Nicolai, "Die Aufgabe des Verwaltungsbeamten" (1934), with further references. Regarding the studies from the viewpoint of the NSRB, see details in "Thesen des NSRB, Reichsgruppenwalter Junge Rechtwahrer" (undated) (studies to be as short as possible, reduction of course to four semesters, etc.) (BA R 22/4446, Bl. 34–36). On training courses, cf. the report of October 18, 1937, from the justice senator of Hamburg (Rothenberger) to State Secretary Freisler, on a weekend meeting of Greater Hamburg judges at the Gauführer School, Barsbüttel (Nuremberg doc. NG-2249), according to which the weekend meetings were an innovation by Rothenberger. More details on training camps in Johe, *Die gleichgeschaltete Justiz*, 210 ff.; an enthusiastic report by Hedemann, "Juristen im Schulungslager" (1934).

11. The most important training camp was the one for junior lawyers in Jüterbog (Hans-Kerrl Camp); a training camp was set up for junior government lawyers at Bad Tölz. The Hans-Kerrl Camp was established in 1934, after camps for junior lawyers had been set up in the individual *Län-*

der (see "Das 'Hans-Frank-Lager' in Rastatt," *DR* [1934]: 184). In the first phase, 1934–38, in the two months immediately before the assistant judge examinations, the training was almost exclusively military. From about 1938 on, numerous complaints by participants gave rise to a change of policy whereby in addition to "defense drill," political and technical training was incorporated for an equal amount of time. Politically, tension reigned between the camp directors and the junior lawyers, who found the political drill irksome. Spying and consequent reprimands were common, and students were occasionally expelled for "political unreliability." For (positive) reports on the communal camps during the period, see H. Vogatzky, in Rothenberger, *Das Hanseatische Oberlandesgericht* (1939), 15 f., 100 f.: Schwister, "Gemeinschaftsdienst und Große Staatsprüfung" (1933); Friedrich, "Das Gemeinschaftslager Hans Kerrl" (1935), 24; Freisler, "Hans-Kerrl-Lager" (1936); Palandt, "Die sachliche Auswirkung der Gemeinschaftserziehung" (1936); Hildebrandt, "Grundsätzliches zum Dienst im Gemeinschaftslager Hans Kerrl" (1936).(Hildebrandt was the commander of the *Gemeinschaftslager* Hans Kerrl.) More details in Johe, *Die gleichgeschaltete Justiz*, 219 f.; Ostler, *Die deutschen Rechtsanwälte*, 239 f.; Weinkauff and Wagner, *Die deutsche Justiz*, 238; report by M. Hirsch to the author, July 22, 1974; he stressed the improved conditions in 1939 from the technical point of view and the critical attitude of the junior lawyers to the political training (MS).

For legal training, see the Lawyer Training Code of July 22, 1934 (RGBl. I 727 in the new version of January 4, 1939, RGBl. I 5); see Ostler, *Die deutschen Rechtsanwälte*, 239 ff., with further references; Weinkauff and Wagner, *Die deutsche Justiz*, 237 f.; Jescheck, "Die juristische Ausbildung" (1939); Reich Ministry of Justice, ed., "Die Ausbildung des deutschen Rechtswahrers," Stand 1.9.38, BA R 22/4430, Bl. 87 f.

The legal foundation for "*Volk* studies" was sec. 5 of the Lawyer Training Code of July 22, 1934 (RGBl. I 727), and sec. 5 of the new version of the Lawyer Training Code of January 4, 1939 (RGBl. I 5). Judges, ministerial officials, Party functionaries, municipal officials, professors from other disciplines, school inspectors, and assistant teachers acted as "*Volk* studies examiners" (internally known as "brown examiners"; see letter from the Reich Ministry of the Interior to the Reich Ministry of Justice of September 27, 1941 [BA R 22/4532]): see the list of members of the Law Examination Board, Stuttgart, of March 22, 1944 (BA R 22/10954). For details of the structure, scope, and content of the examination in the subject "*Volk* studies," see the communication of September 17, 1941, from the Reich Ministry of the Interior to the Reich Ministry of Justice (BA R 22/4532). Examples of examination subjects in history taken from the Reich Ministry of the Interior guidelines of March 2, 1936, issued to the Reich Ministry of Justice are "Attacks on Germany by France since the Thirty Years War," "What Germany Had to Suffer" (BA R 22/4533, Bl. 147 f.); see also the list of examination subjects for the examinations in July and August 1936, compiled by the president of the Reich Law Examination Board (Bl. 214 f.). Individual examples of examinations in *Volk* studies for the year 1936, ibid., 162 f., and in "Material für die Besprechung mit den Prüfern der Prüfungsstelle Berlin am 4.3.1936" (undated, BA R 22/4533), with detailed explanations and many complaints on the ignorance of the examinees in ideological subjects ("trite phrases learned by rote," "appalling helplessness," lack of "inner integration" of National Socialism) (ibid., Bl. 167 f., 172). For the subject under discussion, there were some forty questions, ranging from Theoderich the Great to basic geographical (e.g., What is the course of the Gulf Stream?) and historical questions (What were Napoleon's intentions in Egypt?).

12. For example, the majority of participants of the Hans Kerrl Communal Camp were in principle not opposed to the regime, but they were probably not interested in politics. Jokes about leading National Socialists and demonstrations of dissatisfaction during lectures by Party officials were common (many examples will be found in Ostler, *Die deutschen Rechtsanwälte*); report of July 22, 1974, by M. Hirsch (see note 11 above).

13. Tegtmayer, "Die Rechtsarbeit der Partei" (1939); see also Weinkauff and Wagner, *Die deutsche Justiz*.

14. Exchange of correspondence and material for training judges in criminology, procedural law, race law, marital health law, etc., in BA R 22/4486; Vorl. 20683; Nuremberg doc. NG-346; Reich

Ministry of Justice circular instruction of January 18, 1937 (Erlaßsammlung, BA Koblenz). On materials for the training courses organized by Reich Minister of Justice Thierack on Burg Cochem, see Nuremberg doc. NG-393. Regarding further plans for centralized, more extensive training, see the speech of the Reich minister of justice to the presiding judges of the courts of appeal on February 3, 1944, in Weimar (BA R 22/4405).

15. For general information on the new training functions of the NSRB ("Leadership of men in the field of law"), see the speech of September 30, 1942, by Reich Minister of Justice Thierack to the officials of the Reich NSRB office (*DR* [1942]: 1404); and Reich Ministry of Justice memorandum (undated) regarding the employment of judges and public prosecutors for the training of Party officials (BA R 22/247). In addition, work communities were set up in the universities (Reich Ministry of Justice memorandum [Klemm, undated], 1944, BA R 22/247); see also the communication dated November 17, 1943, from the *Senatspräsident* (head of the Chamber of the Court of Appeal), Dr. Friedrich, to *Kammergerichtsrat* Schmidt-Leichner (Reich Ministry of Justice) regarding preparation of the courses for leaders of student work parties (BA R 22/4513) and training courses in a very wide variety of subjects. In addition, regular NSRB weekend training courses were maintained in the curriculum or added to it (Reich Ministry of Justice circular instruction of May 19, 1944, BA R 22/4215; progress report on weekend camps with study schedule, BA R 22/4214). Regarding technical training by the NSDAP, see the Reich Ministry of Justice memoranda of June 10, 1943, to *Oberlandesgerichtsrat* Meinhof regarding seven-day courses in racial politics for law students by the NSDAP Race Policy Office, with a report on one such course (Nuremberg doc. NG-410), and of March 22, 1943, regarding planning of so-called "*volk*-biological courses" for judges and public prosecutors with a view to the "Aryanization processes and the coming Law on Enemies of the Community" (BA R 22/4488). Regarding further plans for coordination of the training activities of the Party and the ministry, see the instruction by the head of Department 6 of the Reich Ministry of Justice dated May 31, 1944, to his leading officials (BA R 22/4215). On the cooperation between the Reich Ministry of Justice and the NSRB in the *Gaue*, see the note by *Ministerialrat* Dageförde (head of the NSRB training office) of March 18, 1943 (BA R 22/4214). The technical-ideological training of the NSRB was particularly energetic in the Annexed Eastern Territories: see, e.g., the reports in the *Ostdeutscher Beobachter* of August 9, 1940, p. 3; and December 1, 1943, p. 4, on such courses.

16. An Office for Recruitment and Training was established in the Reich Ministry of Justice as late as the spring of 1944 in its temporary office at Leitmeritz (Litoměřice), which held its first work session in June 1944 (internal instruction, Reich Ministry of Justice, March 22, 1933, BA R 22/4449; reports on later sessions, transcripts of papers, etc., in BA R 22/4450) but was soon to cease its activity on August 11, 1944 (Reich Ministry of Justice administrative instructions of August 11, 1944, *DJ* [1944]: 228); see also memorandum by *Ministerialrat* Dr. Haag, Reich Ministry of Justice, on "training objectives in the senior judiciary service" (BA R 22/4449).

17. Thus, as early as October 18, 1937, the justice senator of Hamburg, Rothenberger, wrote to State Secretary Freisler with suggestions for training dependable judges (Nuremberg doc. NG-2249); see also Rothenberger's memorandum of March 31, 1942 (at this time he was state secretary in the Reich Ministry of Justice), on judiciary reform (Nuremberg doc. NH-075) and the schedule of a meeting of the *Referenten* (personnel policy advisers) for the senior service at Cochem, May 5–8, 1944 (BA R 22/20675), on the question of personnel policy in the "new judiciary."

18. Weinkauff and Wagner, *Die deutsche Justiz*, 113, 117.

19. Many references will be found in the Reich Ministry of Justice *Diensttagebuch* for the period November 5, 1934, to December 30, 1935 (Nuremberg doc. PS-3751). See the list from the Bavarian Justice Ministry (director of which at that time was Hans Frank), reproduced in Weinkauff and Wagner, *Die deutsche Justiz*, 113 ff., on interference by the Party in judiciary matters, classified under (a) interference in personnel affairs, (b) interference in the administration of criminal justice (with the note that cases connected with Dachau were not taken into consideration), and (c) inter-

ference in civil justice. Attacks by the Party on individual judges and interference in pending trials were reported especially from the court of appeal districts of Bamberg (117) and Hamm (report of December 4, 1950, by the presiding judge of the Hamm Court of Appeal [118]). Other examples of such pressure tactics in trials involving Party members were the requisitioning of archives without returning them, nonappearance of the accused, intimidation of witnesses, false statements under oath, etc. (more details in 128 f.).

20. More examples in Weinkauff and Wagner, *Die deutsche Justiz*, 117.

21. Circular of May 22, 1935, by the deputy of the Führer (BA R 99/35). Cf. also the notification of September 3, 1935, by the deputy of the Führer in *Verfügungen, Anordnungen, Bekanntmachungen*, 2:394 f., requesting to be briefly informed of all known attacks against the Party and its institutions under the terms of the Treachery Law of December 20, 1943, "notwithstanding the required notification to the public prosecutor's office."

22. Confidential information no. 49/551 of October 18, 1941, by the head of the Party Chancellery to the Gauleiter (*Verfügungen, Anordnungen, Bekanntmachungen*, 2:392).

23. See Party Chancellery directive 15/38 of February 9, 1938 (ibid., 378); also order by the Führer of December 2, 1943 (given in transcript in the State Archive Poznań, *Landgericht Posen*, 16, Bl. 27 and 28, with confidential note of February 10, 1943, from the Reich Ministry of Justice to the higher Reich judicial authorities, ibid.) regarding dealing with Civil Code matters through Party offices, which contains the following:

Direct interference in pending lawsuits is in no case permitted. If it is necessary to influence a lawsuit in a matter of fundamental or political importance, and unless an agreement can be reached between the parties concerned, the head of my Party Chancellery should be informed. He will then take the necessary measures with the Reich minister of justice and obtain my decision as required. . . . If a Party agency is convinced that a court decision justifies serious misgivings on legal or factual grounds, it can apply to the head of my Party Chancellery or to me by way of the latter. All attempts to counter a court decision by exerting pressure on one of the parties involved are forbidden.

24. *DR* (1934): 19; *JW* (1934): 24.

25. In "ordinary" cases the Party did what it could to delay or stop legal proceedings against members of the NSDAP, SA, or SS. With regard to serious cases, see Reich Ministry of Justice memorandum, undated, presumably 1940, regarding the prosecution of the *Kreisleiter* of Bromberg (Bydgoszcz), W. Adolf K.: as head of the Compensation Office, K. was entrusted with "compensating the ethnic Germans for the damages they have suffered through Polish atrocities" and in this capacity passed millions to NSDAP cronies and local officials. The charge against K. was prepared, but K. was covered by the Gauleiter of Danzig–West Prussia, Forster. But, stated the note, K. should be removed from his duties (BA R 22/4087). It is not known from the existing documents whether K. was in fact charged.

26. A Kreisleiter in the Koblenz district, for example, required of a court that his permission be obtained before every dispossession action (Koblenz District Court [*Landgericht*], Akten 313 E 4, quoted in Weinkauff and Wagner, *Die deutsche Justiz*, 139).

27. Weinkauff and Wagner, *Die deutsche Justiz*, 139.

28. On this subject, see ibid., 126.

29. See the statement by a *Kreisleiter* before the Koblenz District Court, Akten 313 E 4, quoted in Weinkauff and Wagner, *Die deutsche Justiz*, 138 f., in a temporary injunction against a Jew: "The Jew must leave the town; a Jew has no rights in Germany."

30. Weinkauff and Wagner, *Die deutsche Justiz*, 139.

31. See the letter of September 9, 1941, from the NSDAP *Kreisleitung* Hohensalza (Inowrocław) to the *Gauleitung* Wartheland: "re: Situation report for August 1941 . . . Judiciary—In one case I observed that the Municipal Court [*Amtsgericht*] responded very quickly and actively on behalf of

a Pole who had made unjustified demands of a German. By my rapid intervention in this affair, I was able to protect the German comrade, an active participant in the national-racial struggle, from being summoned before the Municipal Court by a Polish woman. . . . Steps should be taken there to ensure that such a situation cannot recur in the Wartheland. The Kreisleiter" (State Archive Poznań, NSDAP-*Gauleitung* Wartheland 14, p. 33).

32. See Kaul, *Geschichte des Reichsgerichts* (1971), 226 (who quotes from DZA Potsdam, Bl. 93-197/7): The Bielefeld District Court sentenced a Pole to one year in a penitentiary on September 23, 1940 (5 KLs 7/40), on account of sexual offenses on two occasions. The *Gauleitung* complained to Party headquarters about the "overly lenient" judgment and demanded a plea of nullity. The competent senior public prosecutor stated on January 9, 1941, that following an order by telephone from the Reich minister of justice on December 6, 1940, the convicted person "was put at the disposal of the state police headquarters in Münster i.W and removed from the penitentiary on December 9, 1940."

33. Circular no. 131/42, dated August 27, 1942, from the head of the Party Chancellery, in *Verfügungen, Anordnungen, Bekanntmachungen*, 2:375 ff.

34. Handwritten draft (undated) by Thierack of a speech before the presiding judges of the courts of appeal and chief public prosecutors at a working meeting in Weimar on February 3–4, 1944 (BA R 22/247).

35. In *Verfügungen, Anordnungen, Bekanntmachungen*, 2:375 ff.

36. RGBl. I 535.

37. Circular no. 131/42, August 27, 1942, from Party Chancellery, *Verfügungen, Anordnungen, Bekanntmachungen*, 2:377.

38. Collection in BA R 22/4089.

39. Collection in BA R 22/4002; the material for the *Richterbriefe* came from the individual districts or the various departments of the ministry. In this regard see the internal directive of June 8, 1944, by the Reich minister of justice, in which he requests that material on the *Richterbriefe* and information on major changes in the law and all other such important events "of significance to the administration of justice" should be brought to the attention of the ministry adviser, *Kammergerichtsrat* Schmidt-Leichner (BA R 22/4275). Cf. also the documentation published by Boberach, *Richterbriefe* (1975), which contains the whole collection of *Richterbriefe*.

40. See *Richterbrief* no. 1 of October 1, 1942 (BA R 22/4002, introduction).

41. Circular no. 131/42, dated August 27, 1942, from the Party Chancellery (*Verfügungen*, 2:375 ff.).

42. Letter dated March 6, 1943, from the *Kreisleiter* and head of the *Gau* legislation office of the NSDAP, Dr. Krämer, to the RMJ (BA R 22/vorl. 20301); the writer justified his request by the fact that as the person in charge of the *Gau*, he was responsible for the training of judges. As a handwritten note added to the letter indicates, the letter was not replied to, by order of Thierack.

43. *Richterbrief* no. 1 of October 1, 1942 (BA R 22/4002, introduction).

44. Circular of August 27, 1942, from the Party Chancellery (*Verfügungen*, 2:377).

45. RGBl. I 372.

46. At a meeting of the presiding judges of the courts of appeal and chief public prosecutors in early May 1942 in Berlin (protocol BA R 22/4162), at which the effects of Hitler's invectives against the judiciary in his Reichstag speech of April 26, 1942, were discussed, State Secretary Freisler spoke of the Party Chancellery's complaints, stating, however, that the cases deplored were special cases.

Part Two. Section 1. Excursus. 2. The Influence of Hitler, the SS, and the Police Command

1. Regarding the relations between the police and the judiciary from the viewpoint of the ministry, see the detailed statement by Schlegelberger at the Nuremberg Judiciary Trials (protocol [d], 4315 ff., 4321 f., in BA All Proz. 1, XVII A 58).

2. Eickhoff, "Die Preußische Geheime Staatspolizei" (1936).

3. More details in Maunz, *Gestalt und Recht der Polizei* (1943), 48 f., 53; Schäfer, "Die Verhängung von Schutzhaft" (1936); Prussian Supreme Administrative Court, 97, 103; 99, 85; 103, 137. See Prussian Supreme Administrative Court, *RVerwBl.* (1935): 923; OVGE, 97, 103; 99, 85; 103, 137; Reich Supreme Court, *JW* (1934): 767, which (before the Prussian Law of February 10, 1936, GS 21, forbade the courts access to Gestapo archives) had interpreted the concept of "defense against danger to security and order" by the police extremely broadly in an attempt to formally salvage control by the courts. For this they were reproached by Best (*DR* [1938]: 224) on the grounds that such "wildly enlarged interpretation can but falsify the facts," and he proposed proscribing the authority of the courts in *criminal justice* cases, too. See also Maunz, *Gestalt und Recht der Polizei*; Schäfer, "Die Verhängung von Schutzhaft."

4. Führer decree of June 17, 1936 (*RGBl.* I 487).

5. Prussian statute book, 21. See the references cited in the introduction to this volume, III, 1, "The Führer Principle," regarding the limitation or exclusion of court control of administrative archives.

6. Maunz, *Gestalt und Recht der Polizei*, 53.

7. Picker, *Hitlers Tischgespräche* (1951), 211, 259 f.; see also Hitler in the table talk of August 20, 1942 (quoted in *VjhZ* [1964]: 94 ff.), and the discussion in Gruchmann, *Hitler über die Justiz* (1964), 96 ff.

8. Maunz, *Gestalt und Recht der Polizei*, 8 ff., 51 ff.

9. Full details in Spohr, *Das Recht der Schutzhaft* (1937); Schäfer, "Die Verhängung von Schutzhaft"; Tesmer, "Die Schutzhaft und ihre rechtlichen Grundlagen" (1936); Lüdtke, "Die Schutzhaft gemäß der VO vom 28. 3. 1933" (1933); Boehr, "Nochmals: Die Schutzhaft gem. der Verordnung vom 28. 2. 1933" (1933); Geigenmüller, *Die politische Schutzhaft im nationalsozialistischen Deutschland* (1937), 39 ff.; Daluege, "Der nationalsozialistische Kampf gegen das Verbrechertum" (1936); Böhme, "Die Vorbeugungsaufgabe der Polizei" (1936); Best, "Die Polizei" (1937), 338 ff.; H. Frank, *Nationalsozialistisches Handbuch für Recht und Gesetzgebung* (1934), introduction, xx. From the postwar literature: M. Broszat, *Anatomie des SS-Staates* (1965), 2:11 ff., 41 ff., 88 ff., 97 ff.; Bracher, Sauer, and Schulz, *Die nationalsozialistische Machtergreifung* (1962), 541 f.; Echterhölter, *Das öffentliche Recht im NS-Staat* (1970), 166; Weinkauff and Wagner, *Die deutsche Justiz* (1968), 304.

10. *RGBl.* I 35.

11. *RGBl.* I 83. Cf. the basic decrees issued by the Reich Ministry of the Interior on April 12, 26, 1934 (quoted in Tesmer, "Die Schutzhaft und ihre rechtlichen Grundlagen"), and January 25, 1938 (general statutes of the RSHA, 2 F VIII a, BA R 19/3), regarding protective custody; and the circular decree of December 14, 1937, by the Reich Ministry of the Interior, regarding preventive detention (quoted in M. Broszat, *VjhZ* [1958]: 390 ff., 395). On the extension of the types of people subject to preventive detention, see the circular decree of October 17, 1939, from the head of the Reich Criminal Police Bureau (quoted in Weinkauff and Wagner, *Die deutsche Justiz*, 305), and further details in Broszat, *Anatomie des SS-Staates*, 2:78 ff. Before promulgation of the centralized regulations, the *Länder* had applied their own rules on protective custody; see, e.g., Bayer, *GVOBl.* (1933): 85. Further central regulations followed with the advent of the war (decrees of September 3, 1939, from the head of the Security Police and Security Service to all local Gestapo headquarters regarding "Principles of internal State security," BA, Sammlung Schuhmacher 271; of September 9, 1939, regarding arrest of Polish nationals in the territory of the Reich, ZS, Verschiedenes 82, 134; and of October 24, 1939 [no release of those held in protective custody for the duration of the war], IfZ; circular decree of July 27, 1942, by the RFSSuChddtPol [BA R 22/1144]). The creation of the concentration camps was generally not mentioned in publications; at most they were referred to obliquely or were tacitly taken for granted; although it was recognized that they were not "constitutional installations" (Koellreuter, *Der deutsche Führerstaat* [1934], criticized by Forsthoff, "Besprechung von O. Koellreutler" [1934]), the conclusion that they were unlawful was never expressly

stated; see Best, "Die Polizei," 338 ff., according to whom the authority to order protective custody was vested "exclusively in the nature of the office" of the Gestapo with the aim of inculcating an "attitude of inner commitment to the community" (394); see also Frank, *Handbuch für Recht und Gesetzgebung*, who regards the Reich president's decree of February 28, 1933 (*RGBl*. I 83), as legal basis for protective custody.

12. Spohr, *Das Recht der Schutzhaft*, 67, with references; Prussian Supreme Administrative Court, 97, 103; 99, 85; 103, 137; Supreme Administrative Court, Hamburg, *JW* (1937): 3335; Maunz, *Gestalt und Recht der Polizei*, 48 ff., 51 ff; Neubert, "Die Schranken richterlichen Prüfungsrechts" (1933); Lüdtke, "Die Schutzhaft gemäß der VO vom 28. 3. 1933," 2241; see also the references in note 9 above.

13. See the example given in Fraenkel, *Der Doppelstaat* (1974), 246b.

14. Full details in Weinkauff and Wagner, *Die deutsche Justiz*, 143 ff.

15. Cf. Schlegelberger's statements at the Nuremberg Judiciary Trials (III), 4325 f. (see note 1 above); Schlegelberger also spoke of other arbitrary orders by Hitler. Between September 1939 and Schlegelberger's resignation on August 20, 1942, alone, Hitler *personally* had subsequently "corrected" at least 25 to 30 indefeasible judgments in this manner, quite apart from the *advance* execution of alleged criminals (affidavit by Hitler's adjutant, Schaub, and Schlegelberger's personal adviser, Dr. Hans Gramm, Nuremberg docs. NG-5263, NG-4798). With regard to the judicial foundation for the Führer's right to veto any court decision, see R. Freisler, *DJ* (1939): 1565 ff. (1570) and 1597 ff. (1598).

16. More details in M. Broszat, "Nationalsozialistische Konzentrationslager" (1965), 107, 109; see also the situation reports of February 3, 1940; August 3, 24, 1942, by the chief public prosecutor, Bamberg (BA R 22/3365); the situation report of July 7, 1942, by the chief public prosecutor of Hamm (Nuremberg doc. NG-395); the situation reports of July 31, 1940; May 31, December 1, 1941, by the chief public prosecutor of Celle (quoted in *VjhZ* [1958]: 452 ff.); situation report of March 10, 1942, by the presiding judge of the Brunswick Court of Appeal (BA R 22/3357); situation report of March 28, 1940, by the presiding judge of the Hamburg Court of Appeal (BA R 22/3366).

17. Situation report of January 27, 1942, by the chief public prosecutor to the Prussian Supreme Court, Berlin; report of November 18, 1941, by the president of the Hamburg District Court (*Landgericht*) to the presiding judges of the Hamburg Courts of Appeal (both quoted in Johe, *Die gleichgeschaltete Justiz* [1967], 167).

18. See the collection of documents from Hamburg of November 1939, according to which there was a growing number of killings on escape or "against resistance" (quoted in ibid., 158 ff.). Weinkauff and Wagner, *Die deutsche Justiz*, 125, are somewhat more reserved. According to a Reich Ministry of Justice register dated September 28, 1939 (Nuremberg doc. NG-190), also reproduced in Broszat, "Zur Perversion der Strafjustiz" (1958) (Doc. 6 B), in the period from September 6, 1939, to January 20, 1940, alone, that is, in less than five months, a total of 18 people were shot by the police, either before their trial or following their conviction by the special court, at the order of Hitler, the RFSS, or the head of the Security Police. After 1942 the number of executions of prisoners of justice increased sharply; the reports to the Reich minister of justice by the presiding judges of the courts of appeal and the chief public prosecutors are full of complaints of encroachments on the part of the Gestapo (Weinkauff and Wagner, *Die deutsche Justiz*, 144, 156, with references). In February 1942, 11 people accused of "suppression of evidence" (i.e., looting) were shot by the police without trial on a single day (*Völkischer Beobachter*, February 16, 17, 1942, quoted in the situation report by the chief public prosecutor, Hamm, of February 27, 1942, Nuremberg doc. NG-395a, reproduced in *VjhZ* [1958]: 435 f.).

19. Speech by Ohlendorf to SD personnel, circulated to all the relevant offices of the Security Police and Security Service in the form of "instructions for operations in the domain of the law" (BA R 22/990).

20. An example is a case of unlawful slaughtering in which the special court at Leitmeritz (Litoměřice) had condemned a woman, Irene von E., to four months' imprisonment. She was apparently arrested by the Gestapo before pronouncement of the verdict. A memorandum dated January 6, 1942, from the Reich Ministry of Justice reporting a discussion with the head of the Security Police noted that the latter would ensure that the files of the Dresden Stapo requested by the Reich Ministry of Justice would be made available (BA R 22/4062).

21. Cf. the letter of April 28, 1942, from the senior public prosecutor, Seidel, in Hamburg, to the Reich Ministry of Justice (quoted in Johe, *Die gleichgeschaltete Justiz,* 168 f.), reporting a decision by the Special Court of Bremen in which the accused was condemned to fifteen years' penitentiary in opposition to the public prosecutor's demand. The head of the criminal police office in Bremen had advised him to exert his influence to have the sentence commuted by way of a plea of nullity; "otherwise action might possibly be taken in another place." The threat was successful, as the sender himself lodged a recommendation for a plea of nullity: "Before the execution K. is still needed to serve as a witness." In a letter dated May 14, 1942, the head of the criminal police headquarters in Hamburg informed the presiding judge of the Hamburg Court of Appeal that a judgment by the Hamburg Special Court in which a man had been convicted of looting should be revised to one of petty larceny: the court too "would agree." A plea of nullity was therefore entered with the Reich attorney general (quoted in ibid., 169).

22. Letter dated October 22, 1942, from the head of the Security Police and Security Service to the Party Chancellery (BA R 22/4203).

23. Letter dated January 19, 1943, from the SS judge at the RFSS, Munder, to State Secretary Rothenberger (Nuremberg doc. NG-439). Johe, *Die gleichgeschaltete Justiz,* 169, is not so clear about this, referring to this letter and stating that Himmler made no such concession to Rothenberger, since only Hitler decided on executions and publication.

24. Instruction from the RFSSuChddtPol to all Gestapo posts, January 6, 1943 (ZS, G.J. No. 117, 261; copy).

25. Regarding the personality of Reich Minister of Justice Gürtner, who, until his death in 1941, did his best to avoid direct confrontation between the ministry and the police (especially its directorate), see Reitter, *Franz Gürtner* (1976).

26. Memorandum of January 24, 1939, from the Reich Ministry of Justice (Klemm) on a discussion with the presiding judge of the Court of Appeal in Berlin on that day (Nuremberg doc. NG-366) (full details in Johe, *Die gleichgeschaltete Justiz,* 163 ff.).

27. "No discord" was, e.g., an expression used by the presiding judge of the Graz Court of Appeal at a meeting of chief presidents on January 24, 1939, in Berlin; see the report of January 24, 1939, from the Düsseldorf Court of Appeal district ("good understanding" between the committing magistrates and the Gestapo); memorandum of January 24, 1939, on the meeting of the presiding judges of the courts of appeal in Berlin (see note 26 above). The chief public prosecutor of Posen (Poznań), Drendel, spoke of "close cooperation and trust with the Security Police" (*Ostdeutscher Beobachter,* June 24, 1939); report of July 4, 1941, by the president of the Hamburg District Court to the Reich Ministry of Justice (Johe, *Die gleichgeschaltete Justiz,* 166).

28. See the letter of November 30, 1939, from the Reich Ministry of Justice to the RFSSuChddtPol (Nuremberg doc. NG-190), also reproduced in Broszat, "Zur Perversion der Strafjustiz," 411 ff.).

29. Minutes of a meeting of the presiding judges of the Hamburg courts on February 1, 1939, quoted by Johe, *Die gleichgeschaltete Justiz,* 160.

30. Spohr, *Das Recht der Schutzhaft,* 67, with numerous references; Supreme Administrative Court, Hamburg, *JW* (1937): 3335.

31. Cf. the memorandum of January 24, 1939 (see also note 26 above), from the Reich Ministry of Justice on a meeting of chief public prosecutors on January 23, 1939, in Berlin, at which Gürtner

responded to complaints from the various districts about the countless number of people in protective custody, saying that he regretted the cases in which protective custody could be regarded "as justified criticism" of the judiciary and that nothing could be done about preventive measures.

32. Instruction of July 7, 1939 (BA R 22/1421); it was only possible to keep people temporarily; regarding enforcement, not the enforcement provisions of the judiciary, but police instructions were applied.

33. Report from the court of appeal districts of Düsseldorf and Naumburg; quoted in the memorandum of January 24, 1939, from the Reich Ministry of Justice on a meeting of chief public prosecutors on January 23, 1939, in Berlin (see note 26 above).

34. Report from the court of appeal districts of Düsseldorf and Graz; quoted in the Reich Ministry of Justice memorandum of January 24, 1939 (see note 26 above).

35. Memorandum of January 24, 1939, from the Reich Ministry of Justice (see note 26 above); the Reich Ministry of Justice recommended that the gathered presiding judges of the courts of appeal "cultivate" connections with the Gestapo.

36. Johe, Die gleichgeschaltete Justiz, 165 f., with examples.

37. Report of July 4, 1941, by the presiding judge of the Hamburg District Court, quoted in ibid., 166.

38. See the corresponding instruction of June 23, 1938, from the local Gestapo headquarters, Karlsruhe, to subordinate departments (BA R 22/1463).

39. Circular decree of May 28, 1937, by the Reich Ministry of Justice (BA R 22/1462).

40. The suggestion was made at a meeting of chief public prosecutors of June 28, 1937, in Berlin; see the chief public prosecutors' point of view on the circular decree of May 28, 1937, at the meeting (BA R 22/1462).

41. This was Dr. Joël, said to be a school friend of Freisler's, who was later taken into Security Service headquarters and was rapidly promoted through the ranks. In 1943 the RSHA attested that he had collaborated with the Security Police "in a particularly close and fruitful manner" and had clearly worked in the interests of the RSHA; data will be found in the SS personnel files on Joël (Nuremberg doc. NG-747) and his personnel files in the ministry (NG-587); for the personality of Joël, see H. Heiber, "Der Fall Eliáš," VjhZ (1955): 275 ff., 283, 296.

42. Administrative instructions of August 3, 1942, from the Reich Ministry of Justice (DJ [1942]: 521); in organizational terms, the instruction required that correspondence between the SD and the Reich Ministry of Justice pass exclusively via the head of the Security Police and Security Service, and that between the SD and the other judicial authorities was to pass exclusively via regional SD headquarters.

43. For example, see the situation report of September 30, 1943, by the chief public prosecutor of Jena, extracts of which are found in BA R 22/vorl. 20296.

44. See the secret document from Ministerialdirektor Letz to Ministerialdirektor Vollmer, both at the Reich Ministry of Justice (quoted in Steiniger and Leszczyński, Das Urteil im Juristenprozeß [1969], 1660 f.); see also the situation report of February 27, 1942, by the presiding judge of Hamm Court of Appeal (Nuremberg doc. NG-395a), according to which members of the police force were regularly present at proceedings in order to inform their office of the course of trials and the court decisions.

45. DJ (1942): 521.

46. Situation report by the chief public prosecutor of Celle, September 30, 1942 (BA R 22/3359).

47. Under the administrative instructions issued by the Reich Ministry of Justice on May 21, 1935, the Party and its subdivisions obtained, ex officio, reports on the outcome of all criminal proceedings against members of the NSDAP, the SA, the SS, and the National Socialist Motor Corps. Judgments against members of auxiliary organizations such as the DAF, the NSRB, etc., however, were not communicated to the Party offices (special official issue of DJ [1935]: no. 8, 807 [also BA R

22/4462, Bl. 142]). Communication to the Party of disciplinary decisions against members of the NSDAP and its auxiliaries in public service was effected at the order of the ministry, insofar as a concurrent criminal court judgment existed; in the absence of a criminal court judgment, no report was made on grounds of "work overload" (the real reason was probably a reluctance to refuse the Party openly) (letter of January 20, 1937, from the Reich Ministry of Justice to the Reich Ministry of the Interior, BA R 22/4462). In the same letter, the Reich Ministry of Justice also expressly refused to inform other offices than those of the Party, including auxiliary offices, of disciplinary verdicts. Apart from these arrangements, there were numerous informal ways in which information was passed on to the Party.

48. Administrative instructions dated January 23, 1938 (*DJ* [1938]: 130 f.). Transmission of records was "for the purposes of administrative and juridical assistance," "at the request" of the deputy of the Führer, the Führer's Chancellery, the Reich Treasury Minister at the NSDAP, the SA chief of staff, the RFSSuChddtPol, the *Korpsführer* of the National Socialist Motor Corps, the Reich Youth Leader, the Supreme Party Court, and the other party courts (whereas files on staff and disciplinary court files were sent only to the Supreme Party Court and the *Gau* courts on request) (Ziff. 1, 4 of the administrative instructions of January 23, 1938 [ibid.]). Access to files and information on files was also ensured for these offices and for numerous others "on justified application" (all Reichsleiter and Gauleiter of the NSDAP, subordinate offices of the Party subdivisions down to the middle level [section heads, *Gruppenführer, Abschnittsführer, Gebietsführer*]). The content of general criminal files was not to be passed on to the Party "if the outcome of the investigation is thereby jeopardized or the need for secrecy compromised" (Ziff. 4 of the administrative instructions of January 23, 1938 [ibid.]). Internal documents (such as the reference files of the public prosecutor's office, examination records, records of pardons) were not to be made known to any Party agency.

49. *Führerinformationen* no. 48 of June 19, 1942 (BA R 22/4089).

50. Unpublished circular decree of September 5, 1942, by the RFSSuChddtPol (Allgemeine Erlaßsammlung, 2 A III f., BA RD 19/3).

51. Made known in the fifth series of the Reich Ministry of Justice Information Service, September 1944 (BA R 22/4003).

52. Cf., e.g., the Reich Ministry of Justice circular instruction of July 20, 1935, regarding the struggle against "political catholicism" (Nuremberg doc. NG-630).

53. Decree of May 6, 1933, quoted in Bracher, Sauer, and Schulz, *Die nationalsozialistische Machtergreifung,* 541.

54. Circular instruction of October 29, 1935, quoted in a letter from the chief public prosecutor of Dresden to the Reich Ministry of Justice, February 22, 1937 (BA R 22/1143).

55. Circular instructions of June 3 and October 17, 1936, quoted in the letter from the chief public prosecutor, Dresden, to the Reich Ministry of Justice, February 22, 1937 (ibid.; also in Johe, *Die gleichgeschaltete Justiz,* 139).

56. Quoted in the letter from the chief public prosecutor, Dresden, February 22, 1937 (BA R 22/1143).

57. The circular instruction of January 18, 1937, ibid., probably dates back to the letter of December 14, 1936, from the Secret State Police Office, Berlin, to the Reich Ministry of Justice, where agreement was expressed to a suggestion by the Reich Ministry of Justice that the justice authorities should be obliged to report only in cases of treason. [There are two types of treason in German: *Hochverrat* (high treason) and *Landesverrat* (national betrayal), both of which are referred to here—Trans.]

58. Under the circular decree of June 26, 1936, the criminal police were centralized and put under the authority of the head of the Security Police (*MinibliV* [1936]: 946 ff.).

59. Decree appended to the Reich Ministry of Justice circular instruction of March 9, 1937 (Erlaßsammlung des RMJ, Federal Ministry of Justice, Bonn; since 1990, Berlin).

60. Circular instruction of March 9, 1937, from the Reich Ministry of Justice (ibid.).

61. This circular was also in contravention of secs. 161, 163, par. 1, Code of Criminal Procedure, under which—irrespective of the type of event under investigation or which police authorities were involved—"the police and Security Service authorities and officials [were to] investigate punishable acts and to take all measures necessary to avoid delay with a view to preventing collusion" (quoted in Schwarz, *Strafprozeßordnung* [1943]).

62. This was the import of an instruction dated June 23, 1938, from the Gestapo headquarters in Karlsruhe to all subordinate departments (BA R 22/1463).

63. Reich Ministry of Justice, July 2, 1937, quoted in Johe, *Die gleichgeschaltete Justiz*, 139 (also mentioned in a letter dated February 22, 1937, from the chief public prosecutor, Dresden, to the Reich Ministry of Justice, BA R 22/1143).

64. BA R 22/1143; also quoted in the minutes of the meeting of chief public prosecutors at the Reich Ministry of Justice on January 23–26, 1939 (Nuremberg doc. NG-366; Johe, *Die gleichgeschaltete Justiz*, 139).

65. Reich Ministry of Justice decree dated December 14, 1937, quoted in Maunz, *Gestalt und Recht der Polizei*, 43 ff.

66. See note 56 above.

67. Reports of the chief public prosecutors of Berlin, Jena, Munich, Stettin (Szczecin), and others at a meeting on January 23, 1939, quoted in an Reich Ministry of Justice memorandum dated January 24, 1939 (Nuremberg doc. NG-366).

68. See note 63 above.

69. Circular instruction of March 8, 1938 (BA R 22/1143); see also the instruction from the head of the Security Police and Security Service dated June 12, 1937 (Nuremberg doc. NG-366).

70. Reports of the chief public prosecutors of Berlin, Jena, etc. at the meeting on January 23, 1939 (see note 67 above).

71. This must have been so, since such information was a condition for imposition of protective custody or preventive detention; see details in Broszat, "Zur Perversion der Strafjustiz," 390, 395. Further evidence for this viewpoint is provided by the fact that following the "standardization" of the judiciary, the prisoners' personal files (approximately thirty forms) were made uniform. One of the forms had to be sent to the Gestapo ninety days before release (affidavit by former *Hauptwachmeister* Josef Prey, December 26, 1946, Nuremberg doc. NG-506).

72. Broszat, in Buchheim et al., *Anatomie des SS-Staates*, 2:90 ff.; between 1934 and 1937, preventive detention was pronounced on 6,852 persons (Freisler, "Fragen zur Sicherheitsverwahrung" [1938]); more details in Johe, *Die gleichgeschaltete Justiz*, 144.

73. This emerges from the Reich Ministry of Justice circular instruction of May 4, 1940 (quoted in Johe, *Die gleichgeschaltete Justiz*, 150).

74. Ibid.

75. Reich Ministry of Justice administrative instructions of November 20, 1941, regarding "amendment of the administrative instructions on enforcement matters" (*DJ* [1941]: 1091), which refers to the administrative instructions of March 25, 1941 (*DJ* [1941]: 399 ff.).

76. Reich Ministry of Justice administrative instructions of March 25, 1941 (*DJ* [1941]: 199 ff.), transmitted to the police stations by way of the RSHA circular decree of April 18, 1942 (Allgemeine Erlaßsammlung des RSHA, 2 F VIII f.) (BA R 19/3).

77. Circular decree of April 18, 1942, RSHA (see note 76).

78. BA R 22/1262.

79. According to BVerfGE 6, 132 ff., 186, the decisive discussion of chief public prosecutors took place on February 1, 1939, in Berlin; Johe (*Die gleichgeschaltete Justiz*, 129) gives the date as January 24. In point of fact, however, appropriate instructions had already been made known in November 1938; see the Reich Ministry of Justice decree of November 19, 1938, to the chief public prosecutor of Hamburg (Document Center, Berlin, Rothenberger files), which required only the following to be prosecuted: "murder out of selfish motives, *insofar as* the Gestapo did not order it,

and looting." All other offenses were not to be prosecuted [i.e., not murder for reasons of racial hatred—Author]. The original instruction of the Reich Ministry of Justice to which the decree refers is not known.

80. Excerpt from the affidavit of July 14, 1947, by former SS-*Sturmbahnführer* R. Breder on his activity with the inspector of the Security Police and Security Service in 1941–42 in Hamburg (Nuremberg doc. NO-5134, point 5).

81. The Berlin meeting of chief public prosecutors on November 12–13, 1936, on questions of treason may be mentioned, at which the head of the Security Police and Security Service, Heydrich, read a paper titled "The Communist in Police Investigation Proceedings" and an SS-*Sturmbannführer*, Müller, spoke on "The Comintern and the Communist Movement in Germany" (quoted from the agenda of the meeting, in Nuremberg doc. NG-266).

82. Reich Ministry of Justice memorandum of July 5 1944 (anon.) (BA R 22, vorl. 20675).

83. Similarly, see also Johe, *Die gleichgeschaltete Justiz.*

84. Cf. the Führer decree of June 17, 1936, on placing a head of the German police in the Reich Ministry of the Interior (*RGBl.* I 487).

85. Himmler's speech at the constitutive meeting of the committee on police law at the Academy of German Law on October 11. 1936, reproduced in *Ausgewählte Dokumente zur Geschichte des Nationalsozialismus,* ed. Jacobson and Jochman (1961).

86. See the article by the Reich Ministry of Justice press secretary, K. Doerner, "Gegen unsachliche Angriffe auf die deutsche Rechtspflege," *DJ* (1935): 895, which protests energetically against the inflammatory campaign for convictions in the *Stürmer* "and other newspapers," with a detailed correction of the convictions under fire. The column *Amtliche Erlasse und Verordnungen* (Official decrees and directives) in *DJ* (1939): 175 ff., carried a refutation of criticism by the SS journal, *Das Schwarze Korps.* These arbitrary measures also affected the internal domain of the judiciary. Thus, for example, all the penal records of the Court of Appeal of Vienna were confiscated by the Gestapo in March 1938. The event was reported directly to the ministry, not by the competent presiding judge of the court of appeal, but by a director of a district court (communication of May 20, 1938, from the director of the Vienna District Court, Kuhn, to the Reich Ministry of Justice, BA R 22/1462, B. 143 b).

87. Reich Ministry of Justice memorandum dated January 24, 1939, on a meeting of the chief public prosecutors in Berlin on January 23, 1939 (Nuremberg doc. NG-366), which gives an overview of the situation in the various districts.

88. Ibid.: statements by Gürtner on the treatment of the clergy by the Gestapo and other matters.

89. Ibid.

90. Minutes of a discussion among the presiding judges of the Hamburg courts on February 1, 1939, quoted in Johe, *Die gleichgeschaltete Justiz,* 160.

91. Cf. the reports of July 22 and November 18, 1941, by the presiding judges of the Hamburg district courts (archives of the Hanseatic Court of Appeal [LG (State Court of Appeals) 3130-E], quoted in Johe, *Die gleichschaltete Justiz,* 167).

92. Memorandum of January 24, 1939 (see note 87 above). There was no objection to "purely preventive" protective custody, but "adjustment of decisions" should not be "overzealous."

93. Ibid. (report from the Court of Appeal district of Darmstadt).

94. This applied particularly to prisoners under a preventive detention order, for whom the concentration camp appeared to be the most suitable place to be held. The police therefore interpreted the term *habitual offender* referred in the law of November 24, 1933 (*RGBl.* I 995), in an extremely broad fashion as that of a potential prisoner under a preventive detention order.

95. This practice is, for example, evident in a confidential circular instruction from the Reich Ministry of Justice dated August 18, 1942, in which the courts had to be expressly ordered not to neglect "serious consideration" of the question whether preventive detention under the terms of

sec. 42e of the Penal Code [where it was called *Sicherungsverwahrung*—Trans.] should be imposed in the conviction of so-called dangerous habitual offenders, because *Vorbeugehaft* [another form of preventive detention—Trans.] was possibly called for (Erlaßsammlung, BA Koblenz). The instruction, one of Schlegelberger's last official actions, was an attempt to prevent complete control by the police over this category of people.

96. Reich Ministry of Justice memorandum of January 24, 1939 (see note 87 above) (report from the Court of Appeal district of Hamm); see also Celle Court of Appeal, December 5, 1947 (*MDR* [1940]: 174). Ostler, *Die deutschen Rechtsanwälte* (1971), 279 n. 76, with references, and Schorn, *Der Richter im Dritten Reich* (1959), 593.

97. Cf. the report by the presiding judges of the courts of appeal and chief public prosecutors dated December 3, 1941, in which the complaint about the execution of people suspected by the Gestapo of high treason is claimed to be based on RFSS orders: the judiciary was quite capable of rapid adjudication.

98. Reports of November 18 and July 22, 1941, quoted by Johe, *Die gleichgeschaltete Justiz*, 167.

99. Cf., for example, Hitler's criticism of the decision of October 21, 1940, by the Lüneburg Court of Appeal against a Pole who had been convicted and sentenced to *one* year's imprisonment for rape (sec. 176, par. 1 of the Penal Code) on account of the "lack of inhibition" of the Poles with regard to such offenses. Although the Führer only had the Reich Ministry of Justice "requested" to ensure that "this would not be *repeated* in *other* courts" (author's emphasis) (letter of March 29, 1941, from the RMuChdRkzlei to the Reich Ministry of Justice, Nuremberg doc. NG-280), the judges of the criminal court in question were immediately transferred and no longer employed in penal matters; the competent presiding judge of the Court of Appeal and the judges involved were taken to task by the Reich Ministry of Justice. The "ineptness" of the ruling was further circulated to all the judicial authorities of the Reich by way of a circular instruction (letter of April 3, 1941, from the Reich Ministry of Justice to the RMuChdRkzlei [ibid.]). In the case of A. Scharff, too, a youth who was convicted to a lengthy term of imprisonment for acts of collusion, Schlegelberger originally acknowledged Hitler's principle of severe punishment (see the letter of May 25, 1941, from the "Führer's secretary" [Bormann] to the RMuChdRkzlei, Nuremberg doc. NG-611, also *VjhZ* [1958]: 419), before putting forward the attenuating circumstances of the case (the young age and good previous record of the offender), on the basis of which he believed that "we should stay with the judgment as passed" (letter of June 28, 1941, to the RMuChdRkzlei, ibid.). When Hitler criticized the sentencing of Luftglass, a 74-year-old Jew accused of hoarding eggs (violation of the War Economy Decree) to "mere" imprisonment (letter of October 25, 1941, from the RMuChdRkzlei to the Reich Ministry of Justice, Nuremberg doc. NG-287A, quoted in *VjhZ* [1958]: 422), Schlegelberger immediately capitulated. By his own personal order (letter of October 29, 1941, to the RMuChdRkzlei, Nuremberg doc. NG-287 B, quoted in *VjhZ* [1958]: 423), the prisoner was put into the hands of the Gestapo (for execution), whereby the Reich Ministry of Justice was spared the embarrassment of having to amend the judgment itself. In contrast, there is evidence of other rulings that gave rise to the disapproval of Hitler or the police and were "adjusted" by the judicial authority itself—with the aid of a plea of nullity (examples in Johe, *Die gleichgeschaltete Justiz*, 168 f.). Regarding the plea of nullity, see sec. 34, art. 5, of the so-called Jurisdiction Decree of February 21, 1940 (*RGBl.* I 405); sec. 7 of the decree of August 13, 1941 (*RGBl.* I 508); RGSt (Supreme Court for Criminal Cases) 74, 75 f., 307; affidavit of December 7, 1946, by the lawyer Ernst Escher (Nuremberg doc. NG-677); statistics in the report of August 29, 1944, from the Reich attorney general at the Reich Supreme Court to the Reich Ministry of Justice (BA R 22/1112). See also *Richterbriefe* no. 16 of January 1 and February 1, 1944, item 39 (BA R 22/4002, Bl. 138, 149); Fraenkel, "Die Nichtigkeitsbeschwerde in der Praxis" (1941); Schwarz, "Reichsgericht als Tatsacheninstanz" (1940); Weinkauff and Wagner, *Die deutsche Justiz*, 271 ff., with numerous examples.

100. Statement made by State Secretary Schlegelberger on March 10, 1936, quoted in Steiniger and Leszczyński, *Das Urteil im Juristenprozeß*, 158.

101. The explanation given by Weinkauff and Wagner, *Die deutsche Justiz*, 143, that the severity of the judgments was based on Hitler's own repeated threats and emotional fits, to which the ministry deferred, is not a satisfactory one. Hitler's supply of information and his outbursts against the judiciary were sporadic and had no influence on judicial practice. Hitler's mind was taken up with quite different, more important matters. The fact that the political leadership was able to gain such direct influence is due above all to the passivity of the ministry.

102. Hitler quoted in *Der Großdeutsche Freiheitskampf, Reden A. Hitlers* (1943), 147 f. For Schlegelberger's decree, see Nuremberg doc. NG-507 (also quoted by Johe, *Die gleichgeschaltete Justiz*, 53). The circulated passage read, verbatim, "Just as we have been mercilessly severe in the struggle for power, so we will be equally merciless and equally strict in the struggle for the preservation of our people. At a time in which thousands of our best men are falling, nobody who slurs the victims of the front at home can count on his life" (quoted from the Reich Ministry of Justice decree of December 15, 1941, Johe, *Die gleichgeschaltete Justiz*, 53 n. 139).

103. Letter of May 21, 1942, from the RMuChdRkzlei to the head of the Party Chancellery (Nuremberg doc. NG-236).

104. Letter dated May 6, 1942, by way of the RMuChdRkzlei to the Führer and Reich Chancellor containing the draft of such a decree (Nuremberg doc. NG-102, quoted in *VjhZ* [1958]: 426 f., 428; also in Weinkauff and Wagner, *Die deutsche Justiz*, 149).

105. Letter of June 10, 1942, from the head of the Party Chancellery to the Reich Ministry of Justice (Nuremberg doc. NG-102; also in Weinkauff and Wagner, *Die deutsche Justiz*, 150) (the Führer should have the final say over decisions).

106. *RGBl.* I 995.

107. "Preventive detention matters," *DJ* (1938): 626.

108. *RGBl.* I 995.

109. In the early years of the Third Reich, political motives were doubtless at the bottom of the relatively large number of preventive detentions. There were 6,835 cases between 1933 and 1937 (Freisler, "Fragen zur Sicherheitsverwahrung"), or 6,898 (of which 3,723 were pronounced in 1934 alone), according to the Reich criminal statistics (*DJ* [1943]: 377 n). The figures in the text are also from this source.

110. *RGBl.* I 539.

111. Hitler in Picker, *Hitlers Tischgespräche* (1951), 203.

112. *DJ* (1938): 323.

113. In the Reich Ministry of Justice circular instruction of May 4, 1940 (quoted in Johe, *Die gleichgeschaltete Justiz*, 150), the courts were forbidden to release prisoners for the duration of the war.

114. Letter dated June 10, 1942, from the head of the Party Chancellery to the Reich Ministry of Justice (Nuremberg doc. NG-102).

115. Statement by Schlegelberger on June 27, 1947, before Military Court 3 in Nuremberg, Nuremberg Trials III, Prot. (d), 4324, BA All. Proz. 1, XVII A 58; according to him, Hitler was informed about the judiciary by Bormann only when he was already in a rage for some other reason and needed a "lightning conductor."

116. Schlegelberger in a letter dated May 15, 1942, to the RMuChdRkzlei (BA R 22/4089, Bl. 3).

117. An almost complete collection of issues of *Führerinformationen* exists in BA R 22/4089 (nos. 36, 66, 181, and 189 are missing). Discussed in detail in Gribbohm, "Die Führerinformationen des RMJ" (1971).

118. The collection ceases with issue 191 dated February 15, 1945. Letter of May 15, 1942, to the head of the Party Chancellery (quoted by Gribbohm, "Die Führerinformationen des RMJ").

119. The top copy was intended for Hitler, and one copy each for the Reich Ministry of Justice, the Party Chancellery, and the Reich Chancellery.

120. In connection with the purpose of the publication, see the affidavit by Schlegelberger's

right-hand man, Dr. Gramm, of July 3, 1947 (Nuremberg doc. NG-1884). Quotation in a letter dated May 15, 1942, from Schlegelberger to the RMuChdRkzlei, quoted by Gribbohm, "Die Führerinformationen des RMJ."

121. See Gribbohm, "Die Führerinformationen des RMJ," 153, for details.

122. The reports were devoted primarily to proceedings against prominent people, such as those instituted by the People's Court against the former *Ministerpräsident* of the Protectorate, Beran, and against H. Grynszpan, who in 1938 shot a member of the staff of the German Embassy in Paris, Ernst v. Rath (report of May 15, 1942); details in Heiber, "Der Fall Grynszpan" (1957). Further relevant reports will be found in nos. 172, 173, and 190 (BA R 22/4089).

123. *Führerinformationen* nos. 18, 23, 65, 68, 136, and 160 (see note 117 above). According to a communication in no. 132, more than two thousand sexual offenders had been castrated by order of the courts as of January 1, 1941.

124. The minister of justice reported that a total of 3,641 death sentences (2,760 in the Reich and 881 in the Annexed Eastern Territories from July 1 to December 31, 1942) had been pronounced and a petition for clemency submitted, two and a half times as many as all the death sentences (1,400) pronounced between 1907 and 1932 (this last figure in Leber, *Das Gewissen entscheidet* [1957], 20 f.). In January and February 1943 alone, the *Führerinformationen* reported 806 death sentences (Reich, 615; Annexed Eastern Territories, 191).

125. On the prisons, cf. nos. 11, 34, 41, 57, 83, 93, 103, 138, 185, and 187 (BA R 22/4089). On the execution of sentences, see *Führerinformationen,* December 9, 1944 (ibid.), according to which 197,867 individuals (including 48,017 women) had been detained as of December 1944; these included 72,804 held in penitentiaries, 47,098 in prisons, 2,757 in preventive detention, and 15,774 Poles in prison camps). The large number of penitentiary inmates evidences the increased severity of the jurisdiction. See *Führerinformationen* of November 4, 1942 (ibid.), according to which the number of "employable" prisoners was 152,700 as of October 1, 1942. On May 21, 1942, the minister of justice reported that he had imposed the "obligation to inflict decisive and severe punishment above all on war criminals" on all the presiding judges of the courts of appeal and chief public prosecutors (ibid.). The report dated May 29, 1942 (ibid.), states that "Communist high treason" (*kommunistischer Hochverrat*) should regularly be punished by death, "because today it also has the character of *Landesverrat.*" [A distinction is drawn in German between two types of high treason, *Hochverrat* and *Landesverrat,* the first meaning betrayal by means of violence, the second, without violence—Trans.] On July 10, 1942, the Reich Ministry of Justice pointed out that in the wake of instructions it had issued, the courts were frequently criticized in official Party quarters for excessively harsh penal practice (ibid.).

126. There is certainly some evidence that the *Führerinformationen* were submitted to Hitler in 1942 at least, since in a letter from the Party Chancellery to the Reich Ministry of Justice dated October 31, 1942, Bormann explains the Führer's position regarding certain points in the *Führerinformationen* (BA R 22/4089).

127. See the letter of June 10, 1942, to the Reich Ministry of Justice (Nuremberg doc. NG-102) claiming to represent Hitler's view.

128. Statement by Schlegelberger in Nuremberg on September 6, 1946 (Nuremberg doc. NG-097), that he "did not want to sit at the same table" as Thierack (note by Schlegelberger dated August 30, 1946, Nuremberg doc. NG-125).

129. According to the press release in *DJ* (1942): 551, at the time of his inauguration, Thierack (b. 1889), a lawyer from Saxony, was minister of justice there from 1933 on, and then minister of justice of Thuringia as of 1935. After the judicial administration had passed into the hands of the Reich, he was made deputy presiding judge of the Reich Supreme Court in 1935 and presiding judge of the People's Court on June 1, 1936. In the spring of 1932, he joined the Party and climbed to the rank of *Oberbefehlsleiter* and *SA-Brigadeführer.* He held a high position in the Academy for Ger-

man Law, and when Hans Frank fell into disfavor on account of his sharp criticism of SS and police policy in the General Government, he took over the leadership of the NSRB and the chairmanship of the Academy for German Law. With his nomination to the post of Reich minister of justice on August 20, 1942, Thierack held power of the highest state and Party offices in the judicial domain.

His appointment was due not least to his conduct in the "Eliáš case," where as presiding judge of the People's Court, in complicity with Heydrich, he maneuvered to replace the Reich attorney general by the SS as representative of the prosecution, thus gaining the favor of Hitler and the Security Police. After that he was known at Führer headquarters as the "alert judge," although he lost the confidence of most of his colleagues in the judiciary (at least according to Heiber, "Der Fall Eliáš," *VjhZ* [1955]: 275 ff., 277, 295).

130. Affidavit by the former public prosecutor of Wiesbaden, Dr. Hans Quambusch, November 22, 1946 (Nuremberg doc. NG-397). It appears that not only legally convicted prisoners fell victim to such actions, but also individuals held in custody who had been charged with offenses punishable by death (defeatist statements, etc.). Quotation in Heiber, "Der Fall Eliáš," 277, 295.

131. Situation report of November 30, 1942, from the Brunswick Court of Appeal (BA R 22/3357); the reception of the change among the judiciary authorities was not reported.

132. See Thierack's memorandum of September 18, 1942, on the discussion (Nuremberg doc. PS-654; BA R 22/4062; copy also in ZS, G.J. no. 104, 255 f.).

133. Memorandum of September 18, 1942 (ibid.); it was proposed to lower the age of criminal responsibility to 12 years and to introduce flogging, which reputedly had been ordered by Hitler, as a general measure (point 6: "the RFSS is completely in agreement with the proposed regulations for flogging as ordered by the Führer").

134. The judgments contested by the RFSS were generally those by the regular courts (district courts and municipal courts) but also judgments by special and military courts, which were submitted to the Reich Ministry of Justice *without* a request for adjustment having been made (see letters of November 28, 1942; June 9, December 2, 1943; February 13, October 6, 1944, from the head of the Security Police and Security Service; and of October 22, 1942, from the head of the Security Police and Security Service to the Party Chancellery, BA R 22/4203). The Reich Ministry of Justice investigated each case and then communicated "the action taken" to the head of the Security Police and Security Service: either an instruction to the Reich attorney general to lodge a plea of nullity, a "suggestion" of police custody (that is, transfer to a concentration camp) in the case of people who had been discharged, or a thorough exposition of the facts of the case, if it was desired that the judgment remain (see, e.g., the letter of February 23, 1943, from the Reich Ministry of Justice to the head of the Security Police and Security Service [ibid.]; in three of the eight cases contested by the head of the Security Police and Security Service in his letter of November 28, 1942 [ibid.], the Reich Ministry of Justice arranged for a plea of nullity to be lodged) (see note 99 above). In the great majority of all cases, the Reich Ministry of Justice acceded to formal "applications" for "adjustment." In October 1942 alone, no less than 72 such "applications" were made (applications of October 1942 [precise date unknown] from the head of the Security Police and Security Service to the Reich Ministry of Justice by way of the Party Chancellery [Klemm], in some cases with a handwritten note in the margin, "to Dept XV," BA R 22/4202 [Dept. 15 of the Reich Ministry of Justice was responsible for selection of the prisoners to be handed over to the Gestapo]); reply of February 2, 1943, to the head of the Security Police and Security Service (ibid.): in 43 cases the prisoners were ordered to be "handed over to the Gestapo" for work in concentration camps; in 10 cases the Reich Ministry of Justice arranged for a plea of nullity to be lodged; in 3 cases the pretrial confinement period was not counted; in 5 the order was to hand over the prisoners for "special military use"; in the case of 2 prisoners who had been released, the Reich Ministry of Justice suggested preventive police custody (i.e., transfer to a concentration camp). In 9 cases the original judgment was maintained.

135. Minutes of meeting, September 18, 1942 (BA R 22/4062).

136. See the letter of October 1942 from the head of the Security Police and Security Service to the Reich Ministry of Justice (BA R 22/4202), containing a total of sixteen applications for "special treatment."

137. Note by the Reich Ministry of Justice on a discussion with the RMuChdRkzlei (Lammers) on October 1, 1942 (BA R 22/4062). Statements by Hitler on so-called habitual offenders, quoted in Picker, *Hitlers Tischgespräche* (1951), 203. Such people were "put into concentration camps or done away with."

138. Thierack's memorandum of September 18, 1942 (BA R 22/4062; Nuremberg doc. PS-654).

139. Memorandum from the Reich Ministry of Justice (no author, undated), presumably spring 1943 (BA R 22/1262), according to which 7,600 people were in protective custody in German prisons, 31,000 "ethnic Poles" and approx. 1,200 Jews.

140. *Führerinformationen* no. 41 of June 12, 1942 (BA R 22/4089) (males under a preventive detention order only).

141. Memorandum of September 18, 1942 (ibid.). See also the secret Reich Ministry of Justice decree of October 27, 1942, to all chief public prosecutors (prison authorities) (Nuremberg doc. PS-648).

Part Two. Section 1. Excursus. 3. Police "Rectification" Measures. and 4. Judicial Consequences of the Usurpation of the Prosecution of "Non-Germans" by the Police

1. Reich Ministry of Justice memorandum of September 18, 1942 (BA R 22/4062; Nuremberg doc. PS-674).

2. Reich Ministry of Justice memorandum, undated (spring 1943) (ibid.).

3. Urgent memorandum of November 5, 1942, from the RSHA to all subordinate offices (Nuremberg doc. PS-1850). Any national of one of the powers at war with Germany, especially the people of the Eastern European states, was considered "hostile" and an "alien"; the prosecution of citizens of allied or neutral states should remain in the hands of the judiciary.

4. Letter from the Reich Ministry of Justice of November 16, 1942, to the head of the Party Chancellery (BA R 43 II/1512).

5. Memorandum dated December 13, 1942, by Thierack (BA R 22/4062; also as Nuremberg doc. PS-1750; L-316 [copy also in ZS, Versch. 250 I, 256]). Broszat, *Nationalsozialistische Polenpolitik* (1961), 140, is of a different opinion, considering that Thierack dropped the matter of his own accord.

6. *RGBl.* I 352.

7. Memorandum of December 13, 1942, by Thierack (see note 5 above).

8. Decree referred to in statements by Thierack at the meeting of presiding judges of the courts of appeal and chief public prosecutors on February 10–11, 1943, in Berlin (minutes of meeting, BA R 22/4200; speech by the minister, Bl. 28 ff.).

9. Instruction quoted in the minutes (ibid., Ziff. 3, Bl. 24). The date of the instruction is not given.

10. Report by *Ministerialdirigent* Schäfer, Reich Ministry of Justice, at the meeting of February 10–11, 1943 (minutes of meeting, ibid., Ziff. 3).

11. More details in Broszat, in Buchheim et al., *Anatomie des SS-Staates* (1965), 2:103 ff. From 1939 on, this measure was based on the circular decree of September 3, 1939, issued by the head of the Security Police and Security Service on "principles of internal State security during the war" ("if ordered by a high authority, brutal liquidation of such elements ['hostile to the nation and Reich']," BA Sammlung Schuhmacher, 271), with implementing decree of September 20, 1939 (Nuremberg doc. NO-2263).

12. Regarding the illegality (under international law) of the *Nacht und Nebel* provisions, see Steiniger and Leszczyński, *Das Urteil im Juristenprozeß* (1969), 73; BVerfGE 26, 132 ff., 187.

13. Nuremberg doc. WA-503, NG-246, L-90 (also in *Dok. der Deutschen Politik und Geschichte*, 5:349). All *Nacht und Nebel* operations are also reported in BA R 22/20198. See also Wagner, *Der Volksgerichtshof* (1974), 416 f., esp. 417 n. 303.

14. Nuremberg Doc. L-90, in conjunction with the administrative regulations of December 12, 1941 by the chief of the Armed Forces High Command (Nuremberg doc. PS-669). Regarding the Occupied Eastern Territories, the SIPO had in any case largely usurped the prosecution proceedings against "aliens" (see below, section 2, excursus, 1, "Efforts by the Police to Create a Police 'Penal Law for Alien Peoples' "). Under the implementing regulations referred to, the *Nacht und Nebel* provisions covered "attacks against life and limb, spying, sabotage, Communist activities, criminal offenses likely to give rise to unrest, support of enemies . . . unauthorized possession of weapons." Adjudication by the military court should be carried out only when the death sentence was probable and its rapid execution possible. See also the Reich Ministry of Justice decree of October 14, 1942, and the Reich Ministry of Justice circular instruction of the same date on implementation of the *Nacht und Nebel* decree (BA R 22/20198); Reich Ministry of Justice instruction of July 3, 1943, on sentencing by the special courts of accomplices from other regions than the territories mentioned or participants in offenses against the *Nacht und Nebel* provisions (Nuremberg doc. NG-243).

15. Hitler's wish was communicated to the Reich ministries involved by Keitel in a letter dated December 12, 1941, to which the implementing regulations referred to were appended (Nuremberg doc. PS-669). Letter of April 1944 from Dr. Hülle of the legal department of the Armed Forces High Command to *Ministerialrat* von Ammon at the Reich Ministry of Justice (Nuremberg doc. NG-230).

16. According to the letter of December 12, 1943, from the head of the Armed Forces High Command (Keitel), suspected persons were to disappear without trace. No information on their whereabouts was allowed to be given to relatives or other persons. (The Reich Ministry of Justice addressed a corresponding instruction in early 1942 to the attorneys general of the special courts dealing with *Nacht und Nebel* matters in Cologne, Dortmund, Kiel, and Berlin, quoted in Steiniger and Leszczyński, *Das Urteil im Juristenprozeß*, 53). Those accused of crimes under the *Nacht und Nebel* provisions were bereft of all rights of due process: no choice of defense counsel; appointment of defense counsel at the discretion of the court (see the letter of February 9, 1942, from the competent officials at the Reich Ministry of Justice [von Ammon and Mettenberg] in response to various inquiries from the special courts of Hamm, Kiel, and Cologne; letter of February 9, 1942, from the Reich Ministry of Justice to the competent special courts, Nuremberg doc. NG-253). As a rule the accused did not learn what they were charged with until the court hearing, *provided* they understood German or their defense counsel translated the indictment. No ex officio translation was provided (memorandum of October 2, 1943, by *Ministerialrat* von Ammon of the Reich Ministry of Justice, Nuremberg doc. NG-281). Foreign witnesses could be heard only with the agreement of the SS. The special courts had to give the public prosecutor a clear indication of how far they were willing to deviate from their demand (executive decree of February 6, 1942, by the Reich Ministry of Justice, mentioned in the affidavit by von Ammon, Nuremberg doc. NG-232). Enforcement of the penalty was equally inhuman: under the terms of a secret Reich Ministry of Justice decree of March 16, 1943, persons imprisoned under the *Nacht und Nebel* provisions were forbidden visits, parcels, or letters, and they were not allowed to write, themselves. It was forbidden to inform relatives of the execution or to give them the prisoner's belongings; graves were not to be marked (quoted after BVerfGE 6, 132 ff, 187; see also the instruction of December 1942 by Reich Attorney General Lautz, Nuremberg doc. NG-708).

17. Conrad, *Deutsche Rechtsgeschichte* (1962), 26.

18. Circular instruction of October 28, 1942 (Nuremberg doc. NG-737), according to which the

"other measures" taken by the Gestapo were either "detention" "for the duration of the war" (i.e., in a concentration camp) or "release to the occupied territories"; there was of course no guarantee that such releases actually took place. See also the affidavit by von Ammon (Nuremberg doc. NG-232), according to whom this instruction further amended the executive decree of December 6, 1942 (ibid.), in that the court could at its discretion deviate from the public prosecutor's demand. See also the letter of February 20, 1943, from the senior public prosecutor of the Essen special court to the Reich Ministry of Justice (Nuremberg doc. NG-267) and an earlier Reich Ministry of Justice instruction on the handing over of *Nacht und Nebel* prisoners to the Gestapo (Nuremberg doc. NG-205).

19. Reich Ministry of Justice instruction of early 1942 (Nuremberg doc. NG-232, quoted in Steiniger and Leszczyński, *Das Urteil im Juristenprozeß*, 53). In the overviews by the Reich Ministry of Justice dated September 1, 1942 (Nuremberg doc. NG-228), and November 1, 1943 (Nuremberg doc. NG-282), however, only the special courts of Kiel, Essen, and Cologne are mentioned.

20. Reich Ministry of Justice overviews of September 1, 1942 (1,456 cases pending before the special courts of Kiel, Essen, Cologne); November 1, 1943 (see the preceding note) (pending before these special courts and the People's Court: 1,786 cases involving 5,240 accused, 1,230 of which led to a conviction); and April 30, 1944 (Nuremberg doc. NG-232): proceedings against 6,639 accused were pending, of whom 1,793 were convicted; the number of *Nacht und Nebel* cases is, however, higher, since the activities of the special courts continued until August 1944 (indictment in the Judiciary Trials, quoted in Steiniger and Leszczyński, *Das Urteil im Juristenprozeß*, 72); in addition, the figures cover only proceedings that were passed on by the military courts, i.e., not those they dealt with themselves. The People's Court was in session virtually without interruption, especially in the years 1933 and 1934. As of August 1, 1944, it used more than 172 honorary associate judges, for the most part high-ranking military, SS and SA officers, and Party functionaries (Nuremberg doc. NG-184).

21. Steiniger and Leszczyński, *Das Urteil im Juristenprozeß*, 191, name 304 demonstrable death sentences in *Nacht und Nebel* cases at the People's Court by 1944 alone (see also the indictment document at the Nuremberg Judiciary Trials, quoted in ibid., 72). More recently, see Wagner, *Der Volksgerichtshof*, 416 f., on the judgment practice of the courts.

22. The grip of the Gestapo was clearly established since the middle of 1943, however. Cf. the RSHA decree of May 31, 1943, under which "old" *Nacht und Nebel* prisoners were defined as those whom the military courts had "handed over to the transfer agencies to be brought into the Reich," whereas "new" *Nacht und Nebel* prisoners were arrested on the spot by the SIPO and taken directly to the Reich concentration camps (quoted from the decree by the Central Economic and Administrative Office of the SS to the commanders of various concentration camps, ZS, G.J. no. 158). The decree of May 31, 1943, coincides with the Reich Ministry of Justice secret decree of March 16, 1943, with respect to the ban on receiving and writing mail for *Nacht und Nebel* prisoners (see note 16).

23. Either he was condemned by the special court or, after 1944, the proceedings were officially passed over to the Gestapo, which could mean nothing other than liquidation or transportation to a concentration camp. If he was acquitted or had served his term of imprisonment, he was to be handed over to the Gestapo on the instructions of the Reich Ministry of Justice (see note 18) and incur the same sanctions. The best that a prisoner under the *Nacht und Nebel* provisions could hope for, and as was frequently practiced by the courts, was to serve a long term of imprisonment in a prison run by the judiciary.

24. Decree of March 11, 1942, quoted in the situation report of August 11, 1942, by the chief public prosecutor of Königsberg (BA R 22/3375).

25. Cf. the RFSS decree of February 10, 1944, and the decrees of December 10, 1940, and July 5, 1941, cited there, quoted by Weinkauff and Wagner, *Die deutsche Justiz* (1968), 306.

26. After about 1941, a "refined" procedure was applied for Poles, whereby execution was made to depend on racial investigation of the accused. The "racial judgment," which was pronounced purely on the basis of external appearances, was, according to the testimony of former

members of the SIPO, "enormously important" and "decisive" for the fate of the "culprit," for whom a negative judgment meant the death penalty. If the racial judgment was positive, the "culprit" was sent to a concentration camp. The German woman involved was also sent to a concentration camp (affidavit of July 14, 1947, by Breder, Nuremberg doc. NO-5134; and affidavit of August 8, 1947, by Paucke, Nuremberg Doc. NO-5132). The police leadership even went so far as to issue decrees forbidding the so-called Eastern workers, i.e., the labor force from the Occupied Soviet Territories, *all* sexual intercourse. In the event of sexual intercourse with Germans, Soviet Russians were not subjected to a racial investigation, as was the case with Poles, but male Russians were immediately executed, and Russian women were put into concentration camp (unpublished circular decree of February 20, 1942 by the RFSSuChddtPol, letter A, Allgemeine Erlaßsammlung des RSHA, 2 A III f.; repeated in the circular decree of February 10, 1944, II, Ziff. 6; the latter decree prohibited only the racial judgment, with "special treatment" as consequence). In the event of sexual intercourse between Soviet Russians and other foreign workers, the threat of concentration camp hung over both parties (decree of February 20, 1942).

27. Allgemeine Erlaßsammlung des RSHA, 2 A III (BA R 19/3).

28. Directives dated September 3, 1940, and July 5, 1941, from the RFSSuChddtPol, quoted in *Doc. Occ.* 10:108 ff. (also in Weinkauff and Wagner, *Die deutsche Justiz,* 306).

29. Urgent memorandum of August 5, 1940, from the head of the Security Police and Security Service to Stapo headquarters (B, no. 3642/40 g—IV A 1 c, BA Koblenz).

30. See Steiniger and Leszczyński, *Das Urteil im Juristenprozeß,* 69, with references; *Führerinformationen* no. 66 of July 3, 1942 (BA R 22/4089).

31. See the situation report of November 4, 1941, by the presiding judge of the Brunswick Court of Appeal (BA R 22/3357); situation reports of July 31, 1940; May 31, December 1, 1941, by the chief public prosecutor of Celle (hanging of Polish agricultural workers on account of "indecent acts"), in *VjhZ* (1958): 452; situation report of May 23, 1941, by the senior public prosecutor of Mosbach, annexed to the situation report of June 3, 1941, by the chief public prosecutor of Karlsruhe (BA R 22/3370, fol. 44 ff.); reports by the higher SS and police leader, Stuttgart, to the Reich governor of Baden (ZS, Versch. 9/2341, excerpts); see also the circular dated May 20, 1942, from the RSHA to the state police headquarters of the Annexed Eastern Territories, according to which sexual intercourse between Germans and "aliens" would be dealt with not by the judiciary but by the Gestapo (Nuremberg doc. NO-3296). Regarding the actual execution, which was generally carried out by compatriots of the victim or fellow prisoners, extremely detailed instructions were issued for selection of the site, the presence of spectators, police measures, the photographs to be taken, etc. The earliest RFSSuChddtPol decree (no longer extant) dates back to December 10, 1940, followed by the decrees of July 5, 1941 (see note 28), May 4, 1943 (Allgemeine Erlaßsammlung des RSHA, II F VII a), and February 10, 1944 (quoted in Weinkauff and Wagner, *Die deutsche Justiz,* 306).

32. See Weinkauff and Wagner, *Die deutsche Justiz,* 298, for more details.

33. See ibid. for further details.

34. Allgemeine Erlaßsammlung des RSHA, 2 A III f. (BA R 19/3).

35. See the statements by *Ministerialdirektor* Schäfer of the Reich Ministry of Justice at the meeting of senior presiding judges and chief public prosecutors in Berlin, February 10 – 11, 1943 (minutes of meeting, BA R 22/4200).

36. *RGBl.* I 759.

37. Allgemeine Erlaßsammlung des RSHA, 2 A III f. (BA R 19/3).

38. Letter 8 of the circular decree of February 20, 1942 (see note 26 above).

39. Note dated December 13, 1942, from the Reich minister of justice on a discussion with Himmler (BA R 22/4062).

40. RSHA circular decree dated June 30, 1943 (Allgemeine Erlaßsammlung des RSHA, 2 A III, 131 ff., BA R 19/3).

41. ZS, Versch. 26, 86, 127 f., 131.

42. A secret RSHA circular decree dated August 10, 1943 (Allgemeine Erlaßsammlung, BA R 19/3, 2 A III f., 148 f.), contains the following definition of this group of people: The term *Polish civilian workers* covered all Poles wearing a P employed in the Altreich (virtually no Polish civilian workers were engaged in the Annexed Eastern Territories). Regarding Soviet Russian civilian workers, see the circular decree of June 30, 1943 (see note 40), according to which criminal prosecution throughout the territory of the Reich (including the Annexed Eastern Territories) was incumbent on the police. Penal jurisdiction by the police over Poles living in the Annexed Eastern Territories ("persons of Polish nationality with protected status," unless they were registered in the German Ethnic Classification List) was covered by the circular decree of October 23, 1942 (not included in the general collection of RSHA circular decrees; quoted only in the decrees of June 30 and October 30, 1943, Allgemeine Erlaßsammlung des RSHA, 2 A III, 131 ff., BA R 19/3). Evidence that such questions of delimitation regarding the "nationality" of the people involved caused no few problems for the Gestapo bureaus is provided by the fact that just four weeks later, on September 10, 1943, a further circular decree was issued by the RFSSuChddtPol (Allgemeine Erlaßsammlung, 2 A III f., 150 ff., ibid.) with detailed administrative regulations (159 ff.) canceling the earlier decrees of and March 8, 20, April 8, July 10, and September 3, 1940; December 10, 1941; and July 26, 1942, and repeating once again the fundamental authority of the Gestapo in matters of criminal offenses and violations of work contracts by Polish civilian workers in the territory of the Altreich.

43. ZS, Versch. 26, 86, 127 f., 131; also quoted in the situation report dated November 29, 1943, by the presiding judge of the Königsberg Court of Appeal (BA R 22/3375).

44. See the situation report by the presiding judge of the Königsberg Court of Appeal (BA R 22/3375).

45. Situation report dated January 29, 1941, by the chief public prosecutor, Hamm (Nuremberg doc. NG-685), referring to the punishment by the Gestapo of Polish workers who had broken their work contract; information on Polish workers was no longer passed on to the public prosecutor's office, but went straight to the Gestapo.

46. Reich Ministry of Justice memorandum of December 13, 1942, by Thierack on a discussion with Himmler (BA R 22/4062): Thierack reported achieving agreement with the *Reichsführer-SS* such that these decrees (issued by the head of the Security Police and RSHA) would serve as the basis for the prosecution of "aliens"; Germans, however, should continue to be dealt with by the judicial system; the *Reichsführer*-SS is said to have made no comment on this.

47. The situation report of May 23, 1941, by the senior public prosecutor of Mosbach (see note 31) urgently requested communication of the "unpublished" authority of the police.

48. Quoted from information by Thierack, Reich Ministry of Justice (Bl. 28 ff.), at the meeting of the presiding judges of the courts of appeal and chief public prosecutors in Berlin, February 10–11, 1943 (minutes of meeting, BA R 22/4200).

49. Reich Ministry of Justice memorandum of December 13, 1942, on a discussion with the *Reichsführer*-SS (BA R 22/4062).

50. Minutes of meeting (BA R 22/4200).

51. Ibid., Ziff. 3, Bl. 24 ff.

52. See Heiber, "Der Fall Eliáš," *VjhZ* (1955): 257 ff.

53. Reported by Schäfer in minutes of meeting (BA R 22/4200).

54. Statements by Thierack and *Ministerialdirektor* E. Schäfer (minutes of meeting, ibid., Ziff. 3, Bl. 24 f.).

55. Statements by Thierack, minutes of meeting (ibid.).

56. See Reich Ministry of Justice memorandum on the discussion of September 18, 1942 (BA R 22/4062).

57. On this question see Broszat, "Zur Perversion der Strafjustiz" (1958), 390 ff.

58. Letter of October 13, 1942; for this reason the RFSS would take over criminal prosecution "untrammeled by legal constraints" (Nuremberg doc. NG-558; also ZS, Eichmann, no. 454).

59. Minutes of the meeting of February 10 – 11, 1943, in Berlin (BA R 22/4200, Bl. 30).

60. Ibid.

61. "And if some get excited about the hanging of Poles, I personally see nothing special about the fact that the chief of police finds it necessary to hang people as a deterrent" (ibid., Bl. 31).

62. "If a Pole who is employed by a farmer exhibits refractory behavior and breaks the pitchfork or axe, he must be destroyed" (ibid., Bl. 32).

63. Ibid., Bl. 23 ff.

64. Ibid.

65. Ibid., Bl. 26 ff, 33 ff.

66. No. XIII, Decree on Penal Law for Poles of December 4, 1941.

67. Circular decree of June 15, 1942, by the RFSSuChddtPol (*MinbliV* [1942]: 1309).

68. Minutes of meeting (BA R 22/4200, Bl. 27).

69. Ibid.

70. Ibid., Bl. 26 f. (Schäfer).

71. See situation report of May 23, 1941, by the senior public prosecutor of Mosbach (see note 31).

72. Minutes of meeting (BA R 22/4200) (Schäfer).

73. *RGBl.* I 352.

Part Two. Section 1. B. I. Main Elements of the Transformation of Civil Law on an Ethnic Basis

1. Schönke, "Einige Grundlinien der Entwicklung des Zivilprozessrechts seit 1933" (1943).

2. The academy's activity has been sorely underrated in the past (Weinkauff and Wagner, *Die deutsche Justiz* [1968], 110; Johe, *Die gleichgeschaltete Justiz* [1967], 23 ff.). Almost all jurists of repute worked on their committees; they included important names—see, e.g., the list of participants at a meeting of the "Theory and Practice" group held in Cochem on August 1, 1944 (BA R 22/4514), at which virtually all the leading legal authorities of the time participated. The work of the committees, of which there were forty-five active in every province of the law (see the enumeration in K. Lasch, in *Handwörterbuch der Rechtswissenschaft,* ed. Erich Volkmar, Alexander Elster, and Günther Küchenhoff [1937], vol. 8), had a decisive influence on the interpretation of the law by students, junior attorneys, and judges, since their publications were obligatorily to be found on the shelves of the universities and courts. Much of the content of the speeches of the Reich Ministry of Justice representatives was taken directly from articles in these publications.

The function of the academy, in the words of the *Reichsrechtsführer,* H. Frank, was to deal with all the "fundamental problems" of the law "from the higher perspective of a general view and scientific method"; the academy served as "a refuge . . . for the creation of a truly German law." For details of the structure, functions, and staff of the academy, see Frank, *Nationalsozialistisches Handbuch für Recht und Gesetzgebung* (1934), introduction, xxii, 1572 ff.; Johe, *Die gleichgeschaltete Justiz,* 23 ff.; *DR* (1933): 205 f.; *DJ* (1942): 724; see also Weinkauff and Wagner, *Die deutsche Justiz,* 110.

3. Full details in Kluge and Krüger, *Verfassung und Verwaltung* (1941), "Reform des BGB," 425 ff.; Lange, "Wesen und Gestalt des Volksgesetzbuches" (1943), 208 ff., 223 ff., also 234 ff., 252 ff.

4. More details in Lange, "Wesen und Gestalt des Volksgesetzbuches," 208 ff.; Lange, "Die Arbeiten der Akademie für Deutsches Recht an der Erneuerung des bürgerlichen Rechts" (1939); Lange, "Einzelgesetze oder Gesetzeseinheit" (1939); on the reform status, H. Frank, *ZAKfDtRecht* (1939): 262; Hedemann, "Wert der Entwürfe" (1943); see also the academy's official material: Hedemann, Lehmann, Siebert, "Volksgesetzbuch, Grundregeln und Buch I," *Arbeitsberichte der*

Akademie für deutsches Recht (1942), no. 22; Hedemann, *Das Volksgesetzbuch der Deutschen,* special issue of *Arbeitsberichte der Akademie für deutsches Recht* (1941). The work was begun in 1936; the Reich Ministry of Justice was also working on a reform of the German Civil Code, but it published only small amendments (see also note 8 below).

5. Schlegelberger, *Abschied vom BGB* (1937).

6. See Reich Labor Court, *JW* (1936): 2945; Reich Disciplinary Court, *DVerw.* (1939): 281; Reich Supreme Court, *DJ* (1936): 1941 ff. (1943); RGZ 153, 71; Breslau *Landgericht* (District Court), *DJ* (1935): 413, annotated; Pätzold, *DJ* (1935): (414); Fraenkel, *Der Doppelstaat* (1974), 102 f., 107 ff., with further references; see also H. Frank, *Rechtsgrundlegung des nationalsozialistischen Führerstaats* (Munich, 1938), 21.

7. For example, the decree dated September 19, 1939 (*RGBl.* I 1956); Simplification Decrees of September 1, 1939 (*RGBl.* I 1658), September 18, 1940 (*RGBl.* I 1253), May 16, 1942 (*RGBl.* I 333), and January 12, 1943 (*RGBl.* I 7); also the War Measures Decrees of May 12, 1943 (*RGBl.* I 290), and September 27, 1944 (*RGBl.* I 229).

8. Marriage Law of July 6, 1938 (*RGBl.* I 807). Testament Law of July 31, 1938 (*RGBl.* I 973); see especially the preamble. The Law of Entail of September 29, 1933 (*RGBl.* I 685), with the Decree of Entail of December 21, 1936 (*RGBl.* I 1069). Law on the Regulation of National Labor of January 20, 1934 (*RGBl.* I 7); Law on the Regulation of the Forced Labor Service of May 15, 1934 (*RGBl.* I 381); Decree on the German Labor Front of October 24, 1934 (*Dokumente der deutschen Politik,* 5:187). Decree of June 25, 1938, on Wage Structure issued by the administrator of the Four Year Plan (Wage Freeze Decree, *RGBl.* I 691); Decree of October 3, 1941, on the Employment of Jews (*RGBl.* I 675), with executive decree of October 31, 1941 (*RGBl.* I 681); Führer Decree of March 21, 1942, on the Appointment of a Plenipotentiary for the Forced Labor Service (*RGBl.* I 179); directives issued by the plenipotentiary for the Forced Labor Service dated July 1, 1940; July 20, August 22, November 27, 1942 (quoted in Melies, *Das Arbeitsrecht des GG* [1943], 13 ff.). More details on labor legislation reform in Siebert, *Die Deutsche Arbeitsverfassung* (1942); Siebert, "Die Entwicklung der staatlichen Arbeitsverwaltung," in *Reich-Volksordnung-Lebensraum* (1942). Regarding the changes, see also Altstötter, "Die nationalsozialistische Rechtserneuerung" (1943); Volkmar, "Die Arbeiten der Abteilung IV" (1939); Regarding the changes in procedural law, see the ZPO amendment of October 27, 1933 (*RGBl.* I 780), and in more detail Volkmar, "Die Neugestaltung des Zivilrechts," in Frank, *Nationalsozialistisches Handbuch für Recht und Gesetzgebung* (1934); A. Schönke, "Einige Grundlinien der Entwicklung des Zivilprozessrechts seit 1933"; Weinkauff and Wagner, *Die deutsche Justiz,* 308. Enumerations of all changes up to 1939 in Sauer, *Das Reichsjustizministerium* (1939), 23.

9. More details in Rüthers, *Die unbegrenzte Auslegung* (1973); Grunsky, "Gesetzesauslegung durch die Zivilgerichte im Dritten Reich" (1969).

10. Tax Adjustment Law, sec. 1, October 16, 1934 (*RGBl.* I 925).

11. See Böhmer, "Die 'Guten Sitten' im Zeichen nationalsozialistischer Familienpflicht" (1941); and the Reich Supreme Court decisions of September 17, 19, 1940, cited there (84 f.).

12. Published by the League of National Socialist German Jurists Press and Periodicals Office, Berlin, 1933, Principle 4.

13. See Rüthers, *Die unbegrenzte Auslegung,* 210 ff., 145 ff.; Maus, *Bürgerliche Rechtstheorie und Faschismus* (1976), 146.

14. H. Lange, *Liberalismus, Nationalsozialismus und bürgerliches Recht* (Tübingen, 1933), 5.

15. Annotation to the judgment by the Breslau District Court, October 20, 1933, *DJ* (1933): 662.

16. See note 4 above.

17. More details in particular in Lange, "Wesen und Gestalt des Volksgesetzbuches" (1943), 232.

18. More details in B. Rüthers, *Die unbegrenzte Auslegung,* secs. 12 – 17.

19. K. Michaelis, "Ständische Ehrengerichtsbarkeit," *DR* (1935): 572. This had nothing to do

with the Independent States Law of earlier times; see Maus, *Bürgerliche Rechtstheorie und Faschismus*, 140 f., for more details.

20. Wieacker, "Der Stand der Rechtserneuerung" (1937). In this connection see also Maus, *Bürgerliche Rechtstheorie und Faschismus*, 136 ff., 140 f.; Weinkauff and Wagner, *Die deutsche Justiz*, 223 ff; Schorn, *Die Gesetzgebung des Nationalsozialismus als Mittel der Machtpolitik* (1963), 19.

Part Two. Section 1. B. II. The Principle of *Völkisch* Inequality in the Domain of Substantive Law

1. Naumburg Court of Appeal, April 20, 1937, *ZAKfDRecht* (1937): 539; see also the Reich Supreme Court decision of November 23, 1937, on the question of contestation of paternity, which under the terms of the German Civil Code could only be brought within one year of the child's birth and ran counter to the family concept of the National Socialists (RGZ 152, 390 ff., 395).

2. See Adami, "Das Kündigungsrecht wegen eines jüdischen Mieters" (1938); and the declaration by the Reich Ministry of Justice in *DJ* (1939): 175.

3. *JW* (1938): 3242.

4. Reich Supreme Court, November 2, 1936, *JW* (1937): 99 f.; in a discussion in *ZAKfDRecht* (1937): 119, the expert at the Reich Ministry of Justice, Maßfeller, contended that there was no more to be said, since "no other decision was possible." A similar instance is the decision of August 12, 1936, by the Berlin *Amtsgericht* (Municipal Court), quoted by Fraenkel, *Der Doppelstaat* (1974), 117.

5. *Land* Labor Court, Düsseldorf, judgment of July 7, 1939, *Deutsches Gemein- und Wirtschaftsrecht* (1939), 194, quoted by Rüthers, *Die unbegrenzte Auslegung*, 188.

6. "Given that point 6 of the screenplay contract . . . refers to the fact that [a right of withdrawal is agreed if] C. is prevented from undertaking his function as director on account of illness, death, or similar causes, a change in the legal standing of the person based on legally recognized politico-racial considerations should unhesitatingly be given equal weight, provided that it prevents performance of the director's function in a manner similar to that in which *death* or *illness* would have done" (my emphasis). (Under the contract between the plaintiff, a Swiss film company, and the defendant, the German film company UFA, a screenplay by C., a Jewish film director, was to be made available to UFA, for a film that C. was also to direct.)

7. Cologne Municipal Court, December 21, 1936, and Halberstadt Municipal Court, June 16, 1937, *DJ* (1937): 1192 f.

8. Wanne-Eickel Municipal Court, May 5, 1936, *DJ* (1936): 936 f.

9. Mainz Municipal Court, May 27, 1936, *DJ* (1936): 1017 f.

10. Jena Municipal Court, September 14, 1937, *DJ* (1937): 3306.

11. Nürnberg-Fürth District Court, March 21, 1938 (Az. 4013/38), *DJ* (1938): 905 ff.

12. Worms Municipal Court, November 16, 1939, *DR* (1940) (A): 295.

13. Reich Labor Court, September 22, 1937, *DJ* (1937): 1989 ff.

14. Reich Supreme Court, February 16, 1934, *JW* (1934): 1963 f.; guiding principle: for the important grounds to be accepted, the evolution of the government's standpoint as regards the treatment of non-Aryan firms with respect to the granting of contracts, the fact that the non-Aryan party was not active in the war, and, finally, that the party giving notice is also a non-Aryan, is of legal significance.

15. German Court of Appeal, Prague, September 2, 1941, *DR* (1942) (A): 394 f.

16. Breslau (Wrocław) District Court, October 20, 1933, *DJ* (1933): 662 f.; the statutes of the association prevented it from appointing another director; the Breslau Municipal Court had refused the commissar nominated on the grounds of "not being a member"; the court of appeal allowed the claim.

17. Annotation to the judgment of October 20, 1933, by the Breslau District Court, ibid.

(anon.) (see part 2, section 1, B, I. "Main Elements of the Transformation of Civil Law on an Ethnic Basis," note 15 above).

18. Reich Supreme Court, April 16, 1942, HRR 1942, 529.

19. Bad-Sübre Municipal Court, July 8, 1935, *JW* (1935): 2309 (under sec. 110f the Civil Status Law, old version, the registrar was *obliged* to receive the application if there was no obstacle to the intended marriage).

20. Sec. 45 of the Civil Status Law of November 3, 1937 (*RGBl.* I 1146), in conjunction with the first implementing regulation of May 19, 1938 (*RGBl.* I 533); an immediate appeal by the supervisory authority (lower administrative authority, higher administrative authority, Reich Ministry of the Interior) against such an instruction by the Municipal Court was permitted under sec. 49.

21. Königsberg District Court, East Prussia, August 26, 1935 (Az. 3 T 687/35), *DJ* (1935): 1387 f.

22. Decision of November 2, 1936, *JW* (1937): 98 f.

23. Reich Supreme Court, November 2, 1936, RGZ 152, 301,

24. *RGBl.* I 1146.

25. Regarding the term *Jew*, see sec. 1, par. 3, of the Implementing Regulation of November 14, 1935, to the Law for the Protection of German Blood and German Honor (*RGBl.* I 1334) and sec. 5 of the First Decree of November 14, 1935, to the Reich Citizenship Law (*RGBl.* I 1333); further details in Palandt, *Bürgerliches Gesetzbuch* (1942), appendixes 1 and 2 on Marriage Law 4, note 1 on sec. 3 of the implementing regulation, 2009 f., and note 1 on sec. 4 of the implementing regulation. See sec. 6 of the implementing regulation; this referred to undesirable "blood mixtures," such as marriage with "Gypsies, Negroes, and their *Mischlinge*"; previously contracted marriages remained valid, however; petitions to annul marriages were possible under secs. 37 and 38 of the Marriage Law (ibid., note 1 on sec. 6 of the implementing regulation, 2012).

26. Reich Supreme Court, February 18, 1937, *DJ* (1937): 589 f.

27. *RGBl.* I 807.

28. See Mössmer, "Neugestaltung des deutschen Ehescheidungsrechts" (1936).

29. See full details in Fauck, "Behandlung von deutsch-jüdischen Mischehen."

30. In the departments of the Reich Ministry of the Interior and other agencies responsible for race matters, there certainly was a later intention to dissolve all "*mixed marriages*" by new legislation, a plan whose execution was probably prevented only by the advent of the war (minutes of a discussion on March 6, 1942, at the RSHA, Nuremberg Doc. ND-2586; excerpts in Poliakov and Wulf, *Das Dritte Reich und die Juden* [1961], 383 f.).

31. Cf. Mössmer, "Rassenmischehe und geltendes Recht" (1934), which reports numerous court decisions; Maßfeller, "Grundsätze der Erb- und Rassenpflege" (1935); Olczewski, "Rassengebundene Rechtsprechung" (1941).

32. Sec. 37 of the Marriage Law stated: "(1) One of the marriage partners can apply for annulment of the marriage if he had been mistaken about such *circumstances* relating to the person of the other partner . . . [sec. 1333, German Civil Code: 'such *characteristics* relating to the person of the other partner' (my emphasis)] that, given a knowledge of the facts and in the event of correct (sec. 1333, German Civil Code: 'reasonable') appreciation of the nature of the marriage, would have prevented him from contracting the marriage. (2) Annulment is excluded if, after discovery of the mistake, the partner has given to understand that he wishes to maintain the marriage, or if his request to annul the marriage is not morally justified in the light of the previous nature of the married life of the partners."

33. *DJ* (1938): 1107. Palandt, *Bürgerliches Gesetzbuch* (see note 25 above), notes 4 and 5 on sec. 37 of the Marriage Law, with reference to RGZ 1958, 275; in contrast to the interpretation of sec. 1333 of the German Civil Code, relating to the individuals affected, the emphasis was now placed more "on generally valid moral and *völkisch* standpoints rather than on rational considerations re-

lating to the interests of the individual case." The "circumstances relating to the person of the other partner" included race.

34. Wiesbaden District Court, March 27, 1935, *JW* (1935): 3127.

35. Reich Supreme Court, decision of November 2, 1933, *DJ* (1933): 818 f.; Reich Supreme Court, July 12, 1934, RGZ 145, 1 (or *JW* [1934]: 2613 f.).

36. Reich Supreme Court, April 29, 1937, *JW* (1937): 901; see also Reich Supreme Court, April 20, 1936, *JW* (1936): 1958, Ziff. 17, Karlsruhe Court of Appeal, March 2, 1934, *JW* (1934): 1371; Cologne District Court, quoted in Prussian Supreme Court, Berlin, *DJ* (1933): 818 f.; Celle Court of Appeal, *DJ* (1935): 573.

37. See, for example, the judgment of the Karlsruhe Court of Appeal, *JW* (1934): 1371; Prussian Supreme Court, Berlin, December 2, 1933, *DJ* (1934): 134; see also Wöhrmann, "Die Auflösung der Ehe zwischen Juden und Ariern" (1933); Palandt, *Bürgerliches Gesetzbuch* (1942), notes 5 and 8 on sec. 37 of the Marriage Law, catchword "Rasse," with further references.

38. Palandt, *Bürgerliches Gesetzbuch*, note 8 on sec. 37 of the Marriage Law; Prussian Supreme Court, Berlin, December 2, 1933, *DJ* (1934): 134.

39. Reich Supreme Court, April 17, 1939, RGZ 160, 146.

40. Reich Supreme Court, March 23, 1939, RGZ 160, 41.

41. Reich Supreme Court, July 12, 1934, RGZ 145, 1 ("Therefore, so long as the provision under sec. 1333 BGB is not amended—retroactively—there can be no objection to mixed marriages").

42. *RGBl.* I 175.

43. Prussian Supreme Court, Berlin, July 12, 1934, 134; for this reason nullification was no longer possible after April 7, 1934.

44. Nuremberg Court of Appeal, *DR* (1940): 33.

45. Sec. 1337, par. 2, German Civil Code. A forfeiture was not taken for granted and an application for divorce was permitted if married life had taken place in a period "when a petition for divorce . . . still had no likelihood of success" (i.e., the Weimar period) (Celle Court of Appeal, November 5, 1934, *DJ* [1935]: 573 f.), whereas continuation of a "mixed marriage" after January 30, 1933 with knowledge of the racial characteristic served as a reason for forfeiture (RGZ 145, 8 f.; Maßfeller, note on Prussian Supreme Court, February 8, 1934, *DJ* [1934]: 395 f.).

46. Breslau Court of Appeal, September 8, 1942, *DR* (1943) (A): 84.

47. Decision of June 5, 1935, quoted in Fraenkel, *Der Doppelstaat*, 82.

48. Decision of May 4, 1937, *DR* (1937): 466; see also Breslau Special Court, *DRiZ* (1935): no. 554, which sentenced a Catholic priest who warned a mother not to send her child to the year in the country, since the children lost their faith there, to six months' imprisonment for malicious attacks against the government.

49. Decision of April 15, 1935, *Das Recht* (1935): no. 8016.

50. Decision of February 26, 1938, *JW* (1938): 1264.

51. Decision of April 15, 1935, *Das Recht* (1935): no. 8016.

52. Berlin District Court, May 14, 1934, *JW* (1934): 1516 f.

53. Dresden Court of Appeal, January 29, 1936, *DJ* (1936): 692.

54. Prussian Supreme Court, Berlin, decision of May 22, 1936, *JW* (1936): 2562.

55. Prussian Supreme Court, Berlin, decision of August 7, 1936, *JW* (1936): 3065 f.; Prussian Supreme Court, decision of April 17, 1936, *JW* (1936): 1998.

56. Dresden District Court, decision of December 19, 1935, *JW* (1936): 286 f.

57. Torgau District Court, November 27, 1935, *DJ* (1936): 1092.

58. Berlin Municipal Court, August 12, 1936, *Zentralblatt für Jugendrecht und Jugendwohlfahrt* (1936): 283, quoted in Fraenkel, *Der Doppelstaat*, 177.

59. Prussian Supreme Court, Berlin, August 7, 1936, *JW* (1936): 3065 f.

60. Prussian Supreme Court, Berlin, January 31, 1936, *DJ* (1936): 522.

61. Decision of July 16, 1935, *JW* (1935): 2762 f.

62. Breslau Court of Appeal, September 27, 1940, HRR 1941, 320.

63. Reich Supreme Court, November 23, 1936, RGZ 152, 390.

64. Reich Supreme Court—Fourth Civil Senate—judgment of July 13, 1940, *DR* (1940) (A): 1960 ff.

65. Administrative instructions issued by the Reich Ministry of Justice, May 24, 1941, *DJ* (1941): 629; and July 15, 1942, *DJ* (1942): 489.

66. Berlin District Court, May 20, 1936, *JW* (1936): 2010.

67. Zwickau District Court, February 25, 1938, *DJ* (1938): 909 f.

68. Reich Supreme Court—Fourth Senate—February 11, 1935, 824 (also RGZ 147, 65).

69. Prussian Supreme Court, Berlin, November 23, 1934, *DJ* (1935): 786 f. In the case in point, an assistant judge was designated as guardian of the children of a pharmacist living with their mother. The father's application for dismissal of the guardian was successful, since the latter was non-Aryan.

70. Prussian Supreme Court, Berlin, August 29, 1941, HRR 1942, no. 99 (also *DR* [1942] [A]: 2564 f.).

71. Hamburg District Court, decision of November 9, 1936, *JW* (1937): 338.

72. Prussian Supreme Court, Berlin (see note 70).

73. Reich Supreme Court, *JW* (1936): 100; the Reich Ministry of the Interior decree of August 6, 1937, instructed the competent authorities to refuse to confirm adoption contracts if one of the parties was of non-Aryan descent (*MinbliV* [1937]: 1345). Dresden District Court, December 19, 1935, *JW* (1936): 286 f.

74. Cf. Himmler's memorandum, "Some Thoughts on the Treatment of Aliens in Eastern Europe," of May 15, 1940 (reproduced in *VjhZ* [1957]: 194 ff.): plans included an annual racial investigation of Polish children in the General Government aged between 6 and 10 years, importation of children "selected as valuable" into the Reich, and attendance at German primary school, with the decision after four years whether the child should continue at primary school or be transferred to a national political education establishment. The memorandum apparently takes up ideas that had been presented in the memorandum of November 25, 1939, by the NSDAP Race Policy Office on the question of the treatment of the populations of the former Polish territories (Nuremberg doc. NO-3734).

75. Himmler's speech of October 14, 1943 (Nuremberg doc. PS-1919).

76. There is proof of Germanization actions in the occupied territories of Croatia, Slovenia, Russia, Ukraine, Czechoslovakia, Estonia, Lithuania, Romania, and Norway (Sosnowski, *The Tragedy of Children under Nazi Rule* [1952], 50; similarly, the affidavits of August 9, 1947, by M. M. Heinze-Wisswede in Nuremberg, Nuremberg doc. NO-4822; G. Küster, undated, Nuremberg doc. NO-4820; and K. Schafhauser, undated, Nuremberg docs. NO-5003 and 5004 [reproduced as appendixes 23-25 in Sosnowski, *The Tragedy of Children under Nazi Rule*, 394 ff.]); regarding the Germanization of children of Czechs executed following a drumhead court-martial, see the secret communication of June 13, 1944, from the German state minister for Bohemia and Moravia (personal) to the RFSS/Personal Staff (Nuremberg doc. PS-435).

77. For example, the plan of the so-called *Heuaktion* (hay action). In this connection, see the memorandum of April 12, 1944, from the head of the RFSS Political Staff headquarters—personnel policy adviser—(secret Reich business), whereby the *Heeresgruppe Mitte* intended to bring 40,000 to 50,000 adolescents from the Occupied Eastern Territories into the Reich, since they presented too much of a burden and strengthened the military potential of the enemy. A similar operation was reported as being undertaken at the time in the area of the *Heeresgruppe Ukraine-Nord*, in the course of which all youths over 17 years of age were to be detailed to the SS-*Division* and those un-

der 17 years to the SS-*Hilfsaktion* (SS Relief Campaign) (Nuremberg doc. PS-031; also as appendix 22 in Sosnowski, *The Tragedy of Children under Nazi Rule,* 392 f.). See also the RFSS order of May 20, 1944 to SS-*Obergruppenführer* Phleps, to round up "alien" orphans throughout the Balkans and to send them into the Reich territory, so that "the Croatian State . . . gets back decent people and valuable citizens" (as is noted at the bottom, the letter originally contained the following addition: "While the Reich has in them loyal followers of the Führer and future soldiers of the old defense border of the Reich") (Nuremberg doc. NO-2218, 4000).

78. *RGBl.* I 118.

79. Based on RFSS/RFK directive 67/I of February 19, 1942, under which Polish children living in Polish orphanages in the Warthegau who were judged "capable of Germanization" (even if the parents did not wish to be included in the German Ethnic Classification List), were to be brought into the Altreich and there to be put into "German state boarding schools" (*Deutsche Heimschulen*) (6–12 years), or if aged 2–6 years to be taken care of by SS families designated by the "*Lebensborn e. V.*" with a view to subsequent adoption (Nuremberg doc. NO-1615; also as an appendix in Sosnowski, *The Tragedy of Children under Nazi Rule,* 375 ff.); see also the affidavit by Dr. E. Schulz, undated (Nuremberg doc. NO-5235). A note dated February 12, 1944, from the head of the Central Settlement Office to the head of the SS Race Bureau to the effect that the RFSS "hopes for a special educative effect" when taking children away from Poles who were reluctant to have their names in the German Ethnic Classification List (Nuremberg doc. NO-1404)—more details in Sosnowski, *The Tragedy of Children under Nazi Rule,* 49 ff.

80. Communication dated June 18, 1941, from the RFSS/RFK to the Reich governor of the Wartheland, in which Himmler pressed for the campaign to be started (reproduced as appendix 7 in Sosnowski, *The Tragedy of Children under Nazi Rule,* 372 f.).

81. Communications dated May 14, 1940, from the Reich Commissar for the Strengthening of German Nationhood to the head of the Security Police (Nuremberg doc. NO-1680); and October 9, 1942, to the Gauleiter and Reich governor of Upper Danube (Nuremberg doc. NO-5007). Communication dated September 17, 1942, from the head of the Central Settlement Office to all higher SS and police leaders, quoted by Sosnowski, *The Tragedy of Children under Nazi Rule,* 50.

82. Directive no. 67/I of February 19, 1942, by the Reich Commissar for the Strengthening of German Nationhood (Nuremberg doc. NO-1615); their status under the law was the same as that of German Reich children; the affidavit by M. Sollmann is in the same vein (Nuremberg doc. NO-4706, undated; also as appendix in Sosnowski, *The Tragedy of Children under Nazi Rule,* 401).

83. See the letter of April 15, 1944, from the higher SS and police leader, Nuremberg, to the NSDAP *Gauleitung,* Mainfranken (Nuremberg doc. NO-4370; more details in Sosnowski, *The Tragedy of Children under Nazi Rule,* 50 ff.). Letter of August 11, 1943, from the Reich leadership—Head Welfare Office—to the RFSS (Nuremberg doc. NO-4665, also as appendix 44 in Sosnowski, *The Tragedy of Children under Nazi Rule,* 433). Regarding the high mortality among the children of Eastern workers, see also the affidavit by L. Schneider, undated (ibid., 433): under SIPO policy the birth of "racially inferior offspring" of Eastern workers and Poles should be prevented as far as possible. Although abortions were only to be performed on a voluntary basis, they were "nevertheless to be forced in all cases" (Nuremberg Doc. L-8; also as appendix 43 in Sosnowski, *The Tragedy of Children under Nazi Rule,* 432).

84. Communication of October 9, 1942, from the RFSS to the Gauleiter and Reich governor of Upper Danube ("In exceptional cases . . . when the foreigner . . . is particularly inferior . . . I had the child removed during pregnancy") (Nuremberg doc. NO-5007, also as appendix 14 in Sosnowski, *The Tragedy of Children under Nazi Rule,* 383).

85. See also the report of October 6, 1942, from the head of the Race Bureau at the Central Settlement Office (Nuremberg doc. NO-1600; also as appendix 13 in Sosnowski, *The Tragedy of Children under Nazi Rule,* 380 ff.). Confidential report by the NSDAP *Gauleitung* Wartheland—Office

for Nationhood Affairs—"Überblick über die Rückdeutschungsarbeit. Erfahrungen und Anregungen," 1944 (*Doc. Occ.* 4:132; also as appendix 18 in Sosnowski, *The Tragedy of Children under Nazi Rule*, 389); K. Zlukowski, "Zbrodnie niemieckie w Zamojszczyźnie," *Bulletin der Hauptkommission Warschau* 2:44 ff.; see also Sosnowski, *The Tragedy of Children under Nazi Rule*, 62 f. and appendix 29 there (401 ff.).

86. More details in Sosnowski, *The Tragedy of Children under Nazi Rule*, 52 n. 48, with references (212 ff.); R. D. Koehl, *RKFDV. German Resettlement and Population Policy 1939–1943* (Cambridge, Mass., 1957), 220. According to these, the number of "alien" children must have run into the tens of thousands.

87. Directive of February 19, 1942 (no. 67/I), by the Reich Commissar for the Strengthening of German Nationhood (Nuremberg doc. NO-1615), regarding the Germanization action in the *Reichsgau* Wartheland, according to which the RKF made a final decision with the Reich governor of the Wartheland on Germanization, before bringing the child into the Altreich.

88. Such a prohibition was already called for by the memorandum of November 25, 1939, from the NSDAP Office of Racial Affairs (Nuremberg doc. NO-3732), and was probably also applied, since adoption of racially "undesirable" Polish children by Poles would obviously have publicly contradicted the Germanization policy.

89. It may be presumed that the competent guardianship courts were not involved in the appointment of the guardian, since they would have been obliged to undertake research on the origin of the child and the whereabouts of the parents. This would certainly have been conflicted with the purposes of the SS agencies responsible for Germanization.

90. *RGBl.* I 722.

91. *Richterbrief* of June 1, 1943, Ziff. 9. Cf. also the case described in *Richterbrief* no. 5 of February 1, 1943, Ziff. 26 (BA R 22/4002), in which a Jewish testatrix had provided for her husband and his family and had disinherited her children living abroad to the extent that if they were "capable of inheriting" again after ten years, they should inherit as the legal heirs. Although in the first instance the court had not opposed the will, the Reich Supreme Court reversed the original judgment at the demand of the senior public prosecutor at the Reich Supreme Court. In the *Richterbriefe* the will was described as being "in contradiction to the healthy sense of justice of the people" and "truly Jewish" and so declared null and void, because its intention was to preserve the estate for the testatrix's children; their succession, it was stated, was excluded under the terms of the Eleventh Decree of November 25, 1941, implementing the Reich Citizenship Law, since Jews living abroad could no longer inherit German nationality. The point of view of conditional reversionary succession taken by the court of first instance was not upheld.

92. Prussian Supreme Court, Berlin, November 2, 1941, *DJ* (1941): 433 ff. In this case the second, Jewish wife was sole heir. The grandchild from the first marriage successfully contested the will.

93. Leipzig Municipal Court, September 29, 1936, *DJ* (1936): 1579 f.

94. Reich Supreme Court, April 5, 1939, HRR 1939, 826.

95. Reich Supreme Court, November 16, 1937, *DJ* (1939): 309 ff.

96. Reich Supreme Court, January 14, 1937, *DJ* (1937): 402 ff.

97. Reich Supreme Court, September 22, 1938, *JW* (1938): 2972 f.

98. See Adami, "Das Kündigungsrecht wegen eines jüdischen Mieters."

99. Protection of Tenants Law of February 17, 1928 (*RGBl.* I 25), in the version of the law dated April 27 1933 (*RGBl.* I 235); Decree on Protection of Leaseholders of August 28, 1937 (*RGBl.* I 917), with first and second implementing regulations of December 4, 1937 (*RGBl.* I 1325), and August 31, 1938 (*RGBl.* I 1070), respectively.

100. Adami, "Das Kündigungsrecht wegen eines jüdischen Mieters," 3217 f., 3218 f.

101. For eviction by private landlords, see Halle Municipal Court, August 18, 1938, *DJ* (1938):

512; Schönberg Municipal Court, September 16, 1938, *JW* (1938): 3045 f.; and October 18, 1938, *DR* (1938): 512; Berlin District Court, November 7, 1938, *JW* (1938): 3242 f.; Nuremberg Municipal Court, November 26 1938, *JW* (1938): 3243 f.; further judgments in Köhler, "Wohngemeinschaft mit Juden?" (1938). For eviction by public landlords, see Charlottenburg Municipal Court, September 3, 1938, *JW* (1938): 3172 f.

102. Cologne District Court, May 11, 1938, *DJ* (1938): 907 ff.

103. For more details see Köhler, "Wohngemeinschaft mit Juden?" with judicial references.

104. Adami, "Das Kündigungsrecht wegen eines jüdischen Mieters."

105. Decision of August 18, 1938, *DR* (1938): 512. Similarly, Schöneberg Municipal Court, September 16, 1938, *JW* (1938): 3045 f.

106. *JW* (1938): 3242 f.

107. Ibid., 3243 f.

108. Decision of October 18, 1939, *DR* (1938): 512: "No legal provision exists that permits Aryan landlords to give notice to Jewish tenants on account of their racial appartenance."

109. Adami, "Das Kündigungsrecht wegen eines jüdischen Mieters," 3218.

110. Ibid., 3219.

111. Decision of October 1, 1938, quoted in ibid. n. 91.

112. Decision of September 12, 1938, quoted in ibid.

113. Decision of May 6, 1938, quoted in ibid.

114. *RGBl.* I 864; in this connection see Buchwald, "Neugestaltung des Mietrechts" (1938).

115. Prussian Supreme Court, Berlin, June 20, 1940, *DR* (1940) (A): 1577 f. The certificate had "to clearly indicate the assurance (of the accommodation)."

116. Prussian Supreme Court, Berlin, November 9, 1940, *DR* (1940) (A): 2111 f.

117. Decision of November 8, 1939, HRR 1940, 430.

118. Rohlfing, "Rechtsfragen aus der Zugehörigkeit zur jüdischen Rasse" (1933): 2098 ff., with references.

119. Wiesbaden Municipal Court, March 4, 1935, *DJ* (1935): 1038 f.

120. Reich Labor Court, November 25, 1933, *DJ* (1934): 229 f.

121. *RGBl.* I 1580.

122. Leipzig Labor Court, March 3, 1939, *DJ* (1939): 970; Reich Labor Court, January 9, 1940, *DR* (1940) (B): Rechtsprechung p. 62, no. 207.

123. Wuppertal Labor Court, German Labor Front compendium of decisions 1939, 134; *Land* Labor Court, Düsseldorf, ibid., 194, quoted in R. Freisler, "Ein arbeitsrechtlicher Einzelfall," *Deutsches Gemein- und Wirtschaftsrecht* (1940): 265 ff, 268; *Land* Labor Court, Koblenz, *JW* (1940): 87. Reich Labor Court, decision of July 24, 1940, *DJ* (1940): 1035 f.

124. Malz, "Richtertum im nationalsozialistischen Staat" (1941), 2220.

125. Reich Labor Court, *DJ* (1940): 1035 f.

126. *RGBl.* I 681.

127. See part 1, section 1, V, 3 ("Labor Law").

128. Reich Labor Court, February 7, 1940, *DR* (1940) (A): 1326 f.; guiding principle: "For what is to be regarded as right and fair is decided by the sense of justice of the German people inspired by National Socialism, where the concept of race has priority over purely economic considerations. The judge must give weight to this on the foundation of the prevailing law" (sec. 242, German Civil Code).

129. Reich Labor Court, February 7, 1940, *DR* (1940) (A): 1246 f.

130. *RGBl.* I 1580.

131. Reich Labor Court (see note 129).

132. Reich Supreme Court, July 12, 1939, *DJ* (1939): 1666 f.

133. Erlaßsammlung des RMJ, Federal Ministry of Justice, Bonn.

134. Hamburg Court of Appeal, November 27, 1935, *DJ* (1936): 775 f.

135. Prussian Supreme Court, Berlin, November 21, 1935, *JW* (1936): 333 f.

136. Munich Court of Appeal, May 19, 1937, 2417 f.

137. Prussian Supreme Court, Berlin, August 29, 1935, *JW* (1935): 3164.

138. Prussian Supreme Court, Berlin, October 25, 1934, *JW* (1935): 436 ff., for the case of the company name Deutsche Lederindustrie.

139. Berlin District Court, May 15, 1938, *DJ* (1938): 1195 f.

140. Reich Supreme Court, February 9, 1942, *DR* (1942) (A): 1060 f.

141. *RGBl.* I 404.

142. Reich Supreme Court, December 14, 1939, HRR 1940, 476.

143. *RGBl.* I 627; sec. 3: "A business is considered Jewish if it is de facto under the dominating influence of Jews."

144. Reich Supreme Court, April 7, 1941, HRR 1941, 1066.

145. Reich Supreme Court, October 10, 1939, HRR 1940, 276; and May 23, 1939, *DJ* (1939): 1367 ff.

146. *RGBl.* I 1709.

147. A limited company was regarded as a "Jewish firm" even if the Jewish associates were only trustees of an Aryan (Prussian Supreme Court, Berlin, January 25, 1940, HRR 1940 677). The forced liquidation of Jewish businesses was facilitated by the fact that in the bankruptcy of the Jewish owner following compulsory sale, the claims of the liquidator were included in the costs of the administration of the estate, which had to be paid out of the estate in advance (secs. 57, 58, KO) (Berlin District Court, July 6, 1939, *DJ* [1940]: 487 f.). If, as a consequence of the liquidation of a Jewish company, the use of the property rented by it was not possible, the company continued to be responsible as tenant toward the landlord, since the liquidation (or, more precisely, the obstacle to its use) was attributed to grounds "residing in the person of the tenant" (sec. 552, German Civil Code), i.e., in this case the racial characteristic, even if the rented object was destroyed "as a result of the events of the night of November 9, 1938 (*Kristallnacht*)" (Düsseldorf Court of Appeal, October 29, 1940, HRR 1941, 192). Following the decision of the Prussian Supreme Court in Berlin, Jews who were obliged to sell their property under the decree of December 3, 1938, were refused a mortgage for the balance of the purchase (decision of March 16, 1939, *DR* [1939] [B]: 316 f.), or indeed any mortgage at all (sec. 7, par. 1), since Jews could not "acquire real title to German property" (decision of January 18, 1940, HRR 1940, 672). A conveyance registered in the name of a Jew could therefore be canceled on grounds of being "null and void" (sec. 84, Land Register Code) after the decree came into force (decision of February 8, 1940, *DR* [1940] [A]: 648), whereby the rightful owners lost all real safeguards, i.e., under land register law, to their claims.

148. If a Jew permitted registration of a real right to his property, this did not initially require authorization in the view of the Prussian Supreme Court (KG Berlin, May 11, 1939, HRR 1939, 891). In 1943, however, the Supreme Court held that authorization or registration of such a disposition was necessary: the previous decision of May 11, 1939, tacitly supposed that the Jew would remain owner of the property until its subsequent sale; the property may well, however, have come into the hands of the Reich since promulgation of the Eleventh Regulation of November 25, 1941, to the Reich Citizenship Law (*RGBl.* I 722), which ordered the forfeiture of the property of Jews who had emigrated abroad. If by way of a notice in the land register reservation or an option to buy, the Jew favored a third party, registration of the transaction in the land register was ruled to have been in error. All dispositions requiring registration were now subject to official authorization (decision of November 11, 1943, *DR* [1944] [A]: 252).

149. Prussian Supreme Court, Berlin, February 13, 1941, *DR* (1941) (A): 1001 f. (Nießbrauch); February 22, 1940, *DR* (1940) (A): 820; November 9, 1939, *DJ* (1940): 36 f.

150. Prussian Supreme Court, Berlin, May 23, 1941, *DR* (1941) (A): 2132 f. (under sec. 868 ZPO

the owner of the property acquired the judicial mortgage if the decision was annulled or its execution was declared inadmissible or an order for distraint was issued).

151. Prussian Supreme Court, Berlin, May 4, 1939, HRR 1939, 892.

Part Two. Section 1. B. III. Discriminatory Principles in Procedural Law

1. Volkmar, "Die Neugestaltung des Zivilprozeßrechts" (1934), 1498 ff. For the development of civil procedural law under the Civil Code in the National Socialist period, see A. Schönke, "Einige Grundlinien der Entwicklung des Zivilprozessrechts seit 1933" (1943); in particular, Schönke emphasizes the increased influence of the "community" concept, the strengthened position of judges, and the increased obligation of the parties to accelerate the process in civil proceedings.

2. Berlin District Court (*Landgericht*), decision of November 10, 1933, *JW* (1934): 442.

3. Berlin District Court, 86th Civil Court Division, decision of February 23, 1934, *JW* (1934): 924.

4. Hanover District Court, June 26, 1934, *JW* (1934): 1684.

5. *RGBl.* I 1524. Under the terms of the Second Decree, official acts taken after November 14, 1935, by those in an official post remained effective even when the official was de jure (i.e., on grounds of race law) no longer in office at that time. Reich Supreme Court, May 16, 1938 (IV 2/38), *JW* (1938): 2018 f.

6. *RGBl.* I 1403.

7. Frankfurt Court of Appeal, May 24, 1934 (3 W 107/34), *JW* (1934): 1509.

8. Hamm Court of Appeal, Seventh Civil Senate, March 23 1935 (7 W 44/35), *JW* (1935): 1446. Also Naumburg Court of Appeal, Fourth Civil Senate, decision of July 5, 1935 (4 W 195/35), *JW* (1935): 2216; Frankfurt am Main Court of Appeal, decision of May 24, 1934 (3 W 107/34), *JW* (1934): 1509.

9. Naumburg Court of Appeal, Fourth Civil Senate, decision of July 5, 1935 (4 W 194/35), *JW* (1935): 2216.

10. Dresden District Court, Eighteenth Civil Court Division, decision of March 8, 1937 (18 T 250/37), *JW* (1937): 1650 f.

11. Under sec. 157, ZPO, proxies and legal advisers professionally involved in foreign legal matters, with the exception of lawyers, were not permitted in oral hearings.

12. Charlottenburg *Amtsgericht* (Municipal Court), decision of May 17, 1935 (48 C 682/35), *JW* (1935): 1729.

13. Sec. 90, par. 1, ZPO: "Insofar as representation by lawyers is not required, a party may appear with any person as adviser who is legally entitled to appear in court."

14. Under the then valid version of sec. 91, par. 2, subpar. 2, ZPO, the fees of multiple lawyers were "refundable only insofar as they did not exceed the fees of a single lawyer, or if a change of lawyer was necessary." Prussian Supreme Court, Berlin, Twentieth Civil Senate, decision of November 18, 1933 (20 W 8932/33), *JW* (1933): 2778 f.

15. Decision of February 27, 1933 (101 T 135/33), *DJ* (1933): 612.

16. Decision of December 6, 1933 (101 T 208/33), *DJ* (1933): 30 f.

17. Berlin Labor Court, June 20, 1933 (9 10 A C 527/33), *JW* (1933): 1794; Magdeburg Labor Court, August 1, 1936 (5 CA 170/36), *JW* (1937): 275 f.

18. SD-Bericht zu Inlandsfragen, November 1941 to December 1943, Bl. 215 ff.

19. Reich Supreme Court decision, April 19, 1941 (VII A 75/40, VII 13/40), *DR* (1941) (A): 1994 f.

20. Situation report of May 1, 1942, from the presiding judges of the Court of Appeal, Hamburg ("the courts of first instance refuse to grant legal aid to Jews. In one such case the district court reversed a decision"; quoted in Steiniger and Leszczyński, *Das Urteil im Juristenprozeß* [1969], 238).

21. In a speech to judges of the Hamburg Court of First Instance, the presiding judge of the court stated that legal aid for Jews should be limited as far as possible (minutes of meeting, Nuremburg doc. NG-632 [Ziff. 11]).

22. Situation report of May 1, 1942, by the presiding judge of the Hamburg Court of Appeal (see note 20 above).

23. Nuremburg doc. NG-589, 151.

24. Speech, quoted without date in Steiniger and Leszczyński, *Das Urteil im Juristenprozeß*, 237.

25. Minutes of meeting (BA R 22/4200); statements by *Ministerialrat* Grau, Reich Ministry of Justice.

26. Berlin District Court, decision of May 10, 1939 (201 T 3531/33), *JW* (1933): 1275.

27. *RGBl.* I 302.

28. Berlin District Court, March 15, 1940 (20 T 1556/40), *DJ* (1940): 656 f.

29. *RGBl.* I 1234.

30. Schöneberg Municipal Court, decision of October 11, 1938 (61 M 3660/38), *JW* (1938): 3063.

31. Altona District Court, decision of November 16, 1936 (7 T 5/36), *JW* (1936): 1393 f.

32. Schöneberg Municipal Court, decision of March 22, 1938 (8 M 1885/38), *JW* (1938): 1917.

33. Schöneberg Municipal Court, decision of September 3, 1938 (60 M 1075/38), *JW* (1938): 2910.

34. *SD-Bericht zu Inlandsfragen,* November 1941 to December 1943, Bl. 215 ff., referring to the alleged opinion of "national comrades" and "jurists" that a "general cleaning up of Jewish entries in the land register" was desirable "in order to simplify real estate transactions."

Part Two. Section 2. Introduction

Nazi laws in the occupied territories often had no sections, only "numbers." This was done on purpose, to show that these territories were of juridically minor status and not worthy of the "gift" of normal German rules, not even of the outfit. It is therefore important to show this disdain in the quoting of the regulations. Sections and paragraphs indicate normal leegal status; numbers indicate something much more inferior. The reader not familiar with details will see, in the manner of quoting the German original exactly, the trace of discriminatory law.

1. *RGBl.* I 2042.

2. Figures compiled and published for official use only in *Das Deutsche Reich und das GG der besetzten polnischen Gebiete in statistischen Angaben* (Berlin: Publikationsstelle Berlin-Dahlem [government's own imprint], 1940).

3. Cf. Huber, *Verfassungsrecht des Großdeutschen Reiches* (1939), 181.

4. Figures from the memorandum of November 25, 1939, from the Race Policy Office of the NSDAP (Nuremberg doc. NO-3732, 6; reproduced in *Doc. Occ.* 5:2 ff., 8); these concur with Reich Ministry of the Interior data transmitted confidentially to the Supreme Reich Authorities on November 13, 1939 (Geheimes Staatsarchiv Berlin-Dahlem, State Secretary Pfundtner, Rep.; 320/125). The absolute figures show minor variations among the different sources.

5. According to the memorandum referred to in note 4, there were 3.6 million Poles (85.1%), 323,000 Jews (7.6%), and 309,000 Germans (7.3%) living in the Wartheland as of fall 1939.

6. The extermination campaigns carried out by the *Einsatzgruppen* (special operations squads) of the SIPO began in the very first days of the war; more details in Adam, *Judenpolitik im Dritten Reich* (1972), 247 ff. By 1940 the Jewish population had already been almost completely deported from the Annexed Eastern Territories or concentrated in the ghetto of Łódź, which was administered exclusively by the SS and the police; more details in Broszat, *Nationalsozialistische Polenpolitik* (1961), 68 f.; a number of Jews in the Wartheland (especially the eastern part) lived under

close surveillance in ghettos without walls until spring 1942; see Hohenstein, *Wartheländisches Tagebuch* (1963), 144 f., 214 f., 233.

7. See the memorandum of November 25, 1939, by the Race Policy Office of the NSDAP (see note 4 above); also the secret report dated January 1940 by the Academy for German Law, "Rechtsgestaltung deutscher Polenpolitik nach volkspolitischen Gesichtspunkten" (Nuremberg doc. PS-661; IMT XXVI, 206 ff., 208, 210 f.). Full details can be found in Greiser, *Der Aufbau im Osten* (1942), in which the Gauleiter of the Wartheland boasts of a future "German East."

8. Summary in Huber, *Verfassungsrecht des Großdeutschen Reiches* (1939), 181 ff.; and Blau, *Das Ausnahmerecht für die Juden in Deutschland* (1965).

9. See, e.g., the statements by the Reich minister of justice in *Richterbriefe* nos. 19 and 26 (BA R 22/4002).

10. Tautphaeus, "Der Richter im Reichsgau Wartheland" (1941).

11. On the illegality of the treatment of the Polish population under international law, especially in the field of penal law, see Steiniger and Leszczyński, *Das Urteil im Juristenprozeß*, 64 ff.

12. See the statements by Reich Minister of Justice Thierack on the position of judges and the public prosecutor on the occasion of the inauguration of a new chief public prosecutor (Steinberg) in Posen (Poznań). According to Thierack, the public saw the judge as the person responsible for the administration of justice. His job was to make judicial decisions, and therefore he needed freedom of judgment. His standing in the judicial establishment was based on the fact that he drew his authority from the power of the Führer as supreme judge of the nation. Thus, only the Führer could hand down directives to a judge, who furthermore was answerable only to his conscience (*Ostdeutscher Beobachter*, January 13, 1944, 1–2).

13. Speech in February 1942 on the duties of the public prosecutor in the Warthegau (*DJ* [1942]: 188); similarly, Tautphaeus, "Der Richter im Reichsgau Wartheland," 1941, 2467.

14. Speech by the Reich governor of the Wartheland, A. Greiser, before the presiding judges of the courts of appeal and special courts and members of the Posen Court of Appeal (*DJ* [1942]: 532; undated, presumably August 1942).

15. Report on a meeting of the attorneys general and prison directors of the Wartheland, *Ostdeutscher Beobachter*, July 25, 1943, 5.

16. Chief public prosecutor, Posen, *DJ* (1942): 188.

17. Chief public prosecutor, Posen, *Ostdeutscher Beobachter*, June 24, 1940.

18. Froböß, "Zwei Jahre Justiz im Warthegau" (1941).

19. Speech by R. Freisler on the occasion of the inauguration of the presiding judge of the court of appeal (Block) and the chief public prosecutor (Dr. Steimer) on June 12, 1941, in the new court of appeal district of Kattowitz (Katowice), *DJ* (1941): 716 f.

20. The Warthegau was described by the presiding judge of the Posen Court of Appeal, for example, as the "*Gau* of the soldiers on the front" (*Ostdeutscher Beobachter*, January 13, 1944, 1).

21. Statements by Reich Minister of Justice Thierack on the occasion of the inauguration of Chief Public Prosecutor Steinberg in Posen (*Ostdeutscher Beobachter*, January 13, 1944, 1–2). In his situation report of January 8, 1941, the presiding judge of the Danzig (Gdańsk) Court of Appeal recommended that judges from the East be used in the Annexed Eastern Territories as far as possible in order to avoid passing overly lenient judgments on Poles. Anyone "who has grown up in the national-racial struggle in the East knows better than the judges of the Altreich that Poles are to be treated differently from Germans" (BA R 22/3360). (On account of a shortage of law officers, however, the majority of judges and public prosecutors did come from the Altreich.) The careers of the senior judiciary certainly largely followed these ideas. The presiding judge of the court of appeal and the chief public prosecutor of Danzig; the presiding judge of the Königsberg Court of Appeal, who was also responsible for the Zichenau District Court (*Landgericht*); and the chief public prosecutor of Königsberg and the presiding judge of the Posen Court of Appeal all had several years or even

decades of "Eastern experience" in the administration and judiciary (more details in *Handbuch der Justizverwaltung* [1942]; regarding the presiding judge of the Posen Court of Appeal, see also the *Ostdeutscher Beobachter* of April 3, 1942; Fröboß personal files, State Archive Poznań, OLG [State Superior Court] Posen, 264, 265; and report on the inauguration in *DJ* [1940]: 409 f., R. Freisler, *DJ* [1940]: II, 1125 ff.) and were considered radical "stalwarts of the national-racial struggle." This also goes for the chief public prosecutors of Posen (there were three in all) (see *Ostdeutscher Beobachter*, April 30, 1940, p. 5; June 18, 1940, p. 5; July 29, 1943, p. 3; January 13, 1944). Only the chief public prosecutor of Kattowitz was without "Eastern experience," and he requested transfer to the Reich territory on grounds of health in the spring of 1943, after the Reich Ministry of Justice had already taken steps to transfer him (presumably on account of his critical reports on police practices).

22. According to information by Freisler in *DJ* (1940): II, 1125 ff., 1127, the judges and public prosecutors came from the court of appeal districts of Berlin, Brunswick, Breslau (Wrocław), Celle, Darmstadt, Dresden, Düsseldorf, Frankfurt am Main, Hamburg, Hamm, Kassel, Kiel, Munich, Naumburg, Stettin (Szczecin), and Zweibrücken, plus staff who had worked in Posen before 1918 or had been born in the old province of Posen, and a few "upholders of the law" from Bessarabia and Burgenland. Later the judiciary took on a "whole new look" as a result of the "return of the Baltic Germans" (1130). Personal details and material on the careers and Party-political activity of judges from the Warthegau will be found in the State Archive Poznań—(a) municipal courts: *Signatur Landgericht* Posen (64, 65, 70, 71, 73, 74, 80, 83, 84, 86, 89 et passim; Posen Court of Appeal, 1232, 1143, 1355); (b) district courts: *Signatur Oberlandesgericht* Posen 1286 (regarding the presiding judge of the Kalisch [Kalisz] District Court), 285 (regarding the presiding judge of the Gnesen [Gniezno] District Court), 1352 (regarding the presiding judge of the Leslau District Court), 560 (regarding the presiding judge of the Ostrowo [Ostrów Wielkopolski] District Court), 582 (regarding the presiding judge of the Łódź District Court), 1168 (regarding the presiding judge of the Lissa [Leszno] District Court), 191 (regarding the presiding judge of the Hohensalza [Inowrocław] District Court); also Posen District Court, 78 and *Gauamtsblatt der NSDAP—Gau Wartheland*—1/40, of May 1, 1940, p. 12 (regarding the presiding judge of the Posen District Court). Personnel records of the court of appeal directors from the Warthegau district courts: *Signatur Landgericht* 62, 63, 82, 87; *Oberlandesgericht* Posen 103a; 1204, 1187, 177, 907, 1251, Bl. 1, 5, 83, 90; 414; 405, 663; 865; 1363, 324; 540; 1387; (c) Posen Court of Appeal, *Signatur* Posen Court of Appeal 85 and 1311, 265, Bl. 3.

23. Freisler, "Deutscher Osten" (1941) ("All those who have proved themselves in the East will leave their mark on the judicial practice of the entire Reich. Each one who feels a calling to the higher should therefore pass through this eminent school of responsible constructive work!").

24. Freisler, "Das deutsche Polenstrafrecht" (1941); similarly, Drendel, *DJ* (1942): 188.

25. Full details in von Rosen–von Hoevel, "Das Polenstatut" (1942).

26. See. e.g., art. 2 of the Decree on the Implementation of German Penal Law of June 6, 1940 (*RGBl.* I, 844); secs. 4 and 5 of the Decree on the Administration of Justice in the Eastern Territories of September 25, 1941 (*RGBl.* I, 597 ff.); the Decree on Penal Law for Poles of December 4, 1941 (*RGBl.* I 759).

27. See von Rosen–von Hoevel, "Das Polenstatut," who says: "Although we have not yet finalized a Polish statute book, many special regulations exist for Poles in many legal domains." (Von Rosen–von Hoevel was a *Regierungsrat* in the Reich Ministry of the Interior.)

28. Ibid.

29. See, among many others, the article by Freisler, "Psychische Grundlagen der Polengreuel" (1940).

30. Memorandum of November 25, 1939, from the Race Policy Office of the NSDAP (Nuremberg doc. NO-3732).

31. Drendel, "Aus der Praxis der Strafverfolgung im Warthegau" (1941). (Drendel was chief public prosecutor of Posen.)

32. See notes 24, 29, 31 and 33.

33. Drendel, "Aus der Praxis der Strafverfolgung im Warthegau." See also Pungs, "Die bürgerliche Rechtspflege im Warthegau" (1941) (Pungs was head of the Chamber of the Court of Appeal, Posen); Froböß, "Zwei Jahre Justiz im Warthegau," 2465 (Froböß was presiding judge at the Posen Court of Appeal); Tautphaeus, "Der Richter im Reichsgau Wartheland," 2466 ff. (Tautphaeus was assistant presiding judge at the Posen Court of Appeal); Thiemann, "Anwendung und Fortbildung" (1941) (Thiemann was a public prosecutor in Posen); Fechner, "Das bürgerliche Recht in den eingegliederten Ostgebieten" (1941), 2481 ff., 2482 (Fechner was OLG-Rat [councillor of the State Superior Court] and responsible for the civil law desk at the Reich Ministry of Justice; see letter dated February 8, 1940, from Reich Ministry of Justice to Reich Ministry of the Interior, BA R 43 II/1520).

Part Two. Section 2. A. Stages in the Implementation of *Völkisch* Inequality

1. For more details see Broszat, *Nationalsozialistische Polenpolitik* (1961), 29 ff.

2. Cf. two decrees issued by the commander in chief of the army concerning the establishment of special courts in the occupied Polish territories, September 5, 1939 (*VOBl. Polen*, 2 f.; reproduced in *Doc. Occ.* 5:40 ff., 40). Decree on Possession of Weapons of September 12, 1939 (*VO Bl. Polen*, 32, reproduced in first and second supplementary decrees dated September 21 and October 10, 1939; *VOBl. Polen*, 32, reproduced in *Doc. Occ.* 5:45 ff.); decree of September 10, 1939 (*VOBl. Polen*, 8 f.).

3. *RGBl.* I 2042

4. "News from the Reich," June 27, 1940 (BA R 58/151).

5. Cf. the collection of essays in *DR* (1941) (A): 2465 ff. (see part 2, section 2, introduction, note 33).

6. Tautphaeus, "Richter im Reichsgau Wartheland" (1941).

7. The regulation agreed literally or in general meaning with the existing Führer decrees on the incorporation of territories, according to which the principle of continued validity of local legislation was the rule (cf. art. 2 of the Law on the Reunification of Austria with the German Reich of March 13, 1938, *RGBl.* I 237; decrees issued by the Führer and Reich Chancellor on the incorporation of the Sudetenland and the Protectorate of Bohemia and Moravia of October 1, 1938, *RGBl.* I 1331; and March 16, 1939, *RGBl.* I 485, respectively). In these areas the existing law (usually that of the Austrian statute book) was not fundamentally affected by the incorporation (Fechner, "Das bürgerliche Recht in den eingegliederten Ostgebieten" [1941]; cf. also minutes of a meeting of presiding judges and chief public prosecutors on February 10–11, 1943, in Berlin, BA R 22/4200, 51 ff.). The same is true for the General Government, where—as a matter of principle—Polish law continued to be in effect (sec. 4 of the Decree of the Führer and Reich Chancellor on the Administration of the Occupied Polish Territories, October 12, 1939, *RGBl.* I 2077).

8. Hitler in a speech on July 30, 1932, in Kempten, quoted from Tautphaeus, "Richter im Reichsgau Wartheland"; in this sense see also Buchholz, "Zur Ostrechtspflegeverordnung" (1941); Froböß, "Zwei Jahre Justiz im Warthegau" (1941).

9. Tautphaeus, "Richter im Reichsgau Wartheland"; Froböß, "Zwei Jahre Justiz im Warthegau"; Buchholz and Wolany, "Zum Grundstücksverkehrsrecht in den eingegliederten Ostgebieten" (1941), 682 ff.; Thiemann, "Anwendung und Fortbildung," 2473; Buchholz, "Zur Ostrechtspflegeverordnung," 2477. The reasoning was that international law (art. 43 of the Hague Warfare Convention, according to which, in principle, the law of the occupied territory was to be respected) was not applicable since the Eastern lands were no longer "occupied territory" but an integral part of the Reich (Froböß, "Zwei Jahre Justiz im Warthegau"; Pungs, "Die bürgerliche Rechtspflege im Warthegau" [1941]; see also part 1, section 2, introduction); cf. also verdict of the Supreme People's Court of Poland vs. Artur Greiser, July 9, 1946 ("quod *ab initio turpe* est, non potest tractu temporis

escere"), quoted from a working translation of the ZS (Az. I 110 AR 655/73). Or purely "political" arguments were used: the annulment of Polish law was justified merely on the grounds that "in many instances it had been conceived—or at least had served—as a means of opposing German-ness in the reconquered ('*wiedergewonnene*') territories" (Fechner, "Das bürgerliche Recht in den eingegliederten Ostgebieten"; Buchholz, "Zur Ostrechtspflegeverordnung," 2477); the continuation of Polish law "would have destroyed the political objectives" and would only have been "seen by the Poles themselves as a sign of political weakness and the transience of German domination." There were also practical reasons, such as ignorance of Polish law and the "impossibility" of allowing Pol-ish judges to remain in office (Froböß, "Zwei Jahre Justiz im Warthegau"; Tautphaeus, "Richter im Reichsgau Wartheland").

10. Cf. Spanner, "Fragen der Verwaltung besetzter Gebiete" (1944), 96 ff. (101 ff.), which ex-plains that the occupying power had the right to alter the political system and laws of the occupied territory as it saw fit. If this discretion existed for territories administered according to interna-tional law, it must be all the more valid for territories that—in the German view—were incorpo-rated into the Reich.

11. Tautphaeus (see note 6). See also Buchholz (see note 8), 2477 (exception: cases dealt with under earlier law); Buchholz and Wolany, "Zum Grundstücksverkehrsrecht in den eingegliederten Ostgebieten"; Pungs, "Die bürgerliche Rechtspflege im Warthegau," 2491. The idea of applying Ger-man law did not arise spontaneously but had been prepared for well in advance. As early as 1935, a *Reichsgrenzausschuß* (Reich Border Committee) in the Reich Ministry of the Interior ascertained that, in all newly acquired territories, "only the will of the Reich" was to prevail (minutes of a com-mittee meeting, November 21–22, 1935, BA R 22/5, Bl. 49–51).

12. Froböß, "Zwei Jahre Justiz im Warthegau."

13. Cf., for example, a report by the *Regierungspräsident* of Hohensalza (Inowrocław) dated March 18, 1941, Bl. 17 (Posen University Library), objecting to a verdict of the *Amtsgericht* Dietfurt that commanded a *Volksdeutscher* to return a horse to its Polish owner in accordance with sec. 985 of the Civil Code. The horse had been allocated to the accused after the German invasion. The *Regierungspräsident* explained that this verdict was not an isolated instance. "It was only at my prompting that the *Reichsstatthalter* notified the courts that their standpoint would not be toler-ated." At any rate, "the overarching legal principle that 'justice is what serves the German people as a whole, everything else is injustice' has been completely ignored."

14. Tautphaeus (see note 6).

15. Enke, "Die Rechtspflege im Volkstumskampf" (1941).

16. Tautphaeus, "Richter im Reichsgau Wartheland," 2467.

17. Ibid.

18. Cf. "News from the Reich" (BA R 58/150): "In legal circles there is a desire to see the rapid introduction of German law in the Annexed Eastern Territories."

19. The position of the *Reichgrenzausschuß* in the Reich Ministry of the Interior was stated on November 21–22, 1935, recommending, on grounds of Reich security, that "in all future territorial acquisitions, German law should be introduced in an appropriate degree by legal prescription relat-ing to each specific case" (BA R 22/5).

20. Express letter from Reich Ministry of the Interior (signed by State Secretary Pfundtner) to the Supreme Reich Authorities, November 16, 1939 (BA R 43 II/694).

21. Enke, "Die Rechtspflege im Volkstumskampf," 2489. Enke was, as is apparent from the minutes of a discussion between representatives of the Party Chancellery and the Reich Ministry of Justice held on June 22, 1943, *Oberregierungsrat* in the Party Chancellery (Nuremberg doc. NG-889). His remarks can therefore be considered as representing the official Party line.

22. Fechner, "Das bürgerliche Recht in den eingegliederten Ostgebieten," 2482.

23. A complete list is given in the "Supplement to the Official Gazetteer of the *Reichsstatthal-ter* Wartheland" (IfZ).

24. *RGBl.* I 844.

25. *RGBl.* I 587 ff.

26. See part 1, section 2.

27. *RGBl.* I 759.

Part Two. Section 2. B. I. Principles of Substantive Special Penal Law

1. Drendel, "Aus der Praxis der Strafverfolgung im Warthegau" (1941), 2472.

2. More in R. Freisler, "Ein Jahr Aufbau der Rechtspflege im Reichsgau Wartheland," *DJ* (1940): II, 1125 ff.

3. Drendel, "Aus der Praxis der Strafverfolgung im Warthegau."

4. For details, cf. Klinge, "Bemerkungen zur Begriffsbildung im Polenstrafrecht" (1942), 324 f. (325); Thiemann, "Anwendung und Fortbildung" (1941), 2473.

5. More in Freisler, "Ein Jahr Aufbau der Rechtspflege im Reichsgau Wartheland," 1126.

6. Official Gazetteer of Poland, p. 2 (reproduced in *Doc. Occ.* 5:40 ff., 44).

7. Thiemann, "Anwendung und Fortbildung," 2473.

8. Beurmann, in "Das Sondergericht Danzig," *DR* (1942) (B): 77 ff. (78), also assumes that the decree of September 5, 1939, would continue in force.

9. Drendel, "Aus der Praxis der Strafverfolgung im Warthegau," 2472.

10. Thiemann, "Anwendung und Fortbildung," 2474.

11. *VOBl. Polen*, 24, reproduced in *Doc. Occ.* 5:48; the decree was considered still effective, even after October 26, 1939 (Beurmann, see note 8).

12. Beurmann (see note 8).

13. Letter from the staff of the deputy Führer to the *Gauleitung* Wartheland of the NSDAP, February 24, 1941 (Institute for Western Studies, Poznań, Doc., I-1; unsigned; reproduced in *Doc. Occ.* 5:335).

14. On the same lines, legally binding sentences by Polish courts against *Volksdeutsche* were carried out only in extreme cases; in most cases, they were not carried out because "the motive for the wrongdoing . . . [was] the economic hardship resulting from the political situation of the time" (cf. report of the Reich Ministry of Justice to the deputy Führer on November 28, 1940, BA R 22/848). Regarding the incorporated territories of Silesia, the chief public prosecutor of Breslau (Wrocław) reported that he knew of no "untoward occurrences" (*Unzuträglichkeiten*) resulting from the execution of sentences passed by Polish courts against *Volksdeutsche* (BA R 22/848).

15. More in Freisler, "Ein Jahr Aufbau der Rechtspflege im Reichsgau Wartheland."

16. The text of sec. 125 of the Penal Code at that time was: "When a crowd of people gang together in public and join forces in acts of violence against persons or property, each individual perpetrator of this mob violence shall be punished with prison sentences of no less than three months for breach of the peace. The ringleaders and anybody perpetrating acts of violence against persons or guilty of plundering, damaging, or destroying property will be punished with up to ten years in a penitentiary; also the admissibility of police supervision can be recognized. If there are mitigating circumstances, a prison sentence of no less than six months will be passed."

17. A. Schönke, *Strafgesetzbuch*, commentary, 2d ed., 1944, sec. 125, note 3.

18. Thiemann, "Anwendung und Fortbildung," 2474.

19. Ibid.

20. *RGBl.* I 83.

21. Regarding the concept of the "dangerous instrument," cf. Schönke, *Strafgesetzbuch*, 473. Thiemann, "Anwendung und Fortbildung."

22. Thiemann, "Anwendung und Fortbildung."

23. Concerning the admissibility of the reinterpretation, see, e.g., Schönke, *Strafgesetzbuch*, sec. 2, no. III 2; Mezger, *Deutsches Strafrecht* (1938), 26; Dalcke, *Strafrecht und Strafverfahren* (1940),

sec. 2, 2a; Schaffstein, "Rechtswidrigkeit und Schuld im Aufbau des neuen Strafrechtssystems" (1938), 295 ff. (316); a contrasting view is expressed in Kohlrausch, *Strafgesetzbuch* (1941), sec. 2, note IV 5c; Wachinger, "Rechtsschöpferische Rechtsprechung des Reichsgerichts auf materiell-strafrechtlichem Gebiet" (1939).

24. Thiemann, "Anwendung und Fortbildung," *DR* (A) (1941): 2474.

25. Drendel, "Aus der Praxis der Strafverfolgung im Warthegau"; in this sense see also Froböß, "Zwei Jahre Justiz im Warthegau," 2465 f.; Tautphaeus, "Der Richter im Reichsgau Warthe-land" (1941), 2467.

26. Thiemann, "Anwendung und Fortbildung," 2473. This work is the source for the examples given.

27. *RGBl.* I 1683.

28. *RGBl.* I 694.

29. Decree circulated by GstA (chief public prosecutor) Posen (Poznań), January 9, 1940 (BA R 22/52).

30. *RGBl.* I 61.

31. *RGBl.* I 83.

32. *RGBl.* I 162.

33. *RGBl.* I 723.

34. *RGBl.* I 1269.

35. *RGBl.* I 999.

36. *RGBl.* I 1679.

37. *RGBl.* I 2378.

38. *RGBl.* I 1146.

39. Cf. decree circulated by the chief public prosecutor Posen on January 9, 1940 (BA R 22/52). Another standpoint was adopted by the *Reichsführer*-SS; he took the view that admixture of the Polish and Jewish population should be avoided and consequently that the Law for the Protection of German Blood and German Honor should also be applicable to the Poles (letter from *Reichsführer*-SS to Reich Ministry of the Interior, June 21, 1940, Nuremberg doc., NG-1916, English summary).

40. Second Implementing Regulation to the Law for the Protection of German Blood and German Honor of May 31, 1941 (*VOBl. Reichsstatthalter* Wartheland, supplement no. 12, 37), explic-itly restricted to German citizens and nationals.

41. Thiemann, "Anwendung und Fortbildung," 2473.

42. Legal Gazette, July 15, 1932, no. 60, 571, quoted from Kodeks Karny I Prawo o Wykrocze-niach (penal code and law of torts), 1968, 51.

43. Thiemann, "Anwendung und Fortbildung."

44. Froböß, "Zwei Jahre Justiz im Warthegau."

45. Beurmann, in "Das Sondergericht Danzig," *DR* (1942) (B).

46. RGSt (Supreme Court for Criminal Cases) 73, 38; 73, 379, 386.

47. Thiemann, "Anwendung und Fortbildung," 2475.

48. Ibid.

49. *RGBl.* I 844.

50. Regarding the origins of the implementing decree, cf. Broszat, *Nationalsozialistische Po-lenpolitik* (1961), 130 ff., with further examples.

51. Sec. 1, no. I, 1–14; nos. II and III.

52. Thiemann, "Anwendung und Fortbildung," 2475; Beurmann, in "Das Sondergericht Dan-zig," *DR* (1942) (B): 78.

53. *RGBl.* I 135.

54. An example of the uncertainty of practice is revealed in a letter from the Reich minister of justice to the Reich minister of the interior dated August 22, 1940. The Reich Ministry of Justice

states that the special courts in the Eastern Territories had already been passing sentences under sec. 5 of the Law for the Protection of German Blood and German Honor (on grounds of "racial defilement"). Since coming into force there, the introductory regulation had given rise to misgivings because it had not been presented as part of the decree. He requests that an appropriate retroactive clause be included (BA R 22/51). (However, no such clause was included in the Second Implementing Regulation to the Law for the Protection of German Blood and German Honor of May 31, 1941, *RGBl.* I 297.)

55. In the draft of the law amending the Penal Code of June 26, 1935 (*RGBl.* I 839).

56. Schönke, *Strafgesetzbuch* (see note 17), sec. 2, no. II.

57. There was general agreement that this decree did not contain a "complete list" of all the regulations applied in the Annexed Eastern Territories; consequently, it could not "mislead" courts concerned with the application of regulations not specifically named in the decree (Thiemann, "Anwendung und Fortbildung," 2475).

58. *RGBl.* I 1679.

59. This was a departure from the principle that the regulation covered only those criminal offenses committed in "abnormal" wartime conditions; sec. 4 included not only the "evacuation" of Polish apartments, the closing down of Polish and Jewish businesses, and the nighttime curfew for Poles, but also the "unusual overall situation" in the Annexed Eastern Territories, the shortage of German police, and "the extremely high level of criminality among the Poles," which the authorities had so far failed to bring under control as a result of the war—all these were considered "extraordinary conditions" under the terms of the Decree on Parasites upon the *Volk* (Thiemann, "Anwendung und Fortbildung," 2475); accordingly, every criminal act committed in the context of this "overall situation" was potentially a capital offense.

60. *RGBl.* I 1269.

61. For example, the offense of "public abuse of the Reich," which was punishable under sec. 134a of the Penal Code, was extended to cover "malicious slander of ethnic Germans and their blood sacrifice," the people being "the human essence of the Reich" (Special Court Danzig, *DJ* [1941]: 945), and the singing of the Polish national anthem and public slander of the German armed forces (Thiemann, "Anwendung und Fortbildung," 2475; Beurmann, "Das Sondergericht Danzig," *DJ* [1942] [B]: 78). The clauses of the Treachery Law (*Heimtückegesetz*) of December 20, 1934, were constantly invoked and very broadly applied to "constant carping criticism" of "German construction" by the Poles. Sec. 1, which referred only to the *public* dissemination of falsehoods directed against the Reich, in other words not as part of a "whispering campaign," was used in conjunction with sec. 2, par. 2 (prosecutability of *non-public* utterances hostile to the party, so as to cover "whispered" propaganda) (Special Court 1, Leslau, verdict of July 25, 1941, SD 4 Kms 10/41, quoted from Thiemann, "Anwendung und Fortbildung," 2475 n. 14).

62. Special Court 1, Posen, June 20, 27, 1941; Special Court 2, Posen, August 19, 26, 1941; all judgments quoted from Thiemann, "Anwendung und Fortbildung," 2476 nn. 19, 21; in Danzig–West Prussia, such cases were treated more leniently (analogous to the application of the Law on Titles, Honors, and Medals of July 1, 1937, RGBl. I 725; Special Court Danzig, June 20, 1941, *DJ* [1941]: 945).

63. The special regulations were taken almost verbatim from the draft of a decree from the *Reichsführer*-SS and chief of the German police "concerning measures against acts of violence in the Annexed Eastern Territories" of February 21, 1940 (BA R 43 II/647), which Himmler originally wanted to issue in his own right as a separate police ordinance outside of the general penal code. For a detailed account of the tensions that arose between Reich administration and police leadership concerning the introduction of this legislation, see Broszat, *Nationalsozialistische Polenpolitik*, 132 ff., with numerous examples.

64. According to sec. 16 of the implementing order, the circle of privileged ethnic groups was determined by the *Reichsstatthalter* (*Oberpräsident*). As a result of this discretionary power, the

following groups were excluded from the special regulations set out in secs. 8–15 of the implementing order in Wartheland and Danzig–West Prussia: Ukrainians, Russians (except Soviet Russians), White Russians, refugees from the Caucasus, and "non-German returnees from the ethnic German areas" (decrees issued by the *Reichsstatthalter* in Wartheland, August 9, 1940, and August 15, 1941, *VOBl. Wartheland*, 1940, 630; 1941, 468; decree issued by the *Reichsstatthalter* in Danzig–West Prussia, 1941, 652)—in other words, the special regulations applied only to Poles and Jews.

65. For more details, see Broszat, *Nationalsozialistische Polenpolitik*, 134 ff., with numerous examples.

66. Cf. letter from the deputy Führer's chief of staff to the Reich minister and head of the Reich Chancellery of November 20, 1940 (BA R 43 II/1549; Nuremberg doc. NG-227). Bormann did not hesitate to pass off his own ideas about the shaping of the Polish Penal Code as "the views of the Führer," thus getting his way; cf. Broszat, *Nationalsozialistische Polenpolitik*, 206 f. n. 97.

67. Letter from Reich Ministry of Justice (State Secretary Freisler) to the Reich minister and head of the Reich Chancellery, November 20, 1940 (BA R 43 II/1549; Nuremberg doc., NG-127, my emphasis).

68. *RGBl.* I 759.

69. R. Freisler at a conference of appeal court presiding judges and chief public prosecutors (probably in May 1942) in Berlin, minutes (no date) (BA R 22/4162). The draft is dated April 17, 1941.

70. In the preamble to the draft of April 17, 1941, State Secretary Schlegelberger praised the "rapid and effective working of the special courts" and the "extremely impressive rate at which cases were processed." He was pleased with the courts' efforts to counter moves by the Party and police to displace the judiciary altogether from the administration of the criminal law in cases involving "non-Germans" and to replace them with summary police courts. Nevertheless, he came down in favor of the Party line. He gave as an example the Special Court in Bromberg (Bydgoszcz), which had up to that point sentenced a total of 201 defendants to death, given life sentences to 11 more, and condemned 93 further defendants to a total of 912 years in the penitentiary, an average sentence of 10 years (BA R 43 II/1549; also Nuremberg doc. NG-144).

71. BA R 43 II/1549. The only thing the ministry did not agree with was Bormann's proposal to introduce corporal punishment for Poles, a pet idea of the Party and police leadership, stating that this "was incompatible with cultural standing of the German people." Under a later plan devised by Minister of Justice Thierack in consultation with the *Reichsführer*-SS, corporal punishment was to be introduced into the Altreich by decree; cf. Thierack's note on a discussion with Lammers on October 1, 1942. Lammers pressed for a presentation of the case by the Reich minister of justice to the Führer (BA R 22/4062). I do not know whether the presentation ever took place.

72. Broszat, *Nationalsozialistische Polenpolitik*, 139.

73. Indictment in trial of lawyers before the American Military Court in Nuremberg, quoted from Steiniger and Leszczyński, *Das Urteil im Juristenprozeß* (1969), 62 f., 64 f., 66.

74. Ibid.

75. Situation report, chief public prosecutor Kattowitz (Katowice), March 2, 1942 (BA R 22/3372).

76. The decree therefore contained no regulations concerned with the cessation of validity of the criminal justice implementing order of June 6, 1940 (*RGBl.* I 844), for Poles and Jews. Only the "special penal provision" contained in secs. 8–16 of the implementing order were declared to be no longer applicable to Poles and Jews (Decree on Penal Law for Poles, clause 16). Thus, with regard to the procedural provisions that contained essential legal guarantees (legal remedy procedures) also for "non-Germans," the implementing order should have remained in force. It was, however, effectively abrogated by clause 2 of the Decree on Penal Law for Poles (proceedings only "on the basis" of the German criminal code at the court's discretion).

Whereas the 1940 implementing order (*RGBl.* I 844) was still drafted in the customary "legal style," the implementing regulations contained brutal and indiscriminate language that made it clear that it was no longer a question of making law but of combating political enemies by every means available. For example, clause 1, par. 1, of the Decree on Penal Law for Poles said: "Poles and Jews in the Annexed Eastern Territories are to conduct themselves in accordance with German law and the instructions issued to them by the German authorities. They must desist from any conduct that is detrimental to the sovereignty of the German Reich and the name of the German people."

77. See also the commentary to the Decree on Penal Law for Poles in the situation report of the Kattowitz chief public prosecutor of March 2, 1942 (BA R 22/3372).

78. Clause 3, par. 1, Decree on Penal Law for Poles. These detention camps (*Straflager*) are not to be confused with the concentration camps, although the conditions were to some extent similar. The detention camps only received convicted prisoners for sentences of a set length, whereas Poles were usually sent to the concentration camps for indefinite periods (for the duration of the war). Nor should they be confused with the "work training camps" (*Arbeitserziehungslager*) of the SS and police—frequently referred to as detention camps—where summary sentences passed by penal order were served (see also decree circulated by the *Reichsführer*-SS and chief of the German police on December 28, 1942, reproduced in *Doc. Occ.* 5:348 f.).

79. In accordance with the so-called Decree on the Execution of Sentences for Poles (*DJ* [1942]: 35; slightly modified by the implementing regulation of the Reich Ministry of Justice of May 31, 1944, *DJ* [1944]: 160), the execution of sentences imposed on Poles was characterized by "absolute discipline"; the labor had to be "particularly arduous" and the "productive capacity of the convict exploited to the full"; the working day was an hour longer than in the penitentiary; no visits were permitted; letters were only allowed when adjudged "necessary" by the overseer. No "remuneration" was allowed, not even for prisoners on remand (letter from Reich Ministry of Justice to all chief public prosecutors, January 16, 1942, BA R 22/1431, 135). Nonetheless, compared with the SS and police-run "work training camps," these camps were the lesser evil ("prisoners' health and ability to work must be safeguarded," clause 4, Decree on the Execution of Sentences for Poles, *DJ* [1942]: 35), since the former lacked any sort of clause concerning prisoners' well-being ("convicts . . . [are] to be detailed for particularly strenuous work," circular decree from *Reichsführer*-SS and chief of the German police dated December 28, 1942, reproduced in *Doc. Occ.* 5:348 f.). It is doubtful whether such detention camps were established throughout the Eastern Territories. In Warthegau, for example, simple detention camp sentences were served either in special camps or in normal penal institutions (cf. circular from chief public prosecutor Posen, January 8, 1942, State Archive Poznań, Posen District Court 13). In his report on activities for the year 1943, *Reichsstatthalter* Greiser ("Der Tag der Freiheit, 1943," 29, Library of Institute for Western Studies, Poznań, Sign. II 75778) also speaks of (39) penal institutions (*Vollzugsanstalten*), in which 10,514 Polish and German prisoners were working. For further details on execution of sentences on Poles in Warthegau and Danzig–West Prussia, see also circular decree from the Reich Ministry of Justice of December 11, 1942 (Erlaßsammlung BA); a list of penal institutions in Wartheland is given in the *Ostdeutscher Beobachter* of January 30, 1940 (State Archive Poznań), and in an overview of penal institutions in the court of appeal districts (no date) (BA R 22/1266, 246 ff.); see also *Handbuch der Justizverwaltung* (1942), 264, 272. For the administrative district of Kattowitz, see situation report by chief public prosecutor, Kattowitz, May 3, 1942 (BA R 22/3372).

80. Similarly, the decree—under Reich law—concerning the setting up of courts-martial, February 15, 1945 (*RGBl.* I 30), under the terms of which the death sentence could be passed for any criminal offense.

81. The condition for applicability of the Penal Code for Poles was that the person in question should have had his or her place of residence within the territory of the "former Polish state" on September 1, 1939.

82. Further details in comments by Posen chief public prosecutor in the *Ostdeutscher*

Beobachter of June 24, 1940 (State Archive Poznań). Poles were treated as Germans only if they were on the *Deutsche Volksliste* (German Ethnic Classification List) *and* had been resettled in the Altreich (implementing order of Reich Ministry of Justice, June 5, 1943, *DJ* [1943]: 520). What was never cleared up beyond doubt was the question of the treatment under criminal law of those Poles who were on the list but had not been resettled in the Altreich and of those who qualified for registration on the list but whose names had not yet been entered. The SS and police leadership wanted to treat such people as Poles, the judicial system as Germans. See also letter from Reich Ministry of the Interior to Reich Ministry of Justice, July 10, 1942; letter from RFSS/RKF to Reich Ministry of Justice, September 25, 1942 (BA R 22/851); situation report from presiding judge of Danzig Court of Appeal, March 10, 1942; report from presiding judge of Bromberg District Court to presiding judge of Danzig Court of Appeal of July 18, 1944 (BA R 22/3360); regarding the precarious situation in Upper Silesia, where there was a strong mix of population groups, see situation report from the Kattowitz chief public prosecutor of September 2, 1942 (BA R 22/3372, 10).

83. *RGBl.* I 844.

84. More details in Freisler, "Grundsätzliches zur Ministerratsverordnung" (1941), 2629 ff. (2632).

85. Von Rosen–von Hoevel, "Das Polenstatut" (1942), 111.

86. Freisler, "Grundsätzliches zur Ministerratsverordnung," 2631.

87. Freisler, "Das deutsche Polenstrafrecht" (1941), 1129; (1942), 25 f. (29).

88. Freisler, "Grundsätzliches zur Ministerratsverordnung," 2631.

89. See the letter from State Secretary Freisler (Reich Ministry of Justice) to RMuChdRkzlei (BA R 43 II/1549; also Nuremberg doc. NG-127).

90. Drendel, "Aus der Praxis der Strafverfolgung im Warthegau"; Thiemann, "Anwendung und Fortbildung," 2473.

91. Examples in Drendel, "Aus der Praxis der Strafverfolgung im Warthegau," 2471; Buchholz, "Zur Ostrechtspflege VO" (1941), 2480; Enke, "Die Rechtspflege im Volkstumskampf" (1941), 2489; Pungs, "Die bürgerliche Rechtspflege im Warthegau" (1941).

92. Cf. Pungs, "Die bürgerliche Rechtspflege im Warthegau," 2491, who states that "not all plaintiffs are equal before the judge of the Warthegau" and that "rather a distinction should be drawn between Poles and Germans. This . . . should not be understood as meaning that Poles should have no rights. . . . Provided that he is designated to serve German development and is ready to cooperate in it, the Pole should find justice before the courts as a person with protected status of the German Reich."

93. Only the paragraphs printed in *DR* (1941) (A): 2465 ff., insofar as they are clear, provide any details.

94. Freisler (see notes 84 and 87 above).

95. A very few definitions in penal law for Poles will be found in Klinge, "Bemerkungen zur Begriffsbildung im Polenstrafrecht"; and in von Rosen–von Hoevel, "Das Polenstatut."

96. The articles by Drendel, "Aus der Praxis der Strafverfolgung im Warthegau"; and Thiemann, "Anwendung und Fortbildung," appeared in no. 48 of the journal *Deutsches Recht* of November 29, 1941 (the Decree on Penal Law for Poles was promulgated on December 4, 1941), and hinted at a (forthcoming) new legislative arrangement ("The development of legal practice in the Annexed Eastern Territories is not yet terminated with respect to penal law. Precedents alone are not sufficient to carry it. Further legislative measures can therefore be expected—perhaps in the near future," Thiemann, "Anwendung und Fortbildung").

97. Meeting of the presiding judges of the courts of appeal and chief public prosecutors with State Secretary Schlegelberger in Berlin (undated minutes, presumably May 1942) (BA R 22/4162).

98. Freisler (see notes 82 and 85). The statements in *DJ* (1942): 25 ff., in particular, show how confused and impossible to dissociate law and politics were, the two even being used as synonymous

terms, for example in the following: "The guideline for reaching a just decision in the penal jurisdiction for Poles is achieved when the judge considers the totality of the interests of the German
people and of the Reich and the respective political necessities, whose legal interpretation arises
from the political objectives of German work in the Annexed Eastern Territories."

99. Speech before the chief public prosecutors on October 28—29, 1941 (Institute for Western
Studies, Poznań, doc. I-804; transcript).

100. Minutes (see note 97 above).

101. Thus, nepotism and preparatory acts should be "interpreted flexibly" as reprehensible
acts in order to ensure that they too were punished (minutes, see note 97 above).

102. The introduction stated, "They [Poles and Jews] shall be punished by death, in less serious cases by imprisonment, if they exhibit an anti-German attitude through malicious or inflammatory activity, and in particular make hostile statements or tear down or deface official notices
put up by the German authorities or offices, or if through any acts they disparage or harm the reputation or the welfare of the German Reich or the German nation."

103. Minutes (see note 97 above).

104. This is supported by the fact that Freisler had used the term as early as 1940 in an article,
"Psychische Grundlagen der Polengreuel" (*DJ* [1940]: 557 ff.), in which he presents Polish history as
one of continual struggles and divisions and the Poles themselves as incapable of creating a nation
and unworthy of the European community.

105. See also Stolleis, *Gemeinwohlformeln im Nationalsozialistischen Recht* (1974).

106. Full details in Frank, *Nationalsozialistische Strafrechtpolitik* (1938), especially 35 ff.; Frank,
Nationalsozialistisches Handbuch für Recht und Gesetzgebung (1934), introduction, xxi; Exner, "Wie
erkennt man den gemeingefährlichen Gewohnheitsverbrecher?" (1943); Reich Supreme Court, *DJ*
(1943): 527 (on the term *habitual offender*); Reich Supreme Court, May 22,1942, *DJ* (1942): 529 (the
term *violent criminal*); *Richterbrief* no. 1 of October 1, 1942, p. 4 (the term *antisocial parasite*);
Richterbrief of June 1, 1943, point 24 (BA R 22/4002) (the term *asocial element*).

107. Freisler, *DJ* (1940): 557; and Freisler, "Ein Jahr Aufbau der Rechtspflege im Reichsgau
Wartheland," *DJ* 1940: II, 1125 ff.; the article by Beurmann, "Das Sondergericht Danzig," *DR* (1942)
(B), also gives an example of the rich fantasy of the judiciary with respect to Poles: "The tranquility,
the studied seriousness, the clear eye, the straight posture, the almost melancholic reticence of the
East German contrasts with the restless, talkative, easily excited character, the bent body posture,
the shifty eyes, the playful superficiality of the Poles." The "lack of love for the truth, a tendency to
fantasize, which sometimes borders on compulsive lying," and "an underhand way in politics" are
emphasized as particular character traits of the Poles, corresponding to their "slyness in military
action." "The judge should therefore not allow himself to be influenced by the excessive politeness
and submissiveness on the part of Polish accused prisoners; they are generally not authentic but
merely the expression of inner cunning."

108. The official number of ethnic Germans killed and missing was multiplied by ten, apparently at Hitler's personal order (according to Hitler's former military adjutant, *Hauptmann* Engel,
quoted in Broszat, *Nationalsozialistische Polenpolitik*, 51). Documentation from the Foreign Office
dated November 1939, which spoke of "approximately 5,400 murders," was recalled, and instead all
the relevant offices received instructions to quote the number of murdered and missing ethnic Germans as 58,000 in future (radio broadcast by the Reich minister of the interior, transcribed by the
Posen police radio unit, February 7, 1940, photocopy at the IfZ). At the meeting of the Reichstag on
December 11, 1941, Hitler even claimed that 62,000 ethnic Germans had died "as a result of Polish
atrocities" (quoted in Freisler, "Das deutsche Polenstrafrecht," *DJ* [1941]: 1129).

109. This was above all true of the special courts, which had already been set up in the first
weeks of the occupation in order to deal with the so-called September crimes. Most of these cases
came before the Bromberg Special Court (Beurmann, "Das Sondergericht Danzig," *DR* [1942] (B):

78), which had already been installed by Freisler personally on September 11, 1939, during the Polish campaign (Freisler, "Das deutsche Polenstrafrecht," *DJ* [1941]: 1130; Thiemann, "Anwendung und Fortbildung," 2474) and which actually passed the first three death sentences on that date; they were immediately carried out (Az. KLs Sd. 2/39, quoted in J. Gumbowski and R. Kuczma, *Zbrodnie Hitlerowskie, Bydgoszcz 1939* [Warsaw, 1967], 60 ff.).

110. Freisler, "Ein Jahr Aufbau der Rechtspflege im Reichsgau Wartheland," *DJ* (1941): 1125 ff., according to whom responsibility for the "September crimes" fell to (a) "the culprits," (b) "the leadership of the Polish State," (c) "the Polish intelligentsia," and (d) the whole Polish people, "because demonstrably once again the underlying pathological nature of the Polish character has shown itself in a primitive manner."

111. Freisler, "Ein Jahr Aufbau der Rechtspflege im Reichsgau Wartheland," 1130.

112. Freisler, "Das deutsche Polenstrafrecht," *DJ* (1942): 25 ff.

113. *RGBl.* I 844.

114. The regulations on unauthorized possession of arms were simplified (clause 1, par. 4, sentence 5, Decree on Penal Law for Poles; sec. 15, pars. 1 and 3, Implementing Decree of June 6, 1940). The actions of collusion, incitement to commission of the offenses named in the special regulations, and failure to report such offenses were brought together under a single title (clause 1, par. 4, sentence 4, Decree on Penal Law for Poles).

115. State Secretary Schlegelberger at a meeting of the presiding judges of the courts of appeal and chief public prosecutors in Berlin (minutes, undated, presumably May 1942, BA R 22/4162).

116. Thus, e.g., the offense of "associating with prisoners of war" (punishable under the decree of May 11, 1940, *RGBl.* I 769, in conjunction with sec. 4 of the Decree on Supplementing the Penal Code for the Protection of the Defense of the German People of November 25, 1939, *RGBl.* I 2319) was punished as an "anti-German attitude" under the terms of clause 1, par. 3, of the Decree on Penal Law for Poles (cf. Łuczak, *Dyskryminacja Polaków* [1966], 128 f.).

117. Unauthorized listening to foreign radio stations, for example, was punished as "anti-German behavior" under the terms of the Decree on Exceptional Radio Measures of September 1, 1939 (*RGBl.* I 1683) (enacted by the decree of April 29, 1940, *RGBl.* I 694), in conjunction with clause 1, par. 3, of the Decree on Penal Law for Poles.

118. Situation report of March 2, 1942, by the chief public prosecutor of Kattowitz (BA R 22/3372, my emphasis).

119. See Klinge, "Bemerkungen zur Begriffsbildung im Polenstrafrecht," 325 f., who regarded such acts as the sale of "scarce goods" to Poles by Polish shopkeepers and the wearing of badges by Poles ("masquerading as a German") as punishable under clause 1, par. 3, on account of "damage to the development" of the East. (Similarly, Freisler, "Das deutsche Polenstrafrecht," *DJ* [1942]: 28). The same ought to be true of a Pole who lived in a new building and took the locks from the doors. Telling political jokes was also to be most severely punished on account of the "basically different Polish mentality," compared with the German mentality. Sexual offenses were to be punished not, as under sec. 176 of the Penal Code, by penitentiary, but in conjunction with sec. 1 of the law of September 4, 1941, amending the penal code, by death (thus the verdict of the special criminal tribunal of the Reich Supreme Court of November 20, 1941, *DJ* [1942]: 265).

120. Administrative instructions of May 19, 1943, issued by the Reich Minister of Justice, *DJ* (1943): 287.

121. Situation report of March 2, 1942, by the chief public prosecutor of Kattowitz: the concurrence regulation under sec. 43 of the Penal Code (nominal concurrence) was no longer valid, since the commission of several punishable offenses merely strengthened the "infringement of the obligation of obedience, which could not be divided"; sec. 74 of the Penal Code (real concurrence) could also not be applied to Poles, since it was exclusively a protective clause in favor of Germans. Concurrent offenses by Poles thus always attracted the maximum penalty. A regulation from the

Civil Code, sec. 4, par. 2, of the Decree on the Administration of Justice in the Eastern Territories of September 25, 1941 (*RGBl.* I 597), which was claimed to serve as a general basis of law in the Eastern Territories (BA R 22/3372), was cited as legal justification. (The regulation was worded as follows: "If the application of a regulation in an individual case gives rise to a result that is incompatible with the spirit of the assimilation in the Reich, the regulation should not be used, and such decision should be taken as corresponds with this spirit.")

122. Situation report of March 2, 1942 (BA R 22/3372).

123. Ibid.

124. Commentary of September 9, 1942, by the presiding judges of the courts of appeal and chief public prosecutors, Posen, on a draft by the Reich Ministry of Justice of a Decree on the Participation of Germans in Punishable Offenses by Poles and Jews of August 11, 1942 (State Archive Poznań, *Reichsstatthalter* 816, Bl. 8–11).

125. Preamble to the Reich Ministry of Justice draft of August 11 1942 (ibid., Bl. 2).

126. Draft of August 11, 1942, ibid.

127. Administrative instructions of July 23, 1942, *DJ* (1942): 510 (*Doc. Occ.* 5:342). The responsibility limit of 14 years was, however, also applicable in Polish penal law; see the letter from the Posen chief public prosecutor to the presiding judges of the district courts and the senior public prosecutors of the district (State Archive Poznań, *Landgericht* Posen, 15, 104), according to which the decision to place Polish youths in "work training camps" could no longer be legally challenged by the tutelage judge (sec. 67, Reich Youth Welfare Law), but was subject to an *incontestable* provisional order by the juvenile judge under sec. 45 of the Procedural Law on Juveniles.

128. This included plans to amend clause 11 of the Decree on Penal Law for Poles, according to which false statements made while not under oath in penal procedures were punishable under the regulations on "perjury and unintentional false statements," such that false statements made while not under oath in *civil* suits, as well as false statements made under oath, were to become punishable under these regulations. It was further planned to extend the procedural regulations of the Decree on Penal Law for Poles, which were effective only in the Annexed Eastern Territories, to the entire Reich territory in the future (minutes of a discussion between representatives of the Reich Ministry of Justice and the executive officials of the Annexed Eastern Territories, July 28, 1942, BA R 22/850).

129. Reich Ministry of Justice draft of August 11, 1940 (State Archive Poznań, *Reichsstatthalter* 816, 18).

130. Above all, it was a matter of declaring incitement of Poles by Germans to so-called anti-German behavior punishable under the terms of clause 1A, par. 3, of the Decree on Penal Law for Poles, since this was "reprehensible behavior," "which offends the sense of justice of the general public in the gravest manner" (commentary of September 9, 1942, by the presiding judges of the courts of appeal and chief public prosecutors on the Reich Ministry of Justice draft of August 11, 1942, State Archive Poznań, *Reichsstatthalter* 816, 6–11).

131. See the examples cited in the commentary (ibid.): allowing a Pole to tell German jokes, because the German thereby "stabbed his compatriots in the back"; an invitation to a Pole to have sexual intercourse by a German woman whose husband was at the front, under the threat of denouncing him (punishable for the Pole as an "offense against the entire German national honor" under clause 1, par. 3, of the Decree on Penal Law for Poles; for the German woman it was a matter of "giving herself away to a member of a people that had proved itself to be inferior"); secret transportation of Jews to East Prussia by a German transport company for payment of a large sum, to give them an opportunity to flee to Russia ("Doing business" in "the most distasteful manner imaginable"); good treatment of Polish domestic staff by German employers ("*völkisch*-unworthy behavior"). "Pole-friendly behavior" by Party members was particularly disapproved of (for example: "the head of a German public office, a Party member, a war veteran and fighter against the Polish

insurrection movement, openly declares that he disapproves of the entire political measures regarding the treatment of Poles. He therefore demonstratively treats his Polish servant girl in such a way that the German population of the small town is generally outraged by his behavior. He has special charwomen to do the girl's menial work. He takes his meals together with her; when he has guests, he allows the girl to be present and treats her like a guest. He goes for walks with her, helps her over ditches like a gentleman, stretching out his hand to her, goes shopping together with her and carries her shopping bag, etc. Remonstrances by the authorities have been of no avail," ibid.). A further example of "Pole-friendly behavior" was to help Poles with the "unauthorized mailing of parcels" (letter from the Wartheland Gauleiter and Reich governor to the Party Chancellery and the Reich Ministry of Justice, May 27, 1943, State Archive Poznań, *Reichsstatthalter* 816, Bl. 35–36).

132. Commentary of September 9, 1942 (see note 130 above).

133. Minutes of July 28, 1942 (see note 128 above); Reich Ministry of Justice circular of May 29, 1942 (Az. II a 2–812/42, quoted in the minutes, see note 126). Draft with preamble by State Secretary Freisler, with a letter from the Reich Ministry of the Interior of August 25, 1942 to the governors (*Oberpräsidenten*) of the Annexed Eastern Territories (State Archive Poznań, *Reichsstatthalter* 816, Bl. 1–3).

134. Commentary of September 9, 1942, on the Reich Ministry of Justice draft, by the presiding judges of the Posen courts of appeal and chief public prosecutors, which was supported by the presiding judges of the courts of appeal of Königsberg, Danzig, and Kattowitz (State Archive Poznań, *Reichsstatthalter* 816, 6–11).

135. Letter of October 1942 (precise date unknown) from the Wartheland Reich governor to the Reich Ministry of the Interior (ibid., Bl. 24–25); for a detailed discussion of the drafts, see memorandum from Policy Desk I/23 at the office of the Reich governor, October 1942 (no precise date) (Bl. 22–23).

136. Unsigned memorandum of September 1942 (precise date unknown) (ibid., Bl. 18) from the office of the Reich governor of Posen and letter of October 1942 (no day given) with the same content from the Wartheland Reich governor to the presiding judges of the courts of appeal and chief public prosecutors (Bl. 26).

137. Letter of November 5, 1942, from the Wartheland Reich governor—personal adviser—to the head of Policy Desk I/50 (personal); letter of November 26, 1942, from the Wartheland Reich governor to the head of Policy Desk I/50 (ibid., Bl. 27).

138. Thus, the head of the Security Service of the *Leitabschnitt* Posen and adviser for nationhood questions to the Wartheland Reich governor, SS-*Sturmbannführer* Höppner, expressed the opinion in September 1942 that it appeared "extremely questionable whether we should not leave as it is the previous punishment by the Security Police of offenses that, under the terms of the new draft [by the presiding judge of the court of appeal and chief public prosecutor, Posen], would be brought before the courts" (memorandum by Höppner dated September 26, 1942, ibid., Bl. 20).

139. Letter of November 5, 1942, from the Wartheland Reich governor—personal adviser—to the head of Policy Desk I/50 (ibid., Bl. 27).

140. See the situation report of July 1942 by the chief public prosecutor of Kattowitz (BA R 22/3372).

141. Letter of March 20, 1943, from the Reich Ministry of Justice to the Wartheland Reich governor (State Archive Poznań, *Reichsstatthalter* 816, Bl. 32).

142. Telegram of May 27, 1943, from the Wartheland Gauleiter and Reich governor to the head of the Party Chancellery, Reich Ministry of the Interior, and Reich Ministry of Justice (ibid., Bl. 35–36).

143. In his telegram of June 4, 1943, Dr. Klemm of the Party Chancellery stated that in place of the Reich Ministry of Justice draft, a change in the Treachery Law of December 1, 1934, was being examined, the wording of which corresponded almost exactly to that proposed by the Reich governor,

but which was "somewhat more elastic." Discussions were close to completion, he said, so that the issue of a decree by the Reich governor was "not appropriate" (ibid., Bl. 37).

Part Two. Section 2. B. II. The Status of "Non-German" Individuals in Procedural Law

1. Instead, special introductory decrees were necessary, which selectively enacted German organizational and procedural law; see, e.g., the Decree on the Introduction of the Court Constitution Law and Coordination of the Courts of June 13, 1940 (*RGBl.* I 907).

2. Decree of September 5, 1939, by the commander in chief of the army (*VOBl. Polen,* 2, quoted in *Doc. Occ.* 5:40 ff.).

3. On the self-defense corps, see full details in H. von Krannhals, *Die Einsatzgruppen der Sicherheitspolizei in Polen, 1.9.1939–31.10.1939* (BA R 58, 1082); Broszat, *Nationalsozialistische Polenpolitik* (1961), 29 ff., 41 ff.; Nawrocki, *Policja hitlerowska w tzw. kraju warty* (1970), 35 ff., 51 ff.; see also the decision of July 23, 1940, by the Posen Special Court against the commissary *Landrat* and SA leader, von Hirschfeld (excerpts in *Doc. Occ.* 5:41 n.9).

4. More details in Broszat, *Nationalsozialistische Polenpolitik,* 50 f.

5. Thiemann, "Anwendung und Fortbildung" (1941), 2474; State Secretary Freisler had already personally set up a special court in Bromberg (Bydgoszcz) designed to punish the activities that took place on the so-called "Bromberg bloody Sunday" (September 3, 1939), Freisler, "Das deutsche Polenstrafrecht" (1941), 1130 (see K. M. Pospieszalski in *Doc. Occ.* 5:40 n. 9; referring to the corresponding instruction in *VOBlatt des Militärbefehlshabers Danzig-Westpreußen,* p. 91, he dates the establishment of the special court at September 27, 1939). In the ten months up to April 1941, the Bromberg Special Court condemned no fewer than 201 people to death, 11 to penitentiary for life, and 93 to penitentiary sentences totaling 912 years (letter of April 17, 1941, from State Secretary Schlegelberger to the RMuChdRkzlei, Nuremberg doc. NG-144). In Posen a special court was already operative on September 20, 1939 (by order of the military commander, Posen, of that date, ZS, Polen-Film 56, Bl. 461)—it passed its first death sentence on September 27, 1939 (K. M. Pospieszalski, *Doc. Occ.* 5:41 n. 9)—and in Kattowitz (Katowice) since September 22, 1939 (notification regarding jurisdiction of September 22, 1939, *VOBl. Grenzschutz,* no. 10, quoted in *Doc. Occ.* 5:40 f. n. 9); in the regional district of Zichenau, the Gauleiter and supreme president of East Prussia, Erich Koch, had already abolished the special court in the late fall of 1939, because "a German jurisdiction is an obstacle to the development of the district" (as Koch said at a meeting with the Königsberg Court of Appeal presiding judge on May 27, 1940, minutes in BA R 22/848). It was able to resume its activity only on March 15, 1940 (Reich Ministry of Justice administrative instructions of March 11, 1940, *DJ* [1940]: 323), but was stopped once again after a short time, since Koch again forbade the activity of *all* judicial bodies until the German Penal Code came into effect in the Annexed Eastern Territories in June 1940. (See the report of the former head of the public prosecutor's office in the regional district of Zichenau, quoted by Broszat, *Nationalsozialistische Polenpolitik,* 128 ff. [no date or source], and the minutes of May 27, 1940, BA R 22/848).

6. Decree of June 6, 1940, *RGBl.* I 844.

7. In the Reich each court of appeal district originally had one special court (sec. 1 of the decree of March 21, 1933, *RGBl.* I 137), and their number increased only gradually (sec. 10, par. 1, of the Jurisdiction Decree of February 21, 1940, *RGBl.* I 405) (list of all special courts of the Reich in Reich Ministry of Justice administrative instructions of March 11, 1940, *DJ* [1941]: 323), but in the Annexed Eastern Territories several special courts were instituted in each court of appeal district from the start: the court of appeal districts of Danzig and Posen each had five (*Doc. Occ.* 5:329 ff.; see also the letter of April 23, 1940, from the presiding judge of the Posen Court of Appeal to the Reich governor of Posen, State Archive Poznań, *Reichsstatthalter* Posen 896, Bl. 59). In the incorporated territories of Silesia, there was one special court each in Kattowitz and Bielitz (Bielsko-Biała),

and in the administrative district of Zichenau, which belonged to the court of appeal district of Königsberg, there was one special court at the Zichenau District Court.

8. The members of the special courts and the representatives of the prosecuting authorities there were initially appointed directly by the Reich Ministry of Justice (sec. 4 of the decree of September 5, 1939, by the commander in chief of the army, *VOBl. Polen*, p. 2; reproduced in *Doc. Occ.* 5:40 ff., 43), later, as in the Altreich, by the competent presiding judges of the courts of appeal or the chief public prosecutors (sec. 2 of the decree of June 13, 1940, *RGBl.* I 907, in conjunction with secs. 11, par. 2, and 17 of the Jurisdiction Decree of February 21, 1940, *RGBl.* I 405; and the Law on Allocation of Business of the Courts of November 24, 1937, *RGBl.* I 1286). Care was taken that only officials with special-court duties were appointed, who exercised the penal procedures against aliens with expedience and severity. In this connection, see the evaluation by the Reich governor of the head of the prosecuting authority at the Posen Special Court, whom he describes as having "deserved particular merit, especially in his energetic action during the events of September 1939" (proposals list for the award of the Wartime Cross of Merit, second class without swords, of October 2, 1941, State Archive Poznań *Reichsstatthalter* 936, Bl. 14–15).

9. Letter to the RMuChdRkzlei of April 17, 1941 (Nuremberg doc. NG-144).

10. See the decree of February 21, 1940 (*RGBl.* I 405), which put all so-called political offenses, among other things, under the remit of the special courts, with the exception of high treason and major criminality (secs. 5, 13, 14).

11. *VOBl. Polen*, 2, quoted in *Doc. Occ.* 5:42.

12. This was the basis of the decree of March 21, 1933 (*RGBl.* I 136), which made the special courts competent to prosecute all punishable activity of any importance having political implications (Reich President's Decree on the Protection of the People and State of February 28, 1933, *RGBl.* I 83; and on Defense against Malicious Attacks against the Government of the National Revolution of March 21, 1933, *RGBl.* I 135).

13. An exception was that acts against the German armed forces were prosecuted by military courts (sec. 1 of the decree of September 5, 1939, *VOBl. Polen*, p. 2; reproduced in *Doc. Occ.* 5:40 ff., 43).

14. See the instruction of October 5, 1939, by the Posen military commander (State Archive Poznań, *Landgericht* Posen 11, Bl. 4).

15. The Reich Ministry of Justice showed no compunction in exercising the analogy principle in procedural law, too, and wanted to apply the Reich Jurisdiction Decree of February 21, 1940 (*RGBl.* I 405), either directly or analogously (Reich Ministry of Justice decree of April 10, 1940, to the presiding judge of the Court of Appeal and chief public prosecutor of Königsberg, Institute for Western Studies, Poznań, doc. I-151; also included in the minutes of May 27, 1940, by the presiding judge of the Königsberg Court of Appeal, BA R 22/848); the Reich Ministry of the Interior took the position that the decree of February 21, 1940, "is not or not yet valid" in the Annexed Eastern Territories (letter of May 21, 1940, from the Reich Ministry of the Interior to the Wartheland Reich governor, Institute for Western Studies, Poznań, doc. I-150).

16. *RGBl.* I 844.

17. *RGBl.* I 405.

18. Letter of August 6, 1940, from the presiding judge of the Court of Appeal and chief public prosecutor of Posen to the presiding judges of the district courts, the senior public prosecutors, the supervisory judges of the municipal courts, and the heads of the district public prosecutor offices (State Archive Poznań, *Landgericht* Posen 17, Bl. 53).

19. Secs. 13 and 14, par. 2; sec. 14, par. 1.

20. *RGBl.* I 759.

21. *RGBl.* I 136.

22. Sec. 3 of the decree of September 5, 1939 (*VOBl. Polen*, 2, quoted in *Doc. Occ.* 5:42).

23. Sec. 16, par. 2, of the decree of March 21, 1933 (*RGBl.* I 136).

24. Drendel, "Aus der Praxis der Strafverfolgung im Warthegau" (1941), 2472.

25. *VOBl. Polen*, 24 (reproduced in *Doc. Occ.* 5:48).

26. The retroactive clause already contained many loopholes in the Reich territory, too (see the laws of March 29 1933, *RGBl.* I 151; of June 22, 1935, *RGBl.* I 493; and of June 22, 1938 *RGBl.* I 651; the decrees of December 5, 1939, *RGBl.* I 2378; and of October 4, 1939, *RGBl.* I 2000).

27. Thiemann, "Anwendung und Fortbildung," 2473.

28. Drendel, "Aus der Praxis der Strafverfolgung im Warthegau," 2472. Thiemann, "Anwendung und Fortbildung," 2473.

29. From statements by Reich Minister of Justice Thierack before the chief presiding judges and chief public prosecutors on February 10–11, 1943, in Berlin (minutes, BA R 22/4200).

30. Decree of October 5, 1939, on Implementation of the Pardon Decree of October 4 1939 (ZS, Ordner 57, pp. 0192 f.); regulations on security and reform were not affected by the Pardon Decree; records of acts designated by the decree were removed from the penal register (secs. 3 and 5).

31. Memorandum by Dr. Kritzinger, Reich Chancellery, April 11, 1940 (BA R 43 II/1549).

32. Drendel, "Aus der Praxis der Strafverfolgung im Warthegau," 2472.

33. Decree of February 21, 1940, *RGBl.* I 405.

34. *RGBl.* I 759.

35. Situation report of March 2, 1942, by the chief public prosecutor of Kattowitz (BA R 22/3372).

36. Situation report of January 3, 1942 (BA R 22/3372), by the chief public prosecutor of Kattowitz (whence "in my opinion the question of appropriateness should be adjusted according to the nationhood and type of offense and offender").

37. Letter of February 20, 1942, from the presiding judge of the Posen Court of Appeal to all district court presiding judges (ZS, Polen Film 57, 199 ff.).

38. Letter of February 20, 1942, from the presiding judge of the Posen Court of Appeal (ibid.), demanding cooperation on the part of all judges in the development of "a procedure worthy of German jurisdiction."

39. Sec. 16, par. 1, of the decree of March 21, 1933 (*RGBl.* I 136); sec. 26, par. 1, of the decree of February 21, 1940 (*RGBl.* I 405).

40. *RGBl.* I 844.

41. In his situation report of July 25, 1942, the chief public prosecutor of Posen stated that the abolition of the oath for Jews and Poles was widely regretted, since on account of the religiousness of the Poles, the oath had been a way to get at the truth; according to the chief public prosecutor, this standpoint was "erroneous"; rather, the incapacity of Poles to take the oath should also be introduced in the Altreich, too (BA R 22/3383).

42. See the letter of July 3, 1941, from the senior public prosecutor at the Posen District Court to the presiding judge of the Posen District Court (State Archive Poznań, *Landgericht* Posen 14, Bl. 127 f.).

43. Decision of May 19, 1942, *DJ* (1942): 547.

44. *RGBl.* I 52; implementing provisions in the Reich Ministry of Justice decree of August 7, 1942 (Nuremberg doc. NG-744).

45. Situation report dated March 18, 1941, by the president of the Hohensalza (Inowrocław) Administrative District (Posen University library).

46. Cf. the report of January 23, 1943, by the presiding judge of the Königsberg Court of Appeal (Nuremberg doc. PS-672; also BA R 22/20993).

47. Content of the decree reproduced in the report of January 23, 1943 (see the preceding note), and the circular of May 30, 1942, by the presiding judge of the Danzig Court of Appeal to subordinate offices (BA R 22/20993).

48. Report of January 23, 1943 (Nuremberg doc. PS-672; also BA R 22/20993).

49. Ibid.

50. This was true at least in Danzig–West Prussia; see the instruction from the presiding judge of the Court of Appeal, Danzig, in a circular to subordinate offices, July 4, 1942 (BA R 22/20993).

51. Ibid.

52. Instruction dated April 3, 1940, from the presiding judge of the Danzig Court of Appeal to the presiding judges of the district courts and supervisory judges at the municipal courts (ibid.).

53. The administrative instruction was announced by Reich Minister of Justice Thierack at the meeting of the chief presiding judges and supervisory judges at the municipal courts (minutes, speech by Thierack, Bl. 54, BA R 22/4200).

54. Circular of May 30, 1942, by the presiding judge of the Danzig Court of Appeal (BA R 22/20993).

55. Instead of the maximum permissible punishment of one year's imprisonment, up to five or six years' prison camp was imposed in isolated cases. The Reich Ministry of Justice attempted by way of internal arrangements to limit penal orders to three years' prison camp (minutes of a discussion of representatives of the Reich Justice Ministry with the executive officials of the Annexed Eastern Territories in Berlin, July 28, 1942, BA R 22/850, 5).

56. Letter of March 27, 1942, to State Secretary Freisler/Reich Justice Ministry (BA R 22/850).

57. See Freisler, "Das Deutsche Polenstrafrecht," *DJ* (1941): 1129 ff.

58. *RGBl.* I 405.

59. The number of penal proceedings before the courts of appeal did increase, however, as the Polish resistance movement became more effective.

60. Führer decree of September 3, 1939 (Nuremberg doc. NG-700; also in Broszat, "Zur Perversion der Strafjustiz" [1958], 411 n. 18). As early as May 1941, Greiser had asked the Reich Minister of Justice for such delegation of the right to pardon, referring to the "growing number of sabotage acts by Poles"; see the letter of May 24, 1941, from the Reich leadership NSDAP (Bormann) to the RMuChdRkzlei (BA R 43/1543). See the letter of July 19, 1941, from the Reich Ministry of Justice to the Wartheland Reich governor accompanying the corresponding decree. Delegation was granted to the Reich governor (chief public prosecutor) (BA R 22/850), it being initially understood by the Reich Ministry of Justice to include only *confirmation* of death sentences by the Reich governor; in cases in which the latter approved the commutation of a death sentence to imprisonment, this was to be considered only as a suggestion, which still required the approval of the Führer. Following a complaint by Greiser (letter of November 13, 1941, to the RMuChdRkzlei, BA R 22/850) he was accorded the full right of pardon (letter of December 11, 1941, from the state minister and head of the Presidential Bureau of the Chancellery of the president of the Reich, Dr. Meißner, to the Reich Ministry of Justice, according to which proposals for pardon for Poles and Jews in the Wartheland no longer needed to be submitted to the Führer, BA R 43 II/1549).

Reich Ministry of Justice decree of May 28, 1942 (Nuremberg doc. NG-126). Minister of Justice Thierack expressed strong disapproval of the publication of this decree in the official journal *Deutsche Justiz*, since now all the other Gauleiters demanded the right of pardon for their *Gaue* (discussion between the chief presiding judges and chief public prosecutors on September 29, 1942, in Berlin, BA R 22/850).

Part 2. Section Two. B. III. The Elaboration of Special Law by the Courts

1. See the report by the Security Service (SD) for domestic questions for November 1941 to December 1943, point 6, pp. 402 ff.

2. Situation report by the Posen chief public prosecutor, July 25, 1942 (BA R 22/3383).

3. Full details in Freisler, "Das Deutsche Polenstrafrecht," *DJ* (1941): 1129.

4. See sec. 2, Decree on the Implementation of German Penal Law of June 6, 1940 (*RGBl.* I 844).

5. Some 30% of the verdicts of the Posen Special Court have been preserved and are to be found partly at the Main Commission Warsaw, partly at the Institute for Western Studies, Poznań, and partly at the Main Commission Warsaw (Poznań Office); the State Archive Bydgoszcz contains the almost complete records of the special courts of Bromberg, Leslau, Hohensalza (Inowrocław) and Thorn (Toruń); the judgments of the Łódź special courts, publication of which is in preparation, are at the State Archive Łódź; those of the Zichenau Special Court, insofar as they remain extant, are at the Main Commission Warsaw. (This was the situation as of 1975.)

6. For example, see the report "Strafverfolgung und Strafvollstreckung" in the *Ostdeutscher Beobachter* of June 24, 1940, 3.

7. Beurmann, *DR* (1942) (B): 77 ff. (81).

8. R. Freisler, in *Ostdeutscher Beobachter*, February 7, 1942.

9. Some of the judges of the first "detachment wave" had themselves volunteered for detachment (Tautphaeus, "Der Richter im Reichsgau Wartheland" [1941]).

10. According to a statement by the former general judge of the Luftwaffe, the criminal judges at the *special courts* were culled above all in the Eastern provinces of the Reich, as they were probably considered politically reliable from the start and offered a guarantee for a firm anti-Polish course (information by Dr. Manfred Röder, Nuremberg doc. NG-711).

11. See letter of February 17, 1942, from the Posen senior public prosecutor to the *Gendarmeriekreisführer* of Schrimm (State Archive Poznań, Gend. Kreis Schrimm, 197, Bl. 1, 2).

12. Thus, on September 28, 1940, the chief public prosecutor of Danzig reported to the Reich Ministry of Justice about a suggestion by a government official to mitigate the provision in the Implementing Decree of June 6, 1940, concerning the death penalty for violent acts against Germans on account of their German nationality, "since the death penalty frequently is out of proportion to the mild nature of the act." He (the chief public prosecutor) did not agree, "given that the attitude of a large part of the population of Polish origin is still hostile to everything German" (IfZ, Fa 75/1).

13. See the situation reports of January 19 and February 19, 1942, by the chief public prosecutor, Königsberg (BA R 22/3375), who states that according to a report by the senior public prosecutor in Zichenau, the introduction of the Polish Penal Code was received with satisfaction, "since the German penal laws cannot sufficiently take into account the idiosyncrasies inherent in a foreign people." The introduction of the Polish Penal Code would take the "particular Polish character" into consideration. Situation report of March 2, 1942 (BA R 22/3372): "As a weapon . . . in the fight against the foreign destroyers of German defense in the war," the Decree on Penal Law for Poles "gives the judiciary . . . a welcome task that brings them closer to the immediate political purpose."

14. See the situation reports of July 10, 1940, and May 31, 1943, by the chief public prosecutor of Posen (BA R 22/3383); situation report of May 4, 1942, by the presiding judge of the Königsberg Court of Appeal (BA R 22/3375); also the situation report of January 8, 1941, by the presiding judge of the Danzig Court of Appeal (BA R 22/3360).

15. Report of September 28, 1941, by the chief public prosecutor of Danzig (IfZ, FA 85/1, photocopy); report of July 10, 1942, by the presiding judge of the Danzig Court of Appeal (Nuremberg doc. NG-432).

16. See, e.g., the situation report by the chief public prosecutor of Posen of August 14, 1942 (BA R 22/3383), and of the Kattowitz (Katowice) chief public prosecutor of September 3, 1942 (BA R 22/3372).

17. Thiemann, "Anwendung und Fortbildung" (1941), 2474.

18. Ibid., 2473; Drendel, "Aus der Praxis der Strafverfolgung im Warthegau" (1941), 2472.

19. Freisler expressed the instruction orally in his speech "The Penal Code and Alien Peoples in the Reich," situation report of March 2, 1942, by the chief public prosecutor of Kattowitz (BA R 22/3372).

20. See the judgments by the Wartheland Municipal Court reported in the *Amtliche Mitteilungen*

of the Labor Unit at the office of the Warthegau Reich governor, September 30, 1942 (State Archive Poznań, quoted in Łuczak, *Dyskryminacja Polaków* [1966], 132 f.).

21. Of the various special courts, those of Łódź, Kalisch (Kalisz), and Leslau were particularly harsh in their jurisdiction. In this connection see the excerpts from a total of 71 judgments of Wartheland special courts reprinted in *Doc. Occ.* 5:351 ff. Of the judgments against a total of 19 persons at the Leslau Special Court, as many as 13 were condemned to death, whereas 3 were condemned to one, 1 to four, and 2 to five years' detention in prison camp. Regarding the verdicts of the Łódź Special Court against Poles, see, for example, those of October 27, 1942 (4 death sentences for offenses against the war economy), August 18, 1942 (a death sentence for violence against a German), August 24, 1942 (2 death sentences for serious revertible theft), August 25, 1942 (a death sentence for arson), August 27, 1942 (a death sentence for continued offenses against the war economy), and July 22, 1943 (one death sentence each for "posing as an official, receiving stolen goods, fraud and blackmail," and violence against a German official), from promulgations by the senior public prosecutor of Łódź on the execution on December 3, 1942, of these judgments, undated, presumably August–September 1942, and of October 7, 1943 (Main Commission Warsaw, Plakatsammlung XIV, 111 t/1–3); see also the judgment of April 1943 (the death penalty for a Pole who had stolen four army postal parcels, *Litzmannstädter Zeitung* of April 3, 1943); some 20% of the verdicts of the Łódź Special Court were said to be death sentences (according to Cygański, *Z dziejów okupacji w Łodzi* [1964], 134).

22. See the preceding note; cf. also the selection of death sentences in Nuremberg doc. NG-2467, compiled from East German newspaper reports, from which it emerges that death sentences were imposed in most cases for relatively minor offenses. See also the notification of February 15, 1943, by the senior public prosecutor of Posen on the execution of death sentences pronounced by the Posen Special Court against two Poles branded as "dangerous habitual criminals" (Main Commission Warsaw, Plakatsammlung XIV, 103 t/7); the judgment of the Posen Special Court of June 1943, condemning a Pole to death for burglary (*Ostdeutscher Beobachter,* June 9, 1943); judgments of the Posen Special Court of April 1942 (*Ostdeutscher Beobachter,* April 11, 1942, reproduced in *Doc. Occ.* 5:362); judgments of the Hohensalza Special Court of June 1943 (*Ostdeutscher Beobachter,* June 28, 1943, reproduced in *Doc. Occ.* 5:366), condemning three Poles to death for very minor theft of textile fibers, classing them as "parasites upon the *Volk,*" in accordance with sec. 1 of the Decree on Parasites upon the *Volk* of September 5, 1939 (*RGBl.* I 1679). The courts managed to pronounce the death sentence in these cases only by interpreting such thefts as "looting in the liberated zone" under the terms of the Decree on Parasites upon the *Volk* (although looting was classified as an offense against property only in the blackout during or after air-raid attacks). Almost all death sentences pronounced by the special courts were regularly published by the competent senior public prosecutor on red posters at the seat of the special court in question, but only after the executions had taken place.

23. Broszat, *Nationalsozialistische Polenpolitik* (1961), 142 f.

24. Situation report by the chief public prosecutor of Kattowitz, January 3, 1942 (BA R 22/3372).

25. Ibid.

26. Greiser, *Der Tag der Freiheit* (1943), 29.

27. Letter of September 11, 1942, from the Reich Ministry of Justice to *Reichsmarschall* Göring (Nuremberg doc. NO-241).

28. The applications, which contained detailed qualifications of the applicant (irreproachability, "steady hand," "sure hand," etc.) fill two large files (BA Koblenz).

29. Cf. the situation report of May 21, 1941, by the president of the Hohensalza Administrative District, Bl. 13, which contains the following passage: "The public execution of the death sentences of the Special Court in Leslau, during which, among others, three Poles were publicly hanged in the

marketplace in Kutno, has been received with disapproval by the Poles. Polish circles have stated that the Poles know how to die for their country. The public execution of a Jew in Leslau as a deterrent measure against violations of the War Economy Decree, on the other hand, was welcomed by the Poles" (Posen University library).

30. Situation report of February 19, 1942, by the chief public prosecutor of Kattowitz (BA R 22/3375).

31. Secret memorandum dated October 14, 1940, from Public Prosecutor Stephan, Danzig, according to which the *Kreisleiter* of Bromberg in a discussion with Stephan had spoken of a series of "errors of judgment and wrong decisions," of which he "gave a long list and which provided evidence of conscious favoring of Poles" (ZS, Polen Film, 24, 580). Decisions of the special courts in which Polish accused prisoners were considered to have been treated too leniently and Germans too harshly also provoked the disapproval of the Party; cf. the situation report of September 29, 1941, by the chief public prosecutor of Danzig (BA R 22/3360).

32. Situation report of January 8, 1941, by the presiding judge of the Danzig Court of Appeal (BA R 22/3360).

33. Situation report of July 16, 1942, by the presiding judge of the Danzig Court of Appeal; report of February 10, 1941, by the presiding judge of the Bromberg District Court to the presiding judge of the Danzig Court of Appeal (BA R 22/3360).

34. Situation report of February 5, 1941, by the presiding judge of the Posen Court of Appeal (BA R 22/3383).

35. Thiemann, "Anwendung und Fortbildung," 2474.

36. Ibid.

37. Examples: 3 death sentences against Poles for the murder of a German in the first days of the September incidents (Posen Special Court, June 10, 1941, Institute for Western Studies, Poznań, doc. I-68); 4 death sentences and 1 stiff penitentiary sentence on account of reprisals against ethnic Germans in early September 1939 (Posen Special Court, June 4, 1940, ibid., doc. I-88); 28 death sentences for the murder of Germans in early September 1939 (Posen Special Court 1, August 25, 30, September 2–4, 1940, ZS); death sentences against 5 Poles for maltreatment of Germans in early September 1939 (Posen Special Court, *Ostdeutscher Beobachter*, December 6, 1941); sentences to fourteen years' penitentiary for involvement in the murder of ethnic Germans in 1939 (Kalisch Special Court, October 10, 1940, *Litzmannstädter Zeitung*, December 2, 1940, Institute for Western Studies, Poznań, doc. I-844); promulgation by the senior public prosecutor, Kattowitz, on June 30, 1942, on the execution of a Pole condemned to death by the Kattowitz Special Court, found guilty for "sniping at German soldiers" (Main Commission Warsaw, Plakatsammlung XIII 98 6/2); 16 death sentences by Warthegau Special Courts, submitted to the Reich Ministry of Justice for confirmation on April 30, 1940 (Nuremberg doc. NG-221).

38. In this connection see the decisions listed in *Doc. Occ.* 5:353 ff., insofar as they were pronounced before the issue of the Decree on Penal Law for Poles. Some of the few statistics available will be found in Beurmann, "Das Sondergericht Danzig," *DR* (1942) (B): 77 ff. (78). According to this, the court pronounced 83 judgments in 1940, including 13 death sentences, which is a ratio of only 1 to 5.3; in 1941, out of a total of 171 judgments, 14 were death sentences.

39. Examples: in August 1941 the Posen Special Court sentenced a Pole who had punched a German to "only" two years' imprisonment because he had not intended to insult "Germanness" with his action (*Ostdeutscher Beobachter*, August 18, 1941, quoted in *Doc. Occ.* 5:353 f.), thus saving him from the death sentence, foreseen for such acts (sec. 11, Introductory Decree, *RGBl.* I 1940, 844; clause 1, par. 2, Decree on Penal Law for Poles of December 4, 1941, *RGBl.* I 759).

40. Regarding amendment, see the situation report of September 28, 1940, by the chief public prosecutor of Danzig, telling of a proposal by a government official to mitigate the provision concerning the death penalty for violent acts against Germans on account of their German nationality,

punishable by death under sec. 11 of the Implementing Decree of June 6, 1940 (IfZ, FA 85/1). Regarding interpretation, the term *act of violence* (sec. 8 of the Implementing Decree of June 6, 1940) was made subject to special requirements; i.e., such acts had to go beyond simple bodily harm or acts of resistance under the terms of secs. 223, 113 of the Penal Code (Thiemann, "Anwendung und Fortbildung," 2474).

41. Following the decision of the Reich Supreme Court of July 7, 1941, "violence is not only an act of particular severity . . . which threatens the stability of German authority in the Annexed Eastern Territories, but so is any punishable act that is carried out with the use of violence." As a result the Supreme Court condemned to death a Pole whom the special court had found guilty of resistance against authority in combination with bodily harm (secs. 113, 223, 73, Penal Code) but refused a conviction (death sentence) under sec. 8 of the Implementing Decree of June 6, 1940 (*DJ* [1942]: 75; see also Reich Supreme Court, *DJ* [1940]: 69; *DR* [1941]: 1888). In a memorandum accompanying the decision, *Ministerialrat* Grau of the Reich Ministry of Justice stated that the decision was also of significance for the new penal law for Poles of December 4, 1941. The term *act of violence* was now extended even to include acts that would otherwise not be punishable, such as attempted bodily harm or attempted duress (*DJ* [1942]: 75). The Reich Supreme Court expressed itself in a similarly extensive manner with respect to the subjective facts in the Polish emergency code. Thus, in pursuance of the decision of August 21, 1941 (Az. C 505/41, 5 Sts 18/41), the criminal act did not have to have been perpetrated for its own sake but could also derive from other motives (e.g., damage to a prison cell with a view to escaping), without a more lenient judgment being appropriate on account of the presumption of "a less serious case"; i.e., such damage would be subject to the death penalty under the terms of sec. 9 of the Penal Law Implementing Decree of June 6, 1940 (quoted from Thiemann, "Anwendung und Fortbildung," note 11).

42. *RGBl.* I 2378.

43. Cf. the judgment of October 10, 1941, by the Kalisch Special Court, noted for its harshness (AZ Sd 7 KLS 187/41, quoted in E. Herterich, *Die Nazi-Justiz* [Würzburg, 1963], 58 f.). A Pole had been caught in the act of burglary and had defended himself with a sharp object. The court ruled that this was an offense under the Violent Crimes Decree of December 5, 1939. Not only offenses under sec. 1, Penal Code, were considered "violent acts"; it was sufficient for a criminal act to have "a certain weight." This was the case for theft (of food) that had continued for a year. The sharp object that the accused had carried was a "dangerous weapon" and therefore carried the death sentence.

44. *RGBl.* I 1269.

45. Beurmann, *DR* (1942) (B): 77 ff. (81).

46. Situation report of July 25, 1942, by the chief public prosecutor of Posen (BA R 22/3383): this corresponded precisely with Hitler's wishes; in his opinion a person who remained in prison for more then ten years was lost to "society"; such people were put into concentration camp or killed. In the present period (of war), death was preferable as a deterrent (quote in Picker, *Hitlers Tischgespräche* [1951], 203).

47. The Kattowitz chief public prosecutor in his situation report of March 2, 1942 (BA R 22/3372).

48. Commentary on the judgment of the Reich Supreme Court of July 7, 1941, by *Ministerialrat* Grau of the Reich Ministry of Justice (*DJ* [1942]: 75; see also note 41 above).

49. See the letter of July 14, 1942, by the presiding judge of the District Court, Posen (State Archive Poznań, *Landgericht* Posen 14, Bl. 198):

It is my opinion that the criteria of the Secret State Police in its supervision of the mail and its interpretation of the term "disparage the reputation of the German nation or expression of an anti-German attitude" are somewhat too strict, and that the results may even be detrimental to the German reputation. As necessary as it may be to react with the severest measures in all cases in which Poles intentionally attempt to undermine the reputation of the German people or the German authorities by statements, slander, etc., as the special courts of the Posen District Court regularly do in the desirable degree, it nevertheless appears dangerous if, as apparently is sometimes the case, such intentions are attributed to private remarks in letters written by Poles who do not seem to have this motivation and are merely expressing an opinion in passing, and who are then prosecuted. The presidents of the special courts have on many occasions brought themselves to pronouncing a conviction only with some reluctance in such cases, and apparently sometimes did so purely for reasons of expediency, since in the event of an acquittal the accused would possibly have been dealt with by the state police in a similar or even more rigorous form.

50. Situation report of September 6, 1941, by the chief public prosecutor of Kattowitz (BA R 22/3372). Before the Decree on Penal Law for Poles came into effect, the singing of the Polish national anthem was punished under the Treachery Law of December 1, 1934 (situation report of September 29, 1941, by the chief public prosecutor of Danzig, BA R 22/3360; situation report of September 6, 1941, by the chief public prosecutor of Kattowitz, BA R 22/3372). Decree of May 11, 1940 (*RGBl.* I 769), in conjunction with the Amending Decree on Penal Provisions for the Protection of the Defense of the German People (*RGBl.* I 2319). If Poles were involved in the contact with prisoners of war, however, *only* the Decree on Penal Law for Poles was applied. Situation report of May 3, 1940, by the presiding judge of the Court of Appeal, Königsberg (BA R 22/3375), which speaks of thirty-five cases before the Zichenau Special Court, in which nineteen women were given stiff penitentiary sentences for having had sexual intercourse with prisoners of war.

51. The decisions of Leslau Special Court 3 of September 23, 1942, reproduced in *Doc. Occ.* 10:218 ff., 223 ff., relating to a Polish cowherd, and of October 20, 1942, by the Łódź Special Court against a Polish servant girl, are particularly instructive in this regard.

52. See the judgments of September 23, 1942, by the Leslau Special Court against a number of Poles and Jews, published in the *Ostdeutscher Beobachter*, June 10, 1941 (quoted in *Doc. Occ.* 5:351 ff., where further decisions will be found).

53. Situation report of September 29, 1941, by the chief public prosecutor, Danzig (BA R 22/3360).

54. Under the terms of this instruction, all so-called war crimes, that is to say, offenses against the Decree on Parasites upon the *Volk*, the Decree on the War Economy, the Decree against Violent Crimes, and the Decree on Exceptional Radio Measures were in principle to be brought before the special courts (quoted in the letter of June 13, 1941, from the presiding judge of the Hamburg Court of Appeal to State Secretary Freisler, Reich Ministry of Justice, Nuremberg doc. NG-2215).

55. See the selection of court (mainly special-court) judgments against Poles and Jews reproduced in *Doc. Occ.* 5:351 ff., which probably reflect the average judiciary practice in the Warthegau. The convictions among the 71 judgments reported were as follows: 30 for violent acts or assault against Germans (of which 20 were death sentences); 21 for an "anti-German attitude" under clause 1, par. 3, of the Decree on Penal Law for Poles (3 death sentences); 18 for war economy offenses (8 death sentences); 7 for associating with prisoners of war (4 death sentences [assisting evasion]), 2 death sentences for "sabotage" (cutting the drive belt of a machine, rendering an agricultural machine unusable), under clause 1, par. 3, of the Decree on Penal Law for Poles; 3 death sentences as "parasites upon the *Volk*" for mild offenses against the textile collection of the Winter Aid Fund. There is also no lack of "curiosities," such as stiff penalties for unauthorized attendance at the German theater in Posen (*Doc. Occ.* 5:357), hiding two fire hoses (death sentence by the Posen Special Court [364]), "bad plowing" (judgment of the Posen Special Court: six years' prison camp [405]). The minimal sentence of three months' prison camp provided for in the Decree on Penal Law for Poles was applied on only two occasions, and a four-month sentence was pronounced twice (Posen Municipal Court), but always with reference to the particularly mitigating circumstances (young age of the accused).

56. Letter of September 25, 1942, from the Reich Ministry of the Interior to the Reich Ministry of Justice (BA R 22/850), and situation reports of September 29, 1941, by the chief public prosecutor of Danzig (BA R 22/3360); and of September 6, 1941, by the chief public prosecutor of Kattowitz (BA R 22/3372).

57. In the court of appeal district of Kattowitz, for example, unlawful slaughtering increased the business of the special courts by 60% (!) (situation report of September 6, 1941, by the Kattowitz chief public prosecutor, BA R 22/3372). Situation report of September 29, 1941, by the chief public prosecutor of Danzig (BA R 22/3360). This is a field in which the development toward pure deterrent justice is particularly apparent. Whereas initially, as corresponding Security Service reports deplored, sentences in similar circumstances ranged from eight years' penitentiary to six months' imprisonment (*Meldungen aus dem Reich,* January 30, 1941, BA R 58/166), convictions became more uniform in that certain "sentencing scales" were established according to the seriousness of the unlawful slaughtering; the "sentencing scales" applied in the Eastern Territories (for "alien" perpetrators) differed considerably from those of the Reich (for Germans, see the "sentencing scales" of the Reich Ministry of Justice in *Richterbrief* no. 16 of January 1 and February 1, 1944, BA R 22/4002). In mild cases, i.e., slaughtering of a pig up to 50 kg or a calf for personal use in cases of need, the "standard penalty" in the Eastern Territories was two years' imprisonment, whereas the sale of illegally slaughtered meat attracted a minimum sentence of three years. If there was no case of need, the unlawful slaughtering thus occurred for the purpose of sale, and the death penalty was incurred, it being of no consequence how many animals were slaughtered. The court of appeal district of Königsberg made considerable use of this last possibility. Between May 10 and 16, 1942, no fewer than six Poles were sentenced to death by the special courts (situation report of June 11, 1942, by the chief public prosecutor of Königsberg, BA R 22/3375). Furthermore, Königsberg demanded even greater severity: in future every person found guilty of unlawful slaughtering, indeed *every offense* by a Pole or a Jew against the war economy regulations, should be punished by death. It was intended to add the following warning to the posters announcing the execution of death sentences in unlawful slaughtering cases: "Every unlawful slaughterer and every Pole and Jew who in some way violates the German war economy laws can expect to be sentenced to death" (situation report of June 11, 1942, by the chief public prosecutor of Königsberg, ibid.).

58. See, for example, the decisions of March 31, 1942, by the Hohensalza Special Court (listening to foreign radio stations) (quoted in Łuczak, *Dyskriminacja Polaków*); of March 18, 1942 (Az. Ds 178/72), July 2, 1941 (Az. Ds 76/72), and August 8, 1941 (Institute for Western Studies, Poznań), by the Bromberg Municipal Court; and of June 30, 1943, by the Lissa (Leszno), Warthegau, Municipal Court. The commentary to the decision mentioned as an exacerbating factor that "the accused, a Pole, . . . had the temerity to write two petitions in a short space of time for other Poles and thus burden the public prosecution with unnecessary applications" (quoted by Łuczak, *Dyskryminacja Polaków,* 129 f.); see also the decisions of June 23, 1942, by the Kutno Municipal Court (quoted in ibid., 249 f.), and May 11, 1943, by the Posen District Court (Institute for Western Studies, Poznań, doc I-160).

59. Official communications from the Labor Section at the office of the Wartheland Reich governor, no. 18 of September 30, 1942, 220, quoted in Łuczak, *Dyskryminacja Polaków,* 132 f.

60. Cf. the judgments reproduced in the (strictly confidential) information broadsheet of February 20, 1942, issued by the Wartheland *Gau* press office (Institute for Western Studies, Poznań).

61. *Meldungen aus dem Reich,* April 3, 1940 (BA R 58/150).

62. Situation report of November 6, 1941, by the presiding judge of the Königsberg Court of Appeal (BA R 22/3375), who explains this on the one hand by the "Polish character" and on the other by the long absence of condemned Poles from home.

63. Situation reports of May 3 and July 3, 1942, by the chief public prosecutor of Kattowitz (BA R 22/3372), who attributes the increase to the mixed German-Polish population of the district.

64. Situation report of September 6, 1941, by the Kattowitz chief public prosecutor (ibid.); see also notes 53, 54, and 57 above.

65. Cf. the situation reports of January 3 and February 2, 1942, by the chief public prosecutor of Kattowitz (BA R 22/3372). For the Wartheland, see Greiser, *Der große Rechenschaftsbericht* (1944), 32:

> The success of German efforts to create order is visible in the domain of the police and justice in a felicitous reduction in the number of offenses and criminal acts. Whereas in the first year of the war, criminality in the *Reichsgau* Wartheland was the second highest in the Greater German Reich, the broad, energetic measures undertaken by the police produced such a diminution that criminality in our *Gau* has now fallen to eighth place among the nineteen existing police directorates. . . . Generally speaking, the continued heavy punishments inflicted on war economy criminals have lead to a further reduction in such acts.

66. Situation report of August 14, 1940, by the Könisberg chief public prosecutor (BA R 22/3375).

67. Situation report of January 31, 1943, by the Posen chief public prosecutor (4, BA R 22/3383): "it is just like the dishonest way of the Pole to incite Germans to be accomplices in order to make things easier for themselves if they are caught." According to him, the simpler employees who lived with Poles and lower-grade officials working in remote villages or near the border of the General Government were particularly exposed to this danger.

68. Situation report of July 31, 1940, by the chief public prosecutor of Posen; and of February 5, 1941 (ibid.): "it has repeatedly happened of late that Germans resort to criminal acts, out of a belief that the German is the absolute master of the Poles." Situation reports of January 3 and March 2, 1942, by the Kattowitz chief public prosecutor (BA R 22/3372); and of June 6, 1941, by the Königsberg chief public prosecutor (BA R 22/3375); report of February 10, 1941, from the presiding judge of the Bromberg District Court to the presiding judge of the Danzig Court of Appeal (BA R 22/3360); all of these complained that the Germans had the impression that they could do anything they liked with the Poles: nepotism, fraud, and sexual offenses abounded; see also the decisions of March 18 and August 20, 1943, by the District Court of Thorn (Institute for Western Studies, Poznań, doc. I-83).

69. See the report of February 16, 1942, by the presiding judge of the Posen Court of Appeal to the Wartheland Reich governor, summarizing the basis of this "flogging right" (State Archive Poznań, *Landgericht* Posen 14, Bl. 185 f.). See also the report of a meeting in Posen of the Reich trustees of labor in the Eastern Territories on October 9 1941 (*Doc. Occ.* 5:274), where Dr. Derichsweiler, Posen, says, "The Pole who feels secure in the crowd basically responds to our decency with sabotage and a refusal to work, because he sees it as a sign of weakness. The efficacy of a harsh policy against Poles is illustrated by the experience of the German arms and ammunition factories (Deutsche Waffen- und Munitionsfabriken, D.W.M.), where the punishment of flogging was introduced and regularly applied whenever a Pole had an industrial accident. . . . The accident curve has since declined quite amazingly" (277). The head of the labor office in Gnesen (Gniezno), Danzig–West Prussia, stated: "He has set up his own motorized punishment squad, which travels the country and breaks every refusal to work by a Pole with the severest measures. It works miracles" (279). Reich Governor Greiser: "A Pole should never be beaten because he is a Pole, because the individual can do nothing about that. But if one beats him for other material reasons he must always be told why, so that he sees the justice of the measure. He has a fine feeling of justice for such things" (280). See also the letter of July 20, 1943, from the Posen Reich governor to the *Kreisleiter* of Chodziaz (Łuczak, *Dyskryminacja Polaków,* 149 f.).

70. This was because the evidence of the victims at court was proved ineffective on account of their unfitness to plead (clause 9, Decree on Penal Law for Poles) and indeed provoked criminal acts on the part of Germans ("for some Germans, especially settlers, the lack of credibility in statements by Poles is a passport to criminal acts") (situation report of May 31, 1943, by the Posen chief public prosecutor, BA R 22/3383). Above all, public flogging of Polish workers was the order of the day and had sometimes (for example, in the administrative district of Bromberg) already taken "the form of a breach of the national peace," against which the judiciary was powerless (*Meldungen aus dem Reich*, January 31, 1941, BA R 58/166); for the practice itself had given Germans a general right to beat up Poles "in order to break rebellion . . . resistance, refractoriness, and impertinence in their personal behavior," indeed to punish all "cheekiness by the Pole in his everyday life" (letter of February 16, 1942, from the presiding judge of the Posen Court of Appeal to the Wartheland Reich governor, State Archive Poznań, *Landgericht* Posen 14, Bl. 185 f.). The practice of the police authorities to drag out criminal proceedings against Germans, especially Party members, also encouraged criminality (cf. the situation report of August 2, 1941, by the chief public prosecutor of Königsberg, BA R 22/3375). See also the report of the justice administration over the Wartheland (undated, approx. May 1942) on the plan to establish the lower station of Poles in the regulations, so as to avoid their being "completely without rights, particularly as workers, and at the mercy of their employer's arbitrariness" (State Archive Poznań, *Reichsstatthalter* 896, Bl. 126). No such regulations were enacted because the Wartheland Reich governor felt that to establish the "flogging right" and other such rights would be a "national-political mistake"; he called for a continuation of the previous policy (it was all right to flog, but not "senselessly") (letter of July 20, 1943, to the *Kreisleiter* of Chodziaz, ibid.).

71. See the letter of February 16, 1942, from the presiding judge of the Posen Court of Appeal, State Archive Poznań, *Landgericht* Posen 14, Bl. 185 f.

72. The official statistics give only absolute figures, no classification by group of offense or perpetrator. Up to May 1942, a total of some 60,000 criminal cases were on record, about 30,000 of which reached adjudication; cf. the report of the Wartheland justice administration (undated, c. May 1942, State Archive Poznań, *Reichsstatthalter* 896, Bl. 126); in 1943, 84,000 investigation proceedings were pending in the Warthegau; of these, some 12,000 gave rise to a charge, 21,000 to a penal order, and 35,000 to no action. The special courts dealt with 2,262 charges (Greiser, *Der Tag der Freiheit*, 28 ff.). In 1944, 73,400 investigation proceedings were pending, including some 25,000 against Germans and 47,000 against Poles. Sixty-eight thousand proceedings were concluded, 18,500 in the form of penal orders, of which 15,000 were written against Poles. Of the 7,500 charges, 4,700 were directed against Poles; 1,300 charges were brought before the special court (Greiser, *Der große Rechenschaftsbericht*, 32).

73. The execution lists were to be submitted in monthly reports to the Reich Ministry of Justice by the chief public prosecutors with a brief description of the facts of the case from 1942 on; further, the decision of the Reich governor (*Oberpräsident*) regarding a pardon was to be reported in each individual case in which a death sentence was pronounced (BA R 22/1320, 1321; excerpts also in BA R 22/3358, book 5). The execution lists were established by the Reich Ministry of Justice on the basis of these documents. Situation report of June 29, 1942, by the presiding judge of the Königsberg Court of Appeal (BA R 22/3375). According to the official figures, the administrative district of Zichenau had a population of 842,819 in 1940 (figures from *Die Ostgebiete des Deutschen Reiches und des Generalgouvernements* [Berlin-Dahlem, 1940], ZS). Dr. Alfred Funk, presiding judge of the district court, was born in Königsberg in 1897. He had held a post in the judiciary since 1927 and in 1939 was appointed head of the Chamber of the Court of Appeal in Königsberg and then commissar for the transfer of the administration of justice for the Memel district at the Memel District Court; in 1943 he was appointed presiding judge of the District Court in Zichenau. Finally Funk became head of the Central Department of Justice of the Reich Commissariat for the Ukraine

and head of the German Superior Court in Rowno, Ukraine. He was a long-standing Party member and climbed to the rank of SA-*Oberführer*. He was killed by partisans in the vicinity of Rowno on November 16, 1943. Reich Commissar Erich Koch described him as one of his "most trustworthy and conscientious officers" (from Funk's obituary notice in *DJ* [1943]: 568).

74. Execution lists of the Reich governor (chief public prosecutor), Wartheland (BA R 22/1321).

75. Report of February 8, 1942, from the chief public prosecutor, Posen, to the Reich Ministry of Justice (Nuremberg doc. NG-360).

76. Execution lists (BA R 22/1321). The number of death sentences *pronounced* is somewhat higher, since the lists contained only cases in which the Reich governor had refused a pardon, even though he made very rare use of the pardon.

77. Almost all these death sentences were from the Zichenau Special Court, mostly for unlawful slaughtering (execution lists of the Königsberg chief public prosecutor, BA R 22/1320). See also his situation report of August 1943 (BA R 22/3375).

78. Situation report of June 29, 1942, by the presiding judge of the Königsberg Court of Appeal (BA R 22/3375).

79. Execution lists of the Danzig chief public prosecutor (BA R 22/1320).

80. Execution lists of the chief public prosecutor, Posen (BA R 22/1321); of the chief public prosecutor, Königsberg (BA R 22/1320, 1321); of the chief public prosecutor, Danzig (BA R 22/1320); of the chief public prosecutor, Kattowitz (BA R 22/1320, 1321) (but only 21 death sentences, according to the list in Nuremberg doc. NG-309). The relatively low figures are, however, also due to the fact that the police (Gestapo) increasingly appropriated the administration of justice for "aliens" for itself from mid-1942 at the latest; see part 2, section 2, excursus.

81. Greiser, *Der große Rechenschaftsbericht*, 32. Execution lists of the chief public prosecutor, Posen (BA R 22/1321); of the chief public prosecutor, Königsberg; of the chief public prosecutor, Danzig; of the chief public prosecutor, Kattowitz (BA R 22/1320, 1321).

82. See also the statistical report by the Wartheland Reich governor, according to which 555 of the 589 death sentences pronounced in 1942 were against Poles (94.2%), and 34 against Germans (5.8%) (Greiser, *Der Tag der Freiheit*, 29).

83. Ibid. According to Greiser, 569 death sentences were passed in the Eastern Territories and 566 (including 34 against Germans) executed. Reich criminal statistics, 1942, Nuremberg doc. NG-767 (2,199 pronounced, including 930 under the Decree on Penal Law for Poles). Contribution by Reich Minister of Justice Thierack to the internal information service *Die Lage*, on "administration of penal justice in the fifth year of the war," August 1944 (Nuremberg doc. NG-252) and September 1944 (BA R 22/4003); total death sentences in 1942: 3,360, including 894 in Eastern Territories.

84. *Führerinformationen* of July 23, September 9, and November 17, 1942; and January 15, 1943 (BA R 22/4089). Figures also found in Schorn, *Der Richter im Dritten Reich* (1959), 942.

85. BA R 22/1320, 1321.

86. Ibid.

87. Criticism was directed above all against decisions of the regular courts; see the situation report of January 8, 1941, by the presiding judge of the Danzig Court of Appeal (BA R 22/3360); disapproval was also expressed regarding decisions against Reich Germans and ethnic Germans for criminal acts against Poles; see, for example, the situation report of September 10, 1940, by the presiding judge of the Danzig Court of Appeal and that of the presiding judge of the Bromberg District Court to the presiding judge of the Danzig Court of Appeal of February 10, 1941 (ibid.). Quotation in situation report of April 16, 1942, by the chief public prosecutor of Königsberg (BA R 22/3375); also the situation report of March 10, 1942, by the presiding judge of the Court of Appeal, Danzig (BA R 22/3360) ("a useful basis in the fight against Polish law-breakers"); and that of July 25, 1942, by the Posen chief public prosecutor (BA R 22/850) ("a considerable improvement").

88. Situation report of May 4, 1942. Situation report of November 26, 1942 (BA R 22/3375); in East Prussia about one judge in four (61 of a total of 246) was over 60 years old; according to the presiding judge of the court of appeal, it was difficult to eliminate superannuated and "otherwise unsuitable people" on account of the personnel situation (p. 2 of the report of November 26, 1942, ibid.).

89. Situation report of March 8, 1941, by the presiding judge of the Danzig Court of Appeal (BA R 22/3360).

90. Situation report of July 25, 1942 (BA R 22/3383).

91. Ibid., Bl. 12.

Part Two. Section 2. Excursus: Encroachment upon the Jurisdiction of the Judiciary

1. *RGBl.* I 295.

2. Sec. 2 of the Implementing Order of January 16, 1942, to the Decree of the Führer and Reich Chancellor on the Position of the Head of the Party Chancellery (*RGBl.* I 35); even before this, the cooperation of the Party in the legislation was essential: no intended legislation could be enacted without its consent.

3. Letter of April 22, 1942; see also the position statement of the Reich Ministry of Justice to the RFSSuChddtPol, June 13, 1942 (BA R 22/851).

4. Letter of April 17, 1941, from the Reich Ministry of Justice to the RMuChdRkzlei (BA R 22/1549).

5. Letter of November 20, 1940, to the RMuChdRkzlei (ibid.; also available as Nuremberg doc. NG-227).

6. *RGBl.* I 844.

7. Letter of October 9, 1940, from the head of the Security Police and the Security Service to the Reich Ministry of Justice (BA R 43 II/1549).

8. Letter of November 20, 1940 (see note 5 above).

9. See the letter of February 16, 1942, from the presiding judge of the Posen (Poznań) Court of Appeal to the Posen Reich governor (State Archive Poznań, *Landgericht* Posen 14, Bl. 185–86); and part 2, section 2, B, III ("The Elaboration of Special Law by the Courts"), notes 69 and 70 above.

10. Broszat, *Nationalsozialistische Polenpolitik* (1961), 41 ff.

11. Such "programs" included, for example, the instruction of October 30, 1939, by Himmler, ordering that "all Jews" from Danzig–West Prussia, all "congress Poles," the "leading anti-German Poles," and the Polish intelligentsia of Danzig and the Warthegau be "resettled" from the new Eastern Territories by February 1940 (instruction of November 30, 1939, no. 1/II, by the RKF, BA R 49/2, also Nuremberg doc. NG-5586). Full details in Broszat, *Nationalsozialistische Polenpolitik*, 84 ff.; and Łuczak, *Wysziedlenia Ludności Polskiej* (1969) (*Doc. Occ. 8*).

12. See H. von Krannhals, *Die Tätigkeit der Einsatzgruppen der Sicherheitspolizei*, 1.9.31.10.1939 (manuscript, BA R 58/1082); Wrzosek, "Deutsche Polizei in Oberschlesien" (1967); Datner, Gumbowski, and Leszczyński, "Der Einsatzgruppenprozeß (Urteil und Begründung)" (1962).

13. See *Doc. Occ.* 5:40 ff. n. 9.

14. Thus, the Security Police Command, Subcommand, Schroda, in its situation report of October 9, 1939, to Detachment 14/VI in Posen, requested "to apply for a court-martial execution . . . in the local marketplace for the criminals Tomaszewski and Stachowiak, . . . since a deterrent example needed to be established again for Schroda" (State Archive Poznań, *Sicherheitsdienst* Posen 2, Bl. 57). Regarding the "national-political" situation in the Schroda district, see the situation report of October 1, 1939, by the Security Police Command, Subcommand, Schroda, which says: "*Senatspräsident* Greiser told Pg. Körner (Bürgermeister), that three hundred executions were still not enough" (Institute for Western Studies, Poznań). There is a list of execution sites in the Annexed

Eastern Territories in *Przegląd Zachodni* nos. 1–2 (1955): 298–394. Broszat, *Nationalsozialistische Polenpolitik*, 48.

15. See the letter of February 16, 1942, from the head of the Security Police and the Security Service to the Reich Ministry of Justice (BA R 22/309), in which Heydrich requests presumption of "missing on account of the war" in cases for which a public report could be dispensed with (Decree on Amendment of the Law on Missing Persons, etc., of January 17, 1942, *RGBl.* I 31); in its letter of February 24, 1942, the Reich Ministry of Justice answered that this decree could hardly be applied here but that the courts should be instructed not to publish, in accordance with sec. 20, par. 3, of the Missing Persons Law, whereby no report was to be issued if serious circumstances went against the public order (BA R 22/309, Bl. 57a).

16. According to the report by a public prosecutor from Posen, the court-martial in Lissa (Leszno) had tried 53 prisoners on October 21, 1939, dealing a death sentence in 20 of them. The trial lasted twenty minutes (!), and one witness was heard (Institute for Western Studies, Poznań, doc I-857). Cf. one of the records, dated November 25, 1939 (4 names are marked with an X, doubtless signifying the death sentence) (Posen University library).

17. See the record of the October 2, 1939, sitting of the Security Police Detachment 14/VI court-martial ("the court-martial has ruled that the following Poles are to be shot") (District Commission for the Investigation of Hitlerian Crimes in Poland, Posen, Akt. II/4/21, K 73).

18. See, for example, the notification of November 2, 1939, by the *Landrat* of Plozk (Płock) (administrative district Zichenau), on the court-martial executions of several Poles on account of theft, dealing in stolen goods, "denigration of Germandom," etc. (*Kreisblatt Płock* of March 28 and May 5, 1940, Institute for Western Studies, Poznań, doc. I-706).

19. Letter of April 22, 1940, from the commander of the gendarmerie with the district president of Zichenau, to the commander of the regular uniformed police in Soldau (Dziadowo) (Tgb. Nr. A 666/400, Institute for Western Studies, Poznań).

20. See the report of April 21, 1940, by the senior public prosecutor at the Zichenau District Court to the Reich Ministry of Justice (BA R 22/848). Regarding the conditions in the administrative district of Zichenau, in which the police authorities were instructed by the higher SS and police leader not to pass on investigation proceedings to the public prosecutor, and the Gauleiter and *Oberpräsident* of East Prussia, E. Koch, had forbidden the judiciary all activity, see the record of a discussion between the presiding judge of the Königsberg Court of Appeal, the district president of Zichenau, and the higher SS and police leader of Königsberg on May 27, 1940 (BA R 22/1082).

21. See the letter of November 6, 1939, from the gendarmerie station of Wiesenthal (Fabianowo) to the *Gendarmeriekreis* Posen: "On November 2, 1939, the owner Adam Schneider of E. was acquitted of the charge of breach of a mortgage contract in the proceedings before the municipal court of Posen.... The court's decision is incomprehensible to me.... This acquittal does nothing to improve the standing of the gendarmerie in the public eye.... As a result of this case, the congress Poles, who in any case are reluctant to bow to the present administration, have the upper hand again and are encouraged . . . to resist future instructions by the German administration." Letter of November 8, 1939, from the *Landrat* of Posen to the Posen senior public prosecutor: "Since Schneider has been found guilty of a breach of mortgage contract, his acquittal is incomprehensible.... In the state interest, I therefore consider it essential that Schneider be condemned . . . request that the case be taken up again and an appeal lodged against the decision." The municipal court sent the files the very same day to the senior public prosecutor; further documents are lacking (State Archive Poznań, *Landgericht* Posen 11, Bl. 5–6).

22. Decree on the Possession of Weapons of September 12, 1939, *VOBl. Polen* 8 (reproduced in *Doc. Occ.* 5:45 f.). Secs. 1 and 2 of the decree of September 21, 1939, *VOBl. Polen* 9 (reproduced in *Doc. Occ.* 5:47).

23. See the letter of September 20, 1939, from the head of the Security Police and the Security

Service to all Stapo headquarters, in which these "principles" are explained in more detail; it was expressly forbidden to pass on the decree of September 3, 1939, to the district and local police authorities (quoted in Broszat, "Zur Perversion der Strafjustiz" [1958]: 390 ff. [405, doc. 1]; also as Nuremberg doc. NO-2263); the decree of September 3, 1939, itself has not been preserved. See also the minutes of a discussion of Gestapo advisers in Berlin on September 26, 1939, dealing with the division of jurisdiction between the police and the judiciary (Nuremberg doc. NO-905).

24. This emerges from a memorandum by Gürtner dated September 28, 1939, on a discussion with police representatives (reproduced in Broszat, "Zur Perversion der Strafjustiz," 408, doc. 3; Nuremberg doc. NG-190).

25. Statement by Hitler at the discussion on October 17, 1939, with the chief of the high command, West, on the future form of the Polish relationship with Germany (Nuremberg doc. PS-864; reproduced in Doc. Occ. 5:27 ff.).

26. Memorandum by Gürtner on a discussion with Lammers on October 14, 1939 (Nuremberg doc. NG-190, reproduced in Broszat, "Zur Perversion der Strafjustiz," 411, doc. 5). The minister of justice was nevertheless not informed in more detail of either the decree of September 3, 1939, or Hitler's order to Himmler, in spite of a request for such notification; the head of the Security Police, Heydrich, who was present at the meeting of September 28, 1939, directed him instead to Hitler personally (memorandum by Gürtner dated September 28, 1939) (see note 24 above).

27. See note 22 above.

28. This emerges from a notification by the Landrat of Plozk (administrative district of Zichenau) on the execution of judgments by the Gestapo court-martial of March 27 and April 4, 1940 (Kreisblatt Płock of March 28 and April 5, 1940, Institute for Western Studies, Poznań, doc. I-706).

29. See notes 16 and 18 above.

30. Memorandum by Minister of Justice Gürtner dated September 28, 1939, point 4 (see note 24 above).

31. Draft of February 21, 1940 (BA R 43 II/647).

32. See the explanation of the draft by Himmler (ibid.).

33. More details in Broszat, Nationalsozialistische Polenpolitik, 132 ff., and the references there; memorandum dated February 27, 1940, by Ministerialdir. Kritzinger, Reich Chancellery (BA R 43 II/647; Nuremberg doc. NG-944).

34. Letter of May 4, 1940, from Himmler to Göring (BA R 43 II/647).

35. Letter of March 31, 1940, from the state secretary of the plenipotentiary for the Four Year Plan and the Prussian prime minister (Körner) to the RMuChdRkzlei (BA R 43 II/647). In the General Government, in contrast, Himmler's concept prevailed completely; see part 2, section 3, excursus, 2 ("The Extension of Police Summary Jurisdiction").

36. RGBl. I 844.

37. According to the (radioed) instruction by the RFSSuChddtPol of June 14, 1940, to the higher SS and police leader in the Annexed Eastern Territories, all procedures still pending before the police courts on June 15, 1940, should be temporarily suspended or passed on to the regular criminal courts (BA R 22/848).

38. RFSS instruction of June 18, 1940 (ibid.).

39. Thus, for example, in his situation report of September 4, 1940, the presiding judge of the Königsberg Court of Appeal speaks of the "immediate cessation" of court-martial activity as of June 15, 1940 (BA R 22/3357).

40. Order of March 25, 1940, by the commander of the regular uniformed police (quoted in "Geheime Anordnung des Kommandeurs der Gendarmerie beim Regierungspräsidenten Posen vom 6.5.1940," State Archive Poznań, Gendarmerie Kreis Rawitsch 3, Bl. 5), whereby one court-martial in Posen should be set up under the regular police and one under the Gestapo; higher SS and police leader order of the day of May 9, 1940, no. 37, point 4, according to which permanent

courts-martial were to be established under the staff officers in Posen, Hohensalza (Inowrocław), and Łódź (quoted in "Anordnung BdO" of June 13, 1940, State Archive Poznań Befehlhaber der Ordnungspolizei 3). The courts-martial of the regular police were composed of the commander of a police regiment or battalion and two further members of the staff (instruction of October 14, 1939, by the commander of the Security Police, Posen, State Archive Poznań, Gendarmerie Kreis Schrimm 3, Bl. 20).

41. Secs. 1 and 2 of the decree of September 21, 1939 (*VOBl. Polen* 9, reproduced in *Doc. Occ.* 5:47). According to order of the day no. 10 by the commander of the regular uniformed police in Posen dated June 13, 1940, the police had instructions to hand over all information on illegal possession of weapons to the police courts-martial, which would then decide on submission to the courts. A case was to be passed on only if from the outset a death sentence was *not* to be expected.

42. Order of April 25, 1940, by the commander of the regular uniformed police, Posen (quoted in note 40 above).

43. Cf. the situation report of September 6, 1941, by the chief public prosecutor of Kattowitz (Katowice) (BA R 22/3372, Bl. 7); secret report dated December 3, 1941, by the presiding judge of the Court of Appeal and chief public prosecutor of Kattowitz to the Reich Ministry of Justice (Nuremberg doc. PS-674). Public proclamation of August 2, 1941, by the *Landrat* of the *Land* of Posen, "Sabotage means death," on the execution of a Pole by the Gestapo court-martial in Posen in September 1941 for "damaging harvest trucks" and an attempted attack on his employer (Main Commission Warsaw, Plakatsammlung XIV, 103 t/5, photocopy); telegram of August 6, 1941, from the Wartheland Reich governor to the administrative president of Hohensalza (State Archive Poznań, *Reichsstatthalter* 1232, Bl. 1) on the death sentence by the court-martial on a Polish agricultural worker for attempted murder (the Reich governor had decided against a pardon from the start).

44. At least as far as the Wartheland is concerned, nothing is known about court-martial proceedings against Jews (from information by public prosecutor Lehmann, Posen, October 1971). According to a letter dated October 11, 1941, from the Posen Gestapo to that of Lissa (A 7 B No. II B-Wi, Institute for Western Studies, Poznań), the "special measures" (i.e., summary execution) for Jews were not limited to cases of escape from the camp (by which concentration camp is doubtless meant) but were also applied to other punishable acts such as "sedition," "incitement," etc. Description of details of so-called Jewish operations (executions, etc.) in the notes on the trial of an ethnic German accused of raping a Jewish girl, June 1940 (Institute for Western Studies, Poznań, doc. I-849).

45. Cf., for example, the public proclamation of August 8, 1940, by the higher SS and police leader southwest (von dem Bach-Zelewski) in Kattowitz on the execution by court-martial of twenty Poles ("professional criminals, fences, thieves, violent criminals, etc.") and on shootings in August 1940 as reprisals for "murder and attacks by Polish professional criminals" (Main Commission Warsaw, Plakatsammlung XIII, 98 t/7). Situation report of October 11, 1940, by the chief public prosecutor of Königsberg (BA R 22/3375, 11 f.) on the execution of Poles by the Gestapo in October 1940. Report of November 7, 1940, by the *Landrat* of Tuchel (Tuchola) to the Bromberg (Bydgoszcz) Gestapo on the execution by court-martial of ten Poles as "retribution" for an attack on an SS man in Danzig–West Prussia in fall 1940 (Institute for Western Studies, Poznań, doc I-598). On May 19, 1941, the Bromberg Secret State Police publicly announced that on that day twenty Poles had been executed by court-martial in Thorn (Toruń) "for setting fire to vital factories and incitement to terrorist acts," and in Bromberg itself ten Poles had been executed by court-martial on account of an attack with explosives (Main Commission Warsaw, Plakatsammlung XIV 103 t/5). See also the report of May 23, 1941, from the district president of Posen to the Wartheland Reich governor on the execution on May 22, 1941, of twenty-five Poles in Kleinberg, Schroda district, in reprisal for an arson attack on the property of a German returnee (State Archive Poznań, *Reichsstatthalter* 1232, Bl. 102). See also note 91 below.

46. See, for example, the report of May 1941 by the inspector of the Security Police and the

Security Service in Posen on the shooting of thirteen Polish hostages (and one alleged perpetrator) in Wiskitno (administrative district Łódź) at the order of Reich Governor Greiser for the killing of a German police officer by two Poles (archives of the Polish Interior Ministry [AMSW], Łódź Gestapo Archives, Mappe 234, quoted in Madajczyk, *Hitlerowski terror na wsi polskiej* [1965], 151). The report contains the passage,

> For implementation of the execution, the help of the police president in Łódź was requested, who put a company of Security Police at our disposal, which . . . undertook to round up the Polish population of the neighboring villages around the scene of the crime and to keep them in check during the execution. In addition, the police president of Łódź prepared a firing squad that carried out the execution according to military principles. . . . [Before that] the district president . . . addressed the . . . Polish population, indicating to them the abominable nature of the act. . . After this speech, the head of the Gestapo gave the order for the execution to begin. . . . The Polish population present was at first impressed by the measure undertaken but later showed increased indifference to events. The execution had an unmistakably positive effect on the German population present, a large part of which . . . had also been brought there. The Germans spontaneously gave fervent expression to their approval (clapping and so on) after the salvo. There is no doubt that the measures taken gave them confidence that everything . . . would be done to protect them.

An example of an execution on direct order of the RFSS is the execution of twenty-five hostages in Kleinberg (see the preceding note), which was undertaken *without* a court-martial procedure (memorandum in the archives of Dept. 1 of the Wartheland Reich governor's office, dated May 28, 1941, State Archive Poznań, *Reichsstatthalter* 1232, Bl. 103), and the execution of forty-eight hostages in Kalisch (Kalisz) in the spring of 1941 for "attacking and murdering police officers" (report of May 1941 by the inspector of the Security Police and the Security Service [see the beginning of this note]). See also note 91 below.

47. See notes 45 and 46.

48. See, for example, the lists of about one hundred "people suitable" as hostages, generally from intelligentsia circles, compiled by the Ostrowo (Ostrów Wielkopolski) Security Police in November–December 1939 (Institute for Western Studies, Poznań, doc. I-903).

49. See the example in note 46.

50. See the letter of September 24, 1940, from the district president of Posen to all *Landräte* of the district (State Archive Poznań, Gendarmerie Schrimm 103, Bl. 76–79).

51. Thus, pertinent instructions provided that communication of the execution to the family of the victims should not be in writing but only by word of mouth; death certificates were not sent to the registry office responsible for the victim's residence but were issued by the registry office of the district in which the execution took place; see the letter of August 20, 1941, from the Posen Gestapo to the *Landrat* of Wollstein (Wolsztyn) (AZ B no. II D-[2], Institute for Western Studies, Poznań). "Heart failure" was often given as cause of death, and sometimes, accurately, "strangulation" or "hanging" (see the death certificates for two Jews from the Annexed Eastern Territories, ZS, Polen Film 58, Bl. 87 ff.). The graves of Poles executed by court-martial were kept secret, "in order to ensure *for all time* that there are no investigations on any such corpses found" (see the letter of April 8, 1941, from the Wollstein Higher Municipal Court to the *Landrat* of Wollstein, State Archive Poznań, *Landgericht* Posen 14, Bl. 107, my emphasis).

52. Letter of April 20, 1941, from the chief public prosecutor, Posen, to the Reich Ministry of Justice (BA R 22/1463).

53. Letter of May 5, 1941, from the Reich Ministry of Justice to the chief public prosecutor, Posen (ibid.).

54. See note 46.

55. Letter of May 24, 1941, from the chief of staff of the deputy Führer's office to the RMuChdRkzlei (BA R 43 II/1549).

56. Circular letter of July 26, 1941, from the Reich governor of Posen, according to which the courts-martial were composed of the "local Party authority" as president and one leader each of the Security Police and the regular police as jurors (BA R 22/850). This authorization in some measure anticipates the general authorization of the establishment of police courts-martial under clause 13 of the Decree on Penal Law for Poles; see section 3 of this excursus, below. See, for example, the circular letter of September 24, 1940, from the district president of Posen, according to which there was an "agreement" with the Gestapo to try as many Poles as possible in a single sitting by a rapid procedure (State Archive Poznań, Gendarmerie Schrimm 103, Bl. 76–79).

57. Situation report of October 1, 1941, by the chief public prosecutor of Posen (BA R 22/3383).

58. Full details in Broszat, *Nationalsozialistische Polenpolitik*, 134 ff.

59. *RGBl.* I 759.

60. See the letter of January 9, 1941, from the presiding judge of the Posen Court of Appeal to the Reich Ministry of Justice (BA R 22/850).

61. See the letter of May 16, 1941, from the head of the Security Police and the Security Service (signed Heydrich) to the RMuChdRkzlei (BA R 43 II/1549). Letter of June 7, 1941, from the Reich Ministry of Justice (State Secretary Freisler) to the RMuChdRkzlei (no answer exists) and of June 24, 1941, to the Wartheland Reich governor (ibid.; also as Nuremberg doc. NG-135).

62. Letter of July 8, 1943, from the RFSS to the head of the Party Chancellery (Nuremberg doc. NG-2718).

63. The regulation was worded, "They [the authorities and officials of the Police and Security Service] are to send their reports immediately to the public prosecutor's office."

64. Full overview of these practices in the situation report of September 25, 1943, by the Posen chief public prosecutor (BA R 22/3383).

65. Cf., for example, the instruction of February 18, 1941, by the Posen Gestapo headquarters to the *Landräte* of the administrative district of Posen (State Archive Poznań, Landsratsamt Grätz 30, Bl. 29).

66. Situation report of April 16, 1942, by the Königsberg chief public prosecutor (BA R 22/3375).

67. Situation report of April 13, 1942, by the Posen chief public prosecutor (BA R 22/3383). Situation report of August 11, 1942, by the Königsberg chief public prosecutor (BA R 22/3375).

68. Report of May 10, 1941, from the presiding judge of the Bromberg District Court to the presiding judge of the Danzig Court of Appeal (BA R 22/3360).

69. Thus, the gendarmerie of Wollstein reported the public execution of fifteen hostages in the village of Tuchorza near Wollstein as retribution for the killing of an auxiliary gendarme on July 9, 1942 (State Archive Poznań, Gendarmerie Kreis Wollstein 4, Bl. 83, and the District Commission for the Investigation of Hitlerian Crimes in Posen, Koppe archives with commentary by Prof. Pospieszalski, 1966); see also the memorandum of November 17, 1942, by the Posen Criminal Police on the handing over to the Gestapo of a Pole (who was fit for "extermination") for court-martial on account of an economic offense (State Archive Poznań, Kriminalpolizei Posen 16, Bl. 65). In Upper Silesia the practice was "simply to hang" criminals (situation report of January 3, 1942, by the chief public prosecutor of Kattowitz, BA R 22/3372).

70. Notification of April 13, 1942 (Main Commission Warsaw, Plakatsammlung XIV, 103 t/5, in German and Polish).

71. BA R 22/3372.

72. *Verordnungsblatt des Reichsstatthalters im Wartheland*, no. 26 (1942): 282.

73. Clause 4 of the decree of August 3, 1942 (ibid.).

74. Closing speech, quoted from a working translation at the ZS (Az I 110 AR 655/73).

75. See the minutes of a meeting of the chief presiding judges on September 29, 1942, in Berlin (BA R 22/4199), according to which an unnamed participant, designated XXX (perhaps the presiding judge of the Posen Court of Appeal?) informed the meeting that there were still no courts-

martial in the Warthegau because the Reich governor did not want to make use of them. However, he continued, the Gestapo carried out numerous executions of hostages.

76. Nuremberg doc. PS-1249. The establishment of the courts-martial is also announced in the situation report of August 3, 1942, 4 f., by the chief public prosecutor of Kattowitz (BA R 22/3372).

77. BA R 22/3372; also in the situation report (ibid., Bl. 21).

78. The catalog contained in the instruction of June 1, 1942 (ibid.), included treason and high treason; resistance against state authority; offenses against the public order; false coinage; sexual offenses against Germans; homicide against Germans; bodily harm against Germans; crimes against personal freedom; theft and embezzlement; robbery and blackmail; abetment and dealing in stolen goods; fraud and perfidy; damage to property; criminal actions against or to the disadvantage of Germans; malicious acts; radio offenses; economic crimes; offenses against the Venereal Diseases Law of February 18, 1927, insofar as the act is directed against Germans; crimes with explosives; and violations of the weapons regulations. According to the situation report of July 3, 1942, by the chief public prosecutor of Kattowitz (ibid.), this list was not even exhaustive but served only as a directive providing examples. The offenses mentioned could also lead to deletion from the German Ethnic Classification List, so that the perpetrator was treated as a Pole. According to the attached recipient list, only the general administrative authorities and the police, but *not* the judiciary authorities, received a copy of this instruction. The decree of June 1, 1942, which spoke only of "serious criminal acts," was sent to all army and Party offices, all offices of the Security Service, the Reich Commissar for the Strengthening of German Nationhood, the relevant chief public prosecutor, but *not* the relevant presiding judge of the court of appeal.

79. According to the situation report of August 6, 1942, by the chief public prosecutor of Kattowitz (BA R 22/3372), information from the *Oberpräsident* and Gauleiter of Upper Silesia put this percentage at only 6–7% of cases.

80. Situation report of September 3, 1942, by the chief public prosecutor of Kattowitz (BA R 22/3372). See also the secret report dated December 3, 1941, from the presiding judge of the Court of Appeal and chief public prosecutor of Kattowitz to the Reich Ministry of Justice (Nuremberg doc. PS-674).

81. Quoted from the situation report of November 26, 1942, by the presiding judge of the Court of Appeal, Königsberg (BA R 22/3375).

82. Ibid.

83. Report by an unnamed speaker, designated by the letters NNNN (presiding judge of the Danzig Court of Appeal?) at the meeting of chief presiding judges in Berlin on September 29, 1942 (minutes in BA R 22/4199).

84. Minutes (ibid.).

85. According to instructions dated March 11, 1943, from the Reich Security Main Office (promulgated via circulars of April 21, 1943 [Nuremberg doc. PS-701; also ZS, Ordner 225 a G.J. No. 96] and March 11, 1944 [Institute for Western Studies, Poznań, doc I-37, reproduced in *Doc. Occ.* 5:346]), these Poles were also to be sent to a concentration camp "for the duration of the war."

86. Situation report of May 31, 1943, by the chief public prosecutor, Posen (BA R 22/3383).

87. More details in part 2, section 1 (Reich), excursus, 1 ("The Influence of the Party"); regarding the penal competence of the police, see also the letter of September 8, 1943, from the Reich governor of Posen to the Reich Ministry of Justice (BA R 22/850).

88. See also full details in the minutes of the meeting of chief public prosecutors and presiding judges of the courts of appeal in Berlin, February 10–11, 1943 (BA R 22/4200).

89. Statements by Thierack at the meeting of chief presiding judges in Berlin, September 29, 1942 (minutes in BA R 22/4199): the judiciary had done a "good political job" in Danzig–West Prussia. Polish affairs occupied 75% of all discussions among judges and constituted the main part of the supervisory activity of the presiding judges of the district courts.

90. Situation reports of January 3, August 6, and September 3, 1942, by the chief public prosecutor of Kattowitz (BA R 22/3372); situation reports of February 19 and April 16, 1942, and January 31, 1943, 23 ff., by the chief public prosecutor of Königsberg; situation report of November 26, 1942, by the presiding judge of the Königsberg Court of Appeal (BA R 22/3375); report of July 2, 1941, by the chief public prosecutor of Posen to the Reich Ministry of Justice (BA R 22/1463); situation reports of August 14, 1942, and May 31, 1943, by the chief public prosecutor of Posen, whereas that of September 25, 1943, contains the following (all three reports are in BA R 22/3383):

> There is reason to believe that the police bureaus of the public prosecutor do not pass on all cases that laws and decrees oblige them to. A Stapo station of the district makes no secret of first checking whether the most important political and other penal cases cannot be dealt with by a court-martial or police measures and passes only such cases on to the public prosecutor as *it* thinks appropriate. . . . There are even *Landrat* offices that have received such instructions from the State Police. Furthermore, I have been informed in confidence that similar instructions by the present minister of the interior [i.e., Himmler, who had taken over the post as Frick's successor] exist, about which the judiciary is to know nothing. (p. 2)

In this context, see also the situation report of January 26, 1944, by the chief public prosecutor of Posen (BA R 22/3385): "Apart from this [not passing on investigation cases to the public prosecutor]," cooperation between the judiciary and the Party and State is "not only without friction, but is comradely" (p. 5).

91. It may be presumed here that the justice authorities had cognizance of only a fraction of the arbitrary operations of the police. For example: situation report of April 27, 1940, by the chief public prosecutor of Posen (difficulties in prosecuting on account of unilateral action on the part of the police, which "is able to curtail freedom in a considerable measure on its own authority," BA R 22/3383); similarly, the situation report of October 1, 1941 (ibid.); the situation report of May 30, 1940, by the chief public prosecutor of Danzig states that in addition to evacuations, internments, and the sudden searching of entire apartment houses, the shooting of hostages had helped "to suppress any Polish intentions to attack" and thus "to calm the situation" (BA R 22/3360); situation report of October 11, 1940 (11 f.), by the chief public prosecutor of Königsberg (BA R 22/3375), reporting on the public execution of Poles (twenty in Makow, four in Schirpo) as "preventive measures" against "restiveness," about which all authorities except the judiciary had been informed. In Zichenau the Gestapo had refused all information and indicated the next higher authority, adding, however, that there had been absolutely no signs of "restiveness." Situation report of November 25, 1940 (BA R 22/3360), on the public execution of hostages in Lipno and (at the order of the *Reichsführer*-SS) in Tuchel as reprisals for attacks on German officials. See also the secret report of December 3, 1941, by the presiding judge of the court of appeal and chief public prosecutor of Kattowitz to the Reich Ministry of Justice regarding the summary execution by the Gestapo of persons suspected of belonging to the resistance movement (Nuremberg doc. PS-647).

92. Situation report of October 1, 1941, by the chief public prosecutor of Posen (BA R 22/3383).

93. See note 98 below, for example.

94. Letters of September 11, 1942, from the Reich Ministry of Justice to the chairman of the Ministerial Council for the Defense of the Reich, and of October 6, 1942, to Reich Governor Greiser; answer of October 6, 1942, from the Reich Ministry of Justice, in which he expresses thanks for à corresponding instruction on the part of Greiser to the presiding judges of the courts of appeal and chief public prosecutors in Posen, to hand over the condemned prisoners to the Gestapo (Nuremberg doc. NG-241). The work of execution "could not be expected" of the justice officers on account of their advanced age.

95. Cf., for example, the situation report of October 1, 1941, by the Posen chief public prosecutor (BA R 22/3383): the special court had pronounced and executed a death sentence against a Pole in the space of two days, whereas the court-martial (of the Gestapo) had needed a week for the same purpose; situation report of February 19, 1942, by the chief public prosecutor of Königsberg

(BA R 22/3375) (stating that six weeks had elapsed between the death sentence by the court-martial on a Polish worker who had murdered the widow of a German soldier and the execution of the sentence; a court would have needed much less time).

96. Cf. the situation report of August 2, 1941, by the chief public prosecutor of Königsberg (BA R 22/3375).

97. Situation report of September 3, 1942, by the chief public prosecutor of Kattowitz (BA R 22/3372). Also see, for example, the secret report of December 3, 1941, by the presiding judge of the Court of Appeal and chief public prosecutor of Kattowitz (Nuremberg doc. PS-674), containing the suggestion to establish a "lightning special court" at which no more than three days should elapse between passing on the procedure to the public prosecutor and the execution (it was apparently the rule that the special courts pronounced virtually only death sentences). The Reich Ministry of Justice's answer is not known.

98. Thus, for example, the situation reports of January 3, 1942, and of May 3, 1942 (BA R 22/3372), by the chief public prosecutor of Kattowitz, requesting clarification of the competence of the police and courts-martial "by Reich standards" (!). See also the situation report of August 6, 1942, and especially that of September 3, 1942 (ibid.): "The great activity of the State Police leaves no room for doubt that a large part of the proceedings that the State Police courts-martial have appropriated for themselves have either never been submitted to the *Oberpräsident* for a decision on the competence of the court-martial to deal with them, or despite a refusal have nevertheless remained in the hands of the State Police—not for adjudication by court-martial." In this context see also the situation report of June 8, 1944, 13 f. (ibid.): "The judiciary has for years fought to keep its powers. Again and again its competence is curtailed, particularly the cases of Poles and Eastern workers."

99. Situation report of September 3, 1942, and June 8, 1944 (BA R 22/3372). The former is one of the most impressive testimonies to the reversal of the relations between judiciary and police. See, for example, the situation report of September 10, 1940, by the presiding judge of the Danzig Court of Appeal, with vivid examples (BA R 22/3360).

100. See notes 78 and 90 above.

101. See, for example, the commentary by the Reich Ministry of Justice appended to the situation report of September 3, 1942, by the chief public prosecutor of Kattowitz (BA R 22/3372): "In answer to a request on the telephone, the chief public prosecutor of Katowice stated that he could not produce documents [which the Reich Ministry of Justice had invited him to do] on the subjection of *Germans* to the State Police procedures and on the failure to pass them on to the prosecuting authorities, because they involved confidential information from other offices. These offices have further requested that their communications be not dealt with officially." (The chief public prosecutor also mentioned several concrete cases of the treatment of Germans by the Gestapo.) Below the commentary there is a handwritten note by the head of the Criminal Justice Department at the Reich Ministry of Justice (Dr. Crohne), dated October 7, 1942: "The above information confirms my . . . supposition that it is apparently here a matter of general [next word illegible] without a [next word illegible] basis. The competent expert at the Kattowitz chief public prosecutor's office is known to be a prolific writer." There follows a handwritten remark dated October 13, 1942, by Reich Ministry of Justice Thierack: "Today, October 12, I passed on the content of the memorandum Ref. 2 to the chief public prosecutor in Kattowitz." See also note 133 below.

102. See the controversy in this connection between the Reich Ministry of Justice and the Reich Security Main Office (RSHA), initiated as a result of a complaint by the chief public prosecutor of Posen about the interference of "third parties" in investigation proceedings against so-called prominent individuals; letter of June 6, 1941, from the RSHA (Heydrich) to the Reich Ministry of Justice, proposing for such cases a "police investigation procedure," which "for tactical reasons" should be exercised by the competent authority of the Security Police, and requesting the issue of an appropriate directive to the chief public prosecutors; answer of July 18, 1941, by the Reich Minis-

try of Justice that such a directive was not necessary, since the basic situation was that public prosecutor's office charged the police with investigations in pursuance of the legal requirements (BA R 22/1463).

103. For example, the letter of March 25, 1941, from the senior public prosecutor of Kalisch to the Kalisch Gestapo (AZ Sd 7 Js 187/41), with which a Polish priest who was not demonstrably guilty of illegal possession of weapons was handed over to the Gestapo (reproduced in Herterich, *Die Nazi-Justiz* [1963], 57). See also the letter of June 5, 1942, from the senior public prosecutor of Kalisch to the Kalisch Gestapo (AZ Sd 7 Js 390/41), with which a Polish woman arrested for anti-German remarks, but against whom nothing could be proved, was handed over to the Gestapo together with her files ("The accused is at your disposal") and "State Police measures" were proposed (reproduced in Herterich, *Die Nazi-Justiz*, 54 f.).

104. See the secret report dated December 3, 1941, from the presiding judge of the Court of Appeal and chief public prosecutor of Kattowitz to the Reich Ministry of Justice (Nuremberg doc. PS-674), which closes with the words: "These considerations do not represent a stand on the competence of a court-martial functioning for Poles and Jews."

105. See the situation reports of September 25, 1943, and January 26, 1944, from the chief public prosecutor of Posen (BA R 22/3383); situation report of June 8, 1944, by the chief public prosecutor of Kattowitz (BA R 22/3372).

106. Situation reports of January 3 and September 3, 1942, by the chief public prosecutor of Kattowitz (BA R 22/3372).

107. See the situation report of September 3, 1942, by the chief public prosecutor of Kattowitz (ibid.).

108. Circular of January 28, 1943, from the Posen Gestapo to the *Landräte* of the district (State Archive Poznań, Polizeipräsidium Posen 15, Bl. 10–11).

109. Sec. 5 of the Second Implementing Order of November 2, 1939, by the Reich Ministry of Justice (*RGBl.* I 2133) to the Führer Decree on the Structure and Administration of the Eastern Territories of October 8, 1939 (*RGBl.* I 2042).

110. Cf. the report of April 16, 1942, by the chief public prosecutor of Königsberg (BA R 22/3375) and that of September 3, 1942, by the chief public prosecutor of Kattowitz (BA R 22/3372): "It is difficult to obtain an overview on account of the great interference in criminal prosecution by bodies external to the judiciary. Since the decision as to which cases . . . are to be adjudicated by the courts-martial or the police devolves on the police alone, the judiciary . . . deals only with those that for some reason are not of interest to the police." It further stated that it was not possible to obtain even information on printed forms as prescribed by sec. 163, par. 2, of the Code of Criminal Procedure.

111. Sec. 413 of the Code of Criminal Procedure, old version.

112. Secs. 413, par. 3, and 417, Code of Criminal Procedure, old version, in conjunction with sec. 16 of the decree of September 1, 1939 (*RGBl.* I 39), on measures in the field of the constitution of the courts and administration of justice.

113. *MinbliV* (1942): 1309 (reproduced in *Doc. Occ.* 5:341).

114. In the Warthegau, compulsory fines and compulsory imprisonment, which for more than a year had been permissible without an upper limit (instruction of August 23, 1941, by the Reich governor in the Warthegau, ZS, Film Posen 14, 772 ff.), were thus limited to the maximum penalties provided for in the decree of June 15, 1942.

115. Letter of May 29, 1942, from the Reich Ministry of Justice to the Reich Security Main Office (BA R 22/850).

116. Drews, *Preußisches Polizeirecht* (1936), 113.

117. For the handling of this decree, see the decree of December 21, 1942, by the RFSSuChddtPol (Az. O-Vu R II 3991/42, Institute for Western Studies, Poznań).

118. Cf. the situation reports of July 25 and August 14, 1942, by the Posen chief public prosecutor ("another blow against justice") (BA R 22/3383); in the same context, see also the situation report of September 3, 1942, by the Kattowitz chief public prosecutor (BA R 22/3372). See the minutes of a meeting between representatives of the Reich Ministry of Justice and the top officials of the Annexed Eastern Territories on July 28, 1942, in Berlin (BA R 22/850, p. 5), according to which the Reich Ministry of Justice should study whether a further approach to the Reich Ministry of the Interior as the formally superior authority of the police administration was "expedient." (There are no documents testifying to such an approach.)

119. Memorandum by the Reich Ministry of Justice added at the bottom of a letter dated May 29, 1942, from the Reich Ministry of the Interior to the Reich Ministry of Justice (BA R 22/850).

120. *Ministerialrat* Grau (Reich Ministry of Justice) at the meeting of presiding judges of the courts of appeal and chief public prosecutors, Berlin, February 10–11, 1943 (minutes, p. 51, BA R 22/4200).

121. State Archive Poznań, *Reichsstatthalter* 487, Bl. 14.

122. See the instruction of August 23, 1941, by the Reich governor in the Warthegau to the subordinate authorities (ZS, Posen Film 14, 772 f.).

123. *MinbliV* (1943): 1507 (reproduced in *Doc. Occ.* 5:345).

124. The decree contained the laconic instruction to delete the words "and Jews" "throughout" the First Decree of June 15, 1942, on Police Penal Measures (see note 113).

125. In the Warthegau, the instruction of April 24, 1942, by the Reich governor of Posen to the district president of Posen had already reduced the local police authority to issuing sentences of up to *three* months' prison camp (penal framework under the Police Decree of June 15, 1942: *six* months) (State Archive Poznań, *Reichsstatthalter* 487, Bl. 14).

126. See, for example, the RFSSuChddtPol decree of February 20, 1942, under the terms of which all such "criminal acts" "by aliens" "from the East" were to be prosecuted by the Gestapo (Allgemeine Erlaßsammlung des RSHA, A III f.); see also the situation report of November 28, 1942, by the presiding judge of the Court of Appeal of Königsberg (BA R 22/3375), which speaks of this instruction: the presiding judge states: "The German women—until the Führer forbade this—were often branded by having their hair shorn, being led through the streets, etc."

127. Reports of September 3, 1942, and June 8, 1944, by the chief public prosecutor of Kattowitz (BA R 22/3372, p. 2). Also the situation reports of September 25, 1943, and January 26, 1944, by the chief public prosecutor of Posen (BA R 22/3383); situation report of February 10, 1944, by the chief public prosecutor of Danzig (BA R 22/3360).

128. Situation report of January 31, 1943, by the chief public prosecutor of Königsberg (BA R 22/3375, Bl. 23); situation report of May 31, 1943, by the chief public prosecutor of Posen (BA R 22/3383).

129. Situation report of August 6, 1942, by the chief public prosecutor of Kattowitz (BA R 22/3372), which speaks of a discussion on public executions between the Gauleiter of Upper Silesia and the *Reichsführer*-SS.

130. Situation report of January 31, 1943, by the chief public prosecutor of Königsberg: public execution no longer had a deterrent effect, but only increased the "restiveness" of the Poles (BA R 22/3375).

131. Cf. the situation report of April 11, 1944 (BA R 22/3372), which states, among other things, that the work of the judiciary "is duly appreciated by leading personalities in that it in no way lags behind other such state authorities. For this reason I regret that none of the presiding judges under me . . . have received a mark of honor."

132. Situation report of July 10, 1942, by the presiding judge of the Court of Appeal of Danzig (Nuremberg doc. NG-432). See the situation reports by the chief public prosecutors from 1941 on, especially that of July 26, 1941, by the chief public prosecutor of Marienwerder (Kwidzyn) (BA R 22/

G 5/5 -18), according to which, in the course of an investigation procedure, a Pole was handed over to the Gestapo for trial; on July 2, 1941, the public prosecutor requested the Pole's return. The Pole was executed by the Gestapo on July 8, 1941.

133. More on this subject in part 2, section 1, excursus, 3, a ("Collaboration between the Reich Ministry of Justice and the Police"), above; see also the significant but completely unsatisfying reaction of the Reich Ministry of Justice to the remark by the presiding judge of the Kattowitz Court of Appeal at the meeting of presiding judges of the courts of appeal and chief public prosecutors, Berlin, February 10–11, 1943, that the police courts-martial in Upper Silesia were increasingly taking over the whole administration of justice against Poles, but also against *Germans*. The minister demanded documentary evidence and claimed to be against such practice in principle. He knew of no case in which a German had been condemned by a court-martial, but there were cases in which individuals had been erroneously included in the German Ethnic Classification List in Upper Silesia and had then been treated as Poles by the Gestapo, and also cases of sexual intercourse between Poles and Germans. Poles were dealt with according to the Decree on Penal Law for Poles; Germans were not. It "did happen that the police put the German(s) into concentration camp," and this was right, but in no case was this tantamount to adjudication by a court-martial (minutes, BA R 22/4200; see also note 101 above).

134. An example are the conditions in Łódź, where in certain cases the police themselves intended to decide as a "court." See the situation report of August 14, 1942, by the chief public prosecutor of Posen (BA R 22/3383): "In Łódź it has even come about that the police president let the judge of the court of summary jurisdiction know by a messenger that the police themselves now wished to deal with all criminal cases not liable to a penalty of more than six months, and that such cases should be taken away from the public prosecutor or the court. With this the thought looms in people's minds that the broadening of the retributive powers of the police . . . also includes the possibility to try the accused in an oral hearing. The senior public prosecutor in Łódź has so far managed to prevent this development."

Part Two. Section 2. C. Civil Law

1. *RGBl.* I 2042.

2. See also Pungs, Buchholz, and Wolany, *Ostrechtspflegeverordnung* (1943), 3 f., 6; Klee, *Die bürgerliche Rechtspflege* (1942), 17, 49; Fechner, "Das bürgerliche Recht in den eingegliederten Ostgebieten" (1941), 2481; von Rozycki, "Über den Geltungsbereich des Reichsrechts im Großdeutschen Reich" (1941), 54 ff., 57.

3. Pungs, Buchholz, and Wolany, *Ostrechtspflegeverordnung*, 6 f. (The authors were judges at the Posen Court of Appeal.)

4. Ibid., 6 f., 161; Klee, *Die bürgerliche Rechtspflege*, 17, 47; Fechner, "Das bürgerliche Recht in den eingegliederten Ostgebieten," 2482; see also Enke, "Die Rechtspflege im Volkstumskampf" (1941).

5. Fechner, "Das bürgerliche Recht in den eingegliederten Ostgebieten," 2482; Klee, *Die bürgerliche Rechtspflege*, 47.

6. BA R 43/II/694.

7. Pungs, Buchholz, and Wolany, *Ostrechtspflegeverordnung*, 33.

8. Fechner, "Das bürgerliche Recht in den eingegliederten Ostgebieten," 2485.

9. For example, it was disputed whether sec. 7 of the Führer decree merely propounded that German law as practiced by the courts was to remain valid, or whether, generally speaking, all the regulations under Reich law that conflicted with the National Socialist ideology should become ineffective in the Annexed Eastern Territories (see *Meldungen aus dem Reich*, June 27, 1940, BA R 58/ 151).

10. Fechner, "Das bürgerliche Recht in den eingegliederten Ostgebieten," 2485.

11. Ibid. See also the (undated) list drawn up by the presiding judge of the Posen Court of Appeal regarding the "jurisdiction to be applied in the Annexed Eastern Territories" (Institute for Western Studies, Poznań).

12. Note at Referat II/2 of the Office of the Reich Governor on a discussion with the deputy presiding judge of the Posen Court of Appeal, Dr. Tautphaeus (State Archive Poznań, *Reichsstatthalter 857*, Bl. 80–81).

13. These directives were made known via notification of court of appeal decisions (see circular of November 19, 1940, from the presiding judge of the Posen Court of Appeal to the presiding judge of the District Court [*Landgericht*] there, State Archive Poznań, *Landgericht* Posen 10) or by way of personal instructions to the *Instanzgerichte*, which then adhered to them (Pungs, "Die bürgerliche Rechtspflege im Warthegau" [1941], 2492). See also the letter of October 8, 1942, from the presiding judge of the Posen District Court to the president of the special courts and the criminal and civil courts requesting that the presiding judges of the courts of appeal be sent a report directly—*before* the trial date—of important criminal and civil cases (State Archive Poznań, *Landgericht* Posen 11, Blatt 33).

14. Third-party motor insurance: decree of March 2, 1940 (*RGBl.* I, 495); foreign exchange and checks: decree of December 9, 1940 (*RGBl.* I, 1585); commercial law: decree of June 14, 1941 (*RGBl.* I, 319). The German labor code was not introduced (see Altmann, "Die Entwicklung des Arbeitsrechts im Reichsgau Wartheland" [1941], 2503 ff.), "in order to ensure that they [the Poles] cannot participate in the social advances of the new Germany" (von Rosen–von Hoevel, "Das Polenstatut" [1942], 109 ff., 111). With regard to social security law, see the decrees of November 6, 1940, and March 17, 1941 (*RGBl.* 1940 I, 1511; and 1941 I, 147). Full details of Reich legislation as introduced in the Annexed Eastern Territories in Klee, *Die bürgerliche Rechtspflege*, 18 ff., summary).

15. The corresponding rules on pay were published in the *Reichsarbeitsblatt* 4, no. 2 (1940): 38, 211, 727, 1338, laying down lower wages and a special procedure in the event of labor disputes for Poles. *Deutscher Rechtsanzeiger*, October 5, 1941, no. 235.

16. More details in Buchholz and Wolany, "Zum Grundstücksverkehrsrecht in den eingegliederten Ostgebieten" (1941).

17. Decree of January 15, 1940, on the Protection of the Assets of the Former Polish State (*RGBl.* I, 174); decree of February 12, 1940, on the Public Management of Agricultural and Forestry Operations and Land (*RGBl.* I 355); first and second executive decrees of January 24 and February 1, 1941 (*RGBl.* I 67); decree of September 17, 1940, on the Treatment of the Assets of the Citizens of the Former Polish State, the so-called Polish Assets Decree (*RGBl.* I 1270) (more details in part 1, section 2; see also Klee, *Die bürgerliche Rechtspflege*, 38 f., 55 ff.; Buchholz and Wolany, "Zum Grundstücksverkehrsrecht in den eingegliederten Ostgebieten," 682); decree of August 3, 1941, on the Settlement of Outstanding Claims and Debts of Polish Capital (*RGBl.* I 516).

18. Decree of March 30, 1942 (*RGBl.* I 166) (adoption of the anti-Jewish legislation of the Altreich). The need for "development of the German economic order," "to ensure food supplies to the people," etc., quoted in Klee, *Die bürgerliche Rechtspflege*, 55 ff.

19. Letter of February 8, 1940, from the Reich Ministry of Justice to the Reich Ministry of the Interior (BA R 43 II/1520); also *Meldungen aus dem Reich* (Security service), June 27, 1940 (BA R 58/151).

20. Fechner, "Das bürgerliche Recht in den eingegliederten Ostgebieten," 2482. In this connection, see also Pungs, Buchholz, and Wolany, *Ostrechtspflegeverordnung*, 7.

21. See *Meldungen aus dem Reich*, April 3, 1940 (BA R 58/150) ("the desire to introduce German law is becoming increasingly stronger in judicial circles"). Letter of February 8, 1940, from the Reich Ministry of Justice to the Reich Ministry of the Interior (BA R 43 II/1520), to which various draft laws were appended.

22. Decree of June 6, 1940, on the Implementation of German Penal Law (*RGBl.* I 844); the Decree of December 4, 1941, on Penal Law for Poles (*RGBl.* I 759); more details in Broszat, *Nationalsozialistische Polenpolitik* (1961), 130 ff.

23. Letter of July 12, 1940, from the deputy of the Führer (Bormann) to the Reich Ministry of Justice (BA R 22/1520).

24. Letter of September 18, 1940, from the Reich Ministry of Justice to the RMuChdRkzlei (ibid.).

25. Letter of August 14, 1940, from the Reich Ministry of Justice to the deputy of the Führer (ibid.). "If necessary," the Civil Code should be applicable only to Germans.

26. Letter of July 12, 1940, from the deputy of the Führer to the Reich Ministry of Justice (ibid.).

27. Letter of August 21, 1940, from the deputy of the Führer to the Reich Ministry of Justice (ibid.).

28. Note dated September 11, 1940, from the Reich Chancellery on the point of view of the deputy of the Führer (ibid.).

29. Letter of September 2, 1940, from the deputy of the Führer to the Reich minister and head of the Reich Chancellery (ibid.).

30. Letter of November 1, 1940, from the Reich governor of the Wartheland to the deputy of the Führer (ibid.).

31. Letter of August 21, 1940, from the deputy of the Führer to the Reich Ministry of Justice (ibid.).

32. Note by an official of the Office of the Reich Governor of Posen on a meeting with the deputy of the Führer (apparently without the participation of the Reich Ministry of Justice) on July 19–20, 1940, in Berlin (State Archive Poznań, Reichsstatthalter 857, Bl. 9–10).

33. Note on the discussion (see note 12 above); see also von Rosen–von Hoevel, "Das Polenstatut," 113: "The aim of all the special regulations is to make the distinction between Poles and Germans that the circumstances require. Accordingly, care is taken in the regulations that the Poles should not acquire any legal rights and that they remain limited in their recourse to the law."

34. Letter of November 1, 1940, from the Wartheland Gauleiter to the deputy of the Führer; letter of October 21, 1940, from the Reich minister and head of the Reich Chancellery (BA R 43 II/1520).

35. According to the letter of October 21, 1940, from Bormann (ibid.), the clause in question was worded as follows: "If a claim against a German by an ethnic Pole comes to court, the court shall submit the plea to the *Kreisleiter* of the NSDAP to investigate whether allowing the appeal does not conflict with state or *völkisch* interests. The result of the investigation shall be announced within a week. If the decision is in the negative or the findings are not communicated within the required time limit, the court shall allow the plea; otherwise it shall notify the plaintiff that it is not allowable in that court. If the court finds that a positive or negative answer to the submission is clearly incorrect, it shall submit the proceedings through the official channels to the Gauleiter for a final decision."

36. Notes dated September 23 and December 19, 1940, from the Reich Chancellery (*Ministerialdirektor* Kritzinger) (ibid.).

37. Letter of September 18, 1940, from the Reich Ministry of Justice to the RMuChdRkzlei (ibid.).

38. See the letter of October 21, 1940, from the deputy of the Führer to the RMuChdRkzlei (ibid.).

39. Letters of November 26, 1940, from the head of the Security Police and the Security Service to the deputy of the Führer; and of December 14, 1940, to the RMuChdRkzlei; Reich Chancellery note of December 19, 1940 (ibid.).

40. Letter of December 14, 1940, from the RFSSuChddtPol to the RMuChdRkzlei (ibid.).

41. *RGBl.* I 597 f., 599 ff. (also BA R 43 II/1520); excerpts in *Doc. Occ.* 5:323 f.).

42. More details in Gebert, "Das Handelsrecht in den eingegliederten Ostgebieten" (1942).

43. See Buchholz, "Zur Ostrechtspflege VO" (1941), 2476 ff, 2481; Fechner, "Das bürgerliche Recht in den eingegliederten Ostgebieten," 2481 ff. (2485).

44. Klee, *Die bügerliche Rechtspflege,* 48.

45. Ibid.

46. Buchholz, "Zur Ostrechtspflege VO," 2481. (Buchholz was *OLG-Rat* [councillor of the State Superior Court] at the Posen Court of Appeal.)

47. Enke, "Die Rechtspflege im Volkstumskampf," 2490.

48. Klee, *Die bürgerliche Rechtspflege,* 67.

49. Ibid., 48 f.

50. Pungs, Buchholz, and Wolany, *Ostrechtspflegeverordnung,* 34.

51. Fechner, "Das bürgerliche Recht in den eingegliederten Ostgebieten," 2485 (Fechner was an official in Abt. IV/civil code, of the Reich Ministry of the Interior); cf. letter of February 8, 1940, from the Reich Ministry of Justice to the Reich Ministry of the Interior (BA R 43 II/1520).

52. Klinge, "Bemerkungen zur Begriffsbildung im Polenstrafrecht"; although his comments refer to criminal law, they also correspond to the line taken in the field of the civil code. See also Tautphaeus, "Der Richter im Reichsgau Wartheland" (1941), 2466.

53. See Pungs, Buchholz, and Wolany, *Ostrechtspflegeverordnung,* 34.

54. Ibid.

55. Ibid.; Klee, *Die bürgerliche Rechtspflege;* Schütze, *Das Recht der Ostgebiete* (1942), with appendix 1 (1942) and appendix 2 (1943). Decisions by courts in the Annexed Eastern Territories were only occasionally reported in the legal press, and generally they were related to "normal" Civil Code cases (Posen District Court, November 28, 1940, *DR* [1941] [A]: 2523; Posen Court of Appeal, February 26, 1941 [2519]; April 23, 1941 [2525]; July 30, 1941 [2519]; and January 30, 1942, *DR* [1942] [A]: 938 f.); further examples and material in the State Archive Poznań, *Landgericht* Posen 10 ff.

56. *DJ* (1942): 928.

57. For specific cases, see Pungs, Buchholz, and Wolany, *Ostrechtspflegeverordnung,* 35, Ziff. III. According to them, this interpretation was designed "to combat a possible effort, by *adhering to the letter of the term* 'in the individual case,' to limit the judge's freedom of decision granted to him in the legislation. Everything else should be left to the administration of justice, which already shows gratifying signs that it is worthy of the trust placed in it by its broad but also, in the best sense of the term, moderate use of the provision under sec. 4."

58. This included the exclusion of Poles from relief from the Settlement of Debts Law in its version of September 3, 1940 (*RGBl.* I 1209) (sec. 7, first executive decree), and their exclusion from exemption from the obligation of advance payment of costs in labor court proceedings (sec. 35, first executive decree, in conjunction with sec. 12, par. 3, 2, Labor Court Law) (for more details, see Pungs, Buchholz, and Wolany, *Ostrechtspflegeverordnung,* Ziff. IV, on sec. 35), and the fundamental nonapplication to Poles of the legal distraint limit (sec. 48, first executive decree). Furthermore, the understanding of practice under sec. 4, Decree on the Administration of Justice in the Eastern Territories, was such that Poles were not permitted to be reinstated in the previous situation if exclusion deadlines were missed (sec. 2, first executive decree); the adaptation regulations of the Marriage Law (secs. 19 and 29, first executive decree), the regulations on the coming into effect of Polish decisions after August 26, 1939 (sec. 45, first executive decree), and the regulations on the technical investigation of an order to carry out a Polish sentence (sec. 47, par. 4, no. 3, first executive decree) were to be so interpreted that under no circumstances could "non-Germans" enjoy privileged legal status (see also Pungs, Buchholz, and Wolany, *Ostrechtspflegeverordnung,* and Ziff. IV 2 regarding sec. 48; I 3, II regarding secs. 19, 20; V 1 regarding sec. 45; II 1 regarding sec. 47 of the first executive decree).

59. See Pungs, Buchholz, and Wolany, *Ostrechtspflegeverordnung*, 161, for more details.

60. Klee, *Die bürgerliche Rechtspflege*.

61. Ibid.

62. Pungs, Buchholz, and Wolany, *Ostrechtspflegeverordnung*, 36.

63. Cf. the report by the Wartheland judicial administration (undated, around May 1942) (State Archive Poznań, *Reichsstatthalter* 896, Blatt 126): "Matrimonial procedures played a special role in some localities, where it was generally a matter of disputing the validity of racially mixed marriages. The annulment of such mixed marriages, which are to be regarded as highly undesirable from the standpoint of racial policy, should be particularly encouraged in the interest of the state."

64. Cf. the circular of September 15, 1943, from the *Gau* Office for National Affairs in the *Reichsgau* Wartheland (*Gauamtsblatt der NSDAP, Gau Wartheland*, pp. 18/43): "According to the directives of the *Reichsführer*-SS—Central Settlement Office—pressure should be exerted on the spouse of German nationality or origin to petition for annulment of the marriage if the partner of Polish origin refuses to be registered in the German Ethnic Classification List. . . . Needless to say, an error regarding the nationality of the other spouse justifies annulment of the marriage. But also an error with respect to the true significance of the nationality should always be given considerable weight in the judgment of the Warthegau courts in the light of the national-racial struggle." Regarding application of sec. 4 of the Decree on the Administration of Justice in the Eastern Territories in marriage law, see also Posen Court of Appeal, *DR* (1942) (A): 938.

65. Material in State Archive Poznań, *Landgericht* Posen 10 ff.

66. Pungs, Buchholz, and Wolany, *Ostrechtspflegeverordnung*, Ziff. V, regarding sec. 19, first executive decree (162 f.).

67. Other provisions that were not to be implemented were secs. 84, 85, and 93 of the Marriage Law; further, secs. 86–92 and 94–98 were applicable analogously (ibid., 165 f.).

68. Most associations had long been dissolved before the Decree on the Administration of Justice in the Eastern Territories came into effect (probably by way of a simple implementing regulation) and deleted from the register of associations. In Danzig–West Prussia, all *Polish* associations had been dissolved through the Decree on Associations and Meetings of September 10, 1939 (*Verordnungsbl. Militärbefehlshaber Danzig-Westpreußen* no. 11, p. 11) (Pungs, Buchholz, and Wolany, *Ostrechtspflegeverordnung*, Ziff. II regarding sec. 3, first executive decree).

69. *RGBl.* I 83.

70. *RGBl.* I 444.

71. Pungs, Buchholz, and Wolany, *Ostrechtspflegeverordnung*.

72. Prussian Supreme Administrative Court, December 15, 1938, *JW* (1939): 717.

73. Pungs, Buchholz, and Wolany, *Ostrechtspflegeverordnung*, Ziff. V regarding sec. 3, first executive decree (84).

74. Ibid., 83.

75. Ibid.

76. Letter of November 26, 1940, from the head of the Security Police and the Security Service to the deputy of the Führer (BA R 4 II/1520).

77. Buchholz, "Zur Ostrechtspflege VO," 2480.

78. Enke, "Die Rechtspflege im Volkstumskampf," 2489 ff., 2491 f.

79. Buchholz, "Zur Ostrechtspflege VO," 2480.

80. Ibid.; this quotation is one of the few in which the "German interest" is also explicitly mentioned from the standpoint of the judges; see also Fechner, "Das bürgerliche Recht in den eingegliederten Ostgebieten," 2481 f. (2485), who reaches the same conclusion but on the basis of sec. 4, Decree on the Administration of Justice in the Eastern Territories.

81. Enke, "Die Rechtspflege im Volkstumskampf," 2490.

82. For more details see Fechner, "Das bürgerliche Recht in den eingegliederten Ostgebieten," 2485.

83. Sec. 5 included, for example, "appeals and objections by Poles against a judgment by default, since they were in contradiction with the 'demands of the State and *Volk*'; opposition on the part of Poles to an order for arrest or a temporary injunction; petitions by Poles to reopen an earlier Polish judicial dispute; petitions by Poles to permit execution . . . of a ruling of a [former] Polish court . . . if it favored a Pole against a German; petitions by a Pole in voluntary jurisdiction cases that could go against a German" (see Pungs, Buchholz, and Wolany, *Ostrechtspflegeverordnung*, 40).

84. Buchholz, "Zur Ostrechtspflege VO," 2480.

85. Pungs, Buchholz, and Wolany, *Ostrechtspflegeverordnung*, 41.

86. Buchholz, "Zur Ostrechtspflege VO," 2480.

87. *RGBl.* I 383.

88. Pungs, Buchholz, and Wolany, *Ostrechtspflegeverordnung*, 37 f.

89. Fechner, "Das bürgerliche Recht in den eingegliederten Ostgebieten"; Pungs, Buchholz, and Wolany, *Ostrechtspflegeverordnung*, Ziff I H 6 regarding sec. 5 (40).

90. See Fechner, "Das bürgerliche Recht in den eingegliederten Ostgebieten," for more details.

91. The reason for this may have been the decision to annul to the benefit of the German defendant, the term of limitation—which had been interrupted by the prosecution (sec. 209, par. 1, Civil Code)—of the plea that had been allowed, which was not automatically terminated by interruption of the proceedings. Interruption of the procedure was probably equivalent here to a verdict rejecting the plea without interrupting the term of limitation (sec. 212, Civil Code). Cf. Pungs, Buchholz, and Wolany, *Ostrechtspflegeverordnung*, 40.

92. Pungs, Buchholz, and Wolany, *Ostrechtspflegeverordnung*, 36 f. With this the Reich minister of justice relinquished the principle of equality before the law for "aliens" and Germans; the only principle remaining was that "some legal basis must remain for Poles," but only insofar as this corresponded with the "spirit of the assimilation into the Reich" (letter of September 18, 1940, from the Reich Ministry of Justice to the RMuChdRkzlei, BA R 43 II/1520).

93. Fechner, "Das bürgerliche Recht in den eingegliederten Ostgebieten," 2488.

94. Clause 1, pars. 1–3, and clause 2, Decree on Penal Law for Poles of December 4, 1941 (*RGBl.* I 759).

Part Two. Section 3. The Implementation of *Völkisch* Inequality in the General Government; Introduction

1. See sec. 1 of the Decree on the Development of the Judiciary in the General Government of October 26, 1939 (*VBl. GG* 1939, 4) (reproduced in *Doc. Occ.* 6:102 ff.). Weh, "Das Recht des Generalgouvernements" (1940), 100: "A German and a Polish court system exists in the General Government." The idea of separation also comes out clearly in the terms *German courts* and *non-German courts*.

2. Report of July 1, 1940, 1:44 ff. (BA R 52 II/247).

3. Governor General Frank at a reception for the president of the German Superior Courts in the General Government, September 15, 1943 ("Diensttagebuch," 1943, V, September 15, 1943, BA R 52 II/207).

4. Wille, "Aufbau der Sondergerrichte" (1942), 5 ff. (6) (University Library, Warsaw, Sign. 011249). (Wille was head of the Central Department of Justice in the General Government.)

5. See part 2, section 3, B ("Criminal Law as the Principal Tool of Discriminatory Law"), notes 75–77.

6. *Bericht über den Aufbau im Generalgouvernement* 1 (1940): 51 (BA R 52 II/247).

7. Wille, "Aufbau der Sondergerrichte," 5 ff. (6).

8. Speech by the governor general at the inauguration of the German judiciary in the General Government on April 9, 1940 ("Diensttagebuch," 1940, I, 280 ff., BA R 52 II/176).

9. For more details, see Best, "Grundfragen einer deutschen Großraumverwaltung" (1941).

10. This was true only in the field of the judiciary, since the whole Polish judicial organization (with the exception of the Supreme Court in Warsaw) remained intact (Decree of October 26, 1939, on Polish Jurisdiction in the General Government, *VBl.GG* I, 64), but not for the general administration, which, with the exception of the municipal administration, was destroyed.

11. Cf. sec. 2, par. 1, of the Decree of October 26, 1939, on the Development of the Judiciary in the General Government (*VBl.GG* 1939, 4; also published in *Doc. Occ.* 6:102 ff.), under which it was incumbent on the German judiciary to protect against attacks on the security and reputation of the German Reich and people and on the life, well-being, and property of German citizens.

12. Decree on Polish Jurisdiction in the General Government of February 19, 1940 (*VBl.GG* 1940 I, 64).

13. "Diensttagebuch," January 19, 1940 (quoted from a copy at the IfZ).

14. At the occasion of the inauguration of the German Superior Court in Radom on May 25, 1940, Governor General Frank stated:

A further thought is that this court organization [whereby he means the German organization—Author] of the General Government does not have to be the model for the Polish jurisdiction. It goes without saying that we must compare this jurisdiction with the native [!] jurisdiction in other parts of the world. The internal conflicts of the Polish people should be dealt with in the particular Polish manner. But even in this smallest domain, anything that could be detrimental . . . to the German power structure must be ruled out. The German judiciary . . . is therefore bound to a certain activity that both safeguards Germanness . . . and oversees the Polish administration of justice and in a certain sense develops it. ("Diensttagebuch," 1940, II, May 25, 1940, 525 ff., quoted from the copy at the IfZ).

15. Broszat, *Nationalsozialistische Polenpolitik* (1961), 158.

16. *RGBl.* I 2077.

17. Tautphaeus, "Der Richter im Reichsgau Wartheland" (1941), 2466.

18. These included, inter alia, penal law, economic management, labor law, currency regulations, wage and price control, police law, the church and cultural spheres, prices, etc.

19. Cf. sec. 1, par. 2, of the Decree of February 19, 1940, on Polish Jurisdiction in the General Government (*VBl.GG* 1940 I, 64).

20. For more details, see Thiesing, "Ein Jahr deutsche Gerichte im GG" (1941); Hubernagel, "Aufbau und Aufgabe der deutschen Gerichte im GG" (1941). A detailed description of the German and Polish judicial apparatuses will be found in Wille, "Drei Jahre Aufbauarbeit in der Justiz des GG" (1942). For a full treatment of the structure of the special courts, see Wille, "Aufbau der Sondergerichte"; and Wille, "Die Rechtspflege im Generalgouvernement" (1942); also K. Wille, *Das Generalgouvernement, Seine Verwaltung und seine Wirtschaft* (Kraków, 1943), 106.

21. Thus, the head of the Central Department of Justice in the General Government, K. Wille, like his colleague Dr. Ganser, acted as adviser for political crimes in the Reich Ministry of Justice; a list of political advisers in the Reich Ministry of Justice for 1938 includes these two names (BA R 22/1462). See also part 2, section 3, A ("The Function and Structure of the German Judiciary"), note 24.

Part Two. Section 3. A. The Function and Structure of the German Judiciary

1. Cf. in this connection the statements by Frank at a reception for the president of the German Superior Courts in the General Government on September 15, 1943: The principle of "letting alien justice be administered by alien personnel" was correct; the Polish judiciary had functioned "satisfactorily," and the German leadership could "safely leave it with a certain degree of independence" ("Diensttagebuch," 1943, V, September 15, 1943, BA R 52 II/207).

2. Frank in a speech to German judges at the inauguration of the German Superior Court in

the General Government on April 9, 1940 ("Diensttagebuch," 1940, II, April 9, 1940, excerpts in *Doc. Occ.* 6:108 n. 15).

3. Statements by Governor General Frank at the occasion of the inauguration of the German Superior Court in Radom on May 25, 1940, where he said, "We cannot fall into the error of those jurists of the eighteenth century who praised *Rechtsfindung* as the highest purpose and acted on the principle of *fiat justitia, pereat mundus*" (ibid., May 25, 1940, 525 ff.).

4. Decree of February 19, 1940, on Polish Jurisdiction in the General Government (*VBl.GG* 1940 I, 64, reproduced in *Doc. Occ.* 6:116 ff.).

5. Decree of October 19, 1942, on Non-German Jurisdiction in the Galicia District (*VBl.GG* 1942, 653).

6. Secs. 4–6 of the decree cited in note 4 above.

7. Courts of appeal existed in Warsaw, Kraków, and Lublin before September 1, 1939, so that a court of appeal needed to be established only in Radom and later (1941) also in Lemberg (L'viv) (Wille, "Die Rechtspflege im Generalgouvernement" [1942]).

8. See full details in ibid.

9. By the end of March 1940, all the Polish courts were once again functioning in the district of Warsaw, for example (progress report of the Justice Department in the district of Warsaw dated April 9, 1940, Archives of the Main Commission Warsaw, Regierung des GG/Hauptabteilung Justiz V/87); by the end of June, the Polish judiciary employed a total of 4,145 people, 998 of whom were judges and public prosecutors (approx. ten times as many as the number of German judges and public prosecutors), 2,455 office staff, and 692 ushers and prison officers (*Bericht über den Aufbau im Generalgouvernement* 1 [1940]: 55, BA R 52 II/247).

As of the end of 1942, the General Government possessed 5 courts of appeal, 22 district courts, 239 *Burg* courts and 29 public prosecutors' offices (Wille, "Aufbau der Sondergerichte" [1942], 14). In 1942 the "non-German judicial service" employed 4,293 officials, and 807 employees (1,700 in the Warsaw district alone); the "non-German penal service" employed 1,550 officials and employees (a total of 6,650) (progress report of November 4, 1940, by the head of the office of the Warsaw district, Justice Department, IfZ, MA-158/1, Fasz. 14, p. 2).

10. Secs. 4, 7, 10, 11 of the decree of February 19, 1940 (*VBl.GG* 1940 I, 64); see also the report in the *Krakauer Zeitung* of January 7, 1943. Decree of July 23, 1940 (*VBl.GG* 1940 I, 222).

11. Secs. 8 and 9 of the decree of February 19, 1940 (*VBl.GG* 1940 I, 64).

12. Executive decree of August 1, 1940 (*VBl.GG* 1940 II, 411).

13. *VBl.GG* 1940 I, 68 (reproduced in *Doc. Occ.* 6:121 ff.).

14. Secs. 1–3 of the decree of February 19, 1940 (*VBl.GG* 1940 I, 64); see also sec. 1, par. 2, of the Decree of February 19, 1940, on Polish Jurisdiction in the General Government (*VBl.GG* 1940 I, 64), within the terms of which transfer of criminal cases to the Polish judicial authorities was at the discretion of the German prosecuting authority.

15. Archives of the Main Commission Warsaw, Regierung des GG/Hauptabteilung Justiz V/6.

16. Sec. 4 of the Decree of February 19, 1940, on Transfer of Judicial Matters in the German and Polish Jurisdiction (*VBl.GG* 1940 I, 68), in conjunction with sec. 4 of the Decree on Polish Jurisdiction, February 19, 1940 (*VBl.GG* 1940 I, 64), and sec. 19 of the Decree on German Jurisdiction in the General Government, February 19, 1940 (*VBl.GG* 1940 I, 57).

17. Secs. 5, 6, 8, 9 of the Decree of February 19, 1940, on Transfer of Judicial Matters in the German and Polish Jurisdiction (*VBl.GG* 1940 I, 68).

18. Sec. 8 of the Decree of February 19, 1940, on Polish Jurisdiction (*VBl.GG* 1940 I, 64).

19. *Bericht über den Aufbau im Generalgouvernement* 1 (1940): 55 (BA R 52 II/247).

20. Secs. 16 and 17, par. 1, sentence 1, of the Decree of February 19, 1940, on Polish Jurisdiction in the General Government (*VBl.GG* 1940 I, 64).

21. Ibid., sec. 18, par. 2.

22. Ibid., sec. 18, par. 1. If the decision was already effective when this decree came into force, the time allowed was counted from the coming into force of the decree (sec. 17, par. 1, sentence 2).

23. In this connection, see *Meldungen aus dem Reich* (Security Service) of June 12, 1941 (no. 193) (IfZ Ma-441/4 ff.). In the district of Warsaw, for example, only four judgments were examined by the German supervisory authority before 1942 (Gollert, *Warschau unter deutscher Herrschaft* [1942], 124).

24. *Ministerialrat* Kurt Wille was the representative of the general adviser for political crimes from April 1938 on and was responsible for questions concerning the death sentence in the Reich Ministry of Justice (Reich Ministry of Justice organization plan, BA R 22/4223). On the evidence of the Reich Ministry of Justice staff list, Wille was appointed president of the Central Department of Justice, effective March 15, 1942, and transferred to the General Government (BA R 22/4378). See also the list of political officials in the Reich Ministry of Justice for 1938 (BA R 22/1462), which includes Wille's name.

25. The archives of the General Government were largely destroyed or, if they were still intact at the time of writing, not fully available for scientific research. The above conclusion is corroborated by the few documents from the former Central Department of Justice of the General Government still remaining.

26. A notable example is the circular dated July 18, 1943, issued by the Central Department of Justice (ZS, Poland 342, 204 f.) on the interpretation of the Third Decree on Residence Restrictions for Jews in the General Government of October 15, 1941 (*VBl.GG* 1941, 595), which prescribed the death penalty for any who left the ghetto without permission and those who helped to hide Jews. See also the circular dated May 9, 1942, issued by the Central Department of Justice, which directed the courts to punish the departure of minors as having been set up by the parents(!), who were to be sentenced to death (ZS, Poland 342, 880), sec. 2 of the Juvenile Courts Law notwithstanding (prosecution from the age of 14 years), and the principles of accessory acts.

27. Cf., for example, the circular of September 8, 1941, issued by the Central Department of Justice on the applicability of the Blood Protection Law in the General Government (Archives of the Main Commission Warsaw, Regierung des GG/Hauptabteilung Justiz V/6); see also the circular of March 28, 1944, by the Central Department of Justice, on the applicability of the German juvenile penal law in the General Government: since the education of young Poles was not encouraged, criminal acts on their part were to be dealt with by the Polish judiciary (ibid., V/126, Bl. 8).

28. Cf., for example, the circular of December 8, 1941, on the application of the accelerated procedure under the (Reich) Jurisdiction Decree of February 21, 1940 (*RGBl.* I 405), in penal trials (Main Commission Warsaw, Regierung des GG/Hauptabteilung Justiz V/6).

29. According to the *Bericht über den Aufbau im Generalgouvernement* 1 (1940): 52, a total of 95 German judges and public prosecutors were working in the General Government in the year 1940; in addition there were 56 junior, middle, and senior officials and 143 employees. See H. Frank in the "Diensttagebuch," 1940, I, January 8, 1940, 50 ff. (quoted from the copy in the IfZ).

30. Law of September 16, 1939 (*RGBl.* I 1841). Exceptional opposition was a clear violation of the the rule prohibiting double jeopardy. The Reich attorney general had the right to intervene if he had "serious doubts" about the soundness of the decision. The "Special Senate" at the Reich Supreme Court, which was composed of particularly reliable members, decided on the objection; see Wagner, "Die Umgestaltung der Gerichtsverfassung" (1968), 269 f.

31. *VBl.GG* 1940 I, 57.

32. Files in the Archives of the Main Commission Warsaw, Bestand Sondergericht Kraków, no registration code. The German Superior Court had not recommended a pardon "on principle," even though several German bodies spoke on behalf of the condemned doctor. It is possible, however, that a pardon was nevertheless granted by Governor General Frank and that the sentence was not executed. Certainly the records contain no notice of its execution.

33. Decree by the Führer and Reich Chancellor on the Granting of the Right of Pardon in the General Government of January 30, 1940 (*RGBl.* I, 399). Frank did not want the decree to be published in the official organs under any circumstances ("Diensttagebuch," 1940, I, March 19, 1940 [see note 29 above]).

34. Decree of March 16, 1940, issued by the governor general (*VBl.GG* 1940 I, no. 19).

35. Second Decree by the governor general of April 6, 1940, on the Granting of the Right of Pardon (Main Commission Warsaw, Archives of the General Government, Hauptabteilung Innere Verwaltung II/384).

36. Decree of March 16, 1940, issued by the governor general (*VBl.GG* 1940 I, no. 19); see also the governor general's "Diensttagebuch" of January 18, 1940 (text of five death sentences pronounced by the Warsaw Special Court confirmed and published by the governor general); of January 31, 1940 (confirmation of four death sentences pronounced by the Kraków Special Court); March 8, 1940 (confirmation of four death sentences pronounced by the police court-martial for unauthorized possession of weapons); and March 16, 1940 (text of death sentences pronounced by the courts-martial and special courts of Czenstochau [Częstochowa] and Kraków) (BA R 52 II/175, Bl. 19, 60, 188, 207).

37. The authority entitled to grant pardons under the German jurisdiction within the terms of sec. 33 of the Decree on Pardons of February 6, 1935, in the version of September 1, 1939 (*DJ* [1939]: 96), was vested in the head of the German public prosecutor's office at the special court, and for "non-German" jurisdiction in the governor of the district (the justice department) (governor general's decree of March 16, 1940, *VBl.GG* 1940 I, no. 19; and circular of February 8, 1940, by the Central Department of Justice, quoted in circular of February 1, 1944, by the Central Department of Justice, Archives of the Main Commission Warsaw, Regierung des GG/Hauptabteilung Justiz V/126).

38. "Diensttagebuch," December 1, 1939, quoted from a copy in the IfZ.

39. Decree of January 26, 1940, on Jurisdiction by the Wehrmacht over Civilians in the General Government (*VBl.GG* 1940 I, 41); secs. 2–4, 76 of the Code of Criminal Procedure in Wartime of August 17, 1938 (*RGBl.* 1939 I, 1457 ff.); and sec. 1 of the Decree of August 17, 1938, on the Special War Penal Code (*RGBl.* 1939 I, 1455 ff.).

40. *VBl.GG* 1940 I, 57 (reproduced in *Doc. Occ.* 6:107 ff.).

41. As early as March 1940, a month before the decree of February 19, 1940, came into effect, all the German courts had begun their activities (*Krakauer Zeitung,* March 5 and 11, 1940); in the Lublin district, German courts were already operating in February 1940, with a staff of twenty officials (ibid., April 3, 1940).

42. The German court at Żyrardów was later amalgamated with the German court in Warsaw (*Doc. Occ.* 6:109 n. 18).

43. Cf. the Decree of August 1, 1941, on the Development of the Judiciary in Galicia (*VBl.GG* 1941, 445 f.), which introduced German jurisdiction into Galicia (decrees of November 15, 1939, *VBl.GG* 1939, 34; and of February 19, 1940, *VBl.GG* 1940 I, 57).

44. Sec. 7 of the Decree of November 15, 1939, on Special Courts in the General Government (*VBl.GG* 1939, 34).

45. The first sitting of the Kraków Special Court took place on September 27, 1939 (*Krakauer Zeitung,* November 23, 1939, University Library, Warsaw, Sign. 05763). The court of Czenstochau functioned from September 16, 1939, on which day its first judgment was pronounced; see H. von Krannhals, *Die Tätigkeit der Einsatzgruppen der Sicherheitspolizei in Polen, 1.9.1939–31.10.1939* (1965), manuscript, 100 (BA R 58/1082). For the Petrikau (Piotrków Trybunalski) court, see Wille, "Aufbau der Sondergerichte." The Warsaw Special Court ceased to function at the end of November 1939 (*Krakauer Zeitung,* June 30–July 1, 1940, University Library, Warsaw, Sign. 05763).

46. Decree of September 5, 1939, on Special Courts in the Occupied Polish Territories, issued

by the commander in chief of the army, *Verordungsblatt für die besetzten Gebiete in Polen*, 2 (reproduced in *Doc. Occ.* 5:40 ff.).

47. *VBl.GG* 1939, 34 (reproduced in *Doc. Occ.* 6:104 ff.).

48. Secs. 1, 4, 10 of the decree of November 15, 1939 (*VBl.GG* 1939, 34).

49. Du Prel, *Das Generalgouvernement* (1942), 157.

50. Decree of August 1, 1941, on the Development of the Judiciary in Galicia (*VBl. GG* 1941, 445 ff.); directives of October 13, 1941, on the establishment of special courts in the Galicia district (*VBl.GG* 1941, 603); and January 23, 1942 (*VBl.GG* 1942, 79).

51. Decree of February 19, 1940, on German Jurisdiction in the General Government (*VBl.GG* 1940 I, 57).

52. See note 29 above.

53. *Bericht über den Aufbau im Generalgouvernement* 1 (July 1, 1940): 52 (BA R 52 II/2471).

54. Administration instruction no. 2 (Ziff. 9 and 3-B-3) of March 1, 1941, to the decree of December 1, 1940 (Weh, *Übersicht über das Recht des Generalgouvernements* [1943], A 121 b); see Wille, "Drei Jahre Aufbauarbeit in der Justiz des Generalgouvernements" (1942), 1425 ff., for more details.

55. Secs. 1, 7, pars. 3, 17, of the Decree of December 1, 1940, on the Unified Administration (*VBl.GG* 1940, 357; reproduced in *Doc. Occ.* 6:58 ff.), in conjunction with Ziff. I B, no. 3, of administration instruction no. 1 of April 7, 1941 (Weh, *Übersicht über das Recht des Generalgouvernements*, A 122a, reproduced in *Doc. Occ.* 6:65 ff.).

56. Thus, the attorney general at the Kraków Special Court, who had reported to the Central Department of Justice at the office of the governor general on the treason cases pending there, received a strong reprimand from the Justice Department of the Kraków district for not having gone through the official channels (secret communication from the Justice Department [Kraków district] to the Central Department of Justice, dated June 13, 1942, ZS, Poland 342, 1036).

57. The following were under the obligation to report in the district: the presiding judges of the German courts, the presidents of the special courts, the heads of the Polish courts, the director of the patent office in Warsaw, and the head of the chamber of notaries and lawyers (progress report of the Justice Department at the Office of the District Governor of Warsaw, dated August 8, 1940, Archives of the Main Commission Warsaw, Regierung des GG/Hauptabteilung Justiz V 87). Beginning in March 1941, the progress reports by the courts were supplemented by monthly so-called business reports by the heads of the public prosecutors' offices, special courts, and German courts, which contained brief summaries of business that had come in and had been dealt with, and which were to be submitted by the Justice Department to the Central Department of Justice (directives of the Central Department of Justice dated March 4, 1941 [ibid., V/6], and of February 28, 1944 [ibid., V/126, Bl. 7]).

58. Under the terms of the circular of November 21, 1941, from the Central Department of Justice, the public prosecutors' offices were to report directly to the Central Department of Justice at the office of the governor general, with a copy to the Justice Department of the district concerned. Instructions and directives concerning penal matters went directly to the public prosecutors (ibid., V/6). In matters concerning pardons, the public prosecutors' offices were to submit their proposals as before to the Justice Department of the district, but they were directed by the Central Department of Justice to file a report immediately in addition. Reports to the Central Department of Justice on death sentences were to be sent to the Justice Department of the district as before (circular dated February 8, 1940, from the Central Department of Justice, quoted in the circular of February 1, 1944, ibid., V/126). Regarding reports on so-called ghetto affairs, that is criminal proceedings against Jews condemned to death for leaving the ghetto, a special regulation came into force in March 1942: whereas hitherto regular reports had been filed in such matters, the public prosecutors were instructed to report only in cases in which the governor general was required to

make a decision on a pardon (directives of the Central Department of Justice, January 2, March 30, 1942, ZS, Poland, Film 64, 158).

Part Two. Section 3. B. Criminal Law as the Principal Tool of Discriminatory Law (Special Law) against "Non-Germans"

1. Klein, "Zur Stellung des GG" (1941); Giese, "Die gegenwärtige Staatsangehörigkeit."

2. See part 1, section 3, introduction.

3. Circular dated September 8, 1941, from the Central Department of Justice (Archives of the Main Commission Warsaw, Regierung des GG [Hauptabteilung Justiz V/6]).

4. Cf. sec. 7, par. 2, Decree of June 6, 1940, on the Introduction of the German Penal Code in the Annexed Eastern Territories (*RGBl.* I 844); clause 1, pars. 1, 3; clauses 2, 12, Decree on Penal Law for Poles of December 4, 1941 (*RGBl.* I 759); secs. 4, 5, Decree on the Judiciary in the Eastern Territories of September 25, 1941 (*RGBl.* I, 597).

5. *VBl.GG* 1939, 4.

6. Decree of November 30, 1941, on the Rights of Persons of German Descent in the General Government (*VBl.GG* 1942, 739 f.).

7. Sec. 2, par. 2, of the Decree of October 26, 1939, on the Development of the Judiciary in the General Government (*VBl.GG* 1939, 4; also published in *Doc. Occ.* 6:102 ff.).

8. Sec. 2 of the Decree on Special Courts of November 15, 1939 (*VBl.GG* 1939, 34), in conjunction with sec. 7, par. 2, of the Decree on German Jurisdiction of February 19, 1940 (*VBl.GG* 1940 I, 57).

9. Sec. 1, par. 2, of the Decree on Polish Jurisdiction in the General Government of February 19, 1940 (*VBl.GG* 1940 I, 64).

10. Statements by the head of the Justice Department at the office of the governor general (K. Wille, "Diensttagebuch," 1940, I, 93, BA R 52 II/175).

11. The Wehrmacht courts, though, being directed centrally from Berlin, were instructed to apply the section on substantive law of the Decree on Penal Law for Poles. For full details, see the situation report of May 27, 1942, by the chief public prosecutor, Posen (Poznań), according to which the appropriate instruction was issued on the basis of a decision of the Reich Court-Martial with the agreement of the Reich Ministry of Justice and the Armed Forces High Command (BA R 22/850).

12. See Freisler, "Das deutsche Polenstrafrecht" (1942), 25 ff.

13. *VBl.GG* 1939, 34 (sec. 3).

14. *VBl.GG* 1940 I, 57 (secs. 7 and 8); see also note 7 above.

15. Statements made at the occasion of the introduction of German jurisdiction in the General Government ("Diensttagebuch," 1940, II, April 9, 1940, 279; reproduced in *Doc. Occ.* 6: 108 n. 15).

16. Circular dated March 28, 1944, from the Central Department of Justice (Archives of the Main Commission Warsaw, Regierung des GG/Hauptabteilung Justiz V/126, Bl. 8).

17. Implementing Regulation of May 31, 1941, to the Blood Protection Law (*RGBl.* I 297). Under the terms of the decree, that law was to be applied in racial offenses by German nationals, assimilated nationals, and Jews. According to a note in the "Diensttagebuch" of February 19, 1940, I, 84 ff., the courts were instructed to call for the decision of the governor general in all cases of "racial defilement," by analogy to the Reich regulations, under which the approval of the Reich minister of justice and the Reich minister of the interior was required before sentences against Germans could be implemented. According to a circular dated September 8, 1941, from the Central Department of Justice to the district justice departments, however, only the male German (not the Jewish) party was liable to punishment (the reason probably being the relatively large proportion of Jews in

the General Government, although sec. 5, par. 2, of the Blood Protection Law held the male party to be punishable without distinction [circular of March 28, 1944 (see note 16 above), V/6]). See the report of June 1943 by the commander of the Security Police, Lemberg (L'viv), to the Reich Security Main Office—III (the number of racial defilement cases was "remarkably high") (ZS, Ordner 36, Bl. 49 ff.).

18. Decree of March 20, 1942, on Protection against Major Criminals and Habitual Offenders (*VBl.GG* 1942, 143) (preventive detention or death penalty for major habitual offenders).

19. *VBl.GG* 1941, 595 (reproduced in *Doc. Occ.* 6:542), and circular dated July 18, 1943, from the Central Department of Justice (ZS, Poland 342, 204 f.).

20. Regarding the term *unauthorized leaving* of the ghetto, see the circular of May 9, 1942 (ZS, Poland 342, 880 ff., and Poland Film 64, 166). More on the persecution of those who helped escaped Jews will be found in Bartoszewski and Lewin, *Righteous among Nations* (1969); Szymon Datner, "Niektóre dane o zbrodni Hitlerowskich na Polakach ratujących Żydów" (Some notes on the persecution by the Nazis of Poles who helped the Jews), *Bulletin der Hauptkommission Warschau* 16 (1967): 158 ff.

21. Cf. circular of July 18, 1943, Central Department of Justice (ZS, Poland 342, 204 f.).

22. See part 2, section 3, A ("The Function and Structure of the German Judiciary"), note 26.

23. This was true for the Galicia district, where Poles and Ukrainians lived in close proximity and the judiciary found itself in difficulties on account of the frequent lack of subjective evidence (report of October 7, 1943, by the higher SS and police leader in the General Government, Institute for Western Studies, Poznań, doc. 1–7, excerpts in *Doc. Occ.* 6:452); see also the following note.

24. For example, at the cabinet meeting of March 11, 1942, the governor of the Radom district, Kundt, stated that the public prosecutor's office had for too long neglected to apply the decree on unauthorized departure from the ghetto in the special court at Petrikau (Piotrków Trybunalski) and that therefore no deterrent existed for the Jews emigrating from the Warsaw district. That had now changed ("Diensttagebuch," 1942, BA R 52 II/242).

25. As stated by the head of the office of the district governor of Warsaw, Dr. Hummel, at the cabinet meeting of December 16, 1941; only death sentences had been pronounced in Warsaw; a further six hundred demands for judgment (from the public prosecutor's office?) were pending. For the reasons named, it was impossible to close the ghetto by judicial means. The procedures needed to be "simplified"—for example by using court-martial procedures ("Diensttagebuch," 1941, II/2, BA R 52 II/241).

26. Letter dated February 20, 1942, from the head of the Warsaw district (office chief: Dr. Hummel) to the General Government Legislative Office (ZS, Verschiedenes 69, Bl. 312).

27. See "Die Arbeit der Sondergerichte in der Kriegszeit" (a summary report on the meeting of the special-court presidents and experts on special-court questions to the chief public prosecutors, held in the Reich Ministry of Justice on October 24, 1939) (BA R 22/4158, also Archives of the Main Commission Warsaw; paper by *Ministerialrat* Rietzsch, Reich Ministry of Justice, Bl. 8).

28. Details from *Die Ostgebiete des Deutschen Reiches und des Generalgouvernements* (Berlin-Dahlem, 1940) (ZS, Bl. 9).

29. See the Decree on Violent Acts in the General Government of October 31, 1939 (*VBl.GG* 1939, 10); sec. 2, par. 2, of the decree by the supreme commander of the army on the special courts, September 5, 1939 (*VOBlatt für die besetzten polnischen Gebiete*, 2).

30. Sec. 2, par. 2, of the decree by the supreme commander of the army on the special courts, September 5, 1939 (*VOBlatt für die besetzten polnischen Gebiete*, 2).

31. *VBl.GG* 1939, 34.

32. *RGBl.* I 844.

33. *RGBl.* I 759.

34. *RGBl.* I 405.

35. Wille, "Aufbau der Sondergerichte" (1942).

36. More details in Wille, *Das Generalgouvernement. Seine Verwaltung und Wirtschaft* (Kraków, 1943), 106.

37. A list of all decrees can be found in Pfeiffer, Büttner, and Heubner, *Das Generalgouvernement und seine Wirtschaft* (1942), 6 (BA E 7 a [bibl.]).

38. See Wille, "Die Rechtspflege im Generalgouvernement" (1942); Wille, "Aufbau der Sondergerichte."

39. *RGBl.* I 136.

40. *RGBl.* I 405. With the abrogation of the Reich decree by this decree, the latter now became the basis for proceedings in the special courts, too (cf. sec. 4 of the Decree on Special Courts in the General Government of November 15, 1939, *VBl.GG* 1939, 34; also the circular of December 4, 1941, issued by the head of the Central Department of Justice, Archives of the Main Commission Warsaw, Regierung des GG/Hauptabteilung Justiz V/6).

41. *VBl.GG* 1939, 34 (sec. 4).

42. Cf. "Die Arbeit der Sondergerichte in der Kriegszeit" (1939), manuscript, papers by *Ministerialrat* Rietzsch and *Ministerialdirektor* Crohne of the Reich Ministry of Justice (BA R 22/4158).

43. See, for example, Krieser, "Die Deutsche Gerichtsbarkeit im Protektorat Böhmen und Mähren, Ausübung und Umfang" (1940); Broszat, "Tätigkeit der früheren deutschen Gerichte in der Ukraine."

44. Sec. 16, par. 2, of the Decree on Special Courts of March 21, 1933 (*RGBl.* I 136); and sec. 24 of the Jurisdiction Decree of February 21, 1940 (*RGBl.* I, 405). According, the case was taken up by the regular justice system on appeal by the condemned prisoner, when the circumstances "appeared to necessitate . . . investigating the matter by regular process."

45. Sec. 5 of the Decree on Special Courts in the General Government (*VBl.GG* 1939, 34).

46. Sec. 16, par. 2, of the Decree on Special Courts of March 21, 1933 (*RGBl.* I, 136).

47. Sec. 14 of the Decree on German Jurisdiction in the General Government of February 19, 1940 (*VBl.GG* 1940 I, 57); see also the same wording under clause 10, par. 1, sentence 2, of the Decree on Penal Law for Poles of December 4, 1941 (*RGBl.* I, 759); in this case, however, only the attorney, not the condemned prisoner, had the right to have the case taken up again.

48. Circular of December 4, 1941, by the head of the Central Department of Justice (Archives of the Main Commission Warsaw, Regierung des GG/Hauptabteilung Justiz V/6).

49. Sec. 407, par. 2, of the Code of Criminal Procedure, in conjunction with sec. 23 of the so-called Simplification Decree of September 1, 1939 (*RGBl.* I, 1658).

50. *VBl.GG* 1939, 34; in the territory of the Reich, the powers of the municipal court judges were considerably broadened by the Second Decree of August 13, 1942, on Simplification of Judicial Practice (*RGBl.* I, 508), in that sentences of up to five years' imprisonment and written penal orders could also be imposed in the case of criminal acts. There is no evidence of formal authorization of these competences to the individual judges of the special courts in the General Government.

51. *VBl.GG* 1942, 667 (*Doc. Occ.* 6:123).

52. Fourth Decree of December 13, 1944, on Simplification of Judicial Practice (*RGBl.* I, 339); in this connection see Grau, "Die 4. Verordnung zur Vereinfachung der Strafrechtspflege im Kriege von 13. 12 1944."

53. See the directives of the Central Department of Justice dated February 17, 1942 (Archives of the Main Commission Warsaw, Regierung des GG/Hauptabteilung Justiz V/7).

54. *VBl.GG* 1939, 10.

55. See, for example, the judgment of the Warsaw Special Court of April 15, 1943, by which a Pole was sentenced to two years' imprisonment for violation of the Law against Malicious Acts ("That fucking Hitler will come to grief soon enough") (Archives of the Main Commission Warsaw, Bestand Sondergericht Warschau).

56. Sec. 1, par. 3, Decree on Penal Procedures in Wartime; this included acts to the advantage

of the Soviet Union by Polish civilians committed before June 22, 1941 (the beginning of the Russian war) (see the letter of January 16, 1942, from the Armed Forces High Command to the General Government, ZS, Poland 342, 1018 f.). The Wehrmacht courts first passed on such cases to the Reich Court-Martial on the basis of an agreement with the military commander in the General Government (see letter of December 22, 1941, from the presiding judge of the Reich Court-Martial to the Armed Forces High Command [1020 f.]).

57. Note by the head of the Central Department of Justice written in February 1942 (ibid., 1022); see, further, the discussion of June 5, 1942, between Governor General Frank and the head of the Central Department of Justice ("Diensttagebuch," 1942).

58. Secs. 1–3 of the Decree of January 26, 1940, on Jurisdiction by the Wehrmacht in the General Government (*VBl.GG* I, 41, *Doc. Occ.* 6:106 f.), under which the Wehrmacht courts were empowered to pass on cases to the special courts.

59. Instruction by the Central Department of Justice, May 5, 1942 (ZS, Poland 342, Bl. 1026 f.).

60. Wille, "Aufbau der Sondergerichte."

61. *VBl.GG* 1940 I, 57.

62. According to information supplied to the author by the relevant responsible official (Mag. Solski) at the Archives of the Main Commission Warsaw, September 29, 1971.

63. Wille, "Die Rechtspflege im Generalgouvernement."

64. Secs. 9, 25, of the decree of February 19, 1940 (*RGBl.* I, 405; also in Weh, *Übersicht über das Recht des Generalgouvernements* [1943], C 120); see also the First and Second Implementing Regulations of August 1, 1940 (ibid., C 121), and November 13, 1940 (C 122), respectively.

65. Secs. 28 ff., Jurisdiction Decree of February 21, 1940 (*RGBl.* I, 405). Archives of the Main Commission Warsaw, Regierung des GG/Hauptabteilung Justiz V/6.

66. See Wille, "Aufbau der Sondergerichte," and Wille, "Die Rechtspflege im Generalgouvernement," for details.

67. *VBl.GG* 1942, 667 (reproduced in *Doc. Occ.* 6:123 ff.).

68. With the coming into effect of the Thirteenth Decree to the Reich Citizenship Law of July 1, 1943 (*RGBl.* I, 372), which transferred jurisdiction over Jews to the police, Jews became "unfit to appear before the court" and could thus never take the oath; see Schwarz, *Strafprozeßordnung* (1943), 960, Ziff. 4.

69. ZS, Poland 342, 88.

70. By virtue of this regulation, "the public prosecutor could refrain from pursuing an offense if a punishment had already been served abroad for the same act and the expected punishment at home [was] not heavy."

71. *VBl.GG* 1939, 34; 1940 I, 57, 64.

72. Thus, for example, in May 1944 the Warsaw Special Court sentenced two Germans to two and a half years' and two years' imprisonment, respectively, for severe bribery (accepting presents) (decision of May 4–5, 1944, quoted from the author's statistics; see note 89 below), and in January 1944 an ethnic German, who as head of the finance department of the Warsaw Gas Company had illegally sold two hundred tons of coke, to imprisonment for a year and a half and a fine of 75,000 złoty for an offense against the war economy (decision of January 28, 1944, author's statistics); the Kraków Special Court sentenced a German national by the penal order of April 10, 1943, to the extremely mild term of five months' imprisonment, and as late as January 10, 1945, a Reich German to three months' imprisonment for breaking a work contract (Archives of the Main Commission Warsaw, Akten Sondergericht Kraków, no registration code); cf. the thirteen cases for "racial defilement" by the Lemberg Special Court discussed in the report of June 1943 by the commander of the Security Police, Lemberg, of which (following pressure by the police), two were sentenced to 3 years, one to 4 years, one to 5 years, and 1 to 8½(!) years' imprisonment (ZS, Ordner 36, 49 ff.). See also note 17 above and note 34 to the excursus below.

73. Cf. the pronouncement of the death sentence by the Stanislau (Ivano-Frankivs'k) Special

Court on the *Land* commissar in Nadworna (*Kreishauptmannschaft* [prefecture] Stanislau [Stanisławów], Galicia district), Hozzel, for embezzlement of "considerable quantities" of silver and gold objects handed over by Jews, on the basis of the so-called Parasites upon the *Volk* Decree of September 5, 1939 (report of the commander of the Security Police, Radom, 1943, IfZ, MA-641, 2217–20); see also the death sentence prononouced by the Kraków Special Court (decision of July 3, 1944) on a 19-year-old ethnic German for major theft with violence (author's statistics; see note 89 below). See further report of the commander of the Security Police, Radom (ibid.; also in ZS, Ordner 36, 49 ff.): three death sentences on account of "racial defilement" with rape and looting.

74. "Diensttagebuch," 1940, I, March 16, 1940, 207 (BA R 52 II/175).

75. See the circulars issued by the Central Department of Justice on August 16, 1940 (ZS, Poland 342, 837 f.); October 8 and November 4, 1941 (Archives of the Main Commission Warsaw, Regierung des GG/Hauptabteilung Justiz, V/6).

76. In a discussion on February 10, 1944, the president of the Central Department of Justice, Wille, reported to Governor General Frank on the trial of a German police official who had shot Jews in the course of an operation in the Jewish quarter, ostensibly on account of resistance, authorizing annulment of the proceedings; Frank acquiesced, but wanted it to be put on record that he disapproved "most strongly" with the fact that the annulment was not carried out "by way of the pardon process" but as a matter of mere convenience. In the same discussion, Wille reported on the case of the leader of a forestry protection commando who had killed four Poles under the influence of alcohol because his comrade had been shot down by "bandits," requesting annulment on account of the effects of shock (sec. 5, par. 2, Penal Code); Frank refused, however: "brutalization of morality" could not be tolerated, but the penalty could be served in the Reich ("Diensttagebuch," 1944, February 10, 1944, BA R 52 II/213).

77. Circular dated January 15, 1941, from the head of the Central Department of Justice to the subordinate justice departments of the district (Archives of the Main Commission Warsaw, Regierung des GG/Hauptabteilung Justiz, V/6).

78. ZS, Poland, Film 58, 841 ff.

79. Archives of the Main Commission Warsaw, Regierung des GG/Hauptabteilung Justiz, V/7.

80. Statements by Higher SS and Police Leader Krüger at the meeting in the office of the governor general on January 21, 1940: imprisonment "was not working" and had "lost all character of a deterrent. Everybody wants to go to prison, where they expect to be taken care of and be out of the cold." The death penalty should also be used in the economic sector, for example in cases of profiteering ("Diensttagebuch," vol. I, 78, quoted from a copy in the IfZ).

81. Decision of the Lublin Special Court, November 1941 (Main Commission Warsaw, poster collection, V/32 t/4).

82. Decision of the Radom Special Court, March 5, 1943 (Institute for Western Studies, Poznań).

83. Decision of the German Superior Court, Kraków, June 18, 1943 (case of Zygmunt Walczyński) (original documents in the Archives of the Main Commission Warsaw, Sondergericht Kraków, no registration code); the German court of first instance had pronounced a sentence of two years' imprisonment (see part 2, section 3, A "The Function and Structure of the German Judiciary"], note 32).

84. Thus, by the penal order of March 27, 1941 (ZS, Poland 342, 889 ff.), the Warsaw Special Court condemned a Jew to one year's penitentiary for leaving the workplace without permission, notwithstanding that under sec. 8 of the Decree of November 15, 1939, on Special Courts in the General Government (*VBl.GG* 1939, 34), the maximum sentence that could be imposed by way of a written penal order was one year's imprisonment. By way of the penal order of April 15, 1941 (ZS, Poland 342, 889 ff.), the Warsaw Special Court sentenced a Jew to three months' imprisonment for

not wearing the yellow star. The fee for issue of a written penal order was set at 1, 250 RM(!), a sum that, unless a printing error was at fault, can only be regarded as a draconian fine.

85. Some 80% of the records of the Warsaw Special Court (approx. 10 meters of floor space) have been preserved, as have records of the Kraków Special Court for 1944 (some fifty volumes) and a hundred general files (administration, accounts) (all at the Archives of the Main Commission Warsaw, no registration code). Apart from a few remnants (kept in the Görlitz archives), the records of the special courts of Radom, Lemberg, and Lublin are no longer extant (although indications as to their judgment practice can be gleaned from press notices in the *Krakauer Zeitung*; see the following note). (Information obtained by the author from the responsible official at the Archives of the Main Commission Warsaw, September 29, 1971.)

86. At a meeting of department heads on May 10, 1940, the governor general expressed his astonishment that according to reports in the press, two Jews were fined only 1,500 złoty for profiteering. In his opinion, the verdict in the case of such minor offenses should not be published: publication was meaningful only when the persons concerned were condemned to death ("Diensttagebuch," 1940, I, quoted from a copy in the IfZ).

87. Cf. the statements by Frank at the occasion of the reception of the presiding judge of the German Superior Courts on September 15, 1943, in which he stressed the independence of judges. He, the governor general, and the offices of the General Government could well demand "that we refrain from any interference in the administration of justice by our independent judges." He would defend any attempt to interfere in the process of justice against anybody. No Party office should interfere. The "Germanic ideal of justice" of the independent judge should remain intact ("Diensttagebuch," 1943, V, September 15, 1943, BA R 52 II/207). Cf. the discussion between Governor General Frank and the head of the Justice Department, Wille, on April 18, 1940. The question raised by Wille, whether the National Socialist Association of Law Officers (NSRB) should have a say in the General Government regarding the appointment of lawyers, judges, and public prosecutors, was refused by Frank, since no Party organs whatsoever were allowed to be active in the General Government ("Diensttagebuch," April 18, 1940, vol. 2/1, p. 314, BA R 52 II/217). The relations between Party and Administration in the GG therefore were tense from the beginning (see "Diensttagebuch" 1944 III, 602, BA R 52 II [217]).

88. Speech on the occasion of the introduction of German jurisdiction in the General Government: "Let no one hold any hope that we will be weak, let no one hope that we will allow resistance under the guise of bureaucratic paragraphs. . . . So jurisdiction in the General Government will be hard, but it will be human" ("Diensttagebuch," 1940, II, April 9, 1940,; excerpts in *Doc. Occ.* 6:108 n. 15).

89. The author studied a total of eighty judgments from 1940 to 1944 in the archives of the Warsaw Special Court referred to in note 85 above, a random selection of some 10% of the material, and established statistics on circumstances, charges, and penalties. The decisions of the Kraków Special Court for the year 1944 in the Main Commission archives were also studied. Details of a number of decisions by the special courts of Radom, Kielce, Czenstochau (Częstochowa), Zamość, and Reichshof were gleaned from notices in the official German-language newspaper, *Krakauer Zeitung* (IfZ, also University Library, Warsaw, Sign. 05764); see also note 85 above.

90. The figures were as follows: no death sentences in 1939, 26 in 1940, 16 in 1941, 30 in 1942, 1 in 1943, and none in 1944.

91. Notification by the director of the Brehm District Court at a meeting with representatives of the governor general's office on March 1, 1940: he had only two public prosecutors at his disposal for German jurisdiction but needed at least twenty ("Diensttagebuch," 1940, I, IfZ).

92. *Krakauer Zeitung*, April 25, 1940.

93. Report dated June 15, 1942, by the governor of the Warsaw district (Institute for Western Studies, Poznań, doc. 1–10).

94. Information in the report of June 15, 1942, by the governor of the Warsaw district for May 1942 (Institute for Western Studies, Poznań, doc. 1–10). The 187 death sentences against Jews are probably included in the figure of 192 death sentences.

95. Data from author's statistics and notices in the *Krakauer Zeitung* (see note 89 above).

96. Ibid. Worthy of note is the decision of July 25, 1942, by the Warsaw Special Court, sentencing a Pole who had harbored a Russian prisoner of war to the minimum of one month's imprisonment(!), in spite of the fact that sec. 3 of the Decree on Prisoners of War in the General Government of October 23, 1941 (*VBl.GG* 1941, 601), provided for confinement in a prison or penitentiary.

97. Data from author's statistics (note 89 above).

98. *Bericht über den Aufbau im Generalgouvernement,* vol. I, 49 f. (BA R 52 II/247).

99. As stated by the head of the Justice Department at the governor general's office at a meeting on January 26, 1940 ("Diensttagebuch," 1940, I, IfZ).

100. Tautphaeus, "Der Richter im Reichsgau Wartheland" (1941), 2466 ff. (2477).

101. Gollert, *Warschau unter deutscher Herrschaft* (1942), 122 ff.

102. *VBl.GG* 1940 I, 64; also sec. 3 of the Decree of February 19, 1940, on Transfer of Judicial Matters in German and Polish Jurisdiction (*VBl.GG* 1940 I, 57).

Part Two. Section 3. Excursus: The Criminal Jurisdiction of the Police

1. *VBl.GG* 1939, 10.

2. See, for example, the proclamation of November 13, 1939, by the *Land* commissar for the Chełm district on the execution of eight Poles by the "Lublin Court-Martial" for "murder of an ethnic German" (Main Commission Warsaw, poster collection XIII, 97 t/2).

3. In the spring of 1943, these differences reached their peak with complete rupture of relations. More details in Broszat, *Nationalsozialistische Polenpolitik* (1961), 77 ff.

4. *VBl.GG* 1939, 5.

5. "Diensttagebuch," III/2, September 23, 1941, Bl. 880 (BA R 52 II/185).

6. Draft and explanation of this text, dated February 1, 1942, in ZS, Poland 342, Bl. 911 ff.; it was proposed that the court-martial could also be composed of the *Kreishauptmann* as president and two members of the administration of his district, since the *Kreishauptmann* was the "representative of the German government and the primary representative of the interest of the state in his district."

7. Statement by Governor Zörner, who had incorporated the negative standpoint of the head of the Justice Department of his district, *Kammergerichtsrat* Dr. Zippel, into the draft (position statement of March 1, 1940, in ibid., Bl. 909 f.).

8. Note of March 1940 (no precise date) from the Justice Department at the office of the governor general and letter of March 1940 (presumably March 28) from the Justice Department to the legislation department (ibid., Bl. 913).

9. Letter of November 8, 1941, from the legislation department to the Central Department of Justice (ibid., Bl. 936).

10. Sec. 5, par. 2, of the decree of November 26, 1941 (*VBl.GG* 1941, 662).

11. *VBl.GG* 1939, 10.

12. The courts-martial applied the later Polish penal code in matters of substantive law in this sense. In this connection, see full details in the situation report of July 25, 1942, by the chief public prosecutor, Posen, and the letter of August 4, 1943, from the Reich minister of justice to the *Reichsführer*-SS/SS court (BA R 22/850, Bl. 347 ff.).

13. Cf. the proclamation of the execution by court-martial of two Poles who had looted the homes of Jews who had emigrated, dated August 30, 1942, published by the *Kreishauptmann* of

Neumarkt (Nowy Targ) in the Kraków district. The competence of the court-martial was based on the premise that all houses and equipment of Jewish quarters were regarded or defined as "serving German interests," so that all offenses involving these objects were punishable under the decree on violent criminality (Main Commission Warsaw, poster collection V, 34 t/2).

14. Sec. 10 of the Decree on Violent Criminality, in conjunction with secs. 1 and 2 of the Decree on Possession of Weapons of September 12, 1939 (*VOBl.* Polen, Bl. 8; also in Weh, *Das Recht des GG* [1943], C 300). As early as 1940, the exclusive competence for sentencing for illegal possession of weapons had been transferred to the police courts-martial.

15. *VBl.GG* 1941, 663.

16. Secs. 11 and 12, par. 3, Decree on Violent Criminality.

17. See, for example, the decision of July 19, 1940, by the Kraków police court-martial and the documents appended to it (Main Commission Warsaw, archives, department 01, Sign. 997) and the decision of the military court-martial of January 12, 1940, at Minsk, Masovia (AZ 4 KWs 1/40) (ibid., dept. *Landgericht*).

18. *VBl.GG* 1942, 409.

19. Cf. the proclamation of the execution by the court-martial of six Poles for unlawful slaughtering, January 18, 1943, published by the *Kreishauptmann* of Jasło (Kraków district) (Main Commission Warsaw, Abt. II, 17 t/1). See also the proclamation of November 24, 1942, by the *Kreishauptmann* of Przemyśl: "By order of the General Government, cattle are now subject to the decree on protection of the harvest of July 11, 1942 [*VBl.GG* 409]. Be warned: from now on I will hand over all cases of unlawful slaughtering made known to me . . . to the Court-Martial" (Main Commission Warsaw, poster collection V, 39 t/4).

20. See the report by the governor of Radom, Kundt, at the cabinet meeting of March 11, 1942 ("Diensttagebuch," 1942, BA R 52 II/242). According to this, the following procedure was followed as a rule in rural areas: if the farmers did not deliver, their horse and cart, their only means to bring in the harvest, were taken away. A fine was also imposed through an administrative penalty procedure. If they were unable to pay, they were sent to a so-called *Verwaltungsstraflager* (work camp for minor offenders). See part 2, section 3, C ("Civil Law"), note 13.

21. See note 19 above and the proclamation of August 27 by the *Kreishauptmann* of Sochaczew, in which the hanging of a Pole for setting fire to a stack of grain was announced (Main Commission Warsaw, poster collection VI, 45 t/15).

22. See note 3 above.

23. "Diensttagebuch," October 19, 1943 (1943, quoted from a copy in the IfZ).

24. *VBl.GG* 1943, 589 (*Doc. Occ.* 6:517 f.).

25. In this connection see also Broszat, *Nationalsozialistische Polenpolitik*, 172.

26. Directives on the application of the Decree on Combating Attacks on the German Development Effort in the General Government, October 2, 1943, published by the *Kommandeur* (more correctly, *Befehlhaber*) of the Security Police and the Security Service in the General Government (Archives of the Main Commission Warsaw. 962, vol. 43, quoted in Bartoszweski, *Der Todesring um Warschau* [1966], 195 f. n. 3).

27. Announced to the public by posters.

28. Cf., for example, the death sentences pronounced by the Warsaw Court-Martial on March 27, 1944 (Main Commission Warsaw, Abt. M, Signatur 996), the Kraków Court-Martial on May 11, 1944 (District Commission for the Investigation of Nazi Crimes, Kraków, transcript), and the Petrikau (Piotrków Trybunalski) Court-Martial on July 25, 1944 (Main Commission Warsaw, Abt. II, Sig. 466).

29. Sec. 13, Decree on Violent Criminality (*VBl.GG* 1939, 10). See also the confidential letter of February 22, 1940, from the Central Department, Internal Administration (signed, Siebert) to the *Kreishauptleute* and *Stadthauptleute*: "The governor general has decreed that execution of

court-martial sentences shall until further notice be subject to his approval. Notice is hereby given"
(Main Commission Warsaw, Archiv, Reg. des GG, Hauptabteilung Innere Verwaltung II/453).

30. Discussion of May 31, 1944. As a further reason for his refusal, Wille gave the fact that a
whole series of death sentences had come before the Pardons Commission of the governor general
in which execution had always been carried out in the past ("Diensttagebuch," 1944, III, 607 ff., 610,
BA R 52 II/217).

31. In a discussion with Wille on June 6, 1944, Frank vehemently opposed the final pardoning
of condemned prisoners by the Pardons Commission in order that they should be sent to concentration camp. He refused to support such decisions, since he did not want an official confirmation of
the concentration camps. In his opinion, a pardon was only possible against a certain type of imprisonment, and this was exclusively a matter for the judiciary ("Diensttagebuch," 1944, IV, ibid.).

32. In the discussion of June 6, 1940, Wille named cases in which the judiciary had undertaken the enforcement of imprisonment sentences from which the condemned prisoners had been
pardoned. He no longer had an influence in the case of the others who had been sent to concentration camp ("Diensttagebuch," June 6, 1944, ibid.).

33. See W. Jacobmeyer, "Polnischer Widerstand im deutschen Urteil," VjhZ 4 (1977): 658 ff.,
with many references.

34. See the report of June 1943 by the commander of the Security Police, Lemberg, to the
Reich Security Main Office—III (ZS, Ordner 36, 49 ff.; see part 2, section 3, B ["Criminal Law as the
Principal Tool of Discriminatory Law"], note 72): Since the Lemburg Special Court in part stayed
proceedings because the (German) accused denied sexual intercourse, "influence [was] exerted directly on both the public prosecutors and the Lemburg Special Court in individual cases in order to
counter these exceptional circumstances." The result: of 13 proceedings, 3 ended with the death
penalty, 5 with heavy penitentiary sentences, and 5 were stayed.

35. Thus, according to a proclamation dated June 3, 1941, by the governor of the Warsaw district, hostages had been taken on account of damage to Wehrmacht installations, with the threat
that they would be shot if the sabotage continued (Main Commission Warsaw, poster collection,
68 t/5).

36. The proclamations were generally worded as follows:
On account of an offense under secs. 1 and 2 of the Decree . . . of . . . [VBl.GG no. 82 of October 9, 1943], the court-martial of the Security Police and Security Service for the . . . district
condemned the following to death: [list of names]. The sentence has been carried out in the
case of those named under figure . . . on account of recent murders and robbery with violence
in. . . . Those named under figure . . . are eligible for pardon. Should acts of violence continue
in the next three months, however, especially attacks against Germans, members of states allied with the Greater German Reich, or non-Germans working in the interest of the development work in the General Government, and unless the culprits are immediately apprehended,
the judgment will be carried out also in the case of those eligible for pardon, in such a way
that for each act of violence against anyone under the protection of the Greater German
Reich, the intended pardon will be annulled for at least ten condemned prisoners. In the
event of attacks or acts of violence against installations useful to the German development
work, as many of those named above will be executed as is appropriate to the seriousness of
the action. It is therefore up to the non-German population to bring the pardons into effect by
a corresponding cooperation in preventing acts of violence and a search for the culprits. . . .
[place]. The SS and Police Leader in the district of. . . . Signature.

37. From the collection of proclamations by the respective commanders of the Security Police
and the Security Service in the various districts, some 80% of which have been preserved (according to information from the Main Commission Warsaw, in September 1971) and approx. 70% of
which are housed in the archives of the Main Commission Warsaw, it emerges that above all from

fall 1942 onward, thousands of members of the resistance movement, but also people taken hostage for alleged "illegal activities," "sabotage," "economic crimes," "participation in attacks by gangs," "robbery," etc. were executed by the police courts-martial. The actual number of victims is therefore higher.

38. See the preceding note; and Bartoszewski, *Der Todesring um Warschau* (1968), 195–334; IMT, Nuremberg doc., vol. 36, D-956. In addition there were innumerable executions without trial by the police (so-called street executions), and execution of Jews who were *suspected* of any "offense," without court-martial proceedings. Since the enactment of the Third Decree on Residence Restrictions in the General Government of October 15, 1941 (*VBl.GG* 1941, 595), such "offenses" included leaving the ghetto, which was in fact to be judged by the special courts but was usurped by the police by virtue of a secret order by the commander of the regular uniformed police; see part 2, section 3, B ("Criminal Law as the Principal Tool of Discriminatory Law"), notes 23 and 24. A proclamation by the Security Police unit of Petrikau (Radom district, undated, presumably 1942) indicates that Jews were liable to be shot "without legal proceedings"—here meaning without court-martial proceedings, for the following "offenses": "buying, selling, bartering, or giving presents without permission," "noncompliance with camp or factory regulations," etc. (Main Commission Warsaw, poster collection V, t/3).

39. According to the proclamations (see note 37 above), between June 1942 and December 1943, 777 people were executed by court-martial there alone. To this was added the extermination of whole villages (e.g., in August 1942, shooting of the inhabitants of two villages; shooting of the "male inhabitants" of three villages). (The district came under the administration of the *Oberpräsident* of East Prussia and Reich commissar for the Ukraine, Erich Koch.)

40. Statistics from documents at the Main Commission Warsaw (see note 37 above). For the Warsaw district, see also the proclamations of August 27 and November 4, 1942, by the *Kreishauptmann* of Sochaczew (VI, 45 t/15, 18) and of October 1943 by the *Kreishauptmann* of Sokolow (46, t/21) on a total of 17 executions; for the Kraków district, the proclamation of January 18, 1943, by the *Kreishauptmann* of Jasło (II 17 t/2) on 6 executions. See also the following proclamations (all Institute for Western Studies, Poznań): SS and police leader of the Warsaw district, October 3 and December 15, 17, 20, 1943 (a total of 439 executions); commander of the Security Police, Warsaw, February 28, 1944 (80 executions); SS and police leader, Lublin, December 1943 (18 executions); and commander of the Security Police, Lublin, December 14, 1943 (18 executions). It has not been established whether the last two proclamations refer to the same people and whether those in the Institute for Western Studies, Poznań, are identical with those of the Main Commission as cited in note 37 (copies of proclamations also in ZS, Polen Film 25, Bl. 257 ff.). Full references also in Bartoszewski, *Der Todesring um Warschau*, 195 ff., 357 ff.

41. See note 38 above.

42. Collection of such reports in Institute for Western Studies, Poznań; the execution of *any Jew* outside of the ghetto was considered such a "normal" thing that the regular police (*Ordnungspolizei*), not the Security Police (Gestapo, criminal police) were charged with it. The reports contain neither names nor locations, nor the circumstances of the executions, but only the number of people shot (for example "3 Jews, male," "1 Jew, female"), without any further details. Occasionally there is the appended note: "By order," whereby the secret order of the commander of the uniformed police is meant. Example: The reports of February 16 and 22, 1943, by the *Gendarmeriezug*, Warsaw, to the *Gendarmerie-Hauptmannschaft*, Warsaw (commander of the gendarmerie), announcing the liquidation of a total of 24 "Jews, male" and "Jews, female."

43. More details in Bartoszewski, *Der Todesring um Warschau*, 158 ff., 195 ff.

44. For Kraków, see Zaborowski and Posnański, *Sonderaktion Krakau* (1964), 49 ff.

45. Following a suggestion by the head of the Justice Department at the office of the governor general, a schedule should be appended to the Decree on Violent Criminality transferring the

"immediate" execution of "elements with a heavy record" to the police (draft of March 20, 1940) (ZS, Poland 342, 908 ff.). He brought up the subject again in a discussion with the governor general, whose answer was evasive, stating that an arrangement still needed to be found ("Diensttagebuch," April 18, 1940, vol. 2/I, Bl. 314, BA R 52 II/176).

46. Not only actual resistance, but "any *possible* or *conceivable* resistance, as long as there are groups that offer resistance to the German administration," was defined as a "hostile element" or a "resistance movement" (*Brigadeführer* Streckenbach at the police meeting of May 10, 1940, "Diensttagebuch," 1940, II, Nuremberg doc. PS-2233, 440 ff.; excerpts in *Doc. Occ.* 6:496 ff.).

47. "Diensttagebuch," May 16, 1940 (ibid.), from which it emerges that the security situation was in no way "extremely serious."

48. See the minutes of the police meeting of May 30, 1940 (ibid.), at which the governor general stated:

We don't have to drag these elements first to the concentration camps of the Reich, because that would only cause trouble and unnecessary correspondence with the families, so rather we liquidate the business in this country. Gentlemen, we are not murderers. . . . Any police and SS leader who has the difficult duty of carrying out these executions must be one hundred per cent certain that what is happening is in accord with the judgment of the German nation. For these cases . . . too, the . . . police court-martial proceedings will be maintained so that no impression of arbitrary action or a similar action can possibly arise. The Pardons Commission introduced under my auspices has nothing to do with these matters.

Regarding the AB operation, see Broszat, *Nationalsozialistische Polenpolitik*, 162 f.

49. Police meeting of May 30, 1940 ("Diensttagebuch," 1940, II, Nuremberg doc. PS-2233, 440 ff.; excerpts in *Doc. Occ.* 6:496 ff.).

50. Police meeting of May 30, 1940 (ibid.): "If a judiciary office were crazy enough to subject the actions of any police agency in connection with an important political operation to judicial proceedings and possibly press a charge . . . of dereliction of duty, such an action could be construed as a severe violation of the community interest."

51. Discussion between Wille and Frank, July 12, 1940 ("Diensttagebuch," 1940, III; excerpts in *Doc. Occ.* 6:502 f.).

52. Ibid.

53. See the instruction dated December 17, 1942, by the head of the Gestapo, SS-*Gruppenführer* Müller, to the subordinate Stapo offices, "approx. 35,000 prisoners . . . to be sent immediately to the concentration camps" (Nuremberg doc. NO-1523), if possible young people, and above all "only people fit for work, as otherwise we would defeat the purpose and overload the concentration camp" (Nuremberg doc. NO-2131).

54. Information from the adviser on protective custody at the Reich Security Main Office, Dr. Bernstorff, dated November 4, 1943 (Nuremberg doc. NO-1967). The best-known example is the major raid undertaken in Warsaw and other large cities between January 15 and 22, 1943, for "asocial elements suspected of resistance activities"; according to November 1942 reports by the Reich Security Main Office on heightened activity of Polish resistance groups, the operation was based on an order by Himmler, "to bring a large number of Poles involved in such riots to the concentration camps immediately" (Nuremberg doc. NO-3206).

55. Circulars of October 29, 1940, and March 12, 1941, by the head of the Central Department of Justice (not received; their content is, however, reproduced in the circular of July 10, 1941) (Archives of the Main Commission Warsaw, Regierung des GG/Hauptabteilung Justiz V/6).

56. See, for example, the communication of April 11, 1942, "Deutsches Gericht," Warsaw, to the commander of the Security Police, Warsaw (ZS, Film Polen 62, 187).

57. ZS, Polen 342, 881; sec. 154a, par. 3, Code of Criminal Procedure, stated: "It is possible to refrain from bringing a public accusation if the suspect is banished from the Reich territory." Sec. 456a, par. 1, Code of Criminal Procedure, stated: "The execution authority can . . . refrain from the

execution if the convicted person is extradited to a foreign government on account of another act or is banished from the Reich territory."

58. Letter of October 7, 1942, from the Central Department of Justice to the Polish Appellate Court (ZS, Polen 342, 998).

59. Governor General Frank to the president of the Central Department of Justice in a discussion on May 31, 1944; he was in favor of appearances and "a certain independence of the judiciary from the general government" ("Diensttagebuch," 1944, III, 607 ff., BA R 52 II/217).

60. Discussion with the president of the Central Department of Justice, Wille, on May 31, 1944 (ibid.), and June 6, 1944 (ibid., IV, June 6, 1944); see also note 31 above.

61. Circular of February 12, 1943, from the head of the Central Department of Justice (Archives of the Main Commission Warsaw, Regierung des GG/Hauptabteilung Justiz, V/6), with reference to a decree dated December 30, 1942, that had not been received.

62. Regarding the execution of sentences in the General Government, see the directives of the Central Department of Justice (ZS, Poland 342, Bl. 976 ff.); letter of October 26, 1940, from the Internal Administration Department to the Justice Department at the office of the governor general (Poland 257, Bl. 6). Decree of January 25, 1941, from the Central Department of Justice to the Justice Department of the Radom district on the fundamental application of the penal execution regulations of the Reich in the General Government (Main Commission Warsaw, Regierung des GG/Hauptabteilung Justiz, V/128, Bl. 9). See also full details in the Bericht über den Aufbau im Generalgouvernement 1 (1940): 49 (BA R 52 II/247); Krakauer Zeitung no. 79 of April 5, 1940; Wille, "Aufbau der Sondergerichte" (1942), 5 ff. (13); regarding the clearing of the prisons and the transfer of the prisoners to the Reich at the end of the war, see the note dated August 20, 1943, by the Reich Chancellery (BA R 43 II/1341 a); decree of August 12, 1944, from the Reich Ministry of Justice to the chief public prosecutor, Posen (Main Commission Warsaw V/68, Bl. 25); regarding the clearing of the police prisons and liquidation of prisoners in the event of "unexpected development of the situation," see the letter of July 21, 1944, from the commander of the Security Police, Radom, to the outside office, Tomaschow (Tomaszów Mazowiecki) (ZS, Versch. 10, Bl. 603, reproduced in Doc. Occ. 6:519). For the liquidation of 812 prisoners at the Warsaw remand prison (Rakowiecka Street) under horrible circumstances at the order of the commandant of Warsaw as a consequence of the Warsaw insurrection (after the building had been formally handed over to the SS, so that "the institution would no longer be involved"), see the reports by the deputy head of the prison, Justizinspektor Kirchner, and the head (Regierungsrat Langenbartels), both of August 20, 1944, to the Central Department of Justice (Main Commission Warsaw, Regierung des GG/Hauptabteilung Justiz, V/68, Bl. 27/1–8, 12–14), who forwarded them to the Reich minister of justice (letter of August 25, 1944, ibid., Bl. 27/15).

63. Main Commission Warsaw, Regierung des GG/Hauptabteilung Justiz, V/6 (also in ZS, Poland 342, Bl. 843).

64. This instruction is quoted in the letter of March 20, 1943, from the Warsaw district governor, Department of Justice, to the Polish Appellate Court in Kraków (ZS, Poland 342, Bl. 1002).

65. Circular of March 15, 1941 (Main Commission Warsaw, Regierung des GG/Hauptabteilung Justiz, V/68; also ZS, Poland 342, Bl. 973 f.).

66. Ibid.

67. Circular of May 22, 1941, ibid.

68. Circular instruction of February 28, 1944, from the Central Department of Justice (ZS, Poland 342, 843 ff.).

69. See note 63 above.

70. See note 61 above.

71. Circular instruction of February 28, 1944, from the Central Department of Justice (ZS, Poland 342, 843 ff.).

72. Letter of July 8, 1943, to the head of the Party Chancellery (Nuremberg doc. NO-2718).

Part Two. Section 3. C. Civil Law

1. Details in Wengler, "Das deutsche Privatrecht im Protektorat Böhmen und Mähren und im Generalgouvernement Polen" (1940).

2. See the collection of Civil Code regulations enacted by way of decrees of the governor general in Weh, *Übersicht über das Recht des Generalgouvernements* (1943), C 205 ff.

3. Sec. 19, pars. 1 and 3, of the Decree on German Jurisdiction in the General Government, February 19, 1940 (*VBl.GG* 1940 I, 57).

4. Sec. 19, par. 1, nos. 1–3, ibid.

5. See the Decree of March 16, 1940, on Civil Status Affairs in the General Government (*VBl. GG* 1940, I, 104).

6. Secs. 22–24 of the Decree on German Jurisdiction in the General Government, February 19, 1940 (*VBl.GG* 1940 I, 57), in the version of the amending decree of December 14, 1940 (*VBl.GG* 1940 I, 364).

7. Secs. 19, 20, 30, 2 of the decree of February 19, 1940 (*VBl.GG* 1940 I, 57); regarding the establishment of German trading companies in the General Government, see the decree of November 15, 1939 (*VBl.GG* 1939, 38).

8. Sec. 31 of the decree of February 19, 1940 (*VBl.GG* 1940 I, 57).

9. Sec. 1, par. 1, of the Decree on Polish Jurisdiction in the General Government of February 19, 1940 (*VBl.GG* 1940 I, 64), in conjunction with sec. 19 of the Decree on German Jurisdiction in the General Government of February 19, 1940 (*VBl.GG* 1940 I, 57).

10. A rare example of a special arrangement is a decree enacted in 1942 by the governor general whereby in those cases in which under the disunified Polish law (Austrian law was partly still valid in the south, Prussian law partly in the region that until 1918 belonged to the Prussian province Posen, and the old Russian law partly valid in the other regions occupied by Russia), the "jurisdiction practiced in the capital" was to be applied, not the Warsaw but the Kraków law (containing Austrian-German elements) should obtain. This regulation was intended to have a disunifying effect on the nationality and emphasize the primacy of the German-Austrian law.

11. Secs. 26, 31 of the Decree of February 19, 1940, on German Jurisdiction (*VBl.GG* 1940 I, 57).

12. Sec. 16 of the Decree of February 19, 1940, on Polish Jurisdiction in the General Government.

13. There is evidence for such camps in the Radom district (instruction dated February 3, 1942, by the district governor; letter of May 20, 1942, from the *Kreishauptmann* of Kielce with *subsequent* approval of such a camp by the *Kreishauptmann* [ZS, Ordner 365b]); in the Warsaw district (proclamations of December 5, 1940, and October 1941 by the *Kreishauptmann* of Łowicz); the latter contains the passage, "After several threats of punishment, I arrested three hundred farmers and sent them . . . to a work camp . . . for not having delivered their quotas. I will not hesitate to evacuate whole villages, if need be" (Main Commission Warsaw, poster collection V, 33 t/1–3); a further proclamation of March 20, 1942, announced that a mill had been burned down because the Polish miller had ground wheat without permission (t/5) (see also the proclamations of October 1941 by the *Kreishauptmann* of Sokolow regarding the threat of internment, and the internment of a total of fifty-three farmers at the "Treblinka work training camp" [46 t/10, 13; 56 t/15]); such a camp also existed in the Lublin district (proclamation of November 3, 1942, by the *Kreishauptmann* of Przemyśl [39 t/1]). See also note 20 to the part 2, section 3, excursus.

Conclusion

1. The General Government budget and all sections of the Reich budget were managed in this way: not, as would have been consistent, centrally, but separately for each department. The detach-

ment of officials occurred via the Reich; the governor general had only formal powers of appointment *after* the official had been detached. The General Government was increasingly treated as a territory of the Reich (see the discussion between Hitler and Rosenberg, Lammers, Keitel, and Göring on July 16, 1941, Nuremberg doc. L-221).

2. Cf. the governor general's decree on legislation in the General Government of January 18, 1940 (Weh, *Das Recht des GG* [1943], A 170 n. 6), which named the *Verordnungsblatt für das Generalgouvernement* the official record of legislative acts of the governor general (see also sec. 10 of the First Decree on the Development of the Administration of October 26, 1939 [A 120]). For legislative acts of the governor general, see the individual regulations in Weh, *Das Recht des GG*, A 170 n. 546. Regarding the publication of official proclamations in the *Amtlicher Anzeiger des GG*, see the decrees of July 23 and October 18, 1940 (*VBl.GG* 1940 I, 223, 321; also in Weh, *Das Recht des GG*, A 170).

3. Governor General Frank had always made this painfully clear: "The idea that it is possible to make important political decisions and wage an ideological war at the same time is erroneous... I must postpone the question of what I will do from the *völkisch*-ideological standpoint until after the war. The resettlement maneuvers in the Wartheland remain with us as a horrific memory of one of the most serious violations of this principle. To change this policy would require an enormous effort." "So they shouldn't come with reproaches that we are coddling the Poles if they are doing exactly the same thing in the Reich" (press meeting in Kraków on April 14, 1942, "Diensttagebuch," 1942, I, 297, excerpts in Doc. Occ. 6:437 ff., 443).

4. See note 3.

5. See full details in Ilnytzkyj, *Deutschland und die Ukraine* (1956), 1:152 ff., with further references; also the memoranda of June 22 and August 25, 1941, from the Union of Ukrainian Nationalists (OUNR) to Governor General Frank (reproduced in ibid., 1:150 ff.; 2:386 ff.). See further the secret position paper of September 5, 1942, by Dr. Markull, Ministry for the Occupied Eastern Territories, submitted to Reich Minister Rosenberg (reproduced in ibid., 2:293 ff.)

6. See Bormann's note on a meeting between Hitler and Rosenberg, Lammers, Keitel, and Göring at the Führer's headquarters on July 16, 1941. Among other things, Hitler stated that the partisan war behind the front ordered by the Russians had one advantage: "It gives us the possibility of exterminating whatever is against us."

7. See also the position paper by Markull (see note 5 above, 2:293 ff.), with numerous examples ("District commissars who choose to forbid ethnic Germans to go to church or who confiscate church money from the Ukrainians are just as out of place as those who make a sport of shooting prisoners they have brought in personally"). The terror, which was above all directed against "Jews and Communists," was justified by the atrocities of the NKWD against the Ukrainians before the retreat of the Soviets in 1941 (cf. the eyewitness accounts of June 1941 by German war reporters in Ilnytzkyj, *Deutschland und die Ukraine*, 2:262–72). For details, see the so-called Commissar Decree of May 6, 1941 (elimination of all "political dignitaries" and "political leaders") (Nuremberg doc. PS-884); the Hostage Decree of October 1, 1941, under which hostages were to be taken as a precautionary measure "in nationalist, democratic, middle-class, and Communist circles" (reproduced in Ilnytzkyj, *Deutschland und die Ukraine*, 1:70); the so-called Communist Decree of September 16, 1941, according to which fifty to one hundred "Communists" were to be shot for every German soldier killed in the rear (1:69); and finally the decree on the "ruthless struggle against bandits" of December 16, 1941 (quoted from Kordt, *Wahn und Wirklichkeit* [1947], 104).

8. See Hitler's statements on the policy toward the Soviet Russians (quoted in Picker, *Hitlers Tischgespräche* [1951], 52, 72 ff., 115 f.). See also the *Mitteilungsblatt des Reichssicherheitshauptamtes*, no. 6, of July 10, 1942 (administration of this area "with a colonial approach and by colonial methods") (BA R 58/225, 75 f.). The administrative principles are summarized in the Markull memorandum of September 5, 1942 (see note 5, 2:293 ff.).

9. The Markull memorandum (see note 5, 2:293 ff.) quotes statements by a Kreisleiter, Krütz, claiming that Kiev should be depopulated by a plague. It would be best if the superfluous section of

the population were to die of hunger. Markull remarked in reply that these principles were already a reality.

10. Cf. the Markull memorandum (note 5 above), which quotes everyday statements by German administration officials in the Ukraine; they indicate that the Soviet Russians were treated like a colonial people, comparable to the blacks in Africa (e.g., "when all is said and done, we're among Negroes here" [a statement from a discussion at the Culture Department of the Reich Ukraine Commissariat in April 1942, ibid., 2:297]; "the population is just dirty and lazy," a point of view in the winter of 1941; "anyone who shows any intelligence here will be shot immediately" [*Gebietskommissar Kreisleiter* Becher, Galicia]).

11. See notes 5–8 in part 1, section 2, introduction, I ("Objectives and Outlines of the Implementation of National Socialist Policy")

12. Report by Dr. F. Siebert, "Zur Polenpolitik im GG," of May 4, 1959 (BA Ostdok. 13 GG I b/3).

13. See Hitler in the table talk of July 27, 1942, quoted by Picker, *Hitlers Tischgeschpräche* (1968), 257 f.

14. Cf. Hitler's ideas on the "pacification of the huge territory," which was best brought about by "shooting anybody who looks at all suspicious" (Hitler at a discussion on July 16, 1941, Nuremberg doc. L-221). "The people of the East" must "feel" that the German soldier (or the German generally) was "the master" (circular by the commander in chief of the army [undated], quoted in the report of the commander in chief of the Italian Expeditionary Corps, G. Messe, October 1942, quoted in Ilnytzkyi, *Deutschland und die Ukraine*, 1:71 f.). See also Bormann's notes on a discussion with Hitler, Rosenberg, and Gauleiter E. Koch, who was also Reich commissar for the Ukraine, on May 19, 1942 (BA R 58/1005, 3f.). Regarding the powerlessness of the government vis-à-vis the superiority of leading forces close to the Reich government, see the Markull memorandum (note 5 above).

15. See Fraenkel, *Der Doppelstaat* (1974), 29, 51, 81 ff., with respect to the Anglo-American concept of law. At about the same time as the Reich Labor Court was stating: "In the first half of 1933 the structure of the National Socialist state could not yet be regarded as securely established . . . so long as the Communist threat was not removed, the . . . dangerous situation persisted and made political measures necessary that went beyond their previous judicial limits" (decision of October 17, 1934, *JW* [1935]: 379), the American Supreme Court had to decide whether a constitutional body could claim exceptional circumstances may make the use of exceptional measures necessary, no actions that go beyond constitutional powers could be justified by such an argument; exceptional circumstances did not create or extend the constitutional powers (*Schlechter vs. United States,* 295 US 495, 528; decision of May 27, 1935).

16. Regarding the establishment of constitutional jurisdiction, see the overview in M. Hirsch, "Verfassungsgerichtsbarkeit und Verfassungsgerichte in der Bundesrepublik Deutschland sowie in anderen Staaten," in W. Däubler and G. Küsel, eds., *Verfassungsgericht und Politik* (Hamburg, 1979), paperback, edition ro-ro-ro (this is a series of the editors' house) aktuell, 4439.

Glossary of Traditional German Legal Terms and National Socialist Legal Terminology

This glossary is designed to acquaint the reader with the principal traditional German legal terminology, the formal National Socialist legal terminology, and other terms adopted into the legal language of the time. To a great extent the Nazi terms do not correspond to the traditional German legal terminology, nor do they correspond to legal terms in other languages. For example, the Nazi term *Rechtstaat* (legal state) corresponds neither to that concept in traditional German law nor to the concept of rule of law as it is understood today. Most of the Nazi terms were coinages, new creations, or a misuse of older terms. They often were couched in excessively bureaucratic language and founded on a "racial" basis. When no English-language term corresponding to the German notion exists, the translation is rendered according to the literal meaning of the word. Abbreviations such as RG, RMJ, and the like are explained in the list of abbreviations following the table of contents.

Adlerbrief. Honorary Prussian citizenship

Ahnenerbe. Ancestral Heritage (the National Socialist Society for Research in the Spiritual Roots of Germany's Ancestral Heritage)

Ahnenpaß. Certificate of Ancestry (proving pure "Aryan" descent)

Akademie für Deutsches Recht. Academy of German Law (an academic institution under Nazi Party administration that worked for legal reform outside the Reich Ministry of Justice and to which most leading German professors of law belonged)

Aktion Erntefest. Operation Harvest Festival (SS code name for the mass shootings of some 40,000 Jews in the Lublin District in November 1943)

Alldeutscher Verband. Pan-German League (nationalistic and anti-Semitic association formed during the *Kaiserreich*)

Allgemeines Recht. General (written) law (applicable to all citizens—as contrary to special law; common law is not synonymous, because it contains also the unwritten rules of law)

Allgemeine und innere Verwaltung. General and internal administration (competent for all sectors not assigned to other special authorities)

Allgemeinverfügung(-en). Administrative instruction(-s)

Altreich. Germany in its 1937 borders

Amt des Generalgouverneurs. Office of the governor general (1939–45 in Kraków)

Amt für Beamte. Office of the NSDAP for the Civil Service (as distinguished from the *Reichsbund der deutschen Beamten)*

Amt für Gesetzgebung. Legislative Office (of the NSDAP)

Amtsarzt. (Chief) medical officer

Amtsgericht. District court (court of first instance)

Amtsgerichtsräte, Amtsrichter. District or municipal court judges

Amtsleiter. Head of a local or state administrative office

Änderungsgesetz. Amending law

Angeschlossener Verband. Association or organization affiliated with the Nazi Party

Anordnung. Directive

Anschluss. Annexation, union; in historical terms, the annexation of Austria to Germany, which occurred in March 1938

Anweisung. Instruction or directive

Arbeitsamt. Labor Office

Arbeitsdienst. (German) Labor Service (obligatory for German citizens over the age of 18)

Arbeitseinsatz. Labor allocation, Nazi term for forced labor by nationals of occupied territories

Arbeitserziehungslager. Labor reeducation camp(s)

Arbeitsgericht. Labor court

Ariernachweis. Certificate of "Aryan" descent or Aryan certificate

Arierparagraph. Aryan Paragraph (regulation to exclude Jews from organizations, federations, political parties, and other spheres of public life. First appeared in the Third Reich with the Law for the Restoration of the Professional Civil Service of April 7, 1933)

Arisierung. "Aryanization" (confiscation of Jewish assets and enterprises, which were purchased, usually at low cost, by German individuals and businesses) (Nazi term)

Artverwandt. Racially akin (Nazi term)

Ärztekammer. Physicians' Chamber

Asoziale, asozial. Asocial person, asocial

Auslandsbürger, Auslandsdeutscher, Auslandsreichsdeutsche. German citizen residing abroad

Aussiedlung. Evacuation (transfer of population, e.g., from coastal or bombed areas); in Nazi terminology, deportation of parts of the Polish population of the Annexed Eastern Territories to the General Government

Auswärtiges Amt. German Foreign Ministry

Autoritäres Strafrecht. Authoritarian penal law (a part of legal theory, which focuses on the principle of deterrence and the "objective circumstances" of the offense, not on the subjective will of the offender, and which favors harsh punishment)

Bagatellgericht. Small-claims court

Bandenüberfälle. "Gang attacks" (Nazi term for partisan attacks in occupied territories)

Bauernbund, Deutscher. German Peasants' League

Bayerische Volkspartei. Bavarian People's Party (Weimar Republic)

Beauftragter für den Vierjahresplan. Plenipotentiary for the Four Year Plan

Befehlshaber der Sicherheitspolizei und des Sicherheitsdienstes (= Befehlshaber der SIPO und des SD) (im Generalgouvernement). Commander of the Security Police and the Security Service (also, commander of the SIPO and SD (BdS) in the General Government)

Bekanntmachung. Proclamation

Beratungsstelle für Erb- und Rassenpflege. Counseling Bureau for Heredity and Racial Hygiene (established by the German authorities)

Berufsbeamtengesetz. Professional Civil Service Code

Berufsrecht. Professional Law

Betriebsgemeinschaft. Working community (employers and employees of a firm or plant according to the National Socialist Labor Law)

Betriebsrat. Works council (prescribed by law in every plant employing a certain number of employees)

Betriebszelle. Factory cell (cell of the German Labor Front in an commercial or industrial plant)

Bezirk. District

Bezirksverwaltungsgericht (= Oberverwaltungsgericht). District administrative court, higher administrative court) (court of second instance)

Blutsbewußtsein. "Blood-consciousness" (i.e., race consciousness, a Nazi term)

Blutschutzgesetz. Blood Protection Law (short for Law for the Protection of German Blood and German Honor)

Blutsgemeinschaft. Community of blood purity (Nazi term)

Braunes Haus (Zentrale der NSDAP in Munich). Brown House (Central Office of the NSDAP in Munich)

Bundesdisziplinarhof. Federal disciplinary court (a court of second instance)

Bundesgerichtshof (BGH). (German) Federal Supreme Court

Bundesverfassungsgericht. (German) Federal Constitutional Court

Bund Nationalsozialistischer Deutscher Juristen (seit 1936 Nationalsozialistischer Rechtswahrerbund [NSRB]). League of National Socialist German Jurists (after 1936, National Socialists Jurists' League [NSRB])

Bürgerliches Gesetzbuch (BGB) (1896). (German) Civil Code (1896) (in force since January 1, 1900)

Bürgermeister. Mayor

Chef der Deutschen Polizei im Reichsministerium des Innern (seit 1936 in Personalunion mit

Reichsführer-SS, Heinrich Himmler). Chief of the German police in the Reich Ministry of the Interior (since 1936 in personal union with the *Reichsführer*-SS, Heinrich Himmler)

Denkschrift. Memorandum

Deutschblütigkeit. German-bloodedness (Nazi term)

Deutsche Arbeitsfront (DAF). German Labor Front

Deutscher Dozentenbund. German Lecturers' Association (professional federation affiliated with the NSDAP)

Deutsche Rechtsfront. German Law Front (organization of all jurists under the control of the NSDAP)

Deutsches Beamtengesetz (DBG). German Civil Service Code (1936)

Deutsches Obergericht. German Superior Court (court of second instance in the General Government)

Deutsches oder artverwandtes Blut. Of German or related blood (Nazi term)

Deutsche Volksliste (DVL). German Ethnic Classification List (established in the Annexed Eastern Territories for the racial classification of persons of German descent)

Deutsche Volkspartei (DVP). German People's Party (a liberal party in the Weimar Republic)

Deutschstämmige. (Polish or other) nationals of German descent (Nazi term)

Deutschtum. "Germanness" (Nazi term)

Distrikt, Kreis. District (orig. Austrian), the grouping of several counties (*Kreise*); the General Government was divided into five districts

Doppelstaat, Der. The Dual State (a formulation used by the German lawyer Ernst Fraenkel, who was forced to emigrate during the Nazi era. By this term Fraenkel wanted to show the peculiarity of the National Socialist state: the normative side, the world of written law, on one hand, and the unrestricted powers of the executive, without any legal basis, on the other hand)

Durchführungsverordnung (ident. mit Ausführungsverordnung) (DVO). Implementing decree (an executive decree providing detailed regulations in the execution of a law)

Ehedarlehen. Marriage loan(s)

Ehefähigkeitszeugnis. Certificate of Marriageability (a certificate proving eligibility for marriage within the Nazi racial context)

Ehegesundheitsgesetz. Marital Hygiene Law

Ehetauglichkeitszeugnis. Certificate of fitness for marriage

Eheunbedenklichkeitsbescheinigung. Certificate of nonobjection to marriage

Ehrenbrief. Document conferring honorary citizenship

Ehrengericht. Disciplinary court

Einheitsgesetz (Gesetz über die Einheit von Partei und Statt) (1934). Unity Law (Law to Secure the Unity of Party and State) (1934)

Einsatzgruppe(n). lit. Special duty squad(s) of the Security Police and SD in the Occupied Eastern Territories; in the Soviet Union these were mobile killing units that murdered Jews, Gypsies, political functionaries, and the mentally handicapped

Erbgesundheitsamt. Office for Hereditary Health

Erbgesundheitsgericht. Hereditary Health Court

Erbhof. Farmer's entailed estate, a hereditary farm (in the Nazi context, an agricultural holding reserved to farmers of "German descent")

Erbkrank. Congenitally ill, afflicted with an hereditary disease

Erlaß. Administrative decree, administrative order, administrative directive

Ermächtigungsgesetz vom 23. März 1933. Enabling Act of March 23, 1933

Ernste Bibelforscher. Jehovah's Witness(es)

Freikorps. lit. Free Corps (a voluntary military organization not attached to a larger body of troops; in the German context, those volunteer bands, largely composed of nationalistic officers who coalesced after the dissolution of *the German Imperial Army in 1918*)

Fremdarbeiter. Foreign workers (used for all "non-German" workers in the Third Reich)

Fremdvölkisch. Alien (i.e., "non-German," Nazi term)

Frontkämpfer. Frontline soldier, here a participant in World War I

Führererlaß. Führer

Führererlass über die Gliederung und Verwaltung der Ostgebiete. Führer Decree on the Division and Administration of the Eastern Territories

Führerprinzip. Führer Principle (Fascist principle of authoritarian leadership with unrestricted, absolute powers)

Gau. Regional unit of the Nazi Party organization (Nazi term)

Gauamt für Volkstumspolitik. Gau Office for Ethnic Policy (Nazi term)

Gauführer. Party leader in a *Gau* (Nazi term)

Gaugruppenwalter. Party functionary responsible for certain member groups (Nazi term)

Gauleiter. Leading Nazi Party official in a *Gau* (Nazi term)

Gauleitung. Party's office of a *Gau* (Nazi term)

Gaurechtsamt (der NSDAP). Gau office for legal affairs of the NSDAP (Nazi term)

Gaurechtsamtsleiter. Chief of a Party office for judicial matters in a *Gau* (Nazi term)

Geheime Staatspolizei (Gestapo). Secret State Police (Gestapo)

Geltungsjude. Person counting as a Jew under Nazi law

Gemeinschaft. Community

Gemeinschaftsfremd. Foreign to the community (Nazi term)

Gemeinschaftsfremdengesetz. Law on Aliens to the Community (draft, 1944) (Nazi term)

Gemeinschaftsgefährlichkeit, -schädlich. Danger to the community, harmful to the community (Nazi term)

Generalbevollmächtigter für den Arbeitseinsatz (GBA). Plenipotentiary general for labor allocation

Generalgouvernement. General Government (territory of German-occupied Poland not annexed to the Reich; term originally from the Austrian administration before 1914)

Generalkommissariat. General commissariat (Nazi administration district in the Occupied Soviet Territories)

Generalstaatsanwalt (GStA). Chief public prosecutor

Gerichtsverfassungsgesetz (GVG). Judicature Code

Gesetz gegen gefährliche Gewohnheitsverbrecher. Law against Dangerous Habitual Criminals

Gesetz über den Widerruf von Einbürgerungen und die Aberkennung der deutschen Staatsangehörigkeit. Law on the Revocation of Naturalization and the Deprivation of German Citizenship

Gesetz über die Änderung von Familiennamen und Vornamen. Law on Changes to Surnames and Forenames

Gesetz über die Einziehung volks- und staatsfeindlichen Vermögens. Law on the Seizure of Assets of Enemies of the People and State

Gesetz über die Reichsverweisungen. Law on Expulsions from the Reich

Gesetz über die Zulassung zur Rechtsanwaltschaft. Law on Admission to the Profession of Attorney

Gesetz zum Schutz der Erbgesundheit des deutschen Volkes. Law for the Protection of the Hereditary Health of the German People

Gesetz zum Schutz des deutschen Blutes und der deutschen Ehre. Law for the Protection of German Blood and German Honor (Blood Protection Law)

Gesetz zur Änderung der Strafprozessordnung. Law to Amend the Code of Criminal Procedure

Gesetz zur Sicherung der Einheit von Partei und Staat. Law to Secure the Unity of Party and State

Gesetz zur Verhütung erbkranken Nachwuchses. Law for the Prevention of Progeny with Hereditary Diseases

Gesetz zur Wiederherstellung des Berufsbeamtentums. Law for the Restoration of the Professional Civil Service

Gesundheitsamt. Public Health Office

Gewalttatenverordnung (1939). Decree on Acts of Violence (1939)

Gleichschaltung. lit. Coordination (here, the alignment of political organizations, cultural and professional associations by law to the goals of National Socialist policy)

Großdeutsches Reich, Großdeutschland. Greater German Reich, Greater Germany (which included the occupied and annexed territories of Austria, Czechoslovakia, and Poland) (Nazi term)

Grundrechtsvorbehalt. Reservations of basic constitutional legal rights (i.e., that such rights can be restricted by legislative acts, which, however, may not affect the very essence of these rights; see art. 19, clause 2, of the Constitution [*Grundgesetz*] of the Federal Republic of Germany)

Haager Landkriegsordnung (1907). Hague Convention on the Rules of Land Warfare (1907)

Hauptabteilung Innere Verwaltung (in der Regierung des Generalgouvernements). Central Department of Internal Administration (in the General Government)

Hauptabteilung Justiz (im Generalgouvernement). Central Department of Justice (in the General Government)

Hauptkommission Warschau. Main Commission (for the Investigation of Nazi Crimes in Poland) Warsaw

Haupttreuhandstelle Ost (HTO). Main Trustee Office East (agency established for the confiscation and administration of Polish and Jewish property in occupied Poland)

Heimtückegesetz (Gesetz gegen heimtückische Angriffe auf Staat und Partei). Treachery Law (Law against Treacherous Attacks on State and Party), concerning minor political offenses against the state

Hitlerjugend (HJ). Hitler Youth (youth organization of the NSDAP with the status of a *Parteigliederung*, or structural division)

Höherer SS und Polizeiführer (HSSPF). Higher SS and police leader

Inlandsjude. German Jew (Nazi term for a Jew of German nationality or of German descent)

Innere Mission. Charitable agency of the Protestant Church in Germany

Judenrat (Judenräte). Jewish Council(s)

Judenrein. Purged of Jews (Nazi term)

Jüdische Unterstützungsstelle für das Generalgouvernement. Jewish Aid Office for the General Government

Jüdisch versippt. Related to Jews through marriage (Nazi term)

Jugendgericht. Juvenile court

Kaiserreich. German Empire (1871–1918)

Kammer. Chamber, as Literature Chamber, Film Chamber

Kammergericht. Prussian Supreme Court

Kämpfer, alter. "Old Fighter," an early Nazi Party member (before 1933)

Kennkarte. Identification card

Kollegialgericht. Court composed of several judges (as opposed to a single judge)

Kommandeur der SIPO und des SD (in einem Distrikt des Generalgouvernements) (KdS). Commander of the Security Police and the Security Service (KdS) in a district of the General Government, under control of the *Befehlshaber der SIPO und des SD* in the General Government)

Kommunalverwaltung. Municipal administration

Kommunistische Partei Deutschlands (KPD). German Communist Party

Kreis. Administrative entity (roughly equivalent to a British or American county and comprising several local communities)

Kreishauptmann (pl. Kreishauptleute). Administrative chief of a *Kreis* in the General Government

Kreisleiter. Party leader of a *Kreis*

Kultusgemeinde, jüdische. Jewish community

Lagebericht. Situation report

Land (pl. Länder). State or province (as in a federal nation-state)

Landgericht. State court, of the second instance (dealing with more important criminal and civil cases than an *Amtsgericht*)

Landjägerei. Local police office

Landrat. Prefect (of a *Kreis*)

Machtergreifung. Seizure of power, the takeover of governing power by Hitler and the Nazi Party on January 30, 1933, and especially after the Enabling Act of March 23, 1933

Militärstandgericht. Summary court-martial

Ministerialblatt: Reich Ministerial Gazette

Mischling. Person of mixed descent, half-breed (in Nazi terminology, a descendant of Jewish and Gentile parents or grandparents)

Nachlaßgericht. Probate court

Nacht-und-Nebel-Aktion. Night and Fog Action (secret actions of Wehrmacht and judiciary officials against foreign nationals accused of "punishable offenses against the Reich." Such persons were brought secretly ["by night and fog"] and adjudged by special courts.) (Nazi term)

Nationalsozialistischer Deutscher Studentenbund. National Socialist German Students' League (affiliated organization of the NSDAP)

Nationalsozialistischer Rechtswahrerbund (NSRB). League of National Socialist German Jurists (affiliated organization of the NSDAP) (NSRB)

Nationalsozialistische Volkswohlfahrt (NSV). National Socialist Welfare Organization (affiliated organization of the NSDAP) (NSV)

NS-Frauenschaft. Nazi Women's League (affiliated organization of the NSDAP)

NS-Gliederung. Structural division of the NSDAP (e.g., the Hitler Youth or the SS)

NS-Kraftfahrerkorps (NSKK). National Socialist Motor Corps

Oberbürgermeister. Lord mayor

Obergericht. Superior Court (Court of appeal in the General Government)

Oberkommando des Heeres (OKH). Army High Command

Oberkommando der Wehrmacht (OKW). Armed Forces High Command

Oberlandesgericht (OLG). State Superior Court (also depending on function: appellate court or court of appeal

Oberlandesgerichtspräsident (OLGP). Presiding judge of *Oberlandesgericht*

Oberregierungsrat. Senior high official

Oberreichsanwalt. Reich attorney general

Oberstaatsanwalt. Senior public prosecutor

Oberster Gerichtsherr. lit. Supreme ruler over the judiciary (Nazi term for the Führer as supreme power with unlimited authority and not bound by the law)

Oberster Gerichtshof der Wehrmacht. Supreme Court-Martial of the Wehrmacht

Oberster Prüfungshof für Volkszugehörigkeitsfragen. Supreme Court of Review for Nationality Questions

Oberverwaltungsgericht (OVG). Prussian Administrative Supreme Court

Ordensburgen. Elite Nazi Party schools named after the castles of the Teutonic Order (a term applied by Nazis to schools devoted to training of members of the Hitler Youth destined for political leadership)

Ordnungspolizei. Order police: regular uniformed police; also constabulary in contrast to Security Police, which comprised the Gestapo and the criminal police

Ortsgruppenleiter. Local section head of the Nazi Party (Nazi term)

Ostjuden. Eastern European Jews

Ostraum. Eastern territories (Nazi term for Eastern European countries to be ruled by the Nazis)

Parteigenossen (Pg.). lit. Party comrade, a member of the Nazi Party

Parteigericht. Nazi Party court

Polendelikt. Crime committed by Poles (Nazi term)

Polenstrafrechtsverordnung (1941). Decree on Penal Law for Poles

Polizeidirektion. Police directorate, police headquarters

Polizeirichter. Magistrate

Polizeistandgericht. Police summary court

Polizeiverwaltungsgesetz (1931) (PVG). (Prussian) Law of Police Administration

Positives Recht. Statutory law

Präsidialkanzlei. Presidential Chancellery (united in 1934 with the Chancellery of the Führer)

Privatrecht. Civil law

Protektoratsangehörige. Citizens of the Protectorate (of Bohemia and Moravia)

Rassenpflege. Cultivation of race (eugenics) (Nazi term)

Rassenreferat (im Reichsministerium des Innern). Race Policy section (as in the Reich Ministry of the Interior)

Rassenschande. Race defilement, or miscegenation (as defined by the Nuremberg laws, which declared marriage and sexual relations between "Aryans" and Jews illegal and punishable by law) (Nazi term)

Rassensonderrecht. Special racial laws (especially anti-Jewish legislation)

Rasse- und Siedlungshauptamt (RuSHA). Race and Settlement Main Office of the SS

Razzia. Raid or roundup (as of Jews for deportation)

Recht, formelles. Formal (statutory) law (e.g., procedural law)

Recht, materielles. Substantive law

Recht, öffentliches. Public law (relation between public authorities and between individual and state authorities)

Rechtsstaat. In the context of German legal conceptualization, a state that stands under rule of law and which recognizes legal limitations to its sovereignty

Rechtsverordnung. A decree issued by the executive branch

Referat, Referent. Section, or department, of an agency; section chief

Regierungsbezirk. Administrative district (comprising several *Kreise*)

Regierungspräsident. District president (also the title of the representative of the Reich in Sudetenland)

Regierungsrat. Governmental councilor

Reichsamtsleiter. Head of a Reich office of the NSDAP (Nazi term)

Reichsanwalt. Public prosecutor (at the Reich Supreme Court)

Reichsanzeiger: Reich Gazette (publishing all relevant legal acts of the Reich authorities except laws and decrees, those being published in the *Reich Law Gazette*)

Reichsarbeitsgericht. Supreme Labor Court

Reichsbahn, Deutsche. German National Railroad

Reichsbund der Deutschen Beamten. National League of German Civil Servants (an affiliated organization of the NSDAP founded in 1933 and reorganized by the law of May 27, 1937, as the only organization of Reich, state, and municipal civil servants)

Reichsbürger. Citizen of the Reich (first category of subjects with full political status) (Nazi term)

Reichsbürgergesetz. Reich Citizenship Law (one of the so-called Nuremberg Laws; it created two categories of subjects: *Reichsbürger,* that is, persons of "German" descent with full political status, and *Staatsangehörige,* with minor status, for example, Jews in Germany)

Reichsdeutscher, Reichsdeutsche. Reich German citizen (in contrast to Germans in other countries or annexed territories, e.g., Austria)

Reichsdienststrafhof, Reichsdisziplinarhof. Supreme Disciplinary Court (established by the *Reichsdienststrafordnung* of January 26, 1937, as supreme disciplinary court for civil servants)

Reichsdienststrafordnung. Reich Code of Disciplinary Procedure

Reichserbhofgesetz. Reich Entailment Law

Reichsfinanzhof. Reich Finance Court

Reichsfluchtsteuer. Reich abandonment tax (a tax levied in 1931 on all emigrating Germans to deter emigration and the flight of capital during the Depression; repeatedly amended after 1934 to take advantage of the wave of emigration, especially of Jews, from the Reich)

*Reichsführer-SS und Chef der deutschen Polizei. Reichsführer-*SS and chief of the German police

Reichsgericht (RG). Reich Supreme Court (the highest tribunal in Germany, established in Leipzig by the Judiciary Act of 1877)

Reichsgesetzblatt (RGBl.). Reich Law Gazette (legal register for the Reich since 1871)

Reichskanzlei. Reich Chancellery (established in 1878 as a special bureau for the Reich chancellor, it became important after 1934, with the unitary position of Hitler, to coordinate the intercourse between the chancellor and the Reich ministries)

Reichskommissar für die Festigung des deutschen Volkstums (RKF or RKFDV). Reich Commissar for the Strengthening of German Nationhood (established by the edict of October 7, 1939, in order to resettle those Germans in the conquered areas of Poland who were transferred to Germany from southwestern Europe and the Baltic States)

Reichskriegsgericht. Reich Court-Martial

Reichskriminalpolizeiamt (RKPA). Reich Criminal Police Office (since 1939 part of the Security Police in the RSHA)

Reichsleiter. Party leader at the Reich level

Reichsleitung. Reich administration of the NSDAP (central administration of the NSDAP in Munich)

Reichsrechtsamt (der NSDAP). Reich Legal Office (of the NSDAP)

Reichsrechtsanwaltkammer. Reich Chamber of Attorneys

Reichssicherheitshauptamt (RSHA). Reich Security Main Office (founded 1939; comprised the Security Police [Gestapo and criminal police] and the regular police or order police)

Reichssippenamt. Reich Office for Ancestry Research

Reichsstatthalter. Reich governor, representative of the Führer in the German states as a supervisory authority of their administration, often in merging of office with the NSDAP *Gauleiter* in the *Reichsgaue)*

Reichs- und Staatsangehörigskeitsgesetz (1913) (RuStAG). Reich Nationality Law (1913)

Reichsvereinigung der Juden in Deutschland. Reich Association of Jews in Germany (compulsory association established by decree of July 4, 1939; responsible for Jewish welfare)

Renegaten. Renegades (used in connection with the Deutsche Volksliste to designate persons of German descent who remained loyal citizens of their native country and defended its institutions)

Richterbriefe. Instructions to presiding judges from the Reich Ministry of Justice

Runderlaß. Circular decree, circular order

Schöffengericht. Lay assessor's court

Schutzangehörige, Schutzangehöriger. lit. Protected nationals; politically reliable foreign nationals living in the German Reich and enjoying limited indigenous rights

Schutzgelder. Money paid for protection by an organization

Schutzhaft. Protective custody (euphemism for arbitrary imprisonment by the police, formally based on emergency decree of February 28, 1933)

Sicherheitsdienst (SD). Security Service (an intelligence division of the SS; it also took over executive tasks, e.g., in the *Einsatzgruppen* in occupied Eastern Europe)

Sicherheitspolizei (SIPO). Security Police (comprising criminal police and Gestapo)

Sonderbehandlung. Special treatment (Nazi euphemism for execution or killing)

Sondergericht (SG). Special court (for minor political crimes, established on March 21, 1933, in each district of the *Oberlandesgericht)*

Sonderrecht. The principle of inequality under special law (author's term)

SPD. Social Democratic Party of Germany

SS-Totenkopfverbände (TV). SS "Death's Head Units" (special formations of the SS Guards, used for guarding concentration camps)

SS und Polizeiführer (SSPF). SS and police leader

SS-Verfügungstruppen (VT). SS troops available for special tasks (e.g., as in formations of the SS Guards; the most important of these was the SS-Leibstandarte Adolf Hitler)

Staatsangehöriger. Subject of the German state (not possessing full right of citizenship, based on *Reichsbürgergesetz*; to be distinguished from *Reichsbürger*)

Staatsanwalt. Public prosecutor

Staatsanwaltschaft (StA). Public prosecutor's office

Stadthauptmann (pl. Stadthauptleute). Head of a municipal administration in the General Government

Stahlhelm. lit. Steel Helmets, right-wing soldiers' league founded in late 1918 to combat Communist and socialist uprisings

Stalag. Abbreviation for *Stammlager*, men's prisoners camp

Standesamt. Registry office, where changes in civil status (births, marriages, deaths) are registered

Standgericht. Court-martial

Stellvertreter des Führers. Deputy of the Führer (chief of the Party administration)

Strafgesetzbuch. Penal Code

Strafprozessordnung. Code of Criminal Procedure

Strafregister. Penal or criminal register (method of registry regulated by a decree of February 17, 1934, in which a list is kept at every *Landgericht* of all criminals born in the district and of the sentences they received)

Strafsenat (eines Oberlandesgerichts). Chamber of a high criminal court (i.e., of an *Oberlandesgericht*)

Umwandererzentralstelle. Central Transfer Office (for the resettlement of ethnic German settlers from the Baltic states in the Reich); part of the office of *Reichskommissar für die Festigung deutschen Volkstums*

Untersuchungshaft. Pretrial confinement

Untersuchungsrichter. Examining judge (for a mandatory preliminary judicial investigation, provided by the traditional criminal procedure in all cases in which appeal on questions of fact was excluded)

Verjudung. Spreading of Jewish influence among non-Jews (Nazi term)

Vermögensrecht. Property Law

Verordnung (VO). Decree (subordinate legislation issued by the executive on entitlement in a law with the character of a norm, in contrast to administrative orders without legal value) (equivalent to Rechtsverordnung)

Verordnung über den Aufbau der Verwaltung des Generalgouvernement. Decree on the Administration of Justice in the General Government

Verordnung über den Einsatz jüdischen Vermögens. Decree on the Utilization of Jewish Property

Verordnung über die Anmeldung des Vermögens von Juden. Decree on the Registration of Jewish Property

Verordnung über die Beschlagnahme von privaten Vermögen im Generalgouvernement. Decree on the Seizure of Private Assets in the General Government

Verordnung über die Einführung des bürgerlichen Rechts in den eingegliederten Ostgebieten (Ostrechtspflegeverordnung). Decree on the Implementation of Civil Law in the Annexed Eastern Territories (Decree on the Administration of Justice in the East)

Verordnung über die Strafrechtspflege gegen Polen und Juden. Decree on the Administration of Penal Justice against Poles and Jews

Verordnung über die Veröffentlichung von Bekanntmachungen im Generalgouvernement. Decree on the Publication of Proclamations in the General Government

Verordnung über Sicherheit und Ordnung im Generalgouvernement. Decree on Security and Public Order in the General Government

Verordnung zur Ausschaltung der Juden aus dem deutschen Wirtschaftsleben. Decree on the Exclusion of the Jews from German Economic Life

Volk. Nation, people (in Nazi interpretation, *Volk* in ethnic or racial sense)

völkisch. Synonym for *German* in ethnic or racial sense in the Nazi era

Volksdeutsche. Ethnic German ("racial Germans" with foreign citizenship living outside German frontiers)

volksfremd. Alien to the spirit of the *Volk* (Nazi term)

Volksgemeinschaft. Ethnic or racial community (interpreted in Nazi terminology as the "truly" national community of interests, as opposed to the "artificial" community of civilization or of law)

Volksgenosse. "Ethnic" or "racial" comrade

Volksgerichtshof. People's Court (established in Berlin by laws of April 24, 1934, and April 18, 1936, for cases of political crimes [treason and high treason])

Volksschädling. Antisocial parasite upon the *Volk* (Nazi term)

Volksschule. Elementary school

Volkstum. The entity or characteristics of a *Volk* (in Nazi era, used in an ethnic or racial sense)

Volljude, volljüdisch. Full Jew, fully Jewish (Nazi term)

Vorbeugehaft. Preventive detention (Nazi term for arrest by Gestapo)

Vormundschaftsgericht. Guardianship court

Vorschrift. Regulation

Wachtmeister. Lowest rank in the police

Wandervogelbewegung. A youth movement group in Weimar Germany

Wehrkreisbefehlshaber. Commander of the Military District

Wehrkreiskommando. District Military Command

Wehrmachtsgerichtsbarkeit. Military jurisdiction

Winterhilfe. Winter Relief Fund (Nazi organization that collected clothing and other goods during the war years)

Wirtschaftsrecht. Commercial law

Wirtschafts- und Verwaltungshauptamt der SS. Economic and Administrative Main Office of the SS

Zentrum. Catholic Center Party (in the Weimar Republic)
Zivilpole. Polish civilian working in Nazi Germany
Zivilprozessordnung (ZPO). Code of Civil Procedure
Zuständigkeitsverordnung (1940). Jurisdiction Decree
Zwangsarbeiter. Forced laborer

SS Ranks and American/British Military Ranks

SS	American/British
Reichsführer-SS	
	General of the Army/Field Marshal
Oberstgruppenführer	General
Obergruppenführer	Lieutenant General
Gruppenführer	Major General
Brigadeführer	Brigadier General/Brigadier
Oberführer	
Standartenführer	Colonel
Obersturmbannführer	Lieutenant Colonel
Sturmbannführer	Major
Hauptsturmführer	Captain
Obersturmführer	First Lieutenant
Untersturmführer	Second Lieutenant
SS-Standartenoberjunker	
SS-Standartenjunker	Senior Cadet
SS-Junker	
SS-Führerbewerber	Cadet

The following sources have been consulted:

British Special Legal Research Unit. "Outline of Statutes and Other Legal Enactments Whereby the Nazis Established the Totalitarian State and Obtained Complete Control of Germany." July 2, 1945. Wiener Library, London. Typescript.

Dietl, Clara-Erika, and Egon Lorenz. *Dictionary of Legal, Commercial and Political Terms.* 2 vols. Munich: Beck, 1992.

Gutman, Israel, ed. *Encyclopedia of the Holocaust.* New York: Macmillan, 1990.

Hamilton, L. *The BBC German Vocabulary.* London: Longmans, 1947.

Melland, Brian. Glossary appended to *Anatomy of the SS State,* ed. Helmut Krausnick. New York: Walker, 1968.

Mendelsohn, J., ed. *The Holocaust.* New York: Garland, 1982.

Muret, E., and D. Sanders. *Langenscheidts enzyklopädisches Wörterbuch der englishchen und deutschen Sprache.* Ed. Otto Springer. Vols. 1–2. Munich: Langenscheidt, 1974–75.

Neuburger, Otto. *German-English Dictionary of German Administrative Terms: Civil Affairs Guide.* War Department Pamphlet no. 31–169. Washington, D.C.: Government Printing Office, 1944.

When these sources did not supply sufficient explanations, terms were defined by the author and the translators.

Bibliography

This bibliography has three parts: the first lists unpublished sources; the second reflects scholarship available in 1981, when the first German edition of this book was edited by the Federal Archive in Koblenz, Germany; the third part originally was updated to the end of 1992, just before the second German edition appeared in 1993. Since 1993 a great deal of specialized literature has been published, the citation of which would have been too numerous. It does in any case not affect the basic outlines and conclusions of this book, but is rather a confirmation of these conclusions—or these works refer to very special topics of National Socialist policy, topics that are not discussed in this book, or are not discussed in detail. The third part of the bibliography also includes citations of some detailed studies that were published before 1981 but that were not available then. All of these texts open the way for further studies in many fields—areas of inquiry that are pointed out or mentioned in or even motivated by this book.

UNPUBLISHED SOURCES

Archiwum Państwowe Bydgoszcz (State Archive Bydgoszcz)

Archiwum Państwowe Łódź (State Archive Łódź)

Archiwum Państwowe Poznań (State Archive Poznań)

    Akten des Befehlshabers der Ordnungspolizei
    Akten des Chefs der Zivilverwaltung
    Akten der Gauleitung Wartheland der NSDAP
    Akten der Gendarmeriekreisführer in Rawitsch, Schrimm und Wollstein
    Akten der Kreisleitung Lissa der NSDAP
    Akten der Kriminalpolizeistelle Posen
    Akten des Landgerichts Posen
    Akten der Landsratsämter Grätz, Kempen, Kosten und Lissa

Akten des Polizeipräsidiums Posen
Akten des Reichsstatthalters im Reichsgau Wartheland
Akten der Schutzpolizei Rawitsch
Akten des SD-Abschnitts Posen
Akten der Treuhandstelle Posen
Plakatsammlung

Bundesarchiv (Federal Archive), Koblenz (since 1997, in Berlin)
(abbreviated BA in notes)

R 2	Akten des Reichsfinanzministeriums
R 18	Akten des Reichsministeriums des Innern (einschließlich des früheren Repertoirs 320 des Geheimen Staatsarchivs Preußischer Kulturbesitz)
R 19	Akten des Hauptamtes Ordnungspolizei
R 22	Akten des Reichsjustizministeriums
R 26 IV	Akten des Beauftragten für den Vierjahresplan, Geschäfts- gruppe Ernährung
R 33 II	Akten der Zentralhandelsgesellschaft Ost
R 43 I and II	Akten der Reichskanzlei
R 49	Akten des Reichskommissars für die Festigung deutschen Volkstums
R 52 II	Akten der Regierung des Generalgouvernements, Kanzlei des Generalgouverneurs
R 52 III	Akten der Regierung des Generalgouvernements, Hauptab- teilung Innere Verwaltung
R 58	Akten des Reichssicherheitshauptamtes
R 70/Polen	Akten deutscher Polizeidienststellen in Polen
Allierte Prozesse (1 XVII)	Protokolle und Dokumente der Nürnberger Prozesse; Pro- zeß vor dem amerikanischen Militärgericht gegen Schlegel- berger u. a. (Juristenprozeß)
Ostdokumentation (13)	Berichte über die Tätigkeit der deutschen Verwaltung in östlichen Besatzungsgebieten während des 2. Weltkriegs

Geschäftsverteilungspläne (organizational charts) des Reichsministeriums des Innern

Aktenzeichen 283/39/5231, September 14, 1939
Aktenzeichen Z 6616/4352.31, July 1, 1943
Aktenzeichen ZHB 1001/15.1.1945, January 15, 1945
Sammlung Schumacher zur Geschichte des Nationalsozialismus
Sammlung von Erlassen und allgemeinen Verfügungen des Reichsjustizminister-
iums

Bundesministerium der Justiz (Federal Ministry of Justice), Bonn (since 1997, in Berlin)

Personalakten der Oberlandesgerichtspräsidenten und Generalstaatsanwälte 1933–1945

Sammlung von Erlassen und allgemeinen Verfügungen des Reichsjustizministeriums

Główna Komisja Badania Zbrodni Hitlerowskich w Polsce (Main Commission for the Investigation of Nazi Crimes in Poland), Warsaw (abbreviated Main Commission Warsaw in notes). In 1991 the name was changed to Główna Komisja Badania Zbrodni przeciwko polskiemi narodowi (Main Commission for the Investigation of Crimes against the Polish Nation); in 1998 it was changed to Główna Komisja Ścigania Zbrodni przeciwko polskiemi narodowi (Main Commission for the Prosecution of Crimes against the Polish Nation).

Akten der Regierung des Genralgouvernements, Hauptabteilungen Innere Verwaltung und Justiz, und der Sondergerichte Krakau und Warschau

Plakatsammlung

Institut für Zeitgeschichte (Institute for Contemporary History), Munich (abbreviated IfZ in notes)

Da 056	Drucksachen der Publikationsstelle Berlin-Dahlem
Fa 85	Kopien von Lageberichten der Oberlandespräsidenten an das Reichsjustizministerium (Originale im Bundesarchiv, Bestand R 22)
Fb 85	Kopien von Dokumenten aus dem Prozeß gegen Heuser u. a. vor dem Landgericht Koblenz
Ma 158	Mikrofilme deutscher Akten aus dem Westinstitut Posen
Ma 289, 300, 305, 325, 441, 641	Mikrofilme von Akten von Dienststellen der SS und Polizei (Mikrofilmbestand T 175 des amerikanischen Nationalarchivs, Originale überwiegend im Bundesarchiv in den Beständen R 58, NS 19 und R 70)
Ma 679, 682, 1017	Mikrofilme von Akten militärischer Dienststellen in besetzten Gebieten (Mikrofilmbestand 501 des amerikanischen Nationalarchivs, Originale im Bundesarchiv-Militärarchiv Freiburg/Potsdam)
Ma 708	Mikrofilme von Dokumenten der Zentralen Stelle der Landesjustizverwaltungen in Ludwigsburg

Instytut Zachodni Poznań (Institute for Western Studies, Poznań)

Collection of individual files of German agencies in Poland, in particular of orders and reports of the police (including the *Umwandererzentralen*) and the Security Service (Sicherheitsdienst), of agencies on all levels of general administration and the NSDAP in the incorporated Eastern Territories, also of verdicts of the District Court

Bromberg and the situation reports of the district and municipal civilian administration in the General Government.

Komisja Okręgowa (Regional Office of the Main Commission Warsaw), Poznań (abbreviated Main Commission Warsaw [Poznań Office] in notes)

Serien von Dokumenten aus den Prozessen vor dem Internationalen Militärgerichtsh of und den amerikanischen Militärgerichtshöfen in Nürnberg (Series of documents of the International Military Tribunal and of the U.S. military courts in Nuremberg) (abbreviated Nuremberg doc. in notes)

Series D	Dokumente der britischen Anklagebehörde betr. Sklavenarbeit in der deutschen IndustrieSeries
EC	Dokumente betreffend die deutsche Wirtschaftspolitik und Ausbeutung der Wirtschaft in den besetzten Gebieten
Series L	in London zusammengestellte Dokumente
Series NG	NS-Government, Dokumente von Behörden, insbesondere zur Außenpolitik
Series NO	NS-Organizations, Dokumente betreffend die NSDAP und ihre Gliederungen
Series PS	in Paris von Oberst Storey gesammelte Dokumente
Series WA	in Washington zusammengestellte Dokumente

Zentrale Stelle der Landesjustizverwaltungen (Central Office of the Administrations of Justice of the *Länder*), Ludwigsburg (abbreviated ZS in notes)

Copies of documents, particularly from foreign archives as evidence for investigations in the trials of Nazi capital crimes, among others from the trial against Eichmann in Jerusalem and from the files of the commissar for the Jewish residential area in Warsaw (Auerswald).

SOURCES PUBLISHED BEFORE 1981

Abendroth, Wolfgang, ed. *Faschismus und Kapitalismus.* Frankfurt/Main, 1967. 39 ff.
Ackermann, Josef. *Heinrich Himmler als Ideologe.* Göttingen, 1972.
Adam. "Die rechtlichen Handhaben zur Wahrung der Arbeitsdisziplin." *DVerw* (1940): 289 ff.
———. "Beschäftigung ausländischer Arbeitskräfte," *DVerw* (1941): 321 ff.
Adam, Uwe Dietrich. *Judenpolitik im Dritten Reich.* Düsseldorf, 1972.
Adami, Friedrich Wilhelm. "Das Kündigungsrecht wegen eines jüdischen Mieters." *JW* (1938): 3217 ff.
———. "Das Programm der NSDAP und die Rechtsprechung." *DR* (1939) (A): 486 ff.
———. "Die Gesetzgebungsarbeit im Generalgouvernement." *DR* (1940): 604 ff.
Adler, Hans-Günther. *Der verwaltete Mensch, Studien zur Deportation der Juden aus Deutschland.* Tübingen, 1974.

Ahemm, Hilde. Review of Adler, *Der verwaltete Mensch*. *Stuttgarter Zeitung*, February 23, 1974, 50.

Aldag, Heinrich. *Die Gleichheit vor dem Gesetz in der Reichsverfassung*. Berlin, 1925.

Allen, William Sheridan. *"Das haben wir nicht gewollt": Die nationalsozialistische Machtergreifung in einer Kleinstadt 1930–1935*. Gütersloh, 1966.

Altmann. "Die Entwicklung des Arbeitsrechts im Reichsgau Wartheland." *DR* (1941) (A): 2503–5.

Altstötter, Josef. "Die nationalsozialistische Rechtserneuerung auf dem Gebiete des Bürgerlichen Rechts und der Bürgerlichen Rechtspflege." *DJ* (1943): 83 ff.

Amlacher, G. "Über die Richterreform zur Rechtsreform." *DJ* (1943): 459 ff.

Anschütz, Gerhard. *Die Verfassung des deutschen Reiches*. 14th ed. Berlin, 1933.

Anzilotti, Dionisio. *Lehrbuch des Völkerrechts*. Vol. 1. Leipzig, Berlin, 1929.

Arendt, Hannah. *Ursprünge und Elemente totaler Herrschaft*. Frankfurt/Main, 1958.

Argyle, Michael. *Judenaktion*. Ed. Friedrich Grau. Trans. from the English by W. R. Arndt. Cologne, 1972.

Arndt, Adolf. *Kommentar zum Reichsbeamtengesetz*. 3d ed. Berlin, 1923.

Arndt, J. "Entziehung und Verbringung jüdischen Vermögens (Ausland und Deutschland)." *Gutachten des IfZ* 2 (1966): 92 ff.

Auerbach, H. "Der Begriff 'Sonderbehandlung' im Sprachgebrauch der SS." *Gutachten des IfZ*, Stuttgart, 2 (1966): 182 ff.

———. "Arbeitserziehungslager 1940–1944 mit besonderer Berücksichtigung der im Befehlsbereich des Inspekteurs der Sicherheitspolizei und des SD Düsseldorf liegenden, speziell des Lagers Hunswinkel bei Lüdenscheid." *Gutachten des IfZ* 2:196 ff.

Auswärtiges Amt, ed. *Dokumente polnischer Grausamkeit*. Berlin, 1940.

Bahne, Siegfried. "Sozialfaschismus in Deutschland: Zur Geschichte eines politischen Begriffs." *International Review of Social History* 10 (1965): 211 ff., 245.

Bartoszewski, Władisław. *Der Todesring um Warschau 1939–1944*. Warsaw, 1968.

Bartoszewski, Władisław, and Zofia Lewin, eds. *Righteous among Nations: How Poles Helped the Jews 1939–1945*. London, 1969.

Bauer, Otto. *Zwischen zwei Weltkriegen? Die Krise der Weltwirtschaft, der Demokratie und des Sozialismus*. Bratislava, 1936.

———. "Der Faschismus." In Abendroth, *Faschismus und Kapitalismus*, 113–42.

Bauer, Otto, Herbert Marcuse, and A. Rosenberg. *Faschismus und Kapitalismus: Theorie über die sozialen Ursprünge und die Funktionen des Faschismus*. Frankfurt, 1967.

Baumbach et al. *Zivilprozeßordnung, Kommentar*. 33d ed. Munich, 1975.

Baumgart, Winfried. "Zur Ansprache Hitlers vor den Führern der Wehrmacht am 22. 8. 1939," *VjhZ* (1968): 120 ff.

Bayle, François. *Psychologie et ethique du National-Socialisme: Etude anthropologique des dirigeantes SS*. Paris, 1953.

Becker, Werner. "Das Verhältnis der Staatsanwaltschaft zur Kriminalpolizei im neuen Strafverfahren." *Deutsches Strafrecht* (1938): 167 ff.

——. "Gaurechtsamt und NS-Rechtswehrbund." In Rothenberger, *Das Hanseatische Oberlandesgericht*, 287 ff.

Bein, Alexander. "Der jüdische Parasit: Bemerkungen zur Semantik der Judenfrage." *VjhZ* (1965): 121 ff.

Bennet, George, ed. *The Concept of Empire, from Burke to Attlee, 1776–1947*. London. 1953.

Berenstein, T., A. Eisenbach, and A. Rutkowski, eds. *Eksterminacja Z ydów na Ziemiach polskich w okresie okupacji hitlerowskiej*. Warsaw, 1957.

Berger, Hans Hermann. "Die Deutsche Volksliste in den eingegliederten Ostgebieten." *DVerw* (1941): 327 ff.

Berning, Kornelia. *Vom Abstammungsnachweis zum Zuchtwert (Vokabular des National-sozialismus)*. Berlin, 1964.

Best, Werner. "Der Reichsführer und Chef der Deutschen Polizei." *DR* (1936): 257 ff.

——. "Werdendes Polizeirecht." *DR* (1936): 224.

——. "Die Geheime Staatspolizei." In Frank, *Deutsches Verwaltungsrecht*. Munich, 1937.

——. "Die Polizei." In Frank, *Deutsches Verwaltungsrecht*. Munich, 1937.

——. "Neubegründung des Polizeirechts." *Jahrbuch der Akademie für Deutsches Recht* (1937): 132 ff.

——. "Die bisherige polnische Verwaltung." *DR* (1939) (A): 1805 ff.

——. "Die Schutzstaffel der NSDAP und die Deutsche Polizei." *DR* (1939) (A): 44.

——. "Die Weimarer Verfassung, ein Nachwort zum 11. August 1919." *RVerwBl.* (1939): 757 ff.

——. "Neue Gliederung und Verwaltung des ehemaligen polnischen Staatsgebietes." *DR* (1939) (A): 2089 ff.

——. "Volksordnung und Polizei." *DVerw* (1939): 240 ff.

——. *Die Verwaltung in Polen vor und nach dem Zusammenbruch der polnischen Republik*. Berlin, 1940.

——. "Die deutsche Militärverwaltung in Frankreich." *Reich-Volksordnung-Lebensraum* 1 (1941): 29 ff.

——. *Die Deutsche Polizei*. Darmstadt, 1941.

——. "Grundfragen einer deutschen Großraumverwaltung." In *Festgabe für Heinrich Himmler*, 33 ff. Darmstadt, 1941.

——. "Nochmals: Völkische Großraumordnung statt völkerrechtlicher Großraumordnung." *DR* (1941) (A): 1533 f.

Bindewald, Helmut. *Der Gleichheitsgedanke im Rechtsstaat der Gegenwart*. Bamberg, 1931.

Blanke, Bernhard, Reimut Reiche, and Jürgen Wirth. "Die Faschismus-Theorie der DDR." *Das Argument* 33 (1965): 33 ff.

Blau, Bruno. *Das Ausnahmerecht für die Juden in Deutschland 1933–1945*. 3d ed. Düsseldorf, 1965.

Bloch, Ernst. "Der Faschismus als Erscheinungsform der Ungleichzeitigkeit." In Nolte, *Theorien über den Faschismus*.

Boberach, Heinz. *Meldungen aus dem Reich: Auswahl aus den geheimen Lageberichten des Sicherheitsdienstes der SS 1939–1944.* Munich, 1968.

——, ed. *Meldungen aus dem Reich.* Neuwied, Berlin, 1965.

——, ed. *Richterbriefe. Dokumente zur Beeinflussung der deutschen Rechtsprechung 1942–1944.* Vol. 21. of *Schriften des Bundesarchivs.* Boppard, Rhine, 1975.

Boehr. "Nochmals: Die Schutzhaft gem. der Verordnung vom 28. 2. 1933." *JW* (1933): 2499 ff.

Böhme, Albrecht. "Die Vorbeugungsaufgaben der Polizei." *DR* (1936): 142 ff.

Böhmer, Gustav. "Die 'Guten Sitten' im Zeichen Nationalsozialistischer Familienpflicht." *ZAKfDtRecht* (1941): 73.

Bollmus, Reinhard. *Das Amt Rosenberg und seine Gegner.* Stuttgart, 1970.

Bossowski, J. J., et al. "Uniwersytet Poznánski na początku Hitlerowskiej okupacij." *Przegląd Zachodni* 7–8 (1935).

Bracher, Karl Dietrich. *Die Auflösung der Weimarer Republik.* 3d ed. Villingen, 1960.

——. "Stufen totalitärer Gleichschaltung: Die Befestigung der nationalsozialistischen Herrschaft." *VjhZ* 4 (1966).

——. *Die deutsche Diktatur: Entstehung, Struktur, Folgen des Nationalsozialismus.* 2d ed. Cologne, Berlin, 1969.

——. *Zeitgeschichtliche Kontroversen im Faschismus, Totalitarismus, Demokratie.* Munich, 1976.

Bracher, Karl Dietrich, Wolfgang Sauer, and Gerhard Schulz. *Die nationalsozialistische Machtergreifung.* 2d ed. Cologne, 1962 (1st ed., 1960).

Brandt, Edmund, ed. *Die politische Treuepflicht: Rechtsquellen zur Geschichte des deutschen Berufsbeamtentums.* Karlsruhe, 1976.

Brecht, Arnold. "Civil Service." In *Social Research*, vol. 3. New York, 1936.

——. "Bureaucratic Sabotage." In *The Annals of the American Academy of Political and Social Science*, vol. 189, 49 ff. Philadelphia, 1937.

——. "How Bureaucracies Develop and Function." In *The Annals of the American Academy of Political and Social Science*, vol. 292, 49 ff. Philadelphia, 1954.

Brecht, Harald, and Glaser Glemstock. *The Art and Technique of Administration in German Ministries.* Cambridge, Mass., 1940.

Breitling, Rupert. *Die nationalsozialistische Rassenlehre: Entstehung, Ausbreitung, Nutzen und Schaden einer politischen Ideologie.* Meisenheim, Glan, 1971.

Bresser, Hildegard. *Die Kunstpolitik des Nationalsozialismus.* Hamburg, Reinbek, 1963.

Brettle. "Ein Jahr Nichtigkeitsbeschwerde." *DJ* (1941): 561 ff.

Breusing, Rolf. "Die Juden, ihre Rechtsstellung in Preußen und Deutschland in der geschichtlichen Entwicklung." *DVerw* (1936): 149 ff.

Bristler, Eduard. *Die Völkerrechtslehre des Nationalsozialismus.* Zurich, 1938.

Brohl. "Polenvermögen im Altreich." *DR* (1942) (A): 60 ff.

Broszat, Martin. "Zur Perversion der Strafjustiz im Dritten Reich." *VjhZ* (1958): 390 ff.

——. "Betrachtungen zu Hitlers Zweitem Buch." *VjhZ* (1961): 417 ff.

——. *Die nationalsozialistische Weltanschauung, Programm und Wirklichkeit.* 4th ed. Stuttgart, 1961.

——. *Nationalsozialistische Polenpolitik.* Stuttgart, 1961.

——. "Erfassung und Rechtsstellung von Volksdeutschen und Deutschstämmigen im GG." *Gutachten des IfZ,* Stuttgart, 1966, 2:243 ff.

——. "Nationalsozialistische Konzentrationslager: 1933–1945." In *Anatomie des SS-Staates,* vol. 2. Olten, Freiburg, 1965.

——. "Soziale Motivation und Führerbindung des Nationalsozialismus." *VjhZ* (1970): 392 ff.

——. *Der Staat Hitlers, Grundlegung und Entwicklung seiner inneren Verfassung.* Munich, 1969; 2d ed., vol. 9 in the series Weltgeschichte des 20. Jahrhunderts, Munich, 1971.

——. *200 Jahre deutsche Polenpolitik.* Rev. and expanded ed. Frankfurt/Main, 1972.

——. "Kompetenzen und Befugnisse der Haupttreuhandstelle Ost." *Gutachten des IfZ,* 2:235 ff.

——. "Tätigkeit der früheren deutschen Gerichte in der Ukraine." *Gutachten des IfZ,* 2:332 ff.

Brzeziński, Friedrich. *Totalitäre Diktatur.* Stuttgart, 1957.

Buch, Walter. "Parteigerichtsbarkeit." *DR* (1934): 4 ff.

Buchheim, Hans. "Struktur der totalitären Herrschaft und Ansätze totalitären Denkens." *VjhZ* 8 (1960): 163 ff.

——. *Totalitäre Herrschaft, Wesen und Merkmale.* Munich, 1962.

——. "Die Höheren SS- und Polizeiführer." *VjhZ* (1963): 362 f.

——. *SS und Polizei im NS-Staat.* Düsseldorf, 1964.

——. "Die Struktur der nationalsozialistischen Herrschaft." In *Anatomie des SS- Staates,* vol. 1, 13 ff. Olten, Freiburg, 1965,

——. "Gliederungen und angeschlossene Verbände." *Gutachten des IfZ,* vol. 1, Munich, 1958.

Buchheim, Hans, Martin Broszat, Helmut Jacobsen, and Helmut Krausnick, eds. *Anatomie des SS-Staates.* Vol. 1, *Polizei und SS,* and vol. 2, *Konzentrationslager, Kommisionsbefehl, Judenverfolgung.* Olten, Freiburg, 1965.

Buchholz, Fritz. *Gleichheit und Gleichberechtigung im Staats-und Vökerrecht.* Göttingen, Bleicherode, 1937.

Buchholz, Karl. "Zur Ostrechtspflege VO." *DR* (1941) (A): 2476 ff.

Buchholz, Karl, and Joseph Wolany. "Zum Grundstücksverkehrsrecht in den eingegliederten Ostgebieten." *DR* (1941) (A): 682 ff.

Buchwald, Martin. "Neugestaltung des Mietrechts." *ZAKfDtRecht* 13, no. 3 (1938).

Bühler, Joseph. "Das GG und seine Wirtschaft." Loseblattsammlung, Berlin, 1941 (BA/BA 102).

——, ed. *Das Generalgouvernement, seine Verwaltung und seine Wirtschaft.* Kraków, 1943.

Bühler, Joseph, and H. Frank. "Nationalsozialistische Strafrechtspolitik." *ZAKfDtRecht* (1939): 232 ff.

Bullock, Allan. *Hitler: Eine Studie über Tyrannei.* Düsseldorf, 1960.

Bund Nationalsozialistischer Deutscher Juristen. "Aus der Arbeit für das neue deutsche Völkerrecht." *JW* (1944): 823.

Burckhardt, Carl Jacob. *Meine Danziger Mission 1937 bis 1939.* Munich, 1960.

Campe, J. H. *Wörterbuch der deutschen Sprache.* Pt. 3. Braunschweig, 1809.

Claßen, Hans-Kurt. "Der Judeneid." *Deutsche Rechtswissenschaft* (1937): 166 ff.

Clemen, Paul. "Kunstdenkmäler und Denkmalschutz im GG." Kraków, 1941 (BA BR II/ 46 [Bibl.]).

Coblitz, Wilhelm. *Bibliographie des deutschen Rechtsschrifttums.* Munich, 1938.

Conrad, Hermann. *Deutsche Rechtsgeschichte.* Vol. 1. Karlsruhe, 1962.

Coudenhouve-Kalergi, Heinrich Graf. *Das Wesen des Antisemitismus.* Leipzig, Vienna, 1932.

Coulon. "Nationalsozialistische Volkstumspolitik." *DR* (1941) (A): 2468 ff.

Crohne. "Die Strafrechtspflege 1936." *DJ* (1937): 9 ff.

———. "Die Strafrechtspflegeabteilung 1938." *DJ* (1939): 11 ff.

Cygański, Mirosław. *Z dziejów okupacji w Łodzi, Wydawnictwo Łódzkie.* Łódź, 1964.

———. "Powiat Łódzki w latach okupacji hitlerowskiej 1939–1945." *Rocznik Łódżki* 16 (19) (1972): 101 ff.

———. "Urząd Tajnej Policji Hitlerowskiej (Gestapo) w Łodzi w Latach 1935–1944 i pozostałe po nim akta." *Archeion*, vol. 43: 165 ff.

Dahm, Georg. "Verrat und Verbrechen." *ZStW* 95 (1935): 283 ff.

———. "Staatsanwaltschaft und Kriminalpolizei." *DtRechtsw* (1938): 148 ff.

———. "Richtermacht und Gerichtsverfassung im Strafrecht." *ZStW* 101 (1941): 287 ff.

———. *Völkerrecht.* Vols. 1–5. Stuttgart, 1958–61.

Dahm, Georg, and Friedrich Schaffstein. *Liberales oder autoritäres Strafrecht.* Hamburg, 1933.

Daitz, Werner. "Echte und unechte Großräume." *Reich-Volksordnung-Lebensraum* 2 (1942): 75 ff.

Dalcke, Albert. *Strafrecht und Strafverfahren.* 31st ed. Berlin, 1940.

Dallinger. "Amtseinführung des Oberlandesgerichtspräsidenten und Generalstaatsanwaltes in Kattowitz." *DJ* (1941): 716 ff.

Daluege, Kurt. "Der nationalsozialistische Kampf gegen das Verbrechertum." *DR* (1936): 123.

Dammeyer, Manfred. "Nationalsozialistische Filme im historisch-politischen Unterricht." *Aus Politik und Zeitgeschichte* 16–17 (1977): 1 ff.

Datner, Sz., J. Gumbowski, and St. Leszczyński. "Wysiedlanie ludności polskiej z ziem polskich wcielonych do Rzeszy." *Bulletin of the Main Commission Warsaw* 12 (1960).

———. "Der Einsatzgruppenprozeß (Urteil und Begründung)." *Bulletin of the Main Commission Warsaw* 14 (1962).

Dennewitz, Bodo. *Das nationale Deutschland, ein Rechtsstaat: Die Rechtsgrundlagen des neuen deutschen Staates.* Berlin, 1933.

Der Großdeutsche Freiheitskampf, Reden Adolf Hitlers. Vol. 3. Munich, 1943.

Der polnische Blutterror (ed. for Reichsstatthalter Forster). Danzig, 1940.

Diehl-Thiele, Peter. *Partei und Staat im Dritten Reich: Untersuchungen zum Verhältnis von NSDAP und allgemeiner innerer Staatsverwaltung 1933–1945.* Münchner Studien zur Politik, vol. 9. Munich, 1969.

Diener, Roger. "Das System der Staatsverbrechen." *DR* (1934): 329 ff.

"Diensttagebuch des deutschen Generalgouverneurs in Polen 1939–1945." Ed. W. Präg and W. Jacobmeyer, 1975. Manuscript in the form of an enlarged positive copy from microfilm in the IfZ, FB 105 (copy of the daily activity reports also in the Federal Archives Koblenz; original in Main Commission Warsaw).

Dietze, Hans Helmut. "Die Entwicklung des Sonderrechts im Kriege." *DR* (1944): 306 ff.

Doblanski, T. *Die Entwicklung zum Menschen.* Hamburg, Berlin, 1948.

Documenta Occupationis Teutonicae (Hitlerowskie "Prawo" Okupacyjne w Polsce). Wybór dokumentów, Instytut Zachodni, Poznań. Vols. 5–7, ed. and rev. by Cz. Łuczak, Posen, 1975. Vol. 10, rev. by A. Konieczny and H. Szurgacz, Poznań, 1976.

Doerner, Karl. "Gegen unsachliche Angriffe auf die deutsche Rechtspflege." *DJ* (1935): 895 ff.

Draht, Martin. "Totalitarismus in der Volksdemokratie." Introduction to *Macht ohne Mandat: Der Staatsapparat der sowjetischen Besatzungszone Deutschland,* by Ernst Richert. Cologne, Opladen, 1963.

Drendel. "Aus der Praxis der Strafverfolgung im Warthegau." *DR* (1941) (A): 2471 ff.

Dresler, Adolf. "Die Reprivatisierung in Galizien." *DVerw* (1942): 347 ff.

Drews, Bill. *Preußisches Polizeirecht.* Vol. 1. 5th ed. Berlin, 1936.

du Prel, Max. *Das Generalgouvernement.* Kraków, 1942.

Dürr. "Der Vollzug der Freiheitsstrafe." In *Nationalsozialistisches Handbuch für Recht und Gesetzgebung,* 1477. Munich, 1934.

Echterhölter, Rudolf. *Das öffentliche Recht im Nationalsozialismus. Quellen und Darstellungen zur Zeitgeschichte,* vol. 16, pt. 2. Stuttgart, 1970.

Eichholtz, Dietrich, and Kurt Grossweiler. "Noch einmal: Politik und Wirtschaft 1933–1945." *Das Argument* 47 (1968): 210 ff.

Eickhoff, Ludwig. "Die Preußische Geheime Staatspolizei." *DVerw* (1936): 90 ff.

"Ein Jahr Rechtsprechung des Reichsverwaltungsgerichtes." *DR* (1943): 1127 ff.

Eisenblätter, Gerhard. "Grundlinien der Politik des Reiches gegenüber dem Generalgouvernement, 1939–1945,." Ph.D. diss., Düsseldorf, Frankfurt/Main, 1969.

Eltzbucher, Paul. *Totes und lebendes Völkerrecht.* Munich, Leipzig, 1916.

Engert, Karl. "Stellung und Aufgaben des Volksgerichtshofs." *DR* (1939) (A): 485.

Enke, Paul. "Die Rechtspflege im Volkstumskampf." *DR* (1941): 2489.

Ernst, Waldemar. "Erlebnis und Gestaltung deutscher Großraumverwaltung." *Reich-Volksordnung-Lebensraum* 5 (1943): 269 ff.

Esch, Peter. *Polen kurz und quer.* Berlin, 1939.

Euller, M. "Die Hitlerjugend im Generalgouvernement." *Das Generalgouvernement*, no. 2 (1940): 24.

Exner. "Wie erkennt man den gemeingefährlichen Gewohnheitsverbrecher." *DJ* (1943): 377.

Fauck. "Behandlung von deutsch-jüdischen Mischehen." *Gutachten des IfZ*, 2:26–28. Munich, 1966.

———. "Mitnahme von Devisen und Schmuckstücken bei Auswanderungen von Juden." *Gutachten des IfZ*, 2:23 f. Munich.

———. "Verfolgung von Mischlingen in Deutschland und im Reichsgau Wartheland." *Gutachten des IfZ*, 2:29 ff. Munich.

———. "Vermögensbeschlagnahmen an jüdischem Eigentum vor dem Erlaß der 11. Durchführungsverordnung zum Reichsbürgergesetz." *Gutachten des IfZ*, 2:25 f. Munich.

Fauser. "Verwaltungsverfahren und verwaltungsgerichtliches Verfahren nach dem Führererlaß vom 28. 8. 1939." *AöR*, NF 31 (1940): 186 ff.

Fechner, Fritz. "Das bürgerliche Recht in den eingegliederten Ostgebieten: Zu den Verordnungen vom 25. September 1941." *DR* (1941) (A): 2481 ff.

Feder, Gottfried. *Das Programm der NSDAP und seine weltanschaulichen Grundgedanken*. Munich, 1932.

Feldscher, Werner. "Rassenpflege und Erbpflege im deutschen Recht." In *Reichsrechtspflege und Verwaltung, 1943: Die Juden und die Justiz*, ed. S. Lorenzen, no. 3. 2d ed. Berlin, 1943.

Fest, Joachim. *Das Gesicht des Dritten Reiches, Profile einer totalitären Herrschaft*. Munich, 1964.

———. *Hitler: Eine Biographie*. Frankfurt/Main, 1973.

Fetscher, Iring. "Faschismus und Nationalsozialismus: Zur Kritik des sowjet-marxistischen Faschismusbegriffs." *PVS* 3 (1962): 42–63.

Finke, Alfred. "Die Unverbesserlichen." In *Pressedienst des Generalgouvernements*, May 22, 1942, ser. 169, ZSt Ludwigsburg, binder 108, 402 ff.

Fischbach, Oskar Georg. *Deutsche Beamtengesetze: Kommentar*. 2d ed. Berlin, 1942.

Flitner, Andreas, ed. *Deutsches Geistesleben und Nationalsozialismus*. Tübingen, 1965.

Florian-Herz, J. H. "Bolshevist and National Socialist Doctrines of International Law." *Social Research* (1940): 1 ff.

Forsthoff, Ernst. *Der totale Staat*. Hamburg, 1933.

———. "Besprechung von O. Koellreutler: Der deutsche Führerstaat." *JW* (1934): 538.

———. "Formalismus im öffentlichen Dienst." *DR* (1934): 347 ff.

Fournier. "La Conception nationalsocialiste du droit de gens." Ph. D. diss., Paris, 1938.

Fraenkel, Ernst. "Die Nichtigkeitsbeschwerde in der Praxis." *DR* (1941) (A): 2305.

———. *The Dual State: A Contribution to the Theory of Dictatorship*. London, 1941; German translation, *Der Doppelstaat* (Frankfurt/Main, 1974).

Frank, Hans. "Die staatsrechtliche Bedeutung des 30. Januar 1933." *DR* (1934): 25 ff.

———. "Die Zeit des Rechts." *DR* (1936): 14 ff.

———. "Leitsätze des Reichsjuristenführers zur richterlichen Unabhängigkeit." *DJZ* (1936): 179 ff.; *JW* (1936): 309.

———. "Der Führer und das Recht." *ZAKfDtRecht* (1937): 289 ff.

———. *Nationalsozialistische Strafrechstpolitik.* Munich, 1938.

———. "Das Generalgouvernement Polen." *Europäische Revue* (1940): 384.

———. "Der Aufbau der Verwaltung im Generalgouvernement." In *Die nationalsozialistische Gemeinde 1940, 97* ff.

———. "Der Deutsche Aufbau im Generalgouvernement." *DR* (1941) (A): 2417 ff.

———. "Der Nationalsozialismus und die Wissenschaft der Wirtschaftslehr." *Schmollers Jahrbuch*, vol. 58, 641 ff.

———. "Diensttagebuch 1940–1944." Copy in the Federal Archives Koblenz and in the IfZ, Munich (original at the Main Commission Warsaw).

———, ed. *Nationalsozialistisches Handbuch für Recht und Gesetzgebung.* Munich, 1934.

———, ed. *Nationalsozialistische Leitsätze für ein neues deutsches Strafrecht, Allgemeiner und Besonderer Teil.* Berlin, 1935, 1936.

———, ed. *Deutsches Verwaltungsrecht.* Munich, 1937.

———, ed. *Die beiden Grundprobleme des Rechts. Schriften der Akademie für deutsches Recht.* Hamburg, 1938.

Franz, Günther. "Der Jude im katholischen Kirchenrecht." *Dt. Rechtswiss.* (1937): 157 ff.

Franzen, Hans. *Gesetz und Richter: Eine Abgrenzung nach den Grundsätzen des NS-Staates.* Hamburg, 1935.

Franzen, Wilhelm. *Die Polizei im neuen Staat: Grundriß des Polizeirechts.* Marburg, n.d.

Frauendorfer, Max. "Arbeits- und Sozialpolitik im Generalgouvernement." *Das GG*, ser. 13/14 (1941): 58 ff.

Freisler, Roland. "Die Ausbildung des Juristen." *DJ* (1933): 462 ff.

———. "Recht, Richter, Gesetz." *DJ* (1934): 694.

———. "Volksverrat im Lichte des Nationalsozialismus." *DJZ* (1935): 907.

———. "Ein Jahr Blutschutzsprechung in Deutschland." *Deutsches Strafrecht.* (1936): 385 ff.

———"Gedanken über Strafvollzug an jüngsten Gefangenen." *Beiträge zur Rechtserneuerung*, no. 1. Berlin, 1936.

———. "Hans Kerrl Lager: Weltanschauliche Schulung und Volksgemeinschaft." *DJ* (1936): 1750 ff.

———. "Schutz von Rasse und Erbgut im werdenden deutschen Recht." *ZAKfDtRecht* (1936): 14 ff.

———. "Fragen zur Sicherheitsverwahrung." *DJ* (1938): 626 ff.

———. "Justiz und Politik." In *200 Jahre Dienst am Recht*, 197 ff. Berlin, 1938.

———. "Das Gesetz zur Änderung von Vorschriften des allgemeinen Strafverfahrens, des Wehrstrafverfahrens und des Strafgesetzbuches und seine Stellung in der Strafverfahrenserneuerung." *DJ* (1939): 1565 ff., 1597 ff.

———. "Personalpolitik im höheren Justizdienst." *DJ* (1939): 1342 ff.

———. "Arbeitseinsatz im Strafvollzug." *DJ* (1940): 1021 ff.

——. "Die Handhabung des Jugendarrestes." *DJ* (1940): 1405 ff.

——. "Die Idee des Reiches." *DJ* (1940): 253 ff.

——. "Nichtigkeitsbeschwerde." *DJ* (1940): 341 ff.

——. "Psychische Grundlagen der Polengreuel, dargestellt an der Entwicklung des polnischen Volksgeistes." *DJ* (1940): 557 ff.

——. "Das deutsche Polenstrafrecht." *DJ* (1941): 1129 ff.; *DJ* (1942): 25 ff.

——. "Deutscher Osten, ein Wort an die deutsche Rechtswahrerjugend." *DJ* (1941): 737 ff.

——. "Grundsätzliches zur Ministerratsverordnung über das Strafrecht gegen Polen und Juden." *DR* (1941) (A): 2629 ff.

Freyer, Hans. *Der Staat.* Leipzig, 1925.

Frick, Wilhelm. "Partei und Staat." *DVerw* (1934): 289 ff.

——. "Wiedergeburt des deutschen Beamten." *DR* (1934): 26 f.

——. "Die Rassenpolitik des Dritten Reiches." *ZAKfDtRecht* (1936): 2 ff.

——. "Die Verwaltungsgerichtsbarkeit im nationalsozialistischen Staat." *DVerw* (1936): 332.

——. "Probleme des neuen Verwaltungsrechts." *DVerw* (1936): 329 ff.

——. "Reden auf dem Deutschen Beamtentag 1937 in München." *DVerw* (1937): 321 ff.

——. "Die Rassenfrage in der deutschen Gesetzgebung." *DJZ* (1939): 1934.

——. "Geschehen der Zeit." *DVerw* (1939): 222.

——. "Über grundsätzliche Verwaltungsaufgaben." *DVerw* (1939): 33 ff., 38.

——. "Das Reichsbürgergesetz und das Gesetz zum Schutze des Blutes und der deutschen Ehre vom 15. 9. 1935." *DJZ* (1940): 1935.

——. "Der Oberpräsident als Organ der Zentralgewalt des Reiches." *DVerw* (1941): 133 ff.

Friedrich. "Das Gemeinschaftslager Hanns Kerrl." *DJ* (1935): 24 f.

Friedrich, Carl Joachim. "The German and the Prussian Civil Service." In *Civil Service in the Modern State,* ed. L. D. White. Chicago, 1930.

Friedrich, Carl Joachim, and Z. K. Brzeziński. *Totalitäre Diktatur.* Stuttgart, 1957.

——. *Totalitarian Dictatorship and Autocracy.* 2d ed. Cambridge, 1965.

Fritzsche, Fritz. "Was ist ein Eingriff in die Berufsaufgaben des Rechtsanwalts?" *JW* (1937): 525.

Froböß, Hellmut. "Zwei Jahre Justiz im Warthegau." *DR* (1941) (A): 2465.

Fröde, Paul. "Das Urlaubsrecht im Kriege." *DVerw* (1940): 87 ff.

——. "Die Verordnung über den Arbeitsschutz." *DVerw* (1940): 25 f.

Fugger, Ernst-Rudolf. "Die Deutsche Polizei: Bemerkungen zum Schrifttum des Polizeirechts." *ZStW* 104 (1941): 723 ff.

"Führung als Rechtsprinzip." *DR* (1934): 327.

Gassner, E. "Die Presse." *Das GG,* ser. 15 (1941): 12 ff.

Gebert. "Das Handelsrecht in den eingegliederten Ostgebieten." *DR* (1942) (A): 700 ff.

Geigenmüller, Otto. *Die politische Schutzhaft im nationalsozialistischen Deutschland.* 2d ed. Leipzig, 1937.

Geiß, Emmanuel, *Der polnische Grenzstreifen, 1914–1918: Ein Beitrag zur deutschen Kriegs-zielpolitik im Ersten Weltkrieg.* Historische Studien no. 378. Lübeck, 1960.

Genschel, Helmut. *Die Verdrängung der Juden aus der Wirtschaft im Dritten Reich.* Göttingen, 1966.

Gerber, Hans. *Politische Erziehung des Beamten im nationalsozialistischen Staat.* Tübingen, 1933.

——. *Staatsrechtliche Grundlinien des neuen Reiches.* Tübingen, 1933.

——. "Der politische Begriff des Volkes." *AöR*, n.s., 31 (1940): 129 ff.

Gernhuber, Joachim. *Das völkische Recht: Ein Beitrag zur Rechtstheorie des Nationalsozialismus, Festschrift für Kern.* Tübingen, 1968.

Giese, Friedrich. "Die gegenwärtige Staatsangehörigkeit der aus ehemals polnischen Gebieten stammenden Juden in Deutschland." *ZÖR*, vol. 21, no. 1, 53 ff.

Glaser, Kurt. *Der Zweite Weltkrieg und die Kriegsschuldfrage.* Würzburg, 1965.

Goebbels, Joseph. *Tagebücher 1942–43.* Ed. L. P. Lochner. Zürich, 1948.

——. "Außerordentliche Rundfunkmaßnahmen: Dokumentation." *VjhZ* 11 (1963): 418 ff.

Goldhagen, Erich. "Weltanschauung und Erlösung: Zum Antisemitismus der nationalsozialistischen Führungsschicht." *VjhZ* (1976): 379 ff.

Gollert, Friedrich. *Warschau unter deutscher Herrschaft.* 2d. ed., with map. Kraków, 1942.

Göppinger, Horst. *Die Verfolgung der Juristen jüdischer Abstammung durch den Nationalsozialismus.* Villingen, 1963.

——. Review of Schorn, *Die Gesetzgebung des Nationalsozialismus als Mittel der Machtpolitik. JZ* (1965): 783.

Göring, Hermann. *Die Rechtssicherheit als Grundlage der Volksgemeinschaft: Schriften der Akademie für Deutsches Recht.* Hamburg, 1935.

Gott. "The National-Socialist Theory of International Law." *American Journal of International Law* 32 (1938): 704 ff.

——. *Völkerrechtsordnung und Nationalsozialismus.* Berlin, 1941.

Graf, G., and M. Dietherr. *Deutsche Rechtssprichwörter.* Nördlingen, 1869.

Grau. "Die 4. Verordnung zur Vereinfachung der Strafrechtspflege im Kriege von 13. 12 1944." *DJ* (1944): 309.

Grau, Heinrich. "Zur Stellung der Mischlinge 1. Grades." *Gutachten des IfZ*, 2:31 f.

Greifelt. "Festigung deutschen Volkstums in den Ostgebieten." *DVerw* (1940): 17 ff.

Greiffenhagen, Martin. "Der Totalitarismusbegriff in der Regimelehre." *PVS* (1968): 372 ff.

Greiffenhagen, Martin, Reinhard Kühnl, and Johann Baptist Müller. *Totalitarismus: Zur Problematik eines politischen Begriffs.* Munich, 1972.

Greiser, Artur. *Der Aufbau im Osten.* Jena, 1942. Kieler Addresses, no. 68; Library of Institute for Western Studies, Poznań, sig. 40903/68.

——. *Der Tag der Freiheit 1943. Der große Rechenschaftsbericht.* 1943. Library of Federal Archives, Poznań.

——. *Der große Rechenschaftsbericht.* 1944. Library of Federal Archives, Poznań.

Grewe, Wilhelm. "Der Reichsbegriff im Völkerrecht." *Monatshefte für Auswärtige Politik* (1939): 798 ff.

Gribbohm, Günter. "Der Volksgerichtshof." *JuS* (1969): 109 ff.

———. "Die Führerinformationen des RMJ." *DRiZ* (1971): 152 ff.

Grimm. "Das Reichsgesetz über die Zulassung zur Rechtsanwaltschaft vom 7. April 1933." *DJZ* (1933): 651.

Grimm, J., and Wilhelm. *Deutsches Wörterbuch*. Vol. 8. Leipzig, 1889.

Groß, Walter. "Die rassenpolitischen Voraussetzungen zur Lösung der Judenfrage." *DR* (1942) (A): 2 ff.

Gruchmann, Lothar. "Nationalsozialistische Großraumpolitik: Die Konstruktion einer Deutschen Monroedoktrin." *VjhZ* (1962).

———. "Hitler über die Justiz: Das Tischgespräch vom 20. August 1942." *VjhZ* (1964): 96 ff.

———. *Der Zweite Weltkrieg: Kriegsführung und Politik*. Vol. 10 in the series Weltgeschichte des 20. Jahrhunderts, ed. Martin Broszat and Helmut Heiber. Munich, 1967; paperback dtr. no. 4010.

Grunberger, Richard. *Das zwölfjährige Reich: Der deutsche Alltag unter Hitler*. Vienna, Munich, Zürich, 1973.

Grundmann, Siegfried. "Die richterliche Nachprüfung von politischen Führungsakten nach geltendem deutschen Verfassungsrecht." *ZStW* 100 (1940): 511 ff.

———. "Deutsches Kulturleben in Warschau." *Das Generalgouvernement* (March 1941), issue 6, 3 ff. (University Library, Warsaw, Sign. 011248).

Grunsky, Wolfgang. "Gesetzesauslegung durch die Zivilgerichte im Dritten Reich." *KJ* (1969): 146 ff.

———. *Grenzen der Rückwirkung bei einer Änderung der Rechtsprechung*. Karlsruhe, 1970.

Guggenheim, Paul. *Beiträge zur völkerrechtlichen Lehre vom Staatenwechsel*. Berlin, 1925.

———. *Lehrbuch des Völkerrechts*. Vol. 1. Basel, 1948.

Gumbowski, Janusz, and Kazimierz Leszczyński. "Generalne Gubernatorstwo w Oczach Niemca." *Bulletin der Hauptkommission Warschau* 15 (1965): 129 ff., 135 ff.

Günther, Hans F. K. *Rassenkunde des deutschen Volkes*. 2d ed. Munich, 1930 (1st ed., 1922).

Gürtner, Franz. "Richter und Rechtsanwalt im neuen Staat." *DJ* (1934): 369 ff.

Gürtner, Franz, and Roland Freisler. *Das neue Strafrecht (Grundsätzliche Gedanken zum Geleit)*. Berlin, 1936.

Gütt, Arthur. "Gesundheits- und Rassenpflege im Dritten Reich." *Reich und Ostmark* (1940) (B): 131 ff.

Gütt, Arthur, and Herbert Linden. *Kommentar zum Ehegesundheitsgesetz*. Munich, 1936.

Gütt, Arthur, Herbert Linden, and Franz Maßfeller. *Blutschutz und Ehegesundheitsgesetz, Kommentar*. 2d ed. Munich, 1937. (The first edition is Gütt and Linden, *Kommentar zum Ehegesundheitsgesetz* [1936].)

Haenich, Walter. "Der organisierte Weg zur einheitlichen Reichspolizei seit 1933." Legal diss., Berlin, 1939.

Hamel, Walter. "Die Polizei im neuen Reich." *DR* (1935): 412 ff.

———. "Die Aufgabe der Polizei im nationalsozialistischen Staat." *DJZ* (1936): 1465 f.

Handbuch der Entscheidungen des Ständigen Internationalen Schiedsgerichtshofes 1922–1935. 2 vols. 1931–34; Cologne, Berlin, Munich, Bonn, 1961.

Handbuch der Justizverwaltung. Berlin, 1942.

Handbuch für die Dienststellen des Generalbevollmächtigte des Arbeitseinsatzes im Großdeutschen Reich. Ed. plenipotentiary general for the allocation of labor. Berlin, 1944.

Hankins, F. H. *The Racial Basis of Civillzation.* New York, 1926.

Hannover, Heinrich, and Elisabeth Hannover-Drück. *Politische Justiz 1918–1933.* Frankfurt/Main, Hamburg, 1966.

Hartshorne, Edward J. *The German Universities and National Socialism.* Cambridge, Mass., 1937.

Hasche, Walter. *Der Reichsstatthalter in der Entwicklung der Reichsmittelinstanz.* Hansische University, no. 31. Würzburg, 1938.

Hayes, Paul M. *Fascism.* London, 1973.

Hedemann, Justus Wilhelm. "Juristen im Schulungslager." *DR* (1934): 181 f.

———. "Arbeit am Volksgesetzbuch." *DR* (1941): 1913.

———. *Das Volksgesetzbuch der Deutschen.* Special Issue of *ZAKfDtRecht.* 1941.

———. "Wert der Entwürfe-Arbeit am Volksgesetzbuch." *ZAKfDtRecht* (1943): 3 ff.

Hedemann, Justus Wilhelm, Heinrich Lehmann, and Wolfgagng Siebert. "Volksgesetzbuch: Grundregeln und Buch I." *ZAKfDtRecht* (1942).

Hegel, G. W. Friedrich. Selected by and with an introduction by Friedrich Heer. Fischer-Bücherei no. 86. Frankfurt/Main, Hamburg, 1955.

Hegel, G. W. Friedrich. *Grundlinien der Philosophie des Rechts.* Ed. Johannes Hoffmeister. Vol. 12. Hamburg, 1955.

———. *Vorlesungen über die Philosophie der Geschichte.* Stuttgart, 1961.

Heiber, Helmut. "Zur Justiz im Dritten Reich: Der Fall Eliáš," *VjhZ* 3 (1955): 275 ff.

———. "Der Fall Grünszpan." *VjhZ* 5 (1957): 134 ff.

———. *Walter Frank und sein Reichsinstitut für die Geschichte des neuen Deutschland.* Stuttgart, 1966.

Held, H. J. *Volk, Recht und Staat im Lichte deutscher Rechtserneuerung.* Berlin, 1935.

Heldrich, Karl. "Die Form des Vertrages: Vorschläge zur Neugestaltung des Rechts auf Grund eines Referates." *AcP*, vol. 147, 89 ff.

Hempfer, Walter. *Die nationalsozialistische Staatsauffassung in der Rechtsprechung des Preußischen Oberverwaltungsgerichts, dargelegt an ausgewählten Beispielen rechtsstaatlicher Grundsätze.* Schriften zum öffentlichen Recht, vol. 241. Berlin, 1974.

Henkys, Reinhard. *Die nationalsozialistischen Gewaltverbrechen.* Ed. Dietrich Goldschmidt. Stuttgart, Berlin, 1964.

"Herrenschicht oder Führungsrolle." *Reich-Volksordnung-Lebensraum* 3 (1942): 122 ff.

Herrfahrdt, Heinrich. *Die Verfassungsgesetze des nationalsozialistischen Staates dem Text der Weimarer Verfassung gegenübergestellt.* Marburg, 1935.

———. "Politische Verfassungslehre." *Archiv für Rechts- und Sozialphilosophie*, vol. 30, 107 ff.

Heydecker, Joe J., and Johannes Leeb. *Der Nürnberger Prozeß (Bilanz der tausend Jahre).* 6th ed. Cologne, 1962.

Heydrich, Reinhard. "Die Bekämpfung der Staatsfeinde." *DR* (1936): 121 ff.

Hildebrand, Klaus. *Deutsche Außenpolitik 1933–1945.* Stuttgart, Berlin, Cologne, Mainz, 1971.

Hildebrandt, Heinz. "Formalismus im bürgerlichen Recht." *DR* (1934): 353 ff.

———. *Rechtsfindung im neuen deutschen Staate: Ein Beitrag zur Rezeption und den Rechtsquellen, zur Auslegung und Ergänzung des Gesetzes.* Berlin, 1935.

———. "Grundsätzliches zum Dienst im Gemeinschaftslager Hanns Kerrl." *DJ* (1936): 1757 ff.

———. "Rechtsquellen." In *Handwörterbuch der Rechtswissenschaft*, ed. Erich Volkmar, Alexander Elster, and Günther Küchenhoff. Berlin, 1937.

Hilferding, Rudolf. "Das historische Problem." *Zeitschrift für Politik*, NF (1954): 293 ff.

Hill, Werner. *Artgleichheit und Gleichartigkeit.* Berlin, 1966.

Hillgruber, Andreas. *Hitlers Strategie 1940–1941.* Frankfurt, 1965.

———. "Die 'Endlösung' und das deutsche Ostimperium als Kernstück des rasseideologischen Programms des Nationalsozialismus." *VjhZ* (1972): 133 ff.

Himmler, Heinrich. *Dr. Wilhelm Frick und sein Ministerium.* Festschrift. Munich, 1937.

Hintze, Otto. "Der Commissarius, und seine Bedeutung in der allgemeinen Verwaltungsgeschichte." In *Festschrift für Karl Zeuner: Historische Aufsätze.* Weimar, 1919.

———. *Staat und Verfassung (Gesammelte Abhandlungen zur allgemeinen Verfassungsgeschichte).* Vol. 1, ed. Fritz Hartung. Leipzig, 1941.

Hitler, Adolf. *Reden am Parteitag der Freiheit.* Munich, 1936.

———. *Mein Kampf.* 74th ed. Munich, 1934; anniversary ed., Munich, 1939 (all citations are to the 1939 edition).

———. *Der großdeutsche Freiheitskampf: Reden A. Hitlers.* Vols. 1 and 2. Munich, 1942.

———. *Hitlers zweites Buch: Ein Dokument aus dem Jahre 1928.* With an introduction and commentary by Gerhard L. Weinberg. Vol. 7 of *Quellen und Darstellungen zur Zeitgeschichte.* Stuttgart, 1961.

———. *Weisungen für die Kriegsführung 1939–1945, Dokumente des Oberkommandos der Wehrmacht.* Ed. Walther Hubatsch. Frankfurt/Main, 1962.

———. "Über die Justiz: Das Tischgespräch vom 20. 8. 1942." *VjhZ* (1964): 86 ff.

Hoche, Werner. *Die Gesetzgebung des Kabinetts Hitler.* Berlin, 1933–39.

———. "Grundsätze, Aufbau und Verwaltung des nationalsozialistischen Staates." *Amtliches Jahrbuch des deutschen Rechts*, n.s., 1 (1934): 1 ff.

Hohlfeld, Johannes, ed. *Dokumente der deutschen Politik und Geschichte.* Vols. 1–5. Berlin, 1951.

Höhn, Reinhard. "Form und Formalismus im Rechtsleben." *DR* (1934): 346 f.

——. "Rechtsgemeinschaft und Volksgemeinschaft." In *Der deutsche Staat der Gegenwart*, ed. Carl Schmitt, no. 14. Hamburg, 1935.

——. "Staat und Rechtsgemeinschaft." *ZStW* 95 (1935): 656 ff.

——. "Das Führerprinzip in der Verwaltung." *DR* (1936): 304.

——. "Volk und Verfassung." *Dt. Rechtswiss.* 2 (1937): 193 ff., 212.

——. "Reich-Großraum-Großmacht." *Reich-Volksordnung-Lebensraum* 2 (1942): 97 ff., 184 ff.

Höhn, Reinhard, and Helmut Seydel. "Der Kampf um die Wiedergewinnung des Deutschen Ostens: Erfahrungen der preußischen Ostsiedler 1886–1914." In *Festgabe für Heinrich Himmler*, 61 ff. Darmstadt, 1941.

Höhne, Heinz. *Der Orden unter dem Totenkopf: Die Geschichte der SS*. Hamburg, 1966.

Hollstein, Dorothea. *Antisemitische Filmpropaganda: Die Darstellung des Juden im nationalsozialistischen Spielfilm*. Munich, Pullach, 1971.

Holtz, Dietrich. "Zur Volksgeschichte der Ostgebiete." *DVerw* (1940): 182 ff.

Horn, Wolfgang. *Führerideologie und Parteiorganisation der NSDAP 1919 bis 1933*. Düsseldorf, 1969.

Höver. "Entjudungsfragen." *DR* (1941) (A): 12 ff.

Hubatsch, Walther, ed. *Hitlers Weisungen für die Kriegsführung 1939-1945: Dokumente des Oberkomanndos der Wehrmacht*. Frankfurt/Main, 1962.

Huber, Ernst Rudolf. "Bedeutungswandel der Grundrechte." *AöR*, NF 23 (1932): 1 ff.

——. "Besprechung von Leibholz, Gerhard: Die Auflösung der liberalen Demokratie in Deutschland und das autoritäre Staatbild, Munich, Leipzig 1933." *AöR*, NF 24 (1933/34): 246 ff.

——. "Das Staatsoberhaupt des Deutschen Reiches." *ZStW* 95 (1935): 202 ff.

——. *Neue Grundbegriffe des hoheitlichen Rechts*. Hamburg, 1935.

——. *Vom Sinn der Verfassung*. Hamburg, 1935.

——. "Die Rechtsstellung der Volksgenossen." *ZStW* 96 (1936): 438 ff.

——. "Politik und Justiz: Zu Hans Peter Ipsens Schrift über das Problem der 'justizlosen Hoheitsakte.' " *ZStW* 98 (1938): 193 ff.

——. "Die Rechtsgestalt der NSDAP." *DtRechtsw* (1939): 314 ff.

——. *Verfassungsrecht des Großdeutschen Reiches*. 2d ed. Hamburg, 1939.

——. "Das richterliche Prüfungsrecht und seine Künftige Gestaltung." *ZAKfDtRecht* (1940): 216 ff.

——. "Die verfassungsrechtliche Stellung des Beamtentums." In *Festschrift der Leipziger Juristen-Fakultät für Heinrich Siber zum 10. April 1940*, 2 vols., 1 ff. Leipzig, 1941–43; reprint, 1970.

——. "Bau und Gefüge des Reiches." In Huber, *Idee und Ordnung des Reiches*, 1:5 ff.

——. "Das Reichsbürgerrecht." In Huber, *Idee und Ordnung des Reiches*, 1:15 ff.

——, ed. *Idee und Ordnung des Reiches*. Vol. 1. Hamburg, 1941.

Hubernagel, G. "Aufbau und Aufgabe der deutschen Gerichte im Generalgouvernement." *DR* (1941) (A): 8 ff.

Hubrich, Georg. "Gliederung und Verwaltung der Ostgebiete." *DVerw* (1939): 605 ff.

Hueber. "Justiz im Führerstaat." *DJ* (1942): 5 ff.

Ilnytzkyj, Roman. *Deutschland und die Ukraine, 1934–1945.* 2 vols. Institut für Osteuropa, Munich, 1956.

Ipsen, Hans Peter. *Das Problem der justizlosen Hoheitsakte.* Hamburg, 1937.

Jacobsen, Hans Adolf. *1939–1945, Der Zweite Weltkrieg in Chronik und Dokumenten.* Darmstadt, 1961.

———. *Zur Konzeption einer Geschichte des Zweiten Weltkrieges.* Frankfurt/Main, 1964.

———. *Nationalsozialistische Außenpolitik 1933–1938.* Frankfurt, Berlin, 1968.

———. "Vom Wandel des Polenbildes in Deutschland (1772–1972)." *Aus Politik und Zeitgeschichte* (supplement to *Das Parlament*), May 26, 1973, (B) 21 (1973): 3 ff.

Jacobsen, Hans Adolf, and Werner Jochmann, eds. *Ausgewählte Dokumente zur Geschichte des Nationalsozialismus 1933–1945.* Bielefeld, 1961.

Jacoby, Henry. *Die Bürokratisierung der Welt.* Vol. 64 in the series Soziologische Texte. Neuwied, Berlin, 1969.

Jaenicke, E. "Propaganda und Kulturarbeit." *Das Generalgouvernement*, ser. 15 (1941): 3 ff.

Jaenicke, Martin. "Totalitäre Herrschaft." Ph.D. diss., Berlin, 1971.

Jakels, Otto. "Totalitarismus-Begriff und Ostrechtsforschung." In *Recht in Ost und West*, 95 ff. Berlin, 1970.

Jarmer. "Die Einräumigkeit: Ein Beitrag zur Förderung der Einheit der Verwaltung." *DVerw* (1940): 225 ff.

Jerusalem, Franz. *Das Verwaltungsrecht und der neue Staat.* Jena, 1935.

Jescheck, Hans-Heinrich. "Die juristische Ausbildung in Preußen und im Reich— Vergangenheit und Gegenwart." Vol. 2 of *Neue deutsche Forschung, Abt. bürgerliches Recht.* Berlin, 1939.

Johanny, Carl, and Oskar Redelberger. *Volk, Partei, Reich.* Berlin, 1943.

Johe, Werner. *Die gleichgeschaltete Justiz: Organisation des Rechtswesens und Politisierung der Rechtsprechung 1933 bis 1945, dargestellt am Beispiel des Oberlandesgerichts Hamburg.* Frankfurt/Main, 1967.

Jońca, Karol. *Polityka Narodowościowa III Rzeszy na śląsku Opolskim w latach 1933–1940.* Instytut śląski w Opolu, 1970.

Jürgens, Adolf, ed. *Ergebnisse deutscher Wissenschaft: Eine bibliographische Auswahl aus der deutschen wissenschaftlichen Literatur der Jahre 1933–1938.* Essen, 1939.

Just, Helmut. "Das Ende des Paragraf 14 Polizeiverwaltungsgesetz in der Rechtsprechung des Preußischen Oberverwaltungsgerichts." *Reich-Volksordnung-Lebensraum* 2 (1942).

———. "65 Jahre Reichskanzlei." *DR* (1943) (A): 637 ff.

Kaliski, T. "Pierwszwe dni Okupacji hitlerowskiej w Inowrocławiu." *Przegląd Zachodni* 5 (1959): 112 ff.

Kater, Michael A. "Das Ahnenerbe: Die Forschungs- und Lehrgemeinschaft der SS." Ph.D. diss., Heidelberg, 1966.

Kaufmann, Erich. "Die Gleichheit vor dem Gesetz im Sinne des Art. 109 der Reichsverfassung." *VVdStRL.* no. 3 (1926): 1 ff.

Kaul, Friedrich Karl. *Geschichte des Reichsgerichts 1933–1945.* Vol. 4. Glashütten i. T., 1971.

Kelsen, Hans. "Théorié générale du droit international publique." *Recueil des Cours* 42 (1932): 121 ff.

Kelz. "Zur Anrechnung von Schutzhaft auf die Strafe." *DJ* (1936): 1609 ff.

Kempner, Robert M. W. *Das Dritte Reich im* Kreuzverhör. Munich, Eßlingen, 1969.

Kern, Eduard. *Geschichte des Gerichtsverfassungsrechts.* Munich, 1954.

Keßler. "Die bürgerliche Rechtspflege im Kriege unter besonderer Berücksichtigung der Amts-und Landgerichte." *DR* (1940) (B): 114 ff.

Kirchheimer, Otto. *Politische Justiz: Verwendung juristischer Verfahrensmöglichkeiten zu politischen Zwecken.* Neuwied, 1965.

———. "Die Rechtsordnung des Nationalsozialismus." *KJ* (1971): 366 ff.

———. "Staatsgefüge und Recht des Dritten Reiches (1935)." *KJ* (1976): 33 ff.

Kirn, Michael. *Verfassungsumsturz oder Rechtskontinuität: Die Stellung der Jurisprudenz nach 1945 zum Dritten Reich, insbesondere die Konflikte um die Kontinuität der Beamtenrechte und Art. 131 Grundgesetz.* Schriften zum öffentlichen Recht, vol. 194. Berlin, 1972.

Kirschenmann, Dietrich. *Gesetz im Staatsrecht und in der Staatsrechtslehre des Nationalsozialismus.* Schriften zum öffentlichen Recht, vol. 135. Berlin, 1971.

Klappenbach-Steinitz, ed. *Wörterbuch der deutschen Gegenwartssprache.* Vol. 33. Lieferung, Berlin, 1971.

Klee, Hans Joachim. *Die bürgerliche Rechtspflege in den eingegliederten Ostgebieten.* Berlin, 1942.

Klein, Friedrich. "Die staats- und völkerrechtliche Stellung des Protektorats Böhmen und Mähren." *AöR* 31 (1940): 255 ff.

———. *Theorie und Praxis des Völkerrechts: Die mittelbare Haftung im Völkerrecht.* Frankfurt/Main, 1941.

———. "Zur Stellung des Generalgouvernements in der Verfassung des Großdeutschen Reiches." *AöR*, NF, 32 (1941): 227 ff.

Klinge. "Bemerkungen zur Begriffsbildung im Polenstrafrecht." *DJ* (1942): 324.

Kluge, Rudolf, and Heinrich Krüger. *Verfassung und Verwaltung im Großdeutschen Reich.* 3d rev. ed. Berlin, 1941.

Kneppers-Bannier, Hans. *Arbeitsrecht der Polen im Deutschen Reich.* Berlin, 1942.

Kobelt. "Einzelfragen der Rechtseinführung in den eingegliederten Ostgebieten." *DVerw* (1940): 167 ff.

Kodeks Karny i Prawo o Wykroczeniach. *Wydawnictwo Prawnicze.* Warsaw, 1968.

Koellreuter, Otto. *Grundriß der allgemeinen Staatslehre.* Tübingen, 1933.

———. *Vom Sinn und Wesen der nationalen Revolution.* Tübingen, 1933.

———. *Der deutsche Führerstaat.* Tübingen, 1934.

———. *Grundfragen des völkischen und staatlichen Lebens im deutschen Volksstaat.* Berlin, 1935.

———. *Volk und Staat in der Weltanschauung des Nationalsozialismus.* Berlin, 1935.

———. *Zur Entwicklung der Deutschen Rechtseinheit.* Jena, 1935.

──. *Deutsches Verfassungsrecht: Ein Grundriß.* 2d ed. Berlin, 1938.

──. *Deutsches Verwaltungsrecht.* 2d ed. Berlin, 1938.

Kogon, Eugen. *Der SS-Staat: Das System der deutschen Konzentrationslager.* 3d ed. Frankfurt/Main, 1948.

Köhler, H. *Lebenserinnerungen des Politikers und Staatsmannes 1878–1949.* Ed. J. Becker. Stuttgart, 1964.

Köhler, Heinz-Dieter. "Die Juden in Deutschland." *Deutsche Rechtswissenschaft* (1937): 190 ff.

──. "Wohngemeinschaft mit Juden?" *DR* (1938): 512.

Köhler, Ludwig. *Grundlehren deutschen Verwaltungsrechts.* Stuttgart, 1935.

Kohlrausch, Eduard. *Strafgesetzbuch mit Nebengesetzen und Erläuterungen.* 36th ed. Berlin, 1941.

Kolbe, Dieter. *Reichsgerichtspräsident Dr. Erwin Bumke: Studien zum Niedergang des Reichsgerichts und der deutschen Rechtspflege.* Karlsruhe, 1975.

Kordt, Erich. *Wahn und Wirklichkeit: Die Außenpolitik des Dritten Reiches. Versuch einer Darstellung.* Stuttgart, 1947.

Köttgen, Arnold. "Der Führer." In A. Köttgen, *Vom deutschen Staatsleben, Jahrbuch des öffentlichen Rechts,* vol. 24, sec. C, "Der Staat des deutschen Volkes," no. 1, 58 ff. 1937.

──. "Die Nationalsozialistische Deutsche Arbeiterpartei als Trägerin des deutschen Staatsgedankens." In A. Köttgen, *Vom deutschen Staatsleben, Jahrbuch des öffentlichen Rechts,* vol. 24, sec. C, "Der Staat des deutschen Volkes," no. 1. 1937.

Krause, Hermann. "Rechtseinheit und ständiges Recht." *Deutsche Rechtswiss* (1936): 300.

Krausnick, Helmut. "Hitler und die Morde in Polen, Dokumentation." *VjhZ* (1963): 196 ff.

──. "Judenverfolgung." In Buchheim et al., *Anatomie des SS-Staates,* vol. 2.

Krebs, A. *Tendenzen und Gestalten der NSDAP: Erinnerungen an die Frühzeit der NSDAP. Quellen und Darstellungen zur Zeitgeschichte,* vol. 6. Stuttgart, 1959 (Publications of the IfZ).

Krieck, Ernst. "Der Weg zum völkisch-politischen Richter." *DR* (1936): 434.

Krieser. "Die deutsche Gerichtsbarkeit im Protektorat Böhmen und Mähren, Ausübung und Umfang." *DR* (1940) (A): 1745 ff.

Kröning, Volker, and Jacob Schiszler. "Die Exekutivgewalt in der Bonapartismus- und Faschismustheorie." In "Hypothesen zum nationaisozialistischen Herrschaftssystem," *KJ* (1970): 1 ff.

Krosigk, Graf Schwerin von. *Es geschah in Deutschland.* Tübingen, 1961.

Krüger, Heinrich. *Die Verfassung der nationalsozialistischen Revolution.* 2d ed. Dresden, 1933.

──. "Verfassungsrecht und Verfassungswirklichkeit." *Reich-Volksordnung-Lebensraum* 5 (1943): 221 ff.

Krüger, Herbert. *Führer und Führung.* Breslau, 1935.

──. "Volksgemeinschaft statt subjektiver Rechte." *DVerw* (1935): 37 ff.

————. "Der Raum als Aufgabe der inneren Verwaltung." *DVerw* (1941): 281 ff..;; *DVerw* (1942): 21 ff.

————. "Die Bedeutung des Raumes für die innere Verwaltung." *DVerw* (1941): 281 ff.

————. "Der Wille des Gesetzgebers." *Reich-Volksordnung-Lebensraum* 5 (1943): 108 ff.

Kübler, Friedrich Karl. "Der deutsche Richter und das demokratische Gesetz." *AcP* 162 (1963): 104 ff.

Küchenhoff, Günther. "Führung und Verwaltung im Dritten Reich." *DJ* (1936): 1682 ff.

————. "Der Umbruch 1933–36, Die Rechtsentwicklung der Jahre 1933–35–36." In *Handwörterbuch der Rechtswissenschaft*, vol. 8, ed. Erich Volkmar, Alexander Elster, and Günther Küchenhoff, 207 ff. Berlin, 1937.

Kühn, Friedrich. "Der Führergedanke in der neuen Arbeitsverfassung: Zugleich ein Beitrag zu den Rechtsreformen der Führerverfassung im allgemeinen." In *Festschrift der Leipziger Juristenfakultät für Richard Schmidt zum 1. 11. 1934*. Leipziger rechtswissenschaftl: Studien, vol. 7. Leipzig, 1936; Neudruck, 1970.

Kühnl, Reinhard. *Formen bürgerlicher Herrschaft: Liberalismus-Faschismus*. Hamburg, 1973.

————. "Aspekte der Faschismusdiskussion: Historische Aufarbeitung und aktuelle Bedeutung." *Blätter für deutsche und internationale Politik* (1976): 531 ff.

Külz, Helmut R. "Verwaltungskontrolle unter dem Nationalsozialismus." *KJ* (1969): 367 ff.

Kümmerlein. "Das neue Reichsjugendgerichtsgesetz." *DJ* (1943): 529 ff., 553 ff.

Kundt, Ernst. "Entstehung, Probleme, Grundsätze und Form der Verwaltung des Generalgouvernements." In Bühler, *Das Generalgouvernement, seine Verwaltung und seine Wirtschaft*.

————. "Regierung des Generalgouvernements: Entstehung, Probleme, Grundsätze und Form der Verwaltung des Generalgouvernements." *Die Burg*, no. 2 (1944): 47 ff. (University Library, Warsaw).

Labs, Walter. "Die Verwaltung der besetzten Ostgebiete." *Reich-Volksordnung-Lebensraum* 5 (1943): 132 ff.

Lammers, Hans Heinrich. "Die Staatsführung im Dritten Reich." *DJ* (1934): 1296.

————. "Zum 30. Januar 1942." *RVerwBl.* (1943): 43.

Lämmle. "Aus der Rechtsprechung des Volksgerichtshofs zum Allgemeinen Teil des Strafgesetzbuches." *DR* (1944) (A): 505 ff.

Landau, Ludwig. *Kronika lat wojny i okupacji*. 3 vols. Warsaw, 1962. In author's possession.

Lange, Heinrich. "Die Arbeiten der Akademie für Deutsches Recht an der Erneuerung des bürgerlichen Rechts." *ZAKfDtRecht* (1939): 469 ff.

————. "Einzelgesetze oder Gesetzeseinheit auf dem Gebiet des völkischen Rechtslebens?" *Dt. Rechtswiss.* (1939): 222 ff.

————. "Wesen und Gestalt des Volksgesetzbuches." *ZStW* 103 (1943): 208 ff.

————. "Rechtsgrundabhängigkeit der Verfügung im Boden- und Fahrnisrecht." *AcP*, vol. 146, 28 ff.

Larenz, Karl. "Deutsche Rechtserneuerung und Rechtsphilosophie." *Recht und Staat* 109 (1934): 34 ff.

Lasch, Karl. "Die deutsche Aufgabe im Osten." *ZAKfDtRecht* (1940): 350 ff.

Lassar, Gerhard. "Reichseigene Verwaltung unter der Weimarer Verfassung, Zwei Studien." In *Jahrbuch des öffentlichen Rechts*, 14:4 ff. 1926.

———. *Recht und Staat im neuen Deutschland*. Ed. Ares. Berlin, 1929.

Lauer, Klaus. "Die Polizei im Nationalsozialistischen Staat." Legal diss., Hamburg, 1935.

Leber, Annedore, ed. *Das Gewissen entscheidet: Bereiche des deutschen Widerstandes von 1933–1945 in Lebensbildern*. Berlin, Frankfurt/Main. 1957.

Lehmann, Heinrich. "Vom Werden des Volksgesetzbuches." *DR* (1942) (A): 1492.

Leibholz, Gerhard. *Die Gleichheit vor dem Gesetz*. Berlin, 1925.

———. *Die Auflösung der liberalen Demokratie in Deutschland und das autoritäre Staatsbild*. Munich, 1933.

Leppin, Rudolf. "Der Schutz des Deutschen Blutes und der Deutschen Ehre: Ein Überblick über Rechtsprechung und Schrifttum." *JW* (1937): 3076 ff.

Lerner, Daniel. *The Nazi Elite*. Stanford, 1951.

Lewald, Walter. "Schlußbetrachtung der Schriftleitung zu den Beamtenurteilen des BVerfG." *NJW* (1954): 1275.

Lichter, Matthias. *Das Staatsangehörigkeitsrecht im Großdeutschen Reich*. Berlin, 1943.

Liepelt, Adolf. *Über Umfang und Bedeutung der Polizeigewalt im nationalsozialistischen Staat*. Würzburg, 1938.

Lingg, Anton. *Die Verwaltung der NSDAP*. 2d ed. Munich, 1940.

Locher, Eugen. *Die Neugestaltung des Liegenschaftsrechts*. Berlin, Leipzig, Vienna, 1942.

Lochner, L. P., ed. *Goebbels Tagebücher 1942–43*. Zurich, 1948.

Loewenfeld, Philipp. *Das Strafrecht als politische Waffe*. Berlin, 1933.

Loewenthal, Richard. "Totalitäre und demokratische Revolution." *Der Monat* 13, no. 146 (1960–61): 29 ff.

Lorenzen, Sievert. "Die Rechtsstellung der Juden vor der Emanzipation." *DJ* (1938): 1949 ff.

———."Das Eindringen der Juden in die Justiz vor 1933: Ein historischer Rückblick." *DJ* (1939): 731 ff., 768 ff., 956 ff.

———. "Judentum und Judenfrage." *DJ* (1939): 235.

———. *Die Juden und die Justiz*. 2d ed. Berlin, 1943.

Losacker, Ludwig. "Aufbau der Verwaltung im neuen Distrikt Galizien." *DVerw* (1942): 5 ff.

Lösener, Bernhard. "Die Hauptprobleme der Nürnberger Grundgesetze und ihrer Ersten Ausführungsverordnung." *RVerwBl.* (1935): 929 ff.

———. "Als Rassereferent im Reichsinnenministerium." *VjhZ* 2, no. 3 (1961): 264 ff.

Löwenstein, Karl. "Law in the Third Reich." *Yale Law Journal* 45 (1936): 779 ff.

Löwenstein, Rudolph M. *Psychoanalyse des Antisemitismus*. Trans. from the French by Lothar Baier. Vol. 241 in the Edition Suhrkamp. Frankfurt, 1968.

Łuczak, Czesław. *Dyskryminacja Polaków w Wielkopolsce w Okresie okupacji Hitlerowskiej*

(Discrimination against Poles in Greater Poland during the Hitler Occupation). Posen, 1966.

———. "Wysziedlenia Ludności Polskiej na tzw." In *Ziemiach Wcielonych do Rzesy* 1939–1945. Instytut Zachodni, Poznań, 1969.

———, ed. *Grabież polskiego mienia na ziemiach zachodnich rzeczypospolitiej "wcielonych" do rzeszy 1939-1945.* Poznań, 1969.

Lüdtke. "Die Schutzhaft gemäß der VO vom 28. 3. 1933." *JW* (1933): 2241 ff.

Ludwig, H. "Ethische Grundzüge zukünftiger deutscher Kolonialpolitik und Kolonialrechtspolitik." *DR* (1937): 499 ff.

Ludz, P. Chr. "Offene Fragen in der Totalitarismus-Forschung." *PVS* 2 (1961): 319 ff.

———. "Entwurf einer soziologischen Theorie totalitär verfaßter Gesellschaft." In *Soziologie der DDR*, ed. P. Chr. Ludz. Cologne, Opladen, 1964.

Lufft, Hermann. *Das britische Weltreich.* Leipzig, 1930.

Madajczyk, Czesław. *Hitlerowski terror na wsi polskiej 1939–1945.* Warsaw, 1965.

———. *Polityka III Rzeszy w Okupwanej Polsce.* 2 vols. Warsaw, 1970.

Maier, Hans. *Politische Wissenschaft in Deutschland.* Munich, 1969.

Malz, Heinrich. "Der Weg zur deutschen Polizei." *DR* (1936): 461 ff.

———. "Richtertum im nationalsozialistischen Staat." *DR* (1941) (A): 2217 ff.

Marcuse, Herbert. "Der Kampf gegen den Liberalismus in der totalitären Staatsauffassung." In *Zeitschrift für Sozialforschung*, vol. 3. Paris, 1934.

———. *Vernunft und Revolution.* Neuwied, Berlin, 1968.

Martin, Ludwig. "Die Bundesanwaltschaft beim Bundesgerichtshof." *DRiZ* (1975): 314 ff.

Marx. "Der Strafvollzug." *DJ* (1943): 80 ff.

Masing, Tim. "Der Primat der Politik: Politik und Wirtschaft im Nationalsozialismus." *Das Argument* 41 (1966): 473 ff.

Maßfeller, Franz. "Anmerkung zum Urteil des Reichgerichts vom 12. 7. 1934." *JW* (1934): 2613 f.; *DJ* (1934): 1102.

———. "Wann läuft die Frist zur Anfechtung einer Mischehe ab, wenn die Bedeutung der Rassenfrage schon im Jahre 1926 erkannt worden ist?" *DJ* (1934): 355 ff.

———. "Das Reichsbürgerrecht und das Gesetz zum Schutz des deutschen Blutes und der deutschen Ehre." *JW* (1935): 3417 ff.

———. "Grundsätze der Erb- und Rassenpflege im deutschen Familienrecht." *DR* (1935): 763 f.

Massing, Paul W. *Vorgeschichte des politischen Antisemitismus.* Trans. and edited for the German edition by Felix J. Weil. Frankfurter Beiträge zur Soziologie, vol. 8. Frankfurt, 1959.

Matzerath, Horst. *Nationalsozialismus und kommunale Selbstverwaltung.* Stuttgart, Berlin, Cologne, Mainz, 1970.

Maunz, Theodor. "Neue Grundlage des Verwaltungsrechts." In *Der Deutsche Staat der Gegenwart*, no. 9. Hamburg, 1934.

———. "Das Ende des subjektiven öffentlichen Rechts." *ZStW* 96 (1935/1): 71 ff.

———. "Die Zukunft der Verwaltungsgerichtsbarkeit." *DR* (1936): 478.

———. *Deutsche Verwaltung*. Hamburg, 1937.

———. *Die Staatsaufsicht*. Munich, 1938.

———. "Die Polizei im Reichsgefüge." *DVerw* (1941): 93 ff.

———. "Verfassung und Organisation im Großraum." *DVerw* (1941): 456 ff.

———. "Die Auslese in der deutschen Beamtengesetzgebung seit 1933." *Reich-Volksordnung-Lebensraum* 3 (1942): 315 f.

———. *Gestalt und Recht der Polizei*. Hamburg, 1943.

Maus, Ingeborg. *Bürgerliche Rechtstheorie und Faschismus: Zur sozialen Funktion und aktuellen Wirkung der Theorie Carl Schmitts*. Munich, 1976.

Mayer, Otto. *Lehrbuch des deutschen Verwaltungsrechts*. Vol. 1. 3d ed. Munich, 1924.

Medicus, Franz Albrecht. "Das Reichsministerium des Innern—Geschichte und Aufbau." *Schriften zum Staatsaufbau*, nos. 41–42. Berlin, 1940.

Meissner, O., and G. Kaiserberg. *Staats- und Verwaltungsrecht im Dritten Reich*. Berlin, 1935.

Melies, Heinz. *Das Arbeitsrecht des Generalgouvernements*. Kraków, 1943.

Menard, Hermann. "Rechtsfragen zur Abwicklung der Organisationen der polnischen Volksgruppen im Reich." *DJ* (1941): 572.

Menzel, Curt. *Minderheitenrecht und Judenfrage*. Berlin, 1934.

Merkl, Peter H. "Die alten Kämpfer der NSDAP." In *Sozialwissenschaftliches Jahrbuch für Politik*, ed. Rudolf Wildemann, vol. 2. Munich, Vienna, 1971.

Mettenberg, Wolfgang, ed. for the Reich Ministry of Justice. *Erwin Bumke zum 65. Geburtstage*. Berlin, 1939.

Meyer, Herbert. "Das jüdische Hehlerrecht." *Dt. Rechtswiss.* (1937): 97 ff.

———. *Rasse und Recht bei den Germanen und Indogermanen. Schriften der Akademie für Deutsches Recht*, group 2, *Deutsche Rechtsgeschichte. Forschungen zum deutschen Recht*, vols. 2–3. 1937.

Mezger, Edmund. *Deutsches Strafrecht: Ein Grundriß*. Munich, 1938.

Mieses, Matthias. *Der Ursprung des Judenhasses*. Berlin, Vienna, 1923.

Mitteis, Heinrich. *Deutsche Rechtsgeschichte*. 13th ed. Munich, 1974.

Möhring, Philipp. "Die Behandlung feindlichen Vermögens im Inland." *ZAKfDtRecht* (1940): 125 ff.

Mohrmann, Walter. *Antisemitismus: Ideologie und Geschichte im Kaiserreich und in der Weimarer Republik*. East Berlin, 1972.

Mommsen, Hans. "Der nationalsozialistische Polizeistaat und die Judenverfolgungen vor 1938." *VjhZ* (1962): 68 ff.

———. "Aufgabenkreis und Verantwortlichkeit des Staatssekretärs der Reichskanzlei Dr. Wilhelm Kritzinger." In *Gutachten des IfZ*, 2:369 ff. Munich, 1960.

———. *Beamtentum im Dritten Reich: Mit ausgewählten Quellen zur nationalsozialistischen Beamtenpolitik*. Stuttgart, 1966.

———. "Die Rechtsstellung des Reichskommissariats Ukraine." In *Gutachten des IfZ*, 2:328 ff.

Mössmer, Ferdinand. "Rassenmischehe und geltendes Recht." *ZAKfDtRecht* (1934): 86 ff.

————. *Neugestaltung des deutschen Ehescheidungsrechts. Schriften der Akademie für Deutsches Recht*, group 11, "Personen-, Familien- und Erbrecht," No. 1, Berlin, 1936.

Mueller, B., and Hildebrand. *Das Heer 1933-1945*. 2 vols. Darmstadt, 1954; Frankfurt, 1956.

Müllerheim, Fritz. *Die gesetzlichen und außergesetzlichen Maßnahmen zur wirtschaftlichen Vernichtung der Juden Deutschlands 1933-1945*. Hamburg, 1962.

Müller-Payer, Albert. *Die deutsche Sünde wider das Recht*. Stuttgart, 1946.

Muth, Heinrich. "Liberalismus und Verwaltungsgerichtsbarkeit." *DR* (1936): 407.

————. "Die verfassungsrechtliche Stellung des Beamtentums." *Reich-Volksordnung-Lebensraum* 3 (1942): 328 f.

Nair, Arnold D. Mc. *Legal Effects of War*. 2d ed. Cambridge, 1944.

Nawiasky, Hans. *Die Stellung des Berufsbeamtentums im parlamentarischen Staat*. Munich, 1926.

————. "Programm der Nationalsozialistischen Deutschen Arbeiter Partei Deutschlands vom 24. 3. 1920." Reprinted in Sartorius, *Verfassungs- und Verwaltungsrecht*, appendix 1. Munich, 1944.

Nawrocki, Stanisław. *Hitlerowska okupacja wielkopolski w okresie zarządu wojskowego*. Instytut Zachodni, Poznań, 1966.

————. *Policja hitlerowska w tzw. kraju warty w latach 1939-1945*. Instytut Zachodni, Poznań, 1970.

————. *Terror Policyjny w. "kraju warty" 1939-1945*. Wydawnictwo Poznańskie, 1973.

Neese, G. "Die Rechtsnatur der NSDAP." *ZStW* 95 (1935): 709 ff.

————. "Die verfassungsrechtliche Gestaltung der Einheitspartei." *ZStW* 98 (1938): 673 ff.

Nef, Hans. *Gleichheit und Gerechtigkeit*. Zürich, 1941.

Neubert, Reinhard. "Die Schranken richterlichen Prüfungsrechts bei staatspolitischen Handlungen der Verwaltung." *JW* (1933): 2426 ff.

————. "Neue Richtlinien für die Ausübung des Anwaltsberufes." *JW* (1934): 1763 f.

————. "Anwaltliche Ehrenrechtsprechung in der Spruchpraxis des Dienststrafsenats." *DR* (1944) (A): 425 f.

Neufeldt, H. J., J. Huck, and G. Tessin. *Zur Geschichte der Ordnungspolizei 1936-1945*. Koblenz, 1957.

Neumann, Franz. *Behemoth: The Structure and Practice of National Socialism 1933-1945*. 2d ed. New York, 1963.

————. *Demokratischer und autoritärer Staat: Beiträge zur Soziologie der Politik*. Frankfurt/Main, 1967. Originally published as *The Democratic and the Authoritarian State* (New York, 1957).

————. "Notizen zur Theorie der Diktatur." In Neumann, *Demokratischer und autoritärer Staat*.

Neumann, Siegfried. "Vom Kaiserhoch zur Austreibung: Aus den Aufzeichnungen eines jüdischen Rechtsanwalts." *Aus Politik und Zeitgeschichte* (B) 45 (1976).

Neumann, Siegmund. *Permanent Revolution: The Total State in a World War*. New York, 1942.

Neurohr, Jean. *Der Mythos vom Dritten Reich: Zur Geistesgeschichte des Nationalsozialismus.* Stuttgart, 1957.

Nicolai, Helmut. *Grundlagen der kommenden Verfassung.* Berlin, 1933.

———. *Der Neuaufbau des Reiches nach dem Reichsreformgesetz vom 30. 1. 1934.* Berlin, 1934.

———. "Die Aufgabe des Verwaltungsbeamten und die fachliche Arbeit der Fachgruppe Verwaltungsbeamte." *DR* (1934): 2 ff.

———. *Die Rassengesetzliche Rechtslehre: Grundzüge einer nationalsozialistischen Rechtsphilosophie.* 3d ed. Munich, 1934.

———. "Grundsätzliches über den Zusammenhang von Rasse und Recht." *DR* (1934): 74.

———. *Rasse und Recht.* 2d ed. Berlin, 1934.

Noack, Erich. "Die Stellung des Anwalts sowie der freien Berufe im Staat." *JW* (1933): 2185 ff.

———. "Formalismus im Strafprozeß." *DR* (1934): 353 f.

———. "Der freie Anwalt im Dritten Reich." *JW* (1936): 1746 ff.

———. *Kommentar zur Rechtsanwaltschaftsordnung i.d.F. vom 21.2.1936.* 2d ed. Leipzig, 1937.

———. "Die Entjudung der deutschen Anwaltschaft." *JW* (1938): 2796 ff.

———. "Das deutsche Kriegsrecht-Kriegsgesetzgebung." *DR* (1940) (A): 1 ff.

Noack, Erwin. "Die Stellung des Rechtsanwalts im nationalsozialistischen Staat." In *Nationalsozialistisches Handbuch für Recht und Gesetzgebung,* 1525 ff. Munich, 1934.

Noam, Ernst, and Wolf Arno Kropat. *Juden vor Gericht.* Kommission für die Geschichte der Juden in Hessen. Wiesbaden, 1975.

Nolte, Ernst. *Der Faschismus in seiner Epoche: Die Action francaise: Der italienische Faschismus: Der Nationalsozialismus.* 2d ed. Munich, 1965.

———. "Vierzig Jahre Theorien über den Faschismus." Introduction to Nolte, *Theorien über den Faschismus.*

———. *Die Krise des liberalen Systems und die faschistischen Bewegungen.* Munich, 1968.

———. ed. *Theorien über den Faschismus.* Cologne, Berlin, 1967.

NSDAP. *Parteistatistik der NSDAP.* Vol. 1. Munich, 1935.

Nußbaum, Arthur. *Geschichte des Völkerrechts.* Munich, Berlin, 1960.

Oetker, Friedrich. "Grundprobleme der nationalsozialistischen Strafrechtreform." In Frank, *Nationalsozialistisches Handbuch für Recht und Gesetzgebung,* 1317 ff.

Olczewski. "Rassengebundene Rechtsprechung." *DR* (1941) (A): 36 f.

Oppenheim. L. F. L., and H. Lauterpacht. *International Law: A Treatise.* 8th ed. London, 1955.

Ostforschung, Deutsche. *Ergebnisse und Aufgaben seit dem 2. Weltkrieg,* 1943 (BA D I 1024 [Bibl.]).

Ostler, Fritz. *Die deutschen Rechtsanwälte, 1871–1971.* Essen, Ellinghaus, 1971.

OUNR, "Denkschrift zur Autonomie der Ukraine." In Ilnytzkyj, *Deutschland und die Ukraine 1934–45,* vol. 2, 386 ff.

Palandt, Otto. "Drei Monate Prüflinge aus dem Gemeinschaftslager der preußischen Referendare." *DJ* (1933): 640 f.

———. "Die sachliche Auswirkung der Gemeinschaftserziehung." *DJ* (1936): 1751 ff.

———. "Die Arbeit der Ausbildungsabteilung im Jahre 1937." *DJ* (1938): 22 ff.

———, ed. *Bürgerliches Gesetzbuch, Beck'sche Kurzkommentare.* Vol. 7. 2d ed., 1939; 5th ed. Munich, Berlin, 1942.

Peters, Karl. "Die Umgestaltung des Strafgesetzes 1933–1945." In Flitner, *Deutsches Geistesleben und Nationalsozialismus.*

Pfeiffer, Helfried. *Rechtsvereinheitlichung und Verwaltungsvereinfachung im Großdeutschen Reich.* Hamburg, Wandsbek. 1942.

Pfeiffer, Büttner, and Heuber. *Das Generalgouvernement und seine Wirtschaft.* 1942.

Pfundtner, Hans, ed. *Das neue deutsche Reichsrecht.* Berlin, 1933–44.

———, ed. *Dr. Wilhelm Frick und sein Ministerium: Aus Anlaß des 60. Geburtstages des Reichs- und Preußischen Ministers des Innern Dr. Wilhelm Frick am 12. 3. 1937.* Munich, 1937.

———, ed. *Beamtenrecht.* 3d ed. Berlin, 1944.

———, ed. *Die Bücher der Verwaltung.* Berlin, 1944.

Pfundtner and Warnak. *Taschenbuch für Verwaltungsbeamte.* Berlin, 1941.

Phelps, Reginald. "Hitlers 'grundlegende' Rede über den Antisemitismus." *VjhZ* 16 (1968): 390 ff.

Picker, Henry, ed. *Hitlers Tischgespräche im Führerhauptquartier, 1941–42.* Bonn, 1951; Munich, 1968; revised and expanded ed., Stuttgart, 1976.

Piotrowski, Stanislaw. *Hans Franks Tagebuch.* Warsaw, 1963.

Pirker Theo, ed. "Komintern und Faschismus: Dokumente zur Geschichte und Theorie des Faschismus." Stuttgart, 1965; *VjhZ*, no. 10, 124.

Plum, Günter. "Staatspolizei und Innere Verwaltung 1934–1936." *VjhZ* 2 (1965): 191 ff.

Poetzsch-Heffter, F., C. H. Ule, and C. Dernedde. "Autoritäres volksverbundenes Führertum," "Volksverbundenheit des Führertums und ihre organisatorische Sicherung," and "Der völkische Staat." *Vom deutschen Staatsleben, Jahrbuch für öffentliches Recht* 22 (1935): 1 ff., 50 ff.

Poliakov, Leon, and Josef Wulf. *Das Dritte Reich und seine Diener: Dokumente.* Berlin, 1956.

———. "Information und Propaganda." In *Das Dritte Reich und seine Diener.* Berlin, 1959.

———. *Das Dritte Reich und die Juden: Dokumente und Aufsätze.* Berlin, 1961.

Polnische Akademie der Wissenschaften, ed. *Dzieje najnowsze Polski* (Materials and Studies from the Second World War). 4 vols. Warsaw, 1959–60.

Popitz, Johannes. "Die Verwaltungsgerichtsbarkeit im Kriege." In Huber, *Idee und Ordnung des Reiches,* vol. 1.

———. "Die Anfänge der Verwaltungsgerichtsbarkeit." *AöR*, NF, 33 (1943): 158 ff.; *AöR*, NF, 34 (1944): 3 ff.

Pospieszalski, Karel Marian. *Polska pod niemieckiem prawem, 1939–1945.* Poznań, 1946.

————. "Poznań pod okupacja hitlerowska." *Przegląd Zachodni* (1953): 403 ff.

Pross, Harry. *Literatur und Politik*. Freiburg, 1963.

Prussian Ministry of Justice. *Nationalsozialistisches Strafrecht, Denkschrift*. Berlin, 1933.

Publikationsstelle Berlin-Dahlem. *Das Deutsche Reich und das Generalgouvernement der besetzten polnischen Gebiete in statistischen Angaben*. Berlin, 1940.

Pulzer, Peter P. *Die Entstehung des politischen Antisemitismus in Deutschland und Österreich 1867–1914*. Trans. from the English. Gütersloh, 1966.

Pungs, Wilhelm. "Die bürgerliche Rechtspflege im Warthegau: Rückblick und Ausblick." *DR* (1941) (A): 2491 ff.

Pungs, Wilhelm, Karl Buchholz, and Joseph Wolany. *Ostrechtspflegeverordnung und Ostrechtspflegedurchführungsverordnung*. Berlin, 1943.

Püschel, Wilhelm. *Der Niedergang des Rechts im Dritten Reich*. 2d ed. Reutlingen, 1947.

Raeke, Neubert. "Gemeinsame Mitteilung des Reichsfachgruppenleiters Rechtsanwälte und des Präsidiums der Reichsrechtsanwaltskammer." *JW* (1934): 3049.

Ramm, Thilo, "Nationalsozialismus und Arbeitsrecht." *KJ* (1968): 108 ff.

Rasch, Ernst. "Die Organisation der Polizei (Geschichtliche Entwicklung und jetziger Stand)." *DÖV* (1960): 81 ff.

Rauchfuß, Kurt. "Studien zur außerordentlichen Kündigung von Arbeitsverhältnissen unter besonderer Berücksichtigung der Rechtsprechung des Reichsarbeitsgerichts: Ein Beitrag zur Lehre von der Kündigung." Legal diss., Leipzig, 1936.

Rauschning, Hermann. *Die Revolution des Nihilismus: Kulisse und Wirklichkeit des Dritten Reiches*. Zurich, 1938.

————. *Gespräche mit Hitler*. Zurich, 1950.

Rave, Paul Ortwin. *Kunstdiktatur im Dritten Reich*. Hamburg, 1949.

Redeker, Konrad. "Bewältigung der Vergangenheit als Aufgabe der Justiz." *NJW* (1964): 1097 ff.

"Referendare in Uniform: Ein Film aus dem Gemeinschaftslager Hanns-Kerrl." *DJ* (1937): 558 f.

Reich, Wilhelm. *Massenpsychologie des Faschismus*. 1942; Cologne, Berlin, 1971.

Reichmann, Eva G. *Die Flucht in den Haß: Die Ursache der deutschen Judenkatastrophe*. Frankfurt/Main, n.d.

Reich Ministry of Justice. "Übersicht über die Zahl der am 1. 5. 1934 zugelassenen arischen und nichtarischen Rechtsanwälte und Notare." *DJ* (1934): 950.

————. "Übersicht über die zahlenmäßige Auswirkung des Gesetzes über die Zulassung zur Rechtsanwaltschaft im Jahre 1934." *JW* (1935): 758.

Reich Security Main Office (RSHA) (Amt III), ed. "Zur Rechtssicherheit und Unabhängigkeit der Richter." In *Beiträge zur Aussprache über Lebensgebietsfragen*. N.p., n.d.

Reich-Volksordnung-Lebensraum. Ed. W. Stuckart et al. Review for *völkisch* constitution and administration; organ of the Reich research council, department of state and administration science; preliminary organ of the International Academy for State and Administration Science. 6 vols. 1941–43.

Reimers, Erich. *Der Kampf um den deutschen Osten.* Leipzig, 1943.

———. *Deutsche Ostforschung, Ergebnisse und Aufgaben seit dem 2. Weltkrieg.* 1943.

Reitter, Ekkehard. *Franz Gürtner: Politische Biographie eines deutschen Juristen 1881–1941.* Berlin, 1976.

Reuß, Hermann. "Die Verwaltungsgerichtsbarkeit im neuen Reich." *JW* (1935): 2025 ff.

———. "Partei und Staat im Dritten Reich." *JW* (1935): 2314 ff.

———. "Der Krieg und die Verwaltungsgerichtsbarkei." *ZAKfDtRecht* (1940): 10 ff.

———. "Zuständigkeit und Verfahren der Verwaltungsgerichte." *DR* (1942) (A): 1345 f.

Rhode, Gotthold. *Kleine Geschichte Polens.* Darmstadt, 1965.

Ridder, Helmut. "Zur Verfassungsdoktrin des nationalsozialistischen Staates." *KJ* (1969): 221 ff.

Riefersauer, Fritz. "Die Juden in der deutschen Grundstücks- und Wohnungswirtschaft." *DJ* (1939): 1270 ff.

Rietzsch and Crohne. "Die Arbeit der Sondergerichte im Kriege: Abgekürzter Bericht über die Tagung der Sondergerichtsvorsitzenden und Sachbearbeiter für Sondergerichtsstrafsachen bei den Generalstaatsanwälten im RMJ am 24.10.1939." Typewritten manuscript in Archives of the Main Commission Warsaw, also BA R 22/4158.

Rilk, Otto. "Judentum und Wirtschaft in der neuen deutschen Rechtsprechung." *JW* (1938): 2533 ff.

Ritterbusch, Paul, ed. *Politische Wissenschaft.* Berlin, 1940.

Roesen, Anton. "Rechtsfragen der Einsatzgruppenprozesse." *NJW* (1964): 133.

Rogge, Heinrich. "Der Begriff des "Völkischen." *Deutsche Rechtswissenschaft* (1941): 271 ff.

Rohlfing. "Rechtsfragen aus der Zugehörigkeit zur jüdischen Rasse im Arbeitsrecht." *JW* (1933): 2098 ff.

Roos, H. "Der Feldzug in Polen September 1939." *Wehrwissenschaftliche Rundschau* 9 (1959): 491 ff.

Rosen, G. "Die Entwicklung der Handels- und Genossenschaftsregister im Warthegau." *DR* (1941) (A): 2500 ff.

Rosenberg, Alfred. *Die Protokolle der Weisen von Zion und die jüdische Weltpolitik.* Munich, 1923.

———. *Der Mythos des 20. Jahrhundert.* 1st ed. Munich, 1933.

Rößiger, Herbert. "Führertum und Verwaltungsgerichtsbarkeit." *Leipziger rechtswissenschaftliche Studien,* no. 98. Leipzig, 1936.

Rothenberger, Curt. "Die Rechtsquellen im neuen Staat." *DJZ* (1936): 22.

———. "Die Stellung des Richters im Führerstaat." *DR* (1939): 831 ff.

———. "Die ersten Gedanken über den Aufbau einer nationalsozialistischen Rechtspflege." *DJ* (1942): 365 ff.

———. "Zum Problem 'Friedensrichter.' " *DR* (1942) (A): 1521.

———. "Der Aufbau der Gerichte." *DR* (1943) (A): 465 ff.

———. *Der deutsche Richter.* Hamburg, 1943.

———. "Der Richter im nationalsozialistischem Staat." *DJ* (1943): 257 ff.

————. "Die ersten fachlichen Maßnahmen zum Aufbau einer nationalsozialistischen Rechtspflege." *DJ* (1943): 66 ff.

————, ed. *Das Hanseatische Oberlandesgericht: Gedenkschrift zu seinem 60jährigen Bestehen.* Hamburg, 1939.

Rousseau, Jean Jacques. *Du contrat social ou principes du droit politique.* Paris, 1960.

Rückerl, Adalbert. *NS-Vernichtungslager im Spiegel deutscher Strafprozesse: Belzec, Sobibor, Treblinka, Chelmno.* Munich, 1977.

Rühle, Gerd. *Das Dritte Reich (Dokumentarische Darstellung des Aufbaues der Nation).* Berlin, 1935.

Rümelin, Max. *Die Gleichheit vor dem Gesetz.* Tübingen, 1928.

Runte, Ludwig. "Die Verwaltung der besetzten Ostgebiete." *DVerw* (1942): 226 ff.

Rusiński, Władisław. *Położenie robotników Polskich w czasie wojny 1939–1945, Poznań 1948/1949* (The situation of Polish workers in the German Reich and in the Annexed Eastern Territories during the war years). Vols 1–2. Posen, 1949–55.

Ruth, Rudolf. "Wucher- und Wucherrecht der Juden im Mittelalter." *Dt. Rechtswiss.* (1937): 111 ff.

Rüthers, Bernd. *Die unbegrenzte Auslegung: Zum Wandel der Privatrechtsordnung im Nationalsozialismus.* 2d ed. Frankfurt/Main, 1973.

Ruthfelder, Herbert Philipps. "A Study of Alfred Rosenberg's Organizations for National Socialist Ideology," Ph.D. diss., Michigan, 1963. Microfilm.

Ryszka, Franciszek. *Państwo i stanu wyjątkowego.* Wrocław, 1964 (from Griese's review in *KJ* [1976]: 116 ff.).

Sachweh, Kurt. "Die Verwaltung der deutschen afrikanischen Kolonien vor dem Weltkrieg." *DVerw* (1941): 344 ff.

Saller, K. *Die Rassenlehre des Nationalsozialismus in Wissenschaft und Propaganda.* Darmstadt, 1961.

Salomon, Albert. "Leadership in Democracy." In *Political and Economic Democracy,* ed. Max Ascoli and Fritz Lehmann. New York, 1937.

Sartorius, Carl, ed. *Verfassungs- und Verwaltungsrecht.* 15th ed. Munich, Berlin, 1944.

Sassen, Franz Josef. "Das Gesetzgebungs- und Verordnungsrecht in den deutschen Kolonien." Vol. 5, 2, in the series Abhandlungen aus dem Staats-, Verwaltungs- und Völkerrecht, ed. Philipp Zorn and Fritz Stier-Somlo. Tübingen, 1909.

Sattelmacher. "Richter und Rechtsfindung." *DJ* (1942): 93 ff.

Sauckel, Fritz. "Das Wesen des Großdeutschen Arbeitseinsatzes—Allgemeingültige und verpflichtende Grundsätze." In Sauckel, *Handbuch,* 51 ff.

————. "Manifest des Generalbevollmächtigten für den Arbeitseinsatz vom 20.4.1943." In Sauckel, *Handbuch,* 41 ff.

————. "Programm des Generalbevollmächtigten für den Arbeitseinsatz." In Sauckel, *Handbuch,* 27 ff.

————. "Totaler Arbeitseinsatz für den Krieg." In Sauckel, *Handbuch,* 227 ff.

————. "Totaler Arbeitseinsatz für den Sieg: Rede am 6.1.1943." In Sauckel, *Handbuch.*

———. "Der Arbeitseinsatz im Jahre 1942: Geheimer Bericht des GBA vom 23. 12. 1942." In *Dokumente der Deutschen Politik und Geschichte*, 5:392 ff. Berlin, Munich, 1953.

———, ed. *Handbuch für den Dienst des Generalbevollmächtigten für den Arbeitseinsatz und die interessierten Reichsstellen im Großdeutschen Reich und den besetzten Gebieten*. Vol. 1. Berlin, 1944.

Sauer, Franz. *Das Reichsjustizministerium*. Schriften der Hochschule für Politik, nos. 36–37. Berlin, 1939.

Sauer, Wilhelm. "Rechtsprechung und Regierung: Zur Frage der Unabhängigkeit des Richters." *DJ* (1935): 181 ff.

Schacht, Konrad, and Lutz Unterseher. "Versuch zur Systematisierung des Chaos." *KJ* (1970): 9 ff.

Schäfer, Friedrich. "Anspruch auf Ruhegeld im Arbeitsrecht." Legal diss., Tübingen, 1939.

Schäfer, G. "Demokratie und Totalitarismus." In *Politikwissenschaft: Eine Einführung in ihre Probleme*, ed. G. Kress and D. Senghaas, 105 ff. Frankfurt, 1969.

Schäfer, Leopold. "Die Verhängung von Schutzhaft." *DR* (1936): 377.

———. "Zehn Jahre nationalsozialistische Strafgesetzgebung." *DJ* (1943): 73 ff.

Schäfer, Wolfgang. *NSDAP: Entwicklung und Struktur der Staatspartei des Dritten Reiches*. Hannover, Frankfurt/Main, 1956.

Schaffstein, Friedrich. "Formalismus im Strafrecht." *DR* (1934): 349 ff.

———. "Rechtswidrigkeit und Schuld im Aufbau des neuen Strafrechtssystems." *ZStW* 57 (1958): 295 ff.

Schauwecker. "Der Volksgerichtshof für das Deutsche Reich." *JW* (1936): 1569 f.

Scheerbarth, Walter. "Polizeirecht, Feuer- und Fremdenpolizei, Bau- und Siedlungswesen, Gesundheitswesen." In *Die Bücher der Verwaltung*, vol. 5. Berlin, Vienna, 1942.

Scheffler, Wolfgang. "Nationalsozialistische Judenpolitik." In *Zur Politik und Zeitgeschichte*, nos. 4–5. Berlin, 1960.

———. *Judenverfolgung im Dritten Reich 1933–1945*. 2d ed. Frankfurt/Main, Vienna, Zurich, 1964.

Schemann, L. *Briefwechsel Toqueville an Gobineau 1843–1859*. Berlin, 1908.

Scheuermann, Alfred. *Der deutsche Osten ruft*. Berlin, 1942.

Scheuner, Ulrich. "Die nationale Revolution." *AöR*, NF 24 (1933–34): 166 ff., 261 ff.

———. "Die Gerichte und die Prüfung politischer Staatshandlungen." *RVerwBl.*, no. 21 (1936): 437 ff.

———. "Der Gleichheitsgedanke in der völkischen Verfassungsordnung." *ZStW* 99 (1939): 245 ff.

———. "Die deutsche Staatsführung im Kriege." *Dt. Rechtswiss.* (1940): 1 ff.

———. "Die Machstellung der Vereinigten Staaten in Zentralamerika." *ZAKfDtRecht* (1940): 304 ff.

Schieder, Theodor. *Hermann Rauschnings "Gespräche mit Hitler" als Geschichtsquelle*. Opladen, 1972.

Schlangen, Walter. "Der Totalitarismusbegriff (Grundzüge seiner Entstehung, Wandlung und Kritik)." In *Politik und Zeitgeschichte* (supplement to *Das Parlament*), B 44/70, from October 31, 1970.

Schlegelberger, Franz. *Abschied vom BGB*. Berlin, 1937.

———. "Kriegszivilrecht einst und jetzt." *DJ* (1939): 1881.

Schmidt, A. M. "Polizeiverwaltungsrecht." *DVerw* (1937): 9 ff.

Schmidt, Eberhard. *Einführung in die Geschichte der deutschen Strafrechtspflege*. 2d ed. Göttingen, 1951.

Schmidt, Carl. *Politische Theologie*. Munich, 1922.

———. "Das Reichsstatthaltergesetz." In *Das Recht der nationalen Revolution*, no. 3. Berlin, 1933.

———. "Neue Leitsätze für die Rechtspraxis." *JW* (1933): 2793; *DR* (1933): 201 f.

———. "Ein Jahr nationalsozialistischer Verfassungsstaat." *DR* (1934): 27 ff.

———. "Nationalsozialismus und Rechtsstaat." *JW* (1934): 713 ff.

———. "Richter und Gesetz: Zur Reichstagserklärung Hitlers vom 13. 7. 1934 zur Röhm-Affaire." *DJZ* (1934): 691 ff., 945.

———. *Über die drei Arten rechtswissenschaftlichen Denkens*. Berlin, 1934.

———. *Staat, Bewegung, Volk*. 3d ed. Hamburg, 1935 (from Reuß's review in *JW* [1935]: 2254).

———. "Was bedeutet der Streit um den Rechtsstaat." *ZStW* 95 (1935): 189 ff.

———. "Die deutsche Rechtswissenschaft im Kampf gegen den jüdischen Geist." *DJZ* (1936): 1194 ff.

———. "Großraum gegen Universalismus." *ZAKfDtRecht* (1939): 333 ff.

———. "Die Raumrevolution: Durch den totalen Krieg zu einem totalen Frieden." *Das Reich*, no. 192 (September 29, 1940).

———. "Reich und Raum: Elemente eines neuen Völkerrechts." *ZAKfDtRecht* (1940): 201 ff.

———. "Raum und Großraum im Völkerrecht." *ZVR* 24 (1941): 145 ff.

———. "Völkerrechtliche Großraumordnung mit Interventionsverbot raumfremder Mächte: Ein Beitrag zum Reichsbegriff im Völkerrecht." In *Schriften des Instituts für Politik und Internationales Recht an der Universität Kiel*, vol. 7. 1939; 3d ed., Berlin, Leipzig, Vienna, 1941.

———. *Verfassungsrechtliche Aufsätze aus den Jahren 1924–1954: Materialien zu einer Verfassungslehre*. Berlin, 1958.

Scholl, Albert. *Die Entjudung des deutschen Grundbesitzes: Die Verantwortung über den Einsatz des jüdischen Vermögens vom 3. Dezember 1938 nebst Durchführungsverornung vom 16. 7. 1939 und dem ministeriellen Durchführungsbestimmungen vom 6. Februar 1939*. 2d ed. Berlin, 1940.

Scholte, Harald. "Die NS-Ordensburgen." *VjhZ* 15 (1967): 269 ff.

Scholz, Franz. "Nationalsozialismus und Rechtsstaat." *JW* (1934): 713 ff.

———. "Die Rechtssicherheit." *DVerw* (1944): 28 ff.

Schönbaum, D. *Die braune Revolution: Eine Sozialgeschichte des Dritten Reiches*. Cologne, Berlin, 1968.

Schönke, Adolf. "Die bürgerliche Rechtspflege seit Kriegsbeginn." *DR* (1942) (A): 564 f.

———. *Strafgesetzbuch, Kommentar.* Munich, 1942.

———. "Einige Grundlinien der Entwicklung des Zivilprozeßrechts seit 1933." *DR* (1943) (A): 113 ff.

Schorn, Hubert. *Der Richter im Dritten Reich: Geschichte und Dokumente.* Frankfurt/ Main, 1959.

———. *Die Gesetzgebung des Nationalsozialismus als Mittel der Machtpolitik.* Frankfurt/ Main, 1963.

Schramm, Percy. ed. *Hitlers Tischgespräche 1941–1942.* Stuttgart, 1943.

Schraut, Rudolf. "Blutgebundenes Recht." *DR* (1934): 73 ff.

———. "Ein Jahr Reichsjustizkommissariat." *DR* (1943): 269 ff.

Schröder, Sebastian. "Die Heeresverwaltung." *Reich-Volksordnung-Lebensraum* 6 (1943): 383 ff.

Schulz and Arno Brachmann, eds. *Die Oststeuerhilfe.* Berlin, 1941.

Schulz, Gerhard. "Der Begriff des Totalitarismus und des Nationalismus." *Soziale Welt* 12 (1961): 116 ff.

———. *Faschismus und Nationalsozialismus: Versionen und theoretische Kontroversen 1922–1972.* Berlin, 1974.

———. *Aufstieg des Nationalsozialismus: Krise und Revolution in Deutschland.* Frankfurt/ Main, 1975.

Schulze, Alfred, Walter Simons, and Fritz Förster. *Die Rechtsprechung des Reichs-disziplinarhofes.* Berlin, 1935.

Schürmann, Adolf. "Festigung deutschen Volkstums in den eingegliederten Ostge-bieten." *Reich-Volksordnung-Lebensraum.* 6 (1943): 475 ff.

Schütze, Hermann. *Das Recht der Ostgebiete.* Berlin, 1942; supplement 1 (1942), 2 (1943).

Schwarz, Otto. "Der nationalsozialistische Strafprozeß." In Frank, *Nationalsozialistisches Handbuch für Recht und Gesetzgebung,* 1460 ff.

———. "Reichsgericht als Tatsacheninstanz." *ZAKfDtRecht* (1940): 139 ff.

———. *Strafprozeßordnung.* 12th ed. Munich, Berlin, 1943.

Schwinge, Erich. *Wesenschau und konkretes Ordnungsdenken im Strafrecht.* Bonn, 1937.

Schwister. "Gemeinschaftdienst und große Staatsprüfung." *JW* (1933): 1747 ff.

Seeber, Eva. *Zwangsarbeiter in der faschistischen Kriegswirtschaft: Die Deportation und Ausbeutung polnischer Bürger unter besonderer Berücksichtigung der Lage der Arbeiter aus dem sog. Generalgouvernement (1939–1945).* East Berlin, 1964.

Seel, Hans. "Die Gestaltung des deutschen Beamtenrechts seit dem 30. Januar 1933." In Frank, *Deutsches Verwaltungsrecht,* 154 ff.

Seeley, Y. R. *Die Ausbreitung Englands.* Frankfurt, 1954.

Sehn, Jan. "Zur Organisation der Polizei im Reich und im GG." *Bulletin of the Main Commission Warsaw* 3 (1947): 175 ff.

Seidel, Bruno. *Totalitarian Dictatorship.* Cambridge, 1965.

Seidel, Bruno, and Siegfried Jenker, eds. *Wege der Totalitarismus-Forschung.* Darmstadt, 1968.

Seidl and Ignaz Hohenveldern. "Beseitigung der Verfolgungshindernisse für NS-Verbrechen." *Zeitschrift für Rechtspolitik* (1974): 225.

Seraphim, Hans-Günther, ed. *Das politische Tagebuch Alfred Rosenbergs 1934–1935 und 1939–1940.* Munich, 1964.

Serwański, Edward. *Wielkopolska w cieniu swastyki.* Instytut Zachodni, Posen, 1970.

Siebert, Wolfgang. "Gemeinschaft und bürgerliches Recht." *DR* (1934): 303 ff.

———. *Die deutsche Arbeitsverfassung.* Hamburg, 1942.

———. "Die Entwicklung der staatlichen Arbeitsverwaltung." *Reich-Volksordnung-Lebensraum* 2 (1942): 227 ff.

———. "Wandlungen im bürgerlichen Recht seit 1933." *DR* (1944): 5 ff.

Sievers, R. "Maßnahmen der Polizei außerhalb ihrer sonstigen Grenzen." *DVerw* (1940): 243.

Silbermann, Alphons. "Exkurs über die Aufgaben der Soziologie zur Bekämpfung des Antisemitismus." *Kölner Zeitschrift für Soziologie und Sozialpsychologie* (1967): 736 ff.

Six, F. A., ed. *Dokumente der Deutschen Politik und Geschichte, 1942–1944.* Ed. Hans Volz.

Smend, Rudolf. *Die politische Gewalt im Verfassungsstaat und das Problem der Staatsform: Festgabe für Wilhelm Kahl.* Tübingen, 1923.

———. *Verfassung und Verfassungsrecht.* Munich, 1928.

Sobczak, Janusz. *Hitlerowskie przesiedlenia ludności niemieckiej w dobie II wojny światowej.* Instytut Zachodni, Poznań, 1966.

Sommer, Walter. "Partei und Staat." *DJZ* (1936): 593 ff.

———. "Justiz und Verwaltung." *DVerw* (1942): 83 ff.

Sosnowki, Kiryl. *The Tragedy of Children under Nazi Rule.* Posen, Warsaw, 1962.

Spanner, Hans. "Fragen der Verwaltung besetzter Gebiete unter besonderer Berücksichtigung der besetzten niederländischen Gebiete." *AöR*, NF 34 (1944): 96 ff.

Spieler. "Preußischer Geist im Gemeinschaftslager Jüterbog." *DJ* (1933): 641 ff.

Spohr, Werner. *Das Recht der Schutzhaft.* Berlin, 1937.

Stach, J. "Polenreservate im Warthegau." *Bulletin of the Main Commission Warsaw* 17 (1967): 151.

Staff, Ilse, ed. *Justiz im Dritten Reich: Eine Dokumentation.* Frankfurt, Hamburg, 1964; 2d ed., 1978.

Stamati, C. Graf. "Zur Kulturpolitik des Ostministeriums." *VjhZ* (1958): 78 ff.

Stamm. "Sozialversicherung im Generalgouvernement und ihre Einordnung in die Arbeits- und Gesundheitsverwaltung." *ZAKfDtRecht* (1942): 37 ff.

Stammer, Otto. "Aspekte der Totalitarismusforschung." In *Politische Soziologie und Demokratieforschung,* by O. Stammer. Berlin, 1965.

Steffens, Heinz. "Die rechtliche Vertretung der Juden im Reich." *DR* (1942) (A): 9 ff.

Steiner, W. H. "Verändertes Tarnow." Press Service of the General Government, June 9, 1942, ZS.

Steinert, Marlis. *Hitlers Krieg und die Deutschen.* Düsseldorf, 1971.

Steiniger, Peter Alfons, and Kazimierz Leszczyński. *Fall 3: Das Urteil im Juristenprozeß, gefällt am 4. Dezember 1947 von dem Militärgerichtshof III der Vereinigten Staaten von Nordamerika.* East Berlin, 1969.

Steinlechner, Wolfgang. "Anmerkung zu BGH NJW 1968, 1339 (Rehse-Verdict)." *NJW* (1968): 1790.

Stolleis, Michael. "Gemeinschaft und Volksgemeinschaft." *VjhZ* 20 (1972): 16 ff.

———. *Gemeinwohlformeln im nationalsozialstischen Recht.* Berlin, 1974.

Strauß, Leo. *Naturrecht und Geschichte.* Stuttgart, 1953.

Streicher, Julius, ed. *Die Judengesetze Großdeutschlands.* Ed. Peter Meg. Nuremberg, 1939.

Strothmann, Dietrich. *Nationalsozialistische Literaturpolitik.* 2d ed. Bonn, 1963.

Strupp and Schlochauer. *Wörterbuch des Völkerrechts.* 2d ed. Berlin, 1960–61.

Strupp, Karl. *Grundzüge des positiven Völkerrechts.* 5th ed. Bonn, 1932.

Stuckart, Wilhelm. *Nationalsozialistische Rechtserziehung.* Frankfurt/Main, 1935.

———. "Nationalsozialistischer Staat und Verwaltungsgerichtsbarkeit." *DVerw* (1935): 161 ff.

———. "Partei und Staat." *DJ* (1936): 815 ff.

———. "Verwaltungsrecht." 4th ed. Leipzig, 1939.

———. "Das Reichsverwaltunggericht." *DVerw* (1941): 189 ff.

———. "Die Neuordnung der Kontinente und die Zusammenarbeit auf dem Gebiet der Verwaltung." *Reich-Volksordnung-Lebensraum* 1 (1941): 3 ff.

———. "Die Staatsangehörigkeit in den eingegliederten Ostgebieten." *ZAKfDtRecht* 8 (1941): 223 ff.

———. "Zentralgewalt, Dezentralisation und Verwaltungseinheit." In *Festgabe für Heinrich Himmler.* Darmstadt, 1941.

———. "Die europäische Neuordnung im Hinblick auf Verfassung und Verwaltung." *DVerw* (1942): 161 ff.

———. *Der Staatsaufbau des Deutschen Reiches.* Leipzig, 1943.

———. "Staatsangehörigkeit und Reichsgestaltung." *Reich-Volksordnung-Lebensraum* 5 (1943): 57 ff.

———, ed. *Neues Staatsrecht: I. Der neue Reichsaufbau, Leipzig 1944. Neues Staatsrecht: II. Die Errichtung des Großdeutschen Reiches.* Leipzig, 1943.

Stuckart, Wilhelm, and Hans Globke. *Reichsbürgergesetz vom 15. 9. 1935: Gesetz zum Schutz des deutschen Blutes und der deutschen Ehre vom 15. 9. 1935. Gesetz zum Schutz der Erbgesundheit des deutschen Volkes (Ehegesundheitsgesetz) vom 18. 10. 1935: Kommentare zur deutschen Rassengesetzgebung.* Vol. 1. Munich, 1936.

Stuckart, Wilhelm, and Horst Hoffmann, eds. *Handbuch des Beamtenrechts.* Berlin, 1938.

Stuckart, Wilhelm, and R. Schiedermair. *Rasse- und Erbpflege in der Gesetzgebung des Reiches.* 3d ed. Leipzig, 1942.

Stuckart, Wilhelm, and Harry von Rozycki. *Die Reichsverteidigung (Wehrrecht).* Leipzig, 1940.

Sülwald, P. "Grundsätzliches Verbot der Vertretung von Juden in Rechtsangelegenheiten." *JW* (1939): 84 ff.

Suthoff and Groß. "Deutsche Großraumlehre und Großraumpolitik." *DR* (1943): 625 ff.

Syrup, Friedrich. "Gegenwartsaufgaben im Arbeitseinsatz." *DVerw* (1940): 81 ff.

Tannenberg, Otto Richard. *Großdeutschland: Die Arbeit des 20. Jahrhunderts.* Leipzig, 1911.

Tautphaeus. "Der Richter im Reichsgau Wartheland." *DR* (1941) (A): 2466 ff.

Teffelmann. "Die Rechtsprechung des Reichsfinanzhofes unter nationalsozialistischem Einfluß in den Jahren 1933–1943." Legal diss., Cologne, 1943.

Tegtmeyer. "Die Rechtsarbeit der Partei." *DR* (1939) (A): 1942 f.

Tenenbaum, Joseph. *Race and Reich: The Story of an Epoch.* New York, 1956.

Teppe, Karl. "Die NSDAP und die Ministerialbürokratie: Zum Machtkampf zwischen dem Reichsministerium des Inneren und der NSDAP um die Entscheidungsgewalt in den annektierten Gebieten am Beispiel der Kontroverse um die Einsetzung der Gauräte 1940/41." *Der Staat* (1976): 367 ff.

Tesmer, Hans. "Die Schutzhaft und ihre rechtlichen Grundlagen." *DR* (1936): 135 ff.

Tessin, G. *Zur Geschichte der Ordnungspolizei 1936–1945.* Koblenz, 1957.

Thalheimer, August. "Der sog. Sozialfaschismus." *Gegen den Strom* 2, no. 16 (1929).

———. "Über den Faschismus." *Gegen den Strom* 3, nos. 1–4 (1930); shortened version in Abendroth, *Faschismus und Kapitalismus*, 19 ff.

Thiemann. "Anwendung und Fortbildung des deutschen Strafrechts in den eingegliederten Ostgebieten." *DR* (1941) (A): 2473 ff.

Thieme, Hans. "Führerprinzip in der Arbeitsverfassung." *DR* (1935): 215 ff.

Thierack. "Gedanken zum Neuaufbau der deutschen Rechtspflege." *DJ* (1942): 661 ff.

———. "Menschenführung auf dem Gebiete des Rechts." *DR* (1942): 1404.

Thiesing, Jochen. "Ein Jahr deutsche Gerichte im Generalgouvernement." *DR* (1941) (A): 980 f.

Toeche-Mittler, Theodor. *Kommissare: Eine Staats- und Verwaltungsrechtliche Studie.* Berlin, 1934.

Tönnies, Ferdinand. *Gemeinschaft und Gesellschaft.* Berlin, 1926.

Treue, Wolfgang. *Deutsche Parteiprogramme 1861–1945.* 3d ed. Göttingen, 1961. 146 ff.

Trials of War Criminals, Nuernberg Oct. 46–April 49: The Justice Case. Vol. 3.

Triepel, Heinrich. *Goldbilanzenverordnung und Vorzugsaktien.* Berlin, 1924.

Ulbricht, Walter. *Der faschistische deutsche Imperialismus 1933–1945.* 4th ed. Berlin, 1956.

Ule, Carl Herrmann. Review of "Autoritärer und totaler Staat," by Heinz O. Ziegler, in *Recht und Staat in Geschichte und Gegenwart* (Tübingen, 1932). *AöR,* n.s., 24 (1934): 122.

Ulrich, Arthur. "Das Recht der Patentanwälte im neuen Staat." In Frank, *Nationalsozialistisches Handbuch für Recht und Gesetzgebung,* 1935 ff.

Urban, H. "Krakauer gegenwärtige und zukünftige Neubauten." *Das Generalgouvernement,* ser. 8 (1940): 27 ff. (University Library, Warsaw, Sign. 011248).

Verdross, Alfred. *Völkerrecht.* Vienna, 1937.

Verfügungen, Anordnungen, Bekanntmachungen. Vols. 2, 6. Ed. the Party Chancellery, Zentralverlag der NSDAP. Munich, n.d.

Voegelin, Eric. *The New Science of Politics.* Chicago, 1954.

Vogel, Christian. *Vom Wesen des ständischen Rechts*. Berlin, 1937.

Volkmar, Erich. "Die Neugestaltung des Zivilrechts im Geiste nationalsozialistischer Auffassung." In Frank, *Nationalsozialistisches Handbuch für Recht und Gesetzgebung*, 1498 ff.

――――. "Die Arbeiten der Abteilung IV." *DJ* (1939): 13 ff.

von Bayer-Katte, Wanda. "Das Verlockende im nationalsozialistischen Führerprinzip." In *Autoritorismus und Nationalsozialismus: Ein deutsches Problem*, vol. 2 of *Politische Psychologie*. Frankfurt/Main, 1963.

von Gagern. "Ursachen und Auswirkungen der VO über die Abwicklung der Forderungen und Schulden polnischer Vermögen vom 15. August 1941." *DR* (1941): 2505.

von Hippel, Fritz. *Die nationalsozialistische Herrschaftsordnung als Warnung und Lehre*. 2d ed. Tübingen, 1947.

――――. *Die Perversion von Rechtsordnungen*. Tübingen, 1955.

von Hohenstein, Alexander. *Wartheländisches Tagebuch 1941–42*. Munich, 1963.

von Krannhals, Hans. *Der Warschauer Aufstand 1944*. Frankfurt/Main, 1962.

――――. "Die Tätigkeiten der Einsatzgruppen der Sicherheitspolizei 1. 9.-31. 10. 1939." Ms., 1965, BA R 58/1082. Original in the archives of the Polish Ministry of the Interior in Warsaw.

von Massow, Detlef. "Die Tragweite der bisherigen Begriffe 'Gleichheit vor dem Gesetz' und 'Gewährleistung des Eigentums' im Dritten Reich." Legal diss., Marburg, 1936.

von Medeazza, Julius. "Ein Jahr Generalgouvernement." *DR* (1940) (A): 1793 ff.

――――. "Ein Jahr Verwaltung im Generalgouvernement." *DVerw* (1940): 308 ff.

――――. "Die jüdischen Wohnbezirke im Generalgouvernement." *DR* (1941) (A): 1441.

――――. "Die Partei im Generalgouvernement." *DR* (1941) (A): 1648 ff.

――――. "Judenfrage und Judengesetzgebung in Europa." *DR* (1941) (A): 673 f.

von Münch, Ingo, ed. *Gesetze des NS-Staates (Gehlen-Texte 2)*. Bad Homburg, Berlin, Zurich, 1968.

von Olenhausen, Albrecht Götz. "Die 'nichtarischen' Studenten an den deutschen Hochschulen: Zur nationalsozialistischen Rassenpolitik 1933–45." *VjhZ* (1966): 175 ff.

von Repkow, Eike [Robert M. W. Kempner]. *Justizdämmerung: Auftakt zum 3. Reich*. Berlin, 1932.

von Rosen–von Hoevel, Harry. "Das Polenstatut." *DVerw* (1942): 109 ff.

von Rozycki, Harry. "Über den Geltungsbereich des Reichsrechts im Großdeutschen Reich." *DVerw* (1941): 54 ff.

von Scheurl, Eberhard. "Grundsätze deutscher Verwaltung." *DR* (1934): 34 ff.

von Schwerin-Krosigk, Lutz Graf. *Freiheit und Gebundenheit im germanischen Staat*. Berlin, 1933.

von Seckendorff, V. L.. *Teutscher Fürstenstaat*. Frankfurt/Main, 1956. Expanded from the 1737 ed.

von Stutterheim. *Die Reichskanzlei*. Berlin, 1940.

von Zeska, Theo. *Der großdeutsche Freiheitskrieg: Der Feldzug in Polen 1939*. Berlin, 1940.

von zur Mühlen, Patrick. *Rassenideologien: Geschichte und Hintergründe.* Berlin, Bad Godesberg, 1977.

Vormann, N. *Der Feldzug in Polen.* Weissenberg, 1958.

Waag, Heinrich. *Die Verwirklichung des Reiches: Zur Handlung des politischen und juristischen Denkens.* Berlin, 1936.

Wachinger, Michael. "Rechtsschöpferische Rechtsprechung des Reichsgerichts auf materiellstrafrechtlichem Gebiet." In *Erwin Bumke zum 65. Geburtstag,* 53 ff. Berlin, 1939.

Wagner. "Formalismus in der bürgerlichen Rechtspraxis." *DR* (1934): 359 ff.

Wagner, Albrecht. "Die Umgestaltung der Gerichtsverfassung und des Verfahrens- und Richterrechts im nationalsozialistischen Staat." In *Die deutsche Justiz und der Nationalsozialismus,* ed. W. Weinkauff and A. Wagner. Vol. 16, 1, of *Quellen und Darstellungen zur Zeitgeschichte.* Stuttgart, 1968.

Wagner, Walter. *Der Volksgerichtshof im nationalsozialistischen Staat.* Stuttgart, 1974.

Walk, Joseph, ed. *Als Jude in Breslau, 1941: Aus den Tagebüchern von Studienrat a. D. Dr. Willy Israel Cohn.* Jerusalem, 1975.

Walz, Gustav Adolf. "Der Führerstaat: Vortrag auf dem deutschen Juristentag." *DJ* (1936): 813 ff.

———. *Volkstum, Recht und Staat.* Berlin, 1937.

———. *Artgleichheit gegen Gleichartigkeit. Schriften der ZAKfDtRecht, Gruppe Rechtgrundlagen und Rechtsphilosophie,* no. 8. Hamburg, 1938.

———. "Neue Grundlagen des Volksgruppenrechts." In Ritterbusch, *Politische Wissenschaft,* 71 ff.

———. "Gleichheit und Rangordnung im Recht." *DR* (1941) (A): 2209 ff.

———. *Der Begriff der Verfassung. Schriften der Ak. f. Dt. Recht,* group 4, *Verfassung und Verwaltungsrecht,* no. 4. Berlin, 1942.

———. *Völkerrechtsordnung und Nationalsozialismus: Untersuchungen zur Erneuerung des Völkerrechts.* Munich, 1942.

Walz, Heinz. *Das britische Kolonialreich.* Stuttgart, 1935.

———. "Die Inflation im Völkerrecht der Nachkriegszeit." In *Zeitschrift für öffentliches Recht,* appendix. 1939.

Weber, Max. "Der Reichspräsident (1918)." In *Gesammelte politische Schriften,* ed. J. Winkelmann. Tübingen, 1958.

———. "Parlament und Regierung im neugeordneten Deutschland (1918)." In *Gesammelte politische Schriften,* ed. J. Winkelmann. Tübingen, 1958.

Weber, Werner, "Zuständigkeit und Zukunft der Verwaltungsgerichte." *ZStW* 104 (1944): 424 ff.

Wegener, Ulrich. "Der Grundsatz der Gleichheit im Weimarer Staat und seine Wandlung im nationalsozialistischen Reich." Legal diss., Munich, 1940.

Weh, Albert. "Das Recht des Generalgouvernements." *DR* (1940) (A): 1393 ff.

———. "2 Jahre Gesetzgebungsarbeit." *Das Generalgouvernement,* ser. 15 (1941): 27 ff.

———. "Galizien, Bestandteil des Generalgouvernements." *DR* (1941) (A): 1857 ff.

———. *Übersicht über das Recht des Generalgouvernements.* Kraków, 1943 (collection of laws).

Wehner, Bernd. *Die polnischen Greueltaten.* Berlin, 1942.

Weidemann. "Gemeinde und Staat." in *DR* (1936): 310 ff.

Weinkauff, Hermann, and Albrecht Wagner, eds. *Die deutsche Justiz und der Nationalsozialsimus.* Vol. 16, 1, of *Quellen und Darstellungen zur Zeitgeschichte.* Stuttgart, 1968.

Welzel, Hans. "Gesetzmäßige Judentötungen?" *NJW* (1964): 521 ff.

Wengler, Wilhelm. "Das deutsche Privatrecht im Protektorat Böhmen und Mähren und im Generalgouvernement Polen." *ZAKfDtRecht* (1940): 105 ff.

Weniger, Helmut. "Die zahlenmäßige Entwicklung der Anwaltschaft seit 1933." *JW* (1937): 1391.

Westerkamp, Eberhard. "Die Einheit der Verwaltung als Vorbedingung einer Führung und eines Dienstes." *DVerw* (1941): 69 f.

———. "Ein Jahr Einheit der Verwaltung im Generalgouvernement." *DVerw* (1941): 438 ff.

Wetzel, E., and G. Hecht, eds. "Zur Frage der Behandlung der ehemaligen polnischen Gebiete nach rassepolitischen Gesichtspunkten: Denkschrift des Rassepolitischen Amtes der NSDAP vom 25. 11. 1939." *Doc. Occ.* 5:2 ff.

Wieacker, Franz. "Der Stand der Rechtserneuerung auf dem Gebiete bürgerlichen Rechts." *Dt. Rechtswiss.* (1937): 3 ff.

Więtrzykowski, Albin. *Powrót Artura Greisera*, Poznań, 1946; reprint, 1971.

Wilhelmi, Walter. "Die Rechtspflege in den besetzten Ostgebieten." *DR* (A) (1942): 1617 ff.

Wille, Kurt. "Aufbau der Sondergerichte." In *Die Burg, Vierteljahreshefte des Instituts für Deutsche Ostarbeit*, no. 11, 5 ff. Kraków, 1942.

———. "Drei Jahre Aufbauarbeit in der Justiz des Generalgouvernements." *DR* (A) (1942): 1425 ff.

———. "Die Rechtsflege im Generalgouvernement." In *Die Burg, Vierteljahreshefte des Instituts für Deutsche Ostarbeit*, no. 1, 5 ff. Kraków, 1942.

Winkler, Heinrich August. "Extremismus der Mitte? Sozialgeschichtliche Aspekte der nationalsozialistischen Machtergreifung." *VjhZ* 2 (1972): 175 ff.

Wippermann, Wolfgang. *Faschismustheorien.* 2d ed. Darmstadt, 1975.

Wogatzky, Hans. "120 Jahre oberste Hanseatische Gerichte." In Rothenberger, *Das Hanseatische Oberlandesgericht*, 15 ff.

Wöhrmann. "Die Auflösung der Ehe zwischen Juden und Ariern." *JW* (1933): 2041.

Wojan, R. *Bydgoszcz, Sonntag, den 3. 9. 1939.* Poznań, 1959.

Wojciechowska, Janina. "Przyczynek do udziału mniejszości Niemiecki w Hitlerowskiej akcji eksterminacynej w Bydgoszczy." *Przegląd Zachodni* (1958).

Wolany, Joseph, "Das Zwangsvollstreckungsrecht in den eingegliederten Ostgebieten aufgrund der verschiedenen Beschlagnahmen." *DR* (A) (1941): 2494 ff.

Wolf, Erik. "Das Rechtsideal des nationalsozialistischen Staates." *Archiv für Rechtsphilosophie und Sozialphilosophie* 28 (1934–35): 348 ff.

Wolfgramm, Lothar. "Deutsche Rechtsanwälte und deutsche Notare im GG." *DR (A)* (1942): 1428 ff.

Wolfram, Josef, and Adolf Klein, eds. *Recht und Rechtspflege in den Rheinlanden (Festschrift zum 150-jährigen Bestehen des Oberlandesgerichts Köln).* Cologne, 1969.

Wolgers. "Das Notariatsrecht." In Frank, *Nationalsozialistisches Handbuch für Recht und Gesetzgebung,* 1440 ff.

Wrzosek, Mieczysław. "Deutsche Polizei in Oberschlesien." *Bulletin of the Main Commission Warsaw* 15 (1967): 101 ff.

Wulf, Josef. "Lodz, das letzte Ghetto auf polnischem Boden." In *Schriftenreihe der Bundeszentrale für Heimatdienst,* no. 59. Bonn, 1962.

———. *Die bildenden Künste im Dritten Reich.* Hamburg, 1966.

———. *Literatur und Dichtung im Dritten Reich.* Hamburg, 1966.

———. *Musik im Dritten Reich.* Hamburg, 1966.

———. *Presse und Funk im Dritten Reich.* Hamburg, 1966.

———. *Theater und Film im Dritten Reich: Eine Dokumentation.* Hamburg, 1966.

Wuttke. "Der deutsche Verwaltungsaufbau in der Ukraine." *DVerw* (1942): 201 ff.

Zaborowski, Jan, and Stanislaw Poznański. *Sonderaktion Krakau.* Warsaw, 1964.

Ziegler, Heinz O. "Autoritärer und totaler Staat." In *Recht und Staat in Geschichte und Gegenwart.* Tübingen, 1932.

Zorn, Philipp. *Deutsche Kolonialgesetzgebung* (text edition with notes and index). Berlin, 1901.

Zunker, Albrecht. "Institutionengeschichte und Regierungslehre." *DVBl.* (1975): 57 ff.

ADDITIONS TO THE BIBLIOGRAPHY (1993)

Adam, Uwe Dietrich. "Zur Entstehung und Auswirkung des Reichsbürgergesetzes." *Aus Politik und Zeitgeschichte* (B) 48 (1985): 14 ff.

Adlerstein, Leo. "Die Justiz und der Nationalsozialismus: Ursachen und Folgen einer Perversion des Rechtsdenkens." *Protokolldienst der Evangelischen Akademie Bad-Boll* 25 (1982): 1 ff.

Albrecht, Dietmar, and Holger Clausen, eds. *Justiz und Drittes Reich.* Schriftenreihe der Akademie Sankelmark, no. 57. 1984.

Anderbrügge, Klaus. "Verwaltungsrechtliche Aspekte der volksgenössischen Rechtsstellung." In Rottleuthner, *Recht, Rechtsphilosophie und Nationalsozialismus,* 128 ff.

Angermund, Ralph. *Deutsche Richterschaft 1919–1945.* Frankfurt/Main, 1990.

Azzola, Axel. "Die rechtliche Ausschaltung der Juden aus dem öffentlichen Leben im Jahre 1933: Ein Beitrag zur Vorgeschichte eines Genozids." In Dreier and Sellert, *Recht und Justiz im "Dritten Reich,"* 104 ff.

Bästlein, Klaus. "Als Recht zu Unrecht wurde: Zur Entwicklung der Strafjustiz im Nationalsozialismus." *Aus Politik und Zeitgeschichte* 13–14 (1989): 3 ff.

Benz, Wolfgang. "Wissenschaft oder Alibi? Die Etablierung der Zeitgeschichte." In Pehle and Sillem, *Wissenschaft im geteilten Deutschland,* 11 ff.

Böckenförde, Ernst-Wolfgang, ed. *Staatsrecht und Staatsrechtslehre im Dritten Reich*, 212 ff. Heidelberg, 1985.

Böhm, Peter. "Zivilprozeß und Ideologie im nationalsozialistischen Staat." In Davy et al., *Nationalsozialismus und Recht*, 149 ff.

Börner, Fritjof. *Die Bedeutung der Generalklauseln für die Umgestaltung der Rechtsordnung in der nationalsozialistischen Zeit*. Frankfurt/Main, 1989.

Borst, Otto, ed. *Das Dritte Reich in Baden und Württemberg*. Stuttgart, 1988.

Brandt, Martin. "Eigentum und Eigentumsbindung." In Böckenförde, *Staatsrecht und Staatsrechtslehre im Dritten Reich*, 212 ff.

Brünneck, Alexander von. "Die Eigentumsordnung im Nationalsozialismus." *KJ* (1979): 151 ff.

———. "Die Justiz im deutschen Faschismus." *KJ* (1983): 108 ff.

———. "Die Eigentumsordnung im Nationalsozialismus." *KJ* (1984) 9 ff.

Buchner, Herbert. "Das Wirtschaftsrecht im Nationalsozialismus." In Rottleuthner, *Recht, Rechtsphilosophie und Nationalsozialismus*, 92 ff.

Cheim, Hans-Gerhard. "Die Verfolgung jüdischer Rechtsanwälte in der Nazi-Zeit." *Neue Justiz* (1988): 438 f.

Comité des Délégations Juives. *Die Lage der Juden in Deutschland 1933: Das Schwarzbuch—Tatsachen und Dokumente*. Paris, 1934; new ed., Frankfurt/Main, 1983.

Däubler, Wolfgang. "Arbeitsrechtsideologie im deutschen Faschismus: Einige Thesen." In Rottleuthner, *Recht, Rechtsphilosophie und Nationalsozialismus*, 120 ff.

Davy et al., eds. *Nationalsozialismus und Recht: Rechtssetzung und Rechtswissenschaft in Österreich unter der Herrschaft des Nationalsozialismus*. Vienna, 1990.

Deutsche Richterakademie, Trier. *Das Oberlandesgericht Celle im Dritten Reich—Justizverwaltung und Personalwesen—Dokumentation anläßlich der Tagungen "Recht im Nationalsozialismus" vom 3.-9.12.1989 und 2.-8.12.1990*, 148 S.

Diederichsen, Uwe. "Nationalsozialistische Ideologie in der Rechtsprechung des Reichsgerichts zum Ehe- und Familienrecht." In Dreier and Sellert, *Recht und Justiz im "Dritten Reich*," 241 ff.

Diestelkamp, Bernhard, and Michael Stolleis, eds. *Justizalltag im Dritten Reich*, Frankfurt/Main, 1988.

Dölling, Dieter. "Kriminologie im 'Dritten Reich.' " In Dreier and Sellert, *Recht und Justiz im "Dritten Reich*," 194 ff.

Dreier, Ralf, and Wolfgang Sellert, eds. *Recht und Justiz im "Dritten Reich*." Frankfurt/Main, 1989.

Drobisch, Klaus, and Günther Wieland. *System der NS-Konzentrationslager 1933–1945*. Berlin, 1993.

Dürkop, Marlies. "Zur Funktion der Kriminologie im Nationalsozialismus." In Reifner and Bernd-Rüdeger, *Strafjustiz und Polizei im Dritten Reich*, 97 ff.

Erichsen, Hans-Uwe, Werner Hoppe, and Albert von Mutius. *System des verwaltungs-*

gerichtlichen Rechtsschutzes: Festschrift für Christian-Friedrich Menger. Cologne, 1985.

Fachhochschule für öffentliche Verwaltung, Kehl. *Recht und Verwaltung im Nationalsozialismus.* Kehl, 1986.

Fahrenbach, Helmut. "Nationalsozialismus und der Neuanfang 'westdeutscher Philosophie' 1945–1950." In Pehle and Sillem, *Wissenschaft im geteilten Deutschland,* 99 ff.

Falk, Georg-Dietrich. "Vom alltäglichen Funktionieren der Justiz im Nationalsozialismns." *Betrifft Justiz* 2 (1985): 39 ff.

Fangmann, Helmut D., and Norman Paech. "Faschistische Justiz." In Fangmann and Paech, *Recht, Justiz und Faschismus,* 17 ff.

——, eds. *Recht, Justiz und Faschismus: Nach 1933 und heute.* Cologne, 1984.

Faulenbach, Bernd. "Historische Tradition und politische Neuorientierung: Zur Geschichtswissenschaft nach der 'deutschen Katastrophe.' " In Pehle and Sillem, *Wissenschaft im geteilten Deutschland,* 191 ff.

Fieberg, Gerhard. *Justiz im nationalsozialistischen Deutschland.* Cologne, 1984.

Flechtheim, Ossip K. "Recht und Unrecht im Nationalsozialismus." In Schoeps and Hillermann, *Justiz und Nationalsozialismus,* 178 ff.

Frommel, Monika. "Von der Strafrechtsreform zur 'Rechtserneuerung.' " In Rottleuthner, *Recht, Rechtsphilosophie und Nationalsozialismus,* 45 ff.

——. "Verbrechensbekämpfung im Nationalsozialismus." In Säcker, *Recht und Rechtslehre im Nationalsozialismus,* 185 ff.

Fürst, Michael. "Reformen im politischen Strafrecht in der Zeit des Dritten Reiches— unter besonderer Berücksichtigung der Sondergerichte für politische Strafsachen und deren Arbeit." Legal diss., Augsburg, 1990.

Godau-Schüttke, Klaus-Detlef. *Ich habe nur dem Recht gedient: Zur "Renazifizierung" der Schleswig-Holsteinischen Justiz nach 1945.* Baden-Baden, 1993.

Göppinger, Horst. *Juristen jüdischer Abstammung im "Dritten Reich": Entrechtung und Verfolgung.* 2d ed. Munich, 1990 (1st ed., *Die Verfolgung der Juristen jüdischer Abstammung durch den Nationalsozialismus* [Villingen, 1963]).

Graue, Eugen. "Das Zivilrecht im Nationalsozialismus." In Säcker, *Recht und Rechtslehre im Nationalsozialismus,* 103 ff.

Gribbohm, Günter. "Richter und Strafrechtspflege im Dritten Reich." In Albrecht and Clausen, *Justiz und Drittes Reich,* 15 ff.

——. "Nationalsozialismus und Strafrechtspraxis—Versuch einer Bilanz." *NJW* (1988): 2842 ff.

Gruchmann, Lothar. "Das 'Blutschutzgesetz' vom 15.9.1935 und die Justiz." *VjhZ* (1983): 418 ff.

——. " 'Blutschutzgesetz' und Justiz: Entstehung und Anwendung des Nürnberger Gesetzes vom 15. September 1935." *Aus Politik und Zeitgeschichte* 48 (1985): 28 ff.

——. *Justiz im Dritten Reich 1933–1940: Anpassung und Unterwerfung in der Ära Gürtner.* Munich, 1988.

———. " 'Reichskristallnacht' und Justiz im Dritten Reich." *NJW* (1988): 2856 ff.

Heller, Kurt. "Die Rechtsgrundlagen für die Verfolgung von 'entarteter Kunst' im Dritten Reich." In Davy et al., *Nationalsozialismus und Recht*, 285 ff.

Henning, Karl, and Josef Kestler. "Die Rechtsstellung der Juden." In Böckenförde, *Staatsrecht und Staatsrechtslehre im Dritten Reich*, 191 ff.

Herbert, Ulrich. *Fremdarbeiter: Politik und Praxis des "Ausländer-Einsatzes" in der Kriegswirtschaft des Dritten Reiches.* Bonn, 1985.

———. *Geschichte der Ausländerbeschäftigung in Deutschland 1880–1980: Saisonarbeiter, Zwangsarbeiter, Gastarbeiter.* Bonn, 1986.

Hillermeier, Heinz. *"Im Namen des deutschen Volkes!" Todesurteile des Volksgerichtshofs.* Darmstadt, 1980.

Hirsch, Martin, Diemut Majer, and Jürgen Meinck. *Recht, Verwaltung und Justiz im Nationalsozialismus: Ausgewählte Schriften, Gesetze und Gerichtsentscheidungen mit ausführlichen Erläuterungen und Kommentierungen.* Cologne, 1984; 2d ed., Baden-Baden, 1997.

Hofer, Walther. "Stufen der Judenverfolgung im Dritten Reich 1933–1939." In Strauss and Kampe, *Antisemitismus*, 172 ff.

Hofmeister, Herbert. "Privatrechtsgesetzgebung für Österreich unter der Herrschaft des Nationalsozialismus." In Davy et al., *Nationalsozialismus und Recht*, 124 ff.

Höver, Ulrich. "Politische Justiz im Dritten Reich: Das Heimtückegesetz." *IfdT* 12 (1989): 48 ff.

Im Namen des deutschen Volkes: Justiz und Nationalsozialismus. Catalog of the exhibit of the Federal ministry of Justice. Cologne, 1989.

Jonca, Karol. "Die Rechtslage der Juden und die 'Endlösung der Judenfrage' in Schlesien (1938–1945): Begutachtung der antijüdischen Gesetzgebung 1933–1936." In *Hauptkommission zur Untersuchung der Naziverbrechen, Internationale wissenschaftliche Session: Naziverbrechen gegen die Menschlichkeit in Polen und Europa 1939–1945.* Warsaw, 1983.

———. "Nationalsozialistisches Recht im besetzten Polen (1939–1945)." *Polnische Weststudien* 3, no. 2 (1984): 239 ff.

Jung, Susanne. *Die Rechtsprobleme der Nürnberger Prozesse dargestellt am Verfahren gegen Friedrich Flick.* Tübingen, 1992.

Justizakademie Nordrhein-Westfalen, ed. *Die Auflösung des Rechtsstaates 1933–1936: Dokumentation mit einer Einführung.* Recklinghausen, 1991.

Kąkol, Kazimierz. "NS-Verbrechen in Polen und Probleme der Rechtshilfe." In Schoeps and Hillermann, *Justiz und Nationalsozialismus*, 71 ff.

Kaufmann, Arthur. "Rechtsphilosophie und Nationalsozialismus." In Rottleuthner, *Recht, Rechtsphilosophie und Nationalsozialismus*, 1 ff.

Kirchberg, Christian. *Der badische Verwaltungsgerichtshof im Dritten Reich: Eine Quellenstudie zur Justiz- und Verwaltungsgeschichte des ehemaligen Landes Baden unter dem Nationalsozialismus.* Berlin, 1982.

Kirchheimer, Otto. "Die Rechtsordnung des Nationalsozialismus." In *Redaktion Kritische Justiz: Der Unrechts-Staat: Recht und Justiz im Nationalsozialismus*, 9 ff.

Koch, Hannsjoachim W. *Volksgerichtshof: Politische Justiz im 3. Reich.* Munich, 1988.

Kohl, Wolfgang. *Das Reichsverwaltungsgericht: Ein Beitrag zur Entwicklung der Verwaltungsgerichtsbarkeit in Deutschland.* Tübingen, 1991.

Kohl, Wolfgang, and Michael Stolleis. "Im Bauch des Leviathan: Zur Staats- und Verwaltungsrechtslehre im Nationalsozialismus." *NJW* (1988): 2849 ff.

König, Stefan. *Vom Dienst am Recht: Rechtsanwälte als Strafverteidiger im Nationalsozialismus.* Berlin, 1987.

Koppel, Wolfgang. *Ungesühnte Nazijustiz—Hundert Urteile klagen ihre Richter an.* Karlsruhe, 1960.

Kranig, Andreas. "Arbeitsrecht und Nationalsozialismus." In Rottleuthner, *Recht, Rechtsphilosophie und Nationalsozialismus*, 105 ff.

———. "Treue gegen Fürsorge: Arbeitsrichter unter dem Nationalsozialismus." In Diestelkamp and Stolleis, *Justizalltag im Dritten Reich*, 63 ff.

Kregel, Volker. "Die Personalpolitik der Justiz im 'Dritten Reich' am Beispiel des Oberlandesgerichts Celle." In Dreier and Sellert, *Recht und Justiz im "Dritten Reich,"* 226 ff.

Kriele, Martin. "Staatsphilosophische Lehren aus dem Nationalsozialismus." In Rottleuthner, *Recht, Rechtsphilosophie und Nationalsozialismus*, 210 ff.

Kritische Justiz: Der Unrechts-Staat: Recht und Justiz im Nationalsozialismus, vol. 1. Baden-Baden, 1983.

———. *Der Unrechts-Staat*, vol. 2. *Recht und Justiz im Nationalsozialismus*, Baden-Baden, 1984.

Kroeschell, Karl. "Die nationalsozialistische Eigentumslehre: Vorgeschichte und Nachwirkung." In Stolleis and Simon, *Rechtsgeschichte im Nationalsozialismus*, 43 ff.

Krumsiek, Rolf. "Justiz und Nationalsozialismus." *Recht und Politik* (1990): 58 ff.

Kumpf, Johann Heinrich. "Die Finanzgerichtsbarkeit im Dritten Reich." In Diestelkamp and Stolleis, *Justizalltag im Dritten Reich*, 81 ff.

Landau, Peter. "Römisches Recht und deutsches Gemeinrecht: Zur rechtspolitischen Zielsetzung im nationalsozialistischen Parteiprogramm." In Stolleis and Simon, *Rechtsgeschichte im Nationalsozialismus*, 11 ff.

Lehmann, Joachim. "Repressive Ausländerpolitik im faschistischen Deutschland: Die Ausländerpolizei-Verordnungen von 1932 und 1938." *Wissenschaftliche Zeitschrift der Wilhelm-Pieck-Universität Rostock*, no. 2 (1984): 47 ff.

Loebenstein, Herbert. "Strafrecht und Strafenpraxis im nationalsozialistischen Staat." In Davy et al., *Nationalsozialismus und Recht*, 200 ff.

Loewe, Josef. *Befreite Justiz: Rechtsfälle rings um den Nationalsozialismus.* Reutlingen, 1947.

Lübbe, Anna. "Die deutsche Verfassungsgeschichtsschreibung unter dem Einfluß der nationalsozialistischen Machtergreifung." In Stolleis and Simon, *Rechtsgeschichte im Nationalsozialismus*, 63 ff.

Luthardt, Wolfgang. "Unrechtsstaat oder Doppelstaat? Kritisch-theoretische Reflexionen über die Struktur des Nationalsozialismus aus der Sicht demokratischer Sozialisten." In Rottleuthner, *Recht, Rechtsphilosophie und Nationalsozialismus*, 197 ff.

Majer, Diemut. "Der Kampf um die Einführung des preußischen Polizeiverwaltungsgesetzes in den 'engegliederten Ostgebieten'." *Der Staat* (1978): 49 ff.

———. "Justiz und NS Staat: Zum Einfluß der NSDAP auf die Organisation und Personalpolitik der Justiz." *DRiZ* (1978): 47 ff.

———. "Der Einfluß der NSDAP auf die Justiz." *Protokolldienst der Evangelischen Akademie Bad-Boll* 16 (1980): 59 ff.

———. " 'Rechts'-Prinzipien des nationalsozialistischen Staates am Beispiel der Verfolgung Andersdenkender." *Aus Politik und Zeitgeschichte* (B) 30 (1983): 11 ff.

———. "Rechtstheoretische Funktionsbestimmugen der Justiz im Nationalsozialismus am Beispiel der 'Völkischen Ungleichheit'." In Rottleuthner, *Recht, Rechtsphilosophie und Nationalsozialismus*, 163 ff.

———. "Das Verhältnis von Staatsanwaltschaft und Polizei." In Reifner and Sonnen, *Strafjustiz und Polizei im Dritten Reich*, 121 ff.

———. "Der Wahn von Reich und 'Großraum': Ein Beitrag zur Völkerrechtslehre des Nationalsozialismus." *Studia historica slavo-germanica* (Breslau) 13 (1984): 11 ff.

———. "Die ideologischen Grundlagen des nationalsozialistischen Rechtsdenkens dargestellt am Beispiel der NSDAP (Justiz und NSDAP)." In Albrecht and Clausen, *Justiz und Drittes Reich*, 43 ff.

———. "Racial Inequality and the Nazification of the Law in Nazi Germany." *Israel Yearbook on Human Rights* 14 (1984): 111 ff.

———. "Die Perversion des Völkerrechts unter dem NS." *Jahrbuch für Deutsche Geschichte* (Tel Aviv) 14 (1985): 311 ff.

———. "Führerunmittelbare Sondergewalten in den besetzten Ostgebieten." In Rebentisch and Teppe, *Verwaltung contra Menschenführung im Staat Hitlers*, 374 ff.

———. *Grundlagen des nationalsozialistischen Rechtssystems: Führerprinzip, Sonderrecht, Einheitspartei*. Stuttgart, 1987.

———. "Justiz zwischen Anpassung und Konflikt." In Schoeps and Hillermann, *Justiz und Nationalsozialismus*, 118 ff.

———. "Richter und Rechtswesen." In Borst, *Das Dritte Reich in Baden und Württemberg*, 46 ff.

———. "Justiz und Polizei im 'Dritten Reich'." In Dreier and Sellert, *Recht und Justiz im "Dritten Reich,"* 136 ff.

———. "Der allgemeine Gleichheitssatz und seine Umwandlung zum Sonderrecht im nationalsozialistischen Staat." In Davy et al., *Nationalsozialismus und Recht*, 55 ff.

———. "Systeme des Besatzungsrechts 1939–1948." In *Tel Aviver Jahrbuch für deutsche Geschichte*, 139 ff. 1990.

———. "Die Frage der Entschädigung für ehemalige NS-Zwangsarbeiter in völkerrechtlicher Sicht." *Archiv des Völkerrechts* (1991): 1 ff. (with in-depth documentation).

———. "Die Verführbarkeit der Juristen: Zur Restauration der Rechtswissenschaft nach 1945." In Pehle and Sillem, *Wissenschaft im geteilten Deutschland*, 86 ff.

———. "NS-Verwaltung im besetzten Europa 1939–1945." *Verwaltungsarchiv* (1999): 163 ff.

Marxen, Klaus. "Die rechtsphilosophische Begründung der Straftatlehre im Nationalsozialismus—Zur Frage der Kontinuität strafrechtswissenschaftlichen Denkens." In Rottleuthner, *Recht, Rechtsphilosophie und Nationalsozialismus*, 55 ff.

———. "Zum Verhältnis von Strafrechtsdogmatik und Strafrechtspraxis im Nationalsozialismus." In Reifner and Sonnen, *Strafjustiz und Polizei im Dritten Reich*, 77 ff.

———. "Strafjustiz im Nationalsozialismus: Vorschläge für eine Erweiterung der historischen Perspektive." In Diestelkamp and Stolleis, *Justizalltag im Dritten Reich*, 101 ff.

Maus, Ingeborg. "Juristische Methodik und Justizfunktion im Nationalsozialismus." In Rottleuthner, *Recht, Rechtsphilosophie und Nationalsozialismus*, 176 ff.

———. "'Gesetzesbindung' der Justiz und die Struktur der nationalsozialistischen Rechtsnormen." In Dreier and Sellert, *Recht und Justiz im "Dritten Reich,"* 80 ff.

Mayer-Maly, Theo. "Nationalsozialismus und Arbeitsrecht." In Davy et al., *Nationalsozialismus und Recht*, 173 ff.

———. "Arbeitsrecht, Arbeitsgerichtsbarkeit und Nationalsozialismus." In Säcker, *Recht und Rechtslehre im Nationalsozialismus*, 125 ff.

Meinck, Jürgen. "Die Rechtsprechung des Reichsgerichts in der Zeit von 1933 bis 1945." *Protokolldienst der Evangelischen Akademie Bad-Boll* 16 (1980): 34 ff.

Meyer-Hesemann, Wolfgang. "Modernisierungstendenzen in der nationalsozialistischen Verwaltungsrechtswissenschaft." In Rottleuthner, *Recht, Rechtsphilosophie und Nationalsozialismus*, 140 ff.

Michaelis, Karl. "Die außerordentliche Wiederaufnahme rechtskräftig abgeschlossener Verfahren in der Praxis des Reichsgerichts 1941–1945." In Dreier and Sellert, *Recht und Justiz im "Dritten Reich,"* 273 ff.

Michel, Bertram. "Die Entwicklung der Arbeitsgerichtsbarkeit in den Faschismus." In Reifner, *Das Recht des Unrechtsstaates*, 154 ff.

Michelberger, Hans. *Berichte aus der Justiz des Dritten Reiches.* Tübingen, 1989.

Müller, Ingo. "Das Strafprozeßrecht des Dritten Reiches." In Reifner and Sonnen, *Strafjustiz und Polizei im Dritten Reich*, 59 ff.

———. *Furchtbare Juristen.* Munich, 1987.

Neumann, Franz. *Behemoth: Struktur und Praxis des Nationalsozialismus 1933–1945.* Frankfurt/Main, 1984.

Neumann, Volker. "Vom Entscheidungs—zum Ordnungsdenken. Carl Schmitts Rechts- und Staatstheorie in der nationalsozialistischen Herausforderung." In Rottleuthner, *Recht, Rechtsphilosophie und Nationalsozialismus*, 152 ff.

Niedersächsische Landeszentrale für politische Bildung. "Dokumentation zum Seminar 'Recht im Nationalsozialismus.'" Hannover, n.d.

Ostler, Fritz. "Rechtsanwälte in der NS-Zeit: Fakten und Erinnerungen." *AnwBl.* (1983): 50 ff.

Otte, Gerhard. "Die zivilrechtliche Gesetzgebung im 'Dritten Reich.' " *NJW* (1988): 2836 ff.

Pehle, Walter, ed. *Der historische Ort des Nationalsozialismus: Annäherungen.* Frankfurt/ Main, 1990.

Pehle, Walter, and Peter Sillem, eds. *Wissenschaft im geteilten Deutschland: Restauration oder Neubeginn nach 1945?* Frankfurt/Main, 1992.

Petrovic, Gabriela. "Des Sozialversicherungsrecht in der 'Ostmark.' " In Davy et al., *Nationalsozialismus und Recht,* 307 ff.

Potz, Richard. "Nationalsozialismus und Staatskirchenrecht." In Davy et al., *Nationalsozialismus und Recht,* 266 ff.

Rabofsky, Eduard, and Gerhard Oberkofler. *Verborgene Wurzeln der NS-Justiz: Strafrechtliche Rüstung für zwei Weltkriege.* Vienna, 1985.

Ramm, Thilo. "Nationalsozialismus und Arbeitsrecht." *KJ* (1968): 82 ff., 108 ff.

———. "Familien-und Jugendrecht im Nationalsozialismus." In Rottleuthner, *Recht, Rechtsphilosophie und Nationalsozialismus,* 75 ff.

———. *Das nationalsozialistische Familien-und Jugendrecht.* Heidelberg, 1984.

Rapp, Gertrud. *Die Stellung der Juden in der nationalsozialistischen Staatsrechtslehre: Die Emanzipation der Juden im 19. Jahrhundert und die Haltung der deutschen Staatsrechtslehre zur staatsrechtlichen Stellung der Juden im Nationalsozialismus.* Baden-Baden, 1990.

Rau, Johannes. "Justiz und Nationalsozialismus." In Schoeps and Hillermann, *Justiz und Nationalsozialismus,* 9 ff.

Rebentisch, Dieter. *Führerstaat und Verwaltung im Zweiten Weltkrieg: Verfassungsentwicklung und Verwaltungspolitik 1939–1945.* Stuttgart, 1989.

Rebentisch, Dieter, and Karl Teppe, eds. *Verwaltung contra Menschenführung im Staat Hitlers.* Göttingen, 1986.

Reifner, Udo. "Institutionen des faschistischen Rechtssystems." In Reifner, *Das Recht das Unrechtsstaates,* 11 ff.

———. "NS-Rechtsbetreuungsstellen und die Rechtsberatung der Deutschen Arbeitsfront Theorie und Praxis sozial befriedender Rechtsberatung." In Reifner, *Das Recht des Unrechtsstaates,* 178 ff.

———, ed. *Das Recht des Unrechtsstaates: Arbeitsrecht und Staatsrechtswissenschaften im Faschismus.* Frankfurt/Main, 1981.

Reifner, Udo, and Bernd-Rüdeger Sonnen, eds. *Strafjustiz und Polizei im Dritten Reich.* Frankfurt/Main, 1984.

Ridder, Helmut, "Zur Verfassungsdoktrin des NS-Staates." In *Redaktion Kritische Justiz: Der Unrechts-Staat: Recht und Justiz im Nationalsozialismus,* 24 ff.

Robinsohn, Hans. *Justiz als politische Verfolgung: Die Rechtsprechung in "Rassenschandefällen" beim Landgericht Hamburg 1936–1943.* Stuttgart, 1977.

Rottleuthner, Hubert. "Substanzieller Dezisionismus—Zur Funktion der Rechtsphilosophie im Nationalsozialismus." In Rottleuthner, *Recht, Rechtsphilosophie und Nationalsozialismus*, 20 ff.

——. "Rechtsphilosophie und Rechtssoziologie im Nationalsozialismus." In Dreier and Sellert, *Recht und Justiz im "Dritten Reich,"* 295 ff.

——, ed. *Recht, Rechtsphilosophie und Nationalsozialismus: Vorträge aus der Tagung der deutschen Sektion der Internationalen Vereinigung für Rechts- und Sozialphilosophie (IVR) in der Bundesrepublik Deutschland vom 11. und 12.10.1982 in Berlin (West).* Supplement 18, Archiv für Rechts- und Sozialphilosophie. 1983.

Rüping, Hinrich. " 'Auflockerung' im Strafverfahrensrecht—Grundsätzliche Entwicklung zwischen Liberalismus, 'deutschem Gemeinrecht' und Naturrecht." In Rottleuthner, *Recht, Rechtsphilosophie und Nationalsozialismus*, 65 ff.

——. "Nationalsozialistische Rechtsprechung am Beispiel der SS und Polizei-Gerichte." *Neue Zeitschrift für Strafrecht* (1983): 112 ff.

——. "Zur Praxis der Strafjustiz im 'Dritten Reich.' " In Dreier and Sellert, *Recht und Justiz im "Dritten Reich,"* 180 ff.

Rüthers, Bernd. *Entartetes Recht: Rechtslehren und Kronjuristen im Dritten Reich.* Munich, 1988.

——. "Recht als Waffe des Unrechts—Juristische Instrumente im Dienst des NS-Rassenwahns." *NJW* (1988): 2825 ff.

——. "Die Ideologie des Nationalsozialismus in der Entwicklung des deutschen Rechts von 1933 bis 1945." In Säcker, *Recht und Rechtslehre im Nationalsozialismus*, 17 ff.

Säcker, Franz Jürgen, ed. *Recht und Rechtslehre im Nationalsozialismus: Ringvorlesung der Rechtswissenschaftlichen Fakultät der Christian-Albrechts-Universität zu Kiel.* Baden-Baden, 1992.

Schäfer, Herwig. "Die Rechtsstellung des Einzelnen—Von den Grundrechten zur volksgenössischen Gleichstellung." In Böckenförde, *Staatsrecht und Staatsrechtslehre im Dritten Reich*, 106 ff.

Schellenberg, Ulrich. "Die Rechtsstaatskritik: Vom liberalen zum nationalen und nationalsozialistischen Rechtsstaat." In Böckenförde, *Staatsrecht und Staatsrechtslehre im Dritten Reich*, 71 ff.

Schleier, Hans. "Vergangenheitsbewältigung und Traditionserneuerung? Geschichtswissenschaft nach 1945." In Pehle and Sillem, *Wissenschaft im geteilten Deutschland*, 205 ff.

Schminck-Gustavus, Christoph U. "Zwangsarbeitsrecht und Faschismus: Zur 'Polenpolitik' im 'Dritten Reich.' " *KJ* (1980): 1 ff., 184 ff.

——. "Zwangsarbeit und Faschismus: Zur 'Polenpolitik' im 'Dritten Reich.' " In Redaktion Kritische Justiz: *Der Unrechts-Staat*, vol. 2, *Recht und Justiz im Nationalsozialismus*, 155 ff.

Schneider, Otmar. *Rechtsgedanken und Rechtstechniken totalitärer Herrschaft: Aufgezeigt am Recht des öffentlichen Dienstes im Dritten Reich und der DDR.* Berlin, 1988.

Schoeps, Julius H., and Horst Hillermann, eds. *Justiz und Nationalsozialismus.* Stuttgart, 1987.

Schreiber, Hans-Ludwig. "Die Strafgesetzgebung im 'Dritten Reich.' " In Dreier and Sellert, *Recht und Justiz im "Dritten Reich,"* 151 ff.

Schröder, Rainer. ". . . *aber im Zivilrecht sind die Richter standhaft geblieben!" Die Urteile des OLG [State Superior Court] Celle aus dem Dritten Reich.* Baden-Baden, 1988.

———. "Der zivilrechtliche Alltag des Volksgenossen: Beispiele aus der Praxis des Oberlandesgerichts Celle im Dritten Reich." In Diestelkamp and Stolleis, *Justizalltag im Dritten Reich,* 39 ff.

Schubert, Werner, et al. *Abteilung NS-Zeit (1933–1939)—Strafgesetzbuch.* Vol. 2, *Protokolle der Strafrechtskommission des Reichsjustizministeriums.* Ed. Jürgen Regge and Werner Schubert. Berlin, 1988–90.

Schütz, Hans. *Justiz im "Dritten Reich": Dokumentation aus dem Bezirk des Oberlandesgerichts Bamberg.* Bamberg, 1984.

Schwerdtner, Peter. "Personen Persönlichkeitsschutz und Rechtsfähigkeit im Nationalsozialismus." In Rottleuthner, *Recht, Rechtsphilosophie und Nationalsozialismus,* 82 ff.

Simon, Dieter. "Waren die NS-Richter 'unabhängige Richter' im Sinne des § 1 GVG?" In Diestelkamp and Stolleis, *Justizalltag im Dritten Reich,* 11 ff.

———. "Die deutsche Wissenschaft vom römischen Recht nach 1933." In Stolleis and Simon, *Rechtsgeschichte im Nationalsozialismus,* 161 ff.

Sombart, Nicolaus. *Die deutschen Männer und ihre Feinde: Carl Schmitt—ein deutsches Schicksal zwischen Männerbund und Matriarchatsmythos.* Munich, 1991.

Sonnen, Bernd-Rüdeger. "Strafjustiz im Nationalsozialismus." In Fangmann and Paech, *Recht, Justiz und Faschismus,* 33 ff.

Stolleis, Michael. "Die Verwaltungsgerichtsbarkeit im Nationalsozialismus." In Erichsen, Hoppe, and von Mutius, *System des verwaltungsgerichtlichen Rechtsschutzes,* 57 ff.

———. "Die Verwaltungsgerichtsbarkeit im Nationalsozialismus." In Diestelkamp and Stolleis, *Justizalltag im Dritten Reich,* 26 ff.

———. "Die Rechtsgeschichte im Nationalsozialismus: Umrisse eines wissenschaftsgeschichtlichen Themas." In Stolleis and Simon, *Rechtsgeschichte im Nationalsozialismus,* 1 ff.

———. " 'Fortschritte der Rechtsgeschichte' in der Zeit des Nationalsozialismus." In Stolleis and Simon, *Rechtsgeschichte im Nationalsozialismus,* 177 ff.

Stolleis, Michael, and Dieter Simon, eds. *Rechtsgeschichte im Nationalsozialismus: Beiträge zur Geschichte einer Disziplin.* Tübingen, 1989.

Strauss, Herbert A., and Norbert Kampe, eds. *Antisemitismus: Von der Judenfeindschaft zum Holocaust.* Bonn, 1984.

Sunnus, Michael. *Der NS-Rechtswahrerbund (1928–1945): Zur Geschichte der nationalsozialistischen Juristenorganisation.* Frankfurt/Main, 1990.

Tanzer, Michael. "Steuerrecht im nationalsozialistischen Staat." In Davy et al., *Nationalsozialismus und Recht,* 331 ff.

Terhorst, Karl-Leo. *Polizeiliche planmäßige Überwachung und polizeiliche Vorbeugungshaft im Dritten Reich: Ein Beitrag zur Rechtsgeschichte vorbeugender Verbrechensbekämpfung.* Heidelberg, 1985.

Urner, Klaus. "Das Schicksal jüdischer Firmen im Nationalsozialismus." *Neue Zürcher Zeitung,* May 27, 1989, 33.

Verein für Hamburgische Geschichte. *Schicksal jüdischer Juristen in Hamburg im Dritten Reich.* Hamburg, 1985.

von Dickhut-Harrach, Hans-Jürgen. *"Gerechtigkeit statt Formalismus": Die Rechtskraft in der nationalsozialistischen Privatrechtspraxis.* Cologne, 1986.

von Münch, Ingo, and Uwe Brodersen. *Gesetze des NS-Staates: Dokumente eines Unrechtssystems.* 2d ed. Paderborn, 1982.

Wagner, Heinz. "Das Strafrecht im Nationalsozialismus." In Säcker, *Recht und Rechtslehre im Nationalsozialismus,* 141 ff.

Washner, Roderich. "Faschismus und Arbeitsrecht." In Reifner, *Das Recht des Unrechtsstaates,* 86 ff.

——. "Die deutsche Rechtsgeschichte und der Faschismus." In *Redaktion Kritische Justiz: Der Unrechts-Staat: Recht und Justiz im Nationalsozialismus,* 95 ff. 1983.

——. "Arbeitsrecht und Arbeitsgerichtsbarkeit im Dritten Reich." In Fangmann and Paech, *Recht, Justiz und Faschismus,* 40 ff.

Walk, Joseph. *Das Sonderrecht für die Juden im NS-Staat: Eine Sammlung der gesetzlichen Maßnahmen und Richtlinien—Inhalt und Bedeutung.* Karlsruhe, 1981.

Walther, Manfred. "Hat der juristische Positivismus die deutschen Juristen im 'Dritten Reich' wehrlos gemacht?" In Dreier and Sellert, *Recht und Justiz im "Dritten Reich,"* 323 ff.

Wassermann, Rudolf. "Die Justiz als Instrument eines rechtsfeindlichen Herrschaftssystems." *Recht und Politik* (1988): 129 ff.

Werle, Gerhard. "Zur Reform des Strafrechts in der NS-Zeit: Der Entwurf eines Deutschen Strafgesetzbuchs 1936." *NJW* (1988): 2865 ff.

Willoweit, Dietmar. "Deutsche Rechtsgeschichte und 'nationalsozialistische Weltanschauung': Das Beispiel Hans Frank." In Stolleis and Simon, *Rechtsgeschichte im Nationalsozialismus,* 25 ff.

Wrobel, Hans. "Die Anfechtung der Rassenmischehe: Diskriminierung und Entrechtung der Juden in den Jahren 1933–1935." *KJ* (1983): 349 ff.

——. *Strafjustiz im totalen Krieg: Aus den Akten des Sondergerichts Bremen 1940–1945.* Vol. 1. Ed. Senator for Justice und Constitution of Freien Hansestadt Bremen. Bremen, 1991.

Index

Italic *n* following page numbers refers to notes; italic *t* refers to tables.

102-3, 106-7, 124; police law on, 180-83, 367,
370-72, 687-91n; "resettlement" from east,
124-25, 254-55, 305, 804-5n, 896n; restrictions on, 178-83; sentencing of, 345, 367-69,
421; and "social compensation tax," 151, 152,
168, 679n; statistics on, 667n, 736n; violence
against, 79, 629n; as witnesses, 343-45, 834n.
See also "alien" workers in Altreich
Poles in Annexed Eastern Territories: administrative policy toward, 195-97, 204-6, 700-
703n; applicability of German law to, 406-
10, 476-80; citizenship/legal statuses of, 121,
123-27, 236-46, 461, 740-43n; civil law for
(see civil law in Annexed Eastern Territories); in Civil Service, 230-31, 732-33n; communications restrictions for, 255-56, 751-52n;
court-appointed defense for, prohibition of,
343, 435-36; criminal offenses by, prosecution of, 432-33, 443; cultural goods restrictions for, 256-57, 752-53n; "disfranchisement" of, 422-25, 434, 487; duty of
obedience, 425-27; educational policy for,
224-25, 726-27n; food supply policy for,
257-59, 753-56n; freedom of movement restrictions for, 249-55, 745-48n; German
crimes against, dismissal of, 432; on German
Ethnic Classification List, 239-46, 461, 740-
43n; Germans friendly toward, prosecution
of, 428-29, 881-82n; insubordination by, 418,
452, 875n; labor law and work conditions for,
232-35, 700n; legal claims by, 481-84; legal
rights against police orders, dispute over,
216-21, 721n, 722n; marriage law for, 102-3,
124, 246-48, 479, 744n; penal law for (see penal law in Annexed Eastern Territories); political comments by, 417; professionals, 231;
property law for, 226-30, 255-57, 728n, 729-
31n, 751-53n; public life restrictions for, 223;
punishment goals for, 413-14, 439; religious
restrictions for, 223-24; resettlement/depor-
tation of, 254-55, 749-50n; segregation of,
206-13, 711-15n; sentencing standards for,
415, 421, 425-27, 441-46, 452, 886n; sexual
liaisons with Germans, 209-10, 212, 230, 333,
369, 714n; as "threat to community," 424;
welfare policy for, 222, 723n; as witnesses,
434
Poles in General Government: attitudes toward
Jews, 778n; civil law for (see civil law in General Government); cultural policy for, 289-
91, 783-90n; educational policy for, 290,
786-88n; food supply policy for, 272-73, 306,
757n, 806n; freedom of movement restrictions for, 316-17, 819n; in German adminis-

tration, 275, 297-99, 797n; health care policy
for, 300-301, 311; labor policy for, 302-3,
305-6, 800-802n, 804-5n; legal status of,
308-9; marriage policy for, 310; "of German
extraction," 308-9, 812n; penal law for (see
penal law in General Government); professionals, 299-300, 311, 798n, 813-14n; property policy for, 292-94, 318-19, 792n, 793n;
tax policy for, 296-97; treatment of, 206-10,
261, 271-74, 286-87, 711-15n, 757n, 764n,
765n, 766n, 775n, 776n, 780n, 786n; welfare
policy, 306-7, 807-8n; workers, 301-3, 305-6,
800-802n, 804-5n
police, 3, 174-77, 541, 683-85n; actions by, 68,
541; chief of German, 179, 180, 182, 684n; expansion of powers of, 542-45; in occupied
Eastern Europe, 192, 697n; organization of,
685n; relationship to law, 174-75, 219, 684n,
721n; separation from administration, 75,
541-42, 544-45. See also Gestapo; police in
Altreich; police in Annexed Eastern Territories; police in General Government; SD; Security Police; SS
police actions, 68, 541-42, 544-45; in General
Government, 305, 517-18, 775n, 776n
police acts, administrative, immunity to judicial
review, 20-21
police camps (concentration camps), 70, 449,
456, 824n, 847n
police courts, 513
police courts-martial, 449-55, 877n, 896-901n;
in Annexed Eastern Territories, 449-59; empowerment of, 456-59, 467-68, 902n, 904n;
in General Government, 513-15; mobile, 449,
453; reaction of judiciary to, 460-62
police custody. See protective custody
Police Decree on the Appearance of Jews in
Public (Sept. 1, 1941), 170
Police Decree on Foreigners (Aug. 22, 1938), 119
police in Altreich, 174-77, 183-84, 683-86n; and
"alien" workers, 154, 177-83; expansion of
powers of, 68, 107-8, 154, 174-77, 345-78,
439, 447-48, 542-43, 835n, 854n; and judiciary, 353-58, 372-78, 832n, 844-45n, 903n;
unification with SS, 175, 355-56; wartime
function of, 351
police in Annexed Eastern Territories, 198, 203,
221-22; and citizenship policy, 237-38, 243-
44; courts-martial by, 449-59; dispute over
regulation of, 213-22, 721n, 722n; illegal executions by, 450-53, 457; jurisdiction and
powers of, 107-8, 376, 446-69, 527-29, 543;
local, reporting of Polish crimes to Gestapo,
456-57, 528, 897n

About the Author

Born in West Germany, Diemut Majer studied law and political science at various German universities and at the Johns Hopkins School of Advanced International Studies in Bologna, Italy; she obtained a Ph.D. degree in public law at the University of Freiburg (Germany). Having served six years as a judge and attorney at an administrative court and three years as an assistant to the Constitutional Court of (West) Germany in Karlsruhe, she was until 2001 a professor of administrative law at the Federal College of Public Administration in Mannheim, Germany. She is a professor of public law, constitutional legal history, and comparative law at the University of Bern and a lecturer in European law at the University of Karlsruhe.

Professor Majer's works include *"Fremdvölkische" im Dritten Reich* (Boppard am Rhein: Bundesarchiv Koblenz, 1981, 1993); *Recht, Verwaltung und Justiz im Nationalsozialismus* (with M. Hirsch and J. Meinck) (Cologne/Baden-Baden: NOMOS-Verlag, 1984, 1997); *Neutralitätsrecht und Neutralitätspolitik am Beispiel Österreichs und der Schweiz* (Heidelberg: Deckers-Verlag, 1987); *Grundlagen des nationalsozialistischen Rechtssystems: Führerprinzip, Sonderrecht, Einheitspartei* (Stuttgart: W. Kohlhammer, 1987); *Der lange Weg zu Freiheit und Gleichheit: 14 Vorlesungen zur Rechtsstellung der Frau in der Geschichte* (Vienna: Wiener Universitätsverlag, 1995); two other monographs in the field of constitutional law (1966, 1981); and numerous articles and book reviews in the fields of constitutional history, constitutional law, environmental law, comparative law, and European law.